North

The Laffites' Louisiana, 1803–1820

MISSISSIPPI TERRITORY
(post 1813)

(Statehood Boundary, 1812)

Bayou Manchac

Lake
Maurepas

Lake
Ponchartrain

Rigolets Channel

Donaldsonville

Mississippi River

GERMAN COAST

Bayou Sauvage

Bayou St. John
Carrollton

New Orleans

Bayou Bienvenue

Lake
Borgne

Napoleonville

Attakapas Canal

Lac des
Allemandes

Bayou
des Allemandes

English
Turn

Bayou Terre
Boeuf

Chandeleur Island

Bayou Lafourche

Lake Salvador
(Big Lake Barataria)

Bayou Perot
Temple

Bayou Rigolets

Grand
Lake

Barataria Bayou

Bayou
St. Denis

Wilkinson
Bayou

Breton Harbor

Bayou Terrebonne

Little Lake Barataria

Barataria
Bay

Fort St. Philip

Round
Bay

Grand Terre

Terrebonne
Bay

Timbalier
Bay

Grand Bayou

Little Bayou

Chenier Caminada

Barataria Pass

Grand Isle

Fort Plaquemine

Balize

Cat Is.

The

PIRATES
LAFFITE

ALSO BY WILLIAM C. DAVIS

An Honorable Defeat:
The Last Days of the Confederate Government

Lincoln's Men:
How President Lincoln Became Father to an Army and a Nation

Three Roads to the Alamo:
The Lives and Fortunes of David Crockett, James Bowie,
and William Barret Travis

A Way Through the Wilderness:
The Natchez Trace and the Civilization
of the Southern Frontier

"A Government of Our Own":
The Making of the Confederacy

Jefferson Davis: The Man and His Hour

WILLIAM C. DAVIS

The
PIRATES
LAFFITE

The Treacherous World of the Corsairs of the Gulf

HARCOURT, INC.

Orlando Austin New York San Diego Toronto London

Requests for permission to make copies of any part of the work should be
mailed to the following address: Permissions Department, Harcourt, Inc.,
6277 Sea Harbor Drive, Orlando, Florida 32887-6777.

www.HarcourtBooks.com

Library of Congress Cataloging-in-Publication Data
Davis, William C., 1946–
The pirates Laffite: the treacherous world of the corsairs
of the Gulf/William C. Davis.—1st ed.
p.   cm.
Includes bibliographical references and index.
1. Laffite, Jean. 2. Laffite, Pierre, d. 1826? 3. Pirates—Louisiana—
Biography. 4. Pirates—Mexico, Gulf of—Biography. 5. Privateering—
Mexico, Gulf of—History—19th century. 6. New Orleans, Battle of,
New Orleans, La., 1815. 7. Louisiana—History—1803–1865—Biography.
8. Mexico, Gulf of—History—19th century.   I. Title.
F374.L2D385   2005
976.3'05'0922—dc22   2004029150
ISBN-13: 978-0-15-100403-4
ISBN-10: 0-15-100403-X

Text set in Adobe Caslon
Designed by Linda Lockowitz

Printed in the United States of America
First edition
A C E G I K J H F D B

For Bird, again

In the days of d'Arraguette,
He Ho He Ho!
It was the good old times.
You ruled the world with a switch—
He Ho He Ho!

—Old French Creole song, Anonymous

Why, sir, it will be very difficult to get at particulars,
some of them being of a strange character!
But there are some still living who had a hand in those matters.

—John Lambert, circa 1840

I found in my researches, twenty years ago, romantic
legends so interwoven with facts that it was extremely difficult
to separate the historical truth from the traditional.
I am sure that the same cause will make it impossible
to arrive at the truth of his life.
His only biographer at last must be the romancer.

—Joseph H. Ingraham, September 1, 1852

CONTENTS

He left a corsair's name to other times,
Linked with one virtue and a thousand crimes.

—LORD BYRON, "THE CORSAIR," 1816

PREFACE

A Corsair's Name

O N FEBRUARY 1, 1814, his publisher issued ten thousand copies of the great English poet Lord Byron's newest creation, "The Corsair," three cantos of brilliant imagination that quickly sold out and went into a second printing. In an age that thrilled at the idea of bold buccaneers defying authority and convention, the poet's tale of the gallant Captain Conrad, a pirate risking even his beloved ship *Medora* for the love of a slave girl forced into a *pasha's* harem, fed the appetite of a generation hungry for romance and adventure. How much more appealing was it when Conrad, having the cruel pasha at his mercy, refused to take his life even to save his own. It was his one "virtue," amid the life of crime.

It is poetically typical of the lives of the brothers Pierre and Jean Laffite, smugglers, merchants of contraband, revolutionaries, spies, privateers, and pirates as well, that so little in their memory fits their lives, and nothing less so than their persistent association with Byron's poetic epic. When he wrote it, the Laffites were nothing more than minor figures on the crowded criminal landscape of early Louisiana. The poet likely never heard of

either, and certainly his corsair was not patterned after Jean Laffite. Conrad's single virtue was a romantic device, and had nothing to do with the Laffites' celebrated and much exaggerated act
of patriotism in aiding American forces in repelling the British at
the Battle of New Orleans, which took place three weeks short of
a year after publication of "The Corsair." And yet, romance and
legend will not yield to break the bond between poem and pirate.

Throughout history, circumstances having nothing to do
with poetry and romance occasionally conspire to produce an environment perfect for the explosion and spread of privateering
and piracy, conditions that can vanish just as quickly as they appear. Never in the history of the United States were the times so
right for it as in the years of young nationhood, when an adoles-
cent America was beginning its spread across the continent amid
the clash of immigrant colonial cultures, and a European war of
gigantic proportions whose tremors upset the New World as
well. In unsettled times, enterprising men found opportunity to
build their own fortunes and wrest new nations away from old.
Many tried. Few succeeded. Some became legends. The privateer-
smugglers from Bordeaux and their ilk could not have flourished
at their craft anywhere other than there and then, any more than
the experience of the corsairs of the Gulf would have been the
same without the brothers Laffite. In the virtues and crimes of
them all lay not just the stuff of romance, but zephyrs to fill the
sails of the nascent American character.

The
PIRATES
LAFFITE

O'er the glad waters of the dark blue sea,
Our thoughts as boundless, and our soul's as free
Far as the breeze can bear, the billows foam,
Survey our empire, and behold our home!

ONE

Vintage Bordeaux
1770-1803

P ERHAPS IT IS FITTING for men whose lives so lent themselves to adventure and melodrama that their name traced its origins to a word meaning something like "the song." For centuries men named Lafitte inhabited the fertile reaches between the river Garonne and the Pyrenees Mountains that separated France from Spain. Proximity to the often lawless Pyrenees, and life in the part of France most remote from the center of politics and culture in Paris, encouraged a spirit of independence in the region's inhabitants, and a tendency to look as much to the world as to their country for opportunity. Among those named for "the song," that independence appeared in their stubborn refusal of a uniform spelling of their name. Lafitte, Lafit, Laffitt, Laffite, and more, all emerged between the river and the mountains, and for many the song in their name was a Siren's call to the broader world. Immediate access to the sea on the Bay of Biscay tied many of them to trade and seafaring. The lush vineyards on either side of the Garonne, and the Gironde estuary formed at its confluence with the Dordogne River, turned more of them into vintners.

The ancient village of Pauillac perched on the west bank of the Gironde estuary exactly midway between Bordeaux and the Bay of Biscay at Pointe de Grave some thirty miles distant.[1] It was about as far up the estuary as the limited maneuverability of sail could bring oceangoing ships, making it a natural port for the merchants of Bordeaux and the surrounding region. Though small, it was already the informal capital of the Medoc, and just now starting to blossom thanks to the produce of its vineyards. One Laffite family, and apparently only one of that spelling, lived in the village.[2] Jean Laffite and his wife, Anne Denis, saw their son Pierre marry Marie Lagrange in 1769, but the young woman died, perhaps giving birth to a son Pierre around 1770.[3] In 1775 the father Pierre remarried, this time to Marguerite Desteil, who bore six children at their home in the little village of Bages just south of Pauillac. Three daughters lived to maturity, as did a son Jean, born around 1782 or later but not baptized until 1786.[4]

Most of the Laffites living in the Bordeaux were solidly middle-class merchants and traders, and the elder Pierre Laffite appears to have been in trade himself.[5] Certainly he was able to give his two sons at least rudimentary schooling, though their written grammar, spelling, and syntax would never be better than mediocre.[6] Whoever taught them to write—parent, priest, or schoolmaster—could not keep a natural independence out of their developing handwriting, for neither boy learned very good penmanship, but their teacher left some artifacts of his rote with them. All their lives, the half brothers signed their surname in identical fashion, lifting the pen from the paper midway and leaving a barely perceptible space before finishing, to produce "Laff ite."

What they might have made of themselves in France would never be known, for they were born into a changing and uncertain world. The Bourbon kings of France, living in increasing isolation among an in-bred and calcified aristocracy, had long since lost touch with the people and the times. The emergent middle class, especially merchants like the Laffites of the Bordeaux, felt crushed under the weight of taxation and church levies imposed to provide for the outrageous extravagance of the aristocracy and clergy. The Gironde became a seedbed of antipathy, and the Laffites would not have been men of their class if they did not share the general outrage.

It all came to an explosion in the summer of 1789, and by the fall of 1795 the people of the Bordeaux, like all Frenchmen, felt nervous exhaustion after six years of constant turmoil. By the time elections were held in October for delegates to a new Convention to rule in Paris until a regular government should take over under a new constitution, Pierre Laffite may well have been financially ruined as were so many other merchants. Even as an ardent young captain named Napoleon Bonaparte saved both the Convention and the new constitution by turning away an uprising that sought to disrupt the elections, Laffite's sons Pierre and Jean could only look on what must have seemed a blighted future landscape.[7]

The son Pierre, his schooling long over, lived and probably worked with his father at Number 49 Rue de la Deliverance in Bordeaux, trying to keep their business alive. Jean, perhaps aged about fourteen, likely saw his education disrupted by the turmoil that he had lived with for fully half his life. Just what each of them felt about it all he never said, but like many others of their class they imbibed a general—if not passionate—belief in local autonomy as preferable to central rule from afar, and from the turmoil and dissolution in their immediate region they learned the lesson that in troublous times, on the frontiers of civil authority, the wise man took care of himself first.

They may even have seen object lessons in how a man could profit during times of political and social upheaval if he was smart, daring, and none too scrupulous. A later acquaintance of

the Laffites' recalled being told that the brothers had been contraband smugglers on the Spanish border during the times of
scarcity, which would have been one way to combat severe price
controls.[8] And they were anyhow close enough to the Pyrenees to
fall under the age-old lure of smuggling as a remedy from the
greedy excise man.

Whatever the Laffites learned of making their way in the
world, by the end of the decade it was evident to them that they
would not make it in their native country. Economic recovery
would take years, and even with a new constitution and with the
Terror at an end, civil affairs remained shaky or dependent on a
military that was now embroiled in contests of arms all across
Europe, and with England as well. Then in December 1796 their
father Pierre died. Thousands of Frenchmen from their region
had emigrated, reestablishing themselves in the colonies in the
New World far from the reach of the Jacobins and the guillotine.
Many a royalist had gone to Spanish Louisiana, and other
colonies thrived on the islands of San Domingue, Martinique,
and Guadaloupe in the Caribbean. It was a natural direction to
turn their eyes.

And so sometime in the last of that decade they began disap-
pearing, and completely. For years barely a trace of them survives.
A third brother, name unknown, may have left France first, or
Jean may have gone about the turn of the century. Then on May
24, 1802, Pierre obtained a passport, saying he was "going to
Louisiana to join one of his brothers."[9] Perhaps he was the same
Pierre Laffite from Pauillac, and his 1802 departure from Bour-
deaux was only the return from a visit home from the colony.
Two-thirds of French commercial trade was with the island
which was half French and half Spanish until 1795 when France
got it all. French merchant ships called first at Cap Français, and
some then went on to New Orleans despite an official edict from
Madrid prohibiting trade with the colonies of other powers as

well as restrictions imposed by Paris. If Pierre Laffite was involved in trade at Port-au-Prince, then he might have had cause to know of and perhaps even to visit New Orleans. Nevertheless, he found that he could not escape the Revolution. Once again, inept and corrupt rule from a great distance created unrest, here compounded by a large and resentful black population. San Domingue had only 20,000 white inhabitants, while more than 100,000 free blacks and mulattoes owned one-third of the land and a fourth of the half million slaves in the colony, creating a hierarchy in which whites looked down on free blacks and mulattoes, who in turn looked down on slaves.[10]

A series of slave rebellions beginning in 1790 sent waves of white planters fleeing the island. Whenever he first arrived in San Domingue, Pierre Laffite spent at least some time in Le Cap, as Cap Français was called. He may have been there to witness the fighting on June 20, 1793, when about two thousand mariners and political prisoners on ships in the harbor rose and landed under arms to attack the government buildings. French commander Leger Felicité Sonthonax won a temporary victory, but by the summer of 1794 the British, now at war with France, held Port-au-Prince, and the Pierre Laffite living there left for Savannah, Georgia, with the flood of émigrés.[11] But then, lured by Sonthonax's declaration of emancipation, former slave Toussaint Louverture, now commanding most of the free black and slave forces, joined forces with the French to eject the British. By this time the Spanish were also involved, and in time both Britain and Spain would entrench themselves trying to keep what they could of San Domingue.

Meanwhile the Pierre Laffite who left Port-au-Prince in 1794 returned once the British were contained. He may have been back in Le Cap in May 1800 when black workers rebelled in the north and thousands marched on Le Cap to take it back from the Spanish. Or he may have been there later in October 1801 when farm workers rose up and killed three hundred white colonists.[12] But most likely he was there in 1802 after sailing under his passport and making a stop on his way to Louisiana. In January 1802 Napoleon, now risen to emperor in France, sent an army under General Charles Leclerc to reestablish control. Instead the French met disaster. Leclerc was soon all but besieged in Cap Français, and that summer he burned most of the town. In November he died of yellow fever and his successor, General Donathien Rochambeau, resorted to wholesale extermination of blacks and mulattoes. Napoleon could not help him as he had gone to war with Britain again in May, and in March 1803 the black population of San Domingue rose again in revolt. Rochambeau holed up in Le Cap after losing control of the countryside, and was besieged, while British ships returned to establish a blockade of the harbor.

By that time Pierre Laffite was most certainly gone for good. What role he took, if any, in the upheavals on the island is unknown. On May 10, 1802, as Pierre prepared to leave Bordeaux, an Antoine Lafitte was waylaid at Port-Republicain and marched off with a number of other white citizens and was murdered.[13] He may even have been the brother Pierre was going to visit. When Pierre arrived, he was himself caught in the street fighting in Cap Français. One day on the Place St. Pierre, Laffite and his friend Bernard Narieu and others found themselves in the middle of the deadly swirl. Laffite and Narieu escaped to safety, but not before they saw one of their acquaintances, a Mr. Gabauriau whom Pierre may have known back in France,[14] fall victim to the mob. It was a good time for Laffite to be leaving, and where else to go but a place so many he knew had gone before him, a place with which he may well have had some acquaintance already, New Orleans.[15]

That spring and summer of 1803 French privateers began ferrying refugees to Cuba and New Orleans, getting out as many of the white French as possible before Rochambeau surrendered on November 29, 1803. Among the exiles was Jean Joseph Amable Humbert, a somewhat unstable visionary who went back to France, though his life would intertwine with the Laffites in years to come.[16] Also fleeing San Domingue were a promising young architect named Arsené Latour, only recently arrived to take a position as engineer on Rochambeau's staff, and Barthelemey Lafon, a gifted surveyor who mixed privateering with mapmaking. Lafon escaped to Havana in 1802, and Latour got out sometime before November 1803, and perhaps escaped on a privateer, first to Cuba, then to New Orleans. Like Humbert and many another refugees from San Domingue, they would reappear in the Laffite story, though nothing suggests that Pierre was acquainted with them in Cap Français.[17]

Pierre Laffite left on one of those refugee ships no later than early March 1803, and if he went that late then he did not go alone.[18] By the time he put San Domingue permanently behind him, Pierre Laffite had an infant son.[19]

These are our realms, no limits to their sway—
Our flag the sceptre all who meet obey.
Ours the wild life in tumult still to range
From toil to rest, and joy in every change.

TWO

New Men in a New World
1803-1806

I N 1803 NEW ORLEANS was overwhelmingly a French community, though so many languages and colors were to be seen on
its streets that it was truly a city of the world. It had changed
hands often since its founding by the French in 1718. France had
ceded the vast inland empire known as Louisiana to Spain in
1762, but in 1801 in the Treaty of Madrid, Napoleon reclaimed
Louisiana as part of the spoils of his reduction of Spain to a vas-
sal state. Now, even as Laffite walked the streets of New Orleans,
Napoleon was negotiating the sale of the Louisiana Territory to
the infant United States.

New Orleans itself made up several dozen square blocks of
creole and colonial houses on the northwest side of a crescent
bend in the Mississippi River, all still encased in the remnants of
an earthen rampart remaining from its earlier defenses. The
Place d'Arms sat just back from the river, an open square on
which stood the Cathedral Church of St. Louis, with the territorial prison and guardhouse to one side and an ecclesiastical charity house on the other. Street names redolent of French and
Spanish history—Chartres, Royal, Bourbon, Dauphine, Bur-

gundy, and Rampart—paralleled the levee road at the river's edge. Intersecting them were others of equal association—Bienville, St. Louis, Conti, Toulouse, St. Pierre, Orleans, St. Anne, Dumaine, St. Philip, and more. Many of the blocks at the outer periphery close to the rampart were yet vacant, while to the east, beyond the rampart, already Faubourg Marigny was growing, mainly the home of the large free black and mulatto community.

Pierre Laffite may not have found reestablishing himself in New Orleans to be as easy as he could have hoped. In 1803 an arriving refugee faced paying $10 to $20 a month for lodging in a quiet suburb of town.[1] Pierre first took rented quarters on Royal Street, probably near the intersection with Dumaine, while looking for a suitable venue to go into business. A newcomer had to pay $25 to $80 a month to rent a well-located commercial building.[2] Instead of renting, however, on March 21, and at a cost of 8,000 silver Spanish pesos, Pierre bought from the widow Marguerite Landreaux a city lot one block east of the Place d'Arms, at the intersection of Royal and Dumaine. It came with a substantial house and outbuildings, including probably a small warehouse, if the selling price be any measure. The site had a mercantile history, having belonged until 1800 to the late Julian Vienne, an importer with San Domingue connections who had operated two merchant vessels prior to his death, and who may well have done business with Laffite in years past.[3] Laffite bought it in partnership with Joseph Maria Bourguignon, a member of a New Orleans family dating back at least to 1728. Bourguignon lived on Dumaine, and he and Pierre may have become acquainted when Laffite took lodgings around the corner. Evidently they did not have much by way of cash in hand, however, for they promised to pay the widow half of the purchase price at the end of June, and the balance at the end of 1804.[4]

Within a few weeks Laffite had to borrow 320 pesos from an innkeeper, the Spaniard Pedro Alarcon, who was known to conduct an unlawful gambling table that might have increased

Pierre's indebtedness.[5] Thereafter Pierre's financial affairs reveal a chronic shortage of ready cash, and with it a tendency to live beyond either his means or his ability to manage his money.[6] Indeed, only eleven weeks after signing the papers for the Royal Street property, Laffite and Bourguignon returned it to Landreaux in return for cancellation of their debt on June 6, probably after finding that they could not make the first installment due at the end of that month.[7] Pierre Laffite had been a property owner for less than three months, and would never own a house or land again.

The exact nature of Laffite's mercantile enterprise is unclear but, despite later myth and recollection to the contrary, it almost certainly was not ironworking.[8] Dumaine in that period was known as the "Street of the Stores," and would have been the place to be if Laffite, like fully one-fourth of the other refugees from San Domingue, was a merchant.[9] He may have expected to import goods from abroad or perhaps from Havana, but with so many newly arrived merchants in New Orleans added to the established houses, competition would have been keen, especially for a man of limited resources. In 1803 merchants led all other professions in the city, selling chiefly cargoes imported by ship. Most were middlemen who did not own the ships themselves, but already it was evident that the real fortunes would be made by men who controlled both the importation and sale of their wares.[10] Doing that would require more capital than Pierre Laffite could command at the moment, however, and more likely, he hoped to trade in goods from the Louisiana Territory interior, a market still being developed. Indeed, the crowding in New Orleans just then may have forced him to that alternative.[11]

Unfortunately for Pierre Laffite, he arrived near the end of the massive immigration from San Domingue. Refugees from the Haitian revolts arrived in New Orleans at a steady rate, starting at a trickle of about one hundred per year from 1791 to 1797 and reaching more than 1,000 by 1803. The French-speaking community in the city welcomed the white arrivals, and at first they did not mind lots of San Domingue slaves coming with them. By 1803, though, just under 4,000 whites were barely out-numbered by 4,100 blacks, a third of them free.[12] Already under-currents of fear were palpable in the white community, especially with the example of San Domingue if not on their doorstep then certainly in their front yard. Then there was the question of changing nationalities. Americans spreading into the Ohio and upper Mississippi River valleys needed the Mississippi for access to markets. The Spaniards had closed the port of New Orleans to them, effectively stifling trade, at the same time leaving America's back door vulnerable to European aggression. When Spain turned the Louisiana Territory over to an aggressive Napoleonic France in 1801 President Thomas Jefferson's anxiety for the infant United States' western border only heightened, as he expected Napoleon to keep the river closed. Moreover, with France at war with Britain, a British victory could put America's onetime colo-nial master in control of the Mississippi, with every manner of foreseeable unfortunate consequence. Rumors of an expedition being readied to invade Louisiana and take it from France only spurred Jefferson to action.[13]

Jefferson sent Robert Livingston and James Monroe to France to negotiate an open port at New Orleans and free trade for the United States. But changing circumstances in Europe made Napoleon amenable to much more than that, and in April 1803 Jefferson's emissaries were asked point-blank what they would pay for the Louisiana Territory. By the end of that month Jefferson had all of it from the Gulf of Mexico to the Pacific northwest, in-cluding the so-called island of New Orleans—that small portion of land east of the Mississippi running from the Gulf through Lake Borgne, west through Lake Pontchartrain on the city's northern outskirts, and thence through Lake Maurepas and along the Amite River and Bayou Manchac to its mouth on the Mississippi seventy miles upstream from New Orleans. Above that lay the parishes of Spanish West Florida.

Pierre Laffite was probably in New Orleans on December 20, 1803, when the formal ceremony turning over the government of Louisiana took place on the Place d'Arms. General James Wilkinson and new territorial governor William C. C. Claiborne accepted the keys of the city from the French commissioner and then raised the flag of the United States, "amidst the acclamations of the inhabitants" according to an American present.[14] Many of the French and Spanish citizens saw the reaction rather differently, however, and one spoke of "the lugubriousness of the silence and immobility" among the Frenchmen and Spaniards and the locally born European Creoles.[15] It would not be the last mark of a subdivision in the white community, nor of conflicting loyalties among the Europeans that would one day make the livelihood of Pierre Laffite and ultimately direct his destiny. Significantly, Jefferson sent several gunboats to New Orleans to protect order among what their naval commander David Porter regarded as "a very turbulent population."[16]

Claiborne had already promised to the European community in New Orleans all the protections of United States citizens, and the carryover of all previous laws and civil officers except those who collected the customs, who would now be federal appointees.[17]

Within months of the American takeover, the character of the city began to change as its new masters imposed order on its chaotic streets and in its civil affairs. More new shops opened almost overnight as American merchants rushed to the city to capitalize on the new world marketplace. The influx increased the population to twelve thousand. What the influx meant for Pierre Laffite and other San Domingue refugee merchants was even more competition in a crowded market. They had almost monopolized trading to this point, even spreading out over the rural sections of lower Louisiana and along the inland bayous.[18] Many turned peddler, getting a year's credit from wholesale suppliers in New Orleans and then taking their goods to the interior and accepting payment in furs and agricultural goods that they returned to sell in the city's marketplace to pay their debt and outfit for the next trading trip.[19]

Pierre Laffite decided to become one of them, or at least to seek prosperity outside the immediate orbit of New Orleans. Sometime prior to the fall of 1804, he settled at the post of Baton Rouge in Spanish West Florida, some seventy-five miles upriver from New Orleans, and there went into business as a merchant once more.[20] Baton Rouge sat on the east bank of the river, home to a small garrison and a regional commandant under orders from the administrative center at Pensacola, 250 miles to the east. Aside from the Spaniards in the garrison, the locals were mostly German, Irish, and French-speaking Acadian immigrants from Canada. Baton Rouge was truly a frontier, for beyond it living conditions became increasingly primitive with the exception of the community thirty miles upstream at Point Coupée.

Point Coupée had been in 1766 a string of settlements running about twenty miles along the west bank of the Mississippi, augmented by others on a nearby "false river"—a former bend of the Mississippi cut off and isolated as a lake when the river changed its course. A fort, a four-bastioned quadrangle, with stockade and commandant's house, barracks, storehouses, and a prison stood there. Spain kept barely more than a dozen soldiers stationed there in 1766, along with a capuchin father to operate the church near the fort. About two thousand white inhabitants and seven thousand slaves grew tobacco, indigo, and corn and raised poultry that they sold in New Orleans to victuallers from the merchant ships. They also cut timber and sent lumber and staves downriver in rafts. After 1762 and the Spanish takeover,

most of the planters who were cultivating on the east side moved
to the west bank.[21]

Now Point Coupée was an enclave of wealth without the os-
tentation of New Orleans. Its planters, proud and jealous of each
other, eschewed dancing, gambling, and fine clothes. The English-
speaking planters lived on the east bank of the Mississippi and
traded more with Natchez upstream than with New Orleans. In
earlier years they produced furs, indigo, bear oil, and game, as
well as salt beef and pork. Now, however, they planted cotton,
which accounted for their advancing affluence. Their money attracted merchants, and by 1804 new stores appeared constantly,
offering credit to the planters and saving them a trip to Natchez
or New Orleans for goods. Itinerant merchants called *caboteurs*
peddled from their boats, moving on the river and bayous plantation by plantation in their flat-bottomed pirogues. Most were
French sailors stuck in Louisiana by the current war. They sold
poor quality merchandise at low prices due to the intense competition among them, and became so numerous that travelers met
them at all times on the river. The *caboteurs* bartered goods for
chickens, eggs, hides, grease and tallow, honey, corn and rice,
beans, and anything else they could sell in New Orleans, in the
process becoming the chief source of fresh produce in the city.
They also traded illicitly with the slaves, selling *tafia*—a cheap
rum substitute—and oddments in return for chickens and other
stolen items. The whites frequently complained of the thefts encouraged by the *caboteurs,* but to no avail. Meanwhile itinerant
peddlers competed by working their trade on foot or in carriages.[22]

Point Coupée was more than a planter community. River
travelers stopped there en route to Natchez. Those moving into
the western Louisiana interior via the Red River used the river-
bank there as a staging place, providing a trade in fur, horses, tallow, and Indian produce. By the time Pierre Laffite came to the
area, the population of Point Coupée—also called False River—

had declined, but still maintained a typically imbalanced population in which two-thirds were slaves.[23]

Seemingly unable to avoid turmoil wherever he moved, Pierre Laffite arrived in the Baton Rouge–Point Coupée vicinity in the middle of a brief revolution. In August 1804 Nathan and Samuel Kemper, brothers from a perpetually turbulent family, led about thirty men in a march on Baton Rouge to throw out the Spanish and declare West Florida independent. They maintained that the so-called West Florida Parishes were really part of the Louisiana Territory and should have been ceded to the United States. The people refused to rise up with them, however, and so the Kempers simply plundered the countryside then retreated northward into the United States' newly created Mississippi Territory, pursued by Spanish militia. Spain's officials protested to Claiborne, who acted as governor of Mississippi as well as interim governor of Louisiana, but he declined to extradite the Kempers and their followers. To protect Spain's interests and discourage any further outbreaks, Vicente Folche, governor of West Florida, collected a professional garrison and brought it to Baton Rouge.[24]

Folche arrived not long after Laffite went into business, and in the days ahead the two became at least passingly acquainted as the governor oversaw even the most minor legal transactions. Indeed, soon after his arrival Laffite became well known to local officials including Don Carlos de Grand-Pré, colonel of the Spanish Royal Army commanding the post of Baton Rouge, and on the other side of the river Julian Poydras, the new American civil judge representing the United States in Point Coupée. By October 1804 Pierre had other connections in Point Coupée as well, sufficient that a local widow engaged him as her attorney to sell, exchange, or otherwise dispose of for her profit two of her slaves who had been imprisoned in Pensacola. The prison term of one of them was about to expire, and now she authorized Laffite to act on her behalf in New Orleans, or in any Spanish court in Havana, or even distant Vera Cruz, Mexico, or wherever else the slaves might be found after their release, to reclaim and dispose of them. In the process, she transferred all her rights in the slaves to Pierre, evidence of his ability not only to instill trust in her, but also to convince her that he had connections far beyond the sphere of rural Louisiana.[25] Her confidence in Pierre was well placed, for within two weeks he sold one of the slaves several months in advance of his anticipated release, and the buyer was none other than Folche.[26] The transaction reveals the effort that Laffite put into establishing good connections with both Spanish and American authorities, something that was always good for a businessman, and a pattern he continued in the years ahead. More than that, though, this was his first experience in the New World at profiting by the sale of a slave.[27]

Pierre's transaction for the widow touched upon another tension in the region, for her slaves had been imprisoned for taking part in a rebellion against white control. Real and imagined insurrection plots, some inspired by the San Domingue example, unsettled Point Coupée and West Florida from the 1790s onward.[28] By 1804, isolated from one another, whites lived in constant fear of slave uprisings and mounted nightly patrols of their plantation environs.[29] On November 9 inhabitants of Point Coupée drafted a petition asking Claiborne to send militia to protect them from yet another feared slave uprising. Laffite did not sign, but as a resident of Baton Rouge he would certainly have shared their apprehension.[30]

By July 1804 Claiborne felt sufficient concern for the public safety that he had ships stopped at the Balize, a customs point covering the intersection of the three delta channels that connected the Mississippi with the Gulf to keep San Domingue slaves from coming into Louisiana.[31] This fear of introducing insurrection from San Domingue made the importation of slaves to

Louisiana difficult at a time when the demand to put more and more land under cultivation was driving up the price of slaves. A slaveowner could make up to $30 a month by renting a slave. Slaves fresh from Africa sold for $500 or more, while a skilled Louisiana slave could bring up to $1,400.[32]

Pierre Laffite was in Baton Rouge when the apprehension at Point Coupée reached its height. Indeed, as a resident merchant he could be expected to be in Baton Rouge most of the time, though like other traders he may not have depended entirely upon the *caboteurs* to bring him goods.[33] Most likely he made buying trips into the interior to barter for goods to sell downriver. The trading boats used by merchants like Laffite were open, with only a *tendelet*—usually just a pole frame with canvas over it for shelter—raised above the deck at the stern for the owner, the captain, and his friends. Some pirogues carried up to one hundred barrels under their canvas covering, with rowers crowded on either side of the cargo. They could row six leagues a day, as much as eighteen miles, and farther with a current behind them. Traders hired the boatmen by the trip or by the month at about a dollar a day.[34]

If Laffite made any of these buying trips himself, he could not have helped but learn something of the geography of the immediate interior, from the tiny Spanish settlement of Galvezton to the east, to the system of bayous on the west side of the Mississippi below Point Coupée.[35] Most important of all was Bayou Lafourche, a distributary that took high water from the Mississippi from a point thirty miles downriver from Baton Rouge all the way to the Gulf, bypassing New Orleans. It was too narrow for sailing vessels to navigate, and often too shallow in summer drought, but with only a few feet of water in it the light draft pirogues could easily row up and down its entire length. That made it ideal not only for trading with Indians and the more reclusive trappers and hunters in the backcountry, but also for smuggling goods past New Orleans to Baton Rouge, or else for evading United States customs inspectors at the Mississippi's mouth by bringing commodities up the Lafourche to the big river, then downstream to New Orleans by the back door. Pierre Laffite may not have used Bayou Lafourche for that purpose, for smuggling did not offer very rich rewards in 1804 and 1805, but before long it would, and the knowledge gained here now would be very useful one day.

West Florida's administrative center at Pensacola also offered a profitable market for goods the merchants at Baton Rouge acquired in the region, especially now when the Pensacola merchants John Forbes and Company, successors to Panton and Leslie Company, began expanding eastward.[36] Pierre Laffite might have found that prospect attractive, and certainly developed some contacts for future exploitation in Pensacola, but taking goods to the Pensacola market himself would have been a long and costly journey.

Indeed, sometime in 1805, and perhaps within less than a year of moving to Baton Rouge, Pierre decided that his fortune was not to be made in this backwater. The continuing political turbulence may have helped persuade him to leave, for in August 1805 the Kempers tried and failed once more to take Baton Rouge. Spanish officials sent reinforcements at the same time that relations between the United States and Spain began to deteriorate. A clear threat of war loomed. Jefferson had wanted to acquire Florida from Spain when he bought Louisiana from France, believing those parishes essential to protecting New Orleans from above.[37] Robert Livingston had advised on May 20, 1803, that if necessary the United States should take West Florida by force before Britain did. Following the Louisiana Purchase, Livingston continued to argue that West Florida had been included in what France originally understood it received from Spain, but Spain refused to sell.[38] In the growing discord, Folche felt such concern that he tried to get West Florida and the province of Texas immediately west of Louisiana heavily reinforced by Spain.[39]

The tense atmosphere threatened to make Baton Rouge an unhealthy place for a merchant should war erupt, and Laffite turned once more to New Orleans. He was back in the city as early as March 1805, though not yet on a permanent basis.[40] Indeed, since he owned no property in the city, he well could have divided his time between rented lodging in New Orleans and Baton Rouge as he continued bringing upstream trade to the city marketplace. By July his associates knew that he did not intend to stay indefinitely, and perhaps had even contemplated leaving not only New Orleans, but the territory itself.[41]

At that very moment an unfounded rumor that the diplomatic crisis might result in ceding Louisiana back to the Spaniards circulated, which in itself could have suggested to Laffite that he look elsewhere.[42] But his first allegiance now and in the future was to his trade and livelihood, and he was already thinking of strengthening his ties in Pensacola. A much more powerful inducement for him to think about leaving New Orleans was debt, for yet again he could not pay what he owed. How much was due and to how many creditors is uncertain, but in July merchant Stephen Carraby filed a civil suit against him in the parish court for a mere $122 after Pierre repeatedly ignored demands for payment. Carraby demanded Laffite's arrest if he did not pay.[43] Carraby may have been one of those who extended credit to Laffite for trade goods to be sent upriver, but since Carraby also traded in slaves, the debt may have been owed from a slave purchase.[44] It may even have been money borrowed for an earlier slave purchase that went awry, when Pierre Laffite had what was probably his first direct experience with both smuggling and illegal slaves.

In November 1804 the Spanish merchant schooner *Nuestra Senora del Carmen,* out of the port of Campeche on Mexico's

Yucatán peninsula, anchored at the Balize. She had regularly brought slave cargoes to New Orleans for the past twenty years or more, but now supposedly carried only a cargo of logwood and a rowdy crew of Spaniards and other "rabble" that the customs inspector thought were "mostly a lot of ill looking Wretches, and a medley of all the Indies and Campeache included." They promised to be a challenge to keeping the peace if they reached New Orleans, he warned. More to the point, he found them in concert with the denizens of a house near English Turn, a tight bend in the river a few miles downstream from New Orleans, where a Spaniard kept a tavern on the east bank, and from which smugglers used a bayou for landing and transporting to the city illicit goods secreted past the inspector at the Balize.[45]

The inspector managed to keep the schooner at anchor for several weeks, but Captain Jean Baptiste Deyrem landed several slaves without his knowing it and got them to New Orleans for sale.[46] More than that, after the inspector duly recorded a free black woman named Marie Zabeth and her infant child as passengers, a privateer named Juan Buatista Elie came aboard the detained ship and simply took them, either by force or with the collusion of Deyrem.[47] As soon as Elie's vessel reached New Orleans, he sold mother and child into slavery. The buyer was Pierre Laffite. Zabeth, however, almost immediately turned to the parish superior court, where in December 1805 she won her suit and their freedom.[48] Laffite almost certainly did not get his money back from Elie, money that he may well have borrowed from Carraby.

Just why Laffite bought Zabeth is unclear. He was not dealing commercially in slaves, at least not in 1805. Though he had no established home of his own in New Orleans, however, Laffite may have needed a woman with housekeeping experience, which Zabeth had from her time in Port-au-Prince. Whoever mothered his son born in San Domingue, by 1805 she seems to have been out of the picture and Pierre needed someone to take care of his boy, who presumably stayed with him whether here or in Baton Rouge. Moreover, by this time he was involved with a woman who could use a housekeeper, as there would be others on the way to care for as well.

A three-tiered racial structure—white, free black and mulatto, and slave—prevailed in New Orleans, as did a gender imbalance imported with the influx of white men from San Domingue. Whites and free blacks could not marry by law, and free blacks and slaves could not marry. However, if a working or merchant class white male wanted to have feminine company on a stable basis, a mulatto mistress offered an acceptable alternative to participating in the heavy competition for the few eligible white women in the city. As a result, color lines blurred in New Orleans more than anywhere else in the young United States.

A visitor to the city the same year that Laffite first arrived complained that there were taverns seemingly on every corner, open all hours, with white and black, free and slave, mingling indiscriminately. Best known of them was "the famous house of Coquet," as the proprietor called it, "where all the scum is to be seen publicly." Three years earlier Bernardo Coquet opened his dance hall on St. Philip between Bourbon and Royal Streets, only a few blocks from Pierre Laffite's first residence in town. He originally intended it for white and free black revelers, but quickly slaves in the city gathered there as well. Coquet held dances every Sunday night, and twice a week during the annual Shrove Tuesday carnival in February.

In 1805 Coquet rented the St. Philip Street ballroom to Auguste Tessier, and in November Tessier renamed the hall the Salle Chinoise and began holding two balls a week for white men and free colored women. His operation would last until the summer of 1807 when Coquet returned to continue the business under a succession of names, but maintained Tessier's practice of allowing no colored men to attend the dances. The intention that they be a setting for liaisons was clear.

The "quadroon balls" promoted a custom called *plaçage*, very likely imported to New Orleans by the refugees from San Domingue, in which free mixed-blood women paraded themselves before eligible white men hoping to make a match of convenience and, if possible, romance.[49] Meaning essentially "placement," *plaçage* was economically far more advantageous for a free black woman than a marriage with a free black male, and because many quadroons had so little African blood that they were nearly white, they would not marry full blacks or mulattoes, whom they considered socially inferior. Mothers sometimes contractually placed their daughters at ages as young as thirteen or fourteen with white men, including married men looking for mistresses. A virtual business arrangement was reached whereby the woman became the man's mistress and bore and raised his children, but he did not get to cohabit with her until he had bought her a house, preferably near Rampart Street, and all the trappings of domesticity, sometimes including slaves. (In New Orleans many free blacks owned slaves, and 70 percent of those black slaveowners were women, who also owned much more real estate than black men thanks to the gifts of their *plaçage* mates.[50]) He also agreed to provide for her for life and for their children, and to give her a settlement if they separated. Any children were regarded as "natural," and were set apart from bastards. The men often gave the young women some education, and taught their brothers a trade.

Socially, New Orleans in 1805 disappointed some visitors, one complaining that there was scarcely a pane of window glass in the city, and the streets were little more than rivulets of mud and water with decaying rats and house pets in the puddles. "The eternal jabbering of French in the street was a sealed book to us," recalled Thomas Nicholls in 1840.[51] Many of those French "jabberers" were the San Domingue refugees who gathered at the "Café des Refugiés" or "Café des Émigrés" run by Jean Thiot on Chartres Street, next door to the Hôtel de la Marine, the haunt of gamblers and more disreputable elements.[52] Pierre Laffite probably visited there with his friends from earlier days when in New Orleans, though most likely he did not meet Marie Louise Villard there, but at one of Coquet's or Tessier's balls.[53] She was about twenty-one years old, a free mulatto or quadroon born in New Orleans about 1784 to a white father and a free black or mulatto mother Marie Villard, who was of a family of free mixed blood Villards who had been in Louisiana since the 1760s.[54] Pierre may not have entered into a formal *plaçage* arrangement with Marie Villard, for among other things he seems hardly able to afford the upkeep of a woman in New Orleans, but very soon she and Laffite began a relationship that would last for the next sixteen years.

With fear of slave revolt making refugees from San Domingue unwelcome in Louisiana, Laffite may well have faced a coolness that made New Orleans less than hospitable, a situation only compounded by his problems with Stephen Carraby. When Carraby determined that Pierre had no real property in New Orleans that he could seize to satisfy his debt, he demanded that Laffite be arrested and held to bail until he paid. Judge Thomas Kennedy summoned Pierre to appear at the courthouse in the first week of August or else face judgment by default, but when the sheriff, George Ross, tried to locate Pierre to serve the summons, he reported that Laffite was nowhere to be found and had no known address.[55]

Pierre Laffite may have taken his son and Marie Villard with him, for now she was pregnant and dependent upon him, and he had not installed her in a house of her own in New Orleans.[56] Or more likely she remained in the city living with relatives and keeping Pierre's boy with her. Pierre probably went back to Baton

Rouge, where he had trading connections, and apparently he profited well enough on the trip that he returned to New Orleans by November, openly and presumably without fear of arrest.

That was because he also came back with a new calling— slave dealer. Where he acquired the slaves, or the money to buy them, is unclear, but that same November he sold two young males for more than enough to satisfy the debt to Carraby and several hundred dollars to spare.[57] In the next five months he sold nine more slaves for a combined $4,880.[58] It was a small fortune to a man who the year before almost went to jail for a debt of $122. It was also a revelation, as if Laffite needed one, that a man could spend months making pennies trading upriver for hides and tallow, or acquire substantial affluence almost overnight by bringing black gold from Africa to a hungry New Orleans marketplace. Of course one had to buy one's stock cheaply in order to realize a good profit, and to do that could mean stepping outside the law. But then, seemingly everyone else was doing it, or looking the other way in order to realize their own bargains.

He might even have a partner in his brother Jean.

Oh, who can tell, save he whose heart hath tried,
And danced in triumph o'er the waters wide,
The exulting sense—the pulse's maddening play,
That thrills the wanderer of that trackless way?

THREE

Brothers United
1806-1809

FROM THE MOMENT of his birth in Pauillac to more than
twenty years thereafter, Jean Laffite's life is a complete mystery, though it is virtually certain that at some point he chose the
sea for his livelihood. Unlike his brother Pierre, who would always
be a land-bound merchant dependent upon trade from the oceans,
Jean walked the decks of the ships, and by early manhood acquired enough experience before the mast to command merchant
vessels at least. He felt at home on the small sailing feluccas with
their mainmast and triangular sails, the single-masted schooners,
and even the larger merchant brigantines that carried most of the
oceanic and Gulf trade. Where and how he acquired his seamanship is part of his mystery, though likely he started on the Gironde
estuary on vessels owned by or trading with his father. After that
he may have shipped on merchantmen, or even entered the
French navy, but here, too, the page is blank. He may just possibly
have been in San Domingue in the merchant trade with Pierre by
1802.[1] What is certain, though, is that by 1806 more than one
"Captain Lafitte," under varying spellings, commanded merchant

and privateering vessels in American waters, and one of them was probably Pierre's brother.[2]

The most tantalizing possibility among them is the commander of the French privateer *La Soeur Cherie*. She appeared off Louisiana in April 1804 accompanied by two prize vessels. Her captain knew the locale well enough, or had aboard a sufficiently knowledgeable pilot, to avoid the customs inspector at the Balize by entering the Mississippi from a less used side channel. Territorial officials stopped her at the tiny post at Fort Plaquemine a dozen miles upstream. The unarmed prizes were allowed to pass on, while the captain sent word to the authorities in New Orleans that his ship was in distress. He asked permission to take on fresh water and provisions and to come upriver to the city for refitting and repairs.[3] Permission granted, he tied up at the city wharf after dawn on April 25.

In New Orleans in 1804 the customshouse was run by about six people. Unlike their Spanish predecessors, American officials did not yet search ships carefully. A ship arrived and the captain made his declaration of the contents of his cargo and then unloaded it without problems. The passengers likewise made their personal declarations, and then went on their way. If an irregularity were discovered later, the ship could be seized, but by that time it was often gone.[4] Now, once in port, the captain of *La Soeur Cherie* told the governor that his ship was a French privateer outfitted and commissioned at Aux Cayes on San Domingue in late September, and departed to cruise on October 7, 1803. Claiborne seems to have believed him, though the beleaguered French on the island at that time were probably no longer issuing letters of marque—privateering commissions. In fact, the French commander at Aux Cayes, General Jean Baptiste Brunet, had surrendered his command to the British just five days after the supposed departure of *La Soeur Cherie*. A week later France and Spain signed an alliance, meaning that French private armed vessels—

privateers—could no longer prey on Spanish shipping, and certainly not out of San Domingue, which by January had been declared independent and renamed Haiti. Hereafter privateer activity for the French would only be against British shipping, and out of the Caribbean island ports of Martinique and Guadeloupe.

The captain's story included taking the two prizes that had accompanied him to the Mississippi, but then, he said, he nearly lost his vessel in a storm that cost several crewmen their lives, and lost more men in desertions when the ship made landfall. This, too, Claiborne apparently believed, though guardedly, for pleading damage at sea and a need to refit was on its way to becoming a popular ploy for privateers wanting to come into port to unload smuggled goods or to take on men and arms to continue privateering. Consequently Claiborne ordered an inspection of the ship, including her armament, and forbade her from taking aboard either arms or men. He also brought in an inspector, who reported back that since landing, *La Soeur Cherie* had indeed lost more than a dozen men as deserters, but that most of them were slaves from San Domingue. The story smelled of chicanery. The importation of foreign slaves into the United States and its territories had been outlawed everywhere by 1803. The so-called desertions sounded very much like a subterfuge for illegally bringing San Domingue slaves into the territory for sale.

This finally aroused enough suspicion in Claiborne that he held the vessel in port until August. By then he had conclusive proof that the captain was enlisting men, though not Americans, to fill out his crew, and that one of the two prizes in convoy had tied up before reaching the city and sold her cargo, thus evading customs at the Balize and New Orleans alike. Worse, though presented as being a Spanish prize, this vessel was in fact an American ship taken while she traded with British Jamaica.[5] Before Claiborne could take action, however, *La Soeur Cherie* and her elusive captain had set sail and were gone.

During the time he spent in New Orleans, the commander of the mystery ship was known to the governor only as "Captain La fette."[6] Nothing more is known of him.[7] He might not have been Jean Laffite, but it is certainly interesting that the same summer, only a few weeks before Claiborne allowed *La Soeur Cherie* to leave in early August, Stephen Carraby believed that Pierre Laffite was about to leave the territory, and on July 30, as the privateer made ready to leave port, Pierre could not be found in the city. Of course, two months later Pierre was in Baton Rouge, but there exists at least the possibility that the "Captain La fette" of *La Soeur Cherie* was Jean, and Pierre left with him to escape his creditors, then made his way back to Spanish West Florida by another route. And there exists as well the possibility that this brother freebooter was the source of Pierre Laffite's sudden supply of marketable slaves in late 1805 and early 1806.

If Jean Laffite was the commander of *La Soeur Cherie*, he might have been sailing out of San Domingue while Pierre lived there, or even have helped in the ferrying of refugees to New Orleans. If he was a privateer in 1804 or earlier, then he plied one of the growth industries of the Indies. Piracy had been a problem in the Caribbean and the Gulf for two centuries, and in antiquity to prehistoric times. Rather as beauty dwells in the eyes of the beholder, so piracy tended to lie in the point of view of the victim. Broadly defined, piracy was the unlawful taking of one privately owned vessel by another one. It was simple highway robbery on the seas. In time of war, however, the merchant trade of each combatant became the legitimate prey not only of its opponents' warships, but also of private armed vessels, or privateers. In order to help finance its war effort while damaging the economy of its enemies, a government issued letters of marque and reprisal to qualified private vessels. The owners—and often they were whole syndicates of investors—armed, equipped, and crewed their ships at their own expense, and posted a hefty cash bond as guarantee that they would observe the rules of warfare and re-spect civilian life. The vessels were supposed to be commissioned in a home port of the commission-granting country. Their crews were supposed to be made up of a majority of men native to that country. They were to bring their prizes into ports of the com-missioning nation or a friendly nation, where a court of admiralty was to hear testimony and examine ship's papers and other evi-dence to decide whether the prize was eligible for capture and lawfully taken. If the court awarded possession of the prize to its captors, the prize ship and its cargo were sold and the proceeds shared between the crew, the investors, and the government whose flag the privateer flew.

Piracy was largely on the wane in the Caribbean in 1800, but when war erupted in Europe as Napoleon set the continent on fire, ripples extended to the west. Colonial possessions far from the protection of the mother countries, and scattered and isolated amid tens of thousands of square miles of ocean, offered tempt-ing targets for entrepreneurs. As late as early 1804 a pirate vessel called the *Favorite* fell to American naval arms off the Louisiana coast.[8] However, after 1800 piracy was almost unnecessary, for any men so disposed could easily legitimize their calling and pro-tect themselves from the hangman by taking letters of marque. Piracy did escalate modestly, chiefly out of Cuba, and continued for another two decades before its demise, but the overwhelming activity during this period would be by privateers. The English preyed on the French, the French upon the English, and every-one went after the Spaniards' vessels as Spain shifted from one side to the other and back in Europe's diplomatic waltz.

Much as the United States tried to stay out of the European imbroglio, domestic affairs in America encouraged privateering. For one thing, America offered a market for privateers' goods. The acquisition of vast new territory in the Louisiana Purchase, the Industrial Revolution with its voracious appetite for textiles, and the invention of the cotton gin that quickly and economically readied raw cotton for the loom together created a huge demand for slave labor to till and harvest existing Southern fields and the ones to be carved from Louisiana. A ban on the importation of foreign slaves could not have come at a worse time for the Spanish slave ships plying a constant route from Africa to the colonies of New Spain, especially Mexico and the islands. The ships were easy targets, and it was no great challenge to smuggle the slaves into Louisiana for sale. Many an enterprising American captain also took commissions from foreign governments, and the uprising on San Domingue created an independent Haiti close to home.

The revolution in San Domingue spawned the heyday of the privateer. Once the insurgents drove out the French, Napoleon's agents commissioned virtually all who applied out of the French colonies Guadaloupe and Martinique.[9] Many of these privateers stopped American ships trading with the newly independent Haitians, and some became justly famed, none more so than Captain Dominique, or Frederick Youx. He began appearing in the West Indies prize courts in 1805 as captain of *La Superbe,* an armed privateer owned by Jacques Plaideau, when he took three American ships condemned in the prize court at Basseterre, Guadaloupe, and then sold them in Cuba. Dominique lost his ship in action in October 1806 and escaped to his home in Baracoa, where he would prove to be a hero of the defense of the port against British attack the following year.[10] Also operating out of Guadaloupe was yet another Captain Lafitte, this one commanding a corsair called *Le Regulateur,* which captured the American vessel *Maria Mischief* late in 1805.[11]

This Lafitte may or may not have been Governor Claiborne's nemesis of the year before, but he represented a cause for grave concern all the same. By taking an American merchantman, "Captain La fette" chose not to scruple overmuch on the nationality of his prizes when there was profit at the end of the day. After 1803 British and French privateers frequently took Yankee vessels, simply ignoring the rights of the weak, neutral United States. By 1805 British privateers cruised off the Balize waiting for any vessel, French or American, that offered a good target. Claiborne warned Secretary of State James Madison that if the war in Europe continued much longer, "I am fearful that the Gulph will be crowded with Privateers and that much Spoliation on our Commerce will be committed."[12]

Claiborne's words proved prophetic when a number of ships out of New Orleans were taken by Spanish and English privateers in late 1805 and early 1806, but the real explosion lay around the corner.[13] Once again events in Europe would be the spark. In 1806 Napoleon issued the Berlin Decree forbidding neutral ships to enter or leave British ports, thus making them subject to his privateers. Britain responded with its Orders in Council, forbidding neutral ships from using ports that excluded British shipping unless they were carrying British goods from a British port. Between the English and French actions, America's merchant trade faced danger of extinction. Her vessels were at risk of seizure no matter with whom she traded, and Britain was soon boarding Yankee ships at will and impressing their crewmen into the Royal Navy. Jefferson responded that year with the Nonimportation Act, banning the import of a range of British goods, and thus creating shortages and demands that privateers and smugglers were all too ready to supply.

Even before this the privateers and amenable city merchants explored ways of getting goods to an increasingly hungry market. A few less scrupulous New Orleans merchants such as Jean Blanque engaged sailors who plied both sides of the law.[14] Indeed, Blanque was the supposed consignee of the cargo of "Captain La fette's" prize British merchantman *Hector*, revealed later to be an impostor smuggling goods under forged ship's papers. In 1806

Blanque would be taken to federal court for buying twenty-seven thousand pounds of coffee taken from an American vessel by a privateer.[15] The same Bartholomy Lafon who had been on San Domingue when Pierre Laffite was there was selling ships in New Orleans in 1803, and was mixing his surveying and map-making work with questionable commerce with Vera Cruz, Havana, and Charleston on his large copper-bottomed privateer the *Bellona*.[16] Renato Beluche, yet another veteran of the San Domingue upheaval, ran his brig the *Thomas* to several Caribbean ports, generally to bring in merchandise that some regarded as suspicious.[17] Even the more upright merchants such as Paul Lanusse traded in illegal slaves, in his case many more than he could have acquired domestically. As the privateering trade grew, these merchants needed a place to warehouse goods away from the eyes of customs and excise officials.[18] Their Caribbean home bases were too far away, but by the time "Captain La fette" came to New Orleans, some thought a closer place looked promising.

The spot lay fifty miles due south of the city in a wild and scarcely inhabited place called Barataria Bay. The name itself is redolent of mystery and romance. In Miguel de Cervantes's *Don Quixote*, Sancho Panza received the gift of an island called Barataria. The Spaniards used words such as *barato* and *baratura* and *baratillo* to describe cheap goods and bargain sales, which would certainly apply to the contraband being sold there. Yet the name Barataria predates the establishment of smugglers on the bay. Perhaps it came from barratry, or even from the French word for deceit, *barat*. A single pass, scarcely navigable except to those who knew it well, led between two low sandy barrier islands, Grand Terre and Grand Isle, into the bay itself. From there a series of bayous and lakes gave shallow-draft rowing pirogues access to several points just below New Orleans, to the Mississippi several miles upstream, or to Bayou Lafourche. This bayou, which did not have a protected harbor of its own at its mouth, could transport goods far into the interior. In 1804 Grand Isle had at least one resident, Jacques Reynard, a Revolutionary War veteran who called his sandy island "Grand Ille Des Baratariare."[19] Yet for twenty years or more Barataria had been known to the French and Spanish as something else, a sometime refuge for runaway slaves and what the Spaniards called *famosos picarónes*—notorious scoundrels—a place where fugitives could lose themselves for months.[20] Smugglers and privateers could well make use of this bay as a base for the operation Governor Claiborne so feared.

If Jean Laffite spent some of his lost years gaining experience in this murky privateering environment, his brother Pierre faced far more mundane challenges in Louisiana, though his introduction to slave dealing showed him that he did not have to live in penury. After his sudden flurry of slave sales, Pierre briefly disappeared again, though he was hardly inactive. He may have made another visit to Baton Rouge, where Elias Beauregard had engaged the engineer and fellow refugee Arsené Latour to survey town lots for sale.[21] But by April he was back in New Orleans with a new horizon in mind, Pensacola.[22]

Pierre spent almost three months intermittently making preparations, though whether he was taking trade goods to the West Florida capital or intending to buy them there to export back cannot be determined. Certainly he was not fleeing debt this time, for he had several thousand dollars in hand. Surely, too, he meant to take the pregnant Marie and his son with him, as he planned an extended residence in Pensacola.[23] Amid the activity of readying his family for the trip, he found time for a few routine bits of business, including appearing before notary public Pierre Pedesclaux on April 21 to file a "to whom it may concern" affidavit that he had witnessed the murder of his acquaintance Gabauriau at Cap Français some years before.[24] All too many refugees had to file such statements to establish deaths on San Domingue, and help to settle estates back in France.

In May Pierre went to Pensacola, probably to arrange for lodgings for his family, and remained at least through the end of the month, but by early June he was back in New Orleans.[25] In his absence he arranged to spend $700 to buy a twenty-six-year-old Congolese slave woman named Therese, probably to help Marie take care of the household.[26] Then he called on the Chartres Street merchant William St. Marc and leased a slave man named Lubin to go to Pensacola as a cook.[27]

It remained only to engage passage. There were two ways to get from New Orleans to Pensacola. One was much the faster, an inland waterway passage beginning outside the city at Lake Pontchartrain at the end of Bayou St. Jean, then traveling eastward to Lake Borgne through a channel known as the Rigolets, and on east into the Mississippi Sound and behind the protection of Cat, Ship, Horn, and Dauphin Islands, to Mobile Bay, and thence to Pensacola. In the small, broad, flat-bottomed vessels that plied the route, the trip was two to four days long and did not risk the Gulf hazards of storms and privateers, though going through the Rigolets required a good pilot, and sailing Lake Pontchartrain demanded skill at low water. The fare was usually five or six dollars per head, but passengers also had to pay for their food. The boats sometimes made stops at Dauphin Island or at Biloxi.[28]

The alternative was to go via the mouth of the Mississippi and across the Gulf, which could take three weeks due to the vagaries of water levels and the difficulty of navigating the twists of the river with only wind power for headway and control. Loss of wind at the Balize could halt a vessel for days or even weeks. Yet for a merchant traveling with goods, or a household's furniture and family, the longer passage was the more practical.

In any event, the only vessel scheduled for Pensacola the last half of June was the modest *Louisa*, owned and operated by Captain Jean LaCoste, who sometimes dealt in slaves at Pensacola.[29] Pierre probably knew her captain and her quarters from his trip to Pensacola the month before.[30] The single-decked, two-masted schooner was cramped, just over forty-eight feet long and a mere fourteen feet wide on the deck with no gallery to separate passengers from crew.[31] But the voyage would be brief, as she was small enough to take either route and the weather was good.[32] By June 27 they were aboard, and once in open water, with the prevailing westerly winds, they could have put into the capital of Spanish West Florida as early as July 1.

Pensacola in 1806 presented a dramatic contrast to the New Orleans they left behind them. Pensacola lay on a sandy plain stretching about a mile along the bay from which it took its name. Much of the plain was not built on, and the town had fewer than fifteen hundred inhabitants, many of them French and Canary Islanders, but mostly Spaniards who had left New Orleans a few years earlier when Spain turned Louisiana over to Napoleon.[33] Pensacola had been in decline since the Spaniards took control from the British in 1784. It was a place of modest one-story Spanish and two-story English houses, spread intermittently along Spanish-named streets so randomly laid out that some were forty feet wide and others measured two hundred feet across, streets that were sandy in dry weather and absolute mires when it rained. Most of the houses seemed under constant threat of encroachment from the surrounding swamps. A visitor described even the governor's house as "wretched," and the rest of the town as decaying.[34] The only brick structure in town was the mansion of merchant William Panton.[35]

Pensacola afforded perhaps the best harbor on the Gulf. It lay only two days from New Orleans in the best of times, three days' sail from Havana, five or six from Vera Cruz, and a day or so more to Jamaica, with numerous ports even closer.[36] Hence the surprise with which many travelers beheld its current torpid economic climate. The English had established trades, and harvested masts and timber and naval stores and furs from Indians as their main commerce. They had built numerous jetties, warehouses, and wharfs, but under the Spanish only the mast and stores trade continued. With no wharves, unloading ships' cargoes was difficult, "lighters" being required to convey cargo from ship to shore.[37] Moreover, Pensacola had no industry other than brickmaking and some lumbering, and there was scant trade and almost no local market. Inhabitants had no steady supply of foodstuffs except locally raised beef, seafood from the Gulf, and truck vegetables grown in private gardens. Even chickens and corn had to be imported from Mobile, while rice and flour and all European provisions and wine came from New Orleans. The cost of their transport doubled their price.[38]

A few carpenters and artisans provided skilled work when they felt like it, but there were no printers or tailors, nor blacksmiths, and no makers of consumer products, and residents depended heavily on imports from Havana and New Orleans for any hard goods. Even that foreign trade found no official encouragement from local Spanish rulers. The port had been all but empty for several years, and Laffite would have found barely half a dozen ships in the harbor when he arrived. Four or five schooners of ten to twenty-five tons, such as the *Louisa*, brought passengers and freight from New Orleans, but that was about all.[39] There was little or no hard currency in circulation, and what wealth existed lay almost exclusively in land.[40]

Virtually all commerce revolved around the Panton, Leslie Company. The company exported cotton and yellow earth for stucco used in New Orleans, and enjoyed a monopoly on the fur trade in the region. It had offices in London and the Bahamas and its agents were Englishmen who traded with the local Indians for rum, muskets, powder, blankets, cloth, and more. Even after the Spanish takeover, Panton, Leslie kept its monopoly, so the benefit of local trade went to the English firms that sold goods to Panton, and the profits went to the company. The company also imported merchandise for the town's inhabitants, pretending it was trade goods, which were exempt from import duty, and thus Spain got nothing though there were customs inspectors at the port. Indeed, with so little trade otherwise, the inspectors collected almost nothing. As a result, Panton had most of the hard cash in the colony in 1806.[41]

Pensacola's civil government was run by Vicente Folche, who doubled as mayor of the town after Pensacola became capital of West Florida in 1803 following the Louisiana Purchase. Spain maintained a garrison of about five hundred *soldados,* but only two hundred were ready or fit for duty. Folche held a colonel's rank as their military commander, and was aided by several officers of staff rank. He also had the artisans, coopers, and carpenters needed to maintain the vessels of a naval fleet, but Folche's "fleet" was one small sloop.[42] The governor at least made efforts to revitalize Pensacola after 1803 when it stood on its own. He legalized general commerce and abolished the import duty on goods from New Orleans, hoping to foster trade. Now in 1806 Folche opened Pensacola to trade with all neutral nations, and the Americans began to trickle in.[43]

Most likely it was Folche's liberalization of trade restrictions that brought Pierre Laffite to Pensacola. Certainly it would not have been the social attractions. The gender imbalance was even greater here than in New Orleans, with a third of the population white males, more than four hundred of them unmarried.[44] These male inhabitants, having few chances for feminine companionship, passed their time playing, gambling, drinking at the town's one small tavern, and engaging in endless conversation at the billiard room that became the social center of the place. Perhaps their boredom was the reason Pensacolans enjoyed a reputation for being very hospitable to visitors.[45]

Just how welcome Laffite felt is unknown. He at least had an acquaintance with Governor Folche, and had probably developed some contacts with Panton, Leslie during his merchant days at Baton Rouge. The lure for a man of his entrepreneurial instincts was obvious. Panton, Leslie's stranglehold on the economy may not have left much hard cash for a merchant to squeeze out of local hands, but with more and more Americans coming in and the liberalization of trade restrictions, money could be made. Moreover, Spain's hold on mainland North America appeared to be dramatically weakened after Spain lost Louisiana to France and then to the Yankees. East and West Florida were now clearly isolated by an American Georgia on the east and the Mississippi Territory on the west, with British Alabama in between. The activities of men like the Kempers threatened to wrest West Florida from Spain, especially with the encouragement of outside American supporters. If West Florida became American, attached either to Louisiana or Mississippi, then those who were in place early on could hope to reap fortunes.

Probably most persuasive was Pierre's realization of the money to be made in slaves. The prohibitions against importing foreign slaves to Louisiana and elsewhere in the United States presented a serious obstacle to him. The Constitution prevented Congress from taking any all-encompassing action against the African slave trade through the end of 1807, but everyone could anticipate that as soon as that restriction expired, statute legislation would be passed abolishing slave importation everywhere and permanently. Spain observed no such ban, however, meaning that Laffite could acquire as many Africans as he wished in Pensacola, and then use his expanding grasp of the back roads and bayous of Louisiana to introduce them into the territory for the sort of profit he had realized so recently in New Orleans. Indeed, on July 6, within a week of his arrival, the largest public slave sale to date in Pensacola occurred. Eighteen blacks just arrived from Africa aboard the *Success* went on the block, some bringing as much as $350.[46] Most likely the buyers were not the cash-strapped Pensacolans, but men from

Louisiana come to buy illicit stock that they could then smuggle home either to work their plantations or else to sell.

The public demonstration of the money to be made inspired Pierre to a spontaneous, and ill-advised, attempt to capitalize on the presence of eager buyers who had cash left after the sale. On July 10 he engaged to sell the slave cook Lubin to François Bellestre of New Orleans. The fact that Bellestre paid $700, double the best price realized for any slave at the recent auction, apparently overcame any qualms Pierre might have had about selling what was not his to sell. After the fact he sent a letter to St. Marc asking permission to sell the cook. When St. Marc refused, Laffite was trapped by his own hasty action, but being outside the jurisdiction of a Louisiana court now and for the foreseeable future, he probably felt little fear of the repercussions.[47]

For the next three years Pierre Laffite remained in Pensacola all or most of the time, and Marie Villard with him.[48] Indeed, they were not there long before the little family began to grow. First, probably before the end of the year, Marie gave birth to a daughter they named Catherine Coralie Laffite. Barely a year later in late 1807 or early 1808 appeared a younger brother Martial—or Martin—Firmin Laffite.[49] Marie may have given birth to yet another child, Jean Baptiste, late in 1808 or early 1809.[50] And at some point their home took in Marie's sister Catherine or Catarina, whom they called Catiche—a common nickname for girls of her name, especially if diminutive in stature.[51]

If his family prospered, Pierre may not have done so well commercially. On September 17, 1806, a devastating hurricane hit the Gulf coast, the worst storm for thirteen years and likely Pierre's first experience with the potential fury of the region's weather. In New Orleans it damaged every vessel in port but one, and flattened the sugarcane fields for miles around.[52] Then in 1807 Enrique, the Chevalier de Peytavin, drew the eyes of the authorities looking into unlawful slaves being smuggled into Baton

Rouge. Peytavin and his family did a lot of slave buying and selling in this period, and if an operator of his scale attracted attention, it could hardly make the efforts of smaller entrepreneurs like
Laffite any easier.[53] Nor does Pierre appear to have done much
business with Panton, Leslie, or the other principal local merchants.[54] If he did, especially in slaves, then most probably it was
of the sort that he had by now learned required subterfuge and
discretion.

More important, events on a broader stage would soon persuade him that the marketplace was shifting. Aaron Burr's 1806
effort to carve out a new empire in Spanish Texas had failed, but
it attracted the attention of men across the region, for with Spain
weakening, Texas offered cheap land and resources for the taking
and, in the right hands, a plump market for slaves.

More immediately, after the failure of the Nonimportation
Act, Jefferson began considering an outright embargo prohibiting all American trade with foreign ports. Congress passed the
measure in December 1807, virtually closing all lawful commerce
with other nations. Despite the enforcement acts that followed,
the embargo would completely fail to accomplish its purpose of
ending trade with England and France. Rather, it fostered the
eruption of the nascent smuggling trade on the Gulf. Meanwhile
Britain wound up with all but a monopoly on the Atlantic carrying trade.

If the embargo and nonintercourse laws made smuggling
lucrative, the contraband trade led naturally to privateering, and
ultimately to piracy. Congress on March 1, 1807, directed that
piracy be suppressed, and looked to the navy to do so, but even
before then Washington realized that the United States Navy was
too small to be effectual.[55] When Congress inaugurated a new
year with the January 1, 1808, abolition of America's African slave
trade, the legislators only added one more incentive to those who
sought to profit by circumventing the laws of the United States.

Most immediately affected was Louisiana, where planters feared that the abolition would ruin them because sugar, cotton, and indigo could not be cultivated without cheap labor. Neither could the planters keep the levees repaired to hold back the river while the climate made it impossible to get white men to do the work ordinarily performed by slaves. In several years interstate trade would begin to address the slave shortage, but until then smuggling was the only answer, and Louisiana's complex and virtually unpolicable coastline and interior waterways worked to the advantage of those willing to take great risks for great rewards. Indeed, on April 14, 1808, two American ships brought ninety-eight blacks to New Orleans in brazen defiance of the ban.[56] It was only the beginning, and hereafter the illicit slave trade on the Gulf would be inextricably linked with the corsairs.

Seemingly every available French vessel turned to privateering. Louis Aury, a career adventurer from France who came to the New World determined to make himself a fortune and a name, was in San Domingue serving on privateers prior to the French being driven out. "Corsairs are the only French boats, war or merchant, in this country," he wrote in September 1808. "They wage war as loyally as the ships of his imperial majesty."[57] Though French privateers were officially commissioned to act against British vessels, they wanted the fat Spanish ships laden with slaves and Mexican gold, and took advantage of Spain's alliance with Britain after 1808 when she revolted against and briefly deposed Napoleon's brother Joseph to restore her own monarchy. Meanwhile the United States and Spain all but severed relations that year as a result of the British alliance and Jefferson's embargo, which threatened to starve Baton Rouge and West Florida. Hostility to Spain grew rapidly in American minds, and rumors of war spread. Just as when Pierre Laffite was living in Baton Rouge, war between Spain and the United States did not promise to be good for business. Besides, the slave market was now in New Orleans, as Pierre well knew, and the explosion of privateers bringing much wanted goods to a hungry market that did not scruple at buying outside the law suggested that the enterprising man move his base once again.

In a futile effort to put down privateering, Congress passed a Restriction Act forbidding all vessels in United States waters from interfering with the vessels of any other nation's commerce in those waters. Thanks to the wording of the legislation, however, the privateers had no trouble evading the law, and soon they made New Orleans the point of sale for their takings. "The sea, in fact, at that time swarmed with legalized pirates," recalled Commodore David Porter, whom Jefferson charged with suppressing piracy in the Gulf in 1808. Spain and the United States did cooperate to the extent of offering large rewards for the capture of certain members of the freebooter community, especially the Frenchmen, but to little avail. Porter took command in New Orleans with twenty gunboats and a naval station ashore, only to find that the bays and inlets of the coast were already the resort of smugglers and pirates under British, French, and Spanish flags.

"These gentlemen were continually hovering on our coasts, and in default of finding enemy's ships would seize upon our own, upon one pretext or another, for which outrages our people obtained little redress," he complained. Many privateers chose to refit and resupply in New Orleans since the city had no garrison and foreign warships did not go there. "As they spent their money freely, the local authorities rather encouraged their presence," Porter discovered. "These desperadoes, mixing with the dissolute part of the population, kept the town in a continual state of turmoil."[58] In fact, just after Porter took command in August, several mob fights erupted on the city levee between American sailors and those of France, Spain, and Italy. A number of men were killed or injured in the melees, and Porter concluded that "there was certainly a large number of dangerous characters in New Orleans requiring the utmost vigilance." It presented a serious challenge to any commander to preserve law and order, for "there were so many 'choice spirits' in and around New Orleans always ready for desperate enterprises, that the forces of the army and navy were always in readiness to preserve order."[59]

Worse, the local authorities, animated by the sympathies of a populace that wanted to keep slaves and consumer goods coming into Louisiana, seemed happy to encourage the violations of the embargo. "The district attorney evidently winked at piracies committed in our waters and at the open communication kept up between these depredators and the citizens of New Orleans," Porter complained.[60] He discovered that he could not interfere without colliding with the civil authorities and merchants who had connections in Washington that could cost him his position, or even career.

The ingredients were all in place: a market starving for slaves and luxury goods regardless of the source; a district attorney and court system inclined to cast blind eyes on malefactors who provided consumer goods; a large population primarily of French origin who felt hostility toward their new American masters and a corresponding disregard of their laws; a Gulf teeming with newly made privateers anxious to prey on any vessel they could take; an international political climate sufficiently fluid that any privateer could find *some* flag under which to claim legitimate service; and Spain's New World colonies on the verge of widespread revolt. It was a recipe for opportunity, primarily at Spain's expense, from which everyone else could benefit, even the officially opposed United States, which secretly hoped to take more of the New World away from Spain—a cause in which the privateers could be excellent unofficial and unpaid allies.

All that was needed were daring men to grasp the opportunity. By 1809 Pierre Laffite decided that he would be one of them, though it meant his return to New Orleans. Surely it was no coincidence that at virtually the same time his brother Jean finally came to Louisiana.

No matter where—their chief's allotment this;
Theirs, to believe no prey nor plan amiss.
But who that CHIEF? his name on every shore
Is famed and fear'd—they ask and know no more.

FOUR

Brothers in Business
1809-1811

ONCE AGAIN affairs beyond their immediate horizon guided the Laffite brothers, finally bringing them together once and for all. Pierre may not have been back to New Orleans after leaving for Pensacola, though during those years he may have made a visit or two to Baton Rouge and Point Coupée to buy and sell slaves.[1] Then on March 25, 1809, Congress repealed the unpopular Embargo and replaced it with a Non-Intercourse Act that opened the United States to trade with all nations except Britain and France, and thus made trade with Spain legal once more. To the extent that Laffite had moved to Pensacola in order to evade the Embargo and deal in Spanish goods, that reason was gone.

In May 1809 something much more dramatic happened that helped to draw him back to New Orleans. When San Domingue finally fell to the insurgents in 1803, Cuba was the closest place for refugees, and they began streaming there early that year. More than twenty-seven thousand of them came, and for several years they were welcome. But in March 1808 Napoleon occupied

Madrid and put his brother Joseph on the throne of Spain, and in Cuba the Spaniards reacted against the refugees. On April 11, 1809, the colonial governor issued a proclamation evicting all Frenchmen who were not naturalized citizens, giving them no more than forty days to leave.[2] Most of the refugees had no choice but to sell their property at the mercy of speculators, and then began the parade of vessel after vessel, many of them French privateers, transporting the fugitives to Charleston, Baltimore, Norfolk, and Louisiana. Between May 10 and August 19 at least fifty-five ships landed in New Orleans, forty-eight of them from Santiago, six from Baracoa, and one from Havana.[3]

In 1805 New Orleans had 8,475 people. By December 1809, 9,059 refugees had stepped ashore at the levee. Of them, 2,731 were white, 3,102 were free colored, and 3,226 were slaves. Another thousand came in the early months of 1810, and one thousand others remained from the 1803 wave of refugees. This influx affected an already unbalanced population makeup.[4] Whereas previously in New Orleans less than one-fifth of the population were free colored, over a third of the refugees were such. In fact, the largest single group of refugees were free women of color, some 1,377. These new free women of color had fewer children, allowing them more freedom to earn employment, and thus compete with the existing population. As for competing for men, the arrivers only made a poor situation worse. In 1809 the city had 195 white men over fifteen for every 100 white women of the same age. However, in the free colored community, there were only 31 adult men for every 100 women, leaving even more unattached free colored women to seek livelihood and partners.[5]

Initially the mayor and civic leaders thought this new influx of free blacks to be quite desirable. Some had money and the rest had needed skills.[6] American authorities, too, welcomed the exiles at first. The local army commander General James Wilkinson told a deputation of them just a week before the eviction order that they had American sympathy, and promised them sanctuary in America.

At the same time, however, he reminded them of the recent and absolute ban on importing slaves into the country. The navy had vessels cruising the Louisiana coast from March to May 1809 looking for smugglers, and as illicit activity went on the rise, reduced the distance between patrolling stations for more careful scrutiny.[7] In March Porter took two vessels, the USS *Vesuvius* and the USS *Alligator*, on an extensive patrol to acquaint himself with the coastline. He spotted one French corsair and pursued it to Barataria, where he lost the quarry.[8]

Not all of them got away, however, and that July the United States District Court tried the owners of the schooner *Santa Rita* for bringing slaves in from Cuba the previous summer.[9] Even earlier, on May 25, during the first wave of refugee arrivals, the same schooner *Louisa* that took Laffite to Pensacola was detained and searched by Collector of Customs William Brown when he caught it coming in the river with fifteen slaves from Santiago that the captain intended to sell. The United States attorney Philip Grymes filed a charge against her at the District Court, and on June 20 authorities seized her and her cargo at anchor. Her owner made the pettifogging plea that as he had not actually sold any slaves in the United States, he had not technically violated the law.[10] As evidence that Commodore Porter's complaint about the local district attorney had some substance, the owner's frail plea saved him his ship, for within a week the *Louisa* was back on her way to Pensacola on her old route.[11]

The exiles could come, but they could not legally import their slaves. For refugees forced practically to give away most other property, slaves, if they had them, were their only transportable capital assets other than currency. When their ships arrived, Governor Claiborne allowed the refugees, including free colored people, to come ashore, but their slaves had to remain aboard the

THE PIRATES LAFFITE · 47

ships. He then ordered the vessels impounded to prevent them from either departing with the property of the refugees or secretly allowing that property to come ashore. For several months many of the refugees lived on the charity of sympathetic New Orleanians while their slaves lived on the ships.

At last in July Claiborne allowed the slaves to come ashore if their owners posted bond guaranteeing that the blacks would be produced if and when required as the local federal court or Washington decided whether or not they could stay as exceptions to the recent law. In November when the British took San Domingue, leading U.S. authorities to expect even more French refugees, Claiborne wanted them to be told to go elsewhere.[12] For the moment, however, Claiborne asked that the law be relaxed to allow the refugees to bring their slaves with them, and Congress passed such an exception that summer.[13]

Many of the refugees had nothing else, and found themselves forced to sell their slaves to the anxious market, sometimes at prices lower than real value. This alone might have lured Pierre Laffite back to New Orleans. In either case, he did not need long to take advantage of the situation. On July 29 he bought his first slave from Pierre Bourg, and two days later sold the slave for $425.[14] Within a few weeks he made $600 more from the sale of another black, an Islamic Mandingan quite certainly from Africa via one of the San Domingue refugees.[15]

Marie Villard may have had some relatives among the new arrivals, for an Antoine Villard, a mulatto "gaboteur" or seaman from Mole, San Domingue, came that summer.[16] Perhaps some Laffite cousins were also among the exiles.[17] What is certain is that sometime during this influx of San Domingue refugees, Jean Laffite came to Louisiana intent on remaining. His arrival now, combined with his unquestionable experience at sea, put him in the mainstream of a number of other men of his stamp who were coming to Louisiana.

French privateers were still off American shores, and still attacking United States shipping in the Caribbean. Baracoa and other Cuban ports had been their bases until the expulsion of the refugees that spring.[18] Some of these sailors, remnants of the naval and military forces evicted from San Domingue in 1803, had become little more than freelance pirates. Some French privateers had also operated out of San Domingue, now sharing the island with Haiti, until this year, when San Domingue fell to the British and they, too, sought new bases at Guadaloupe, the last remaining French colony in the West Indies. Within a year Guadaloupe, too, would fall to the British.[19] With no French ports to call home, the corsairs turned to the coast of Louisiana where even if the authorities were not amenable, the chiefly French and Creole population welcomed the wares they could provide. San Domingue refugees in New Orleans such as Henri de Ste. Gême financially backed some of the corsairs.[20] Moreover, the wild coastline afforded both hiding and good anchorages, especially at Barataria. One who made the change of base was Louis Aury, by this time an experienced privateer commander and almost certainly a Laffite acquaintance.[21] Many free men of color from San Domingue also made the move, most notably Lieutenant Colonel Joseph Savary.[22]

When the United States and Spain severed diplomatic relations in 1809, it was an open door for privateers, for now taking Spaniards' property was almost patriotic, if still not legal. In fact, the corsairs were essentially pirates, for their prizes had to be taken to an admiralty court run by the corsairs' commissioning nation for adjudication to declare them lawful seizures, but now there were no French admiralty courts in the Caribbean and France was too far to take the prizes. The privateers seized upon the expedient tried by "Captain La fette" back in 1804 by transferring captured cargo to their holds, then bringing their ships to New Orleans pretending to be making emergency stops for repairs. Once there, they secretly sold their goods. They flew the French flag because Spain was then allied with Britain and at war with France, and because most merchant vessels in the Caribbean were Spaniards, and they made easy prizes. But the privateers were not necessarily French ships or crews. Some managed to outfit and crew themselves in New Orleans in spite of neutrality laws, and it was well known what they are doing.[23]

Just when Jean Laffite arrived in Louisiana is uncertain, but he was there very close to the time that Pierre returned, and may have come to New Orleans captaining a corsair vessel bringing a load of refugees.[24] However, he appeared in New Orleans rarely if at all during his first year or two in Louisiana, choosing instead to base himself at Barataria. The pass into the bay lay at the west end of the island, usually running nine or ten feet of water at good tide, deep enough for most of the privateer vessels but too shallow for more substantial warships. Behind the island sat the best harbor on the coast, remote and difficult of access from New Orleans, and almost unsettled.[25] Looking inland, the bay extended about eighteen miles and ended on the horizon, so it was a good sail to get to the bayous. Small islands covered with weeds, marsh grass, and brush pocked the bay's waters.

Grand Terre, one of the barrier islands on either side of the pass, was six miles long and one to three miles wide, and barely more than marsh in most places. Indians once made use of it, though they may have been gone by this time. The highest point on the island rose to not more than five feet. A few groves of large live oaks provided some shade, and a so-called oak ridge ran along the island. Masses of driftwood washed up on the shore, brought down the Mississippi to the Gulf. Southerly winds prevailed, especially in summer, making the few small trees lean permanently toward the north. Perhaps due to the wind, there were no really bothersome insects, though the few mosquitoes were big and ferocious. The bay boasted an abundance of redfish and spotted trout, with oysters, crabs, terrapin, and shrimp all to be taken easily in the surrounding waters. Fruit and vegetables grew well.[26] An island aptly called Petite Isle sat just behind Grand Terre, the two being separated by a brackish bayou.

A scattering of salvagers, scavengers, and coastal recluses lived on a semipermanent basis either on Grand Isle across the pass or in the vicinity. After the Embargo, a few of the fishermen there began operating a contraband trade from Grand Terre, chiefly off-loading goods from captured vessels onto American ships and then taking their cargoes under false shipping papers to New Orleans.[27] Following the foreign slave trade prohibitions these men began smuggling in a modest fashion. But until the influx of privateers denied French ports, the operations on Grand Terre were never extensive or organized. That would change once the Laffite brothers reunited.

It may not have happened overnight, but by the fall of 1809 men in New Orleans knew that a man seeking slaves could get them fresh from Africa at a good price at Grand Terre if he felt no unease about circumventing the law. Even men of prominence such as attorney John Randolph Grymes had no qualms about referring buyers to the *barracón*, or slave barracks, on the island where privateers kept blacks pending sales. By November Grymes was suggesting that customers get in touch with the man one buyer's son called "the notorious Captain Lafitte."[28]

He had to mean Jean, for Pierre was neither a captain nor notorious. Just what Jean Laffite had done to achieve notoriety can only be surmised, but if he was the captain of *La Soeur Cherie,* then he might still be remembered in New Orleans, and as "notorious," and more so now for his known association with the growing band of miscreants at Barataria.[29] If he had been a privateer captain, he seems to have abandoned the trade for something more lucrative and less hazardous, and there lay the entrepreneurial genius of the Laffites. Privateers risked the hazards of the sea, capture or death at the hands of the Spaniards, and arrest and prosecution by the United States. Here Pierre's experience as a merchant came into play. If the privateers limited their risk by landing their goods on Grand Terre rather than trying to bring their ships into New Orleans, the Laffites could act as middlemen between supply and market, either bringing buyers to the island in the case of slaves, or else getting the merchandise to New Orleans via means less dangerous than coming in through the port and its customs officers.[30] By the fall of 1809 the Laffites had a modest smuggling operation well founded, matching buyers with well-established slave importers. Jean took buyers to Grand Terre to make the sales, while Pierre stayed in New Orleans to handle the Laffites' business affairs there.[31]

For the moment, their notoriety cannot have been great, for their names were entirely absent from the public press and the private correspondence of those charged with apprehending violators of the customs and slave laws. Indeed, complaints about Barataria were few as yet. Both Pierre and Jean moved freely in and out of the city. Pierre rented a house for himself and his family, probably on St. Ann Street, and Jean stayed with them when he was in town.[32] People started to take note of Pierre. He was thirty-nine years old. Visitors saw a robust, powerfully built man of above middle height—about five feet, ten inches tall—with a light complexion and light brown hair growing or combed low over his forehead. Piercing dark eyes that were just a little crossed flashed from his face. When he spoke English with his heavy French accent, his teeth were brilliantly white.[33]

Jean began to be noticed, too, and he presented a different aspect from his brother. He was tall, perhaps as much as an inch or two over six feet, and well proportioned. He wore side whiskers down his chin, and the pale cast of his skin despite his time at sea created an arresting contrast with his large dark hazel eyes and dark hair.[34] He, too, showed unusually white teeth, and where

Pierre may have been rather ungainly, Jean liked to dress in style and displayed some grace and elegance in his manner in spite of unusually narrow feet and small hands. He impressed people as an easy and genial conversationalist, and liked to tell stories of his experiences, no doubt with embellishments. "He would stand and talk upon any serious matter, with one eye shut, for hours, and at such times had rather a harsh look," recalled an acquaintance. "But he was tall and finely formed; his manners were highly polished, and in his pleasant moods, one who did not know him would have suspected him for being anything but a pirate."[35]

Jean had no trouble finding company among the many quadroon women of the town. That fall he was seen at Coquet's St. Philip Street Ballroom in the company of a woman so slender she seemed barely out of girlhood, whose "liquid black eyes" dazzled one of Jean's acquaintances. Jean and Pierre appeared together, too, both playing occasionally at the ballroom's gaming tables.[36] Jean's sociability worked to the brothers' benefit, for there were good connections to be made in New Orleans. Latour, a fellow refugee from San Domingue, now divided his time between the city and Baton Rouge making surveys for Livingston and other landowners. Before long Latour opened an office at the intersection of Royal and Orleans and began moving in important city circles, as well as buying slaves, including five masons in a single day, possibly from the Baratarian establishment. Soon he and both Laffite brothers knew one another.[37] The Laffites may also have had some passing acquaintance with the lawyer Livingston, who was not universally popular just now, having been attacked as a Jefferson favorite and thus linked with the hated Embargo and Non-Intercourse acts.[38]

Much broader cultural forces favored the success of the Laffites. The social mix of New Orleans worked in their interest. By 1810 the population was 24,552, of whom a mere 3,200 were En-

glish or American and the rest all French and Spanish. This refugee community and the French-Spanish creoles were generally
in unison politically, arrayed often bitterly against the American
element in the city. Since the American authorities opposed the
nascent Baratarian enterprise, the refugee-Creole alliance naturally favored it.[39] "The foreign Frenchmen residing among us take
great interest in favour of their countrymen, and the sympathies
of the Creoles of the Country (the descendants of the French)
seem also to be much excited," complained one of the Americans
to whom the French were much less welcoming.[40] More frank
was the secretary of the Louisiana Territory, Thomas Robertson,
who complained in April that the most recent arrivals from San
Domingue were "desperadoes from St. Yago de Cuba accustomed to piracies and connected with the parties who furnish
them with every facility to escape forfeitures or punishment."[41]

The Laffites could not help but benefit from such sympathies. Besides hanging out with gamblers and the rougher sort at
the Café des Refugiés and the Hôtel de la Marine, the Laffites
likely spent time at Turpin's cabaret at Marigny and the levee,
which sold groceries and liquor, had accommodations, and became the regular haunt of the Baratarians when in town.[42] In such
environs, the brothers became well known to a population who
were refugees like them, driven to make common cause in their
effort to survive in their new home. It helped that Claiborne continued trying to keep slaves and free men of color out of Louisiana, never losing his fear of an outbreak of violence.

The first privateers caught attempting to smuggle goods into
New Orleans under the pretext of needing repairs came early that
year. The *Duc de Montebello* was sighted in February off the
mouth of the Mississippi, followed by *L'Epine*, and then *L'Intrépide*.[43] Aboard the first Porter found a number of blank privateering commissions, making it evident that commissions were to be
filled out in New Orleans for vessels fitted out there, in violation

of the international requirement that corsairs be commissioned in a home port of their commissioning nation. Porter learned at the same time that more than half a dozen other privateers were cruising off his coast, some expecting to come into New Orleans on similar pretenses. They were taking on their cannon unlawfully within Louisiana territorial waters at Breton Island, barely ten miles from the mouth of one of the passes into the Mississippi. With the dull and sluggish sailing ketches that made up most of his fleet, Porter had little hope of catching them at sea.[44]

When the three privateer ships came into the river and anchored in the stream, Porter took his modest gunboats out to confront them and demanded their surrender for violations of the laws. They asked to be allowed simply to leave, and then New Orleans friends of the privateers asked him to let them go. Porter refused both requests, at last threatening to open fire on the corsairs if they did not surrender. They yielded and were taken to the city, though not incarcerated. Immediately the townspeople rose in an uproar, outraged that the privateers roamed the city at will, expecting that the district attorney would get their vessels released. Philip Grymes told Porter that he had no authority to interfere with the privateers, but Porter insisted that he had properly libeled the vessels as prizes before the United States District Court on Royal Street, and that Grymes had no alternative but to try the privateers on the government's behalf. He even threatened to send them to another jurisdiction in Savannah, Georgia, and the district attorney finally agreed to try the case. The ships' crews stayed relatively peaceful while the issue remained unsettled, but when the case went to trial they came to the courthouse and acted in a threatening manner. The court charged the vessels' owners with unlawfully fitting out a privateer within the United States, and the intimidation seemed to work as Judge Dominic Hall decided that no proper nonintercourse law existed between the United States and Britain, and thus there were no restrictions on British goods coming into the country. In July the accused won an acquittal.[45]

Incensed, Porter complained to his superiors of "the many embarrassments thrown in my way by publick officers here." Disgusted, and castigating both Claiborne and district attorney Grymes, he announced almost petulantly in May that he would "decline making any further exertions to break up the system of iniquity that has been attempted by the privateers," including efforts to prevent illicit privateers being fitted out in New Orleans. If the government replaced Grymes, however, Porter would renew his efforts.[46]

Porter found himself so reviled in New Orleans that he began watching where he walked and keeping a guard at his home at night. Bitterly he quipped that he would be safer in the corsair lair at Guadaloupe than in Louisiana. Finally the court condemned the boats and ordered their sale as legitimate prizes taken for violation of the Embargo and other laws, but their captains and owners began to hound Porter. Porter asked Judge Hall to take steps to protect him, but Hall showed either little interest or little ability to do so, and finally late in May Porter and his family returned to Washington.[47] Even then, for years afterward the privateer captains badgered him with personal suits for detaining them and for their loss of property, forcing Porter eventually to engage attorney Edward Livingston, the brother of Robert Livingston, to defend him.[48] This was a delicious irony, in that Robert Livingston had successfully defended the owners of the *Duc de Montebello*. It was his first, though not his last, case in the pay of privateers and smugglers, which would not have escaped the notice of the Laffites.[49] Porter finally resigned in July 1810, sick of what he saw as Claiborne's vanity, General Wilkinson's pomposity, and the attitude of the local officials and leading townsmen, convinced that "they all looked upon the country as a big orange which they had a good right to squeeze."[50]

Thus the corsairs fooled no one for long. Almost immediately complaints of their deceptions appeared in that segment of the city's press that was more attached to the laws than to the French community.[51] Privateers sailing under Napoleon's flag and letters of marquee were pathetically obvious, complained an editor in April. Napoleon had not a foot of land in the West Indies nor was his flag permitted to enter any port on the continents of South or North America.[52] A few New Orleans merchants such as Joseph Sauvinet even armed and equipped their own privateers pretending French service, directly in violation of the neutrality laws. Sauvinet's brig *L'Intrépide* sailed from New Orleans in February 1810 bound to the Leeward Islands, where she took aboard a French captain who then brought her back to New Orleans pretending to be a French privateer.[53]

Shifts in the Caribbean's balance of power set off a four-year heyday for privateering out of Barataria.[54] It began even before the fall of Guadaloupe. In December 1809 the 250-ton brig *Constance* had been run aground off the mouth of the Lafourche by privateers who then stripped her down to her hull, leaving only several hundred barrels of salt too heavy to carry away. After taking the plundered goods up the Lafourche to the tiny village of Donaldsonville, where the bayou met the Mississippi, they got the brig back afloat and brought her to the Balize early in January. Authorities in New Orleans tried to prevent the prize brig from being sold as a legitimate capture in their port, and meanwhile alerted the temporary customs collector at Donaldsonville, Walker Gilbert, to be on the alert for the hidden booty before it could be raised from its hiding place and smuggled into New Orleans.[55]

Once the French privateers began to base themselves at Barataria and its environs, they would follow essentially the same course. There were four main smuggling routes from Barataria Bay to New Orleans. One went up Bayou St. Denis or Grand

Bayou through Lake Salvador to the Mississippi at Carrolton. Another went up Wilkinson's Bayou north then east. A third followed the Big Bayou Barataria, and the fourth used Little Bayou Barataria through Bayou Rigolets.[56] All of them brought the goods to points on the Mississippi well below New Orleans, yet well above the customs inspector at the Balize, and from these points either buyers or the smugglers could take them into the city for disposal. These Barataria routes and the Lafourche were virtually modus operandi that the Laffites would use for at least the next three years.

Since the Laffites were already on the scene and knew the routes to and from Grand Terre, visiting French corsairs naturally turned to them to dispose of prize goods and share in the proceeds. Thus, the supply probably initially came to the Laffites without their seeking it, but word of mouth among the corsairs only guaranteed that their business would grow. Latour commented on a sale by public auction at Grand Terre at which he saw people from all over lower Louisiana. Nor did the buyers make any attempt to hide the business they were at. In the streets of New Orleans Latour saw traders giving and receiving orders for goods purchased at Barataria, with no more care for secrecy than if they were ordering from Philadelphia or New York. "The most respectable inhabitants of the state, especially those living in the country, were in the habit of purchasing smuggled goods coming from Barataria," observed Latour. The goods were subject to official confiscation if discovered, but this hardly retarded the trade, for what got by the customs officers was highly profitable for the traders, as they bought the goods cheaply due to the quantity brought in by the privateers and the fact that no duty was attached. The privateers were usually anxious to sell so they could get on another cruise, which made them dispose of their goods even more cheaply, and all to the benefit of the Laffites and the others who plied their trade.[57]

Early in May Treasury Secretary Albert Gallatin advised Thomas Williams, the customs collector in New Orleans, that the Non-Intercourse Act had expired and a new law enacted that excluded from American ports any British and French privateers, whether publicly or privately owned. Any French corsairs already in New Orleans in violation of the Non-Intercourse Act prior to its expiration were still to be prosecuted, which only guaranteed that the freebooters would continue to haunt Barataria instead.[58] Officials increased their watchfulness, and at the Balize, though he knew of no specific cargoes of contraband goods being smuggled, customs officer Chauncey Pettibone told Williams that he had no doubt but that "vast quantities of them are carried to New Orleans every week."[59] Meanwhile, when French privateers and their Spanish prizes were impounded in New Orleans, the federal officials were altogether lax in prosecuting the cases, allowing many if not most of the privateers to sell their cargoes and leave. The Spanish consul in the city, Diego Morphy, began to lodge protests with Williams as early as May, and thereafter his complaints became commonplace as he vainly demanded that the captured goods be returned to the Spaniards who claimed rightful ownership.[60] The blind eye in New Orleans was already lazily at work, one more silent ally of the Laffites and their associates.

At the time there were perhaps several leading men called "*bos*" at Barataria, and while neither of the brothers could be said to dominate the others, their combination of marketing skill in New Orleans was already attracting more and more of the privateers to deal first with them.[61]

Before the summer was out Pierre had disposed of nineteen slaves and realized a total of $7,903. One slave had come from San Domingue, and another had been brought from Cuba, but fully a dozen came directly from Africa, though by what means Pierre did not say. Everyone knew.[62] In seven months he took in on behalf of himself, Jean, and André Robin, one of the biggest slave merchants in the territory,[63] just over $12,000 from slaves alone. He could even afford to buy slaves on the legal market now, and in April he and another man paid his partner Robin $4,025 for eight young blacks, and the next month spent $400 for a seventeen-year-old mulatto girl.[64]

The revenue from their smuggling allowed the Laffites to live rather well by the end of the year. Having owned a warehouse on Royal Street, however briefly, Pierre knew the area well and he and Jean leased or rented another on the same street. While Pierre probably remained with Marie practically full-time, Jean sometimes stayed at a boardinghouse in the city. Fellow boarders found him excellent company at the dinner table, and at least rudimentarily conversant in English and Spanish, though he was most comfortable in *Bordelaise*, a regional patois French. It seemed apparent from his conversation and good grammar that he had received some education in his youth.[65]

Meanwhile the number of corsairs hoping to profit from the Louisiana trade steadily grew. One of them was Louis Aury, who arrived in May off Barataria having left Guadaloupe aboard his vessel the *William* just two weeks ahead of Guadaloupe's capture. He unloaded 208 slaves at Grand Terre and engaged three Baratarians to take 105 of them up Bayou Barataria to a place known as McLarange's Vacherie on Bayou Lafourche, from which point Joseph Mendoza took them farther up the Lafourche to be sold for $17,000 to Eugene Fortier, a man with whom Pierre Laffite had transacted slave deals a few years before. They were discovered, however, and soon depositions and statements were taken in the federal district court.[66] Meanwhile, thinking himself safe after unloading his cargo, Aury sailed into the Mississippi claiming distress from weather damage. The United States marshal promptly impounded the *William*, and when the case went to the federal district court, the judge ordered Aury's arrest on $50,000 bond, and had his vessel seized and sold, the proceeds going to the government. Aury was eventually acquitted on charges of piracy. Accompanying Aury to Louisiana was the experienced privateersman Jean Jannet—alias Janny, Jeanette, and Jannetty.[67] Given their later close association with both Aury and Jannet, the Laffites very likely had some involvement with arranging the transportation of the *William's* slaves. Indeed, this may have been their first meeting with Aury and Jannet.

Soon after Aury's misfortune, Pierre became a direct participant in the smuggling, perhaps for the first time and very nearly the last. Early that year Vincent Dordoigaite, a Spanish merchant in Pensacola, fitted out a felucca, a small sailing vessel also powered by oars and well adapted for the coastal waters, to make a slaving run to Africa. He called the ship *El Bolador* and she made a successful voyage early that summer. On the return trip his ship had just cleared the Straits of Florida on July 5, with a straight sail to Pensacola, when an armed felucca appeared, identified herself as the privateer *Carolina*, raised the flag of France, and ordered *El Bolador* to stop. She was commanded by Jan Leloupe and Ange Michel Brouard, and the latter, at least, was no Frenchman, but a sometime resident of New Orleans. In fact, he was part owner and sometime captain of the *Duc de Montebello*. Dordoigaite had no doubt that the corsair was unlawfully fitted out and crewed in Louisiana, but had no choice but to yield. The "pirates," as Dordoigaite called them, imprisoned the felucca's crew on the corsair, then put a crew aboard *El Bolador* and sailed her to an inlet called Round Bay some miles east of the Balize. Brouard pillaged the brig of everything including seventy slaves, then burned her. That done, he sailed west to the mouth of Bayou Lafourche and then started the slaves on the underground trade route up the Lafourche to the New Orleans market, only releasing the crew of *El Bolador* after the slaves were gone.

Dordoigaite was not a man to take his loss genially. On his way to New Orleans he got word of the direction his slaves had been taken, and immediately reported it to the marshal, who found and recovered some of them before long. Dordoigaite continued using the law to reclaim more slaves as he learned of their locations.[68] He informed the secretary of the New Orleans Territory, Thomas Robertson, then acting governor during Claiborne's absence, and Robertson issued a proclamation condemning the "set of brigands" who brought this cargo into the territory via Barataria and Lafourche, and asserting that "an extensive and well-laid plan exists, to evade or to defeat the operation of the laws of the United States." He believed there were more than one hundred slaves now held illegally by citizens, and he called on the public to help find them and crush the lawbreakers. Not surprisingly, the people ignored him almost completely.[69]

But not completely. By late August, hearing that what one editor called "those *piratical smugglers*" had secreted some twenty of the slaves up the Lafourche and sold them to various planters, Sheriff Robert Walker of Lafourche Parish seized the slaves and marched them to another plantation where he found some of their companions, then brought them all to New Orleans.[70] Dordoigaite filed charges against Brouard, whom Hall's court ordered to post $40,000 bond while the matter of ownership of the slaves was settled, and got a warrant for the arrest of all of the blacks wherever found.[71] Then, in a surprising twist, the sheriff of Ascension Parish summoned Pierre Laffite to assist him in the parish seat, Donaldsonville. It was a young little community, founded by William Donaldson, a New Orleans merchant and builder. In February 1806 he bought the site of a defunct village called l'Ascension, and commissioned none other than the San Domingue refugee and sometime privateer Lafon to survey its lots and produce a town plan. Lafon himself owned property where the river and the bayou met, and it can hardly be coincidental that privateers now smuggled their goods on a stream that passed directly by the bayou bank property of their occasional comrade.[72] Certainly the Laffites used the Lafourche route, and even if they had not known Lafon on San Domingue, they became well-established associates now.

Somehow the sheriff in Donaldsonville suspected that one A. Bayonne and Louis Bourdier, in addition to having purchased some of the slaves through knowing them to be illegally imported, had forcibly taken four of the recently recovered slaves out of the local jail where they were being held temporarily, and then hidden them on Bourdier's plantation in the parish. In a delicious irony, the sheriff made Pierre a deputy marshal, and sent him to recover the blacks if he could. Laffite knew Bourdier, who was at this time an officer of the court and a frequent witness to legal acts in the parish. Bourdier also bought and sold a lot of property on the Lafourche, and was clearly a man of some prominence. Laffite took with him Captain Peter Paillet of *El Bolador*, who might be able to identify the missing slaves, and in mid-September they reached the Bourdier plantation to find the owner absent or in hiding. They found one young boy hidden in an outhouse, and Paillet claimed to recognize him. Then they found three more slaves concealed in a garret, and these, too, Paillet recognized. They seized all four and handed them over to the sheriff.[73] After Laffite and Paillet gave sworn depositions, the sheriff ordered Bourdier's arrest and Laffite, still a deputy marshal, served the writ on Bourdier in Donaldsonville and brought him in to be held on bail.[74]

Yet it may not have been as simple as that. Following the official abolition of the foreign slave trade, statute law provided a means of dealing with the slaves who were now undeniably in the country. If identified, they were to be seized, then sold at public auction—which made them lawful domestic slaves thereafter—with half of the proceeds going to the government and the balance going to the person who identified or recovered them. Slave sellers like the Laffites may have realized that they could use the law to "launder" Africans by importing them and then arranging for them to be turned over to the authorities. Thereafter they could buy the slaves at a sheriff's auction, usually for much less than their market value, and not only have lawful slaves to dispose of, but also recover half of what they paid at auction as their reward.

Moreover, if slave recovery led to a prosecution and fines for those involved, the informant was entitled to half of those fines. Paillet immediately filed claims for the slaves recovered by him and Laffite, as well as many others once they were found. The fine for trading in illegal Africans was $800 per slave, and Paillet eventually got his half.[75] In other similar claims filed on behalf of Dordoigaite, Paillet sought to collect $57,600.60 as the purchase price of all seventy-two of the slaves taken from his vessel.[76] Ultimately all of them were found and restored to Dordoigaite.[77] What Pierre Laffite got for his trouble is unknown, but the fact that he was a temporarily deputized officer of the court did not exclude him from a share of fines and rewards. Pierre appeared in court twice in September to file testimony and affidavits in the case, but by September 28 he was finished with the matter, at least officially.[78]

Yet the question remains of why the court brought him into it in the first place, especially since his brother was surely known in Ascension as well as New Orleans for his smuggling connections, and Pierre likely was, too. Pierre may have inserted himself into the matter, informing on Bourdier and others purely for profit. Almost certainly the Laffites were not parties to the smuggling of the *El Bolador* slaves, and if Jean had been the middleman in the operation, Pierre would hardly have helped in its disruption. If it became known that the Laffites sold slaves and then aided in their recovery, costing buyers the purchase price plus legal fines, buyers would not continue to deal with them for long. It is far more likely that Leloupe and Brouard were outsiders trying to bypass the growing Laffite operation at Grand

Terre, and that in aiding in the recovery of the slaves and the prosecution of buyers, Pierre was attempting to eliminate competition, and at the same time sending a none-too-subtle message both to privateers and to buyers that all parties would be wise to deal through the Laffites. The Laffites were stretching their tendons to take control of the Baratarian operation, as well as the Lafourche and other avenues of trade.

Within weeks of the *El Bolador* business, Pierre Laffite may have been unable to stretch anything else. Though only forty, sometime that fall or winter, perhaps as early as October, he suffered a thrombosis or stroke.[79] It attacked his left side, resulting in partial paralysis and fits of trembling that recurred again and again in the years to come, and perhaps the rest of his life. That December, for the first time, he failed to appear before a notary or to sign an instrument for a slave sale, leaving it to Robin to sign for both of them.[80] He may not have been feeling well enough to travel or leave New Orleans again until March 1811.[81] More to the point, though he was mobile most of the time, his permanent impairment meant that he could no longer be as active. From now on he would limit himself almost exclusively to being the brothers' New Orleans presence, leaving more and more of the active operation and management of their affairs elsewhere to his brother. Within a few months it would be general knowledge among Louisianans that the younger brother Jean Laffite was now in charge.

Not now my theme—why turn my thoughts to thee?
Oh! who can look along thy native sea.
Nor dwell upon thy name, whate'er the tale
So much its magic must o'er all prevail?

FIVE

Dawn of the Corsairs
1810-1811

B Y THE TIME Pierre Laffite finished his one and only stint enforcing the law, Louisiana was to experience more upheaval.
Since the spring of that year some of the Anglos living north of
Baton Rouge had let their discontent at being subject to Spain
erupt once more. Rebellion again threatened, the Kempers always at the forefront. They secured permission to hold a convention in Baton Rouge that September, and almost at once the
majority faction proposed declaring independence. The independence bloc stopped short of an outright declaration, but began
steps to enact a civil code that virtually stripped Spanish officials
of authority, even though most of the inhabitants of West Florida
were not in sympathy with the effort. When the convention adjourned, it seemed clear that any second meeting would try to
evict the Spaniards from West Florida and claim independence.

The complaints against Spain were the same as everywhere
else in her colonial empire. Pay for her soldiers habitually arrived
a year late, corruption riddled the administration of every government department, and justice was venal and capricious. "The

Reins of Government are held with a loose & careless hand & the public distress & discontent are every where conspicuous," complained a Pensacola merchant.[1] After *soldados* led by Folche marched toward Baton Rouge to enforce order, outbursts of resistance appeared in several places. On September 23, the day Pierre Laffite made his final appearance in court at Donaldsonville, a force of rebels attacked and easily took the fort at Baton Rouge. Then the insurgents set out to take Mobile, which Folche attempted to fortify while Pensacola girded itself. Meanwhile veterans of the capture of Baton Rouge met at St. Francisville some miles up the Mississippi and formally declared the independent Republic of West Florida under a blue flag with a single white star. At once some sent an appeal to President James Madison in Washington to annex West Florida to the United States, either for future statehood, or else to become a part of Louisiana.

Madison was all too ready to seize the opportunity. The United States had maintained since 1803 that the so-called Florida Parishes north of New Orleans between the Mississippi on the west and the Pearl River on the east were included in the Louisiana Purchase. Responding to the increasing appeals and violations, as well as complaints from authorities in Louisiana, on October 27, 1810, Madison issued a proclamation condemning the smuggling and slave trade on the Gulf coast in general, and instructing Claiborne as governor of the Louisiana Territory to take steps to assume control of West Florida preparatory to its being absorbed into Louisiana.[2]

The result was electric. "The Star of the West for such is the flag of the people of Baton Rouge, has shed its baleful influence as far as Tombigbie & Tensaw," grumbled an Englishman who preferred to remain under Spanish dominion. Americans clearly bent on aiding the rebellion began flocking to Pensacola on the pretext of business, and soon Mobile expected an army of five hundred rebels to attack.[3] Rumor rapidly increased their number to over one thousand, backed by artillery taken at Baton Rouge, but some thought another objective beckoned. "Pensacola will afford more plunder & be more convenient," wrote a man in Gainesville far to the east. "I wish them success in the great object (if it be object) of rendering Florida [a] republic as an American,—but I would endeavor to convince them—if they w[oul]d listen one moment to the voice of reason amidst the tempest of ambition,—that outrage and plunder will not lead to republicanism, or to peace, or to honour." When no attack materialized and the coup was accomplished with relatively little bloodshed, most Floridians felt relief.[4] On December 7, 1810, Claiborne and Governor David Holmes of the Mississippi Territory assumed control of St. Francisville, and the blue lone star flag went down. Soon they established control in Baton Rouge as well, and the Republic of West Florida ended its all-too-brief existence.

The event would have far-reaching significance for the Laffites and the rest of the privateering community. With West Florida as far as the Pearl now in American hands and the Spaniards on their way out, use of those parishes as a back door for smuggling slaves or other goods into Louisiana became more difficult. And this sudden change came virtually at the same moment as an event even farther away that would have an even greater impact. In May 1810 Cartagena, a formidable fortress city on the coast of Colombia, rose in open resistance. Within weeks the independence movement spread all the way to the Venezuelan capital at Bogotá, where a junta deposed the governor in July and declared Cartagena an open port.[5] Just as quickly the movement began to sputter, though not in Cartagena, where a mercenary, the former French officer Pierre Labatut, took over as all-but-dictator. Meanwhile Francisco de Miranda liberated Caracas and declared a Venezuelan republic in December 1810, and a young revolutionary named Simon Bolívar began making plans for a broader new republic he wanted to call Gran Colombia.

More than a decade of infectious rebellion in Spain's New World possessions thus saw its dawn. Not surprisingly, as an old corsair himself, Labatut anticipated the value privateers could provide to Cartagena now. Nearly alone at the moment, it did not need a navy, but it did need supply and finances. As luck would have it, dozens of privateers had just lost the last of their French bases with the fall of Guadaloupe. By now their commissions were expiring, even if they could find a lawful port. Thus as soon as the word spread through the Caribbean that Cartagena was in rebellion, corsairs flocked to the port, among them Dominique Youx. When the privateers sailed away, they took with them letters of marque signed by *Presidente-Gobernador* Manuel Rodríguez Torices and Secretary of War Joseph Axnazola y Vonay, as well as a code of conduct that they probably ignored entirely now that they were back in business.[6]

However, prizes could hardly be taken back to Cartagena for sale or for safekeeping. The money to be realized from selling prize goods lay in other places not strapped for cash by the cost of sustaining a rebellion. The corsairs might be sailing under legitimate commissions at the moment, but there were no other safe ports in the Caribbean or on the Gulf. There was Louisiana, however. The United States still maintained its neutrality toward France and Spain, meaning that vessels of an unrecognized insurgent Spanish city could not be received in New Orleans. But there was always the growing mercantile and smuggling establishment loosely managed by the Laffites.[7] As early as August 1810 Spanish authorities began to complain of the "unlucky incident" of their vessels being captured and "taken by the French pirates to the Great Land of Barataria."[8]

By the fall more Spanish vessels than ever were being taken by privateers, and their goods unloaded at Grand Isle for introduction into Louisiana. All their owners could do, through their agents or the Spanish consul Morphy in New Orleans, was protest and seek action in the federal court. An officer of Spain's ministry in Philadelphia complained to Secretary of State Robert Smith in Washington, specifying, "I also understand that the most frequented rendezvous of these Pirates is at Barataria, and have even been assured, that they have fortified themselves at that place, threatening vengeance with daring arrogance to whomever attempts disturbing them." He demanded that the president make efforts to dislodge and prosecute "this nest of pirates."[9]

For the next several years Madison would pursue an equivocal course. U.S. policy was to maintain neutrality and respect the rights of other nations—meaning Spain. Washington often offered assurances of sympathy along with promises to put an end to depredations on Spanish shipping by vessels fitted out or operating from American waters. Unofficially, anything that irritated or weakened Spain in North America worked to Madison's purpose, for his administration, like Jefferson's before it, wanted Spain out of the Floridas. Madison had encouraged the revolt in West Florida that now saw it a part of Louisiana, and his administration would be none too diligent in discouraging similar grassroots movements in East Florida, though support for independence there was weak as yet. When privately raised and funded schemes emerged to lead filibustering assaults on East Florida, Washington officially condemned them, but quietly willed them to succeed. For the next decade Spain would find Madison and his secretaries of state Smith and James Monroe to be duplicitous friends at best.

When it came to the privateers, however, Washington faced an internal dilemma. Their depredations hurt Spain and worked toward a laudable end. But the volume of the prize goods that came in by way of the Laffites and their like cost the government vast sums in unpaid customs duty. Aside from public condemnation, Madison was not certain what to do. Outright pirates were one thing, but these Americans and outcasts from a host of other nations now flying the flag of Cartagena—and soon other insurgent Spanish colonies—presented a more complex problem. Their defiance of Commodore Porter revealed their boldness. Their victory over him demonstrated their strength and the support for them in Louisiana.

New Orleans was an enormously important city to the United States, far out of proportion to its size, though already it was the largest city in the South. It commanded the Mississippi, and the river was the key to opening and exploiting the central part of the continent. Madison knew all too well how divided was the population, and how great the suspicion and resentment on the part of the French and Creole majority toward their new American townsmen and rulers. He need have no fear of an uprising among them, but with relations with Britain deteriorating rapidly, and with a strong and assertive British naval presence in the Caribbean, he could imagine a scenario in which a disaffected French population would choose Britain as the lesser of evils in a contest with the United States. He could not afford to lose even the lukewarm support of that population, especially when his own navy was so weak that Porter and his successors would complain for years of not having the proper vessels to do their job. Put the privateers out of business, and many of the merchants of Louisiana would suffer as well, and all of the citizens would pay more for their goods, not to mention the effect of removing the only source of new slaves capable of meeting expanding demand.

And so Washington would continue making a show of trying to quell violations, and naval authorities would continue to bring in a questionable privateer from time to time, while the district attorney steadily filed libels in the federal court against ships and cargoes believed to be improperly commissioned or unlawfully fitted out in American jurisdiction. But nearly as often, Judge Hall's court found in favor of the privateers. As a result, men who had been aboard ships taken and plundered at sea often encountered their robbers walking the streets of New Orleans, yet could do nothing about it.[10] At worst, the smugglers and privateers were an embarrassment to the American community. The French regarded them as colorful heroes who brought them bargains while thumbing a nose at Spain, Washington, and the resented local Americans at the same time.

Amid such an indulgent population, Jean was able to pursue as active a social life as he chose. Pierre, too, enjoyed that freedom, and not being married he may have allowed his social sport to extend beyond Marie Villard before his stroke restricted his activity.[11] The Laffites may have shared with other smugglers in the supply and operation of retail sales establishments on Conti and Toulouse streets in the city itself.[12] It was not a good time for Pierre's unauthorized sale of the slave that he leased when he went to Pensacola to come back to haunt him. In 1808 the slave was jailed in New Orleans as a runaway using an assumed name. His original owner, William St. Marc, paid for his release, only to have the man to whom Laffite sold the slave file a suit two years later, charging St. Marc for $125 in lease revenue for the time St. Marc had the slave after his release from jail. When he lost the suit and had to pay, St. Marc in turn filed a suit against Pierre Laffite to recover his loss.[13] By the end of the year Pierre was borrowing money from the Bank of Louisiana.[14] Then, just after the first of the year, something happened that threatened to bring the Laffites more directly under the gaze of the authorities for the first time, and at the same moment risked costing them the goodwill even of their French-Creole sympathizers.

Slave rebellions did not occur that often in Louisiana. The first came in 1730, an unsuccessful uprising led by a slave named Samba. In 1795 Point Coupée Parish experienced a brief slave revolt linked to the unrest in San Domingue. Three whites and twenty-five blacks were arrested, and twenty-three of them were put in a boat and floated downstream toward New Orleans, stopping in each parish church along the way for one of them to be hanged as an example.[15] Thereafter the fear that the San Domingue influence could lead to a serious revolt in Louisiana remained constant.

But now it happened. On January 8, 1811, at the plantation of Manuel Andry in St. Charles Parish, thirty-six miles south of New Orleans, Charles Deslondes, a San Domingue refugee, organized the other slaves on the plantation. Joined by a handful of "maroons," or runaway slaves living in the swamps close by, Deslondes's band wounded Andry and killed his son, then armed themselves and set off down the river road toward New Orleans, gathering recruits and burning plantations as they went. Eventually their force grew to somewhere over one hundred, though panicked reports soon inflated the number to five hundred or more. White families fled before their advance, and the families' carriages arriving in New Orleans spread the alarm. "The whole city was convulsed," a naval officer reported a few days later. Commodore John Shaw, Porter's successor, sent forty men and officers on shore to cooperate with General Wade Hampton and twenty-eight of his army regulars, augmented by volunteers and city militia under Captain George Ross, in an expedition to stop the insurgents.[16] While awaiting military support, white planters organized and on the evening of January 9 attacked the blacks on the François Bernoudi plantation and drove them into the woods. The next morning Hampton's detachment arrived, attacked, and stopped the rebels at Jacques Fortier's plantation in St. Charles Parish.

The first report said that sixty-six had been killed or executed on the spot, another sixteen taken prisoner, and seventeen escaped. The number killed was higher, as bodies continued to be found after this report, and soon more fugitives were found in the woods. On January 13 trials began at the Destrehan plantation and thirty blacks were brought before a tribunal of plantation owners. Two days later the tribunal condemned twenty-one of them to death and released the rest. The condemned were taken to their home plantations, and then shot and beheaded, the heads placed on poles to be a continuing admonition to other blacks thinking of freedom.[17] Meanwhile, others who escaped the soldiers fled to New Orleans, but several were caught and tried, and at least thirteen more were executed.[18]

Had they not moved quickly, Shaw concluded, "the whole coast would have exhibited one general scene of devastation." He trained the guns of his brig USS *Syren* on the city and the powder magazine in the Place d'Arms, and ordered guards to patrol the city for four nights. Even after the uprising was quelled on January 10, New Orleanians remained in a panic. "I have never before been witness to such general confusion and dismay, as prevailed throughout the city," said Shaw. Few men had their own guns, and he doled out weapons and ammunition from his own stores. Once the trials commenced, he observed that "condemnations, and executions by hanging and beheading are going on daily."[19]

Several theories about what caused the revolt emerged in Louisiana and the United States. Some blamed disgruntled Spanish planters in Louisiana. The most persistent suspicion, however, laid it at the feet of the San Domingue slaves, since the assumed leader Deslondes and several of the other offenders came from San Domingue. Of course, the community had been conditioned to fear a revolt by these people for fully a decade. Governor Claiborne certainly shared this view, though none of the evidence brought forward at the trials suggested that the rebellion was instigated specifically by recent arrivals from San Domingue.

As a result of the 1811 revolt, the Louisiana legislature passed stringent slave control laws. In New Orleans the city council enacted ordinances restricting the movement of slaves in the city, and banning from the city slaves not owned or temporarily hired by New Orleans residents. Slaves could not gather in the streets except for funerals and dances with mayoral sanction, and neither were they to be in the public squares, the markets, or coffee-houses. That the revolt hit just as Congress was debating state-hood for Louisiana came as a severe embarrassment, while word of the revolt spread renewed fear of slave insurrection throughout the Union. Small though it was, in numbers involved it was the largest revolt ever to occur in the United States.

Some influential leaders and some of the population wondered whether it was possible to absorb a large slave population and enclaves of foreign-born people such as the refugees without borrowing trouble. Everyone knew that in 1809 and 1810 the Laffites brought smuggled San Domingue slaves into the territory. No evidence emerged that slaves smuggled in through Barataria by the Laffites participated in the uprising.[20] But fear was far more persuasive than fact, and suddenly the perception of the Laffites in New Orleans shifted. Hereafter the authorities began to take greater notice of their activities, and to take efforts to hinder them.[21]

Certainly the Laffites did not let up in their growing trade, though Jean probably had to absorb more of the New Orleans share of their business until Pierre recovered. Moreover, Pierre's domestic responsibilities continued to expand. Sometime early in the year Pierre and Marie added to their brood with the birth of Jean Baptiste Laffite.[22] But if Pierre's health was yet too frail, all too many of the locals were happy to aid in the enterprise.[23] Walker Gilbert at Donaldsonville, empowered to seize smuggled goods if he could find them, declared in January 1811 that "it is astonishing the interest the inhabitants take in aiding those persons to carry on that shameful trade. I am certain that there is goods now secreted on the bayou to the amt. of $15,000 or 20,000$." That month he learned of three prizes being unloaded at the mouth of the Lafourche, probably of slave cargoes. Gilbert suspected that a justice of the peace in Lafourche Parish was involved in the trade, and learned that a few months before the owners of a boat carrying $20,000 worth of contraband goods had paid a $2,000 bribe to be allowed to go on their way when stopped in a canal above New Orleans.[24] In May a single French privateer brought in four prizes and ninety-one slaves that he offered to sell cheaply at $5,000 for the lot.[25]

The efforts of the authorities seemed as futile as ever. On March 14 one of Shaw's armed boats, *Gun Vessel No. 15*, took the privateer *La Sirena*—sailing under a French captain, yet carrying both Spanish and French papers—and a cargo of slaves. Shaw consulted with Governor Claiborne and District Attorney Grymes and they decided to try to make an example of her "for the purpose of breaking down the Piratical outrages committed by plunderers of this description, on our commerce." They took the offenders before Judge Hall on charges of piracy, but already Shaw expressed pessimism as to whether a fair trial could be obtained. He suggested that in the future captured pirates be taken to some other port in the United States where they could be tried. Meanwhile, remembering the experience of Porter before him, he predicted that "I shall acquire myself a host of enemies in this city; the population of which is made up of an influx of beings, from all countries, and of all descriptions, three fourths of whom, possessing the very worst principles. In a word, New Orleans, may with propriety, be stated the Botany Bay of America."[26] He proved to be a prophet, for when the accused came to trial before Judge Hall, despite good evidence of piracy against them, a jury composed almost entirely of Frenchmen gave them an acquittal.[27]

The Laffites had the Bayou Lafourche route firmly established now, and had thoroughly familiarized themselves with other available avenues to introduce goods. Timbalier and Terrebonne bays a few miles west of the mouth of the Lafourche were even larger than Barataria, and Timbalier offered good anchorages and a short overland portage to the Lafourche. Terrebonne Bay had a direct connection thanks to Bayou Terrebonne, which flowed out of the Lafourche some fifty miles above the bay. And the Laffites found other spots like Cat Island that were good for running prize ships aground for unloading.

Still Grand Isle dominated the Baratarians' enterprise. The fact that the pass at the east end of the island was the only one wide and deep enough to allow oceangoing vessels to pass meant that by commanding it the smugglers could enjoy safe haven inside the bay. Those vessels too deep of draft to make the pass anchored on the seaward side of the island.[28] The smugglers and the visiting privateers lived in rude quarters among the oaks, but also had camps at Cheniére Caminada on the mainland just opposite the western tip of the island, as well as at a few other points inside the bay.[29] Their scattered encampments bespoke the fact that no one really commanded them, however much the Laffites increasingly dominated their business.

The full scale of the brothers' business is elusive, but they certainly did well in slave sales early in the year. In five weeks in March and April 1811 Pierre sold twenty-five blacks, mostly Africans, for $15,275.[30] Most likely they represented all or part of a single cargo brought in that spring. But thereafter the Laffites' slave sales declined dramatically. In the next six months Pierre sold a single slave, and then five in three days at the end of October. Another three brought the Laffites some money in November, then four more sold in December, but for more than eight months of the year the Laffites sold just thirteen slaves for a total of $4,955. Moreover, for those six sold after April they realized prices per head that were down by a third over what slaves brought them earlier in the year.[31]

Finally the authorities had begun to erode the slave supply. Certainly the privateers continued taking vessels frequently, and just as often the court let them off when they were caught, but more and more they were losing their cargoes to the government if they had not unloaded at Barataria before capture. In August

Shaw's gunboats took two privateers off Mobile. In at least one case the naval vessels managed to take forty crewmen with a four-pounder cannon and a chest of muskets while they waited to be picked up by a privateer at Chandeleur Island outside Lake Borgne in the Gulf.[32] Then in September 1811, Lieutenant Thomas ap Catesby Jones took a privateer ship between Lake Barataria and Lake Perdido, and found it manned with French men who had earlier violated the neutrality act by signing on with a French privateer.[33]

That month the navy finally came after the trade at its source when it attacked Barataria. The reason for the change in policy was probably a combination of Shaw's frustration and the arrival at the New Orleans Naval Station of twenty-five-year-old Lieutenant Daniel Tod Patterson, a man with two driving motivations—a hunger for prize money, and an antipathy toward freebooters no doubt encouraged when he spent some time as the prisoner of Tripolitan pirates.

Under Shaw's orders, Lieutenant Francis Gregory took his *Gunboat No. 162* to the vicinity of Grand Terre, and there on September 5 met a man willing to inform on the privateers in return for a bribe, demonstrating the proverbial absence of honor among thieves. The informant told Gregory of the privateers' routes and said he expected some pirogues to be leaving the coast shortly with prize goods for the interior. The next morning Gregory followed up on the information, and soon he saw about twenty pirogues behind a sandbar. He opened fire on them and they immediately scattered. He then sailed on until shortly after noon when he came up on Grand Terre and spied the three-masted polacre *La Divina Pastora* aground in about six feet of water inside the bay with her masts taken down, clearly being stripped prior to destruction.

Gregory sent a shot toward her, and the men aboard raised the French flag in hopes of fooling him into thinking she was a friendly vessel in distress. But the lieutenant spotted privateer schooners tied to either side of her. One was the *Sophie* and the other *La Vengeance,* one of them yet another investment of the indefatigable Sauvinet, and crewmen from both vessels were even then unloading cargo from their prize. The twenty pirogues he had seen earlier floated nearby, loaded with prize cargo and guarded by perhaps one hundred men. Gregory tried to take his vessel through the pass but became stuck on a sandbar, and night had almost fallen by the time he got afloat and inside the bay. By then it was too late to attack, and he decided to wait until morning. But then he saw flames and realized that the privateers were setting fire to their prize. He sent an officer and several men in a launch into the bay to try to save the ship.

When they got to the scene they found one of the privateer schooners burning and adrift, while the other lay lashed to *La Divina Pastora,* itself just starting to catch the blaze. Gregory's men cut loose the burning schooner, then boarded the *La Divina.* Her cargo included more than sixty-three hundred packages of writing paper, which the boarders now found littered over the decks to spread the fire, brandy casks knocked open to expose their flammable spirits, and gunpowder strewn about waiting to go off. Miraculously, they doused the fire before the flames hit a half barrel of powder lying open in the magazine surrounded by bottles of powder, in turn ringed with slow-burning matches, and powder trails leading to yet more powder and paper. All that saved the vessel was that the privateers had fled in their pirogues so hurriedly that no one thought to light the fuses, and the flames from the burning schooner tied alongside moved slowly. Even then some of the privateers were close enough to shoot at the rescue party from the mainland, and the naval seamen sent scores of rounds into the darkness.[34]

Gregory's men saved two-thirds of the prize's cargo, and the prize herself, which they brought back to New Orleans, much to the delight of Spanish consul Morphy.[35] With Livingston representing him, Patterson libeled the vessel as a lawful prize in the district court in November, and by February 18, 1812, she had been ordered sold and the proceeds shared between Patterson and his sailors and the owners of the ship.[36] Nevertheless, this blow to the smugglers proved little more than an inconvenience compared to the profits to be made.

The open trade of some merchants with the smugglers was evidence enough of that. In January 1812 a newly empanelled grand jury made a statement to the court, and through it to all revenue officials, decrying the fact that "many facilities have been afforded to the persons engaged in this violation of the laws of the United States by characters considered respectable in this Community." It brought disgrace and dishonor upon them all, the grand jury declared, as well as injuring the revenue of the nation at a time when relations with Great Britain approached the point of war.[37] No doubt the grand jury declaration was prompted by President Madison's annual message on November 5, 1811, when he complained of "the practice of smuggling, which is odious everywhere, and particularly criminal in free governments." It was worse, he said, "when it blends with a pursuit of ignominious gain a treacherous subserviency, in the transgressors, to a foreign policy adverse to that of their own country."

Yet the privateers and their retail merchants in New Orleans were bold enough to confront their critics in the city's press. On December 18 one of them who signed himself only as "The Agent of the Freebooters" sent a letter arguing that the privateers were patriots, too, simply trying to punish the British and the Spanish, and at the same time do a civic benefaction to the people of Louisiana by introducing cheap goods to "prevent the total stagnation of trade during the existence of the Nonintercourse Act." Indeed, he declared, "without us there would not be a bale of goods at market." Warming to his theme, he cited "the open manner in which our business is done," and concluded from the ineffectual attempts at control and policing by the authorities, that "the government of the United States has no objection either to the fitting out of our prizes and the sale of their cargoes, without troubling ourselves about the payment of duties." The inaction of the authorities proved "the protection and license we enjoy, to plunder when we please, and import without entry what we think proper."

Pointing out that they sold their goods at low prices in return for cash "in these hard times," he even dared to promote their business by publishing an announcement that "the association company of free booters have recommended their calling, and have formed depots at Barrataria, the mouths of Fourche, and Teche, at the Chandeliers, and Breton Islands, where they sell ships and cargoes by wholesale; and if their old stands in Conde and Toulouse streets can be obtained, will there open by retail." He then referred to the recent sale of some of the smuggled goods from *La Divina Pastora* and the fact that the men who handled the sales—Sauvinet probably being one of them—made over $30,000, which ought to be an encouragement to other merchants to join in the contraband business. "There are still a vast quantity of goods for sale; ships, brigs, schooners, and several hulls, to be disposed of," he added. Even the weather wanted people to trade with the contrabandists, for the annual rise in the Mississippi would make it easy to reach their depots in Barataria.[38]

Who this "Agent of the Freebooters" was is uncertain, though it is easy to see in it the taunting hand that would characterize a few products of the pens of both Laffites before long. Now might not have been a good time for a Laffite to be thumbing his nose at authorities, however. The grand jury claimed not to know the identities of "the persons engaged in this nefarious practice." Yet by now rumor must have associated the brothers with the trade. Else how would people in town have known where to direct prospective slave buyers as early as 1809?

Certainly there would be enough privateers to continue the business. On November 11, 1811, Cartagena officially declared its independence and became the headquarters of the newly declared United Provinces of New Granada, including portions of Colombia and Venezuela. Though no nation recognized Cartagena's independence, and Spain retook most of Venezuela by the following summer, New Granada's President Manuel Rodríguez Torices would in time resort to handing out privateering commissions to men willing to prey on Spanish shipping and that of Spain's ally Britain.[39] French and San Domingue sailors filled Cartagena's streets, and soon *Cartageñeros* and San Domingans became privateers and pirates almost interchangeably.[40] Aury and Renato Beluche went to Cartagena to take their commissions as lieutenants in the Granadan service early in 1813, and some among the Barataria-based privateers soon followed.[41]

Ironically, newly independent Cartagena granted equal rights to whites and free blacks and outlawed the slave trade, but did not outlaw slavery. While sailing under Cartagena's colors and commissions, the privateers who would bring slave cargoes into Louisiana in the years ahead were participating in a trade outlawed in Cartagena itself.[42] Oblivious of that, when Torices sent agents to Louisiana some months hence, they would seek out the Baratarians, as well as the free colored men from San Domingue and the privateers ejected from Cuba in 1809, all of whom provided natural targets of opportunity. Well before then, however, an even more attractive prize appealed to privateers' hunger for plunder when rumors spread briefly that an expedition would fit out in New Orleans to sail to Cuba and attack Baracoa.[43]

It was the signal for the explosion of privateering on the Gulf, and with it the rise of a class operating in the gray area between legitimate corsairing and rank piracy. A small army of men stood poised to reap the profits the new trade promised, the Laffites among them, though as yet they were only faces in a crowd. Within the next eighteen months all that would change. The United States would be presented with an organization and daring never before seen, and the challenge of dealing with two impending wars—one with the British, and the other with the privateers.

This said, his brother Pirate's hand he wrung,
Then to his boat with haughty gesture sprung.
Flash'd the dipt oars, and sparkling with the stroke,
Around the waves' phosphoric brightness broke

SIX

Origins of the Laffite Fleet
1811-1813

T HE ILLICIT ENTERPRISE had two arms that must be severed if the government was to control the problem. First, the illegal fitting out, arming, and manning of privateers in New Orleans had to be stopped, primarily by the United States Navy; second, the internal trade in contraband goods smuggled from the coast to New Orleans had to be curtailed, and this was the job of the customs and revenue authorities. The difficulty was compounded by the fact that lawful privateers—or at least vessels that could show commissions obtained in Cartagena—also sailed the Gulf.

The privateers bringing goods into Barataria and elsewhere to the Laffite smugglers gave Captain Shaw constant frustration. "The whole of the coast from Vermilion Bay westwardly, round to the Rigolets on the east, appears, in fact, to swarm with pirates,—fitted out, for the most part, at New Orleans," he complained to Washington. He needed vessels capable of cruising on the Gulf, and his were not up to it. The gun vessels were "dull sailors," and not fast enough to compete with the privateers.[1]

Still he had to try. Vessels in Shaw's flotilla cruised often along the west coast of Louisiana, even stopping at Barataria, though sometimes they could find scarcely a vestige of the Grand Terre operations when they went ashore.[2] On December 27 Shaw sent one of his gunboats after the privateer vessels *Mary* and *Adeline,* and it briefly exchanged shots with them a few days later. The privateers forced the gunboat to back off, and went on to take on arms at the mouth of the Lafourche on or about January 26. At virtually the same time Catesby Jones, commanding *Gun Vessel No. 156,* came upon a privateer schooner anchored at Grand Terre with a crew of eighty or ninety. He fired on her, whereupon she raised sail. But though Jones put several shots through her and her crew was seen throwing guns overboard to lighten ship to keep from sinking, the privateer finally left him behind.[3] Jones returned to Barataria and captured a crew belonging to the French privateer *Marengo.* He discovered that the crew were almost all Americans, enlisted at New York.[4] More encounters with French corsairs took place off Grand Terre in February, but with no happy result.[5]

Meanwhile, the Treasury Department's Revenue Service tried their best. Early in the year Captain George Gibson and his men seized $7,000 to $8,000 worth of contraband goods on Bayou Lafourche.[6] Lieutenant Angus Fraser commanding the revenue cutter the *Louisiana* chased and took a privateer in the Mississippi in February. Her captain, Pierre Cadet, had earlier cleared a ship out of New Orleans under Swedish colors, but once in the Gulf "went directly a privateering," as Fraser put it.[7] The next month Fraser took another privateer, the *Two Brothers,* which had come into New Orleans listing a cargo of rice and flour on her manifest. When he opened the barrels aboard her, he found wine, brandy, and gin hidden within.[8]

The hapless Louis Aury also fell afoul of the authorities once more. In the past three years he had failed at almost everything. When San Domingue fell to the British, he lost his vessel there in port and escaped to Guadaloupe, where he equipped another.

When the British took Guadaloupe he lost that vessel, too, and came to Louisiana, where he spent $4,500 to buy a boat—only to have it confiscated when authorities caught him illegally outfitting it for privateering. Aury had already sworn vengeance on the British and Spaniards, and now took a share in a French corsair for $2,000. But when he brought her into a United States port, Americans attacked and killed or wounded a dozen of his crew, then burned the boat. Now he hated Americans, too.[9]

Despite the discomfiture of Aury and Cadet, Captain Shaw continued to report his gunboats "altogether inadequate" to the task of protecting commerce from the pirates and smugglers of the coast. By the summer of 1812, with war with Britain brewing, Shaw had only two brigs and eleven gunboats to guard the coastline under his care. He assigned five of the gunboats to a patrol west of the Balize, a hopelessly outnumbered force as he—and the smugglers—well knew. Experience showed that if his vessels could not stop a privateer on the first fire, the lighter craft quickly outdistanced the navy ships, and he acknowledged grudgingly that the smugglers and pirates were also better sailors than his own. If proof were needed, in May Jones and his gunboat came up against two privateers off Bayou Lafourche, where they had brought in a Spanish prize, but he could not catch them.[10] A month later, on June 16, Jones attacked two French privateers and their Spanish prize off Barataria, but was beaten off.[11]

Philip Grymes died suddenly the previous year, leaving the office of district attorney to be filled on May 4, 1811, by his brother John R. Grymes. But the new Grymes and Judge Hall were no more successful in stopping privateers than the navy.

Meanwhile, another familiar name resurfaced, the determined corsair Dominique. He had been in port the previous spring, purchasing ship's victuals and apparently observing every stipulation of the regulations covering legal privateers in American waters.[12] Now, late in August, he brought his vessel the *Pandoure* up the river to Fort Plaquemines, where the commandant stopped him and Dominique gave the officer a packet addressed to the French consul in New Orleans.[13] He claimed to be out of Bordeaux, with a cargo of sugar and cotton, and explained that in a terrible hurricane on August 19 and 20 he had lost his masts and was nearly killed, and now needed repairs for his ship and a doctor for himself.[14] Following procedure, he filed a statement of the damage done to his vessel, and at the same time claimed that his commission was about to expire, and that he needed to get a letter of permission from the consul allowing him to return to France after repairing his ship and removing her armaments.[15]

Dominique, for a change, appeared to be a lawful privateer with a genuine commission. At least, the authorities did not interfere with him. He prepared a careful list of his prizes taken since he left Bordeaux, and valued his cargo at $36,921, for which sales brought in $20,721.38. He even set aside the prescribed percentages of his profits for the expenses of the local consulate, for invalids from the French navy, and for the care of French prisoners of war in England.[16] He inventoried everything on his ship, from armaments to barrels of biscuits, prior to liquidation.[17] Then on October 15 he sold the *Pandoure* for $7,500.[18] Her commission being expired, she was of no more use to him, and with the profits from his voyage he could buy another vessel when he was ready to put to sea once more.[19]

All of this activity meant trade for the Laffites—who, incredibly, had not yet appeared in any charges for smuggling.[20] Certainly the district court prosecuted merchants who tried to bring merchandise into the city without paying proper customs duty, as José La Rionde found out when he was sued for failure to pay duty on a cargo of coffee and brown sugar from Mexico.[21] But perhaps the Laffites had a friend in a high place, for rumor said that Daniel Clark, currently with the United States consular office in New Orleans, was in their pay, and that was why Pierre could sell goods with impunity out of their reputed warehouse on Chartres Street.[22]

When customs officials tried to go after the shipments, they had little better fortune than Shaw's gunboats. "The nature of the coast is peculiarly favourable to their schooners; and the disposition of a very great proportion of the population are unfortunately too favourable to the execution," customs collector Thomas Williams had reported to the secretary of the treasury in March.[23] In mid-October 1812 revenue agents did go down a bayou from English Turn to Barataria Bayou, where they encountered several smuggler craft. The smugglers fled and the revenue officers took their booty, but the smugglers attacked that night and recovered their goods—embarrassing to say the least. Perhaps it was this humiliation that led a few weeks later to the first really successful assault on the Laffite enterprise, and the introduction of the Laffites' name on the court docket in New Orleans.

A factor in the smugglers' assault may have been the Laffites' own embarrassment of a sort, or at least Pierre's. He seemed in the main recovered from his stroke, though fits of palsy still struck him, affecting his mood as much as his body. There was good news in his household when Marie presented him with another child, his daughter Rosa, born August 28, but he would scarcely be in New Orleans to see her during the next several months, for his old problems with money haunted him.[24] In fact, before long he would have no known residence in the city, meaning that he spent most of his time either with Jean at Grand Isle, or at Donaldsonville, or in one of a few safe homes of associates on the outskirts of New Orleans.[25] Throughout 1812 slave sales continued to bring in cash that the Laffites needed to build their enterprise, though seemingly not nearly as much as before. In the first half of the year Pierre lawfully disposed of just eight blacks for $4,270, though he and Jean certainly sold many more at

Grand Isle for much greater sums.[26] Still Pierre was no longer sharing the proceeds of legal sales with Robin, with whom his informal partnership had all but ended. Moreover, despite the substantial sums the brothers realized from their smuggled goods, theirs was a costly operation. Proceeds had to be shared with others, supplies had to be purchased for their employees at Barataria, money was needed from one sale to buy the goods for the next, and from time to time cash flow presented a problem, especially given Pierre's history of poor money management and Jean's taste for expensive living and entertainment, which earned him the sobriquet "Gentleman Lafitte" in New Orleans.[27]

It did not help that Pierre lost his pocketbook in May, and with it several promissory notes on which they had yet to collect,[28] including a large one for $500. In April Pierre put $146.30 on account with merchant Antoine Lanaux to buy twenty-three barrels of ship's biscuit, no doubt for Jean to take to Barataria, yet five months later he had not paid the debt and Lanaux filed suit for collection.[29] In October shortly after Lanaux filed his suit, Pierre sold a slave cook he had owned for six years to raise $500, then borrowed $217.50 from his old partner Robin, and in November borrowed $500 more from another acquaintance, pledging two slaves as surety. In five months' time he had not paid this debt either. When Robin went looking for Pierre at Bernard Tremoulet's Exchange Coffee House at the corner of Chartres and St. Louis and other haunts, no one knew his whereabouts. Indeed, no one admitted even to knowing him, or offered to settle the debt on his behalf.[30] Meanwhile Pierre's ill-advised sale of that leased slave in 1806 caught up with him yet again. Already in March of this year William St. Marc had sued him and Pierre was forced to post a bond for $2,000 to guarantee his appearance in court. Pierre lost the suit and the judge levied a settlement of $1,133.39 against him. By December Laffite had paid barely more than $500 of the debt, and so the original owner of the slave filed another suit against Pierre for $611.68, which forced Pierre to post another $1,000 with the court even though he denied the debt.[31] If the courts wanted money from the Laffites, they would have to stand in line, but before long the courts would be interested in the Laffites for reasons other than debt, for Pierre's absence from New Orleans that fall involved much more than evading his creditors.

Part of the problem, of course, was the outbreak of war with Britain on June 18, 1812. General James Wilkinson arrived to take command of the defenses of New Orleans and that region of the Gulf coast on July 9, 1812, but found it ill-prepared. Immediately he began strengthening existing fortifications, including works at English Turn, and trying to inspire the local American and Creole population to volunteer, with discouraging results. With all this on his hands, his dispatches to the war department in Washington made virtually no mention of smugglers.[32]

Mounting debt may have forced them to it, but most likely the Laffite brothers could not resist the opportunity they saw. Never before had the same individuals controlled the acquisition of prize goods through piracy or privateering, their delivery to the market vicinity, subsequent smuggling or transport of the goods to the waiting market, and then their wholesale and retail sale. The potential for profit in controlling every phase of the operation beckoned, and now the brothers resolved to do just that, taking advantage of the shortages caused by the war and the British blockade, and the distraction of the authorities thanks to the war.

The endeavor required only the organization and imagination of sophisticated entrepreneurial minds, and the Laffites had those to be sure. Around October the brothers purchased a prize schooner brought into Barataria by a corsair, very possibly Captain Aury, for now the Laffites engaged Aury's old hand, the forty-year-old Italian Jean Jannet, to go to New Orleans to enlist a crew. The schooner was a workhorse privateer vessel, simple and efficient to operate with its two masts, and infinitely adaptable into variations such as the topsail schooner, the foretopsail schooner, and the hermaphrodite brig.[33] The brothers had to arm the vessel, which was easy enough with a schooner. Privateer schooners and feluccas—small, wide, three-masted boats that were light drafted and fast, yet held a lot of cargo—usually carried only muskets rather than cannon, few being large enough to mount any artillery other than an eighteen-pounder, a gun tube nine feet long and thirty-nine hundred pounds, with a five-inch bore. Some carried long cannon called "long Toms" regardless of their weight or bore, often on swivels. Larger vessels might have two or more carronades, which fired through ports on the gunwales.[34]

Meanwhile Jannet hired a man named Antonio to scour the town for likely hands, then bring them to a house on the outskirts where Jannet signed them on and paid each an advance of $10 against future shares of prize spoils. This outlay alone probably explained some of the money Pierre was borrowing that fall. When Jannet had about forty men engaged, he sent them to Grand Isle by way of Donaldsonville and Bayou Lafourche to avoid attracting the attention of the port authorities or customs and naval officers downriver. Jannet took another route to Barataria, and was there to meet the crew when they arrived. Also waiting was the schooner, now fitted out at Laffite expense with two small cannon mounted on deck. What she did not have, apparently, was a commission.[35]

Before the ship could sail early in November, both Laffite brothers arrived to see Captain Jannet take her out on her—and their—maiden corsairing voyage. That done, the brothers had other things to do. Another privateer had dropped anchor and unloaded twenty-six bales of cinnamon, fifty-four linen shirts, three pieces of Russian sheeting for making bed linen, seven pieces of canvas, one bundle of twine, and one handkerchief, goods worth an estimated $4,004.89.[36] Five pirogues and twenty-two men waiting nearby took on the cargo—an ordinary transaction, only Pierre would be with Jean for the return to New Orleans. It was probably his first smuggling run, and one that both brothers expected to be routine.[37]

The boats loaded, the Laffites raised sails and started northward up the bay, picking their way through innumerable small islets and into Little Lake Barataria. By nightfall on November 16 they were still under sail approaching the northern end of the lake, where they would pass a spot known locally as the Temple and enter Bayou Rigolett, which they would follow, relying on their oars, on their way to Bayou Barataria and the rest of the way to the back door to New Orleans. Suddenly in the bright moonlight the Laffites made out the dim shapes of boats ahead of them, sailing without identifying flags. At once the brothers decided to flee, but the wind was against them. They ordered their crews to drop sails and pull at their oars as they turned to run for the distant shore. The other boats gained on them in the time this took, and the chase continued for only a few minutes before the lead boat behind them came within eighty yards, close enough to hail.

One of the Laffites called out, demanding to know who followed them, and out of the darkness came the reply "United States Troops." One of the Laffites yelled back to the pursuers that if they came any closer he would "fire into them & kill them every one." Meanwhile the smugglers continued pulling feverishly, while others began throwing their incriminating cargo overboard, one man carelessly tossing away his gun in the confusion. Finally they reached the shore and fled the boat, only to see that some of their pursuers were about to run ashore a short distance away. In the moonlight the smugglers could see that many of the men wore the regulation army summer uniform of white roundabouts and pantaloons, with black bayonet scabbards and cartridge boxes attached to black leather belts, and some wore dragoon helmets with plumes. A few even wore dragoon uniforms of blue trimmed with white, while others wore the winter uniform of blue with red facings. It was impossible to mistake them for anything other than the military.[38]

When the soldiers started to get out of their boats, some of the smugglers yelled at them not to set foot on land or they would "put every man to instant death."[39] Then the Laffites saw another boat loaded with fifteen armed men approaching their beached pirogues, and the trap became evident. Their pursuers had split up, and now had the Laffites between two fires if they started shooting. Seeing this, some of the smugglers ran into the woods, while others headed back to their pirogues. It was quickly apparent that a water escape attempt would be futile, but a few smugglers tried to jump into a pirogue and row away in the darkness. Their captors fired a volley into the boat, killing one man and persuading the rest to give up. Almost beyond question, it was the first time that Jean and Pierre Laffite suffered or witnessed a fatality in their business.[40]

The Laffites discovered that they had fallen prisoner to Lieutenant Andrew Hunter Holmes, onetime Natchez lawyer and Mississippi militia commander who now in the war with Britain took a commission in the 24th United States Infantry. He was the very man they had embarrassed a few weeks earlier. Following that debacle, his superiors had ordered him to take a detachment of thirty or forty men to assist revenue officers in suppressing smuggling via Little Lake Barataria. Holmes was aided now by a report received just days earlier from John Ballinger, whom Wilkinson had ordered out the month before to perform a thorough investigation of the passes and rumored defenses at Barataria and the mouth of the Lafourche. Ballinger had discovered that at Barataria vessels drawing less than three feet of water could approach within two leagues—about six miles—of New

Orleans, though sometimes the vessels would have to pole because the bayou was too narrow for rowing and too swampy to cordelle by towing from the banks. In high water vessels could come all the way to the Mississippi.

With an eye toward the possibility of British invasion, Ballinger concluded that it would be practicable for troops to advance on New Orleans by this route, and to guard against that he suggested that a post be built at the Temple, a mound of shells and Indian bones on the shore of Lake Salvadore that sat five feet above the highest tide and had a bluff with a command of any approach for three-fourths of a mile. "No other place can come in competition with it," he believed. All water routes to New Orleans by Barataria Bay came together below the Temple, so a battery there would oversee everything. Still, the land was low and subject to flooding at every uncommon tide and was commanded by higher ground on the same island. Meanwhile Ballinger found that the Lafourche had two mouths, a narrow one on the east called the Little Bayou one league west of the west pass of Grand Isle, and a bigger one called the Grand Bayou that opened three leagues farther west. A battery of three cannon at the fork of the Lafourche would command the latter, he thought. He suggested that local Creole volunteers would be best suited to garrison such a battery, "as I consider it a very unhealthy situation."[41]

Holmes had come twenty-five miles through the bayous from New Orleans without sighting anything suspicious, but he now knew the best spots to catch smugglers in action. The night before encountering the Laffites, he had spotted a single pirogue that refused to stop when hailed. A shot persuaded the occupants to come ashore and surrender, and Holmes confiscated a small amount of contraband but let the crew go because of their cooperativeness after capture—meaning they probably told him he could expect to find much larger spoils if he kept moving down Bayou Barataria.[42]

Holmes's men rowed their own and the smugglers' boats back across the lake to a temporary camp, and there they searched their captures carefully, finding among other things the cinnamon, two finely sharpened swords, three loaded muskets with their hammers cocked ready to fire, and a variety of dirks and daggers. Holmes asked each of the captives to identify himself, and probably for the first time learned that Pierre and Jean Laffite were present. When he spoke with Jean Laffite, who was clearly in command, he asked him where the contraband came from, and Laffite frankly admitted that it came in aboard a very powerful privateer currently near Grand Isle.[43]

Holmes took the captured boats, cargo, and prisoners back to New Orleans, losing a smuggler who escaped along the way, and turned them over to the district court. Despite the protests of the Spanish owners who appeared to identify their property, Judge Hall's court ordered the goods sold and the proceeds distributed among the captors and the government.[44] Still, consul Diego Morphy considered the outcome of the expedition encouraging enough that he advised Spain's governor-general in Havana of the affair, and asked him to publicize there and in Vera Cruz the capture of the smugglers and their goods as inducement to merchants to continue shipping merchandise. He did not mention the Laffites by name, however.[45] The Laffites and their companions escaped immediate charges and were apparently released pending introduction of any formal charges, free to go about town unmolested. Jean, at least, hurried back to Grand Isle, and soon after his return he saw something to make the loss of the cinnamon a pittance.

His enterprise was growing. In January Jannet brought the brothers' corsair schooner into Barataria with a Spanish prize taken several miles from Campeche on the Yucatán peninsula. The vessel had been outbound from Campeche for Havana with a cargo of slaves, logwood, indigo, and cochineal. Jannet put her crew ashore at Sisal, near Campeche, then sailed her back to Barataria.⁴⁶ She was named the *Dorada*—the Golden One—a so-called hermaphrodite brig owned by Francisco Ajuria. No one much liked the traditional brig, but the Spaniards sometimes sailed polacres that could be altered into hermaphrodite brigs, with square sails on the foremast and the mainmast rigged with triangular sails like a schooner. This was a very effective adaptation for the wind and waters of the Gulf and the coastal trade. A big hermaphrodite brig might displace 150 tons and measure 80 feet at the keel.⁴⁷

Laffite sold the seventy-seven slaves aboard the *Dorada* on the spot to Sauvinet, who paid $170 a head. That alone brought in just over $13,000, probably more than enough to pay for the corsair and its first voyage and to give the brothers a taste of what they could expect. The cargo was worth another $5,000.⁴⁸ Almost at once Pierre and Jean began buying the goods and arms necessary to convert their new prize into a second privateer. She had a single deck, measured sixty-two and one-half feet in length, just over eighteen feet in the beam, and displaced sixty-nine tons. There were no frills, no galleries or figurehead, but she was fast and strong enough to mount eight guns.⁴⁹ Before long the *Dorada* was ready, and the Laffites sent her out with Jannet in command. Neither Jean nor Pierre went along. Their proper place was ashore overseeing the entire operation, not off on the Gulf hunting prizes. They had engaged Jannet, a professional, to do that for them, and he did it well.

Not many days out the *Dorada* took a Spanish schooner and by late February Jannet had her back at Barataria, where the Laffites found aboard her $8,460 in silver coin, forty-nine gold doubloons worth $784, a jewel box valued at $150, and two boxes of wine worth $24. All told, their second haul made them $9,418. The captured schooner was of no use to them, but rather than burn her, they turned her over to her captain and crew and let them sail away, having shown considerable courtesy to the

Spaniards temporarily in their custody. It was a course they would follow frequently hereafter. Everyone shared in the prize, including a new arrival, Vincent Gambi, who would become a frequent denizen of Grand Isle and an associate, if not a close friend, of the Laffites.[50] Not ones to waste time or opportunity, the Laffites sent the *Dorada* out again before the end of the month, this time with Pierre Cadet in command. The Laffites had something else in mind for Jannet. They were going to build a fleet.

Late in March 1812 the French privateer *La Diligent* had arrived at the Balize and tried to come up the river under the familiar plea of distress.[51] Denied, she attempted to land several trunks of foreign goods clearly intended for smugglers, but customs men caught her in the act. Fraser took possession of the contraband, then searched the vessel and found more, plus ten slaves from Africa. He put an officer aboard and had her taken first to Fort St. Phillip upstream, and later to New Orleans. She had been built in Bermuda in 1808, and was recently out of Charleston, South Carolina, under command of Captain John Anthony Gariscan, and one thing not found aboard her was a commission or other papers to establish her as a lawful privateer. Gariscan, who had been a corsair based in Guadaloupe until 1810, and in Cuba before that, claimed that he had his letter of marque from the French consul in Charleston, and had sent his commission and ship's papers to New Orleans ahead of the vessel.[52] Fraser knew enough to be suspicious of Gariscan, inasmuch as he believed the fellow had landed some ninety illegal blacks on Breton Island the year before.[53]

Even if the court was inclined to favor the privateers, men such as Gariscan made it hard. No sooner was *La Diligent* in port under Fraser's care than Gariscan began enlisting as crewmen some of the men recently discharged from the privateer *Marengo* after Jones brought her into port, making *La Diligent* liable for seizure for being outfitted within the United States. Gariscan even openly engaged locals to act as guides, which he hardly needed if he intended to put back to sea on legitimate business. Grymes was convinced that if *La Diligent* were allowed to leave port with her cargo of goods and Africans intact, the cargo would be landed on the coast and smuggled back into New Orleans within days. Still, Gariscan's commission from the French consul in Charleston appeared to be in order, and Grymes had to let *La Diligent* go. But he communicated his suspicions to Jones of the navy and Fraser of the revenue service, and Fraser vowed to watch the ship all the way down the Mississippi until she sailed out of sight on the Gulf.[54]

Beyond question, Gariscan brought his ship into Barataria as soon as he was beyond Fraser's grip. There he unloaded his cargo and became well acquainted with the Laffites if he had not already made a deal with Pierre in New Orleans. By the end of the year Gariscan had sold or traded *La Diligent* to Jean and Pierre Laffite.[55]

It was time to escalate their business. Jean engaged Antoine Lavergne, currently a baker in New Orleans but a man with privateering experience, to come to Grand Isle and oversee fitting out the ship that winter. Like many another corsair, Lavergne was often known to his crew by an alias, in his case Cadet Patte Grasse, or just Captain Cadet. Shortly after the turn of the year, he had the massive 136-ton, single-decked schooner ready.[56] Significantly, the Laffites seem not to have considered trying to secure a legitimate American letter of marque for her. The federal government had authorized a limited number of such commissions to be issued at New Orleans, as at Charleston, Boston, and elsewhere, and by the late spring of 1813 eleven were granted—one of them to Beluche for his vessel the *Spy*.[57] There were too many restrictions, however, too much oversight for the Laffites' liking, and a share of the takings had to go to the government, which would depress profits unacceptably. It was easier and more expedient to buy a commission from Gariscan, or to buy his commission with his ship.[58] If they acquired *La Diligent* about the same time that their first schooner was ready to sail under Jannet, then they may have used Gariscan's commission to try to legitimize prizes taken by the schooner, but the one commission could hardly cover the schooner, the *Dorada*, and now *La Diligent*. And despite Pierre's later claim that they paid for a commission in New Orleans, probably purchased from Gariscan, the possibility remains that they simply did not have one, which made them pirates.[59]

Meanwhile the Laffites assigned Jannet as master of the vessel, and then began enlistments in New Orleans to make up the eighty-four common seamen needed to run the ship. Among them were Laurent Maire, the helmsman whom the Laffites already knew, and artillerists, quartermasters, cooks, and six officers besides Jannet and Jean, including another experienced corsair, Pierre François Laméson. All told, the Laffites had to pay out more than $1,000 by the time they completed the ship's crew.[60] The outfitting would be expensive as well. In addition to the cost of the vessel herself, the price of a set of anchors could be $192 or more, sufficient cable for anchoring might run $338, and then pork for the crew cost $18 a barrel, and sugar twenty cents a pound for the coffee that cost thirty.[61] While the profit from the Laffites' slave sales should have been more than sufficient to cover the expense, apparently it was not, for Pierre was still borrowing several hundred dollars in the middle of February, most likely to meet the debts incurred in victualing and crewing the ship.[62]

Armed with a dozen fourteen-pounder cannon, eighty muskets, an equal number of cutlasses, and twenty pairs of pistols, *La Diligent* was formidable. Jean had gone to New Orleans late in January, probably to pay debts and to raise more money for outfitting, by disposing of some of the latest cargo as well as selling a slave, but soon he was back on the coast.[63] Perhaps the ship's strength made the Laffites more daring, for now Jean decided to take command of *La Diligent* himself and to take her with the prize cargo from the *Dorada* directly to New Orleans.

Late in February Jean sailed *La Diligent* to the Balize, and then dropped anchor. He knew that the harbor officials were well on to the trick of pleading damage at sea. Instead, he wrote a letter to the French consul in the city, identifying his ship as a French privateer whose commission had expired on her way to New York. Claiming that he was aware of the harbor officials' "persecutions" of French corsairs who tried to refit or supply in New Orleans, or to sell their prize merchandise, he sent his ship's papers to the consul—no doubt including Gariscan's genuine expired commission—and asked the consul to keep them secure for him and to get him permission to come into port to sell his goods. Laffite added that his crew's enlistments were expiring and he feared they would not stay with him, as they had not been paid. He appealed to the consul for an advance on the money due his crewmen and a letter authorizing payment of the balance that he could present for redemption to the French consul general in New York, as well as a recommendation to issue him letters of marque for a "new expedition" or else to return to a port in France itself.

Laffite sent the letter and ship's papers by one of his officers who delivered them in the city before the end of the month.[64] The ruse appears to have worked. J. B. Laporte, the interim French consul in New Orleans, apparently got the vessel permission to come upriver, though perhaps not all the way to New Orleans, then sent his vice consul to visit the ship, bringing with him the necessary forms. Jean Laffite, however, was not aboard. He went ashore somewhere on the river, knowing that by this time a warrant might have been issued for him in connection with his arrest by Holmes in November. Jannet simply told Laporte that Laffite had fallen ill and gone ashore, putting Jannet in charge.[65]

Pierre Laffite met with them now, and told the official that *La Diligent* belonged to him and that he had paid for her outfitting in New Orleans, a half-truth at best. The consular official accepted it all the same. He assembled the crew and told them that other French privateers were also in the river, then took down the names of the crewmen, mustered them into French service, read them the articles of war, and explained to them the proportion of any future prize money to which they would be entitled—all of which was necessary if the consul was to authorize their being paid.[66] He then reported back to Laporte, who allowed disbursement of $732 to the crew as one month's pay in advance, pending their arrival in New York.

Laporte had just unwittingly helped to defray most of the enlistment costs paid out of the Laffites' pockets. He also gave the Laffites what amounted to a one-month extension on the already expired commission, which was not theirs in the first place. Had he paid careful attention to their birthplaces, he might have noted that the crew formed a perfect cross section of the privateers then working the Gulf: France, Germany, Italy, San Domingue, Greece, Portugal, Buenos Aires, England, Holland, Mexico, and Guatemala, as well as the United States.[67] And there was more to it than that, for Pierre also turned over to the vice consul a share approaching one-third of the proceeds of the latest sale of contraband in the city. This may have been legitimate fees; more likely it was a bribe for the vice consul and perhaps for Laporte himself.[68]

The extension on the letter of marque would allow *La Diligent* to pass by United States authorities long enough to get to Cartagena, where the Laffites could hope to get a new and legitimate commission—or as legitimate as any Cartagenan commission might be. However, the customs officials were keeping an eye on the vessel. Fraser put an officer aboard *La Diligent* as soon as she came upriver after he discovered that she had prize goods and several slaves aboard. He also kept an eye on the comings and goings of the crewmen, noting that most of the men aboard were discharged, while new crewmen were coming aboard as late as April 21 preparatory to her making sail. He was not sufficiently vigilant to catch the fact that Laffite and Jannet commanded, though, for Fraser believed that Gariscan was still captain when that corsair was even then in Cartagena.[69]

In fact, on April 22 in New Orleans Pierre wrote a letter to Gariscan, to be taken to Cartagena aboard *La Diligent*. He told Gariscan that he had two prizes to send to Cartagena, and asked his help in seeing them through the bureaucracy of the admiralty court for condemnation, either for sale or for commissioning as more Laffite corsairs. *La Diligent* had not brought any prizes with her into the Mississippi, so these must have been vessels held at Barataria that *La Diligent* could pick up and convoy after she left New Orleans. The fact that Pierre asked Gariscan for his help with the authorities in Cartagena made it evident that this would be a new experience for the Laffites.[70]

Pierre went on to add that "my intention is fixed to leave this country." He begged Gariscan to send him commissions to cover all of his vessels, the *Dorada, La Diligent*, and a third prize he expected to outfit as a corsair, and promised to place them under Cartagena's new flag—three concentric rectangles of red, yellow, and green in descending sizes, with an eight-pointed white star in the center—as soon as he received the letters of marque. "This would be doing for me the exceptional service of a friend," Pierre said, "on account of which I would give you proof of my appreciation," a scarcely veiled promise of a bribe. Pierre also revealed where his sentiments lay in the warfare that had engulfed Europe. He cheered the October defeat of Wellington's army at Burgos, Spain, and said that from what he saw of political affairs as related in the New Orleans press, he anticipated "a happy future."[71]

It is the only political sentiment ever known uttered by one of the Laffites. It may have been the patriotic feeling of a French-born supporter of Napoleon, or it may just as well have been the business judgment of a man who realized that so long as Napoleon held out over the powers arrayed against him, privateering against British and Spanish ships could continue.

Pierre's decision to abandon Louisiana grew out of several factors, and may have been rather sudden. The encounter with Holmes was a warning that the authorities now knew some of their smuggling routes, and might interfere with their business more regularly hereafter. Indeed, the past December the secretary of the navy had rebuked Commodore Shaw for not putting down the Baratarian enterprise.[72] Moreover, shots had been fired and a man killed, the brothers' first confrontation with the potential cost of doing their sort of business. If they needed further object lessons, it appeared that the district court was finally taking piracy seriously. On February 15 a grand jury returned several indictments for piracy, and throughout the ensuing months the court docket would be crowded with piracy trials. Though they all ended in acquittal, they were a warning.[73]

Perhaps most immediately of concern, however, was the fact that criminal and civil law had caught up with the Laffites. As early as April 7 Grymes asked that the district court order the brothers' arrest for the November smuggling episode, charging that their actions warranted fines totaling $24,025.04.[74] The next day the arrest order went out, summoning them to appear in court on April 19 to make their plea and present their defense, if any, or else face judgment by default. The court demanded bail in the amount of the total anticipated fine plus $500 for each brother. When the appointed day came, neither appeared, and when an officer of the court went to their presumed lodgings and known haunts in the city, he could find neither man.[75] The next day the court ordered them to appear on July 19, or again face judgment by default.[76]

Jean was probably on Grand Isle as usual, but Pierre had been in the city. In fact, three days before Hall ordered his arrest, he was arrested, though not by the district court. On April 5, before Grymes approached Judge Hall's bench, an order went out from the local judicial court to take into custody on charges of armed robbery several men including Laméson, Jannet, Gambi, and "Peter Laffite, and Laffite, Junior, brother of the latter." The men from whom they had taken the silver on their first prize had filed suit. Again Jean eluded arrest by his absence, and Pierre spent no more than a few hours in jail before his old friend Robin and Paul Gaudin posted an $18,000 bond—rather surprising since Robin had not collected on the debt already owed him by Pierre.[77]

Perhaps already anticipating the need to leave town, Pierre had borrowed another $1,500 from the ever-accommodating Robin less than a week before his arrest.[78] Laffite may have planned to leave aboard his ship before the arrest order, but now everything changed. *La Diligent's* departure was imminent, but given the possibility that civil and federal authorities would search her—especially as it was known that he owned the vessel—taking that route was now too risky. Thus he had to write to Gariscan, as he would not be able to state his case in person when the ship reached Cartagena. That done, a few days before the end of the month Pierre quietly stole out of New Orleans with about ten newly recruited crewmen, chiefly mulattoes, and headed up the Mississippi. Neither he nor Jean would be seen openly in the city streets again for more than a year, though Pierre soon abandoned the notion of going to Cartagena, and would never set foot in the privateer haven.[79]

Pierre went as far as Donaldsonville, where he arrived April 30, making little or no effort to hide his presence once beyond the confines of New Orleans. Indeed, one of the few people living in the village took special note of the arrival of "the Celebrated M. La Fite" that day, not least because there had been a good bit of recent Laffite activity in the vicinity. In fact, Pierre found Jean waiting for him, probably by prearrangement, Jean having arrived only the day before. Jean had been busy since leaving *La Diligent.* At the beginning of April he turned up in Donaldsonville with a motley assemblage of about forty free blacks and mulattoes, Spaniards, Americans, and more. He had reportedly fled from the seacoast of St. Mary Parish, one hundred miles west of Grand Isle, an area that many residents still called the Attakapas. With naval surveillance off Barataria and the Lafourche increasing, the corsairs sometimes tried unloading their prizes at other anchorages and beaches.

Indeed, in May 1813 a privateer bringing a prize into Barataria Bay found not fellow corsairs there but American authorities, who chased and captured him and his prize.[80] The St. Mary coast, chiefly Atchafalaya Bay, afforded an excellent alternative. Bayou Atchafalaya flowed into it, and via that waterway pirogues could pass northward some thirty miles to Lake Verret. On the eastern shore of the lake the old Attakapas Canal gave access to Bayou Lafourche less than ten miles distant, at a little settlement called Canal that would soon be renamed Napoleonville. From there it was a short trip to Donaldsonville, and on to the markets of New Orleans.

Jean sent the men to the city right away while he stayed in Donaldsonville for a week, possibly cementing business arrangements with local men who would help him in the future by hiding contraband on their plantations. Then he went downriver to New Orleans, arriving within a day or two of the issuance of Grymes's arrest order. Jean did not wait for the court date, of course, or to be arrested. He may have left aboard *La Diligent,* but more likely he found another way back to the coast, for by April 29 he was in Donaldsonville again, followed by rumors that he had taken another prize. Now as soon as Pierre arrived, Jean informed him of the arrangements made in Donaldsonville, and the brothers and Pierre's recruits left in pirogues to go down the Lafourche to bring the latest cargo up the bayou.[81]

The prize that Pierre wanted to commission as a third privateer for the brothers' fleet was waiting for them, too. On May 1 the *Dorada* had hoisted French colors and taken another Spaniard, the schooner *Louisa Antonia*, four days out of Vera Cruz with coin and cargo worth about $30,000. Prize, crew, and passengers were brought back to Barataria, and there buyers from New Orleans snapped up the cargo of cochineal. The corsairs held the sale on the deck of the prize, bale by bale, and then distributed the crew's shares to each man according to his rank.[82] Pierre and Jean kept the silver and the indigo found aboard for themselves, and soon smuggled the merchandise into New Orleans, where they kept it hidden at the home of one of their associates. They then put yet more recruits from New Orleans aboard the *Louisa Antonia*, which they armed partially by stripping a smaller, less seaworthy privateer schooner. They convinced a Spaniard captured with one of their prizes to enlist aboard her for a cruise and make a new set of Cartagenan colors for her, and when she was ready they renamed her the *Petit Milan*. With pardonable pride, the Laffites looked on to see their newest corsair riding at anchor alongside the *Dorada*, now commanded by Louis Fougard, and Jannet's *La Diligent*.[83] Their three vessels probably comprised one of the largest privately owned corsair fleets operating on the coast, and the most versatile. With the large *La Diligent*, the hermaphrodite brig *Dorada*, and the smaller schooner *Petit Milan*, their flotilla included vessels suited to every condition on the Gulf.

The new schooner went out on sortie before summer, the Laffites sending her in tandem with the *Dorada*. In command of the schooner was the Italian Vincent Gambi, who would prove to be as aggressive as any man working for them, and before long he took a Spanish schooner loaded with dry goods that he brought back to sell at Cat Island some fifteen miles west of the mouth of the Lafourche. The Laffites took half the proceeds as their share of the profits, while the rest went to the crews of their ships.[84]

When the *Dorada* went out on her own and came in again, she brought a schooner laden with tobacco taken off Cuba, and again the brothers outfitted the prize for privateering, giving her two six-pounder cannon and twenty-nine men. This time they fitted her out at Terrebonne Bay, thirty-five miles west along the coast from Grand Isle, since Captain Shaw's gunboats were showing themselves off Barataria[85]—though perhaps the Laffites need not have bothered, for Shaw continued to complain that his little flotilla was entirely inadequate for dealing with the "Marine Banditti."[86] The Laffites called their new ship *Sarpis,* and put their helmsman Laurent Maire in command.

Gaze where some distant sail a speck supplies
With all the 'thirsting eve of Enterprise:
Tell o'er the tales of many a night of toil,
And marvel where they next shall seize a spoil.

SEVEN

Lords of Barataria
1813-1814

PRIVATEERING WAS going to be very profitable indeed. The establishment on Grand Isle was taking shape as the Laffites
steadily took over. One French privateer came in regularly just to
sell beef and other supplies to the privateers gathered there, while
other prizes often included flour and bacon that augmented the
corsairs' provisions. The corsair vessels coming in now brought
some familiar faces, not the least Lafon, whose *La Misere* brought
in the prize the *Cometa* in August and unloaded her cargo.[1]
Beluche appeared with captures taken by his privateer the *Spy*, one
of the few corsairs officially commissioned in New Orleans by the
United States, though by law he should have brought his captures
to that port.[2] It was believed the privateers were operating a court
of admiralty on Grand Isle, thus legitimizing their captures at
least in their own minds, for the *Petit Milan*, and probably the
Laffites' other vessels, never landed at Cartagena in spite of flying its colors.[3] It was faster and more profitable to smuggle their
goods into Louisiana instead. On a regular basis, sometimes twice
weekly, the Laffites held sales and auctions at places generally

known and not far from the island. Rumors began to exaggerate the size and strength of the establishment until some believed that the Laffites had erected a fort on Grand Terre to protect their operation. Eventually foolish word of mouth expanded the number of men at Grand Isle to two thousand, and the number of Laffite vessels to a dozen or more.

Complaints of the operation began to appear in the press with increasing frequency. "The pirates, at and near the Island of Barrataria have received strong reinforcements, and if not soon dislodged, will do serious injury to any little trade that may be opened to this city," one citizen wrote to an editor in March. "Every article is sold cheap for cash—they give no credit, having no banks of discount." He complained that recently the schooner the *Arrow*, owned by New Orleans merchants, went out under Spanish colors in hopes of getting through the British blockade, but instead fell prey to the privateers, who then took her to Barataria and their admiralty court. Not surprisingly, its judge condemned her as a lawful prize, but afterward he came to New Orleans to buy some books on the maritime laws of nations, and while there promised the hapless owners of the schooner that if they paid the costs of "salvage" they would get their vessel back. In short, having sold the cargo at auction, and having no need for the schooner itself, the Baratarians would now ransom the boat to its owners. Sarcastically, the author commented that "the commercial people of this city must feel happy in having such accommodating neighbors."

The writer did not name the Laffites or anyone else, though by now the Laffites' names were surely associated with the trade. But then he did not give his own name, either, wisely fearing retaliation. He simply signed himself "Prudence," but did offer to give the authorities more information "should it be *deemed good policy* to break up this nest of robbers." It may have been the first detailed news that New Orleanians had of the operation, whatever rumors they had heard, and it raised a new theme in complaints about the corsair merchants. By refusing to take bank notes or give credit, they were creating a shortage of hard money in the midst of the inflationary problems being caused by the war. Vincent Nolte, one of the leading merchants of the city, complained that planters, mostly French Creole, went to Barataria to buy slaves at $150 to $200 each, whereas in the city legal slaves cost up to $700. The money did not leave the country, but it was believed that the agents of the smugglers hoarded it, thus withdrawing it from circulation. This argument ignored the fact that most of the corsairs spent that same specie with New Orleans merchants in buying supplies and outfitting their ships, but some remained convinced that if not stopped, the contrabandists could corner currency and dominate the economy of Louisiana.[4] Moreover, the scarcity of hard cash exacerbated partisanship between French and American citizens, as the latter blamed the former's open business dealings with the contrabandists in part for the state of virtual anarchy on the coast.[5]

"Prudence" reported one more rumor, probably no more than an idle boast by a Baratarian in his cups, but worrying to the authorities in time of war. "The new government at Barrataria declare that in the Cession of Louisiana by France to the United States, this Island was not included, and in consequence thereof they have named it *The Isle of France*." Tongue in cheek, "Prudence" suggested that the authorities send a message to the commander of the British squadron in the Gulf asking him to "look into" the rightful authority of the Baratarians, broadly hinting that if they claimed to be an outpost of Napoleon's empire, then they entitled themselves to some attention from British guns.[6]

Certainly Governor Claiborne paid heed. He could not ignore the mounting complaints from the legitimate merchants of New Orleans, nor the damage the corsair merchants were doing to the local economy and to the United States, much in need of cash in time of war. He also could not ignore the diplomatic problems caused with Spain, with whom the United States was not at war. Diego Morphy, the Spanish consul in New Orleans, complained on March 11 that French and American privateers were taking Spanish vessels, carrying their prizes to Grand Isle, and from there smuggling their cargoes into New Orleans. He confidentially reported to his superiors that there were two hundred to three hundred Frenchmen fortified at Barataria, with fourteen cannon in place to discourage unwelcome callers. Echoing "Prudence," he said he'd heard it said in the streets that the corsairs now called their lair "New France," and were occupying Cat Island as well as Barataria. It was an open secret, he lamented, adding that "the government here is not unaware of this, but I do not know why they have not taken any provisions." He had complained repeatedly to the collector at New Orleans, warning that if the Americans did not stop this business, "the day will come when these pirates will raise the English flag attacking and capturing American ships, and they will do to them the same they do now with the Spanish."[7]

It was an embarrassment to the Union's newest state to be known as a haven for freebooters. Governor Claiborne attempted to increase the vigilance of state and federal officers alike days after Morphy's private and "Prudence's" public complaints, when on March 15 he issued a proclamation. Having learned that "a considerable Banditti composed of Individuals of different nations, have armed and equipped several Vessels for the avowed purpose of cruising on the high Seas, and committing depredations and piracies of the Vessels of Nations at peace with the United States, and carrying on an illicit trade in goods, Wares and Merchandize with the Inhabitants of this State," he said, he feared that these lawless men would eventually start to prey on citizens of Louisiana. He commanded the pirates to cease, and required civil and military officials within each of the districts to

apprehend them. He also cautioned the people not to have anything to do with them or be "in any manner concerned with such
high offenders." Rather, he called on citizens to aid officials in
putting them down "to rescue Louisiana from the foul reproach
which would attach to its character should her shores afford an
assylum or her Citizens countenance, to an association of Individuals, whose practices are so subversive to all Laws human and
divine, & of whose ill begotten treasure, no Man can partake,
without being forever dishonored."[8]

Claiborne admitted that he did not expect the proclamation to
make the smugglers disperse, but he hoped that it would excite the
citizenry to boycott their sales, and impel officers of the law to be
more vigilant. "As regards the principal offenders I am persuaded
that nothing short of the most vigorous measures will put a stop to
their evil practices and a resort to force is in my opinion indespen-
sible," Claiborne told General Wilkinson.[9] That same day the
customs collector for the port of New Orleans, echoing Claiborne's plea, formally asked the army and navy for help in putting
down the Baratarian smugglers. When the agents of the Laffites
and others then in New Orleans learned of it that day, "Prudence"
heard them say that Claiborne "has overleaped his powers." After
this, interestingly and perhaps ominously, "Prudence" went silent,
and was not to be heard from again.[10] Both Claiborne's and the
customs collector's efforts failed embarrassingly.[11]

Part of the hazard posed by the corsairs was their flimsy allegiance to the United States. Certainly the Laffites felt themselves
to be Frenchmen first, but loyalties were fluid, and should they
choose to aid the British the privateers and the smugglers could
seriously compromise the security of New Orleans and south
Louisiana. Within weeks of Claiborne's proclamation, the United
States marshal for the New Orleans district issued an order requiring anyone not a citizen of the city doing legitimate commerce in town to withdraw at least forty miles from the Gulf coast

and tidewater areas. Those who disobeyed faced arrest.[12] Meanwhile, at least a few citizens began to share the outrage of "Prudence." In June an anonymous tip revealed that Pierre's sometime partner Robin had $10,000 worth of indigo and other goods hidden in flour barrels in the cellar of the house of Jean Baptiste Soubie on Dumaine Street.[13] Part of this cache was the Laffites' share of the spoils from the *Louisa Antonia*, still awaiting sale. Soubie was a close associate, having been with the brothers, Jannet, Gambi, Laméson, and others in February when they looted the first prize brought in by *Dorada*. Now his association with the Laffites caught up with him.[14]

If Claiborne expected vigorous measures from Wilkinson, he was to be disappointed. A dissatisfied Washington had ordered General Wilkinson to give up his command in New Orleans in March, but he only handed it over on June 10.[15] A thoroughly unsavory character, Wilkinson was tainted with connection to the failed Burr plot, and was suspected, accurately, to be in the pay of Spain as well as the United States, and serving his own interests ahead of both nations. Major General Thomas Flournoy took over the command of the 7th Military District that same June, but auguries that he would be successful were few. Though Claiborne regarded him as a man of good character, and along with Patterson, Livingston, and other leaders gave him his support, Flournoy enjoyed wretched health and had few manpower resources at hand and less money. Flournoy knew he faced an uphill struggle. "I had enemies in [New] Orleans," he would recall, mostly foreigners, "smugglers, & men engaged in illicit commerce with the enemy, supplying them with provisions &c."

Flournoy realized that stopping them required stronger means than the law allowed. Nevertheless, when Governor Claiborne asked the general to declare martial law in New Orleans soon after he assumed the command, Flournoy thought he could do the job by less drastic means. He posted guards around town at what he thought were suitable places, and ordered that no vessels be allowed out of port without his permission. The smugglers only took this as a challenge, and quickly he learned that his foes were forging his signature on passports. He responded by ordering his officer at the Balize to search every vessel regardless of its documents. Even that did not provide much by way of security, for during the time that a British squadron lay off the Balize observing American movements, a British officer visited the city as a spy more than once, and sometimes ate in the same dining room with Flournoy. Of course the general did not know that until afterward, when he learned that others in that dining room had known the spy as an enemy officer, but said nothing. No wonder he concluded that "I was beset *within* & *without*, by *spies, Traitors,* & *bad* men."

Among the bad men Flournoy now resolved to stop were the Laffites, wanted by the federal court and, in the case of Pierre at least, the civil court as well. The brothers appear to have stayed landsmen through the spring and summer, though Jean may have gone on cruise very occasionally. In the main he managed affairs at Barataria, and oversaw the transportation of goods up the Lafourche and other routes. Prior to his arrest order in April he dealt openly with merchants friendly to his prices, among them François Duplessis on Conti Street, Laurence Millaudon on St. Louis, and especially Leblanc and Sons, who kept their warehouse on the road to Bayou St. Jean, the route used to smuggle goods into the city from the north. Jean might remain in the city for two or three weeks at a time, and then return to Grand Isle.[16] While in the city, he and Sauvinet, Beluche, Dominique, Gambi, and others "were time and again, seen walking about, publicly, in the streets of New Orleans," complained Nolte. "They had their friends and acquaintances, their depots of goods, &c., in the city, and sold, almost openly, the wares they had obtained by piracy, particularly English manufactured goods."[17] The Laffites got their wares to market by night and then distributed them among the stores in town and on the levee. Men recalled them as being liberal and genial, "and only slightly demoralized by an incurable antipathy . . . to revenue laws, restrictive tariffs, and other impediments to free trade."[18] After Claiborne's proclamation, the attention in the newspapers, and the arrest orders, however, neither Jean nor Pierre was able to venture into New Orleans in safety, at least openly.[19]

Nevertheless, Pierre stayed at a safe location very close to the city, probably with a friend on the Bayou St. John road, and almost nightly went into town to visit Marie Villard and the children. It did not require much inquiry for Flournoy to learn of Pierre's nocturnal visits, and even of a certain night that summer when he was expected. Flournoy posted a company of soldiers to arrest Pierre during the night, but Pierre heard their approach in the street and in the little time available he opened a back window and jumped out to the courtyard, then let himself down into an open well with only his head above water. There he stayed until the soldiers moved on, after which he climbed out and got out of town. But he was not to be chased out of New Orleans or his mistress's bed so lightly. He sent a message to Flournoy informing him that he knew the general on sight, and in fact passed him undetected almost nightly when Flournoy walked home from discussions with Claiborne or Shaw. Pierre boasted that at any time he wished he had only to say the word to friends and the general would be abducted in the street or even in his quarters. According to Flournoy, Laffite capped his braggadocio by saying that "as he supposed I acted from a sense of duty, he would spare me if I would give myself no further trouble on his account.— That I had much more to fear from him, than he from me."[20]

In fact, for the next several months Flournoy did not trouble himself overmuch about the smuggling operation at Barataria, because by August he was convinced by reports that the privateers had abandoned the place. One of his officers, Major Henry

Peire, advised him from an outpost at "Cantonment Caminada" on the coast west of Barataria, that he believed the corsairs had moved to Cartagena, abandoning Cat Island, too. Moreover, he predicted that they would not return for fear of harassment. It was a piece of hopeless misinformation, evidence only of how lax Peire was at his job. When he went on to complain that policing the bays and bayous and hundreds of inlets with connections to New Orleans was impossible, he may have revealed his own weariness with trying. Still, acting on Peire's intelligence, Flournoy asked permission to move Peire's little company elsewhere, where they were needed.[21] Relocated closer to New Orleans, Peire was soon making seizures of brandy and wine by the barrel.[22] From now on watching the Gulf Coast and the smugglers would be up to the Navy and the Revenue service.

For the next several months, in fact, while privateers continued to bring prizes into Cat Island and Grand Isle in spite of what Major Peire said, attention refocused on Bayou Lafourche and the inland routes of transportation. Holmes's raid and Ballinger's exploration and report equipped the revenue people with enough information to try to stop the illicit trade in the middle of its course, since the navy seemed unable to curtail it at its inception on the coast. Thomas Copping, temporary customs inspector for the port of New Orleans in the absence of Thomas Williams, took his work seriously, and on July 10 ventured down the Lafourche, where he seized a pirogue loaded with goods that the occupants said came from Cat Island. The men aboard included several known associates of the Laffites whom Copping brought before the district court.[23]

Meanwhile planter John Foley maintained a steady correspondence with customs officials in New Orleans, in part to report on the movements of smugglers past his plantation on the upper Lafourche, and in part to suggest that he be appointed a customs inspector so that he would be authorized to seize the goods. Wine, brandy, and a host of other things floated past his house almost daily, he wrote, and nothing came or went from the Gulf without him seeing it.[24] Armed with such information, Copping and then his successor Pierre Dubourg advised the Treasury Department in July of "the smuggling & Piratical establishment made by certain persons in defiance of the laws at & near Lake Barataria." In return they got a promise that Shaw would be instructed to cooperate with revenue officers in curtailing the trade, and were told that they should go after smuggled merchandise and slaves. The secretary of the treasury told Dubourg to ask Claiborne for help, too, then promised that if he needed more revenue cutters, he need only ask. At last someone in high authority seemed willing to commit resources to the chore, even if it was the tiny and hardly powerful Revenue Service of the Treasury Department.[25] Unfortunately, they were only promises.

Every office in Washington seemed to get reports of the smuggling operations on the Lafourche and the Gulf. Even Thomas Freeman, surveyor general of the United States and hardly a man whose official purview included concerns about contraband, heard from his old friend Walker Gilbert, customs inspector at Donaldsonville, of the state of affairs. Four or five hundred privateers occupied Cat Island and others, Gilbert said in a considerable contradiction of Major Peire's report. "They are an out lawd set," Gilbert said in August, and he feared they were going to give him trouble as he surveyed for Freeman along the Lafourche. "It is astonishing to what length this piratical business is carried on," he continued. "It would seem truly to confirm the opinion that we were free; yes free to comit the most heinous crimes with impunity. I saw a person lately from there who informed me that they have regular auctions and from eighty to one hundred persons of New Orleans attend them regularly and so anxious were those speculators to encorage the business that they had paid higher in some instances for dry goods than the New Orleans market."[26]

The Laffites used several bases for hiding and transporting their wares along the route from Cat Island through the Lafourche, and paid several agents to help them. Cat Island itself was ideal. Summer hurricanes washed completely over the island, meaning it had no inhabitants but for occasional fishermen and a stubborn family of Spaniards living intermittently in a rude cabin of wattle and straw thatching.[27] At the other end of the smuggling route in the Donaldsonville area the Laffites hid goods on the Viala plantation and on the land of Godefroi Dumon, employing a man variously called Martin, Morrin, or Mayronne as their local agent. This may have been the François Mayronne who owned the plantation a few miles above New Orleans where the tailrace of a sawmill ran into a bayou, allowing a route for pirogues from there down the bayou to Barataria.[28] The agent was also a very large buyer of goods at Grand Isle, and almost certainly the same Mayronne who owned land in the mangrove swamps on the landward side of Grand Isle.[29] Typically when one of the Laffites brought a shipment to the vicinity, Mayronne met them some distance ahead of their destination and then took them to the bank of the Lafourche opposite Donaldsonville to hide their contraband.[30]

"The quantity of goods which passed my House during the High Water is incredible," Foley complained on September 27. "Day and night continually passed Pirogues on Topp covered with Cockel Shells, and I am convinced, as you justly observe that wealthy Planters and others from their situation in life ought not be concerned in business injurious to the community and contrary to the Laws." Local report said that Jean Laffite or some of his men had recently landed three prizes at Cat Island, and were now passing up and down the Lafourche continually as they convoyed the prize goods to hiding or on to buyers. The brothers' Donaldsonville agents were also actively traveling the bayou, though "Mr Dumon who is a great friend of Lafites" was stopped by a small company of soldiers camped lower down on the

Lafourche and denied further passage. He simply took another route. Meanwhile another agent, probably Mayronne—"He is notorious as well as Dumon"—successfully passed the guard and brought back a pirogue loaded with goods.

Perhaps this increasingly blatant flouting of the law is what finally escalated the contest between the Laffites and the authorities. Of course, by the fall they were quite definitely wanted men. Both had failed to appear in court in July. Judge Hall set another court date for October, saying this would be their last chance. But neither made an appearance then, either.[31] Any bond they had posted in April was now forfeit, and they would be prosecuted as smugglers if caught.

The Laffites did not try to hide their guilt. They were committed to their trade, and had accepted that it made them outlaws. On September 28 inspector Walker Gilbert saw three men across the Lafourche from Donaldsonville boldly taking something out of hiding in daylight. For the past several days boats loaded with contraband had been passing, including one very heavy and low in the water that Foley had seen that morning. He assumed its cargo had been deposited somewhere along the bayou, and now Gilbert had seen it. Gilbert went across the Lafourche and demanded the men halt. The men loading a pirogue tossed their goods into the bayou and then jumped into the stream and swam to safety. Gilbert found a quantity of coarse linen, now well soaked and partially ruined but still, he thought, worth bringing to New Orleans for sale once dry.[32]

Both Laffites had been in the neighborhood for some days. Pierre was staying at Lake Verret, where he received stores and provisions, especially ship's biscuit, sent up the Mississippi to Dumon, whose wagons then carted it to the Lafourche, and thence through the Attakapas Canal. Pierre was building up supplies to get to Cat Island for another cruise. Jean, whom locals referred to as "the Captain," kept a more public profile in and around Donaldsonville. There he received privateering recruits, men described by residents as having "the appearance of Brigands," whom he funneled to Pierre for assignment to the Laffite vessels. He also spent much time on open and intimate terms both with Dumon and, more disturbingly, county Judge B. Hubbard. Foley learned that it was Hubbard's cart and slaves that had transported the most recent load of provisions to Lake Verret.

Early in October Foley heard stories of a very large store of accumulated merchandise hidden in the woods and long grass at a plantation on the Attakapas Canal. That Gilbert now posed a threat to those goods after his seizure on September 28 irritated Jean. Moreover, rumors—false as yet—claimed that a reward had been offered for the apprehension of one of the Laffites, though which was unknown. This spurred a new resolve with Jean, and he and his friends did not attempt to conceal it. "The Contrabandists & their friends insinuate that as the Merchandise which Mr Gilbert seized is going to New Orleans that it will be taken by them," Foley learned. Jean probably made the open threat in the hope of dissuading the overzealous Gilbert from further interference. If it was more than a stratagem, however, the Laffites were changing the equation. In November 1812 they had run from Holmes and then surrendered without resistance. They would not do so again. Now they themselves would take action, and if Gilbert resisted, the confrontation could lead to violence. The ancient imperatives of their trade were finally catching up with them.

Foley sent word to Gilbert to be careful if he tried to take the captured goods to New Orleans, then continued his surveillance.[33] Gilbert, far from being frightened by Laffite's threats, continued uncovering and seizing goods—including nine bales of fabric on the evening of October 7—at the same time notifying New Orleans that more loads were getting past him regularly from his want of men to take them.[34] Perhaps what finally drove

Jean to action was the loss of another small boat loaded with goods as it moved down the Mississippi from Donaldsonville, taken from some of his men in a nighttime attack. The rest of the smugglers' boats escaped, and the men aboard ran them ashore and landed their goods, which they hid in the woods under brush and wood. That done, Jean Laffite and the men with him crossed to the other side of the river to hide, but returned the next day after a rain made them fear their merchandise had gotten wet. Indeed it had, and Laffite set the men to laying it out on the shore to dry for two or three days, all the while fearful of discovery. On the evening of October 12, the smugglers were walking a few miles downshore to contact the man to whom Laffite was selling the shipment, probably Mayronne, when a horseman rode up from the Lafourche and called for Jean, then gave him a letter most likely sent by Dumon or Hubbard. It informed Laffite that Gilbert was expected to be moving his captured goods down the river to New Orleans that very evening. Now was Jean's opportunity to make good on his threat to retake his merchandise. He reassured his men that few men would be on the boat, and that only Gilbert was to be feared. They lay in wait, but Gilbert did not pass that night. The next morning they walked farther downriver to the house of a Mr. Gaudins on the west bank, perhaps only six miles upstream of New Orleans, where they found Mayronne waiting for them.

Jean and his men stayed at Gaudins's all day and all that night, and on the morning of October 14 saw Gilbert approach. He was in a keelboat, a wide-bottomed cargo craft with a boxlike cabin amidships, usually propelled by men walking along the side pushing poles against the river bottom, or else by cordelling, men walking along the levee pulling the boat along with ropes. Laffite could see two black men cordelling the boat, and another three men on top of the cabin, none of them Gilbert. Laffite stepped to the levee and stopped the cordellers, and the keelboat floated by with Gilbert in the cabin. Jean sent Andrew Whiteman, a man named Scott, and a mulatto after him in a pirogue. As the men left, Jean gave Whiteman peremptory orders to "fire in case of being fired at," and instructions to demand the boat's surrender with the threat that Jean would fire upon it from the shore. Then Laffite and two mulatto associates ran along the levee to catch up with the keelboat, which was drifting close enough to shore that they could probably leap aboard if they caught it.

Whiteman and the pirogue were no sooner on the water than they saw a chicken fall overboard from the keelboat and heard one of the men on its cabin, who clearly did not yet apprehend the situation, yell to them to catch the bird for him. Whiteman had a bigger catch in mind, however. He rowed up to the boat and started to board it, Scott calling in French for Gilbert's men to give up. William Randall, one of the men on the cabin, quickly ducked inside to load his musket, but Gilbert had his gun ready. A pistol in each hand, Scott stuck his head in the cabin and Gilbert fired, but his musket was loaded with buckshot, and so he only succeeded in wounding Scott in the head, and not seriously. Scott fired back and hit Randall in the thigh, and then Whiteman fired his musket into the cabin and demanded that Gilbert give up "Mr Lafite's" goods. At the same moment, Laffite and the mulattoes leapt aboard from the shore, and at that, Gilbert surrendered the boat.

Randall was wounded, and at first it looked serious. As was characteristic of the solicitude the Laffites showed toward the Spaniards on the prizes they took, Jean left to find a physician while the rest of his men hauled the keelboat back to Gaudins's, then took Randall to a neighboring house. The next day the firing of a signal gun told Laffite that buyers from New Orleans were on the other side of the river, and he had his men row the merchandise across for sale. Jean, meanwhile, stayed at Gaudins's house, and when some men he had been expecting arrived, he led them up the west bank to return to the Lafourche.[35]

News of the attack aroused immediate indignation. "This is

an outrage I can scarcely believe," Foley declared, "although there is nothing these Pirates are not capable of."[36] It certainly left Gilbert and Randall frustrated. It took Gilbert more than six months to collect the $2 a day due him for his time in bringing the contraband as far as he got it and another $20 reimbursement for the hire of the black deckhands. He paid Randall's doctor out of his own pocket, care that ran to $100 in addition to the $68 he had to pay to board the wounded man for some time at the house where he recuperated. But Randall, who had volunteered to help Gilbert, was not a revenue service employee, and therefore was not eligible for compensation for his time lost due to his injury. No one attached any blame to their loss of the cargo, but still each was a loser in the event.[37]

Gilbert was angry. He felt he was risking his health and even his life in combating the smugglers. Worse, in the days after his return to Donaldsonville, several more pirogues came up the bayou and he simply could not find anyone to assist him in taking them.[38] Two weeks after the affair, the Laffite brothers had made a list of people such as Randall whom they knew to have assisted Gilbert in his seizures. They left the list in the hands of friends in Donaldsonville, who showed it about town and in the immediate area, passing along the Laffites' promise to kill anyone on the list who helped the revenue collector again. Even Gilbert felt the shadow of the threat, for he begged his superior in New Orleans, Pierre Dubourg, to keep what he said about the Laffites in confidence.[39]

Jean was not the only brother now using force. At almost the same time that Jean confronted Gilbert, Pierre had as many as ninety men with him on Bayou St. Denis in six pirogues heavily loaded with contraband. Suddenly they saw a longboat full of unidentified men approach. Pierre fired a pistol shot in the air and yelled out *"pavillon Francais,"* indicating that they were under French colors and implying a French privateer commission.

Then the smugglers unleashed a ragged volley of musket and pistol fire at the boat. A voice came from the boat begging them to stop and saying the strangers meant no harm. The voice identified himself as Captain Amelerq of the United States service, saying he was visiting points along the coast where contraband was believed to be coming ashore. Nevertheless, Laffite and his men continued firing, and Amelerq ordered his men to return a volley. Three of Amelerq's men went down with wounds, and Pierre called out again to ask who his adversaries were. Now Amelerq identified his men as United States soldiers. At once Pierre replied that if he had known he would not have opened fire, and volunteered to take the three wounded men into the city for care.[40] But he added that he preferred to lose his life rather than lose his merchandise.

The Laffite operation grew increasingly sophisticated. The brothers even devised a means of introducing contraband goods directly into New Orleans aboard their own ships in broad daylight. It was deceptively simple. They would send *La Diligent* into port with a safe cargo or perhaps none at all, allowing a thorough search of the vessel without fear. Then the captain made out a manifest to cover the outgoing cargo he was taking on in port. However, whatever he loaded in his hold—and most likely it was innocent provisions for a voyage—on his manifest he listed goods the Laffites had in hand at Cat Island, counting on port authorities not to compare the inventory with the cargo when he left port. After all, the revenue agents were interested in what came into New Orleans, not what went out of it. Then the vessel sailed to the mouth of the Lafourche and took on the contraband, which now matched a cargo manifest signed and approved by the port inspector. The ship took the goods back to New Orleans, where all the paperwork was in order and there was nothing to show that the goods were prize merchandise taken by the privateers. The ploy also worked in reverse. A vessel coming into the Mississippi with a legitimate cargo would stop at the Balize for inspection, but once cleared to go on to New Orleans, the boat went some distance upriver where smugglers loaded contraband they had brought through the bayous, counting on inspectors in port not to check too carefully a manifest that had already passed once.[41]

Authorities caught on before long, however. Just ten days after Jean attacked Gilbert on the Mississippi, Shaw's *Gun Vessel No. 5* stopped *La Diligent* and performed an exhaustive search of the vessel, comparing the findings to the manifest and then seizing her cargo.[42]

Meanwhile the Laffites and their associates expanded their network of Gulf shore landing places and inland storage and auction sites. They sent goods from the Lafourche landing places into the Bayou Teche country to the hungry planters there.[43] They sometimes held sales on the shores of Bayous Villars, Barataria, Rigolets, Perot, and Lake Salvador. The Temple, on the western shore of Lake Salvadore, was their principal trading post, but they also sold and auctioned merchandise at the "Little Temple" where Bayous Rigolets and Perot met.[44] The Laffites also used Bayou Sauvage, which flowed into the rear of the Bretonne, or Indian Market, on Bayou Road just outside New Orleans, passed on through the Gentilly to Bayou Bienvenue, and continued to the Gulf. It was usable only by small boats. Daniel Clark lived and had his depot on the bank of the bayou near the junction of Esplanade and Bayou Road streets, making his place a convenient conduit into the city.[45] Thus the smugglers could get their goods to customers from virtually every point of the compass: northward from Barataria to the Temple or on to the city directly; from the east via the lakes and then in the St. John Bayou road or by Clark's place; from the northwest by bringing it down the Mississippi from Donaldsonville; and from the west and southwest by several routes connected to the Lafourche.

Whenever one route began attracting too much attention, they could let it lie fallow and concentrate on one or more of the others for a while.

Once they got their goods to the vicinity of New Orleans, sale posed little problem, for seemingly everyone was interested in bargains. When he came to New Orleans after the Gilbert affair, Andrew Whiteman recognized a frequent customer at the Grand Isle sales, only now he was in uniform with the epaulettes of an officer in charge of the city guardhouse.[46] Nevertheless, smuggled goods were just as vulnerable to seizure in the city as on the bayous. On October 9 officials raided Patton and Murphy's auction house and removed a considerable quantity of contraband.[47]

For the time being, the Lafourche remained the favored artery, though when low water made it too shallow, the Laffites used another route through the Atchafalaya to Bayou Boeuf to Grand Lake and on to Plaquemine.

Late in October, with the repercussions of the attack on Gilbert only starting to be felt, Dumon was helping to plunder a prize schooner off the mouth of the Teche and moving the booty to the Lafourche for hiding.[48] Suddenly the men Gilbert called "the Cat Island boys" disappeared from Donaldsonville, though Jean Laffite stayed in the village for a few days before going down the Mississippi to an area called the German Coast to protect goods purchased at one of his auctions from a repeat of Gilbert's recent interference.[49] Dumon seemed almost constantly away from home doing the brothers' business.[50]

Then, just before the end of the month, large pirogues began passing down the bayou loaded with barrels for packing goods and more than twenty-five men, all locals well known in the community, and some of them rather prominent, such as the son-in-law of the Ascension Parish judge. The Laffites had hired them to unload a new prize off the Atchafalaya's mouth, this time a haul of woolens. They were well armed and made no secret of their determination to resist if challenged on their return passage with their contraband, and Foley complained to collector Dubourg that "the Inhabitants generally are friendly towards them & assist and give them every information in their power."[51] The brothers' share of the latest prize went to New Orleans for sale, while the crew's portion of the goods went on sale at a two-day auction on the banks of the Lafourche at Valentine Solent's plantation. Hundreds of people attended. Merchant I. Hart of New Orleans spent nearly $7,000, and others from the city almost as much, and within days the wares were in the stores of the city.[52] The impunity with which the transactions were carried on almost challenged a response. "It will be impossible without a force (Military) to put a stop to the contraband in this Neighbour-hood," Foley told Dubourg. He knew of a cache of merchandise hidden on Bayou Boeuf not far from Donaldsonville, under the guard of "from 16 to 20 of these ruffians." Nor was that all authorities would have to contend with, for "the inhabitants are likewise interested so it is impossible to go near them."[53]

Collector Dubourg could add to the problem, for on at least one occasion in October when he asked a local military commander to furnish him with a squad of soldiers for an expedition inland to seize goods, the officer provided the men but Dubourg failed to show up. The officer chided Dubourg that while he was happy to cooperate when he could, he did not have enough men available to be able to divert any of them from their duties for nothing.[54] Meanwhile Dubourg had sent repeated complaints about the smuggling problem to his superiors, begging to have more revenue cutters to patrol the coast and more men assigned as inspectors inland. Secretary of the Treasury William Jones was not unsympathetic, but he was relatively powerless during the war emergency. He acknowledged being fully aware of "the frequent violation of the revenue laws of the United States, by a daring & unprincipled band of pirates & smugglers." Jones had ordered Dubourg's predecessor Thomas Williams to ask Claiborne for help, but to little avail. "I will not dissemble however that whilst the inhabitants of Louisiana continue to countenance this illegal commerce and the courts of justice forbear to enforce the laws against the offenders, little or no benefit can be expected to result from the best concerted measures," he now told Dubourg. "The appointment even of Inspectors unless they are proof to the temptation of bribes, so far from operating as a check upon smuggling, will only contribute to diminish the chances of detection."

Jones concluded that the best means of achieving success would be to make seizures more profitable to inspectors than the bribes they might get, by giving the inspectors a share of what the collector received on behalf of the government when contraband was seized and sold. This procedure had worked on the Canadian frontier. Of course, Dubourg must also encourage district attorney Grymes to prosecute vigorously all cases with sufficient evidence. Jones could not go to the length of authorizing purchase of another revenue cutter, but he did approve the appointment of up to six new temporary inspectors, and if Dubourg wanted he could buy a cutter on his own and take his chances on the government covering the cost.[55]

It was half a loaf, and not very encouraging at that, but Dubourg took it. He granted temporary appointments as customs inspectors to several men besides Gilbert, though they would work solely for a percentage of the contraband they seized. Foley finally got his appointment on October 17, almost the instant that Dubourg would have learned of the attack on Gilbert.[56] John Hughes received a similar appointment soon thereafter. The problem was that Dubourg could hardly know whom to trust. The situation became absurd late in October when Judge Hubbard secured a temporary appointment as a customs inspector on the Lafourche. Gilbert angrily complained that it was well known locally that Hubbard had a "friendship to those villens," and asked his superiors to suspend the appointment.[57] Foley seconded the complaint, reporting that a recent shipment of ship's biscuit that passed through the area for the privateers was transported to Lake Verret by a cart and a slave belonging to Hubbard, "who I believe to be concerned as he has on all occasions been very intimate with the Lafites."[58]

Gilbert gave the temporary commission to Hubbard, but told him to his face that he knew that Hubbard was close with Dumon and was suspected of dealings with the Laffites. Hubbard pretended outrage and refused to accept the appointment, even complaining to Dubourg. Told of the accusation that he had loaned his cart to Dumon for use in transporting contraband, Hubbard responded indignantly that Dumon was his near neighbor and that Hubbard's overseer had standing orders to loan Dumon anything he needed without asking how it was to be employed. "I have always made it a maxim never to believe more than one half of what the world says," Hubbard protested in denying the rumors. "I disclaim all converse with contrabandists." That said, he went on rather impudently to assert the "me too" defense by commenting that rumor put him in good company, since Claiborne and one of his militia generals were also rumored to be involved with the smugglers.[59]

In early November Donaldsonville became quieter with the "Cat Island boys" still elsewhere. "I have heard nothing of those people who have infested the vicinity of Lafourche for sometime," John Hughes reported on November 5.[60] But they were hardly inactive. On the evening of November 14 Gilbert learned of a large cache of goods on a bayou not far from Donaldsonville, but under a heavy guard. He confessed that unable as he was to enlist help, he could do nothing about it. He did know of a person on the Lafourche who owed the Laffites $1,000 secured by a note in the hands of a third party, and it occurred to him that he could seize the note and hold it as an indemnification to cover a portion of the goods Jean had taken back from Gilbert in October, but it was a paltry gesture in the face of the scale of the smuggling operation.[61]

Some believed that Jean Laffite was more than a mere smuggler, and might even be an exiled general from Napoleon's defeated armies.[62] They were wrong, of course, but by the end of the year Jean and Pierre presided over an establishment worthy of a general. Having shifted their base from Barataria, they had now built Cat Island into a seemingly formidable position for their trade. Rumor said they had five or six vessels constantly coming and going, which may have been true, though nothing suggests that the Laffites themselves owned or operated more than their squadron of three—*La Diligent*, the *Dorada*, and the *Petit Milan*. Rumor also said their vessels were each crewed by sixty to ninety men and mounted a dozen cannon or more, which in fact only applied to *La Diligent*. Cat Island received the prizes of other owners and captains, including Dominique, who also took goods up the Lafourche on his way to New Orleans. Contrary to perceptions, Dominique was not an employee of the Laffites, but an independent corsair who sold prize goods to them from time to time.[63] Gilbert, understandably prejudiced where the Laffites entered the picture, referred to them and their followers as "this banditti, the most base and daring ever known in any country on Earth." All told, the exaggerated reports that came up the Lafourche to him indicated that there were five hundred to six hundred men on the island with a shore battery of fourteen guns to protect their base, and that the brothers had sunk a prize brig in the main pass into the island to deter deep draft naval warships from getting too close.

"The quantity of goods brought in by this banditti is immense: I have not a doubt but they have entered & secured far more than a million of dollars within this last six months," he told his superiors. Up to five hundred citizens at a time could be found on Cat Island buying from them. "What depravity!—Men in office; Citizens hitherto of undoubted integrity and first respectability, uniting with a piratical band and sharing with them their ill gotten booty." When legal officers did not try to apprehend the smugglers or stop the trade, law-abiding citizens got the wrong message.[64] Even fines of up to three times the value of contraband purchased could not deter the bargain hunters from buying Laffite goods.[65] Meanwhile those citizens who objected to smuggling complained that the smugglers had become "the strongest force in Louisiana," as one declared. "Such a nest of pyrates had never been known on the continent."[66]

Finally other forces came into play. The day after Gilbert learned of the guarded store of contraband, Patterson received orders to relieve the hapless Shaw of command of United States naval forces headquartered at New Orleans.[67] Patterson had already sparred with the Laffites once. Moreover, he had the motivation of knowing a proportion of whatever vessels and goods he seized from them would be awarded to him in prize courts. There is no question that the contrabandists had been on his mind before he took his new command, and he made them a priority now. Within days of relieving Shaw, Patterson reported to the secretary of the navy that the smugglers "have now arrived to such a pitch of insolence and confidence from their numbers as to set the revenue laws and force at defence, and should they not be soon destroyed, it will be extremely hazardous for an unarmed vessel even American to approach this coast." He reported Jean Laffite's attack on Gilbert, and the damage the corsairs were doing to the local economy. "The honest merchant cannot obtain a livelihood, by his sales while those robbers robe in riches piratically captured on the high seas and brought and sold in face of day in this place," he declared.[68] Patterson took over on December 13, 1813, and on inspecting his new post he felt hopeful that he could put down the smugglers. He made it clear to Jones, however, that this could not be done with the men and vessels currently available at New Orleans. The secretary, belatedly responding to Shaw's pleas for faster ships to chase down the privateers, suggested sending in a force of speedy vessels, and Patterson felt encouraged.[69]

The governor shared Patterson's indignation and embarrassment. He encountered the sympathetic attitude of the French and Creole people of New Orleans personally when he denounced smugglers as criminals to ladies on social occasions, and they only replied, as he put it, that "that is impossible; for my grandfather, or my father, or my husband, was, under the Spanish government, a great smuggler, and he was always esteemed an honest man."[70] Patterson's appointment may have given the governor a renewed incentive to do something. On November 24 Claiborne issued another proclamation. Smuggling had lately increased, he said, and the brazen smugglers no longer tried to conceal their activities, selling their wares in open daylight. He referred to the attack on Gilbert, and for the first time specifically named the chief culprit as Jean Laffite. He now charged state, civil, and military officials to prevent these violations and apprehend those engaged in the smuggling, and issued an order for Laffite's arrest. Claiborne warned that the apathy of the people could only further disgrace Louisiana, and instructed the people to give no aid to Laffite or his men, but to help arrest them. He offered a $500 reward to anyone delivering Laffite to the sheriff in New Orleans, or any other sheriff in the state.[71]

Now at last Jean Laffite had a price on his head, even if $500 was not much of a reward given his transgressions, or much of an inducement to his associates to turn him in. Indeed, Jean was in the city when Claiborne issued his proclamation, and any number of associates could have claimed the quick reward—at later risk of their lives, of course. Laffite's own response revealed yet again the combination of bravado and impish humor in his personality. That day he hired a printer to produce some handbills of his own that his associates put up in the night. When New Orleans awoke the next morning, citizens saw posted at the Exchange Coffee House and elsewhere a $1,000 reward offered for apprehending Governor Claiborne and delivering him to Cat Island.[72] It was signed simply "Laffite." A memorandum at the bottom of the broadside stated that he was "only *jesting* & desired that no one would do violence to his Excellency."[73]

While most citizens saw the humor in it, Gilbert at least took it very seriously. "Le Fitte & Party," as he called them, were dangerous men. He believed that Claiborne was not personally safe. "I firmly believe that the Gov. runs a greater risk of being taken to Cat Island and tried for his life than Le Fitte does of being punished for his crimes in the State of Louisiana," Gilbert moaned. The signs of impending anarchy could hardly be worse than the fact that Governor Claiborne could not count on his own authorities for his protection.[74]

With these he mingles not but to command;
Few are his words, but keen his eye and hand.
Ne'er seasons he with mirth their jovial mess
But they forgive his silence for success.

EIGHT

The Rise of the Filibusters
1814

THE NEW YEAR brought an escalation both in the complaints against the smuggling and in the Laffites' brazenness and determination to hazard any risk. On the evening of January 14 some thirty or more armed men came into Donaldsonville to move a cargo, and when Walker Gilbert approached them they simply sneered at him. Two days later John Foley reported signs of a major sale approaching. The word was that a cargo of 415 slaves from Guinea had arrived at Cat Island, and that the wealthy sugarcane planters were going down to make their purchases. He knew at least four of the prominent men who had passed his place heading south, and heard also that a cargo of sugar and coffee had come into Lake Verret.[1] In New Orleans Spanish consul Diego Morphy knew of that cargo, too, some three hundred barrels of coffee and two hundred boxes of sugar. He sent a warning to the Spaniard in command at Pensacola, cautioning him that every ship coming from there to New Orleans needed to have a precise manifest to prevent smugglers from trying to sneak goods into the city aboard her.[2]

The reports were right. In fact, the Laffites boldly advertised that they had a cargo of slaves they intended to auction within a few days. Gilbert pleaded to his superior in New Orleans that if he had only fifteen men he could stop the slaves en route.[3] Gilbert's and Foley's warnings got the attention of Pierre Dubourg, who was about to succeed to the post of collector of customs for the port of New Orleans, and had already begun some of his duties. He informed Claiborne on January 20, and taking Gilbert at his word, asked for men to help Gilbert halt the proceeding.[4] By then, however, events had come to a tragic, and inevitable, collision. In October 1813 Dubourg swore into service as a temporary revenue inspector John B. Stout, an experienced man who came highly recommended by concerned citizens thanks to his recent service as a city constable in New Orleans.[5]

Dubourg had stationed Stout and a dozen customs officers at the Temple, where they made camp and stood ready to halt traffic of contraband going northward or potential buyers going south. On or about January 16 Stout saw a substantial party of smugglers approaching in pirogues, most likely the same aggressive band that Gilbert met in Donaldsonville a few days earlier. The customs men took to their boats to give chase, but it is unclear who became the prey. Soon the smugglers opened fire. Two customs men went down with wounds, and then a musket ball hit Stout, who was either killed instantly or else drowned when he fell overboard and disappeared.[6] The smugglers swarmed the officers and took them prisoner. News of the skirmish reached New Orleans on January 18 or 19, and with it began rumors that the privateers would take the captured officers to Cartagena.[7] Within two weeks of the outrage news reached Donaldsonville that the smugglers had the captured men in close confinement, and one of them "sentenced" to ten years' hard labor with a fifty-six-pound weight chained to his leg.[8]

Surely this would be more than enough to stimulate a definitive response. At the first word of the incident, Governor Claiborne denounced the act, and on January 24 he attributed these "horrible violations of the Laws" to "Lafite & his associates," adding that "some thing must be done to arrest the progress of these lawless men." Apparently one or more of the customs officers had escaped after recognizing Jean or Pierre in the attacking party, or else smuggling in Louisiana had become so dominated by the Laffites that Claiborne and others now attributed all of it to them. Either way, the Laffites were now wanted not only for smuggling, but possibly for murder. "It is high time that these contrabandists, dispersed throughout the State, should be taught to respect our laws," Dubourg declared. The problem was that General Flournoy did not have enough men available to detach some to deal with the problem, and federal authorities were too distracted with the war. Dubourg suggested to the governor that he order out militia, which Claiborne could do under his own authority. Afraid of the risk of failure, Claiborne prudently submitted the question to the legislature on January 25.

Claiborne confessed hesitance. The militia had failed before in dealing with the smugglers, and he suspected that loyalties to the Baratarians on the part of men in the state service could compromise the effort. "So numerous and bold are the followers of Lafitte, and, I grieve to say it, such is the countenance afforded him by some of our citizens, to me unknown—that all efforts to apprehend this high offender have hitherto been baffled." Nevertheless, "the evil requires a strong corrective," he demanded. "Force must be resorted to. These lawless men can soon be operated on by their fears and the certainty of punishment." The legislature showed even more hesitance than the governor, and simply tabled his appeal.

Which made it all the more irritating that, having consistently escaped the federal criminal court, Pierre Laffite could not stay out of trouble with the petty civil bench. Though he kept out of New Orleans by day to avoid arrest, he transacted business there through his attorney, Louis Morel, who coincidentally lived on the Bayou St. John smuggling route. Now the April 1813 suit that resulted in Pierre's brief arrest resurfaced. In June 1813 the plaintiff had transferred all claims in the suit to prominent Toulouse Street merchant Paul Lanusse, a thirty-year-old civic leader born on the French side of the Pyrenees. When Pierre failed to appear in court, he defaulted on the case, and now Lanusse came to collect. On February 21, 1814, he or a court officer searched the city but could find no known residence of Pierre Laffite, and no Pierre Laffite.[9]

Lanusse and three other parties to the claim went to district court and obtained a judgment against Laffite for $9,557.62 for "money robbed by him from them." The judgment allowed them to seize any and all property belonging to Pierre, and a week later, on February 28, he responded in court—no doubt through Morel—with, of all things, a petition for bankruptcy. Being nothing if not brazen, Pierre claimed that he owned "nothing but his industry"—no house, no carriage, no assets in banks—in spite of the common knowledge that he and his brother were acquiring substantial assets. The court issued an order calling his creditors to meet, meanwhile staying execution against Laffite or his property.

Lanusse was not to be put off so easily, for he knew better. "In the fact," said Lanusse, "he is part owner of several armed vessels or privateers and of Ladiligente and he does also possess within the jurisdiction of your honorable court valuable effects and other moveable property, which he concealed from his creditors." Lanusse and the other parties also protested that since the stay of execution, Pierre had kept himself concealed, and they had strong reasons to fear that he was "about to depart fraudulently and permanently from this state and carry with him his concealed property." Thus they asked for a sequestration order against him and his arrest unless he posted bond of $21,454.62, representing the total amount that Pierre owed his creditors in his bankruptcy declaration.[10]

The court approved Lanusse's appeal, and on March 9 ordered the sheriff to sequester "all and singular the property of the said Lafitte, wheresoever the said property may be found in the Parish aforesaid," and that Pierre be arrested and held until he posted the security. Not surprisingly, when the sheriff went to serve the orders, he had to report that "after diligent search I have neither been able to find the body of the within named Peter Lafete nor any of the property to him belonging."[11] All he could do was leave a copy of the court petition and citation, along with orders to appear or file a response within eight days, "at the ordinary place of residence of the defendant"—meaning that even court officials knew where Pierre was likely to be found when he risked coming to town, just as Flournoy had known to no avail.[12] On March 15, the day before the deadline, Morel appeared in court and moved that the court order Pierre's creditors to show cause within ten days why his bankruptcy petition should not be ratified.[13] Despite their knowledge of Pierre's deception, Lanusse and his associates could not offer definitive proof of Laffite having property within the jurisdiction of the court, and so the judge granted Pierre bankruptcy. Lanusse would not forget.

Where the sheriff expected to find Pierre is unclear, though most likely it was at the house on Dumaine Street that Marie Louise Villard purchased on April 9 from Pierre Delaronde, and almost unquestionably with money provided by Pierre. If Laffite did not legally own property in New Orleans, then it could not be seized.[14] That Pierre would risk being in the city at all while the authorities groped toward a way to arrest both Laffites, and charge at least Jean with a capital crime, seemed incredible. Pierre's visits to Marie in spite of such danger suggest more than a casual relationship between the two. At the same time, Lanusse's belief that Pierre was about to leave the state raises the possibility that once again both Laffites thought of departing Louisiana.

While Pierre's legal and possible financial embarrassments occupied his lawyer, Pierre's and Jean's attention were directed to their business, current and future. Willful failure to pay debts was not good practice for a merchant, even a crooked one, for today's creditors could be tomorrow's customers. Pierre's bankruptcy may have been a legal dodge to avoid paying his debts, but more likely he did not have as much money available to him as rumor said. After all, his was a costly and uncertain business. For all their failures, the customs men did make seizures from time to time, and what they confiscated in New Orleans was almost certainly the Laffites' share of cargoes sold and distributed at Cat Island and elsewhere. Just as Lanusse was in court going after Pierre, Major Peire seized a substantial cache of contraband at Barataria.[15]

But most of the merchandise continued going through, and the local inspectors could only report it to New Orleans and perhaps send lists of the names of men trading with the smugglers to be charged as abettors.[16] Helpful citizens were so cowed after Gilbert's experience and Stout's death, that when they did furnish information it often as not came anonymously.[17] Claiborne told Dubourg that if the Laffite operation were to be disrupted, it would have to be United States forces that did it.

Flournoy came up with a means of breaking the logjam. Since Dubourg was a federal official, he said, if the collector asked the governor for help, then officially it would be a request from the United States government, and the governor could station a company of state militia at Donaldsonville without risk to his own prestige.[18] That worked for the governor, who promised on March 1 to order one hundred militia to report to Dubourg.[19] The next day Claiborne addressed the legislature once more, asking for a volunteer force of one hundred and four men and officers to serve for up to six months. He got around fiscal objections by averring that since the force would be used to enforce United States laws, Washington would reimburse any expenses.

Once again the assembly was not moved. Even if the assembly failed to act, though, encouraged by this glimmer of cooperation from Claiborne, the collector approached Commodore Patterson to ask if he could spare an armed vessel for an expedition against the smugglers, and though Patterson had to respond that he could not at the moment, he promised that he would help as soon as he could free one of his ships from more pressing duty off the coast.[20] At the same time, Flournoy detailed a sergeant's guard of United States soldiers—not much, but an encouraging start—for Dubourg's anticipated strike.[21] The collector was marshaling forces to hit the smugglers, and in their small ways the governor, the army, and the navy were contributing and cooperating for the first time. It would not be the end of the Laffites, but it would be the beginning of the demise of their enterprise.

Meanwhile their privateering continued to bring in the goods for their sales. On April 9 the Spanish schooner the *Amiable Maria* sailed from Havana with a cargo of wax, paper, and dry goods, bound for Vera Cruz. Thirty miles from her destination Pierre Cadet and the *Dorada,* now mounting five cannon, came upon her on April 15 and raised the French flag. After capturing the merchantman, however, Cadet ran up the flag of Cartagena, and took the prize to Grand Terre, arriving May 15 to be detained a month while Jean Laffite oversaw sale of the cargo to buyers from New Orleans.[22] Cadet proved himself to be "without comparison in kindness and attentions," according to a Spanish civil officer aboard. The privateers did not touch the passengers' personal luggage and possessions when they brought the *Amiable Maria* into Barataria, and shortly thereafter Cadet provided the Spaniards with passage back to Havana.[23]

This civility was standard procedure for Laffite captains, and in time the Laffites' consideration toward Spanish seamen would work to their advantage. Indeed, there may have been some calculation in their attentions to Spaniards, for in the roiling world of Spanish America, allegiances shifted constantly. For the rest of

their lives the brothers would find their fortunes linked both pas-
sively and actively to Spain's affairs in the New World. Of course
they made their living preying on Spanish shipping, but far more
was to be made by capitalizing on the political quicksands around
them. Cartagena, Chile, Buenos Aires, and Venezuela had all declared independence by now, and Bolívar led revolutionary forces
in New Granada in campaigns from Caracas to Cartagena. Their
fortunes ebbed and flowed, Spain sometimes retaking lost ground,
but the revolutionaries had the taste of independence in their
mouths and were not to be dissuaded. At this moment Bolívar
was in retreat, the revolutionaries under Bernardo O'Higgins had
been defeated in Chile, and José Maria Morelos y Pavon, who
had been leading a revolt in Mexico since 1810, was besieged just
short of his goal of Mexico City.

The message to men of enterprise was not that Spain had the
rebels on the run almost everywhere in mid-1814. Rather it was
that with the mother country so distracted and so distant, there
was opportunity in the vastness of New Spain. Eastern Florida
seemed ripe, as did the province of Texas immediately west of the
Sabine River. Moreover, Texas afforded a back door to northern
Mexico that hopeful revolutionaries might use. The fabulous
wealth that Spain had siphoned from Mexico and South America for centuries may have made the dons rich, but it also fed the
dreams of adventurers, and the weakening of Spain during the
Napoleonic wars in Europe, along with its defensive position on
so many fronts in the New World, naturally gave daring men
ideas of opportunity.

One such man was Louis Aury, now operating as a corsair out
of Cartagena. He owned and commanded three privateers by
February, and nearly three hundred men answered to his orders.
He regularly sent prizes into Louisiana, and his agent in New
Orleans, the merchant François Dupuis, held several thousand
dollars of Aury's money in safekeeping at any given time. The

junta at Cartagena had been good to Aury, and he to them with the money he brought them from his prizes. They gave him distinction and "have filled my strong box," he boasted. Speaking for Cartagena, Spanish America, and New Orleans he said, "Homage is paid here as in all times and countries to the strongest."[24]

The privateers produced by European wars and New World upheavals were among the first to attach themselves both to the independence movements like Cartagena's and to the shadier enterprises that soon took their name from the Dutch *vrijbuiter,* which sounded like and essentially meant "freebooter." It would have been strange if New Orleans had not become a seedbed for these "filibusters," for its access to the sea, the convenience and privacy of the coastal ports at Barataria, Cat Island, and elsewhere, and Louisiana's proximity to Texas, virtually dictated that the Creole city on the Mississippi be the center of plots against Texas, Mexico, and much of the rest of New Spain.

As early as 1791 Philip Nolan and the ever-scheming General James Wilkinson cast eyes toward exploiting Texas, and possibly something more, but Nolan lost his life in a skirmish with Spaniard *soldados* in 1801, and by that time Wilkinson was on Spain's payroll as a spy while also acting as commanding general of the United States Army. Another army officer, Augustus Magee, resigned his commission in 1812 and with José Bernardo Maximiliano Gutiérrez de Lara led an abortive invasion of Texas that resulted in Magee's death in February 1813, followed by Gutiérrez's brief success and then rapid descent into brutality. José Alvarez de Toledo, a Havana-born former officer in Spain's navy, maneuvered Gutiérrez out of his command, but led the army to disaster at the Battle of the Medina on August 18, 1813, after which Toledo escaped to New Orleans, arriving in early November 1813.

The hallmark of filibustering, however, was that defeat and disaster only seemed to whet the appetite of adventurers. After all, Gutiérrez had taken most of Texas before his downfall. A more able leader should do even better. The next would-be liberator on the scene appeared to be such a leader. Jean Joseph Amable Humbert had commanded a company in Napoleon's Imperial Guard in 1796, and thereafter rose rapidly in the emperor's esteem. A veteran of campaigns in Ireland and San Domingue, he asked Bonaparte in June 1812 to send him to the United States on a mission probably having to do with distracting Spain from Europe by starting insurrections in Mexico. Carrying a bogus passport identifying him as Jean Berthum—a transparent anagram of Humbert—he arrived in Philadelphia in November, where he established an uneasy partnership with the refugee plotter Toledo before Toledo departed to join Gutiérrez and Magee's ill-fated expedition.

In Philadelphia, Humbert also became acquainted with Juan Mariano Buatista de Picornell y Gomila. The fifty-three-year-old Picornell had been a revolutionary in Madrid, and had tried to incite revolt in Venezuela as early as 1798. In about 1806 he came to Philadelphia and started hatching plots to take Texas that saw him spending some time in New Orleans, but to no avail. He returned to Philadelphia by 1812, when he allied himself with Toledo, but after the Medina he returned to New Orleans, and then rejoined the remnants of the invading force at Natchitoches.

The fifty-eight-year-old Humbert was a man of commanding presence and personality. Slender and above-average height, he presented a long swarthy face and heavy beard that seemed dominated by a red drinker's nose like a plump strawberry. In mid-August 1813 he boarded ship for New Orleans, taking with him a number of French and Spanish officers whom he had enlisted in his enterprise. Their task was to maneuver Gutiérrez out of command of those remaining loyal to him, establish a base in Texas, and then encourage revolt in Mexico. Unfortunately, one of Humbert's hallmarks was his indiscretion, and while in Philadelphia he tried to persuade the Spanish minister Luis Onís to his cause. Onís had been in Philadelphia since about 1809, running a shadow legation because Washington refused to recognize his appointment as minister until King Ferdinand VII was restored to the throne taken from him by Napoleon. Onís constantly lobbied the State Department and other officials in Washington on behalf of Spanish interests, at the same time running an intelligence system in the United States, the Caribbean, and New Spain. A masterful politician and diplomat, Onís played along with the guileless Humbert, and as a result had word of his plans on the way to the viceroy in Havana even as Humbert sailed.[25]

As soon as Humbert reached New Orleans he began fomenting filibusters, and approaching the Baratarians to link them with his schemes. His contacts with the Laffites at this stage, if any, would have been few and probably indirect, for the brothers were seldom in the city, and then only clandestinely. But certainly they knew of his presence and probably his mission, and he could not have been in the city long without learning that they exercised more authority than anyone else over the loose brotherhood of corsairs and smugglers operating on the coast. Their bases at Grand Isle and Cat Island would be ideal staging points for any maritime arm of his Texas plan. First he had to deal with Gutiérrez, however, but that did not take long. After the debacle of his 1812–1813 expedition, Gutiérrez commanded little respect. Indeed, when Humbert reached New Orleans, Gutiérrez had gone underground and was nowhere to be found. Toledo was out with the remainder of the beaten volunteers from the Medina, and Picornell's ambitions were political rather than military. That left the field in New Orleans to Humbert.

He actively began enlisting men for his new "army," and found hundreds of Frenchmen and Creoles interested in following his guidon. Unfortunately, he both exaggerated his support

and outright misled the men in telling them that he acted with
Toledo's blessing, for Toledo soon disavowed Humbert entirely.
Each presumed to be entitled to command the next "invasion" of
Texas. Humbert apparently did achieve one thing, however. As
early as mid-September the rumor spread outward from New
Orleans that some Barataria-based privateers had agreed to make
their ships available to convoy men and supplies to the Texas
coast to support Humbert, no doubt in hopes of making new
bases for their own operations. Gutiérrez had reportedly come to
a similar understanding with them earlier that year, though nothing came of it.[26]

Nothing specifically links the Laffites with these first interac-
tions between the privateers and the filibusters, but it is incon-
ceivable that such an alliance would have been made without at
least their knowledge and more likely their involvement. It made
good business sense for them to shift their base outside United
States territory now that being seen in New Orleans was no
longer safe for them. Humbert's "army" would offer them a measure of protection against Spanish interference by land. Sailing
from a base outside the United States on the Sabine River—or
even closer on the Calcasieu, whose upper tributaries reached almost to the Red River—they should not be subject to harassment from Patterson and the navy, yet would be close enough to
Louisiana to smuggle their goods in by the usual means.

Humbert worked on his plans and his recruiting until November, when he went to Natchitoches, the overland gateway to
east Texas. On November 25 the motley remnant of earlier expeditions and new recruits created a Provisional Government of the
Interior Provinces of Mexico and chose Picornell as president.
Five days later Picornell gave Humbert a general's commission,
and Humbert accepted.[27] With Toledo absent and maneuvered
out of influence, Humbert took command of the so-called Republican Army of the North, and appointed none other than

Arsené Latour an officer on his staff.[28] But it was evident that
they would continue to be paper tigers without more men and
money, and Picornell and Humbert soon after returned to New
Orleans, hoping to win the cooperation of prominent filibuster
leaders like the Kempers, Henry Perry, who commanded much
of the remnant after the Medina, and Dr. John Robinson, another would-be giant who had compromised Magee's operations
prior to the Medina. Rumors spread that some three thousand
men and one thousand Indians were ready and waiting to follow
Humbert's lead.[29]

The reality was vastly different, the plan doomed to failure,
for by February 1814 an important participant in the filibusters'
meetings had been "turned" and was feeding information to the
Spaniards through the most unlikely of intermediaries, the Capuchin Fray Antonio de Sedella, the parish priest of New Orleans who lived behind the Cathedral of St. Louis on the Place
d'Arms. Known to his parishioners as Père Antoine, Sedella was
a fierce-looking and combustible cleric with an unyielding loyalty
to his flock and an equally tenacious devotion to Spain, regardless
of Louisiana's American ownership. In the past he had fed information on revolutionaries to Spanish authorities, and now with
the filibuster leaders in New Orleans, he was determined to crack
one of them open. Incredibly, he decided to start at the top, and
on February 4 wrote to Juan Ruíz de Apodaca, the captain general in Cuba, that he intended to make a traitor of none other
than Picornell.[30] More amazing still, within a week Sedella
succeeded.

Apparently Picornell had been an uncertain revolutionary
for some time, and after almost two decades of one insurrec-
tionary plot after another he was tired, and no doubt disillusioned by the chancers and opportunists who filled his ranks. He
had approached Onís about a pardon and resumption of allegiance to Spain a couple of years earlier, but the Texas dream had

lured him back to the revolutionary fold. Now Picornell fell out with the bumptious and impractical Humbert, the vain Toledo, Perry, the treacherous Robinson, the brutal Gutiérrez, and the sort who followed them. Despite his title as president, he had lost control of the enterprise. Within a month Claiborne would issue a proclamation that made Picornell an outlaw in the United States as well as a traitor to Spain, and thus a man without a country. He was easy prey for Sedella, who approached with promises of a pardon. By February 11 Picornell had been turned, and the next day he officially resigned his presidency and submitted an application for pardon.[31] Hereafter he would work with Sedella in trying to compromise the efforts of the filibusters, and though henceforth he would be outside the inner circle of plotters, still Picornell knew much and could find out more.

Thus it is almost certain that Picornell was the source of the first piece of useful information about Humbert's plans that Sedella was able to feed Apodaca. Only days after Picornell's resignation, Sedella learned "through a person present in the meetings held to this respect," that the privateers and pirates of Barataria, soon to be joined by others out of Cartagena, intended to surprise and ransack Tampico, midway down the Mexican Gulf coast, and then sail up the coastline to Matagorda Bay, midway between the mouths of the Sabine and the Rio Grande rivers on the Texas coast. There, in a fine bay sheltered by barrier islands, they would remain in strength to establish a new base. Tabasco, on the southernmost Mexican Gulf coast shore, was another possible target.[32]

Picornell's information did not mention the Laffites, but soon Sedella and Spanish consul Diego Morphy learned more that made the brothers' involvement unquestionable. On April 12, 1814, with Picornell and Toledo effectively out of the affair, Gutiérrez formed a new junta in New Orleans and held a meeting. This council included prominent merchants such as Abner Duncan and John K. West, the ambitious attorney Edward Livingston, and adventurers of the stamp of Ellis P. Bean and Henry Perry. One of the members of the council was Pierre Laffite. They discussed a combined land and naval expedition against Matagorda and Tampico, with Gutiérrez and Humbert to be in command of seven hundred men, assisted, as the Spaniards put it, "by the pirates of Barataria."[33] This assistance was what put Pierre in a seat on the council.

Morphy passed along the information to minister Onís, who immediately protested to Secretary of State Monroe. President Madison had issued a proclamation on June 29 proclaiming neutrality toward Spanish affairs, but people in New Orleans flagrantly violated that doctrine, he complained. Robinson and Toledo and Humbert were at large making their nefarious plans, as was "the traitor Picornel and even the monster Bernardo Gutierres the perpetrator of the atrocious assassinations committed in the Province of Texas." Louisiana citizens—the men on the council—were aiding "these convicted Traitors, these high way Robbers." He told Monroe of the anticipated expedition against Mexico, "assisted by the Pirates of Barataria who furnished five armed vessels and a portion of their People to carry the expedition into effect." Indeed, he went on, the plans were hardly a secret in New Orleans. Referring to the "ascendancy acquired by the Pirates of Barataria," he went on to ask the administration "to destroy that nest of Robbers."[34]

The Onís protest put its finger on just one of the reasons that the initial Gutiérrez-Humbert plan came to nothing. Everyone knew about it. Moreover, typical of the short-range thinking of most of the filibusters, they soon discovered that money was a problem. Even the merchants on the council who subscribed personal funds wound up unable or unwilling to meet their obligations. That probably did not apply to the Laffites, since their contribution would have been the vessels and crew to carry the expedition.[35] Nevertheless, the council had little choice but to postpone their grand plan. Meanwhile the experience of a Laffite privateer suggested an alternative approach.

The passengers of the *Amiable Maria* watched "with a lot of pain in our hearts" as Jean Laffite supervised the dismantling of their taken vessel, removing her equipment and landing her cargo. Morphy was quick to send word to Apodaca of the capture of the *Amiable Maria*.[36] The import of the rich prize could not be overlooked. While Humbert and Gutiérrez bumbled about in search of money, the Laffites could finance their own operation against Tampico or elsewhere. The Laffites learned the same lesson, but applied it differently, for soon a new plan emerged. This time Humbert would sail with a few score men on two of the Laffite *goletas*, to command the men in action if they attacked a city by land, and the Laffites would have at least three more vessels available in Barataria to join him if necessary. The corsairs' chief mission would be to prey on more of the Havana–Vera Cruz trade, especially money ships bringing soldiers' pay to the mainland. Once they had captured enough to meet the needs of the grander overland expedition, the original plan of April could be revived.

Men and events stopped them. Morphy feared that the resources of the privateers were sufficient that they might launch the attack even if Humbert and Gutiérrez could not deliver their end of the men and money. He knew from observing Humbert and Gutiérrez that this gang, or *"pandilla"* as he called them, was ineffectual. "They are always resolved to carry out their diabolic plans," he commented to Apodaca, "without considering all the big problems they have to overcome in order to fulfill them." But the Baratarians were another matter, for he saw firsthand in New Orleans how effective they could be, and how substantial were their military resources. By late May he believed the privateers were ready to start on their own by hitting Tampico and preying on Spanish money ships bound for Vera Cruz.[37]

Morphy had likely already taken steps to meet this eventuality. He contacted Patterson about his concerns, and the commodore told Morphy that he would keep a ship cruising Lake Borgne to stop the pirates from using that avenue to New Orleans, and would place at least one cannon, if not a whole battery, on shore to help.[38] In addition to the damage being done to customs revenues and the continuing entreaties of Governor Claiborne, Patterson had reasons to find the privateers inconvenient. Following the defeat and abdication of Napoleon that spring, Spain was once more a neutral nation, and the privateers' attacks on Spanish shipping caused diplomatic problems. Patterson was obligated to protect neutral commerce in American waters, making every Laffite prize an embarrassment.[39]

Other events converged to stop the plan. On April 30, after years of dithering, the grand jury called by the district court issued the first of what would be a series of indictments for piracy, this one against a close Laffite associate, Manuel Joachim. It was the testimony of Andrew Whiteman that made the case, and he was testifying against many others, including both Laffites.[40] Meanwhile the number of seizures and surveillance increased by late spring, and authorities were becoming more resourceful at finding prize goods that the Laffites hid in the homes of friends, especially in the Faubourg Marigny section of New Orleans where most of the San Domingue refugees settled.[41]

Of course the prizes still came in. Dominique and his *Tigre* brought in a modest one at Cat Island early in May, and two or three more came into Grand Isle. Walker Gilbert believed that most of the population along the lower Lafourche were in motion toward the coast to participate in the *Amiable Maria* sale, or to do some illegal business with British ships briefly landing in order to trade goods for supplies.[42] The Laffites' *Dorada* brought a prize loaded with dry goods into Barataria that month. Meanwhile Gambi and his *Philanthrope,* apparently following the revised plan for funding Humbert's campaign, took two prizes off Tampico in May and brought them to Grand Isle on June 1. One was filled with silver ingots, and both with cocoa and more dry goods, all of which the Baratarians landed and sold to yet another concourse of buyers from New Orleans. Unlike the Laffites, Gambi paid little attention to the welfare of captured crew and passengers. He kept them for four weeks in what one described as "the most cruel situation," before he sent them home in one of the prize vessels.[43]

Matters had changed by the time Gambi brought in these prizes. Within days after Gambi's arrival the cross-purposes, miscommunication, and organizational ineptitude of the filibuster leaders upset their plans once more. Gutiérrez announced on June 7 that he and Humbert intended to leave New Orleans for Barataria, then sail with several ships for the anticipated attack on Matagorda. But Gutiérrez never left the city, probably thanks to news that Toledo had a mere 120 men on the Sabine, and Robinson even fewer, with no cooperation between the two camps. This and maneuvering by Morphy, plus Picornell changing allegiances so suddenly, convinced Gutiérrez as of June 10 that the revised invasion plan was compromised. Undaunted, Humbert went to Grand Isle. He arrived at Barataria early that month, and there found Dominique in port after an eventful and embarrassing cruise.

Youx had returned to cruising the Mexican Gulf coast after delivering the prize to Cat Island early in May. Running under Cartagenan colors, he passed Nautla, some seventy-five miles north of Vera Cruz, and there saw signals from the shore that were intended to get him to land. Instead he continued on his way toward Vera Cruz, only to run into an armed British merchantman that chased him back past Nautla two days later. The

Englishman opened fire and brought down one of *Tigre*'s masts, then sent two boats to board her, but the privateers fought them off and the ships separated. Unfortunately Dominique allowed his crew to celebrate their narrow escape rather intemperately, and everyone aboard got so drunk that they accidentally ran the crippled *Tigre* ashore near Nautla. Word of their situation reached Nautla soon enough, and before long Dominique saw a schooner approaching his beached corsair.

In it was Ellis P. Bean, the man who had signaled Dominique from shore several days earlier. General José Maria Morelos of the Mexican revolutionary junta had engaged Bean to acquire arms in the United States for his insurgency, and to aid and encourage the several competing filibuster plans for invading Texas, which would make his own task of defeating Spain in Mexico that much less difficult. Bean had raised something approaching $10,000 from wealthy patrons, but on reaching the coast at Nautla he had been unable to get anything better than a little schooner to take him to New Orleans. This was why he tried to signal Dominique to his aid, but now he went to Dominique's. The *Tigre* had to be abandoned. Bean transported the privateer crew to Nautla, where they made his schooner more seaworthy, and then they sailed to Grand Isle. Jean Laffite welcomed Bean ashore and entertained him generously, then gave him a guide for the journey through the bayous to New Orleans. In the process Laffite learned that Bean had money for arms, and that there was more to be had.[44]

Humbert probably arrived at Barataria before Bean left, and what he learned would have encouraged him. The Mexicans could raise enough money to buy substantial arms, and that promised good business for the Laffites and their merchant associates in New Orleans. Morelos was anxious to cooperate with Texan ventures, which appealed to Humbert. Rather than act on their own as filibusters, with all the attendant risks of Spanish and American retaliation, perhaps Humbert, the Laffites, and their cohorts could legitimize their several ambitions under the aegis of the Mexican rebel regime, which included a congress and all the other forms of a working government. For the Laffites, the Morelos insurgency could offer legitimacy on the high seas, while his army afforded protection of any privateering base the Laffites established on the Mexican coast. This base would be essential, for even with Mexican letters of marque, the Laffites and their brethren risked prosecution in the United States if they operated out of Louisiana in taking neutral Spanish ships.

Between them, Humbert, the Laffites, and perhaps Bean decided that a chastened Dominique would carry Humbert to the Mexican coast in an unarmed Laffite felucca. His intentions were not yet entirely clear to the Spanish authorities in New Orleans.[45] Sedella, for instance, believed that Dominique was taking Humbert to Tampico or Vera Cruz bent on a pillaging raid.[46] Sedella passed the information along to Apodaca in Cuba using as a secret courier the merchant Francisco Brunetti, whose three-year-old mulatto daughter Silvania Catherina would fourteen years hence marry Pierre Laffite's son Martin.[47]

However, Humbert's real intent was to meet with leaders of the insurgency and to obtain a commission to legitimize his Texas intentions, letters of marque for the corsairs involved in his plan, and some immediate profit to finance their efforts. The last they would achieve by Dominique taking along a cargo of several tons of gunpowder to sell to the rebels. On June 19 Humbert landed at Nautla, where he first posed as an envoy from the United States in order to make contact with the insurgent leaders. In fact, there were two rival leaders, Ignacio Rayón and Juan Rosains, and each had sent a representative to see Humbert. He met with both of them, José Antonio Pedroza and Juan Pablo Anaya. Each sought to take Humbert to his leader, especially after Humbert falsely presented himself as a United States agent authorized to discuss an alliance with the junta. His cargo of gun-powder was also most attractive, and even more so was his prom-ise that other Laffite ships including the *Dorada* and Gambi's *Philanthrope* would be coming with more.[48]

On July 12 Anaya struck first when he gave Humbert a pass-port allowing him to travel inland to meet with Rosains.[49] While Humbert was gone, Anaya and Dominique sold the gunpowder for $5,000 and a variety of silver and gold jewelry. On hearing that the Rayón faction had taken control of the congress and or-dered his arrest, Anaya decided it was time to leave Mexico. He manufactured for himself a bogus commission as emissary to the United States, then virtually kidnapped his enemy Pedroza, put the money and jewelry aboard Dominique's felucca, and set sail as soon as Humbert returned, reaching Barataria about the first of September. On their arrival they met Bean, who joined them for the trip to New Orleans. Dominique dropped them off in the city on September 6 and returned immediately to Grand Isle, for he had learned disturbing news on reaching Barataria.[50] During their absence the landscape had changed dramatically for the fil-ibusters, for the progress of the American war with Britain, and most of all for the Laffites, beginning not least with the fact that Pierre Laffite was in jail.

Is this my skill? my craft? to set at last
Hope, power, and life upon a single cast?
Oh' Fate!—accuse thy folly, not thy fate!
She may redeem thee still, not yet too late.

NINE

Patriots for a Price
1814

SUGGESTIONS OF A stiffening attitude by federal, state, and local authorities earlier in the year proved to be no aberration, but representative of a genuine resolve at last to attack the problems posed by Louisiana's smugglers, privateers, and outright pirates. On April 30, 1812, Louisiana became a state, and in 1814 Claiborne ceased to be an appointed territorial governor with amorphous powers when Louisianans elected him their first state governor. He had long complained of the embarrassment the Baratarian enterprise brought on the area, and more specifically of the Laffites since Holmes's arrest of the brothers brought them to his attention. The April 7, 1813, legal case brought against them for violation of the revenue and neutrality laws made no mention of piracy. These were misdemeanor charges, and nothing came of them. Though under threat of arrest, the brothers continued to operate at large, merely showing circumspection when they made their sporadic nocturnal visits to New Orleans.

By the summer of 1814 the flagrant flouting of the revenue laws by the virtual bazaars at Grand Isle and Cat Island had become well known throughout the Mississippi Valley. "The smuggling at Barataria has greatly injured all honest traders," opined a newspaper in St. Louis, Missouri. Nor was there any question in the public mind who oversaw the enterprise, though the brothers were sometimes merged into one, for the journal added that "in consequence of his [Laffite's] piracy and smuggling, a great variety of goods are very cheap here."[1] Both Jean and Pierre were constantly at Barataria now, and most visitors agreed that they directed the operation. Jean, referred to as "the younger," exercised the greater overall command of the men and personally supervised the auction sales and the collection of the money from the buyers.[2] "There was always a great collection of people on shore of whom Lafitte the younger had command," one privateer observed.[3] Mariner William Godfrey agreed, reporting, "There were two persons named Lafitte who appeared to command the people on shore, the chief command being in the youngest person of that name."[4]

Yet Gambi also had influence.[5] To some it appeared that Jean Laffite and Gambi shared control of the operation, while others thought Gambi was Jean's second-in-command.[6] Some privateersmen acknowledged Laffite's primacy by referring to him as "the Governor," while others used sailors' convention in calling him "the old man."[7] Many merely addressed him by the nickname "Fita."[8] Jean exercised some executive powers such as issuing and signing passports into and out of Barataria for visiting merchants and traders from New Orleans.[9] He also imposed at least a few laws that he and Pierre conceived for all to observe. While the Laffites were in the business of selling illegal African slaves, they discouraged harboring runaway slaves. That was a legal offense that no real or pretended privateering commission could excuse, and only promised to alienate their planter customers. When Jean found a runaway in the Dorada's crew, or in the crew of a vessel belonging to Gambi or another privateer, he arrested the black for return to its owner.[10] One story survived for years claiming that Gambi and some of his men felt aggrieved that Laffite rather than he commanded, and that Jean only cemented his control when he shot one of Gambi's followers for disobeying orders.[11] The story may have had a grain of truth, for Gambi's own vicious nature was well enough known, one Spanish agent warning Apodaca that Gambi was "the cruelest and greatest assassin among all the pirates."[12] Some recalled Jean's rule as being absolute, and the punishment he imposed on rule breakers severe, but none of it seemed unjust. Most of all, in an enterprise of independent, unruly, quarrelsome, and basically criminal men, he kept order.[13]

The smuggler community extended to perhaps forty huts and makeshift houses, most poorly constructed with simple roofs of thatched palmetto fronds. It was a fluid population, consisting primarily of the crews of privateers then in port, their occasional prisoners from prizes, and the visiting buyers from New Orleans. The only long-term residents were a handful of Laffite employees, for few employees were needed. The corsair crews did the work of off-loading cargoes, and often helped run the pirogues into the interior, from which they returned with provisions for the next cruise. A few vendors may have provided outlets for the crewmen to spend their shares, but stories that reached the outside of a thriving commercial community with billiard halls and the like were pure exaggeration. Life on Grand Isle was temporary and rude, of the sort men could create for themselves anywhere they stopped for a few days. Only the Laffites lived in an actual house, at the eastern end of the island overlooking the pass into the bay.

The island had a few permanent residents—a Mr. Dugas, for one, and François Rigaud, who owned some of its land—and their relations with the privateers were excellent, neither interfering with the other.[14] The privateers erected log signal towers in order to communicate with vessels seeking entry into the bay, and the Laffites built one or more warehouses for storing goods prior to auction.[15] Despite exaggerated reports of forts and artillery to protect the pass, they built none, though it is possible that they ran *La Diligent* aground to use as defensive battery, as was reported.[16]

Few had any illusion about the contents of the warehouses. Daniel McMullin spent enough time on Grand Isle to satisfy himself that summer that "Lafitte Vincent & all the others concerned with them were plunderers & smugglers."[17] James Hoskins agreed that "they all appeared to this deponent to be robbers & smugglers," and John Oliver, who came to take passage aboard *La Misere,* frankly admitted afterward in remarkably similar language, that "Lafitte, Gambio & their associates appeared to be sea robbers & plunderers."

"There was a great concourse of people at Grand Terre, sometimes as many as twelve hundred, buying, and selling prize Goods brought in, and supplies procured from New Orleans," one sailor found that summer. Less exaggerated eyewitness accounts put the number at a steady three hundred or four hundred people.[18] When Laffite goods were seized en route to market by agents such as Gilbert, or confiscated from cache houses in New Orleans, the smugglers simply established other "warehouses" in the city's environs.[19] People in New Orleans suspected that the customs agents did not want to put the Laffites out of business, for the agents were making too much money from their shares of the proceeds on the confiscated goods they seized.[20]

Yet it was not all this enterprise that ultimately triggered the decline in Baratarian fortunes, but the old 1813 misdemeanor charge for violation of the revenue laws. Both Laffites were known to visit the city by night or in disguise for business and pleasure. Certainly Pierre paid conjugal visits to Marie at the house on Dumaine that she bought in April. Almost certainly he bought it for her, though it was in her name and he was not present for the transaction for obvious reasons.[21] Jean, too, was seen in the city enough that citizens came to refer to him as "Gentleman Lafitte" to differentiate him from the better known yet rough-hewn and now partly impaired Pierre.[22] Most likely too many successful visits probably bred complacence—for on July 8 word of Pierre being in town reached the wrong ears. Almost at once Hall's court issued an order for his arrest on bail of $12,514.52 as a result of the outstanding judgment from the year before. The United States marshal acted swiftly, probably taking Pierre unawares at home. When Pierre could not post the bail immediately, he was locked in the city jail behind the Cabildo, the old administrative building on the Place d'Arms, and shackled in leg irons, with orders to go before the judge in ten days.[23]

The reaction was swift. The city press exulted. "ANOTHER EMPEROR FALLEN," ran one headline, comparing Pierre to the exiled Napoleon at Elba. Now a cell confined the man they dubbed "Emperor of Baratraria [sic], King of the smugglers." Jean's primacy among the privateers at Grand Isle was not so well known in New Orleans,[24] where Pierre had been the public face of the brothers' enterprise. Spaniards in town felt equally exultant. "The infamous and mean Pirate Lafitte," Mateo Gonzalez Manrique reported to Apodaca, "has been arrested and jailed for the enormous crimes, offenses and other complaints against him."[25] Pierre sat confined in a narrow and windowless ground-floor cell of the three-story *calabozo*, the door locked from the outside by a swing bolt.

Perceptive observers recognized that the old judgment and Pierre's failure to appear in court were merely pretext for getting him in jail when the opportunity presented itself. The real reason for Pierre's arrest was the death of John Stout, for which no indictment had been forthcoming for want of proof of who pulled the trigger. Manrique acknowledged this to Apodaca. "We do not ignore that the main complaint which caused his arrest and

THE PIRATES LAFFITE · 159

jail, is the American's spent blood, when firing against them," he reported.[26] From the Spaniards' viewpoint, it would have been much better had Laffite been arrested for violations of neutrality, which would have shown some acknowledgment by the Americans of Spanish rights. But an arrest was an arrest.

Moreover, the court now had witnesses who were willing to talk about what they had seen and done on Grand Isle and Cat Island. Since the indictment of Joachim in April, more had come forward, and to bring a serious indictment against Pierre and a number of others the authorities had merely to hold Laffite behind bars long enough for a grand jury to hear testimony. With ironclad evidence of not merely revenue violations, but outright piracy, the court could strike at the heart of the smugglers' enterprise, and perhaps get a conviction serious enough to make Pierre pay for Stout's death, even if they could not indict him for the crime.

On July 18 the federal court empanelled a new grand jury, with Paul Lanusse as chairman. This did not bode well for Pierre, for Lanusse still had pending a civil case against Pierre for his interest in the goods taken from the first prize captured by the *Dorada* the year before. Moreover, Lanusse had unsuccessfully attempted to gain a legitimate privateering commission from the government for his vessel the *Cora,* and thus had cause to resent unlawful corsairs such as the Laffites.[27] He was a onetime president of the chamber of commerce, and a current director of the Bank of Louisiana and a leading merchant, and his business suffered proportionately from the unfair competition of the Laffites' contraband. Pierre could hardly expect leniency from Lanusse or a grand jury under his authority.[28]

The court told the grand jury that district attorney Grymes had no presentments for indictment in hand for them to consider, but went on to open the door for them to initiate presentments for possible indictments if they so chose. It was an invitation to bypass Grymes, who may have been perceived as too friendly toward the corsairs. Lanusse's jury retired, obviously prepared for this, and heard testimony from Whiteman and two others, then returned and offered its first preliminary presentment, a charge against "a certain Pierre Lafite now detained in the prison of this City, as a pirate & a notorious Smuggler."[29] By mentioning piracy they were saddling Pierre with a serious federal charge. The only good news was that in spite of long-standing custom in the world, piracy was not a capital crime under federal jurisdiction—though that could change at any minute with Washington's increasing awareness of the problem.

Two days later the jury heard more testimony and returned a formal presentment against Pierre "for having knowingly & wittingly aided & assisted, procured, commanded, counselled & advised . . . acts of piracy & robbery upon the high seas . . . and for having received & repeatedly introduced goods, wares & merchandise arising from such piratical captures into this District."[30] A week later the grand jury issued to the court a general statement making it clear that its action against Pierre was only the first shot of a battle it would wage against the Laffite establishment. It began by decrying the "piracy & smuggling so long established & so systematically practiced by many of the inhabitants of this state." The indulgence of the smugglers and privateers undermined local credit, injured the honest fair trader, drained the country of hard currency in wartime, and corrupted the morals of their citizens. Finally, the jury said, it "stamped disgrace on our state." The jury called on the public to suppress the illicit trade by "pointed disapprobation of every individual who may be concerned." Condemning "the feeble efforts that have been made by those whose immediate duty it was to correct the evil," the jury stopped short of questioning the motives of Governor Claiborne or United States revenue and military authorities, but did charge that had they used the full means available to them the criminals would have been stopped long since.[31]

Seeing the temper of the grand jury, Pierre's friends, probably managed by Jean, began efforts to get him out of jail. Posting the $12,514.52 would have posed no problem for them, but that covered only the original arresting charge. The court had not set bail on the new charges, and would not, for it knew the Laffites' history of jumping bail. The Laffites' lawyer at the moment was Louis Marie Elisabeth Moreau Lislet, a French refugee from San Domingue and former judge of Orleans Parish.[32] On August 6 he filed an "ex Parte Pierre Lafitte" argument before the court, basing the plea for bail on a presumed recurrence of Laffite's physical disability that made incarceration an intolerable hardship for him. Two days later Moreau brought in Dr. J. B. Trabue of Bourbon Street, who had probably treated Pierre for his symptoms in the past, and he testified on behalf of Pierre's medical plea.[33]

But Lanusse had been prepared for this and engaged two independent physicians to examine Pierre in his cell. On August 10 the jury received their written statement and testimony. They confirmed that at some time in the past Pierre had suffered a seizure or stroke, and was subject to intermittent fits of palsy and shaking on his left side. However, they found him entirely free of symptoms suggesting a relapse, and stated that his only apparent problem was depression, no doubt the result of the situation of the moment. Consequently, they saw no reason to recommend releasing him on bail or for removing the manacles "which have been applied as a means of security." Occasional exercise outside his cell was all he needed.[34] The next day the jury denied bail.[35] They would take no chances with Pierre Laffite.

Meanwhile the seriousness of the jury's intent became evident. Two days earlier the jury had indicted a privateer variously called Johanness or Johnny on a charge of piracy for his first prize taken while working for the Laffites, and with him "a certain Peter Lafite of the city of New Orleans, mariner" in that he "knowingly & willingly did assist, procure, command, counsel & advise the said Johanness the said Robbery piracy and felony to do & commit." Also cited in the indictment was Jannet for the capture in February 1813 of the ship owned by Julian Ybarra and loaded with copper and coin, a matter on which Lanusse still sought restitution from Pierre. The specification listed thirteen others as codefendants, including Gambi, Lamé-son, and both Laffites.[36]

From the moment he heard of Pierre's arrest, his brother's safety became Jean Laffite's first concern. With bail out of the question, however, Jean found his options limited. In ordinary times his friends might have stormed the jail and taken Pierre to safety, and this was still an option, but with a growing military presence in New Orleans thanks to the war, such a move carried risks. Jean first tried a far subtler approach that revealed his sure grasp of the social and political situation in New Orleans. He went to the press.

Some in the city believed that the Laffites, especially Pierre, enjoyed close relations with newspapermen, such as Hilaire Leclerc, a San Domingue refugee and ardent supporter of Napoleon who published and edited *L'Ami des Lois*.[37] In this paper's pages sometimes appeared parodies defending the smugglers in the wake of public proclamations, and rumor said that Pierre Laffite was their author.[38] Another refugee editor was Joseph C. de St. Romes, who published the *Courier de la Louisiane*. However, Jean decided to contact David McKeehan, the new owner and publisher of the *Louisiana Gazette and New-Orleans Advertiser*. It was a perceptive choice. As the names of their papers suggested, St. Romes and Leclerc published primarily for the Creole and refugee community, though each issue carried texts in both French and English. The *Gazette*, however, appeared only in English and was clearly aimed at the American population.

In a court run by Hall and Grymes, in a state run by Claiborne, and with a grand jury that had several American members as well as French, civil and legal power belonged to the Americans. Moreover, the French community was already sympathetic to the Laffites and their enterprise; it was the Americans whose favor Laffite needed to win.[39]

A week after the indictments Jean Laffite wrote a letter to McKeehan. He wrote it in English, which presented a challenge, since even his written French was ungrammatical. Writing had always been Pierre's realm. "I am not accustomed to write for public eyes, nor well acquainted with the English language," Jean confessed, asking the editor to correct his text where necessary "and publish it for the benefit of our worthy friends." Then, rather than addressing the subject of Pierre, he aimed his words directly at the self-interest of New Orleans' consumers and at some of the allegations in the recent grand jury statement.

"It is the duty of every good man to prevent *monopoly*, as far as in his power," he opened, and therefore he begged to inform the public that "several rich prizes have lately been brought to Grand Isle (vulgarly called Barrataria) by the remains of *my uncle's faithful band of loyal subjects*," a reference to the Frenchmen among the privateers whom Laffite now tried to link to Napoleon, though few if any of them had served the emperor. In a veiled barb at Lanusse, he went on to say that "a certain class of monopolizing gentry in and near this city" had tried to keep the arrival of the prizes a secret from the public, while themselves going to Grand Isle in search of bargains. "Now, sir," he continued, "as the public ought to generally share the profits of this advantageous trade, I have thought proper thus to address you." He emphasized that specie was not the only currency accepted at his auctions. "Bank note money of the Banks of New Orleans will be received for goods sold," he added, in spite of the "blind and stupid opinion of the late Grand Jury of this city, who stated that *our trade* contributed to drain the country of its specie." Exactly the opposite was the truth, he said. "We deal in specie instead of carrying it away."

Laffite could not close without impishly adding a suggestion. "Would it not be *pro bono*," he asked, "to establish a press in the Empire of Barrataria?" That way the public could regularly be informed of the latest arrivals and sales. He finished by signing himself "Napoleon, Junior." McKeehan published Jean's letter on August 18, but there seems to have been no immediate reaction or repercussion, nor would Jean have expected any.[40] His best hope in writing the letter was to sway public opinion, his missive's none too subtle subtext being that if Pierre were convicted and Barataria broken up, everyone would be the poorer for paying more for their imported goods thereafter. Favorable opinion might make it difficult to assemble a jury that would convict, buying Jean some time to arrange to break his brother out of jail if necessary and move on, for Jean Laffite had come to the conclusion that his Barataria operation was finished.

The authorities in New Orleans were becoming too aggressive, with the American naval and military establishment increasingly a threat. Only the distraction of the war with Britain kept them from being even more vigilant. Business with New Orleans had been good, and could continue to be so even if the Laffites left Louisiana. Indeed, an affiliation with the new Mexican revolutionaries could give them genuine corsair commissions, and allow them a Mexican coastal base outside the reach of American interference. A court of admiralty there could condemn and clear for sale whatever their ships brought in, and then the Laffites and their brethren would be free to transport their goods to New Orleans and trade on the open market. Even if they paid customs duties, they could undersell the city's merchants since they would have paid nothing for the goods. Or Jean may have considered simply establishing a market on the Texas side of the Sabine River and inducing Louisiana buyers to come to sales there, meaning he and his associates could avoid American waters altogether. The Laffites had been planning since April to establish a new base outside the United States, and even now Jean daily expected the return of Humbert and Dominique with news, and perhaps money and a Mexican rebel commitment of cooperation. Pierre might not go to trial for months as the court gathered more evidence. Thus, though he felt concern for his brother's physical condition, Jean had time, or so he thought.

While he may have gone close to New Orleans to contact McKeehan and arrange for publication of his letter, as well as to orchestrate attempts to get bail set for Pierre, by late August Jean was back at Grand Isle assessing what he needed to do for the pending relocation, and waiting for Humbert.[41] By September 2 Humbert and Dominique had returned, and with them Anaya and Pedroza. But as interesting as the news they brought with them was, almost immediately another sail showed on the horizon, introducing an entirely new dimension to the decisions facing Laffite.[42] On September 3 at about 10 o'clock in the morning, a strange warship appeared outside the pass between Grand Terre and Grand Isle. The warship sent a few shots at a ship heading for the pass into the bay. The smaller vessel ran aground and shortly the warship dropped anchor inside the pass, leaving Jean uncertain of its intent. He decided to find out for himself.[43]

Laffite could see the vessel from his rude house on the eastern end of the island.[44] He put out in a pirogue pulled by four oarsmen and rowed toward the mysterious vessel.[45] At the same time, about noon, a pinnace showing a white flag of truce was lowered from the vessel, which began rowing toward Laffite.[46] Soon he recognized the British naval pennant flying from the pinnace, and while he might have been inclined to rush back to shore, the boat was too close by now for him to get away.[47] When they came abreast, Captain Nicholas Lockyer identified himself as commander of the HMS *Sophie* and asked to be introduced to Laffite. Jean remained wary, and did not identify himself. Lockyer asked if Laffite were ashore, and Jean said that he was not certain but believed that he was.[48] At that Lockyer handed him a packet addressed "To Mr. Lafitte—Barataria," and asked him to deliver it.

Instead, Laffite persuaded Lockyer to row back to Grand Isle with him to present the packet in person. Moments before they reached the shore Laffite finally identified himself. By this time two hundred or more privateers had gathered to see what was going on, and Laffite advised Lockyer not to say anything of his reasons for coming. British warships had fired on some of these men during the past year, and though they were largely outlaws, the island's predominantly French population had no love for Britain. This was made clear when the two boats landed amid an uproar, as some of the mob wanted revenge while others demanded that the visitors be arrested and taken to New Orleans as spies. Laffite calmed the mob, telling the privateer captains present to tell their men that he needed to cajole the British officers in order to learn their intentions, and perhaps find out the names of their spies in New Orleans.[49] Then he took Lockyer by the hand and conducted the officers away from the milling crowd to his house, thinking that both they and the secrets of his establishment would be safer with them there.[50]

Laffite later claimed that even before he opened it, he thought the packet might contain important information. This was a reasonable enough assumption, for he could hardly be unaware that the British had been paying some attention to what happened at Grand Isle. English merchants on Jamaica had protested the refugee corsairs from Cuba and San Domingue sailing under their real and imaginary papers from Cartagena.[51] And as Britain tried to pull Spain from the French yoke and make it an ally, corsairs preying on Spanish merchant trade and the filibustering adventures were equally unwelcome.[52] In July the Spanish foreign minister asked the British foreign secretary Lord Castlereagh to have British ships in the Gulf destroy the nest of pirates to protect the navigation of the three allied nations, Britain, Spain, and Portugal.[53] Spain also asked England to blockade Cartagena to help interdict the privateer trade.[54] By the end of 1813 Spain complained of "continual depredations" in the Caribbean by pirates, some of them taking shelter in English colonies.[55]

Britain soon came to view the Baratarians from another vantage, however, suspecting that for the moment they might be useful. As early as March 1813 British spies had a copy of General Wilkinson's earlier report on the state of defenses on the lower Mississippi, and deduced from it that the Baratarian fleet could be invaluable in blockading New Orleans.[56] The past June Captain Hugh Pigot of HMS *Orpheus,* then off Florida trying to convince Indian tribes to assist the British, and even then arming them for the anticipated attack on New Orleans, received intelligence suggesting that the Baratarians "would cheerfully assist in any operations against the Americans if afterward protected by Great Britain." He believed there were eight hundred of them, "Pirates to all Nations," and that New Orleans lived in fear of them.[57] Pigot and others got exaggerated reports that the Laffites had a fort on Grand Terre and more than a dozen cannon emplaced for defense, an echo of the report on *La Diligent*'s final employment.[58] Thus there could be good cause in approaching the Laffites.

While he later claimed that he first suspected that Lockyer's packet might be of use to the United States, it is more likely that Laffite's initial instinct was that it might be useful to himself. He opened it and found inside four documents.[59] The first was a copy of a proclamation dated August 29, issued by Lieutenant Colonel Edward Nicholls, then commanding British land forces operating in and off Florida. In it he exhorted Louisianans to assist in liberating themselves from "a faithless, imbecile Government," calling especially on the Spaniards, Frenchmen, Italians, and British in the area to abolish "the American *usurpation in this country.*" If they rose to his standard, he promised help from the numerous Indians under his command, well armed and trained and commanded by British officers, and the backing of squadrons of British and Spanish ships. Men coming to his aid need have no fear of onerous taxes to carry on an unjust war, and British arms would protect their property and laws. As for the Indians, they were pledged not to harm friends, for "these Brave red men only burn with an ardent desire of satisfaction, for the wrongs they have suffered, to join you in liberating these Southern Provinces from their Yoke, and drive them into those limits formerly prescribed by my Sovereign."[60]

Next was a letter from Nicholls addressed directly to "Monsieur Lafite or the Commandant at Barataria." Written three days earlier from Nicholls's headquarters in Pensacola, it called on Laffite "with your Brave followers to enter into the service of Great Britain." In return, Nicholls promised that Laffite would be given the rank of captain in the army, and that after a British victory in the war Laffite and his men would receive generous grants of land. He also guaranteed the security of their persons and property, presumably against retaliation for acts against British shipping, asking only that they immediately cease taking British and Spanish merchantmen. Instead, the Baratarian fleet would be turned over to the command of the naval commodore in the Gulf, Captain William H. Percy. In short, Laffite and his men must become soldiers and abandon their maritime endeavors completely.

Nicholls also asked that Laffite circulate his proclamation. "Be expeditious in your resolves," he said, enjoining Laffite to make his decision quickly. "You may be a useful assistant to me." Nicholls hinted that he expected soon to mount a serious threat to Louisiana, which to date had seen little of the British other than blockades off the Mississippi. Nicholls's reference to a substantial soldier reinforcement on the way, however, could only mean land operations, and of course the only target on the mainland in Louisiana would be New Orleans.[61]

Laffite also found a letter from Captain Percy directing Lockyer to sail his ship to Barataria to contact Laffite, and substantially reiterating Nicholls's terms, though Percy emphasized that the land bounty would come from "His *Majestys colonies in America.*" Percy, at least, did not expect the United States to survive as a nation. If the Baratarians declined to join in the coming offensive against the Americans, Percy suggested that they be urged to remain neutral and cease their preying on Spanish shipping. If Laffite agreed, Percy ordered Lockyer to coordinate their efforts in annoying the enemy and made it clear that he wanted the Baratarian fleet to join with his own for an attack on Mobile.[62]

The fourth document was a letter from Percy to Laffite, dated the previous day. In it Percy revealed a rather less accommodating spirit, and more of the traditional attitude of professional naval officers toward pirates and privateers. Having heard that Laffite had taken and sold British merchantmen, he demanded immediate restitution, and informed Laffite that, should he refuse, Lockyer had orders "to destroy, to his utmost every vessel there, as well as to carry destruction over the whole place," adding that he would give Lockyer all the additional force he might need to do the job. "I trust at the same time that the Inhabitants of Barataria consulting their own interest, will not make it necessary to proceed to such Extremities," he went on to say. They had now the choice of "a war instantly Destructive to them," or cooperation that would only be to their gain. Percy would pay them for their vessels, and any of the privateers who wished to enlist in His Majesty's military or naval forces would be welcomed. If any of them were British subjects, he promised pardon for their offenses against the Crown as soon as they enlisted.[63]

As Laffite read the papers, Lockyer elaborated on their intent, emphatically urging Laffite not to let this opportunity escape him. If he did, said Lockyer, he would regret it.[64] Laffite asked for a few days to consider and consult with his associates, but Lockyer pressed him, arguing that there should be no need for time to think, as the offer was too good. France and Britain were friends again, and so Frenchmen like Laffite should side with the British. Laffite was an outlaw in America and at this very moment his brother was in jail, quite possibly with the gallows awaiting.[65] Laffite would get ahead in the British service, even win promotion perhaps.[66] Lockyer also suggested that Nicholls wanted permission to land troops at Grand Isle, using it as a base for a campaign against New Orleans, to which Laffite replied that though he was a smuggler, he "did not intend to fight against the Americans."[67] He refused to be pushed, committing himself only to providing an answer in a few days.

Jean then raised a pretext to leave his house for a short time. Once he was gone, some of the men outside reassembled, rushed in, arrested Lockyer and a marine officer with him, and took them to a cell used for keeping rule breakers and perhaps Spanish prisoners from prizes. According to Lockyer, the men threatened and insulted him, then took from him the papers he had brought and tore them up in front of his face—though they must have been copies as Laffite had the originals in hand.[68] John Oliver heard Dominique, feeling vengeful over the British crippling of the *Tigre*, say he wanted to take the British ship.[69] A few called for Lockyer to be hanged—which must have galled him, since the captain was known for his kind and attentive treatment of prisoners who fell into his hands.[70]

Somehow Lockyer sent an appeal to Laffite, but Jean could see the temper of his men. He had prevailed over them at the waterline, but now they had ignored his wishes and were clearly in a mood to challenge his authority, even mutiny, if he interfered. Better not to create a situation that could compromise his future sway over them, he concluded, but to wait until he found them more manageable. Consequently, Laffite did not acknowledge that the Englishmen had been arrested, and sent Lockyer's pinnace back to the *Sophie* with instructions to return in the morning.[71]

Laffite spent the balance of the daylight hours at other tasks as if nothing had happened, and that evening met with the leaders of the disaffected men. Speaking as if Lockyer had not been taken, he reminded them that if the officers were harmed, the Baratarians would all be liable to reprisals when they crossed paths with British vessels at sea. Moreover, they would forfeit the chance to learn British intentions and perhaps identify England's spies and collaborators in Louisiana. Laffite left the men to consider what best served their interests, and left Lockyer to spend a very uncomfortable night.

The next morning, September 4, when the British pinnace returned, the mob arrested its crew as well, and threatened to send them to New Orleans as spies. But as Laffite expected, the unruly men then had what Lockyer described as "a sudden change of mind," and they released the officers.[72] Seizing the moment, Laffite immediately walked Lockyer and the others to their pinnace and saw them off. Within the hour the *Sophie* weighed anchor and stood out of the pass and back into the Gulf, there to await a reply.[73]

That afternoon Laffite drafted a letter that he sent to Lockyer, first apologizing for the treatment of the visitors. As for the British offer, he told Lockyer that "indeed, at present, I cannot give you the satisfaction you wish." However, if the British could give him fifteen days, thereafter "I will be entirely at your service." He needed the time to reestablish his control over the men by dealing with three of the ringleaders in the near mutiny, who would be leaving Grand Isle in little more than a week. One of the three, who may have been Dominique, he said would be going to New Orleans, as indeed Dominique did that day, along with Humbert and the rest. Jean needed the second week to get his affairs in order, but he was essentially accepting the British offer, and with a little flattery thrown in. "You have inspired me with more confidence than perhaps the admiral, your superior, would have done," he told Lockyer. "Therefore it is with you that I would treat; and from you I shall claim, in my term, those services which I may now render you, at proper time and place." Meanwhile Lockyer could communicate with him by sending messages to his house overlooking the pass.[74]

Beyond question Jean had no intention of keeping this bargain. He was buying time to consider a complicated situation. In itself, the British proposal offered him nothing, and even that predicated on American defeat in the war. The pay that the British offered for service as an army captain was scarcely a fraction of what he made from a single good prize. He would be paid for his vessels, but would thereby be out of a frequently lucrative profession. A land bounty was no use to him. He certainly did not intend to become a planter, and he could not sell the land for much as land was cheap just then and could be obtained from the government for almost nothing. Most of all, the Baratarian enterprise would be out of business.

Laffite already knew that no matter which side won, American or British, his operation within the United States was doomed. This is what made Dominique's coincidental arrival with Humbert, Anaya, and Pedroza so fortuitous, troublesome though Youx might have been with Lockyer. Before they went on to New Orleans, probably within hours of Laffite's letter to Lockyer, Anaya informed Laffite of his new commission as agent, which Jean could not know had little or no validity. Anaya said that soon under the authority of the Mexican congress he would provide privateering commissions for the Baratarian captains, meaning that for perhaps the first time Laffite ships could sail under legitimate papers. He would start work on it as soon as he reached New Orleans and contacted those backers still willing to support Humbert.[75] The old Tampico plan would be on again, and this time legitimized by the Mexican insurgency. It needed only a little time, yet another reason for Laffite to stall Lockyer for a fortnight.

Jean also needed to bargain some delay from the Americans, and the Britons' approach could serve a purpose. If he turned Lockyer's papers and what he had learned in conversation with the British captain over to authorities in New Orleans, he might win favor, if only temporarily. Laffite surely knew from his informants in the city that Patterson was preparing an expedition to destroy the Baratarian establishment. Anything that delayed this would give him more time to prepare the shift of base to the Mexican coast. The Laffites remained almost entirely silent as to their sympathies in the current war. Certainly they felt no patriotic affection for the United States sufficient to make them obey its laws. Yet like most of French blood, they felt an ancestral enmity for Britain. The Baratarians included many men who had fought against the British on Santiago and Baracoa prior to 1809.[76] While most of the brothers' personal and business associates in New Orleans were Frenchmen, they enjoyed good relations with some Americans as well. From a purely pragmatic viewpoint, there was still a hungry market for slaves in the United States, while Britain had outlawed the slave trade in its colonies in 1807 and was considering complete abolition throughout the empire—which would not bode well for Laffite business. Thus, even if self-exiled from their adopted home, the Laffites had a strong self-interest in American victory.

All things considered, the scale tipped toward informing authorities in New Orleans of the British visit. The choice of whom to approach may not have been difficult. Claiborne or Flournoy would have been the most logical, but Laffite might not expect either to credit something coming from him. He must contact someone who had their ear, and the name that came to mind was Jean Blanque. An immigrant to New Orleans in 1803, the same year Pierre arrived, Blanque was a merchant, onetime slave dealer, and banker who had held successive offices in the territorial government, and at the moment sat in the legislature then in session in New Orleans. Blanque was also an investor in more than one privateer, which likely led to an acquaintance with the Laffites. A few months later a Creole planter would frankly state that "Blanque is regarded as one of the persons financially interested in the piracies of Barataria, which he openly protects." He had also recently been admitted to practice before the federal district court, which might prove useful.[77] It helped, of course, that Blanque was bilingual, and thus Laffite could communicate precisely with him and leave it to Blanque to translate his communications for the Americans.

Almost immediately after sending Lockyer his temporizing letter, Laffite addressed a letter to Blanque. "Though proscribed by my adoptive country," he claimed, he wrote to prove his loyalty and to demonstrate that "she has never ceased to be dear to me." Informing Blanque of Lockyer's visit, he enclosed the documents handed him by Lockyer. "You will see from their contents the advantages I might have derived from that kind of association," he pointed out, then went on to declare, somewhat tongue in cheek, that "I may have evaded the payment of duties to the custom house; but I have never ceased to be a good citizen; and all the offence I have committed, I was forced to by certain vices in our laws." Warming to hyperbole, he declared that he was making Blanque "the depository of the secret on which perhaps depends the tranquility of our country." Then, having called attention to his patriotism and the importance of his action, he protested that he would be content to let both speak for themselves.

A second motive for turning the documents over to the Americans emerged. "Our enemies have endeavored to work on me by a motive which few men would have resisted," he said. "They represented to me a brother in irons, a brother who is to me very dear! Whose deliverer I might become." Laffite expressed the hope that in providing this information to the Americans, he might gain Pierre's release. "Well persuaded of his innocence, I am free from apprehension as to the issue of a trial," Jean averred, "but he is sick and not in a place where he can receive the assistance his state requires." In the "name of humanity," Jean asked Blanque to use his influence to free Pierre, resorting to the same type of flattery he used on Lockyer when he added that he thought Blanque to be "a just man, a true American, endowed with all other qualities that are honored in society." Laffite lied outright when he told Blanque that he had refused Nicholls's offer, though of course he had lied to Lockyer when he indicated that he would accept. He told Blanque that he had asked for fifteen days to settle his plans, and expected that the grace period would be granted.[78] He sent the letter and accompanying documents to New Orleans by the fastest means, possibly unaware that unfolding events would negate his proposal before Blanque learned of it.

That night a person or persons unknown crept into the courtyard behind the Cabildo and stopped outside Pierre Laffite's cell. They swung open the bolt that locked the door from the outside and in a matter of seconds Pierre walked out a free man. Not content with this, he and his rescuers released three slave men being held in another cell and stole off into the night to begin the journey to Barataria, though not before Pierre sent a message of his own to Jean Blanque, who may well have assisted the escape.[79] When the cells were found empty the next morning, an immediate outcry arose. Few had any doubts as to who had managed the escape. McKeehan took it for granted that smugglers had done the deed, remarking that the jail was well situated for such a clandestine action, being behind the Cabildo and out of sight from the Place d'Arms or the city streets. Indeed, he had predicted when Pierre was arrested months before that someone would break him out whenever the time came that Pierre felt genuinely threatened by the charges against him.[80]

The jailbreak was embarrassing for Sheriff J. H. Holland, especially when the press implied that he had connived in the breakout. McKeehan commented rather pointedly that Laffite *"is said to have broken and escaped from prison?—!!!"* though he later apologized for the innuendo.[81] Still the editor thought "it is not a very pleasant joke on the jailor" to post a mere $1,000 reward for retaking "such a man as this." He regarded the reward offer as nothing but a mockery, and assumed it was done for form's sake rather than from an expectation that anyone would bring Pierre in. It was all part and parcel of the defective way the laws were enforced and justice administered in Louisiana, he complained.[82]

Spaniards in town had little doubt, too, that Laffite's confederates had freed him. When the break was discovered, Morphy immediately wrote of it to Apodaca, indication that they regarded Laffite as an important component in the filibustering enemy facing them. "With the aid of his companions, [he] was able to climb the walls of the jail and escape," Morphy explained. "It is not rare that this happened, because unfortunately in this city are many individuals involved in the pirate acts he committed and therefore many are interested in saving him at all costs, in order to avoid being discovered." In short, Morphy believed it was city merchants who got Pierre out of jail.[83] He may have been right. Even if Jean had plans for getting his brother out, he was not likely behind this break, or he would hardly have bothered to ask Blanque for his assistance. So far as the Spaniards were concerned, the how and who of Pierre's escape were immaterial, for now, "even with all his offenses and enormous crimes,"

Manrique complained to Apodaca, "he is already walking and free to get back to his horrific practices as he is the meanest of all pirates."[84]

While Pierre was making his way to Grand Isle, and surely before word that he was at large arrived ahead of him, Jean Laffite received information that he thought might be useful in his bargain with Blanque. Somehow he came into possession of a letter from Havana, written August 8 to a recipient in Pensacola, probably taken on a prize brought in on September 6 or 7. The letter contained some details of a British expedition bent on taking Mobile, but told little that Laffite—and now Blanque—did not know from Lockyer's papers. However, the letter went on to say that after taking Mobile, Nicholls intended to push for New Orleans, and place forces at Plaquemine to isolate the Mississippi from the Gulf.[85]

On September 7 Laffite enclosed the letter in another missive to Blanque, noting that Lockyer's ship still sat at anchor in sight from his house, and was now joined by two others. Jean had held no further communication with Lockyer, waiting for instructions from Blanque.[86] "We have hitherto kept on a respectable defensive," Laffite added, but then dropped the hint that "if, however, the British attach to the possession of this place, the importance they give us room to suspect they do, they may employ means above our strength." If the British warships were there to carry out Percy's threat to destroy Barataria if Laffite refused to aid them, as Jean suggested, then the enemy would have a foothold at the back door to New Orleans. This being the case, Jean suspected that Claiborne and the military might now be very receptive to receiving intelligence from him, even at the cost of a favor to Pierre.[87] Then, perhaps within hours of writing to Blanque, Laffite saw the *Sophie* and the other vessels raise anchor and sail out of sight. Lockyer had gotten tired of waiting, though Jean could not know whether this meant a reprieve from danger, or that Lockyer was going to inform Percy that Laffite was playing with them and it was time to attack.[88]

By this time Blanque had received Jean's first package, and by his own account he thought this a "strange communication" from Laffite. After he read the documents he immediately determined to turn them over to Claiborne.[89] Meanwhile he sent a verbal message back via Laffite's courier, a Mr. Rancher, telling Jean to remain calm and do nothing until he heard more from Blanque or from the governor.[90] Blanque's response probably took two or three days to reach Grand Isle, meaning it arrived on or about September 10. But the perfunctory message would have been far overshadowed when a pirogue came down the bay that day and Pierre Laffite stepped ashore and into his brother's arms.

It required but a few minutes for Jean to inform his brother of the past week's events. Both quick thinkers, they now dealt with the shift in circumstances caused by Pierre's escape. Jean's requests from Blanque were now moot, of course. In effect, they had given the authorities information for nothing. The information was of little value, for there was nothing in the Lockyer papers not already known in New Orleans, but now they had nothing with which to bargain. Meanwhile Percy might send a force to destroy Barataria at any time in the next few weeks, and they could not ignore the rumors coming out of New Orleans that Patterson was preparing to do the same thing. They needed time, and Pierre came up with a new carrot to dangle before Claiborne and the American authorities.

The Baratarians would offer to defend Barataria against a British attack if it came, and in return Jean would ask Claiborne for a cessation of the prosecutions against them, which implied a halt to Patterson's intended attack as well. This plan was brilliant in its way, for the governor was not necessarily to know that in effect the Laffites were offering nothing. Jean already accepted, and as much as admitted to Blanque, that he could not defend

Barataria against a British attack. He had several privateers in the harbor and three hundred to five hundred men at any given time, but this was no match for English warships. But of course the British might not come. If they did not, then he would have forestalled Patterson's attack at no expense to himself, and he could still leave for the Mexican coast when ready. If the British did come, he could try to stop an attack by sending out word accepting their terms, which he had conditionally accepted already. In the worst case, if the British proved intractable, he could simply evacuate earlier than he intended and move to the Calcasieu or the Sabine.

Pierre wrote a letter to Claiborne the same day, and once more resorted to flattery, telling Claiborne that he had been elected governor thanks to his merit and the esteem of the people. Then he portentously broached a matter "on which may depend the safety of this country." Offering to restore to Louisiana "several citizens, who perhaps in your eyes have lost that sacred title," he proffered the Baratarians "such as you could wish to find them, ready to exert their utmost efforts in defence of the country." Asserting the strategic importance of his position on Grand Isle, he offered to defend it, asking in return that the current prosecutions and indictments against him and his men be quashed, and that a general pardon be granted for all they had done in the past.

"I am the stray sheep, wishing to return to the sheepfold," he went on. "If you were thoroughly acquainted with my offences, I should appear to you much less guilty." He had never sailed under any flag except Cartagena's, he protested, adding disingenuously that "my vessels are perfectly regular in that respect." Indeed, he would have brought his prizes into New Orleans if he could have, since they were lawful, but he stopped at that, saying, "I decline saying more on the subject." Should Claiborne refuse his offer, he concluded, "I declare to you that I will instantly leave the country, to avoid the imputation of having co-operated towards an invasion on this point, which cannot fail to take place, and to rest secure in the acquittal of my own conscience." Laffite did not offer to aid in the defense of New Orleans, or to join the American army, or to do any other service where needed, but only to defend Grand Isle.[91] What remained to be seen was whether the shepherd was willing to let these black sheep join his flock.

How speed the outlaws? stand they well prepared,
Their plunder'd wealth, and robber's rock, to guard?
Dream they of this our preparation, doom'd
To view with fire their scorpion nest consumed?

TEN

The End of Barataria
1814

G OVERNOR CLAIBORNE had the Laffites on his mind even before the moment, probably the morning of September 7,
when Jean Blanque asked for an audience.[1] The diplomatic situation created by the privateers had only gotten stickier as General
Andrew Jackson sought to defend Mobile and southern Alabama, which were made particularly vulnerable by the Spanish
occupation of Pensacola and East Florida. Jackson feared that af-
fronts to Spain's neutrality could make the Spaniards amenable to
the British using Florida as a base for an attack on Mobile and,
ultimately, New Orleans. Early in July reports conjectured that
the British would launch an invasion from Apalachicola.[2] At the
same time Jackson upbraided Governor Gonzalez Manrique of
Florida for allowing the British to land men and guns in their effort to inflame the Indians against the Americans. Manrique
countered by noting the "scandalous notoriety" of the United
States harboring "the piracies of Lafite and his party, at Barrataria." Their enterprise, he suggested, could be seen as sufficient reason to help the British make war against a nation so
indulgent of violations on Spain's commerce.[3]

Thus Jackson had been delighted when Claiborne informed him of Pierre Laffite's capture, though several weeks elapsed before Jackson wrote to Manrique to declare that "Monsieur Le Fitte, commander of the band of pirates, was arrested some time ago and now is being prosecuted for the enormous crimes, piracies, and complaints which there have been against him." That, he suggested, should be proof enough of American good intentions, and he went on to challenge Manrique for providing a haven for American deserters and English renegades who raided American communities. Manrique was swallowing none of that, however. Advised by his friends in New Orleans, he shot back that Pierre had been arrested for the Stout killing and not for his attacks on Spanish ships, "and that for his piracies and enormous crimes he is now at liberty to return to his honorable occupation, that of the vilest of pirates."[4] Meanwhile in New Orleans, Fray Sedella had pressed steadily with Claiborne for legal action to be taken against the Baratarians, though this put him at risk of retaliation from the smugglers, or so he thought.[5] The governor, in turn, persistently took his case to the military authorities. In mid-August he wrote to General Jackson that "the Pirates and Smugglers who have so long infested the shores of Barataria . . . Are still in force and, in the daily violation of all laws human and divine." His legislature would not authorize the means to deal with the problem, and he begged the United States to do so. Patterson had told him he was disposed to act, and Colonel George Ross of the 44th United States Infantry was in accord.[6] By the beginning of September, General Jackson was every bit as anxious as Claiborne, Patterson, and Washington to make an end of the Baratarians.

The growing focus on the Laffite problem was about to produce results. On July 8 Secretary of the Navy William Jones had sent Commodore Patterson a direct order to break up the Grand Isle operation.[7] To that end, Jones assigned to him the armed schooner USS *Carolina*, which arrived in New Orleans in mid-

August. Patterson feared that the British naval presence in the Gulf would make it unsafe to take his little fleet on a sortie, but then he learned that enemy warships were moving toward Mobile, and this gave him an opportunity.[8] By the beginning of September Patterson had his expedition ready, expecting it would take no more than a fortnight.[9] At the last moment, though, one of his brigs lost a mast, necessitating repair. On September 4 Patterson expected to be able to leave in two days, his anxiety heightened that day by the news of Pierre Laffite's escape from jail.[10]

The day after Pierre's escape, Claiborne ordered two divisions of state militia to be ready to march and to muster at Baton Rouge October 1. This had little or nothing to do with Barataria, and more with the beginning perceptions that New Orleans might be a British target after Mobile, if not before. But it was amid the flurry of activity among officials in New Orleans that Jean Blanque appeared at Claiborne's quarters asking for an audience.[11] When they met, Blanque handed the governor the packet of correspondence he had received from Laffite, and immediately tried to disassociate himself from the Baratarians by protesting curiosity as to why Laffite sent it to him when he had "no acquaintance with Lafite." Still, he told the governor that he knew on reading the documents what he should do with them. Claiborne read the letters in Blanque's presence, and then at Blanque's request returned to him the one addressed from Jean to Blanque, Blanque likely thinking he might need it later to establish that he was only an intermediary.[12]

Here was a pretty quandary. Commodore Patterson was ready to launch his expedition, and now Jean Laffite confirmed that the British had solicited the Baratarians' assistance. While this could have added urgency to Patterson's enterprise, the governor's understanding from Jean's letter to Blanque was, as he put it, that Laffite felt determined to "take no part with the English."[13] Laffite's sending the material to Blanque suggested that if he learned anything more of British intentions, he could be willing to pass it on to Claiborne. Yet Laffite had not explicitly offered aid to the Americans, and the only thing Jean asked for, his brother's release or relief, had been attained with no further need of the deal he proposed. Indeed, Claiborne even thought there was room for doubt that the correspondence proposing the bargain was genuine.

Dealing with the Laffites could have advantages, however, and to discuss what should be done Claiborne that day summoned the informal "Board of Officers," with whom he consulted on matters relating to the defense of Louisiana. The board consisted of Commodore Patterson, Colonel Ross, collector Dubourg, and Major General Jacques Villeré, commander of the state militia. Claiborne put the packet of materials before them, along with his views. "Lafitte and his associates might probably be made useful to us," Claiborne said, but he added his doubts about the propriety and wisdom of "using men of such desperate character in any manner." Caught in his indecision, Claiborne confessed some doubts about Patterson's expedition. "I begin to think it would be advisable, for the present, to postpone it," he said.

Patterson disagreed emphatically, and argued that his orders to attack Barataria left him no alternative. Moreover, he confessed his own anxiety to get at them at last.[14] Unsaid, though certainly a part of his thinking, was the fact that he and his men would be entitled to share the proceeds of sale of whatever his expedition captured in the way of vessels and merchandise. He stood to profit considerably if his raid were a success. Money mattered to Patterson, who was married to the daughter of George Pollock, director of the New Orleans Branch of the Bank of the United States, and the Orleans Navigation Company. Patterson had already engaged an attorney to represent him in the anticipated prize cases to come.

Ross agreed that the raid had to go on. He, too, would share in any contraband seized. Then the question arose of whether the documents were genuine, or simply a ruse to try to negotiate

Pierre Laffite's freedom.[15] Claiborne at first thought them false, as did Patterson, Ross, and Dubourg. Apparently Villeré disagreed, however. Later that day Claiborne met with former collector Pierre Duplessis, who had seen Jean's signature before and confirmed that the one on the letter to Lockyer was genuine, which satisfied the governor.[16]

The weight of the argument to strike Barataria ran against Claiborne. They no longer had Pierre as a guarantee that Jean would honor a bargain, and Jean had not offered anything concrete. Moreover, as Ross pointed out, the letter to Lockyer "shews Lafites acceptation," so for all they knew the smugglers would cooperate with the enemy.[17] That decided it. Indeed, if anything, the meeting hastened the launch of the expedition. The next day, September 8, Claiborne wrote to General Jackson, sending him copies of the documents and expressing his own ambivalence, while Ross notified the general that the expedition would be leaving soon.[18]

Meanwhile the message Blanque had sent to Jean via Rancher may have included a promise that the government would not take action against the Baratarians immediately—though whether that was Claiborne or Blanque speaking is uncertain.[19] What little Rancher was able to report upon reaching the island may have prompted Pierre's "stray sheep" letter to Claiborne. When the brothers were together Pierre exercised the greater authority, and now he wrote to Blanque endorsing Jean's actions and promising that he was "fully determined to follow the plan that may reconcile us with the government." He enclosed his letter to Claiborne, leaving it to Blanque's judgment whether it should be delivered.[20] By this time Blanque had received Jean's September 7 letter, with the captured Havana letter enclosed, which Blanque thought shed "some light on the situation of the English as much as he [Laffite] could furnish." He immediately put it into Claiborne's hands.[21] The accumulating evidence began to argue that the Laffites were sincere in their disavowal of intent to aid the

British. Pierre's September 10 letter to Claiborne could not have made it any more explicit. But by the time the governor got it two days later, Patterson and Ross had launched their expedition hours earlier and it could not now be called back even if Claiborne had had the authority to do so.

At 1 A.M. on September 11, Patterson loaded seventy men under Colonel Ross on three barges above the city, then floated downriver in the darkness to avoid detection—a failed effort since the next day it was well known in New Orleans that the expedition was under way, with no mystery as to its objective. Morphy sent word of it to Havana, along with his conviction that "now there can be no doubt that the Baratarians rob every ship without distinction." There was, he said, no alternative to driving them permanently from their lair.[22] By daylight Patterson had reached English Turn, and by the next day joined the *Carolina* at Plaquemine. Patterson stopped at Fort St. Philip the following morning, and rendezvoused that afternoon with the USS *Sea Horse* and six gunboats at the Balize.[23] He spent more than a day there in final preparations. Finally on the evening of September 15 the flotilla sailed through the southwest pass and into the Gulf. No doubt Patterson delayed sailing until after dark in hopes of slipping past prying eyes, and to time his arrival at Grand Terre for just after dawn.[24] However, he was convinced that word was already on its way to the Laffites. More than that, he fully expected that when he struck Grand Isle in the morning, the smugglers would fight to the last.[25] Meanwhile mere hours after Patterson left Morphy realized that something was going on. He had news that the *Petit Milan* was at Plaquemine—which it was not—and there was a Spanish armed vessel then in New Orleans that he hoped could go out to take Gambi's corsair. The port authorities would not let her leave, however, and he thought that suspicious. He believed it was because they did not want anyone interfering with the *Petit Milan,* but more likely it was because Patterson did not want any competition when he went after the privateers.[26]

It had been an eventful ten days on Grand Isle since Lockyer's visit. The *Sophie* had not returned, though the Laffites might still have expected her if the British honored the fortnight Jean had asked for. Meanwhile several other vessels arrived. On September 9 the *Moon of November* under Captain Thomas Frank came in for repairs after taking a Spanish brig loaded with wine and Spanish rum.[27] The *Cometa* was still there, her owner Lorenzo Oliver having paid her ransom, and he and four helpers were hard at work readying her to leave.[28] The *Harlequin,* a Spanish pilot boat formerly named the *Experiment* taken on a voyage out of Vera Cruz, was in port fitting out.[29] Gambi had finished fitting out the *Petit Milan,* which he had bought from the Laffites, and would be leaving soon for another cruise.[30] Dominique was there, too, now without a command other than the little felucca that had brought him, Humbert, and the others from Mexico. Though an independent privateer, Dominique was generally understood to be acknowledging orders from the Laffites.[31] The Cartagenan privateer schooner *Militia* was moored to the shore, half full of water where she had been run ashore to prevent her sinking, her rigging removed and stored in a Laffite warehouse, awaiting repairs. The men had just finished pumping out her hold on September 15.[32]

All told perhaps four hundred men were on the island, in addition to a substantial number of merchants and buyers.[33] Precisely when the Laffites learned of the Patterson raid is unclear. Nothing in the brothers' September 10 letters hints at knowledge of an impending attack, but they must have learned of it very soon thereafter. A careless word from one of the principals after the decisive September 8 meeting of Claiborne's council could have reached Grand Isle within forty-eight hours, and news of Patterson and Ross's movements at any time after that.[34] In any event, there were few secrets in New Orleans.

Once more the brothers had to adapt to rapidly shifting circumstances. They did not wish to fight, and did not likely consider doing so. Most of the men on Grand Isle were ordinary sailors who signed on as privateers hoping to make a swift and risk-free profit by taking defenseless merchantmen. When they encountered an armed vessel willing to fight back, they as a rule weighed their chances and sailed away. Most had never experienced a fight, and certainly not as an organized force. And, in light of the recent near mutiny over Lockyer, Pierre and Jean could not be confident that the men would follow them if they tried to command a defense. There was no fort, contrary to rumor in New Orleans, and only three cannon mounted on logs rather than proper carriages.[35] If *La Diligent* had been posted aground as a battery ship, she was gone now, most likely dismantled for her rigging and equipment. The privateer ships then in port mounted about twenty guns of varying calibers, and the Laffites' men had plenty of small arms, muskets, and cutlasses, but one man among them believed that "they had not men enough to man the privateers & fight their guns if they had had a mind [to do it]" unless some of the shoppers from New Orleans were willing to take a hand at fighting.[36]

Then, too, while one smuggler maintained that in August Jean had referred to the three cannon as being there "to receive the Americans when they arrived,"[37] it was generally assumed among the Baratarians that their leaders did not want to come to blows with the United States. French patriotism aside, defending a base they intended to abandon would simply have been a waste of lives and resources.[38] When word came of the Patterson raid, one Baratarian heard Jean Laffite remind his captains that he "had always said he never would fight against the Americans."[39]

The captains agreed that escape was their best option. But when the officers of the Laffite ships remonstrated with the brothers that they should sail immediately for Cartagena, the Laffites refused. Jean at least professed faith that Patterson would not attack after Jean's offer to defend Barataria against the British. Indeed, he expected at any moment to get instructions from Claiborne to that end. However, he gave no orders for those working for him to stay, but rather told men and officers alike that they were free to take what prize goods were theirs. The contraband belonging to the Laffites he made little attempt to hide, since a sale was already scheduled.[40]

By September 15 a fair concourse of potential buyers was on Grand Isle, and most of the cargo from the *Cometa* and other recent prizes was ashore in the warehouse, stored west of the island on a point of land called Chenier Caminada, or strewn on the beach for sale.[41] Even the houses of the few permanent residents of Grand Terre were host to buyers for the occasion.[42] The Laffites' plan had been to sell as much as they could as quickly as possible, then get their seaworthy ships out of the bay to safety before Patterson and Ross arrived.[43] Any unsold goods were supposed to be concealed inland.[44] In the end the Laffites managed to sequester only a large quantity of pistol flints and perhaps some gunpowder.

The men on Grand Isle were eating breakfast about 8:30 on the morning of September 16 when they saw the fleet's sails on the horizon.[45] The Laffites had left everyone but their crews to their own devices, and panic ensued. Some men wanted to escape into the bayous. Others wanted to make sail if they could, while a few called for them to stand their ground and fight. The buyers from New Orleans immediately fled in their pirogues, though not before leaving some incriminating papers behind.[46] Some of the privateers were flying Cartagenan colors, and at about 9 o'clock they started forming their vessels in what appeared to be line of battle near the entrance of the harbor.

Pierre and Jean left the privateers to make their separate decisions. Calling as many of their crewmen to them as would rally, the brothers abandoned their merchandise and boarded pirogues. They could not risk Pierre's recapture. They had close associates in the sparsely settled areas of St. Charles Parish, known locally as the German Coast. They rowed up the bay into Little Lake, past the Temple, then up a bayou to Lake Salvadore. From there the Bayou Des Allemandes or other waterways, routes they had used for smuggling, led to the marshy wilderness of the German Coast interior, where they would be secure.[47] Behind them they left a disaster.

At 10 o'clock, with a light wind behind him, Patterson moved in to attack. Half an hour later he saw signal smoke columns rising along the coast, probably to alert men inland, perhaps the Laffites, that the attack had come. Soon a white flag went up on one privateer schooner, and then the stars and stripes on its mainmast, and for good measure a Cartagenan flag on the topping lift. Patterson ran a white flag up his mainmast to signify that he would not fire unless fired upon, but then he saw two of the privateer vessels aground set ablaze. This meant the smugglers were destroying valuable prize goods, and at once he raised a signal to attack—at the same time running up a large flag that proclaimed "Pardon to Deserters," since he thought men once serving in the United States Army and Navy might be among the Baratarians.

Two of Patterson's gunboats ran aground on the sandbar outside the pass, as did the *Carolina*, but the rest passed over and crafts from the grounded vessels started rowing into the bay, only to see the privateers abandoning their ships and fleeing in small boats in every direction.[48] Dominique joined a few others and put out in his little felucca hoping to reach New Orleans, but before he could get out of the pass Patterson's gunboats were coming in. One opened fire on him, and he had to run aground and try to flee in a pirogue.[49] Gambi tried to warp the *Petit Milan* to safety by letting out a cable to men in boats and having them row her into deep water, but the cable broke and the boats scattered, leaving the *Petit Milan* adrift.[50]

Quickly the attackers boarded and saved a burning schooner that mounted one twelve-pounder and four smaller cannon.[51] By noon Patterson had possession of six schooners, one felucca, a brig, a prize, and two armed schooners that were captured with their crews still aboard, their guns ready and matches lit as if they had intended to use their cannon.[52] Then commenced the mopping up. The bay was full of fleeing pirogues. The soldiers and sailors began taking prisoners in number, including Dominique and Joseph Martinot, whom they brought directly to Patterson. The commodore personally searched the captives, taking from Martinot $700 in bank notes, his knife, and a telescope. To Martinot's protests that he was only there to get his vessel afloat, and that he had legitimate goods stored in a Laffite warehouse, Patterson turned a deaf ear. He had Martinot's *Cometa* burned since she was not yet seaworthy, and later made an inventory of her rigging in the warehouse, but denied all knowledge of Martinot's other cargo. He had come to serve his country and to make a handsome profit, and he was determined to do both.[53]

Patterson was not the only one plundering. It was systematic, and extended to everything from the merchandise on shore and in the warehouse to the pocket contents of the men and merchants, including four gold doubloons and $50 in bank notes in the trunk of an ailing merchant staying in one of the civilian homes.[54] Once secure ashore and with the smugglers on the run, Ross's soldiers began burning about forty houses, most of them badly built and thatched with palmetto leaves.[55] Ross also torched emptied warehouses, signal towers, two schooners, and a brig.[56] The whole affair lasted no more than a few hours. When it was done, Patterson and Ross began to tally their captures, and they were impressive.

First there were the privateer vessels. Twenty-seven ships had been in the bay that day, several of them recent additions to the Laffite fleet. Most were not worth keeping, nor did Patterson have enough men to crew them all, so he burned several. He kept the Laffites' *Dorada* and *Misere;* the ninety-ton *Harlequin,* which now sailed under the Laffites' friend Laurent Maire; the ninety-ton *Surprise,* a prize taken the previous spring by the *Dorada* and fitted out for privateering; Gambi's fifty-ton *Petit Milan;* a thirty-ton felucca called the *Fly* belonging to the Laffites; the *Comet* of seventy-five tons; the fifteen-ton felucca *Moon of November;* and the Laffites' *Amiable Maria.*[57]

Then there were the dry goods bags of medicinal herbs and flowers, bags of anise seed, boxes and barrels of antimony and bluestone, bags of gum, anchors, bars of iron, barrels of glassware, more than ten thousand gallons of wine, seventy-five demijohns of spirits, ships' sails, a ship's cable, boxes of soap, glass tumblers, a lot of German linen, hundreds of silk stockings, poplin sheeting, sewing thread, coffee, bales of paper, cocoa, rope grass bales, window glass, duck canvas, and more—all the real plunder of pirates rather than the doubloons and jewels of fiction.[58] The flour taken ran to 163 barrels, and that had been Jean Laffite's own goods.[59] The *Santa Rita* had aboard her cloves, coffee, cinnamon, 17,200 cigars, sherry, Málaga wine, 769 gallons of brandy, raisins, candles, 483 pounds of chocolate, cocoa, and more. Just the duty being evaded on such a cargo amounted to $10,776.39. The *President* carried sherry, black pepper, and brandy, and the *Petit Milan* had more sherry, rum, and candles.

There was also a lot of money. Patterson's men found $668 in Spanish cash on the *Petit Milan,* $6,255 on the *President,* and another $1,641 on the *Santa Rita.*[60] They took gold and silver coin and paper banknotes of an indeterminate amount, though one money belt alone had $1,249 in specie.[61] The paper notes of several New Orleans banks were ample evidence that city denizens had come to the island to make purchases. Another cache contained sixteen plates of silver bullion, sixty-two pieces of silver, and $564.43 in Spanish milled dollars. Equally valuable metal came in the form of the artillery seized, for besides what was on the captured ships, there were eight cannon of varying size, all useful to the navy.[62] All the raiders missed were the hidden gun flints.

Patterson gained useful information among the prize goods. In the papers seized were letters of several New Orleans merchants of good standing, documentation of their business with the Laffites that the court could use to institute prosecutions.[63] More useful was the paper, found aboard the *Dorada*, that listed the signals used between Grand Isle and approaching privateer vessels.[64]

Considering that the ships might bring as much as $5,000 each for the larger vessels when sold at public auction, the bounty from the raid would be considerable. Later estimates placed it as high as $500,000—an obvious exaggeration, but it may have run to $200,000.[65] The prize tally went higher on September 20 when a strange sail appeared on the horizon. The *Carolina* gave chase at a distance of five miles, but soon closed the gap, at which point the other vessel opened fire and the *Carolina* returned it. Soon the quarry ran aground outside the pass and broke her rudder. The *Carolina* could not get close, but the gunboats on the bay side of Grand Isle opened fire across the island and in half an hour the chase struck her colors. Patterson's men boarded and found her to be the *General Bolivar,* formerly the *Atalanta,* operating on a letter of marque from Cartagena dated the previous December.[66] After having been chased at the Balize by a British squadron, the *General Bolivar* had mistaken the *Carolina* for an English warship, which was why she opened fire.[67] Aboard her Patterson's sailors took $4,753 worth of goods, not to mention the vessel herself, which would bring another $5,813.[68]

On the afternoon of September 23 Patterson had his booty loaded aboard the eight prize vessels he would keep, and set sail for New Orleans. The schooner *Moon of November* escaped one night along the way, but by October 1 he had the rest safely in the city, and the loss of one small prize did not dampen Patterson's pride.[69] While it stood the Baratarian community had been "alarming from its extent, indiscriminating in its character, and deplorable in its consequences and effects," he declared.[70] The Laffites might have escaped, but he had taken Dominique, who some mistakenly believed to be the second-in-command. Public reaction was muted, thanks to the sympathy the smugglers enjoyed, but some professed pleasure. "The expedition has resulted very fortunately," one New Orleanian declared within hours of learning the news, "and will be the means of giving considerable strength to our naval station."[71]

Between the signal columns of smoke and the hundreds of smugglers, privateersmen, and customers fleeing through the bayous, the Laffites surely learned the extent of the disaster within twenty-four hours. They must have heard or seen some of it in the distance as they fled. Likely they had brought with them little money, since the sales were in process when the attack came. If they truly believed that their offer would forestall Patterson's expedition, then the loss of their ships and goods came as a shock. If *La Diligente* was still afloat somewhere, probably under a different name, then she was safe for the time being, and they knew from experience, they would need only a few prizes brought in to their anticipated Mexican base to recover their fortunes. The damage to their prestige, however, was another matter. The Baratarian enterprise was never more than a loose conglomeration of disparate types, men of a hundred allegiances, some of whom submitted to the Laffites' administration only because it brought them profit. Now Jean and Pierre were fugitives, their empire—and with it their bargaining power with Claiborne and the Americans—gone.

Before long, however, they learned of events in New Orleans that might give them an opportunity to bargain once more. The day before Patterson's attack, a group of citizens had held a meeting at Bernard Tremoulet's Coffee House on Levee Street opposite the public market. It was a popular meeting place, one sometimes frequented by Baratarians. On the first floor was an auction room, and on the second a well-stocked reading room with newspapers, maps and charts for mariners, and a small library of geography, commerce, and travel books. Pierre Maspero was about to take it over and rename it the Exchange Commercial Coffee House.[72]

In addressing the meeting, which he apparently had engineered, Edward Livingston said it was imperative that those assembled maintain control of the Mississippi. If the enemy took Louisiana, they would lose their property, their slaves, even their freedom, and they might be forced at bayonet point to fight their fellow Americans.[73] He proposed that they form a committee to dominate the governor if necessary and work with the army and navy in planning the defense of their city and state. In spite of Claiborne's mobilization of two divisions of the state militia ten days earlier, Livingston did not believe enough was being done, and clearly anticipated going around the governor to deal directly with General Jackson.

Like most community leaders, Livingston knew by this time at least the outline of the correspondence that Blanque had delivered to Claiborne, and had likely heard it virtually verbatim from Blanque himself, who was at the public meeting and had probably helped Livingston with its organization. And though Claiborne studiously kept Pierre's September 10 "stray sheep" letter out of public knowledge for several weeks, Livingston surely knew its contents from Blanque. Thus, Livingston knew what the public did not: The Laffites had offered to defend Barataria against a British advance. That they could not have done so was immaterial, as was the near impossibility of an enemy moving thousands of men and animals, let alone artillery, through sixty miles of lakes and narrow bayous in pirogues. (Indeed, the British do not seem to have considered Barataria as a route of invasion, nor did Jackson seem to fear it.)[74] The point was that the Laffites had offered the services of a force of several hundred, and Claiborne and the local military authorities had answered that offer of assistance with a raid.[75]

Livingston may not have discussed the full purport of the Laffite correspondence, or even mentioned it at the meeting, but he did address the underlying significance of the papers.[76]

Ignoring the fact that Patterson and Ross took their orders from military higher authority and not from the governor, Livingston and other critics could conclude that Claiborne's allowing Patterson to attack Barataria risked driving the smugglers into British arms.[77] Quite possibly someone, most likely Livingston or Blanque, raised the idea of approaching the Baratarians on the basis of Pierre's offer of September 10.

Before the meeting adjourned the assembly elected a Committee of Public Safety, with Livingston as chairman. Among the others picked to serve was Blanque, ensuring that the committee would be well apprised of the Laffite correspondence. Three days later, immediately after learning the result of the Patterson raid, the committee opened communication directly with General Jackson, providing him with its assessment of the approaches the British might use in moving on New Orleans. They closed with the pass into Barataria Bay, noting that until lately it had been in the hands of "a number of Buccanee[r]s under the Carthiginian flag," and recommended that though vessels drawing more than ten feet of water could not enter the bay, a battery of artillery be placed on Grand Isle or Chenier Caminada for protection.[78]

The day after the committee wrote to the general advising defense of Barataria, Claiborne did virtually the same. After informing Jackson of the triumph, Claiborne added that the smugglers could return once Patterson left, and suggested that a military installation protecting Grand Isle and the Temple might be wise.[79] He also expressed fears that some of the smugglers streaming into town, San Domingue blacks "of the most desperate characters and probably no worse than most of their white associates," would provoke a slave rebellion.[80] Patterson, for his part, complained that on his return from Barataria he found the bayous around the city infested with fugitive smugglers and pirates.[81] Morphy was outraged, and complained to Apodaca on September 19 that "a great number of these villains have already found refuge at this city."[82]

The first report of the attack on Barataria had come in a September 19 letter written by Ross at Grand Isle, and appeared in the city press five days later.[83] However, the details of the Laffite correspondence had not been publicized, and no mention of Pierre's September 10 offer printed. In a city in which so many felt sympathy with the smugglers and profited through their business, it would not be politic for Claiborne to let it be known that he had met their offer of assistance with the sword, even if it were not his responsibility. Livingston, however, thought there was still hope of enlisting the Baratarians. As a result, in subsequent sittings of the Committee of Public Safety, he repeatedly raised the prospect of bringing the stray sheep into the fold via a pardon in return for their assistance in defending New Orleans.[84]

While he had not done business with the Laffites, and apparently had no acquaintance with them, Livingston had defended some of the privateer community in court in the past, and the Laffites must have known him by reputation.[85] He was witty, urbane, highly cultured, fluent in French, and married to the sister of Auguste Davezac, refugee from San Domingue and a member of the committee.[86] Moreover, perhaps thanks to Blanque, word of Livingston's agency on their behalf at the supposedly confidential committee meetings filtered back to the German Coast by the end of September. At some point after their flight, the brothers took refuge on the plantation of one of the LaBranche brothers, Alexandre or Jean Baptiste, on the left or east bank of the Mississippi. This put them within twenty land miles of the city, close enough to communicate with friends, yet in an area the authorities were unlikely to search.[87] Word of Livingston's advocacy was the first good news to reach the brothers since Pierre's escape, and Jean wasted no time in sending his thanks. "I have found out directly about your good intentions for me," he wrote to Livingston on October 4. "I find no expressions to explain how touched I was." Passing into the flattery that he almost always used with people in prominent positions, he averred that if his already lofty opinion of Livingston were capable of increase, "then certainly it would have overflowed after the solicitude you have shown for me in the committee sessions over which you preside."

Laffite went on to claim that Livingston was "all my hope in my unhappy position," and prayed that he would continue to speak in the brothers' behalf. "There is only you to pull me out of the trouble where I am." Livingston had done much already, not only arguing in favor of pardoning the Baratarians in exchange for their enlistment, but also directly challenging the basis for the brothers' indictments. More was required, but Laffite expressed confidence that Livingston would stay the course and "that you will be my liberator." Indeed, Jean seemed to believe that Livingston's efforts were the only reason that the brothers had not been further pursued into the German Coast, for his informant on the committee had alerted him that some attempt would have been made but for the committee's intercession. This may or may not have been the case, but what was important was that Laffite believed it. He counted on Livingston to counsel him on his future actions, pending the decisions of the committee and the other authorities. Should some arrangement be proposed that was agreeable to them, he enjoined Livingston to make him immediately aware of his obligations in the bargain. Laffite closed by reiterating his trust in the committee chair, declaring "it is this degree of confidence that has made me more secure in my opinion concerning my present safety."[88]

Interestingly, in his letter Jean Laffite spoke only in the first person and of himself, making no mention of Pierre or the dispersed Baratarians. Of course, in speaking of his own safety, Jean naturally spoke for Pierre, since they faced the same indictments for piracy. His establishment being broken up, Jean could no longer presume to represent the smugglers. However, he and Livingston knew that many if not most would continue to take their lead from the Laffites, and that any deal made by the brothers would likely be embraced by their followers under arrest by Patterson or under indictments of their own. It was the best these men could hope for.

In the weeks following Jean's letter, a flurry of piracy indictments came out of the district court. It began on October 11 with a presentment against Manuel Joachim. A week later came charges against merchant Henri de St. Gême, followed on October 19 by presentments against Jacques Cannon, René Roland, and Alexander St. Helme, all men captured at Barataria.[89] The grand jury called for indictments of the bigger fish on October, starting with Lafon for taking two Spanish vessels. It charged Alexander Bonnival as well, and then addressed the biggest name from those taken at Barataria, Captain Dominique, "alias Frederique Youx."[90] None of these presentments mentioned specific dates or vessels, but were general, counting on testimony to fill in the blanks after indictment. The case against Dominique, however, came with testimony averring $6,000 worth of goods taken by him, and stating that no prizes were taken to Cartagena, and that neither Dominique nor any of the other captains ever displayed commissions from Cartagena, France, or any other nation. Andrew Whiteman was heard from yet again, as well as a deponent who explained how the privateers changed the names of their vessels, sometimes after every cruise, to confound later efforts to recover prize goods and ships in the district court.[91] The grand jury was systematically building a case to penetrate the workings of the Baratarian establishment, and to make its indictments foolproof.

All told, eleven indictments came down by October 29. Patterson turned over to the court the papers captured at Barataria, and based on them the grand jury began issuing presentments against several city merchants, too. The merchants turned primarily to Livingston for their defense, knowing him to be against Claiborne's and Judge Hall's rigid enforcement of the revenue and embargo laws.[92] Then, as if to demonstrate how wide a net it intended to cast, the grand jury struck at the filibusters in the community with a piracy indictment against Toledo for his work against the Spaniards. He was arrested on November 11.[93]

None of this boded well for the Laffites, but apparently they left the issue in Livingston's hands.[94] Meanwhile Claiborne's warnings to both Jackson and Secretary of War James Monroe that a permanent naval force would be necessary to keep Barataria clear proved correct.[95] Soon after Patterson left Grand Isle, and despite the soldiers Ross left there as a guard, many of the smugglers returned, while the privateers merely shifted their operation to Cat Island.[96] Ten days earlier Patterson had sent Lieutenant Thomas Jones with three gunboats and a schooner to drive the smugglers away and take their leaders if possible. Jones reached Grand Isle on October 17, and took charge of the *General Bolivar*, which had been left behind with the military guard. The next day he sighted Cat Island, and thereafter spent some time searching the islands in the vicinity, finding only the litter remaining from the recent landing of the two prizes, including the remains of the vessels themselves. He concluded that the area had not been "much frequented by *Lafitte's* parties for a length of time past," and so returned to Grand Isle and then to Chenier Caminada. On the morrow he came upon Gambi and several others who had escaped Patterson's raid, and they quickly disappeared up the Lafourche with the aid of friends.[97] Patterson resolved to continue sending unannounced sorties after the fugitives attempting to land prizes until they ceased. Toward that end, he proposed that the navy buy three of the vessels he took at Barataria and with them augment his squadron. The Gulf was full of armed privateers under Cartagenan colors who plundered vessels of every nation, and he suspected most of them were connected to the Baratarians. Meanwhile their confederates in and around New Orleans intercepted at least one of his letter bags, and he felt it prudent not to send another until he secured his mail route.[98]

Word from local residents suggested that the Laffites and some of their captains were now in the Lafourche country.[99] Apparently after first withdrawing to the German Coast, Pierre at least used the brothers' old smuggling route from Napoleonville on the Lafourche to pass through the Attakapas canal and Lake Verret down to the hamlet of Brashear City near the mouth of Bayou Teche where it flowed into Berwick Bay. There he stayed in an inn for a time, protected by associates. A traveler to whom the Laffites had once done a good service chanced to meet him there, and was forcefully impressed that "he certainly had many good friends." To remain close to both New Orleans and Pierre, Jean stayed near Napoleonville, and from there kept up correspondence with the city via Donaldsonville.[100] The situation should have brightened a bit for the Laffites as the content of the correspondence sent to Blanque became more widely known. By October 1 news of the Laffite-Lockyer episode, including Pierre's September 10 offer, reached Senator James Brown in Washington, perhaps before it reached Monroe. In fact, Brown misinterpreted Laffite's offer, or Claiborne misstated it, to include volunteering to defend New Orleans.[101]

Yet Patterson apparently still did not know of Pierre's "stray sheep" letter to Claiborne as of October 10, for in sending Washington copies of the Nicholls and Percy materials, along with Jean's September 4 letter to Lockyer, the commodore stated that this was the whole of the documentation in the matter. Claiborne had already sent copies to the State Department, but again without the September 10 offer from Pierre. Singing his own praises a bit, Patterson declared that "this correspondence shews the importance of the expedition, and the important [elements] of force we have prevented the enemy's receiving by their proposed alliance with the Pirates."[102] The day after Patterson wrote his report, news of the episode appeared in the city press, and again no mention was made of the Laffite offer of service in return for pardon. Rather, the report stopped at Jean's request for "fifteen days to decide the subject of *adhesion*" to the British.[103]

Someone was withholding the important September 10 letter, though if Blanque and Livingston knew of the missive, it is strange they did not make it public. The likely reason is that the Laffites' offer was caught up in the contest for control going on between the governor and Livingston. Both also vied for the favor of General Jackson. Livingston clearly identified himself and his Committee of Public Safety with the Laffite offer, and Claiborne was not about to abet anything coming from that quarter. Livingston was trying, so far unsuccessfully, to gain a position as a volunteer aide on Jackson's staff. Claiborne concentrated on posing the perilous state of the city's defenses. The general's initial reaction to news of the Lockyer visit was to send a proclamation on September 21, exhorting Louisianans to their defense, and condemning the British for seeking an alliance with "pirates and robbers." It did not reach New Orleans until October 15.

Just when Claiborne informed Jackson of Pierre's September 10 offer, if he ever did, is unclear, but the general's opinion of those he called "hellish Banditti" remained unchanged for weeks.[104] In fact, he wrote to the governor on the last day of the month, long after he should have been made aware of the letter, scolding Claiborne for not taking action against "those wretches, the refugees from Barataria and its dependencies." He said he was shocked that the refugees from Patterson's raid "should even be permitted to remain in [New Orleans], without being strictly scrutinized under your existing vagrancy laws." He warned Claiborne to arrest them immediately, for the city was at risk of being "reduced to ashes by these incendiaries."[105]

A chastened Claiborne did not write to Jackson again for more than two weeks, until he informed the general on October 17 that the Baratarians had resumed smuggling at Cat Island, which worked against the Laffites and Livingston. The governor told Jackson at the end of the month that he was sending one hundred state militia to the pass at Grand Isle, both to watch for the British and to keep an eye on the smugglers and prevent them from assembling.[106] Meanwhile the court continued to publish in the city press the announcement of the reward for Pierre's recapture, and would do so until the end of November.

By mid-October Livingston changed his approach. Early that month he sent the general several bottles of what he called "Claret of Barataria," probably spoils of Patterson's raid, but possibly a more direct gift from the Laffites now that he and Jean were in communication.[107] Thereafter he probably continued to try to soften Jackson's attitude toward the Laffites and their onetime followers. He was in frequent conference with Dominique and others in the city jail who appealed to him to get them out on terms of military service. Then came the flurry of piracy presentments and indictments.

Perhaps it was more than coincidence that on the day of Dominique's indictment, October 24, Livingston bypassed Jackson and wrote directly to President James Madison. "A number of privateers, first sailing under the French, afterwards under the Carthaginian flag, have for four years past brought their prizes to the Bay of Barataria in this State," he told the chief executive, as if Madison did not already know. Without naming Claiborne, he went on to say that the local government had neglected its obligation to deal with the smugglers, with the result that "they became bold from impunity." Patterson and Ross had destroyed the establishment now, with many of the prisoners in the city jail and their business associates in the city exposed by the captured documents, but "the number of them as well as their influence is great." New Orleans was a city badly divided ethnically and socially, and even Claiborne feared that the citizens might not unite in its defense. Livingston suggested to Madison that a general pardon extended to all the Baratarians would "quiet the public mind." Moreover, making service in arms a condition of pardon would add as many as five hundred sailors to the city's defense. He went so far as to suggest that most of the miscreants were not knowingly pirates, but had "embraced that kind of life more from an idea that their commissions were good than from any piratical design." Knowing of the privateers' experience against Spanish shipping, he also dropped the hint that if the United States and Spain went to war, the Baratarians "will be of the greatest service."[108]

Less than a week later, Claiborne followed Livingston's approach to Madison with his own to Attorney General Richard Rush. Claiborne granted that Barataria should have been taken sooner, as familiarity "led the people here to view their course as less vicious." He had struggled to convince the people that smuggling was an evil, but with scant success. Now Claiborne expected Judge Hall to bring many of the Baratarians to trial. "Justice demands that the most culpable be punished with severity," he averred, but acknowledging the same social dynamics that Livingston cited to Madison, Claiborne proposed that Grymes be instructed to select a few of the most flagrant offenders for prosecution and free the rest. "It will have a salutary effect on the community," he promised.[109]

Though each acted for his own ends against the other, Claiborne and Livingston had unwittingly cooperated in suggesting amnesty for some or all of the Baratarians. Meanwhile, in mid-

October Claiborne gave the local press a "true copy from the original in my possession," of Nicholls's August 31 letter to Laffite, along with Percy's proclamation and his letter to Laffite. Still, he withheld Laffite's September 10 letter, likely knowing the reaction it might spark in the community.[110] By early November the documents appeared in newspapers as far east as Baltimore.[111] In the circumstances, clemency seemed a wise course to the president, and in late November or early December he told Rush to pass this preference along to Claiborne.

Jackson finally arrived in New Orleans on December 1, after a long time of uncertainty for the American cause. The war had not gone well for the United States from its outbreak, punctuated on August 24 when the British took Washington and burned the capitol. Now the enemy planned to take the Mississippi Valley and its cornerstone, New Orleans. On September 18, while the fires on Grand Isle still smoldered, threescore warships left England bound for the Caribbean, and on November 26 they departed Jamaica for the Gulf. The armada mounted more than one thousand cannon and carried some eight thousand experienced soldiers, many of them veterans of victories over Napoleon. Its goal was first the taking of Mobile, and then Baton Rouge and New Orleans.

At Mobile, Jackson assembled a force sufficient to turn back Admiral Percy on September 12 when he made an attempt to take the city in advance of the armada's arrival. Jackson followed his victory by marching on Spanish Pensacola, which the British fleet had used as a base, and occupied the town on November 8. Jackson then returned to Mobile, not knowing that his small twin victories had shifted British plans. Now the armada would go after New Orleans first. Jackson remained in Mobile only three days after his November 19 arrival, however, before receiving intelligence of the new strategy from Secretary of War Monroe. It took the general some time to disabuse himself of his conviction that Mobile was the danger point, but on November 22 he left for the Mississippi, rallying forces and making his plans as he rode.

The Laffites and their "hellish banditti" were hardly on Jackson's mind in these early days in New Orleans. After he made his headquarters on Royal Street, the general conferred with Claiborne and the Committee of Public Safety and then addressed the public from a balcony, Livingston ingratiating himself by acting as translator for the largely French-speaking audience. Jackson and Livingston were old friends, and that plus the lawyer's obvious influence in the city's American and French communities was enough to persuade the general to appoint Livingston to his staff at last. This done, Jackson began acquainting himself with the city's defenses and the land and water approaches the British might use. The day after his arrival he reviewed some local volunteers and then went on an inspection tour to Fort St. Philip, accompanied by another new appointment to his staff, Arsené Latour. For the next week Jackson feverishly directed construction of earthworks and batteries.

Jackson made it clear that he was his own man, neither welcoming persuasion nor giving in to it. After two weeks in New Orleans, he apparently gave no notice to the Laffite question, though now he had two Laffite proponents on his staff. Civic officials and private citizens added their voices to the committee's urgings to take advantage of Pierre's "stray sheep" offer, but Jackson did not budge. On December 13 Major General Villeré of the militia visited Jackson and pled with him to accept the Baratarians into service to man Patterson's understrength warships and help crew the army's land batteries. Villeré left disappointed, but he may have perceived some weakening in the general's resolve and communicated it to the committee. The next day Bernard de Marigny de Mandeville and the committee called on a harried Jackson at his headquarters. Davezac was there, too, and probably Livingston. Still Jackson remained immovable, pointing out that Dominique and many others were in prison under civil prosecution, while many more faced prosecutions in the parish courts. He had neither the inclination nor the authority to interfere with civil officers, and he did not have to add that it hardly served his purpose to enlist men who might be yanked from the ranks at a moment's notice by a summons or a jury verdict.

The discouraged delegation left, but Marigny and committee member Joseph Ruffignac decided to call on Judge Dominic Hall. Informed of the logjam caused by the proceedings of his federal district court, Hall saw a way out of the problem. "I am general in these circumstances," he told his visitors, and then he outlined his campaign. The legislature was in session in the city. He told Marigny and Ruffignac to get before it immediately a resolution asking the federal court to suspend its action against the Baratarians. Once that passed, the judge could attend to the criminal proceedings under way for federal crimes. "I will immediately give my orders to the District Attorney of the United States."[112]

Marigny and Ruffignac acted with dispatch, as did the legislature. The same day it passed a resolution that acknowledged the critical need for experienced seamen at the moment as well as the fact that many of the Baratarians were willing to enlist but feared prosecution. The resolution asked Jackson to "proclaim amnesty" for any who were now in service or enlisted within thirty days, with the promise that the legislature would petition the president for a full pardon of all who served their terms faithfully. The resolution also asked Claiborne to petition Grymes to enter *nolle prosses* in the pending cases of those like Dominique who were already in confinement and under indictment.[113] This would allow for the release of those willing to enlist.

In fact, Grymes did not get the chance to enter the *nolle prosses* because the next day, December 15, Hall simply recessed the federal court until February 20, 1815, citing the current emergency.[114] Grymes could enter the decisions not to prosecute later. By now everyone knew of the talk about a pardon in return for volunteering. Grymes may even have heard from the attorney general that the president favored such a scheme, and so he would not object to Hall's recess. The legislature, meanwhile, had always been sympathetic to the smugglers. In proposing his "campaign," therefore, Hall no doubt assumed that the prosecutions postponed would never be resumed.

Coincidentally, just hours before Hall recessed the court, word arrived of disaster. On December 12 outposts had sighted the enemy fleet approaching Lake Borgne. The only thing to deter the armada was a small squadron consisting of five of Patterson's gunboats under Jones. Two days later the British overwhelmed and captured Jones and his vessels, leaving a clear road to New Orleans. Jackson got the news late that night or early on December 15. Patterson met with Jackson and expressed the severity of his manpower shortage. He had not enough men to crew properly his two warships, the *Carolina* and the *Louisiana*. Meanwhile British regulars were only sixty miles away. Jackson declared martial law on December 16.

Naturally he met with Governor Claiborne before doing so, and Claiborne cooperated by mustering all the local militia not yet under arms. In their meeting Claiborne or Jackson raised once more the subject of the Baratarians. Now even Jackson knew he needed them. Hall had removed the federal impediment to his accepting their services, and the legislature could be expected to follow in kind. Something else also influenced the general. Only a few days earlier, on December 10, he had written to the secretary of war to complain that he had insufficient arms for the men then volunteering, and virtually no gunflints.[115] Gunflints were quirky. A flint might last for weeks, or it could shatter on the first fire. If Jackson did not have sufficient replacements immediately at hand when a fight came, he might as well not have the soldier who held the weapon. Now, probably through Livingston, he learned that the Laffites had thousands of gun-flints as well as other useful supplies, and were willing to hand it all over in exchange for pardon for good conduct in his army.[116]

That was enough. The general consented that those men in confinement who agreed to take arms to defend New Orleans could be released, and the governor said he would issue a procla-mation to the smugglers in hiding. The next day, December 17, Claiborne published a call for them to come forward, announcing that Jackson would join with him afterward in petitioning the president for a full pardon for every man who did his duty.[117] On December 18 the legislature passed an act suspending for 120 days all bankruptcy proceedings, civil suits, and collection of debts, and placing a moratorium on new civil suits.[118] This provided another layer of immunity for the smugglers.

That was all it took. Dominique and virtually all the other men in jail at the Cabildo walked free. Jackson gave Livingston orders to issue a pledge of allegiance to them and then accept all into the militia, where they were amalgamated into several of the volunteer companies of Louisianans already under arms.[119] The men hiding outside the city began to come in as well, and Marigny averred that "the Baratarians hastened to us from all quarters."[120] In the end, as many as four hundred of them took the oath, and 7,500 flints were turned over to Jackson's quarter-master.[121] What Jackson and Claiborne and the rest could not yet know was that Washington had already concluded it would take much the same approach with the Baratarians. Livingston's Oc-tober 24 letter to the president probably won him over, though it would take more than a month, and surely more information from others, before Madison came to a decision.[122] At President Madison's direction, Attorney General Rush's letter of December 10 informed Claiborne that if the governor approved, the United

States attorney would be instructed to divide the pending piracy indictments into "proper" and "improper" cases for application of clemency. The attorney would enter *nolle prosse* decisions before the court, and then promise pardon or aid in applying for presidential pardon in return for service during the invasion and good conduct thereafter.[123] Secretary of War Monroe asked Rush to inform Claiborne that he, too, felt disposed toward lenience.[124] Rush's letter would not reach New Orleans until a week or more after the jail doors opened, but when it came it more than validated the authorities' course of action.

The Laffite brothers appeared in New Orleans no later than the morning of December 22. As of December 15 reports put them in hiding some eighty miles south of Baton Rouge, probably either on the lower Lafourche or else in the vicinity of the inn they used at Brashear City. General John Coffee, then at Baton Rouge, had asked Jackson if he should send men out to try to take the brothers, not to mention the $200,000 they supposedly had secreted nearby. Coffee actually did send a detail to look for a warehouse near Baton Rouge in which the Laffites were believed to have clothing and other desperately needed articles, but then Jackson ordered all outposts into the city after the Lake Borgne defeat.[125] The report that Coffee got of the brothers' whereabouts was probably mistaken, however, for they were close enough to New Orleans to learn of Claiborne's proclamation almost immediately. Two or three days after it was made, about December 20, they summoned their followers and friends to the LaBranche plantation, where Jean spoke to them about the clemency offer and encouraged them to rally to the defense of the city.[126]

The Laffites met with Jackson within hours of their arrival in New Orleans.[127] On December 22 Jackson gave Jean a safe conduct pass signed by Judge Hall and Marshal Duplessis, and sent him to help defend Louisiana.[128]

That for itself can woo the approaching fight,
And turn what some deem danger to delight;
That seeks what cravens shun with more than zeal,
And where the feebler faint can only feel—

ELEVEN

The Fight for New Orleans
1814-1815

ANDREW JACKSON's sound instincts made up for his lack of formal training or extensive practical experience. The bulk of the Baratarians were men accustomed to being commanded, and he wisely concluded to keep most of them in separate companies under their own officers. Thus Dominique became captain of a militia company on December 23, and even men such as Gambi became enlisted in his ranks, all of them promised eight dollars a month for their service.[1] For the Laffite brothers, however, Jackson had other plans.

In the fashion of ancient conquerors who married a local woman in every vanquished province in order to bind its people to his regime, Jackson gave volunteer appointments on his staff to representatives of virtually every faction in New Orleans—Livingston and Claiborne representing their cliques, Sauvinet from the merchants, Humbert standing for the French Napoleonic segment of the community, and Anaya, Toledo, and Ellis P. Bean from among the filibusters and revolutionists. None save Humbert had any military skill or experience. What the Laffites had to offer was their knowledge of Barataria and the lesser traveled water approaches to New Orleans, and their role as a visible representation of the commitment of the Baratarians and a symbol to the substantial part of the Creole community that sympathized with the smugglers.

In short, the Laffites were one of the minor political realities of Louisiana, and now Jackson addressed that reality and bent it to his purpose. He did observe one distinction, however. Whereas Livingston and some others received genuine appointments as aides, others held more honorary or supernumerary positions, acting in the main as couriers. This was how he would use the Laffites. There would be no ranks, no need for uniforms or the trappings of officers, though Jean, in particular, had commanded in a fashion more men that most of the officers in the growing army. It may have been oversight. It may have had no meaning whatsoever. It may just have reflected Jackson's lingering suspicion of the corsair leaders, and an unwillingness to accord to these two "hellish banditti" the honorable station of soldiers, officers and gentlemen.

On the matter of how to use the Laffites, Latour and Livingston could have made useful suggestions. Latour had worked with General Wilkinson a few years before in preparing maps of the water approaches to New Orleans.[2] As Jackson's chief engineer, Latour explained to the general that seven possible water avenues offered an approach on New Orleans, one of them being the smugglers' route from Barataria.[3] It might not have been a practical pathway for a major army with its artillery and impedimenta, but over the years the smuggler pirogues had moved several tons of goods up the bayous. If the British used the same route, they could at the very least move enough men and perhaps light artillery to open a second front on Jackson's flank while the main army occupied him before the city.

Here was where the Laffites should be used. Major Michael Reynolds commanded eighty men posted on Bayou St. Denis south of the city. On December 22 Jackson sent Jean Laffite to Reynolds carrying orders to lead fifty men to the Temple, with their artillery, while the remainder stayed at Bayou St. Denis long enough to fell trees into it to obstruct boat passage before joining their comrades. Learning either from Latour or the Laffites of the strategic importance of the position on Little Lake Barataria that commanded access to the bayous leading to New Orleans' back door, Jackson wanted Reynolds to fortify himself on the slight elevation. The general promised to send three fieldpieces to strengthen the spot, and even advised Reynolds to try to stretch a chain across the bayou just below him to retard any boat approach. Jean volunteered to show Reynolds the way and inform him of geographical features affecting the placement of his men and arms. Jackson showed some sensitivity to the fact that the soldiers might not appreciate having a smuggler in their midst, ordering Reynolds to protect Laffite from "Injury and insult." More to the point, Jackson did not want Laffite to remain at the Temple longer than necessary. As soon as Reynolds learned what he needed to know, he was to give Laffite a safe conduct pass and send him back to Jackson.[4]

While Jean was off on this errand, Pierre remained in or near New Orleans, and was consulted by Jackson and Livingston on matters such as the bayous and plantation irrigation canals in the vicinity. The British finally launched their campaign on December 16, the same day Jackson declared martial law, but it was not until well after dark six days later that the boats transporting the Redcoats reached the mouth of Bayou Bienvenue at the western extremity of Lake Borgne. They were within a dozen miles of the city, and they had gotten there entirely undetected. The next day they turned southwest through a cypress swamp and picked a path along a canal leading to General Villeré's plantation. Finally they came out of the swamp and saw ahead of them the way to the Mississippi and New Orleans. From this point northwestward toward the city the Mississippi posed a barrier on the left, the swamps a barrier on the right, and one thousand yards of good level ground filled in between. On that they would advance, and on that Jackson would have to try to stop them.

Later that day Jackson learned of the enemy's stolen march on him, and a flurry of activity ensued. Thousands of citizens fled the town for fear it might fall in a few hours. At the moment Pierre was apparently four miles north of the city at Fort St. John, where Bayou St. John, one of his old smuggling routes, flowed into Lake Pontchartrain. In aid to his old nemesis Commodore Patterson, he was helping Dominique and Beluche emplace batteries with which they were to hold that approach. Jean, of course, was still on his way to the Temple with Major Reynolds. Now Jackson got a message to Patterson that he planned to make a surprise assault that evening and needed him immediately, leaving the Baratarian artillery companies to finish their work. Jackson may also have asked specifically for Pierre, anticipating that he would need Laffite's knowledge of the ground. When Patterson and Laffite reached Jackson, the general initially kept Pierre with him, along with Livingston and several other volunteer aides. Livingston told Pierre that he had decided not to send his family off in the sudden exodus, but had a carriage waiting at his house. Apparently expecting that he would be with Jackson on the fighting line, and that Pierre would not, he asked the smuggler to get his wife and child to safety should the enemy break through the lines and endanger the city.[5]

But Pierre Laffite would be with the army and in harm's way. Either on his initiative or by Jackson's direction, Pierre went that afternoon to the extreme left of the American line where it met the swamps. He and Denis de Laronde would act as guides for General John Coffee as he advanced that night. Jackson had others who knew the ground along the swamp as well as, and probably better than, Pierre—among them de Laronde, who lived in the area. In fact, the Laffites scarcely used the waterways this side of New Orleans. Still, the Laffites had a reputation as masters of the hidden backways of Louisiana. Locals said that the bayou country known to the brothers was otherwise habitable only "by alligators and wild ducks."[6] Very likely Jackson attributed to the Laffites much greater wilderness wisdom than they possessed, and both brothers were accomplished at overselling themselves.

That evening Pierre and de Laronde led Coffee's eight hundred men to their launch position on the swamp side of Pierre Lacoste's plantation. They were Jackson's left flank, and their mission was to drive the British right flank back on the Mississippi while Jackson and the main line occupied the British front. At 7:30 they heard Patterson's *Carolina* begin a bombardment of the enemy line, and then Jackson launched his attack. Coffee went forward shortly before 8 P.M., and pushed the enemy back all the way to the Villeré plantation. Then he shifted his line to the right and started forcing the Redcoats toward the river as ordered. Through it all, Pierre Laffite was near Coffee, who noted the smuggler's courage in action, and more than once asked him for advice on the ground.[7]

Coffee penetrated into the enemy camps before darkness, fog and mounting confusion left him unsure of his position, and unable to tell what had happened to Jackson's part of the line. Meanwhile Jackson had halted the attack after pushing as far as he could with the main line. It had been a qualified success. Jackson had stalled the British advance and severely upset the enemy, buying himself several days' time, but he decided that his lines were too weak and exposed. He concluded that on the morrow, Christmas Eve, he would withdraw his army two miles to the Rodriguez canal, positioning his lines behind the ditch with the river guarding his right flank and the swamp his left. There he would make his stand.

After the army moved into position, Livingston called on Pierre Laffite once again. Livingston felt uneasy about Bayou

Bienvenue. It was still navigable—with difficulty, to be sure—
to a point well in the rear of Jackson's new line where only a few
hundred yards of admittedly dense cypress swamp would separate an approaching enemy from the Americans' unprotected
left rear. The British had already used the bayou in one embarrassing surprise. Another could be fatal. Livingston consulted
with Sauvinet and Pierre Laffite. Sauvinet agreed that the bayou
presented a weak spot, adding that he thought the ground on its
west bank fronting the swamp was firm enough that soldiers
could maneuver on it as much as half a mile in the direction of
Jackson's flanks.

Laffite disagreed, however, and he knew the waterways better. He suggested that Jackson extend his line on the Rodriguez
canal as far to the east as possible, and where the canal ended at
the edge of the swamp, put his men to work digging an extension
well into the bog. The British might be able to march along the
bank of the Bienvenue, but Pierre was convinced that the swamp
was impassable and would thus protect Jackson's left flank completely.[8] Livingston passed this advice on to the general, and the
army did, indeed, extend its line a few hundred yards into the
swamp.

Now Jackson consolidated his forces, calling in Dominique
and Beluche to take command of two twenty-four-pounder fieldpieces on the right of his line at the levee, protecting the river
road to the city. They arrived December 28, and soon Jackson
added a thirty-two-pounder to their care. Eventually Dominique
and Beluche commanded Battery Number 3, situated about 150
yards from the river, supporting the part of the line held by the
battalion of Major Jean Baptiste Plauché, in which some of the
Baratarians enlisted.[9] The men used cotton bales seized from a
vessel then in the river to build a barricade. As it happened the
bales belonged to the cranky merchant Nolte. His complaints
proved unavailing.[10] A French aristocrat then in New Orleans re-

marked on the general's wisdom in affirming pardon in return for the Baratarians' services. "That is a very politic stroke," said the Chevalier Anne Louis de Tousard, anticipating that the Baratarians would prove to be of "great assistance."[11] Still, perhaps out of mistrust, or more likely out of awareness that artillery could be critical in the coming battle, Jackson thereafter took special interest in the Baratarian gunners, often visiting them in their positions.[12]

From now on there would be desultory fighting almost daily. The night of December 27 a lucky British shell blew up Patterson's *Carolina*, leaving only the *Louisiana* to support Jackson from the river. The next day the British made a general advance, but the fire from the batteries and the *Louisiana* stopped them, convincing the foe to spend several days bringing up heavier artillery of its own. On New Year's Day the British opened a bombardment, sighting directly on Battery Number 3. Dominique was looking at the enemy positions through a small telescope when a shot fragment struck his arm. Bandaging the wound on the spot, he told his gunners, "I will pay them for that!" He personally directed the fire of one of his twenty-four-pounders until it hit and disabled a British fieldpiece.[13]

The British spent the next week preparing to launch their principal assault, and Jackson perfected his arrangements and plugged every available man into his line. Pierre Laffite was probably still with Coffee on the left flank, keeping an eye on the cypress swamp and perhaps Bayou Bienvenue. Jean was simply out of sight, most likely still with Reynolds at the Temple, or perhaps reconnoitering as far south as Grand Isle.[14] Meanwhile Baratarians made up only about fifty of the five thousand men on Jackson's main line.[15] In short, they formed a minuscule portion of the army about to fight a battle for New Orleans. And yet, given the nature of the ground and the fact that the Mississippi and the swamp virtually closed the door to maneuver, the British would have no option but to advance in the open, without cover.

In such a circumstance, artillery could be decisive, and the Baratarians manning Battery Number 3 with their three cannon could speak with a voice far greater than their numbers.

Indeed they did. On January 8 the British launched their attack, and almost from the first it became apparent that everything was against them. Dense fog obscured their view of the Americans in their works behind the canal, while Jackson's artillery poured salvos into the mist and the British ranks. Mismanagement at high levels exacerbated the Redcoats' problems, as did the fall of several high-ranking officers, including the British commanding general. The enemy never even reached the American line, only a few men gaining the canal before being cut down or pushed back. Within half an hour, two-thirds of the three thousand soldiers who began the attack had been killed or injured. Though skirmishing continued for some hours afterward, the battle was over, and the Baratarian gunners had played an important role in breaking up the assault, with Dominique taking a second wound and Gambi shedding his blood as well.[16]

Even as his men began celebrating their victory, Jackson knew half of the battlefield remained in doubt. The British planned to land fourteen hundred men on the west bank of the river during the night, in the hopes of capturing American guns there and turning them on Jackson's line across the river, placing him between two fires when the attack came. However, the crossing had not been completed until the battle on the east bank was under way. Only after Jackson's line had repulsed the main assault did the British on the river's other side approach American defenses commanded by General David Morgan. Jackson's men lined their side of the river expecting to watch an entertaining victory on the other side.

Instead, disaster struck. Morgan was not prepared for a surprise. Once ashore, the British first met exhausted and ill-armed

Kentucky volunteers who had been hurried forward to slow the enemy. In the face of disciplined British fire, the Kentuckians dissolved in near panic and rushed back to Morgan's main line, directly across the river from Jackson. The Redcoats struck as Jackson's men watched helplessly from the other side. The Kentuckians broke again, and the British overran the American line, forcing Morgan to abandon his artillery. Patterson barely saved the *Louisiana* by getting it into the main channel and away from shore before the enemy swarmed past. Jackson hurriedly summoned Pierre Laffite and Humbert and sent them to the other side with a reinforcement of four hundred men. His confidence in Morgan apparently shaken, Jackson wanted the Napoleonic veteran of a dozen fields to lead the reinforcements and any who could be rallied in a bayonet charge against the British. If the enemy held Morgan's position, they could potentially cross upriver and cut the American army off from New Orleans. Laffite's part of the assignment was to advise Morgan of the canals and bayous that might be used to get around the British flank and secure an advantage.[17]

Pierre and Humbert found Morgan trying to reestablish his command a mile and a half behind his original position. Morgan informed Laffite of the situation on the ground and sent him back to Jackson with a plea for more reinforcements, asking at the same time that Pierre return as quickly as possible to advise him on the terrain.[18] Upon hearing Pierre's report, Jackson told his aide Grymes to send Pierre over the river with a promise of reinforcements to come that evening and an address, hastily penned by Jackson, to be read to the troops to boost their morale.[19] By then, however, the crisis had passed, for in the face of the disaster to the main British line, an order soon arrived directing the Redcoats in front of Morgan to return to the east bank. The Americans, perhaps spurred by Humbert, began to pursue, but one show of resolve on the part of the withdrawing

British stopped them and the foe retired without further harassment. The Battle of New Orleans was over.

Jackson remained concerned about the west bank of the river for a day or two, and Pierre Laffite probably remained there with Morgan, with whom he struck up something of a friendship.[20] But in the aftermath of the victory, Jackson had another task for Pierre Laffite. Jackson had sent an order to Major Reynolds to remove the inhabitants from Grand Terre, Barataria, and the whole coastline. Many fled of their own accord and eventually almost all were gone. On December 16, however, Captain David Libby took his Cartagenan corsair the *Estaba* into Grand Isle to escape British pursuit, and then left her while he went to New Orleans for supplies.[21] When Libby's arrival in New Orleans alerted Jackson that privateers might be trying to use Grand Isle, he called on Pierre Laffite no later than January 10 to go down to the coast and bring out all remaining inhabitants who could be collected. The general hoped to remove anyone who might cooperate not only with smugglers but also with the British should they try a thrust at the city by that route. He seems not to have seen the irony in sending one of the leaders of the Baratarian establishment to his old haunts to clear it of new privateers. Pierre reached the coast on January 11 or 12, probably joined by Jean, whom he could have met at the Temple on the way. There in the anchorage he saw the ruins of Libby's *Estaba*, which a British naval raid had burned with its cargo the day before.[22]

Laffite probably already knew that Libby's partner in the *Estaba* was an old friend, Pierre Laméson.[23] What he could not know until he heard it from the corsair's crew was that off Cuba Libby and Laméson had taken a Spanish schooner. Laméson had equipped the prize with seven men and one cannon and some muskets, but then he was separated from the *Estaba* in a storm.[24] Laméson sailed the prize to Cat Island, and then went in a ship's boat to Grand Isle looking for Libby. He arrived about January

12, possibly at the same time as Pierre Laffite, to find the *Estaba* burned and Libby gone, and swore at the moment to kill his partner for abandoning their joint property to its fate.[25] Meanwhile he gathered some of the *Estaba*'s remaining crew from their hiding places on shore, and returned to Cat Island, where he raised two more cannon from the hulk of a prize that Gambi had scuttled there some months before.[26] Laméson had a two-year-old Cartagenan commission from his previous privateer the *President*, questionable though it may have been.[27] Now he reasoned that the commission could be used for the prize if he changed her name, so he dubbed her the *Presidente*. He got sailcloth from some people still at Chenier Caminada and a little gunpowder from other straggling inhabitants, and enlisted crew members from a passing vessel. Then he took to the sea once more, bound for Campeche, where he would take on more crew. Laméson told his crew that he intended to keep taking prizes, though he admitted that Cartagena was virtually out of business, having fallen to the British. Some doubted that he could be serious, but he was.[28]

With what few inhabitants he found, Pierre returned to New Orleans in a few days, probably bringing Jean. While they were absent, the British fleet had come up the river and bombarded Fort St. Philip for several days, but by January 18 the British gave up and returned to the Gulf. Meanwhile Jackson kept the beaten British army off guard with his own bombardment on their camps, and on that same January 18 the Redcoat army began its withdrawal to the safety of its fleet. On the morning of January 27 the British sails disappeared beyond the horizon. Not entirely beaten, the British sailed to Mobile and began efforts to seize it when the fleet got word that a peace treaty signed in Belgium had ended the war on December 24, 1814.

Amid the American euphoria, the Baratarians came in for their full share of accolades. Five days after the battle, while Pierre and Jean were at Grand Isle, one New Orleanian wrote to a friend that "the privateering class, formerly yclept *Baratarians*, have produced a corps of skillful artillerists."[29] Calling them "the amnestied rebels of Barataria," the French consul at New Orleans de Tousard declared on January 20 that they "in truth, performed miracles."[30] Speaking of the "former French filibusters driven from our islands by British conquest or by insurrections excited by the British," he called them "intrepid men, hardened to fatigue and experienced in the work and dangers of war," and echoed the compliments to their skill as artillerists.[31] A man from St. Louis who happened to be in New Orleans when the smugglers stood by Jackson said, "They are very brave men," and referred to "Lafete" as their leader who had gained pardon for them all.[32] Others also personified the Baratarians as Laffite, without saying which man they meant, the public seemingly amalgamating the brothers into one generic Laffite. "I informed you of Lafitte, the famous smuggler and pirate, having joined our forces," a Louisianan told a friend on January 20. Laffite's men had been "of great value, and distinguished themselves," the man went on. "Indeed, it has proven a fortunate circumstance that they were enrolled in our army."[33]

On January 21 Jackson issued a congratulatory address to his army in which he praised Dominique and Beluche, "lately commanding privateers at Barataria." That Livingston wrote the address for Jackson may explain why the Baratarians received special mention.[34] The speech complimented the gallantry with which they had redeemed the pledge they had given at the opening of the campaign, and went on to say that "the brothers Lafitte have exhibited the same courage and fidelity." Jackson thereby renewed his promise to inform the government of their conduct and lend his support to their appeal for pardon.[35]

Men then and later debated the extent of the Laffites' contribution. The Baratarians, making up a scant 2 percent of Jackson's forces, were hardly a decisive factor. Most were stationed elsewhere at Fort St. John or Fort St. Philip, or on Patterson's *Louisiana*, and thus did not take part in the January 8 battle.[36] The roles of Jean and Pierre themselves are so shadowy that it is scarcely possible to evaluate their impact, if any. Pierre's activities were peripheral, though certainly Jackson acknowledged his courage and usefulness. By contrast, no participant recalled with certainty that Jean was present during the battle, and a few testified later that they did not see him anywhere on the battlefield.[37] Almost beyond question, Jean Laffite was not in the action on the east side of the river, and if he had been with Morgan on the other side, there would have been no need for Jackson to send Pierre. Most likely he was still with Reynolds, or more likely still in the vicinity of Grand Isle where there were new affairs about to unfold of interest alike to General Jackson and the Laffites.[38] As for the combined contribution of the brothers to the victory, their greatest influence must have been the moral force of their siding with the Americans, thus bringing French Louisianans over to that side. The seventy-five hundred flints they provided also cannot be discounted,[39] though Jackson would exaggerate their importance. "If it had not been for this providential aid the country must have fallen," the general would say a dozen years later.[40] In fact, in all likelihood, the battle would have been won without them, for it was British mistakes and bad fortune, combined with American artillery, that turned the tide. The Baratarians made an impact on the tide of battle, but no more than a host of other influences.

By March, Jackson's continued martial law began to alienate elements in the city's population. Protests appeared in the press, whereupon Jackson arrested their author. Judge Hall defied Jackson by issuing a *habeas corpus* writ to free the offender, and that provoked Jackson to arrest Hall. Sensing the rebellious current running in the city and through some of his volunteer units, who thought they should be free to go home, Jackson issued a proclamation on March 5 regarding mutiny and its penalties. But then came the news of the Treaty of Ghent, and Jackson freed all those under arrest. A group of citizens gave Hall a triumphant escort to the courthouse, and the judge immediately cited Jackson for interfering with civil authority and commanded him to appear before the court on charges of contempt. Jackson appeared on March 31, heard Hall levy a fine against him of $1,000, paid it, and left.[41] Waiting for him at the door was a crowd of about fifty, including Dominique and Beluche. They lifted Jackson on their shoulders and carried him to the Maspero's Exchange Commercial Coffee House.[42] Before Jackson left the city on April 6 to return home, he took a moment to send Pierre Laffite a personal note of thanks for his "activity and zeal." Pierre was, he said, "one of those to whom the country is most indebted," and closed with an expression of his private friendship and esteem.[43] Of course, in the fullness of victory, Jackson was a bit hyperbolic in praising everyone, but still it was an encomium to be treasured, and perhaps to be made use of before long.

The Laffites were as anxious as everyone else in the city to celebrate the final victory after the peace treaty. When a ball was held for Jackson's officers, the Laffites attended. Pierre was now well acquainted with some of the men there, but Jean knew few of them due to his being elsewhere during most of the campaign. General Coffee arrived late, and when he encountered Pierre, seemed momentarily unable to connect a name with the face. Pierre was offended and introduced himself rather stiffly as "Lafitte, the pirate!" Coffee immediately extended his hand and made amends for his absentmindedness.[44]

The president would not be so forgetful. On February 6 Madison made good on his support for clemency with a proclamation. Referring to the Baratarians as citizens who had formerly forgotten their duty to the law, he acknowledged their "sincere penitence" when they agreed to give up smuggling and defend New Orleans. Without mentioning the Laffites specifically, he also made reference to the attractive British offer they had refused. The Louisiana legislature recommended that they be pardoned, and now the president did so, granting forgiveness for all violations of any acts of Congress touching on commerce or intercourse with foreign nations prior to January 8, 1815, and stays of any and all claims for fines or penalties against them. To obtain pardon each applicant simply had to produce a certificate from Claiborne attesting that the applicant aided in the defense.[45]

Even before Madison's proclamation reached New Orleans, Claiborne and the federal district attorney agreed that the Baratarians' performance at New Orleans, coupled with Jackson's endorsement of clemency and the call from the legislature, smoothed the path to pardon. The governor did his part by asking the prosecutor to enter findings of *nolle prosse* in all cases against the Laffites and others under prosecution when the federal court reopened February 20.[46] Grymes's term as district attorney had expired when the court adjourned in December, but he would continue to act for the government intermittently for a few weeks now.[47] His replacement, the Irishman John Dick, did not wait for the proclamation he knew would be coming. As the first business of the bench when the federal court reopened on February 20, he entered the appropriate findings to halt proceedings against the Laffites.[48] Those facing indictments were Jean for piracy, Pierre and Jannet as accessories before the fact, and fifteen others—including Lafon, Lavergne, and Dominique, "alias Frederick Youx"—for piracy or illegally fitting out a privateer in United States territory. Dick had asked Claiborne to suggest which deserved pardon, and Claiborne opted to recommend everyone under indictment—though, without convictions, no pardons were needed.[49] They were still to present the statement certifying their service for Jackson, but in the end out of the several hundred men eligible, only Humbert and three others did so, and the court chose not to stand on detail.[50]

Their newfound freedom allowed the Laffite brothers to resume the sort of public life that was not possible on Grand Isle.
Once more Jean was found in the coffeehouses and taverns.[51]
Both brothers, Dominique, Beluche, and others were seen in the
streets of New Orleans, walking arm in arm with Livingston and
his brother-in-law Davezac as fellow heroes of the defense.[52]
"Captain Lafitte," Jean, was even solicited to testify on the behalf
of a Baratarian who somehow wound up in jail again.[53]

Before leaving on his mission to Barataria for Jackson, Pierre
had returned briefly to the house on Dumaine where Marie and
the children lived, and Jean no doubt went there with him on
their return. Around this time Jean made a change in his own domestic life. It is safe to assume that Jean Laffite had enjoyed some
degree of romantic experience not limited to the slender young
quadroon with whom Glasscock saw him in 1809. Any liaisons of
his during the ensuing five years, however, failed to attract
enough notice to leave comment.[54] Now, however, he either commenced or resumed an involvement with Marie Villard's younger
sister Catherine, who also lived in the house on Dumaine, and
sometime in February she became pregnant.[55] He did not establish her in a *plaçage* arrangement, though. Rather, it appears that
the two couples shared then and later whatever lodging Pierre
provided, with Jean contributing to its maintenance.[56]

One reason they shared a house may have been their restricted funds, for they had to subsist on what cash they had
when they fled to the German Coast. Pierre had declared bankruptcy the year before, of course, but his flight from the city and
the time spent in hiding, incarceration, escape, and then fighting
the invasion had forestalled his creditors. With the emergency
past and the brothers accessible in the city, the specter of debt
could catch up with them.

Pierre attempted to put the best face on his new public appearance, and advertised his readiness to meet his obligations. He

had declared bankruptcy, he protested, to protect himself from "exorbitant pretentious demands," but he never meant to avoid "just debts due honest creditors." Disingenuously saying that he believed he had satisfied all obligations and owed no one, he invited any who thought they had claims on him to make themselves known to him or his brother.[57]

They came forward soon enough, though the legislature's suspension of civil suit prosecution spared him payment until April. The judgment against him that had originally caused his bankruptcy came forward again, clearly unsatisfied.[58] In March Pierre had to pay $264 on a debt that went back to 1810. Shortly thereafter the owner of one of the slaves that Pierre took with him when he escaped from jail filed a suit against him for refusing to return the black, and obtained a judgment against him for $400. The case would drag on to late in the year, and end with Pierre making an unsuccessful appeal to the state supreme court.[59] Jean meanwhile found himself in a legal dispute over the sale of the *Adventurer* in Mobile as he strove to hold on to the full proceeds.[60] The brothers were not in financial difficulty, to be sure, but with their sources of income interrupted, they had to watch their expenses.

While casting about for the means to renew their fortunes, the Laffites had time to pursue an expanding friendship with Latour.[61] The engineer had decided to write a book about the recent campaign, and while Jackson and many of the officers were still in New Orleans in March, Latour began interviewing them and copying documents in their files.[62] In the process, he spoke with the Laffites about their role, particularly the Lockyer episode, and the brothers gave him copies of all the correspondence, which Latour would include in an appendix to the volume. Jean embellished the details somewhat in his telling, exaggerating Nicholls's monetary offer to a ridiculous $30,000 and implying that the commission he was offered was not in some insignificant militia, but that of a captain in the Royal Navy.

This was more than a sailor telling sea stories, for there was advantage to magnifying Jean's apparent self-sacrifice in turning down the British offer. The brothers hoped to regain some of the property lost at Barataria, and the more they looked like disinterested patriots, the better their chances. Latour's book, if it appeared in time, could advance their cause. Livingston was also an enthusiastic backer of Latour's project, further binding the Laffites with Livingston peripherally.[63] Interestingly enough, Latour showed his initial draft to one or both of the Laffites before it went to the translator late that spring, for the published version contained even more embellishments than the draft, and ones that would only have come from Jean.[64] For his part, Latour exaggerated the importance of the Laffite-Lockyer episode and its ramifications, placing the documents given him by Jean at the beginning of the lengthy appendix, out of chronological order and in the company of documents of far greater weight.[65]

Patterson and Ross had wasted no time in submitting libels to Hall's bench after returning from their September 1814 raid, and the court was as expeditious. It issued the first order for the sale of goods taken at Barataria on October 24, the proceeds to be held by the court until proper disposition could be determined.[66] A month later, on November 29, Hall ordered the sale of all the vessels captured except the *Dorada* and the *Amiable Maria*, which an inspector judged to be in poor condition.[67] The marshal posted an inventory of the boats and their goods at Maspero's and held the sale a week later.[68] The appearance of the British soon thereafter and the closing of the court postponed further action, but when Hall resumed the bench in February the proceedings resumed with vigor.

Immediately after Dick posted the *nolle prosse* findings on February 20, the court ordered the sale of seventy-four casks of perishable wine, more than seventy-seven hundred gallons. Five days later the *Dorada* and the *Amiable Maria* were ordered sold.[69]

Even a claim from the Spaniard from whom the Laffites originally took the *Dorada* could not save her from the auction block.[70] Soon thereafter the court began distributing the proceeds of the sales, and Patterson and Ross and their men started to come into large shares.[71] Jean Laffite submitted depositions in cases involving what he claimed was his property, but by April 24—when Patterson won an important judgment allowing the combination of two of his major libels, each strengthening the case of the other—Laffite's attorney Morel could see the direction of things.[72] Morel withdrew Laffite's claims and depositions.[73] If they could not sway the court, perhaps they could be used to persuade some higher authority.

Testimony continued for another three weeks before the Laffites gained their first minor success on May 13 when Hall dismissed Patterson's libel on 163 barrels of flour, 16 barrels of bread, and a barrel of rice. This did not mean, though, that the Laffites were to get the proceeds from the sale of these goods, which had already taken place, and the bench immediately decreed that all the goods in another case were condemned and their proceeds forfeited to the government.[74] Three days later it added to the injury by ordering the proceeds of the sales of the *Dorada* and the *Amiable Maria* turned over to their Spanish claimants, reserving a one-third share for Patterson.[75] In a few cases in which citizens at Barataria during the raid were relieved of their personal property by overzealous soldiers, the court returned it, including the doubloons taken from St. Helme and some property belonging to Dominique.[76] The court even released the *General Bolivar* when Beluche was able to produce what appeared to be genuine papers from Cartagena.[77]

The only substantial success for the Laffites came on July 12. In the preceding weeks Louis Morel had ceased acting as their counsel. He would seek a seat in the legislature within a few months, and perhaps he regarded his association with the Laffites as a political liability at the moment. Livingston represented them instead as both attorney and procurator. His political connections and personal prestige after the battle added weight to their petitions, and he seemed to entertain no concerns about being the smugglers' lawyer. Indeed, he had acted on behalf of privateers some years earlier, and now took on Gambi and Dominique as clients. Of course, Livingston was first and foremost an opportunist and entrepreneur. He had already taken an interest in the filibustering and Mexican insurgent schemes fermenting in New Orleans, and he knew that the Baratarians, especially the Laffites, had close ties to Humbert, Toledo, and the rest. Being the smugglers' attorney could, in short, be good for his purse well beyond his fees and the fat contingencies he could expect to garner if he won substantial judgments for his clients.[78]

Though Dominique and Jean Laffite were not present in court that day, Livingston acted for both in submitting and winning a judgment that ordered the marshal to pay them the net proceeds from the sale of Dominique's felucca and Laffite's *Fly* and *Wasp* after the deduction of Patterson's salvage share. At the same time he recovered some of the proceeds of goods taken on Gambi's *Petit Milan*.[79] In all of these cases Jean Laffite was prepared to support his claim for restitution on the grounds of his service to Jackson, first with the correspondence relating to the British offer, then with a list of his vessels and copies of their supposed commissions, and not least with the testimonial letter from General Jackson. These documents were not direct evidence in the cases at hand, but he had his attorney keep them ready to be produced in mitigation if necessary. Unfortunately, the bench never admitted them. Laffite would have to find somewhere else to employ their persuasions.[80]

While later estimates put the value of what was lost at Barataria at half a million dollars or more, the sale of the vessels and goods yielded closer to $35,000—no small sum at the time.[81] The *Dorada* and the *Amiable Maria* between them only brought

$6,890 at auction.[82] Still, every article was worth contesting, and the good news on July 12 encouraged Jean to have Livingston submit a petition for recovery of more of the merchandise. Livingston would oblige, but immediately after he got the judgment on the proceeds from the sale of the *Fly* and the *Wasp*, Jean Laffite removed himself permanently from the litigation and thereafter left it to his attorney. Collecting his award immediately, a few thousand dollars at best, he had a journey to make and a use for the money in his purse.

Ho! treachery! my guards! my scimitar!
The galleys feed the flames—and I afar!
Accursed Dervise—these thy tidings—thou
Some villain spy-seize cleave him—slay him now!

TWELVE

Spies for Spain
1815-1816

WITH THE BRITISH THREAT no longer a distraction, Humbert, Toledo, and Gutiérrez had time to try to resuscitate their plan for a combined land campaign against Texas and maritime strike at Tampico. They found ardent support in what Morphy and others referred to as an "association" of men in New Orleans bent on gaining personal profit through encouraging assaults on Spanish property. Never a formal organization, the "association" had a fluid membership in which the constants were Livingston, Davezac, Grymes, Abner Duncan, Nolte, Lafon, merchant John K. West, and of course the Laffite brothers. While most provided financial backing as their investment, the Laffites' contribution was to be transportation. Only now they did not have a fleet.

While the bumptious Humbert published an announcement of the plan's renewal and tried to enlist volunteers in distant Kentucky, Toledo turned his attention, as he had the year before, to the currently ascendant party in the peripatetic insurgent Congress in Mexico. On February 10 he wrote to them saying that he had four hundred men in hand, and another two thousand could be raised. If the Congress funded the enterprise, he could lead these men in a campaign to help drive the Spaniards out of Mexico. At the same time, he suggested that the Congress supply him with letters of marque to commission privateers. There would be plenty of applicants. Tampico or some other point should be opened as a port for steady traffic with New Orleans, and a court of admiralty established to take care of the prickly matter of legalizing prizes. The Congress should send a minister to conclude a treaty of amity with the United States. Most of all, the Congress should send money, lots of it, to make everything happen.[1]

As was typical of the cross-purposes and conflicting ambitions that crippled almost all of these enterprises, Anaya had his own agendum. Anaya had shifted his support to the failed filibuster John H. Robinson's dream of leading an invasion of Texas, and Toledo feared that Anaya was collecting "some bloodthirsty adventurers from Barataria, who have bought a vessel," intending to seize any patriot funds they could get their hands on under the pretext of buying arms.[2] They would be competing with Toledo for Mexican financial support and attention.

It is ironic that Toledo complained about Anaya's courting of "bloodthirsty adventurers from Barataria," for Toledo turned to that very resource. Before his plans could be launched, he had to get his plea to the Congress, and that required a ship. General Jackson, however, refused to let vessels leave port. Anxious not to see privateering restart and not overly trusting of his recent allies, the general held up almost all departures during January and February 1815. Gambi's *Petit Milan* had been taken at Barataria, and subsequently sold to West and renamed the *Aguila* or *Eagle*.[3] Coincidentally, the day that Toledo wrote to the Mexican Congress, word of the peace treaty with Britain reached New Orleans. Immediately Toledo applied for permission to take the *Eagle* to Nautla, ostensibly to carry passengers belonging to, and dispatches for, the revolutionary government, and to return with specie for Toledo's use. People of good reputation endorsed his request, and Toledo affirmed in writing that the voyage had no object other than what he declared, and specifically "no intent to commit hostilities against Spain or her subjects." Further, "no arms should be put on board." On that basis, Jackson approved the request.[4]

Toledo's indictment for violating the neutrality law was outstanding, and Dick did not enter the government's *nolle prosse* in his case until February 20. Toledo had been free on his own recognizance and a posted bond since he volunteered to join in the defense of New Orleans.[5] When Toledo first came to New Orleans, the inhabitants greeted him as a man who "risked every thing, to engage in the perilous task of freeing his countrymen from the yoke that bowed them to the earth." Dick saw that "every eye met him with friendly gratulation; every liberal heart was open to receive him." Recent setbacks to his cause only made Toledo more admired, and when he showed credentials from the Supreme Congress in Mexico identifying him as "generalissimo of the army of the north," people received him as such.

Dick could not conceal his mistrust of the fellow, however. "From the first moment of our knowledge of General Toledo, it was obvious, to those who considered at all the extent of his qualifications, that they were entirely inadequate to his station, that his mental resources were few, when the difficulties he had to overcome required them to be multitudinous," said Dick. It was no secret that the insurgent Congress in Mexico had revoked Toledo's commission when he fled with Anaya and Humbert the previous year, and since then he had done nothing but stay in New Orleans trying unsuccessfully to regain his lost power. The Mexican junta might have used him occasionally as an agent in New Orleans simply because he was there, but he had no authority and Dick doubted that he enjoyed the confidence of genuine higher-ups. The attorney knew most of the important people connected with the failed Gutiérrez-Magee expedition of 1813, and to him they uniformly attributed their defeat "to the incapacity and mismanagement of Toledo."

Dick, himself sympathetic to the independence movements that Toledo espoused, concluded his appraisal of Toledo's fitness to command by saying that "he has neither capacity to plan nor ability to execute; he is incapable of discovering expedients for each exigency or of providing remedies for each disorder; he can have neither dexterity in his means, nor flexibility in varying his measures, without altering his designs." Ultimately, said Dick, "he wants energy, he wants the means of inspiring confidence, and what is worse, I fear he wants integrity." As if it needed saying, he added, "I think him capable of deception and falsehood," and Toledo would immediately prove Dick to be right.[6] Nevertheless, Toledo was able to inspire enough confidence in the "association" for West to lend his ship to Toledo's mission. Toledo's assurances of large amounts of Mexican gold likely helped West take the risk.

To captain the *Eagle*, West engaged Julius Caesar Amigoni, formerly master of the privateer *Esperanza*, itself a prize Amigoni had taken with a corsair out of Barataria the year before.[7] "This Amigoni is well known as an associate of the Baratarian Pirates or smugglers," the district attorney attested.[8] Toledo began boarding some twenty or more crewmen on February 17, and finished fitting out the ship the next day. On February 18 Amigoni cleared the *Eagle* out of the port with half a dozen passengers, supposedly bound for Nautla.[9] Instead, she went straight to Grand Isle.

There Amigoni met Vincent Gambi and Colonel Bean, who had secreted on several oyster boats goods including two six-pounder cannon formerly on the *Petit Milan*, twenty muskets, cutlasses, and gunpowder.[10] The men got past the soldier guard at the Temple by exhibiting a forged pass from Jackson, which Gambi said he had obtained from Livingston. Gambi even removed some of the obstructions that Jackson had ordered placed in the bayous to impede an enemy advance, an action that made Jackson furious when he learned of it early in March as the peace treaty had not yet been ratified.[11]

They had their stories ready. Bean was to say that the two cannon were a gift from him to Amigoni, intended to become fieldpieces. Gambi was to maintain that he was merely a passenger, going to Mexico to settle, notwithstanding the saber and pair of pistols he wore. In fact he replaced Amigoni as captain, and found a nine-pounder hidden in the hold under the ballast and another small pivot gun ready for mounting on deck.[12] After several days spent mounting the guns and loading other weapons and munitions, the *Eagle* made sail once again on February 22, fully equipped as a corsair.[13] With no commission, anything she took made her a pirate.

Thanks to calm winds, almost two weeks passed before they made Boquilla de Piedras, a simple open point on the Mexican coast with a good anchorage. There they learned that Nautla had fallen to the Spaniards, meaning the port was closed to them.[14] Gambi landed the passengers and one of them went some thirty miles into the interior on a pirogue, looking for the insurgent Congress. He returned the next day with twenty or more men from Dominique's crew of the *Tigre* and a packet for Amigoni. Amigoni told the *Eagle*'s crew he had been given a commission as a captain in the Mexican navy and papers for the *Eagle* to cruise as a privateer.[15] In fact, he had been handed several blank commissions to distribute to corsairs in Louisiana.[16] There was also a general's commission for Toledo, signed by insurgent leader Rayón.[17] Dominique's former crew members brought muskets and barrels of powder, which they quickly loaded aboard the *Eagle*.[18] Bean's cannon were not landed, and probably were never meant to be. They would be used to arm the first prize taken by the *Eagle*.[19]

Once the representatives from the Congress had left, the *Eagle* set sail again, clearly on a cruise. Gambi had gone to a house ashore, feeling unwell, before the pirogue returned from the interior, and Amigoni now commanded.[20] Less than a week after leaving Boquilla de Piedras, the *Eagle* returned with a prize, the schooner *Santa Rita* out of Campeche, loaded with salt and dry goods, cargo, and a vessel worth $20,000.[21] Gambi promptly took over the schooner and renamed her the *Mexicana*. He put a crew aboard and spent a few days transferring guns to outfit her, while the *Eagle* left to continue her cruise. Then Gambi set sail under the colors of the Mexican insurgency, the ship's former Spanish flags in the locker just in case, and almost immediately took the *Nuestra Señora de Rosario*. As soon as he took the prize, he re-named the *Santa Rita* again to cover her tracks, this time calling her the *Nonesuch*.[22]

When Gambi's men went through their new prize, they made a startling discovery. Papers aboard the ship revealed that Picornell had become a traitor, and was trying to feed information on insurgent and filibuster plans to Spain.[23] Gambi had plenty of time to peruse them, if he could read, for the return voyage to Barataria for the *Santa Rita* and her prize took more than three weeks thanks to heavy weather, and those aboard were almost drowned when the seas threatened to overwhelm her.[24]

The *Eagle*, heavily loaded with merchandise taken from her own prize, came along the *Santa Rita* near Grand Terre.[25] They reached the island on April 9, and by the next day their arrival was known in New Orleans.[26] As soon as the collector at the customs house learned of it, he asked Patterson to take them, and the commodore readily dispatched Lieutenant Thomas Cunningham and a gunboat.[27] A few days later near Cat Island, Cunningham came up with the *Eagle* at anchor alongside Laméson's newly fitted out *Presidente*, each under the flag of Cartagena, and in Laméson's papers was his old privateering commission.[28] Cunningham took both ships, along with the *Santa Rita/Mexicana/ Nonesuch*, and set out for New Orleans. Gambi was back aboard the *Eagle*, having relieved Amigoni, who was at Barataria looking after some storm damage to the *Nuestra Señora de Rosario*.[29] Unfortunately, Cunningham's small crew found it impossible to keep the prisoners in check. By the time the little flotilla reached the city, all but two of the privateer crewmen had simply run away over the side, and only two crewmen remained from the prize ship.[30]

They returned to a city hearing echoes of trouble some hoped had disappeared. The privateering problem had not evaporated with the destruction of Barataria. Part of the problem lay at Cartagena. The Spaniards had struck back effectively at independence movements everywhere else, but the city held out. Encouraged by the assistance of Aury, Beluche, Jannet, and other corsairs, the ruling elite maintained a welcoming climate for adventurers and privateers. Sauvinet had visited in the summer of 1814 to investigate moving there permanently, most likely acting as a representative of Humbert, Toledo, and others seeking a united front against Spain. Latour had considered relocating there before he became caught up in the war, but a friend advised him to be cautious. "This country is not yet stable," he told Latour. Moreover, as Sauvinet found, "the system is totally changed with regard to foreigners, they are very suspicious of them." Still, American privateers were an important source of revenue, and Cartagena continued to hand out commissions in its port and to print more for extralegal distribution elsewhere.[31]

The instability at Cartagena dogged its affairs for the next several months. But Aury and other corsairs found plenty of opportunity meanwhile. By early 1815 the privateers of the Gulf were active in a small way, sometimes boarding vessels waiting at the Balize or in the channel. Within days of the announcement of peace, however, Morphy observed with disgust that four suspect ships had passed down the river, destined, he was convinced, to be armed at Barataria by some of the "Captains and Old Sailors." A person he trusted had told him of a meeting held by what he called "the main associates of the pirates," at which the assembled discussed raising Cartagenan colors and attacking Florida. While Morphy tried to learn more, on March 26 he warned Apodaca to put out a warning. With the war with Britain at an end, the war with the privateers and filibusters was about to resume.[32]

The customs people, too, realized soon enough that, as collector John Williams put it, "the Barataria Trade is not yet done." The citizens, too, were ready to revert to their old ways. One of his inspectors told Pierre Duplessis early in April that "on the part of the enemy we have to contend with, we behold an extended and organized system of Enterprise, of Ingenuity, of indefatigability and of audacity favoured by a variety of local advantages & supported always by force of arms." It seemed a disgrace that "the old & notorious offenders who have so lately been indulged with a remission of the punishment they merited are already making arrangements to recommence their former nefarious pursuits."[33] Sales of smuggled goods began to take place openly on the lower Lafourche by May if not earlier, though no one seemed to suspect the Laffites of direct involvement. There were even rumors of American merchant vessels being taken, a violation of the one rule the Laffites had strictly observed.[34] Collector Duplessis appealed to the secretary of the treasury to seek assistance from the navy in quelling this lawlessness. He complained bitterly that "the crimes of these men are hightened by their ingratitude to the government" for its recent clemency.[35]

Patterson's response was to promise that additions to his command—including the *Dorada*, which he had purchased at auction and renamed *Firebrand*—would enable him to protect the coast from "the pirates of Barrataria" and those sailing under Mexican and Cartagenian colors. He wanted the authority to use his discretion in dealing with vessels under lawful commissions, but if he found such corsairs acting in cooperation with the Baratarians, he promised to take "effectual measures," even at the cost of damage to legitimate privateers.[36]

Indeed, the question of legitimate privateers proved challenging, thanks chiefly to the Cartagenan commissions. Dick complained that he and the federal court operated in "peculiarly embarrassing" circumstances at times, trying to avoid all interference with those colonies of Spain that claimed to be independent, and at the same time repress the smugglers and illegal corsairs. "Much of this difficulty has arisen from the very improper conduct of the government of Carthagena," he said, citing its habit of distributing blank letters of marque. It was all but impossible for the court to distinguish genuinely commissioned privateers from pirates. He tried to be impartial, as did Judge Hall, but at times he feared impartiality favored the smugglers too much.[37]

Prosecutor Dick got his chance to test the limits of that impartiality when he immediately started proceedings, libeling the *Eagle* for illegally outfitting in the United States and her prize merchandise for violating customs laws, which also applied to the *Santa Rita*.[38] Dick was not fooled by the *Eagle*'s pretended Mexican commission.[39] Indeed, Gambi had initially told him that she sailed under two letters of marque, including one from Cartagena, which was prohibited by international law. Gambi and Laméson posted bond for themselves and their ships, pending adjudication.[40]

The court was in a mood to act quickly. On May 16 the grand jury indicted Gambi, Amigoni, John Robinson, and Romain Verry for piracy. Amigoni had escaped capture, but the marshal arrested the rest and brought them before the bench for arraignment. They heard the indictments read to them, entered pleas of not guilty, and were remanded into custody for trial two days thence. The grand jury also issued indictments against Toledo for illegally fitting out the *Eagle,* and Pierre Laméson for the same with the *Presidente.*[41] Spanish authorities in the city met the news with guarded pleasure, especially regarding Gambi, "the cruelest and the greatest assassin among all the pirates."[42]

The court heard Gambi's trial on May 18. The witnesses called in his defense included Humbert, Toledo, and even collector Pierre Duplessis, while the prosecution relied on the four captured crewmen.[43] Gambi was an experienced dissembler. Besides the sobriquet "Vingt cinq"—it meant "Twenty-five" but was also a pun on his name Vincent—he sometimes did business under the name of Juan or Jean Roux. Indeed, three months later he would tell a notary that Roux was his real name and Gambi an alias, and with a man this shifty none could say for sure.[44] Now he claimed that the *Eagle* had a valid commission from the Mexican junta when she left New Orleans, and actually produced it in court. He consistently protested that he was only a passenger, and that he had been ill ashore when the *Eagle* took the *Santa Rita,* which was the only act listed in the piracy indictment.

But through testimony from the printer, Dick revealed that the commission had been printed in New Orleans at Toledo's order, and was not delivered to him until well after the *Eagle* had sailed. Toledo had somehow gotten the commission to Gambi after his arrest. Dick also demonstrated that prior to the trial Toledo had lured the two captured Spanish crewmen from the *Santa Rita* to the office of a notary, telling them they were seeing the Spanish consul. There Toledo promised each of them $15 if they would make a statement of the affair based on his "suggestions," and they had done so. But they refused to take an oath before the notary, and now in court they swore that they were not present when their supposed testimony was written down and notarized. "These frauds were so palpable, so shame-less, and so base as to fill every mind with indignation, and to call down odium and contempt upon their fabricator Toledo," Dick argued.[45] Yet that same day the jury returned a verdict that "as there has been no *positive proof* that the Prisoner was in any other capacity, on board the Schooner Eagle, than [that] *of a Passenger*, the Jury find him not guilty." Dick entered a *nolle prosse* for the remaining indictments, seeing that further prosecution with such a jury would be pointless.[46] He also had it in mind that by doing so, he might persuade the other men under indictment to become witnesses against Gambi if he could find a new charge to justify resurrecting the case.

Illicit activity at Grand Isle began to increase. Indeed, even while Gambi was awaiting trial, Duplessis got a report that "the notorious pirate Vincent Gemby" had led two dozen men on a quick trip to Barataria to begin fitting out another vessel.[47] Soon the *Cleopatra*, a prize taken by Beluche's privateer *La Popa* under genuine Cartagenan commission, was taken in tandem with another corsair by the *Firebrand* in the *Dorada*'s first act after her change of personality.[48] A vessel believed to belong to Sauvinet brought a prize into Grand Terre early in July.[49] A few weeks later the authorities caught the *Eugenia* trying to fit out as a Cartagenan privateer not far from New Orleans. And that same month a privateer operating under a Mexican commission brought a prize into New Orleans, where Dominique bought her and began outfitting her as a privateer to be called the *Mexicain*.[50]

For his part, Toledo had posted bond April 15 with Livingston as his surety, and his trial, originally scheduled for a few days later, was deferred to July on motion of Livingston.[51] A jury acquitted him, too, regarding the testimony against him to be circumstantial, though Dick felt no doubt of Toledo's guilt. In his defense Toledo denied—probably honestly—that he had any share of ownership in the *Eagle*, and argued as proof that since his arrival in New Orleans he had lived entirely on the charity of friends and simply had no money to outfit a vessel.[52] During the trial Livingston got permission to remove some Spanish documents from Toledo's court file, claiming they were not material.[53] Most likely they were the ones captured with the *Eagle* and the *Presidente*, documents that not only revealed Picornell's treachery but also could have implicated some of the "associates," including Livingston, as Toledo's backers. Indeed, Patterson's sudden support for the return of some proceeds from Barataria to Jean Laffite very likely reflected the fact that sometime this summer he, too, had felt the lure of the "associates'" ambitions, and had become one of them.

After the trials and acquittals, the fight over the vessels and their cargoes commenced. On April 30 the court ordered an inspection of the *Eagle* to determine her value as a legitimate prize taken by Cunningham.[54] By May 20, when no one had come forward to demonstrate ownership of the vessel, Judge Hall pronounced any pretended owners like Amigoni to be in contempt, and decreed the ship to be awarded to sale and distribution by default. The same process was applied to the *Presidente*.[55] Meanwhile on May 31 Morphy filed a claim on behalf of the Spanish owners of the *Santa Rita*, and Amigoni filed his own claim to her as a legitimate prize under his supposed commission. Livingston represented him, demonstrating that he was now clearly the attorney of choice for the corsairs and smugglers.[56]

The resulting litigation continued for months, delaying trials and requiring testimony from Mexico. Pierre Laffite appeared among the witnesses, and even the acquitted Gambi gave testimony, though the court noted that his was to be used "subject to all exceptions as to competency and credit."[57] It finally ended in February 1816, when the court dismissed Amigoni's claim and ordered the *Eagle* sold.[58] Meanwhile Amigoni attempted to protect some of his cargo by claiming it as merchandise belonging to the

Mexican insurgents and put aboard the *Eagle* at Boquilla de Piedras by order of General Morelos.[59] However, the court finally returned the goods taken aboard the *Santa Rita* and the *Eagle* to the original owners, less a one-third share going to Cunningham for their recovery.[60] Later that month Laméson lost the *Presidente* unequivocally, while the prize goods he had on board when captured were turned over to Morphy for return to their owners.[61] Fully a year after the litigation began, Livingston would renew Laméson's and Amigoni's claims, but to no avail, and he finally withdrew them.[62] Long before then, at the auction of the *Eagle*'s cargo, Livingston bought some of the bargains on offer.[63] When the marshal sold the *Presidente* at auction after removing her armament, the buyer was none other than Pierre Laffite.[64]

Livingston complained that this "vexatious business" fully occupied his time. He needed the work, however, for he found himself heavily in debt, with two plantations not paying their way and a new lumber business that did no better. It was this need for money that had helped lure him into the "association," and when its plans took a new direction that fall, they consumed more of his time.[65] These opportunities came at some cost, however, for by now he was so closely and openly attached to the Baratarians that he found his reputation at risk. When he and fellow "associate" Abner Duncan served as defense counsel in the trial of one allegedly unlawful privateer, Duncan became so convinced that their client was a pirate that he withdrew from the case. Collector Duplessis condemned Livingston, "the legal protector of all the Pirates & smugglers who infest this District," for remaining on the case "as usual true at his Post." Duplessis took his complaint against Livingston to the secretary of the treasury in Washington, averring that "if these wretches had not this zealous advocate to support them there is every reason to believe they could ere long be driven from the Country."[66]

Duplessis had to contend with another problem caused by the smugglers and pirates. By aligning themselves loosely with genuine independence movements, they were doing injury to those causes by association. He must punish piracy without punishing honest revolutionaries. "An act of revolt or rebellion against a sovereign must not be confused with an act of Piracy," the secretary of the treasury advised him. Any merchant vessel that had not committed an offense against the law of nations governing piracy, that carried a lawful cargo and conformed to United States law, was entitled to enter American ports regardless of the flag it sailed under. What such a vessel could not do was enlist crewmen other than natives of its own country, fit out to convert from a merchant vessel to a corsair, or take on weapons. Mindful of Toledo and the rest, the secretary also reminded Duplessis that no military enterprise could be raised or launched from American territory against a nation with which the United States was at peace. At the same time, however, a 1795 treaty guaranteed Spanish subjects and their vessels protection in American waters. As Spain had not recognized the independence of her New World colonies in revolt, the United States must continue to regard these Spanish subjects as entitled to the protection of that treaty.[67]

Meanwhile attorney Dick waded through the diplomatic and legal morass trying to get to Gambi. Thanks to testimony provided by the minor defendants whom Dick had released on *nolle prosse* findings, he secured another piracy indictment from the grand jury on July 15. Despite the new evidence, however, and the fact that Livingston called no witnesses for the defense, the trial on July 18 ended in yet another acquittal, meaning that in six months "Vingt cinq" had escaped from three separate indictments for piracy.[68]

Coincidentally, as Gambi was about to face another trial, the Laffites came to a decision. They had been remarkably quiet during the past months, no doubt anxious not to hurt Jean's efforts to reclaim their property or secure restitution, but now one of them must go to the East to pursue their interests. They needed to buy and outfit a new ship or two away from prying eyes in New

Orleans, especially after the loss of the *Eagle* and the *Presidente*.
Baltimore was the place for that. Humbert had contacts with
backers in Philadelphia and Baltimore, and more would-be supporters of the Tampico enterprise made those cities their headquarters. In Washington the Laffites could approach higher
authorities with their case for reparation for their losses to Patterson, money they might need to fund their own involvement in
the plans for Humbert and Mexico. The "associates" in New Orleans were at risk of being compromised. If the brothers were to
prosper, they needed other backing as security, and commissions
more authentic than Toledo's. Pierre being the man of business in
New Orleans, the trip fell to Jean.

A seaborne letter could take almost a month to reach the East
and the brothers planned for the journey well in advance, corresponding with those on whom they hoped to call. The trip would
be costly, but thanks to the court's award of the proceeds of the
sale of the *Fly* and the *Wasp*, Jean could travel with a substantial
government draft that would be negotiable in Philadelphia, the
center of American banking even after the demise of the first National Bank a few years earlier. If the draft was not sufficient for
their needs, major purchases such as ships or rigging could be
made on letters of credit from their associates in New Orleans, or
paid for on delivery with money provided by them or the Mexican Congress if all went well. For out-of-pocket expenses of passage and hotels they had little cash in hand, however, especially
after spending $415 to buy a slave to help Marie with the house
and a family about to grow even more.[69] Jean would have to manage his hard money carefully. Two days before Jean was to leave,
the parish court rendered a judgment against the brothers for
$164 for a debt due to a creditor. Rather than pay the just debt,
Jean appealed his half the next day, and then he and Pierre signed
a joint promissory note while the appeal was pending.[70] It was a
means of postponing the debt while husbanding the cash on
hand for the journey.

John West's ship the *Francis* regularly made the run between New Orleans and Philadelphia, and now she was in port and due to depart July 15.[71] Jean purchased a passage from her captain, Thomas Barns, and then he and Pierre attended to last minute business. Pierre went to attorney George Pollock and drafted a power of attorney empowering his brother to represent his interests in Washington, including presenting petitions and memorials to the president, heads of the executive departments, and Congress in seeking to obtain the return of their property seized by Patterson and Ross. Jean also had his full assent to make unilateral commitments to sell their existing property, or to contract for the purchase of new property, meaning vessels and tackle. Jean could accept money to be collected for both of them, and if he had to go to court to do it, he was fully empowered to speak for Pierre.[72] This day Francis Tomasis, owner of the *Moon of November*, also gave Jean his power of attorney to attempt recovery of his vessel and her cargo taken by Patterson.[73]

Jean also had a court appearance to make. Besides his coming piracy trial, Gambi faced a civil suit over a slave that had run away and served on both the *Dorada* and the *Petit Milan* prior to Patterson's raid. Jean went to the Orleans Parish district court on the morning of July 15 and attested in a deposition that Gambi had not known the slave to be a runaway.[74] Indeed, Jean was so busy that he could not make his court appearance appealing the $164 debt, and had his lawyer Henry Carlton represent him.[75] That done, while Vincent Gambi was hearing his third indictment for piracy, Jean walked to the waterfront and boarded the *Francis*, which cleared the port that evening.[76]

It was August 27 when the *Francis* tied up at the wharf in Philadelphia to disgorge her cargo of cotton, brandy, sugar, and passengers.[77] Jean Laffite stepped ashore to find the city buzzing with word that Guadaloupe had fallen to the British two weeks earlier. More startling yet was the news that after escaping his exile at Elba and conducting a campaign that ended with defeat at Waterloo, Napoleon was once more a prisoner.[78] Philadelphia hummed with rumors of plots to free the emperor, even to bring him to America. Within a few weeks of Jean's arrival, word spread that Joseph Bonaparte had arrived in New York in early September, and suddenly the stories of secret schemes took on greater authenticity.[79]

Of more immediate and personal interest to the Laffites was a proclamation by President Madison, issued September 1, that appeared in the press within a few days.[80] The president was responding to Spanish complaints by condemning the plans in Louisiana to launch a military expedition against Texas and Mexico in aid of the insurgents there. Madison declared that such plotters were "deceiving and seducing honest and well-intentioned citizens to engage in their unlawful enterprises." He warned those duped into participation to withdraw, and ordered that the organizers cease immediately. "They will answer the contrary at their peril," he admonished. He also called on all military and civil authorities, national, state, and local, to be on the watch for such schemers, to seize their arms and vessels, and to try them for violating the neutrality laws.[81] The United States and Spain were close to restoring full diplomatic relations, and violations of Spain's sovereignty worked against that.

The very expedition Madison condemned was one of the reasons Jean Laffite came to the East, and to Baltimore at least once. At that moment the Maryland city was on the verge of becoming more important than New Orleans as a seedbed of filibustering activities against Spain, for would-be revolutionaries found sympathetic ears among the port's merchant investors.[82] One such man was Peter A. Guestier, a merchant and ship chandler doing business at the southwest corner of Frederick and Second streets.[83] Laffite met with him to make arrangements for acquiring and fitting out at least one new vessel to resume privateering against Spanish traders under letters of marque that Jean expected to get from Humbert as an agent of the Mexican junta.[84]

Jean passed most of the fall in Philadelphia, however. There were people in the Quaker City on whom he had to call, perhaps starting with bankers to deposit the money or instruments that he brought from New Orleans. Another likely visit was to the attorney Peter Du Ponceau, a close business associate of the Laffites' new friend and sometime legal counsel Livingston, to whom Livingston referred friends visiting the city.[85] Laffite could need a lawyer if he made any business commitments while there. Latour was also in the city in November to oversee the proofing and printing of his book. He expected to produce six hundred copies and had an agent taking money for advance sales in Louisiana, Livingston acting as surety for their delivery.[86] Latour was also there to cement a new enterprise as an agent for Spain reporting on the condition of its territory north and west of Louisiana and any efforts to interfere with its colonial possessions.

Indeed, he probably discussed with Laffite the advantages to Jean engaging himself with Spain, too. Latour would know that in the wake of the fall of Barataria, the brothers' financial fortunes ran at an uncertain ebb, and their close association with Humbert, Toledo, and other revolutionaries was an open secret. Everyone could see the hopeless impracticality and infighting that crippled the filibustering projects, and there was little reason to expect future efforts to be less disastrous than past. Rather than risk themselves and their means on wild schemes of conquest, the Laffites could earn sure money by feeding Spain information on the insurgents' plans. With no vessels of their own at the moment, they were out of the privateering business, but they could reestablish their fleet with what they earned from Spain, who might even allow them to privateer as a cover for their espionage. In short, they might have it both ways.

Jean soon fell into the perfect means of making the brothers useful to Spain. In December he learned from someone in the French émigré community of a supposed plot by the exiled emperor's brother Joseph to locate a colony of refugees somewhere in Texas. Laffite also heard—or said he heard—rumors of a plan to incite a slave rebellion in Cuba, probably to distract the Spaniards while the new Texas colony was planted. He later claimed that he thought it a fantastical scheme at the time, one that he dismissed out of hand. In fact he may have invented the whole thing in order to have dramatic evidence of the kind of information the brothers could provide. The same day Laffite supposedly learned these things, he met with Latour, who almost certainly took him to see Luis Onís.[87]

Onís had been running his shadow legation in Philadelphia for at least five years. Even so, he remained in constant contact with officials in Washington, lobbying for actions such as Madison's September 1 proclamation—though Onís, like most Spaniards, suspected it was a hollow gesture. Onís and his friends believed that unofficially the Americans wanted Florida and Texas, and preferred that rebel movements evict Spain from the Americas entirely. For this reason, Onís ran the intelligence system in the United States, the Caribbean, and New Spain that engaged Latour, and would be interested in meeting Jean Laffite.[88]

The timing of this meeting was wonderfully coincidental, for on November 17 Pierre had entered into an agreement with Picornell and Sedella for the brothers to spy for Spain. If he sent word at once to his brother, it could have reached Jean at the same time that he met with Onís, and certainly by December 28 Onís knew of Pierre's bargain. Surely Pierre did write to Jean, for there was a spate of good news. Earlier in the year, on July 29 the court awarded Jean the proceeds from the sale of some property seized at Barataria.[89] Better yet, when Livingston filed a petition for the recovery of sixteen pieces of gold plate and eight cannon, Dick assented to the motion, and on July 29 all parties agreed to returning the gold plate, though Patterson would retain the cannon.[90] No one thought it wise to turn artillery back to a man so closely tied to smuggling. Though subsequent judgments went against the Laffites, Pierre could tell Jean well before December that the brothers had more money available for their projects.[91] And on a more personal note, just as he was to leave for Washington, Jean probably got another letter with the news that he had become a father on November 4 when Catherine Villard gave birth to a son she named Jean Pierre.[92]

Jean went to Washington in December to press his case for restitution or reparations for the losses at Barataria. Congress had begun its session four days into the month, and to persuade the representatives from Louisiana on whom he called Jean brought with him copies of the Lockyer documents and his own correspondence with Blanque, which he had retrieved earlier that spring on Livingston's advice.[93] Jean also carried a list of the brothers' vessels taken at Barataria, and the commissions or pretended letters of marque under which they sailed, to demonstrate that the charges of piracy against them were unfounded.[94]

Unfortunately, no one in officialdom was interested. In the wake of normalization of relations with Spain, restoring ships to men who had plundered Spanish vessels under questionable papers, or no papers at all, would have been a prime diplomatic blunder. The Laffites' well-known connection with the invasion plans Madison had condemned made a sympathetic reception even more unlikely. Jean may have gained an interview with Secretary of State Monroe, since Latour visited with Monroe a couple of times this winter.[95] He would have tried to gain audiences with Attorney General Rush, who had been an agent in quashing the piracy indictments, and perhaps with the secretary of the treasury, Alexander Dallas. Members of Louisiana's congressional delegation offered less attractive targets. The Laffites had no known connections with either of the senators, James Brown and Eligius Fromentin, and could expect little sympathy from Representative Thomas Bolling Robertson, a friend of

Judge Hall's who had earlier condemned the Baratarians as "brigands."

Given the boldness with which the brothers customarily approached high officials, Jean probably bypassed everyone initially and took his plea directly to Madison. He drafted a letter in French, and got someone, perhaps Latour, to translate it into passable but awkward English on December 27. Typically, he began with flattery of Madison's "benevolent dispositions," meaning the pardons, and then begged the president's agency in gaining the favor of Dallas, "whose decision could but be in my favour, if he only was well acquainted with my disinterrested conduct during the last attempt of the Britanic fources on Louisiana." Laffite went on to describe how, with utter disregard of his own interests, he acted for the welfare of the nation in the crisis, and declined to let his ships leave Barataria even after he learned of the impending Patterson raid. He told Madison that in spite of his crews' protests about the loss of their property, he assured them that "if my property should be ceised I had not the least apprehention of the equity of the U. S. once they would be convinced of the cinserity of my conduct."

To emphasize his patriotism and self-sacrifice, he averred that he kept his ships at Barataria in order to detain his crews there, and thus "retain about four hundred skillful artillers in the country which could but be of the utmost importance for its defense." Even after the raid, at the LaBranche plantation he had tried to rally the people of the German Coast to defend the state. Showing that Laffite was well aware that service with Jackson had made the "pirate-patriots" celebrities in the national press, he boasted that "my conduct since that period is notorious." The country was now safe and at peace, he went on. "I claim no merit for having like all the inhabitants of the state, cooperated in its wellfair [for] in this my conduct has been dictated by the impulse of my proper centiments." However, now he felt justified in asking for "the equity of the Government of the U. S. upon which I always relied for the restitution of at least that portion of my property which will not deprive the treasury of the U. S. of anny of its own funs."[96]

The president never acknowledged Laffite's letter.[97] There was ample testimony in Hall's court that the commissions of the Laffite vessels were unlawful, making both the ships and their prizes and goods forfeit. The brothers were fortunate to be free of indictments and able to walk the streets of New Orleans unmolested. They could expect nothing more from this administration after the pardon and *nolle prosse* scheme, and it would not interfere with the decisions coming from Hall's bench in prize cases already decided or to come. Madison's failure to respond also reflected his official policy toward the Mexican and South American insurgents and their American sympathizers, as stated in his proclamation. Ultimately, the absence of any indication of aid or sympathy from the president crippled Laffite's hopes of redress from Rush or Dallas, and Jean may not have taken his appeal any further after waiting long enough to realize that the president would not countenance his plea.

It could not have helped Laffite's case that the day he wrote to Madison, the press reported that at the end of October Toledo had returned to New Orleans from another trip to the Mexican coast. He brought with him yet another would-be representative, José Manuel de Herrera, the Mexican junta's newly appointed minister plenipotentiary to the United States. With them came the news that the insurgents now controlled much of the open country in Mexico, leaving the major towns isolated from one another.[98] Washington had no intention of receiving Herrera or acknowledging the revolutionaries until they succeeded on their own, but his arrival with the notorious Toledo in New Orleans, and their obvious intention to raise men and money in Louisiana, made embarrassingly public just how little

Madison's proclamation mattered. Worse, the news arrived only a week after Onís presented his ambassadorial credentials.[99] But at least with both Jean and Onís in the city on December 28 the ambassador gave his blessing to the employment of the Laffite brothers as spies.[100]

General Jackson was in Washington as well, having arrived in early November. Citizens held a grand ball in his honor across the Potomac in Alexandria on December 7, though he was too ill to attend. He remained in the city until Christmas Eve, and Laffite likely attempted to see the general to solicit his support, though if Old Hickory was sympathetic, he appears to have done nothing to further the brothers' cause.[101] Perhaps Laffite even attended the ball if he reached Washington in time. Years later he told people that he lived lavishly, spending thousands of dollars in fashionable pursuits, but the facts of the brothers' financial conditions belie that.[102] He probably spent his days as his limited funds allowed.

While in Washington Laffite learned of the United States Navy's action against the Mediterranean pirates operating out of Algiers. Stephen Decatur returned to the capital to be hailed as a hero. Even more disturbing was the news from New Orleans. Word came that Morelos, the insurgent leader who originally sent Bean to Louisiana for help, had been captured as his Congress retreated, and was executed on December 22. Then came news of a more direct and threatening disaster for those already practicing the corsairing trade. Cartagena had fallen.

Cartagena's role as an incubator for privateers, legal and illicit, ended in early October 1815 when Spanish gunboats attacked. The siege lasted for 106 days, with Jannet and other alumni of Barataria trying to defend the city's water approaches with their small fleet. Aury commanded a dozen vessels, and fought several indecisive engagements with Spanish warships. The factions within the city even united for a time, but on Octo-

ber 8 Aury and others led a revolt against the military commander who had defied Bolívar. By November the Cartagenans
were in a desperate condition, more than twenty-five hundred
dying of hunger and the rest eating beef hides and what Aury described as "a thousand other filthy things." Finally on December
6 Aury abandoned the defense and spent four hours sailing a fleet
of fourteen privateers and merchantmen loaded with refugees
past enemy guns to escape to San Domingue.[103]

Rough seas swamped several of the ships, and the Spaniards
captured others, but some captains made it through. One was
Jannet, who like Beluche and Aury had a legitimate commission
from Cartagena. He was almost the last to leave, carrying the
news to Bolívar that there was no hope for the city. Another was
William Mitchell, commanding the *Cometa* under the city's colors, with the fleeing governor of the city aboard. Once beyond
Spain's guns, he abruptly put ashore and marooned his passengers
on or near the island of San Andres after robbing them and
killing the governor. Not content with that, he attacked San
Andres, killed yet another governor and several others, gathered
plunder estimated at $40,000, and then took twenty slaves.[104] Fi-
nally on December 10 he boarded a Spanish vessel and relieved
her of some $25,000 in specie.[105]

It was a perfect example of how the violence and barbarity
that lay beneath the surface of privateering could suddenly and
frighteningly erupt once the restraints of legal pretense were removed. Given the choice between quitting their calling or continuing without proper commissions, some were willing to choose
the latter, and with it the implicit understanding that their plundering need have no limits, since they would face charges of
piracy anyway. The collapse of Cartagena negated any remaining
legitimacy of its privateering commissions. If the Laffites ever
had legitimate letters of marque from the infant republic, they
evaporated in the flames and the pillaging.[106]

This news shook the revolutionary representatives in Washington, just as it heartened Onís. In the capital Jean Laffite found and probably moved on the fringes of a small circle of insurgent agents, in whom Onís took much interest, and about whom he probably tried to secure information through Laffite. Garcia de Sena, an agent from Bolívar's new Venezuelan republic, was in Washington then, as was José Carrere, an agent from José de San Martín's insurgent Buenos Aires, now meeting with Baltimore privateers in hopes of emulating Cartagena's corsair policy. Pedro Gual was there acting for Bogotá and New Granada, which Bolívar hoped to join with Venezuela as the United Provinces of New Granada, and Manuel Rodríguez Torices, former governor of the now defunct Cartagena, was living in Philadelphia, where old General James Wilkinson spent his time writing his memoirs and probably mixing in the brew of intrigue.

Laffite met more than once with Gual in Washington, and discussed ambitions for several of the insurgent colonies. Gual told him he had high hopes that Washington would recognize New Granada before long. This boded well for the Laffites and their friends, of course, as an independent New Granada could grant letters of marque to privateers. Of more immediate and personal concern to Jean, though, was the news Gual had of Mexican affairs. Gual wrote to Toledo, and probably said to Jean, that if Vera Cruz and Tampico could not be taken soon, then the Congress in Mexico would need to open another port on its Gulf coast in order to establish an admiralty court and properly hand out commissions on its soil. At the same time Gual wrote to Mexican insurgent Luis Iturribarría to encourage his efforts. Ample armaments and everything else awaited them in Baltimore—information that Laffite may have provided after his visit to the city—if only the insurgents could open a port to receive them. The execution of Morelos was a blow, but still Gual felt optimistic. What he did not have was money.[107] On February 8, entirely unaware that Jean was now in the employ of Spain, Gual entrusted his correspondence to Laffite, who promised to deliver it to Toledo.

Laffite quite possibly took the letters directly to Onís, though the Spanish ambassador was already well informed of rebel movements thanks to his other spies. In late January 1816 he demanded that Washington take all measures to punish and disperse a "factious band of insurgents in Louisiana, and especially New Orleans" who were lighting revolutionary flames in Spain's provinces. He wanted Toledo and Herrera arrested, and warned that the two traitors were reviving the old plan for a marine assault on Tampico, along with an overland march into Texas.[108] His source was Sedella, who got his information from Picornell and Pierre Laffite. Pierre may also have written to his brother. In early February, speaking of Pierre Laffite, Onís affirmed to Apodaca "the great value this acquisition presents." He told Picornell to promise Pierre everything he asked.[109]

By the middle of February Jean was ready to return to New Orleans.[110] Jackson had left Washington at the beginning of the month, and it was clear that neither Congress nor the president were going to act on Jean's appeal for restitution. His arrangements for a new vessel or vessels were complete, and, more important now, he had his first assignment from his Spanish employers. Onís and Latour had persuaded him to accompany the engineer on a tour of Spanish land north and west of Louisiana, ostensibly a routine inspection and mapping expedition but really a chance to assess defenses and probe the vulnerability to attack by filibusters. Onís left for Philadelphia on February 13, after which Jean could not expect to receive more instructions in person and was free to depart.

By the middle of March he was back in Louisiana. He gave Pierre the letters from Gual, and Pierre promptly turned them over to Sedella, who would put them in the hands of the viceroy in Havana. It was Jean's first accomplished act of espionage. Now he saw his son for the first time. He also came back to a new home for his sporadic sojourns in New Orleans. In September Pierre and Marie Villard had sold her Dumaine Street house to a free colored woman, though Pierre had to witness the transaction for it to be lawful.[111] At the same time, to satisfy a debt, Marguerite Villard, probably Marie's mother, sold her old picket cabin at the corner of Dauphine and Orleans streets, where the brothers had probably spent some time on the gallery on summer evenings. Indeed, with its latrine and well, this might have been the place where Pierre spent the uncomfortable night in a well hiding from General Flournoy's guard. Marguerite had owned the place for almost twenty years, and Pierre witnessed her transaction, too.[112]

After satisfying Marguerite's debt, Pierre had moved the family to a rented accommodation, but already he was looking for a new house. Such things were apparently of little interest to Jean, for he never had and never would buy property. Even now his stay in the rented home lasted scarcely a fortnight. By the end of March he was gone again, joining Latour for their expedition and his first real mission as a Spanish spy.[113]

The only known alleged portrait from life of Pierre Laffite is this ghostly image, which survives today only in a poor reproduction of the original painted miniature. It surfaced in the hands of New Orleans antique dealer Joseph Pelletier in 1925, supposedly in effects belonging to General Daniel Morgan, with whom Pierre served at New Orleans in 1814-1815. Lyle Saxon saw the miniature in Pelletier's hands in the late 1920s and described it as showing a young man in a green coat with light brown hair drawn back over his ears. He suspected that it was painted in France circa 1797, but that was only a guess. Efforts to locate the original have been fruitless, and in the absence of it or any provenance establishing its authenticity, it can only be said that this *might* be Pierre Laffite.

New Orleans, *Times-Picayune,* August 23, 1925

The only known alleged portrait of Jean Laffite by someone who claimed to have known him, this crude sketch was supposedly done by a man named Lacassinier who said he worked for the Laffites in Galveston circa 1819. Joseph O. Dyer acquired it in 1874. There is no reason to suppose it to be an accurate depiction, and it could be complete invention.

Galveston, *Daily News,* September 19, 1926

In 1879 Homer Thrall published his *Pictorial History of Texas*, and in it included this woodcut by John R. Telfer depicting Jean Laffite. It may be pure imagination, though it shows evidence of being based in part on published descriptions available at the time. Still, regardless of his sources, it was drawn half a century after the fact by someone who never actually saw Laffite in the flesh. It remains the most popular image of the privateer.

Thrall, *Pictorial History of Texas*, 1879

The territories of Louisiana, Mississippi, and Spanish West Florida, as they appeared in 1806 in Barthélémy Lafon's outstanding map published that year, still a masterpiece of historical cartography. This was the America that the Laffites knew on coming to the New World.   Historic New Orleans Collection, Acc. No. 1971.52

UNDER MY WINGS EVERY THING PROSPERS

New Orleans as it looked to Pierre Laffite when he arrived in 1803, in an etching that year by John L. Boqueta de Woiseri. The view is down Levee Street, with the spires of the Cathedral Church of St. Louis at right center marking the location of the Place d'Arms.   Historic New Orleans Collection Acc. No. 1958.42

Governor William C. C. Claiborne endured a rocky relationship with the Laffites, first as their adversary, then as their erstwhile ally in defending New Orleans, but in the end he never regarded them as more than criminals.

George W. Cable, *The Creoles of Louisiana*, 1885

Top: Pierre Laffite's signature in March 1803 soon after his arrival in New Orleans. *Middle:* Pierre's signature in October 1811 when he sold a slave to Adelaide Masclari, showing the effects of his stroke the year before. *Bottom:* Pierre Laffite signs an October 7, 1819, report to Captain General Cagigal with his code name "No 13."

Top and middle, NONA; Bottom, Gobierno Superior Civil, Coleccion de Documentos del Archivo Nacional de Cuba, Havana, Legajo 492, Expediente 18688, microfilm at HNOC

Jean Laffite's earliest known signed document, February 5, 1813.   NONA

General Andrew Jackson
as he appeared when he
met with the brothers
Laffite in 1815.
Arsené Latour, *Historical
Memoir of the War in West
Florida and Louisiana in
1814–1815.* 1816

This crude 1837 woodcut is probably the first attempt to depict Jean Laffite in art.
In this instance he stands at left, looking distinctly unpiratical, while meeting with
Governor Claiborne at center and General Jackson at right.
Charles Ellms, *The Pirates Own Book,* 1837

The only known contemporary eyewitness depiction of a Laffite vessel is this January 7, 1819, watercolor by Benjamin Henry Latrobe entitled "View of the Balize at the Mouth of the Mississippi." As Latrobe's own caption shows, the tall masts with yardarms appearing above the trees at left belong to the USS *Firebrand*. It, of course, was formerly the Laffites' *Dorada*. A captured sloop formerly belonging to the pirate William Mitchell, probably taken in the September 1819 raid on Barataria, is tied up beneath the large signal tower.

Copy from original owned by the Maryland Historical Society, Baltimore

New Orleans as surveyed in 1816 by Barthélémy Lafon, the Laffites' sometime fellow corsair and soon to be their partner in spying for Spain. Bayou St. John, a route sometimes used by the smugglers to bring goods into the city, runs across the top of the map, one of its branches extending down into the western suburb of the city, a haunt of the smugglers after the War of 1812.

Historic New Orleans Collection, Acc. No. 1945.2

PLAN
DE
TROIS LOTS DE TERRE
DANS LA
MUNICIPALITE Nᵒ 1

RUE DAUPHINE.

ST PHILIPPE.

URSULINES.

RUE DES

RUE

RUE

RUE BOURBON.

No image of a Laffite dwelling survives other than this 1848 overhead site plan of the house owned in the name of Marie Louise Villard at the northeast corner of Bourbon and St. Philip Streets. It shows the house at the lower left corner of the lot, along with outbuildings. As of 1848 it had not changed from its 1816-20 appearance when the Laffites intermittently lived there.

Plan de Trois Lots de Terre de La Municipalite No. 1, Plan Book No. 72, Folio No. 27, March 28, 1848

"Père Antoine," Padre Antonio de Sedella, the zealous champion of Spain in the New World, spiritual leader of New Orleans and spymaster who helped enlist and then manage the Numbers 13, Pierre and Jean Laffite.

George W. Cable,
The Creoles of Louisiana, 1885

This crude woodcut depicts the death of Jean Laffite. It is probably based on published accounts from Captain Porter's squadron soon after the actual event in 1823, and while they were themselves inaccurate, still they likely echoed genuine current stories of the corsair's death.   Charles Ellms, *The Pirates Own Book,* 1837

New Orleans artist Edward Arnold's imaginative painting, "Interception by American Navy Frigates of Lafitte's Privateer Attacking A Merchant Vessel," painted in 1858. It is a fictional scene, of course. No privateer, and certainly not the Laffites', flew the skull and crossbones flag so popular in pirate fiction, nor did any of the corsairs risk taking on an armed frigate.   Courtesy of a private collection

He had the skill, when Cunning's gaze would seek
To probe his heart and watch his changing cheek
At once the observer's purpose to espy,
And on himself roll back his scrutiny,

THIRTEEN

A Career of Betrayals
1815-1816

DURING JEAN'S eight-month absence, Pierre maintained the Laffites' interests in New Orleans, as well as their roles in the projects of the "associates" and their emerging double life as Spanish spies. The Spaniards had known of the Laffites' flirtation with the filibusters and revolutionaries when the brothers conspired with Picornell in the abortive Tampico raid the year before.[1] Sedella was ever vigilant, as was Morphy, and the plotters seemed almost comically inept at keeping their plans secret. As early as March 4, 1815, an agent in Pensacola warned Apodaca of the threat to Tampico and Béxar, to be aided by "all of the indolent French, privateers, and Americans who served in the defense of New Orleans, and which Pirates' Crimes have been forgiven by the State Legislature."[2] When Cunningham took the *Eagle,* the *Presidente,* and the *Santa Rita,* the captured correspondence on them revealed the details of Toledo's plans, and hinted at tacit acquiescence by the United States government, which Apodaca's agent condemned for its "shocking dissimulating strategy." Apodaca was advised to halt all maritime communication between

Nautla or Vera Cruz and Barataria after Toledo's captured letters made it clear that the smugglers were involved with the revolutionaries, and that Governor Claiborne gave "very good Audience" to them. Rumor even held that the American government now conspired with the Baratarians to smuggle Spanish prize goods into New Orleans, with the result that insurance companies in the city refused to write policies on Spanish cargoes.[3]

When news arrived of the peace treaty, Apodaca feared that his troubles would only get worse, "because as I see it, these pirates will gain a new strength and vitality, and there is nothing else than the crude activity and braveness of our Royal Navy able to finish once and for all this mob infecting the Mexican essence and entirely annihilating the Spanish Commerce." Even before the return of the *Eagle*, Toledo sent another *goleta* to Nautla seeking money and an official diplomatic envoy to the United States. Apodaca feared that if this trip was successful, the filibusters' little force would experience a "big immigration of privateers and armorers and Military men of every kind."[4]

The capture of the *Eagle* and Toledo's arrest put a halt to the plotters' movements, but by July the men were ready to resume, and Pierre Laffite was to be very much involved. The intrusive Anaya was shunted aside, and Humbert, Toledo, and Gutiérrez took up again their idea of a joint land-sea operation. At first Toledo planned for Humbert and himself to lead the army that ships would convoy to Matagorda, while Gutiérrez would lead another overland from Natchitoches in northwestern Louisiana. They would rendezvous at La Bahía, an important colonial presidio, and then take the Spanish administrative center of Texas at San Antonio de Béxar. At the same time a fleet led by Dominque was to attack Tampico and establish a port on the Gulf coast to be controlled by the Mexican Congress.

But then Toledo fell out with Humbert. Now Major Henry Perry would take over Humbert's army, and Gambi, once free of his legal difficulties, stepped in for Dominique, who seems as usual to have gone his own way. The group made little attempt at secrecy, Perry publishing in New Orleans the call for one thousand men willing to invade Texas, which served as one of the catalysts for President Madison's September 1 proclamation. Soon arms and munitions openly came into New Orleans for Perry, and to Natchez for Gutiérrez, and volunteers passed on the road to Natchitoches. Pierre Laffite's role would be to cooperate in assembling and outfitting the ships, if they could be found.

Still Toledo needed money and a minister from the Congress to give the enterprise official sanction. By the end of May rumors began to circulate that Gambi might be leaving New Orleans suddenly, no doubt to prepare a vessel or vessels for the next part of the campaign.[5] In fact, Gambi was going to leave on the *Eagle*—still free on the bond posted by Amigoni—which Gambi took once more to calling the *Petit Milan*. In July, almost immediately after his acquittal in the district court, Toledo began preparations for a voyage to Boquilla de Piedras. He sent letters ahead to rebel leaders asking that they have an accredited diplomat there for him to bring back to Louisiana, promising that the United States would recognize the junta as soon as it received an envoy. At the same time, Toledo told the leaders to have money ready to pay for the arms he intended to bring.

This time Toledo had no need to worry about his ship being taken, for he had protection from Commodore Patterson. Patterson had agreed to have the *Firebrand* accompany the *Petit Milan* on the voyage. Ostensibly he was providing an escort to an American merchant ship, but the commodore knew the vessel would be carrying dispatches and munitions for the insurgents, and he did not send escorts with other merchant ships. Using a United States naval vessel to bring back the proceeds of a private mercantile transaction was hardly within the mandate of a naval officer. Patterson might have been encouraging the junta in consonance with a general pre–Monroe Doctrine hostility to a European power's presence in the New World. But in sending the *Firebrand* he went against the official neutral policy of his government, and risked something approaching recognition of an unauthorized junta, which could be very embarrassing for Madison if the junta fell, as it did. At the least the action appeared to run counter to the spirit of Madison's September 1815 proclamation, given that the proceeds of the voyage could be expected to help fund a filibustering attack on Mexico.

Patterson may not have been an actual investor or partner with the "associates," but he was doing their work. The investors secured arms and supplies to be loaded on the *Petit Milan,* and Morphy believed that Patterson gave Toledo goods from government storehouses. It seemed perhaps too coincidental that on October 1 someone broke into the federal arsenal and removed muskets and hundreds of uniforms. The *Petit Milan* had left port on September 2, but it was an old trick to load prohibited goods on a vessel somewhere downstream, or even at Barataria. Rendezvoused with the *Firebrand,* the *Petit Milan* sailed across the Gulf and reached Boquilla de Piedras early in October.

While the vessels were at sea, Spanish warships sank several insurgent schooners off Boquilla de Piedras. On October 6 the *Petit Milan* and the *Firebrand* arrived. The priest turned revolutionary José Manuel de Herrera was there to meet them. Better yet from the "associates'" point of view, he had with him $28,000 in specie to pay for the arms and matériel. While Toledo had arranged the voyage, Henry D. Peire had charge of the cargo on behalf of the New Orleans investors and Patterson. A recently discharged officer from the 44th Infantry who before the war had been a revenue agent trying to thwart the Laffites, Peire represented the "associates'" insistence that Herrera pay for the cargo on the spot. Herrera stood his ground, however, and in the end Peire unloaded the goods and agreed to allow Herrera to pay the investors directly once he reached New Orleans. That done, the vessels set sail on October 11, and just over two weeks later tied up at the wharf in New Orleans.[6]

No doubt Herrera felt rather put upon when, before any official reception or welcome, merchant West demanded full payment for the cargo and charged him almost double the value of the twelve hundred muskets delivered. Herrera had almost no choice but to hand over the money though he knew he was being cheated. This incident made it evident that for all their protestations of commitment to Mexican independence, the "associates" were in it for the profit. Even when West agreed to accept part of the payment in cash and the balance on a note, Herrera was left with far too little to accomplish the original purpose for his money, the outfitting of Toledo's expeditions.[7] West persuaded Herrera to ask his Congress for another $100,000, and Patterson obligingly offered the *Firebrand* to carry Herrera and his dispatches to Mexico in order that he might return safely with any messages or money the Mexican junta sent. After landing Herrera at Vera Cruz, the *Firebrand* would wait off the coast for a month. Meanwhile Patterson began fitting out the ketch the *Surprise* to transport a printing press, more correspondence, and printed proclamations that Toledo would write, all designed to incite the insurgents to take Tampico and Vera Cruz to provide a port for more commerce.[8]

When Herrera wrote to his superiors, he kept from them the embarrassing manner of his reception in New Orleans, and instead told them that officials had received him warmly. He dissembled further when he said that he had put together a company "composed of the most respectable & opulent citizens and traders," in order to assist the junta with military aid. He named those he thought most committed to what he called his "Patriotic" association, including Bean, West, Livingston, and Peire, and claimed that Claiborne had orders from Washington to protect the revolutionaries and treat their agents kindly. He said that he had persuaded Patterson to carry his correspondence on the *Firebrand* under pretext of cruising, and to bring back the junta's correspondence and the money he requested. He also asked that letters of marque be sent him to hand out in New Orleans, revealing yet again the concerns of the "associates."[9]

Herrera's stay in New Orleans was necessarily brief before he returned to Mexico on his mission. Meanwhile the "associates" sent the *Petit Milan* on another voyage delivering munitions, and she made a third trip in January 1816 before the court finally seized her for auction.[10] Laméson had lost the *Presidente* by this time, but he took over the schooner *Indiana* and made the voyage to Boquilla de Piedras with more goods for the rebels, a run he would make several times in the next year. Pierre Laffite had also been preparing to put a ship into the business. He had bought the *Presidente* when the court auctioned it late that summer, probably with some of the proceeds from the restitution Jean had secured in July or with financial backing from some of the "associates." By September the ship was his.

Pierre engaged a carpenter to make repairs to the main deck, including removing the base for a pivot gun, which suggested that he intended to use her as a conventional merchantman. His cargo was to be muskets for the revolutionaries, but in the true spirit of profiteering, he would not sell new muskets. Rather, in October he and his backers acquired close to five hundred worn and damaged weapons left over from the war. Pierre took them to gunsmith Theon Barberet on Toulouse Street, showed him a letter from Humbert, and told him the guns were for the general. He gave Barberet a month to repair them and then had them delivered to the house he shared with Marie and Catherine and the children.[11]

In addition to West, Toledo and Herrera met with others of what Morphy later described as "the principal armorers and captains of the Baratarian pirates."[12] One of them was Pierre Laffite. He asked Toledo to pay him in full for the used guns and take charge of sailing them to Mexico, but Toledo declined, not least because Herrera's funds were already depleted and Toledo did not have enough left for his own purposes. Laffite also spoke with Herrera, asking him to undertake to get the *Presidente* to Mexico to deliver dispatches and goods, but he, too, refused.[13] There would be no easy money derived from them now on, and there was no certainty of the depth of the pockets of the Congress in Mexico.

Pierre decided on a change of plan. He engaged his own captain, Louis Fougard, and told Toledo when they met in the city street one day that he planned to sail the *Presidente* to St. Bartholomew's in the Leeward Islands.[14] Yet a few days later on November 6 Pierre had auctioneer Francois Dutillet sell the *Presidente*. Officially the buyer was Charles Parent, and he certainly paid Laffite, and Pierre paid Dutillet his commission. In fact, however, the vessel went to a partnership of shareholders, all of them New Orleans merchants, and they were almost certainly a front for Pierre. Made in a public forum, the sale was meant to divert the prying official eyes that might look into anything with which the Laffites were connected.[15]

By November 25 Herrera was back from Mexico and disillusioned by the mercenary nature of the people with whom he was dealing. In a November 26 letter he advised the Congress that they should "proceed with the greatest caution in the mode of accepting their services and offers," and should withhold the letters of marque, which would be used for rank piracy.[16] The Laffites were just as disappointed in the "associates." West had gobbled up most of Herrera's cash before Laffite could get at him. Duncan had his own vessel now, having bought the *General Bolivar* and converted her to the *General Jackson,* and was pursuing his own interests, as was Sauvinet. The big merchant backers were going to look out for themselves. Once they had enough of their own vessels such as Duncan's, especially with independent mariners such as Gambi and Dominique able to enlist all the crewmen required, they might have no need for the Laffite brothers, and no need to share any increasingly illusory profits.

Someone else in New Orleans perceived this shift. Morphy had watched for a year as enthusiasm for Mexican independence grew in New Orleans. He saw how men such as Toledo or the Baratarians and their backers "hope to make a quick fortune." When Picornell indicated his wish to return to the Spanish fold the past spring, Onís dangled a pardon before him while putting him to work. Onís told him that he could prove himself deserving of clemency if he broke up the Tampico plot and that those involved included the Laffites. To give Picornell some ammunition, Onís lied, telling him 160,000 *soldados* were ready in the mother country, and 25,000 of them would soon be sent to Mexico to put down the rebels. That would make filibustering hopeless, indeed suicidal. "There is nothing more effective for strengthening the good intentions of a man who has just forsaken a bad cause than to persuade him that the plans of the revolutionists will be disrupted and their atrocities punished with the severity they deserve," Onís told an associate in August.[17] Yet the ambassador also held out the clemency that Picornell was to receive as a carrot for winning over others. Speaking for the king, Onís told him to "assure unfaithful ones in his name that they will find his arms open from the day that they submit and forever unless they commit new offenses."[18]

But first Spain had to know what was happening inside the counsels of the plotters. In fact, almost everyone knew the outline of the plot from the outset. John Dick knew something was going on as early as July. Though he felt an ardent sympathy with the liberation movements in Spanish America, he warned the attorney general that up to five hundred well-armed men, including former United States Army officers, were gathered at Belle Isle, a point of land at the mouth of Bayou Atchafalaya. They would be taken by sea to Matagorda and then march on La Bahía and thence to San Antonio. He also heard rumors of a one thousand-strong expedition gathering at Natchitoches, with more men expected from Kentucky and Tennessee. He was not sure who commanded the Belle Isle crowd, but he suspected it was Perry.[19] Claiborne learned of it the same day, and confided his concern to the secretary of state in Washington. "The Civil authority of Louisiana is not competent to the suppression of these Expeditions, and if the Government wants them put down, force must be applied," he advised. As usual, the people of the state seemed in favor of such enterprises, and he confessed that there was an impression among the people that the filibusters "are secretly countenanced by the administration."[20]

Of course, despite official protestations, including Madison's September proclamation, Washington did tacitly approve of the filibusters. Madison hoped for a repeat of the West Florida experience, in which locals wrested territory from Spain in their own name, then affiliated themselves with the United States. Indeed, the United States believed that it rightfully owned Texas, at least as far west as the Nueces River, as part of the Louisiana Purchase. The resumption of full diplomatic relations between the United States and Spain in June had opened negotiations to settle the western boundary of Louisiana, but if filibusters took Texas in the meantime and handed it over to Madison, so much the better in weakening Spain's position at the table.

And so Washington did not respond to advice of the expeditions with celerity. Indeed, for months it did not respond at all. Meanwhile the Spaniards watched in frustration throughout the summer as the preparations continued under their noses. A loyal Spaniard in Vera Cruz had learned of the plot from an insurgent as early as May.[21] When Perry left New Orleans on July 10 with close to four hundred men, a very well-informed Spaniard sent word to officials in Texas of the filibusters' passing down Bayou Lafourche, and warned that they intended to embark on vessels for Matagorda to march on La Bahía. They had no artillery or cavalry with them, and appeared to be poorly organized, he thought. Toledo was not with them, having fallen out with the plot's leaders. Three days later Teodoro Martinez learned of the expedition expected to come overland, and warned of that, too.[22]

More detailed intelligence on the second part of the invasion came from a citizen of Natchitoches who happened to be named Paul Bouet Lafitte, though of no relation to the brothers Laffite. On July 21 his sons Cezar and Luis returned from a visit to Natchitoches, where they had seen Humbert dressed like a herdsman in a deerskin jacket, on foot and passing through in a great hurry with about fifty men on their way to the rendezvous on the Louisiana side of the Sabine. Revealing yet more of the infighting among the filibusters, Humbert let it be known that he thought Toledo an impostor. Displaying his commission as a major general, received from Gutiérrez two weeks earlier before he left New Orleans, Humbert tried to enlist those he encountered by promising that the expedition was well funded, with "plenty of money in Laffites vessels."[23]

Watching the preparations at close range, Morphy divined almost exactly the same details, of which he advised Apodaca on July 20. By mid-August Onís in Philadelphia knew the full outline of the latest scheme "to repeat the horror scenes, robbery and murder" of the 1813 Gutiérrez expedition. He expected a "Corps of Adventurers" from Kentucky and Tennessee to join the Louisianans in a concentration at the Sabine, where they would be led by "the monsters Bernardo Gutiérrez, Toledo, Anaya, Humbert and their gang." He knew that bronze cannon and one thousand muskets had been shipped from New Orleans to Natchez to be taken overland to Natchitoches, and that rations for the soldiers had been sent to the ships to be commanded by "the famous pirate Vincente Gamby." Gambi would transport the "tramp army" to the mouth of the Sabine, and from there it would march upstream to invade. Onís complained to Monroe of the facilities given to rebel privateers in United States ports, but had no illusions that anything would be done.[24]

Dick protested that in recent months Hall's court had seized and returned to their original owners nine Spanish prize ships fitted out in United States ports, but Onís regarded this as a mere gesture, and so it was.[25] All Morphy had to do was stand in the street in New Orleans and watch as merchant banker Benjamin Morgan busily bought all the muskets, pistols, and sabers he could get from private homes and shipped them, along with food, in pirogues to Barataria where the naval contingent was to gather. Convinced that the United States was behind this latest enterprise, Morphy warned Apodaca that it might involve seven or eight vessels mounting more than twenty cannon in all, with additional launches and pirogues transporting six hundred to eight hundred volunteers and another four hundred to five hundred from the United States Army. The good news was that the plotters were squabbling among themselves as usual, all asserting the right to command and "disputing the authority of the Chief." Morphy warned everyone he could, sending word to Apodaca by a special sailboat.[26]

By November 16 Morphy knew that Perry had left the Louisiana coast the month before. When news of Madison's September proclamation reached Louisiana, it made Perry's position precarious. Even before then on September 5 Patterson, satisfied that there was substance to the reports of filibusters massing on Belle Isle, sent Lieutenant Cunningham with his gunboat to disperse them, by force if necessary.[27] Perry knew it was getting too warm for him in Louisiana. Indeed, three Spaniards who wanted to join Perry in his campaign were made so fearful by rumors of

Americans and loyal Spaniards watching the byways, waiting to kill them, that they never left New Orleans, but stayed at Pierre Laffite's home.[28] In October Perry embarked a first contingent of his command and landed them at what he would name Bolívar Point opposite the eastern end of Galveston Island. When the rest of his men had been transported there they would move on to Matagorda, and when Gutiérrez arrived overland, they would attack. Paul Lafitte learned of the movement and advised authorities in Mexico that "Laffite's vessels" were a part of the operation, "but their only object is plunder."[29]

Through the summer and fall Picornell worked with Morphy in trying to penetrate the conspirators and set the leaders against one another. This required little effort, of course. Morphy helped to discredit Anaya, and employed three men to infiltrate the lower ranks of plotters or backers. Picornell, meanwhile, instituted legal proceedings against some Baratarians who cooperated with Toledo, though not against the Laffites, and at some risk to himself harbored witnesses in his home pending their testimony.[30] Even then, however, neither Picornell nor Morphy had enough discretionary cash to buy information, and Onís could not help since his own funds were limited.[31]

Thus Picornell saw with dismay Toledo's return from Mexico with both money and Herrera. Picornell decided he must penetrate their schemes by "attracting to our party one of the persons who were in the secret of all the plans and trusted in part with their execution." Studiously, he considered "the character of each one of those who met in the secret councils"—Livingston, Davezac, Duncan, West, Grymes, Nolte, Patterson, even Duplessis, and of course the Laffites—and concluded that his best option lay with Pierre Laffite, "whom I thought the most proper and the easiest." Picornell's reasons for settling on the elder brother as "the easiest" are not hard to surmise. Because the Laffites did not have the money to be major investors or outfitters, their potential gain would be less than that of their associates, and their role essentially reduced to hired transport. Privateering profit might be available to them if a port issuing commissions were opened on the Mexican coast, but having just escaped from the indictments of the federal court, Pierre and Jean might be reluctant to put themselves at risk again. The risk was twofold since they had taken or been involved in the plunder of enough Spanish vessels to expect summary treatment if they should fall into the hands of Spaniards while corsairing the Gulf. More simply, their Baratarian establishment was gone and the Laffites no longer commanded the authority they once enjoyed. Moreover, Pierre was almost always short of cash.

Picornell hoped to show Pierre that the path of his self-interest led away from the filibusters and toward an alliance with Spain, especially if Apodaca could include cash in return and the promise of royal forgiveness for past acts against Spanish shipping. Picornell first spoke with Pierre on the subject in early fall. Pierre went out of his way to magnify his importance and to make himself a more attractive target. He told the Spaniard that he and Jean were the sons of a Spanish mother and had been raised among Spaniards, which was why they had always shown kindness to their Spanish prisoners. He convinced Picornell that he was "good and honest in meeting his obligations," which many a New Orleans creditor might have challenged, and went on to exaggerate the Laffite brothers' influence among the Creole and San Domingan people of Louisiana while averring that he felt nothing but hatred for the Americans. Picornell left without a commitment from Pierre Laffite but convinced that "this man alone if furnished with means of offering some payment to his people will easily be able to ruin the projects that our enemies are forming in the Gulf."[32]

Picornell had gone fishing, and taken the bait himself. In fact, the Laffites' friend Latour believed that Pierre had initiated the business by offering to spy for Sedella, and Picornell was getting information on insurgent activities from an unidentified source as early as February 1815. Hopes for such a shift in the Laffites' endeavors could even have been behind Jean's trip to Washington, as the brothers adjusted to the changing landscape. Just as likely, Pierre exaggerated his role to Latour as he would to Picornell. Without question, however, Pierre Laffite had long ere this assessed Picornell and Sedella as carefully as they evaluated him now.

Then in mid-November, days after Toledo and Herrera disappointed Pierre's hopes for his shipment of used guns, New Orleans merchant Angel Benito de Ariza returned to town. He had helped to turn Picornell's loyalty the year before, and now he joined him in the courting of Laffite. In a series of meetings over several days Picornell pressed his suit, and finally Laffite let himself be won. Picornell and Ariza arranged to take Laffite to the corner of Orleans Street behind the church, to the rude hut of "Père Antoine" on the evening of November 17. There Sedella, who commanded the confidence of Apodaca far more than they did, would give his approval and witness Laffite's promises. If Pierre later tried to back out, no one would doubt the priest should he speak publicly. Even if they did not come to terms, Pierre could not retreat without risking his willingness to betray his associates becoming known. That could be fatal. The meeting went well. Pierre told the padre, dressed no doubt as usual in a coarse dark brown habit, that "being informed as he was of all secrets, plans and projects that were forming at this time and in this city by the traitor Toledo, the insurgent José Manual Herrera and the rest," he would advise the Spaniards of whatever he learned well in time for them to "not only avoid but destroy these plans entirely." With typical boldness, Pierre offered to confirm for Apodaca what he said "by any required test, over any of the themes he had indicated or he was about to indicate."

In return Pierre asked for a general pardon from Spain for himself and two others, one no doubt Jean and the other probably Fougard, and of course for payment commensurate with his services. He also said that he had two ships, the *Presidente* and likely the one that Jean was purchasing in the East, and for them he wanted safe passes in case they were captured by Spanish warships. He promised to give the Spaniards advance notice of the vessels' sailings including their purposes and destinations. Showing that the business of clandestine operations came naturally to his turn of mind, he also asked that, should his ships be taken, Morphy pursue the usual legal action against them so as not to arouse suspicion. He demanded an early agreement to his terms, or he would regard the deal as void. Then as evidence of good faith, he told them what he knew of Toledo and Herrera's plans, with some embellishment to make his information seem more valuable. They intended to foment and coordinate rebellion in several Spanish provinces in the New World, he said, and had negotiated contracts with several American firms to manufacture arms and artillery. At that very moment, he said, a vessel was outfitting in New Orleans to take the contracts to the Congress for its approval. It was also to deliver two thousand muskets and a printing press to produce proclamations calling citizens to arms in rebellion.

Of course Pierre spoke of the *Surprise,* and on its return it was to bring money from the Congress and any specie that could be captured from Spanish money trains between Vera Cruz and Mexico City. The plotters wanted to open two ports to supply their expeditions, he said, one at Tampico in the coming spring, and the other immediately near Matagorda. Humbert and fifty men had already left for the Sabine, where his force would train and wait for Toledo to arrive with five hundred more recruited for what they were told was a "secret expedition." They would be well armed and organized into companies of infantry, cavalry, and artillery, along with two companies of mechanics and artisans, so that they could fully establish the new port. Meanwhile armed vessels would depart New Orleans to clear Spanish shipping. Toledo was to be commander in chief of the movement, and had fifteen hundred military commissions to hand out and a proclamation being printed in his name calling on men of every nation to join him and promising rich rewards. Pierre had heard Toledo say that he expected to enlist more than two thousand men in Louisiana alone, many of them expelled from Cuba and anxious to get even with Spain and make a new nation. Toledo had also met with the leaders of the "former pirates" of Barataria, said Laffite, and promised to issue them letters of marque from the new Mexican regime. Within six weeks he expected to have a new port established at Boquilla de Piedras, and would furnish them with signals for entering the port safely. Any who came with his letters would be commissioned a state armed privateer. Laffite attested that Toledo was working long hours every day with his ministers preparing the regulations of their enterprise and new regime. That Pierre considerably exaggerated the state of Toledo's preparedness in order to enhance his own value to his listeners is clear. It worked, for they were all the more delighted with their catch, not realizing that they were swallowing his bait as well.

If Spain gave him the protections he asked for, "and could supply the indispensable pecuniary aid" he needed, then even as bad as things were Pierre believed they could thwart Toledo and Herrera. He urged secrecy, and asked that his name not be used in any communication for fear its interception by the wrong parties could compromise him just as Picornell had been compromised. He also now or soon hereafter told Sedella that he thought Spain ought to assign an agent to New Orleans, with the power to make unilateral decisions on behalf of the king, and the financial resources to take action. This made sense operationally for Spain, but it also made sense for Laffite, who could then ply his persuasions directly on a decision maker with instant access to substantial funds. At the end of the meeting Picornell and Sedella thanked Pierre heartily and promised to communicate all he had said to their superiors and to do their best to meet his terms and secure an early decision from Apodaca. Laffite told them this was good enough for him and that, to show his good faith, he would continue to feed them information in the meantime.[33]

Sedella was delighted. A few days later he informed Apodaca that they had secured "a person, that is understood to be very well informed of all up to date plots," and who wanted in return only money and protection. Having taken Pierre's injunction to secrecy seriously, Père Antoine would say no more since "the importance of this project demands the most strict caution and silence." In fact, he sent Ariza to Havana to inform the viceroy orally. He followed this with another urgent petition for acceptance of Laffite, whom he referred to as "the newly converted one," adding, "I am fully persuaded that he will be able to perform most important services for His Majesty in circumstances so critical as those we are in."[34] Onís approved Pierre's terms from Washington and promised to secure them from Madrid.[35]

Within ten days Pierre began sending Sedella information on the supplies and munitions being shipped to the Sabine. On November 27 Laffite sat with the "associates" as they discussed their final preparations and read correspondence from leaders of volunteers coming from Tennessee and Kentucky announcing that they could not reach New Orleans before December 21. The assembled decided to send Toledo upriver one week earlier to meet them on the road and lead them to the Sabine. The council also determined to send word to Gambi and the corsairs that their new port on the Texas coast would be ready in six weeks, meaning the armada could depart in mid-January.

That evening or the next morning Pierre visited Sedella and gave him a detailed account of the meeting. The padre immediately wrote to Apodaca. He suggested that a few Spanish vessels cruise the Texas coast, their presence being perhaps enough to retard or discourage a landing. Since it was a little known coast-line, he also advised that Spanish captains acquaint themselves with its inlets and bays, for the time when the filibusters actually did make a landing. Pierre told the Spanish to keep an eye particularly on the coast from Galveston to Matagorda, including both bays as possibilities. At the same time Laffite told Sedella the names of the men who had contracted with Toledo to provide arms and munitions. The 29,000 muskets alone, at $12 apiece, came to almost $350,000, and they along with 9,000 saddles were to be delivered to the Mexican coast providing that Toledo promised to buy from no one else. The merchants were Nolte, Duncan, John B. Gilly of Gravier Street, and Thomas Harman of Royal Street. Attorneys Livingston and Grymes were also on the list. Grymes was no longer an officer of the federal court, but collector Duplessis and Commodore Patterson brought to their membership in the "associates" a suggestion of conflict with their professional duties.[36] Patterson's use of the *Firebrand* called into question his motives, while as an investor at least Duplessis acted as a private citizen, apparently making no use of public funds or facilities to advance an enterprise from which he would profit. Meanwhile he continued his vigilance against smugglers, for everything he captured from them put a percentage in his pocket. Thus Laffite did not betray only the filibuster leaders, but also his fellow merchants, and it is hard not to suspect that he was evening scores with some like Nolte, who had been the loudest critic of the Laffites during the heyday of their smuggling enterprise.

As Sedella finished his letter to the viceroy, Pierre called on him again, having just learned that the plot's leaders had decided since the meeting of the previous day that an initial landing would take place on the coast between the mouth of the Mermenteau River, thirty miles east of the Sabine, and the mouth of the Nueces, more than 270 miles along the Gulf coast. That span included both Galveston and Matagorda, yet was remarkably unspecific, suggesting that Pierre knew more than he was telling and wanted to parcel out his information in order to exaggerate his usefulness. Indeed, the Spaniards already knew the landing would be at Galveston or Matagorda, and soon enough would know that Perry was already at a place he named Bolívar Point on Galveston Bay. Pierre did tell Sedella, though, that this unspecified point was where Toledo was to bring the Kentucky and Tennessee volunteers when they arrived. In the meeting Toledo said he would decide on the exact landing point after he received word from pilots he sent to investigate the harbors and the depths of the passes connecting them to the Gulf. Pierre promised to pass that news along as soon as he learned of it. Meanwhile he showed Sedella the pattern of the newly designed flag of the Mexican republic, sixteen horizontal oblong blocks of alternating blue and white inside a red border, giving a checkerboard effect. Thus forewarned, Apodaca's vessels ought to be able to identify the filibuster transport and supply ships when they were spotted. And thus Pierre betrayed Gambi and any number of his comrades of past years, many of whom could expect a rope and a yardarm if captured thanks to his information.

Laffite also gave Sedella a growing list of participants in the mix of merchants and businessmen, military authorities, filibusters, and adventurers who made up the guiding hands of the Texas scheme. Livingston appeared to be the overall head of the Louisianans, who included Grymes, Duncan, Duncan's partner West, Duplessis the customs collector, Morgan, Patterson, Perry and Peire, and Aury's financial agent François Dupuis.[37] This only convinced Sedella the more of Laffite's worth, and he implored Apodaca to send a fully empowered confidential aid to New Orleans to satisfy Apodaca of the value of Laffite. This done, Sedella could arrange with Pierre everything they might have to do, as well as arrange for Pierre's payment.[38] Sedella also wanted to have Apodaca's agent in New Orleans now that Toledo had returned from Boquilla de Piedras with Herrera and a return voyage with the *Firebrand* was being planned.[39] Sedella would have been a little less agitated had he known that Herrera's faction in the Mexican Congress had been ousted from power and that, as with Toledo before him, Herrera's credentials were now meaningless. Herrera hoped to leave shortly for Washington, but knew already that the mission would probably be fruitless.[40]

Pierre's request for a "general oblivion" of his past acts against Spain may have been unnecessary. Ferdinand VII had issued a blanket pardon when he regained the throne of Spain late in 1814, and that had been sufficient for some revolutionaries such as Picornell to switch sides. Never having been a Spanish subject and having been involved with Cartagena, Pierre might have believed he needed a more specific clemency. Probably what he wanted was a pardon that cleared the way for the Laffites if circumstances required that they emigrate to a Spanish possession.

Within days of Pierre's agreement with Picornell and Sedella, his action in selling the *Presidente* became more suspect. The ship changed name to the *Dos Hermanos,* a phrase conveniently Spanish that meant in English *Two Brothers,* a popular merchant ship name and an almost unmistakable reference to the Laffites. She flew the flag of Cartagena, the republic that had but days to live, and prepared to put out of New Orleans under Fougard for her announced destination St. Bartholomew's. Unfortunately, the authorities suspected ship and cargo.

On December 5 a mysterious man whom many recognized but could not name approached a drayman on the levee and asked him if he would use his wagon to transport a shipment of arms to Belle Isle off the coast, where the *Two Brothers* would pick it up. It was probably Pierre Laffite. The next day, Duplessis warned Patterson of the vessel. Though she cleared the customs house identified as the property of Charles Parent, the collector was convinced that the vessel "belongs to Laffite." He thought it likely that she would fit out within United States territorial waters for corsairing, and he asked the commodore to loan him a boat to use in inspecting her before she left.[41] On inspection officers found two arms chests, a magazine, and space for a cannon, but no weapons. There were no separate cabins for officers, a common feature of privateers.[42] As for Fougard, it soon became known that he had boasted that he was going to privateer for Cartagena and would not discriminate in taking British and Spanish prizes, though America was at peace with both. This was enough; the authorities seized the vessel on suspicion of unlawfully fitting out.[43]

This was not what Pierre had expected. Fougard's comments about taking Spanish ships may well have been part of Laffite's strategy to conceal his arrangement with Spain. Almost at once Laffite and Parent approached Toledo and asked him to buy the ship on behalf of the Mexican junta, which would have legitimized the craft and protected it in court. When Toledo found that the court had no intention of releasing the vessel, however, he pursued the matter no further. What he and Herrera could and did do was to testify that Pierre had not asked them for a Mexican commission.[44] That, plus the absence of weapons, would eventually beat the charge of intent to privateer, and the *Dos Hermanos* would be released to Laffite before the winter was out.

Meanwhile the information furnished by Laffite percolated throughout Spanish officialdom. By January 6, 1816, all the officials in Cuba knew of the Toledo scheme, and of the role of what Apodaca called "a Frenchman named Laffite" in uncovering it.[45] They knew, too, that the *Firebrand* returned from her second, clearly unlawful voyage to Boquilla de Piedras carrying contracts signed by the Mexican Congress for the purchase of arms. Laffite told Sedella that Toledo and the *Petit Milan* were scheduled to fulfill the contracts with another arms shipment to Boquilla de Piedras. Meanwhile he reported that Toledo had five vessels preparing for the landing, which he now confirmed was to be at Matagorda, and that Toledo had also contracted for the manufacture of torches and rockets to set Spanish-held towns ablaze. Pierre assured Sedella that he and Picornell could do a lot in the city to stall these preparations if he had money, even convincing the padre that with enough financial support he could single-handedly defeat the planned landing.[46] The news that the *Surprise* had reached New Orleans on December 20, 1815, with another $13,000 for Herrera only added weight to Pierre's argument that he needed Spanish money to fight rebel money.[47] To leaven this diet of bad news, Laffite could only add that the reinforcement of the awaiting invasion forces had slowed, and even suffered one disaster. On November 20 some eighty men were sailing to join Perry at Bolívar Point when their vessel lost its bottom in the shallows around Galveston and most went down with their ship.[48]

By early January 1816 the information Pierre gave Sedella and Picornell had also reached Onís in Washington.[49] Onís now mounted an offensive against the American State Department, showing damning evidence of the involvement of Patterson, Duplessis, and others. The problem was that negotiations over the Louisiana boundary had resumed along with diplomatic relations between Spain and the United States, making it inopportune to be too strident. In this situation full and accurate intelligence on conditions in that part of Spain's colonies, as well as on the schemes of the filibusters, was absolutely vital. Chance and calculation had placed the Laffites in exactly the right spot at the right time.

The lip's least curl, the lightest paleness thrown
Along the govern'd aspect, speak alone
Of deeper passions; and to judge their mien,
He, who would see, must be himself unseen.

FOURTEEN

Distant Horizons
1816

WHEN Onís AND Latour engaged Jean Laffite to accompany the engineer on his expedition into the interior beyond Louisiana, they may not have shared with Jean the full background of the trip. The enemies of Spain—including the United States—might make use of this area to stage or support campaigns against Texas. Spain also hoped to recover some of its lost territory in the vast Louisiana region, an important topic in the coming boundary negotiations, and feared especially the spread of Americans into the portion of the territory to the north called the Arkansas. Already traders from that region were journeying several hundred miles westward to the Spanish mercantile outpost at Santa Fe. Spain needed the post's rich fur and mineral trade. Moreover, Santa Fe was the vital link for trade and communications with Spanish territory in California and with the Pacific. The settlers in Arkansas could well be the first wave of a tide of Americans that would sweep westward, ignoring Spain's territorial rights, and fomenting in Santa Fe the same unrest that now threatened uprisings in Texas and Mexico.

Spain could not afford to lose Santa Fe, and to that end Onís and his masters needed to ascertain the sentiments of the Spaniards and the Indians there, the extent of the Americans' inroads, and what support, if any, filibusters could expect from the inhabitants. This was Latour's assignment, guised as a geographical survey—though the survey was real, for Spain needed to know more about the defensible parts of the empire and its resources. Latour was the right man for the job, and he needed a job, as he was virtually bankrupt, his architectural business in New Orleans foundering and his as-yet-unpublished book showing little promise of making him rich. And though Laffite may have been recruited chiefly because he was handy and he was Latour's friend, he was for some of the information Latour needed to gather the right man to accompany him.[1]

Latour and Laffite probably spent much of their time prior to departure engaging boats and boatmen, waiting for spring rains to raise the river, and devising an itinerary based on Onís's instructions and what they learned talking with Indians and trappers.[2] During this brief time in New Orleans, Pierre and Jean exchanged their separate views and experiences leading to their liaison with Spain, Pierre having much to impart on the filibusters' plans and activities during Jean's absence. This update would inform Jean's observations during the expedition, and while Jean was gone, Pierre would continue listening on behalf of both the brothers and Spain, for each could profit from what he heard.[3]

Sometime in March Jean left New Orleans, either with Latour or else with plans to meet him up the Mississippi.[4] They went to the mouth of the Arkansas, and then up that stream a few miles to the old Spanish settlement of Arkansas Post. Arkansas Post had originally been not much more than a rectangular stockade, sitting about two hundred yards back from the bank, but the fort had been in ruin for fifty years. Now fewer than three hundred people lived in the outpost, and because the low sandy soil was subject to annual flooding and not very good for cultivation, they subsisted mainly by hunting. Each year they sent bear oil, tallow, salted bison, and pelts to New Orleans.[5] The Arkansas River was being intensely worked by trappers, and Arkansas Post attracted ambitious men from all quarters. Even Pierre might have made it this far up the Mississippi during his days as a merchant at Point Coupée, for that Louisiana post received furs from the far west brought down via the Arkansas.[6] Arkansas Post was a good place to sound the temper of men living in the region, and those passing farther through, and Laffite and Latour remained through the rest of the spring gathering information from trappers and travelers coming east.

This trade in furs made the settlement important despite its small population. Most of the permanent residents were French Canadians and Americans, though some distinguished Spaniards remained, none more distinguished than Don Carlos de Villemont, commander of Arkansas Post until the turnover to the United States in 1803. Now he owned more than twelve thousand acres along the Mississippi, and he and his wife and several children were American citizens. Universally liked and respected, he displayed impeccable manners and high principles, and was a sociable and cheerful host to visitors, as Laffite and Latour found on their arrival.[7] They also became acquainted with Frederick Notrebe, the township justice for Arkansas County.[8] Indeed, since Notrebe traded frequently in New Orleans, he and Laffite may have been acquainted already.[9]

Latour and Laffite tried to keep their mission a secret, even adopting false names—Laffite calling himself "Captain Hillare" and Latour becoming John Williams—but the people at Arkansas Post soon realized who Jean was, possibly because Notrebe recognized him. Latour and Laffite noted the frustration people expressed with Washington. The Creoles among them had been lax in registering their old French and Spanish land grants with the new American regime, and now found themselves at risk of losing their land and feeling aggrieved at the United States. "They know the Americans and cordially hate them," said Latour. They would welcome a return of Spanish authority.[10]

By early July Latour and Laffite had moved upriver to Pine Bluff, where they visited with the widower François Catejan de Vaugine, a native of Bayou Teche who had been appointed judge of the court of common pleas by the governor of the territory in 1804, William Clark. Laffite and Vaugine became friendly enough that the judge engaged Jean to witness a property transaction on July 4.[11] Sometime after July 4 Laffite and Latour were ready to go on. By this time they had another companion on the journey, the surveyor Louis Bringier. Pierre Laffite may have known him slightly, for Bringier lived on Canal Street in New Orleans until 1810 and was frequently sighted at the city's gaming parlors. He had also taken part in some business transactions in Ascension at the time Pierre was moving *El Bolador*'s slaves through that parish. Bringier left Louisiana to explore the Arkansas and Missouri territory, chiefly scouting for spots to mine gold on public lands.

Not too many months ago Bringier had petitioned Congress to enact legislation allowing citizens to exploit minerals on public lands west of the Mississippi, and though Congress did not respond to his entreaty, the Public Lands Committee did report on February 13, 1816, a recommendation for a bill allowing the president to grant leases or permits on an ad hoc basis. This was enough to encourage Bringier to pursue his prospecting. Interestingly, if Bringier made his petition in person, then he was in Washington at the same time as Laffite and Latour, and the three meeting now in Arkansas Post may not have been mere serendipity. By joining together, Bringier gained company and possible assistance on his prospecting, and Latour and Laffite had the advantage of Bringier's prior travels up the Arkansas.[12]

The three set out in keelboats and barges with crews to pole their way up the Arkansas, bringing provisions to last them several months, as well as arms for protection and some of Bringier's mining equipment and tools. They stopped first at the plantation of Daniel Wright, located a few miles below a land feature known as the Little Rock. Laffite and Wright became acquainted enough that a year later Wright entrusted Jean with his power of attorney to sell a slave for him in New Orleans.[13] From Wright's they moved upstream, a dozen miles past the Little Rock until they came to Crystal Hill on the north bank.[14] Bringier lived there, and here they made camp. Over the next few weeks they assembled a lumber mill, then cut and milled timber to erect shanties in which they set up Bringier's mining machinery. They prospected in the vicinity for a time, but it proved an unhealthy stop, for a few of the boatmen took sick and died.[15]

Bringier remained there looking for silver or gold while Laffite and Latour continued their journey.[16] From Crystal Hill they poled upriver, stopping at Cadron. The new American settlement was nothing more than a blockhouse and half a dozen scattered farming families, and so remote that its leading citizen, Major James Pyeatt, maintained that he only learned of the War of 1812 after it was over.[17] That degree of isolation was gone, as Latour noted that United States mail now came to Cadron, brought by mail riders who then traveled southwest past the Hot Springs on the Ouachita, and down to Natchitoches. If Washington would deliver the mail to this far-flung outpost, then the government clearly expected it to endure and to grow.

Equally significant, at Cadron Latour and Laffite met a trapper who told them he had several times made the seven-hundred-mile overland trip across the plains to Taos and the pass through the Sangre de Cristo Mountains into the Rio Grande Valley. It took just fifteen days, and from Taos it was a mere seventy miles to Santa Fe. If a man on horseback could make this journey in such a time, then an army could do it in a month. If the Americans took Santa Fe, then they could cut off California, and at the same time have the Rio Grande as a highway into Texas.[18]

While at Cadron, Latour's expedition traded with Indians who told them of rich fields of ore near the Caddo River, perhaps seventy-five miles away. This was enough to persuade some in the group to set out overland on ponies purchased from the Indians. After riding several days southwest through heavily wooded and hilly country they made camp at the Caddo, and were ready to prospect again when they were attacked by a roving party of Lipan Indians. At first the prospectors repulsed them, but in a few days the Lipan returned in strength and the whites abandoned their camp and made their way back to the Arkansas, and then down to Major Pyeatt's home at Cadron, as quickly as they could.[19]

Laffite and Latour did not participate in the prospecting for long, if at all, though the promised gold would have appealed to both. They had a clear mission from Onís, and limited time to accomplish it. They also had the recently published maps made by Major Zebulon Pike of the United States Army as a result of his exploration of the territory a few years earlier.[20] Leaving the prospectors behind to their digging, Laffite and Latour continued the arduous voyage up the Arkansas until they reached its confluence with the Poteau River, and a village of about thirty families where Fort Smith would be established the following year. The expedition leaders saw the area's fertile soil and agreed that the nascent settlement was likely to swell rapidly with Americans. Moving up the Arkansas another hundred miles or more they came to a grand village of the Osage Indians, where they found a substantial saltworks with mills, evaporating vats, and all the machinery necessary to extract salt from local deposits.[21] The Poteau settlement and its saltworks would be further aids to any American army on the march.

Latour was finding that the Pike maps were not very accurate, however.[22] As he and Laffite traveled, he drew his own, his chief concern being potential avenues of American invasion.[23] A day or two beyond the Osage village the Arkansas ceased to be navigable, but by then Latour and Laffite were no more than eight days overland from Santa Fe. This was one line of advance. Another was via an upper fork of the Red River in Caddo country not far from where their prospecting comrades encountered the Lipan. The Red then flowed southerly into western Louisiana, to Natchitoches, from which the overland trail into Texas was well established. Laffite and Latour did not have to travel that route to learn of its practicality. Finally, invaders could move up the Mississippi to the Red, and then up to Caddo Lake, from which Cypress Bayou led a few miles to an established trace that would take them directly south over the headwaters of the Sabine to Nacogdoches, and then southwest across the Trinity and Brazos rivers straight to Béxar.[24]

Laffite and Latour probably did not stray far from their boats or the river, relying on information gathered from locals and travelers to fill in their picture of the region as well as their maps. If they did venture down to the Red River they did not go far, for by November 5 they were back at Arkansas Post with Bringier, who had found ore samples that Notrebe thought were gold, but proved not to be.[25] Latour and Laffite were also there to witness settlers casting their votes in local races at the same time as presidential balloting, though territorial voters did not participate in James Monroe's landslide election to the Oval Office. Of more interest to them than the outcome was the turnout. From the electoral count Latour drew an idea of the population and concluded that, though a mere ten years earlier it had been a wilderness, the banks of the Arkansas River were proportionately more settled than Spanish New Mexico.[26] Calculating how the population would grow at its present rate of expansion, or what dangers this posed for Spain's hold on Texas, was not hard. Neither did they overlook the settlers' petition that year to have Arkansas separated from the Missouri Territory to become a territory in its own right, the first step to statehood. Moreover, Congress had promised to give veterans of the recent war a million acres of land as a bounty, and once there, the veterans would themselves constitute a potential army of conquest.[27]

Following the election, Laffite and Latour did not tarry long before taking their boats down the Arkansas to the Mississippi, and thence to New Orleans. They reached home in the last days of the month. By their estimate, in a journey lasting eight months they had covered a round trip of some 540 leagues between New Orleans and the navigable headwaters of the Arkansas, more than 1,500 miles.[28] What they had seen ought to alarm Spain. The Americans moving into the Arkansas country were greater in number than they had expected, and endured hardship cheerfully. "They have strength of character, courage, and skill in the use of guns rarely seen among civilized people," declared Latour. From what Latour and Laffite had heard, even more were settling on the Red River. The land there was excellent and suitable to growing sugar, cotton, indigo, tobacco, corn, and other produce. Already beaver had begun to disappear because of the onslaught of trappers, and Latour and Laffite had seen many hunters leave for the Rio Grande Valley even in late autumn, at the risk of being caught in the mountains in winter. Excess "adventurers" from the eastern United States were pouring into this public land, their eyes fixed on Mexico. "They will gladly join any expedition that is proposed in that direction," Latour concluded.

Worse, the Americans were prepared to incite the Indian peoples to aid them in fighting the Spanish. Latour and Laffite saw traders ready to import guns to the Indians up the Red and Arkansas, and from St. Louis through to the Osage. They also saw a brisk contraband trade in leather, harness, spurs, stirrups, buckles, and more, carried on between the Spaniards in New Mexico and the American traders on the Arkansas and Red, who sold to the Indians. The profits were simply too tempting. The Indians traded furs at the exchange rate of 25 cents per pound. Laffite and Latour witnessed a carbine that would sell for $15 to $20 in Kentucky being exchanged with Indians for 250 pounds in furs, which could then be sold in New Orleans for 35 to 40 cents a pound. A $15 investment in Kentucky could be turned into a profit of $75 or more in New Orleans.[29]

Latour returned to find copies of his book on the Battle of New Orleans done at last, though not before their delay in coming off the presses resulted in a legal imbroglio for Livingston over his failure to deliver them in time to be sold by subscription.[30] No sooner did Latour see his words in print than he began work on a report of the expedition, but to complete a full outline of the hazards Spain faced in its territories he needed more than his own observations. He asked the Laffites for their opinions on the filibusters and revolutionary movements. For all the sympathy the revolutionary movements had in the East, it was in the West, and particularly Louisiana, that the rebels received their greatest encouragement and succor. The Laffites knew this as intimately as anyone, and they knew leaders such as Herrera, Toledo, and Humbert even better than Latour. It was all too evident that the Americans sympathized with them, and that some invested heavily in their enterprises. To prevent harboring an enemy within,[31] Spain must fight further immigration by Americans into its lands and win back the allegiance of the original inhabitants of the settlements on the Ouachita, White, Red, and Arkansas rivers, and up the Mississippi at New Madrid and St. Louis. The dissatisfaction Latour and Laffite had seen among some of the Americans could be put to good use, and the even greater discontent of many of the settlers from the days of French and Spanish reign was a considerable asset. The spread of Americans westward was "inevitable," Latour warned. "The Spanish government cannot prevent it, but at least it can put off the time." Spain must firmly establish the Louisiana boundary as far east as possible, and then militarize that border to stop American infiltration and control the Indians. If Spain could hold on long enough, other factors might save her possessions later, for Latour at least believed that there were signs of an incipient sectional rivalry that could one day lead to the breakup of the Union. When that happened, none of the separate sections would be strong enough to threaten Spain's grip on her colonies.[32]

While Latour considered population changes, the Laffite family continued to expand. Besides Pierre's daughters Catherine Coralie and Rosa and his sons Pierre, possibly Eugene, Jean Baptiste, and Martin, Pierre's household also contained Catherine and her infant Jean Pierre.[33] By August Marie was six months pregnant with another child. This would mean at least ten in the home not counting any slaves or the absent adult Jean. They needed a larger house, and thanks to the money coming in from Spain, Pierre could move them. Of course he bought no property in his name. *Plaçage* protected him as much as it did Marie, for a property purchased in her name could not be confiscated on his account though he had paid for it.

On August 17, while Jean was still away, Pierre sent Marie to Claude Treme to buy a house and lot at the northeast corner of Bourbon and St. Philip streets. It represented a considerable step up in the Laffites' living standard, for the house cost $5,500, more than six times the $900 their previous home had sold for the year before. Marie took out a mortgage for $1,120, and Pierre must have given her the rest of the cash down payment of $2,500, the property itself being security for payment. It was a standard sized lot for the quarter, 60 feet along Bourbon and 120 along St. Philip.[34] The house was twenty-six years old, having been built by Juan Moore under a contract with Don Carlos Parent, coincidentally the father of the Charles Parent to whom Pierre made the sham sale of the *Presidente*. Moore had built a wood and brick house fifty-two feet wide on Bourbon and forty-two feet deep, with a ten-foot-wide wraparound gallery fronting both streets. Inside were six rooms or "apartments," with three fireplaces for heat.[35] Behind the house sat two outbuildings, one a kitchen and the other either a well or an outhouse.[36] Despite the price, the property was not situated in the most desirable section of the old quarter or Vieux Carré. Next door on St. Philip sat the charity hospital, while on the opposite corner were two groups of dilapidated wooden buildings, and next to them two more buildings in nearly as bad condition.[37] The Laffite family would remain in this house for several years.[38]

The money from Spain also allowed Pierre to extricate himself from his creditors, and for a change it was now Pierre Laffite who recovered money from others. The executors of his onetime business associate Robin had spent months trying to collect on $2,297 in notes Pierre had given for loans, but in April he was able to show proof of having paid them and a jury awarded him its verdict, with court costs to be paid by Robin's heirs.[39] Laffite went after $3,075.50 due him from the brothers' former accomplice in the Lafourche smuggling, Godefroi Dumon, and tried to foreclose on Dumon's land near Donaldsonville as compensation.[40]

For the first time in more than a year Pierre Laffite dealt in slaves again, though clearly not as a supplier as before. In April and May he took in $1,400 from the sale of two, but then on August 15, only two days before buying the Bourbon and St. Philip house, Pierre bought a black from San Domingue for $700, most likely as a house servant. If so, the young man must not have given satisfaction, for four months later Pierre sold him.[41] Meanwhile Pierre gave almost perfect satisfaction to his new employers, not least because of his ability to lie convincingly. Picornell found Laffite to be "of attractive appearance and distinguished manners," and learned in talking with townspeople that "no one who has known him before and after his activities in Barataria fails to regret that a man otherwise so good and so honest in meeting his obligations should have lent himself to a business so detestable as that." Given Pierre's history with creditors, this statement alone revealed Picornell's gullibility. He also somehow confused Pierre with Jean, or else Pierre convinced him that he and not Jean directed affairs on Grand Isle, for the Spaniard told his superiors that it was well known "among the rabble that surrounded him in the island" that Pierre "made himself notable by the good treatment that he gave to those who had the misfortune of falling into the hands of the privateersmen." Moreover, Pierre threatened severe punishment to any who failed to treat captives well, and Picornell had only to recall the testimony of several Spanish captains and crewmen in the federal court cases of the past three years to know that they affirmed that at Grand Isle they received "all assistance they could desire." Laffite sometimes bought their private goods with his own funds, provided them with new clothing to replace that taken by privateers, and even gave them smaller vessels in which to return home.

The testimony made it clear that the Laffite who did this was Jean, but Pierre had no reason to set Picornell straight. Pierre told his greatest lie when he convinced Picornell that the brothers' mother had been a Spaniard, and that having been raised among her kind the Laffites felt "very friendly towards Spaniards," even preferring their company to that of all others. "It is also remarked," Picornell added, "that he detests and hates with a deadly hatred the English and Americans." At this very moment Pierre would have been assuring his American friends among the "associates" of his hatred of Spain and Spaniards. At least they could all agree on hating the English. Picornell may have viewed Laffite through a roseate glass, but he was not entirely deluded. Picornell warned Onís that though Pierre might call on his men to serve when an opportunity for action arose, neither he nor they were likely to take a risk until they had money in their pockets. Spain must either pay Laffite in advance for preemptive action, or be satisfied with him revealing what had happened after it was too late to take action.[42]

Within days of Jean Laffite's return to New Orleans Pierre's Spanish masters had taken note, no doubt anxious to see what the second brother could tell them.[43] For his part, Jean had new circumstances with which to acquaint himself. First there was his first sight of his son Jean Pierre, only four weeks old.[44] Then there was the spacious new house where they would all live. Jean also had past due business to settle, not least with his attorneys Livingston and Grymes for their services in securing compensation for some of his goods lost at Barataria.[45] The brothers also engaged in their first legitimate maritime trading. Less than a week after Jean's return, on December 2, Pierre paid $2,049 for a new felucca called the *Flora Belle*, a single decked, two-masted boat just over forty-three feet long and thirteen feet in the beam, built in Bayou St. John. Displacing twenty-one tons, she drew barely more than four feet of water, and would be able to go anywhere.[46] The next day Pierre registered her as the *Flying Fish*, owner Pierre Laffite, "merchant of New Orleans."[47] On December 14, however, Pierre gave the captain he employed for the boat, John Deveze or Davis, power of attorney to sell her.[48] Either Pierre lost interest in her very quickly, or else he was already trying to mask his ownership as he had with the *Presidente*. Old habits died hard.

Pierre's actions may, in fact, have had something to do with the *Presidente*, for by this time she was gone for good, a victim of the steadily tightening noose in the hands of Patterson and Duplessis, Pierre's own partners in the "associates." Despite the challenges posed by the loss of Barataria and the increased naval presence off the coastline, the Cartagenan privateers and simple pirates had not abated their efforts to land and sell or smuggle illicit goods, especially after the fall of Cartagena. Britain's mounting efforts to suppress the slave trade helped their business, as did the enactment that year of the United States' first protective tariff, with duties as high as 20 percent on some imported manufactured goods. On April 2 customs inspector John Rollins at the Balize saw the privateer the *Comet* come to anchor and on going aboard met Captain Mitchell. Mitchell told him quite matter of factly that he had twenty slaves on the ship, fourteen of whom had belonged to the governor of San Andres, and that "he had put to death the Governor and eight soldiers," and was taking the slaves to New Orleans as prize goods. He also admitted to having in his hold six brass six-pounders, forty muskets, and five barrels of powder, but Rollins could see that the seventy-five-ton vessel was riding low in the water, and suspected that a lot more cargo was aboard.[49]

Lieutenant William Lowe and the USS *Boxer,* then stationed off the Balize, immediately seized the *Comet,* and on fuller inspection found aboard her about $40,000 of rich plunder and stores taken from the very passengers she had helped to escape Cartagena, and from San Andres, where the "notorious villain" Mitchell committed what Patterson called "the most wanton murders & brutality robbing churches." On May 23 the grand jury handed down three separate piracy indictments against Mitchell and his crew but Patterson gloomily predicted that "like all others who have preceded them they will escape punishment further than a forfeiture of property." He proved to be prescient.[50]

The pressure on the smugglers made itself felt by late spring. When more fugitive vessels from Cartagena appeared in the days after the *Comet*'s capture, some loaded half with white refugees and half with slaves to sell, the *Boxer* sailed after them, then westward along the coast after Lowe heard that "some very suspicious armed vessels" were in the vicinity.[51] Lowe seized a cargo of 150 crates of crockery, and on another vessel took wine from Bordeaux.[52] In New Orleans the government appointed yet another temporary inspector of customs, John Davis Bradburn, a veteran of the Gutiérrez-Magee expedition who had more recently been an officer under Perry assembling volunteers for the Texas invasion.[53] No one seemed to catch the anomaly of entrusting enforcement of the revenue laws to a man deeply associated with filibusters so closely linked with privateers, but Bradburn was as much a zealot for the law as for Mexican independence. As a result, merchants who traded in illicit goods experienced the reach of the law, even lowly tailors such as Bernard Bourdin, who was foolish enough to fund the privateer *Alerta* though his shop sat next door to the customs house.[54]

Patterson, accustomed to complaining of his inadequate resources, believed by April that his naval force was so completely equipped that he closed the naval arsenal in New Orleans as well as the shops that manufactured naval stores.[55] Evidence of the threat the privateers took the authorities to be came that month as well. At dusk one evening in April, as Patterson walked with his wife, his children, and Lieutenant Cunningham, three men came out of the shadows and attacked them. The officers drove them off without injury, but a few days later three more assailants waylaid Cunningham and went at him with dirks, several of which penetrated the lieutenant's coat sleeve without harming him. He drew blood from one of the men with his saber, and that put them to flight. On April 23 Patterson received a threat in the mail, leading him to conclude that in their desperation "the whole connection will I have little doubt put in operation every expedient to get rid of naval force from this station, for reasons too obvious to require naming."[56] "Vexations similar to those you were troubled with when in command here, are in operation against me & my officers, by our Barataria friends," Patterson advised Captain David Porter.

Pierre Laffite would have had nothing to do with these attacks. The brothers never used violence to achieve their ends. Besides, Pierre pursued a more profitable game. When he recovered the *Presidente,* he promised Herrera that she would be at the disposal of the Mexican junta, never mentioning the sham sale to Parent.[57] By February 1816, now called the *Dos Hermanos,* she carried a cargo of guns, brick, lime for mortar, and other necessary materials to Matagorda for construction of the anticipated port there. She then sailed down the coast to reconnoiter Boquilla de Piedras for Sedella,[58] and was back by March 1, after which Pierre agreed to carry a cargo of munitions to Boquilla de

Piedras for Duncan and West, who had already been paid by Herrera.[59] However, Laffite told Morphy and Sedella his plans, and advised that if an armed Spanish vessel should intercept him, his captain would of course turn over the weapons and surrender his ship. Morphy made it clear that Spain could not condone the vessel's mission, and would deny the arms to the rebels. The "associates" would have been paid for the arms, and Laffite would have his share either from their sale or else from advance payment for their freighting. Everyone would win except the insurgents. In conformity to their arrangement, Pierre gave the Spaniards information that would enable them to capture his vessel in such a way that he would be above suspicion, but with the expectation that if the Spanish warship seized the *Dos Hermanos* in addition to the cargo, she would be returned to him. In sending word to Apodaca, Sedella gladly suggested that "our recommended one is worthy of having granted to him what he has asked." Laffite made it clear that his ultimate goal was to disassociate himself forever from the insurgents.

The *Dos Hermanos* cast off with her cargo on April 8, Fougard replaced by the Italian Laurent Maire, known also as Lorenzo Mairo or Lawrence Morgan.[60] However, the Spanish warships did not arrive in time to intercept her, and Maire landed his cargo at Boquilla de Piedras as instructed. From the rump authority there he obtained for the *Dos Hermanos* a commission as a privateer under the name the *Victoria*, in honor of Guadalupe Victoria, who replaced Morelos but would spend the next several years wandering the countryside with little army and no constituency. The *Victoria* then set off after prizes, taking two before a Spanish vessel caught up with her and began a hard chase that left the *Victoria* severely damaged when she escaped.[61] By April 22 Maire had limped into Cat Island, where he unloaded his prize goods, possibly the slaves that Thomas Copping so enthusiastically went to Donaldsonville to buy.[62] After opening her sea cocks to scuttle her, thirty crewmen boarded four pirogues and rowed east along the coast. The next day at the mouth of the Lafourche, the authorities found them with no provisions but some cheese. They were carrying two cases of arms that a customs inspector seized.[63] It appeared that Maire, knowing that neither the "associates" nor his Spanish masters could confirm how many arms were delivered at Boquilla de Piedras for the insurgents, had held back a part of the cargo, which Laffite could sell anew to Herrera. When Maire returned to New Orleans in June, he and Laffite met with Sedella and cunningly explained to him that taking the Spanish prizes was the only way to preserve the *Dos Hermanos'* cover and "keep up appearances." Besides, it was all in service of the greater goal of destroying the insurgency.[64]

Meanwhile the revenue people improved their surveillance of the smuggling routes up the Lafourche and elsewhere. Thomas Copping of New Orleans foolishly boasted to inspector Rollins that great bargains in illicit slaves were to be had upriver. "He seemed to think that it was a very smart business to get them all in without being detected or lossing a single nigro," Rollins told Duplessis. "He expressed himself very much in favor of such an active business as smuggling Negroes without being detected in it." In fact, the authorities were soon onto Copping for smuggling a variety of contraband goods.[65]

Customs officials also monitored news of legitimate merchantmen who stopped at Galveston before coming to the Balize, perhaps taking on illicit goods to smuggle in with their regular cargo. The inspector at the Balize filed reports of every ship that passed his inspection before going on to New Orleans, in case another more thorough search should be made.[66] If a regularly commissioned Mexican privateer such as the *Little Napoleon* had made a stop at Galveston, the inspectors tried to track its movements and watch for any chicanery.[67] A fair number of Mexican and Venezuelan privateers entered the Mississippi in the last half of the year, but not many directly from Galveston until December, when three came into the river within five days.[68] In general, privateering activity around Galveston seemed to heat up at the end of the year, and finally Duplessis and the rest discovered why. The filibusters on the Texas coast island were handing out their own commissions. It was Cartagena all over again, with even less legitimacy.

It would have taken Pierre several hours to explain to Jean all that had happened during his absence from the murky world of the revolutionaries, filibusters, and Spanish agents. By February Perry and his small command at Bolívar Point were being closely watched by Spaniards in Texas, who had been anticipating such an event for months. These observers provided accurate intelligence on Perry's numbers and movements, and erred only in reporting that the fleet that transported his men had been commanded by the Laffites.[69] By March, tired of waiting for more men and supplies that never came, Perry gave up and returned with his command to Louisiana.[70] Humbert, whom Onís described as "the chief of a band of robbers armed and equipped in the province of Louisiana," had returned to New Orleans in December, and was once more at loose ends in the city taverns, drinking, boasting, and sulking.[71]

Meanwhile the "associates" flirted with funding an expedition to seize Pensacola. The year before they had the idea that they could arm their Texan and Mexican ventures by taking the twenty thousand muskets reported to be in the Spanish armory at the colonial capital, and obtain funding by taking Florida and selling it to the United States. It was a harebrained scheme from the outset, soon abandoned. Then in late February came word of the fall of Cartagena, and the *Firebrand* returned from Boquilla de Piedras on February 20 with no money for Toledo, only promises and the news that affairs in Mexico were not going well for the insurgents.[72]

Toledo had been trying to buy the *General Bolívar* from the navy in order to outfit her as a Mexican privateer. When the *Fire-*

brand failed to bring back the money needed to complete the purchase, however, Patterson quickly cancelled the deal and sold the vessel to Abner Duncan, who would transform her into the *General Jackson*, though many continued to use the ship's previous name. Just as damaging from the insurgents' and "associates'" point of view was Patterson's refusal to lend the *Firebrand* for more courier voyages to Mexico.

The combined effect was a body blow to the revolutionaries' leaders in New Orleans.[73] The scattered return of Perry's disillusioned men from Bolívar Point punctuated another season of dashed hopes, and the flood of disasters continued. Late in March came news that the *Petit Milan* had gone to the bottom in a storm, carrying arms en route to Boquilla de Piedras, and a month later came the sinking of the *Dos Hermanos* and the seizure of the muskets it carried.[74] It is no wonder that Toledo lost all heart with revolutionaries and filibusters. Late in June he approached Sedella and followed Picornell in seeking pardon from Spain for a renunciation of his former associates. Soon he was telling Sedella everything he knew about the plans and movements of his former comrades and actively sharing information with Picornell—perhaps learning to his amazement that the Laffites had been spying on him for months.

Meanwhile Pierre Laffite, whom Sedella habitually referred to as "the recommended one," provided plenty of information himself.[75] Indeed, Sedella felt moved to commend Laffite's loyalty and usefulness. The spy, he wrote to Apodaca, was "being always attentive to anything that can contribute to inform us of our enemies' strategies and plans." He reported that Pierre said the *General Bolívar*, not yet renamed by Duncan, would soon be leaving for Boquilla de Piedras or Nautla with another cargo of equipment and munitions, and Pierre expected Patterson to detach the *Firebrand* again as an escort. The revolutionaries were still short of money, Pierre added. They would move when they got it, but it was slow in coming.[76]

But then Pierre revealed the two letters from Gual to Herrera
and Toledo that Jean had turned over to him. They laid out the
plans to send a fleet of twenty-six privateers from San Domingue
to Tampico, an expedition that Pierre said Spain could stop if she
posted warships off Cuba to intercept. Pierre gave details of the
ships and their rendezvous, but went on to even bigger news.
Quakers in Philadelphia had hatched a plan to incite a slave rebellion, backed by Bolívar, in all of the Spanish American
colonies simultaneously, and had asked Jean to take a leading
role. Maire also reported that he expected to see Cuba in full-
blown insurrection shortly, the free black population taking part
in a repeat of the San Domingue and Haiti nightmare. Laffite
had a list of the agents in charge of igniting the sparks. Again it
was necessary for Havana to send a fully empowered agent to
New Orleans to assist the Laffites in defeating this diabolical design. The brothers did not want to deal with Onís, whose staff
they believed leaked information. Sedella endorsed the request
for a special agent.[77] In Havana, Apodaca, now viceroy of New
Spain, discussed the matter with his advisory council, but they
were less credulous than the enthusiastic priest, and awaited more
convincing news before taking action. Still, they prepared to send
the special agent as Laffite asked.[78]

That the repeated setbacks put the filibusters in low spirits
cannot be denied. If later legend is to be believed, tensions came
to a head around this time at a celebration of a French holiday at
Jean Turpin's newly acquired New Orleans Theater and Marine
Hotel.[79] The bombastic Humbert celebrated along with several of
his Baratarian colleagues, ate heartily, drank heavily, and listened
to many a tribute to him as the most distinguished Frenchman
among them. Reflecting on what he had been and to what he was
reduced now, he became maudlin. Rising, he declared that he
should not be sitting in indolence among outlaws. His place was
in the field. The unintended insult outraged some of the Baratar-

ians present, and it was later recalled that Pierre Laffite led the inebriated old hero away before trouble could start.[80]

Within three weeks of Toledo's defection, a new would-be leader appeared. Aury had been at Aux Cayes and then Jamaica and Port-au-Prince since his escape from Cartagena, and by March 15 had a flotilla of six vessels, four of them armed corsairs.[81] The French commodore was about twenty-nine now, and had been privateering since 1803, after serving in the French navy. He was a lone wolf, however, unable to subordinate himself to anyone for long.[82] He refused to support Bolívar as sole leader of the insurgency, and thus fell out with Bolívar and others, who were even less friendly when he demanded $25,000 for his expenses in evacuating Cartagena. In the end he got the ship the *Constitucion* instead, but he would never enjoy Bolívar's favor again. Meanwhile, seeing their plans foundering, Herrera persuaded Sauvinet to send his schooner the *Morelos* to Haiti with Joseph Savary, a Haitian mulatto, carrying a dozen privateer commissions from Mexico and a new blue and white checkered flag for Aury to sail under if he accepted the invitation to take over the maritime part of their Texas campaign. The proposition came at a perfect time for Aury.[83] Sailing from Port-au-Prince early in June, he intended to make either Matagorda or Galveston his base. Along the way he took several prizes, but he was now essentially a pirate since he took them under improper Mexican commissions and the flag of the defunct Cartagenan republic. By July 17 he was off the mouth of the Mississippi, waiting for Herrera to reply to a message telling of his plans and asking for several letters of marque from the Mexican junta.[84] Herrera tried to persuade Aury to establish himself at Barataria, where Herrera could more easily reach him and from which Aury could transport a new army, but the young privateer was too anxious and independent. He sailed on, first to Matagorda, and then to Galveston, which he concluded offered a safer anchorage. Unfortunately, it also had a shallower bar at the entrance to the bay, and on August 10 the impetuous Aury ran his fleet aground, losing most of his prize ships and the cargo that he had announced would be sold at the mart he intended to establish.[85]

Apparently Pierre Laffite planned to work with Aury, for either plunder or intelligence, and probably both. After the loss of the *Dos Hermanos,* he bought another ship and named her the *Victoria* in order to make the commission given to Maire appear legitimate. He engaged Gambi to command in June, but they soon had a falling-out.[86] On July 2 Gambi borrowed $250 from Maire, and Maire endorsed the note to Pierre. When the note came due Gambi refused to pay, leading to a court case that virtually ended the already cool relations between Gambi and the Laffites.[87] By the end of the month, under either Gambi or Maire, the *Victoria* set sail along with as many as nine other vessels that sporadically left New Orleans for the Gulf to take prizes and cooperate with Aury. Pierre dutifully informed Sedella, and let it be known that another five ships were preparing for the same business.[88] Meanwhile Toledo seemed to have found financing when he told Herrera he had arranged for a line of credit of 20 million pesos from the republican junta in Mexico. Unfortunately, when Herrera tried to access the credit on July 1, three days after Toledo's defection, the credit line proved worthless.[89] On August 4 some money finally arrived, modest though the amount was. On his way to Matagorda Aury had landed one of his vessels, the *Belona,* at Barataria, and he now sent an agent to New Orleans to meet with the "associates" and to contribute $7,000 to their projects, a sign of good faith but too little to be more than a token.[90]

The young commodore needed some reassurance, for he had heard that in the wake of Morelos's execution, the insurgent Mexican Congress had essentially dissolved. The "associates" did not know it yet, but this particular independence movement was flickering out, a victim of its own factionalism and disorganiza-

tion, and hardly aided by the drain of precious funds to New Orleans. Hereafter there would be only isolated bands of revolutionaries, each loyal to their self-proclaimed strongmen. Mexican
privateering commissions were worthless unless a new resistance
movement could establish itself on Mexican soil with a claim to
sovereignty. Aury expected to make such a claim at Galveston,
with himself as *El Supremo.*

Over two days, August 5 and 6, Aury's agent attended a
meeting of the "associates." Patterson, Duplessis, Livingston,
Duncan, Herrera, Peire, Dupuis, and several others were there to
hear that Aury now had a fleet of fifteen armed vessels and ten
prizes, two of which had been armed. More than 150 captured
crewmen were in custody, and some were joining the privateers.
The agent told the assembled that Aury also had carpenters and
smiths and other skilled artisans to help establish his port at
Matagorda, unaware that Aury would change his mind and go to
Galveston. The interest of the "associates," which had flagged
when Herrera and Toledo could not wring more money out of
Mexico, was revived by Aury's $7,000 and the indication of more
to come. The money also renewed Herrera's influence after the
20 million peso credit line fiasco. Now the "associates" assured
Aury's man that they had five vessels in the Mississippi armed
and ready to join him. Additionally, Duncan's *General Bolívar*
would be leaving in two days for Boquilla de Piedras with twelve
hundred muskets and four field cannon, and Grymes and the
now-returned Perry would go along.

Certainly the collapse of the Mexican Congress was discussed, but while a blow, it would not be a disaster so long as a
port could be established to continue the pretense of a government. Someone suggested that Aury use Matagorda only as a
temporary port and supply base and the old joint attack plan be
dusted off. Herrera was still officially the minister from the all-
but-defunct Mexican junta. They decided to pay off his debts in
New Orleans and send him with a command of 120 whites and

mulattoes, the former led by Peire and the latter under Colonel Joseph Savary, to join Aury. Herrera would take civil control of the port, establish a prize court, issue letters of marque, and rule jointly with Aury, with sufficient support from the "associates" to stay two months on the Texas coast. Meanwhile Perry and Gutiérrez would lead an assembly of men overland to meet them, the "associates" guaranteeing to supply necessary arms and provisions. When everything was in place, after about six weeks, Aury's fleet would transport the army to a point on the Mexican coast from which it would launch an invasion while Aury sailed on to take Tampico or Vera Cruz and establish a permanent port and seat of government. Meanwhile the "associates" would pay Pierre Laffite a fee of $1,000, to keep a small boat running between Matagorda and New Orleans to maintain constant communications.

Pierre negotiated the purchase of such a boat immediately after the meeting adjourned, and was making arrangements for a voyage to Matagorda when he encountered Picornell in the street. Morphy and Picornell knew that something was going on. Throughout the day they had seen men from the meeting making hurried calls on other confederates. Picornell asked Pierre to reveal what was happening, but Laffite was in a rush and told him the street was too public a place to be seen talking. However, he hinted that "a lot was going on and it was big," and agreed to meet with Picornell and Sedella in a few minutes at a private spot. There, Pierre put everything in Sedella's hands and vouched for its accuracy, promising to tell them more when he returned from Matagorda. At once his information was on the way to Morphy and Apodaca.[91]

Sedella still tried to preserve Laffite's anonymity. Picornell had been referring to him as "Number 14" since May, but now Sedella changed the code name to "Number 13," perhaps a conscious echo of the identification given to General Wilkinson when he spied for Spain a decade earlier. Père Antoine need not have bothered. Apodaca had declared in January that "even when he's hiding his name, I know he's a French citizen named Lafite."[92] Number 13's information seriously compromised Patterson, for now the Spaniards knew that the commodore purposely allowed privateers to leave New Orleans, and Duplessis was equally culpable. When the news got to Onís, he renewed his complaints in Washington.[93] As for Pierre Laffite, he got ready to leave for Matagorda. Soon he learned of Aury's shift to Galveston, though, and of the disaster to several of his ships on the bar. This was only the beginning.

Aury managed to get some of his prize goods and artillery safely to shore, and started building huts and repairing the ships. Soon he had about two hundred men, mostly from Haiti, and many of them surly because they had been promised riches and not hard work on a barren island. By September 7 the crew of one ship mutinied. Soon the uprising spread to other crews, and the next day several of Aury's men stepped into his tent and demanded that he give himself up. He reached for a dagger, but pistols went off and Aury went down with bullets through both hands and a wound in his chest. With him incapacitated, the mutineers loaded most of the prize goods onto three ships, set another vessel ablaze to discourage pursuit, and sailed off.[94]

On September 9 Herrera arrived to find not the confident adventurer ready for action that the "associates" expected, but a badly wounded and indignant young man with few remaining ships and even less booty.[95] Herrera had planned to leave New Orleans with Peire, Humbert, Savary, and Sauvinet—an enthusiastic supporter of occupying Galveston—on August 24, leaving Iturribarría in his place. However, it was August 30 before Herrera got around to registering his power of attorney for Iturribarría to transact business on his behalf, and so the others left first.[96] Still, Herrera brought the invalid Aury the cheering news that Francisco Xavier Mina had recently arrived in Baltimore from London with supplies, fifty men, twenty-five hundred muskets, nine cannon, fifty barrels of gunpowder, and boxes of pistols and sabers, harness, and uniforms.[97] A lifelong opponent of the monarchy, Mina had come over to the cause of Mexican independence two years before, and after raising more men and money in Baltimore, he would be sailing for the Gulf coast near the end of September. When he arrived, they could reassemble the Galveston base, and Aury and Mina together could continue the enterprise.[98]

On September 13 Herrera drafted and signed a proclamation declaring Galveston a port under the nonexistent authority of the now-defunct Mexican Congress. A few days later Herrera created Galveston's government, with a collector of customs and revenue to receive and distribute money and merchandise taken by the privateers, and an admiralty court to give a semblance of legitimacy to the condemnation and sale or disposal of goods taken, as well as to settle disputes between the privateers. He also appointed a notary to witness, record, and authenticate documents and commissions, all to give the appearance of legitimacy.[99] Herrera named the convalescent Aury governor, and raised the checkerboard flag.[100] Unfortunately, with the myopia that afflicted all of the filibuster leaders, Aury placed only his Cartagenan cronies in prominent positions in the government. His exclusion of Peire and the Americans was a blow to ambition and vanity alike that divided the men at Galveston into two camps. In October Peire would leave with Herrera for Mexico, Major Perry coming to Galveston in Peire's place, but the tension did not abate. Meanwhile more volunteers arrived. The day that Herrera named Aury governor, Morphy in New Orleans reported that "every day much small shipping sails from this port for Matagorda [Galveston], some with provisions, others with various persons who are speculators in prize goods, and in all of them go passengers who it is said are going to seek their fortune in the Kingdom of Mexico."[101] Indeed they did, and very soon the Laffites would be among them.

These are our realms, no limits to their sway—
Our flag the sceptre all who meet obey.
Ours the wild life in tumult still to range
From toil to rest, and joy in every change.

FIFTEEN

The Birth of Galveston
1816-1817

THE ISLAND HAD been known to sailors for generations, under a number of names. Some called it St. Louis Island. Spaniards shipwrecked there in the sixteenth century referred to it as *Malhado*, or "Isle of Doom,"[1] perhaps because of the rattlesnakes. In fact others labeled it Culebra Island, a name given to more than one of the snake-infested barrier islands along the coast. Galveston, its current name, honored Spanish explorer Bernardo Galvez. The island stretched thirty miles between the Gulf and Galveston Bay, yet was nowhere more than two or three miles in width or ten or twelve feet above sea level. A few clumps of trees near the island's center offered the only cover other than beach grass along the shore and more dense scrub behind the dunes. No one lived there year-round, but Karankawa Indians often came to fish.

Otherwise the island belonged to the snakes, some deer, alligators, and huge seasonal flocks of ducks and geese. "The whole island presents rather a dreary and forbidding aspect, with nothing to relieve the eye," a visitor would say a few years hence.[2] The place did have some attractions, however, not the least the seafood, with oysters thick in the shallows, and abundant fish and turtle and crabs. Brackish water could be had by digging in the sand, while in the canebrakes on the interior wells sometimes produced good water. Moreover, the ground was dry, if low, broken by a few shallow bayous but with none of the miasmic swamps that made Barataria rather unhealthy in places. For Aury, the outstanding feature was, of course, the vast bay behind the island, offering many anchorages despite its frequent shallows. The island protected the bay from the Gulf, making the harbor accessible only by a quarter-mile-wide pass between the island and Bolívar Point. Even then, a bar with only twelve to fifteen feet of water above it ran across the Gulf side of the pass, allowing the privateers in, but not deeply laden craft or heavy warships.[3] The Gulf swell could make it dangerous even for lighter vessels, as Aury learned. A small island that some called Little Campechey sat just inside the pass behind the eastern tip of the big island, separated from it by a narrow channel only six feet deep that made passage very difficult.[4]

When Aury arrived, Galveston was a desert with only three or four huts of boards and sails left from Perry's departed men.[5] Before long, Aury ruled from a small square earthen fort with half a dozen cannon on the bay side near the western end of the island. The flag of the Mexican junta flew over the fort, while within it his "government" seemed quite regular to men on the island. Commercial trade with New Orleans and elsewhere came and went, Aury's customs house collecting duties and making inspections according to form. Aury set up a "court of justice" to try men brought ashore after breaking rules aboard his ships. His court of admiralty ran smoothly, conveniently condemning as prizes virtually everything the privateers brought in, though American vessels were out of bounds. When he sent prize goods to New Orleans, Aury removed all marks from the bales and boxes to prevent their original owners from identifying and claiming them in the federal court.[6] By October vessels were leaving New Orleans almost daily with men and supplies bound for Galveston, and returning with prize goods deposited in or near Barataria to be loaded in two-hundred-pound bales onto mules for transport into the city.[7]

In one cargo Abner Duncan sent to Boquilla de Piedras the *Rebecca,* captained by Laméson, carried ten cases of muskets and rifles, thirty-six thousand gunflints, eighty kegs of gunpowder, two cases of sabers, two cases of cartridges for cannon, a case of dragoon pistols, a cannon, a barrel of other ammunition, shovels and spades, medicines, twenty barrels of salted meat, sixty barrels of biscuit, and nine hundred pounds of cannonballs for "ballast." Excluding the powder, the value of the armament came to $6,316. After delivering her cargo in November, the *Rebecca* stopped at Galveston and was saluted by Aury's vessels as a privateer. There her owners sold her to Laméson, who changed her name to the *Eugenie.* In January 1817, with a crew of forty including Jean Desfarges, a longtime Baratarian, she raised the checkerboard flag of Mexico, though one man aboard saw clearly that what Laméson had was not a genuine commission but a blank one handed to him at Boquilla de Piedras.[8] Legal or not, she joined the offspring of Galveston to prey on the Gulf.

The privateers brought a regular supply of goods to the island almost from the first, most without a formal commission. The indefatigable Captain Mitchell led a little fleet of small privateers funded by the "associates," operating out of Barataria, and equipped in New Orleans—leading Onís to complain to Monroe of "whole Squadrons of Pirates having been fitted out from thence." Mitchell had reportedly taken $320,000 in goods from recent prizes, kept $200,000 for his own and his crews' shares, and sent the rest to Aury's agent François Dupuis to deposit in the Bank of Louisiana, whose president Benjamin Morgan happened to be one of the "associates."[9] By the end of the year the privateers' deposits in Morgan's bank totaled $180,000 or more.[10] Onís's demands and the notoriety of Mitchell's captures frightened American shippers and attracted attention that Patterson could not afford to ignore without exposing his involvement.[11] Before he could react, however, Patterson landed right on the edge of an international controversy.

Patterson had at first refused to lend the *Firebrand* for any more voyages on behalf of the "associates."[12] With some inducement, however, he changed his mind, and both the *Enterprise* and the *General Jackson* went to Nautla in May, the latter with a commission from Herrera on August 6 or 7. The *General Jackson* went to Boquilla de Piedras along with the *Firebrand*, which was now acting as escort for an insurgent privateer. John Grymes went aboard the *General Jackson*, his cover story being that he was inspired by curiosity to see a country of which he had heard so much.[13] He actually went to handle the sale of a cargo of munitions, but he was not able to complete the deal, so the vessels left to look for another port.

They were off Vera Cruz when the *General Jackson* took a small armed Spanish schooner, but then three Spaniard warships came in sight and attacked on August 27. Grymes shifted to the *Firebrand*, which Patterson had refitted after purchase as a two-masted schooner for a crew of fifty-two and armed with one six-pounder cannon and half a dozen twelve-pounders. Under Lieutenant Cunningham, she was one of Patterson's best armed lesser warships, but she was no match for what came at her, and did not resist.[14] Cunningham raised the Stars and Stripes, the commander of the Spanish flotilla held the *Firebrand* for a day and arrested Cunningham briefly before releasing the ships. The *General Jackson* sustained heavy damage, lost a mast, and limped away not to be seen again. Her prize escaped and sailed for New Orleans.

The *Firebrand* returned to New Orleans September 7, the day the mutiny against Aury commenced, and missed by hours encountering Herrera and his little squadron on their way to Galveston.[15] Thanks to the anti-Spanish sentiment prevailing in the city and the nation, Patterson miraculously escaped recrimination for putting a United States Navy ship at risk by escorting a privateer of an unrecognized insurrection, operating against a neutral state, in order to benefit private investors and perhaps himself. Instead, a general expression of indignation over Spaniards firing on an American warship swept New Orleans.

On the morning of September 19 some two hundred men gathered at Maspero's coffeehouse. Grymes presided. The "associates" were well represented, and Morphy noted that several of the Baratarian leaders were present, no doubt Pierre Laffite among them.[16] Duncan's loss was deplored. Speakers demanded that Governor Claiborne mobilize the militia. Others urged that Washington declare war on Spain—a move, of course, that promised unlimited financial benefit to the "associates" in the form of legitimate American privateering against Spanish shipping. The meeting adopted resolutions declaring the attack an affront to American honor that must be redressed. Clearly Spain sought to interfere with free navigation. While they were on the subject, the resolutions averred that Louisianans and Americans should resist any move to return any part of Louisiana to Spain in the negotiations with Onís. The meeting delegated Grymes, Duncan, and Davezac to take the resolutions to President Madison. "Our country is on the eve of a war," said one city editorial.[17]

During this first flush of indignation, Morphy briefly feared that Patterson would order out his squadron to find the Spaniards who attacked the *Firebrand* and bring them in.[18] Elsewhere in the nation tempers were hot. Andrew Jackson told Livingston he wished Patterson had simply sunk the three Spanish warships before notifying the government of what had happened. Sinking them was the only way to cleanse the stain on the flag, even if doing so meant war.[19] Onís was alarmed and feared for a time that the New Orleans resolutions would be effective. He asked

Secretary of State Monroe for an official explanation of the whole affair, but seems never to have gotten one. In the end, an unidentified source reported that despite her flying the American flag the *Firebrand* had been mistaken for the privateer she once was, thanks to her rigging, and that was why the Spaniards attacked. Madison mentioned the incident obliquely in his December 3, 1816, annual message, with no word at all of the *General Jackson* or of the *Firebrand*'s mission. After Madison ordered two warships to the Gulf and Onís assured him that it was all a misunderstanding, both nations were happy to let the matter drop.[20]

Pierre Laffite had alerted the Spaniards in May of the *General Jackson*'s anticipated departure and destination, as well as her expected escort—more than enough time for Sedella and Morphy to warn Havana to watch Boquilla de Piedras and Vera Cruz. However, Laffite's information seems to have done little to help interdict the traffic into and out of Galveston, such as Mitchell's. Indeed, on November 25 one of Aury's privateers, the *Jupiter*, took Spanish vessels so close to the mouth of the Mississippi that Patterson responded to Morphy's protest by sending two ships to hover meaningfully outside the pass into Galveston until Aury's prize court returned the vessels to their owners.[21]

Authorities also tried to more effectively prevent unlawful privateers from fitting out. On September 5 Captain Job Northrop brought in the Spanish schooner captured by Duncan's *General Jackson* just before the *Firebrand* incident. The schooner *Mexicain* had been herself a Spanish privateer, but when Northrop stopped at Boquilla along the way he got Mexican letters of marque for her and a commission as a lieutenant in the insurgent "navy" for himself.[22] Unfortunately, she was in abominable condition and nearly worthless. Northrop sold her to François Deglanne, who wanted to have her refitted into a hermaphrodite brig to go out as a privateer once again, probably to sail with Aury. He turned to Dominique, then at loose ends in New Orleans, and hired him both to oversee the work, and to take her out as captain. Over the next several weeks Dominque did the job, incurring on his own behalf a debt of $1,061.25, but after reimbursing him only $580, Deglanne would pay no more. Dominique placed a lien on the vessel itself for the remainder of his expenditure. In his petition he was coy, saying that the expenses were incurred only for "objects of travel," but when finally she was sold in December she brought only $176.84 even after Dominique's work.[23] Sedella and his friends watched her refitting carefully, relieved at Dominique's financial and legal discouragement.[24] In fact, it left him entirely out of the privateering enterprise for the next three years.

When it came to stopping the privateers on the seas, however, Patterson enjoyed limited success. Aury's Galveston privateers were better armed and equipped than their predecessors on the Gulf. The *Jupiter* came and went as she pleased, armed with three large cannon, fifty muskets, forty cutlasses, twenty pistols, and a quarter ton of gunpowder. Amigoni commanded a new vessel, the *Patriota*, carrying a crew of seventy to man five big guns, eighty muskets, seventy cutlasses, and forty pairs of pistols. The *Hidalgo* sortied out of Galveston in November armed with nearly two muskets per crewman.[25] More powerful than the rest was the *General Arismendi*, carrying six heavy cannon, sixty men, eighty muskets, sixty cutlasses, and eighteen pistols. Guy Champlin had fitted her out in New Orleans under the watchful eyes of district attorney Dick, who knew he intended to violate the neutrality laws by privateering, but could not stop him.[26]

Patterson and Duplessis did try to stop the privateers from smuggling illicit goods, but to mixed effect. The navy began to cooperate with the customs officials in stopping Aury's privateers and scrutinizing their commissions carefully when they came up the Mississippi. Officials usually found the papers correct, "or as much so as the officers at Galveston know how to make them," Rollins wryly observed.[27] On September 26 the inspectors below Fort St.

Philip saw Captain Job Northrop's privateer the *Independence* at anchor under the new Mexican colors. Northrop raised anchor and tried to stall inspection by letting the vessel drift downstream while he raised sail, all the while protesting that he was trying to bring his ship about to let an inspector aboard. When the official finally pulled his barge alongside and boarded, he immediately discovered two large boxes of muskets. Northrop admitted that he knew they were illegal but said that he needed the business. He then occupied the inspector with conversation until the boats had drifted so far that the inspector found himself at a dangerous remove from the fort. There was nothing for him to do but board his barge and return, with Northrop yelling after him that he was sorry for not complying with instructions, but that "he had entered into business that he was determined to go through with at all hazards," and that "imperious necessity compeled him."[28]

Northrop indeed seemed driven by this necessity. A month later he had four prizes, fat with merchandise, off the south pass of the Mississippi, though he knew that the authorities were aware of him and determined to prevent him from landing his goods. Rollins marveled, "I cannot conceive what Capt Northrop is doing on these coasts." When his inability to unload his goods frustrated some of his men to the point that they refused further service with no prospect of profit, Northrop landed thirty of them on Grand Isle and in lieu of payment, gave them watches and other merchandise to try to sell on their own.[29] Later when Patterson sent two of his little vessels, the *Bulldog* and the *Tickler,* after Northrop, Rollins told Duplessis that "he might as well have ordered two sheep to take a wolf."[30]

Patterson's newfound energy may have been spurred by unexpected repercussions of Aury's Galveston enterprise. Slaves were disappearing from New Orleans, and many believed former Baratarians were stealing them for a Galveston slave mart. Editor

J. C. de St. Romes of the *Courier* complained that some of these thieves walked among the townspeople by daylight and no one dared to denounce them. He called for the militia to step in, or New Orleans should steel itself to "be exposed to all the horrors of *Fire, Pillage* and *Murder.*"[31] Unfortunately, St. Romes's attack cut too close to some of the insurgent leaders, and in the *Gazette* they struck back by accusing him of insulting Mexican patriots.[32]

At the end of July the king in Madrid had approved the deal Pierre had struck for a pardon and payment in exchange for information, and by December Pierre was feeding news of yet another plot to Sedella.[33] Besides what he gave them on Aury at Galveston, Pierre kept his handlers informed of new designs on an old target, Pensacola.[34] For some time the "associates" had been raising men and money for a Pensacola strike in case the insurgents in Mexico were unable to reassert themselves. In that event, their resources would be better spent establishing a privateering port in Florida. In late November news came that the Mexican insurgency was all but finished.

On January 2, 1817, the "associates" held a meeting with Livingston, Grymes, Duncan, Beluche, Peire, and Pierre Laffite among those present. They decided that Aury's corsairs should rendezvous at an offshore island while their "army" sailed and rowed in barges to make a joint land and sea attack on Pensacola. With the perpetually hopeful Peire in command,[35] they would plunder the town, especially of slaves. It was perhaps coincidental that two days later Pierre bought a slave woman from Marie Louisa Villard for $500 and the same day sold her for $900, but he may have needed the quick profit for investment with the "associates," or because Jean needed $1,000 for his purchase three days later of a nineteen-year-old black male whose labor might be needed in the days ahead.[36] Pierre also filed a civil suit against his sometime associate Gambi to recover the $250 loaned to him six months earlier.[37] Mina, meanwhile, was in Galveston, but in

January 1817 the "associates" sent Sauvinet there to pose the Pensacola idea and ask him to come to New Orleans to discuss his cooperating in the venture. Mina was interested, and made the voyage east. Even before he arrived, Laffite or someone got to Morphy the idea that Mina was going to hit Pensacola, and that the "associates" had promised financial backing to Mina's emissary Noriega y Guerra Mier on that basis.[38] Morphy warned Governor José Masot in Pensacola to be on his guard. Masot commenced preparations for defense, and in both Pensacola and New Orleans rumors flew that Florida was to be the next privateer center after an attack by forces massing at Galveston.[39]

Even before Mina reached New Orleans on February 22, the "associates" split into two factions. Those motivated by fast gain favored the Pensacola raid as a quick grab. Other "associates" with some commitment to the Mexican independence movement and an eye to long-term profits argued for a commitment to Galveston. If the Tampico operation was no longer viable, then the "associates" should consolidate and enhance their Galveston foothold into the center of a new insurgency.[40] For his part, Mina quickly read the situation. After a flurry of meetings he left disillusioned, concluding that "it was merely a mercantile speculation." The "associates" offered resources that he thought "niggardly," and on usurious terms.[41] On March 1 Mina departed for Galveston, committed to the original joint operation with Aury and his fleet, despite his rancorous recent history with Aury.

When Mina reached Galveston late the previous November, Aury, feeling threatened by Mina's title as a general, for eight days refused to allow Mina to bring his command ashore. When he relented and Mina's men landed, Aury revealed that he had barely enough supplies to feed the 200 men on his ships and Perry's 160 ashore. Mina's 140 men would have to subsist on the salt pork, beef, and bread they had brought with them, or the oysters and fish they could buy from passing fishermen. In a tense atmosphere, Mina's men established a separate camp to the east of Aury's. In time Aury consented to provide for Mina's men, but the two leaders could not agree on their next act. Mina hoped to lead his men in a landing at Matagorda, an advance inland to Béxar, and then a march into Mexico. Aury disagreed, wanting to lead the naval expedition against Tampico. The two quarreled inconclusively until Sauvinet arrived on his embassy and Mina left for New Orleans to consult the "associates."[42]

Meanwhile anxious Spaniards had been keeping an eye on the growing settlement. The information gleaned by one spy, Antonio Aguirre, proved especially accurate. By December 22 he had the outline of the plan,[43] and by February 17 the Spanish commander in Texas, Joaquin de Arredondo, knew with some certainty that "the freebooters that are in Galveston Bay, armed and with seventeen pieces of artillery" intended to land at Matagorda to attack the province.

Arredondo even found out that one of Aury's men, Captain Francisco Rouquier, was issuing passports on Aury's behalf.[44] More than that, however, Aury was able to commission as many privateers as he wanted thanks to the printing press Herrera had provided. In February Aury commissioned the *Musquito* under a Captain Graque, who immediately tried to introduce a cargo of illegal slaves into New Orleans by sailing into the port and claiming the blacks as crewmen, a ruse that did not fool Duplessis or the court. In March, while squabbling with Perry, Aury recommissioned the *Independence,* alias the *Hotspur,* under Captain Northrop, with letters of marque from his own regime. The ship was destined for a short cruise before she was seized by Duplessis on April 24.[45]

Soon Duplessis's complex attitude toward smugglers got him removed from office, however, and replaced by the Virginian Beverly Chew, an important businessman and political leader.

Chew wanted smugglers out of business. "The most shameful violations of the slave act, as well as our revenue laws, continue to
be practised, with impunity, by a motley mixture of freebooters
and smugglers, at Galveston, under the Mexican flag, and being,
in reality, little else than the re-establishment of the Barataria
band," he complained to Secretary of the Treasury William
Crawford. He believed that the privateers took mostly Spanish
vessels but were not entirely discriminating, and when they sent
the vessels to New Orleans for sale under the Mexican flag they
followed the old Baratarian practice of changing their names.
Morphy repeatedly tried to reclaim the ships for their owners,
but though the cases went to the court and the privateer captains
could show no evidence that Galveston was a part of the Mexican Republic, still the privateers generally won their prizes. He
feared that without a substantial strengthening of the revenue
service Aury's corsairs could not be countered.[46]

Someone in New Orleans was even more interested than
Chew in the affairs at Galveston. Pierre Laffite, and possibly
Jean, was surely present at the meetings held with Mina in February. Now he knew of the rift between Mina and Aury, and between the "associates" and each of them. Pierre sensed that this
moment of disunity was the perfect time to disrupt the filibusters. Neither Sedella nor Morphy had the authority or the resources to act, however. Boldly, the Laffites engaged Latour to be
their embassy to Havana, where he was going to deliver his report
of the Arkansas exploration. On February 26 they gave Latour a
letter to José Cienfuegos, recommending Latour to the captain
general. Emphasizing—indeed, exaggerating—their intimate
knowledge of the Texas coast, they reminded Captain Cienfuegos that their information had always been accurate in the
past. They reminded him, too, that time and the distance to Havana were their enemies, as well as the hazard of their letters
being intercepted and compromising "the indispensable mystery

that must surround this matter." They added concern for their safety, as well they should have.

This is why Latour would outline orally their "quick and infallible" plan, "the result of a long and profound reflection," for stopping Aury and Mina. Latour would be able to elaborate on the details. They even got Sedella to suggest that when Latour arrived in Havana, he be allowed to disembark his ship secretly to avoid being seen and recognized. Père Antoine could already testify that supposedly confidential correspondence between Spain and the United States was circulating freely in New Orleans, and few secrets were kept.[47] The brothers claimed that during his visit in the East, Jean had been approached by representatives of most of the insurgent movements, who had begged the Laffites to coordinate their efforts. The brothers told Latour that Jean had shown a "simulated acceptance" in order to penetrate the plans further. The Laffites promised that they could discover all for Spain, and did not "request anything in return." They would be, they told Latour, "sufficiently paid by serving humanity's cause." Pierre offered to meet with the authorities in Havana to develop plans to put down the rebels, but as that seemed impossible, he asked for a special agent to deal with him in New Orleans. Once the agent arrived, the brothers would insert him into the councils of the plotters so that he could learn firsthand their schemes before the Laffites made plans for their disruption. The agent must have the authority and money to take action quickly and definitively.[48] Sedella added his endorsement of the Laffites and their plan. "They are capable of obtaining to our favor the most difficult and hard enterprises," said Père Antoine.[49] No sooner was Latour on his way and Mina departed than the brothers decided that Jean Laffite would sail for Galveston under the guise of a mercantile voyage, but while there evaluate the men in charge and scout the military resources on the island. The trip should take no more than a few weeks, and could yield big results for Spain. It might also offer huge rewards for the brothers Laffite. With both brothers now working for Spain, Pierre became Number 13-*uno* and Jean Number 13-*dos*.

Sometime between his return from Arkansas and January 1817, Jean had formed a loose mercantile "partnership" with Vincent Duparc, probably for the sole purpose of trading with the "associates" and Galveston, or to provide a front for the brothers' surveillance work.[50] Between March 7 and 11, on the only occasion on which Jean Laffite filed proper documents with the customs house, he declared his intention to take two cases of Bordeaux red wine, two cases of white wine, and three dozen loose bottles of claret to Galveston aboard the *Devorador.* He and Duparc had imported the wine from France in January. As for the *Devorador,* her captain happened to be Laurent Maire, the same man who had been a crewman on the Laffites' *La Diligente* four years before, and more recently captain of *Dos Hermanos.*[51]

The *Devorador* was probably the vessel that Pierre bought at the urging of the "associates" for courier duty with Galveston, and Pierre likely changed her name for this voyage, for on several of the customs documents now and later Jean, Duparc, and Maire all first wrote in the name the *Bolador,* then crossed it out to substitute the *Devorador.*[52] Coincidentally, of course, *El Bolador* had been the name of the vessel that may have helped inaugurate the Laffites in the illegal slave business in 1810.[53] Laffite and Duparc would not be the only merchants with a cargo on the *Devorador.* Four days earlier Raymond Espagnol shipped aboard her some eight casks of wine, and both he and Laffite and Duparc claimed from the customs collector the drawback, or refund due them, of import duties paid when the goods arrived originally in New Orleans.[54] The law allowed for a drawback when such goods were exported again outside the country, and this was the reason for Jean Laffite breaking habit and observing customs laws.[55] Doing so got him a refund of $162.71.

Maire cast off on March 16 with Jean Laffite, Espagnol, John Ducoing—who hoped to join Champlin's privateer the *General Artigas*—and a few other merchants aboard.[56] They entered the Gulf on the morning of March 20, and almost at once met with the *Bellona*, an Aury privateer coming from his settlement. The two ships hove to, and from the *Bellona*'s captain Laffite heard a bizarre tale of chaos at Galveston. Four days before, as Mina and his ship approached Galveston on his return from New Orleans, Aury sent orders to the *Bellona* to open fire on Mina. The captain did so, but Mina refused to be driven off, and shortly thereafter Aury allowed him to come ashore. The captain had left immediately and knew little more.[57]

Three days later Laffite sighted Galveston, probably for the first time. The *Devorador* joined six other privateers and prizes anchored outside the bar. The vessels were under flags of Mexico and Buenos Aires, the prizes loaded with beef and tallow, logwood, farm tools, and $13,000 to $14,000 in silver. John Deveze commanded one of them, perhaps the same *Flying Fish* that he had captained for Pierre a few months before. If Jean paid close attention, as surely he did, he noticed that here the vessels could anchor very close together, but only go through the pass one at a time.[58] Laffite stayed aboard his ship for a week, watching as other privateers came and went: one commanded by Johnny Barbafuma, another out of New Orleans run by a Captain Neps, and the large frigate *Campechana* carrying several thousand muskets and a number of cannon and other military equipment.[59]

Finally on March 30 Laffite rowed across to Mina's ship. He delivered some letters from New Orleans and asked about the coming expedition, which opened the floodgate of Mina's frustration. News from Mexico suggested the time was ripe, but he had been held up too long by the wasted trip to New Orleans. He may not have offered the details of his problems with Aury, but there would have been no concealing them. Alert to any means of gathering news, Laffite asked Mina his Mexican sources in case they should prove useful for his own intelligence gathering. Then he went ashore to see Aury, who had no hesitance about unburdening himself. The moment Mina arrived back in November he tried to take over everything, Aury complained. But Herrera had appointed Aury governor, and he would not yield to anyone. Aury told Laffite that he had settled the dispute with Mina and finally they had made an uneasy peace.[60]

On shore Laffite found a community that had grown to about 120 *cabañas* with plank walls and sailcloth roofs for the officers and even cruder reed and wattle huts for the men, in addition to a coffeehouse, dry goods stores, and a few other commercial establishments.[61] The men traded with the local Coushatta Indians, and a few dozen women and a few children were now on the island. For those who could read, Herrera's press turned out a few issues of a newspaper, the only one then published in all of Texas.[62] Aury's and Mina's men still lived in two camps, however, and Laffite would have visited both.[63] When he spoke to the men ashore, Laffite no doubt heard a different and less self-serving story than Aury's. In Mina's absence, Aury and Perry had fallen out when the governor announced that the harbor at Galveston was not suitable and that he would move to Matagorda without waiting for or notifying Mina, and without taking Mina's men. Perry refused to take this command without Mina's consent, and Aury ordered Perry's arrest on March 1. Perry's men rose up and threatened to storm Aury's headquarters if he did not release their commander. Aury ordered his own men to arms in front of his quarters, backed by a fieldpiece, and only a spark was needed to ignite a battle. When Perry's men won Mina's commanders over to their side, however, Aury understood that he would be unwise to persist. Aury agreed to meet in parlay, at which the leaders decided that Mina should command all land troops, and Aury the maritime men and ships. By the time Aury ordered the *Bellona* to open fire on Mina, the men on the island were thoroughly displeased with Aury.[64]

On April 1 and 2 Maire landed Laffite's and Espagnol's cargo, as well as consignments including sixteen kegs of vinegar and four casks and twenty-two cases of wine. Laffite was too busy to attend to the necessary paperwork, and so someone signed for him two days later to certify the delivery, and again had to cross out *Bolador* and insert *Devorador* on the form. Aury's judge of the admiralty court, John Peter Rousselin, approved the documentation on April 8, adding that "we also declare, there is not a consul or public agt. of the U. S. of A. or American merchants now residing in this place."[65] The date was significant, for Rousselin was now the only remaining "authority" on the island, a sort of professional secretary for revolutionaries after witnessing Herrera's credit authorization for Toledo the year before.[66] Mina's new intelligence suggested that the mouth of the Santander River, near Soto la Marina 150 miles north of Tampico, was a better place to land on the Mexican coast, and he decided to start his campaign there. Perry would go with him. Aury, if only to rid himself of the troublesome pair before moving on to Matagorda, agreed to transport them.

Mina set sail April 7, he and Aury taking all the island's cannon with them. Looking on, Jean Laffite counted about three hundred men on the ships, while Aury had left behind between thirty and forty of his followers, including Louis Durieux in charge and Rousselin, who was to continue the sham admiralty court and prize condemnations and then forward them to Matagorda.[67] Aury gave no orders for the rest of his people to leave Galveston, but his intentions were clear when he ordered most of the huts and buildings burned.[68] What he did not bargain for was that Jean Laffite had other plans. Before him lay the perfect opening for a coup. Aury's leaving was not the end of Galveston, Laffite told Rousselin and the others. In fact, Aury had been disavowed by the "associates," who were now backing the Laffites. If these few men on the island transferred their allegiance to him, Jean could promise them more men to reestablish the port and a steady flow of supplies from New Orleans.[69]

Jean Laffite simply took over Galveston on April 8.[70] Recognizing that Durieux might command some loyalty from the few remaining men of Aury's, Laffite offered him sufficient persuasion to shift allegiance, and then appointed him colonel in command of the military forces, such as they were, with Antoine Pirroneau as his adjutant. Laffite turned Rousselin, too, and made him collector of customs. Jean's associate Ducoing, whose brother was Espagnol's business partner in New Orleans, he appointed judge of the admiralty court. Espagnol would act as secretary. The Laffites' old lieutenant Jannet, conveniently in port, became commander both of the port and of the island's "navy."[71] A week later on April 15, after Lafon arrived with the *Carmelita* bringing Iturribarría with him as Herrera's deputy, Laffite arranged for a meeting in Lafon's cabin. Iturribarría administered an oath of allegiance to the Mexican republic to Durieux, and Durieux then swore in the rest, Lafon acting as secretary of the meeting. Significantly, they made no provision for a marshal or officer of the law. They all knew how irregular their proceeding was, establishing a government on behalf of a defunct insurrection on territory it did not control, and on territory to which the United States held claim. Yet past privateering experience, and hopes for its future here, left them somewhat obsessed with the show of legality. They all signed a memorandum justifying their action, as one said "to make it authentic" and to ensure that "at all times it will be legal and valid." Having no seal of the insurgency, they made do with a small nondescript seal.[72]

Thus Laffite, noticeably absent from either office or participation in the meeting, put the semblance of official sanction from the Mexican junta on the operation. Meanwhile he had acquainted himself with the men still on the island, consulted with Espagnol—whose coming on the *Devorador* was now clearly no accident—and waited for a few privateers to come into port to lend more muscle. By April 14 the *General Arismendi* and a few others had arrived.[73] Three days later in a meeting aboard the *Jupiter* the privateer captains agreed to bring in prizes for admiralty hearing and condemnation. From the proceeds of their first prize sales Rousselin should withhold a percentage to turn over to Colonel Durieux for the support of the soldiers and equipment necessary to defend the establishment. Thereafter from each month's proceeds Rousselin should withhold a sum for the following month's expenses, so that they would be steadily funded in advance. Any surplus left after paying the captains and crews their shares was to be applied to relieving the debts of the Mexican Republic incurred prior to April 5, but only those debts owed to men then living on the island—a neat artifice to ensure that no money left Galveston. The officers of the government, as well as Captains Jannet, Jean Guerre, Denis Thomas, Joseph Place, Colonel Savary, and several others, approved the terms on April 20.[74]

Jean Laffite and his associates had created something new in the New World that went far beyond the loose Baratarian operation. Galveston was to be a civil-military community conducted by and for privateers, and funded voluntarily from their prizes. As its own leaders admitted, the forms observing fealty to the Mexican junta were mere sham. Ducoing would make it clear that Galveston's object was "capturing Spanish property under what they called the Mexican flag, but without any idea of aiding the Revolution in Mexico or that of any other of the Spanish Revolted colonies." In fact, he for one did not believe a Mexican Republic existed any longer, and regarded Galveston as having no lawful connection with any government.[75] The Laffites intended that they and their followers would become a law unto themselves.

Such were the notes that from the Pirate's isle
Around the kindling watch-fire rang the while:
Such were the sounds that thrill'd the rocks along,
And unto ears as rugged seem'd a song!

SIXTEEN

A Season of Treachery
1817

THE NEW REGIME's first prizes—two vessels, the *Petronille* and *L'Enrequita*—came in with Champlin's *General Artigas* on April 7, just after Aury's departure. Aboard them were 287 slaves. Champlin's business partner, New Orleans merchant Christopher Adams, had bought an additional three hundred slaves from Aury just before his fleet sailed.[1] These unfortunate blacks were now the inaugural merchandise of an illicit slave trade that would see thousands smuggled from Texas to Louisiana thanks to the supply the privateers could provide and the organizational genius of the Laffites. Ducoing held sham admiralty court proceedings aboard Lafon's *Carmelita* for the time being. When a prize came in, Ducoing simply examined her papers and made a pronouncement of condemnation. Espagnol then drafted a condemnation order, and the formality was done. They kept no court records.[2]

Jean Laffite prepared to leave immediately after that April 17 meeting of the privateer captains. So much had happened unexpectedly in the last ten days that he had to return to New Orleans quickly to report to his several masters: Pierre, the "associates," and Sedella. He needed to consult with his brother on just how to position themselves in the days ahead. The "associates" could perhaps be induced to provide credit for building up the Galveston establishment. The Spaniards, of course, would want to know the particulars of Mina and Aury and to hear the Laffites' proposal on how to capitalize on the situation. Before leaving, Jean arranged that Lafon would bring him information if anything happened on the Texas coast in his absence, and though he could not know it, Spanish authorities in Texas had half a dozen soldiers dressed as civilians on their way to the bay to keep their own watch on Galveston.³ Laffite also authorized someone on the ruling council to make necessary purchases from Champlin's agent on the island by charging them to the Laffites' account.⁴

Even the *Devorador* experienced difficulty in the pass or anchorage, for Laffite had to buy a new anchor and some anchor cable from Champlin before he could leave.⁵ Then contrary wind held the *Devorador* outside the bar for a day, during which three more corsairs and one prize came to anchor beside her, giving Jean an opportunity to study once more the depth of the water above the bar. Vessels had to anchor outside and wait for a pilot to come bring them one at a time through the pass.⁶

By April 22 Jean was back in New Orleans, unwell—as he had been for some time—but soon at work with Pierre on a scheme to present to the Spaniards for taking Galveston with the bay full of corsairs and prizes, and thus close off further supply of men and material to Aury and Mina. Jean wrote a note to Sedella telling him that he had talked with Mina, "who told me things of great importance." Jean said that Mina even asked Jean to accompany him on his expedition. This may or may not have been true, for the Laffites never figured in Mina's plans before this, and any invitation now would have been ad hoc and spontaneous. "I was unwilling to consent," Jean told the priest, "having the intention of reestablishing a new government in Galveston."⁷ The brothers now proposed that Spain provide a corvette, a brig, one or two schooners, and a pair of gunboats, all to sail singly in order not to attract attention and then rendezvous in the harbor at Pensacola no later than July 15. If necessary the corvette, brig, and one schooner could achieve the same end, the schooner being vital for reconnoitering and messenger service. Meanwhile, by the end of June one of the brothers would have returned to Galveston to determine the total strength of corsairs and crews, as well as prizes, and to send back weekly reports of arrivals and departures. At the same time another schooner should be sent to Soto la Marina to determine Mina's situation and the progress of his campaign, if any, while stopping at Matagorda to assess Aury's position and strength there. Then the schooner would return to New Orleans with its intelligence, and the Laffites would dispatch it to Pensacola with final instructions. If they acted quietly, no one would know what they were doing until it was all over.

The brothers' fleet would sail to Galveston with the corvette and brig flying the flag of Spain beneath the colors of the Mexican insurgency, a sign that they were prizes. Then the gunboats and a schooner, their presumed captors, would approach the bar flying the Mexican checkerboard. Jean knew from observation that a pilot would be sent out to bring them over the bar and through the pass, and once they were inside the bay the few men there should easily be overwhelmed by a landing party. Indeed, in designating the leaders he left behind, Laffite may have purposefully chosen men whom he knew would not be effective in a crisis. The corvette and brig should be carrying cannon and men to arm and crew another brig that Jean believed would be anchored outside the bar.

Once Galveston was in their hands, they would keep the schooners and gunboats in the harbor, attracting little or no attention, while the corvette and brig or brigs remained at anchor outside, posing as prizes. As corsairs approached, Jean could signal the armed ships to take them one at a time, which could be done "without firing a single shot" by a few men and only a couple of cannon thanks to the narrowness of the pass and the fact that most privateers only mounted one or two guns themselves. The Laffites stressed in their proposal that they wanted at every cost to avoid violence. Bloodshed had never been an intentional feature of their operations, and many of the privateers they would take were friends and former associates whom they might hope to employ. Privateer captains currently warned crewmen that capture by Spain meant instant death, as indeed it could. The Laffites, however, wanted every captured crew to be informed while being taken into port that they were to be offered service for Spain, and thus they need not resist or fear reprisal. That way "the desperate valor of the corsair crews will be dispersed," and each vessel captured would augment the forces to take the rest as well as Spain's naval force in the region. In such a fashion the Laffites' force could capture every privateer and prize, starving Mina and Aury of forces and supplies while the goods taken from the prizes funded the Laffite plan. Galveston taken, and Aury forced to abandon Matagorda, privateers still at large would be discouraged from continuing their trade on those shores, and the "associates" and other outfitters would lose heart. No privateer base on the Gulf coast would remain. Unsaid in the Laffites' proposal was the probability that Galveston would then be theirs to use as their own private base, backed by the power of the vessels Spain had lent them. Indeed, as if to establish the legitimacy of the rump government he'd left behind him, Jean gave to a local editor for publication a statement of the busy commerce of the port yet in its infancy. It was also a way of announcing generally that privateers had a new place to bring their prizes for a quick and favorable adjudication by the "admiralty court," followed by a speedy sale. "The affair has turned out perfectly well for us," Jean declared. "Moments are precious, and there is no time to lose."[8]

In fact, Jean Laffite believed their plan was perfect. Just then Latour asked him to go back to the East to take up their efforts of the past year with men planning filibustering voyages, but Laffite knew he had more important work before him here and now. Indeed, he wanted Latour to persuade the men in the East to join with them. "I am at the head of an operation a thousand times more honorable than the one they have projected," he said. He had little doubt that he could sway them in person if he had to, being like his brother Pierre, convinced of his craft at persuasion. They would be doing a great boon for humanity.[9]

As the Laffites completed their plan, Lafon arrived with news. After a hard voyage Aury abandoned Mina at Soto la Marina on April 21, and on May 4 returned to Galveston to learn of the coup. The ruling council invited him to sit in on its deliberations, and he did, but only to make it clear that while he did not have the strength to resist what had taken place in his absence he would not countenance their actions, nor give up his now meaningless power as governor, by acknowledging the council's legitimacy. The council repudiated his claims to rule, and the meeting broke up indecisively with Aury going back to his ship to sulk. Aury's presence, with his commission from Herrera, compromised the authority of Laffite's council under Iturribarría's endorsement, and yet the council's refusal to take directions from him made him a cipher.

Lafon told Jean that he expected the impasse not to be broken. Aury tried to resume power, identifying himself as governor of Texas on May 7 when he took $5,000 from Nicholas Aiguette in payment for a commission for a new privateer, the prize the *Diana*, but the council ignored him and Ducoing continued to act as admiralty judge for about a week.[10] Aury ordered him to sign an oath of loyalty but Ducoing refused, and also refused to condemn Lafon's prize the *Evening Post* when he found her papers to be in order—probably a Laffite loyalist's pretext for defying

Aury. Vicente Garros took over after Ducoing resigned on May 8, and condemned the prize. Henceforth Garros's decisions would not be influenced by genuine papers aboard the prizes, because the captors did not risk letting them be seen in the court. Rumors soon reached New Orleans that when merchants from the city bought prize goods from the privateers, the corsairs would not take hard cash for fear of being robbed by their own associates, and instead preferred bills of credit on the city's banks.[11] Meanwhile, Ducoing had condemned prizes brought in by Champlin, Beluche, Lafon, and Sauvinet, and business was brisk, with eight corsairs and prizes at anchor.[12]

Latour had been in Havana for some time, presenting his report and the proposals of the Laffite brothers of New Orleans, whom he described as "merchants of that city," though the Spanish authorities knew well enough who and what they were.[13] Before long copies of the report were on their way to Onís and Apodaca, as well as to the governors of Texas and neighboring provinces.[14] None seemed to take its warning of American expansion seriously. Onís thought it a good exercise, but one offering nothing new.[15] The report did not reach Mexico City until July, and Madrid did not see it until November 1818.

Far more interesting, it seemed, was Latour's oral representation of the Laffites' propositions, and José Cienfuegos granted the brothers' wish for a fully empowered agent in New Orleans. Morphy, while energetic, had been a minor official, with almost no prior experience. Felipe Fatio, however, was a career operative with credentials. He had been in Havana when Latour arrived and presented his report on March 26. Fatio received his orders in April, and with them sufficient funds to pay the Laffites, Picornell, Sedella, and other friends in New Orleans $100 a month.[16] He was to contact the Laffites through Sedella, or at least to get in touch with Pierre, and determine their sincerity. Cienfuegos wanted to know as much as possible about the Laffites, including their moral character, the attitude of the community in New Orleans toward them, their influence if any, their financial condition, and their vessels. Once satisfied, Fatio was authorized to promise them that they would be "greatly compensated" in return for useful information and action. That done, Fatio was to listen to the brothers' plans, evaluate and rank them by importance and practicability, and then adopt those he deemed suitable as well as an agent whom he trusted, being wary of Picornell. Having selected the man, Fatio could employ him on a stipend. All disbursements of funds were to be noted as coming from a cover fund called the "Commission of the Royal Services."[17]

Fatio took office the day after his arrival on May 6, and that evening sent word to Sedella to bring the Laffites to him. When they met on May 7 Jean told Fatio that his observations of the men at Galveston under Aury and Mina convinced him that they had "no other patriotism, other virtue, other object, other plan than that of making themselves rich, than that of robbing and murdering, under the pretext of Independence, every Spaniard they might encounter, in order to make, if they could, a quick and great fortune."[18] Jean said he would bring his diary from the voyage to Galveston to Fatio the following day. He gave Fatio his latest news on Mina and Aury, and added that he believed Aury's (incorrect) suspicion that Perry was an American agent hoping to engineer Texas independence in order to hand it to the United States. Before the meeting adjourned Fatio promised to have a schooner ready to take their plan and his recommendation to Havana and Cienfuegos.

One subject they did not address was the rumored plot for a slave rebellion. Fatio proposed that they could simply expose it and its authors by public letters sent to the East, but the brothers adamantly opposed the idea, first because it would expose their undercover work, and second because it might actually endanger their lives. It may have been nothing but a ruse in the first place, of course, and in time the Spaniards concluded that it had been a hoax from the start. They preferred to blame it on Ariza, whom the Laffites said revealed it to them. It could just as easily have been their own scheme, to raise a specter so dread that Havana would do what they wanted and send a representative. Now that Fatio was here, and with money in his pocket, they no longer needed the ruse, if ruse it had been.[19]

Clearly the brothers were feeling out Fatio, otherwise they would have brought Jean's diary and their plan to this first encounter. Yet they left Fatio feeling comfortable, and the following evening the Laffites and Sedella called on Fatio to turn over Jean's diary and a draft of the plan he and Pierre had formulated. The scheme must be implemented immediately, they urged, before conditions changed. If carried out expeditiously, their proposal could end privateering once and for all.

Fatio saw the sense in their plan and their urgency, but did not commit himself. First he spoke with one or two others familiar with Galveston and spent several days making discreet inquiries into the Laffites' "moral and public conduct" since they started their Barataria operation in 1810. Reports said they were humane and generous with Spanish prisoners. Fatio was no fool. He knew that the Laffites acted in self-interest, and that they could harbor deception while pretending to be friends. Nevertheless, he thought they had to see that the benefits of being honest with him far outweighed the reward of duplicity. In their favor also was the fact that so far everything they had given Sedella had turned out to be true. Sedella had known them for a long time, and he vouched for their sincerity, adding that "from the time they first offered their services," they had complained about the sloth of the government to act on their intelligence.

Finally on May 24 he concluded to recommend their plan to Cienfuegos at face value. "Nevertheless," he told Cienfuegos, "I shall not cease to be on guard constantly; and if, unfortunately, I should observe any contradiction between their promises and their conduct, I shall be able to end the evil at its source." Fatio believed that the plan was the only way "to uproot at one blow the evil that we have so long been suffering; since to go on now and then taking one boat or another would in no wise end the life of this hydra, which would be born again of its own blood." Better yet, "the taking of Galveston is so easy in the present circumstances, without the need for losing even one man on one side or the other," Fatio advised, "and the leaders who live there are all dependent upon No. 13," Pierre's code name. He agreed that Pierre would take the *Devorador* to Galveston at once to get the latest information, and he would send a schooner to Soto la Marina to gather intelligence on Mina and Aury if possible. Fatio was not blind to the hazards involved. The Laffites were betraying a score and more of people in New Orleans, and a number of privateers, any of whom might be happy to see them dead if their betrayal were discovered. Fatio, too, felt the danger to his own life, and warned his superior that secrecy was paramount.

As for the Laffites, Fatio wanted them close to him, no doubt for speed of action as well as to keep an eye on them. Latour might be sent east to discourage more filibuster groups from forming there, but Fatio did not want either of the brothers sent that far away unless absolutely necessary.[20] Meanwhile he gave the brothers countersigns with which to identify themselves to Spanish agents as friends and disbursed to them the funds they said were necessary to put their plan into action. At last the brothers felt Spanish coin in their hands. Two days after their second meeting with Fatio, Marie Villard suddenly paid off the $1,120 mortgage she owed on the house at Bourbon and St. Philip.[21]

In April the brothers had a credit balance of over $13,000 with Champlin and Adams, probably proceeds from Pierre's last shipment to Boquilla de Piedras or investment by the "associates" into the Galveston enterprise. The day of their first meeting with Fatio the brothers deposited another $2,000 in specie, probably a reimbursement to Jean for his voyage. A week later they deposited another $650.[22] Then on May 22 just before Fatio wrote to Cienfuegos informing him of his decision, the Spanish agent paid "No. 13" $4,000 as an "installment" for Pierre's voyage to reconnoiter Galveston and Matagorda.[23] Two days later the brothers deposited another $2,020 in gold with Champlin and Adams.[24] Meanwhile Jean reclaimed the bond he had posted for his modest drawback for the cargo of wine and other things he had taken to Galveston.[25] Any dollars that could be raised from any source were urgent now. To provide the fast schooner that the plan required for running to the Mexican coast and doing courier duty, the Laffites sold Fatio their own little prize *goleta* the *Antonio Bonifacia* for $3,000.[26]

During these busy days the brothers outfitted the *Devorador* for Pierre's trip, drawing heavily on their balance with Champlin. Born in New York, Champlin was a sometime planter on the Mississippi, a smuggler, a ship chandler in New Orleans, and a privateer closely tied to Aury. Now he left most of the New Orleans business to partner Adams while he sailed his corsair in search of prizes.[27] Adams sold the Laffites $1,157 worth of ship's biscuit, thirty barrels of pork and thirty of salt beef, two sacks of coffee beans, six cases of salted cod, three barrels of mackerel and forty-two of potatoes. There was also sugar, cooking oil, three barrels of onions, four barrels each of cider and vinegar, as well as mustard, pepper, and a barrel of cheese, all testimony to the monotony of shipboard fare for corsairs, with only the onions and cider to stave off scurvy. The men must have their drink, too, and thus the Laffites stowed aboard six cases of red wine and six white, and a dozen cases of brandy. Anticipating the vagaries of weather and bottom that often required a vessel to cut its anchor cable, they loaded eighteen lengths of cable as well. This left room for Maire to take on five passengers and their baggage, men to add to the Laffites' cadre of loyal followers at Galveston. On May 27 when Adams totaled the debits against the Laffite balance, the cost of outfitting for the trip came to $4,248.06, a little more than Fatio's installment. The passage for the five men and their equipment added another $1,175 to the voyage.[28]

A couple of near slips caused some minor concern. In the middle of the month several prizes condemned by Ducoing's admiralty court came into New Orleans for sale, and Fatio filed libels on behalf of their owners. Lafon and merchant John B. Laporte were particularly interested in the prizes, however, and applied to go before Judge Hall to prove that the authorities under which these ships had been condemned at Galveston were legally appointed and commissioned by Aury. Espagnol was in town and Lafon asked him to testify on their behalf, yet in spite of being owed $1,200 by Lafon, he declared that if put on the witness stand he would tell the truth of the illegality of Aury's and now Laffite's government. Quite possibly Fatio or Jean Laffite had had a word with him and money changed hands.[29] Meanwhile Jean almost caused a problem. The transactions with Champlin and Adams were aboveboard, but Jean stumbled when his sometime partner Duparc tried to import a shipment of thirty-seven small pivot guns or swivels, of the sort mounted at the prow of a pirogue, for the enterprise. They came from Galveston and were improperly cleared through customs in order to avoid paying duty. It would have been ironic if the whole enterprise had foundered because a foolish effort to save perhaps $400 in duty resulted in a court case.[30] Once a smuggler, always a smuggler, it seemed. The case would dog Laffite for years, but it did not in the end impede outfitting the *Devorador*.

Pierre intended to set sail May 26, in Fatio's words, to gather "the final accounts which we need to execute the stroke safely." Before going he gave Fatio the designs of the insurgent flags of

Mexico, Venezuela, and Buenos Aires so that the Spanish vessels in the plan could copy and fly them as they approached Galveston.[31] Iturribarría had arrived in New Orleans by May 15, and committed revolutionary that he was, he spoke of publicizing the shambles at Galveston. He knew that rich prizes were being taken by Aury, but the money was not getting back to New Orleans to fund the revolution. "If there are no funds there are no soldiers," he wrote to Durieux. Though Iturribarría was on good terms with the Laffites, who had done him favors in the past, his discouragement could inhibit the assembly of privateers and threaten to compromise the Laffite-Fatio plan.[32] Added urgency came when the Laffites learned on May 13 that the "associates" had word of a Spanish fleet sailing from Vera Cruz, bound for Havana and thence to Spain. That meant the Gulf would be less protected for weeks or months to come, and this was the time to sail for prizes.[33] Then came late word that a disgusted Aury had left Galveston on May 18 and moved to Matagorda. This called for a last-minute adjustment making Matagorda the target and delaying Pierre's departure until June 3.[34]

Pierre usually left the sailing to his brother, but Jean remained indisposed for some time.[35] The elder Laffite was also clearly the one in charge, and he needed to appraise conditions on-site. Fatio may even have insisted on it. Jean, the more experienced at ship outfitting, was now entrusted with preparing and supplying the *Antonio Bonifacia* in New Orleans. He needed to have her ready to sail at a moment's notice before the end of the month.[36] Jean Laffite also had personal business to attend to in New Orleans, among other things raising $700 by selling a slave that he had bought from his Arkansas acquaintance Notrebe.[37] When the *Devorador* finally sailed, Jean assured Fatio that if Spain did as the brothers said, she would "have no enemies to fear in this part of the world."

Pierre set sail on June 3, and may not have stopped at Galveston, knowing that Aury had left. By June 14 he and the *Devorador* were at Matagorda, and what he found surely encouraged him. The impetuous Aury had wrecked most of his fleet on sandbars as he entered the harbor behind Matagorda Island, and those that got in found they could not get out again. That was only the first disaster. By June 15, while Pierre was still off Matagorda, the Spaniards had assembled enough soldiers that they could march to meet Mina. Mina and Perry fell out, and Perry led some of his men away, only to be surrounded a few days later by sixty men commanded by a Spanish lieutenant who demanded their surrender. Perry refused, and took his own life to avoid capture.[38]

Meanwhile Mina's base at Soto la Marina was besieged and surrendered on June 15, leaving Mina isolated from support by sea. All he could do was march his men inland until they found a band of rebels, whom they joined, Mina's dreams of personal conquest and liberation disintegrating like those of so many of the filibusters before him. Laffite would not learn of this for some time, but meanwhile there was Aury and his battered fleet at Matagorda. On June 12 a Spanish frigate and accompanying gunboats blockaded Aury's vessels and fired on them in their anchorage, and may still have been doing so when the *Devorador* hove in sight.[39] By the time Pierre arrived, a frustrated Aury was already getting those he could extricate back to sea and setting off for Galveston. Champlin's ship was among those stuck in the bay, and Pierre bought a bunch of crabs that Champlin's men had passed the time netting. Pierre also leased a brig of Champlin's as a dispatch boat and sent it to Galveston with orders to stop only briefly before going on to New Orleans to take word of the latest developments to Fatio as promised. When Pierre's dispatch reached New Orleans on about July 12, Fatio gloated that Aury was in a "rat-trap." All they had to do was take him.

Meanwhile the *Devorador* remained at Matagorda a few days, during which Pierre bought a few barrels of white wine for his men, and two slaves from Champlin.[40] Then the *Devorador* set sail for Galveston, probably in convoy with Aury's remnants. They anchored off Galveston a few days later to find Garros still acting as admiralty judge, which he continued to do until he left for New Orleans on June 30 with no named successor.[41] Aury had brought with him two shiploads of slaves, numbering close to seven hundred in all. One prize had three hundred blacks, most of whom were seriously ill by this time, and the callous commander simply cast the vessel adrift in the Gulf and abandoned them. The other cargo he had Garros condemn according to form. Added to the slaves left by Champlin in April, this made more than six hundred and fifty on Galveston Island, representing a substantial potential profit. More immediately, however, Aury tried to reestablish his government. Pierre did not resist as Aury replaced Jean's appointees, for it suited the brothers' plan to keep Aury at Galveston until the Spanish attack came. There would be opportunity aplenty to reestablish their officers once Aury was out of the way.

When he came ashore to make his camp a short distance from Aury's, Pierre walked up a pathway from the landing through the coarse grass to higher ground dotted with dense brush and a few trees. At high tide he found his site no more than six feet above the water, but generally secure, with a well nearby affording nasty but potable water. There Aury rebuilt a village of huts made of planks and sailcloth, while his men stuck poles in the ground and wove wattles and thatch into them for shelter.[42] No sooner was he established ashore than Pierre began working subtly to undercut Aury's authority. It was not difficult. Aury's unbroken record of failure and high-handedness with his men made many ripe for conversion.

By mid-July Aury decided to abandon hopes for success in Mexico, and told Pierre that he intended to take his fleet to Amelia Island off the Florida coast to join with others seeking to take over that remnant of Spain's North American mainland.

Pierre immediately paid a call on General Sarracin, who commanded some of the soldiers with the fleet, and after Laffite promised provisions for his men, the general agreed to keep his command after Aury left. The next day Sarracin moved his camp from Aury's to the site of Pierre's, a symbolic move that further demoralized Aury and the rest. That was only the first defection. Soon more than a dozen of the sailors came over to Pierre, and following them came Colonel Savary and fourteen of the free mulattoes following him. After a month on the island, Pierre believed that Aury's men were so hungry he could buy them all if only he had provisions enough.

But by July 23 Pierre found himself running out of everything, "to which I am not accustomed," he told Jean. He had no choice, if he was to capitalize on his success to date, but to send the brig *Independence* leased from Champlin to New Orleans with a report to his brother and an urgent plea to send more supplies, along with a good store of drinkable water. Even should the brig be lost on the way due to bad weather, always a possibility now that the hurricane season was upon them, the risk was worth taking. Sending the ship directly to New Orleans had not been his original plan, but his destruction of Aury from within allowed for a shift in thinking.

Besides, he had promised passage to New Orleans to some men on the island defecting from Aury, including Iturribarría. Pierre was only too happy to send him back to New Orleans, as his departure would remove Aury's only vestige of legitimacy and a source of privateering commissions from the revolutionary junta. He also sent an appeal for Jean to come if he was over his illness, for now Pierre felt unwell, perhaps his old malady returning, aggravated by his labor and an attack of something akin to scabies. Pierre was also trying to conclude a deal with Champlin to buy the huge lot of slaves on the island, but had to negotiate through an interpreter since Champlin spoke only English and

Pierre felt his command of the language unequal to the fine points of the deal despite his years in New Orleans. He felt that his brother's English was better. Besides, while he admitted that in slave dealing "there are some doubloons to be earned," he was more interested in their own plans, though he did not say whether he meant the brothers' private scheme or their undertaking for Fatio. No doubt expecting that Fatio would want to see his letter, Pierre declared that he was committed to Spain's cause, had given his word to see it to completion, and would do so even if it cost him his life. He had had as much success on the island as he could have hoped for, but he was willing to stay on until it was finished.

There is little doubt that Pierre held the upper hand on the island by the time he sent the brig to New Orleans. "I am like the Chief and father of Galveston," he told his brother. If their "friends" wanted to own Galveston Island, he could make it theirs. If they wanted it abandoned, he could accomplish that, too. Typical of the double game the Laffites played now, those "friends" could have been the "associates" or the Spaniards.[43]

Finally, on July 28 Aury wrote a letter to Herrera announcing that he was leaving. He disclaimed responsibility for what happened on the island after he left, declaring that any acts by those put in power thereafter would be unlawful, for they would occur without his sanction as governor.[44] That day Pierre either paid his last bribe to lure away more of Aury's men or else gave a party when the commodore announced his decision to leave. Pierre bought from Champlin a "pipe" of white wine, more than one hundred gallons, to fuel the celebration.[45] Three days later Aury sailed away, hands washed of Texas and Mexico forever, his course set for Florida to seek new fortune.

While Fatio and the Laffites readied their enterprise, a steady parade of privateers sailed in and out of New Orleans. The *Hotspur* was in the trade, along with the *Mexican Congress,* the

Couleuvre under Deveze, the *Marie* and the *Rover,* as well as the *Alonzo.*[46] Some of the goods being brought into New Orleans from Galveston had been shipped from Philadelphia and other eastern ports, intended to secure and enhance Aury's establishment. While Aury was absent convoying Mina and foundering at Matagorda, however, the shippers found no one at Galveston to take possession or pay, and so brought tons of cargo into New Orleans. Sugar, liquors, beef, pork, musket and cannon shot, as well as tar, turpentine, pitch and resin, varnish, and 11,500 board feet of lumber—the necessaries for building a village—came in aboard the *Alonzo.*[47]

The volume of the traffic left the customs people asking Washington for instructions on how to deal with the vessels plying the Galveston trade, especially when known former offenders were taking an interest. The collector of customs in the Bayou Teche district had an inkling that "one Dominique a Frenchman that was in Prison in New Orleans in the winter 1814 & 15 for smuggling" was trying to outfit another ship, and asked if "he has not forfeited the Privilege of owning or commanding vessels under the Revenue Law."[48] The new and sudden challenge to the slave trade ban posed by Galveston also raised questions. Beverly Chew learned of the large collection of slaves at Galveston and suspected that the Laffites would soon establish a slave mart somewhere on the west bank of the Sabine, just outside American authority. Early in June there were reports of a number of Louisiana planters on their way to Galveston to buy slaves, and later in the month, as Pierre was beginning his espionage work on the island, the navy dispatched the USS *Boxer* to the mouth of the Sabine to try to intercept the buyers when they came back with their illicit purchases. Officials frankly confessed little optimism about success.[49]

In fact, the legitimate slave market in New Orleans was glutted at the moment, with as many as 650 slaves available in July, and Champlin would sell his cargo to a middleman at very advantageous rates. That summer Pierre charged seventeen blacks to the brothers' account with Champlin and Adams for $4,500, less than half what he could expect to realize from Louisiana planters even in a temporarily glutted market.[50] Champlin had more Africans left, and sailed for the Louisiana coast. He anchored on the coast off St. Mary's Parish late in July, probably off Belle Isle, intending to run his slaves up the Atchafalaya to Bayou Teche. Instead, as his pirogue or launch made for shore, it swamped in the surf, and Champlin drowned.[51] Within days of his death Chew in New Orleans knew that Champlin had been selling slaves to the Laffites, Sauvinet, and others, but doubted that his revenue officers could either find or stop them. Chew was exasperated.

By the end of August, however, he had depositions from Ducoing and Garros to add to Espagnol's in supporting his denunciation of the Aury-Laffite government to the secretary of the treasury. He also, thanks to Espagnol, had a copy of the articles drawn up in Galveston on April 15. He had been for some time sending lists of offending vessels to Dick for seizure and legal action, and the revenue officers were doing their job even though the court often failed them. Chew believed that "these steps of the Officers of the port have irritated the Barratarian Gent. and their connexions in a high degree."

Now when Chew learned of men heading for the Sabine with money to buy slaves, he sent a party to arrest them, intending to attack the receiving end of the trade if he could not get at Galveston. But he wanted the navy to stop a reestablishment at Galveston, "otherwise the Bay will no longer be safe for any flag." Currently armed vessels came into and left the lower Mississippi as they pleased, and some armed boats committed robberies in sight of Fort St. Philip. He counted eleven private armed vessels under either Mexican or Venezuelan colors in port just on August 30 alone. He needed more revenue officers and ships, and more

inspectors all along the coast. In Washington, Secretary Crawford was amazed by Chew's complaint. He was sure the navy had
more than sufficient muscle to put down the pirates without the
revenue service needing to build a virtual navy of its own for the
task. "I cannot conceive why they are not employed in destroying
the Pirates in that section of the Union," Crawford wondered of
the navy.[52]

While complimenting Chew for his dedication to duty,
Crawford told him that additional naval patrols ought to be sufficient to curtail the illicit slave traffic.[53] To that end, Washington
authorized Patterson to borrow money from the United States
branch bank to add another vessel or two to patrol the coast.[54] It
was a faint response, and failed to address the new inland avenue
of slave distribution.

Onís continued his campaign to gain the cooperation of authorities in Washington. Everyone was sympathetic. No one did
anything.[55] In fact, the privateers had become so impudent that
they had an attorney preparing a memorandum to complain to
the United States Treasury about the revenue officers and to ask
Washington to permit the privateers to import their booty on the
grounds that they made large cash outlays to acquire it.[56]

At least Chew was not the only man in New Orleans with
problems at the moment. On July 7 the district court indicted
Jean Laffite, Lafon, and Duparc for failure to pay import duty in
the matter of the pivot guns. Duparc claimed to be their legal
owner and denied any intent to evade customs, but the court required the three to post a bond of $2,225, the goods' appraised
value. The court also seized the pivots and ordered Jean and the
others to appear before the bench on July 19 to show cause why
the pivots should not be condemned. On August 5 Jean and
Lafon presented themselves at the customshouse to give their
notes as sureties for Duparc, and there the matter rested. In fact,
it would not come to a final settlement until 1826, after all three

were dead, when the court went after Lafon's estate to collect the unpaid sureties and nine years' worth of 6 percent interest.[57]

Money remained a prime concern for Jean as he prepared to relieve the pressure on Pierre. Late in July he acted as agent in yet another slave sale for one of his Arkansas acquaintances, but within days thereafter he was on his way to Galveston.[58] By that time Pierre's situation was critical. On August 16, almost four weeks after sending his letter to Jean, he expected that the *Independence* should have returned with provisions. Now his supplies were exhausted, and he was forced to buy goods from incoming privateers at high rates, and on the brothers' credit. He had to borrow money from one man passing through in order to pay cash for some necessaries. Meanwhile his health and the scabies-like itch had not improved either. He needed Jean's help, and soon. Unless resupplied, he could be forced to abandon the port.[59]

Fortunately Fatio gave Jean another $1,400 on August 14, which Jean immediately began spending on provisions.[60] Fatio's payment was especially welcome because Champlin's assets had been frozen pending the settlement of his estate, and now Jean could not charge goods despite a credit balance with Champlin and Adams of $2,879.56. Jean made no attempt to conceal his activity. Chew remarked at the end of the month that "Lafitte is now purchasing a large quantity of provisions, and the first cargo will soon sail."[61]

However, Jean kept encountering delays. Fatio would not release enough money, then by late August protested that the bad weather season was upon them and the warships could not risk the voyage. Meanwhile Cienfuegos had decided that the time was not right and wanted to know more details of the plan. The Spanish fleet was simply too small and too overtaxed to take the kind of risk Jean was proposing. Fatio and Laffite met frequently, and finally Fatio agreed to authorize purchase of enough provisions and materials to hold Galveston while they awaited a more definitive decision from Havana.[62] Fatio gave Laffite $2,658 during the last week of August and the first week of September, and Jean ran up debts to the sum of $14,465, half of which was the cost of the two supply ships purchased for the venture. He told Fatio that he had to take out a mortgage on the house at Bourbon and St. Philip to raise another $2,800 on his own, and incurred considerable debt on the brothers' credit with the expectation of reimbursement, which may have been true or may have been a typical Laffite untruth to impress Fatio with the urgency of the situation and Jean's commitment to the cause.[63]

By late August Pierre could hold out no longer. He left Galveston, arriving in New Orleans on or before September 1. No doubt the brothers conferred, and with Fatio, who told Pierre of Cienfuegos's desire for more information. Frustrated but resigned, Pierre dispatched a report to the captain general that did not skimp in deploring the lost opportunities, nor in blaming sloth and carelessness. Fortunately Pierre still had a spy inside Aury's command keeping him informed of the commodore's plans for Florida. Now, however, they must adjust their schemes yet again.

Pierre proposed that he and Jean reestablish Galveston, capitalizing on the trust they enjoyed from corsair captains across the Gulf and those working for the insurgencies at Buenos Aires and elsewhere. He believed the brothers could be fully in control by the spring of 1818, with a well-established base that would attract others until virtually the whole of the corsairing fleet of the Gulf would be there, ripe for the taking.

But Pierre must be able to get the word to the corsairs at sea quickly, as soon as they finished "weaving our web," if they were to get the captains lined up. "Some funds are necessary," he emphasized, but Spain would profit manyfold for its investment. If Cienfuegos did not want Galveston reestablished as a port, he should say so now, in which case the brothers would take their own measures in dealing with corsairs and prizes that fell into their hands. He and Jean had a number of men in New Orleans ready to work for them, some of whom had been their followers in 1814 when they rejected the British offer. Pierre could not help but refer to that as "a period that, without flattering ourselves, brings us honor, by virtue of our conduct and repulses of the brilliant propositions that they made to us to help them in the conquest." Cienfuegos already knew of the Laffites' aid to the Americans, but Pierre pointed it out now as an example of the fact that "there is no one in the world that can make us break our word."

The Laffites were about to send the *Carmelita* loaded with provisions and other goods to reestablish Galveston, and they had a brig that would be very useful in transporting more men and matériel. Thus far their expenditures more than doubled what Fatio had paid them, however, and he was doling out smaller and more infrequent amounts. They had bought much of the goods on two months' credit, and sold the brig leased from Champlin for $13,000. Pierre appealed to Cienfuegos to trust their sincerity and provide the money they needed. Even after the lost opportunities to date, if only they had sufficient money they could "execute the most beautiful political and military operation that has been conceived until now, since discovery of the Antilles." The "associates," unaware of Mina's whereabouts or plight, were still hoping to hear from him, and Laffite warned that if they got reinforcements to him, Mexico could be in real danger. A secure Galveston could help deter that, of course. "When we see ourselves in a position to give this great stroke," Pierre boasted, they would be able to hand over Humbert, Gutiérrez, Mina, and the rest to Spanish justice. However, Pierre advised the captain general that if the Laffites delivered the leaders to Cienfuegos, it must be on the understanding that they were not to be executed. Otherwise, he said, "no one in the world would be able to bring us to serve the cause of kings." Meanwhile, fearing Aury would return to Galveston if he learned of the Laffite plan, Pierre urged Cienfuegos to neutralize him at Amelia Island. Pierre confessed more personal fears, too, for he believed the longer they delayed, the more inevitable it became that the Numbers 13 would be discovered. The insurgents' followers would surely kill them if they were found out, he argued.[64]

The *Carmelita*, captained by Lafon, sailed on September 1, with Jean Laffite aboard.[65] When she reached Galveston a few days later, the community had been deserted. Another vessel loaded with provisions and building materials, Laporte's *Franklin*, stayed at anchor for a time, then returned to New Orleans early in October.[66] Lafon remained at anchor off Galveston, however.[67] Jean Laffite had brought with him about forty of the old Baratarians, "to consolidate his force and maintain himself master of that place," said Fatio. Number 13-*uno* would turn the island over to Cienfuegos whenever he wanted it, but Pierre advised that they wait until the new plan was well in effect in order that "the harvest will be complete." Fatio felt some unease. He knew the brothers resented not having been paid for their expenses, let alone a profit. Fatio believed they acted in good faith, but he did not delude himself. The Laffites enjoyed enormous authority in the privateering and insurgent community. "The knowledge they possess makes them capable of performing everything they have offered," he told Cienfuegos a few days after Jean departed, but "as enemies they would be most dangerous."[68] He could not pay what the brothers demanded, yet feared putting Pierre off too long could be dangerous. Spain was stringing them along, but it should not cut them loose just yet. Should they feel insulted or abandoned, they could easily make their Spanish associates the first victims of their wrath. Pierre's offer to go to Cuba with his family to meet with authorities, and even to be held as hostage for the brothers' redeeming their promises, did not allay a hint of suspicion.[69] Fatio would be vigilant.[70] Chew, too, knew of Jean's arrival at Galveston, and of his plans to start the community anew. Both Chew and Fatio would be watching.[71]

Slight are the outward signs of evil thought,
Within—within—'twas there the spirit wrought!
Love shows all changes—Hate, Ambition, Guile,
Betray no further than the bitter smile.

SEVENTEEN

Deadly Friends
1817-1818

E VEN AS JEAN LAFFITE sailed west along the Louisiana coast toward Galveston, information that he and Pierre passed to Fatio helped discomfit Aury yet again. When he left Galveston in July, Aury sailed to Old Providence, an island off the east coast of Colombia, where one of his corsairs informed him that the revolutionary juntas of Buenos Aires and Chile had empowered him to take both Old Providence and Santa Catalina islands on their behalf. He raised the flag of the insurgencies and proclaimed himself a governor once more, then sailed on to Florida.[1] When Aury reached Amelia Island on September 15, an adventurer named Gregor McGregor had occupied the place, but had left on September 4 in a huff.[2] Colonel Jared Irvine had taken over from McGregor, and Aury simply pushed Irvine aside upon arrival. He raised the Mexican insurgent flag, and prepared to make the island a base for privateering. A week later he had a dozen ships in the harbor.[3] Nevertheless, the United States was not about to risk Florida going from a Spanish colony to a Mexican one. By early December even the British knew that President Monroe would take action, and later that month American forces occupied Amelia Island. Aury gave it up without a fight. He went to Charleston, then Jamaica, and wound up on Old Providence in July, where he would operate for the rest of his brief life.[4]

The British ambassador in Washington expected Monroe to move against Galveston as well, noting that a squadron of four ships—consisting of the corvette *John Adams*, the brig *Prometheus*, the schooner *Lynx*, and another vessel—had been ordered into the Gulf of Mexico.[5] Indeed, the day that Charles Bagot sent his report to London, Monroe issued a state of the union message in which he said that he intended to suppress the pirates at Amelia and Galveston. Significantly, he referred to Galveston as being "within the limits of the United States, as we contend, under the cession of Louisiana," not failing to get in a subtle complaint about Spain delaying the boundary negotiation.[6]

The week after his message, Monroe told the secretary of war to notify the military to be ready for orders. When Captain John D. Henley of the navy asked for 150 soldiers and officers for a joint operation against Galveston, General Andrew Jackson agreed, and on the last day of the year General Robert Butler, in command of the Division of the South at Nashville, Tennessee, ordered men from the United States Army garrison at New Orleans to be ready to march "to suppress the military establishment" at Galveston Island.[7] When Henley and the squadron led by the *John Adams* got Florida without a fight, though, Monroe decided to cancel the Galveston movement. American soldiers were now occupying Spanish Florida, and one diplomatic crisis with Spain was enough for the moment. They could address Galveston later, especially since Monroe had some hope of getting Texas peacefully through the Onís negotiations. In the interim, if the privateers on the island were a thorn in Spain's side, so much the better.

While all of this played out, Pierre Laffite remained in New Orleans, where even small sums became important until Fatio honored his promises. On November 10 Pierre sold a slave of Jean's to raise $1,000, then paid out $900 of it two days later to buy another, all to net $100.[8] But then he learned of something that could make information from the Laffites very valuable again. For some time Spain had feared an attempt by exiles from the former regime of Napoleon to create a new empire in Texas or Mexico where Napoleon could resume his destiny. Joseph Bonaparte was in Philadelphia at the center of all such intrigues.

General Charles Lallemand also found substantial support when he reached Boston in 1816, having already failed in one attempt to free the emperor. Around him revolved the hopes of a resettlement group calling itself by several names, including the "Society for the Cultivation of the Vine and Olive." Lallemand's aims and their desire to start a new French community in the New World largely coincided, and each could use the other. Lallemand went to New Orleans late in 1816 or early 1817, and quickly established relations with the exile community there, most notably Humbert. Lallemand published a disingenuous manifesto proclaiming peaceful agricultural intentions, and his followers gained land grants in the Alabama territory and set out to settle there in the summer of 1817.[9] Lallemand showed no interest in his part of the grant. He was no farmer. He was a general, and he dreamed a general's dreams. Influenced perhaps by Humbert, he turned his eyes to Texas.

By September Washington knew the outlines of Lallemand's idea of enlisting French exiles as the nucleus of an army to take first Texas, and then Mexico—not to liberate the native peoples, but to substitute French rule for Spanish. Lallemand tried to reassure Secretary of State John Quincy Adams that he had no plans for conquest, yet by January he was buying arms and munitions in New York while he had men enlisting adventurers in Louisiana.[10] He tried to enlist Aury in his cause, but the invitation came ten days after Aury had been expelled from Amelia and washed his hands of the Gulf for good. Lallemand even tried to win over Onís by offering to place himself and his followers in the king's service. Apodaca had no thought of countenancing an armed band of adventurers settling on Spanish soil. He sent orders to authorities throughout New Spain to arrest Lallemand on sight. Well before then, however, Lallemand boarded the first contingent of 150 followers aboard the *Huntress* at Philadelphia, along with six cannon, 600 muskets, 400 sabers, and 12,000 pounds of powder, funded in part by money from Joseph Bonaparte. On December 17, 1817, he set sail for the Gulf and Galveston.[11]

By January 1818 Jean Laffite had been at Galveston three months and had the establishment well in hand. Upon his arrival the previous September he put slaves brought in on the first prizes to work building houses for his men. According to Juan Castro, one of the blacks thus employed, there was no question among the slaves that they worked for "the Commandante of that Island, who was Mr. Lafitte."[12] By January 5, 1818, when Jean's old associate Dominique brought a prize into port, there was the semblance of a community. Youx was back at sea after a series of fiascos.[13] Finally in September 1817 he had managed to get a schooner, the *Louise,* out of Bayou St. John and into the Gulf, soon to be refitted into the privateer *Josephine.*[14] Flying the checkerboard flag of Mexico, Dominique took the Spanish schooner *Marin* off the Tortugas on November 30 and now brought her into Galveston. Only two vessels rode at anchor in the harbor, both prizes and one of them the *Panchita,* taken by Laméson, who had gone to New Orleans to get materials to convert her into a corsair. Not another privateer was in sight at the moment.[15]

Manuel Gonzales served aboard the *Marin,* and when he came ashore on January 6 he was one of the first visitors to see the new establishment. It did not impress him overmuch. He found the island to be little more than a "wild sand bar" with four or five "temporary miserable hovels" for the fifty men, mostly blacks and mulattoes, living there. Laffite built for himself "a tolerably good looking frame house" on a slight elevation. It rose two stories, with a piazza and center hall from front to back, and a parlor to one side. It had no carpets and the simplest furniture, and at first remained unpainted on the exterior, but it was a mansion compared to the huts and shanties.[16] Only two women were on the island. One called herself "Madamoiselle Victoire" and ran a cabaret of sorts. The other was a slave belonging to Colonel Savary, though Gonzales noted that she "was then attending upon Lafitte." As for the men, most were sailors and appeared to be in Laffite's employ. During the eight subsequent months that he lived among them, Gonzales saw no sign of anything like a civil government. They flew no nation's flag, held no military parades, and observed no civil order. Living with Laffite was one Rivard, who acted as secretary and oversaw the large store of muskets, pistols, and sabers in Laffite's house. The people generally acknowledged Rivard as "commandant," though there was no question that "Lafitte was the chief."[17] Those who were more familiar with the social landscape of Louisiana noted that the man in command was "Lafite the younger."[18]

The chief would still have been dealing with Dominique's new prize on the afternoon of January 14 when the *Huntress* hove into view and ran aground on the bar. It had been a miserable passage. The passengers were "pressed like anchovies," said one, forced to sleep four to a bed, and when one turned, all did. A storm had hit them, breaking a mast and spoiling much of their food, then alternate cold and hot weather added to their misery. Tempers were frayed and there had been considerable dissent aboard by the time they reached New Orleans.[19] Now General Antoine Rigaud, senior officer among the passengers, went ashore to find Laffite. The next day Laffite came to them, boarded the *Huntress,* and helped get her afloat. That afternoon, having asked Jean for his protection, the passengers brought their stores ashore.[20] To some the place looked desolate, not a tree in the vicinity for shade. They chose a site some distance from Laffite's settlement and made a temporary camp to await Lallemand, who had stayed in New Orleans buying provisions and materials for planting. They erected tents and made rude huts of reeds and driftwood found on the beach, then dug a trench around the camp to protect them against Indians and Laffite's men, "of whose disposition towards us we were yet ignorant," noted Just Girard.[21]

They could do little but try to resupply their larder by fishing and hunting deer on the island, the beginning of a monotonous six weeks until Lallemand finally arrived.[22] Laffite gave them enough provisions for 120 men and officers to help them through their first shortage, and would continue to help.[23] It was, Pierre would say, "convenient" to win the colonists' trust.[24] Not surprisingly, the boredom, added to the hunger and thirst and exposure, the vermin on their bodies, the mosquitoes, the frequent storms and rain, the clothes rotting as they wore them, left the French settlers miserable and short-tempered. Fear of their neighbors only added to the discomfort. "It was difficult for some of us to live mixed in with a horde of real brigands," said one Frenchman. Mounting dissent soon made "disunity the rule." The enlisted men refused to obey their officers, and arguments led to fights, then duels, with at least one man killed in an altercation. One of their number confessed that "we were more than once on the point of cutting each other's throat."[25]

All of which played quite nicely into the Laffites' plans. In New Orleans Pierre met with Lallemand and his brother Henri when they arrived on February 2, and soon he told Fatio of their plans to create a French enclave in Mexico that would lead to a new empire one day. In several meetings at the house on Bourbon and St. Philip, Lallemand credulously told Pierre that the contingent on the *Huntress* was only the first wave, and that he expected six thousand before long.[26] Anyone connected with filibustering had heard claims of such large numbers before, and knew that the men never materialized. Still, Pierre's information seemed all the more vital when he passed the exaggerated figures on to Fatio, and the consul continued to believe that "No. 13 is very exact in his information."[27] Then Lallemand hired Pierre's new brig the *Intrepide* to take his brother, his officers, and more men and provisions to Galveston. It was exactly the trap Pierre had proposed to effect.

Fatio had at his disposal the Spanish armed brig the *Almirante* at Pensacola, and now he and Pierre plotted that she would meet his ship at sea and take her as a prize. The *Intrepide* would fly the American flag, a conventional privateer ruse, but once she was stopped and boarded, the Spanish officers detaining her would know to go to the cabin door where they would see a box with the initials "J. L." on its lid. Inside would be papers to warrant their seizing her. That done, the Spanish warship would escort its prize to Galveston flying flags that Jean would recognize. He would take a boat with a pilot out to meet them. The Spaniards were to seize Jean and interrogate him privately, thus preserving the Laffites' cover, and once alone Jean would respond to a coded inquiry with a countersign sent him by Fatio, at which confirmation the officers were to follow Jean's direction in bringing the *Intrepide* into port and preparing to capture the *Huntress*. Pierre would be aboard to assist Jean in carrying out the coup.[28]

Before leaving, Pierre thought it wise to reinforce the brothers' cover in New Orleans. Collector Chew provided a convenient pretext when one of his letters to Washington complaining of Galveston and the Laffites by name appeared in the press. On February 6 Pierre published an open letter in the *Louisiana Courier* in response to what he termed the collector's "foolish & tiresome heap of idle words." He played the revolutionary card ably, if rather too heavily, linking the brothers with movements for the independence of Mexico and then accusing Chew of opposing freedom and liberty. "You poor little collector of the port of New Orleans," he said derisively. Americans throughout the Union prayed for the liberation of Mexico and South America. "I have embraced with all my heart, the independence of Mexico," he said, and "with all my pecuniary means, and even at the peril of my life." If the United States had been in the hands of men of Chew's sort during the late war, he accused, they would now be a British colony once more. As for the collector's accusation that the Laffites were or had been pirates, Pierre retorted that "I defy you, and defy any man to whatever nation, to prove that I did ever capture any other vessels but those navigating under the flag of Ferdinand VII." When Chew referred to the Laffites and their followers returning to their old ways in spite of the government's generous pardon, Pierre feigned indignation. "What pardon was I in want of?" he demanded. He had been a patriot, and the offices in Washington had the documents Jean had taken there to demonstrate his response to the British offer in spite of the "wealth" the enemy had offered. He wondered if Chew would have shown such high-toned patriotism in the same situation. Then, with no relation to what Chew had written but in a statement aimed directly at the insurgents, he added that "I never became an informer against any man."[29] In fact, the "associates" were all but defunct now, disillusioned by too many failed enterprises after the destruction of Mina's expedition. To add to his ruse, Pierre often feigned great agitation when talking to people on the street about Spanish injustices. He told those would listen that "his hatred of Spain grew out of persecutions which that nation had afflicted on himself and family," recalled young Samuel May Williams. "He frequently became greatly excited while speaking of the wrongs rec'd from Spain."[30]

Pierre may have thickened his cover by publishing this letter, but he antagonized Chew. When Pierre applied for clearance from the port on February 16, Chew searched the *Intrepide* and, finding munitions belonging to the Frenchmen aboard, refused to let her leave until they had been unloaded. That delayed her three days, meaning she would miss her rendezvous with the *Almirante*. Worse, President Monroe's December message to Congress was in the press by now, and its statement of his intent to clear privateers from Amelia and Galveston discouraged a number of Lallemand's officers who had intended to sail with Laffite. Pierre calmed them by saying that he would be on the voyage himself, but in fact when the *Intrepide* sailed,[31] he sent a teenage boy with letters to Jean.

Pierre's letters were meant to preserve the Laffites' pose as revolutionary supporters and to incriminate Lallemand and his people in Spanish eyes when the ship was captured and the letters read. Pierre went out of his way to state that Lallemand intended to take all of Texas, and then "extend his frontiers farther . . . with no less intention than the conquest of Mexico." No doubt with a smile, Pierre wrote that Lallemand would give the Spaniards much more trouble than Mina had. Pierre went overboard in referencing the incriminating papers placed in the box in the ship's cabin, no doubt in case Fatio's instructions to the Spanish warship were not clear.[32] Not content with one letter, Pierre wrote a second the same day to let Jean—and the Spanish captors—know that Humbert would be aboard the ship, as if Jean would not recognize him.[33] By sending Humbert along either to assist Lallemand or to take some office under Jean at Galveston, Pierre was putting one more revolutionary into the Spaniards' grip.

Pierre told Fatio he was entrusting his letters to his son Eugene to carry, and asked Fatio to write to Cienfuegos in Havana and implore him to be no harsher with the lad than was necessary to keep his cover when he and the rest of those captured on *Intrepide* were eventually brought to Cuba for justice.[34] In fact, it is possible that the boy was not even Pierre's son, and he only made this claim to convince Lallemand's officers of his confidence in the voyage.[35] That done, the *Intrepide* departed February 19, but not before Fatio and Pierre learned that the *Huntress* had already landed at Galveston. Not willing to fight the Frenchmen already on shore and well armed, Fatio directed that they content themselves with capturing the *Intrepide* and with her Humbert and most of the important officers.[36] They could probably starve out the rest on the island, and that would be enough to kill the French threat aborning.

After missing her rendezvous with the *Almirante*, however, the *Intrepide* sailed into Galveston after an uneventful voyage. Pierre's letters to Jean now created a problem. They put Pierre on record as urging his brother to show Lallemand's people every cooperation. Assuming the French officers aboard ship may have seen the letters, and outnumbered by the French exiles, Jean faced the necessity of making good on his brother's false instructions.

General Lallemand arrived at Galveston in early March, to find those on the island fed up and demoralized. The settlers celebrated with a party, and he began to enforce order, telling his men they would leave shortly to establish a permanent settlement.[37] Jean told Lallemand of a bluff about thirty miles up the Trinity River from its mouth on the northeastern extension of Galveston Bay, a place where the relatively higher ground would afford some protection while keeping them within reach of the Coushatta Indians, with whom they could trade for provisions.[38] After only three days, on March 12, Lallemand embarked his people and their provisions in nine pirogues that he bought from Laffite. It was the first of a series of ill-advised decisions by the general. The group left in the dark to cross the pass and row to the mainland, but soon lost their bearing. After a mile of rowing a high wind hit them and waves swamped their boats, capsizing one and drowning all but one of its occupants. The settlers would spend another forty-eight exhausting hours rowing nearly sixty miles up the bay before they came to the Trinity. Meanwhile Lallemand went by land. All told it took six days before his followers reassembled on a low bluff overlooking the Trinity just upstream from a wide lake that it formed before flowing into the bay.[39]

As soon as they landed Lallemand's men began fortifying the bluff, including preparations to mount cannon that Lallemand had on the way. A man from Natchitoches who passed by noticed that Lallemand had them under good discipline again, and one of the French settlers made it clear that they were not privateers and had no connection with Laffite other than having accepted his hospitality. They also professed to have high regard for the United States, a useful sentiment since Washington claimed this area as part of the Louisiana Purchase, and repeated their public avowal that they came strictly to become farmers.[40] Yet other observers, including a French spy, remained convinced that the colony was connected to a Bonapartist plot.[41] Few if any of Lallemand's settlers understood his true objective, which was probably setting up a local government and then associating it with the Mexican revolutionaries.[42]

Unfortunately the slipshod planning that crippled so many filibustering attempts saw the settlers arrive at their new home, which they named "Champ d'Asile," with only eight days' rations. It would take more than two weeks to go back to Galveston and bring up more. They rationed themselves to a single biscuit and four ounces of rice a day per man, and when that foodstuff ran out they were reduced to two handfuls of boiled corn. Boats had gone back to Galveston for more provisions from Laffite as well as newly arrived settlers, but on the return trip, the new arrivals consumed so much of the provender they brought that the colony was reduced to just ten days' victuals.[43] Lallemand left on a mission of his own to bring more supplies, but in his ab-

sence the rest lapsed into growing despondency. For fully a
month they struggled to stay alive before Laffite-sent boats arrived laden with fresh supplies as well as mail and newspapers.[44]

From Galveston Laffite kept a careful eye on the Champ
d'Asile people. Meanwhile Jean continued the assembly of his
own establishment.[45] When Nacogdoches merchant J. Randal
Jones came to buy slaves on behalf of friends in Louisiana, he
found that the men had not yet improved their plank and sailcloth shanties. However, Laffite offered hospitality characteristic of that given to visitors to Barataria. "I was never, however,
treated with more courtesy and kindness than I was by the
dreaded and much abused pirate, Lafitte," Jones recalled. "He
was a fine, well-proportioned man, about six feet high, with the
bearing and manner of a refined and cultivated gentleman, affable and pleasant."[46] Jones found Laffite in the prime of manhood, now in his late thirties, "his hair dark, a little gray."[47]
Laffite rarely left the island except to board the occasional incoming ship to inspect cargo and make arrangements for off-
loading and reshipment of slaves and goods to Louisiana.[48]
Instead, he devoted much of his time to continuing the expansion of the village. He was erecting an earthwork fort to command the pass and the bay, and emplacing a few cannon. He was
working on an arsenal and dockyard and a wooden boarding-
house near the fort. A few good wooden houses would be going
up soon.[49]

In time there would be a vestige of a billiard parlor, a coffeehouse, and a few shops, but the structures were never more than
rough-hewn and crude.[50] The number of men grew, too, and a
few more women arrived. There was even a married couple or
two in the establishment, like newlywed Irishman James Campbell and his wife, Mary.[51] People like Mary Campbell found Laffite to be "of polite and easy manners, generous disposition and
exceedingly winning address."[52] He occasionally dressed in a non-

descript green uniform and an otter skin hat, but just as often in plain civilian garb. He wore no arms day to day. Those who met him most of all remembered his good proportions, dark complexion, small hands, and the brilliant white teeth characteristic of both brothers.[53]

Laffite did not waste time in solidifying the island's primary basis in privateering. After a disillusioned Herrera followed Picornell and Toledo in giving up on the revolution and returning to Mexico to make his peace with the Spaniards, Humbert was about all that remained of the pretense of representation from the junta except for Iturribarría, who now distrusted the whole Galveston crowd. Despite this and the fact that the insurgent congress had disintegrated and was on the run, when Humbert and Pierre's "son" reached Galveston late in February, the old general began issuing privateering commissions, the first going to Laméson and William Mitchell, and another soon after to Gambi.[54] Three vessels had been in port when Jones visited that spring, but the number coming in steadily grew.[55] As privateer Alexandre Danges of the *Vengeance* put it, there was "no other port to which the independent privateers can resort on the Coast of Mexico except Galveztown."[56]

From New Orleans, the authorities looked on the burgeoning Galveston enterprise with dismay. Vessels laden with arms were leaving the port and Dick could do little to stop them since they were being shipped not to the Louisiana coast for outfitting corsairs in violation of the law but outside the country, which was legitimate business, even if he knew that the guns would wind up on privateers.

Meanwhile the slaving system the Laffites had evolved was difficult to thwart. In response to the challenge to selling slaves out of Galveston posed by Chew's practice of sending parties after buyers, the brothers had decided to build a barracks on the west side of the Sabine, where the Atascosita Trace coming from

La Bahía crossed the river about twenty-five miles above the Sabine Lake separating the river from the Gulf.[57] The site, near a Coushatta village, was outside what they took to be United States jurisdiction. Henceforward they required buyers to come to them, do business on the Texas side, and then take the responsibility and risk of getting the blacks back through Louisiana. When a cargo of slaves was ready to be sold, privateers put into New Orleans with the legitimate goods that Chew could not impede. Laffite associates then placed signs on trees, crossroads, and other prominent places, with cryptic expressions such as SABINA 28, which meant that on the twenty eighth of the current month a sale would be held at the Sabine *barracon* outside United States jurisdiction on the Texas side of the river. Agents might also spread the word that for a particular sale Laffite wanted wagonloads of provisions, or cash in hand.

Well before the actual sale, Sauvinet or Gambi or another agent in New Orleans produced false bills of sale made out to buyers living in the so-called Neutral Strip between the Sabine and Calcasieu rivers. They then passed the bills of sale to another intermediary—no slave yet having changed hands—and at the Sabine the bill of sale was finally endorsed over to the actual buyer. Thus the paper trail had been established and the slave rather effectively "laundered."[58] Unlike the sales in the Barataria days, these were not auctions. The agents simply weighed the slaves and charged one dollar a pound.[59] Even the occasional loss could not deter the trade, with prime blacks selling on the revitalized New Orleans market at $1,500.[60]

As for other goods, the Laffites made arrangements with a man named Parker, who ran a trading post at Natchitoches called Halfway House, to provide a snuggery for some of the goods they smuggled into Louisiana by the back door.[61] Under the new protective tariff, the rates of duty charged ran as high as 20 and 30 percent on most items, and on some items even higher. A gallon of whisky might have a base cost of twenty-five cents, yet the duty was up to three times that.[62] With such potential savings before them, many consumers could swallow any hesitation at buying smuggled merchandise, especially if they could buy a $1,500 slave for $150 to carry the goods back to New Orleans. One prize alone, the 450-ton *Campeche*, was brought in with a cargo estimated at a value of $360,000.[63]

All the while Pierre continued to incur more debts to build up the island, unaware that as early as October 1, 1817, Apodaca had decided to halt employment of the Laffites. Valuable as their information appeared to be, it was little that he could not learn otherwise, and Havana did not entirely trust the brothers. Moreover, after Aury slipped away, Apodaca doubted the need for them. Pierre apparently stripped himself of assets, however, even selling a woman who cooked and washed for Marie.[64] And on April 1 Marie sold the Bourbon and St. Philip house to Pierre's associate Antoine Abat, who had assumed the unpaid mortgage on the place, netting only $1,185 after closing the loan.[65] Pierre and Marie and the children probably continued to live in the house, but as renters.

Meanwhile Fatio did pay Pierre some amounts, enough to keep Laffite anxious to please.[66] On January 19, 1818, Cienfuegos finally sent an order canceling the employment of the Numbers 13, but Fatio did not get the news until Onís sent a representative to New Orleans in late June.[67] In May Pierre was still sending proposals to Havana through Fatio, but Cienfuegos simply recommended that they be ignored.[68]

Curiously enough, the Spaniards in Texas knew that the Laffites were no longer to be tolerated well before Fatio got the news. Shortly after Lallemand's arrival at Galveston, Spanish authorities warned the governor of Texas that the Frenchman might have a passport and letters of safe conduct from high officials, but these documents were to be taken from him if possible, and he to be told he was not welcome in the province.⁶⁹ The opportunity did not arise in time to stop the move to Champ d'Asile, but thereafter Spanish surveillance was almost constant from May through October. Antonio Martinez may never have known that the Laffites were agents, but Fatio gave him a hint in May when he told the commander in Texas of the Laffite presence at Galveston, even while sending information on Lallemand gleaned from the Laffites. Clearly Fatio intended that Martinez not confuse the two establishments when he took action.⁷⁰ But at the same time Martinez received Apodaca's order of April 24 to destroy the Galveston commune. The commander in Texas protested late in May, however, that he could not match Lallemand's four cannon, nor the firepower at Galveston.⁷¹ One ploy he could try, however, was to incite the Coushatta and Karankawa Indians to attack the privateers, and that he would attempt.⁷²

At the end of May, still thinking he was a Spanish agent, Pierre left for Galveston aboard the *Intrepide*, now renamed the *New Enterprise*, and arrived early in June.⁷³ When he came ashore he learned the current state of play at Champ d'Asile from Jean. The community was developing. Their stockade, shaped as a pentagon with a ditch outside, was connected by a parapet to a square redoubt overlooking the river. Inside the men erected a barracks and powder magazine for the cannon they mounted, and Jean may have given them a few other old pieces to add to their defense, but nothing they could use in the field. They cast their own ammunition from bar lead brought from New Orleans.⁷⁴ Some distance back from the fort was a village of twenty-eight log houses with loopholes cut in the walls for defense.⁷⁵ Prying eyes could see blacksmiths making picks, shovels, crowbars, and adzes, as well as repairing muskets, making wheels for cannon, and forging lances. Cobblers could be seen turning bearskin into dragoon military shakos with brass star insignia on their front, and deerskin into belts. The infantrymen wore blue helmets with tassels. Tinkers manufactured canteens from tin plates, and tailors turned out uniforms from green fabric, with red ruffles, for Lallemand's "farmers." Lallemand engaged a hunter to catch wild horses in order to create a cavalry as soon as a mounted commander arrived.

Lallemand had perhaps 120 men at Champ d'Asile, divided into corps or cohorts of infantry, artillery, and cavalry.[76] There were also at one time a number of prisoners. One spy gleaned that Laffite and Lallemand intended to enlist as many white prisoners as possible into Lallemand's command, and that those who refused would be taken to New Orleans. About fifty blacks also chose to follow Lallemand, while all other slaves and captured black crewmen would be sold. Every afternoon Lallemand's officers paraded and drilled their men. Conscious of security, Laffite and Lallemand halted trade with the local Indians for fear the natives would take information to the Spaniards.[77] By May Lallemand's command was at the point of starvation and had no horses for his "cavalry," no fleet, an artillery "corps" of two four-pounder iron cannon in poor repair, and to all appearances more officers than soldiers. The men did have new American muskets and bayonets, and one hundred kegs of powder filled the magazine.[78]

As soon as Pierre reached the island, Jean left for New Orleans to make his report to Fatio, arriving early in July. When they met at Sedella's house Laffite proposed a quick and—typically—bloodless coup to rid Texas of the intruders. Since shortages of supplies had held up Lallemand thus far, Jean suggested that they starve Lallemand out by hiding the canoes Indians used to bring goods to the colonists. He also wanted to cut off supply from his fellow privateers on Galveston Island, but for that he would need a pair of schooners and one maneuverable warship equipped with light draft launches in order to go up the Trinity with troops.

Fatio believed Laffite's account of affairs. "He has always transacted with us in the greatest sincerity and shows us now that he desires to cooperate in the destruction of that gang of adventurers," the agent reported to his superiors. Fatio thought Lallemand lied to Laffite when he said he had no support from the United States government, but that was not Laffite's fault. Now Jean was leaving again immediately on June 27 to rejoin Pierre, and promised to sow disaffection in Lallemand's ranks just as Pierre had with Aury's. Once he had a few defectors in his service, Jean thought he could execute his plan in a month to six weeks unless the coming of the September hurricanes delayed the arrival of the anticipated warship. Before he left Fatio, Jean Laffite added his concern that the roles he and his brother were playing not be exposed, nor that Fatio and Spain abandon them to what he called "the greatest dangers that threaten them more and more each day." Discovery could be death, whether from Lallemand's people, or their own.[79]

The fourth day roll'd along, and with the night
Came storm and darkness in their mingling might.
Oh! how he listen'd to the rushing deep,
That ne'er till now so broke upon his sleep.

EIGHTEEN

Winds of Change
1818

IN FARAWAY WASHINGTON, authorities also tried to keep abreast of Champ d'Asile. In June John Quincy Adams spoke of "the landing at Galveston, of a number of adventurers, understood to be chiefly Frenchmen," and of the mystery surrounding recent events that "suggested to the President the expediency of obtaining by the means of a confidential person upon the spot such further information, as it may be useful to the public interest."

It was known that "projects of a wild and extravagant character" were dreamed up by some of those with Lallemand. "They were all marked by features of absurdity & of desperation," said Adams. Joseph Bonaparte was implicated. Onís had remonstrated against them. At a May 13 cabinet meeting the president posed the question of sending military forces to Florida and elsewhere, and asked whether the administration should send a confidential agent to Galveston to look into Lallemand and Laffite and warn them away. Three days later he asked Adams to send the agent. On May 19 Adams summoned to his office the Virginian George Mason Graham, a good friend of both Madison and

Monroe, chief clerk of the War Department, and for a time in 1817 acting secretary of war.[1] Monroe had requested him for the mission.[2] Adams told Graham that he was to go to Lallemand to express Monroe's surprise that Lallemand had settled without permission in territory claimed by the United States. The agent should demand to know under what national authority, if any, Lallemand came there, and warn that the United States would not allow permanent settlement to be made. On June 2 Adams told Graham to leave as soon as possible.[3]

By the time Graham was ready to leave, however, Champ d'Asile was already in serious trouble. A few of Lallemand's men ran away in May when they realized that they had been tricked into joining a military expedition rather than a settlement.[4] Defectors complained of Lallemand's "mysterious expedition," one saying, "since our gathering in Philadelphia with Lallemand and as many destinations as we have had, we have never been able to learn the true purposes that we propose for ourselves, since we were always being deceived."[5] In July spies saw men who came from New Orleans to join the settlers turn around after seeing the conditions in which the colony lived.

By the end of July the colonists had no choice but to give up on Champ d'Asile, worn out and starved out, worried alike by the menace of the Indians and the Spanish. Weeks earlier, in fact, Apodaca in Havana had given orders that the "factious men" at Champ d'Asile must be driven away, and no further reinforcements from Galveston allowed to come ashore.[6] Jean Laffite left New Orleans July 7, and soon after his arrival, on July 20 or 21, he sent notice to Lallemand of the Spanish expedition ordered out to destroy them.[7] Lallemand knew that his people did not stand a chance in their little stockade, especially if the Indians assisted the Spaniards. He ordered an evacuation, and by July 24 the refugees had returned to Galveston Bay, ready to row to the island.[8] They established themselves not far from Laffite's village, and commenced building a small protective earthwork about ninety feet square on a slight three-foot rise near the bay, about four hundred yards from the water's edge.[9] The more high-toned colonists complained that the privateers "gave themselves up to the most shameless debauchery and disgusting immorality," as Just Girard declared.[10] By late July even the Spanish spies detected the hostility between the two camps.[11] It was only Jean Laffite, said Girard, "with his extraordinary strength of limb and his indomitable resolution," who was able to control his men. "Thanks to him the pirates became harmless neighbors to the exiles, with whom they often exchanged words of political sympathy, crying amicably, 'Long live Liberty!'"[12]

The Laffites especially won the gratitude of many of the exiles thanks to the brothers repeatedly saving them from starvation. Thereafter Jean Laffite was the main support of the Champ d'Asile colonists, using his own resources to feed them, in hopes of reimbursement from Spain.[13] The brothers also promised Lallemand to bring further volunteers at their own expense as they assembled in New Orleans, and did deliver three hundred San Domingue exiles that month.[14] That they were concentrating in one place as many of Lallemand's people as possible to hand over to Spain could not be known to the colonists, just as Jean and Pierre did not yet know that Spain was no longer interested in their schemes. All the while, Jean subtly promoted dissent within the French camp.

Pierre left Galveston for New Orleans in mid-July with Laméson, who had been there since May outfitting the *Panchita* for privateering under the name the *Lameson*. On July 16 Laméson received his commission from Humbert, and soon took her out under American colors, armed with ten cannon and bound for Grand Terre.[15] Limping with a broken mast, she was taken within days off the Balize by Cunningham and the *Firebrand*.[16] Pierre was there to suffer the irony of being taken by his former ship.[17] When Cunningham brought in the *Lameson*, observers also saw a boat from the *Surprise* escorting the little sailboat on which one New Orleans denizen saw "the noted Peter Lafitte."[18] Laméson would hire Edward Livingston and argue he was legitimately commissioned by the Mexican government, but Livingston was unable to establish even that there was a functioning government in Mexico in 1818, and in the end Laméson lost. An appeal to the Supreme Court in Washington proved to be of no avail.[19] Pierre was not held, however, and soon ran up more debt sending succor to his brother.

Fatio now received definitive news that he was to cut the Laffites loose when Onís's secretary Luis Noeli arrived from Washington and dressed him down for authorizing "such extraordinary expenses" for the brothers, especially after the Laffites' initial insistence that they were willing to "serve for free and did not require any prize or remuneration until the conclusion of this business."[20] It hurt Fatio to find himself thus criticized, especially because he believed that Pierre had dealt faithfully with him throughout. When Noeli complained that nothing had been accomplished from the brothers' schemes, Fatio protested that it was not Pierre's fault that the naval forces necessary to take Galveston had not been available. "Laffite's plan was a splendid one and offered the most brilliant results," he argued.

As for the Laffites' expenses, Fatio complained that they had not received a dollar of payment for their services, which may have been true technically. He then disingenuously exaggerated the brothers' fealty to Spain by telling Noeli that "the Numbers 13 never have solicited any recompense," though he did admit that they had expected more "participation" from Spain. "In all their conduct, they have shown gracefulness which honors them," argued the consul, "but surely it could not be expected that these brothers should keep an establishment, make the trips and give all the dispositions they gave which were convenient to have a happy result of our projects, under their own expenses." When it came to the apparently imaginary Cuban insurrection plot, he could not provide an explanation, but refused to believe that he had been gulled. Investigation and containment of the supposed slave insurrection had been Latour's assignment, given by Cienfuegos, and not the responsibility of Fatio or the Laffites. Noeli even complained over the expense of maps of Galveston that would have been vital had Spanish warships ever come to take the island. He actually got one of them to the *Almirante,* for all the good that did. And to Noeli's complaint of Fatio's obstinacy in not acknowledging the order to shut down the Commission Reservada, the code name for the Laffite operation, the consul answered with understandable smugness that "it was impossible for me to produce or to answer an Official Document that never reached my hands."[21]

Despite his disappointment and chagrin, Fatio had no choice but to obey the orders now. Just what and when he told Pierre is unknown, but Spain owed the Laffites a minimum of $18,889.68 for which they had billed Fatio. Thinking that the brothers had dealt in good faith with Spain, Onís wanted them to be paid and so did Fatio, who complained that the Laffites were being "abandoned and compromised," as well as exposed "to all the fury of the pirates if they come to know the secret." Still, they would never get the money.[22] In the end Fatio advised Apodaca to change the countersigns used by agents, so that those given to the Laffites would no longer be honored, "since I cannot be responsible for the use to which they might be put."[23]

Other events had an impact on Galveston now. General Jackson invaded Florida that spring and on May 28 Pensacola surrendered. This delayed negotiations over the Louisiana Territory borders until midsummer. Now Adams knew that Spain was willing to cede Florida if it had to but not Texas, and he changed his bargaining position, softening demands for Texas and instead asking for Spain's release of its claims on the Oregon Territory. Anti-Spanish feeling ran high in the capital, and congressmen

called for United States recognition of the South American republican movements. The message to Spain was that it had better give
up what was least important to it rather than risk forfeiting far
more, especially if diplomatic recognition of the juntas in Buenos
Aires, Venezuela, and Mexico led to legalization of the privateering menace. In October Onís would propose a new boundary line,
sparking a counterproposal from Adams.[24] Meanwhile Onís reversed himself and refused to agree to an American military force
expelling the Galveston privateers during the negotiations. Publicly he complained that to do so would constitute an invasion of
Spanish territory. In fact, he feared that once American soldiers
and sailors were on Galveston, they would never leave.

Whether or not the American military appeared off the
shores of Galveston depended largely upon what Graham found
there. He left Washington June 6, days before the eastern press
carried a letter from Natchitoches that told of Laffite having
eight to ten privateers and prizes in port, observing that "this is
carrying on pirating in a bold manner."[25] Graham reached the
Sabine two months later, where he encountered a rider carrying
news from Laffite that Lallemand had ordered the evacuation of
Champ d'Asile. Passing through Nacogdoches, Graham finally
reached Galveston on August 24, and immediately presented
himself at Lallemand's camp. The general appeared to be ill at
ease and embarrassed at the interview, and to Graham's statement that this area was in dispute and that the United States
claimed it, Lallemand disingenuously pleaded that he thought
it belonged to Spain and was now up for the taking since the
Spaniards had abandoned it. He reasserted his peaceful intentions toward everyone, but averred that he would fight if forced.
He also complained that the Indians had cut off his supplies.[26] In
fact, Lallemand was so angry at the Coushatta and Karankawas
that he intended to declare war on them, and showed Graham a
draft of a declaration that he had meant to issue that day but
would not now in light of Graham's warning to leave.

Gainsaying his protest of peaceful pursuits, he went on to tell Graham that he had planned to use Champ d'Asile as a base for military operations against the Spaniards, claiming he had a military commission from the nonexistent Mexican Congress. Lallemand said he had intended to go back to Champ d'Asile when the immediate danger passed and he was stronger, but in the face of what Graham told him, he was resigned to abandoning Texas altogether. Before the interview ended, however, Lallemand also made it clear that he had "no connection whatever with the piratical establishment at Galvezton."²⁷ Graham took Lallemand at his word, but still gave him a written statement that the United States wanted him and his followers out of the area, and demanded a written avowal of his future intentions.²⁸ Lallemand immediately agreed to everything, adding that he and his people would happily acknowledge the authority of the United States in the area if it allowed them to remain.²⁹ He was not yet ready to give up entirely.

The real key to Lallemand and Galveston, of course, was Jean Laffite. From Lallemand's earthwork Graham could see "a large & strangely built Brig" beached on the shore about four hundred yards northeast on the bay side. Her spars and rigging had been dismantled, and Lallemand or his people told Graham that Laffite sometimes used the brig as a dwelling, arsenal, and storehouse. In fact, whatever he told Lallemand, Laffite may have placed her there to command the works of the Champ d'Asile refugees, and to be prepared if or when a Spanish attack on Lallemand materialized. Laffite had secured her in the sand parallel with the shore, and since her gun deck stood higher than the island, her guns could fire across the land at anything on the other side.³⁰ Graham believed she could mount as many as eighteen heavy cannon.

After his meeting with the French general, Graham sent a letter to the Laffite village along with a verbal message that if Laffite would call on him, Graham could orally convey his instructions from Adams. Laffite responded immediately, but cagily, asking that Graham demonstrate his authority to make such an approach, and Graham complied.[31] He told Laffite he was sent by the government of the United States "to call upon you for an explicit avowal of the National authority, if any, by which you have occupied the position & harbour of Galveston, and also to make known to you, that the Government of the United States, claiming the country between the Sabine & the Rio Bravo del Norte, will suffer no establishment, of any kind & more particularly one of so questionable a character as that now existing at this place, to be made within those limits."[32] This left no room for misunderstanding, and the next morning Laffite appeared at Graham's tent.

The meeting was cordial. Graham read his instructions from Adams, and then listened as Laffite rehearsed what was now a well-worn story of the persecution suffered by him and his brother. He admitted smuggling, as he always had, but added that his chief accusers were doing it, too, which he thought ought to excuse the Laffites in some measure. He argued contradictorily that his corsairs took only Spaniards' ships, and that he rigorously eschewed taking vessels of neutral countries. As for the United States, he respected her shipping, and it "afforded him the greatest pleasure to render a service to an American vessel," which he said he had done on many occasions. He only occupied Galveston in the first place so that he could "satisfy the two passions that dominated me imperiously, that of offering an harbor to the battleships of independence and that of being able on account of proximity to fly to the aid of the United States if circumstances required it." Satisfied as to the correctness of his motives, he continued, "I carried out this bold plan." He told Graham that he had repeatedly written to the Mexican Congress to obtain "the legitimation of my taking possession in its name, and the chief authorities' sanction of the organization of a regular and legitimate government." Unfortunately, his letters could not find the peripatetic body, if it even existed, and he never received an answer. There were some grains of truth here, but they would have made a poor loaf. Jean made no mention at all, of course, of his mission on behalf of Spain.

Graham told Laffite that he believed his protestations about taking only Spanish vessels, and assured him that President Monroe knew of and valued the Laffites' service in the recent war. The government had no quarrel with the brothers, but it must put an end to this privateering establishment out of duty to its own dignity, as well as to the respect and protection that it owed the flags of other nations. The admitted smuggling, which Graham thought to be the most extensive and organized in the nation's history, took revenue from the Treasury and degraded the morals of the people of Louisiana, not a difficult task in the best of times. Jean granted the weight of the argument, but then pled that the amount of goods smuggled from Galveston was much exaggerated. Indeed, excepting slaves, it had been negligible, he said, neatly avoiding any quantification of the illicit slave traffic. He was attached to the United States, though, and desired always to give way to its wishes.

At the close of the interview, Laffite promised to give Graham a letter restating all this, including his willingness to give up Galveston. In return he asked for a sufficient period of time—two to three months—to close down the port, call in his privateers, and relocate himself and his property, a request that Graham granted. The next day, August 28, Laffite closed his promised letter to Graham with the sanctimonious declaration that "I know, Sir, that I was calumniated in the lowliest manner by persons possessed of a certain importance; but because of my irreproachable conduct in every respect, my interior tranquillity was not affected and in spite of my enemies, I will obtain (without doubt later) the justice that is due me." The expression of wounded innocence was pure Laffite.[33]

That day Graham drafted a protective order for Laffite and his men and property and gave it to him to display to any United States forces that might appear to take possession of the island before Laffite was gone, the only restriction being that authorities should immediately take steps to curtail any remaining smuggling or slave trading before Laffite left. Graham was not entirely taken in by his gracious host.[34] Thereafter Graham remained on the island for nearly a month, getting to know Laffite even while surreptitiously studying the defenses of the place in case the military had to evict the privateers and the French settlers.[35] Indeed, the day that Laffite accepted Washington's instructions, Graham penned a report on the base's strength which he sent to New Orleans on the next outgoing vessel. He gave the depth of the bar at high tide, pointing out that no large warships could enter, while also delineating the strength of Laffite's beached fortress vessel. "These positions would enable a few desperate men to make an obstinate resistance against a large, and probably a successful one against a moderate force," Graham warned. If the government decided to take Galveston, however, he thought it would not require a large force because he had Laffite's promise that "peaceable possession will be given to any officer acting under the authority of the United States."[36]

In the following days Graham talked with Laffite about the absence of a commission from Mexico. Surely the brothers realized that the Mexican junta was defunct, and not likely to resurrect any time soon. Like most in the government, Graham felt hearty sympathy for the liberation movements so long as they worked to Washington's benefit by weakening Spain. He suggested to Laffite that since the Mexican insurgency was impotent, Laffite should look elsewhere. Graham knew representatives of the rebels in Buenos Aires, and told Jean that he could get privateering commissions from them. Jean asked for a letter recommending the Laffites to the appropriate authority, indicating particularly his interest in establishing a court of admiralty "in any place or Island which he might take from the Spaniards, on the Coast of the Spanish main, or on that of any other part of S. America," and Graham provided one addressed to David C. DeForest in New York.[37] Graham could not know, of course, that by directing Jean to another insurgency, he was giving the Laffites a potential opportunity to perform more espionage for Spain, and sustain or renew their claims to compensation.

Meanwhile, after his meeting with Graham, Lallemand announced that he would be leaving. He promised to return in forty days with more provisions for his people, but instead he abandoned them. Joined by Graham, he boarded a vessel and sailed for New Orleans, leaving behind only enough food to give each man a pound of bread a day.[38]

Lallemand barely missed being caught at sea by the dread of Gulf coast summers. Somewhere in the southern Atlantic a depression began gaining intensity as it headed westward. By September 10 it had pushed through the Caribbean, and all but capsized a vessel carrying the last vestiges of the Spanish administration at Pensacola and its archives to Havana, losing the records forever.[39] Two days later the storm hit the Gulf coast, and raged for two days. Matagorda went underwater. The mission at Bahía and more than sixty houses came down in ruins.[40]

On Galveston, the hurricane struck with little warning. Waves washed higher and higher up the beach, whipped by the winds and storm surge, until they simply washed over the island. Lallemand's earthworks and camp went underwater, and his people waded to two sturdy log cabins on a slight elevation. For the next three days they used oars to fend off uprooted trees and spars from wrecks that the waves sent crashing toward their refuge.[41] Around them the water stood up to four feet deep, and the rushing of the waves prevented them from moving about for fear of being carried off their feet. "Galveston village looked like a fort beaten down by assault," one declared. In all only six houses survived, one of them Laffite's on its higher ground, and scores of panicked people fled to it. The waves continued to climb, destroying six of the vessels at anchor and virtually all of the French settlers' provisions.[42] Before the waters started to recede the whole island was inundated except for perhaps an acre on which Laffite's house sat.[43] Laffite either weathered the storm there or on his brig implanted in the sand.[44]

When the hurricane passed Jean Laffite's control of food and defense made him the only power on the island.[45] Freshwater was gone and the island wells would be contaminated with salt water for weeks. For some time to come the survivors would be entirely dependent on what provisions Laffite could ration from his remaining stores or purchase on his own credit from passing ships.[46] Thanks to damage to his house, Laffite stayed on the brig, faced now with the practical dilemma of whether to try to rebuild from the ruins in light of his recent promise to evacuate the place.

The hurricane did Jean one favor, however. In May Pierre had told Fatio that the privateers were being advised to swarm over the Gulf as the Spanish war fleet would be heading back to Spain shortly.[47] That may have worked against him. The Laffites "are putting themselves under strong suspicion by their double dealing," Cienfuegos frankly told Apodaca on July 17. "It is they who maintain the place called Galveston and its privateers."[48] Two weeks later Apodaca gave the orders for a squadron of one brig, a sloop, and a schooner, all armed, to sortie from Vera Cruz to blockade Galveston and capture or disperse everyone there, Lallemand and Laffite alike. Martinez was to make a supporting attack overland.[49] The storm discouraged the squadron from making the attempt, and by the time the Spaniards were ready to consider another effort, the opportunity had passed. Apodaca's disenchantment with the Laffites had not, however. Lallemand would have been starved out by now, he grumbled, but for "the pirate Juan Lafite" feeding the adventurers. Apodaca was thoroughly tired of filibusters, privateers, Laffites, and all their schemes that never came to fruition.

Less than a week after the hurricane, Laffite sent a courier to New Orleans with verbal and written reports for Pierre, detailing the disaster but also passing along the most recent information about Spanish plans to attack. If the United States was going to claim the island then Laffite would warn Graham that Spain was committing a hostile act against the U.S. land, playing each nation against the other to buy himself some time and perhaps turn a profit. He implored Graham to listen to what Pierre told him about Spanish intentions.[50]

Graham got Jean's letter and met with Pierre,[51] then departed for Washington to arrive in November just as President Monroe was preparing to deliver his annual message to the Congress. Graham reported to Adams on his mission and its success, but did not earn complete approbation. Negotiating with Laffite and Lallemand implied a degree of diplomatic status for them that the United States vigorously denied. Adams especially disapproved of Graham having put Laffite in touch with the Buenos Aires junta, fearing that the United States would be left facing the same problems with pirates at sea and smuggling at home. Graham had acted on his own initiative, "and in my opinion, not much to the credit of its wisdom."[52] Perhaps trusting the promises of the Galveston leaders less than had Graham, Adams began to gather from him copies of all of his correspondence and reports, as well as everything the War Department had on file relating to the "state of things" at Galveston.[53]

The state of things was not good, at least so far as Lallemand's people were concerned. Chaos ensued after his departure, and week by week, singly and in small groups, the men began to scatter.[54] Spanish spies reported that by September nothing remained of Champ d'Asile but two iron cannon that Laffite sent two blacks to retrieve.[55] Finally the much-rumored Spanish threat materialized. Captain Juan de Castañeda started out on September 16 at the head of 250 *soldados*, intending to confirm the abandonment of Champ d'Asile or else destroy it. By October 9 he reached the Trinity, and learned that Lallemand had evacuated. He sent José Sandoval and three others down the river to the bay to Galveston, taking with them letters for Lallemand or whomever commanded the settlers.[56] On October 13 some of the Champ d'Asile refugees indulged what they called "artful necessity in way of amusement" by holding a mock matrimonial ceremony. During the revelry, they spotted a column of smoke rising from the beach at some distance, and a party set off to find the cause. Soon they saw a canoe pulled up on the beach and four men standing beside a white flag. Sandoval, his weapon concealed in his clothing, spoke to them on their approach and said he had a packet with communications for the "Chief of that assemblage." Some discussion ensued and the Frenchmen confessed they were disgusted and looking to leave, and that they expected everyone to abandon the place in time.

Though Lallemand had left Antoine Rigaud in charge, the men took Sandoval to Laffite's brig, where Jean greeted him with some courtesy. On learning Sandoval's embassy, Laffite sent ashore for Rigaud, who shortly appeared with a staff of five officers. Rigaud broke the seal on the packet Sandoval presented him and then passed the contents, written in Spanish, to one of his colonels for translation. Laffite and the others heard a demand to know Lallemand's purpose in bringing his "emigrants or outlaws" filibustering in Texas. Castañeda's letter pointed out the fate of Mina, Gutiérrez, and others as a caution. Castañeda was ready to drive the invaders out, and more squads were on the march from Mexico if needed. There was nowhere on Spanish soil that Lallemand could go. If Lallemand wanted legitimately to settle somewhere, he could make application to Castañeda, who would negotiate with him. If he sought to make his own state or nation, however, it was beyond discussion. He would be allowed to leave, even to travel across Spanish territory if he sought to march rather than sail, but he would have to leave behind all armament. All other hopes the French might have, Castañeda said, were "groundless expectations."[57]

The junta spoke in French among themselves, and questioned Sandoval. Finally they told him he would have to stay the night on the brig, for the hurricane had destroyed any accommodations ashore. Even confined as he was, however, Sandoval could tell the poor condition of affairs. There were now only about 150 on the island. They had little good water and no other vessels, and their only serviceable artillery appeared to be two pivot guns, their powder soaked and useless.[58]

While Sandoval observed what he could, Rigaud and the others pondered their response, but Laffite distanced himself from the proceeding. The demand spoke only of the settlers, and he did not want to confuse his establishment with them more than it was already. Rigaud finally prepared a statement reiterating the settlers' peaceful intent to make a colony on the Trinity for Napoleonic exiles. They had arms, but only for hunting and protection. The land they tried to settle was abandoned and unused, but when they learned of the Spaniards' approach, they gave it up and retreated to the island. They would settle here on Galveston but found that "this island does not promise anything other than asylums and difficulties to those that would wish to possess it and cultivate it." Rigaud protested that they were only there now while waiting for Lallemand to make arrangements to settle them elsewhere. Castañeda's ultimatum had shattered their remaining peace of mind, but they could do nothing until they heard from Lallemand. Rigaud asked to be allowed to remain a little longer but refused to hand over their arms. The settlers had never used them against the Spaniards, and needed them for protection.[59]

The next morning an officer handed Sandoval a packet containing the Galveston junta's response and took him back to his canoe. Within a few days Sandoval reached Castañeda's camp, but when the captain read Rigaud's response, he found it unsatisfactory and sent a messenger back to demand that a high-ranking member of the junta come to negotiate with him. "Not only you and your subjects are included in my parley," he wrote to Rigaud, "but the head of the privateer[s], Monsieur Lafitte, of which person and his operations I ought to have knowledge for the concession or denial that his circumstances occasion." Castañeda demanded a reply within three days or he would take steps "that may be fatal to you."[60] To cover himself, Castañeda had already sent a letter eastward to "The First Authority Depending on the Congress of the United States," to inform American authorities of his intentions at Galveston. Spain had the right to evict filibusters seeking to invade Spanish provinces. He wanted the United States to understand that any action he took would not be a hostile act against Americans, and he promised not to cross the border into the Neutral Zone.[61]

Whatever they thought of Castañeda's ultimatum, neither Rigaud nor Laffite sent a reply. Without the boats to make an assault on Galveston Island, he could do little more than destroy the remaining structures at Champ d'Asile and march back to his base.[62] He knew there was no need for the Spaniards to attack, however. Lallemand's people had reached their last extremity. By late October Lallemand's forty days were up and the promised supplies did not appear. Deserters from the island began to seek sanctuary at Spanish camps, often two at a time, and as many as six on one occasion.[63] Three officers handed themselves over to Castañeda before he was too far distant, and happily reported to him the disarray on the island.[64]

One settler, disgusted with the confusion and the hunger, simply walked over to the privateer settlement and signed on to serve aboard a corsair. Soon others would do the same.[65] Laffite continued to provide food sufficient to sustain life, but not to maintain morale. Finally, in November Lallemand sent word that Congress had made another land grant in Alabama and the settlers were to return to New Orleans at once. This was easier to say than to do, for they had no transportation. Laffite had a small prize sloop, the *St. Antonio de Campeche,* but it was so small that only the sick could be embarked. She left on October 24 with Humbert in command and fearing that another awful month would pass on the island before the sloop returned, about sixty of Lallemand's people opted to walk. Despite the heavy debt Lallemand owed him for all the supplies advanced, Laffite ferried them to the mainland and capitalized on his good relations with the Coushatta to trade for horses and guides to get the settlers to Nacogdoches without attracting the attention of Spanish authorities.[66]

In a couple of weeks the sick refugees reached New Orleans, only to find yellow fever. Most became victims. Those who waited on Galveston for the boat to come back arrived a month later and some of them also died, but the rest went on to Alabama to become genuine tillers of the soil.[67] Lallemand became embroiled in legal and financial difficulties over $1,200 he owed Laméson for chartering the *Golden Age* to bring the colony a load of food, a cannon or two, and ammunition. On December 17, 1818, Lallemand appeared before the federal court to state his intention to become an American citizen and take the oath required. His dreams of conquest were over.[68] No doubt too embarrassed to face his former followers, he stayed in Louisiana to become a farmer not far from New Orleans.[69]

By the end of November only seven of Lallemand's men remained on Galveston, but it became evident that the damage from the hurricane, short rations, and uncertainty over the future in the face of what was known of the Graham visit and Castañeda's ultimatum had done their work on Laffite's men, too.

Their numbers were reduced, and they lived once more in brush and sailcloth huts. Laffite's slave mistress remained with him, but in ill health.[70] Laffite stayed aboard the brig with three or four trusted lieutenants to guard merchandise rumored to be worth $200,000—if it could be gotten to market. Sometime around the end of the year a cabal of thirty to forty of the privateers decided to take it for themselves, even if they had to slit Laffite's throat to do so. Jean, who did not customarily carry sidearms, got word of the plot and prepared to defend himself, engaging the seven remaining Frenchmen from Lallemand's band to add to his defense. They must have been sufficient, for though Laffite believed they all ran a risk of assassination that winter, no attempts were made. When the seven finally left on March 3, 1819, he could not pay them, but handed over merchandise that they could smuggle into Louisiana.[71] The Laffites exited the Champ d'Asile episode no better off than the settlers.

Yet they did not give up hope of capitalizing on their skills at espionage. They had failed with Aury and Mina and Lallemand, and by now the "associates" were all but out of the filibustering business. Nevertheless, Graham's good offices with DeForest opened another two-way door. The game never changed, only the players. And so the brothers boldly tried to shift the game to Washington. Leaving Jean behind to press their futile claims for compensation before a sympathetic but hamstrung Fatio, and with Graham's introduction to DeForest in hand, Pierre took ship for the East and arrived by the middle of November.[72]

Pierre Laffite's first and only visit to Washington put him there during what residents would recall as "the period of the best society in Washington." Congress abounded with "gentlemen of high character and high breeding." Already Willard's Hotel on Pennsylvania Avenue was a major hostelry, though Pierre stayed at Washington Hall not far away. If the city's cooks were not outstanding, still the proximity to the Chesapeake left no fine ingredients to be desired.[73] But Pierre was in town on business, and would not remain for months as had his brother. He sent their old associate Vicente Garros to Philadelphia to meet DeForest with Graham's recommendation and the Laffites' own entreaty in hand. Garros met with DeForest on November 16. DeForest was a United States citizen who had applied in May 1818 to be recognized as consul general representing the Buenos Aires junta. Secretary of State Adams had responded by citing "the excesses and outrages committed by Privateers having commissions from Buenos Ayres, but fitted out, armed and manned in the ports of the United States." He did not hesitate to attribute these unlawful privateers to commissions DeForest was giving out in Philadelphia. Indeed, a recognized agent from Buenos Aires admitted to Adams that not one of the corsairs known to be sailing under his junta's commissions was captained or crewed by natives. Thereafter Adams had no further communication with DeForest, so when Garros met with him, he encountered a man who had no official standing at all.[74]

During the conference Garros listed the men whom the brothers would appoint to create an admiralty court, customs administration, and civil and military authorities should they have to leave Galveston and form a new establishment. DeForest was curious to know what location the Laffites might choose for a new base, but Garros evaded a direct answer. Garros gave away nothing by observing, however, that one good spot would be someplace on the coast opposite the Isla Mugeres, the so-called Island of Women off the northeastern tip of the Yucatán peninsula. Indeed, the island itself would leave the corsairs perched on a virtual promontory thrust into the middle of the Gulf directly in the path of Spanish shipping from Cuba to Vera Cruz. In all the region, it was the land base best situated for speedy raid and return. Garros suggested that if DeForest could persuade President Monroe, who was friendly to Buenos Aires interests, to delay closing Galveston for a year, the Laffites could use the time to establish a new base without unnecessary interruption, benefiting both Buenos Aires and the brothers. DeForest agreed to approach Monroe on the subject. It may only be coincidental that Monroe's message to Congress, delivered two days after this meeting, pointedly omitted any reference to Galveston, but thereafter the pressure on Galveston from Washington relaxed for several months.

Garros told DeForest that when he left Galveston in September, Jean Laffite had six unarmed vessels to fit out. Pierre could have informed him that probably not more than two or three vessels were seaworthy after the hurricane, but there was no need to understate the Laffites' need for finance. DeForest asked Garros to go with him to Baltimore to meet with the merchant Thomas Tenant, presumably to help outfit the boats, but Garros pled that as he was in charge of Laffite affairs in Philadelphia, he could not leave. DeForest spoke much of his desire to meet Pierre, and seemed to believe that the Laffite presence at Galveston was considerably more formidable than it was after the storm. He expressed, in fact, the expectation that had the Laffites joined with Aury, they could have conquered Puerto Rico or San Domingue. Garros politely did not disabuse him of the delusion, saying only that they might have taken those islands but could not have held on to them, whereas there were other places where the privateers' numbers could be used to greater effect. For the current enterprise, he said, their hopes for success lay with Tenant and the other Baltimore businessmen who still had an interest in funding revolution against Spain. After he finished his business with Tenant at Baltimore, DeForest decided to travel to Washington to talk with Pierre. Garros wrote to Laffite at once, both to tell him the encouraging news and to detail what he had said to DeForest so that Pierre's version of things would agree with his emissary's.[75]

At virtually the same time that Garros met with DeForest, Pierre had an audience with Onís in Washington on November 25. The ambassador was still fighting his routine battle to demonstrate American duplicity,[76] but he was making a case no one wanted to hear. Thus he could afford to listen to what Laffite had to say. After presenting his statement of over $18,000 in expenses incurred on behalf of Spain, Pierre outlined the brothers' latest plan for Galveston. He confessed that the Spanish fleet might have finally taken possession of the island, in which case Pierre offered to defy the corsairs and transport supplies to the new tenants so that they could start operating against the privateers. Pierre feared no interference from American officials, even should he take arms to fit out privateers for Spain. However, if the Americans had forced Lallemand out by this time—as indeed Lallemand's people were all but gone now—then Pierre offered to evict the Americans, too, which he promised he could do "by my own means and with the help that you give me."

And the Americans were likely to be a problem, he said. Pierre craftily embellished Jean's discussions with Graham, saying that far from abandoning Galveston, Graham had urged Jean to join forces with Aury and Lallemand to resist any Spanish attempt to take the island. Jean had pretended to go along, and then Graham revealed that the United States wanted to assist the Laffites in taking the Gulf coast all the way to the mouth of the Rio Grande in order to effect a repeat of West Florida. An American naval squadron would make a false show of attacking the Laffite forces and they would surrender it all to the United States. Finally Pierre told Onís that Graham had insisted he could offer "very considerable compensations" from the government in return for their complicity. It was the litany that the brothers had rehearsed before Fatio and Morphy in the past: exaggerating their strength, setting Spain against a real or imaginary antagonist, and offering to make the difference for the

Spaniards in spite of "very considerable compensations" from the other side, the perpetual hint that men who could be bought might like to hear a higher offer.[77]

Pierre told Onís it should be easy for the Laffites to gain the confidence of American authorities on the Gulf and pass their plans on to Fatio, reiterating as before that he had "no other aim than that of serving His Catholic Majesty." Whether the Americans or the Spaniards took Galveston, the privateers had to find a new base soon, perhaps on the coast of Spanish Florida if Onís did not give it up. In that event, Pierre offered a new plan for capturing the corsairs then cruising the Gulf, thus stopping piracy at a single blow. The Laffites would hold Galveston and seize all matériel sent there from Buenos Aires for arming corsairs. They would also infiltrate DeForest's circle and pass on information to Fatio and Apodaca. Yet again Pierre wanted to communicate personally with Apodaca, and would do so under the cover of being a merchant selling the supplies and arms seized from Buenos Aires, for which Pierre should be paid in person in Havana, along with the compensation for his information. He added a new demand, one that perhaps reflected a growing realization that time was running out for the Laffites on the Gulf. Spain did not want them there, and neither did the United States, and Pierre knew his secret life as a spy was not so secret. As a result, he told Onís that he wanted a pardon from King Ferdinand for himself and Jean, since there had been no action on his similar request in 1815. He wanted, in fact, to go to Spain, raising once more the untruth that he was Spanish born, and once there he wanted to be provided suitable employment for himself and his brother.[78]

He suggested that he remain in Washington to perfect the scheme with Onís and also to meet and ingratiate himself with the Americans in order to learn their plans and report on them.[79] Efficiency demanded that Onís designate a special agent who would deal directly with Pierre in Washington as Fatio had in New Orleans. Pierre also suggested that his code name be changed. Too many people connected with Cienfuegos's "Reserved Commission" in New Orleans knew the identity of Number 13, and he asked that Onís devise to circulate the word to "the majority of those who knew this number" that he was in fact "no longer added to any of Your Catholic Majesty's business."[80] Pierre diplomatically refrained from saying to Onís what Jean had confided to Sedella and Fatio, that the brothers did not want to be directly involved with Onís and his legation "because everything that happens at this office is later known by the Ministers of the Association."[81]

Onís found Laffite persuasive, and engaged to pass his plans along to Cienfuegos. Reflecting a few days on the matter, however, Onís advised Laffite that he did not need to stay in Washington and that his presence could arouse suspicion. It would be better for him to conduct his other business elsewhere in the East while they awaited a decision from the captain general in Havana.[82] Onís sent a dispatch to Cienfuegos days after meeting with Pierre, attesting at the outset that Laffite "seems to act on good faith." Like Sedella and Fatio and others before him, Onís was partly charmed by Pierre's personality and partly victimized by his own wishful thinking. "There is no doubt that they could serve us greatly under these circumstances," he told Cienfuegos. Agreeing with Pierre's concern for security, Onís notified the captain general that hereafter he would refer to Pierre as Number 19.[83]

Pierre would remain in the capital long enough for Congress to reconvene in December. He hoped to gain an audience with Speaker of the House Henry Clay in tandem with DeForest and other representatives of the Buenos Aires and Venezuelan juntas. Clay outspokenly supported the independence movements in Spanish America. He had tried to kill the legislation outlawing arming and outfitting privateers for the insurgencies in American ports, and in the past year had attempted to repeal the neutrality law. Clay, in fact, was making a bid to take control of foreign policy away from the secretary of state, and sensing the possible shift in power, Laffite and the others wanted to talk with him about the United States granting formal recognition to Buenos Aires. They hoped also to present plans for taking over the rest of Spain's North American holdings.

Sometime in December they probably did get the meeting with Clay, for Pierre afterward gave Onís to understand that Graham, President Monroe, and presumably Clay, remembering his loyalty in the period 1814–1815, wanted to place Laffite in charge of such an enterprise. Of course Laffite protested his devotion to Spain. Stalled in the negotiations with Adams over the Louisiana boundary, Onís could easily believe that the president would be willing to break the stalemate by encouraging filibusters to do the job for him.

Yet there was another side to the matter. For all their puffery, the Laffites were nearly paper tigers on the Gulf coast by now. The hurricane had badly weakened the remainder of the Laffite concern, and at present Onís was less than two months away from final agreement with Adams on a treaty. Negotiations were stalled, but it was obvious that an end was in sight and that they would set the Louisiana border on the Sabine, making Texas and Galveston unequivocally Spanish. If a meeting did take place with Clay, it produced no further action on his part, and most of the Congress did not share Clay's enthusiasm for the insurrections, or at least not so far as to get the United States overtly involved.

The United States was not going to recognize Buenos Aires or Venezuela, at least not yet. America would not send its military to Texas to support the Laffites after the treaty was signed. If there was any remaining use for the Numbers 13 or 19, it was not in Texas. They might be useful elsewhere on the Gulf, but that was a matter for Apodaca and Cienfuegos once the Laffite irritant was removed from Texas. Thus when he received another proposal from Pierre in January offering to reestablish a port at Galveston, Onís passed it on to Apodaca with little expectation. The viceroy had heard it all before, especially the demands for money.[84]

At this time privateering commissions from Buenos Aires would have been a godsend to the Laffites, and there were plenty of them about. In the fall of 1817 alone some fourteen corsairs commissioned by the insurgency had brought forty-two prizes into port. One captain took twenty-four prizes during the summer, and boarded ninety-three vessels of all nations in search of Spanish goods.[85] In discussions with Buenos Aires representatives, perhaps including DeForest, Pierre told Onís that he worked out an arrangement whereby the Laffites would reestablish an admiralty court at Galveston, appoint a governor, name their friend Garros admiralty judge, and then insurgents would split with them the proceeds of all prizes, DeForest getting 1 percent as his fee for issuing the letters of marque. Pierre further said he would persuade the privateers of the insurgencies to rendezvous at Galveston in March 1819 to begin operations, which would concentrate them for an easy conquest by a Spanish fleet. All that was needed was approval from Apodaca, and a commitment of ships, and funds, for the brothers' expenses.[86] But whatever DeForest may have suggested or promised at their meetings, the Laffites would never get commissions from Buenos Aires or from Bolívar, nor apparently from any of the other insurgencies while the brothers remained at Galveston. In the end, the Laffites were not going to get what they needed to operate against Spain, and Spain was disinclined to give them agency against the rebels. The United States wanted nothing to do with them. The brothers, it seemed, were about to be cast into the universe on their own.

Unaware of this as yet, Pierre told people he met socially that he was in the capital to negotiate with Onís for the exchange of some of his corsairs held in Cuba for Spaniards captured on prizes brought into Galveston, probably a cover since it had always been the Laffites' policy simply to release them. Ransom may have made them some money over ships, but they never ransomed people. Pierre probably met with other insurgent representatives while in Washington, men such as Don Lino de Clemente, who arrived there in December 1818 as representative of Venezuela, though without credentials or commission, which did not stop him from issuing letters of marque all the same. After his meetings in Washington, Pierre Laffite left the capital, apparently still unaware that the brothers would have to abandon Galveston.[87] Under the impression, then, that he had made good progress, he traveled to Baltimore to meet with merchants there. At Nathaniel Williams's chandlery on Bowly's Wharf he bought sails to ship to Galveston for refitting the damaged Laffite corsairs, and he probably called on Tenant and others as well.[88] Baltimore was certainly a port of choice for privateers and their agents. Laporte of New Orleans, more than once involved in dealings with the Laffites, frequently sent his prize cargoes there for sale, and Pierre could expect an interested and sympathetic hearing to any business proposals.[89] His business there concluded, he went on to Philadelphia to see DeForest, and then to Charleston, South Carolina, another center of privateering investors, with some of whom the brothers may have had dealings in the past.[90] In all, Pierre stayed in the East almost as long as his brother had three years before, and it was not until the late spring or early summer of 1819 that he returned to New Orleans. He was in no position at all to know what lay ahead for the Laffites.[91]

He knew himself a villain—but he deem'd
The rest no better than the thing he seem'd
And scorn'd the best as hypocrites who hid
Those deeds the bolder spirit plainly did.

NINETEEN

The Dying Dream
1819

By mid-February of 1819 affairs at Galveston were quiet enough that Jean found time to return to New Orleans for a short visit, probably to purchase supplies and building materials with some of the money brought in from the slave sales. He felt flush enough to loan $4,800 to an associate in the city, and then worked with Marie Villard to repurchase the Bourbon and St. Philip house.[1] He negotiated a price of $9,000 with Antoine Abat, a considerable step-up from what Marie and Pierre had paid for it a few years before. No cash changed hands, however. Instead, Jean gave Abat nine promissory notes due in six months, mid-August, himself being security for one of them.[2] After mid-March he returned to Galveston to continue the rebuilding. Before leaving, he made arrangements for Laméson's the *Panchita*, now renamed the *Two Friends,* to bring back Humbert and Dominique and about thirty other men with whom the Laffites intended to get the Galveston operation going once more. It was a move that initially made Fatio fear that forces were marshaling to make another try at Tampico,[3] an idea Jean may have planted if only to manufacture a crisis in which his inside information could be valuable. In fact, the "associates" had long since given up filibustering.

Still, as he departed, Jean may have heard the first rumblings of the unrest from a different quarter that would inspire one final filibustering adventure. By 1819 Spain seemed firmly in control of Texas and Mexico with a treaty establishing the western boundary of Louisiana at the Sabine finally signed and on every front, it seemed, a frenzied decade of agitation laid to rest.

Not for Dr. James Long of Natchez, however, or for the frontier people in the Mississippi Valley who believed that Texas had been theirs and that they had been robbed when Adams gave it away. Worse, Washington had given it away to Spaniards, whose brutality and treachery were by now accepted frontier dogma. As soon as the Adams-Onís Treaty became known in Natchez, Long and others gathered to protest. Among them were familiar names from the filibustering years, such as the Kemper brothers and Gutiérrez, along with new names like James Gaines, Warren D. C. Hall, and the Bowie brothers, James and Rezin.

In May a group of these men gathered in Natchez to plan an invasion army to take back what Adams had given away. Perhaps because his uncle-in-law had been a general, Long was given command of the venture. Once more the merchants and investors hoping to profit pledged their financial support. Once more adventurous and avaricious young men turned out to become soldiers of "liberation." Long established his rendezvous at the old filibuster base of Natchitoches, and the first contingent of them arrived early in June. By June 21 Long had about two hundred men across the line into Texas at Nacogdoches. That day he and his officers decreed a new government, with Long as President of the Supreme Council of Twenty-one. Two days later, in a declaration of independence in which he hoped to speak to the world, Long announced that Texas was now and henceforward an independent republic.

The enterprise was never much more than a landgrab at its root, however, and the public at large saw through the group. In Natchitoches, shortly after Long left for Texas, John Jamison likened Long's followers to puppies riding on a chariot, looking back and telling themselves "what a dust we make." He advised Secretary of War John C. Calhoun in Washington that "the whole is a ridiculos [*sic*] farce and will end like all bubbles."⁴

The day after issuing the declaration of independence, Long sent two men, one of them James Gaines, south along the trace to Galveston to meet with Jean Laffite. When Laffite read the letter they gave him he saw that President Long was offering him an office in the new government and a commission to privateer in its name out of Galveston. In return, he asked for Laffite's fealty and assistance.⁵ To Laffite this was an opportunity. Spain would easily defeat Long, but the Long threat offered the Laffites a chance to infiltrate a plot and pass along information to Fatio and Apodaca. Now as before, assisting the failure of others could bring profit to the Laffites.

Pierre had not returned from the East when Jean received Long's embassy, but the younger brother knew what to do. It was an old story by now. He sent a copy of Long's June 24 letter to Fatio, and meanwhile addressed a reply, sending a copy of that, too, to Havana.⁶ As so often before, Laffite pledged his long devotion to "the emancipation of the Mexican provinces," and assured the filibuster that the Laffites wished to advance his efforts in any way possible. However, he could not help but remind Long that the Laffites had seen Gutiérrez and Magee, Mina and Perry, and Lallemand all try and fail before him. "I have done all in my power to help them along and should not regret the sacrifices they have cost me had they happily succeeded," he said. Now might be a good time for another effort, for Spain was tired and weak in the New World. Indeed, Jean represented his Galveston enclave as a torch keeping alive the flame of freedom in the region. "The spirit of liberty budding out under my care in these fertile provinces is growing rapidly," he said, "and it is no longer necessary to stimulate the heads of those young and brave Creoles but only to lead them wisely."

But he wanted to know the particulars of Long's intentions and immediate plans, and if he was to ally himself with the filibuster, he needed a formal agreement between them of the Laffites' roles and the benefits to accrue to them. He asked Long to tell him "exactly what your resources are, and give me a letter explaining the means you must have to commence the campaign so that I can second you," information that would go straight to Fatio. Jean went on, "Do not keep anything from me that would enable me to cooperate with you." With customary self-aggrandizement, Laffite dangled a morsel before Long and hinted that he knew accurate information on Mexican strength in the region, referring to agents he claimed to have in Béxar who kept him apprised of sentiment there, and of the support for resistance awaiting release.

Jean also bargained for the time he would need to notify Fatio in New Orleans and perhaps strike a new deal with Spain. Jean also expected Pierre at Galveston in a few days and wanted, as always, to confer with his older brother. Meanwhile he offered some advice to Long. Galveston privateers still flew the flag of the Mexican insurgency, but Long entertained no idea of seizing Texas for an illusory independent Mexico and had raised his own banner at Natchitoches. Jean thought it blunted their efforts to be under different flags and for the Laffites to switch now would look like indecision. "It would be a bad policy to take one different from the one under which we have been fighting for the last eight years," he argued. Besides, their flag was recognized by Buenos Aires and Venezuela "and our privateers under such colors are received there in a friendly manner by the authorities of those provinces."

He also told Long that they should establish an admiralty court at Galveston, though neither had the authorization to do so. No doubt that is something he hoped Pierre would bring back with him from one of the several meetings with revolutionary representatives in Philadelphia or Baltimore that had kept him on the East Coast. Meanwhile Jean's suggestion that Long fly the flag of the Mexican insurgency may have been an attempt at insurance. If Pierre came back empty-handed, then even a show of embracing the revolutionary cause would allow Long to justify letters of marque and an admiralty court under his rump council.

Long asked to meet personally with Laffite, but Jean protested that he could not leave Galveston before Pierre returned. Long had also asked for some ammunition, and Jean could spare a little of that, but only a little, as he was fortifying Galveston once more in the wake of the hurricane. Once he had more, he promised to give Long all he asked.[7] It was a typical Laffite response, seeming to promise much in return for a lot of information, but giving little or nothing in effect. Typical of the filibusters, however, Long had not brought adequate supplies, and in July had to disperse his men in small parties to subsist from the land until he could somehow bring in substantial provisions from Louisiana.

Pierre had arrived back in New Orleans by mid-July if not earlier, and the necessity of conferring with him persuaded Jean to leave the island shortly after responding to Long.[8] The brothers returned to Galveston during the first weeks of August,[9] and were there when new emissaries from Long stepped ashore. They came to seek supplies, which they may have gotten in some measure, but also to move on to the steps Jean had suggested of establishing an admiralty court and issuing letters of marque under the authority of what Long would call the Republic of Texas. The Laffites put them off, at least on the admiralty court, for that would have required them to swear fealty to Long, and thus abrogate their ability to operate under the rotting cloak of the Mexican insurgency. Humbert had been back since April, when the

Two Friends dropped anchor in the bay, and now the old warrior began issuing commissions in his role as "lieutenant general and chief of the Province of Texas" under authority from the Mexican Congress. He granted the first on August 18 to Juan Salvador de Torres for *Le Brave,* captained by Jean Desfarges.[10]

Typically, the official governmental letter of marque was a document that had been signed in advance in blank by a member of the junta and as such, had no validity.[11] Laffite's commissions to his vessels, of which he probably never issued more than a half dozen, were written in duplicate in longhand by a secretary, one copy for the vessel and the other for retention, and signed by Laffite. He authorized his captains to stop neutral vessels and take supplies as needed, paying with a warrant negotiable with Laurent Maire, who was now a merchant in New Orleans. When bringing a prize into Galveston, the corsair should fly no flag but a white one on the mizzenmast, and approach from west of the pass. Laffite would respond by showing a white flag from the signal tower atop his house, or else fly a flag on the beach. All friendly ships lying at anchor would display white flags while in port, and when a corsair entered the bay it should fire one shot and receive an answering shot from shore. His captains were prohibited from making landing with their prizes anywhere except Galveston.[12]

The overriding concern with profit was evident in another document handed to captains by Laffite and Humbert, a "charter for partition" that detailed the division of spoils taken from prizes, a touchy subject since the dawn of piracy. Half of everything went to the ship owner and outfitter, together with a 5 percent commission on the balance of the cargo brought into Galveston. The captain was to hold back another 5 percent of what was due to the crew pending dispensation of everything. If the crew took a vessel better than their own and abandoned their own as a result, then the new prize became entirely the property of the owner of the original privateer in order to cover his loss. All arms also went to the owner. Thereafter, in something resembling an insurance policy, Laffite detailed the special shares of profit to be given to a man should he lose an arm or a leg. The first man to spot a prize was to get an extra share, as was the first man to board one. The captain controlled four discretionary shares to hand out to men who performed particularly well, whereas any men who deserted or were caught stealing from their mates should lose their shares. Then in descending order from the captain to the common crewmen, a division by shares by rank was detailed.[13]

Whether Humbert was doing this on the basis of his old commission, or if Pierre secured some new authorization for him in the East, is unclear, but it would not have mattered to the Laffites either way. Before long the word was out that Humbert, "an outcast and a wanderer on the face of the earth," as Patterson called him a few weeks hence, had washed ashore at Galveston yet again to issue commissions for the Laffites.[14] So long as he was doing that, it did not suit the brothers' purposes to make Galveston submit itself to Long's presumed authority.

By late September, however, the Laffites had rethought their situation. The brothers could not expect to be able to hold their island base too much longer. With their corsairs back on the Gulf making money, the brothers could consider ostensibly changing allegiances to Long, putting them in a position to be more valuable to Spain, with the hope for remuneration, or else toleration of their Galveston establishment.

By this time, however, Apodaca had decided he wanted nothing further to do with the double-dealing Laffites. Pierre's plan proposed to Onís in Washington appeared pointless to the viceroy. Given the time it took for information to get from Galveston to Havana, it would be old and obsolete before it could be acted upon, and thus not worth the expense. Besides, Apodaca did not trust the Laffites, and felt convinced that they had been double-dealing with Fatio and Onís. "In spite of whatever the Minister Onís says in favor of LaFit, I do not have any confidence in him," Apodaca told Madrid. He could not forget that while supposedly helping to disrupt Lallemand's enterprise with Fatio, Jean Laffite was also feeding Lallemand's people and thus apparently prolonging their stay. The Champ d'Asile settlement would never have gotten started had Jean not saved the colonists when they first landed at Galveston, and the Laffite argument that they were lulling the colonists to make them easy prey did not carry weight in Havana. "The Lafite person is only concerned with his own affairs," Apodaca railed, "and double-dealing with us and the adventurers."

As for Pierre's offer to sell munitions and supplies to Havana, it was pointless, for Apodaca now had means to secure all he needed from other more reliable sources. Worse, any such dealing with Pierre would be ill advised because it would enable him to provide information on Spanish strength to other filibusters or rebels. Moreover, it would entrench Galveston as a smuggling haven. "Lafit is a lost man, reduced to poverty and without the means of subsistence," said Apodaca. The Laffites would say or do anything for money, and honor no loyalty. As for Galveston, it should be destroyed and the Laffite operation dispersed. Apodaca wanted the Laffites erased from the Spanish coast throughout his viceregal domain.[15] Weather and circumstances had stopped the fleet from attacking in 1818, but in February of this year Apodaca had requested ships for another assault and waited only for official approval. At the same time he sent fifteen thousand pesos to the military commander in Texas to pay for an overland expedition to Galveston, though summer floods and other problems would sap the funds before they could be used.[16]

Unaware of the Spanish sword poised over him, or that his sometime ally Onís had been ordered back to Spain in May, on

September 30 Jean sent another letter to Long, this time borne by John Davis and Jean Lacaze. Laffite was simply gulling the fili-buster.[17] Protesting once again that he could not leave Galveston, Jean said these two "lawyers" from New Orleans came to repre-sent the Laffites' willingness to enter into an agreement whereby they would aid Long in establishing and maintaining Mexican authority at Galveston. To that end, Laffite sent a draft of such an agreement.[18] Long took the Laffite proposal before his coun-cil, and by October 7 Long had come to Galveston to meet with Jean. On that day he appointed Jean "governor and commander-in-chief of the Island of St. Luis and Port of Galveston," empow-ered to grant letters of marque against Spanish shipping.[19] He also declared Galveston a port of entry for the Republic. Jean Laffite began commissioning privateers under his power as gov-ernor, including that month the *Jupiter*, which sailed under the new "Mexican" colors of a white star in the center of a red field.[20] Once again the Laffites were serving two masters, and preparing to betray one.

That day, in New Orleans, Pierre wrote a report on affairs at Galveston to Cienfuegos's successor in Havana, Captain General Juan Cagigal. It recounted the recent misfortunes suffered by the Laffites, and presented an exaggerated portrait of Long's arrival and his undoubted links to American expansionists, as well as his intention of taking La Bahía when his command was strong enough. Of course Pierre would not know until sometime later of the events on Galveston Island that day or what hap-pened immediately thereafter.[21]

Long decided to take a party of his followers from Natchi-toches to Galveston to help establish his sovereignty on the is-land, but he got only as far as the Coushatta Trace when he learned that Spanish *soldados* were on their way to attack. Long ordered a retreat to Nacogdoches, but when he recrossed the Bra-zos River the Spaniards caught him with a surprise attack that sent him reeling back in confusion. Meanwhile a post on the Trinity commanded by Long's brother David was also attacked, and the brother was killed. Fleeing refugees spread panic in Nacogdoches, and when Long reached his base he found it evacuated. He abandoned the town on October 26, just two days before Spaniards occupied the village,[22] and retreated to Louisiana. It had been in part Jean's July warning to Fatio, and information sent subsequently, that resulted in the successful expulsion of the filibusters—this being the only occasion when intelligence furnished by the Laffites influenced Spain's campaign against invaders and revolutionaries. Their information on Long also helped persuade Spain to delay ratification of the Adams-Onís Treaty, by making the Spaniards feel that the United States was trying through Long to take by force what it had agreed to give up in diplomacy.[23]

Long was in disgrace at the fiasco. As his fragmented army crossed the Sabine, one of his officers grumbled that the general had deceived his followers as to their prospects, and might be in danger from his own people if he appeared on the Sabine. A rumor soon spread along the river that Long fled south to Galveston to seek refuge with Laffite.[24] In Béxar Spanish authorities believed the same, and ordered a regimental detachment to reconnoiter the strength of "Genl. Long and the Pirate Lafit."[25]

At this moment, the word "pirate" was finally to carry real peril for the Laffites. When Congress passed new legislation to protect commerce and punish piracy as part of the bargain in the Adams-Onís Treaty, even Onís for a change took heart. The act did not precisely define who should be regarded as pirates, however. Onís wanted it to include those who fitted out privateers in the United States to prey on Spanish shipping under Latin American insurgent flags, and who did so without being commissioned in a home port of that flag, or who took their prizes to insurgent ports for adjudication. In short, Onís wanted Galveston ruled illegal as well as Old Providence and all other corsair outposts on "some desert Island, where under colour of giving a sanction to their robberies, they have established a tribunal bearing the semblance of an Admiralty court." He also wanted it stipulated that the captain and two-thirds of the crew of a privateer must be native to the nation whose flag they flew.[26]

Further definition would be forthcoming, as would a renewed assault on the illicit corsairs and their nests. In May Washington sent Commodore Oliver Hazard Perry aboard the *John Adams* to cruise between Venezuela and Buenos Aires and San Domingue to protect American commerce in those waters. Privately Adams also wanted Perry to meet with the leaders of the insurgencies and assure them of unofficial American support.[27] The message was clear enough. The United States would honor privateers properly commissioned, but would regard all others as pirates. Adams was especially concerned with those commissioned by DeForest for Buenos Aires.[28]

Meanwhile on the Gulf coast, Patterson began the year with his squadron in poor condition. His ketch the *Surprise* was in such bad shape that he thought it might be cheaper to replace her than to repair her. "In her present condition she is unsafe as a cruising vessel," he reported the previous November.[29] The *Enterprise* needed extensive repairs and her sails and rigging were much worn. He also had the *Prometheus*, too decayed to be worth repairing. The *Firebrand*, mounting four twelve-pounder medium guns and four twelve-pounder carronades, was in perfect condition in all respects, however, and his only seaworthy vessel with substantial armament. Otherwise he had the revenue cutter the *Louisiana*, in bad shape generally and unarmed; the little felucca the *Bull Dog* with its two twelve-pounder carronades, in excellent shape; and two small launches each mounting a single carronade.[30]

Still Patterson tightened his grip on the Gulf coast, on July 18 capturing nine men who had attacked and plundered several vessels at anchor below New Orleans and then retreated to Big Bayou Barataria. Washington gave him more muscle, and by late September when rumor had the brutal pirate William Mitchell fortified at Barataria with 150 men, Patterson stationed the *Hornet*, the *Lynx*, the *Surprise*, and the *Bull Dog* off Barataria and the passes leading in from the sea, and sent an expedition in to destroy the remnant of a renascent pirate base.[31] The Laffites' old associate Dominique had already given up on Gulf coast privateering, shortly after appearing in court in New Orleans to contest his right to three boxes of prize goods. When he put out from Galveston the previous March, he left again bound for Aury and Old Providence, stepping out of the Laffite orbit for good.[32]

Less than a month earlier, however, Patterson struck a blow that sent a shiver throughout the corsairing community, and signaled the beginning of its end. On August 29 the Laffite-owned privateer *Le Brave* under Desfarges took the *Filomena* bound from Pensacola to Havana, laden with a cargo of raisins, flour, lard, beef, peas, and $3,000 in gold and silver coin. The next day about one hundred miles west of the Florida Keys the vessels encountered the cutters the *Alabama*, commanded by Don Gomez Taylor, and the *Louisiana*, with Lieutenant Harris Loomis in command. Desfarges had his men fire a musket volley at the *Louisiana*, but after a return volley he quickly surrendered. Loomis brought both the privateer and her prize back to Bayou St. John above New Orleans.[33] Taken aboard *Le Brave* were seventeen men including Captain Desfarges, and with them Loomis captured the articles of agreement prepared at Jean Laffite's order, a blank commission signed by Humbert, and other documents going back to the days of Aury, John Ducoing, and John Peter Rousselin. In a trunk in the cabin Loomis also found some table silver and assorted items including a flag of the Mexican republic.[34]

Perhaps for the first time, federal authorities had in their hands the letters of marque and other relevant documents of a

Laffite privateer out of Galveston, and it was immediately apparent how bogus was any claim to legitimacy. The federal court had
a perfect opportunity with an ironclad case to send a message to
the corsair community. On November 12 a grand jury indicted
Desfarges and his crew on charges of piracy.[35]

It was not a good time to be called a pirate. On August 27, 1819,
three days before the taking of *Le Brave,* Judge Richard Peters
handed down a decision in a case involving one of DeForest's
privateers that brought a Spanish prize into Philadelphia after
being fitted out illegally in Baltimore. What he said bore directly
on the Laffite operation as well as American corsairs everywhere:

It is a disgrace to the character of American citizens, thus to
prostitute themselves in nefarious acts of robbery and plunder,
under the mask of assisting the Spanish patriots of South
America, as those are termed whose cause many of our deluded
or vitiated citizens effect to espouse; when in fact they are pursuing selfish and sordid objects, for their private emolument.
Such base and hypocritical depravity, gives to those who envy
our national character and unexampled success in our republican and highly estimable form of government, the opportunity
of uncandidly generalizing the foul propensities of culpable
individuals, into stains on our national reputation; although
those who are guilty of such unworthy and base crimes and
misdemeanors, are, as in all civilized nations they should be,
subjected to punishment by our laws, (which if defective in a
case will no doubt be made more perfect), and are held in merited detestation by the great body of our citizens. It is the duty
of those to whom the execution of our laws is committed, to
correct these abuses, by punishing the perpetrators, and rendering their enormities unprofitable to them, by restoring their
plunder to those who have suffered by their depredations. Such
unwarrantable misbehavior becomes unsatiable and boundless,
and spreads itself into acts of piracy, murder, and robbery

committed on the persons and property even of our own citizens, as well as those of all countries who navigate the seas, emphatically styled the high road or nations. The Buenos Ayres flag, or even the flag or commission of a nation acknowledged by our government to be sovereign and independent, would not justify to our laws, any acts of capture or depredation committed on the high seas, by an armed vessel fitted and furnished in any of our ports either wholly or partially, on the property or persons of the subjects of a power in amity with us. Such fitting and furnishing, would be a breach of our laws, even if the whole of the officers and crew were subjects of a foreign nation, originally belonging to, and arriving in the vessel thus furnished, equipped or fitted. But it is highly criminal in our citizens to engage on board such vessel, or otherwise to commit hostilities against a friendly power under any pretext.[36]

The Peters decision set a precedent for dealing with questionable privateers and meant trouble for the Laffites, especially once initial reports saying that *Le Brave* belonged to one "Le Fage" were corrected to identify the owner as Jean Laffite. More sobering to the accused was the fact that finally, on the previous March 3, Congress had made piracy a capital crime.

Of course, many men, including the Laffites, had gotten to this point in the past. But hereafter it was not to be so easy. Grymes was engaged, apparently by Pierre Laffite, to defend Desfarges and the others. The crux of the case would be the legitimacy of the Laffite commissions.[37] Until this time, life in New Orleans had assumed a more orderly pace for Pierre than his brother's life at Galveston. When he returned from the East he found the good news that he had won his suit against the estate of Champlin, though instead of getting all Pierre had sought, Livingston secured only $2,879.50 for his client.[38] One of Marie's relations had bought a house two doors away on St. Philip.[39] The family in the house on the corner may have grown yet again, for on Pierre's return he bought a slave girl aged just twelve, and in late August a grown male from the wife of Laurent Maire.[40] The old problems between Pierre and Paul Lanusse seemed to have been forgotten, and Pierre now conducted much of his business on behalf of Galveston through Lanusse's mercantile house.[41] Indeed, when Jean helped Marie Villard repurchase the Bourbon and St. Philip house from Abat, one of the men subscribing himself as security for her notes was Lanusse.[42]

Nevertheless money was tight. On September 6, two weeks after the $9,000 in notes for the repurchase of their house came due, Marie had been able to pay off barely more than $2,000.[43] Meanwhile Pierre's health probably remained indifferent, and the growing fear of exposure and uncertainty over the brothers' future employment by Spain contributed to a time of upset and uncertainty.[44]

Now the plight of Desfarges and his crew added to the stress. The defendants had entered pleas of not guilty and Pierre and the rest had set about their defense.[45] They wanted to call Humbert to testify to his supposed authority in issuing Le Brave's commission, but Humbert had decided it would be prudent to distance himself from the Laffites and he refused to testify. Ironically, the prosecution called Pierre Laffite and Pierre Laméson as witnesses for the government. On November 19 Laffite was able to testify as to the authority from Herrera, or Iturribarría, or whomever, that might or might not legitimize Humbert's commissions. Laméson could speak to his own earlier commission and corroborate Laffite. But together their testimony could have been damning for the men they wanted to defend, for they could present nothing to convince a jury that Desfarges sailed under legitimate papers. Hardly surprisingly, an attempt to get the men out of jail on a writ of *habeas corpus* was denied, for everyone knew that Desfarges and the rest would disappear as the Laffites had in 1813. On November 22 the jury returned a guilty verdict within minutes.[46]

Judge Hall postponed sentencing for several weeks. Until the Long business was settled, Jean did not dare leave Galveston. Pierre Laffite could often be seen at Maspero's Exchange Commercial Coffee House, alternately protesting that he and his brother were not and had never been pirates, and continuing his cover of railing against the Spaniards—which he could do with some sincerity after the expense he had incurred without reimbursement.[47] Whatever his efforts to free Desfarges, however, he failed. It did not help that the sentiment against piracy continued to escalate as public sympathy for smugglers seemed to dissipate. On December 30, before a courtroom packed with Laffite friends, Judge Hall pronounced the feared sentence of death by hanging. It was time to set stern examples.

This made it all the more important for the Laffites to reestablish themselves with Spain, and James Long could provide the lure. When Long arrived at Bolívar Point in late November or early December after the Brazos River fiasco, he did not immediately meet with Jean. Instead, he sent James Gaines, Warren Hall, and a few followers, and they spent some time on Galveston. Laffite received them in the repaired frame house, and there Gaines passed on Long's request that Laffite join forces with him against Spain. Despite showing every hospitality, Laffite avoided making any commitment.[48] Meanwhile Jean sent word to Pierre in New Orleans, and Pierre in turn informed Fatio and wrote to Cagigal with a report of affairs at Galveston. He twisted the bare facts into a warning that Long surely intended to seize the port from Spain's friends, the Laffites. The intruders must be driven away. "I foresee the most woeful consequences if they take possession," he said, "since it is evident that they are instruments of a Government that seeks means of territorial expansion and that is setting them at work as pioneers." In short, Pierre accused Long of being a United States agent. Naturally the Laffites had a plan whereby Spain, with their help, could get rid of Long if he did take over. Pierre asked for eighty to one hundred men to be sent to Galveston, where Jean would allow them through the pass into the bay by means of "a signal to be agreed upon." He would then enable their commander to seize the place and raise the Spanish flag without difficulty. If the Americans tried to return and take the port by force, the Laffites would not be strong enough to repel them, perhaps, but Pierre promised that thanks to the brothers' knowledge of the coast, "never, never will the American gentlemen be masters of it."[49] Long's presence also irritated some in the United States, who complained that Galveston, which some described as "the present headquarters of the republicans," was nothing more than "a nest of murderers and pirates."[50]

While both Spain and the United States decided what, if anything, to do about Long, Jean Laffite had to deal with his unwelcome new neighbor on Bolívar Point, and he did so with his usual veneer of charm. Warren Hall from Rapides Parish, Louisiana, found the corsair, as had so many before him, to be tall and well formed other than those tiny hands and feet, and a man of appealing manners. If Jean Laffite showed any difference in his dealings with people, it was that he treated his subordinates with a coolness approaching the aloof, while visitors got a warm welcome. He spoke good English, with an accent that left no doubt as to his Bordeaux nativity, and which Hall found gave additional zest to his impressive conversational skill. Laffite entertained his guests with often amusing stories of his past, many of them no doubt invented for their benefit. As he spoke, he habitually kept one eye closed, leading some to believe that he was blind in that eye. The old green uniform was gone, at least for the present, replaced by the simple broadcloth of the fashionable gentleman, a costume that should have seemed out of place on this all-but-desert island among pirates and smugglers.[51]

Hall found Laffite "always affable, but perfectly impenetrable."[52] Gaines thought much the same, finding Laffite gentlemanly, sober, and thoughtful, but distant from his subordinates, rarely smiling. He had the manner and bearing of a leader, and relied on his personality and prestige to maintain control, though he occasionally wore a brace of pistols in his belt when he thought they lent weight to his authority. He did not brook disobedience, and could punish malefactors severely, but apparently with the sort of rude equitability that even the roughest men respected.[53] When one of the men on the island, François Francis, robbed Robert Kuykendall, a traveler from the Cadron settlement in Arkansas, Laffite turned Francis over to Kuykendall and told him to punish Francis as he pleased. Kuykendall hanged him.[54] About the same time occurred a long-remembered incident with a privateer who tried to withhold some of the prize goods from the shares turned over to Laffite. When confronted, he supposedly spat in Laffite's face or offered some other insult, and the governor grabbed him, spun him around, and kicked him in the seat of his pants, which put an end to the insolence.[55] Twenty years later men who had been on Galveston at this time liked to recall of Jean Laffite that "his sailors adored him, for though a strict disciplinarian & one who made no bones of hanging & shooting his subjects when they deserved, yet was he generous withal." There may have been more than a gloss of nostalgia or "sea story" to this, but it is apparent that Laffite knew how to control his men with a judicious mixture of severity and generosity.[56]

Always there to soften the rude edges of Jean's life on the island was Laffite's mulatto mistress. Perhaps she was Catherine, as there were rumors on the island that she had a son by Laffite. More likely his companion was another woman altogether. Catherine probably never visited Galveston, even during the awful summer of 1819 when a yellow fever epidemic swept New Orleans. Pierre had at least two children born in earlier years, Pierre and Jean, who disappear from the record after 1818, in all probability victims of the fever. If Jean felt conscious of the hazard being faced by Catherine and their son Jean Pierre, it was apparently not sufficient for him to bring them to the other dangers of Galveston.[57] Meanwhile he dined from china plate and linen at a well-stocked table, highlighted by excellent wine, and his mistress kept his house neat and orderly as if he were a middle-class Royal Street merchant in New Orleans.[58]

All the while that Jean dealt with Long and Pierre and the Spaniards and their foes, the business of privateering and selling contraband continued. Rebuilding the smuggling operation required Jean to keep the flow of slaves going to the Sabine barracks and on into Louisiana. The market was stronger than ever into mid-1819. "The only prevailing thirst of this country appears to be the accumulation of wealth for the purpose of possessing slaves, the bane of every happy country," observed a United States naval agent on an inspection tour that January.[59] A year earlier, on April 20, 1818, when Congress struck a blow at the illegal African slave trade by passing legislation allowing for the seizure of ships carrying such blacks and a reward of 50 percent of the proceeds to those responsible for such captures, it included the sale of the captured slaves in the proceeds to be divided.

Imaginative investors conceived the idea of sending agents to the West Indies to buy cargoes of blacks at a third of the price they would fetch in Louisiana and then ship them into the Mississippi, stopping at the Balize. From that point the agent left the ship and informed the authorities in New Orleans of an illicit cargo, not mentioning his own role in bringing the slaves into American waters. Beverly Chew's people seized the cargo and sold the slaves at auction, by common consent at a price far below market value. The Treasury took its half of the proceeds and the informing agent the rest for his employers. A slave that cost $200 in the Indies might go to the agent for $300 at auction, being legalized in the process. With his rebate of $150, the agent or original buyer was out of pocket $350 but now had a slave he could sell lawfully for $600 to $1,000 or more. Soon rumors told of a host of such cargoes being brought in and more than 10,000 slaves dispersed, though this was surely an exaggeration. Others in New Orleans swore they knew of only one such cargo by the end of 1818.[60]

That gave some enterprising men an idea. Several would employ the scheme, but it seems to have found its most ardent practitioners in the Bowie brothers of Rapides Parish. Having left Long's campaign and returned home, James and Rezin Bowie received a visit from their former comrade Warren Hall, who made them aware of the money to be made from the slaves coming into Galveston.[61] The brothers realized that if they bought slaves from Laffite, who was still selling them at one dollar a pound, and brought them overland into Louisiana, they did not have to risk selling them to buyers to make a profit. All they had to do was inform the authorities of the slaves' whereabouts and then capitalize on the new Congressional legislation. Once seized, the slaves would be sold at public auction, and half the proceeds would go to the Bowies for being informants. Better yet, at auction the Bowies could afford to buy the slaves themselves, knowing that they would be reimbursed half of the purchase price in their reward. Then the slaves would be legally "laundered," and the brothers would be free to sell them on the open market to anyone. A slave that cost $140 could bring $500 or more at the auction, meaning a $250 rebate to the Bowies. Already they had a profit of $110 on their original investment. Early in 1819 a prime male slave sold for as much as $1,800, meaning that when they resold their new slave on the current market, they could turn a $140 investment into a profit of over $1,400. Even when prices dropped due to a cotton shortage later in the year, the gain to be made was still astronomical.[62]

The Bowies and others put the new variant on the trade into operation in the early part of the year, and continued it intermittently as long as Laffite ruled the island.[63] The Bowies once or twice went to Galveston itself, and James Bowie seems to have struck up something of an acquaintance with Jean Laffite during the visits, and probably learned from him some of the old slaving contacts such as the notorious slave smuggler Charles Mulholland.[64] The practice came at some risk, and Mulholland and another Bowie associate, James Reeves of Opelousas, as well as Champlin's partner Adams, were all soon brought up on charges of illegally importing large numbers of slaves.[65]

Meanwhile the trade in other contraband goods remained brisk, encouraged by high consumer prices in New Orleans due to tariffs. Even staples such as produce commanded strong prices, because the cotton boom so obsessed planters that they would not waste profitable land on growing vegetables. Oysters went for a dollar per hundred, an enormous increase in price. In a renewed effort to curtail the trade, on September 7 the Treasury ordered out of New York a second revenue cutter, the *Louisiana*, for Chew to station off the Teche. Chew could also have the revenue cutter the *Alabama*, originally destined for Mobile, if he needed it.[66] Washington wanted the privateers out of business, for they no longer needed them to distract and weaken Spain.

On the night of September 27 a dozen armed men with blackened faces broke into the home of James Lyons in lower St. Landry Parish. They were led by George Brown, who had sought a privateering commission from Laffite earlier that summer. Laffite kept him waiting six weeks pending new authorization Pierre might deliver from one of the juntas. Finally Humbert gave Brown a commission, but Laffite added to it an admonition to take only Spanish goods. Instead, Brown took two armed boats up the Mermenteau River, and thence into the Bayou Queue de Tortue to the Lyons home. His men tied Lyons and his wife and children, then pretended to be customs inspectors and ransacked the house. When they left, they took anything of value, including Lyons's ten slaves.[67] Despite the men's attempts at disguise, few doubted that they were from Galveston. Impelled by the momentum of events and crackdown on corsairs mandated after the Adams-Onís Treaty, Patterson reacted at once, ordering an armed vessel to patrol the coast between the Balize and Galveston. Its mission was to interdict the smuggling, but if it gleaned information that could justify a strike at Galveston, Patterson would be willing to countenance the idea though the island belonged to Spain.

Patterson gave Lieutenant John R. Madison, commander of the *Lynx,* the assignment. With him was Lieutenant James McIntosh, who lost his ship the *Firebrand* in a severe storm at Pass Christian July 28 and had been onshore awaiting orders ever since.[68] When the *Lynx* made ready to leave Charleston, she carried a long twelve-pounder and half a dozen twelve-pound carronades, with a complement of fifty-seven officers and men. She could face anything the privateers put on the water.[69] Madison soon took several privateer and prize schooners in the Gulf, then headed his ship toward the mouth of the Mermenteau, where he sent McIntosh upstream in ship's boats. McIntosh learned that two pirogues had passed there the night before headed for Galveston, with men aboard who said they served Laffite and had robbed citizens and outraged women. They sounded very much like Lyons's attackers. For the next several days McIntosh hunted for the miscreants, often just missing Brown's force until he surprised them and captured their boats. The fugitives escaped, but McIntosh found Brown's commission, dated August 29, 1819, and signed by Humbert.[70]

On the evening of November 5 someone on Galveston Island saw a large signal fire blazing on Bolívar Point. Laffite ordered an inquiry, and when told that about a dozen hungry, ragged men there wanted aid, sent over a small sailboat. In the process he learned that their leader was George Brown. If Laffite did not know of the Lyons robbery, he did within hours of Brown and three of his companions setting foot on Galveston. Left unpunished, Brown's example could spread and bring untold problems with the United States.

Laffite wasted no time in convening a trial and empanelling a court of three judges and thirteen jurors on the morning of November 6. The accused were allowed to give statements, but the court found them guilty and sentenced them to death. At noon that same day they hanged Brown from a gibbet erected on a point overlooking the pass where all incoming vessels would see him. Then came a test of Laffite's leadership. The population on the island appealed for clemency for the remaining three convicted, but left it to the governor to decide. He knew from experience that his men would stand for justice only to a point, but he could not risk a pardon that might incite others to similar crimes. He put the men in a boat and banished them from the island, sending them as he put it, "out into the wild to repent their crimes."[71]

The next morning, through a dense fog, people on the island saw a ship's masts outside the bar. Madison had intended only to patrol the coastline but offshore winds had driven him toward the island and in that fog on the morning of November 7 he had no choice but to drop anchor.[72] Almost at once he saw a sailboat heading along the coast toward the harbor, and recovered from it a man in tatters who admitted to being one of the Brown fugitives. He told Madison that he and his companions had tossed their weapons into the Mermenteau when they saw McIntosh approach, and then stumbled through the forest until they reached Bolívar Point two nights previous. Four of his companions were now with Laffite. He was on his way to join them when Madison caught him.[73]

Laffite may or may not have observed the sailboat through the fog, but he knew the *Lynx* was there and soon demanded an explanation of why she was anchored off his coastline. Galveston was a port of the Republic of Texas, he was its governor, and the

Lynx was violating its sovereignty. If Madison had any business in being there, he must present his requests directly to Laffite. Should Madison attempt to enter the harbor "in a hostile manner," Laffite would "rebut your intentions at the expense of my life."[74] It was the usual hyperbole, but it bought Jean time to think. Madison, who later claimed that he never got Laffite's letter, sent McIntosh to Laffite with a message[75] demanding answers to questions about the whereabouts and condition of the men he sought. Madison included in his note a peremptory order that they be handed over to him, along with the stolen slaves and other goods.[76]

Laffite bristled and wrote an equally stiff, even threatening, reply that McIntosh refused to deliver until certain expressions were modified. Pleading his imperfect command of English, and no intent to give offense, Laffite altered his response and sent it back via McIntosh.[77] He told Madison of the execution of Brown and the banishment of the others. "I thought, not having here much of a prison, that it would be fitting to send them out among the beasts," Jean said. "I beg your forgiveness, Sir, if this condemnation is not completely according to the rules, but I am waiting every day for the supreme authorities to advise me in giving form to my government." Now, however, at Madison's request he would send a boat after them and hand them over once taken. Still he thought his action of the day before would send abroad a message that "the pirates and those other malefactors will know that it will not be at Galveston that they can seek refuge and be free of punishment for the crimes they commit."

If Madison would care to come ashore and accept the governor's hospitality, Laffite promised to "inform you of all the details you could ask for on the subject of all the infamies that are committed on these shores."[78] He also sent a copy of his commission from Long to establish his authority as governor, and the request that should the *Lynx* pay a call on Long at Bolívar Point to look for the remaining fugitives, Madison would tell the filibuster that Laffite had shown Madison and McIntosh "the most friendly, generous and hospitable" treatment possible and promised them every assistance in capturing the thieves. It was Laffite's acknowledgment of Long as his civil superior in the new republic, but also a suggestion that Long cooperate.[79] The last thing Laffite needed was for Long to give sanctuary to the miscreants, and thus bring down American authorities on both of them.

The weather suddenly became so severe that the *Lynx* did not dare remain close to shore at anchor, and that evening Madison took her out to sea, where for a few days she rode out the storm. Meanwhile Laffite's boat found the three banished fugitives and brought them to Galveston. When Madison and the *Lynx* returned, McIntosh came ashore to take charge of the thieves.[80] The wind prevented McIntosh from returning to the *Lynx* with the prisoners, however, leaving him to enjoy the typical entertainment of Laffite's house. During their conversation, Laffite revealed some of his style of management in dealing with the kind of men under him. "I understand the management of such men perfectly," he said. He knew just how far to go with them without pushing them too far. Indeed, the reason he did not execute all of the men in custody was that he knew his men would stand for one example being made, and that one a ringleader, but to do more would have led to their questioning his use of power. "I made it appear that I considered the example sufficient, and retained my control." Laffite also entertained McIntosh with hunting and games, and more of his fund of stories, and the lieutenant amused himself by gleaning what he could learn of the island's strength and defenses to pass on to his commander. When the guest was at last able to leave with his prisoners, Laffite said he regretted McIntosh could not stay longer. "My friend Lieut. McIntosh was much pleased with the attention and politeness of Lafitte," Madison would tell Patterson, and McIntosh left feeling that he had met a man who "if he had his vices had also his virtues."[81]

By November 23 the *Lynx* and her prisoners were in New Orleans, and soon three more of Brown's men were arrested. Livingston defended one of the men turned over by Laffite, but all were convicted at the same time as Desfarges and the crew of the *Le Brave*. The timing was unfortunate, in that by hanging Brown, Jean Laffite had set the standard of punishment for men guilty of outright piracy.[82] Soon the press gave the details of Jean Laffite's own justice to pirates.[83] Within the published documents and accounts of the episode lurked some troubling issues. Madison was supposed to apprehend the pirates who robbed Lyons and bring them back, not countenance a kangaroo trial by Laffite. For the navy to be seen to be treating with Laffite and Long as if they were recognized authorities of an independent Texan republic embarrassed and compromised United States authorities in both their efforts to crack down on piracy and to enforce the Adams-Onís Treaty. Federal authorities were openly opposed to Long's enterprise, as it threatened the treaty, which Spain had not yet ratified. They also wanted Galveston broken up before it started an international incident that might hazard the treaty. Laffite's request that Madison inform Long of what transpired on Galveston suggested some kind of alliance between the pirates and the filibusters. The apparent alliance was bad for Spain, bad for the United States, and would prove bad for the Laffites.

I had no death to fear, nor wealth to boast
Beyond the wandering freedom which I lost;
At length a fisher's humble boat by night
Afforded hope, and offer'd chance of flight.

TWENTY

Farewell to Galveston
1820

THE LAFFITES HAD played a bold game for more than four years, but by the end of 1819 it was clear that their options were dwindling. With the Adams-Onís Treaty not yet ratified, the American claim to Galveston was not officially extinguished. Even if Spain did ratify, the agreement obligated Washington to prevent American citizens and expeditions backed by Americans from making incursions into Spanish territory. From President Monroe on down, the government was at last seriously cracking down on piracy. In the world at large the story was the same. The Buenos Aires insurgency had repudiated unlawful commissions in its name the year before, and nations such as Britain and Russia were raising a considerable furor about the conditions on the seas of the Gulf and Caribbean. Piracy drove maritime insurance rates up 100 percent in this period, though there were likely never more than two thousand men engaged in it in any one year. Spain alone had lost more than three million dollars in merchant goods in the past few years.[1] Stripped of every vestige of legitimacy, and seeing the course of the *Le Brave* trial, the

Laffites could expect that each new prize brought in by their corsairs might be the one that put them in Judge Hall's court, charged with being accessories to piracy. They were still trying to make a bargain with Spain, but Spain showed no inclination to indulge them.

If they needed another signal that their time on this coast had passed, it came in December. With the taking of Brown's men and the capture of *Le Brave*, Patterson had begun to believe that he was about to rid the western Gulf of privateers at last. Then one of his vessels took yet another privateer schooner commanded by "a man named Gambier, who has been for several years engaged in piracy and smuggling." Of course this was Vincent Gambi, who had been arrested and charged so many times before only to escape the law each time. But he was not able to escape a more direct kind of justice now. Shortly before his ship was captured, his crew discovered that he was holding out on their share of several thousand dollars just taken from a victim. One evening as he slept on deck, his head resting on a spar, one of his man decapitated him "by the very bloody axe which he so often used," according to reports.[2] He was not the last of the Laffite associates to meet a violent end.

That month Pierre Laffite began raising money in New Orleans and making arrangements to relocate the brothers, even while trying to work a last-minute deal with Spain. As he wrote his proposal for a new scheme to betray Long on December 11, Pierre was selling two slaves to raise about $1,600.[3] Sometime late in December or early in January 1820, Jean, too, came to New Orleans. It was only the second time in the previous three years that neither brother was at Galveston to keep charge, a tacit admission that the island establishment was all but a dead issue to them. People in New Orleans saw both brothers on the streets as they set about their business. Pierre stood erect, his hat pulled over one eye to shut out the sun, and the eye partially closed, a vestige of the stroke of years before.[4] He did much of his business at Maspero's Exchange Commercial Coffee House, which visitors that month found to provide excellent dining.[5]

By this time, however, few seemed to believe Pierre's habitual rants against the Spanish or his protests that the brothers were not pirates. The leaks about the brothers' Spanish spying compromised them too widely. The debts they ran up cost them too much credibility. In the city the Laffites no longer enjoyed the goodwill of any but their fellow smugglers. "They live obscurely and without acquaintance among the men of position," observed Manuel García, soon to replace Fatio. They had made a lot of money over the years, but they had wasted a great deal of it, and much of the rest went to their attorneys Grymes and Livingston. Word had gotten around that they were almost broke. No one believed that they were repentant or reformed. "Meanwhile they make use of one thing and another," said García, "and so they go, biding their time until proper and suitable occasion may present itself, so that, without consideration for others concerned or keeping faith with them, they may seize upon whatever suits them and advances their interests."[6]

The brothers put out feelers about finding a new—and most unlikely—patron, the United States. On January 3, 1820, Pierre sent a letter to Patterson's headquarters, a communication typical of the Laffites' approaches to potential masters—hyperbolic, boastful, self-righteous, and dissembling. "Too long since the names of the Lafittes have been the object of general execration, as well here as abroad," he began. They had been attacked in the press, and unjustly accused by association with "the criminal undertakings of a gang of Pirates of all countries." Just to make certain Patterson knew how the brothers felt about their own associates, Pierre condemned those corsairs, "the audacity of which encreases by impunity, and who have lately committed depredations and atrocities of all kind on the Sea coast, and even within the jurisdiction of this State." He could prove that those criminals were never hired, protected, or paid by the Laffites, he said, and reminded Patterson that the hanging of Brown should be ample evidence of their own intolerance toward pirates.

In their old gambit, the Laffites offered to make a bargain by doing something they were going to do anyhow:

> To shew to the whole world that I never contributed to the violation of the sacred rights of nations, or would offer resistance or offense to the Government of the United States; and in the view of restoring all confidence to the foreign trade directing itself towards this place; and to destroy all fears which the Establishment of Galveztown might occasion; I now offer myself to you, Sir, willingly, and at my own risk and expense, to Clear Galveztown, and disband all those which are to be found there; taking the engagement for myself and my Brother, that it shall never serve as a place of Rendez-vous for any undertakings with our consent, or under our authorization.

All Pierre and Jean asked was a permit of safe conduct so that they could remove their vessels and their people and reestablish themselves unmolested somewhere outside American jurisdiction. The Laffites were presenting their evacuation as a patriotic act and a repudiation of their own trade, while also buying themselves a little time.

Pierre asked to meet personally with Patterson to discuss his offer, though the commodore maintained his distance and restricted their contact to written communications.[7] Perhaps he saw that Pierre promised less than met the eye, since Pierre did not actually say the Laffites would leave, but only that they would prevent any further privateering under their authorization.

Pierre's offer was a welcome one, however, and timely. Patterson's squadron was still weak and inadequately supplied and the Laffite offer seemed a long step in accomplishing his duty to suppress piracy and privateers violating the neutrality laws. He took Laffite's letter to Judge Hall, collector Chew, and Governor Jacques Villeré to hear their views. Patterson was not fooled by Pierre's protestations of lofty motivations, but Hall and the others agreed that Patterson should accept the Laffite offer to give up Galveston, and that safe conduct was a small price to pay in return for the opportunity to disrupt the illicit slave trade and remove "men of infamous character" from their environs.[8] Certainly it would be less costly than evicting them at gunpoint, and any move to use force at Galveston risked compromising the still pending treaty ratification in Madrid.

Patterson spent three weeks making certain that he would have the strength at hand to compel the Laffites to leave if it came to that. Finally on January 24, Patterson sent a response to Pierre. Whenever Pierre or Jean was ready to return to Galveston, Patterson would send along a letter of safe conduct that would be respected by his vessels and the United States Navy. Nevertheless, Patterson informed Pierre that he would be sending one of his warships before long to make certain of the "faithful and prompt fulfilling of your proposals."[9] He was not going to trust the Laffites without keeping an eye on them.

Patterson was still holding the safe conduct pass when his father-in-law George Pollock, a prominent merchant and officer of the New Orleans branch of the Bank of the United States who had close contacts with the Spaniards in New Orleans, told him that he had been approached by Pierre Laffite. Pierre wanted to meet with the commodore, but if that was not possible, he had some documents he thought might interest Patterson. Pierre sent a packet of papers to Pollock to be shared with his son-in-law. They dealt with something that the Laffites thought might help them with the United States, almost certainly Pierre's December 11 proposal to Cagigal for a Spanish armed expedition to seize Galveston and Long's men. If Cagigal went for it, then Spain would be attacking a position that as of January 1820 still lay within the unsettled territorial claim of the United States. Thus the Laffites could turn Spain's failure to ratify the recent treaty to their advantage.

Patterson saw enough in the documents that he sent Pollock on January 30 to ask Pierre to hand over a complete dossier of the documents he had in the matter in order that Patterson might inform Washington. Pierre replied cagily that he had already destroyed the rest of the documents because "I did not attach any importance to this affair other than what I told you." However, as soon as he returned to Galveston and surveyed the situation—and heard more from Fatio and Apodaca—he would return to New Orleans and inform Patterson of all the particulars in the matter, which of course he already knew.

Informed that Pierre anticipated leaving for Galveston early in February "to fill my pocket," as he put it, Patterson sent the safe conduct on the third, granting permission to "John Laffite and others now occupants of the post and fort of Galveston" to leave with their vessels and goods and any other belongings, without interference or molestation, and to go where they chose so long as it was outside the jurisdiction of the United States. As long as they committed no acts of violence, they were to be allowed to go their way. Patterson made it clear that Pierre and Jean had promised that "the *residences, buildings* &c. there erected, shall be razed to the ground, that every means shall be removed from thence which has hitherto rendered it the retreat and security of Aury and others who have from thence preyed upon the commerce of the Gulf of Mexico." Pierre got the note the same day he told Patterson that he had no more documents to reveal to him in the other matter, and replied to the commodore with typically obsequious thanks, saying that he felt so anxious to prove his gratitude that he wished someone could witness how grateful he felt.[10]

The hint was that Pierre's gratitude would be expressed in information that Patterson might find useful, but Patterson had already lost interest. There was little the Laffites could tell him of Long that he did not know, and as for the Spaniards threatening to take Galveston, he knew as well as anyone how weak Spain's fleet in the Gulf was at the moment. Indeed, he decided that Pierre's information was of so little consequence that he did not mention it to Washington. The Laffites were so compromised as double agents by now that no one could trust them, and their reputation as merchants in old and useless intelligence would have made the commodore even more skeptical. He just wanted them gone from his coast. Deceptive to the end, sometime during the course of the communications, Pierre gave Patterson to understand that he and Jean had decided to go to Venezuela "where they intend selling their vessels and abandoning the nefarious life they have led for so many years."[11] As if to punctuate the close of the Laffites' brief career as spies, the day that Pierre got his safe conduct, Felipe Fatio lay dying in New Orleans. He passed away the next day, making way for García to substitute his utter disdain for the Laffites for Fatio's sympathy.

Despite what he told Patterson, Pierre did not leave New Orleans, but remained while Jean returned to Galveston, and for Jean it was a final parting. Whatever the nature of his relationship with Catherine Villard and their four-year-old son Jean Pierre, it ended now, for he would never set foot in New Orleans again. Once on the island, he honored the brothers' pledge. He burned the frame house and most of the other structures in the community, leaving standing only enough to provide shelter to the men before they left. What defensive earthworks stood to command the pass into the bay he had dismantled. The Laffites' sailors set to work preparing to evacuate aboard a small squadron of the brig the *New Enterprise*, now renamed the *General Victoria*, and two small schooners, the *Minerva* and the *Blanque*, the latter no doubt named for Jean's sometime associate.[12] In the process, Jean found that he needed a number of items from New Orleans, so on February 19 he sent the small schooner the *Pegasus*, commanded by the ubiquitous William Mitchell, with a list. It included cooking ware, anchors, and the like, but also materials, such as cannon cleaning tools and grappling hooks, that were clearly designed for fitting out a vessel for privateering. The Laffites were close to violating their pledge to Patterson. As soon as the *Pegasus* returned with the merchandise and with Pierre, Jean intended to leave Galveston and put to sea.[13]

On her way up the Mississippi to New Orleans, the *Pegasus* may have passed the brig the *Enterprise* coming from the Balize on a mission from Patterson. Lieutenant Lawrence Kearny had commanded the *Enterprise* since 1815. He had left New York late in December 1819, but only after demanding precise instructions on how he was to determine who were pirates and who were not.[14] When Kearny arrived at the New Orleans station in February, Jean had recently left for Galveston, and Patterson almost immediately ordered the *Enterprise* to proceed to the island to see if the Laffites and their associates were carrying out their promise.[15] On February 27 Jean Laffite saw the *Enterprise* bearing down on the island.

Kearny anchored outside the bar and rowed over to the *General Victoria* to meet Laffite, who showed his usual hospitality and unctuous manners, and over refreshments detailed his preparations. He then took Kearny ashore and showed him the work done thus far. All about lay the signs of dismantling, with piles of nautical supplies and equipment strewn on the sand for loading.[16] Now, he said, he awaited only the return of the *Pegasus* and the right weather to take his squadron out the pass and over the bar and "cruise no more the Bay of Mexico." He told Kearny that before he left he would set fire to the remaining houses on the island, as well as burning a small felucca being used as a lighter to transfer supplies to the brig. Their discussion left Kearny convinced that the Laffites were acting in good faith.[17] Laffite then gave Kearny and his officers a dinner aboard his brig, and regaled them with his well-worn cover story of hatred for Spain and Spaniards. The Americans also met, however briefly, the mulatto woman often seen with Laffite on Galveston.

Pierre's continued presence in the city was believed by some to have more than a little to do with the Le Brave crewmen awaiting their sentences. On February 16 Governor Villeré received an anonymous warning that elements then in town intended to set fires throughout the city in order to distract authorities while friends of Desfarges and the rest robbed banks and freed the pirates from their prison. Acknowledging that the warning might be a hoax, the governor doubled the civil patrols at night just the same.[18] The additional guards at the jail prevented any effort to break out the condemned, but soon enough a mysterious fire erupted, the first of a series, mostly at private homes, over the next several weeks. As the date set for the execution of the pirates grew closer, the number of fires increased, and with it the fear and outrage in the city. Every day, complained one editor with exaggeration indicative of the fear, one could see in the city streets "wretches covered with the blood of the unfortunate whom they have murdered at Barataria or Galveston and on the ocean." Some feared that if the rabble did not succeed in freeing their friends, they would destroy the city.[19] This sentiment was one good reason for Jean not to return, and for Pierre to maintain a low profile.[20]

Still, Pierre did not completely evade the authorities' gaze. The Pegasus, bearing Jean's list of necessities, reached New Orleans in a few days, and quickly chandler Guillaume Malus provided the items requested.[21] Being a fast sailor, in fact, the Pegasus was back at Galveston by the beginning of March with Pierre aboard. Once more Mitchell took her back to New Orleans, arriving March 7, this time with several of the brothers' sailors, among them Antonin Ballarda and the Canadian George Bankhead Schumph.[22] The port inspector had given her the customary inspection at English Turn on March 4 and found nothing suspicious about her other than several Spanish swords that the passengers claimed as their own. He did learn that "one Lafitte" was among the passengers, which should have raised an eyebrow.[23] The ship showed no signs of preparations to fit her out for unlawful service. Her rigging and sails seemed in poor condition, and in the opinion of the officer she was good for little but coastal freighting, better for carrying firewood than mounting guns. Yet anyone who knew that Mitchell commanded and that Pierre Laffite was aboard had cause to suspect that all was not as it seemed. And one man recalled that the *Pegasus* had once been a United States gunboat, with a flat bottom for shallow water, and a deck better calculated to carry artillery than those of ordinary schooners of her size.[24]

Within days of the *Pegasus* tying up at the wharf, a man named Nickerson and another named John Wood began to approach sailors in the city asking if they would like to "go a privateering." They were told to meet at Harvey Norton's Jackson Inn on Tchopitoulas Street in the lower Faubourg St. Mary, a spot very close to the river on the outskirts of the city. There on March 15 some 102 men signed on, at least one of them a sailor serving on a United States revenue cutter. They learned that their captain was to be the same Ballarda who came with Pierre, and that they were to rendezvous at Galveston to crew Laffite's twenty-gun brig for a four-month cruise under the defunct red, white, and blue "patriot" flag of Humbert and the Mexican insurgency. Nickerson and a "tall portly & stout man" who was probably Pierre Laffite did not tell them what country's ships they were to capture, but gave each man a $30 enlistment bounty and promised him a share of the prize proceeds amounting to $1,000 before the cruise was done.[25]

Other men gathered by night at Pierre's lodgings on Bourbon, unaware that García knew they were there and suspected they were being recruited to reinforce Long for an attack on Texas.[26] On the morning of March 17 the men began to appear at the wharf beside the *Pegasus*. Some went aboard while others stood about onshore, an assorted group including Americans, Spaniards, and Frenchmen. There they learned that Captain Ballarda would not sail with them but would follow on another vessel. When they boarded they soon saw the evidence of stealthy preparations for privateering.

A revenue inspector boarded her and found the deserter from the revenue cutter, along with others repeating a cover story about being passengers for St. Thomas in the Virgin Islands. The large number of new water casks, far too many for a boat of the *Pegasus*'s size on such a voyage, raised his suspicion. On further inspection he found a cargo manifest listing grappling hooks, bilge pumps too large for the *Pegasus*, more musket and cannon tools, and three hundred shot "for Great Guns." The men told him that the cannonballs were for ballast, but he could see well enough that they were not stored in the ship's bottom as they should be for that purpose but instead stuffed in cabin lockers, in the wings under the deck beams, on top of the water and provision casks, and elsewhere.

Not surprisingly, the United States Marshal John Nicholson seized the *Pegasus* on March 18 and John Dick presented a libel against her in Judge Hall's court charging her with illegally attempting to fit out for privateering against Spain. Though Pierre engaged Grymes right away to represent Mitchell's claim for her return, the court would not release her for three months.[27] Meanwhile, on March 29, a consular official showed Pierre a letter from Cagigal that made it all too clear that Spain was cutting the Laffites loose.

In response Pierre confirmed that he and Jean were abandoning Galveston and suggested that the brothers would move wherever Cagigal wanted them to go, a transparent appeal for Spain to allow them to make a base in her colonial dominion.[28] Indeed, García even knew that Pierre had proposed the move to Patterson, though perhaps not that the old schemer had tried to make some capital of his offer by suggesting that the Laffites might provide information to the United States. "I do not know what he will do," García said of Pierre on April 9, "but I do know that Laffite and his brother have played their game well with the Spanish government."[29]

By May the preparations on Galveston were as complete as they were likely to be, and Jean had to know that he had pushed Patterson's goodwill in remaining on the island more than two months since the *Enterprise*'s visit. It was time to leave. He had his three ships ready, the *General Victoria*, the *Minerva*, and the *Blanque*. The detaining of Pierre and the *Pegasus* left him with less armament than he had anticipated, but he knew from experience that he could find what he needed elsewhere. Indeed, when Pierre contacted him after the arrest of the *Pegasus*, the brothers agreed that Pierre would remain in New Orleans and make another attempt to get men and matériel out of the city and to a convenient spot on the coast where Jean might take them aboard. Either Pierre would get word to him of the rendezvous, or else Jean would hover off the coast at a safe remove, looking for a sign that it was time to come in.

A taunting last echo of the failed attempts to profit by the filibusters and the revolutionaries arrived as Laffite was on the eve of departing. James Long appeared at Bolívar Point on April 6 to join his small coterie of followers there, this time bringing his wife, Jane Wilkinson Long.[30] Learning of their arrival, Laffite invited them to join him for dinner a few weeks later aboard the *General Victoria* before he left. Seventeen years later Jane Long recalled that evening, unwittingly providing not only the last eyewitness description of Jean Laffite, but also testimony of what was apparently one of his final days on the continent.[31] "He was, in every particular the very reverse of what her imagination had pictured him," a friend remembered her saying in 1837:

> He was of middle stature—perhaps a little above it—grace-ful . . . dark hair, brown complexion and a pair of eyes as vivid as the lightning and as black as ebony—In conversation he was mild, placable and polite; but altogether unjocular and free from levity. There was something noble and attractive in his aspect in spite of its occasional severity; and between the fierceness of his glance, and the softness of his speech, the disparity was striking. . . . The only complaint which his fair guest could urge against him, was one which it was natural for her sex to make—his want of communicativeness. . . . The dinner was sumptuous; & many entertaining as well as thrilling adventures were related by several of the party; but all attempts of Mrs. Long to obtain any important information from the host, respecting himself were adroitly and politely parried; and she was compelled to return with as little knowledge as she came, concerning his future operations.[32]

He hauled out the old stories of persecutions by Spain and his unyielding hatred of the dons, of how he had been a prosperous sugar planter in the West Indies until forced into a life of privateering. He may even have told them that Laffite was not his real name. After all, what was a name to a man who had spent years as numbers, first 13 and then 19? Deception was a game to the Laffites, and he may well have practiced it for his own amusement by now, in the process self-consciously shaping his own legend.[33]

If Mrs. Long saw much of the remnant of the Galveston commune, what she saw was desolation—the burned buildings, the destroyed storehouses, the remains of other vessels stripped and grounded. Warren Hall, who was still with the Longs, re-called that Laffite's men were demoralized after the losses from the hurricane and Patterson's inroads on their takings. Many felt unsure about leaving Galveston for unknown shores, and even Laffite's store of charm had lost its luster. Laffite kept to himself, more aloof than usual.[34]

When the day came to set sail on May 7, Laffite left a few of the huts and some lumber for Hall and Long to use in building Mrs. Long decent quarters on Bolívar Point. That done, Jean set fire to the rest. Some refused to leave with him, such as James Sherwood and James Campbell and his wife.[35] Some may have had to resist heavy-handed persuasion in order to stay behind. But in the end Laffite seems to have let each man make his own decision, though he persuaded a few of Long's men to come with him, without making it clear that he did not have valid letters of marque.[36] One man who chose to go with Jean was George Schumph, who had failed to reach him on the *Pegasus*.[37] Jean may also have received reinforcements brought in a few days earlier by Pierre, who was reported seen on Bayou Lafourche with five boats loaded with men on their way to Galveston. Jean's mulatto mistress apparently went, too, and a few of Laffite's men who stayed behind recalled twenty years later that when she and Jean left, an infant son went with them.[38] When the little squadron of three vessels lifted anchor and sailed through the pass out into the Gulf, the spires of smoke fading in the distance behind them testified not only to the ashes of Galveston, but to the ruination of all that Jean and Pierre Laffite had tried to achieve for a dec-ade. They were cast out to sea by a failed past and about to face an uncertain future.

Back in New Orleans, there was no future for some of the Laffites' former associates. Pierre was in the city to witness the denouement of the *Le Brave* case, and the potential fate awaiting all who "go a privateering."[39] In March President Monroe faced dealing with convictions in piracy cases at Baltimore, Charleston, Richmond, Savannah, and the eighteen men under sentence at New Orleans. In an attempt to mix charity with a necessary example, he decided that two of the condemned would be executed at each city, and the rest reprieved for sixty days, except for one man to be pardoned in New Orleans.[40] On April 17 he sent an executive order that Desfarges and his lieutenant Robert Johnson were to forfeit their lives in Louisiana.[41] Livingston moved for a suspension of the sentence on May 16, perhaps still at the instigation of Pierre Laffite, and Judge Hall heard arguments a week later. On May 24, however, he affirmed the sentence to be carried out the next day.[42]

Meanwhile the outbursts of unrest had continued, and by the date of execution there was a common expectation that the condemned would be sprung. Every night through late April to May 24 an armed cadre of two hundred citizens patrolled the streets, in addition to the established city guard, all with orders to shoot if anyone ran from them. The jumpy guards did shoot one man and stabbed another late in April, and soon they were augmented by three companies of United States troops. Then on the morning of April 23 a woman brought a loaf of bread for the condemned, but suspicious jailors broke it apart and found inside a letter telling the prisoners not to despair as their friends were going to set twenty fires in the city and free them within the week. Mysterious fires began to appear almost nightly, all of them some distance away from the jail, in order to draw the guards away. One evening two flares arched over the city. Citizens thought they might have been a signal for an assault on the jail, but apparently its guard refused to be decoyed. On April 25 several officers observed a house where reports said pirates were gathering to plot a jailbreak, only to be discovered and fired on themselves. The same night three fires erupted, but were extinguished before they could do much harm. On May 13 a building on Conti Street erupted in flame, soon spreading to destroy several buildings on either side, including the Conti Ballroom, which backed on the United States Navy arsenal, whose own roof took flame. Soon several grenades exploded, which could be heard throughout the city, leading some to think that the jailbreak had commenced. But no attempt was made after all, and the only result was a somewhat embarrassed Patterson, who was accused of negligence for storing explosives in the city.[43]

An execution was high entertainment for the rougher element in the city. The year before thousands had crowded around the gallows where a Spaniard hanged for murder still dangled, and then the free blacks hurled themselves into Congo dances that a visitor found "shocking to virtue modesty and decency."[44] There were no dancers on May 24 when at noon the marshal brought the two condemned to the riverfront. A rumor held that a family had been abducted out in the bayous to be ransomed for the lives of the condemned, but the ceremony went ahead. The doomed men stepped aboard a navy barge, and a substantial crowd, including the biggest military assembly since the war and perhaps Pierre Laffite, looked on as a distraught Desfarges first asked a marshal for a pistol to shoot himself. Then, though bound, he jumped overboard, perhaps hoping to drown rather than hang. Sailors fished him out of the water and he and Johnson met their ends without further incident.[45]

In time most of the others would be hanged as well. Meanwhile, ten days earlier Congress approved a new act reinforcing the death penalty both for piracy and violation of the slave trade prohibition, and decreeing that any American citizen serving on a foreign ship in the slave trade or crewing any vessel wholly or partly owned by United States citizens engaged in that trade should also suffer death.[46] After the executions in New Orleans and elsewhere, John Quincy Adams declared his hope that others tempted into questionable privateering "might be made to know the difference between South American patriotism and piracy."[47] Clearly there would be no more leniency with pirates.

By the time Desfarges and Johnson stopped swinging, Jean Laffite's small squadron was well on its way southward. As so often before, he said many things to many people as to his intentions on leaving Galveston. He told some who remained behind on the island that he had a commission in the infant navy of the Colombian insurgency, which he indeed may have hoped to secure.[48] What he told his own men mirrored what Pierre said to Patterson, that the squadron would sail under the flag of Venezuela or Buenos Aires, or perhaps for Bolívar. Men aboard the *General Victoria* believed they were on their way to Old Providence to corsair with Aury, and Laffite told the same thing to Warren Hall and others.[49] At this moment at least one of Aury's privateers was briefly active on the Louisiana coast. The availability of Aury commissions as close as Bayou St. John could not have avoided the Laffites' attention.

What Jean probably did not tell anyone was that he had no commissions from any of these places as yet.[50] Laffite probably intended to take a few Spaniards if possible on his way to seeing whether the situation in Mexico allowed for a secure port. If he had a goal beyond that, it was to go to the Isla de Mugeres off Yucatán to see about creating a new base, and then to Old Providence.[51]

Otherwise he could make no definite plans, for he did not know the situation he would find anywhere. Ten days out, on May 22, he came upon the Spanish felucca the *Constitution* out of Vera Cruz, sailing up the coast to Tampico with a cargo of whisky, oil, quicksilver, indigo, iron, and other goods worth about $10,000. He sent his schooner the *Minerva* to take her and dispatched both vessels to Galveston, expecting that Long's followers or the remnants of his own people would be able to smuggle her cargo into Louisiana.[52] With Pierre still in New Orleans, Jean probably planned for his brother to dispose of this cargo, and maybe others, to add to their coffers and finance their next establishment.

The *Minerva* escorted the *Constitution* to Soto la Marina, where they landed all of the Spaniard's crew except a slave boy, Juan Morales, whom they kept to sell. They continued to Galveston, where early in June they ran her aground on a sandbar inside the bay and stripped her of her cargo. They loaded a portion aboard the *Minerva*, and buried the rest in the sand on the shore, though some perishable items would quickly rot in the heat and damp. They also left Morales behind, presumably intending to come back for him and the rest of the cargo after disposing of what they had put on the *Minerva*. But on June 19 Lieutenant Madison anchored the *Lynx* offshore and sent an officer to examine the *Constitution's* wreck. After four days spent pumping out her hold and refloating her, Madison towed her to deep water at high tide. That done, his men explored the beach and found the buried cargo, some of which had been uncovered by wind and surf and plundered by passing Indians. They found dry goods, coffee, liquor, cocoa, and, wandering alone, the slave Morales.[53] They also found five men from the *Minerva's* crew who had, once aware of the bogus nature of the Humbert commission, denounced the taking of the *Constitution* to their fellow crewmen and then attempted to escape ashore. Madison put them in irons aboard the *Constitution* and escorted her and the remnant of her cargo to New Orleans.[54]

The men went before Judge Hall's bench, where they were indicted on July 19, and soon convicted of piracy. However, their pleas of innocence eventually reached Washington, and on November 21 President Monroe granted them a pardon because of their alleged ignorance of the piratical intent of the *Minerva's* owners when they sailed. Of more immediate importance, however, their testimony made it generally known by July 1820 that "John Lafitte's squadron" was taking prizes in the Gulf, and that they were doing so as pirates.[55]

Meanwhile Jean Laffite continued along the Mexican coastline, cruising off Campeche and taking a few prizes, most of which he gave back to their captains after seizing any valuable cargo. On at least one occasion he took a Spanish merchantman while himself flying Spanish colors, a sure route to the gallows if caught, but then he ran into bigger problems.[56] The *General Victoria* was his biggest ship, a brig with seven-gun broadsides port and starboard, and more swivel guns mounted on her deck. She had been the Spanish hermaphrodite the *Intrepido* when taken as a prize two years before, then she was run into Galveston to fit out as a corsair, and for a time she sailed as the *New Enterprise* before being renamed.[57] Now off Sisal on the northwestern corner of Yucatán she took a slave ship, but instead of continuing around to the eastern corner of the Yucatán peninsula to Mugeres, Laffite set their course northeast for Cape Antonio, the westernmost tip of Cuba.

By late July his two ships, rejoined by the *Minerva*, sighted a small fleet of Spanish merchantmen escorted by a single armed frigate. He signaled for his captains to come alongside for a consultation, and then moved from boat to boat asking the crews if they were willing to fight for the prizes, something privateers rarely did. He left the men to discuss the question among themselves and inform him of their decision. Soon James Rollins came forward as spokesman and told Laffite that, inasmuch as they had taken nothing more than the *Constitution* and the slaver in two months at sea, they were ready to fight. Only now, as the men had the smell of profit in their nostrils, did Laffite tell them what the five deserters from the *Minerva* had discovered, that they sailed under worthless commissions. If they attacked the Spaniards, they would do so as pirates.[58]

The men had not bargained for this, and another parlay re-
vealed that thirty-nine were not willing to take the risk. More
than that, they wanted to leave the squadron. For once, Jean had
misjudged his men. Significantly, not one of the mutineers was
French, Spanish, or Italian. Every one of them bore an Anglo-
Irish surname, and every one was an American. To stay with
Laffite would likely make them near-permanent exiles in some
Spanish-speaking tropical wilderness. They wanted to go home.
Backed by the strength of their numbers, they demanded one of
his ships to take them back to New Orleans.

It was a virtual mutiny by nearly half of his command, and
Laffite could do little or nothing without risking a battle that
would damage him sorely even if he won. He was left in a
quandary. Neither of the schooners would be big enough to hold
the deserting men. At the same time, the remaining men might
be too few to man both the larger brig and a schooner. The best
solution was to give the mutineers the *General Victoria*. Besides,
brigs had always been a little too large and cumbersome for corsairing in the shallow coastal waters. Having made the decision,
he agreed, then sailed all three vessels to Mugeres where he transferred the guns from the brig to the shore and his schooners.
That done, the mutineers set sail northward on a port wind for
Louisiana. However, Jean Laffite was not done with them yet. By
bringing them back to Mugeres on the pretext of off-loading the
General Victoria's guns, he took them far from their destination,
and now they were at sea unarmed. That night he set sail in one
of the faster and well-armed schooners, and by next day's light
the mutineers found Laffite bearing down on them from the
northwest with the wind at his back. They had no choice but to
come to when he shouted the order, and then he demanded that
Rollins and a mulatto named Long whom he thought to be a
ringleader be sent aboard his ship. Rollins was sent back with orders to cripple the brig's rigging and throw most of her masts and

spars overboard. Laffite did not send Long back, however, announcing that he intended to send the man to Africa as punishment. Laffite sailed away from the crippled brig and left the men to get to Louisiana the best they could.

The *General Victoria* limped northward for more than two weeks before she sighted the Balize on August 11. The men were all but starving by the time Rollins, nominally in command, turned her over to customs officer G. B. Duplessis and told him the story of the mutiny. Duplessis viewed their story with skepticism, but stocked the brig with enough food to sustain the men for several days, then sent her and her crew upriver to New Orleans to the marshal, with the word already going out that she belonged to Laffite.[59] Soon thereafter District Attorney Dick presented the case against her to Judge Hall. The *General Victoria* was a vessel from which "sundry piratical aggressions . . . restraints, depredations & seizures have been first attempted and made upon the high seas at divers times within the last two years by a notorious Pirate called John Lafitte," he said. He successfully applied to have her forfeited to the court and sold.[60] Meanwhile the crew tried to salvage something from their misadventure. They engaged attorney Isaac Preston and through him protested to the court that they had "at considerable risk of their lives induced the said Lafitte to give her up to them." They had not been a party to the original taking of the *Intrepido,* but they felt entitled to shares from her sale under the 1818 legislation covering rewards for those exposing or turning in unlawful privateers.[61] In the end the court awarded prize shares to Rollins, James McHenry, and the rest, and Jean Laffite joined the small fraternity of corsairs who learned the hard way the truth of the prediction that the 1818 legislation would turn one pirate against another.

It would be some time before Jean Laffite learned the fate of the *General Victoria,* if he ever did. After parting with her, he returned to cruise off Vera Cruz and on August 12, the day after

Rollins turned the brig over to Duplessis, Laffite took the merchant frigate the *Castor Limena*. His luck continued to run against him, however, for an armed vessel put out after him and retook the prize, though Laffite managed to escape.[62] He had a rendezvous to make, and so passed up the coast to Galveston once more, to find the *Two Friends*, which Pierre had taken out of New Orleans on August 5 with a cargo of provisions on a supposed merchant voyage to Cuba.

Pierre had to wait a few days for Jean to reach the island, and then they determined on a plan. Pierre would return to New Orleans to bring their affairs in the city to a close, and then meet Jean at Old Providence or the vicinity. Neither Laffite could hope any longer to accomplish anything in secret in the Louisiana metropolis, but in Charleston Pierre was less likely to be recognized. There he could contact agents of the insurgencies, and perhaps raise a new crew to replace the defectors and also obtain a ship for fitting out to continue their trade under whatever colors they could acquire. Jean, meanwhile, would venture back onto the Gulf, taking prizes when it was safe to do so and bringing the goods to Galveston if possible. He would also sound out Aury at Old Providence about securing letters of marque. It would be a dangerous game, for in the interim they would irrefutably be pirates. A Humbert commission had not saved Desfarges from the noose, and it would not save a Laffite. By August 31 Pierre was back in New Orleans, and his brother was on the main.[63]

Even if he could no longer stay at Galveston, Jean could risk making landing for a few days at a time, either to take on provisions from New Orleans or to unload cargo to be sold by the old channels. Spanish officials in Texas kept a wary eye on Galveston and believed that Laffite was making at least periodic appearances. As early as June, Martinez received reports of mysterious ships on the coast near Matagorda. "I infer it may be people from the Pirate Lafitte," he reported to Apodaca. In September a

Spanish investigation reported that "La Fitte, the notorious pirate, has returned, it is said, under the colors of South America, and was bearer of commissions for Long and the officers of his party." This was probably a delayed echo of the brothers' rendezvous in August.[64] By the end of the year the Spaniards heard reports that Laffite had gone to South America, exaggerated with rumors that after leaving Galveston he had attacked an American ship and killed all its crew except two men who escaped.[65] From now on, the farther the brothers Laffite ventured from New Orleans and Galveston, the more rumor and misinformation would warp their story. Neither could know it, but even while living, they were starting a voyage into legend.

At some time that fall Jean and his tiny squadron passed Mugeres again, perhaps stopping to leave men and materials to start erecting a modest base. Then he turned south around Cabo Catoche and sailed southward across the western Caribbean to Old Providence. Aury had established himself there on July 4, 1818.[66] The island sat just over 450 miles northwest of Cartagena and 150 miles east of the Colombian mainland. It had an excellent harbor, and lay very close to the Spanish trade routes to and from Panama and Cuba. Over the next two years Aury and his corsairs variously flew the flags of the juntas of Mexico, Venezuela, Buenos Aires, and Bolívar's New Granada. He did well for some months and tried to secure legitimate commissions, but none of the revolutionary governments would officially countenance him. Even now Aury's haughty manner and his record made revolutionary leaders suspicious of him. By the time Jean Laffite hove in sight of Old Providence, Aury was a pirate in everything but name, sailing under dubious letters of marque from José Cortes de Madariaga of the combined insurgencies of Buenos Aires and Chile. Any meeting between Laffite and Aury, when or if it came, could have been chilly in light of events at Galveston, but Laffite believed Aury would grant him commissions all the same.

Laffite deposited on the island some prisoners he held from his recent prizes, and perhaps did get commissions from Aury for his two vessels.[67] Nevertheless, he still had his eye on Mugeres, as did Pierre. Aury had a history of rising and falling, and it would not be wise to tie themselves too closely to him. Indeed, the brothers may still have had hopes of spying on Aury for Spain.

Whatever business Pierre had to conduct before he could rejoin his brother, there were personal matters to attend to as well, and it is clear he understood that he was leaving Louisiana for good. His feelings about putting his family behind him permanently, for that is apparently what he intended, remain a mystery. On July 27, a week before he took the *Two Friends* to meet Jean, he sold Marie's Bourbon and St. Philip house to his friend Abat for $10,000.[68] On August 2 Marie borrowed another $600 from Abat, pledging a slave as security.[69] Pierre probably used most of the proceeds to finance the supplies he took to his brother. If he left anything for Marie and Catherine and their children, it was not enough for them to live on as they had for the last few years.

Though Bourbon and St. Philip was hardly a fashionable address, now the families moved a few blocks northeast in a shift that symbolized far more than the distance implies. Pierre reestablished them on Esplanade Street in an area known as the Faubourg Marigny,[70] a large and relatively poor suburb inhabited by Spaniards, Portuguese, and Mexicans, the artifacts of former European masters and the refugees from San Domingue and other upheavals. It was an area messy and neglected, and lagging behind the rest of the city, though still proud and resentful of the Americans.[71] Most of all, it was the home of the bulk of the free colored population of New Orleans. Pierre was turning Marie and their children back to her own people, and there was no indication now or later that he or Jean intended their families to join them once they were established elsewhere.[72] Pierre's family with Marie included the living children: Rosa, Catherine Coralie, Martin Firmin, Adele, born in 1819, and probably a daughter. The son Pierre and the possibly imaginary Eugene were old enough to be out on their own, perhaps even with their uncle Jean. It was another summer of yellow fever, and though the epidemic was not as bad as that of the year before, it hit the Faubourg Marigny hard. Pierre could hardly expect that he would see all of his children again, even if he so desired.

Behind him Pierre also left many old associates. Beluche now owned a home in the city, thanks to help from Sauvinet. Maire had married and given up seafaring with the Laffites, and was on his way to becoming a modestly successful merchant.[73] Even Dominique was back on the coast that summer, having abandoned serving under Aury. Before long he would be a fixed resident and a privateer no more.[74] Others were gone or going. Fatio was dead, and Judge Hall would die in December, to be replaced on the bench by John Dick. Sauvinet and Sedella, Livingston and Grymes, and many more the Laffites would never see again. And there was one very close to Pierre whom he would never get to see, for—though he might not have known it—early in August, just before he took the *Two Friends* to resupply Jean, Marie conceived their last child.[75]

In early October the schooner the *Hiram*, commanded by a Captain Lambert, embarked from Dutch-held Curaçao on its way to a stop in Honduras and points beyond. Its course took the vessel past Old Providence, and there it took on a cargo of gum copal, logwood, sarsaparilla, tallow, leather, and more, mostly the produce of Yucatán brought in by a privateer, possibly Jean Laffite. Along with the cargo, the *Hiram* took on a passenger, Pierre Laffite, who had come from New Orleans sometime in September to meet his brother. When the *Hiram* tied up at the wharf in Charleston, South Carolina, several weeks later on November 15, Pierre Laffite stepped off her deck. In keeping with his years as a number, he now took another alias, introducing himself as "Mr. Francisco."[76] When Lambert took the *Hiram* out again for the Gulf of Honduras on Christmas Eve, Pierre remained behind, ready to launch the next phase of the Laffite brothers' quest for place and fortune. It would be their last.[77]

'Tis morn, and o'er his alter'd features play
The beams—without the hope of yester-day.
What shall he be ere night? perchance a thing
O'er which the raven flaps her funeral wing

TWENTY-ONE

The Last Voyage
1820-1823

M R. FRANCISCO remained in Charleston for more than three months. Among his first contacts was the dry goods merchant John B. Lemaitre, who partially owned the *Hiram*.[1] The Laffites may have known Lemaitre indirectly since Captain Lambert and his wife, Marie Lemaitre, lived in New Orleans, and the merchant sometimes shipped slaves to the Louisiana port.[2] From him Pierre would get the provisions to supply a new vessel. For the next several weeks Laffite tried to maintain a low profile, but tongues were loose and his alias could not hide an appearance well known in privateering circles. His associations with the outfitters and financiers of corsairs called attention to him, too, and it was not difficult to divine his purpose in the city, especially when he met with talkative veterans of the Galveston enterprise such as John Lambert, and an associate from the Baratarian days, Manuel López. To them he frankly admitted his purpose to fit out a new privateer for corsairing against Spanish shipping on the Caribbean, meaning the Laffites intended to continue operating out of Old Providence.[3]

Before long the editor of the principal newspaper, the *Courier*, made it his business to watch Pierre's movements, and they were easy to track. Laffite hired a house near the waterfront for the men he hoped to enlist, and then advertised by word of mouth that he would pay a bounty of fourteen dollars to every man who signed on. By February he had about fifteen men staying at the house, including López. Meanwhile, soon after arriving in Charleston, Laffite contacted a Captain Corby of Norfolk, Virginia, to purchase the schooner the *Nancy Eleanor*. A problem arose when Laffite/Francisco could not show that he was an American citizen, for the people at the customshouse already suspected Pierre, and the law did not allow foreign nationals to fit out ships for corsairing in American waters. Finally he completed the purchase by using yet another name, then paid Corby with one thousand dollars in cash and the balance in dressed leather from the *Hiram* cargo. At the same time he spent more precious money on the rigging and sails needed to convert a merchantman for service as a corsair.

Laffite had sent the *Hiram* back to Old Providence on December 24, and by mid-February he was ready to take the *Nancy Eleanor* out to sea. In her hold he stowed ten casks of rice, five hundred gallons of wine, and thirty barrels of flour and provisions. The port inspector came aboard and found only the usual complement of men to crew a vessel of her size, and no sign of arms. Laffite engaged a Captain Anthony to take her out, and the captain told the authorities that he was bound for the Gulf of Honduras. However, the editor of the *Courier* learned easily enough that her real destination was Old Providence, which was known to be a nest of pirates.[4]

On February 17 the *Nancy Eleanor* cleared the customs inspection and was ready to sail.[5] She did not leave right away, though, but apparently tried the old trick of taking on crewmen and armament elsewhere after the inspection. She did not set sail until just before noon on February 21. Two days later the rumor was current in Charleston that Laffite had taken her out secretly, raising suspicions that he was on a privateering cruise. The editor of the *Courier* had no doubt of it, and said so in his paper the next day, referring to Pierre as "brother to the celebrated pirate of that name."[6]

Finding himself associated with Laffite in the press, Lemaitre kept faith with him and denounced the accusation of piratical intent in a published letter.[7] Few were fooled, but it was too late, for by this time Pierre Laffite and the *Nancy Eleanor*, with a cargo of provisions, arms, and enlisted privateersmen, were well on their way south for the Caribbean.

The schooner made the passage down the Atlantic seaboard, then west through the Florida Straits, around Cape Antonio, and south. In March 1821 Pierre made landing at Isla de Mugeres, where he expected to rendezvous with Jean. He unloaded the men and arms and reloaded the *Nancy Eleanor* with a cargo of dyewood and salt and sent her back to Charleston. Pierre stayed behind with the men to oversee the beginning of the new base.[8] The perfectly situated island was virtually uninhabited but for a few Indians who sometimes came from the mainland by canoe to make salt by evaporating seawater in ponds on the interior. Dense woods made it difficult to get about, especially inland, but the island had good freshwater and an excellent harbor.[9]

Just as in Louisiana and Texas, Jean took the more active role in the brothers' business while Pierre kept to the shore, though life on land at Mugeres was considerably more rigorous than what Pierre had known in New Orleans. He and the men lived in such huts as they could build. They bartered and bought provisions from the fishermen along the coast, with whom Pierre cultivated good relations since they were essential to survival and might also pass on information about likely prizes in the vicinity, as well as prying Spaniards. The coasters regarded him as "a nice gentleman" who "never harmed any poor person," though when

Jean was on the island they found him rather more severe, a strict disciplinarian who was hard to approach, just as he had been on Galveston.[10] Pierre was also generous to men marooned by the loss of their ships, continuing that streak of humanity evidenced so often with Spanish prisoners. By that fall it was evident to visitors that Pierre was the man in charge.[11] Before long Pierre also found female companionship in an American woman named Lucia Allen, whom he may have brought with him from Charleston.[12] Almost certainly he did not know that on May 2, in New Orleans, Marie Villard gave birth to his last son, Joseph.[13]

If Jean Laffite received any commissions from Aury, he soon learned that he had dropped anchor in the wrong harbor. Aury was all but discredited, and on January 18, 1821, Bolívar told Aury to take his ships and leave Colombian waters. "The Republic of Colombia has no more need for more corsairs to degrade its flag on all the seas of the world," Bolívar wrote to him.[14] After he retook Cartagena on October 10, 1821, Bolívar would abolish Colombian privateering entirely, though he would continue to hire private armed schooners to act against pirates and former privateers, not Spanish merchantmen.

By this time the other republican juntas were disassociating themselves from privateering, too, with the result that no one wanted Aury and his corsairs. Aury held on at Old Providence, pretending to be a governor, but on August 20, after a severe fall, he died at the age of just thirty-three.[15] Only a month after Bolívar ended Aury's legitimate career, an internal coup in the Spanish army in Mexico began the process of achieving what a decade of revolution had failed to do. An independent Mexico finally removed any vestige of legitimacy to prior privateering commissions. By October, when Buenos Aires called in its letters of marque, only Venezuela maintained lawful privateers operating out of Margarita Island. Vessels flying Venezuelan colors were regularly boarded by American warships, but if their papers proved to be in order, they were allowed to proceed on their business.[16]

Would-be privateers could find virtually no home port or agreeable junta to allow them to carry on their trade, yet carry it on they would. Many other than the Laffites shifted their bases to Cuba, chiefly the port of Regla close to Havana Bay, as well as St. Bartholomew's in the British West Indies. Soon privateers flying a variety of rebel flags under multiple commissions, all of them suspect, stopped in these ports to bring in prizes and refit. Most of them were American and British vessels and crews.[17] Forced to the far side of the law, they became more brazen, and some began to prey on American shipping as well as Spanish. Captain José Gaspar sailed the *Jupiter* out of St. Bartholomew's under a worthless commission from Uruguay, and on August 19 took and plundered the Yankee ship the *Orleans*. He held her for two days, abusing the crew to some degree, then before releasing her sent aboard a crude attempt at humor in a letter that he signed "Richard Coeur de Lion."[18] Whether trying to hide his own identity or settling a grudge against Laffite, he tried to persuade people that the author was Jean Laffite.[19] Gaspar's panache would not last long, for in October the USS *Grampus* found his ship at St. Bartholomew's and put her out of business.[20]

The taking of Gaspar was merely one example of the noose steadily tightening around the freebooters. Officials of the new Mexican regime kept a watchful eye on Galveston, not only because of Long's return and anticipated invasion, but also wary that the Laffites might come back. Long took La Bahía on October 4 sure enough, but was forced to give up when surrounded by soldiers of the newly independent nation, who felt no more kindly toward invaders than the Spaniards before them. Sent first as a prisoner to Mexico City, he was later allowed the freedom of the capital, only to be killed in April 1822 under mysterious circumstances. It was the end of filibustering.

At the same time that Long took La Bahía, the Mexicans were alarmed by reports of "los Piratas de Galveston" and their recent capture of the *goleta Salio del Refugio*. It may or may not have been Jean Laffite who took the *goleta*, but by the end of the year when Long had been captured and his expedition ended, the authorities decided to depopulate the island and shift everyone remaining, whether smuggler or filibuster, to Nacogdoches. By late December a reconnaissance found Galveston uninhabited.[21]

Slaves were still being smuggled into Louisiana by way of Texas, however, and with the promise of Texas being opened to American settlement starting in 1821 thanks to a grant to Moses Austin, there was the possibility of a local market. John Sibley of Natchitoches warned Senator J. Stoddard Johnston in Washington in June that "Lafitte is still going on in Privateering," and had recently landed on the coast some two hundred blacks taken on a ship off Havana.[22] Just how Sibley was certain it was Laffite who brought in the cargo he did not say, and it may have been no more than rumor, but if Jean Laffite did take any slave ships as prizes, the most profitable market for him was still the United States. Spain's final ratification of the Adams-Onís Treaty on February 19, 1821, had made landing goods at Galveston too dangerous even before the island was depopulated, so Jean probably landed them at Cat Island or one of the other old haunts. That smuggling slaves was still very profitable is evident from the high risks the buyers took. In the summer of 1821 a group of six men in Louisiana, at least one of whom appeared to be a former Laffite associate, were fined a total of $115,000 for smuggling over ninety Africans.[23]

At the end of the year Louisiana's congressional delegation wrote a joint letter to Calhoun to call Washington's attention to the continuing violation of the revenue laws on the state's western border, and to demand suppression of the smugglers. They suggested assigning one hundred dragoons to patrol the Sabine.[24]

Instead, Senator Johnston got the navy to post more armed vessels to patrol the Gulf.[25] By the fall the navy had the *Enterprise*, the *Hornet*, the *Spark*, the *Shark*, the *Grampus*, and the *Porpoise* in the West Indies, and within a few more months the *John Adams*, the *Peacock*, and the *Alligator* joined them. The result was a dramatic increase in pirates put out of business and the press took note that Gulf commerce had been mostly unmolested "since John Lafitte abandoned and destroyed Galveston." In September 1821 two pirate attacks on ships headed for New Orleans were the first in almost two years.[26] Three more corsairs were taken in October, and in early November the *Hornet* captured the Colombian privateer the *Centinella* and a French slave ship prize, the *La Pensee*, with 240 blacks.[27] That month the *Porpoise* hit pirates off Cuba and forced them to abandon their ship and flee into the woods.[28] In December yet another corsair fell victim to the naval might.

The war against the pirates came at a cost, though. Lieutenant Kearney had to finance victualing his ship from his own pocket at times. Lieutenant Madison and his *Lynx*, still embarrassed over the Galveston incident, joined in the pirate hunt off Cuba. Madison raised anchor off St. Mary's, Georgia, on January 21, 1821, and set out on yet another cruise, but neither he nor the *Lynx* were ever seen again. The pirates began to thin out, too, including William Mitchell, who supposedly died May 1, 1821, on Great Corn Island, off Nicaragua. By the fall of the year, however, it was time for a much larger feature in the corsairing firmament to leave the scene.

Pierre Laffite may not have owned the *Nancy Eleanor*, and if he did, he changed his mind about converting her into an armed vessel to prey on Spanish shipping. Instead, ironically, she became prey herself. On August 31, on a voyage to Panama, she was taken off Trinidad by a pirate, plundered, and then ransomed for four thousand dollars before being allowed to complete her voyage.[29] For whatever reason, with the *Nancy Eleanor* no longer at his command, and Jean off cruising with his other ships, Pierre had only a small vessel, probably a felucca, that Jean had taken from Pedro Cupull off Campeche that summer. On her deck the Laffites mounted an eight-pounder, and a Spaniard who saw her described her as a "small, unworthy Mediterranean-type coasting vessel." Laffite had a crew of about seventeen men to work her, almost all Italians except for a Spaniard pilot. They were all pirates so far as Spanish authorities were concerned.[30]

Small though she might be, Pierre's vessel was enough to take prizes, and on June 17 off Campeche, with Pierre in command and his old associate George Schumph as master-at-arms, she captured the schooner the *Constitution* out of Cadiz and bound for Vera Cruz.[31] Aboard her Pierre found twelve hundred barrels of liquor, nine hundred bottles of oil, lace and leather goods, and silver to the value of $50,000 to $60,000. The silver he could keep and use anywhere, of course, but Pierre did not have access to a market for other merchandise. He discovered, however, that local fishermen on the island of Cancun just south of Mugeres were inclined to assist him, and that Clemente Cámara had a small farm on the island where Pierre could hoard goods pending sale. Pierre delivered the bulk of the *Constitution*'s cargo to the farm in October and then entered into a contract whereby he gave Cámara half of the goods for his own use in return for $6,500 and Cámara's agreement to sell the rest in Yucatán's principal city Campeche across the peninsula. By the end of the month Cámara had taken sixty barrels of whisky and a trunk of belts and handkerchiefs to Campeche, and Pierre was staying at Cámara's farm with Lucia Allen and others awaiting their host's return with the proceeds.[32]

Pierre also expected more men to join him at the farm, for he had conceived a plan for substantially greater takings. A relatively new Spanish community had begun at Yalahau, on the Yalahau

Lagoon just west of Cabo Catoche, protected from the sea by a couple of barrier islands almost like Galveston. Apparently Pierre believed there was enough wealth in the village to be worth his sailing in and taking it, but he would need more than his small crew to make a successful landing, and more guns than his single eight-pounder. On the evening of October 30 Pierre was waiting at the small farm on Cancun when well after dark, about 10 o'clock, he heard a small group approaching. He sent out men of his own to challenge the strangers, perhaps thinking they were the expected reinforcement, but when Laffite's men heard the leader identify himself as Miguel Molas, commanding a dozen *soldados* and civilian volunteers, the privateers opened fire in the darkness.

After hearing several warnings of the pirate gathering, Molas had come to investigate. In the barrage he sustained four superficial wounds, and his nephew was also hit, but the Spaniards soon forced their attackers back. A few privateers were killed, and others wounded. Those who could get away, among them George Schumph, ran into the hilly interior or fled in a canoe. Molas took only five prisoners, but they included Pierre Laffite and his mistress. Full of spirit as always, Pierre told Molas that his armed ship was between the island and the mainland and that Molas's line of withdrawal was cut off. In spite of this the Spaniard loaded his men and his prisoners on his boats and prepared to make for the mainland early the next morning, but at dawn he was barely embarked when he saw that Laffite had not been bluffing. The corsair vessel was in his path. Molas quickly ran his boats to the beach and took refuge behind a sand dune. The ship came in close to shore and sent five charges of grapeshot from her cannon, hitting no one. Nevertheless, all but two of the men with Molas panicked and ran, leaving him outnumbered by his prisoners and with no choice but to abandon them on the beach in order to get away.[33]

Pierre may already have been ill when Molas attacked on October 30. Certainly Lucia Allen was unwell. Pierre may even have been one of the wounded.[34] In any case, the Spaniards clearly knew their whereabouts, and Cancun would no longer be safe for them. Collecting those of their scattered party that they could, including Schumph, López, and a *mestizo* named Gregorio, Pierre and Lucia boarded a small fishing boat in order to avoid attention. They sailed north and then west around the peninsula to a small protected lagoon known as Las Bocas, about ten miles from the *pueblo* of Dzilam de Bravo, a string of houses stretching from the lagoon to the village of Santa Clara.[35] By the time they arrived in a tiny village called Telyas, Pierre was terribly ill with a fever, perhaps suffering the same illness as Lucia. For the next several days Gregorio, López, Schumph, and the ailing Allen tended her dying lover. Then, on or about November 9, within sight and sound of thousands of pink flamingos feeding in the lagoon, Pierre Laffite breathed his last.[36] He died the pirate he always claimed he never was, and though he escaped the noose or bullet that would have been his fate if captured, his death was the direct result of his chosen trade.[37] The others took Pierre's body into the town of Dzilam de Bravo on November 10, and Schumph presented himself before the mayor to get permission to have Laffite buried in the churchyard of Santa Clara of Dzidzantún, an old Franciscan convent that had been attacked by pirates several times in the century past. That day López and Gregorio laid the dead pirate in the ground "with honor" as López remembered it, and with appropriate words from the curate José Gregorio Cervera. When they were done they placed over his grave a rude stone marked with his name, the date, and the hour of his death. That done, Schumph left Lucia in the care of locals while he found a room at an inn.[38]

As soon as it was learned who had been buried, Schumph came under suspicion and was quickly arrested. He had to scramble to explain his connection with Laffite without incriminating himself as a pirate. He was a Canadian merchant, he told the authorities, and he had only just come to the island Cancun to discuss some business with Laffite when Molas attacked. Schumph told a dramatic story of jumping into the water to escape the attack, and thereby leaving his trunk behind with his passport in it, to explain his not having traveling papers. No, he had never served on Pierre's vessel, though he did admit being with Jean aboard the *General Victoria* when Galveston was abandoned. He knew nothing first-hand of the cargo of the *Constitution,* but had heard that there might be whiskey and other goods hidden on Cancun. To deflect suspicion from Mugeres, he said that he believed he had heard that Laffite's pirate ship normally anchored near Yalahau, the town Laffite supposedly intended to loot. The court was inclined not to believe him, especially when witnesses identified him as having served on Laffite ships. He was held for several weeks until he agreed to provide information on the location of hidden Laffite prize goods. On December 4 Schumph was finally released and sent to the capital at Mérida. Lucia Allen chose to remain in Dzilam until she recovered, where she may have died in childbirth delivering yet another daughter of Pierre Laffite's.[39]

Jean Laffite probably did not learn of his brother's death for months, and perhaps not until March or April of 1822, because he had suffered a disaster of his own. Sometime in late October or early November, aboard the *Minerva* or the *Blanque,* Jean took on a large ship off Jamaica or the Cayman Islands. Instead of feebly striking her colors, she fought back. Still he took the prize, at the cost of several of his men killed or wounded, and possibly an injury to himself. As had happened with the *Nancy Eleanor,* he held the prize for a day or two and then ransomed her to her owners, who agreed to make payment on Cuba near Santa Cruz del Sur on the south coast. When he approached the port, however, two armed vessels came out of the harbor and retook the prize. In the skirmish, Laffite lost his own ship and most of the rest of his crew, barely escaping with a few others when the Spaniards boarded his vessel.⁴⁰

Jean's trials only began with his escape. Either by swimming or in a small launch, he and his companions made the shore close to Santa Cruz del Sur. They were without food or arms, apparently without funds, and in a definitely hostile land. Before long locals spotted them and they were taken prisoner. Jean was fortunate not to be hanged at once, but the Spaniards were devoted to the law, and took him some miles inland to the provincial capital at Porto Principe, where he and his companions were jailed. After a few weeks he either took ill or his wound became worse, and the Spaniards moved him to the hospital of San Juan de Dios. Laffite spent more weeks in the infirmary, where security was considerably less rigid than at the prison. There, a former acquaintance recognized him or he was able to get word of his predicament to someone he knew to be in the community, perhaps even Picornell, who happened to be practicing in town as a physician. On February 13, 1822, with outside help, Jean Laffite escaped from the hospital and hurried back to the coast.⁴¹

Less than fifty miles directly north of Porto Principe Cayo Romano sat off the coast, with a settlement of Cuban pirates operating out of the Old Bahama Channel, chiefly preying on slave ships. If Laffite and his liberators did not know the people at Cayo Romano, they surely knew of them, and within two or three days Laffite could have been safely on the island. Laffite's friends may even have had a ship waiting for him there, for less than a month after he fled the hospital, reports reached Porto Principe that Jean commanded a schooner followed by several small launches and perhaps thirty men operating out of Rincon Grande and cruising the Old Bahama Channel.⁴²

It was not a good time or place to try to reestablish himself as a corsair. With the gains that the United States Navy had made on pirates from 1819 to 1821, Washington was unwilling to relax the pressure, especially after any sign of an attempted resurgence such as two piratical attacks on New Orleans merchantmen in January.⁴³ A few weeks later Kearny and the *Enterprise* took a pirate off Havana, and on a single morning in April he took eight pirate ships and 160 crewmen off Cape Antonio.⁴⁴ Lieutenant James Ramage cruised the Cuban coast in the *Porpoise* and took the *El Bravo* in early February, meanwhile burning the free-booters' shore establishments and destroying three other pirate vessels. Several of the pirates he captured and sent to New Orleans in chains.⁴⁵ By April the navy had a squadron built around the frigate *Macedonian,* including four smaller vessels and two hundred marines, ready to sail from Baltimore to deal with the pirates operating out of Cuba. If the government of Cuba would not or could not put an end to the outrages, Washington announced, then the United States would, even if it had to violate Spanish sovereignty by operating in Cuban waters. Washington ordered the navy to establish several small stations from which to watch traffic around Cuban shores, and cut off the pirates.⁴⁶

Thus the navy was watching for Laffite when reports came in that he was operating in the vicinity of the Old Bahama Channel in a fleet of four corsairs that included the legitimate Colombian private armed schooner the *Cienago.* On April 11 Laffite finally stepped across the line he had observed for fully a decade when he took and plundered an American ship, the *Jay,* off Gibara, on the north coast some distance southeast of the Old Bahama Channel. He also took an English sloop that day, unaware of just how close by was the cordon of American warships. His action was known two days later to the commander of the armed sloop the *Alligator,* which took the *Cienago.* Laffite and the rest had retired to the haven of Gibara, where local authorities gave them sanctuary in return for the cheap merchandise they provided.⁴⁷

The New York merchantman the *Abigail* was chasing Laffite when she encountered the *Alligator* two days later and they joined forces in the pursuit.[48] The next day they cruised the coastline so closely that Laffite's schooner and the smaller boats with him could not get out to sea, and then the Americans followed in two launches as the pirate schooner retreated up a river. Three days later they caught it at anchor and took Laffite and seven of his men.[49] It was a delicate diplomatic situation, and the Americans unwittingly turned their prisoners over to the same local authorities who were so indulgent of the pirates. When Lieutenant Richard Stockton, commanding the *Alligator,* sailed into Gibara to meet with the *soldados* he soon realized that the pirates would likely be allowed to escape, and sent a request to the province's governor at Holguin that the malefactors be turned over to the Americans. The governor let the Gibaran leaders hold on to their prisoners, however, and Laffite was soon at large.[50]

By May 1 Laffite was again trying to get his vessels away from the coast only to find the *Alligator* blocking his passage, this time reinforced by the *Grampus.* At about 8:30 that morning Laffite saw the *Alligator* coming after him in a chase that lasted ninety minutes until Laffite ran into shoal water too shallow for the American vessel. As soon as the *Alligator* dropped anchor, Laffite opened fire and the ships exchanged several shots inconclusively.[51] The Americans had already taken three prizes from their captors, and the next day went in close to shore in a light draft vessel with more than seventy men, exchanging volleys with what they believed to be Laffite's men aboard his schooner.[52] Once again Laffite escaped.

Laffite had been captured twice, probably wounded once, and nearly taken again. There was a lesson to be learned from this season of near disasters, and Jean Laffite was no fool. If he needed any further admonition, the news of Pierre's death when it reached him sometime that spring should have been enough.

However prepared each brother must have been for such an event given the hazard of their careers, the loss was the greatest of Jean's life. The two had been inseparable for the past decade and more. They thought alike and acted alike, a symbiotic pairing of complementary opposites. The loss of Pierre cost Jean his spiritual anchor, though they had not seen each other for many months.

It was time to try another tack. Laffite learned that Bolívar was commissioning private armed vessels into the Colombian state service, though no longer granting letters of marque. The distinction was a subtle one. The captains took prizes and shared in the proceeds, but they and their vessels were not free agents, but servants in a naval auxiliary of Colombia. Beluche was in the service now, and so was Laméson.[53] By this time most of the surviving old corsairs who had not become outright pirates had been commissioned regular navy officers for Colombia, their vessels nationalized as public property. Jean's notoriety spoke for itself. A commission from Colombia would give him legitimacy and protection, and if he did not make his fortune from prize goods by observing Bolívar's rules, what he did at sea outside the gaze of officials could reward him handsomely.

After escaping the *Alligator* in early May, Laffite decided that the Cuban coast was too hot for him, and sailed his remaining schooner south to Cartagena, a bustling metropolis of 170,000 people.[54] He probably arrived early in June, within days of the arrival of the forty-ton schooner the *General Santander,* a Spanish vessel seized and nationalized by Colombia.[55] She was named for General Francisco de Paula Santander, vice president of Colombia, and on August 19 she received her commission as a private armed vessel in service of Colombia.[56] The Colombian naval authorities gave her to Jean Laffite to outfit, perhaps requiring him to post a bond and absorb some of the cost of converting her. By the first week of September he had her almost ready to leave on her first cruise, armed with a powerful eighteen-pounder, a brass four-pounder swivel gun, and thirty men. Americans in Cartagena who watched her outfitting sent warnings to the United States that "the famous Lafitte" would be on the seas again, and could be expected to prey not only on Spanish vessels but perhaps on American merchantmen.[57]

Why they would expect Laffite to take American ships they did not say, but Laffite soon demonstrated much less than his former punctiliousness in dealing with American shipping. Less than three weeks after embarking, he had the *General Santander* off the Dry Tortugas in the Straits of Florida, one hundred miles north of Havana. There on September 28 he sighted the brig the *Sampson* out of Mobile and boarded her at sea. For eight hours Laffite held the vessel while unloading her cargo, and according to her captain mistreated him physically before releasing the ship.[58] If it was Laffite, as the corsair claimed to be, then it was an act of wanton piracy against a merchant vessel of a nation that enjoyed friendly relations with Bolívar and favored his nation building. Had he learned of it, Bolívar would have repudiated the action and rescinded Laffite's commission just as he had spurned Aury the year before.

After leaving the *Sampson*, Laffite continued to haunt the Cuban shipping lanes, and by November 26 was about fifty miles south of Grand Cayman and due west of Jamaica, having taken two Spanish ships and sent one back to Cartagena as his commission required. Now he encountered the American schooner the *Columbus Ross* out of Jamaica and bound for New Orleans. He showed a remarkably different disposition toward her than he had to the *Sampson*, if indeed it was Laffite who robbed the latter. "Captain Laffite treated us with the greatest politeness," the *Columbia Ross*'s captain reported, and finding her in a lane frequented by pirates, escorted her some distance west until she was through the Yucatán Straits where he himself had preyed on shipping. On parting, Laffite gave the *Columbus Ross* some balls for her four-pounder cannon, and spare provisions as well.[59] His act of kindness found its way into the American press, mitigating a little the chagrin evidenced in the New Orleans journals that month when they learned that "the famous LAFITTE of piratical memory" had been captured the previous year, then escaped. "We cannot too deeply regret, that the monster who had shed so much innocent blood, should have, perhaps for the hunderth [*sic*] time, escaped the sword of justice which has been so long hanging on his guilty head," lamented the editor of the *Courier*.[60]

With the pirates on the run throughout the Caribbean, the merchants whose trade the corsairs preyed on maintained the pressure on Washington to suppress the criminals. Several New Orleans merchants wrote to Senator Johnston on November 26, 1822, that they wanted the government to make the seas safe "if it should require the whole navy of the U. States to effect it—we require it and think we have a right to expect it."[61] As if to punctuate their urgency, something happened a few days prior that made the navy's campaign against the pirates take on a personal tone. The captain of the *Alligator*, ashore chasing pirates on Cuba, was shot and killed in a skirmish. It sparked a storm of protest in Congress.[62] Exaggerated complaints of four thousand pirates operating in the Caribbean led to calls for stern means of putting them down, even if the United States had to occupy by force the places where they were based.[63] On December 31 Captain David Porter offered to resign his position as a naval commissioner to go to the Gulf to root out the problem. Soon the word went out that early in 1823 Captain Porter would take command of a fleet of eight warships mounting 178 cannon and numbering 1,330 seamen. They would overwhelm the pirates by main force if necessary.[64] Sensitive to the potential violation of their sovereignty if they did not make a better effort themselves, Spanish authorities on Cuba started to mount greater patrols against the buccaneers, occasionally taking a corsair. In November the

Marte cooperated with the *Alligator* in its search for the murderers of the American captain.[65]

They would not take Jean Laffite now that he was at last, and probably for the first time in his career, an unquestionably legitimate privateer. The years of specious commissions were over, and so were the awkward months of barely disguised piracy. Ironically, Laffite attained his legitimate commission just as the author of so many of his bogus letters of marque came to a transition. On January 2, 1823, General Humbert was found dead in his room in New Orleans, probably killed by alcoholism. Some eulogized what he had been, but none could fail to see what he had become: a sad, foolish parody of what he and the other filibusters had been in their dreams. "His life, public and private, was and has been the most indecorous and vagrant, forever in the taverns, surrounded by a rabble and attending them in their crimes," Spanish consul García had written Apodaca. "Because of him much innocent blood has been shed."[66]

Unfortunately, Jean Laffite's days of legitimate privateering would last scarcely five months. On February 4, 1823, his *General Santander* was cruising in the Gulf of Honduras. He was off the coast about forty miles west of La Cieba, opposite a point of land called Triunfo de la Cruz—Triumph of the Cross—when the first glimmers of light at 5 A.M. revealed a schooner and a brigantine. When he saw the vessels turn to run, he assumed they were Spanish merchantmen and set his sails for a chase. He dogged them for almost seventeen hours until he caught up to the brig well after dark and for an hour traded shots with her. She appeared to be on the verge of striking her colors when instead her captain raised signal lanterns in his rigging calling the faster schooner back to his assistance. It began to be become apparent that Laffite had been decoyed.

When the schooner opened fire, Laffite and those aboard his ship realized that they were outgunned. Counting the muzzle flashes, men on the *General Santander* made out a dozen cannon on the brig, and another six on the schooner, including a powerful swivel gun whose sound or shot hitting the *General Santander* told them it was a fat sixteen-pounder. Laffite had unwittingly taken on either Spanish privateers or warships, or perhaps elements of a British squadron patrolling for pirates. They might even have been pirates themselves, though, if so, they were unusually well armed.

In one of the exchanges, a direct hit from grapeshot or a splinter of wood from the *General Santander* struck Jean Laffite a desperate wound. He may not have known the extent of his injury, but he turned command over to his chief lieutenant, though he was conscious enough to shout encouragement to his crewmen. Soon the executive officer fell with a mortal wound, and petty officer Francisco Similien took over. The flashing of the guns in the darkness continued until one o'clock in the morning before Similien broke off the action. He ordered the *General Santander*'s course changed to an easterly bearing to start for Cartagena, while their antagonists sailed off to the north.

During the night the men on the *General Santander* stopped her leaks and tended to their wounded. It is unlikely that a ship's surgeon was aboard, but any man experienced at naval action could have seen that Laffite's wound was mortal. He probably knew so, too, though he had experienced no more than one or two combats. Sometime after dawn on February 5, 1823, he died, aged forty-one.[67] A few weeks later, on March 10, the *General Santander* limped into Portobello, Panama, on her way back to Cartagena. A body could not be saved for that long aboard ship, and on the day he died, his crew had buried Captain Jean Laffite at sea. Somewhere in the Gulf of Honduras, probably not far from the Islas de la Bahía, his grave was as lost to time as Pierre's four hundred miles to the north. Perhaps it was fitting for a man who never owned a home or had a country that he died fighting for a people not his own, and that his only epitaph appeared in Cartagena, whose legitimate commissions he never carried, and in Colombia, a place he never lived. "The loss of this brave naval official is moving," said the *Gaceta de Cartajena* when it learned the news. "The boldness with which he confronted the superior forces which hit him manifests well that, as an enthusiast of honor, he wished to follow it down the road to death rather than abandon it in flight." In a final grim irony, the epitaph appeared only in Spanish, the language of his enemies.[68]

The death of Jean Laffite punctuated the demise of privateering in the Caribbean. By the end of 1822 the United States Navy had taken at least thirty-four pirate vessels, and it continued the captures during the next year or so, taking the war against the corsairs to their land bases on Cuba and elsewhere. Five days before Laffite's death Porter was assigned a command in the Caribbean to suppress piracy and protect American shipping, much of which was afraid to sail except when convoyed. He was also to suppress the illegal slave trade. If he took his men ashore in pursuit of pirates, he would so do on his own responsibility, though he was to give any pirates he captured to local Spanish authorities.[69] Porter cut corners, and even interfered with the legitimate privateers in the Colombian service, but Porter was not to be deterred by diplomatic niceties.[70]

The war against the corsairs came at a price, as when pirates took the *Alert* of Portsmouth, New Hampshire, and killed her captain, or when Porter lost a lieutenant on the *Fox* to a cannon shot off Puerto Rico. "The work of piracy and murder still goes on," complained the press, but Porter did not relent.[71] The *Alligator* revenged herself in May by taking one pirate schooner and burning another, and the British were as ruthless.[72] Reports that winter said thirty-nine pirate vessels operated off the coast of Cuba. By March 1823 the British took half of them, killed twenty pirates, and captured forty more. Meanwhile the Spaniards, too, were taking vessels and killing corsairs. Someone among these various forces had killed Jean Laffite.[73]

Porter made his first captures in April, and within forty-three days he had broken up piracy in the Caribbean and forced most of the freebooters to flee inland on Cuba where they would have to face local authorities. By May he sent word home that he had "nearly destroyed all the pirates in the West Indian seas."[74] A month later, its privateering days at an end with the close of hostilities against Spain, Laffite's *General Santander* performed one last official mission. On June 1 she dropped anchor in New York harbor to deliver Leandro Palaceos, Colombia's new consul general, to the United States.[75] The brothers Laffite had died at precisely the right moments. With Mexico independent and virtually all of the republican movements in Central and South American successful, a Spanish Main at peace was a world they would not have known.

For him they raise not the recording stone—
His death yet dubious, deeds too widely known;
He left a Corsair's name to other times,
Link'd with one virtue, and a thousand crimes.

TWENTY-TWO

The Legend of the Laffites

PIRACY DID ENJOY a brief resurgence after Jean's death. In
April 1824 even Colombian naval privateers, especially Beluche and his *General Bolívar,* were aiding in the suppression of
Cuban pirates.[1] By the summer the corsairs were attacking everything that passed. Those claiming to be privateers took Spanish
ships; those who were outright pirates robbed everyone, and it
became all but impossible to tell the difference. Reports from
Cuba in July said that scarcely a vessel came into Havana without
being stopped and plundered by one or the other.[2] By October
the reassertion of the pirates was such that Secretary of State
Adams received a caution that "the temporary cessation of piracies some time before, caused by the presence of a large force on
the coast, seems to have induced a delusive and fatal opinion, that
the evil was extinguished."[3]

It was a bubble, however, for by 1825 piracy was all but finished, especially since Spanish merchantmen were now arming
heavily. The few remaining privateers in the now-independent
Latin American republics were decommissioned, and the gov-

ernments stopped issuing letters of marque. With the new nations at peace with the rest of the world, Spanish commerce was no longer a legitimate target by any definition and there was no remaining pretext for privateering against anyone else. The pressure against outright piracy soon ended it altogether.

Thus the Laffites' trade survived them by barely two years. Had they outlived their occupation, there is little to suggest they could have adapted to another one. Smuggling died out on the United States Gulf coast thanks to falling tariff rates, and when rates went up again dramatically in 1828, smuggling did not return. Pierre had been a merchant many years before, of course, and perhaps the brothers could have gone completely legitimate, but the rise in tariff rates would have hurt them. Filibustering was dead, and though Americans were starting to pour into Texas as sanctioned settlers, neither Laffite had ever owned a piece of ground to plant. Slave smuggling still had some life in Louisiana and Texas, though Mexican authorities would try several expedients to keep slavery in Texas to a minimum, and in any case, no more Spanish slave ships could be taken legitimately. In short, the brothers would have been frozen out on almost every front. The world they had known and in which they could hope to flourish had left them behind, and the new world of the Gulf simply had no room for their kind.

The obscurity in which the Laffites died naturally gave rise to uncertainty. Stories of Pierre's demise got back to Texas in the 1830s and continued to appear thereafter, but since the popular imagination never seized upon him as it did his brother, less time was spent imagining his death. One story did surface that he was privateering with José Gaspar in the spring of 1822, some months after his actual death, and had been caught in a British trap that resulted in Gaspar's suicide and the sinking of Pierre's vessel.[4] Yet in the main, it was his brother about whom everyone wanted to know. Only the dimmest echoes of Jean's death reached the

United States, however, and no American journal picked up his obituary from the Bogotá *Gaceta*. Speculation and eventually fantasy filled the void. Eyebrows in South Carolina rose briefly when a "Captain Lafitte" stepped off the brig *Mary* from Havana in 1827, though he was too young to have been either of the corsairs. By 1840, as Laffite stories began to be told in growing volume in taverns and on decks along the Gulf coast, some doubted that he was dead.[5] In Galveston that year some men who claimed to have known him said they believed he still lived.[6] Other stories emerged that the absence of definitive word of Jean's death was proof that, ashamed of his past crimes, he had changed his name and profession after leaving Galveston and begun a new life.[7] As if to prove this, in 1842 a Texan traveling in upstate New York met a man who told him that Jean had been a native of Orange County and returned there after leaving Galveston to live incognito as a farmer.[8]

Most assumed Jean was dead, though. In 1843 Texan founding father Mirabeau B. Lamar began looking into the Laffite stories and concluded that there were no authentic records of the pirate's death but that he could be assumed to be no longer living. The British visitor William Bollaert, who spent some time at Galveston in the early 1840s, also concluded that Jean was almost surely dead "not many years since, in poor circumstances."[9] This still left room for imagination in accounting for his last years. One rumor held that Laffite was killed by his own men after they left Galveston.[10] Others knew with certainty that Jean Laffite had succeeded in rescuing Napoleon from St. Helena, and the two of them lived and died in Louisiana, being buried at the Temple. Laffite and Napoleon were cousins, and Jean's uncle John Paul Jones was also buried with them. Laffite, in fact, had fought with Jones on the *Bonhomme Richard* when she defeated the British *Serapis* in 1778, about three years before Jean was born.[11] Laffite's death in 1823 would have surprised the distinguished Shakespearean actor Junius Brutus Booth, father of Edwin and John Wilkes Booth. Playing Hamlet in Natchez, Mississippi, he went to the seamier part of town by the riverside and there met a dark stranger who robbed him. It was Jean Laffite. Twenty years later Booth was in New Orleans, where he received a summons from Jean, who was then in jail awaiting hanging. Remorseful over robbing the actor so long before, and aware that his days were at an end, Laffite told Booth that he wanted Booth to have his skull after his death. For the rest of his career, whenever Booth played the troubled prince of Denmark and raised from the grave the skull of "poor Yorick," it was the corsair's skull in his hand.[12]

The Laffites' old friends and associates escaped the myth-making that dogged the brothers, but in other regards time was little better to them. Of most of their men, Bollaert found in 1840 that "they could not very well go back into the world again, but they will all soon be dead."[13] Laurent Maire, who gave up privateering before the fall of Galveston, never achieved much wealth as a city merchant, though he could afford a few slaves for himself and his wife, Adeline Godon.[14] He lived in a rented house on Peace Street in the Faubourg Marigny, hardly a fashionable address for a white merchant, and when he died in 1827, leaving three minor children, all his worldly possessions came to $2,475, the bulk of it five slaves valued at $2,150. One of them had run away, and another would escape before the estate auction. His household goods—some old clothes, a canopy bed, six chairs, two tables, a mirror, and an armoire—together were worth $40.[15] His widow would survive him by seventy years, and live to be 103, later telling stories of her late husband, the "wealthy planter."

Dominique, who never learned to read or write or sign his name, gave up the sea and privateering entirely by 1823, and took a modest home in the Faubourg Marigny.[16] In his last years he became something of a local character. When he died on the morning of November 15, he was destitute and had to be buried on the charity of the city. People remembered "Captain Dominique" as a man "to whom fortune had never been very favorable."[17] Pierre's sometime partner in slave sales Antoine Abat lived only two years beyond Dominique. Only Beluche prospered to some extent. He owned several properties in New Orleans, but he left the city to serve under Bolívar and never came back. His wife would die days before the state legislature granted her a divorce on grounds of abandonment, while he lived in South America until his death in 1860. He, at least, ended his days an honored man of influence.[18]

Time erased most physical signs of the Laffites' passing. Nothing remained of the warehouses at Barataria even in their lifetime. By 1835 a traveler passing through the hamlet of Deweyville, Texas, saw only an old ruined shed when locals pointed out the remains of "one of Lafitte's old stations" where slaves were kept on the west bank of the Sabine.[19] Four years later on Galveston only a few little hillocks revealed where the brothers' community had stood. The bleached ribs of an old hull on the beach were commonly mistaken for the remains of one of their vessels, though more likely it was the *Constitution,* that last prize brought in by the *Minerva.* Now seacoasters living nearby dismantled what was left for firewood.[20] The curious who visited Galveston in the 1830s and 1840s were directed to old characters such as James Campbell, John Lambert, Stephen Churchill, Ben Dolivar, and others who claimed to have served under the brothers.[21] When the USS *Jackall* made a stop on Mugeres in 1824 seeking pirates, she found none, and no sign of them having been there. Local Indians said none had called since early 1822.[22]

As for the remains of the Laffites, Jean's became a part of the Caribbean, and as early as 1840 no one could or would point out Pierre's grave at Dzilam de Bravo. An old woman said to have been Lucia Allen's servant supposedly knew the place, but she was habitually too drunk to show anyone.[23] More than a century later, visitors to Dzilam de Bravo heard the story of Pierre's burial and began searching for a marker in the cemetery. Finding nothing, someone in 1948 erected a wooden cross where lore said an earlier marker had been placed. On the marker the letters *tte* had been legible before a hurricane washed over the cemetery and obliterated the site of the tomb. Of course if there had been such a vestige on a marker, it misspelled the brothers' name. Now, in the eternal conflation of the brothers, those setting the wooden cross carved Jean's name into it rather than Pierre's. By 1960, when locals decided to erect a marble monument to Dzilam de Bravo's most famous recumbent resident, it was commonly assumed to be Jean who lay there somewhere.[24]

In an era fed on Alexandre Dumas's *Count of Monte Cristo* and the poetry of Lord Byron, romantic notions of corsairs were a fixed part of popular culture, and the Laffites were well cast to fill the role. Novelists and writers of serial romances for the press seized upon Jean Laffite as a vehicle for their formulaic potboilers. Almost every known aspect of the brothers' career became exaggerated. They and almost they alone would be given credit for saving New Orleans in 1815. The $1,000 reward that Jean jokingly offered for Claiborne grew until by 1839 it was 10,000 British pounds, the episode dated to before the American Revolution. Stories had Jean leaving Galveston to set up his operation in Barataria rather than the other way round.[25]

Probably the first novel appeared in 1826, only three years after Jean's death, when an author listed only as "Intruder Tar" published *The Memoirs of Lafitte, or The Baratarian Pirate; A Narrative Founded on Fact*, a fictional romance that went through at least six editions under different titles in book and serial form by 1836.[26] Then in 1829 an American newspaper made the erroneous connection between Jean Laffite and Byron's poem "The Corsair" that would ever after confuse readers. Charlotte Barnes hauled Jean out on stage in her play "La Fitte, the Pirate of the

Gulf," which premiered at the Louisville Theatre in Kentucky on November 30, 1836, its author promising that her play was "founded upon the history of an extraordinary man."[27] The previous year Joseph Holt Ingraham published a small edition of his two-volume novel *The Pirate; or, Lafitte of the Gulph of Mexico*, which in numerous subsequent editions became the grandfather of all future Laffite romances, increasingly removed from fact. By 1840 Jean Laffite was depicted as a fatal lothario with women, and a cold-blooded murderer of men who yet observed some forms of honor.[28] Everything from hatred of Spain, to unrequited love, to simple bloodlust had driven him to be a corsair. "I like blood," one author had him declare before taking a prize and slaying its crew.[29]

Hand in hand with the romances went the stories of lost and buried treasure. The prosaic reality is that pirates and privateers lived hand to mouth, were improvident when they had money, and kept plying their trade because they saved none. Pierre Laffite had been bankrupt at least once and in almost constant legal difficulty over debt and disputed claims. The brothers together lost much in the 1818 hurricane, and they never did recover the $18,000 or more they spent on behalf of Spain. When they abandoned Galveston they had nothing more than their three ships, and soon lost one of those. When Pierre tried to raise new crewmen in Charleston, he offered to pay less than half the rate he had paid in New Orleans only two years before. When Englishman William Bollaert visited Galveston in 1840 and met with a few remnants of the Laffite days, one of them told him that "the Lafittes [meaning his men] squandered their money."[30]

That did not stop the march of fantasy. Starting in the 1840s, Laffite treasure was known to be buried all along the Gulf coast from Barataria to Galveston, and every few years a new story appeared of a mysterious stranger who had more money than he should, or of clandestine diggings and lights in the darkness on

the beaches.[31] Sometimes the searcher was one of the brothers'
former companions. On one occasion it was Pierre Laffite himself, raised from the dead.[32] Or one of the former associates, with
his dying words, would reveal the whereabouts of chests of gold.
Once the information came from a former slave of the Laffites,'
complete with lurid tales of how "Marse Lafitte, when he bury
dat money, kilt a nigger and put him in de hole too."[33] In 1853 Jean
Laffite manifested himself at a séance at Galveston, and promised to lead astonished participants to the hiding place of some of
his treasure, though they never seemed to have found it.[34]

In 1875 there came a report that someone had found $75,000
off Bayou La Battre.[35] Others said that Jean—it was nearly always Jean—built a brick vault on the Calcasieu and hid a fortune
there.[36] In 1878 a seventy-eight-year-old man in Galveston called
"Crazy Ben" Dolivar, supposedly known to produce antique gold
coins from time to time to buy his drink, suddenly disappeared
with a nephew of Jean Laffite after revealing to him the location
of Laffite's treasure.[37] Six years later one editor was so perplexed
by the plethora of treasure stories that he wondered that "one
would suppose that this idea of Laffite's having buried treasure
promiscuously about in every odd looking spot, would exist only
with ignorant and superstitious persons," whereas "men of known
good sense have been drawn in this foolish search." More than
that, said the editor, "the whole truth is, that Laffite never had
any treasure at all." Those looking for it, like those seeking the secret of perpetual motion, "will founder on the banks of insanity."[38]

Still men looked for the treasure, and inevitably criminals
capitalized on the lure, as in 1909 when Joseph Choate swindled
$10,000 from gullible investors by claiming to know the cave near
Lake Charles, Louisiana, where Laffite's treasure lay hidden. He
never found the money, of course, but did discover a six-year
prison sentence for fraud.[39] Then in 1936 a woman revealed that
Laffite sank his treasure ship in the Trinity River, and only she

and her father knew where. They had known for fifty years, but never got around to recovering the gold they knew to be aboard, which was why they could not reveal its location.[40] But, no, in 1981 Laffite's treasure had moved to Cameron, Louisiana. Not so, said others twenty years later, who knew it to be back at Lake Charles.[41] Laffite's gold even had magical powers, as Captain J. E. Fehann could attest. He had sailed on a vessel with the unfortunate name the *Miasma*, whose captain was a descendant of a man who had served the Laffites, and always wore around his neck a gold doubloon given him by Jean. It gave him good luck at sea. If ever a storm arose, he said, he had merely to touch the coin to the mainmast and say, "Jean LaFitte banish this wind," and the storm went away. Fehann saw it work in a Caribbean squall when a quarter of an hour after the words were spoken, the storm abated.[42]

Through all the myth and legend, Americans were trying to settle for themselves the place of the Laffites in their history and their folk pantheon. One thing is certain. The brothers were emblems of their time and place. Throughout the settlement of North America, there always appeared at the latest fringe of civilization a species of entrepreneur daring, resourceful, uninhibited by the restrictions of the scanty law available, and imaginative in devising means to get around even those. Once Americans established independence and pursued their inexorable spread westward, the numbers of such men exploded with the dramatically expanding opportunity. Wherever there was a borderland beyond the efficient imposition of the law, they appeared. Wherever there was a population with a need not adequately supplied by conventional means of commerce, they flourished. And once the vacuum of laws and regulation was filled, they disappeared and moved on, unable and unwilling to adapt to existence in the new environment. This was the story of Samuel Mason and the famed "land pirates" of the Ohio and

Mississippi valleys in the early 1800s, the story of James Bowie and his phenomenal land frauds in Louisiana and Arkansas in the 1820s, and the story of the Laffites and the Gulf corsairs. They could not have appeared at any other time or place in America's story, and when the conjunctions of history that created them disappeared, so did they.

Judged by the measure of their achievements, the Laffites were men of temporal success but lifetime failure. First from smuggling, then from privateering and piracy, they often took in large sums of money, and nothing suggests that either entertained any higher ambition. Yet like virtually all of the men in their trades, they kept little for very long, neither did they use their gains to acquire or establish anything lasting. They were chancers who lived for the moment. As for their influence on the course of filibustering efforts to wrest New World colonies from the grip of Spain, none of the enterprises that they supported succeeded, and none of those that failed once the Laffites began to work for Spain owed their demise to the brothers' schemes. Like the filibusters and their opponents, none of them individually, nor the lot of them as a whole, exerted any decisive influence on the revolutionary movements in Latin America or the fate of Texas. While the committed native revolutionaries like Bolívar and San Martín succeeded, Gutiérrez, Humbert, Toledo, Picornell, Aury, Lallemand, Long, and all the other opportunistic "patriots" failed. The damage the corsairs did to Spanish shipping was never enough to keep Spanish merchantmen off the Gulf and Caribbean, or to make the difference in Spain finally losing its New World colonies.

Of course the Laffites represented a special case among their brethren. If their first loyalty was to themselves, still as smugglers and privateers they proved more principled than the rest, solicitous of life, loyal to friends, and operating according to ethical values that often seemed out of place amid a thicket of thieves.

Thus it is ironic that one of the earliest stories told of them, one that appeared in print while they were yet living, portrayed them as murderously bloodthirsty. A story appeared in New Orleans the same month as Jean's abandonment of Galveston that told of a passenger ship bound from New Orleans to France in 1812. A wealthy French lady was among those aboard, and word of the riches with which she traveled reached the corsairs. The ship vanished and nothing was ever heard of it or its passengers, but months later the daughter of the affluent woman was stunned while walking on a New Orleans street to see her mother's jewelry around the neck of Marie Villard. Pierre Laffite indignantly denied any involvement in the disappearance of the ship, and claimed he won the baubles at cards with his associates at Barataria. That the story first appeared immediately after the near panic in New Orleans and the temporary reprieve of Desfarges and Johnson's associates is hardly coincidental. It is certainly a myth, though one that would crop up in Laffite novels, plays, and romances for more than a century.[43]

Beyond their lack of bloodlust, they showed the skills to create and build, even if only for purposes of exploitation. First the Barataria community, and then the commune at Galveston, revealed that they had the organizational sense and the personal presence to establish and govern their rough associates, and to conceive and manage an enterprise directed toward the greater and more efficient profit of all. Most of the pirate communities of the world operated in some degree as egalitarian enterprises in which leaders ruled—to the degree that they governed at all—by common consent rather than election, and only after they had demonstrated an ability to take command and direct for the mutual benefit.

The community had to take care of its own. Every man on a ship that took a prize was entitled to a share regardless of his role in the taking, and when a man suffered a serious or disabling injury, he was entitled to something extra from the commonweal to compensate him for his loss. It was not a "social safety net," but the men who sailed the Laffite vessels out of Galveston did have by right a degree of welfare protection not yet known to ordinary workers. And they recognized the irony that a community of thieves could only flourish by adhering to its own body of laws, laws that the Laffites enforced even to the death. Certainly this is how the Laffites rose to authority among the corsairs for whom they provided a service, and their service was as vertical as that of the largest corporation, from supplying letters of marque to sail under and the ships to take prizes, to providing a port to receive prize goods, and then the means to get the goods to market.

That the scheme did not always work perfectly, or that it did not work for long, takes nothing away from the novelty and magnitude of the Laffites' conception. Their place lies in a portrait of motives and attempts, not lasting achievements. In the end, the importance of the Laffites and the corsairs lies in the impact they had on Americans' perceptions of their country in the first quarter of the nineteenth century, in their attitude toward just who had the right to capitalize on the bounty of the hemisphere, and on the development of nascent Manifest Destiny west of the Mississippi. In an era when dreams were limited only by the size of men's imaginations, the Laffites dreamed large.

In the larger realm of loyalties removed from potential profit, however, the brothers remain an enigma. As spies they were never motivated by more than the hope of gain, of which Jean's final service privateering against Spanish ships after Spain had dispensed with the brothers' services is proof enough. Neither can self-interest be removed from their aid to Claiborne and Jackson at New Orleans. Theirs was a patriotism limited by convenience, and when maintaining a connection to the United States had no further benefit to them, no bonds of sympathy or loyalty held them. Real patriots would have changed profession to remain Americans. The Laffites preferred to remain corsairs and become citizens of the sea.

In the city they had once helped to save, two sisters and several children either waited in hope for the return of the brothers Laffite or else swallowed grief at their abandonment and got on about the business of living. Accurate word of the time and manner of Jean's death may never have come to Catherine, and there is no telling how long it took for news of Pierre's passing to find its way to Marie Villard. George Schumph may never have set foot in Louisiana again after he left Yucatán. Most probably the news came by word of mouth, perhaps via Jean before his own last fight, or from rumors picked up by merchant visitors to Campeche and Cartagena. All that can be said with certainty is that Marie Villard knew or assumed her lover was dead by March 19, 1825, when the marriage record of their daughter Catherine Coralie Laffite listed the father of the bride as "Pierre, dec[eased]."[44]

Marie Louise Villard lived on in the Faubourg Marigny. She was still there in the 1830s, living on Bagatelle Street between Esplanade and the Canal Marigny, with her daughter Rose and two of her surviving younger sons, probably Jean and Joseph.[45] By that time her other children by Pierre had gone on to varying fortunes. In 1833 Rose Laffite married the son of the owner of the St. Philip Street Ballroom, the free mulatto André Tessier, and began several generations of a large family.[46] Pierre's son Martin Firmin Laffite married the mulattress Silvania Catherina Brunetti on April 14, 1828, but he died within a few years, before they could begin a family, and she remarried.[47] Her father Francisco Brunetti was a merchant in New Orleans and an occasional associate of the Laffites.[48] He had been one of Sedella's couriers to Havana, and was robbed at sea by Aury in 1817. He regularly traveled to Campeche as late as 1820, perhaps still doing a little business with the Laffites.

Catherine Coralie Laffite married the mulatto Pierre Roup of San Domingue, a man of prominence in the free black community, a Masonic leader who founded Perseverance Lodge #4, and in time became a prosperous builder who erected several fine houses on Rampart and Esplanade streets.[49] She may even have maintained a connection to that possible earlier liaison of Pierre's with Adelaide Maseleri. The surname existed in a bewildering variety of at least forty-five spellings, one of them being Demasilieres, and in 1825 a Catherina Laffit, probably this same Catherine Coralie Laffite, was godmother at the baptism of Marie Demasilieres.[50] Of Adelaide Maseleri's daughter Marie Josephe Laffite, however, not another trace remains.[51] Of Pierre's sons Joseph, Jean, Pierre, and/or the possibly mythical Eugene, no definitive trace was left after 1830. The elder may have gone with Pierre to Mugeres. The younger could have succumbed to the annual fevers. They may simply have merged into the growing population of Laffites of all spellings and other blood, and disappeared through the documentary cracks.

As for their mother, sometime before her death on October 27, 1833, at forty-eight, Marie married or took another common-law husband named Ramos, probably the father of Feliciano Ramos.[52] Her family buried her in the St. Louis Cemetery Number 2.[53] Her sister Catarina or Catherine Villard lived on another quarter century and somehow kept much of the family together. By August 1850 she resided in the Faubourg Marigny, and P. Ramos, probably Marie's last mate, lived with her. In the same household lived Adele Laffite, born in 1819 and probably a daughter of Jean's or Pierre's, and several of Catherine's children, including two by Feliciano Ramos. Next door lived Marie's daughter Coralie Laffite Roup and one of her sons, as well as a young man named Alexandre Laffite whose relation to the family is unclear.[54] Catherine lived on, never marrying, until she died, aged about sixty-five, on July 2, 1858.[55] Years before she had buried Jean Laffite's only known son, Jean Pierre Laffite, who died during an epidemic in October 1832.[56]

The children of Pierre Laffite lived quietly. Indeed, within two generations his descendants had different surnames, thanks largely to the fact that only his daughters Rose and Coralie, and his possible daughter Adele, seem to have had children. Even in the close-knit free black community where they lived, their connection with the famous pirates passed into hearsay. By 1863 a rumor said a Laffite daughter was still living in New Orleans. Catherine Roup had died on July 22, 1855, aged about fifty.[57] Adele Laffite Grant Ramos was still alive, however, as were most of her nine children, and Rose Laffite Tessier lived until November 10, 1870.[58]

Rose and her husband André Tessier lived on Esplanade, and raised at least five children.[59] Pierre Laffite had left little behind for them to remember him by. His name disappeared when his daughters married, and none of his grandchildren bore it. All that remained in the family by way of mementos were a buckle and a small cross said to have been Pierre's, though they were probably Tessier's.[60]

One thing that Pierre Laffite undeniably left to his progeny, however, was his white skin. Though sometimes referred to as "colored," Marie Villard was almost certainly a mulatto, meaning that in the mathematics of blood, her children with Pierre were three-fourths white and one-quarter black. In the equations of race in Louisiana at that time, however, they were colored before the law if they had a single drop of Negro blood in their veins. They could not vote or hold office, enlist in military service, marry whites, or enjoy a number of other privileges, and the records to establish their legal race were several, including the birth, marriage, and death certificates required in the city, as well as the baptismal, marriage, and funeral records in the Sacramental Archives of the Cathedral Church of St. Louis. Thus the baptisms of the children of Pierre and Jean Laffite were recorded in the sacramental books for free blacks and slaves.

But they had white blood, and like thousands of other mixed-race free people in the city, their skin was lighter than that of full-blooded blacks, and their features more Caucasian. With each succeeding generation, as they married or cohabited with other mulattoes or quadroons, they became more and more white to all appearances. All of Rose and André Tessier's children were recorded as "colored" at the registration of their births.[61] Their daughter Laura Emilie probably married Auguste Allnet around 1860, and gave birth to five children who grew to adulthood, and their birth and death certificates listed them, too, as "colored." But then in 1880 came the census enumerator, and when he called at the Allnet home on Marais Street in New Orleans, its inhabitants told him they were "white" and what he saw did not raise any question in his mind.[62] Pierre's descendants had commenced the risky business of "passing."

On June 14, 1890, Auguste and Laura Emilie's son Edward Andrew Allnet married a white woman, Bertha Eugenie Emuy, and soon they began a family.[63] In the office of vital statistics, every one of their children would be registered as "white" at birth.[64] Laura Emilie's sister Alexandrine did the same thing after she married a white Canadian merchant, Edward Farr. The husband had to know of his wife's dollop of black blood, for at least two of their four children listed their own children as colored at birth. Their oldest son, Edward Robert Louis Farr, would have nine children by his wife, Marie Lacoste. Two of them were listed as colored, another as white, and no race at all was given for the rest, meaning a presumption that they were white.

One of Edward and Marie's children listed as colored at birth was their daughter Alexandrine Mirielle, born December 23, 1891.[65] When she married a white man, George Renton, on March 18, 1911, the family was actively passing as white. As part of the subterfuge, the Farrs told Renton of the several vital records on file in the city and with the cathedral, and explained that they were the result of errors and carelessness, which he seemed to accept. Unfortunately something happened that they could not have anticipated. Renton turned out to be a brute. He abused Mirielle, and, according to her, he "contracted loathsome venereal diseases as a result of his promiscuous adulteries." After four years she left him and moved herself and their furniture into her parents' home.[66]

An angry and vengeful Renton filed for an annulment on October 1, 1915, claiming that he had just learned that his wife had colored blood, making their marriage illegal and she and her family deceivers. A divorce entitled her to a half share of their joint property, whereas an annulment would mean that all property he purchased for them while together remained lawfully his. It came down to parlor furniture, a dining room set, a china closet, a gas stove, clocks, pictures, and even "bric-a-brac" that he had no intention of sharing with the woman who rejected him.[67]

The ensuing legal fight lasted over a decade, turning first to last on the composition of Mirielle's blood. The question went far beyond the matter of divorce or annulment, for if she were adjudged to be colored, then so were all her family. They stood to lose voting rights, legal rights, what social status they had as members of the white working community, and perhaps even their employment. The outcome could be catastrophic for scores of aunts, uncles, and cousins. It all hinged on the documents, and soon archivists appeared in the district court carrying a mountain of certified copies of birth, marriage, and death certificates from the city archives, while the custodian of the Sacramental Archives produced the baptismal books going back to the late 1700s.

The family's case rested on one essential claim.[68] Marie Louise Villard was not their ancestor. Rather, Pierre Laffite had married a white woman, Marie Delas, and Rose Laffite was her daughter. That left the problem of the marriage record of Rose Laffite and André Tessier, which was recorded in a book of marriages of free blacks and showed both Rose and her husband to be mulattoes. The solution was one to which other "passing" New Orleanians had resorted—vandalizing the cathedral records. Sometime shortly after the first suit was filed, if not before, a member of Mirielle's family went into the cathedral archives, which were open to the public, and pulled out part one of the second volume of Marriages of Free Persons of Color for the years 1830 to 1835. The index clearly referenced the Tessier-Laffite marriage on page thirty-five.

A careful slash with a penknife removed the page with the offending record. Showing some forethought, the vandal cut out the index page, too, and inserted in its place a duplicate on which was listed every reference from the removed index page but that to the Tessier-Laffite marriage on page thirty-five. It seemed very clever, but not quite clever enough. For a start, the new index page was obviously a different paper from the rest of the volume, and the entries in a different hand. More careless than that, the vandal did not notice that it was a double entry index, meaning that every marriage was listed twice, once under each surname involved. The page with a reference under Tessier was taken out, but the vandal overlooked the page with the reference listed under Laffite. No one would be fooled, and no one was. When the archivist began gathering the records in December 1915 for the Renton case, he immediately saw what had been done.[69]

Several members of the family filed a joint suit against the New Orleans Board of Health to have the vital statistics records declared void, claiming that court clerks and undertakers, and everyone else who filled out the forms, either made mistakes or perpetuated an earlier error. The archivists testified to the story contained in their records, however, and the trail back to Marie Villard became indelibly clear, while none at all could be established to Marie Delas. Other embarrassing revelations unwittingly came out, as in the discovery that Mirielle's grandfather

Edward Farr had had a mulatto mistress, and several children born to her, all recorded as colored.[70]

The family did not deny that their ancestor Pierre Laffite was the pirate and smuggler of Barataria, though their testimony revealed that after the passage of only three generations, they knew virtually nothing more about him. One, Rosalie DuHart, could only say that her mother told her "he was a pirate."[71] Horace Farr recalled in May 1921 that "we always spoke about Pierre Lafitte and the family," and that "[his] being a pirate, I was interested in knowing his life."[72] Edward Allnet, who led the descendants in their suit against the Board of Health, could only recall his mother Laura Emilie speaking vaguely of the grandfather she never knew as a wandering man. "He never stopped," her mother Rose had told her, but was "always on the go." When she saw her son Edward showing a penchant for travel, she chided him that he was "another one [who] will come out just like Pierre Lafitte." In her motherly jibes there was a sad echo of very different emotions suffered by her grandmother Marie Villard when she teased that Edward was "another one like Pierre Lafitte, gone away and don't know when he will come back."[73]

There was another Pierre Lafitte, of course, as indeed there were several in early New Orleans. He, too, was from Bordeaux, and the cathedral archives revealed that he and a Jeanne Delas had a son Pierre born about 1800. On December 16, 1820, the son married Marie Berret, and both his mother and his wife were certainly white. However, in their court pleadings the family never made any attempt by documents to prove a link between these Laffites and their ancestress Rose. They could not. In all probability, the idea of claiming Delas as an ancestor came to them when they started tracing the documentation at the cathedral on their genuine ancestry and serendipitously chanced upon a Pierre Lafitte with a different spelling of the name but with a wife conveniently white.

The assertion that Pierre married a Delas—they were confused as to whether her name was Marie or Jeanne, a result of
conflating the records of Pierre Lafitte and Jeanne Delas with
those of the couple's son Pierre and his wife Marie Berret—was
attributed to Rose Laffite. Rose's daughter Alexandrine Farr so
claimed in a statement taken in 1918, and she also said that Rose
had only one sibling, a Pierre Laffite who went to France, then
returned to New Orleans to marry.[74] Testimony was introduced
from an elderly woman who had known Rose Laffite Tessier in
her last years in the 1860s, and who said she recalled Rose talking
about her father as "this man Lafitte," and saying that her mother
had been French, which, of course, applied to Marie Villard's
background as well as that of any Delas.[75] Three years later Rosalie DuHart, daughter of Emilie Louise Tessier, repeated the
claim that Rose Laffite said her mother was Marie Delas. She
also produced the buckle and the cross in the hope that they provided some sort of evidence, claiming that Pierre had given them
to Rose, but then her testimony made it clear that they came
from her grandfather Tessier's family. It was hinted that the "D"
in the initials "C. D." on the cross stood for Delas, but again
DuHart compromised her own testimony when she went on to
say that she had put the initials on the cross herself.[76]

In the end the testimony went on for months, and filled more
than five hundred pages of transcripts, none of it convincing anyone that there had been official errors. It was a sad tableau of a
working-class family fighting to retain what position they had in
their community and society, and they were bound to lose. There
had been a number of similar cases in recent years, and the unusually complete vital records kept in New Orleans since early in the
past century defeated most of them. Renton got his annulment,
and in November 1922 the court handed down the inevitable decision in the suit against the Board of Health.[77] Mirielle responded
in December by filing for a divorce, but it was a hopeless effort,

especially after her family appealed the lower court's decision in their suit to the state supreme court, alleging that it came under that bench's purview due to the damages that the family would suffer to their political rights as a result of being adjudged to be of colored blood. On March 10, 1924, the Supreme Court heard arguments, but quickly declined to hear the case or consider overturning the lower court's ruling.[78] In November 1925, giving up all hope, Mirielle filed a motion to withdraw her petition for a divorce, and at last, almost exactly ten years after her legal nightmare began, it was all over.[79]

The family were devastated. For those living out of the state, as many did, it was not so bad, but for those in New Orleans there was no hiding the sudden change in their status. Mirielle Renton went back to being Mirielle Farr, an embittered woman who soon disappeared from New Orleans, doing her best to keep herself and her ancestry a secret.[80] Only after the turn of the millennium would descendants of Pierre and Marie begin to emerge once more from the shadows imposed on them by the mores and prejudices of a distant time. Thus, in a last, sad, irony, when the Laffites disappeared into the Gulf, they were forgotten by their own family just as, apparently, they forgot that family themselves. Instead, as the generations ensued, their descendants preferred to remember their ancestress Marie as the white Delas rather than the mulatto Villard who had held the family together when her man went away and did not return. As for memories of the Laffites themselves, of Jean not a jot of recall survived in the family, and of Pierre little more than that he was a pirate and a vagabond.

There was one thing more, though: vague stories redolent of adventure and mystery all conjured by the name of a place. Asked what Rose told her of her grandfather Pierre Lafitte, Alexandrine Farr could summon only a single ancient recollection that "my mother often spoke to me of Bayou Barataria."[81]

ACKNOWLEDGMENTS

ARCHIVISTS EVERYWHERE without exception have been anxious to help with the research for this work. From among those who have contributed so extensively, several stand out, and all are deserving of thanks. Sally Reeves, now retired from the fabulous New Orleans Notarial Archives, made the rich untapped resources of that unique collection available on many occasions, and with it gave her unrestrained aid with copies and translations. At Fort Worth, Texas, Barbara Rust, Meg Hacker, and Nakita Gore of the National Archives Southwest Region never recoiled from requests for assistance in the wonderful case files of the United States District Court for Eastern Louisiana housed there. The always-helpful staff at the National Archives in Washington did not fail to help, notably Michael Musick, Rebecca Livingston, and Rick Peuser, as well as volunteer staff Russ and Budge Weidman. James Sefcik and Katherine Page were most cooperative at the Louisiana State Museum in New Orleans, as was Pamela Arceneaux of the Historic New Orleans Collection. Belinda Lassalle at the New Orleans Civil Court

was very patient, and Bobby Freyou and Geneva Welch in the
Louisiana State Archives in Baton Rouge were equally helpful.
Wayne Everard of the Louisiana Division, New Orleans Public
Library, gave attention to every request for material from that
underappreciated resource for early New Orleans legal records.

Other state and local government archivists lent invaluable
aid, among them Shirley Perry of the Arkansas County Courthouse, DeWitt, Arkansas; Donaly E. Brice of the Texas State Library and Archives Commission at Austin; Dimitrious Gartrell
at the East Baton Rouge Parish Courthouse in Baton Rouge,
Louisiana; and Ann Lipscomb-Webster of the Mississippi Department of Archives and History in Jackson. University special
collections archivists also contributed, particularly Dean DeBolt
of the University of West Florida at Pensacola, Wilbur Menery
of the Howard Tilton Library at New Orleans' Tulane University, and Ralph Elder at the Center for American History, University of Texas at Austin. Marie E. Windell of the Louisiana
Supreme Court Archives at the University of New Orleans was
most obliging in the matter of the long-lost court record of the
early 1900s trial involving descendants of Pierre Laffite. Dr.
Charles Nolan cordially opened the voluminous Archdiocesan
Archives of the Archdiocese of New Orleans, containing the vital
records of St. Louis Cathedral, and in Houston, Texas, Karen
Clingan of the TORCH Collection was most cooperative.
Françoise Durand-Evrard of the Archives Nationales, Centre
des Archives d'Outre-Mer, in Aix-en-Provence, France, very
cordially helped with documents relating to San Domingue. Special thanks are due to the consideration of Dr. Robert L. Schaadt
of the Sam Houston Regional Library and Research Center at
Liberty, Texas, for granting unrestricted access to the original of
the disputed Jean Laffite Journal, as well as the rest of the Laffite
collections there.

In a work dealing with so many documents in other languages, translations are vital, and several people lent invaluable

aid, led by Nancy Lopez of Blacksburg, Virginia, who dealt with all of the documents in Spanish from the Archives of the Indies materials. Dr. Linda Arnold of Virginia Tech in Blacksburg also assisted with some Spanish readings, while Christina Vella of New Orleans cheerfully allowed translating several documents in French to distract her from her own valuable work. Other aid with French came from Amelia Rodrigue and Dr. Harry Redman, Jr., of New Orleans.

Several members of the Laffite Society of Galveston, themselves interested and active in Laffite research, gave unstintingly of their time and expertise. Two stand out in deserving special gratitude. Pam Keyes of Miami, Oklahoma, has been on the Laffite trail for more than two decades, and went out of her way to make herself and her research materials available. For several years she has been an almost daily sounding board. We have not always agreed, for that is the way of historians, but always differed with mutual respect. Her generosity has been unmatched, and the interest she has taken in this work has undoubtedly made it the better. Similarly, Robert Vogel of New Brighton, Minnesota, author of several important articles on the Laffites and the filibustering community, delved into his own voluminous files to share otherwise elusive documents, and he, too, was ever ready, sometimes on a daily basis, to take on the odd question or help address a conundrum. His encyclopedic knowledge of many of the Laffite associates has been invaluable. Both Keyes and Vogel read this work in manuscript, and offered comments and corrections from which it has benefited immeasurably.

Members of the Laffite Society helped measurably, among them Dr. Reginald Wilson, Jean Epperson, Betje Klier, Jeff and Kathy Modjelewski, and Don Marler. Sylvie Feuillie of France made available some of the findings from her Laffite research, and Patrick Lafitte of Corneilla Del Vercol, France, kindly provided Pierre Lafitte's newly discovered 1802 passport. Fellow historians have been unstintingly gracious, including Dr. Stewart

King of Mt. Angel Seminary, St. Benedict, Oregon, Benjamin Maygarden of New Orleans, and Richard McMurry of Roanoke, Virginia. A number of other friends not already named gave their time on errands great and small. Some like Dennis Brown of St. Louis, Missouri, and Anthony Hall of Stoke-on-Trent, England, performed some distant research, while old friend Thomas Lindley of Austin, Texas, more than once spontaneously sent a document unearthed in his own indefatigable research. Deborah Petite of Alexandria, Virginia, put in many hours running down documents in the National Archives, while Judith Bethea of New Orleans proved invaluable in locating documents in the several archives in New Orleans, particularly the Public Library. Edmée Chanay of Paris, France, went after Laffite origins in Pauillac, Bordeaux, and William Reeves of New Orleans helped with some local sources, while Harold Holzer of New York proved decisive in running down an 1819 sketch of the Laffite ship *Dorada* in its then guise as the USS *Firebrand*.

To each and all, sincere thanks, and for her patience during the writing of this, and her own reading of the manuscript during a terribly busy time for her, the greatest gratitude of all must go to the pirate who stole the author's heart, Sandra Davis.

NOTES

Abbreviations Used in the Notes

AGI-Newberry   Ayer Collection of Transcripts from the
Archivo General de Indias, Newberry Library,
Chicago, IL

AGN   Archivo General de la Nación, Mexico City

Blake   Nacogdoches Archives Transcripts, Robert
Bruce Blake Collection, East Texas Research
Center, Stephen F. Austin State University,
Nacogdoches

CAHUT   Center for American History, University of
Texas at Austin

HNOC   Historic New Orleans Collection, New
Orleans, LA

LBRI   Louisiana Birth Records Index, 1790–1899,
Louisiana Division of Archives, Records
Management, and History, Baton Rouge

LDRI   Louisiana Death Records Index, 1804–1949,
Louisiana Division of Archives, Records
Management, and History, Baton Rouge

LSM   Louisiana State Museum, New Orleans

LSU   Louisiana State University, Baton Rouge

NAFW	National Archives Southwest Region, Ft. Worth, TX
NONA	New Orleans Notarial Archives
NOPL	New Orleans Public Library
NSUL	Northwestern State University of Louisiana, Natchitoches
SAANO	Sacramental Archives of the Archdiocese of New Orleans
TSL	Texas State Library and Archives, Austin

ONE

1. A number of different birthplaces have been offered for the brothers over the years, but most sources are secondhand at best, and all appeared decades after the Laffites' deaths. The earliest source was Texas pioneer Samuel Williams, who stated on one occasion in the 1830s that one of the brothers—context suggests that he was speaking of Pierre—was born in Brest around 1776. But Williams did not know the Laffites more than passingly, having met Pierre in Baltimore, and again on the street in New Orleans ("Lafitte," undated notes in Mirabeau B. Lamar Papers, Texas State Library, Austin [TSL]). And on another occasion in the 1830s Williams said he believed the Laffites were born in Bayonne. (Information derived from Col. S. M. Williams respecting Lafitte, n.d., Lamar Papers, TSL.)

On October 27, 1810, Adelaide Maseleri gave birth to a daughter named Marie Josephe Lafite, the father being a Pierre Lafite, "native of Bayonne in France." For generations it has been assumed that this was Pierre Laffite, the smuggler, and the possibility cannot be entirely dismissed. Nevertheless, in the absence of any other evidence linking Pierre Laffite the smuggler with Adelaide Maseleri, and considering that there were at least one or two other men of the same name in New Orleans at the time, the linkage of this baptismal record to Pierre Laffite seems inconclusive.

The Bayonne claim apparently first appeared in print in 1852 in an account by William Bollaert that gained early and wide currency. Admitting that Williams was one of his sources during his visit to Texas in the years 1842–44, Bollaert cited another man identified as "Old L," in fact an old Galveston denizen named John Lambert who claimed to have served under the Laffites and who told him that there were three brothers, Pierre, Jean, and Marc (also known as Henri or Antoine), and that they were originally from Bordeaux or Bayonne (William Bollaert, "Life of Jean Lafitte, the Pirate of the Mexican Gulf," *Littell's Living Age*, XXXII [March 1852], pp. 434–35). This is also the earliest reference to a third brother, which cannot be entirely discounted, though in this instance Bollaert's source was confusing as a sibling Marc Lafitte, the notary of New Orleans, who was no relation to the Laffites. In 1854 New Orleans merchant Vincent Nolte also stated that the Laffites were from Bayonne (Vincent Nolte, *The Memoirs of Vincent Nolte. Reminiscences in the Period of Anthony Adverse or Fifty Years in Both Hemispheres* [New York, 1934], p. 207). As his text makes clear, though, Nolte was no intimate of the Laffites', and he likely was only repeating from memory what he had read in Bollaert.

Nolte is also apparently the earliest source for the recurrent myth that the Laffites and the privateer Frederick Dominique or Dominique Youx were brothers, but he offers no evidence of what is clearly a canard. Charles Hunt repeated it in his 1864 *Life of Edward Livingston* (New York, p. 203), when he referred to "Jean Lafitte, [and] his brothers Pierre and Dominique, and of their band," and may have been influenced by Nolte. This whole business of Dominique being a brother probably grew out of a mid-nineteenth-century American misunderstanding of the more common Gallic and still English usage of "brother" as a singular of "brethren" or "brotherhood," no blood relation implied. Moreover, Dominique Youx may have had brothers named Pierre and Jean, and this may be the origin of the misconception that he was a Laffite brother (Winston C. Babb, French Refugees from Saint Domingue to the Southern United States: 1791–1810. [PhD dissertation, University of Virginia, Charlottesville, n.d.], p. 314).

Based in part on these sources, Stanley Faye, "The Great Stroke of Pierre Laffite," *Louisiana Historical Quarterly*, XXIII (July 1940), p. 744, concludes that the Laffites came from Bayonne, where Pierre was born in 1776 and Jean four or five years later. Before that, he says, the family lived in Boscay and the Pyrenees valley of Orduna twenty miles south of Bilbao, Spain, their mother being a Spaniard. His source for this is Juan Mariano Picornell to Luis Onís, February 16, 1816 (Legajo 42, Archivo de Su Magestad Católica en Philadelphia, State Department, Madrid, Spain), but in fact that source says nothing of the sort, only saying of Pierre that he was "the son of a Spanish woman and brought up among us." It would have been quite in character for Pierre to tell Picornell something of this sort at the time in attempting to convince him of the duplicitous brothers' sympathies with Spain.

Another early birthplace attribution appeared in J. H. Ingraham, "Life and Times of Lafitte," *DeBow's Southern and Western Review*, XI (October

1851), pp. 372–87, wherein Ingraham without citing a source maintained that the Laffites were born in St. Malo, France. Meanwhile, in the early 1850s Marseilles also became a candidate ("Editorial and Literary Department—History of Lafitte," *DeBow's Southern and Western Review*, XIII [July 1852], p. 102).

Galveston journalist and amateur historian John Dyer was almost certainly the source for perhaps the most novel origin story of all in a Galveston, *Daily News* article on May 9, 1920, which said that Jean Laffite told Warren D. C. Hall, Mrs. James Campbell, Jane Long, J. Randal Jones, and others that he was born in Haute Pyrenees, France, and that Laffite was in fact an assumed name taken from an old servant who brought him to Louisiana in 1807, and that Pierre was the son of the servant, not Jean's real brother. Most of Dyer's sources appear to have been old Galveston loungers with little or no verifiable connection to the Laffites during their days on the island.

In articles on March 5 and May 21, 1933, France even lost claim to the Laffites entirely when the New Orleans *States* carried the story of the confusion of Jean Laffite with a Juan Enrico Lafite whose birth record showed him being born in New Orleans December 27, 1778, the son of Elizabeth Roche and John Lafite, then expounded on his Irish ancestry and finished with a discussion of his star sign as a Capricorn.

These interesting nativity myths to the contrary, and with only the one possible exception of the Maseleri baptism record, virtually every source directly contemporaneous with the Laffites and reflecting statements made by the brothers themselves, reveals them to be entirely consistent over a fourteen-year period in placing their births in the Bordeaux region in the Department of the Gironde in France. The earliest statement in this regard, and also the most specific, came from Pierre in his affidavit dated April 21, 1806, in which he identified himself as a "native of Pauillac, France" (Notary Pierre Pedesclaux, Volume 52, item 335, New Orleans Notarial Archives [NONA]).

The next evidence came from Jean Laffite on March 2, 1813, when he listed his birthplace as Bordeaux on a muster roll of his brother's ship *La Diligente* (Certificate of Inspection, March 2, 1813, Pierre and Jean Laffite Collection, Historic New Orleans Collection [HNOC]). Such a statement, on a document done for and clearly to be scrutinized by Pierre, logically qualifies as a confirmation from both of them of the accuracy of Jean's attestation to his Bordeaux nativity. Finally, among the very last records of the brothers in New Orleans are baptisms of their children in 1820 in which each Laffite gave his birthplace as "the jurisdiction of Bordeaux [Dept. of Gironde]" (Charles E. Nolan and Dorenda Dupont, eds., *Sacramental Records of the Roman Catholic Church of the Archdiocese of New Orleans, Volume 14, 1820–1821* [New Orleans, 1999], pp. 228–29).

2. These findings and conclusions on the parentage of Jean and Pierre Laffite derive from research performed in the birth and death registers at Pauillac by Edmée Chanay in 2003, at the author's commission. One, and only one, Laffite family in Pauillac in the late 1700s, from 1760–1807, spelled their name in the distinctive fashion that Jean and Pierre Laffite used throughout their lives. If Pierre Laffite's statement in the 1806 Notarial affidavit was correct, placing his birth in Pauillac, and these Laffites are the only family of that name and spelling in Pauillac at that time, then almost certainly they are the family of Pierre and Jean of Louisiana. Ms. Chanay also found acts in the parish archives suggesting that this Jean Laffite, son of Pierre, left for the United States, which in some degree corroborates this conclusion. Edmée Chanay to author, November 15, 2003. One potential problem with this scenario, however, is the statement by Jean Laffite in 1813 on the *La Diligente* roll, that he was thirty-two, which would argue for a birth year of 1781 rather than 1786. People of the time seemed remarkably cavalier about their ages, giving different years at different times, and rarely seeming in agreement with themselves, though still for Jean to be off by five years is difficult to accept. In the absence of discovering any other Laffite family in Pauillac at this time, however, the relation herein seems the best one to fit the known facts, the virtually unique spelling of the surname being especially persuasive.

For other speculations on the Laffites' ancestry, none of it conclusive, see Emery De Sidney, "Laffite, Frères et Cie, Filibustiers," *Généalogie et Histoire de la Caraïbe* (Bulletin 85, September 1996), p. 1720; Michel Camus, "Miettes et Pistes pour la Saga Laffite," *Généalogie et Histoire de la Caraïbe* (Bulletin 91, March 1997), p. 1917; Pierre Bardin, "Laffite ou L'art de la Dissimulation," *Généalogie et Histoire de la Caraïbe* (Bulletin 85, September 1996), pp. 1718–19.

3. There is no certainty that this supposition of a son Pierre born to Pierre and Marie is correct. It is a speculation based on the fact that Pierre's son Pierre by his second wife Marguerite appears to have died in 1804, thereby disqualifying him from being the Pierre Laffite of Louisiana and Texas. That Pierre, Sr., would have named a son by his second wife Pierre while already having a living son Pierre by his first is not unusual. Pierre Laffite of Louisiana fathered two sons named Jean by his mistress Marie Villard, presumably differentiating them by their middle names, which are not

known for any of these Pierres. If this speculation is correct, then Pierre and Jean Laffite of Louisiana were half brothers. Attribution of Pierre Laffite's birth year to 1770 derives from his statement in March 1820 that he was fifty years of age, but that of course can be taken as approximate (Rieder and Rieder, *New Orleans Ship Lists*, p. 8). In February 1816 Pierre Laffite's Spanish espionage contact described him as being forty years old, which would have meant a birth year of 1775–76, but again such age references tended to be approximate (Picornell to Onís, February 16, 1816, Legajo 42, Archivo de Su Magestad Católica en Philadelphia, State Department, Madrid. Cited in Stanley Faye, "Privateersmen of the Gulf and Their Prizes," *Louisiana Historical Quarterly*, XXII (October 1939), p. 1035; translation in Stanley Faye Papers, Rosenberg Library, Galveston, TX).

4. Baptismal and Birth Register, Pauillac.

5. James Campbell, latter-day associate of the Laffites' at Galveston, told William Bollaert in 1842–44 that the brothers came from Bordeaux and were the sons of a merchant. That is hardly conclusive, but considering the time and place of their upbringing, the fact that both brothers were literate, and that from their first appearances in the public record in Louisiana they were engaged in trade—albeit often illicit—it seems reasonable to assume that their education and their affinity for commerce are evidence of a middle-class mercantile home environment. Bollaert, "Lafitte," p. 435.

6. This conclusion on the extent of the brothers' education is based on an evaluation of the dozen or so surviving letters in their hand that can definitely be attributed to them and not to clerks. There are a few surviving original letters demonstrably written by Pierre, and half a dozen certainly attributable to Jean. Translator Christina Vella to the author, July 11, 2004, concludes that they wrote with "horrible French grammar and spelling." However, both were certainly literate by the definitions of the day.

7. John Dyer in Galveston, *Daily News*, September 19, 1926, maintains on no stated authority that the Laffites' parents were guillotined in the Terror, almost certainly a romanticization based purely on imagination.

8. Bollaert, "Lafitte," p. 434; Pierre Laffite passport, May 21, 1802, Sevie Passeports, Archives départmentales de la Gironde, Bordeaux, France. This important document has just been discovered by Laffite researcher Patrick Lafitte. Its authenticity is established by the perfect match of the signature on it with 1803 Laffite documents cited hereafter.

9. A Captain Lafite serving in the French army disappeared around 1800, but there is no reason for supposing that he was either of the brothers. Half

a century later one acquaintance thought that Jean might have served in the French navy or army and was perhaps a good swordsman, but could recall nothing more. (Bollaert, "Lafitte," p. 435 and n; "Lafitte," undated notes in Lamar Papers, TSL. The source for this latter account is unnamed, but has the sound of James Campbell, as he told others substantially the same story. There is little reason to believe it to be accurate.) At the same time a man who was certainly at least acquainted with Jean recalled being told that at age nine he ran away from home and joined a British warship. His father brought him back but he ran away again and shipped on the British HMS *Fox*, rising to rank of man before the mast. Then after a difficulty in port at Deptford, he deserted, lived with a French family there for a time, then took ship for South America. After visiting Cartagena and Santa Maria he caught the privateering bug and fitted out a republican privateer under Cartagenan colors. Visiting Charleston, South Carolina, frequently, he fought a duel there over favors of a woman and killed his rival, forcing him to flee. (M. B. Lamar notes ca. 1839, Lamar Papers, TSL.)

More persistent rumors made Laffite the victim of the Spaniards. Recollection averred that he was a trader in Málaga, on the Mediterranean coast, and captured there by Spaniards and imprisoned for seven years before he tunneled out of his prison and escaped. Hiding on an American vessel, he only revealed himself when at sea, and thus remained aboard until he arrived at Charleston, where again he competed with another for a woman and killed his opponent on the dueling field. ("Lafitte," undated notes in Lamar Papers, TSL.) There is no more reason to believe that story any more than another version in which Spaniards captured Jean at sea in a French vessel, and imprisoned him in Cuba for several years, then forgot the reason for his original arrest and so released him. Contradicting this, yet another story maintained that Jean Laffite served during the French Revolution on a privateer and was captured and imprisoned for several years by the English before he escaped. ("Editorial and Literary Department—History of Lafitte," *DeBow's Southern and Western Review*, XIII [July 1852], p. 102.) As evidence that this rumor is clearly ill-informed, it goes on to say that his imprisonment engendered a hatred of the English in Laffite, and that later he preyed only on English ships—which is nonsense—and that after the Battle of New Orleans he returned to France. Perhaps the silliest of these imprisonment stories is in Charles Ramsdell, Jr., "Why Jean Lafitte Became a Pirate," *Southwestern Historical Quarterly*, XLIII (April 1940), p. 468, which maintains that he was a prisoner in Mexico City for many years prior to 1795, and that he was twenty years older than he stated himself to be in later documents. Ramsdell has confused Laffite with another man entirely.

Other belated accounts suggest that Jean Laffite, as evidence of his experience of seamanship in France, went to the Caribbean and shipped aboard privateers operating out of Martinique and Guadeloupe, preying on Spanish shipping, yet if so he left no trace of his service. (Sylvie Feuillie to the author, March 2, 2004, testifies that in her extensive researches in French archives, she found "no proof they [the Laffites] were privateers from Martinique nor Guadeloupe, and in my opinion, they were not.") A later acquaintance recalled being told that Jean, whom he mistakenly thought to be the eldest of the brothers, might have visited the Spanish Main in this period. He did not recall the reason, but believed that the Spaniards captured Jean and imprisoned him at an early age in one of the colonies. (Bollaert, "Lafitte," p. 435. The informant was James Gaines.) One informant decades after the fact attested that Laffite actually ran away from home at an early age, served on a man-of-war for several voyages, and ended at Santa Martha where he fitted out a privateer. (W. A. Fayman and T. W. Reilly, *Fayman & Reilly's Galveston City Directory for 1875–6* [Galveston, TX, 1875], pp. 15–16.) A Louis Lafitte captained the corsair *Dermide* out of Cap Français on San Domingue in 1803, yet even though some think that he might actually be the Laffites' father and that they were serving with him, again nothing connects the brothers with him. (Michel Camus, "Miettes et Pistes pour la Saga Laffite," *Généalogie et Histoire de la Caraïbe* [Bulletin 91, March 1997], p. 1917; Faye, "Stroke," p. 745, says their father might be Louis Laffite, a French privateer out of Cap Français commanding the privateer *Dorada,* but clearly he means the same Laffite who commanded the *Dermide.*)

If the privateering rumors are unsupported, still most stories agree that either singly or together the brothers washed up on Caribbean shores after they left home, either Martinique or San Domingue. One long after-the-fact memory claimed that Laffite told several late acquaintances that he had been a planter in the West Indies until 1809. The brothers settled on Martinique and lived on a sugar plantation, but the Spaniards confiscated his plantation and arrested both him and his wife. Jean was imprisoned, his wife taken by a Spaniard for his mistress, and she soon committed suicide, thus forging his lifelong—and mythical—hatred for Spain. (Faye, "Stroke," p. 745, on the authority of James Gaines, who did meet with and visit Jean Laffite in 1819, and later told what he heard from Laffite to Bollaert in 1842–44, said they went to San Domingue. Much more was written about this in several articles by Joseph O. Dyer in the Galveston, *Daily News,* May 9, 1920, October 1, 1921, and September 19, 1926. Dyer, whose sources were always suspect though they claimed to have known the Laffites, seemed himself to embroider his stories with retelling.)

What most of these stories have in common is that they came from men who actually did have some much later acquaintance with Jean Laffite in 1818–20, but they did not set down their recollections of him until twenty years later or more, when they themselves were elderly, of fallible memory, and perhaps influenced by legends and romances that had grown up around their subject. They may also have been recalling very accurately just what Jean Laffite told them, only to be the victims of a penchant for impish humor and broad storytelling that seemed to be a part of his personality. In short, to cover the gap of these years after he left France, he may well have invented and reinvented his own story, both to amuse himself and his friends.

10. Babb, French Refugees, p. 19.

11. Moreau de Saint-Méry, *Description Topographique,* III, p. 1506.

12. Fick, *The Making of Haiti,* p. 208.

13. Pierre Bardin, "Lafitte, Myth or Reality?" *Généalogie et Histoire de la Caraïbe* (Bulletin 64, October 1994), p. 1149. The author found this information in documents at Port-au-Prince.

14. Pierre Laffite statement, April 21, 1806, Pierre Pedesclaux, Vol. 52, item 335, NONA. An attempt to more precisely date this episode, and to fully identify the victim Gabauriau, has been unsuccessful. There are records of indemnity applications made to the French government by the Saint-Domingue exiles in the 1840s, grouped together in the "Fonds de l'Indemnite de Saint-Domingue" in the Archives d'Outremer in Aix-en-Provence, however, a search failed to produce anything matching this episode. Stewart R. King, Mt. Angel Seminary, St. Benedict, Oregon, was very helpful in this attempt.

15. It is worth noting that in "The Cruise of the Enterprise. A Day with La Fitte," *United States Magazine and Democratic Review,* VI (July 1839), p. 42, the author—identified only as "T"—has Laffite—which one is not stated, but the inference is that it is Jean, who was the well-known one by 1839—saying that "eighteen years ago I was a merchant in San Domingo." As will be discussed later, this is a questionable source. However, it is the

only early source to state that a Laffite had been a merchant in San Domingue, as Pierre almost certainly was. Certainly, as will be demonstrated later, the *Enterprise* did visit Galveston in February 1820 and there were discussions with a Laffite, probably Jean, as Pierre was likely still in New Orleans at the time. So it is just possible that this is an echo of a genuine conversation and statement by a Laffite.

16. A captain of artillery named Laffite also came with the expedition, but nothing suggests that this was Jean, as some have speculated. The identity of this man has not been determined.

17. Gene A. Smith, "Editor's Introduction," Arsené Lacarriere Latour, *Historical Memoir of the War in West Florida and Louisiana in 1814–1815* (1999 reprint, Gainesville, FL, 1999), pp. xiii–xv.

18. Pierre's first recorded appearance in New Orleans on March 21, 1803, and his apparent residence there afterward, places the outside date of early March 1803 on his departure from San Domingue.

19. In the Esau Glasscock letter dated November 1809, the writer speaks of visiting Pierre Laffite and meeting his son. Since only one child is mentioned, it was possibly—but not necessarily—this son, sometimes called Eugene. "He is the son of this Mr. Lafitte by a previous marriage," Glasscock wrote, possibly referring to Adelaide Maseleri as Pierre's first common-law wife. Lyle Saxon, in quoting the letter, says that the boy was Pierre, Jr., however, this does not appear in the quoted material from Glasscock's letter, and thus may be Saxon's embellishment (Esau Glasscock to Ned Glasscock, November 1809, in Lyle Saxon, *Lafitte the Pirate* [New York, 1930], p. 9; for the question of the authenticity of the Glasscock letter see below). Or if the boy was only four or five years old, then he could be a second son actually named Pierre. Other sources to be cited subsequently do establish that as of November 1809, Pierre had to have at least one or two children, a son Martin Firmin and/or his daughter Catherine Coralie, and perhaps even the first of his two sons named Jean, none of whom Glasscock seems to mention. Eugene might actually be this Jean, since phonetically the names are similar and may even come from the same root. If not a Pierre, Jr., then the boy Glasscock saw could have been Martin or Eugene.

A Eugene Laffite does not identifiably appear in the archives anywhere, but there is one reference to him in Pierre's own words. Writing to Jean Laffite on February 17, 1818, Pierre said that "my son Eugene is going to present himself to you" (Pierre Laffite to Jean Laffite, February 17, 1818,

Legajo 1900, Papeles de Cuba, Archivo General des Indias, Ayer Collection of Transcripts, Newberry Library, Chicago, IL [AGI-Newberry]). Clearly speaking of this same son at the same time, and in the same context, Felipe Fatio referred to "[Laffite's] son, a boy of 16 years," which places his birth circa 1802 (Fatio to captain general, February 18, 1818, Legajo 1900, AGI-Newberry).

Then there is the situation with Pierre's daughter Catherine, who later became known as Coralie Laffite, or his son Martin Firmin Laffite who in one document is listed—or misinterpreted—as Martial. So it could actually be that the boy Glasscock met was named Pierre Eugene, but in later years he was called Eugene to avoid confusion with his father. As suggested hereinafter, it is also possible that the son Eugene was an invention of Pierre's for a particular purpose in 1818.

TWO

1. C. C. Robin, *Voyages to the Interior of Louisiana, West Florida, and to the Islands of Martinique and Saint-Domingue During the Years 1802, 1803, 1804, 1805 and 1806* (Paris, France, 1807; edited and translated by Stuart O. Landry as *Voyage to Louisiana* [Gretna, LA, 2000]), p. 32.

2. Babb, French Refugees, p. 157.

3. Pierre Pedesclaux, Vol. 28, item 557, October 22, 1796, Vol. 5, item 588, December 10, 1800, Vol. 59, item 348, July 29, 1809, NONA; Square 48, Lot 18561, 18560, 18559, for 902–912 Royal Street, Vieux Carré Commission Archives, HNOC; "Index to Spanish Judicial Records of Louisiana," *Louisiana Historical Quarterly*, XII (April 1929), pp. 349–50, 353.

4. Marguerite Landreaux to Pierre Laffite and Joseph Maria Bourguignon, March 21, 1803, Notary Pierre Pedesclaux, Vol. 43, act 222-bis; Cancellation of obligation, June 6, 1803, Vol. 44, item 476, NONA. The former document refers to Laffite as being a resident of Royal Street in March. The latter document refers to Laffite and Bourguignon as "neighbors." Since the 1805 City Directory places Bourguignon on Dumaine Street, it seems reasonable to conclude that if they were neighbors, then Pierre's Royal Street residence was close to the Dumaine intersection.

5. The Works Projects Administration Index to Colonial Court Records, Louisiana State Museum, New Orleans (LSM), shows that Pedro Alarcon, innkeeper, shoemaker, and militiaman in March 21, 1791, had proceedings

instituted against him in 1803 for allowing gambling in his house. The reference is to an 1803 document, which was missing as of a 1980s inventory. It is
indexed to the same bound book as the Lafitte document detailed in note 8.

6. Pierre Laffite to Pedro Alarcon, Pierre Pedesclaux, Vol. 45, item 646,
NONA.

7. Cancellation of obligation, June 6, 1803, Notary Pierre Pedesclaux, Vol.
44, item 476, NONA. This document, in Spanish, is not easy to read and
interpret, but it seems apparent that it acknowledges the return of the
property and erasure of the debt. This is confirmed by the fact that on July
29, 1809, Marguerite Landreaux sold the same property to Louis Mil-
tenberger, demonstrating that she retained ownership long after 1803 (Notary Pierre Pedesclaux, Vol. 59, item 348, NONA). The survey for this lot
in the Vieux Carré Commission Archives at HNOC also fails to note any
Laffite-Bourguignon ownership, but confirms Landreaux's possession
throughout this period.

8. The origin of the idea that the Laffites kept a smithy when they first
came to New Orleans lies in an advertisement on the front page of the
New Orleans, *Le Moniteur de la Louisiane,* September 18, 1802, in which
Hearico and Lafitte, "blacksmiths and toolmakers," newly arrived in the
city, offer their services, especially for sugar and lumber mills, at their shop
near the church at the corner of the Place d'Arms. No Lafitte is listed in
the city directory at that time, nor any Hearico, though it is interesting
that in Spanish *"herrero"* meant blacksmith (Pierre Pedesclaux, Vol. 60,
item 497, October 9, 1810, NONA).

Further early advancement of the misconception may lie in an 1803
document indexed to Box 83, Book 4087, WPA Index, LSM. At the time
of indexing in the 1930s, the document stated that a "Pierre Lafitte," an
innkeeper, bought a slave at auction from an unidentified seller. There followed the two-word sentence "master blacksmith," which could mean that
either Lafitte or the slave was the blacksmith. Unfortunately, since being
indexed the original document has disappeared. Nevertheless, this does
show that in 1803, the same year that Pierre Laffite bought property in
New Orleans, there was an innkeeper named Pierre Lafitte who had a
smithing connection, and was perhaps Hearico's partner. Thereafter in
recollection a conflation of the two would have been natural.

By 1851 John R. Grymes, onetime Laffite attorney, and Kilby Smith
both thought they recalled that the Laffites had been blacksmiths, and
other old-timers agreed (New Orleans, *Daily Delta,* November 9, 1851;

"Editorial and Literary Department—Life and Times of Lafitte," *DeBow's Southern and Western Review*, XII [January 1852], p. 112). This appears to be the earliest published statement of the erroneous smithing. After that the acceptance of the misconception became virtually universal. The influential nineteenth-century Louisiana historian Charles E. A. Gayarré said that in his youth he knew well some of Laffites' former companions, clients, and moneyed associates, and he accepted the blacksmith tradition. That virtually implanted it in the Laffite story thereafter. The smithy, he said, had disappeared by the time of his lecture, which was delivered circa 1886, but he recalled that it was on the north side of St. Philip between Bourbon and Dauphine. This is the erroneous site traditionally associated with a Laffite smithy, which will be discussed hereafter ("Lecture on the Lafittes, No. 1," n.d., Gayarré Selected Papers, Louisiana State University, Baton Rouge [LSU]; Charles E. A. Gayarré, *The Story of Jean and Pierre Lafitte, The Pirate-Patriots* [New Orleans, 1938], p. 46). The imaginative John O. Dyer embellished the myth in the Galveston, *Daily News*, September 19, 1926, when he maintained—on no verifiable evidence—that the Laffite brothers formed a company in New Orleans called "Lafitte Freres," and bought slaves at auction and trained the better males to be blacksmiths. Early and influential Texas historian John Henry Brown actually declared in 1892 that the Laffite blacksmith shop "was standing until a few years ago" (John Henry Brown, *History of Texas From 1685 to 1892* [St. Louis, 1892], I, pp. 68–69).

Even before then, however, some saw through the confusion, like early Galveston historian Charles Hayes, who concluded in 1879 that there was a confusion between the Laffites and another Lafitte who was a blacksmith in New Orleans (Charles Hayes, *History of the Island and the City of Galveston* [Austin, Texas, 1974; reprint of destroyed Cincinnati, 1879 edition], p. 84). And if further evidence were needed, the Vieux Carré Survey for the intersection of Bourbon and St. Philip, the long-held traditional site of the supposed blacksmith shop, reveals that the property has an unbroken title from 1791 to 1833 with no Laffite mentioned (Square 76, Lot 18806, HNOC). The Survey report concludes that it is an ancient building but was never a forge and makes no connection other than lore to the Laffites. It does appear that the sometime Laffite associate Renato Beluche was the grandson of a onetime owner of the property, Jean Baptiste Laporte. A map survey indicates that the existing building today identified as "Lafitte's Blacksmith Shop" may have been built between 1722 and 1731.

9. 6.3 percent of the refugee males were mariners and one-fourth were merchants. Paul F. Lachance, "The 1809 Immigration of Saint Domingue Refugees to New Orleans," *Louisiana History,* XXIX (Spring 1988), p. 133.

10. Robin, *Voyages,* p. 36.

11. Francisco Mota, "The Adventures of Lafitte and the Pirates of Barataria," *Laffite Society Chronicles,* VI (August 1998), n.p., says without supporting documentation that Pierre opened a "boutique" on Royal Street to sell luxury goods.

12. Robin, *Voyages,* p. 97.

13. Rufus King to James Madison, March 17, 1803, *State Papers and Correspondence Bearing upon the Purchase of the Territory of Louisiana* (Washington, 1903), p. 146.

14. Ibid., pp. 286–88.

15. Robin, *Voyages,* p. 66.

16. David D. Porter, *Memoir of Commodore David Porter of the United States Navy* (Albany, NY, 1875), p. 73.

17. Proclamation, December 2, 1803, *State Papers and Correspondence,* pp. 288–89.

18. Babb, French Refugees, p. 161.

19. Robin, *Voyages,* p. 36.

20. Josephine Patin gave Laffite her power of attorney in a document, dated and signed at Baton Rouge by Laffite, which refers to him as "a merchant of this post." Power of Attorney, October 16, 1804, Archives of the Spanish Government of West Florida, Clerk of Court's Office, East Baton Rouge Parish Courthouse, Baton Rouge, LA.

21. Philip Pittman, *The Present State of the European Settlements on the Mississippi* (London, 1770), pp. 33–34.

22. Robin, *Voyages,* pp. 116–19.

23. Ibid., p. 98.

24. Alexander DeConde, *"This Affair of Louisiana"* (New York, 1976), pp. 220, 228.

25. Josephine Patin Power of Attorney, October 16, 1804, Archives of the Spanish Government of West Florida, Clerk of Court's Office, East Baton Rouge Parish Courthouse, Baton Rouge, LA.

26. Sale of slave, October 30, 1804, Archives of the Spanish Government of West Florida, Clerk of Court's Office, East Baton Rouge Parish Courthouse, Baton Rouge, LA. In these documents Folche and Grand-Pré both attest that they know Pierre Laffite and recognize his signature.

27. An inferential additional argument to support Pierre Laffite's being a resident of the Point Coupée area at this time is a statement in the New Orleans, *Daily Delta,* October 21, 1851, that there were at that time at Point Coupée a Colonel Morgan and a Colonel White who told many old stories of a Laffite. The newspaper no doubt meant Jean, but he was already often confused with Pierre.

28. Paul Lachance, "Repercussions of the Haitian revolution in Louisiana," David P. Geggus, ed., *The Impact of the Haitian Revolution in the Atlantic World* (Columbia, SC, 2001), pp. 211–12.

29. Robin, *Voyages,* pp. 116–19.

30. Petition to Governor Claiborne by Inhabitants of Point Coupée, November 9, 1804, Clarence Edwin Carter, ed., *The Territorial Papers of the United States, Volume IX: The Territory of Orleans 1803–1812* (Washington, 1940), pp. 326–27.

31. John Williams to William Brown, December 10, 1804, RG 36, Entry 1627, Records of Customs Houses in the Gulf States, New Orleans, LA, Letters Received, 1804–1899, NA.

32. Robin, *Voyages,* p. 53.

33. Laffite witnessed a slave sale in Baton Rouge, Julian Guedri to Clement Lacour, Record of sale, November 3, 1804, Archives of the Spanish Government of West Florida, Clerk of Court's Office, East Baton Rouge Parish Courthouse, Baton Rouge, LA.

34. Robin, *Voyages,* pp. 101–103.

35. This Galvezton is not to be confused with the Laffites' later haunts on Galveston Island in Texas.

36. Paul E. Hoffman, *Florida's Frontiers* (Bloomington, IN, 2002), p. 259.

37. Isaac Joslin Cox, *The West Florida Controversy, 1798–1813* (Baltimore, MD, 1918), p. 101; DeConde, *This Affair of Louisiana,* pp. 220, 228.

38. *State Papers and Correspondence,* p. 201.

39. Thomas Maitland Marshall, *A History of the Western Boundary of the Louisiana Purchase, 1819–1841* (Berkeley, CA, 1914), pp. 23–24.

40. Laffite's presence in New Orleans in February–March 1805 is established in the testimony in Marie Zabeth and infant vs. Pierre Lafitte, Case #131, Superior Court Suit Records 1804–1813, Louisiana Division, New Orleans Public Library (NOPL).

41. In the Petition of Stephen Carraby, July 29, 1805, Carraby refers to "Peter Lafitte a trader," and states that Laffite had no known property in the Orleans territory and was believed to be about "to depart from this country & territory." Stephen Carraby vs. Peter Lafitte, 1805, Civil Suit #71, County Court Records of Civil Suits, New Orleans City Archives, Louisiana Division, NOPL. The fact that Laffite does not appear in any of the extensive records of shipping duties and drawbacks in Entry 1656, Record of Drawbacks, 1795–1849, Record Group 36, Records of the U.S. Customs Service, New Orleans Collection District, National Archives, Washington, DC (citations from this source hereinafter are listed as RG for Record Group, and NA for National Archives), suggests that he was not importing or shipping goods abroad out of the port of New Orleans, but was limited to the upriver internal trade. The fact of his having no fixed domicile nor of owning any property is further established by the absence of any listing for him on Royal and Dumaine or anywhere else in New Orleans in 1805. *A Directory and A Census, Together With Resolutions Authorizing Same Now Printed For The First Time From The Original Manuscript* (Facsimile: New Orleans, 1936).

42. Marshall, *Western Boundary*, p. 22.

43. Stephen Carraby vs Peter Lafitte, 1805, Civil Suit #71, County Court Records of Civil Suits, New Orleans City Archives, Louisiana Division, NOPL.

44. "Stephen Caraby" advertised slaves for sale in the New Orleans, *Moniteur de la Louisiane,* February 18, 1804.

45. Williams to Brown, November 20, 1804, RG 36, Entry 1627, NA.

46. Notary Pierre Pedesclaux, Vol. 51, item 422, May 1, 1805, and Notary Narcisse Broutin, Vol. 11, item 418, May 27, 1815, NONA.

47. Juan Buatista Elie imported slaves from Havana as early as 1803. Notary Narcissus Broutin, Vol. 1, item 108, March 14, 1803, NONA.

48. Marie Zabeth and infant vs. Pierre Lafitte, Case #131, Superior Court Suit Records 1804–1813, NOPL.

49. Henry A. Kmen, *Music in New Orleans: The Formative Years 1791–1841* (Baton Rouge, 1966), pp. 43–48.

50. Sybil Kein, ed., *Creole: The History and Legacy of Louisiana's Free People of Color* (Baton Rouge, LA, 2000), pp. 66–69.

51. Lyle Saxon, *Old Louisiana* (New York, 1929), pp. 107, 109.

52. Ibid., p. 125.

53. It is evident that Marie and Pierre started their liaison as early as 1805, possibly even 1804, but no earlier than 1803, as Pierre only arrived in that year and Marie was a native and resident of Louisiana, and thus would not have come with him from San Domingue. One source covered hereinafter suggests that their first child, Catherine Coralie Laffite, was born in 1804–5, but it was probably somewhat later. Their son Martin Firmin or Martial Laffite was born about 1807–8. The Esau Glasscock letter in Saxon, *Lafitte*, p. 9, says that Pierre had a young son by a previous mistress living with him in November 1809, the boy who was almost certainly Pierre/Eugene Laffite, probably born in San Domingue. Glasscock also apparently wrote about Pierre's mistress at this time, but Saxon quotes nothing from the letter directly, and any text that Saxon himself inserted other than quotations is suspect as being susceptible to influence from other unreliable sources and Saxon's own imagination. For instance, he alleges that Glasscock commented on Laffite's mistress being unable to speak English "as she had lately come from Santo Domingo." Marie Louisa Villard was demonstrably Pierre's mistress as of November, as she had already had one and probably two children by him, yet she was a Louisiana native who had never been in San Domingue. Saxon is almost certainly embellishing the account in this instance by the assumption that Pierre's mistress at this time was Adelaide Maseleri, who was from San Domingue.

54. Marie Louise Villard's age and birth year are approximate. When she was buried on October 28, 1833, in the cemetery l'Eglise Cathedral and Parish of St. Louis, she was recorded as being aged "about 50," a native of the parish and the daughter of Marie Vilard, a free woman of color of the parish. (Funerals S-FPC Volume 10, Part 2 1833–1834, p. 219, entry #1426, Sacramental Archives of Archdiocese of New Orleans [SAANO].) That would place her birth circa 1783. On October 27, 1833, her death was recorded in the civil record both as Louise Marie Villard and also under the name Louise Marie Villard Ramos, and her age listed as forty-eight, which would place her birth in 1784–85 (New Orleans, Louisiana Death Records Index, 1804–1949, Vol. 4, p. 101, Vital Records Indices, State of Louisiana, Secretary of State, Division of Archives, Records Management, and History, Baton Rouge, LA [LDRI]). The 1830 Census for New

Orleans lists her as being between the ages of thirty-six and fifty-four, which does not help narrow her year of birth unfortunately (United States Census, 1830, Orleans Parish, North New Orleans, p. 28). Thus a birth year of 1784, and an age of twenty-one in 1805, represent a compromise among the sources available. She is sometimes confused with a Marie Louise Villars who was born in 1791 and baptized March 14, 1793, at St. Louis Cathedral (Book 5, folio 36, entry 131, SAANO). The evidence of earlier Villards includes a power of attorney by a Margarite or Marguerite Villard on December 24, 1799, on behalf of her infant son Juan Bautista Villard, as well as property dealings showing that this Marguerite owned a house on Orleans Street since about 1800 if not before. It is possible that she is one and the same with Marie Villard's mother Marie, as given names at the time were somewhat fluid in the polyglot culture of New Orleans (Margarita Villard, free mulatto, power of attorney to Celestino Lavergne, Notary Narcisse Broutin, Vol. 1, item 282; Margueritte Villard to Joseph Defaucheux, February 24, 1813, Notary Pierre Pedesclaux, Vol. 66, item 55, NONA). The Villards/Villars may have come originally from San Domingue prior to the revolutions there (Babb, French Refugees, p. 147).

55. Petition of Stephen Carraby, July 29, 1805, Peter Lafitte summons, July 30, 1805, Stephen Carraby vs. Peter Lafitte, 1805, Civil Suit #71, County Court Records of Civil Suits, New Orleans City Archives, NOPL.

56. This is an assumption based on the absence of any New Orleans notarial documents showing a property ownership by Marie Villard or Pierre Laffite during this time.

57. Pierre Laffite to Simon Marin, November 8, 1805, Pierre Laffite to Sebastian Giriare, November 18, 1805, Pierre Pedesclaux, Vol. 51, item 879, NONA.

58. Laffite to Joseph Hotard, January 8, 1806, Pierre Pedesclaux, Vol. 52, item 15; Laffite to Eugene Fortier, January 16, 1806, item 32; Laffite to Abraham Guitrau, February 1805, item 86; Laffite to Nicholas Le Blanc, February 5, 1806, item 90; Laffite to Fortier, February 14, 1806, item 120; Laffite to Paul F. DuBourg, April 7, 1806, Narcisse Broutin, Vol. 12, item 164, NONA.

THREE

1. In "The Cruise of the Enterprise," p. 42, the author—identified only as "T"—has what is presumed to be Jean Laffite saying that "eighteen years

ago I was a merchant in San Domingo." Much of the article is clearly imaginary, however, and this statement is too thin to serve as basis for a definite assertion that Jean, like Pierre, was in business in San Domingue.

2. One of the earliest accounts of Jean Laffite's pre-Louisiana years has him sailing the Indian Ocean and elsewhere and amassing huge booty as an outright pirate before coming to Barataria, after which he was less audacious. This account is very imaginary and it is hard to tell from whence it sprang, as it predates most of the secondhand accounts collected by Lamar and Bollaert in the 1840s. This account also appears to be the origin of the myth that Jean commanded *La Confiance*, a ship that appears in spurious twentieth-century documents allegedly derived from Laffite himself. Charles Ellms, *The Pirates Own Book, or Authentic Narratives of the Lives, Exploits, and Executions of the Most Celebrated Sea Robbers* (Portland, ME, 1837), p. 58.

3. Claiborne to Pierre Lausat, April 14, 1804, Dunbar Rowland, ed., *Official Letter Books of W. C. C. Claiborne 1801–1816* (Jackson, MS, 1917), II, p. 97.

4. Robin, *Voyages*, pp. 267–68.

5. Claiborne to Robert Davis, April 24, 1804, Rowland, *Letter Books*, II, p. 100; John Watkins to Claiborne, April 24, 1804, p. 276; Claiborne to James Madison, April 25, 1804, Carter, *Territorial Papers*, p. 234.

6. Claiborne to Pierre Lausat, April 14, 1804, Rowland, *Letter Books*, II, p. 97.

7. Sylvie Feuillie says that he was Pierre Laffite, but there is no documentary evidence to confirm this (Feuillie, "La Guerre de Course Française," part 3, p. 96). Stanley Clisby Arthur, *Jean Laffite, Gentleman Rover* (New Orleans, 1952), pp. 9–14, also identifies Pierre as being the captain, though Arthur is highly unreliable. As a case in point, on the same page that he identifies Pierre as the ship's captain, Arthur then places Pierre in Baton Rouge in October 1806 based on documents clearly dated 1804. The fact that Pierre Laffite was demonstrably in Baton Rouge in October 1804— not 1806—two months after the vessel left New Orleans eliminates him as a candidate for being its captain. Harris Gaylord Warren, *The Sword was Their Passport: A History of American Filibustering in the Mexican Revolution* (Baton Rouge, LA, 1943), p. 97n, identifies this captain as Louis Laffite, though without authority.

8. New Orleans, *Moniteur de la Louisiane*, February 18, 1804.

9. For more on this see Stanley Faye, "Privateers of Guadaloupe and their Establishment in Barataria," *Louisiana Historical Quarterly*, XXIII (April 1940).

10. Sylvie Feuillie, "Dominique Youx and *La Superbe*," *The Life and Times of Jean Laffite*, IX (Spring 1989), p. 2; Coüet de Montaraud to General Turreau, July 29, 1807, Correspondence Politique, Etats-Unis Supplément, Volume 38, Ministere des Affaires Etrangeres, Paris, France.

11. Feuillie, "Dominique Youx," pp. 2–3.

12. Claiborne to James Madison, April 22, 1805, Jared William Bradley, ed., *Interim Appointment: W. C. C. Claiborne Letter Book, 1804–1805* (Baton Rouge, LA, 2002), p. 237.

13. Several protests over these seizures were filed and will be found in Narcissus Broutin, Vol. II, NONA.

14. Drawbacks, various 1805, Records of the Bureau of Customs, Records of Customs houses in the Gulf States, New Orleans, LA, Record of Drawbacks, 1795–1849, Entry 1656, RG 36, NA.

15. James and David Young vs. Jean Blanque July 10, 1806, Case #0024, United States District Court for the Eastern Region of Louisiana, New Orleans, RG 21, General Case Files, 1806–1932, Entry 21, National Archives—Southwest Region, Fort Worth, TX (NAFW).

16. Drawbacks, May 18, 1805, March 31, 1806, Entry 1656, RG 36, NA; New Orleans, *Louisiana Gazette*, August 3, 19, 1806.

17. New Orleans, *Louisiana Gazette*, July 22, 25, August 5, 1806.

18. John Smith Kendall, "The Huntsmen of Black Ivory," *Louisiana Historical Quarterly*, XXIV (January 1941), pp. 10–11.

19. Jean Louis Fossier to Jacques Reynard, October 8, 1803, Notary St. Amand, item 1894, Afro-Louisiana History and Genealogy, 1718–1820 (Slave), Web site.

20. Orleans Parish tax list, June 3, 1784, Afro-Louisiana History and Genealogy, 1718–1820 (Slave), Web site.

21. Smith, "Editor's Introduction," Latour, *Historical Memoir*, pp. xvii–xviii; Succession of Elias Beauregard, n.d. Records of Spanish West Florida, XIX, p. 495.

22. It is sometimes suggested that the Laffites were involved in Aaron

Burr's celebrated "conspiracy" to conquer the Spanish province of Texas and create a new western empire. In the James Judge Collection, Northwestern State University of Louisiana, Natchitoches (NSUL), an essay entitled "The Great Southwest Pirate," presumably written by Judge, avers that Aaron Burr "was said to have" sought Jean Laffite's aid in his plan. Burr and General James Wilkinson are even supposed to have offered to make Laffite the "Commander of their Naval Fleet," but Laffite refused. No sources are given for these statements, and they may be safely put down to local mythology and overactive imagination. The Laffites almost certainly neither knew of nor participated in the affair. Jean Laffite was seemingly nowhere near Louisiana at the time, and in late 1806 when Burr came down the Ohio River to the Mississippi prior to being stopped and arrested, Pierre Laffite was in Pensacola.

23. It is an assumption that Marie went to Pensacola with Laffite, based on the fact that in the period 1806–9, she bore him at least two children, neither of which had birth or baptism recorded in the registers at St. Louis Cathedral. All of Pierre and Marie's children born after 1812 were so baptized and recorded, however, with both parents invariably present. The most logical explanation for the break in this pattern of baptism is that the parents and the infants were absent from New Orleans at the time of birth and for sometime thereafter. Record of any baptisms in Pensacola, if they took place, were likely lost with the official archives in 1818.

24. Pierre Laffite statement, April 21, 1806, Pierre Pedesclaux, Vol. 52, item 335, NONA.

25. Pierre could have returned to New Orleans on any of several vessels that came in from Pensacola after May 31 but prior to June 15, including the *Bonaparte,* the *Orleans Packet,* the brig *Alert,* or the schooner *Ann.* New Orleans, *Louisiana Gazette,* June 10, 13, 17, 1806.

26. Pedro Laralde to Pedro Lafite, Power of Attorney, May 21, 1806, Pierre Pedesclaux, Vol. 52, item 429, NONA. In this document, filed in Spanish and therefore using the given name Pedro rather than Pierre, Laffite is described as being "actualmente de la Plaza de Pensacola"— "presently in the Post of Pensacola." On May 31, 1806, when Eugene Fortier sold a slave to Laffite, it was done in New Orleans through a representative of Pierre's with power of attorney, noting that he was then still in Pensacola (Fortier to Laffite, May 31, 1806, Pierre Pedesclaux, Vol. 52, item 454, NONA).

27. William St. Marc vs. Lafitte and Garidel, Case #3117, City Court Suit Records, NOPL.

28. Robin, *Voyages*, pp. 4–5, 25, 27–29, 31.

29. Pierre Pedesclaux, Vol. 43, item 524, June 25, 1803, NONA.

30. Pierre was in New Orleans until April 21 at least, and was in Pensacola by May 21, 1806. The New Orleans, *Louisiana Gazette*, April 25, 1806, shows the *Louisa*, Captain LaCoste, having just cleared for Pensacola.

31. Certificate of Registration of schooner *Louisa*, May 1, 1818, New Orleans Certificates of Registration, 1818–1819, Entry 156, Records of the Bureau of Marine Inspection and Navigation, RG 41, NA.

32. Only one ship cleared New Orleans bound for Pensacola between June 15 and July 1 and that was the *Louisa*, under Captain LaCoste. The *Gazette* was published every Tuesday and Friday, and July 1 was a Tuesday, meaning the ship cleared sometime after the previous Friday issue of June 27 went to press, so it could have departed even a day earlier on June 26. New Orleans, *Louisiana Gazette*, July 1, 1806.

33. L. N. McAlister, "Pensacola During the Second Spanish Period," *Florida Historical Quarterly*, XXXVII (January–April 1959), p. 300.

34. Henry M. Brackenridge, *A Topographical Description of Pensacola and Vicinity in 1821* (Bagdad, FL, 1991), p. 6.

35. Pensacola, *Gazette*, December 4, 1824.

36. Brackenridge, *Description*, pp. 10–11.

37. Ibid., p. 6.

38. Bread brought 12.5 cents a pound, double its New Orleans price, and butter ran 37.8 to 50 cents a pound in the summer and more in winter. Robin, *Voyages*, pp. 1–2.

39. Ibid., pp. 4–5.

40. Brackenridge, *Topographical Description*, pp. 1–3.

41. Robin, *Voyages*, pp. 9–11.

42. Ibid., p. 9.

43. McAlister, "Pensacola," pp. 300–7.

44. William Coker and G. Douglas Inglis, *The Spanish Census of Pensacola,*

1784–1820: A Genealogical Guide to Spanish Pensacola (Pensacola, FL, 1980), pp. 89–90.

45. McAlister, "Pensacola," p. 309; Robin, *Voyages,* p. 4.

46. Record of slave sale, July 6, 1806, document #78, Archives of the Spanish Government of West Florida, Volume 11, Clerk of Court's Office, East Baton Rouge Parish Courthouse, Baton Rouge, LA.

47. William St. Marc vs. Pierre Lafitte and Ambroise Garidel, Case #3117, City Court Suit Records, NOPL.

48. When West Florida was being turned over to the United States, the ship *Peggy of Portsmouth* was engaged to carry the governor and sixty-two boxes containing civil and administrative papers from Pensacola to Havana. Unfortunately, virtually all of the official archives were lost overboard in a hurricane on September 10, 1818. Hence, what documentation there might have been of Laffite's time in Pensacola disappeared forever (Notary John Lynd, Vol. 15, item 1005, NONA). What can be determined about Pierre's Pensacola activity derives solely from a handful of New Orleans notarial and court documents, and inference. The fact that he completely disappears from the documentary record from the July 10, 1806, slave sale until a July 1809 transaction in New Orleans, suggests that he spent the intervening three years away from Louisiana, as does the fact that William St. Marc did not seek redress in court for the unlawful sale of Lubin until 1810. Had Laffite been within reach earlier than that, St. Marc presumably would have acted earlier.

49. No record of Catherine Coralie Laffite's birth or baptism have been found, but she is unquestionably the daughter of Pierre and Marie, and her birth has to be traced to this period. She is first mentioned—as Catarina—as a sponsor or godparent at the baptism of her younger sister Rosa Laffite on March 22, 1814 (Baptismal Book 27, item 3, SAANO). She married Pierre Roup in about 1826, and at the birth of their son Charles Roup, November 3, 1827, the boy's maternal grandparents were recorded as being "Pierre Lafitte, dec[eased]. and Marie Louise Vilard" (Charles E. Nolan and Dorenda Dupont, eds., *Sacramental Records of the Roman Catholic Church of the Archdiocese of New Orleans, Volume 18, 1828–1829* [New Orleans, 2003], p. 352). At the baptism of Catherine's daughter Rose Roup on March 8, 1829, the baby was listed as the grandchild of Marie Villard (Baptismal Book 39, p. 265, SAANO). When Catherine's daughter Catherine Roup was born March 25, 1830, her mother is listed as being the daughter

of "Marie Louise Vilard and Pierre Lafitte deceased." The godmother to Catherine was Marie Louise Vilard, her grandmother (Baptismal Book 41, p. 181, act #1070, SAANO).

Sources disagree as to when she was likely born. The official register of her death as "Mrs. Pierre Roup, colored," on July 22, 1855, shows her to be aged fifty, which would put her birth at 1804–5, which seems too early (Louisiana Birth Records Index, 1790–1899, Volume 14, p. 357, Vital Records Indices, Louisiana Division of Archives, Records Management, and History, Baton Rouge [LBRI]). The 1850 Orleans Parish Census, 1st Ward, 3d Municipality, p. 90, lists "Coralie Roupe" as a free woman of color aged thirty-eight, putting her birth at 1811–12, which is clearly unlikely as her younger sister Rosa was born in August 1812. Considering the nonchalance of people of the time about their ages when asked, 1806–7 seems a reasonable birth year for Catherine Laffite.

The birth of Martin Firmin Laffite, Catherine's brother, is even more difficult to fix. He appeared with Catherine as a sponsor at their sister Rosa's baptism, so clearly his birth predated Rosa's. His marriage in 1828 to seventeen-year-old Silvania Brunetti lists him as the son of "Pierre Laffitte and Maria Louisa Vilar," and suggests that he would have been at least the same age as she if not older, putting his birth around 1810 or earlier (Marriage Book 3, p. 91, SAANO; Sylvania Catherine Brunetti death record, August 20, 1844, Vol. 10, p. 286, LDRI). Other than his marriage record and a few appearances as a witness, he disappears from the documentary evidence. However, there are frequent appearances of a Martial Laffite in association with the Roup family. Martial was one of the witnesses to the inventory of Pierre Roup's estate on Catherine Roup's behalf (Succession for Pierre Roup, April 15, 1836, Orleans Parish Court of Probates, Louisiana Division, NOPL). Martial Laffite and Rosa Laffite are the godparents of Catherine Roup's daughter Rose, cited above, strengthening the probability that Martin and Martial are one and the same. Martial Laffite also appeared as godparent at the baptism of Rosa Laffite's daughter Louise Tessier on September 29, 1848 (Baptism Book 28, p. 394, SAANO). Certainly "Martial" and "Martin" could easily be misread for one another in the handwriting of the time. If they are the same person, something happened in the marriage to Silvania Brunetti, for by 1832 she was having children by another man listed as her husband, while Martial Laffite and Celette Durel had a daughter on October 1, 1833 (Vol. 4, p. 93, LDRI). Thereafter "Marshal Lafite," a mulatto, appeared in the 1850 census, Orleans Parish, 1st Ward, 3d Municipality, p. 91, living with his daughter and a Mario Durel, and is listed as age forty-two, meaning birth in about 1807–8. Perhaps significantly, he is living just nineteen doors away from Coralie Roup, and she is living next door to Catiche Villard, who was probably Marie Louisa Villard's sister Catherine, as will be discussed hereafter. Thus 1807–8 seems a likely birth year for Martin/Martial Laffite.

50. The attribution of a Jean Baptiste Laffite to Pierre and Marie is somewhat conjectural. In the Sacramental Archives in New Orleans a record on a page that is now missing can be partially reconstructed from the surviving index. It indicates that a Jean Baptiste Lafitte, a free male of color, was baptized on May 20, 1811, the son of a father whose name does not appear, and a mother named "de Villars" (Baptismal Book 24, p. 47, SAANO). Villard often appears as Villars in the records of this time. It cannot be established definitively that this Jean Baptiste was the son of Pierre Laffite and Marie Villard, but it seems probable, and therefore he is mentioned in the text. He may not have lived more than a few years, hence Pierre and Marie naming another son Jean in 1816.

51. A Marguerite Villard and a Catherine Valiere were then free women of color living in New Orleans, and owning property. They may have been Marie's relations. Antoine Augustin to Catherine Valiere, December 21, 1807, Pierre Pedesclaux, Vol. 57, item 481; Marguerite note to Henry Metzinger, Pierre Pedesclaux, Vol. 56, item 78, NONA. We can only guess when Catherine or Catiche joined the household. Saxon, *Lafitte*, p. 55, says he was told by a descendant of Pierre and Marie's that Catherine was aged thirteen in 1811, and (p. 65) also says that she was called Jeanette. Saxon did not identify this descendant, but it would have been one of the Allnets or their immediate family.

52. Philadelphia, *American Daily Advertiser*, October 31, 1806.

53. Luis Marino Pérez, *Guide to the Materials for American History in Cuban Archives* (Washington, 1907), p. 105.

54. The Heloise Cruzat Papers, University of Florida, Gainesville, contain a listing of debtors for the year 1807 that includes many Pensacola residents, but not Pierre Laffite.

55. Wilburt S. Brown, *The Amphibious Campaign for West Florida and Louisiana, 1814–1815: A Critical Study of Strategy and Tactics at New Orleans* (University, AL, 1969), p. 47.

56. Joe G. Taylor, "The Foreign Slave Trade in Louisiana After 1808," *Louisiana History*, I (Winter 1960), pp. 37–38.

57. Aury to J. Maignet and wife, September 8, 1808, Louis Aury Papers, CAHUT.

58. David D. Porter, *Memoir of Commodore David Porter of the United States Navy* (Albany, NY, 1875), pp. 75, 78.

59. Ibid., p. 76.

60. Ibid., p. 79.

FOUR

1. On March 16, 1809, a Pierre Lafite bought two slaves from the estate of William Dangerfield. The sales instrument is supposed to be on file in the Point Coupée Parish Courthouse at New Roads, LA, but could not be found to verify that the signature is that of Pierre Laffite. It is referenced as document 15-A-036-005-1809, Afro-Louisiana History and Genealogy, 1718–1820 (Slave), Web site http://www.ibiblio.org/laslave/

2. Luis M. Perez, "French Refugees to New Orleans in 1809," *Publications of the Southern History Association,* IX (September 1905), pp. 293–94.

3. Paul Lachance, "The 1809 Immigration of Saint-Domingue Refugees to New Orleans: Reception, Integration, and Impact," *Louisiana History,* XXIX (Spring 1998), p. 112; Babb, French Refugees, p. 76.

4. New Orleans, *Moniteur de la Louisiane,* January 27, 1810.

5. Lachance, "Repercussions of the Haitian revolution in Louisiana," Geggus, *Haitian Revolution,* pp. 213–14.

6. Babb, French Refugees, pp. 190–91, 197.

7. Gene A. Smith, *Thomas ap Catesby Jones, Commodore of Manifest Destiny* (Annapolis, MD, 2000), p. 17.

8. Porter to Hamilton, March 10, April 7, 1810, Letters Received by the Secretary of the Navy from Commanders, 1804–1886, M147, NA.

9. United States vs. Schooner *Santa Rita,* July 10, 1810, Case #0251, NAFW.

10. Libel, June 17, 1809, arrest order June 17, 1809, claim July 3, 1809, United States vs. Schooner *Louisa,* Case #0217, NAFW.

11. New Orleans, *Louisiana Gazette,* July 4, 1809.

12. Perez, "French Refugees," pp. 293, 297–304.

13. Lachance, "Immigration," pp. 119–20.

14. Pierre Laffite to Fernando Alzar, July 31, 1809, Notary Pierre Pedesclaux, Vol. 59, item 354, NONA.

15. Pierre Laffite to Miguel Da Peña, September 28, 1809, Narcissus Broutin, Vol. 20-A, item 510, NONA.

16. Registry of Free Persons of Color, NOPL.

17. In Kingston, Jamaica, in 1810 the children of Alexander Lafitte were the heirs of their late uncle Louis Victor Dufour of Jérémie, San Domingue, who died in Santiago, Cuba, in January 1809. In September 1809, in New Orleans, Alexander Lafitte filed suit to recover some of the estate of more than $150,000. In the suit the Lafitte children are named, and none of them correspond with any known names attached to the family of Pierre and Jean Laffite. Nevertheless, this Alexander may be the origin of the early assumption that there was a third Laffite brother in New Orleans, for which no contemporary proof has been found. Quite certainly this is the wealthy Cuban Lafitte family that has more recently been confused with Jean and Pierre. Alexander Lafitte vs. Laroque and Carlier Doutremer, #2275, #2573, Orleans Territory Superior Court Suit Records, NOPL.

18. Lachance, "Immigration," pp. 116–17.

19. For excellent background on French privateering in the Caribbean in this period, though with little directly relating to the Laffites, see Sylvie Feuillie's articles "La Guerre de Course Française aux Antilles Durant la Revolution et l'Empire," in five parts in *La Revue Maritime*, Numbers 427–430.

20. As early as 1864 Dominique was being confused as a Laffite brother, based apparently on nothing more than the misconception that he was a close associate of the brothers, whereas first to last he appears to have been an independent operator. Charles Havens Hunt, *Life of Edward Livingston* (New York, 1864), p. 203, refers to "the character of Jean Lafitte, of his brothers Pierre and Dominique, and of their band. . . ." Gayarré, "Pierre and Jean Lafitte," lecture no. 2, Gayarré Papers, LSU, says there was a third Laffite brother, unnamed because of his youth, and that all three settled in 1816. He offers no evidence for the claim.

21. Stanley Faye, "Commodore Aury," CAHUT I, pp. 6, 9, 10.

22. Caryn Cossé Bell, *Revolution, Romanticism, and the Afro-Creole Protest Tradition in Louisiana 1718–1868* (Baton Rouge, LA, 1997), pp. 37, 42.

23. Alfred Toledano Wellborn, "The Relations Between New Orleans and Latin America, 1810–1824," *Louisiana Historical Quarterly*, XXII (July 1939), pp. 751–53.

24. Perhaps the earliest explanation of Jean's activities pre-1809 came in Bollaert, "Lafitte," p. 435, when Bollaert said that in 1842 an informant at Galveston, Lambert, told him that Jean came to Barataria in 1807 and that for some time before the operation commenced Jean was taking Spanish ships as a privateer while Pierre acted as his agent in New Orleans and that Jean even occasionally made voyages to Havana. But Lambert was not entirely reliable, for he also said that Jean was the elder of the two, and that Marc Lafitte, New Orleans notary and no relation, was a third brother. The Laffites are not linked by name to the early complaints about smuggling at New Orleans, and though Faye speculates that they were the town agents for merchant Joseph Sauvinet, he offers no evidence. Faye, "Great Stroke," pp. 746–47. Dyer in the Galveston, *Daily News*, May 9, 1920, maintained on no authority that Laffite did not sail because he suffered from seasickness, and had been a sugar planter in the West Indies until 1809. Jean's name does not appear on a list of thirty-four ships and captains that brought refugees to New Orleans prior to July 10, 1809. Robert Smith to Philip Grymes, August 16, 1809, Minutes of the United States District Court for the Eastern District of Louisiana, 1806–1814, II, pp. 130–31, M-1082, RG 21, NA.

25. Arsené Lacarriere Latour, *Historical Memoir of the War in West Florida and Louisiana in 1814–1815* (Philadelphia, 1816), p. 13.

26. New Orleans, *Daily Picayune*, August 27, 1844.

27. Faye, "Stroke," p. 746, says that in 1808 Pierre set up an establishment on Grand Terre to capitalize on this contraband trade, but offers no evidence.

28. Saxon, *Lafitte*, p. 3. Unfortunately, the earliest unmistakable reference to Jean Laffite in Louisiana comes in a document that may no longer survive, and which an extensive search has failed to locate. Thus we are dependent on Saxon, *Lafitte*, pp. 3–11, for what we know of its contents. The problem is that Saxon quoted only selections from the letter, and interspersed those with narrative embellishments. Consequently, some have questioned that the document ever existed, maintaining that the account, including the quotations, was entirely Saxon's fictionalization.

The document was a letter written from eighteen-year-old Esau Glasscock of Concordia Parish, Louisiana, to his brother Edward. Saxon

obtained it from one of two sources. One probability is William Glasscock, a frequent social associate of Saxon's in the bar of the St. Charles
Hotel in New Orleans. The other possibility is Mrs. Elizabeth Dix Perrault of Natchez, who made her family papers available to Lyle Saxon
when he was researching his book *Old Louisiana* (New York, 1929), and he
subsequently credited her with contributing materials for *Lafitte the Pirate*,
published in 1930. She was a great-niece of Thomas's son Esau (Saxon, *Old
Louisiana*, pp. 272ff). Elizabeth Perrault's family papers have passed to her
granddaughter Anna Calhoun, who confirms that the Esau Glasscock letter is not among the things she has, and that she does not now recall the
document (Anna Calhoun to the author, August 19, 2003).

We are left to wonder what might have become of the letter. Of one
thing we may be certain. Saxon did not invent the letter or those portions
of its contents that he *quoted*. Saxon is often derided as a mere fictionalist.
Certainly he was not a historian in our accepted definition of the word.
However, when Saxon dealt with historical documents, his only vice was
correcting spelling and adding punctuation, and when he put such material
in quotations it is clear that he was dealing with an actual document. On balance logic insists that Saxon had a genuine source document in front of him.

29. While Saxon assumes that Glasscock's "notorious Captain Lafitte" was
Jean, nothing in the material quoted indicates which of the brothers young
Esau meant. Moreover, on what basis would he have referred to either as
"captain" in late 1809? There is no evidence that Pierre ever commanded a
vessel, and the earliest firm evidence we have of Jean doing so does not
come until 1813, to be discussed subsequently. Glasscock's use of the title
might indicate that one of the Laffites was commonly known as "captain,"
whether or not he commanded merchant or privateering craft. Since the
Glasscock letter puts Jean on Grand Terre at least occasionally as of late
1809, he might have been acting as overlord or "*bos*" of the smugglers operating there, and thus have been acknowledged as "captain." Moreover,
men in charge of numbers of slaves were sometimes honorifically called
"captain," though this seems the least likely explanation.

With the word "notorious," again questions arise. What had either
Laffite done as of the end of 1809 to be regarded as "notorious"? Moreover,
considering that the Glasscocks came from Concordia Parish, some two
hundred river miles upstream from New Orleans, we have to ask what the
Laffites had done to earn an unsavory reputation so far from home, though
of course Glasscock could mean only that Laffite was notorious in New Orleans. One portion of the Glasscock letter that is paraphrased by Saxon is a

conversation between Thomas Glasscock and John R. Grymes, in which Grymes suggests the Laffites as a source of slaves, and Glasscock protests that he has heard that the Laffites are outlaws. Perhaps this is the origin of their notoriety, though it is interesting that Glasscock might think they were outlaws when neither Laffite would run afoul of the law until 1812.

Is it possible that the notoriety applied to Pierre and that it derived from his dealings in and around Baton Rouge and West Florida a few years earlier? The Glasscock letter thus generates more questions than it answers, yet it remains the earliest really "human" document to get us to grips with the Laffites in the years before they genuinely became notorious.

30. Joseph O. Dyer in Galveston, *Daily News,* September 19, 1926, maintained that Jean Laffite began by "fencing" for the privateers, and while he offered no sources for the assumption, it is certainly what he was doing a year later in 1810. Charles E. A. Gayarré, *History of Louisiana. The American Domination* (New Orleans, 1866), IV, pp. 303–4, maintains that the Laffites began as agents of the Baratarian smugglers, but wound up becoming their leaders.

31. Esau Glasscock's description of his father being taken to Grand Terre by Jean to buy slaves is confirmation that the Laffites were already involved in the illegal importation of slaves. Thus the slave sales conducted by Pierre in the months immediately before and after the Glasscocks' visit are probably documentary proofs of the illicit family business.

32. There is no evidence that Pierre rented a house, but the absence of any land transaction at NONA for a house in either his name or Marie's in the period 1809–13 suggests that he most likely rented or leased. There is a Marie Louise, free woman of color, living on St. Ann in New Orleans (1810 Census, Orleans Parish, p. 232).

33. New Orleans, *Louisiana Courier,* September 26, 1814; Glasscock letter in Saxon, *Lafitte,* p. 9. All references to the Glasscock letter are to direct quotations and not material added or paraphrased by Saxon. These are the earliest directly contemporary descriptions of the two men, and the description of Pierre matches perfectly his description on his 1802 passport. It should be added that they comport well with other contemporary descriptions of the Laffites by those who knew them. An anonymous writer in 1863 penned a portrait of Jean, with whom he said he boarded about this time, and it matches Glasscock's perfectly, stating that Jean was handsome, with black eyes and hair, a fair complexion, and wore narrow whiskers down each cheek and around the chin. New Orleans, *Daily Picayune,* August 20, 1871.

34. Glasscock letter in Saxon, *Lafitte*, p. 11; Deposition of James Connel, July 1813, United States vs. Juan Juanilleo, Case #0774, NAFW. In his testimony Connel speaks of Jean Lafite as "the larger of the two Brothers of that name." Since Pierre was described rather precisely as being five feet, ten inches tall, this would seem to agree with otherwise circumstantial later accounts that have Jean standing six feet tall or even six feet, two inches. Connel's is the earliest known physical description of Jean Laffite that survives in the original. People in Galveston in 1839 recalled that "he was tall and finely formed" (Newark, NJ, *Newark Daily Advertiser*, February 12, 1840). In ca. 1840 James Gaines, who met Jean in 1819, described him to William Bollaert as being well built, six feet, two inches tall, with large hazel eyes, black hair, usually with a mustache (Bollaert, "Lafitte," p. 442). That year John Ijams, who as a boy saw Jean at Galveston, described him as six feet tall "and rather stout" (Galveston, *Weekly News*, October 11, 1883). J. Randal Jones, *A Visit to Galveston Island in 1818*, Rosenberg Library, Galveston, TX, says that Jean "was a man about six feet in height." The date of this fragmentary recollection is unclear, but it was prior to his death in 1873, and more likely in the 1840s or 1850s when Lamar was collecting Laffite information. An anonymous writer in 1863 penned a portrait of Jean, with whom he said he boarded about this time, and it matches Glasscock's perfectly, stating that Jean was handsome, with black eyes and hair, a fair complexion, and wore narrow whiskers down each cheek and around the chin. New Orleans, *Daily Picayune*, August 20, 1871.

35. Galveston *Gazette*, quoted in Newark, NJ, *Daily Advertiser*, February 12, 1840. Though some years after the fact, this is still a very early description of Jean Laffite, and has much to recommend its veracity. For one thing, the writer makes reference to Laffite's 1815–16 winter in Washington, the only such reference to appear in print prior to Saxon in 1930, showing that the description came from a source with at least some firsthand information. The mention of Laffite shutting one eye is also interesting and indicates firsthand observation. This is the first reference to be found until J. H. Ingraham, "Life and Times of Lafitte," *DeBow's Southern and Western Review*, XI (October 1851), pp. 372–87, and was probably the source for Ingraham's otherwise fictionalized account. This 1840 article is the earliest known compilation of the recollections of Charles Cronea, James Campbell, Stephen Churchill, and others who claimed to have known Laffite.

36. Glasscock letter in Saxon, *Lafitte*, p. 11; "Lafitte," undated notes in Lamar Papers, TSL; Kmen, *Music*, pp. 46–48.

37. Smith, "Editor's Introduction," Latour, *Historical Memoir*, pp. xviii–xix; New Orleans, *Louisiana Gazette*, September 21, 1810.

38. New Orleans, *Louisiana Gazette*, Nov. 14, 1809. It is clear from Jean's October 1814 letter to Livingston, dealt with hereafter, that they are not at all close or intimate friends, nor is there any evidence that Livingston did any legal work for the Laffites prior to 1815.

39. Babb, French Refugees, p. 304.

40. Lachance, "Immigration," p. 115.

41. Babb, French Refugees, p. 79.

42. Henry C. Castellanos, *New Orleans as It Was: Episodes of Louisiana Life* (New Orleans, 1895), pp. 39–40.

43. See Cases #0363, 0379, 0380, 0381, and 0401, NAFW; Porter, *Memoir*, pp. 79–81.

44. Porter to Hamilton, April 7, 1810, M147, NA.

45. Porter to Hamilton, May 5, 1810, M147, NA; United States vs. *Duc de Montebello*, verdict, July 24, 1810, Minutes, II, p. 238, M-1082, RG 21, NA.

46. Porter to Hamilton, May 4, 5, 7, 1810, M147, NA.

47. Porter to Hamilton, May 12, 21, 1810, M147, NA.

48. Porter, *Memoir*, pp. 78–81.

49. United States vs. *Amiable Lucy*, October 25, 1810, Minutes, II, p. 265, M-1082, RG 21, NA.

50. Porter, *Memoir*, p. 82.

51. New Orleans, *Louisiana Gazette*, April 12, 17, 1810.

52. New Orleans, *Louisiana Gazette*, April 17, 1810.

53. New Orleans, *Louisiana Gazette*, April 12, 1810.

54. Edward Livingston to James Madison, Oct. 24, 1814, James Madison Papers, Library of Congress, states that privateers had "for four years past brought their prizes to the Bay of Barataria in this State." Latour, *Memoir*, pp. 14–15, 16, agrees on the four-year duration. Felipe Fatio to José Cienfuegos, May 24, 1817, Legajo 1900, AGI-Newberry, also in Harris Gaylord Warren, "Documents Relating to the Establishment of Privateers at Galveston, 1816–1817," *Louisiana Historical Quarterly*, XXI (October 1938), p. 15, states that the Laffites started their Barataria operation in 1810.

55. Walker Gilbert to Thomas Williams, January 20, 1810, Entry 1627, RG 36, NA.

56. Robert C. Vogel, "Jean Laffite, the Baratarians, and the Historical Geography of Piracy in the Gulf of Mexico," *Gulf Coast Historical Review*, V (Spring 1990), pp. 72–73n.

57. Latour, *Memoir*, pp. 14–15, 16.

58. Albert Gallatin to Thomas H. Williams, May 5, 1810, Letters to and from the Collector at New Orleans, La., October 11, 1803–April 11, 1833, M-178, General Records of the Department of the Treasury, RG 56, NA.

59. C. Pettibone to Thomas Williams, May 23, 1810, Entry 1627, RG 36, NA.

60. Morphy to Williams, May 11, 1810, Entry 1627, RG 36, NA.

61. Bollaert, "Lafitte," p. 436. John Smith Kendall claims that Vincent Gambi was the first *bos* at Barataria, and that he appointed agents including the Laffites in New Orleans to arrange disposal of goods. He offers no supporting evidence, nor is there any. Kendall, "The Huntsmen of Black Ivory," pp. 13, 14.

62. Pierre Laffite and A. Robin to J. N. B. D'Abnour, June 12, 1810, Narcissus Broutin, Vol. 23, item 352; Andre Robin and Laffite to George Mayer, June 16, 1810, Vol. 23, item 361; Robin and Pierre Laffite to Simon Croise, June 20, 1810, Vol. 23, item 96; Pierre Laffite and Robin to Etienne LaFebre, June 27, 1810, Vol. 23, item 377; Robin and Pierre Laffite to Francois Charles, July 11, 1810, Vol. 23, item 397; Robin and Pierre Laffite to Laure Freres, July 19, 1810, Vol. 23, item 419; Andre Robin and Pierre Laffite to Marie Laforestrie, July 19, 1810, Vol. 22, item 420; Pierre Laffite to Paul Martin and Paul Savoie, August 24, 1810, Vol. 23, item 475; Robin and Pierre Laffite to Nicholas Godefroy Oliver, September 19, 1810, Vol. 23, item 525, NONA.

63. Pierre Laffite to Jean del Puerto, February 22, 1810, Pierre Pedesclaux, Vol. 60, p. 78; Pierre Laffite and A. Robin, March 3, 1810, Narcissus Broutin, Vol. 22, item 126; Pierre Laffite to Arnaud Bauvais, March 16, 1810, Narcissus Broutin, Vol. 22, item 157; Pierre Laffite and Andre Robin to Ursuline Convent, March 17, 1810, Narcissus Broutin, Vol. 22, item 161; Andre Robin and Pierre Laffite to Etienne Rousset, March 20, 1810, Narcissus Broutin, Vol. 22, item 170, NONA.

64. Andre Robin to Pierre Laffite and Fois Pouche, April 18, 1810, Narcissus Broutin, Vol. 22, item 231; William Liddle to Pierre Laffite and Andre Robin, May 23, 1810, Michele De Armas, Vol. 3, item 144, NONA.

65. New Orleans, *Daily Picayune,* August 20, 1871. This account of Laffite from "a venerable citizen of New Orleans" who cannot be identified, and who claimed to have boarded with Jean at the time, was originally written in 1863. It seems reliable, allowing for some romanticization after the lapse of half a century, and where details are verifiable, the writer has them correct. His physical description of Jean matches Glasscock's 1809 portrait perfectly. The author also states that Laffite was a Bordeaux native and for several years kept a store on Royal Street, one of the earliest examples of the persistent assertion that the Laffites maintained a town warehouse or store on Royal. The source also claimed that Jean was fluent in several languages, while it is apparent that he had to use translators for documents in English and Spanish, though his conversational English was fairly good and better than Pierre's.

66. United States and William Carter vs. Louis Aury, Case #0376, United States vs. Louis Aury, Case #0377, NAFW.

67. Jacques Gueron et al. report on Privateer Schooner *William,* June 4, 1810, Protest, May 29, 1810, Entry 1627, RG, NA; Order for Bond, June 26, 1810, Verdict, July 18, 1810, United States vs. *Guillaume,* Minutes, II, pp. 224, 232–33, M-1082, RG 21, NA.

68. Libel of Vicente Dordoigaite, n.d., Vicente Dordoigaite vs. *El Bolador,* Case #0419; Deposition of Vincente Dordoigaite, August 28, 1810, United States vs. certain slaves late of the cargo of the Spanish brig *El Bolador,* Case #0391, NAFW.

69. Thomas Bolling Robertson, Proclamation, September 6, 1810, Charles E. A. Gayarré, *The Story of Jean and Pierre Lafitte, The Pirate-Patriots* (New Orleans, 1938), p. 47.

70. New Orleans, *Louisiana Gazette,* September 13, 1810.

71. Order for Bond, August 28, 1810, Minutes, II, p. 253, Warrant, September 14, 1810, p. 255, Vincent Dordoigiate vs. Michel Brouard, M-1082, RG 21, NA.

72. Act 276, October 28, 1807, Book 1, p. 220, Conveyance Records, Ascension Parish Courthouse, Donaldsonville, LA.

73. Deposition of Pierre Laffite, September 23, 1810, P. N. Paillet vs. L. Bourdier, Case #0399; Deposition of Pierre Laffite, n.d. [September 28, 1810], United States vs. Pierre Laffite, Case #0574, NAFW.

74. Arrest order, October 11, 1810, Peter N. Paillet vs. L. Bourdier, Case #0399, NAFW.

75. Claim, October 2, 1810, P. N. Paillet vs. L. Bourdier, Case #0399, NAFW.

76. Synopses #0392, 0393, 0394, 0395, September 7, 1810, Works Project Administration, *Synopses of Cases in the U.S. District Court for the Eastern District of Louisiana Cases #1 to #3000 1806–1831* (Baton Rouge, 1941), p. 46.

77. A Summary Statement of Money and Property taken out of Spanish vessels, November 16, 1818, M59, RG 59, NA.

78. Affidavit of Mr. Peter Lafite, Marshal, September 20, 1810, P. N. Paillet vs. L. Bourdier, Case #0399, NAFW.

79. Admittedly, the dating of Pierre's affliction is inductive. The only way in many instances to distinguish between a Pierre or Jean Laffite document and others by men of the same name is the unique double *f,* single *t* spelling used by the brothers, as well as by their signatures. In the case of Pierre, not a single document has been found with this double *f,* single *t* spelling in the signature that does not match his signature. The same is the case with Jean, though a couple of his later signatures do not in all respects match his earlier ones.

Of the dozens of Pierre's signatures available up to September 23, 1810, without exception all are precisely the same, his name written large and boldly, spelled in full, with a lavish rubric, and decorative elements added at either side. The December 22, 1810, slave sale cited hereafter he did not sign at all, which was unusual for him. From March 12, 1811, onward he invariably shortened his given name to "Per" in his signatures, and after March 21 dropped the decorative elements at the sides, reduced the rubric, and overall wrote with a weaker and more diminutive hand, though it is still unquestionably his signature, with the same letter formation and the same lifting of the pen between the second *f* and the *i.* It is a dramatic change, turning a once-forceful signature into something rather meek.

It has generally been accepted that Pierre suffered a stroke in 1812, due to the statement of two examining physicians on August 10, 1814, that "about two years ago" Laffite had experienced "an apoplectic fit" (Opinion of Drs. Lewis Heerman and William Flood with regard to the health of said Lafitte, August 10, 1814, United States vs. Pierre Laffite, Case #0574, NAFW). However, the sudden change in Pierre's signature is almost certainly an artifact of an attack that came much earlier. Though the examiners in 1814 said that it was his left side that suffered the palsy, a stroke could have affected his writing even if he were right-handed. On March 12, 1811, he for the first time signed himself as "Per Laffite," though it was still rather bold, and still with rubric and ornaments. Just nine days later, on March 21, 1811, he commenced the diminutive and unornamented signature that he used in almost all surviving documents for the rest of his life. Given his failure to sign the December 22, 1810, document at all, it seems reasonable to conclude that his attack came prior to that date. Interestingly, without explaining his rationale, Saxon, *Lafitte*, p. 32, also concludes that Pierre suffered the attack in 1810.

80. Robin and Pierre Laffite to Lauve Freret, December 22, 1810, Narcissus Broutin, Vol. 23, item 651, NONA.

81. Pierre Laffite to Charles Lusson, March 12, 1811, Turner's Acts, Book 2K, p. 177, Clerk of Court's Office, Ascension Parish Courthouse, Donaldsonville, LA.

FIVE

1. John Innerarity to John Forbes, November 29, 1810, Heloise Cruzat Papers, University of Florida, Gainesville, FL.

2. James D. Richardson, comp., *A Compilation of the Messages and Papers of the Presidents 1789–1897* (Washington, 1900), I, pp. 480–81.

3. Innerarity to Forbes, November 29, 1810, Cruzat Papers, University of Florida, Gainesville, FL.

4. Henry Toulmin to Innerarity, November 26, December 13, 1810, Greenslade Papers, University of Florida.

5. Isidro A. Beluche Mora, "Privateers of Cartagena," *Louisiana Historical Quarterly*, XXXIX (January 1956), pp. 74–75, 79.

6. Daniel T. Patterson vs. the *General Bolivar*, Case #0760, NAFW. Faye, *Aury*, p. 92, asserts with no evidence that in the winter of 1810–11, when it was learned in New Orleans that privateer commissions were available from Cartagena, the privateers formed something called the "Barataria Association" with the Laffites as its agents. This is surely nothing more than imagination.

7. Kendall, "The Huntsmen of Black Ivory," pp. 10–11; Latour, *Historical Memoir*, pp. 12–13, 15.

8. Blas Moran to Diego Morphy, August 22, 1810, Srs. Llano y Regato to Morphy, December 7, 1810, Legajo 1836, AGI-Newberry.

9. Juan B. Bernaberr to Robert Smith, October 4, 1810, RG 59, M-50, NA.

10. New Orleans, *Louisiana Gazette,* September 24, 1810.

11. On October 27, 1810, just days or weeks before Pierre's stroke, Adelaide Maseleri, the free mulatto from San Domingue who could have been the mother of Eugene Laffite if there was such a person, gave birth to a daughter named Marie Josephe in New Orleans. It has long been assumed that she was the daughter of Pierre Laffite, thanks to the statement in her baptismal record that her parents were "Pierre [Lafitte], native of Bayonne in France, and Adelaide Maseleri, resident of the parish of St. Louis of Jérémie on Santo Domingo, both residents of this city." (Charles E. Nolan and Dorenda Dupont, eds., *Sacramental Records of the Roman Catholic Church of the Archdiocese of New Orleans, Volume 10, 1810–1812* [New Orleans, 1995], p. 254.)

There are immediate contradictions here, however. First, every other contemporary record for which Pierre Laffite was demonstrably present to declare his birthplace states that he came from Bordeaux, not Bayonne. Second, this baptismal record appears in a book to be used exclusively for white births. Only five other records of Adelaide Maseleri have been found, all notarial records, and they show her to be a free woman of color, making the baptismal record of her daughter in the white record book inexplicable.

A further complication comes in another extant record of Adelaide Maseleri, when on October 26, 1811, Pierre Laffite sold a slave to "Adelaide Masclari" (Narcissus Broutin, Vol. 26, item 451, NONA). This is definitely Pierre Laffite, signing himself on the document by his now-distinctive "Per Laffite" signature. Almost a year to the day after the birth of Marie Josephe, Pierre Laffite sold Adelaide a twenty-year-old woman for whom he charged only $50, while on this day Laffite sold another twenty-year-old slave woman to another buyer for $350 (Pierre Laffite to Clarisse Julien, October 26, 1811, Narcissus Broutin, Vol. 26, item 452, NONA). Several factors could explain the seeming discrepancy, including the condition and health of the slaves, or their skills, but the enormous difference in price suggests that Adelaide got a preferential rate because Laffite was the child's father.

The evidence of his long relationship with Marie Louisa Villard is clear. Of course, Pierre could have had more than one relationship, or simply a brief liaison with Adelaide. However, other factors mitigate against this. For one thing, Marie Josephe Lafitte simply disappears from the record after her baptism, and Adelaide Maseleri herself disappears after 1812. Signatures do not appear in the baptismal archives, so it is not possible to identify or disqualify Pierre Laffite by that means.

All things considered, it seems most probable that Marie Josephe's father was another Pierre Lafitte then living in New Orleans and that the smuggler Pierre Laffite's sale of a slave to Adelaide was merely coincidence, since many of the buyers of his slaves were from the free colored community. Similar coincidences abound, including two intermarried Laffite-Ramos families, one of them connected to Jean and Pierre and the other not. And a Maseleri witnessed the baptism of one of Pierre's grandchildren. However, in the mulatto society of the time, concentrated in the Faubourg Marigny section of town, such a close association might not be unusual. There were a host of free black Maseleris under some forty variant spellings.

12. New Orleans, *Louisiana Gazette*, December 20, 1811.

13. William St. Marc vs. Lafitte and Garidel, Case #3117, City Court Suit Records, NOPL.

14. Payment on note, December 29, 1810, Guilledon Cadet vs. Bellurgey, Robin, Pierre Lafitte, and William St. Marc, Case #2560, City Court Suit Records; Judgement, December 19, 1811, Jeane Baptiste Bellestre vs. William St. Marc, Pierre Lafitte et al., Case #2745, Orleans Territory Superior Court Suit Records, NOPL.

15. Babb, French Refugees, p. 231.

16. Shaw to Hamilton, January 18, 1811, Area File of the Naval Collection, 1775–1910, Area 8, M-625, NA.

17. James H. Dorman, "The Persistent Specter: Slave Rebellion in Territorial Louisiana," *Louisiana History*, XVIII (Fall 1977), pp. 394–99.

18. Inventory of the criminal cases tried by Orleans County Court (1805–1807) and City Court (1807–1812), NOPL.

19. Shaw to Hamilton, January 18, 1811, Area File of the Naval Collection, 1775–1910, Area 8, M-625, NA.

20. Dorman, "Persistent Specter," pp. 400–1.

21. John Smith Kendall, "Shadow Over the City," *Louisiana Historical*

Quarterly, XXII (January 1939), pp. 144–46, says without citing any authority that slaves introduced into Louisiana by the Baratarians may have been behind the January 1811 uprising. He goes on to claim that Claiborne's subsequent investigation concluded that this was the case, and as a result the governor determined to stop the Baratarians. In fact, Claiborne's investigation came to no such conclusion. See also John W. Monette, *History of the Discovery and Settlement of the Valley of the Mississippi* (New York, 1846), II, p. 491, for a roughly current assumption that Laffite slaves were involved.

22. Nolan and Dupont, eds., *Sacramental Records of the Roman Catholic Church of the Archdiocese of New Orleans, Volume 10, 1810–1812*, p. 254. The page on which the baptism of Jean Baptiste Laffite was entered is now missing from the original book, having been torn out. The entry can be reconstructed only from the extant index, which indicates that the child was colored, places the date of baptism as May 20, 1811, and the mother as a "De Villars." Villard is often misstated as Villar and Villars in the records, though this is not conclusive. As will appear in the final chapter, descendants of Pierre and Marie did vandalize another book in the Sacramental Archives to remove a reference to Marie being colored, and if this entry dealt with a child of theirs, then the motive to remove this page would have been the same.

23. In the index to Turner's Acts, Book 2K, p. 179, Ascension Parish Clerk of Court, Donaldsonville, Blaze Lacosts/Lacaste is referenced as selling a plantation on the left bank of the Lafourche to Pierre Laffite on February 20, 1811. However, the actual act shows the sale being to the same Louis Bourdier from whom Laffite recovered contraband slaves the previous September. It is perhaps only a coincidence, and it is possible that the indexer at the time saw "Lacaste" and read it as "Laffite." The next month, on March 4, 1812, Louis Bourdier was unable to pay a debt of $327.50 on a one-year note. Protest, Act Book 1, p. 236, West Feliciana Parish Courthouse, St. Francisville, LA. The fact that Bourdier was buying and selling property on the Lafourche in this period raises the possibility that he was a smuggling associate of the Laffites.

24. Gilbert to Williams, January 6, 1811, Entry 1627, RG 36, NA.

25. L. B. Many to Williams, May 28, 1811, Ibid.

26. John Shaw to Paul Hamilton, March 15, 1811, Area File of the Naval Collection, 1775–1910, Area 8, M-625, NA.

27. Shaw to Hamilton, June 7, 1811, Ibid.

28. Vestiges of the Laffite presence on Grand Isle remain, though mostly in lore and legend rather than confirmable association. In 1900 a spot on the north coast in the middle of the island was called Laffite's Cove, and inland a few hundred yards was a wooded spot called Laffite's Meeting Place on a tourist map. This may be today's Laffite's Woods. There was also the home of Nez Coupe, who claimed to be one of Laffite's men, on the island in later years. This was the man also known as Chighizola, and his descendants are there today.

29. Robert Vogel, "Jean Laffite, the Baratarians, and the Historical Geography of Piracy in the Gulf of Mexico," *Gulf Coast Historical Review*, V (Spring 1990), pp. 64–65.

30. Laffite to Charles Lusson, March 12, Turner's Acts, Book 2K, p. 177, Clerk of Court's Office, Ascension Parish Courthouse, Donaldsonville, LA; Laffite to Charles Lusson, March 12, 1811, Notary Narcissus Broutin, Vol. 24, item 176; Laffite and Robin to Jean Baptiste Deblanc, March 29, 1811, Vol. 24, item 74; Laffite to Arnaud Beauvais, March 21, 1811, Vol. 25, item 109; Laffite and Robin to Vincent Fornaud and St. Ville Ternaut, March 23, 1811, Vol. 25, item 114; Laffite and Robin to Jean Baptiste Chichon, March 30, 1811, Vol. 25, item 122; Laffite and Robin to Manette Foucher, April 1, 1811, Vol. 25, item 133; Laffite to Cesar LeBreton des Chapelle, April 5, 1811, Vol. 25, item 144; Laffite to Balthazar Dusnan, April 5, 1811, Vol. 25, item 145; Laffite and Robin to Louis LeBreton des Chapelle, April 19, 1811, Vol. 25, item 178, NONA.

31. Laffite to François Honoré, June 13, 1811, Stephen De Quinones, Vol. 13, item 214; Laffite to Adelaide Masclary, October 26, 1811, Notary Narcissus Broutin, Vol. 26, item 451; Laffite to Clarisse Julien, October 26, 1811, Vol. 26, item 452; Laffite to François Doriocourt, October 29, 1811, Michele DeArmas, Vol. 6, item 506; Laffite and Robin to Andre Candolle, November 23, 1811, Notary Narcissus Broutin, Vol. 23, item 619; Laffite to Dame Marmillon, December 11, 1811, Notary Pierre Pedesclaux, Vol. 63, item 505; Laffite to Françoise Haydel, December 11, 1811, Vol. 63, item 505, NONA.

32. Sea Protest, August 15, 1811, Notary John Lynd, Vol. 7, pp. 525–26, NONA.

33. Smith, *Jones*, p. 19.

34. Libel of Daniel Patterson, November 23, 1811, libel of R. A. Moorhouse, n.d., deposition of William Boyce, January 22, 1812, deposition of John Smith, January 22, 1812, Daniel F. Patterson v. Polacre *La Divina Pas-*

tora, Case #0452, NAFW; P. L. B. Duplessis statement, August 29, 1812, Legajo 1836, AGI-Newberry.

35. Luis Onís to Monroe, November 26, 1811, RG 59, M-50, NA.

36. Patterson vs. *La Divina Pastora*, November 23, 1811, Minutes, III, p. 5, January 28, 1812, p. 28, February 28, 1812, p. 35, M-1082, RG 21, NA.

37. Grand Jury to the Court, January 31, 1812, Minutes, III, pp. 29–32, M-1082, RG 21, NA.

38. New Orleans, *Louisiana Gazette*, December 20, 1811. Unfortunately, the author of this wonderful letter cannot be identified. He signs it from Toulouse Street, but the 1811 New Orleans city directory fails to suggest any obvious candidates. It might be F. L. E. Amelung, who was in trouble in the district court in 1810–11 for dealing in contraband, but this is only speculation.

39. Faye, Aury, pp. 45, 47, CAHUT.

40. Marixa Lasso, "Haiti as an Image of Popular Republicanism in Caribbean Colombia," Geggus, *The Impact of the Haitian Revolution*, pp. 178–79.

41. Vincent Nolte, *The Memoirs of Vincent Nolte. Reminiscences in the Period of Anthony Adverse or Fifty Years in Both Hemispheres* (New York, 1934), p. 189; Bell, *Revolution*, p. 47.

42. Marixa Lasso, "Haiti as an Image of Popular Republicanism in Caribbean Colombia," David P. Geggus, ed., *The Impact of the Haitian Revolution in the Atlantic World* (Columbia, SC, 2001), pp. 178–79.

43. Alfred Toledano Wellborn, "The Relations Between New Orleans and Latin America, 1810–1824," *Louisiana Historical Quarterly*, XXII (July 1939), pp. 755–56.

SIX

1. John Shaw to Paul Hamilton, February 17, 1812, Area File of the Naval Collection, 1775–1910, Area 8, M-625, NA.

2. Angus Fraser to Williams, February 19, 1812, Entry 1627, RG 36, NA.

3. Smith, *Jones*, p. 19.

4. John Shaw to Paul Hamilton, February 17, 1812, Area File of the Naval Collection, 1775–1910, Area 8, M-625, NA.

5. John Shaw to Secretary of the Navy, February 3, 1812, Letters Received by the Secretary of the Navy from Captains 1807–1885, Naval Records Collection of the Office of Naval Records and Library, M-125, RG 45, NA.

6. "The Baratarians vs. the United States: A Chronology, 1812–1815," *Laffite Study Group Newsletter*, VII (Spring 1987), p. 2.

7. Fraser to Williams, February 25, 1812, Entry 1627, RG 36, NA.

8. Fraser to Williams, March 23, 24, 1812, Ibid.

9. Louis Aury to J. Maignet, February 10, 1812, Louis Aury Papers, CAHUT.

10. Smith, *Jones*, p. 20.

11. "The Baratarians vs. the United States: A Chronology, 1812–1815," *Laffite Study Group Newsletter*, VII (Spring 1987), p. 2.

12. Receipts, June 20, 21, 1812, Dominic You Papers, HNOC. The spelling used here is that attached to the collection, even though Youx is apparently the spelling actually preferred by Dominique when using that name.

13. Certificate, August 26, 1812, You Papers, HNOC.

14. Anonymous to Major McRea, August 23, 1812, Anonymous to Anonymous, January 8, 1813, You Papers, HNOC.

15. Dominique to Frederick You, [September 1812], Declaration, August 23, 1812, You Papers, HNOC. The September letter is unclear, but appears to be addressed to Youx, and signed by Dominique, meaning he wrote it to himself, perhaps using his Frederick Youx alias as part of a sham story created to get his ship into port.

16. List of Captures, n.d. [September 1812], Statement of liquidation, September 17, 1812, You Papers, HNOC.

17. Inventaire du Corsaire Francais Le Pandoure, September 17, 1812, You Papers, HNOC.

18. Statement of sale, October 15, 1812, You Papers, HNOC.

19. Certificate, September 17, 1812, You Papers, HNOC.

20. H. W. Palfrey to Editor, November 5, 1851, New Orleans, *Daily Delta*, November 9, 1851.

21. Suit, November 16, 1812, United States vs. José Antonio La Rionde, Case #0537, NAFW.

22. Castellanos, *New Orleans as It Was*, pp. 151–52; John Smith Kendall, "The Huntsmen of Black Ivory," *Louisiana Historical Quarterly*, XXIV (January 1941), p. 15. Kendall gives no source at all for this interesting assertion, but his source is surely Castellanos. It is probably a glimmer of local tradition current in the late 1800s. Clark did live by Bayou St. John, a smuggling route into the city.

23. Thomas Williams to Albert Gallatin, March 15, 1812, July 20, 1813, Collector of Customs Letters, NA.

24. Nolan and Dupont, *Sacramental Records of the Roman Catholic Church of the Archdiocese of New Orleans, Volume 11, 1812–1814* (New Orleans, 1996), p. 433. The baptismal record does not list Pierre as the father, but the child's surname is listed as Villar Lafita and the mother is named as Marie Luisa Villar. Moreover, the sponsors are "Martin and Caterina Lafita," identified as brother and sister of the child, so there is no question that this is a child of the Pierre-Marie liaison.

25. Protest, March 13, 1813, Notary John Lynd, Vol. 10, item, 643, NONA.

26. Laffite to Ursuline Convent, February 12, 1812, Notary Narcissus Broutin, Vol. 22, item 73; Laffite to Louis Demarans, January 3, 1812, Vol. 68, item 2; Laffite to Henri St. Gême, June 9, 1812, Notary Marc Lafitte, Vol. 2, item 130; Laffite to Joseph Foque, February 27, 1812, Notary Michel deArmas, Vol. 8, item 116, NONA.

27. Bollaert, "Lafitte," p. 436.

28. New Orleans, *Courier de la Louisiane*, May 4, 1812.

29. Suit filed September 19, 1812, Antoine Philippe Lanaux vs. Pierre Lafitte, Case #3395, City Court Suit Records, NOPL.

30. Laffite to Marie Rousse, October 28, 1812, Notary Narcissus Broutin, Vol. 27, item 200; Promissory note Pierre Laffite to Andre Robin, October 31, 1812, Protest, March 13, 1813, Notary John Lynd, Vol. 10, item 643; Obligation Pierre Laffite to Pierre Gaillard, November 30, 1812, Notary Narcissus Broutin, Vol. 68, item 381, NONA.

31. William St. Marc vs. Lafitte and Garidel, Case #3177, William St. Marc vs. Peter Lafitte, December 5, 1812, Case #3486, City Court Suit Records, NOPL.

32. Wilkinson, *Memoirs*, III, pp. 335–40.

33. Stanley Faye, "Types of Privateer Vessels, Their Armament and Flags,

in the Gulf of Mexico," *Louisiana Historical Quarterly*, XXIII (January 1940), pp. 118–20.

34. Faye, "Privateer Vessels," pp. 121, 123–24.

35. Andrew Whiteman, who served aboard her, in testimony on April 25, 1814, stated that he had no knowledge of this schooner fitted out and armed at Barataria having a commission from any nationality. United States vs. Certain Goods, etc., Minutes, III, pp. 306–7, M-1082, NA. The fact of Pierre Laffite requesting privateering commissions from Cartagena months later in April 1813—see below—suggests that he had no commissions in the fall of 1812 when this unnamed schooner went cruising for the Laffites. If the brothers had acquired *La Diligent* by this time, then they might have rationalized the remaining time on Gariscan's French commission into covering this schooner, but this is mere speculation.

36. John R. Grymes petition, April 7, 1813, United States vs. Jean Laffite, Case #0573, NAFW. It is interesting that the documents in cases #0573 and 0574 turned up in a woman's hands in New Orleans in 1925 when she tried to sell them to antique dealer James B. Pelletier. It is not known if he bought them or not, but they are now back in the proper case folders at NAFW. New Orleans, *Times-Picayune*, August 23, 1925.

37. Statement of Andrew Hunter Holmes, November 19, 1813 [1812], United States vs. Jean Laffite, Case #0573, NAFW.

38. Cross-examination of Andrew Hunter Holmes, November 20, 1812, United States vs. Pierre Laffite, Case #0574, NAFW.

39. Deposition of James Tyler, November 20, 1812, United States vs. Pierre Laffite, Case #0574, NAFW.

40. Statement of Andrew Hunter Holmes, November 19, 1813 [1812], United States vs. Jean Laffite, Case #0574, Deposition of Andrew Hunter Holmes, November 19, 1813, United States vs. Pierre Laffite, Case #0573, NAFW.

41. John Ballinger report to Gen. James Wilkinson, November 3, 1812, Rosamunde E. and Emile Kuntz Collection, Tulane University.

42. Cross-examination of Andrew Hunter Holmes, November 20, 1812, United States vs. Pierre Laffite, Case #0574, NAFW.

43. Deposition of Andrew Hunter Holmes, November 29, 1812, United States vs. Pierre Laffite, Case #0574, NAFW.

44. Morphy to Apodaca, March 11, 1813, Legajo 1828, AGI-Newberry; United States vs. A Certain Pirogue, 26 Bales of Cinnamon, etc., Verdict, January 25, 1813, Minutes, III, p. 143, M-1082, RG 21, NA.

45. Morphy to Apodaca, November 27, 1812, Legajo 1836, AGI-Newberry.

46. Deposition of Francisco Ajuria, December 5, 1814, Diego Unzaga et al. vs. the Schooner *Dorada* alias *la Rosalia,* Case #0763, NAFW. In testimony given by Andrew Whiteman April 25, 1814, he said that the *Dorada* was taken a year earlier, making this capture circa April 1813, but that is too late to dovetail with other accounts. United States vs Certain Goods, etc., Minutes, III, pp. 306–7, M-1082, NA.

47. Faye, "Privateer Vessels," p. 120.

48. Presentment, October 29, 1814, United States vs. Antoine Lavergne, alias Cadet Patte Grasse, Case #0784, NAFW; Deposition of Andrew Whiteman, November 24, 1813, Entry 949, RG 59, NA; Faye, "Privateer Vessels," p. 120. Whiteman says in this and other statements that the brig was taken off Trinidad, but given the time frame involved and the distance to Trinidad, this is virtually impossible, and thus he must have been speaking of Trinidad, a coastal town on Cuba's south coast.

49. Deposition of Andrew Whiteman, July 11, 1814, Sabourin Papers, Tulane; Certificate of Registration of the *Surprise,* June 7, 1820, Certificates of Registration, 1818–1819, Bureau of Marine Inspection and Navigation, Entry 156, RG 41, NA. The *Surprise* is the name given the captured *Dorada* after she was sold by the navy in 1820.

50. Suit April 3, 1813, Paul Lanusse vs. Jean Jeanetty, Vincent Gambi, et al., Case #10, First Judicial Court Records, NOPL.

51. In 1804 a slave ship named the *Diligent* brought Africans into Louisiana from Havana under a Captain Legue, though it does not seem to be this same *La Diligent,* whose 1813 commission shows her to have been built in 1808. Unnumbered documents of date May 27, 1805, Assumption Parish Courthouse, Napoleonville, LA, in Afro-Louisiana History and Genealogy, 1718–1820 (Slave), Web site http://www.ibiblio.org/laslave/

52. Angus Fraser to Williams, April 3, 6, 1812; African Negroes belonging to the French Privateer *Diligent* Capt. John Antony Gariseon, Entry 1627, RG 36, NA; Sylvie Feuillie, "La Guerre de Course Française aux Antilles Durant la Revolution et l'Empire, III Partie," *La Revue Maritime,* No. 429 (fourth quarter), p. 93. Gariscan's name appears in several alternate forms,

including Alexis Grassan, Garison, Grisson, and so forth. A document dated March 24, 1808, in the French National Archives, Paris, location cited only as 5 mi 1433, supposedly mentions a corsair named Pierre Lafitte and also what appears to be a "Mr. Gariscan," but it has not been possible to check this.

53. Angus Fraser to Williams, April 23, 1812, Entry 1627, RG 36, NA.

54. Angus Fraser to Williams, April 23, 1812, Ibid.

55. No record of the purchase exists, but it is clear from subsequent documents cited that Pierre Laffite claimed and was acknowledged as the owner.

56. Presentment, October 29, 1814, United States vs. Antoine Lavergne, alias Cadet Patte Grasse, Case #0784, NAFW.

57. Abstract of Commissions of Letters of Marque and reprisal issued at the Port of New Orleans, June 7, 1813, Entry 388, RG 45, NA.

58. Pierre Laffite in 1815 stated that he got his privateering commission in New Orleans and had to give a security deposit to Cartagena to get it, a deposit that was never refunded. It seems most likely that he got the commission by taking over Gariscan's and paying the deposit, if any, to Gariscan for delivery in Cartagena. Of course, there may have been no deposit and no legitimate commission, either. Statement of Pierre Laffite, n.d., United States vs. Schooner *Presidente*, Case #0811, NAFW.

59. If the Laffites ever actually held a legitimate Cartagena letter of marque, it was most likely one of the blank commissions carried to the East Coast by the Colombian junta's envoy late in 1812 or early 1813, but no record of them survives.

60. This estimate is based on the fact that a common seaman got $10, and there were sixty men getting that lowest rate. Fifteen others got up to twice the pay, not to mention the officers. Certificate of Inspection, March 2, 1813, Pierre and Jean Laffite Collection, HNOC; Deposition of Andrew Whiteman, November 24, 1813, Records Relating to Privateers and Piracy, Entry 949, General Records of the Department of State, RG 59, NA (copy in the Sabourin Papers, Tulane).

61. Expense inventory, July 1812, William Allan vs. Polacre *San Francisco de Paula*, Case #0509, NAFW.

62. Petition of Davis and Ducatel, April 9, 1816, Executors of André Robin vs. Pierre Laffite, Case #956, Parish Court Civil Suit Records, NOPL.

63. Jean Laffite to Janne Capucin, February 5, 1813, Notary Narcissus Broutin, Vol. 28, item 54, NONA, places Jean in New Orleans on this date.

64. Unsigned letter to Monsieur le Consul, February 1813, Pierre and Jean Laffite Collection, HNOC.

65. Certificate of Inspection, March 2, 1813, Pierre and Jean Laffite Collection, HNOC.

66. Ibid.; Deposition of James Connel, July 1813, United States vs. Juan Juanilleo alias Sapia, Case #0774, NAFW.

67. Certificate of Inspection, March 2, 1813, Pierre and Jean Laffite Collection, HNOC.

68. Deposition of Andrew Whiteman, November 24, 1813, Sabourin Papers, Tulane.

69. Fraser to Williams, April 21, 1813, Entry 1627, RG 36, NA.

70. It is commonly understood that the Laffite brothers had financial interests in privateers sailing under the flags of Cartagena and Mexico. However, while the district court case files in New Orleans establish clear chains of ownership for individual vessels as well as documented connections with the Laffites, there do not appear to be any records of the commissions themselves. Neither is there evidence that any republican junta or revolutionary caudillo ever acknowledged a relation with the Laffites. There is no extant evidence that the Laffites ever got legitimate letters of marque from Cartagena, or at least a search of records during 1812–15 in the files on privateers and mercenaries who came to Gran Colombia fails to reveal any such record. Research by several people in the archives of Colombia and other South American nations finds plenty of references to Barataria and Galveston, but no mention of the Laffite brothers as owners, masters, armorers, or officers of privateers; nor did they or their agents pay any recorded taxes or duties on prizes disposed of in the "patriot" admiralty courts as did Beluche and other legitimately commissioned corsairs. The Colombian junta's envoy brought several blank commissions to the United States late in 1812, but Pierre Laffite's request for such blanks in April 1813 makes it evident that the Laffites did not receive any of those, and the testimony of men serving on their vessels in federal district court cases casts considerable suspicion on the probability that they obtained commissions thereafter before December 1815 when Cartagenan commissions became inoperative in the wake of the sacking of the city. They also do not appear in the archives of Bogotá or Caracas and they do not seem to have been

involved either with privateers in Haiti. Beluche was sailing under a Carta-genan commission, but was not connected with the Laffites at this time. Neither do they appear to have been involved with the Charleston priva-teers, nor with those of Martinique or San Domingue. Robert Vogel spec-ulates that in 1812–13 the Laffites may have had one or two French national privateer commissions, but those were worthless after March 1814, after which the Laffites might have exchanged them for blank commissions is-sued by the agents of the republican junta in Cartagena, which would re-main valid until December 1815.

71. Pierre Laffite to John Anthony Gariscan, April 22, 1813, Edward A. Parsons Collection, CAHUT; Jean L. Epperson, "Flags Flown at Galves-ton by the Corsairs and Filibusters," *Laffite Society Chronicles,* V (February 1999), p. [6–7]; Faye, "Privateer Vessels," pp. 126–28.

72. Shaw to Hamilton, January 18, 1813, M-125, NA.

73. Indictments, February 15, 1813, Minutes, III, pp. 161–62, M-1082, NA.

74. Petition, April 7, 1813, United States vs. Jean Laffite, Case #0573; Peti-tion April 7, 1813, United States vs. Pierre Laffite, Case #0574, NAFW.

75. Arrest order for Jean Laffite, April 8, 1813, United States vs. Jean Laf-fite, Case #0573; Arrest order for Pierre Laffite, April 8, 1813, United States vs. Pierre Laffite, Case #0574, NAFW.

76. Arrest order of Jean Laffite, April 20, 1813, United States vs. Jean Laf-fite, Case #0573; Arrest order of Pierre Laffite, April 20, 1813, United States vs. Pierre Laffite, Case #0574, NAFW.

77. Suit, April 3, 1813, Paul Lanusse vs. Jean Jeanetty, Vincent Gambi, et al., Case #10, First Judicial Court, NOPL.

78. Petition of Davis and Ducatel, April 9, 1816, Executors of André Robin vs. Pierre Laffite, Case #0956, Parish Court Civil Suit Records, NOPL.

79. Statement of Pierre Laffite, n.d., United States vs. Schooner *Presidente,* Case #0811, NAFW.

80. Sea protest, May 11, 1813, Notary John Lynd, Vol. 10, item 182, NONA.

81. John Foley to Pierre Dubourg, May 1, 1813, Entry 1627, RG 36, NA.

82. Deposition of Antonio Ruiz, n.d., United States vs. Juan Juanilleo alias Sapia, Case #0774, NAFW; Andrew Whiteman statement, April 25, 1814, United States vs. Certain Goods, etc., Minutes, III, pp. 306–7, M-1082, NA.

83. Deposition of Bertrande Priella, October 7, 1814, United States vs. Dominique Youx, Case #0779, NAFW.

84. Deposition of Andrew Whiteman, November 24, 1813, Entry 949, RG 59, NA; Deposition of Andrew Whiteman, July 11, 1814, Sabourin Papers, Tulane.

85. Faye, "Privateersmen," p. 1026. Faye refers to this man as "Captain Marcos," but he almost certainly misreads Maire, or Mairo as it was spelled in Spanish, for Maire is hereafter closely associated with the Laffites as one of their captains until 1817.

86. John Shaw to Paul Hamilton, October 27, 1812, M-125, NA.

SEVEN

1. Presentment, October 27, 1814, United States vs. Leverne Cortais, Case #0782; Libel of Jayme Fontenals, October 7, 1814, Jayme Fontenals vs. Schooner *La Cometa*, Case #0730, NAFW; Faye, "Privateersmen," p. 1018.

2. Renato Beluche vs. Ship Jane, Case #0552, NAFW.

3. Deposition of Bertrande Priella, October 7, 1814, United States vs. Dominique Youx, Case #0779, NAFW.

4. Galveston, *Daily News*, September 19, 1926; New Orleans, *Louisiana Gazette and New-Orleans Advertiser*, March 11, 13, 1813.

5. Vincent Nolte, *The Memoirs of Vincent Nolte. Reminiscences in the Period of Anthony Adverse or Fifty Years in Both Hemispheres* (New York, 1934), p. 188–89.

6. New Orleans, *Louisiana Gazette and New-Orleans Advertiser*, March 18, 1813.

7. Morphy to Apodaca, March 11, 1813, Legajo 1828, AGI-Newberry.

8. Proclamation, March 15, 1813, Dunbar Rowland, ed., *Official Letter Books of W. C. C. Claiborne 1801–1816* (Jackson, MS, 1917), VI, pp. 232–33.

9. Claiborne to Wilkinson, March 15, 1813, Rowland, *Letter Books*, VI, p. 216.

10. "The Baratarians vs. the United States: A Chronology, 1812–1815," *Laffite Study Group Newsletter*, VII (Spring 1987), p. 2.

11. New Orleans, *Louisiana Gazette and New-Orleans Advertiser*, March 13, 1813.

12. New Orleans, *Gazette*, May 6, 1813.

13. Anonymous note, June 21, 1813, Entry 1627, RG 36, NA.

14. Suit, April 3, 1813, Jean Baptiste Soubie transfer, June 8, 1813, Paul Lanusse vs. Jean Jannetty, Vincent Gambi, et al., Case #10, First Judicial Court, NOPL; Statement of Andrew Whiteman, April 25, 1814, United States vs. Certain Goods, etc., Minutes, III, pp. 306–7, M-1082, NA. Whiteman specifically states that the goods taken to New Orleans by the Laffites and hidden there were later seized.

15. James Wilkinson, *Memoirs of My Own Times* (Philadelphia, 1816), III, pp. 341–42.

16. Bollaert, "Lafitte," p. 436; Galveston, *Weekly News*, October 11, 1883. This is according to the recollection of John Ijams, who claimed to have spent time with the Laffites as a boy.

17. Nolte, *Memoirs*, pp. 188–89.

18. The Pirate of the Gulf, transcription of unidentified newspaper clipping ca. 1873, Jean Laffite Vertical File, LSM.

19. There are tempting suggestions that Pierre Laffite could have been commanding a privateer out of Charleston this summer. A "Peter Lafete" took command of the privateer the *Eagle*, commissioned June 28, 1813. The same source also records the commissioning of the American privateer the *Hazard* on June 12, 1813, commanded by "Peter Lamason," who is probably the same Laméson who served as an officer aboard the *La Diligent*, and who would have frequent later associations with the Laffites. (Commission 742 issued to Peter Lafete, June 28, 1813, Certificate 740 issued to Peter Lamason, June 12, 1813, Return of Commissions Issued to Private Armed Vessels, from the Month June 1813 to this date, by Simeon Theus, collector, Charleston, S.C., Letters from Collectors of Customs Relating to Commissions of Privateers, 1812–1815, Entry 388, RG 45, NA). The *Eagle* put out on cruise July 5, 1813, bound for Cartagena, and was several times seen thereafter: off Cape Tiburon in July; then Cuba in August, where she encountered Beluche; then in October off Jamaica, where she encountered the *Philanthrope*, a prize taken by Beluche and soon to be commanded by Gambi (Charleston, *Courier*, July 5, August 4, October 29, 1813). Pierre certainly disappears from the record in Louisiana after early June 1813, but the

Charleston Peter Lafete is almost certainly a different character, and one willing to privateer within the law. A Frances Laffatte also had a ship *L'Esperance* seized in New Orleans on May 26, 1813, but there appears to be no connection with the Laffites (Register of Ships Seized in New Orleans, April 26, 1817, Entry 1627, RG 36, NA).

20. Thomas Flournoy to J. F. H. Claiborne, August 3, 1846, J. F. H. Claiborne Papers, Mississippi Department of Archives and History, Jackson, MS. In describing this episode some years later, Flournoy spoke only of "a man called Laffite, (said to be at the head of the smugglers & pirates,)" without identifying whether it was Jean or Pierre. Jean is not known to have had a mistress as of this period, whereas Pierre certainly did, which argues that Pierre was the man in question. He was also at this stage still the public face of the brothers' operation in New Orleans, far better known than Jean. Nor does Flournoy precisely date the episode. It had to have happened between June 1813, when Flournoy took command, and November 4, when Claiborne issued a proclamation mentioned by Flournoy as a subsequent event. J. F. H. Claiborne, *Life and Times of Gen. Sam. Dale, the Mississippi Partisan* (New York, 1860), pp. 87–89n, reproduces this letter but with extensive revision in the wording, considerably changing Flournoy's meaning in places.

21. Henry D. Peire to Flournoy, August 15, 1813, Flournoy to P. Dubourg, August 27, 1813, Entry 1627, RG 36, NA.

22. H. D. Peire to Dubourg, October 3, 1817 [1813], Ibid.

23. Deposition of Thomas Copping, July 1813, Sabourin Papers, Tulane.

24. Foley to Mr. Portier, July 10, 1813, Entry 1627, RG 36, NA.

25. William Jones to P. F. Dubourg, August 24, 1813, Secretary of the Navy Letters, Naval Records, M-175, RG 56, NA.

26. Gilbert to Freeman, August 1813, copy in Laffite Society Research Collection, Sam Houston Regional Library, Liberty, TX.

27. George Robert Gleig, *The Campaigns of the British Army at Washington and New Orleans in the Years 1814–1815* (London, 1847), p. 192; Statement of Pierre Laffite, n.d., United States vs. Schooner *Presidente*, Case #0811, NAFW.

28. Faye, "Privateersmen," p. 1029.

29. Faye, "Privateersmen," p. 1029.

30. Deposition of Andrew Whiteman, November 24, 1813, Entry 949, RG 59, NA.

31. Arrest orders, April 20, July 20, 24, October 18, 1813, United States vs. Pierre Laffite, Case #0574; Arrest orders, April 20, July 24, October 16, 1813, United States vs. Jean Laffite, Case #0573, NAFW.

32. Gilbert to Dubourg, October 1, 1813, List of goods seized by Walker Gilbert, September 28, 1813, Foley to Dubourg, September 28, 1813, Entry 1627, RG 36, NA.

33. Foley to Dubourg, October 4, 1813, Ibid.

34. Gilbert to Dubourg, October 8, 1813, List of goods seized by Walker Gilbert, October 8, 1813, Ibid.

35. Deposition of Andrew Whiteman, November 24, 1813, with interlineations dated December 6, 1813 and July 18, 1814, Sabourin Papers, Tulane; William Randall to Dubourg, December 10, 1813, Entry 1627, RG 36, NA.

36. Foley to Dubourg, October 22, 1813, Entry 1627, RG 36, NA.

37. G. W. Campbell to P. Dubourg, July 22, 1814, M-175, RG 56; Gilbert to Dubourg, December 2, 1813, Entry 1627, RG 36, NA.

38. Gilbert to Dubourg, December 2, 1813, Entry 1627, RG 36, NA.

39. Gilbert to Dubourg, October 29, 1813, Ibid.

40. Deposition of Hypolite Bourgouin, July 11, 1814, Sabourin Papers, Tulane. This episode is also described in Gayarré, *Pirate-Patriots*, p. 57, though Gayarré attributes it to Jean Laffite, which is impossible. In any event, Bourgouin specifically states that it was Pierre whom he encountered.

41. James Miller to Dubourg, October 26, 1813, Entry 1627, RG 36, NA.

42. Shaw to Dubourg, October 24, 1813, Ibid.

43. William W. Kimball to Don C. Seitz, December 26, 1919, Miscellaneous Manuscripts, LSU.

44. Robert C. Vogel, "Jean Laffite, the Baratarians, and the Historical Geography of Piracy in the Gulf of Mexico," *Gulf Coast Historical Review*, V (Spring 1990) pp. 64–65.

45. Castellanos, *New Orleans as It Was*, pp. 151–52.

46. Deposition of Andrew Whiteman, November 24, 1813, Sabourin Papers, Tulane.

47. List of goods taken by Jas. Robinson at Patton and Mossy [Morphy, Murphys] auction house, October 9, 1813, Entry 1627, RG 36, NA.

48. James Miller to Dubourg, October 26, 1813, Ibid.

49. Walker Gilbert to Dubourg, October 29, 1813, Ibid.

50. Foley to Dubourg, October 22, 1813, Ibid. The full extent of the Laffite-Dumon relation is hard to discern. Fragments of a suit against Dumon by Pierre Laffite, including an affidavit dated July 29, 1816, have been interpreted to suggest that Pierre and Dumon were engaged in a contest over control of land fronting the Attakapas Canal that connected Bayou Lafourche with Lake Verret, the vital smuggling route much used by the Laffites in this period. However, the original document, identified as Suit No. 34, Second Judicial Court, August 17, 1816, Clerk of Court, Ascension Parish, Donaldsonville, LA, cannot be found. All that survives is a partial photocopy that says nothing of the canal and only indicates that Dumon owed Laffite $3,075.50 that Pierre sought a seizure order to obtain (copy courtesy of Robert Vogel). John Howells, who found the original and was presumably the last person to see it, said that it dealt with the canal, which is possible. In any case, the suit is evidence of a continuing relationship between the Laffites and Dumon, if not in the end an amicable one.

51. Foley to Dubourg, October 30, 1813, Entry 1627, RG 36, NA.

52. Walker Gilbert to Dubourg, October 29, 1813, Ibid.

53. Foley to Dubourg, October 22, 1813, Ibid.

54. C. Wolstonecraft to Dubourg, October 8, 1813, Ibid.

55. William Jones to Pierre F. Dubourg, September 27, 1813, M-178, RG 56, NA.

56. Oath of John Foley, October 17, 1813, Entry 1627, RG 36, NA.

57. Walker Gilbert to Dubourg, October 29, 1813, Entry 1627, RG 36, NA.

58. Foley to Dubourg, October 15, 1813, Ibid.

59. B. Hubbard to Dubourg, November 10, 1813, Ibid.

60. John Hughes to P. Dubourg, November 5, 1813, Ibid.

61. Gilbert to Dubourg, November 15, 1813, Ibid.

62. J. W. Windship to William Plumer, November [December] 1, 1813, Everett S. Brown, ed., "Letters from Louisiana, 1813–1814," *Mississippi Valley Historical Review*, XI (March 1925), pp. 575–76.

63. Foley to Dubourg, December 7, 1813, Entry 1627, RG 36, NA.

64. Gilbert to Freeman, February 18, 1814, Historical Land Title Records Section, Louisiana State Land Office, Baton Rouge.

65. Fine, July 19, 1813, United States vs. Antonio Ruiz and Francis Lacarter, Case #0596, NAFW.

66. John Brackenridge to William Shaler, December 27, 1813, cited in Warren, *Sword,* p. 100.

67. Patterson to William Jones, November 15, 1813, Letters Received by the Secretary of the Navy from Commanders, 1804–1886, M147, NA.

68. Patterson to Jones, November 22, 1813, Ibid.

69. Daniel Patterson to Secretary of the Navy, November 23, 1813, Ibid.

70. Claiborne to Benjamin Rush, October 30, 1814, Gayarré, *Pirate-Patriots,* p. 68.

71. Proclamation, November 24, 1813, Rowland, *Letter Books,* VI, pp. 279–80.

72. Windship to Plumer, November [December] 1, 1813, Brown, "Letters from Louisiana," pp. 575–76. This letter is clearly misdated as November 1, since it mentions Claiborne's reward of November 25. Obviously, as commonly happens, the writer wrote it on December 1 but neglected to note the new month. Interestingly, he does not name Laffite specifically, and mistakenly refers to him as a French general, but there is no mistaking about whom he writes. This is the earliest verifiable reference to Laffite offering a reward for Claiborne. Over the years the amount of the reward would come to be exaggerated to $5,000 or more.

73. Flournoy to Claiborne, August 3, 1846, Claiborne Papers, Mississippi Department of Archives and History, Jackson.

74. Gilbert to Thomas Freeman, February 18, 1814, Historical Land Title Records Section, Louisiana State Land Office, Baton Rouge.

EIGHT

1. Foley to Dubourg, January 16 1814, Ibid.

2. Morphy to Apodaca, January 19, 1814, Legajo 1836, AGI-Newberry.

3. Gilbert to Dubourg, January 14, 1814, Ibid.

4. William C. C. Claiborne to Dubourg, January 24, 1814, Entry 1627, RG 36, NA.

5. Oath of John Stout, October 4, 1813, Letter of recommendation, September 23, 1813, Ibid.

6. James D. Stout to Dubourg, March 2, 1814, Ibid.

7. Morphy to Apodaca, January 19, 1814, Legajo 1836, AGI-Newberry. Morphy knowing of the captured officers on January 19 suggests that the news had just come into town, likely the day before.

8. Gilbert to Thomas Freeman, February 18, 1814, "Letters from Surveyor to Surveyor General, 1807–1824," Cabinet C-5, Louisiana State Land Office Archives, Baton Rouge, LA.

9. Paul Lanusse vs. Jean Jeanetty, Vincent Gambi, et al., Case #10, First Judicial Court, NOPL.

10. Paul Lanusse et al. vs. Pierre Laffite, Case #300, Parish Court Civil Suit Records, NOPL.

11. Court order, March 8, 1814, notation March 9, 1814, Paul Lanusse et al. vs. Pierre Laffite, Case #300, Parish Court Civil Suit Records, NOPL.

12. Summons, March 8, 1814, notation March 9, 1814, Paul Lanusse et al. vs. Pierre Laffite, Case #300, Parish Court Civil Suit Records, NOPL.

13. New Orleans, *Courier de la Louisiane*, March 16, 1814.

14. Marie Louise Villard to Eugenie Tressanceaux, September 1, 1815, Notary Pierre Pedesclaux, Vol. 71, item 827, NONA.

15. Henry Peire to Dubourg, February 21, 1814, Entry 1627, RG 36, NA.

16. James Miller to Dubourg, February 3, 1814, Ibid.

17. "A–Z Town of Donaldson" to Dubourg, February 25, 1814, Ibid.

18. Claiborne to Dubourg, February 9, 1814, Ibid.

19. Flournoy to Dubourg, March 3, 1814, Ibid.

20. Patterson to Dubourg, March 7, 1814, Entry 1627, RG 36, NA.

21. Flournoy to Dubourg, March 7, 1814, Ibid.

22. Deposition of Jose Rodriguez and Joseph Lor, July 12, 1814, Sabourin Papers, Tulane. Faye, "Privateersmen," p. 1034, mistakenly says it was the *Legislateur* that took the *Amiable Maria*.

23. Mariano Medina y Madrid to Morphy, May 13, 1814, Morphy to Apodaca, May 20, 1814, and enclosure, Legajo 1836, AGI-Newberry.

24. Aury to Victoire Aury, February 24, 1814, Aury to J. Maignet, February 24, 1814, Aury Papers, CAHUT.

25. Luis Onís to Commanding General, August 20, 1813, Nacogdoches Archives Transcripts, Supplement, VIII, pp. 56–58, Robert Bruce Blake Collection, East Texas Research Center, Stephen F. Austin State University, Nacogdoches, TX (Blake).

26. Warren, *Sword*, pp. 79–80.

27. Statement, March 18, 1820, United States vs. John Desfarges et al., Case #1440, NAFW.

28. José L. Franco, *Documentos Para la Historia de Mexico* (Havana, Cuba, 1961), n.p., cited in Robert Vogel to the author, December 20, 2003.

29. New Orleans, *L'Ami des Lois,* January 6, 1814.

30. Antonio de Sedella to Apodaca, February 4, 1814, Legajo 1815, AGI-Newberry.

31. New Orleans, *Le Moniteur de la Louisiane,* February 12, 1814; Petition, February 12, 1814, in Sedella to Apodaca, February 23, 1814, Legajo 1815, AGI-Newberry.

32. Sedella to Apodaca, February 23, 1814, Legajo 1815, AGI-Newberry.

33. Onís to Monroe, July 18, 1814, Notes from the Spanish Legation in the United States to the Department of State, 1790–1906, Vol. 3, M-59, Record Group 59, Department of State, NA.

34. Onís to Monroe, July 18, 1814, M-59, RG 59, NA.

35. Morphy to Apodaca, June 3, 1814, Legajo 1836, AGI-Newberry.

36. Morphy to Apodaca, May 20, 1814, Legajo 1836, AGI-Newberry.

37. Morphy to Apodaca, June 3, 1814, Ibid.

38. Morphy to Apodaca, April 12, 1814, Ibid.

39. Sea protest, May 17, 1813, Notary John Lynd, Vol. 10, item 195, NONA.

40. Minutes, III, April 30, 1814, p. 309, M-1082, RG 21, NA.

41. Affidavit, December 1, 1814, Entry 1627, RG 36, NA.

42. Foley to Dubourg, May 10, 1814, Gilbert to Dubourg, May 3, 1814, Ibid.

43. Deposition of William Hosy, December 5, 1814, United States vs. Jean Laffite, Case #0573, NAFW; Vicente Quintanilla to Morphy, June 29, 1814, Morphy to Captain Intendent of Yucatan, July 7, 1814, Legajo 1836, AGI-Newberry.

44. "Memoir of Ellis P. Bean," Henderson Yoakum, *History of Texas from Its First Settlement in 1685 to Its Annexation to the United States in 1846* (New York, 1856), I, pp. 447–49. Bean wrote this memoir in 1816, so his memory should have been fresh, but there appear to be some errors and confusion in chronology. See also Bennett Lay, *The Lives of Ellis P. Bean* (Austin, 1960), p. 3. The fate of the *Tigre* is covered in testimony of John Oliver, n.d. [December 1814], United States vs. Jean Laffite, Case #0573, Parsons Collection, CAHUT, in which he says that Dominique "went out on the Tiger which was lost & he afterwards in a boat took the Felucca from the Spaniards."

45. Morphy to Apodaca, June 18, 1814, Legajo 1836, AGI-Newberry.

46. Sedella to Apodaca, July 10, 1814, Legajo 1815, AGI-Newberry.

47. Ibid; Marriage Book 3, p. 91, SAANO.

48. Faye, "Privateersmen," p. 1031.

49. Humbert statement, March 18, 1820, United States vs. John Desfarges et al., Case #1440, NAFW.

50. "Memoir of Ellis P. Bean," Yoakum, *Texas,* I, pp. 447–49; Morphy to Apodaca, November 3, 1814, José Antonio Pedroza manifesto, October 30, 1814, Legajo 1836, AGI-Newberry. The arrival of Dominique and Humbert at Barataria is fixed approximately by testimony of John Oliver, n.d. [December 1814], United States vs. Jean Laffite, Case #0573, Parsons Collection, CAHUT, in which he states that Dominique "was at Barataria when the expedition arrived [the Patterson naval attack on Barataria, September 16], he came there about 10 or 12 days or a little more from the coast of Mexico on an unarmed Felucca, & I understood that a Spanish Genl came with him & I think his name was Humbert." This would place Dominique and Humbert's arrival at around September 1–4, 1814, which is confirmed by Bean's October 21, 1814, letter in the New Orleans, *L'Ami des Lois,* October 25, 1814, in which he says he joined them at Barataria and then they sailed to New Orleans, arriving September 6. Isidro A. Beluche Mora, "Privateers of Cartagena," *Louisiana Historical Quarterly,* XXXIX (January 1956), pp. 86–87, places the arrival of Anaya in July, thanks to

dependence on a bogus Jean Laffite journal, which misinterprets chronology thanks to the absence of dates in Bean's memoir, which was undoubtedly the source for this bit of the journal. September is unquestionably established by the Oliver statement.

NINE

1. St. Louis, *Missouri Gazette & Illinois Advertiser,* June 11, 1814.

2. Deposition of Levy Scrivener, July 11, 1814, Ernest Sabourin Papers, Howard Tilton Memorial Library, Tulane University, New Orleans. Even in 1827 in New Orleans it was still widely assumed that Pierre was the man in charge at Barataria. Martin, *Louisiana,* II, p. 362.

3. Testimony of William Hoey, December 5, 1814, Patterson and Ross vs. Certain Goods Seized at Barataria, Case #0734, NAFW.

4. Deposition of William Godfrey, December 3, 1814, Patterson and Ross vs. Certain Good Vessels Seized at Barataria, Case #0734, Parsons Collection, CAHUT.

5. Testimony of William Hoey, December 5, 1814, Patterson and Ross vs. Certain Goods Seized at Barataria, Case #0734, NAFW.

6. Testimony of James Hoskins, December 5, 1814, Testimony of Daniel McMullin, December 5, 1814, Deposition of John Oliver, December 3, 1814, Patterson and Ross vs. Certain Goods Seized at Barataria, Case #0734, NAFW.

7. Deposition of Edward Williams, December 3, 1814, Ibid.; Bollaert, "Lafitte," p. 436.

8. George W. Morgan endorsement, May 7, 1816, on court order, March 26, 1816, Laffite vs. Sylvestre, Case #829, Parish Court Civil Suit Records, NOPL.

9. Paul Dear Borne and Zenon Quenebert passport, August 21, Etienne Derborne and Pierre Louvier passport, August 22, 1814, New Orleans, *Times-Picayune,* August 22, 1937. These documents were originally in the United States District Court files.

10. Deposition of Jean Laffite, July 15, 1815, John Gourjon vs. Vincent Gamby, Suit Records, #751, First Judicial District Court, Orleans Parish, NOPL.

11. "Lafitte, 'The Pirate'—Early Times in the Southwest," *DeBow's Review*, XIX (August 1855), p. 150. The informant for this story was one "Nez Coupe," a man so-called because he had lost a piece of his nose. His actual name was Chighizola. Castellanos, *New Orleans as It Was*, pp. 40–42, claimed that Gambi had that nickname, but was clearly mistaken as Gambi had been dead for almost forty years when this story was told in 1855.

12. Soto to Apodaca, April 25, 1815, Legajo 1796, AGI-Newberry.

13. Bollaert, "Lafitte," p. 436. Bollaert based this information on interviews with former Laffite associates. Though it was twenty years after the fact, and Bollaert's informants were sometimes imaginative, the account fits with what little directly contemporary evidence there is for Laffite's management.

14. Numerous Rigaud family stories about interaction with Laffite survive, including an account of François's daughter Marie winning a gambling prize for Jean by cutting a card for him. They are probably apocryphal or exaggerated, but contemporary records establish that the Rigauds were residents at the time. Ray M. Thompson, *The Land of Lafitte the Pirate* (New Orleans, 1943), p. 44.

15. Daniel Patterson to William Jones, October 10, 1814, M-147, RG 45; George T. Ross to James Monroe, October 3, 1814, RG 107, NA.

16. This speculation, based on a report cited earlier, gains more credibility when it is considered that Jean Laffite did exactly the same thing with a brig at Galveston in 1818.

17. Testimony of Daniel McMullin, December 5, 1814, Patterson and Ross vs. Certain Goods Seized at Barataria, Case #0734, NAFW.

18. Ibid.

19. This comes from John Smith Kendall, "The Huntsmen of Black Ivory," *Louisiana Historical Quarterly*, XXIV (January 1941), p. 15, who offers no authority for the claim.

20. Latour, *Memoir*, pp. 14–15, 16.

21. Marie Louise Villard to Eugenie Tressanceaux, September 1, 1815, Notary Pierre Pedesclaux, Vol. 71, item 827, NONA.

22. Bollaert, "Lafitte," p. 436.

23. Arrest order, July 8, 1814, United States vs. Pierre Laffite, Case #0573, NAFW.

24. New Orleans, *Louisiana Gazette and New-Orleans Advertiser,* July 12, 1814.

25. Mateo Gonzalez Manrique to Apodaca, September 1814, Legajo 1815, AGI-Newberry.

26. Ibid.

27. Lanusse to Dubourg, December 27, 1813, Letters from Collectors of Customs Relating to Commissions of Privateers, 1812–1815, Entry 388, RG 45, NA.

28. Carl A. Brasseaux and Glenn R. Conrad, eds., *The Road to Louisiana: The Saint-Domingue Refugees 1792–1809* (Lafayette, LA, 1992), pp. 221–22.

29. Minutes, July 18, 1814, III, p. 319–22, M-1082, RG 21, NA.

30. Ibid., July 20, 1814, III, pp. 326–27.

31. Ibid., July 27, 1814, III, pp. 338–39.

32. Brasseaux and Conrad, *Road to Louisiana,* p. 205.

33. Ex Parte Pierre Lafitte, August 6, 1814, Minutes, III, p. 350, August 8, 1814, p. 352, M-1082, RG 21, NA.

34. Opinion of Drs. Lewis Heerman and William Flood with regard to the health of said Lafitte, August 10, 1814, United States vs. Pierre Laffite, Case #0574, NAFW.

35. Ex Parte Pierre Lafitte, August 10, 1814, p. 357, August 11, p. 358, Minutes, III, M-1082, RG 21, NA.

36. Indictment, August 9, 1814, ibid., III, pp. 353–56; Presentment of Lafitte and others, August 19, 1814, Sabourin Papers, Tulane, New Orleans.

37. Babb, French Refugees, p. 300.

38. Nolte, *Memoirs,* p. 207.

39. Ibid., p. 207.

40. New Orleans, *Louisiana Gazette and New-Orleans Advertiser,* August 18, 1814. Nolte, *Memoirs,* p. 207, suggests that Pierre wrote this article, and others have accepted that since, but of course Pierre was in jail at the moment and hardly able to write letters to the press. It bears all the signs of a composition of Jean's—the hyperbole, the taunting wit, and the insolence.

41. This is the conclusion of "Lafitte, 'The Pirate'—Early Times in the Southwest," pp. 150–51, and while no source is indicated, it seems probable

that Jean was indeed in the act of making plans and/or preparations for the move as of September 1.

42. Testimony by John Oliver taken in December 1814 stated that Dominique was on Grand Isle when the British arrived on September 3. Patterson and Ross vs. Certain Good Vessels Seized at Barataria, Case #0734, NAFW.

43. Master's Log of the HMS *Sophie,* 1809–1814, September 3, 1814, Ships' Logs, 1799–1974, ADM 51/2791, Records of the Admiralty, and Ministry of Defense, Navy Department, National Archives, Kew, London, England.

44. Laffite to Nicholas Lockyer, September 4, 1814, Parsons Collection, CAHUT.

45. Cross-examination of Edward Williams, December 8, 1814, Patterson and Ross vs. Certain Good Vessels Seized at Barataria, Case #0734, NAFW.

46. Master's log of HMS *Sophie,* September 3, 1814, ADM 51/2791, National Archives, Kew.

47. Manuscript draft of *Historical Memoir of the War in West Florida and Louisiana in 1814–1815,* Arsené Latour Papers, HNOC. Here Latour implies that Laffite wanted to escape from Lockyer's pinnace once he recognized that it was English. This draft, in Latour's hand, contains some significant differences from the final published version. The translation of the original French is by Christina Vella.

48. Cross-examination of Edward Williams, December 8, 1814, Patterson and Ross vs. Certain Good Vessels Seized at Barataria, Case #0734, NAFW.

49. Manuscript of *Historical Memoir,* Latour Papers, HNOC.

50. Cross-examination of Edward Williams, December 8, 1814, Patterson and Ross vs. Certain Good Vessels Seized at Barataria, Case #0734, NAFW.

51. William D. Robinson, *A Cursory View of Spanish America, Particularly the Neighbouring Vice-Royalties of Mexico and New Granada,* (Georgetown, DC, 1815), p. 34.

52. James L. Yeo to Viscount Melville, February 19, 1813, Parsons Collection, CAHUT.

53. Fernan Nuñez to Castlereagh, July 13, 1813, Foreign Office Records, FO72/149, National Archives, Kew, London.

54. Nuñez to Castlereagh, August 17, 1813, Ibid.

55. Nuñez to Castlereagh, December 27, 1813, FO72/180, National Archives, Kew, London.

56. James Stirling, Memorandum by Captain James Stirling Regarding the Condition of Louisiana, March 17, 1813, HNOC.

57. Hugh Pigot to Alexander Cochrane, June 8, 1814, Admiralty Papers, Letters from Captains, 1/2346, National Archives, Kew, London.

58. John Sugden, "Jean Lafitte and the British Offer of 1814," *Louisiana History*, XX (Spring 1979), p. 160.

59. Except where otherwise cited, the basic account of the Laffite-Lockyer encounter that follows is based on Latour, *Memoir*, pp. 17–21.

60. Edward Nicholls, Proclamation, August 29, 1814, Parsons Collection, CAHUT. Many copies of the documents handed to Laffite exist. The ones in the Parsons Collection appear to be the originals, including this one of the Nicholls Proclamation, and evidence suggests that all of these documents were a part of Cases #0573 and/or #0574, NAFW, at one time. They were at the court as late as 1878–79, where they were examined by author Charles Hayes, who believed they were filed by Jean Laffite himself. Charles Hayes, *History of the Island and the City of Galveston* (Austin, 1974; reprint of destroyed Cincinnati, 1879 edition), p. 99n. By the early twentieth century, however, they had been stolen from the district court archives in New Orleans along with most of the other documents making up what is now the Parsons Collection. As of 1930, according to Saxon, *Lafitte*, p. 198, "some years ago these letters turned up in a curio shop in New Orleans." They were purchased by a private collector, presumably Simon J. Shwartz, for they were in his collection when it was auctioned in 1926 and purchased by Parsons (Anderson Galleries Catalog Sale Number 2096, New York, 1926, pp. 77–79). Copies of the documents that Laffite sent to New Orleans for Governor Claiborne are in the Edward Nicholls and William H. Percy Letters, HNOC. In time the Nicholls August 31, 1814, letter to Laffite and the Nicholls August 29 proclamation would appear in *Debates and Proceedings of the Congress of the United States*, Fifteenth Congress, Second Session, Appendix (Washington, 1855), pp. 1948–50.

61. Edward Nicholls to Laffite, August 31, 1814, Parsons Collection, CAHUT. Again the copy in the Parsons Collection appears to be the original, while the Edward Nicholls and William H. Percy Letters, HNOC, contains Claiborne's copy.

62. William H. Percy to Nicholas Lockyer, August 30, 1814, Parsons Collection, CAHUT.

63. Percy to Lafitte, September 1, 1814, Parsons Collection, CAHUT.

64. Manuscript draft of *Historical Memoir*, Latour Papers, HNOC.

65. Lockyer's reference to Pierre being in jail could have been an embellishment added either by Laffite or Latour, though since Spaniards like Sedella and others were writing letters in July informing their superiors of Pierre's arrest, there was no reason the British could not know of it, especially since Spain was now their ally.

66. In both the published version of Latour's *Memoir* and the manuscript draft, he claims that Lockyer also offered Laffite $30,000. If there was a cash offer it might only have been verbal and not mentioned in the letters from Nicholls and Percy, but more likely the money was a later embellishment of Laffite's when he told the story to Latour, or even earlier when he was negotiating amnesty in return for aiding General Jackson. Refusing a large sum of money would make his action look all the more self-sacrificing and patriotic. In fact, Nicholls would not have had to pay any such sum, and he had very little available, and certainly not $30,000. He was already severely taxed providing for thousands of starving Indians who agreed to serve him. He did sometimes recommend paying sums to useful individuals, but nothing like $30,000. In 1815, for instance, he suggested giving one Indian leader £300 and a commission as a militia major, with annual half pay of £146. A captain's half pay—the likely offer to Laffite—would have been £95.16.3. The captain's commission Laffite might have been offered would have been in the militia, with a half pay award, or a lump sum (John Sugden to Vogel, January 24, 1977; John Sugden, "Jean Lafitte and the British Offer of 1814," *Louisiana History*, XX [Spring 1979], p. 164). The only British hint at something substantial being proffered to Laffite comes in a report published in the London *Annual Register*, L (1814), p. 194, which says that Nicholls "addressed a letter to Mons. La Fete, or Fitte, a Frenchman, the chief of a band of outlaws or pirates . . . in which he acquainted La Fete with his arrival, and made him large offers for his assistance." Within a few years the offer became exaggerated by rumor to as much as £75,000, and the British expectation twisted into the Laffites piloting a British fleet to New Orleans (Information derived from Col. S. M. Williams respecting Lafitte, Lamar Papers, TSL).

The case of the invented or exaggerated money offer also raises the question of just how much of the rest of the detail of the episode in

Latour—outside the actual letters involved—Laffite may have invented about the episode. Lockyer's own brief account cited above certainly differs with it in several respects.

67. Cross-examination of Edward Williams, December 8, 1814, Patterson and Ross vs. Certain Good Vessels Seized at Barataria, Case #0734, NAFW.

68. Lockyer to Percy, September 11, 1814, Sugden, "British Offer," p. 165.

69. Testimony of John Oliver, December 1814, Ibid.

70. Charleston, *Courier,* July 1, 1813.

71. Masters' log of HMS *Sophie,* September 3, 1814, ADM 51/2791, National Archives, Kew; Lockyer to Percy, September 11, 1814, Sugden, "British Offer," p. 165. François-Xavier Martin, *The History of Louisiana from the Earliest Period* (New Orleans, 1827), II, p. 362, states in a quirky history written a decade after the fact that Laffite "amused his visitors" while the British officers were with him, and encouraged their hopes. Lockyer likely did not regard arrest and threats of execution as "amusement."

72. Lockyer to Percy, September 11, 1814, Sugden, "British Offer," p. 165.

73. Masters' log of HMS *Sophie,* September 4, 1814, ADM 51/2791, National Archives, Kew.

74. Laffite to Nicholas Lockyer, September 4, 1814, Parsons Collection, CAHUT. While written in French, this is not the original, which would have been kept by Lockyer and has not been found in British archives if it survives. Nor is this copy signed by Laffite, for the signature is misspelled "Lafitte," so it is a secretarial copy perhaps written for Laffite and signed by the scribe, and appears to be in the same hand as other documents written for Laffite at this time also in the Parsons Collection. It is numbered No. 6, so it is perhaps the copy sent to Blanque and handed to Claiborne. This document was also originally in the United States District Court files for Case #0573 or 0574.

75. Morphy to Apodaca, November 3, 11, 1814, Legajo 1836, AGI-Newberry.

76. Lachance, "Repercussions of the Haitian revolution in Louisiana," Geggus, *Haitian Revolution,* p. 223.

77. Stanley Faye, *Privateers of the Gulf* (Hemphill, TX, 2001), p. 54, quoting Louis de Clouet, December 7, 1814. Blanque was admitted to practice before the U.S. court January 17, 1814 (Minutes, III, p. 266, M-1082, RG 21).

78. Laffite to Jean Blanque, September 4, 1814, Parsons Collection, CAHUT. This is the original signed by Laffite, and also came originally from the United States District Court files.

79. In his September 10, 1814, letter to Blanque, written immediately on his arrival at Grand Isle, Pierre stated: "I have not yet been honoured with an answer from you. The moments are precious; pray send me an answer that may serve to direct my measures in the circumstances in which I find myself" (Parsons Collection, CAHUT). There is nothing to suggest the time or content of Pierre's message to Blanque, but it had to have been sent after his escape but before his arrival at Grand Isle. Given that Blanque was an attorney, Pierre was most likely writing about his indictment for piracy.

80. New Orleans, *Gazette and New-Orleans Advertiser*, September 8, 1814.

81. Ibid.

82. Ibid., September 6, 8, 1814.

83. Morphy to Apodaca, September 5, 1814, Legajo 1836, AGI-Newberry.

84. Mateo Gonzalez Manrique to Apodaca, September 1814, Legajo 1815, AGI-Newberry.

85. Anonymous to Dear Sir, August 8, 1814, Latour, *Memoir*, pp. v–vi.

86. Manuscript of *Historical Memoir*, Latour Papers, HNOC.

87. Laffite to Blanque, September 7, 1814, Parsons Collection, CAHUT.

88. The time of Lockyer's departure is uncertain, but September 7 seems the likely date. His laconic report to Percy on September 11 suggests that he left immediately after boarding his ship on September 4, but that is clearly not the case, for Laffite's September 7 letter states that *Sophie* is off the Barataria pass. Moreover, Lockyer's report states that it was written immediately on his arrival at Pensacola, yet it was at best a three- or four-day voyage from Grand Isle. If Lockyer had just arrived at Pensacola on September 11, then he had to have left Barataria September 7 or 8. Lockyer's report, in fact, is very skimpy. It says nothing about Lockyer meeting with Laffite, nor of Laffite's request for two weeks to prepare to aid the British, most probably because he concluded that Nicholls's offer had been rebuffed and his mission had failed, and the less said the better. Lockyer's tone in his report certainly suggests that he regards the matter as closed, and Sugden found nothing in subsequent British correspondence to indicate that they continued to think of the Baratarians (Lockyer to Percy,

September 11, 1814, Sugden, "British Offer," pp. 165, 167). The only other source shedding light is Latour's manuscript of *Historical Memoir*, Latour Papers, HNOC, but it is even less specific, saying only that "after the time fixed"—presumably the fifteen days Laffite asked for, which is clearly wrong—"the English corvette returned, no doubt to have the answer, since it went back and forth several times in front of the pass."

89. Deposition of John Blanque, April 22, 1815, United States vs. Certain Goods taken at Barataria, Case #0746, Parsons Collection, CAHUT.

90. Manuscript of *Historical Memoir*, Latour Papers, HNOC.

91. Jean Laffite to Claiborne, n.d. [September 10, 1814], Parsons Collection, CAHUT. Jack C. Ramsay, Jr., *Jean Laffite, Prince of Pirates* (Austin, TX, 1996), p. 165n, dates this letter to September 4, as does Saxon, *Lafitte*, pp. 143, 145. It is clear from the context, however, that it could not have been written on that date. The failure to mention Pierre being in jail is one clue, for that had been Jean's prime concern in his September 4 letter to Blanque. Conclusive, however, is Pierre's own September 10 letter to Blanque, cited above, in which he mentions the letter his brother has written that day to Claiborne.

TEN

1. No documentation pinpoints the date on which Blanque delivered the Lockyer correspondence to Claiborne, but Claiborne notified Andrew Jackson of it on September 8. He mentioned on that date that he had had time to authenticate Jean Laffite's signature, and also to meet over the correspondence with his council, which suggests September 7 at the latest. Since Laffite could not have dispatched the correspondence to Blanque before the afternoon of September 4, and the bayou water route to New Orleans was more than sixty miles from Grand Terre, much of it requiring rowing, a journey of less than two days is unlikely. Thus late September 6 or the next morning seems the best guess as to Blanque's receipt of the papers. It would require a little more time to hand them to Claiborne.

2. Daniel Patterson to William Jones, July 8, 1814, Area 8, M-625, RG 45, NA.

3. John Reid and John Henry Eaton, *The Life of Andrew Jackson* (Philadelphia, 1817), pp. 201–202; Gonzalez Manrique to Jackson, July 26, 1814, John

Spencer Bassett, ed., *Correspondence of Andrew Jackson* (Washington, DC, 1927), II, p. 21.

4. Jackson to Manrique, August 24, 1814, Bassett, *Correspondence*, II, p. 29, Manrique to Jackson, August 30, 1814, pp. 38–39.

5. Sedella to Onís, September 18, 1815, Papeles de Estado, America en General, Legajo 5558, AGI-Newberry.

6. Claiborne to Jackson, August 21, 1814, Bassett, *Correspondence*, VI, pp. 437.

7. Daniel Patterson to William Jones, July 8, 1814, Letters Received by the Secretary of the Navy from Commanders, "Masters Commandants Letters," 1804–1886, M-147, RG 45, NA.

8. Patterson to Secretary of the Navy, August 20, 1814, M-147, RG 45, NA.

9. Patterson to Jackson, September 2, 1814, Ibid.

10. Patterson to Jones, September 4, 1814, Ibid.

11. Bollaert, "Lafitte," p. 437, speculated that Jean Laffite went to New Orleans to meet with Claiborne, and that while he was away his men seized Lockyer, but this is impossible in the time frame.

12. Deposition of William C. C. Claiborne, n.d., Deposition of John Blanque, April 22, 1815, United States vs. Certain Goods taken at Barataria, Case #0746, Parsons Collection, CAHUT.

13. Deposition of William C. C. Claiborne, n.d., Patterson and Ross vs. Certain Vessels, etc., Case #0734, Parsons Collection, CAHUT.

14. Claiborne to Jackson, September 8, 1814, Bassett, *Correspondence*, VI, pp. 439–40.

15. The authenticity of these documents has received little study, an issue discussed in Robert C. Vogel, "Pierre and Jean Laffite: Going to the Primary Sources," *Laffite Society Chronicles*, VII (October 2001), [p. 9]. However, there seems little cause to doubt them. Certainly Percy's letters and Nicholls's letter and proclamation are genuine. Where question exists, it would have to be with Laffite's September 4 note to Lockyer, which survives only in the copy Jean sent to Blanque, and could thus be his invention. However, since it is the document that most incriminates Jean by its implication that he will cooperate with the British, it would be a foolish document for him to fake.

16. Testimony of P. L. B. Duplessis, December 7, 1814, Minutes, III, pp. 407–8, RG 21, NA.

17. George Ross to Jackson, October 3, 1814, Bassett, *Correspondence,* II, pp. 66–67.

18. Claiborne to Jackson, September 8, 1814, Bassett, *Correspondence,* VI, pp. 439–40, Ross to Jackson, October 3, 1814, VII, pp. 66–67.

19. Latour, *Memoirs,* pp. 22–23. Latour is the only authority for this promise, and it may be an embellishment that Jean Laffite added in telling the story to Latour.

20. Pierre Laffite to Blanque, Grand Terre, September 10, 1814, Parsons Collection, CAHUT.

21. Deposition of John Blanque, April 22, 1815, United States vs. Certain Goods taken at Barataria, Case #0746, Parsons Collection, CAHUT.

22. Morphy to Apodaca, September 12, 1814, Legajo 1836, AGI-Newberry.

23. Libel, October 14, 1814, Patterson and Ross vs. Certain Vessels, Goods and Merchandise, Case #0734, NAFW; George T. Ross to James Monroe, October 3, 1814, RG 107, NA.

24. Patterson to Jones, October 10, 1814, M-147, RG 45, NA.

25. Charles Wollstonecraft to Jackson, September 13, 1814, Harold Moser, David R. Hoth, Sharon Macpherson, and John H. Reinbold, eds., *The Papers of Andrew Jackson. Volume III, 1814–1815* (Knoxville, TN, 1991), p. 136.

26. Morphy to Apodaca, September 12, 1814, Legajo 1836, AGI-Newbury.

27. Deposition of Manuel Ribon, September 27, 1814, United States vs. Joachim Santos, Case #0772, NAFW.

28. Sea protest of Lorenzo Oliver, September 28, 1814, Notary John Lynd, Vol. 11, item 399, NONA.

29. Deposition of Don Miguel Antonio Puentes, December 8, 1814, Miguel Puentes to John B. Laporta, October 29, 1814, Don Miguel Puentes vs. Schooner *Experiment* Alias *Harlequin,* Case #0766, NAFW.

30. Deposition of Edward Williams, December 3, 1814, Parsons Collection, CAHUT.

31. Testimony of John Oliver missing from #0734, but appearing in New Orleans, *Daily Picayune,* April 15, 1880. Faye, "Privateersmen," p. 1032 sug-

gests that the Laffites left Dominique in command at Barataria before Patterson struck, but there is nothing other than Oliver's statement, which could be hearsay, to suggest that Dominique worked for them or was a Baratarian leader.

32. Sea protest, September 29, 1814, Notary John Lynd, Vol. II, item 401, NONA.

33. Deposition of John Oliver, December 3, 1814, Parsons Collection, CAHUT.

34. Latour, *Memoir*, p. 23, states that the Laffites knew Patterson was coming, again information that Latour only would have gotten from Jean Laffite.

35. Deposition of Joseph Siranc, October 7, 1814, United States vs. Dominique alias Frederique Youx, Case #0779, NAFW.

36. Cross-examination of John Oliver, December 8, 1814, Patterson and Ross vs. Certain Goods Seized at Barataria, Case #0734, NAFW.

37. Cross-examination of John Oliver, n.d., United States vs. Jean Laffite, Case #0573, Parsons Collection, CAHUT; Deposition of Joseph Siranc, n.d., United States vs. Dominique alias Frederique Youx, Case #0779, NAFW.

38. J. O. Dyer, whose Laffite researches and articles are almost uniformly unreliable, concluded that Laffite asked Patterson to take Barataria since it had become an unmanageable liability thanks to the number of mulattoes who came with the Haitian refugees. Galveston, *Daily News*, September 19, 1926.

39. Cross-examination of John Oliver, December 8, 1814, Patterson and Ross vs. Certain Good Vessels Seized at Barataria, Case #0734, NAFW.

40. Jean Laffite to Madison, December 27, 1815, James Madison Papers, Library of Congress, Washington, DC.

41. Cross-examination of John Oliver, n.d., United States vs. Jean Laffite, Case #0573, Parsons Collection, CAHUT.

42. Alex St. Helme vs. Captain Jones of United States Navy, April 14, 1815, Case #0801, NAFW.

43. New Orleans, *Times-Picayune*, August 22, 1937.

44. Cross-examination of John Oliver, n.d., United States vs. Jean Laffite,

Case #0573, Parsons Collection, CAHUT; Cross-examination of John Oliver, December 8, 1814, Patterson and Ross vs. Certain Goods Seized at Barataria, Case #0734, NAFW.

45. Sea protest of Lorenzo Oliver, September 28, 1814, Notary John Lynd, Vol. ii, item 399, NONA.

46. Cross-examination of John Oliver, December 8, 1814, Patterson and Ross vs. Certain Goods Seized at Barataria, Case #0734, NAFW.

47. Latour, *Memoir*, p. 23; Manuscript of *Historical Memoir*, Latour Papers, HNOC.

48. Patterson to Jones, October 10, 1814, M-147, RG 45, NA.

49. Sea protest of Joseph Martinot, September 29, 1814, Notary John Lynd, Vol. ii, item 401, NONA; Statement of Joseph Martinot, Patterson, Ross et al. vs. Certain Bank Notes, Case #0754, NAFW.

50. Testimony of Edward Williams, December 3, 1814, Patterson and Ross vs. Certain Goods Seized at Barataria, Case #0734, NAFW.

51. Ross to Monroe, October 3, 1814, RG 107, NA.

52. Patterson to Jones, October 10, 1814, M-146, RG 45, NA.

53. Sea Protest, September 29, 1814, Notary John Lynd, Vol. ii, item 401, NONA.

54. Statement of Joseph Martinot, November 9, 1814, Patterson, Ross et al. vs. Certain Bank Notes, Case #0754; Alex St. Helme vs. Captain Thomas Jones, April 14, 1815, Case #0801, NAFW.

55. Patterson to Jones, October 10, 1814, M-147, RG 45, NA.

56. Ross to Monroe, October 3, 1814, RG 107, NA.

57. Cross-examination of Edward Williams, December 3, 1814, Libel, October 14, 1814, Patterson and Ross vs. Certain Vessels, Goods and Merchandise, Case #0734, NAFW; United States vs. Certain Goods on Board the *Bolivar*, Case #0746, Parsons Collection, CAHUT; List of Vessels reported at the custom house as having been captured at Barataria, Entry 1627, RG 36, NA.

58. Libel, October 22, 1814, United States vs. Certain Goods Taken at Barataria, Case #0746; Deposition, November 25, 1814, William Lawrence, Daniel Patterson et al. vs. Seventy Four Pipes of Wine, etc., Case #0762, NAFW.

59. Petition of Jean Laffite, July 28, 1815, Daniel Patterson vs. 163 Barrels of Flour and Other Articles, Case #0753, Parsons Collection, CAHUT.

60. Goods found onshore at Barataria, Statement of duties in the Above, 1816, Entry 1627, RG 36, NA.

61. Deposition of Daniel Patterson, November 5, 1814, Daniel T. Patterson and George Ross et al. vs. Certain Gold Coin, Case #0750, NAFW.

62. Seizure order, November 10, 1814, Patterson and Ross et al. vs. 16 Plates of bullion &c, Case #0753, NAFW.

63. François-Xavier Martin, *The History of Louisiana from the Earliest Period* (New Orleans, 1827), II, p. 339.

64. Statement, June 23, 1815, Patterson and Ross vs. Certain Goods Seized at Barataria, Case #0746, NAFW.

65. Bollaert, "Lafitte," p. 438; Faye, "Great Stroke," p. 752.

66. Deposition of Patterson, n.d., letter of marque, December 20, 1813, Daniel Patterson vs. the *General Bolivar,* Case #0760, NAFW; Patterson to Jones, October 10, 1814, M-147, RG 45, NA.

67. Protest of Joseph Carpentier, October 1, 1814, Notary John Lynd, Vol. 11, item 404, NONA.

68. United States vs. Certain Goods on Board the Bolivar, Case #0746, Parsons Collection, CAHUT; Statement of sale, July 12, 1815, United States vs. the Proceeds of the Sale of the Schooner *General Bolivar,* Case #0837, NAFW.

69. Patterson to Jones, October 10, 1814, M-147, RG 45, NA; New Orleans, *Times-Picayune,* August 22, 1937.

70. Deposition of Patterson, November 5, 1814, Daniel Patterson, George Ross et al. vs. Certain Gold Coin, Case #0750, NAFW.

71. Kingston, Jamaica, *Gazette,* September 24, 1814.

72. New Orleans, *Louisiana Courier,* September 26, 1814.

73. New Orleans, *Louisiana Gazette and New-Orleans Advertiser,* September 20, 1814.

74. An assessment with which Robert Vogel, "Jean Laffite, the Baratarians, and the Battle of New Orleans: A Reappraisal," *Louisiana History,* XLI (Summer 2000), p. 265, agrees.

75. Charles Havens Hunt, *Life of Edward Livingston* (New York, 1864), p. 203, argues that it was learning of the Laffite correspondence that led Livingston to call the meeting, but offers no evidence.

76. While there are several secondary assertions that the Laffite correspondence was discussed at the meeting, and even that it was the principal reason for the gathering, no contemporary source gives a full account of the topics discussed or decisions taken.

77. William B. Hatcher, *Edward Livingston, Jefferson Republican and Jacksonian Democrat* (Baton Rouge, LA, 1940), pp. 203–4.

78. Committee of Public Safety to Jackson, September 18, 1814, Bassett, *Correspondence*, II, p. 52.

79. Claiborne to Jackson, September 19, 1814, Ibid., pp. 54–55.

80. Claiborne to Jackson, September 20, 1814, Ibid., p. 56.

81. Patterson to Jones, November 18, 1814, M147, RG 45, NA.

82. Morphy to Apodaca, September 19, 1814, Legajo 1836, AGI-Newberry.

83. New Orleans, *Louisiana Gazette and New-Orleans Advertiser,* September 24, 1814.

84. While no contemporary source specifically attests that Livingston championed the idea of enlisting the Baratarians in the committee meetings, Jean Laffite's October 4, 1814, letter to Livingston, cited below, indicates as much.

85. An article in the New Orleans, *Times-Picayune,* January 14, 1918, asserted without authority that Livingston became the Laffites' lawyer in 1811, which is insupportable. There is no evidence of him handling legal business for them prior to 1815.

86. Hunt, *Livingston,* pp. 124–25.

87. Jean Laffite to Madison, December 27, 1815, Madison Papers, Library of Congress. There were two LaBranche plantations on the German Coast at this time, both on the left or east bank, according to the 1810 census for St. Charles Parish, pp. 6–7. Their relative place on the list of inhabitants suggests that they were located between modern-day Destrehan and St. Rose.

88. Jean Laffite to Livingston, October 4, 1814, Edward Livingston Papers, Princeton University, Princeton, NJ.

89. Deposition of John Randolph, October 11, 1814, United States vs. Manuel Joachim, Case #0773; Presentment, October 19, 1814, United States vs. Henri St. Gême, Case #0786; Presentment, October 27, 1814, United States vs. Alexander St. Helme, Case #0781; Presentment, October 27, 1814, United States vs. Jacques Cannon, Case #0777; Presentment, October 27, 1814, United States vs. René Roland, Case #0778; Presentment, October 29, 1814, United States vs. William Fleming, Case #0780, NAFW.

90. Presentment October 24, 1814, United States vs. Benjamin Lafond [*sic*], United States vs. Benjamin Lafond, Case #0775; Presentment, October 24, 1814, United States vs. Alexander Bonnival, Case #0785, NAFW.

91. Presentment of Dominique Youx, October 24, 1814, Deposition of Bertrande Priella, October 7, 1814, Deposition of William Godfrey, n.d., Deposition of Antonio Paras, October 7, 1814, Deposition of Andrew Whiteman, October 7, 1814, Deposition of Joseph Siranc, October 7, 1814, United States vs. Dominique alias Frederique Youx, Case #0779, NAFW.

92. Martin, *History of Louisiana*, p. 367; Claim of José Garcia y Posseda, October 22, 1814, United States vs. Certain Goods Taken at Barataria, Case #0746, NAFW.

93. United States vs. José Toledo, Case #0787, NAFW.

94. In 1830 François Barbé-Marbois, without stating his authority, claimed that Jean Laffite wrote directly to Claiborne from hiding and "sent him the originals of the correspondence with the British officers." That is a clear confusion with the Blanque episode, but then Barbé-Marbois went on to say that Laffite "proposed, at the same time, to surrender himself." It is a possibility, of course, but nothing else supports this statement. François Barbé-Marbois, *The History of Louisiana, Particularly of the Cession of That Colony to the United States of America; With an Introductory Essay on the Constitution and Government of the United States* (Philadelphia, 1830), p. 384.

95. Claiborne to James Monroe, October 24, 1814, Rowland, *Letter Books*, VI, p. 291.

96. Latour, *Memoir*, pp. 16–17.

97. Thomas ap Catesby Jones to Patterson, November 11, 1814, M147, RG 45, NA.

98. Patterson to Jones, October 14, November 18, 1814, Ibid.

99. Thomas ap Catesby Jones to Patterson, November 11, 1814, Ibid.

100. "Memoirs of Mrs. Martha Martin," typescript in Melrose Collection, Bound Vol. 41, NSUL. This is admittedly an interpretation of this source. In the memoir, written some years later, Martin appears to be writing about Jean Laffite, yet it is clear that in dealing with 1814 she is talking about Pierre, for she mentions his capture and escape and the reward offered for him. She also says that she met "Lafitte" at Brashear City when she passed through it, and then again below Donaldsonville, but she would not meet the same man at two places when she was herself traveling. Given that Jean was apparently communicating with Livingston in New Orleans, it would make more sense that it was he whom she met on the Lafourche, and Pierre whom she met at the inn at Brashear City. Her husband was Thomas Martin of Nashville, who made frequent slave deals in the Point Coupée vicinity. Sale May 2, 1817, February 13, 1819, Afro-Louisiana History and Genealogy, 1718–1820 (Slave) site.

101. Brown to Monroe, Oct. 1, 1814, James Monroe Papers, Library of Congress.

102. Patterson to Jones, October 10, 1814, M147, RG 45, NA.

103. New Orleans, Louisiana Gazette and New-Orleans Advertiser, October 11, 1814.

104. Proclamation, September 21, 1814, Bassett, Correspondence, II, pp. 57–59.

105. Jackson to Claiborne, September 30, 1814, Ibid., p. 63.

106. Claiborne to Andrew Jackson, October 28, 1814, Rowland, Letter Books, VI, pp. 296–97.

107. Jackson to Livingston, October 23, 1814, Bassett, Correspondence, II, p. 81.

108. Livingston to Madison, October 24, 1814, Madison Papers, Library of Congress.

109. Claiborne to Richard Rush, October 30, 1814, Gayarré, Pirate-Patriots, pp. 66–69.

110. New Orleans, Louisiana Gazette and New-Orleans Advertiser, October 20, 1814.

111. Baltimore, Nile's Weekly Register, VII, November 5, 1814, pp. 134–35.

112. Marigny, Reflections, pp. 65–66. Marigny is virtually the only knowledgeable eyewitness source for the actions of himself, Villeré, and Hall in

this episode. Unfortunately, he wrote his recollections in 1848, thirty-three years after the fact, and somewhat confuses chronology and clouds his meaning. For instance, Marigny has Judge Hall telling him to "present at once a resolution in the Legislature demanding that the procedures against these men be suspended for four months and I will immediately give my orders to the District Attorney of the United States." This has commonly been interpreted to mean that Hall wanted the legislature to pass a resolution halting the piracy proceedings. However, the legislature had no authority over the federal court, and its December 18 action in fact dealt only with civil suits. It was Hall's recess of the federal court that stopped federal proceedings, along with Grymes's consent no doubt, though no documentation survives of any order at the time from Grymes or any specific statement from the court about quashing prosecutions.

113. Resolution of the Louisiana Legislature Concerning the Baratarians, December 14, 1814, Bassett, *Correspondence*, II, p. 114.

114. Recess order, December 15, 1814, Minutes, III, p. 413, RG 21, NA.

115. Note by Jackson on Monroe to Jackson, December 10, 1814, Bassett, *Correspondence*, II, p. 110, Jackson to James Monroe, February 18, 1815, p. 174.

116. Jackson to Samuel L. Southard, March 6, 1827, Ibid., III, p. 347. There are several versions of the Laffite offer to Jackson, the most bizarre being the assertion that Laffite asked Jackson to surround his establishment at Barataria—which no longer existed—with forces so overwhelming that the smugglers would not dare resist. Then they would surrender and be in place to serve in Jackson's army. New Orleans, *Times-Picayune*, August 20, 1871.

117. Rowland, *Letter Books*, VI, p. 324.

118. Latour, *Historical Memoir*, pp. 226–27 (Smith edition); Marigny, *Reflections*, pp. 65–66. Marigny's chronology is off here, for he says that the legislature passed its resolution "the next day and was passed unanimously." The resolution passed December 18, in fact, but Hall recessed the court December 15.

119. Jackson to Samuel L. Southard, March 6, 1827, Bassett, *Correspondence*, III, p. 347.

120. Marigny, *Reflections*, pp. 65–66.

121. Nolte, *Memoirs* p. 209.

122. Hatcher, *Livingston,* pp. 214–15n.

123. John Dick to Claiborne, February 10, 1815, Entry 9, Records of the Attorney General's Office, General Records—Letters Received 1809–1870, Louisiana 1815 to 1860, Record Group 60, General Records of the Department of Justice, NA.

124. Claiborne to John Dick, February 11, 1815, Rowland, *Letter Books,* VI, p. 338.

125. John Coffee to Jackson, December 15, 1814, Moser et al., *Papers of Andrew Jackson,* III, p. 482; W. H. K. to the editor, May 20, 1852, "Lafitte," *DeBow's Southern and Western Review,* XIII (August 1852), p. 204.

126. Jean Laffite to Madison, December 27, 1815, Madison Papers, Library of Congress. In this letter Laffite says that he held the meeting "where I acquainted them with the nature of the danger which was not far off (as may be seen by the annexed document which is attested by some of the most notorious of the inhabitants which were present) a few days after a proclamation of the Governor of the state permitted us to joyne the army which was organizing for the defence of the country."

127. Vogel argues correctly that there is no contemporary evidence of a meeting between Laffite and Jackson before December 17 and Claiborne's pardon offer proclamation. He says they might have met on Sunday, December 18, the day Jackson ordered the release of the Baratarians who agreed to volunteer, which seems reasonable (Vogel, "Battle of New Orleans," pp. 264–65). With the meeting of Jackson and Jean Laffite, as with other elements of this story, there are wild tales that later appeared in print. Perhaps the most silly is the story in Charles Ellms, *The Pirates Own Book, or Authentic Narratives of the Lives, Exploits, and Executions of the Most Celebrated Sea Robbers* (Portland, ME, 1837), pp. 70–71, which says that Laffite met with Jackson and Claiborne in late September, when Jackson was 140 miles away at Mobile.

128. Latour, *Memoir,* pp. 71–72.

ELEVEN

1. Enrollment December 23, 1814, Vincent Gamby Compiled Service Record, War of 1812, Records of the Adjutant General's Office, Record Group 94, NA.

2. Smith, "Editor's Introduction," Latour, *Historical Memoir*, p. xvi.

3. Ibid., pp. xx–xxi.

4. Jackson to Michael Reynolds, December 22, 1814, Parsons Collection, CAHUT.

5. James Parton, *Life of Andrew Jackson* (Boston, 1860), II, pp. 119–20, is the earliest known source for this claim that Livingston placed his family in Pierre's protection. It was repeated four years later in Hunt, *Livingston*, p. 204. Neither offered authority for the statement, and Hunt may have gotten it from Parton, or from the Livingston family.

6. Letter dated January 30, 1815, "A Junior Officer's Observations from the Field of Battle," *Naval Chronicle*, XXXIII (April–May 1815), pp. 385–88.

7. Jackson to Pierre Laffite, n.d. [March–April 1815], Parsons Collection, CAHUT [a copy of this is also among three items in the Jean Laffite Collection, William R. Perkins Library, Duke University, Durham, NC, but they are all photocopies of items from the Parsons Collection]. There is some ambiguity about this document. The signature certainly appears to be Jackson's. It is not explicitly addressed to Laffite, but merely to "Sir." However, attribution in a different hand says it is a recommendation to a "Lafette." Stanley Clisby Arthur, *Jean Laffite, Gentleman Rover* (New Orleans, 1952), pp. 130–31, reproduces the text of this letter, but cites it as being part of Case #0746, United States vs. Certain Goods and Merchandise, NAFW, a document introduced along with others in establishing the Laffites' services to the country during the crisis. Most of the other documents in the Parsons Collection came from NAFW, and some from Case #0746. Some have suggested that the Jackson letter was addressed to Claiborne, but the burden of logic, and the general provenance of the Parsons documents, leans toward Laffite as the addressee.

8. Livingston to Jackson, December 25, 1814, Bassett, *Correspondence*, II, p. 125. Jane Lucas de Grummond, *The Baratarians and the Battle of New Orleans* (Baton Rouge, LA, 1961), p. 101, incorrectly reads this letter to mean that Jean Laffite advised Livingston.

9. De Grummond, *Baratarians*, p. 104, with no supporting source, says that Jean Laffite supervised the placement and fortifying of this battery. There is, in fact, no evidence that he was even on the field at this time.

10. Nolte, *Memoirs*, p. 216.

11. Le Chevalier de Tousard to John Clement, January 6, 1815, Norman

Wilkinson, ed., "The Assaults on New Orleans, 1814–1815," *Louisiana History*, III (Winter 1962), pp. 47–48.

12. Gayarré, *Pirate-Patriots*, p. 71. Gayarré states that he was told this by an eyewitness.

13. Nolte, *Memoirs*, pp. 217-18.

14. Despite all that has been written, there is not a single reliable contemporary source that mentions Jean Laffite's whereabouts between December 22 and January 8, 1815. There are numerous references to "Mr. Laffite" with the main army, and their context makes it clear that Pierre is the one referenced.

15. Vogel, "New Orleans," p. 274.

16. Nolte, *Fifty Years*, p. 218; Gamby Service Record, RG 94, NA.

17. Jackson to David B. Morgan, January 8, 1815, Bassett, *Correspondence*, II, pp. 132–33.

18. David B. Morgan to Jackson, January 8, 1815, Ibid., VI, pp. 445–46. That the Laffite referred to in this correspondence is Pierre is confirmed by Morgan's reference to him as "Mr. Lafeete senr."

19. John Grymes to Morgan, January 8, 1815, Parsons Collection, CAHUT.

20. There is no certainty of this friendship between Laffite and Morgan, but in the New Orleans, *Times-Picayune* of August 23, 1925, appeared a miniature portrait allegedly of Pierre Laffite that antique dealer Joseph Pelletier of New Orleans claimed to have acquired from a lineal descendant of Morgan.

21. Deposition of Michael Reynolds, July 22, 1815, United States vs. Schooner *Presidente*, Case #0811, NAFW.

22. Deposition of Pierre Laffite, n.d., United States vs. Schooner *Presidente*, Case #0811, NAFW; Sea Protest of David Libby, February 27, 1815, Notary John Lynd, Vol. 12, item 7, NONA.

23. Deposition of John O'Neil, n.d., United States vs. Schooner *Presidente*, Case #0811, NAFW.

24. Deposition of John Antoine, June 24, 1815, United States vs. Schooner *Presidente*, Case #0811, NAFW.

25. Deposition of James Thompson, June 23, 1815, United States vs. Schooner *Presidente*, Case #0811; Laméson statement, n.d., United States vs. Pierre Laméson, Case #0825, NAFW.

26. Deposition of John Antoine, June 24, 1815, United States vs. Schooner *Presidente*, Case #0811, NAFW.

27. Pierre Laméson commission, February 25, 1813, United States vs. Schooner *Presidente*, Case #0811, NAFW.

28. Deposition of James Thompson, June 23, 1815, Deposition of Marco Bashia, June 8, 1815, Deposition of A. Miller, June 24, 1815, United States vs. Schooner *Presidente*, Case #0811, NAFW.

29. Letter from New Orleans, January 13, 1815, Baltimore, *Nile's Weekly Register*, VII, February 11, 1815, p. 375.

30. Letter of Anne Louis de Tousard, January 20, 1815, Wilkinson, "Assaults on New Orleans," p. 51.

31. Lachance, "Immigrants," p. 138.

32. St. Louis, *Missouri Gazette & Illinois Advertiser*, February 4, 1815.

33. Letter dated January 20, 1814, Savannah, GA, *Republican and Savannah Evening Ledger*, February 21, 1815.

34. Hunt, *Livingston*, p. 204.

35. Latour, *Historical Memoirs*, appendix LXIX, pp. clxxxiii–clxxxv.

36. Patterson to B. W. Crowninshield, December 29, 1814, Area 8, M-625, NA.

37. New Orleans, *Daily Delta*, November 5, 1851.

38. It seems especially noteworthy that Latour is silent on the subject of the brothers during the battle, since he clearly got his account of the Lockyer affair and the subsequent pardon-for-service bargain directly from Jean or Pierre Laffite. If they played any active part in the battle, or if Jean was even present on the occasion, they would surely have told their friend when he gathered accounts for the book that he would start writing within a few months after the victory. His silence, especially considering the tendency of both Laffites otherwise to exaggerate their importance, suggests that there was nothing for them to tell.

39. Many years later a story was told that during the battle Plauché's company needed flints. Jean Laffite went aboard one of the schooners that had been taken from him at Barataria and with the help of others rolled off a keg of flints, then passed them out personally along the line. It is surely apocryphal, conflating the Laffite contribution to the battle with the established provision of the flints. New Orleans, *Bulletin*, August 29, 1874.

40. Jackson to Hugh L. White, February 7, 1827, Bassett, *Correspondence*, II, p. 339.

41. Indictment and fine, March 31, 1815, United States vs. Andrew Jackson, Case #0791, Works Project Administration, *Synopses of Cases in the U.S. District Court for the Eastern District of Louisiana Cases #1 to #3000 1806-1831* (Baton Rouge, 1941), p. 91.

42. Nolte, *Memoirs*, pp. 229–31.

43. Andrew Jackson to Pierre Laffite, n.d. [March–April 1815], Parsons Collection, CAHUT.

44. W. H. K. to the editor, May 20, 1852, "Lafitte," *DeBow's Southern and Western Review*, XIII (August 1852), pp. 204–5. Of course this anecdote, published thirty-seven years after the fact as a recollection supplied to an editor, may be apocryphal or embellished. Yet given the association between Pierre and Coffee during the campaign, it has the ring of authenticity. As so often happened by this time, the Laffite involved has been shifted in recollection from Pierre to Jean.

45. James Madison Proclamation, February 6, 1815, Richardson, *Messages and Papers*, I, pp. 558–60.

46. Claiborne to John Dick, February 11, 1815, Rowland, *Letter Books*, VI, p. 338.

47. Later writers sometimes claimed that Grymes resigned in order to represent the Baratarians, but that simply is not true. He did not appear in court as counsel for a privateer or smuggler until the trial of William Mitchell of the *Cometa* in 1816. See, for instance, Gayarré, *Pirate-Patriots*, p. 11, and Arthur, *Laffite*, p. 130. Saxon, *Lafitte*, p. 119, builds on Gayarré, and erroneously has both Grymes and Livingston acting for the Laffites from the summer of 1814. Ramsay, *Laffite*, p. 46, has Livingston working to defend Pierre Laffite from August 1814.

48. *Nolle prosse* entries, February 20, 1815, Cases #0770, 0771, 0772, 0773, 0774, 0775, 0776, 0777, 0778, 0779, 0780, 0781, 0782, 0783, 0784, 0785, 0786, 0787, Minutes, 7RA-119, RG 21, NAFW.

49. Dick to Claiborne, February 10, 1815, Entry 9, RG 60, NA; Claiborne to Dick, February 11, 1815, Rowland, *Letter Books*, VI, p. 338.

50. Discontinuance, May 20, 1815, United States vs. Jean Humbert, Case #0738; Discontinuance, May 16, 1815, United States vs. J. A. De Riano,

Case #0794; same for Cases #0739, 0740, Minutes, 7RA-119, RG 21, NAFW.

51. George W. Morgan endorsement, May 7, 1816, on court order, March 26, 1816, Laffite vs. Sylvestre, Case #829, Parish Court Civil Suit Records, NOPL.

52. Nolte, *Memoirs*, p. 207.

53. Joaquin Provensal to Jackson, February 17, 1815, Moser et al., *Papers*, III, p. 516.

54. During his research in the 1920s Lyle Saxon claimed to have found ten sources touching on Jean Laffite and women, but in his book he did not identify any of them such that they could be found and assessed today. In the quotations he gave, a few sound contemporary to the 1810s, and others more like recollections. In the absence of any original sources for the quotations Saxon presented, they have not been used here. Saxon, *Lafitte*, pp. 191–92.

55. The clear and inferential connections between Catiche Villard and Marie's sister Catherine are many, more than sufficient to risk identifying the two as one and the same. In the 1850 census for Orleans Parish Catiche is found living next door to Pierre and Marie's daughter Catherine Coralie Roup, while in her own household there dwelled Adele Lafite and in the Roup home lived Alexandre Lafite (1st Ward, 3d Municipality, 1850 Census, Orleans Parish, p. 90). The possibility of a liaison with Jean Laffite predating February 1815 lies in Catiche's giving birth to a daughter Marie on November 10, 1813. The sponsors on the occasion of the baby's baptism on June 12, 1814, were Joseph Aicard and Louise Filiosa, who later sponsored Pierre and Marie's son Joseph in 1821 (Nolan and Dupont, eds., *Sacramental Records of the Roman Catholic Church of the Archdiocese of New Orleans, Volume 11, 1812–1814*, p. 434; *Volume 14, 1820–1821*, p. 228). However, with no father identified, and no association of the Laffite name with the baby Marie, this could easily have been a child by a prior liaison. Sources give Catiche's birth year only approximately, as early as 1780 and as late as 1794, the preponderance leaning toward 1792–93.

56. The date of Catherine's conception is derived from the baptismal record of her son by Jean Laffite, which records the date of birth as November 4, 1815. Pierre Laffite and Marie Villard appeared at the baptism as sponsors (Nolan and Dupont, eds., *Sacramental Records of the Roman*

Catholic Church of the Archdiocese of New Orleans, Volume 14, 1820–1821, p. 229).

57. New Orleans, *L'Ami des Lois,* February 28, 1815.

58. Petition of Paul Lanusse, John Francis Meriente, Claude Guillodon, and José Antonio De Riano, November 4, 1814, Paul Lanusse et al. vs. Pierre Laffite, Case #300, Parish Court Civil Suit Records, NOPL.

59. Guilledon Cadet vs. Bellurgey, Robin, Pierre Lafitte, and William St. Marc, #2560, City Court Suit Records; William Thomas vs. Peter Laffite, #729, First Judicial Court Records, NOPL.

60. Agreement between John Lafith and Edward Grant, April 24, 1815, Notary John Lynd, Vol. 12, item 104, NONA.

61. One thing the Laffites definitely did not contemplate doing was going into the retail meat business. Tim Pickles, *New Orleans 1815* (Oxford, UK, 2000), p. 90, reproduces a document dated January 4, 1815, credited only to an unidentified "New Orleans Auction Company." It purports to be a license granted to Pierre Laffite "to have a butcher shop on Bourbon and the intersection with St. Philip" for one year from that date. It is signed by Mayor Nicolas Girod and by Laffite. The Pierre Laffite signature does not even closely resemble his authentic signature. Moreover, the city council did not issue such licenses, and on the date specified the council did not meet, its sessions being suspended for some time because of the pending battle. The document is a forgery of unknown origin and date, and its falsity is further confirmed by its linking Laffite to the Bourbon and St. Philip intersection that tradition identified as the site of the fictional blacksmith shop.

62. New Orleans, *L'Ami des Lois,* March 21, 1815.

63. Livingston to Lewis Livingston, July 1815, Hunt, *Livingston,* p. 215 and n.

64. See the French draft of Latour, *Historical Memoir,* in Latour Papers, HNOC.

65. See, for instance, the Smith edition of *Historical Memoir,* pp. 185–93.

66. Minutes, October 24, 1814, p. 388, M-1082, RG 21, NA.

67. Minutes, November 29, 1814, p. 404, Ibid.

68. Statement of J. Duplessis, December 5, December 8, 1814, Daniel Patterson vs. the *General Bolivar,* Case #0760, NAFW.

69. Court order, February 20, 1815, Patterson et al. vs. 74 Pipes, Case #0762; Court order, February 25, 1815, Patterson and Ross vs. Certain Goods and Vessels Seized at Barataria, Case #0734, Minutes, 7RA-119, RG 21, NAFW.

70. Claim, March 23, 1815, Francisco Ajuria vs. Schooner *La Dorada*, Case #0763, Minutes, 7RA-119, RG 21, NAFW.

71. Court order, April 17, 1815, William Lawrence, Daniel Patterson et al. vs. Seventy Four Pipes of Wine, etc., Case #0762, Minutes, 7RA-119, RG 21, NAFW.

72. Court orders, April 24, 1815, Cases #0746, 0734, Minutes, 7RA-119, RG 21, NAFW.

73. Motion, April 24, 1815, United States vs. Certain Goods and Vessels Taken at Barataria, Case #0746 and 0734, Minutes, 7RA-119, RG 21, NAFW.

74. United States vs. Certain Goods &c Taken at Barataria, Case #0746, Minutes, 7RA-119, RG 21, NAFW.

75. Court order, May 16, 1815, Diego Francisco Unzaga & others vs. *Dorada* alias *Rosalie*, Case #0763, Court order, May 16, 1815, Miguel Barcenas vs. *Amiable Maria*, Case #0764, Minutes, 7RA-119, RG 21, NAFW.

76. Court order, May 27, 1815, Patterson, Ross & others vs. Certain Gold and Silver, Case #0750, Minutes, 7RA-119, RG 21, NAFW.

77. Faye, "Great Stroke," p. 752.

78. The extant Livingston biographies are inadequate, unfortunately, and none explore the relationship with the Laffites beyond a superficial mention.

79. Court order, July 12, 1815, Patterson, Ross et al. vs. Certain Vessels, Goods and Merchandise taken on the *Petit Milan*, Case #0734, Minutes, 7RA-119, RG 21, NAFW.

80. Deposition of John Blanque, April 22, 1815, United States vs. Certain Goods taken at Barataria, Case #0746, Jackson to Pierre Laffite, n.d. [March–April 1815], Parsons Collection, CAHUT; Latour, *Memoir*, p. 16. The surviving originals of the Lockyer documents, in the Parsons Collection, show none of the customary docketing that appears on documents submitted to the district court, suggesting that Laffite did not successfully introduce them as evidence or exhibits.

81. Duplessis to Campbell, January 19, 1816, Entry 1627, RG, NA.

82. Sedella to Apodaca, December 27, 1815, Legajo 1815, AGI-Newberry.

TWELVE

1. Toledo to the Mexican Congress, February 10, 1815, in Warren, *Sword*, pp. 120–21.

2. Toledo to Bean, March 23, 1815, Papeles Dirigos por el Traidor Toledo, Archivo General de Indias Transcripts, CAHUT.

3. John Dick to Richard Rush, August 19, 1815, M-179, RG 59, NA, says she was purchased by Julius Amigoni, but West appears to have been the owner.

4. John Dick to Richard Rush, August 19, 1815, M-179, RG 59, NA; testimony of Abner Duncan, n.d., Diego Morphy for F. Carral et al. vs. Santa Rita and Cargo, Case #0817, NAFW.

5. *Nolle prosse*, February 20, 1815, motion, March 1, 1815, United States vs. José Toledo, Case #0787, Minutes, 7RA-119, RG 21, Ft. Worth.

6. Dick to Rush, August 19, 1815, M-179, RG 59, NA.

7. Deposition of Montero, November 22, 1814, Joseph Montero vs. Schooner *Esperanza*, Case #0761, NAFW.

8. Dick to Rush, August 19, 1815, M-179, RG 59, NA.

9. Statement, United States vs. José A. de Toledo, Case #0824; Deposition of John Robinson, Diego Morphy for F. Carral et al. vs Santa Rita and Cargo, Case #0817, NAFW; Dick to Rush, August 19, 1815, M-179, RG 59, NA.

10. Dick to Rush, August 19, 1815, M-179, RG 59, NA.

11. Deposition of Vincent Gambie, October 26, 1815, United States vs. Schooner *Philanthrope*, Case #0812; Testimony of Abner Duncan, n.d., Diego Morphy for F. Carral et al. vs Santa Rita and Cargo, Case #0817, NAFW.

12. Deposition of Vincent Gambie, October 26, 1815, United States vs. Schooner *Philanthrope*, Case #0812, NAFW; Dick to Rush, August 19, 1815, M-179, RG 59, NA.

13. Deposition of John Robinson, n.d., Diego Morphy for F. Carral et al.

vs. Santa Rita and Cargo, Case #0817, NAFW; Morphy to Soto, March 15, 1815, Legajo 1796, Morphy to Apodaca, April 10, 1815, Legajo 1836, AGI-Newberry; Toledo to Peter Ellis Bean, March 23, 1815, Papeles Dirigos por el Traidor Toledo, Archivo General de Indias Transcripts, CAHUT.

14. Deposition of Vincent Gambie, October 26, 27, 1815, United States vs. Schooner *Philanthrope*, Case #0812, NAFW.

15. Dick to Rush, August 19, 1815, M-179, RG 59, NA; Amigoni statement, January 1816, United States vs. Schooner *Nonesuch*, Case #0814, NAFW.

16. Deposition of General José Toledo, n.d., Diego Morphy for F. Carral et al. vs Santa Rita and Cargo, Case #0817, NAFW.

17. Morphy to Apodaca, April 15, 1815, Legajo 1836, AGI-Newberry.

18. Deposition of Vincent Gambie, October 26, 1815, United States vs. Schooner *Philanthrope*, Case #0812, NAFW.

19. In later testimony Gambi would state that weather did not allow the landing of the fieldpieces at Boquilla de Piedras, a clear falsehood to explain the failure to follow through on the alleged reason that he and Bean took them out of New Orleans in the first place. Deposition of Vincent Gambie, October 26, 1815, United States vs. Schooner *Philanthrope*, #0812, NAFW.

20. Deposition of Vincent Gambie, October 26, 27, 1815, United States vs. Schooner *Philanthrope*, Case #0812, NAFW.

21. Morphy to Apodaca, April 10, September 4, 1815, Legajo 1836, AGI-Newberry; Dick to Rush, August 19, 1815, M-179, RG 59, NA; Indictment, May 1815, United States vs. Julius C. Amigoni, Case #0826; Indictment, April 1815, United States vs. Vincent Gambie, John Robinson, and Romain Very, Case #0821; Deposition of F. Carral, Diego Morphy for F. Carral et al. vs. Santa Rita and Cargo, Case #0817, NAFW. At one place in his letter Dick says that the *Eagle* took a prize loaded with dry goods before she landed at Boquilla de Piedras to take on munitions and her commission, which would unequivocally have been piracy, but elsewhere when he describes a prize loaded with dry goods he makes it pretty clear that it was the *Santa Rita*, and she was almost certainly taken after the Boquilla de Piedras stop.

22. Testimony of Diego Morphy, January 1816, claim filed May 31, 1815, United States vs. Schooner *Nonesuch*, Case #0814; Indictment, April 1815, depositions of José Herrera and Thomas Garcia, United States vs. Vincent

Gambie, John Robinson, Romain Very, Case #0821; Deposition of Vincent Gambie, October 26, 1815, United States vs. Schooner *Philanthrope,* Case #0812, NAFW; Dick to Rush, August 19, 1815, M-179, RG 59, NA.

23. Morphy to Apodaca, April 15, 1815, Legajo 1836, AGI-Newberry; John Dick to Richard Rush, August 19, 1815, Department of State, Miscellaneous Letters, June–August 1815, M-38, RG 59, NA.

24. Deposition of Vincent Gambie, October 26, 27, 1815, United States vs. Schooner *Philanthrope,* Case #0812, NAFW.

25. Dick to Rush, August 19, 1815, M-179, RG 59, NA.

26. Morphy to Apodaca, April 10, September 4, 1815, Legajo 1836, AGI-Newberry.

27. Dick to Rush, August 19, 1815, M-179, RG 59, NA.

28. Deposition of General José Toledo, n.d., Diego Morphy for F. Carral et al. vs. Santa Rita and Cargo, Case #0817; Statement, May 2, 1815, United States vs. Schooner *Presidente,* Case #0811, NAFW.

29. Morphy to Apodaca, April 15, 1815, Legajo 1836, AGI-Newberry.

30. Dick to Rush, August 19, 1815, M-179, RG 59, NA.

31. Henry La Fayette Holstein to Latour, August 20, 1814, Latour Papers, HNOC.

32. Morphy to Apodaca, March 26, 1815, Legajo 1828, AGI-Newberry.

33. Unidentified to Duplessis, April 3, 1815, Entry 1627, RG 36, NA.

34. A. Campbell to Duplessis, May 3, 1815, Gilbert to Duplessis, May 24, 1815, Ibid.

35. A. J. Dallas to P. B. Duplessis, May 19, 1815, M-178, RG 56, NA.

36. Crowninshield to Patterson, June 6, 1815, Notes from the Spanish Legation in the United States to the Department of State, 1790–1906, RG 59, M-50, NA.

37. Dick to Rush, August 19, 1815, M-179, RG 59, NA.

38. Dick to Rush, August 19, 1815, Ibid.

39. Dick to Rush, August 19, 1815, Ibid.

40. Morphy to captain-general, September 4, 1815, Legajo 1836; Miguel de Arambarri statement, October 3, 1815, Legajo 1828, AGI-Newberry; De-

position of Gaston Davezac, January 10, 1816, Diego Morphy for F. Carral et al. vs. Santa Rita and Cargo, Case #0817, NAFW.

41. Indictments, May 16, 1815, Minutes, 7RA-119, RG 21, NAFW.

42. Soto to Apodaca, April 15, 1815, enclosure 5, Legajo 1796, AGI-Newberry.

43. Abstract, May 18, 1815, United States vs. Vincent Gambie, Case #0821, Minutes, 7RA-119, RG 21, NAFW.

44. Power of Attorney of "Juan Roux alias Vicente Gambi," August 14, 1815, Notary Pierre Pedesclaux, Vol. 71, item 802, NONA. Jean Roux bought slaves in New Orleans as late as 1818–19, and maybe earlier as Jean de la Roux.

45. John Dick to Richard Rush, August 19, 1815, M-179, RG 59, NA.

46. Ibid.

47. Duplessis to George T. Ross, May 10, 1815, Entry 1627, RG 36, NA.

48. Diego Morphy vs. Ship *Cleopatra*, Case #0857, Statement, October 12, 1815, United States vs. the Ship *Cleopatra*, Case #0860, NAFW.

49. Duplessis to Patterson, July 13, 1815, Entry 1627, RG 36, NA.

50. Libel, September 4, 1815, United States vs. Schooner *Eugenia* otherwise called *Indiana*, Case #0853, NAFW; Fatio to Apodaca, November 14, 1815, Notas Diplomaticas, III; Morphy to Juan Cienfuegos, September 17, 1816, Legajo 1873, AGI-Newberry.

51. Dick to Rush, August 19, 1815, M-179, RG 59, NA.

52. Dick to Rush, August 19, 1815, Ibid.; Verdict, United States vs. J. A. de Toledo, Case #0824, NAFW.

53. Bond, April 25, 1815, undated note, United States vs. José A. de Toledo, Case #0824, NAFW.

54. Order to ascertain condition of the *President*, April 30, 1815, Entry 1627, RG 36, NA.

55. Minutes, n.d., United States vs. Schooner *Philanthrope* alias *Eagle* alias *Petit Milan*, Case #0812; United States vs. *Presidente*, Case #0811, Minutes, 7RA-119, RG 21, NAFW.

56. Decree, May 1815, Claim of Diego Morphy, May 31, 1815, Claim of Captain Carral, May 25, 1815, United States vs. Schooner *Nonesuch*, Case #0814, NAFW.

57. Claim of Julius Amigoni, May 25, 1815, Deposition of Vincent Gambie, May 27, 1815, United States vs. Schooner *Philanthrope* alias *Eagle* alias *Petit Milan*, Case #0812; Minutes, July 22, 1815, United States vs. *Presidente*, Case #0811, Minutes, 7RA-119, RG 21, NAFW; Dick to Rush, August 19, 1815, M-179, RG 59, NA.

58. Minutes, August 3, 1815, Carral et al. vs. *Santa Rita*, Case #0817; Minutes, August 3, 1815, Vincent Gambi testimony, October 26, 27, 1815, United States vs. *Eagle*, Case #0812; Court order, February 1, 1816, United States vs. *Petit Milan*, Case #0812, Minutes, 7RA-119, RG 21, NAFW.

59. J. Amigoni to Duplessis, May 6, 1815, RG 36, Entry 1627, NA.

60. Finding, February 1, 1816, Morphy for T. Carral et al., Case #0817; Finding, February 1, 1816, United States vs. Goods and Merchandise on the *Nonesuch*, alias *Santa Rita*, Case #0814; Finding, February 1, 1816, United States vs. Goods on the *Eagle* alias *Petit Milan*, Case #0816, Minutes, 7RA-119, RG 21, NAFW.

61. Court order, February 22, 1816, United States vs. Schooner *Presidente*, Case #0811; Court order, February 22, United States vs. Goods on the *Presidente*, Case #0815, Minutes, 7RA-119, RG 21, NAFW.

62. Appeals, April 16, 1816, Cases #0815, #0816, Minutes, 7RA-119, RG 21, NAFW.

63. Account of sales filed February 28, 1816, United States vs. Schooner *Eagle*, alias *Petit Milan*, Case #0816, NAFW.

64. Court order, August 3, 1815, United States vs. *Presidente*, Case #0811; Morphy vs. *Presidente*, Case #0830, Minutes, 7RA-119, RG 21, NAFW.

65. Livingston to Lewis Livingston, October 1, 1815, Hunt, *Livingston*, p. 244.

66. Duplessis to Alexander Dallas, December 1815, Entry 1627, RG 36, NA.

67. Dallas to P. B. Duplessis, July 3, 1815, M-178, RG 56, NA.

68. Indictment, July 15, 1815, Verdict, July 18, 1815, United States vs. Vincent Gambie, Case #0844, Minutes, 7RA-119, RG, 21, NAFW.

69. Louis Dolliole to Marie Louise Villart, July 10, 1815, Notary John Lynd, Vol. 12, item 296, NONA.

70. Citation, July 18, 1815, Petition of Jean Laffite, July 14, 1815, receipt July

18, 1815, Jean Laffite vs. Joseph Sylvestre, Case #829, Parish Court Civil Suit Records, NOPL.

71. New Orleans, *Louisiana Gazette and New-Orleans Mercantile Advertiser,* July 1, 1815, September 26, 1815.

72. Pierre Laffite power of attorney, July 18, 1815, Notary John Lynd, Vol. 12, item 317, NONA. This is the date Pierre filed the power of attorney with the notary. It was actually executed earlier on an unspecified date.

73. Power of attorney, July 15, 1815, Notary Pierre Pedesclaux, Vol. 70, item 738, NONA.

74. Edward Livingston statement, July 15, 1815, Deposition of Jean Laffite, July 15, 1815, John Gourjon vs. Vincent Gamby, Suit Records, #751, First Judicial District Court, Orleans Parish, NOPL.

75. Petition of Jean Laffite, July 14, 1815, Laffite vs. Sylvestre, Case #829, Parish Court Civil Suit Records, NOPL.

76. New Orleans, *Louisiana Gazette and New-Orleans Mercantile Advertiser,* July 20, 1815. The *Francis* is the only vessel clearing the port at the right time, given Livingston's statement on July 15 that Laffite was expected to leave the state immediately. John Dyer later maintained without giving his source that a daughter of Pierre's traveled with Jean on this trip, and then went on to Quebec for education. There seems to be no reason to credit this as anything more than one of the many imaginative stories that Dyer collected from aged and inventive Galveston residents late in the nineteenth century. Galveston, *Daily News,* September 19, 1926.

77. Philadelphia, *United States' Gazette,* August 18, 22, 28, 1815. Laffite does not appear on Philadelphia passenger lists for 1815 and 1816, but that is explained by the fact that the lists contain only immigrants, not travelers from other states.

78. Ibid., August 29, 31, 1815.

79. Washington, *Daily National Intelligencer,* September 12, 1815.

80. Ibid., September 9, 1815.

81. Proclamation, September 1, 1815, Richardson, *Messages and Papers,* I, pp. 561–62.

82. Harris Gaylord Warren, "The Origin of General Mina's Invasion of Mexico," *Southwestern Historical Quarterly,* XLII (July 1938), pp. 6–7.

83. William Fry, *The Baltimore Directory for 1810, containing the Names, Occupations and Residences of the Inhabitants, Alphabetically Arranged; also, A correct List of Streets, Lanes and Alleys Within the City and Precincts. A List of Officers in the General Government of the United States, Government of the State of Maryland, Officers of the Corporation, Custom-House Duties, Banks, Insurance Offices, Turnpike Roads, &c.* (Baltimore, 1810), n.p.

84. Information derived from Col. S. M. Williams respecting Lafitte, n.d. [certainly prior to Williams's death in 1858], Lamar Papers, TSL; Bollaert, "Lafitte," p. 439. Williams recalled that Laffite had a brother and his father with him, clearly an error with regard to the father. As to the brother, Pierre was certainly still in New Orleans, though Williams may have meant Latour, who was in Baltimore at this time and certainly spending some time with Laffite. It should be noted that Williams's recollection is imprecise as to what year he met Laffite in Baltimore, and seems to confuse the two brothers, and also this visit with Pierre's in 1818. However, context suggests that this recollection regarding Peter A. Gustier can only relate to Jean's 1815–16 trip.

85. Hunt, *Livingston*, p. 222.

86. Edward Livingston obligation, August 2, 1815, Notary John Lynd, Vol. 12, item 344, NONA.

87. Latour [John Williams] to Intendant at Havana, March 26, 1817, enclosed in Onís to Pizarro, November 22, 1818, Cienfuegos to Fatio, April 12, 1817, Legajo 1898, AGI-Newberry.

88. On January 29, 1816, Onís made reference in a letter to having met Laffite. Smith, "Editor's Introduction," Latour, *Historical Memoir*, p. xxviii.

89. Petition, July 28, 1815, finding July 29, 1815, Patterson et al. vs. Certain Vessels, Goods and Merchandise, Case #0734, Parsons Collection, CAHUT.

90. Motion, July 28, 1815, Court order, July 29, 1815, Patterson et al. vs. 16 plates of Bullion and 8 pieces of cannon, Case #0734, Minutes, 7RA-119, RG 21, NAFW.

91. See, for instance, court orders on August 3, October 27, and December 4, 1815, Minutes, 7RA-119, RG 21, NAFW.

92. Nolan and Dupont, eds., *Sacramental Records of the Roman Catholic Church of the Archdiocese of New Orleans, Volume 14, 1820–1821*, p. 229. The

baptismal record states only that the son was named Pierre. However, on October 24, 1832, a Jean Lafitte, listed as the son of Catiche Villard and a father identified only as Lafitte, died at the age of sixteen. Taking the record at face value, and cognizant of the idiosyncrasies of stated ages in the records of this period, that would mean he was born after October 25, 1815, and before October 24, 1816. The son Pierre fits that time slot perfectly, suggesting that the two are one and the same, and that the son's full name was Jean Pierre. It is faintly possible that Jean and Catarina could have conceived another son during Jean's brief visit to New Orleans in March 1816, but there is no other evidence of such a second son. Funerals S-Free Persons of Color, Vol. 9 1829–1831, Part 1, page 317, entry #2015, SAANO.

93. Deposition of John Blanque, April 22, 1815, United States vs. Certain Goods taken at Barataria, Case #0746, Parsons Collection, CAHUT.

94. Latour, *Memoir*, p. 16. This is the only source for Jean having such documents to show, and suggests that Laffite must have shown them to Latour during the visit.

95. Smith, "Editor's Introduction," Latour, *Historical Memoir*, p. xxviii.

96. Jean Laffite to Madison, December 27, 1815, Madison Papers, Library of Congress.

97. No record survives of any communication to Laffite from any officials in Washington. Madison's surviving outgoing correspondence is extensive, though he does not seem to have retained copies. However, if any encouraging response was sent to Laffite, Jean would have used it in petitions to Rush, Dallas, and others, and copies would have survived in the archives of the Justice and Treasury departments. Such copies do not exist.

98. Washington, *Daily National Intelligencer*, December 27, 1815.

99. Ibid., December 21, 1815.

100. Onís to Picornell, December 28, 1815, cited in Faye, "Great Stroke," p. 744.

101. Washington, *Daily National Intelligencer*, December 7, 9, 12, 27, 1815.

102. Newark, NJ, *Daily Advertiser*, February 12, 1840. This article, reprinted from an unknown 1840 issue of the Galveston, *Gazette*, has some features that suggest it is an authentic account of recollections by Galvestonians who had known Laffite before he left that island twenty years before. The publisher of the *Gazette* was Hamilton Stuart, who collected stories of

early Texas history later published by his son Benjamin and contained in the Benjamin C. Stuart Papers, Rosenberg Library, Galveston, TX. Certainly in 1840 there were several people still at Galveston who could provide Stuart with such stories as told by Laffite, regardless of their accuracy. Citing no source, Yoakum, *Texas*, I, p. 190, said in 1856 that Laffite went to Washington in 1815 and "squandered his wealth with princely profusion."

103. Marixa Lasso, "Haiti as an Image of Popular Republicanism in Caribbean Colombia," David P. Geggus, ed., *The Impact of the Haitian Revolution in the Atlantic World* (Columbia, SC, 2001), pp. 178–79; Aury to Maignets, March 15, 1816, Aury Papers, CAHUT.

104. Statement of Diego Morphy, May 1816, United States vs. William Mitchell et al., Case #0909, NAFW; Patterson to David D. Porter, April 24, 1816, Parsons, CAHUT. This is possibly the origin of a story that Bollaert encountered in Texas in the 1840s that had Jean Laffite as the protagonist, putting into an unnamed West Indies port to kidnap the governor and others and then threatening them with hanging unless they paid him a $50,000 ransom. Another candidate is the September 1816 capture of the governor of Pensacola by the privateer *General Humbert*, or Job Northrop's December 1816 attempt to demand ransom from Pensacola. See Bollaert, "Lafitte," p. 437, and Faye, *Privateers of the Gulf*, pp. 10–11.

105. United States vs. William Mitchell et al., Case #0909, NAFW.

106. Robert Vogel reports that in research on privateers of Cartagena, Gran Colombia, Artigas, and the United Provinces of South America, he found many references to Barataria and Galveston, but not one mention of the Laffite brothers as owners, masters, armorers, or officers of privateers, nor of them or their agents paying any taxes or duties on prizes disposed of in the "patriot" admiralty courts.

107. Pedro Gual to Toledo, February 8, 1816, Gual to Iturribarría, February 8, 1816, Legajo 1815, AGI-Newberry.

108. Onís to Cienfuegos, January 29, 1816, Sedella to Onís, December 29, 1815, Legajo 1837, AGI-Newberry.

109. Onís to Apodaca, February 8, 1816, in Faye, "Great Stroke," pp. 743–44.

110. Nothing fixes the precise date of his departure, but in Gual to Toledo, February 8, 1816, Legajo 1815, AGI-Newberry, written from Washington, Gual says that Jean Laffite has offered to take this and another letter to New Orleans for him, suggesting a departure soon thereafter.

111. Marie Louise Villars to Eugenie Tressanceaux, September 1, 1815, Notary Pierre Pedesclaux, Vol. 71, item 827, NONA.

112. Marguerite Villard to Joseph Defaucheaux, September 11, 1815, Notary Pierre Pedesclaux, Vol. 71, item 850; Note, February 24, 1813, Marguerite Villard to Joseph Defaucheaux, Vol. 66, item 55, NONA; Vieux Carré Survey, Square 87, Lots 18892–93, HNOC.

113. Certainly Laffite was not back in New Orleans as of February 5, 1816, when a search of the city failed to find him, and could not have, for three days later he was still in Washington taking letters from Gaul. Another search for him on May 7 also failed to find him, the two dates bracketing the period during which he must have returned from Washington and then left with Latour (J. H. Holland endorsement, February 5, 1816, on court order, January 26, 1815; George Morgan endorsement, May 7, 1816, on court order, March 26, 1816, Laffite vs. Sylvestre, Case #0829, Parish Court Civil Suit Records, NOPL). Given the usual three weeks or more for the ocean passage, he should have been in New Orleans by mid-March at the latest. Morphy to Cienfuegos, December 4, 1816, Legajo 1900, AGI-Newberry, says that Jean returned to New Orleans "last week after an absence of eight months." If Morphy is correct, and he would have known firsthand, Jean returned in the last week of November, and an eight-month absence would mean he left on the expedition toward the end of March.

THIRTEEN

1. Morphy to Apodaca, November 3, 1814, Legajo 1836, AGI-Newberry.

2. Antonio Morales to Apodaca, March 13, 1815, Apodaca to José de Soto, March 4, 1815, Legajo 1796, AGI-Newberry.

3. Morales to Apodaca, March 26, 1815, enclosed in Apodaca to de Soto, March 4, 1815, Ibid.

4. Apodaca to de Soto, April 7, 1815, Ibid.

5. Statement, May 30, 1815, John Gourjon vs. Vincent Gamby, Suit Records, #751, First Judicial District Court, Orleans Parish, NOPL.

6. "Memoir of Ellis P. Bean," Yoakum, Texas, I, pp. 447–49; Morphy to Apodaca, November 20, 1815, Legajo 1836, AGI-Newberry.

7. Warren, *Sword,* p. 128.

8. Morphy to Apodaca, November 20, 1815, Legajo 1836, AGI-Newberry.

9. Extracts from the letters of Herrera and Toledo &c &c dated at New Orleans in November & December 1815, United States Department of State Collection, Spanish Affairs, 1810–1816, Library of Congress.

10. "Memoir of Ellis P. Bean," Yoakum, *Texas,* I, pp. 447–49.

11. Deposition of carpenter, December 1815, Deposition of Theon Barberet, December 1815, United States vs. the Schooner *Two Brothers,* alias the *Presidente,* Case #0884, NAFW.

12. Morphy to Apodaca, November 20, 1815, Legajo 1836, AGI-Newberry.

13. Deposition of Toledo, December 1815, Deposition of Herrera, December 1815, United States vs. the Schooner *Two Brothers,* alias the *Presidente,* Case #0884, NAFW.

14. Deposition of Toledo, December 1815, Deposition of Herrera, December 1815, Ibid.

15. Testimony of John Lynd, November 25, 1815, Ibid.

16. Herrera to Toledo, November 25, 1815, Extracts from the letters of Herrera and Toledo &c &c dated at New Orleans in November & December 1815, United States Department of State Collection, Spanish Affairs, 1810–1816, Library of Congress.

17. Onís to Miguel de Lardizábal y Uribe, August 15, 1815, Papeles de Estado, Audiencia de Mexico, Legajo 5558, Expediente 12, AGI-Newberry.

18. Ibid.

19. Dick to Rush, July 20, 1815, M-179, RG 659, NA.

20. Claiborne to Monroe, July 20, 1815, M-179, RG 59, NA.

21. Jose de Quevado to Joaquin de Arredondo, May 5, 1815, Nacogdoches Archives Transcripts, Supplement VIII, p. 100, Robert Bruce Blake Collection, East Texas Research Center, Stephen F. Austin State University, Nacogdoches, TX (Blake).

22. Teodoro Martinez to Benito Armenan, July 18, 20, 21, 1815, Nacogdoches Archives, TSL.

23. Paul Lafite to the Governor, July 21, 1815, Nacogdoches Archives, TSL; Orders from Gutiérrez to Humbert, July 4, 10, 1815, Statement of Gutiérrez,

March 18, 1820, United States vs. John Desfarges et al., Case #1440, NAFW; Picornell to Onís, November 24, 1815, Legajo 1815, AGI-Newberry.

24. Morphy to Apodaca, July 20, 1815, Onís to Apodaca, August 14, 1815, Legajo 1836, AGI-Newberry; Onís to Monroe, August 24, 1815, Notes from the Spanish Legation in the United States to the Department of State, 1790–1906, M59, Record Group 59, Volume 4, NA.

25. Walter Lowrie and Walter S. Franklin, eds., *American State Papers. Documents Legislative and Executive, of the Congress of the United States. . . .: Class I, Foreign Relations, Volume IV* (Washington 1834), p. 432.

26. Morphy to Apodaca, September 4, 1815, Legajo 1836, AGI-Newberry.

27. Patterson to Cunningham, September 5, 1815, M-125, NA.

28. Deposition of Edmund Quirk, February 12, 1816, Blake, Supplement, XV, pp. 216, 220.

29. Onís to Apodaca, November 16, 1815, Legajo 1837, AGI-Newberry; Paul Lafite to Mariano Varela, November 28, 1815, Nacogdoches Archives, TSL.

30. Sedella to Onís, September 18, 1815, Papeles de Estado, Audiencia de Mexico, Legajo 5558, Expediente 12, AGI-Newberry.

31. Morphy to Apodaca, November 3, 1814, Legajo 1836, AGI-Newberry.

32. Picornell to Onís, February 16, 1816, Legajo 42, Archivo de Su Magestad Católica en Philadelphia, Archivo Historico Nacional, Madrid.

33. Picornell to Apodaca, November 28, 1815, Sedella to Apodaca, December 27, 1815, Legajo 1815, AGI-Newberry; Wilson, *Impressions Respecting New Orleans*, p. 166. Harris Gaylord Warren, "Documents Relating to Pierre Laffite's Entrance Into the Service of Spain," *Southwestern Historical Quarterly*, XLIV (July 1940), p. 78, identified the two other recipients of pardons as Jean Laffite and "Laurent Maire, captain of the *Dos Hermanos,*" or *Two Brothers.* Warren repeats this in *Sword,* p. 132n. However, he is mistaken, having borrowed this probably from Stanley Faye. In "Great Stroke," p. 742, Faye repeats the error, then further erroneously identifies Maire as the Laffites' brother-in-law, which most assuredly he was not. Maire was a white Italian, and certainly neither Laffite was married at all, much less to a white European. Maire's wife was Adeline Godon, of an old New Orleans family. Laurent Maire Estate Inventory, September 15, 1827, Orleans Parish Court of Probates, NOPL.

34. Sedella to Apodaca, November 20, 28, 1815, Legajo 1815, AGI-Newberry.

35. Picornell to Onís, February 16, 1816, Legajo 42, Archivo de Su Magestad Católica en Philadelphia, Archivo Historico Nacional, Madrid; Onís
to Apodaca, January 8, 1816, quoted in Warren, *Sword*, p. 132.

36. Juan Ruíz de Apodaca to Francisco Vallesteros, January 16, 18, 1816,
Legajo 1856, AGI-Newberry.

37. Morphy to Apodaca, September 4, 1815, November 20, 1815, Legajo
1836, Morphy to Apodaca, August 10, 1816, Legajo 1877, Morphy to Apodaca, September 17, 1816, Legajo 1873, AGI-Newberry; Faye, "Aury," p. 631.

38. Sedella to Apodaca, November 28, 1815, Legajo 1815, AGI-Newberry;
Faye, "Privateer Vessels," pp. 129–30.

39. Sedella to Apodaca, November 17, 1815, Legajo 1815, AGI-Newberry.

40. Herrera to the Mexican Congress, November 26, 1815, Extracts from
the letters of Herrera and Toledo &c &c dated at New Orleans in November & December 1815, United States Department of State Collection,
Spanish Affairs, 1810–1816, Library of Congress.

41. Duplessis to Patterson, December 6, 1815, Entry 1627, RG 36, NA.

42. Testimony of Robert Fell, December 1815, United States vs. the
Schooner *Two Brothers*, alias the *Presidente*, Case #0884, NAFW; List of
the Crew of the Two Brothers, of NOLA, L. P. Fougard master, December 6, 1815, Entry 1627, RG 36, NA.

43. United States vs. the Schooner *Two Brothers*, alias the *Presidente*, Case
#0884, NAFW.

44. Testimony of John Lynd, November 25, 1815, Deposition of Toledo,
December 1815, Deposition of Herrera, December 1815, Ibid. In fact, no
record has been found of the Mexican insurgent Congress issuing any
commission to the Laffites during its brief existence. There are several
records of letters of marque granted by Rayón, Rosains, Morelos, Anaya,
and Herrera during 1814–15, but searching by Robert Vogel has found
nothing directly related to the Laffites. After the collapse of the Mexican
Congress in 1816, Humbert ran a shirttail provisional government, but no
records of him granting commissions to the Laffites have emerged either.

45. Apodaca to Vallesteros, January 18, 1816, Papeles de Estado, Audiencia
de Mexico, Legajo 5558, Expediente 12, AGI-Newberry; Warren, "Documents," pp. 79–80, 87.

46. Sedella to Apodaca, December 27, 1815, Legajo 1815, AGI-Newberry.

47. Morphy to Captain General, December 27, 1815, Ibid.

48. Morphy to Apodaca, March 8, 1816, Ibid.

49. Onís to Apodaca, January 8, 1816, Legajo 1837, AGI-Newberry.

FOURTEEN

1. Edwin H. Carpenter, Jr., ed., "Latour's Report on Spanish-American Relations in the Southwest," *Louisiana Historical Quarterly*, XXX (July 1947), pp. 715–16, suggests that Jean was already somehow a part of the plan when he went to the East, but erroneously dates Jean's trip to Philadelphia in December rather than July 1815. Certainly Jean did not travel east with Latour, as Carpenter suggests, for Latour was still in New Orleans weeks after Jean's departure.

2. Mr. and Mrs. T. L. Hodges, "Jean Lafitte and Major L. Latour in Arkansas Territory," *Arkansas Historical Quarterly*, VII (Winter 1948), p. 246, mistakenly says Laffite was the leader and Latour his assistant. More likely it was a joint trip of spying and examination, and a look for commercial gain from trade or gold.

3. Lyle Saxon was entirely unaware of Jean Laffite's Arkansas expedition, and mistakenly believed that it was Pierre who went to the East. To explain Jean's whereabouts, Saxon says that he bought a fleet of vessels from Sauvinet in the summer of 1815 and then sailed to Port-au-Prince to make a new privateering base, but was turned away (Saxon, *Lafitte*, pp. 207–10). Saxon probably got this idea—and embellished it—from Yoakum, *Texas*, I, p. 190, who seems to have misinterpreted a statement in Beverly Chew to William Crawford, August 1, 1817, M-38, Miscellaneous Letters of the Department of State August 1–October 31, 1817, RG 59, General Records of the Department of State, NA, as published in the *American State Papers*.

4. Smith suggests that the trip began in May 1816, basing this on the fact that a letter from Benjamin Latrobe was addressed to Latour in New Orleans on May 3, 1816 (Smith, "Editor's Introduction," Latour, *Historical Memoir*, p. xxviii). Of course Latour was not necessarily in New Orleans when Latrobe wrote the letter, and Morphy to Cienfuegos, December 4, 1816, Legajo 1900, AGI-Newberry, clearly says that Jean had been absent

eight months before his late November return, which places his departure in mid to late March.

5. Philip Pittman, *The Present State of the European Settlements on the Mississippi* (London, 1770), p. 40.

6. Josiah H. Shinn, *Pioneers and Makers of Arkansas* (Little Rock, AK, 1908), pp. 79–80; Fay Hempstead, *Pictorial History of Arkansas from Earliest Times to the Year 1890* (St. Louis, 1890), pp. 98, 107.

7. Table of Civil Officers in commission on October 1, 1814, Clarence Edwin Carter, ed., *The Territorial Papers of the United States, Volume XIV: The Territory of Louisiana-Missouri 1806–1814* (Washington, 1949) pp. 792–95.

8. Hodges, "Arkansas Territory," p. 240.

9. Paul Chrisler Phillips, *The Fur Trade* (Norman, OK, 1961), II, pp. 219–22.

10. William F. Pope, *Early Days in Arkansas* (Little Rock, AR, 1895), p. 89; Carpenter, "Latour's Report," pp. 735–36. Shinn, *Pioneers and Makers*, p. 251, agrees that Laffite was recognized, but Shinn could have borrowed this from Pope. However, Laffite's witness under his own name to the July 4 instrument for Vaugine is evidence that at least some knew his real identity.

11. Jean Baptiste Daigl to François Vaugine, July 4, 1816, Deed Book B, 1814–1818, Part 1, pp. 193–95, Arkansas County, Arkansas, Clerk of Court, DeWitt, AR.

12. W. D. Williams, "Louis Bringier and His Description of Arkansas in 1812," *Arkansas Historical Quarterly*, XLVIII (Summer 1989), pp. 109–10, 118. Williams, pp. 113–14, states without giving evidence that Bringier accompanied Latour and Laffite. There is only latter-day testimony to support this, but in this instance, given Bringier's circumstances and motivations, it seems reasonable to assume that he did make the journey with them.

13. Daniel Wright, power of attorney, July 25, 1817, Notary Michele DeArmas, Vol. 13, item 428, July 25, 1817, NONA.

14. Shinn, *Pioneers*, pp. 46–47.

15. Pope, *Early Days*, p. 89. In 1873 Benjamin F. Danley denied there being any evidence of mining at Crystal Hill, but said that old-timers in the

1830s showed him a place called Mine Hill—about three and a half miles above Little Rock on the north bank, between mouths of Big Rock and White Oak bayous—where locals recalled Laffite digging. He had seen an old furnace and broken crucibles said to have been Laffite's. Little Rock, *Arkansas Gazette*, August 16, 1873.

16. Little Rock, *Arkansas Gazette*, April 6, 1873. This account is the recollection of pioneer Daniel T. Witter, as told to him after he moved to Arkansas in 1819. He gets the year wrong, placing it in 1817, but otherwise his account checks out, as in 1820 a suit was filed against Bringier for $1,439.80 plus damages of $2,000, for "work, labor, goods, wares, merchandise, and for money advanced to the defendant" in relation to the mill or the expedition (Williams, "Bringier," p. 119).

17. Shinn, *Pioneers*, pp. 46–47. Shinn locates Pyeatt at Crystal Hill but is mistaken, for Pyeatt moved to Cadron in 1815.

18. Carpenter, "Latour's Report," p. 730.

19. Pope, *Early Days*, pp. 91–93. Pope states that this account was given to him by Pyeatt in 1833.

20. Carpenter, "Latour's Report," p. 723.

21. Ibid., p. 724. This was in the vicinity of present-day Tulsa.

22. Ibid., p. 723.

23. Morphy to Cienfuegos, December 4, 1816, Legajo 1900, AGI-Newberry.

24. Carpenter, "Latour's Report," p. 729.

25. Shinn, *Pioneers*, p. 47. On November 5, 1816, Latour acted as witness to Juninthe Barquaim to Louis Bringier, October 1, 1816, recorded November 5, 1816, Deed Book A, 1819–1823, p. 219, Pulaski County Courthouse, Little Rock, AR.

26. Carpenter, "Latour's Report," p. 724.

27. Ibid., pp. 729–30.

28. Unfortunately, Latour's report is so unspecific about places visited that it can only be stated with certainty that they traveled up and down the Arkansas River. Though his report speaks frequently of the Red River and mentions the Sabine and others, it seems unlikely that the expedition actually touched on them, and more likely that Latour's information was

gleaned from others. Latour had no means to move his boats overland from one river to the other and back. Also, Laffite and Latour are firmly fixed by local documentation on the lower Arkansas on July 4 and November 5, 1816, and the four months in between would not have allowed them to go to the headwaters of the Arkansas and back, nor to go overland to explore other rivers. There was not time between November 5 and their arrival in New Orleans around November 28 to do so, either.

29. Carpenter, "Latour's Report," pp. 725, 728, 729.

30. Ibid., pp. 731, 733–34.

31. D. C. Williams vs. Edward Livingston and Arsené Latour, Protest, July 19, 1816, Notary John Lynd, Vol. 13, item 412, NONA.

32. Carpenter, "Latour's Report," pp. 717–19, 722–23.

33. The precise number and names of Pierre and Marie's children is always problematic, thanks to inadequate records and apparent informal changes in given names. By 1816 the Sacramental Archives definitely establish as theirs Rosa, Jean Baptiste, Catherine Coralie, and Martin Firmin. Of Eugene we have only two references. Felipe Fatio to the Captain General, February 19, 1818, Legajo 1900, AGI-Newberry, refers to Pierre's "son, a boy of 16 years." Pierre, in a letter to Jean, February 17, 1818, Legajo 1900, AGI-Newberry, speaks of "my son Eugene." Combined, these references imply he had a son born circa 1802, almost certainly from a liaison prior to Marie, and that the boy still lived with him. (However, see later discussion of the possibility that the son Eugene was an invention.) In the 1830 Orleans Parish, Louisiana, Census, p. 28, "Marie Louisa Villard" appears living between Esplanade and Canal Marigny in the Faubourg Marigny, her household including one free colored female aged ten to twenty-three, which would be Rosa, then aged eighteen to nineteen. Also living with her was one free colored male aged twenty-four to thirty-six, which would be Eugene, then aged twenty-eight, or Pierre, whose age was uncertain. It is unlikely that it would be Martin Firmin, who married two years earlier and presumably did not live with his mother any longer. Finally, two colored males aged ten to twenty-three appear in the enumeration. One would be Jean, born November 1816, and the other Jean Baptiste, who was born prior to 1811, making him eighteen or older. Marie's last child by Pierre, Joseph, born in 1821, would have been eight to nine in 1830, but no child that age is in the enumeration, suggesting that he had died.

34. Claude Treme to Marie Louise Villard, August 17, 1816, Notary Pierre Pedesclaux, Vol. 73, item 482; John Holland to Marie Louise Villard, May 11, 1817, Notary Phillipe Pedesclaux, Vol. 2, p. 603bis, NONA. The full title history of this property is found in the file for Square 77, lot 22929, Vieux Carré Survey, HNOC.

35. Building contract, October 11, 1790, Notary Felix Broutin, Vol. 7, item 42, NONA.

36. *Plan de Trois Lots de Terre de La Municipalite No. 1,* Plan Book No. 72, Folio No. 27, March 28, 1848, NONA. The subsequent documentation on the house shows no structural changes until 1849, after the 1848 plat was done, so it should be very close to the 1817 appearance of the house.

37. Survey of Square 57, lot 18579, Viaux Carré Commission, HNOC. This corner opposite the Villard house is where later lore believed the Laffite house to have been, and by the twentieth century that lore was firmly established. Today a tavern called "Lafitte's Blacksmith Shop" sits on this site, the brothers' name misspelled. The Laffites never owned or demonstrably had any connection with this property, but the legend persists. Interestingly, while the location of their home has been questioned by some in recent years, the first to hint correctly that it was across St. Philip was Ben C. Stuart in his manuscript "Texas Sea Rovers and Soldiers of Fortune," written in 1913, now in the Stuart papers, Rosenberg Library, Galveston, TX. He may have done so by accident when he said they lived "near" the mythical smithy, but then placed the smithy in the proper location of the Laffite home. He based his manuscript on standard early sources, and ironically may simply have been mistaken in reading a source that put the house in the wrong spot.

Saxon, in his embellishing narrative with the Glasscock letter, suggested that Pierre and Adelaide Maselari were living at the smithy on Bourbon and St. Philip in 1809. Title searches done by the Viaux Carré Commission in the 1930s, and now housed at the Historic New Orleans Collection archives, confirm that this lot has an unbroken title from 1791 to 1833 with no Villard or Laffite ownership, while independent research by the author confirms that there is no record of the Laffites ever owning any property in New Orleans other than the parcel at Royal and Dumaine that briefly belonged in part to Pierre in 1803. Archaeological work at the site traditionally held to be the Laffite smithy revealed none of the debris that would ordinarily be associated with a smithy, suggesting that no such enterprise was ever pursued on that site under any ownership. The Vieux

Carré Survey concluded that it is an ancient building but was never a forge and has no connection to the Laffites other than in folklore. It was owned in 1771 by Jean Baptiste Laporte, grandfather of Renato Beluche (Veaux Carré Survey, Square 76, Lot 18806, HNOC).

The first sure assertion of this true state of affairs came in Edith Elliott Long, "Along the Banquette, Lafitte's Blacksmith Shop Legend or Fact?" an article from an undated issue of the *Vieux Carré Courier*, clipping in Jean Laffite Vertical File, LSM. Yet in a roundabout way the origins of the lore of the Laffite smithy at this site can now also be confirmed. Across St. Philip, where today stands the Lafitte Guest House at 1003 Bourbon Street, Laffite residence is confirmed by Marie Villard's August 16, 1816, purchase. The association of the Laffites with her and the property, even if one does not assume that Pierre bought it for her in their *plaçage* arrangement, is confirmed three years later after she sold and then repurchased it in 1819, paying in part with a promissory note guaranteed by Jean Laffite (April 30, 1819, Notary Philippe Pedesclaux, Vol. 7, item 339, NONA). Documentation also supports a relationship between Jean and Marie's sister Catherine, making Jean's backing of the repurchase in 1819 the more logical. Thus, off and on from the time she first acquired it in 1816, this is where Pierre and Jean Laffite would have stayed when they were in New Orleans.

38. Besides uncertainty on the precise number and names of the Pierre-Marie children, there are conflicting sources on the number of Laffite brothers. Latter-day sources already dealt with erroneously identified Dominique as a third brother, and one refers to an Alexander as an alias of Dominique's. In 1856 Richardson and Company, *The Texas Almanac for 1857, with Statistics, Historical and Biographical Sketches Relating to Texas* (Galveston, 1856), p. 157, said on the authority of Warren Hall, a Laffite associate in 1819, that there were three brothers, with Jean at Galveston, and the other two—unnamed—remaining in New Orleans to merchandise what Jean sent. This is surely a confusion of Pierre and either Pierre's older son Eugene or else one of the unrelated men of that surname then living in the city. Stephen, or Etienne, Lafitte lived in the city then, and was secretary of the Orleans Navigation Company (New Orleans, *L'Ami des Lois*, January 31, 1815). Marc Lafitte was a prominent notary, who sometimes did work for the Laffites. Note, however, that neither spelled his name the way the Laffite brothers did theirs. No other Laffites of any spelling appear in the census or the city directories for the period 1805 to 1822.

39. Summons, February 17, 1816, Pierre Laffite affidavit, February 27, 1816, Petition of Davis and Ducatel, April 9, 1816, Verdict, April 19, 1816, Executors of André Robin vs. Pierre Laffite, Suit #956, Parish Court Civil Suit Records, NOPL.

40. Pierre Laffite affidavit, July 29, 1816, Pierre Laffite vs. Godefroi Dumon, Suit No. 34, Second Judicial Court, August 17, 1816, Clerk of Court, Ascension Parish, Donaldsonville, LA. The original of this transaction has proven elusive. Many years ago researcher John Howells photocopied a portion of it, but the original is not to be found in the location he gave, and diligent hunting has failed to find it. It was in the past interpreted as an attempt by Laffite to gain control of a canal connecting the Mississippi with Bayou Lafourche, but on the evidence of the partial photocopy, it is a simple suit for collection of debt.

41. Pierre Laffite to Joseph Liquet, April 10, 1816, Notary Pierre Pedesclaux, Vol. 72, item 193; Pierre Laffite to François Rillieux, March 11, 1816, Vol. 72, item 262; Jean Grounx to Pierre Laffite, August 15, 1816, Notary Marc Lafitte, Vol. 9, item 360; Pierre Laffite to Sebastian Hiriart, December 20, 1816, Vol. 9, item 520, NONA.

42. Picornell to Onís, February 16, 1816, Legajo 42, Archivo de Su Magestad Católica en Philadelphia, State Department, Madrid, cited in Faye, "Privateers," p. 1035—translation in Stanley Faye Papers, Rosenberg Library, Galveston, TX.

43. Morphy to Cienfuegos, December 4, 1816, Legajo 1900, AGI-Newberry.

44. Charles E. Nolan and Dorenda Dupont, eds., *Sacramental Records of the Roman Catholic Church of the Archdiocese of New Orleans, Volume 14, 1820–1821* (New Orleans, 1999), pp. 228–29.

45. Undoubtedly Laffite would have owed the attorneys either a contingency fee or else a percentage of what they recovered. A quarter century later the garrulous and somewhat bibulous Grymes liked to exaggerate this simple business transaction into tales that one local editor who knew him regarded as one of Grymes's "many ridiculous stories, to which we need not further allude than to pronounce their falsehood." One such account had Jean owing each attorney $5,000, and inviting them to come to his lair at Barataria to be paid. (In 1816, when the cases were settled, Jean was in Arkansas and the Laffites' Barataria establishment no longer existed.) Livingston did not trust Laffite to pay him, said Grymes, and thus sold the claim on his $5,000 fee to Grymes for $2,500. Grymes then went to

Barataria and was royally wined and dined by Laffite for several days, then sent back to New Orleans in a Laffite boat with $10,000 in gold. This story was complete nonsense, just like Grymes's claim that it was he alone who persuaded Jackson to accept the services of the Baratarians. "Many other stories more apocryphal than this are told of the connexion of the distinguished counsel with his distinguished client," said an editor (New Orleans, *Courier,* May 9, 1843). Gayarré, *Pirate-Patriots,* pp. 59–60, took this story and exaggerated the fee to $20,000. In all likelihood, Grymes's stories were simply the tall tales of an old man, getting even with a former legal rival, Livingston, and exaggerating his own importance.

46. John Chambers to Pierre Laffite, December 2, 1816, Notary Pierre Pedesclaux, Vol. 73, item 685-bis, NONA.

47. Entry #318, December 3, 1816, *Ship Registers and Enrollments of New Orleans, Louisiana, Volume 1, 1804–1820* (Baton Rouge, 1941), p. 49.

48. Power of attorney, December 14, 1816, Notary Pierre Pedesclaux, Vol. 73, item 705-bis, NONA.

49. John Rollins to P. L. B. Duplessis, April 2, 1816, Report of all vessels inward bound at the Balize, 1816, Entry 1627, RG 36, NA.

50. Patterson to David D. Porter, April 24, 1816, Parsons, CAHUT; Indictment of William Wilson Mitchell, May 23, 1816, Minutes, 7RA-119, RG 21, NAFW.

51. John Rollins to P. L. B. Duplessis, April 2, 1816, Report of all vessels inward bound at the Balize, 1816, Entry 1627, RG 36, NA; Patterson to David D. Porter, April 24, 1816, Parsons, CAHUT.

52. United States vs. 150 Crates of Earthenware, Case #0912, NAFW.

53. J. D. Bradburn Oath, April 8, 1816, Entry 1627, RG 36, NA.

54. United States vs. Bernard Bourdin, Case #0863, NONA.

55. Patterson to Porter, April 24, 1816, Parsons Collection, CAHUT.

56. Patterson to Porter, April 24, 1816, Ibid.

57. Testimony of Robert Fell, December 1815, Deposition of Herrera, December 1815, United States vs. the Schooner *Two Brothers,* alias the *Presidente,* Case #0884, NAFW.

58. Morphy to Apodaca, March 1, 1816, Legajo 1836, AGI-Newberry.

59. Ibid.

60. Sedella to Apodaca, April 22, 1816, Legajo 1815, AGI-Newberry.

61. Onís to Cienfuegos, August 3, 1816, Legajo 1898, Morphy to Cienfuegos, June 21, 1816, Legajo 1900, AGI-Newberry.

62. Morphy to Apodaca, March 1, 1816, Legajo 1836, AGI-Newberry.

63. William Johnson to Duplessis, September 26, 1816, Entry 1627, RG 36, NA.

64. Onís to Cienfuegos, August 3, 1816, Legajo 1898, AGI-Newberry.

65. Rollins to Duplessis, April 21, 1816, George Fram to Duplessis, June 29, 1816, Entry 1627, RG 36, NA.

66. Report of all vessels inward bound boarded by the Inspr. at the Balize, 1816, Entry 1627, RG 36, NA.

67. Rollins to Duplessis, October 18, 1816, Entry 1627, RG 36, NA.

68. Rollins to Duplessis, December 1816, Ibid.

69. Mariano Varela to the Baron de Bastrop, February 9, 1816, Provincias Internas, Tomo 239, Archivo General de Mexico, AGI-Newberry; Declaration of Edmund Quirk, February 12, 1816, Blake, XVIII, pp. 22–27, Governor Mariano Valera to Arredondo, March 26, 1816, Supplement VIII, p. 123.

70. Morphy to Apodaca, March 8, 1816, Legajo 1836, AGI-Newberry.

71. Onís to Monroe, February 10, 1817, M-50, RG 59, NA.

72. Morphy to Cienfuegos, December 27, 1815, Legajo 1815, AGI-Newberry.

73. Morphy to Apodaca, March 1, 1816, Legajo 1836, AGI-Newberry.

74. Statement, March 23, 1816, Ibid.

75. Sedella, Picornell, and Ariza statement, April 22, 1816, Legajo 1815, AGI-Newberry.

76. Sedella to Apodaca, May 4, 1816, Ibid.

77. Onís to José Pizarro, November 22, 1818, Legajo 1898, AGI-Newberry.

78. Onís to Apodaca, August 3, 1816, Ibid.

79. Purchase contract, November 11, 1815, Notary Michel DeArmas, Vol. 11, item 497, NONA.

80. Castellanos, *New Orleans as It Was*, pp. 40–42. This episode may not have happened at all, but if it did, it has been much adulterated in the

telling. The source has it taking place in 1812–13, yet Humbert was not in Louisiana then, and after his arrival the Laffites could not have been present without risk any time prior to 1815. Saxon, *Lafitte*, pp. 77–80, misstates the source by saying the event was a birthday party, whereas Castellanos clearly says the event was a French national holiday. Bastille Day, July 14, seems the most likely, as it was recognized by Frenchmen though it was not formalized as a national holiday until 1880. The occasion could also have been one of several religious holidays celebrated in France and by the Creoles in New Orleans, such as Ascension Day. If the episode even occurred, and if it happened in either 1815 or 1816, then the Laffite who escorted Humbert out of the hotel had to be Pierre, not Jean, Jean being absent.

81. Aury to Maignets, March 15, 1816, Aury Papers, CAHUT.

82. Robert C. Vogel, "Rebel Without a Cause: The Adventures of Louis Aury," *Laffite Society Chronicles*, VIII (February 2002), p. 3.

83. Morphy to Captain-General, July 9, 1816, Legajo 1900, AGI-Newberry.

84. New Orleans, *Louisiana Gazette*, July 29, 1816.

85. In one of his many unreliable assertions based on the recollections or inventions of old Galveston denizens of the late 1800s, Dyer said that Morin de la Porta originally had the idea of starting the privateer outpost at Galveston in imitation of Barataria, and that in 1815 he sold Aury on this and the pair landed on Galveston November 1, 1816 and established camp and admiralty court. Galveston, *Daily News*, September 19, 1926.

86. Onís to Cienfuegos, August 3, 1816, Legajo 1898, AGI-Newberry.

87. Promissory note, July 2, 1816, Pierre Laffite suit, February 17, 1817, Pierre Lafitte vs. Vincent Gambie or Jean Roup, #1346, First Judicial Court, NOPL.

88. Morphy to Apodaca, July 31, August 2, 1816, Legajo 1900, AGI-Newberry.

89. Line of Credit, July 1, 1816, Notary Marc Lafitte, Vol. 9, Act 310, NONA.

90. Sedella to Apodaca, August 5, 1816, Legajo 1815, AGI-Newberry.

91. Sedella to Apodaca, August 5, 1816, Legajo 1815, Morphy to Apodaca, August 10, 1816, Legajo 1877, AGI-Newberry.

92. Morphy to Apodaca, August 10, 1816, Legajo 1877; Apodaca to Valles-teros, January 16, 1816, Legajo 1856, AGI-Newberry.

93. Luis de Onís to unknown, July 25, 1816, Translation of a Memoir which appears to have been intended for the King of Spain, December 23, 1814, United States Department of State Collection, Spanish Affairs, 1810–1816, Library of Congress.

94. Aury to Victoria Aury, January 14, 1817, Aury Papers, CAHUT.

95. Faye, "Aury," pp. 632–34.

96. Power of Attorney, August 30, 1816, Notary Marc Lafitte, Vol. 9, act 378, NONA.

97. Faye, "Aury," p. 635.

98. In 1929 Stanley Faye concluded that Mina landed on Galveston on August 3, 1816, which would have been before even Aury made landing. Faye to Frank C. Patten, March 29, 1929, Laffite Collection, Rosenberg Library.

99. Washington, *Daily National Intelligencer*, November 21, 1816.

100. Hubert Howe Bancroft, *History of the North Mexican States and Texas* (New York, 1884), II, pp. 34–35.

101. Morphy to Cienfuegos, September 17, 1816, Legajo 1873, AGI-Newberry.

FIFTEEN

1. Vogel, "Baratarians," pp. 68–69.

2. Andrew Forest Muir, ed., *Texas in 1837, an Anonymous, Contemporary Narrative* (Austin, TX, 1958), p. 4.

3. William Davis Robinson, *Memoirs of the Mexican Revolution: Including A Narrative of the Expedition of General Xavier Mina* (Philadelphia, 1820), I, pp. 59–60; Bollaert, "Lafitte," p. 439.

4. Tom Oertling, "Historical Comments and Observations on the Map 'Bahia de Galveston,'" *Laffite Society Chronicles*, II (January 1996), n.p.; Charles Hayes, *History of the Island and the City of Galveston* (Austin, TX, 1974; reprint of destroyed Cincinnati, 1879 edition), p. 36; Galveston, *News*, October 1, 1921. In the 1920s Stanley Faye found in the archives at the

University of Texas in Austin an 1828 map of Galveston by Alexander Thompson, which showed a small island where the causeway leaves Galveston Island. The island has now disappeared.

5. Deposition of John Ducoing, October 7, 1817, United States vs. the cargo of the *Mount Vernon*, Case #1070, NAFW.

6. Harris Gaylord Warren, "Documents Relating to the Establishment of Privateers at Galveston, 1816–1817," *Louisiana Historical Quarterly*, XXI (October 1938), p. 10.

7. San Maxent to Cienfuegos, October 22, 1816, Legajo 1873, AGI-Newberry.

8. Report and Manifest, September 7, 1816, Testimony of Mr. Willson, October 20, 1818, Testimony of Mr. McMellan, October 20, 1818, Testimony of François Raux, August 24, 1818, Testimony of H. Pierre, October 9, 1818, Role d'equipage of the *Lameson*, n.d., United States vs. Schooner *Lameson*, Case File #1227, NAFW.

9. Onís to Monroe, January 2, 1817, M-50, RG 59, NA.

10. Onís to Monroe, February 10, 1817, Ibid.

11. Faye, "Privateersmen," pp. 1054–56. Faye, "Aury," I, p. 126, borrows Saxon's mistaken identification of Sauvinet as a chief agent of the Laffites'.

12. Morphy to Apodaca, March 1, 1816, Legajo 1836, AGI-Newberry.

13. Grymes to Thomas Cunningham, January 11, 1817, M-125, NA.

14. Naval History Division, *Dictionary of American Naval Fighting Ships, Volume II* (Washington, 1963), p. 406.

15. Washington, *National Intelligencer*, October 15, 1816.

16. Morphy to Cienfuegos, September 25, 1816, Legajo 1900, AGI-Newberry.

17. Washington, *National Intelligencer*, October 17, 1816.

18. Morphy to Cienfuegos, September 25, 1816, Legajo 1900, AGI-Newberry. The standard account of this episode is Harris Gaylord Warren, "The Firebrand Affair: A Forgotten Incident of the Mexican Revolution," *Louisiana Historical Quarterly*, XXI (January 1938), pp. 203–12. Warren mistakenly refers to James Monroe as president during the affair, whereas Madison was still in office and Monroe was secretary of state at the time.

19. Jackson to Livingston, October 24, 1816, Bassett, *Correspondence,* VI, pp. 459–60.

20. Eighth Annual Message, December 3, 1816, Richardson, *Messages and Papers,* I, p. 575.

21. New Orleans, *Courier de la Louisiane,* December 16, 1816; Rollins to Duplessis, November 25, 1816, Entry 1627, RG 36, NA; Alfred Toledano Wellborn, "The Relations Between New Orleans and Latin America, 1810–1824," *Louisiana Historical Quarterly,* XXII (July 1939), pp. 760–61.

22. Report of all vessels inward bound & boarded by the Inspector at the Balize, 1816, Entry 1627, RG 36, NA.

23. Petition of Dominique Youx, November 1816, Judgment, December 15, 1816, Result of Sale, December 17, 1816, Dominique Youx vs. Francis Deglanne, #1143, Parish Court Civil Suit Records, NOPL.

24. Harris Gaylord Warren, "Pensacola and the Filibusters, 1816–1817," *Louisiana Historical Quarterly,* XXI (July 1928), p. 816.

25. Rollins to Duplessis, November 25, 1816, Entry 1627, RG 36, NA.

26. Rollins to Duplessis, November 25, December 4, 1816, Dick to Chew, February 1, 1817, Entry 1627, RG 36, NA.

27. Rollins to Duplessis, December 2, 1816, Entry 1627, RG 36, NA.

28. Sam Baldwin to Duplessis, September 26, 1816, Ibid.

29. Rollins to Duplessis, October 28, 1816, Ibid.

30. Rollins to Duplessis, November 25, December 4, 1816, Ibid.

31. New Orleans, *Courier,* November 15, 1816.

32. Ibid., November 20, 1816.

33. Fatio to Cienfuegos, September 28, 1818, Legajo 1900, AGI-Newberry.

34. Morphy to Cienfuegos, December 4, 1816, Ibid.

35. Masot to Captain General, January 11, 1817, Legajo 1874, AGI-Newberry.

36. Marie Louise Villard to Pierre Laffite, January 4, 1817, Notary Phillipe Pedesclaux, Vol. 1, item 8; Pierre Laffite promissory note, January 4, 1817, Vol. 1, item 6; Jean Bonnaux to Jean Laffite, January 7, 1817, Vol. 1, item 11, NONA.

37. On February 17, 1817, Laffite sued Gambi for $250. Pierre Lafitte vs. Vincent Gambie or Jean Roup, #1346, First Judicial Court, NOPL.

38. Robinson, *Memoirs,* I, p. 133; Morphy to Captain General, December 4, 1816, Legajo 1900, Morphy to José Masot, December 23, 1816, Legajo 1874, AGI-Newberry.

39. Warren, "Pensacola and the Filibusters, 1816–1817," p. 816.

40. Faye, "Aury," I 92, CAHUT.

41. Robinson, *Memoirs,* II, p. 127.

42. Robinson, *Memoirs,* I, p. 59; Faye, "Aury," p. 641, CAHUT.

43. Diary of Antonio Aguirre, November 4, 21, 23, December 4, 6, 14, 21, 22, 1816, January 21, 1817, Blake, Supplement VIII, pp. 140–47.

44. Aguirre Diary, January 21, 1817, Blake Supplement VIII, p. 147, X, p. 161.

45. United States vs. the *Independence* alias *Hotspur,* Case #1026, NAFW.

46. Beverly Chew to William Crawford, August 1, 1817, *Message from the President of the United States, Communicating Information of the Proceeding of Certain Persons who took Possession of Amelia Island and of Galvezton, During the Summer of the Present Year, and made Establishments There* (Washington, 1817), pp. 8–9.

47. Sedella to Cienfuegos, March 1, 2, 1817, Ibid.

48. Pierre Laffite and Jean Laffite to Cienfuegos, February 26, 1817, in Dorothy McD. Karilanovic, trans., "Letters from the National Archive of Cuba," *Laffite Society Chronicles,* V (February 1999), n.p. The original is in the Papeles de Cuba, Legajo 492, Expediente 18,688, microfilm at HNOC. A copy is in Legajo 1898, AGI-Newberry.

49. Sedella to Cienfuegos, February 26, 1817, Legajo 1898, AGI-Newberry.

50. The January 1817 shipment to Laffite and Duparc is attested in Manifest of Cargo on Board the Ship *Patterson,* Entry 1657, Record of Fees Paid, Cargo Manifests, RG 36, NA. Not a trace can be found in census, vital statistics, city directories, or other records of the Laffite and Duparc partnership, or of Vincent Duparc himself. He was not fictional, for a federal case cited below involves his estate, but in the absence of evidence of him trading as a merchant except in this voyage to Galveston, and one other, it seems reasonable to assume that the business partnership was brief, and a matter of convenience for a specific purpose, rather than a conventional concern.

51. Again, Maire was certainly not a Laffite brother-in-law as Faye and Warren claimed. In 1815 he married Adeline Godon, born in 1788 of a white family that predated the Laffites in Louisiana. Maire died in 1827, by then a merchant in New Orleans. His widow lived to be 103, and in later years claimed that her husband had been a wealthy planter, but the Maire inventory of 1827 cited earlier shows he was worth just $2,475, and lived not on a plantation but in a house on Peace Street. Years later the widow, or her daughter Mathilde who lived with her, said that Maire was "a gentleman of wealth, who traveled a great deal" (New Orleans, *Daily Picayune*, January 5, 1891). Adelaide Maire lived at 365 North Dolhonde in 1890 and 1891, and in 1832 appeared in the New Orleans City Directory listed as the widow of Lawrence Maire.

52. Drawback Statements, March 11, 25, 1817, Entry 1656, RG 36, NA.

53. The absence of other drawbacks for the *Devorador* suggest that the Laffites may have bought the ship for this voyage alone, or else did not otherwise use *Devorador* for mercantile trading.

54. Drawback, March 7, 1817, Entry 1656, RG 36, NA.

55. Walter Lowrie and Matthew St. Clair Clarke, eds., *American State Papers. Documents Legislative and Executive, of the Congress of the United States. . . .: Class VI, Commerce and Navigation, Volume I* (Washington, 1832), pp. 574–75.

56. Ducoing went to Galveston on March 16 to become first lieutenant on Champlin's privateer under Aury. Deposition of John Ducoing, October 7, 1817, United States vs. the cargo of the *Mount Vernon*, Case #1070, NAFW.

57. Diary of Jean Laffite, March 16, 1817, Legajo 1900, Papeles de Cuba, AGI-Newberry. This is translated in Harris Gaylord Warren, "Documents Relating to the Establishment of Privateers at Galveston, 1816–1817," *Louisiana Historical Quarterly*, XXI (October 1938), pp. 19–20.

58. Laffite Diary, March 23, 1817, Warren, "Documents," p. 20.

59. Ibid., March 27–28, 1817, Warren, "Documents," pp. 20–21.

60. Ibid., March 30, 1817, Warren, "Documents," p. 21.

61. Beverly Chew to William Crawford, August 1, 1817, *American State Papers, Foreign Relations*, IV, pp. 134, 136–37; Robinson, *Memoirs*, p. 59.

62. Statement of J. F. Lamourer, n.d., Felipe Fatio vs. Certain Goods and Merchandise, Case #1033, NAFW. Sadly no issues of this first Texas newspaper seem to have survived.

63. Deposition of Felipe Fatio vs. Certain Goods and Merchandise, Case #1033, NAFW.

64. Robinson, *Memoirs,* I, pp. 75–76.

65. Certificate of delivery, April 4, 1817, with endorsements, Entry 1656, RG 36, NA.

66. Herrera Statement, July 1, 1816, Notary Marc Lafitte, Vol. 9, act 310, NONA.

67. Hayes, *Galveston,* p. 25; Warren, "Documents," p. 12; Deposition of Raymond Espagnol, October 7, 1817, United States vs. the Cargo of the *Mount Vernon,* Case #1070, NAFW.

68. Deposition of Vincent Garros, August 12, 1817, United States vs. cargoes of the *Juana, Eliza, Carmelita,* and *Diana,* Case #1065, NAFW.

69. Laffite Diary, April 7–8, 1817, Warren, "Documents," p. 22.

70. Dyer became acquainted with an elderly man named Jao de la Porta, who told him a story of having been with Aury at Galveston, and then left behind in charge of seven armed men in a camp. Laffite supposedly arrived with Durieux rather than finding him already on the island, and then negotiated with de la Porta and Rousselin for the purchase of the camp. Afterward those on the island formed what they called the St. Louis Company with Rousselin acting as treasurer and de la Porta secretary. Like most of what Dyer gleaned in the later 1800s, this account is probably mostly imagination. Galveston, *Daily News,* March 15, 1920. There are two relevant documents in the J. O. Dyer Collection at the Rosenberg Library in Galveston, one purporting to be signed by de la Porta in 1818, and the other an appointment of de la Porta as "supercargo" to the Karankawa Indians. The latter carries a clearly inauthentic Jean Laffite signature, and both were probably the creations of de la Porta in his later years when he was the sole source of all statements that place him in Laffite's settlement.

71. Registry of Deliberations Made at Galveston April 15, 1817, United States vs. Jean Desfarges et al., Case File #1440, NAFW.

72. Ibid.; Deposition of John Ducoing, October 7, 1817, United States vs. the cargo of the *Mount Vernon,* Case #1070, NAFW.

73. Laffite Diary, April 10–15, 1817, Warren, "Documents," p. 22.

74. Registry of Deliberations Made at Galveston April 15, 1817, United States vs. Jean Desfarges et al., Case File #1440, NAFW.

75. Deposition of John Ducoing, October 7, 1817, United States vs. the cargo of the *Mount Vernon,* Case #1070, NAFW.

SIXTEEN

1. Chew to Crawford, August 1, 1817, M-38, Miscellaneous Letters of the Department of State August 1–October 31, 1817, RG 59, NA.

2. Deposition of John Ducoing, October 7, 1817, United States vs. the cargo of the *Mount Vernon,* Case #1070, NAFW.

3. Martinez to Commandant General, April 17, 1818, Taylor, *Letters of Antonio Martinez,* pp. 116–17.

4. This seems the only way to account for a debit against the Laffite account for a pirogue purchased at Galveston, April 29, when neither Laffite was at Galveston. Goods sold by Champlin to Laffites at Galveston, charged to Pierre Laffite account with firm of Champlin and Adams in New Orleans, Statement of Pierre Laffite Account with Guy Champlin, Pierre Lafitte vs. Estate of Guy Champlin, #1730, First Judicial Court, NOPL.

5. Statement of account of Pierre Laffite, Pierre Laffite vs. Estate of Guy Champlin, #1730, First Judicial Court, NOPL.

6. Laffite Diary, April 17–18, 1817, Warren, "Documents," pp. 22–23, 25.

7. Jean Laffite to Sedella, April 28, 1817, enclosure with Cienfuegos to Apodaca, May 14, 1817, quoted in Faye, "Stroke," p. 769; Jean Laffite to Latour, May 1817, Legajo 1900, AGI-Newberry.

8. Jean Laffite to Sedella, April 28, 1817, enclosure with Cienfuegos to Apodaca, May 14, 1817, quoted in Faye, "Stroke," p. 769.

9. Jean Laffite to Latour, May 1817, Legajo 1900, AGI-Newberry.

10. Louis Aury, Commission to Nicolas Aiguette, May 7, 1817, translation in Elizabeth H. West Papers, University of Florida, Gainesville. The whereabouts of the original of this document are unknown.

11. Charles Morris to Crowninshield, June 10, 1817, *Message of the President,* pp. 34–35.

12. Laffite Diary, April 22–May 2, 1817, Warren, "Documents," p. 23; Deposition of John Ducoing, October 7, 1817, Aury to Ducoing, May 8, 1817,

United States vs. the Cargo of the *Mount Vernon,* Case #1070; Deposition of John Ducoing, August 12, 1817, United States vs. Cargoes of the *Juana, Eliza, Carmelita,* and *Diana,* Case #1065, NAFW.

13. Ramirez to Cienfuegos, April 7, 1817, Papeles de Estado, Audiencia de Mexico, Legajo 5560, Expediente 6, AGI-Newberry.

14. The original is in Gobierno Superior Civil, Coleccion de Documentos del Archivo Nacional de Cuba, Havana, Legajo 492, Expediente 18688, microfilm at HNOC.

15. Onís to Pizarro, November 22, 1818, Legajo 1898, AGI-Newberry.

16. Ibid.

17. Cienfuegos to Fatio, April 12, 1817, Ibid.

18. Fatio to Cienfuegos, May 14, 1817, Legajo 1900, AGI-Newberry.

19. Fatio to Luis Noeli, August 31, 1818, Onís to Pizarro, November 22, 1818, Legajo 1898, AGI-Newberry.

20. Fatio to Cienfuegos, May 24, 1817, September 28, 1818, Legajo 1900, AGI-Newberry.

21. John Holland to Marie Louise Villard, May 11, 1817, Notary Phillipe Pedesclaux, Vol. 2, p. 603-bis, NONA.

22. Statement of Pierre Laffite Account with Guy Champlin, Pierre Lafitte vs. Estate of Guy Champlin, #1730, First Judicial Court, NOPL. The account statement is confused in places between credits and debits, but this seems to be an accurate figure.

23. Felipe Fatio statement of Expenses, September 29, 1817, Gobierno Superior Civil, Coleccion de Documentos del Archivo Nacional de Cuba, Havana, Legajo 492, Expediente 18688, microfilm at HNOC.

24. Statement of Pierre Laffite Account with Guy Champlin, Pierre Lafitte vs. Estate of Guy Champlin, #1730, First Judicial Court, NOPL.

25. Certificate of delivery, April 4, 1817, with endorsements, Entry 1656, RG 36, NA.

26. Fatio to Cienfuegos, June 18, 1817, Legajo 1900, Onís to Pizarro, November 22, 1818, Legajo 1898, AGI-Newberry.

27. Information derived [from] James Campbell now residing on the Galveston Bay, 10th June 1855, Lamar Papers, TSL.

28. Statement of Pierre Laffite Account with Guy Champlin, Pierre Lafitte vs. Estate of Guy Champlin, #1730, First Judicial Court, NOPL.

29. Deposition of Raymond Espagnol, October 7, 1817, United States vs. the Cargo of the *Mount Vernon*, Case #1070, NAFW.

30. Libel of John Dick, n.d. [1817], United States vs. 37 Pivots, Case #1062, NAFW.

31. Fatio to Cienfuegos, May 24, 1817, Legajo 1900, AGI-Newberry.

32. Luís Iturribarría to Luis Durieux, May 15, 1817, Legajo 1900, AGI-Newberry.

33. Fatio to Jose Cienfuegos, May 13, 1817, Legajo 1900, AGI-Newberry.

34. Fatio to Cienfuegos, June 7, 1817, Ibid.

35. Pierre Laffite to Jean Laffite, July 23, 1817, in Dorothy McD. Karilanovic, trans., "Letters from the National Archive of Cuba," *Laffite Society Chronicles*, V (February 1999), n.p. The original is in the Gobierno Superior Civil, Coleccion de Documentos del Archivo Nacional de Cuba, Havana, Legajo 492, Expediente 18688, Archivo Nacional, Havana, and also on microfilm at HNOC. A copy is in Legajo 1900, AGI-Newberry.

36. Fatio to Cienfuegos, June 18, 1817, Legajo 1900, AGI-Newberry.

37. George Lewis to Jean Laffite, June 6, 1817, Notary Michele DeArmas, Vol. 13, June 6, 1817, item 340; Jean Laffite to Louise Patin, June 20, 1817, Vol. 13, item 376, NONA.

38. Fatio to Cienfuegos, May 31, June 7, 1817, Legajo 1900, AGI-Newberry; Martinez to Commandant General, June 11, 1817, Blake, XVI, pp. 280, June 15, 1817, pp. 282–83, June 23, 1817, pp. 284–90. In his May 31 letter Fatio says Pierre left that day, but he must have been delayed.

39. Martinez to Commandant General, July 14, 1817, Blake, XVI, pp. 302–3, Castañeda to the governor, June 13, 1817, Supplement X, p. 265.

40. Statement of Pierre Laffite Account with Guy Champlin, Pierre Lafitte vs. Estate of Guy Champlin, #1730, First Judicial Court, NOPL; Fatio to Cienfuegos, June 18, 1817, July 11, 1817, Legajo 1900, AGI-Newberry.

41. Deposition of Vincent Garros, August 12, 1817, United States vs. Cargoes of the *Juana, Eliza, Carmelita*, and *Diana*, Case #1065, NAFW.

42. Pierre Laffite to Jean Laffite, July 23, 1817, Karilanovic, "Letters from the National Archive of Cuba," n.p.

43. Ibid.

44. Aury to Chew, July 31, 1817, United States vs. Jean Desfarges et al., Case #1440, NAFW.

45. Statement of Pierre Laffite Account with Guy Champlin, Pierre Lafitte vs. Estate of Guy Champlin, #1730, First Judicial Court, NOPL.

46. New Orleans, *Louisiana Gazette and New-Orleans Mercantile Advertiser,* April 24, May 3, 15, 27, 1817.

47. Drawback for the *Pucille,* June 11, 1817, Drawback for *Alonzo,* May 13, 1817, Entry 1656, RG 36, NA.

48. James Miller to Chew, January 30, 1817, Entry 1627, RG 36, NA.

49. Charles Morris to Crowninshield, June 10, 1817, *Message of the President,* pp. 34–35, John Porter to Crowninshield, June 28, 1817, p. 35.

50. Statement of Pierre Laffite Account with Guy Champlin, Pierre Lafitte vs. Estate of Guy Champlin, #1730, First Judicial Court, NOLA.

51. Deposition of Mr. Hennen, January 8, 1818, Henry Coit vs. Jacob Jennings and George W. Morgan, Case File #1701, 1st Judicial District Court, NOPL. Champlin's date of death is unknown, but two bills of exchange from Robert Sprigg dated August 1 and 2, 1817, and one from James Still, dated August 2, 1817, make it clear that Champlin was already dead at their writing. Henry Coit vs. Christopher Adams, Case File #1727, 1st Judicial District Court, NOPL.

52. William Crawford docketing on Chew to Crawford, August 1, 1817, M-38, RG 59, NA.

53. William H. Crawford to Chew, January 31, 1818, Ibid.

54. Patterson to Crowninshield, January 10, 1818, Area 8, M-625, NA.

55. Onís to Adams, September 19, 1817, Ibid.

56. Chew to Crawford, August 30, 1817, *Message of the President,* p. 13.

57. Bond, July 9, 1817, Claim of Vincent Duparc, July 7, 1817, Seizure order, July 5, 1817, Statement of Beverly Chew, August 5, 1817, Court order, February 25, 1826, Libel of Joshua Lewis, December 18, 1826, United States vs. 37 Pivots, Case #1062, NAFW; Dick to Chew, July 8, 1817, Entry 1627, RG 36, NA.

58. Daniel Wright power of attorney, July 25, 1817, Notary Michele DeArmas, Vol. 13, item 428, NONA.

59. Pierre Laffite to Jean Laffite, August 16, 1817, Karilanovic, "Letters from the National Archive of Cuba," n.p. In the article this letter is mistakenly identified as being from Jean to Pierre, whereas internal evidence makes it evident that it is the other way around. The original is in Gobierno Superior Civil, Coleccion de Documentos del Archivo Nacional de Cuba, Havana, Legajo 492, Expediente 18688, microfilm at HNOC. In the translation Pierre says he sends "a thousand things to the brother-in-law," a reference repeated in his October 7, 1819, letter to Cagigal, cited hereafter. There is no evidence of a Laffite brother-in-law, which makes this puzzling, unless it was a colloquialism for a close associate. Both letters would have been in French, calling for the term *"beau frere."* When the 1817 Cagigal letter was sent on to Havana by Fatio, he had it translated to Spanish, and it survives only in this version. If there was a misreading in the transcription of the Spanish version, *"cuñado"* might have been misread from *"cuñada,"* sister-in-law, in which case Pierre could be referring to Catherine though neither brother was married.

60. Felipe Fatio statement of Expenses, September 29, 1817, Gobierno Superior Civil, Coleccion de Documentos del Archivo Nacional, Havana, Legajo 492, Expediente 18688, microfilm in HNOC.

61. Chew to Crawford, August 30, 1817, *Message of the President,* p. 13.

62. Fatio to Cienfuegos, September 29, 1817, Cienfuegos to Fatio, July 10, 1817, Legajo 1900, AGI-Newberry.

63. Fatio to Cienfuegos, September 29, 1817, Ibid.; Statement of Expenses, September 29, 1817, Gobierno Superior Civil, Coleccion de Documentos del Archivo Nacional, Havana, Legajo 492, Expediente 18688, microfilm in HNOC. Jean Laffite may have been lying about the mortgage on the house, for no record of such a transaction survives in NONA.

64. Pierre Laffite to Cienfuegos, September 1, 1817, in Dorothy McD. Karilanovic, trans., "Letters from the National Archive of Cuba," *Laffite Society Chronicles,* V (February 1999), n.p. The original is in Gobierno Superior Civil, Coleccion de Documentos del Archivo Nacional, Havana, Legajo 492, Expediente 18688, microfilm in HNOC.

65. New Orleans, *Louisiana Courier,* September 2, 1817.

66. Ibid., October 8, 1817.

67. Chew to Crawford, October 17, 1817, *Message of the President,* p. 15.

68. Fatio to Cienfuegos, September 29, 1817, Legajo 1900, AGI-Newberry.

69. Fatio to Cienfuegos, September 29, November 1, 5, 1817, Ibid.

70. Fatio to Cienfuegos, September 29, 1817, November 1, 2, 1817, Ibid.

71. Chew to Crawford, October 17, 1817, *Message of the President,* p. 15.

SEVENTEEN

1. "C" to Victoire Aury Dupuis, October 18, 1817, Aury Papers, CAHUT.

2. Charles Bagot to Castlereagh, September 1, 1817, FO5/123, National Archives, London.

3. Bagot to Castlereagh, October 6, 1817, Ibid.

4. Bagot to Castlereagh, December 2, 1817, Ibid.

5. Ibid.

6. James Monroe Message to Congress, December 2, 1817, Walter Lowrie and Walter S. Franklin, eds., *American State Papers. Documents Legislative and Executive, of the Congress of the United States. . . . : Class I, Foreign Relations, Volume IV* (Washington, 1834), pp. 131–32.

7. Robert Butler to William A. Trimble, December 31, 1817, Records of United States Commands, Army Commands, 1784–1821, Entry 72, Letters, Division of the South, 1816–1821, Vol. 2, RG 98, NA.

8. Pierre Laffite to Paullin Fleytas, November 10, 1817, Notary Philippe Pedesclaux, Vol. 3, item 771; Sale of a *griffe* named Francoise, November 12, 1817, item 782, NONA.

9. Jesse S. Reeves, *The Napoleonic Exiles in America: A Study in American Diplomatic History 1815–1819.* (Baltimore, 1905; Johns Hopkins University Studies in History and Political Science, Series XXIII), pp. 85–87.

10. Ines Murat, *Napoleon and the American Dream* (Baton Rouge, LA, 1976), p. 121.

11. Murat, *American Dream,* pp. 121, 125; Just Girard, *The Adventures of a French Captain* (New York, 1878), p. 58.

12. Felipe Roque de la Portilla to Joaquin de Arredondo, May 8, 1818, Blake, Supplement, VIII, p. 187.

13. Antonio de Carion to Diego Morphy, March 21, 1817, Fatio Papers, Rosenberg Library, Galveston; Statement of Pierre Laffite Account with

Guy Champlin, Pierre Lafitte vs. Estate of Guy Champlin, #1730, First Judicial Court, NOPL.

14. Report of all vessels inward bound boarded by the Inspector at the Balize, Entry 1627, RG 36, NA.

15. Bollaert says that Dominique acted as "major-domo, or grand chamberlain" at Galveston, but there is no evidence that he spent much time there or was even a frequent visitor. B[ollaert], "Lafitte," p. 442.

16. Maria Jane McIntosh, *Conquest and Self-Conquest; or, Which Makes the Hero?* (New York, 1843), pp. 163–64. This novel is apparently based on accounts received from the author's brother, who visited Laffite in 1819 and left his own narrative. Thus this detail on Laffite's house is probably from firsthand observation, and is the earliest known description of the house, such as it is. Mary Campbell told John Dyer in 1879 or earlier that Laffite painted his house red. This is the earliest and only eyewitness statement to support the later tradition of a red house called "Maison Rouge," and comes more than half a century after the fact. Galveston, *Daily News*, May 25, 1879.

17. Deposition of Mariano Gonzales, October 9, 20, 1818, United States vs. Schooner *Lameson*, Case #1227, NAFW; Jack Autrey Dabbs, "Additional Notes on the Champ d'Asile," *Southwestern Historical Quarterly*, LIV (January 1951), pp. 351–52.

18. John Sibley to John Robinson, March 16, 1818, Gettysburg, PA, *Adams Centinel*, April 29, 1818.

19. Dabbs, "Additional Notes," p. 350.

20. Fannie E. Ratchford, ed., *The Story of Champ D'Asile as Told by Two of the Colonists* (Dallas, TX, 1937), pp. 123–24.

21. Dabbs, "Additional Notes," pp. 352–53; Girard, *Adventures*, pp. 58–60.

22. Ratchford, *Champ D'Asile*, p. 77.

23. Fatio to Luis Noeli, June 27, 1818, Legajo 1877, AGI-Newberry.

24. Onís to Pizarro, November 22, 1818, Legajo 1898, AGI-Newberry.

25. Dabbs, "Additional Notes," p. 353.

26. Pierre Laffite to Jean Laffite, February 17, 1818, Legajo 1900, AGI-Newberry.

27. Fatio to Cienfuegos, February 19, 1818, Ibid.

28. Ibid.

29. Pierre Laffite to Chew, n.d., New Orleans, *Louisiana Courier,* February 6, 1818. Pierre and Jean both demonstrate a heavy hand with sarcasm in their writings to and about the authorities. Stanley Faye attributed a letter in the Washington, *National Intelligencer,* April 4, 1818, to Pierre Laffite, in which he jokingly talks of making captives "walk the plank."

30. Information derived from Col. S. M. Williams respecting Lafitte, n.d., Lamar Papers, TSL.

31. Fatio to Guillermo Aubarede, January 31, 1818, Legajo 1900, AGI-Newberry.

32. Pierre Laffite to Jean Laffite, February 17, 1818, Ibid.

33. Ibid.

34. Fatio to Cienfuegos, February 19, 1818, Ibid.

35. The letter Pierre wrote to Jean on February 17, 1818 (see below) is the only mention of this son Eugene by name or inference in all the Laffite documentation, though Fatio does apparently confirm it in his February 18, 1818, letter to Cienfuegos, Legajo 1900, AGI-Newberry. It must be considered possible that the boy was not Pierre's son, who would hardly need the introduction that Pierre gives him in his letter, and that he may simply have been a courier whose safe conduct Pierre wanted to guarantee.

36. Fatio to Cienfuegos, February 12, 1818, Legajo 1900, AGI-Newberry.

37. Ratchford, *Champ D'Asile,* p. 124.

38. Fatio to Luis Noeli, June 27, 1818, Legajo 1877, AGI-Newberry.

39. Girard, *Adventures,* p. 61; Dabbs, "Additional Notes," p. 353. Jean Epperson concludes that they probably located themselves on modern-day Moss Bluff overlooking the Trinity River, midway between Liberty and Lake Charlotte. Jean L. Epperson, "Where was Champ D'Asile?" *Laffite Society Chronicles,* V (August 1999), [pp. 16–17].

40. John Sibley to J. H. Robinson, April 25, 1818, New Orleans, *Louisiana Courier,* May 22, 1818.

41. Brivezac, Rapport sur Letat et la Situation Exacte des Colonies Espagnole de L'Amerique a la fin de 1817, Library of Congress.

42. Kent Gardien, "Take Pity on Our Glory: Men of Champ d'Asile," *Southwestern Historical Quarterly,* LXXXVII (January 1984), p. 241.

43. Dabbs, "Additional Notes," p. 354.

44. Girard, *Adventures,* pp. 78–79.

45. Sources disagree on the precise location of the Laffite village in relation to today's Galveston. According to notes in the Anne and Walter Grover Papers, Rosenberg Library, Galveston, his house stood on the west half of 14th Street and Avenue A, and the southeast corner of city Block 714. Christensen, *Pioneers,* p. 72, locates Laffite's fort at 14th Street and Avenue A at #1417, according to the 1845 Sandusky Map. In the twentieth century a retaining wall was found on the site measuring six feet thick and eighteen inches wide, with twelve large cisterns inside the enclosure. Heavy rings of iron on posts suggested boat moorings to some. The best guess for the commune's main location is to the east where the University of Texas Medical Branch was erected in the 1930s. Excavations then and later consistently unearthed construction materials beneath the water table, placing them there at the time of the Laffite occupation.

46. R. J. Calder to J. S. Sullivan, August 15, 1872, Hayes, *Galveston,* pp. 43–44n; Baker, *Scrap-Book,* p. 357n. Note that this is Jones's earliest recorded recollection of Laffite, predating by twenty-two years the 1894 lost memoir of which a fragment survives.

47. J. Randal Jones, A Visit to Galveston Island in 1818, Rosenberg Library, Galveston. This consists of notes taken in 1894 by Philip C. Tucker, from a longer Jones memoir that was lost in the Galveston hurricane of 1900.

48. Warren Hall supposedly told Mary Campbell that Laffite suffered from seasickness, which is always possible, but the source is so latter day as not to be trusted on its own. Galveston, *Daily News,* May 9, 1920.

49. B[ollaert], "Lafitte," p. 442; J. S. Thrasher, *Galveston City Directory, 1857* (Galveston, TX, 1857), p. 61. The tradition is persistent that Laffite painted his house red, though no contemporary source supports this, the earliest known being the circa 1879 statement by Mary Campbell cited previously.

50. L. Hartmann and _____ Millard, *Le Texas, ou Notice Historique sur le Champ d'Asile* (Paris, France, 1819), pp. 27, 83. This source is somewhat questionable, but is at least contemporary. Statements of the nature of the village grew more and more exaggerated with the passage of time, even when attributable to eyewitnesses. Direct contemporary accounts do not paint a very lavish portrait.

51. Information derived [from] James Campbell now residing on the Galveston Bay, 10th June 1855, Lamar Papers, TSL; Mary Campbell Statement, June 20, 1880, James Campbell Pension File, War of 1812, Records Relating to Pension and Bounty Land Claims, 1773–1942, RG 15, NA. A great deal has been made of the accounts of James and Mary Campbell and their life on Galveston. There are several versions, all derivative, and while there is no reason to doubt that the Campbells were there, most of the rest of their recollections are of questionable value, being written decades after the fact and influenced by the Laffite legend and current fiction.

52. W. A. Fayman and T. W. Reilly, *Fayman & Reilly's Galveston City Directory for 1875–6* (Galveston, TX, 1875), [pp. 15–16]. The source of the information in Fayman and Reilly is not identified, but the statements are almost verbatim in an account attributed four years later to Mary Campbell in Galveston, *Daily News*, May 25, 1879.

53. Willis W. Pratt, ed., *Galveston Island, or, A Few Months off the Coast of Texas. The Journal of Francis C. Sheridan, 1839–1840* (Austin, 1954), p. 63.

54. Faye, "Privateersmen," pp. 1038, 1078–79; Navigation Order, April 2, 1818, Alexander Dienst Collection, CAHUT. The latter source purports to be a statement of letters of marque granted to one Nicolai to operate the bateau *Princess* as a privateer on the rivers of Texas. The document is almost certainly a fake, signed by Jao de la Porta as secretary, which he seems never to have been. The Jean Laffite signature is clearly false. This collection also has a document dated May 15, 1818, purporting to be Laffite's appointment of de la Porta to deal with the Karankawas. Laffite signs himself "president" of the commune, but the signature is not genuine. Both of these documents exist in copies in the Dyer Collection, Rosenberg, and were reproduced in the Galveston, *Daily News*, September 19, 1926.

55. R. J. Calder to J. S. Sullivan, August 15, 1872, Hayes, *Galveston*, pp. 43–44n.

56. Deposition of Alexandre Danges, October 10, 1818, United States vs. Schooner *Lameson*, Case #1227, NAFW.

57. William F. Gray, *From Virginia to Texas, 1835: Diary of Col. Wm. F. Gray* (Houston, 1909), p. 170. This is near the site of modern Deweyville.

58. Louis Raphael Nardini, Sr., *My Historic Natchitoches, Louisiana and Its Environment* (Colfax, LA, 1963), pp. 106–107, 133. Nardini is an often

questionable source, but the procedure detailed in this instance matches other accounts of slave laundering from the period.

59. Colfax, LA, *Chronicle*, August 24, 1962. The article identified one of the agents as "Savoldo," which is almost certainly a misstatement of Sauvinet.

60. Joe Gray Taylor, *Negro Slavery in Louisiana* (Baton Rouge, LA, 1963), p. 55.

61. Nardini, *Historic Natchitoches*, pp. 106–7, 133.

62. Tariff rates of the time can be found in Lawrence Furlong, *The American Coast Pilot* (Newburyport, MA, 1817).

63. John Sibley to John Robinson, March 16, 1818, Gettysburg, PA, *Adams Centinel*, April 29, 1818.

64. Pierre Laffite to Nicholas Mioton, April 18, 1818, Notary Philippe Pedesclaux, Vol. 4, item 320, NONA.

65. Marie Louise Villard to Antoine Abat, April 1, 1818, Notary Philippe Pedesclaux, Vol. 4, item 257; Antoine Abat statement, April 1, 1818, Vol. 4, item 256, NONA.

66. Fatio to Cienfuegos, November 1, 2, 1817, Legajo 1900, AGI-Newberry.

67. Noeli to Fatio, July 3, 1818, Fatio to Noeli, August 31, 1818, Legajo 1898, AGI-Newberry.

68. Cienfuegos to Apodaca, Havana, May 26, 1818, Gobierno Superior Civil, Coleccion de Documentos del Archivo Nacional de Cuba, Havana, Legajo 492, Expediente 18688, microfilm at HNOC. In Fatio to Luis Noeli, August 31, 1818, Legajo 1898, AGI-Newberry, Fatio makes reference to $100 that "number 13 received in Havana" for the expenses of a trip.

69. Joaquin de Arredondo to the governor of Texas, April 27, 1818, Nacogdoches Archives, TSL.

70. Fatio to Martinez, May 22, 1818, Blake, Supplement, VIII, p. 196.

71. Martinez to Viceroy, May 19, 1818, Blake, XVI, pp. 4–6.

72. Martinez to Apodaca, Viceroy, May 23, 1818, Blake, XVI, pp. 15–17, Martinez to Cienfuegos, May 18, 1818, Blake XVII, p. 58.

73. Deposition of Mariano Gonzales October 9, 1818, United States vs. Schooner *Lameson*, #1227, NAFW.

74. Martinez to Apodaca, July 29, 1818, Blake, XVI, pp. 42–44; December 21, 1818, report, Gardien, "Champ d'Asile," p. 254.

75. Report of Juan de Castañeda, November 24, 1818, Blake, LIII, pp. 108, 114, 119.

76. Gardien, "Champ d'Asile," p. 252.

77. Felipe Roque de la Portilla to Joaquin de Arredondo, May 8, 1818, Blake, Supplement, VIII, pp. 186–90.

78. Jacobo Tournelle and Vicente Molina to Felipe Fatio, May 22, 1818, Blake, Supplement, VIII, pp. 198–201.

79. Fatio to Noeli, June 27, 1818, Legajo 1877, AGI-Newberry.

EIGHTEEN

1. Adams, *Memoirs*, IV, pp. 15, 91, 97.

2. George Mason Graham Stafford, comp., *General George Mason Graham of Tyrone Plantation and His People* (New Orleans, 1947), pp. 63–64.

3. Adams to George Mason Graham, June 2, 1818, Graham Family Papers, Virginia Historical Society, Richmond, VA. This is also to be found in Domestic Letters of the Department of State, Volume 17, March 3, 1817–February 23, 1820, M-50, RG 59, NA.

4. Jacobo Tournelle and Vicente Molina to Fatio, May 22, 1818, Blake, Supplement, VIII, pp. 198–201.

5. Tournelle and Molina to Fatio, May 22, 1818, Blake, Supplement, VIII, pp. 198–201.

6. Apodaca to Governor of Texas, June 23, 1818, Nacogdoches Archives, TSL.

7. Girard, *Adventures*, p. 84; Fatio and Noeli to Cienfuegos, July 7, 1818, quoted in Faye, *Privateers*, p. 188.

8. Gardien, "Champ d'Asile," p. 256.

9. Graham to Eleazer Ripley, August 28, 1818, Graham Family Papers, Virginia Historical Society.

10. Girard, *Adventures*, pp. 60–61.

11. Martinez to Apodaca, July 29, 1818, Blake, XVI, pp. 42–44.

12. Girard, *Adventures,* pp. 60–61.

13. Klier, "Champ d'Asile," pp. 89–90.

14. Letter dated July 12, 1818, in Reeves, *Napoleonic Exiles,* p. 90.

15. Commission of Pedro Laméson, July 16, 1818, United States vs. Schooner *Lameson,* Case #1227, NAFW.

16. Libel of John Dick August 12, 1818, Ibid.; Protest of Pierre Laméson, August 8, 1818, Notary Michele DeArmas, Vol. 15A, Part 1, act 647, NONA.

17. Deposition of Mariano Gonzales October 9, 1818, United States vs. Schooner *Lameson,* #1227, NAFW.

18. New Orleans, *Orleans Gazette,* August 11, 1818; New York, *Spectator,* September 15, 1818.

19. Protest of Pierre Laméson, August 8, 1818, Notary Michele DeArmas, Vol. 15A, Part 1, act 647, NONA; Claim, August 21, 1818, Admissions and cross questions of Edwin Lorraine and Edward Livingston, n.d., Petition of Pierre Laméson, November 5, 1818, United States vs. Schooner *Lameson,* Case #1227, NAFW.

20. Luis Noeli to Fatio, August 28, 1818, Legajo 1898, AGI-Newberry.

21. Fatio to Noeli, August 31, 1818, Ibid.

22. Fatio to Noeli, August 31, 1818, Onís to the Intendant, November 25, 1818, Ibid.

23. Fatio to Cienfuegos, September 28, 1818, Legajo 1900, AGI-Newberry.

24. Marshall, *Western Boundary,* pp. 55–58.

25. Charleston, *Courier,* June 19, 1818.

26. Apodaca to Martinez, Sept. 22, 1818, Blake, Supplement, VIII, p. 210.

27. George Graham report, n.d. [September 1818], Graham Family Papers, Virginia Historical Society.

28. Graham to Lallemand, August 26, 1818, Ibid.

29. Lallemand to Graham, August 26, 1818, Ibid.

30. Graham to Eleazer Ripley, August 28, 1818, Ibid. The last portion of this letter is missing in the original, but it is printed in its entirety in George Mason Graham, "Political Occurrences on the Island of Galveston in 1818," *Tyler's Historical and Genealogical Magazine,* XXVII (April 1946), p. 272, and in Stafford, *Graham,* p. 82.

31. Jean Laffite to Graham, August 26, 1818, George Mason Graham Papers, LSU.

32. Graham to Laffite, August 26, 1818, [copy] Graham Family Papers, Virginia Historical Society.

33. George Graham report, n.d. [September 1818], Ibid.; Jean Laffite to Graham, August 28, 1818, Graham Papers, LSU.

34. Letter of Protection, August 28, 1818, Graham Family Papers, Virginia Historical Society.

35. John Dyer in Galveston, *Daily News,* September 19, 1926, says his father was in business with Graham in New Orleans in later years, and that Graham said Laffite spoke in pained terms of the fictionalized accounts of his piracy that he saw in the papers. Like all of Dyer's stories, it is probably imaginative, but could be true.

36. Graham to Eleazer Ripley, August 28, 1818, Graham Family Papers, Virginia Historical Society. The last portion of this letter is missing in the original, but it is printed in its entirety in Graham, "Political Occurrences," p. 272, and in Stafford, *Graham,* p. 82.

37. Adams, *Memoirs,* November 20, 1818, IV, pp. 175–76; Graham to David C. DeForest, n.d. [copy], Graham Family Papers, Virginia Historical Society.

38. Ratchford, *Champ D'Asile,* pp. 151–53.

39. Deposition, 1818, Notary John Lynd, Vol. 15, item 1005, NONA.

40. Martinez to Apodaca, October 15, 1818, Blake, XVI, p. 67.

41. Girard, *Adventures,* p. 86.

42. Ratchford, *Champ D'Asile,* pp. 151–53.

43. Galveston, *Gazette* quoted in Newark, NJ, *Daily Advertiser,* February 12, 1840, says that Laffite lost many men, but does not elaborate. Certainly, in such a storm at an unprotected location, fatalities were inevitable; Jones, A Visit to Galveston Island in 1818, Rosenberg Library, Galveston.

44. Saxon, *Lafitte,* pp. 221–22, says that cannon on the upper floor of the house broke through the floor during the hurricane, killing women and children who were sheltering below, and injuring Catherine Villard. As usual, he offers no source for this statement, nor for his assertion that Laffite sat out the storm on a vessel in the bay. There is no contemporary evidence that Catherine was ever on the island.

45. Dyer states in Galveston, *Daily News*, September 19, 1926, that after the hurricane Laffite was virtually "dictator" at Galveston. For once he is probably right.

46. Girard, *Adventures*, p. 86; Ratchford, *Champ D'Asile*, pp. 158–59.

47. Fatio to Cienfuegos, May 13, 1817, Fatio Papers, Rosenberg Library, Galveston.

48. Cienfuegos to Apodaca, July 17, 1818, Historia, Operaciones de Guerra, Notas Diplomaticas, AGI-Newberry.

49. Apodaca to the Governor of Texas, August 13, 1818, Nacogdoches Archives, TSL; Martinez to Commandant General, September 8, 1818, Taylor, *The Letters of Antonio Martinez*, p. 173.

50. Jean Laffite to Graham, September 21, 1818, Graham Family Papers, Virginia Historical Society. This letter, which appears to be a holograph original, has been misinterpreted from time to time as confirmation that there was a third Laffite brother, for in it—in translation—Jean states that he had sent "my young brother" to New Orleans "in order that upon his arrival he may receive the dispatches that I address to my brother who must be quite near you." This appears to mention two brothers, then, the "young" one and the one in New Orleans. The problem lies in the translation, however, and the two brothers are the same and only brother, Pierre. Jean's reference to him as "young" is hard to explain unless it, too, is the result of translation. It should be borne in mind that neither Laffite was an accomplished writer. Sentence structure, syntax, grammar, and more were idiosyncratic and often jumbled in their letters. Jean may simply have misspoken or improperly expressed himself. Then, too, he had impressed Graham with his authority at Galveston, so it may have been in his interest to give the impression that he, Jean, was the elder and senior brother. Perhaps motivated by this misinterpretation of the letter, Stafford, *Graham*, p. 79, states that there was a third brother and that his name was Gabriel. No record of a Gabriel Laffite can be found.

51. Onís to Cienfuegos, November 25, 1818, Legajo 1898, AGI-Newberry.

52. Adams, *Memoirs*, November 20, 1818, IV, pp. 175–76.

53. Adams to Graham, December 4, 1817, M-50, RG 59, NA.

54. Dabbs, "Additional Notes," p. 355.

55. Martinez to Commanding General, September 4, 7, 1818, Blake, XVII, pp. 136–39; Martinez to Apodaca, October 2, 1818, XVI, pp. 66–67.

56. Report of Juan de Castañeda, November 24, 1818, Blake, LIII, pp. 108, 114, 119.

57. Castañeda to General in Chief of the Troops of Galveston, October 13, 1818, Blake, LIII, pp. 133–37.

58. José Sandoval to Martinez, October 20, 1818, Blake, LIII, pp. 128, 129.

59. Rigaud to Castañeda, October 17, 1818, Blake, LIII, pp. 137–40.

60. Castañeda to Antoine Rigaud, October 19, 1818, Blake, LIII, pp. 140–41.

61. Castañeda to "The First Authority Depending on the Congress of the United States," October 13, 1818, Blake, LIII, pp. 141–42.

62. Report of Castañeda, November 24, 1818, Blake, LIII, pp. 108, 114, 119.

63. Martinez to Apodaca, November 11, 1818, Blake, XVI, p. 70, November 12, 1818, pp. 71–73.

64. Martinez to Captain General, November 27, 1818, Taylor, *The Letters of Antonio Martinez,* p. 197.

65. Dabbs, "Additional Notes," p. 356. This comes from a circa 1819 letter by an anonymous refugee.

66. Girard, *Adventures,* pp. 87–88; Ratchford, *Champ D'Asile,* pp. 163–64; Betje Black Klier, "Champ d'Asile, Texas," François Lagarde, *The French in Texas: History, Migration, Culture* (Austin, TX, 2003), p. 89.

67. Girard, *Adventures,* p. 89.

68. Minutes, December 17, 1818, 7RA-119, RG 21, NAFW.

69. Gardien, "Champ d'Asile," pp. 258–59.

70. A story from the Champ d'Asile episode appeared in 1892, apparently originating as a recollection passed on by the son of Dr. Felix Formento, an Italian who acted as a physician for the settlers (Gardien, "Champ d'Asile," p. 268). In its earliest known variant, around November 1818 just prior to the final evacuation, Laffite sent for Formento to come to his dwelling to minister to his daughter, who was suffering a typhoid or similar affliction. Formento stayed with Laffite for several weeks treating the girl, who finally recovered. Laffite rewarded him handsomely and gave him transport to New Orleans, probably on the sloop taking the sick ("Dr. Felix Formento, Sr.," *Biographical and Historical Memoirs of Louisiana* [Chicago, 1892], I, pp. 410–11). By 1892 this was a seventy-four-year-old recollection

if it came directly from Formento himself. Assuming that Formento did indeed tell such a story, and there is no reason to doubt him, as he achieved considerable local and national repute in his medical career, it could still have undergone extensive warping due to frequent retelling and old age. For instance, Jean Laffite is not known to have had a daughter, nor any children but the son Jean Pierre, aged just three in 1818. If an incident like this did take place, then more likely the woman was the young slave earlier seen living with him. The always fertile Dyer collected a story sometime prior to 1926 that Jean had brought to Galveston a daughter of Pierre's by his mulatto "housekeeper" in New Orleans, the same daughter whom Jean supposedly took east with him in 1815 to send to school at Quebec. Unfortunately, she contracted tuberculosis after the hurricane and died (Joseph O. Dyer in "Jean Lafitte, Buccaneer, Had Most Colorful Career," Galveston, *Daily News*, September 19, 1926). Finally, in Simone de la Souchère Deléry's heavily fictionalized *Napoleon's Soldiers in America* (Gretna, LA, 1972), pp. 75–77, the episode took place in New Orleans at Pierre and Marie's house, and again it was Jean's daughter whom Formento saved, this time from yellow fever.

In the end, the story should be taken as little more than confirmation that Laffite still had a female companion with him, as attested earlier in the year by eyewitness contemporary evidence, and as will be reaffirmed in 1819 by others.

71. Dabbs, "Additional Notes," p. 356; Galveston, *Daily News*, May 25, 1879. B[ollaert,] "Lafitte," p. 444, apparently also refers to this incident, though Bollaert's would have been a different informant from the source in Dabbs.

72. Fatio to Noeli, August 31, 1818, Onís to Pizarro, November 22, 1818, Ibid.

73. Benjamin Ogle Tayloe, *Our Neighbors on La Fayette Square, Anecdotes and Reminiscences* (Washington, 1872), pp. 22, 24.

74. Adams to Thompson, May 20, 1819, T829, RG 45, NA.

75. Vincent Garrot [Garros] to Pierre Laffite, November 17, 1818, Legajo 1898, AGI-Newberry.

76. List of Vessels armed or equipped in the Ports of the United States or in their Jurisdiction, agreeably to Documents deposited in the Archives of H. C. Majesty's Ministry, November 16, 1818, List of Spanish vessels

captured by Pirates and brought into the United States, November 16, 1818, enclosure in Onís to Adams, November 16, 1818, M-59, RG 59, NA.

77. Onís to Cienfuegos, November 22, 25, 1818, Legajo 1898, AGI-Newberry.

78. Apodaca to Secretary of State, April 30, 1819, Papeles de Estado, Audiencia de Mexico, Legajo 14, AGI-Newberry.

79. Projects and proposals made by N. 13, n.d., enclosed with Onís to Cienfuegos, November 25, 27, 1818, Legajo 1898, AGI-Newberry.

80. Ibid.

81. Fatio to Noeli, August 31, 1818, Ibid.

82. Onís to Pierre Laffite, November 21, 1818, Ibid.

83. Onís to Cienfuegos, November 25, 1818, Ibid.

84. Apodaca to Venadito, April 30, 1819, in Faye, *Privateers,* p. 203.

85. George Wilson, captain of the privateer *Tucuman,* to the minister of war, September 10, 1817, Buenos Ayres, *Gazette,* November 22, 1817, extracts from the Buenos Ayres *Gazette,* November–December, 1817, M-59, RG 59, NA.

86. Warren, *Sword,* p. 228.

87. Information derived from Col. S. M. Williams respecting Lafitte, n.d., Lamar Papers, TSL.

88. Samuel M. Williams said circa 1850 that "Lafitte, his father & brother, bought the canvass to make his sails of S. M. Williams Uncle in Baltimore" (From Sam M. Williams, n.d., Lamar Papers, TSL). See also Margaret Swett Henson, *Samuel May Williams, Early Texas Entrepreneur* (College Station, TX, 1976), pp. 6–7. Later recollections by James and Mary Campbell maintained that Campbell made the trip to Baltimore to see to the completion of a fast new privateer. It is possibly complete imagination, though the fact of Pierre's being in Baltimore at this time at least in part for this purpose suggests that Campbell's story springs from a germ of truth. Perhaps he actually accompanied Pierre on the journey. W. T. Block, "A Buccaneer Family in Spanish East Texas: A Biographical Sketch of Captain James and Mary Sabinal Campbell," *Texas Gulf Historical & Biographical Record,* XXVII (November 1991), p. 85.

89. A Summary Statement of Money and Property taken out of Spanish vessels, November 16, 1818, M-59, RG 59, NA.

90. DeForest to Manuel Lynch, January 6, 1819, DeForest Family Papers, Yale University Library, New Haven, CT, does not explicitly say that Laffite met with him, but it is implied in the content. Similarly, no source places Pierre Laffite in Charleston at this time. However, the fact that it was a major center for privateering outfitters, coupled with Pierre's period of time spent there the following year, suggest that while in the East he would have made an exploratory trip there to establish necessary business contacts.

91. Jean Laffite to James Long, July 7, 1819, Lamar Papers, TSL, says that Pierre was daily expected in Galveston after his return from the "North." No more precise record of the time of Pierre's return has been found.

NINETEEN

1. Petition of Jean Lafitte, Case file #2289 James Lafitte vs. Juan Gonzales, Parish Court Records, NOPL. The loan was made March 12, 1819, to Juan Gonzales.

2. Antoine Abat to Marie Villard, April 30, 1819, Notary Philippe Pedesclaux, Vol. 7, item 339, NONA.

3. Fatio to Apodaca, May 8, 11, 1819, Papeles de Estado, Audiencia de Mexico, Legajo 14, AGI-Newberry.

4. John Jamison to Calhoun, August 25, 1819, from Natchitoches, W. Edwin Hemphill, ed., *The Papers of John C. Calhoun, Volume IV, 1819–1820* (Columbia, SC, 1969), pp. 274–75.

5. James Long to Jean Laffite, June 24, 1819, Lamar Papers, TSL.

6. Long's June 24 letter to Jean is contained in an August 31, 1819, report by Apodaca, Papeles de Estado, Audiencia de Mexico, Legajo 14, AGI-Newberry.

7. Jean Laffite to Long, July 7, 1819, Lamar Papers, TSL. This is the signed original in French. It is evident that Laffite did not write the body text, but only signed the document.

8. Petition of Jean Lafitte, July 26, 1819, Case file #2289 James Lafitte vs. Juan Gonzales, Parish Court Records, NOPL. The petition is signed and dated in New Orleans and places Jean there at that time.

9. Pierre was in New Orleans as of July 28 (Alexander Choppin to Pierre Laffite, July 28, 1819, Notary Philippe Pedesclaux, Vol. 8, item 559,

NONA), and was back by August 26 (Adelina Maire to Pierre Laffite, August 26, 1819, Notary Michele DeArmas, Vol. 18, Act 25, NONA).

10. Latter-day sources give names for several supposed Laffite corsairs at this time, but there is no contemporary documentary corroboration for most of them. B[ollaert], "Lafitte," p. 442, says that he had the *Pride,* a fourteen-gun schooner; two feluccas; and an armed boat called the *Culebra* that Laffite used to be rowed about the bay. Charles Ellms, *The Pirates Own Book, or Authentic Narratives of the Lives, Exploits, and Executions of the Most Celebrated Sea Robbers* (Portland, ME, 1837), p. 77, appears to be the origin of a tradition that Laffite also had a privateer named the *Jupiter,* but there is no evidence for this. A corsair of that name did call at Galveston at least once, and there are other references at the time to a *Jupiter,* but they make it clear that Laffite was not the owner (Baltimore, *Nile's Weekly Register,* February 5, 1820, pp. 395–96).

11. Commission, n.d. [August 18, 1819], Ibid.; *Nile's Register,* XVII (January 29, 1820), p. 376.

12. Jean Laffite, instructions to Jean Desfarges, August 18, 1819, United States vs. John Desfarges, et al., Case #1440, NAFW.

13. Charter of Partition for the Mexican Corsair named *La Brave,* August 18, 1819, Ibid.

14. Patterson to Lawrence Kearny, October 21, 1819, M-125, RG 45, NA.

15. Apodaca to Secretary of State, January 31, April 30, 1819, Papeles de Estado, Audiencia de Mexico, Legajo 14, AGI-Newberry.

16. Martinez to unknown, August 23, 1819, Taylor, *The Letters of Antonio Martinez,* p. 255.

17. Neither Davis nor Lacaze appear as attorneys in the 1811 or 1822 New Orleans city directories.

18. Jean Laffite to Long, September 30, 1819, Lamar Papers, TSL. A French original and an English translation exist in the Lamar Papers, but the French version appears to be a copy as the signature does not at all resemble Laffite's.

19. Appointment of Jean Laffite, October 7, 1819, RG 45, NA. The document indicates that it was signed in Galveston, meaning Long had to be there. A somewhat questionable document in the Dienst Collection, CAHUT, purports to be an undated circa 1819 note from a John Acogue-

due to Jean Laffite, which Laffite has endorsed with his name and the word "emperor." Walter Benjamin sold it to Dienst in 1927. There is absolutely no evidence of Laffite assuming such a title, even in jest, and certainly not on a monetary document.

20. Faye, "Privateersmen," pp. 1078–79; Stanley Faye, "Types of Privateer Vessels, Their Armament and Flags, in the Gulf of Mexico," *Louisiana Historical Quarterly*, XXIII (January 1940), p. 130.

21. Pierre's October 7, 1819, report seems to exist only in a French version that appears to be in Pierre's handwriting and signed "No 13" in Gobierno Superior Civil, Legajo 492, Expediente 18688, Coleccion de Documentos del Archivo Nacional de Cuba, Havana, microfilm at HNOC. It is referred to in Pierre Laffite to Juan Manuel de Cagigal, December 11, 1819, Historia, Operaciones de Guerra, Notas Diplomaticas, IV, Fondo 50, AGI-Newberry.

22. John Henry Brown, *Long's Expedition* (Houston, TX, 1930), pp. 1–2.

23. Marshall, *Western Boundary*, pp. 66–67.

24. New Orleans, *Orleans Gazette*, November 9, 1819.

25. Order from Béxar, October 21, 1818, Béxar Archives, CAHUT.

26. Onís to Adams, March 9, 1819, M-59, RG 59, NA.

27. Adams to Smith Thompson, May 20, 1819, Miscellaneous Records of the Office of Naval Records and Library, Private Letters, February 1, 1818–March 27, 1822, T829, RG 45, NA.

28. Ibid.

29. Patterson to Rodgers, November 1, 1818, Area 8, M-625, NA.

30. Exhibit Shewing the Names, Force and Present State & Condition of the Vessels of War of every description At New Orleans, November 1, 1818, Area 8, M-625, NA.

31. US Navy Subject File 1775–1910, File SG-Pirates, p. 57; Patterson to Smith Thompson, July 17, 21, 29, 1819, M-125, NA; Baltimore, *Nile's Weekly Register*, September 11, 1819, p. 31.

32. Claim, December 19, 1818, Case #1271; Minutes, 7RA-119, RG 21, NAFW; Faye, "Privateersmen," p. 1033; Faye, "Aury," p. 672.

33. Libel of Lorenzo Bru et al., October 16, 1819, United States vs. *Filomena*, Case #1437; Indictment, November 12, 1819, Bond September 15, 1819,

United States vs. John Desfarges, et al., Case #1440; Libel, December 13, 1819, United States vs. Armed Schooner *Bravo*, Case #1450, NAFW.

34. Inventory of a Trunk captured on board the Privateer Bravo, September 22, 1819, United States vs. *Filomena*, Case #1437, NAFW.

35. Indictment, November 12, 1819, Jury finding, November 12, 1819, United States vs. John Desfarges et al., Case #1440, NAFW.

36. Baltimore, *Nile's Weekly register*, October 2, 1819, pp. 75–76.

37. Margaret Swett Henson, *Samuel May Williams, Early Texas Entrepreneur* (College Station, TX, 1976), pp. 6–7.

38. Pierre Lafitte vs. Estate of Guy Champlin, #1730, First Judicial Court, NOPL.

39. Deed, June 14, 1819, Notary Philippe Pedesclaux, Vol. 8, item 449, NONA. The buyer was Rosette Villard, a free woman of color. She cannot be directly linked to Marie Villard, but as all the Villards in New Orleans at the time seem to be of the same family, and she moved in one lot away from Marie's house, a connection seems a safe speculation.

40. Adelina Maire to Pierre Laffite, August 26, 1819, Notary Michele DeArmas, Vol. 18, Act 25; Alexander Choppin to Pierre Laffite, July 28, 1819, Notary Philippe Pedesclaux, Vol. 8, item 559, NONA.

41. Samuel Wilson, Jr., *Impressions Respecting New Orleans by Benjamin Henry Boneval Latrobe, Diary & Sketches 1818–1820* (New York, 1951), p. 54.

42. Antoine Abat to Marie Villard, April 30, 1819, Notary Philippe Pedesclaux, Vol. 7, item 339, NONA.

43. Note of encumbrance, September 6, 1819, Notary Philippe Pedesclaux, Vol. 9, item 685, NONA.

44. Dyer heard stories that by this time Pierre Laffite was a brutal, cross-eyed ruffian, a gambler, and a drunkard. This is probably as unreliable as the rest of the Dyer tales. Galveston, *Daily News*, September 19, 1926.

45. Minutes, November 12, 1819, United States vs. John Desfarges, et al., Case #1440, Minutes, 7RA-119, RG 21, NAFW.

46. Testimony of John Desfarges, November 19, 1819, United States vs. John Desfarges, et al., Case #1440; Minutes, November 19, 22, 1819, United States vs. John Desfarges, et al., Case #1440. Minutes, 7RA-119, RG 21, NAFW.

47. Information derived from Col. S. M. Williams respecting Lafitte, n.d., Lamar Papers, TSL.

48. B[ollaert], "Lafitte," pp. 441–42.

49. Pierre Laffite to Cagigal, December 11, 1819, Notas Diplomaticas, Vol. 4, pp. 50ff, Mexican National Archives, copy in Lamar Papers, TSL.

50. Baltimore, *Nile's Weekly Register,* November 27, 1819, January 22, 1820.

51. Thrasher, *Galveston City Directory,* p. 61.

52. John H. Heller, comp., *Galveston City Directory for 1870* (Galveston, TX, 1870), p. 122.

53. B[ollaert], "Lafitte," p. 442.

54. Thrasher, *Galveston City Directory,* p. 62n. This will be a story related by Warren Hall.

55. Bollaert, "Lafitte," pp. 442–44; Information derived [from] James Campbell now residing on the Galveston Bay, 10th June 1855, Lamar Papers, TSL.

56. Willis W. Pratt, ed., *Galveston Island, or, A Few Months Off the Coast of Texas. The Journal of Francis C. Sheridan, 1839–1840* (Austin, TX, 1954), p. 56. James Campbell's wife, Mary, recalled of Jean Laffite many years after the fact that "the old man was always on the lookout for the good of those around him." She also remembered that relations between inhabitants of the Galveston community were generally harmonious (Galveston, *Daily News,* May 25, 1879).

57. At an 1839 camp meeting at Caney, near Port Lavaca, Sarah Tone proclaimed herself repentant and saved, saying that in youth and middle age she had been the "wife" of Laffite at Galveston. The only Tone in Texas then was Thomas Tone, who on December 31, 1837, married Sarah Kinsey in Matagorda County. The 1850 census says she was fifty-three and was born in Kentucky. She was dead by 1860. Her story is certainly apocryphal. Journal of Jesse Hord, January 31, 1839, Macum Phelan, *A History of Methodism in Texas* (Nashville, TN, 1924), p. 111.

58. B[ollaert], "Lafitte," p. 442. The portion of this account that undoubtedly comes from Gaines seems to end in the paragraph immediately before mention of the mistress and son, so Bollaert may have gotten those details elsewhere.

59. Journal of John Landreth on an Expedition to the Gulf Coast, November 15, 1818–May 19, 1819, entry for January 12, 1819, T12, NA.

60. Washington, *Daily National Intelligencer*, November 30, 1818; "Negroes Imported," Baltimore, *Nile's Register*, December 12, 1818.

61. Galveston, *Daily News*, March 16, 1920; Thrasher, *Galveston City Directory*, p. 61.

62. Journal of John Landreth on an Expedition to the Gulf Coast, November 15, 1818–May 19, 1819, T12, NA.

63. John Bowie, "Early Life in the Southwest—The Bowies," *DeBow's Review*, I (October 1852), pp. 380–81, is the principal source for the Bowie involvement and their method of operation. Notarial records and the Web site Afro-Louisiana History and Genealogy, 1718–1820 (Slave), show no great number of slave sales by the Bowies, but in March–April 1817 they sold eight; November 1818–February 1819 they sold fifteen for just over $15,000; and February–May 1820 they sold nine for $5,525. Their total slave sales recorded in the site thus amount to $24,360, considerably less than the $65,000 claimed in John Bowie's article. Of course, these are only their recorded sales. Rezin Bowie handled most of the sales, and chiefly in St. Landry Parish. The most likely alternatives for the time when their business with Laffite started would appear to be either November 1818 or March 1820.

64. J. O. Dyer told a friend that Charles Cronea, supposedly a storekeeper in Laffite's establishment, told him in later years that James Bowie visited Galveston in 1819 and "the two men Lafitte & Bowie could readily have passed for brothers" (J. O. Dyer to Beer, February, n.d., William Beer Papers, Tulane University, New Orleans). Like most of Dyer's stories collected from elderly denizens of Galveston in the 1870s and later, Cronea's was probably imagination. According to the 1850 Census, Jefferson County, p. 249, Cronea was born about 1806, and thus would have been about thirteen in 1819, hardly old enough to be running a store. When he filed a claim for a veteran land bounty in 1884, he was telling friends that he had been an unwilling cabin boy aboard a Laffite ship commanded by Campbell, another of the old Galveston storytellers. (Statement of W. D. Ivey, September 8, 1884, Charles Cronea Application File, RV 1153, Veterans Donation Applications, Texas General Land Office, Austin; W. T. Block, "'Uncle Charlie' Cronea: The Last of Lafitte's Pirates," CAHUT). In connection with Laffite, it is interesting to note that a host of prepos-

terous stories about James Bowie's exploits arose after his death at the Alamo, and among them is the one that appeared in the Houston, *Democratic Telegraph and Texas Register* of June 20, 1850. In it, Bowie was traveling on a steamboat on June 4, 1835, when he challenged a cheating gambler to a duel and killed him, the cheat being the son of Jean Laffite. The story exists in several variants.

65. Statement, December 15, 1821, United States vs. Charles Mulholland, Case #1780; Statement, December 14, United States vs. James Reeves, Case #1781; Statement, December 14, 1821, United States vs. Christopher Adams, Case #1778, NAFW.

66. Crawford to Chew, August 11, 1819, M-178, RG 56, NA.

67. New Orleans, *Courier de la Louisiane,* October 22, 1819; B[ollaert], "Lafitte," p. 443.

68. No record has been found of James M. McIntosh serving on the ship *Lynx,* despite the account he wrote of her visit to Laffite that appeared in the March 1847 *Knickerbocker Magazine.* This is not conclusive. Documents in the naval records at the National Archives simply do not account for his time immediately after his being detached from New Orleans and given a six-month furlough on October 11, 1819, virtually the same time that the *Lynx* was preparing for her voyage. This was well in time for his November 1819 visit to Galveston, which must have been in an unofficial capacity. "Mystery of 'LYNX' Visit," *Laffite Study Group Newsletter,* II (Spring 1982), p. 1.

69. J. R. Madison to John Rodgers, November 1, 1818, Area 8, M-625, NA.

70. [James M. McIntosh], "A Visit to Lafitte," *Knickerbocker Magazine,* XXIX (March 1847), pp. 254–55; B[ollaert], "Lafitte," p. 443. Some have questioned the authenticity of the McIntosh article. Certainly it is inaccurate in some particulars, and it may have been heavily influenced by Ingraham's novel *Lafitte, the Pirate of the Gulf.* However, it otherwise agrees overall with contemporary sources. Interestingly, it also agrees with the early 1840s accounts gleaned by Bollaert. Bancroft, *North Mexican States,* II, pp. 43–44n, also accepts it as genuine.

71. Jean Laffite to Madison, November 7, 8, 1819, copy in French in File SG-Pirates, RG 45, NA. Dyer gave a fanciful account of the trial and hanging, maintaining that he had seen a transcript of the trial that was subsequently lost in the great Galveston hurricane of 1900 (Galveston,

News Sun, September 10, 1922). It is worth noting that Dyer apparently turned his Laffite articles and collections into a biography that he tried to get published during World War I, but publishers turned it down citing the shortage of paper during the war. The manuscript seems not to have survived. In fact, Dyer was garrulous and disorganized, unable to tell myth from fact, and very gullible when it came to the imaginative old sea stories of the Galveston denizens who claimed to have been with the Laffites (Dyer to Beer, March 3, n.d., Beer Papers, Rosenberg Library, Galveston).

72. McIntosh to Long, November 10, 1819, *Nile's Register*, XVII (February 5, 1820), p. 396.

73. [McIntosh], "Visit," pp. 258–59.

74. Jean Laffite to Madison, November 7, 1819, copy in File SG-Pirates, NA; Jean Laffite to Madison, November 7, 1819, *Nile's Register*, XVII (February 5, 1820), pp. 395–96.

75. Madison said on February 29, 1820, that he never got the letter from Laffite dated November 7. Baltimore, *Nile's Weekly Register*, XVII, April 22, 1820.

76. Madison to Jean Laffite, Nov. 7, 1819, RG 45, NA.

77. In his later 1847 account, and in what he apparently told his sister as related in Maria Jane McIntosh, *Conquest and Self-Conquest; or, Which Makes the Hero?* (New York, 1843), McIntosh said more than twenty years after the fact that it was on a subsequent visit to the island that he refused to deliver the offensive letter that Laffite then corrected. There was hardly any cause for an aggressive tone with Madison after September 7, whereas Laffite's initial letter to Madison of that date certainly is threatening. It seems most probable that it was Laffite's second letter of that date, in response to Madison's demand for information, that was still aggressive in tone and had to be modified.

78. Jean Laffite to Madison, November 7, 8, 1819, copy in French in File SG-Pirates, RG 45, NA. McIntosh's 1847 account of this is somewhat confused as to chronology and detail. [McIntosh], "Visit," p. 259. James Campbell told much the same story in the 1850s, but confused George Brown with a "Juana," which is probably a dim recollection of Jannet. Information derived [from] James Campbell now residing on the Galveston Bay, 10th June 1855, Lamar Papers, TSL.

79. Patterson to Thompson, November 24, 1819, M-125, NA; McIntosh to Long, November 10, 1819, *Nile's Register*, XVII (February 5, 1820), p. 396.

80. B[ollaert], "Lafitte," p. 443.

81. [McIntosh], "Visit," pp. 260–61; McIntosh, *Conquest and Self-Conquest,* p. 167; Patterson to Thompson, November 24, 1819, M-125, NA; Baltimore, *Nile's Weekly Register,* XVII, April 22, 1820. Though *Conquest and Self-Conquest,* pp. 149–71, has a fictionalized version of the 1819 visit of the *Lynx* to Galveston, the author was the younger sister of Lieutenant James McKay McIntosh of the *Lynx,* and thus would have had the story directly from him. She changed the name of the vessel to the *Enterprise,* the place from Galveston to Barataria, and the date from 1819 to 1812, but some of what she has McIntosh saying and doing in the form of her protagonist, Frederic Stanley, is likely genuine recollection.

82. New Orleans, *Louisiana Courier,* December 3, 1819.

83. Ibid., November 24, 1819.

TWENTY

1. Beardslee, *Piracy,* p. 22.

2. Patterson to Smith Thompson, January 3, 1820, M-125, RG 45, NA; New Orleans, *Louisiana Courier,* November 17, 1819.

3. Pierre Laffite to Isabelle Cheval, December 4, 1819, Notary Michele DeArmas, Vol. 18, Act 131; Pierre Laffite to Baptiste Lafitte, December 28, 1819, attached to Baptiste Lafitte to Antoine Abat, August 2, 1820, Notary Philippe Pedesclaux, Vol. 16, item 425, NONA.

4. Information derived from Col. S. M. Williams respecting Lafitte, n.d., Lamar Papers, TSL. This account is usually read to describe Jean Laffite, but since virtually all of Williams's other recollections indicate that he was speaking of Pierre, this one is probably about him too, especially given the reference to the eye. There is one latter-day statement that Pierre had a bad eye.

5. Journal of John Landreth on an Expedition to the Gulf Coast, November 15, 1818–May 19, 1819, entry for December 27, 1818, T12, NA.

6. Manuel García to Apodaca, April 9, 1820, quoted in Faye, "Stroke," p. 811.

7. Pierre Laffite to Patterson, January 3, 1820, Parsons Collection, CAHUT. This is signed by but not written by Pierre. Copies of this letter are in File SG-Pirates, and in M-125, RG 45, NA.

8. Patterson to Thompson, February 16, 1820, Ibid.

9. Patterson to Pierre Laffite, January 24, 1820, Ibid.

10. Patterson to Commanders of the United States Vessels of War, February 3, 1820, M-125, RG 45, NA.

11. Patterson to Thompson, February 16, 1820, Ibid.

12. [John Henry Brown], "Early Life in the Southwest. No. IV. Captain John McHenry, Pioneer of Texas," *DeBow's Review*, XV (December 1853), p. 572.

13. Jean Laffite to Guillaume Malus, February 13, 1820, United States vs. schooner *Pegasus*, item 13, Case #1509, NAFW. This letter contains not only French words that are misspelled, but also homonyms of the sort a person who spoke the language but rarely read or wrote it might use. The writer also left off the endings of words entirely, writing in a sort of patois that may have reflected his speech. The handwriting is much like that of other letters in Jean's hand, though the signature differs substantially.

14. Kearny to Thompson, December 23, 1819, M-125, RG 45, NA.

15. Patterson to Thompson, March 17, 1820, Ibid.

16. "The Cruise of the Enterprize," pp. 37–40. This article presents something of a conundrum. The unidentified author clearly knows much of the story of the *Enterprise*'s visit, including her mission. He also knows the number and size of Laffite's squadron, as confirmed from other contemporary sources, and describes the stories of antipathy toward Spain that Jean and Pierre had been telling others as part of their "cover." Yet other aspects of the article appear to be considerably fictionalized, including a great deal of conversation. In the end, the article must be judged an authentic account of Kearny's visit, accurate in broad context, but unreliable in some specifics.

17. Kearney to Patterson, March 7, 1820, M-125, RG 45, NA. This report is inaccurately reproduced in Carroll Storrs Alden, *Lawrence Kearny, Sailor Diplomat* (Princeton, NJ, 1936), pp. 35–36. James Campbell gave a considerably garbled version of this meeting in 1855, making it appear that Kearny delivered orders to Laffite to abandon Galveston, and that Laffite entertained Kearny on the island for two weeks. Information derived [from] James Campbell now residing on the Galveston Bay, 10th June 1855, Lamar Papers, TSL.

18. New Orleans, *Louisiana Courier*, February 20, 1820.

19. Ibid., April 12, 1820.

20. Castellanos, *New Orleans as It Was*, pp. 308–9, says that Jean incited the pirates to mob the jail and try to free Desfarges and the others, and when this did not work, the mob then tried to burn the jail and the armory, though there is no evidence of this. Further confusing lore, Castellanos goes on to say that Jean went to Washington to get an audience with the president to plead for clemency, resulting in the pardon of all but Desfarges. Saxon, *Lafitte*, pp. 241–42, substantially repeats this, with embellishments. The story is further exaggerated in John Smith Kendall, "The Successors of Laffite," *Louisiana Historical Quarterly*, XXIV (April 1941), pp. 364–65, which says that the pirates led by Jean plotted to tear down the Cabildo but did not try it because of the strength of the place.

21. Statement of Mr. Malus, [March 1820], United States vs. Schooner *Pegasus*, Case #1509, NAFW.

22. Rieder and Rieder, *New Orleans Ship Lists*, p. 18.

23. Testimony of William Taylor, March 1820, United States vs. Schooner *Pegasus*, Case #1509, NAFW.

24. Statements of James Rinkin, Mr. Marchand, and Mr. Burton, n.d., Statement of Nathaniel Norton, alias Hugh Dunn, [March 1820], Ibid.

25. Statement of John Anderson, March 1820, Statement of Samuel Hughes, March 18, 1820, Ibid.

26. Villavaso to Cagigal, March 29, 1820, Legajo 1945, AGI-Newberry.

27. Order for seizure of the *Pegasus*, March 18, 1820, Libel of John Dick, U.S. attorney, March 18, 1820, John R. Grymes protest, March 22, 1820, Ibid.

28. Villavaso to Cagigal, March 29, 1820, Legajo 1945, AGI-Newberry.

29. García to Apodaca, April 9, 1820, in Faye, *Privateers*, p. 214.

30. Nicolás Villavaso to Cienfuegos, May 30, 1820, Legajo 1945, AGI-Newberry, says Long arrived at Bolívar Point on April 6.

31. B[ollaert], "Lafitte," p. 445, says, based on recollections of Jane Long and others, that the Longs arrived the day Laffite abandoned the island. That would have been April 6, 1820, according to Warren, *Sword*, p. 249, but this clearly does not fit. Long left again on about April 20, taking his

wife and Hall with him, not to return until early June, which means that any dinner with Laffite had to take place before their departure, and not on May 11 as Jane Long's account suggests.

32. Jane Long memoir, circa 1837, Gulick et al., *Lamar Papers*, II, p. 76; Brown, *Long's Expedition*, pp. 2–3. The Long memoir is the origin of the myth that Laffite's principal ship at this time was the *Pride*, a story passed on in her recollections told a few years later to Bollaert (B[ollaert], "Lafitte," p. 445). This confusion of the *General Victoria* has often been continued since, as for instance in Beardslee, *Piracy*, p. 23, Jean L. Epperson, "Jean Laffite and the Schooner *Pegasus*," *Laffite Society Chronicles*, VI (February 2000), [p. 10], agrees that there is no evidence of any vessel of that name being connected with the Laffites.

33. Galveston, *Daily News*, May 9, 1920. This is based on stories told to Dyer by Hall, and is handled with the usual reservations.

34. Galveston, *Daily News*, March 6, 1893, March 14, May 9, 1920. Dyer claimed that he had information that when Laffite destroyed and evacuated Galveston, it was not at the demand of the United States, but because he had to in order to avoid mutiny. Galveston, *Daily News*, March 6, 1893, has the account of Charles Cronea, reprinted as "Charles Cronea of Sabine Pass: Lafitte Buccaneer and Texas Veteran," *Texas Gulf Historical and Biographical Record*, XI (November 1975), pp. 92–93, and later as W. T. Block, "'Uncle Charlie' Cronea: The Last of Lafitte's Pirates," CAHUT. In it Cronea, whose recollection is mainly wild imagination like most of the accounts by Galveston denizens, said he deserted Galveston in 1820, and that much of the account, at least, could be true.

35. Galveston, *Daily News*, December 14, 1919; James Sherwood Statement, March 27, 1880, James Campbell Pension File, War of 1812, Records Relating to Pension and Bounty Land Claims, 1773–1942, RG 15, NA. In June 1820 Madison and *Lynx* arrived at Charleston, South Carolina, and reported that Laffite abandoned Galveston on May 7. This is the only authoritative contemporary account that dates the event. New York, *Spectator*, August 11, 1820.

36. Eli Harris to Lamar, January 18, 1841, Blake, LVIII, p. 179.

37. Interrogation of George Schumph, November 26, 1821, Sumaria Instruida contra el ingles don Jorge Schumph, Notarias Publicas, Protocolos del Año 1821, Archivo de la Cuidad de Merída de Yucatan, Merída, Mexico. The papers in this case were discovered by Rubio Mane in the

1930s, but have since disappeared. Translated transcripts are to be found in the Laffite Society Research Collection, Sam Houston Regional Library and Research Center, Liberty, TX.

38. B[ollaert], "Lafitte," p. 445.

39. Jean L. Epperson, "The Final Years of Jean Laffite," *Laffite Society Chronicles*, VII (October 2001), [p. 2], says that Pierre left New Orleans in March–April for Havana to try to collect pay due the Laffites from their Spanish employers, and that while there he bought a rancho outside town at what is now the intersection of Correa and Calzada de Jesus del Monte. The Laffites never got to live there, but their descendants did. While a well-to-do Lafitte family did live in Cuba thereafter, there is nothing credible uncovered to date to link them with Jean and Pierre Laffite.

40. Adams, *Diary*, V, pp. 55–56.

41. Monroe to John Nicholson, April 17, 1820, United States vs. John Desfarges et al., Case #1440, NAFW.

42. Motion, May 16, 1820, Ruling, May 24, 1820, Minutes, 7RA-119, RG 21, NAFW.

43. New York, *Spectator*, June 1, 8, 1820.

44. Journal of John Landreth on an Expedition to the Gulf Coast, November 15, 1818–May 19, 1819, entry for March 14, 1819, T12, NA.

45. New Orleans, *Louisiana Courier*, May 26, 1820; New York, *Spectator*, June 17, 1820.

46. New Orleans, *Courier de la Louisiane*, August 2, 1820.

47. Adams, *Diary*, V, June 19, 1820, p. 154.

48. This comes from a very well-informed article in the Galveston, *Gazette*, circa 1839, republished in the Newark, NJ, *Daily Advertiser*, February 12, 1840. In it the editor in Galveston says that he has "seen several persons who were here during his [Laffite's] stay, ane [and] who knew him."

49. Interrogation of George Schumph, November 26, 1821, Notarias Publicas, Protocolos del Año 1821, Archivo de la Ciudad de Merída de Yucatan, Merída, Mexico; New York, *Spectator*, August 11, 1820.

50. New Orleans, *Daily Picayune*, August 20, 1871. This very well-informed account, dated in 1863, came from an unidentified source that shows clear indications of personal knowledge, and is entitled to some credence.

51. In 1855 James Campbell, who is not always reliable as to detail, stated that Laffite told him to meet him at Mugeres if he chose to join him. Campbell also stated that in 1836 William Cochrane, supposedly a lieutenant to Laffite when they left Galveston, told him that Laffite sailed south to Cabo Catoche, at the northeastern tip of Yucatán about thirty miles north of Mugeres. Information derived [from] James Campbell now residing on the Galveston Bay, 10th June 1855, Lamar Papers, TSL. Madison of *Lynx* stated in June 1820 that informants told him Laffite stated his intention to go to Old Providence to join Aury. New York, *Spectator,* August 11, 1820.

52. Faye, "Stroke," p. 825, says the *Minerva* deserted Laffite. This seems to be based on Villavaso to Apodaca, July 18, 1820, Legajo 1945, AGI-Newberry, which does not say this.

53. Statement of Romualdo Rodriguez, February 4, 1831, Libel of J. R. Madison, July 15, 1820, Statement of J. R. Madison, August 2, 1820, J. R. Madison vs. Felucca *Constitution,* Case #1581, NAFW.

54. Madison to Patterson, July 10, 1820, Patterson to Secretary of the Navy, July 12, 1820, M-125, RG 45, NA.

55. Baltimore, *Nile's Register,* January 20, 1821, p. 352. B[ollaert], "Lafitte," p. 444, recounts what he was told of the *Constitution* episode, but confused it with the later mutiny aboard the *General Victoria.*

56. Interrogation of George Schumph, November 26, 1821, Notarias Publicas, Protocolos del Año 1821, Archivo de la Ciudad de Mérida de Yucatan, Mérida, Mexico.

57. Libel of Nicholás José Villavaso, September 7, 1820, Don N. J. Villavaso vs. *Intrepido,* Case #1608, NAFW.

58. [John H. Brown], "Early Life in the Southwest, No. IV, Captain John McHenry, Pioneer of Texas," *DeBow's Review,* XV (December 1853), pp. 572–73. This account, though written thirty-three years after the fact, is remarkably accurate. Brown said that when he was young he lived near John McHenry at Indianola, Texas, and "in my home in Indianola, Texas, in 1853" McHenry told him his story of serving with Laffite. Brown wrote it down and showed it to McHenry for his approval before it was published in *DeBow's.* "Only in regard to precise dates did his memory seem uncertain," Brown recalled (Brown, *Texas,* I, pp. 77–78n). McHenry did confuse dates and time spans, and a few names, such as when he referred to James

Rollins as Thomas Rawlins. Otherwise, his account checks out perfectly against contemporary documents cited below, and forms the foundation for the balance of this account of the affair except where other sources are cited. In the original list of mutineers from *General Victoria*, McHenry appears as M'Kendry (Claim of Christian Ardent et al., November 16, 1820, United States vs. Brig *Victoria*, #1609, NAFW). A possible echo of this episode appears in the very well-informed anonymous 1863 account published in New Orleans, *Daily Picayune*, August 20, 1871, attributed to a man who once boarded with one of the Laffites in New Orleans. It states that Jean fitted out three vessels as privateers under Colombian papers. After six months the government changed regime in Colombia and his papers became invalid, and he became a pirate. The basic chronology is wrong, but the element of the expiration of commissions fits with the McHenry account.

59. Statement of G. B. Duplessis, August 12, 1820, N. J. Villavaso vs. *Intrepide*, Case #1608, NAFW.

60. John Dick to Dominic Hall, n.d., United States vs. Brig *Victoria*, Case #1609, NAFW.

61. Isaac T. Preston protest, n.d.,Villavaso vs. *Intrepide*, #1608; Claim of Christian Ardent et al., November 16, 1820, United States vs. Brig *Victoria*, #1609, NAFW.

62. Report January 18, 1821, Independence of the Spanish Colonies Files, Catalogue 3886, Archivos General de Indias, Seville, cited in Gary Fretz, "Laffite's Legacy," *Laffite Society Chronicles*, IX (February 2003), p. 18.

63. Rieder and Rieder, *Ship Lists*, pp. 39, 41.

64. Martinez to Apodaca, October 22, December 22, 1820, Blake, Vol. XVI, pp. 181, 190–91; Martinez to Commandant at La Bahía, October 21, 1820, Supplement, VIII, p. 242; Ramon Quirk and James Gaines to Martinez, September 20, 1820, X, p. 208.

65. Examination of Moses Austin, December 23, 1820, Eugene C. Barker, ed., *The Austin Papers: Annual Report of the American Historical Association for the Year 1919* (Washington, 1924), Part 1, p. 370.

66. Today Old Providence has such landmarks as Buccaneer Point and Aury Channel, vestiges of its colorful past.

67. Interrogation of George Schumph, November 26, 1821, Notarias Publicas, Protocolos del Año 1821, Archivo de la Ciudad de Merída de

Yucatan, Merída, Mexico. Vogel believes that Pierre and Jean went to Old Providence, where both might have served under Aury in his abortive attacks on Central American ports in 1820–21. Robert Vogel, "Some Background Concerning Laffite's Departure from Galveston," *Laffite Society Chronicles*, V (August 1999), [pp. 7–8].

68. Marie Louisa Villard to Antoine Abat, July 27, 1820, Notary Philippe Pedesclaux, Vol. 16, item 411, NONA.

69. Marie Louise Villard to Antoine Abat, August 2, 1820, Philippe Pedesclaux, Vol. 16, item 429, NONA.

70. In the 1822 New Orleans City Directory the corner of Bourbon and St. Philip does not show Marie Louise Villard as an occupant, so she did not stay on as a renter.

71. Joseph G. Tregle, Jr., *Louisiana in the Age of Jackson: A Clash of Cultures and Personalities* (Baton Rouge, LA, 1999), p. 14.

72. It is difficult to tell exactly where Marie Villard made her new home. No transaction of purchase has emerged. There were numerous free women of color named Marie Louise or Maria Louisa who appeared in the 1820 Census for the city, and it is almost impossible to pinpoint which is her, since they are listed merely by given names. Those roughly matching her age lived on Esplanade, Rue de la Quartier, and Dauphine streets. The 1830 Census shows Marie Louise Villard living on Esplanade, however, and that is surely her (United States Census, 1830, Orleans Parish, Louisiana, p. 28).

73. Notary Joseph Arnaud, Vol. 1, item 83; Maire to Rene Broussard, October 30, 1820, Notary Philippe Pedesclaux, Vol. 18, item 1789, NONA.

74. Faye, "Aury," p. 684.

75. Marie gave birth to Joseph Laffite on May 2, 1821 (Nolan and Dupont, eds., *Sacramental Records of the Roman Catholic Church of the Archdiocese of New Orleans, Volume 14, 1820–1821*, p. 228). This means she must have conceived sometime in early August 1820.

76. Charleston, *Courier*, November 16, 1820, February 26, 1821. When the *Hiram* arrived in Charleston in November, three passengers were reported as debarking: Messrs. Oliver, Smith, and Francisco. It seems safe to conclude that with his pronounced accent, Pierre would not have assumed an Anglo-Saxon name like Smith or Oliver.

77. Charleston, *Courier*, December 2, 25, 1820.

TWENTY-ONE

1. James R. Schenck, *The Directory and Stranger's Guide, for the City of Charleston . . . 1822* (Charleston, SC, 1822), n.p.

2. Marie Jeanne Lemaitre Lambert to Joseph Prados, November 4, 1820, Notary Philippe Pedesclaux, Vol. 18, item 1825, NONA; Charleston, *Times,* September 20, 1817; Inward Slave Manifests for the Port of New Orleans, January–March 1822, #631, Schooner *Louisa,* June 1822, Roll 3, RG 36, NA.

3. Bollaert, "Lafitte," p. 435. Lambert, called "Old L" by Bollaert, said that he saw Lafitte at Charleston in 1822 where he was then fitting out a ship to privateer against the Spanish on the Caribbean. Lambert got the year wrong, and like so many confused Pierre for Jean, but otherwise his recollection was accurate. It is tempting to identify this Lambert with the Captain Lambert of the *Hiram,* but there is no evidence to support a connection.

4. Houston, *Morning Star,* February 8, 1842; Charleston, *Courier,* February 26, 1821.

5. Charleston, *Times,* February 19, 1821. Atypically for Charleston, the *Nancy Eleanor's* date of sailing does not appear in the press, which may be a sign that she tried to do so undetected after clearing customs.

6. Charleston, *Courier,* February 26, 1821.

7. John B. Lemaitre to the editor, February 24, 1821, Charleston, *Times,* February 24, 1821.

8. Houston, *Morning Star,* February 8, 1842. This account of an interview with Manuel López came originally from the Matagorda, *Colorado Gazette* of some earlier date. It is very accurate, erring only in recalling the date as "the second year of Mexican independence," which would be 1822, instead of 1821. Thomas Duke to Ferdinand Pinckard, May 1843, in B[ollaert], "Lafitte," p. 445, recounts an 1837 conversation with López in which Duke was given virtually the same account, and Bollaert spoke with López in 1842. In 1841 Duke told the same story of the López interview to J. H. Kuykendall, as recounted in J. H. Kuykendall, "Reminiscences of Early Texans," *Quarterly of the Texas State Historical Association,* VI (January 1903), p. 252.

9. John H. Lee to Porter, May 12, 1824, Charleston, *Southern Patriot,* July 21, 1824.

10. Alice D. Le Plongeon, *Here and There in Yucatan. Miscellanies* (New York, 1885), pp. 6–7. Like most accounts, this one speaks of a single Laffite, the assumption being that it was Jean. However, from the personality traits described, it is evident that the recollections gleaned by the authors have combined both brothers into one.

11. New Orleans, *Louisiana Gazette*, March 14, 1822.

12. Precise identification of Pierre's mistress seems impossible, but it is safe to say that she did exist. George Schumph testified on November 10, 1821, that Pierre was attended by an "American woman" named "Lucia." He did not state her relationship to Laffite, but a romantic liaison can be inferred from the fact that she was with him on Cancún, came with him to Las Bocas, attended him through his illness, and accompanied his body to Dzilam de Bravo. (Statement of George Schumph, November 10, 1821, Sumaria Instruida contra el ingles don Jorge Schumph, Notarias Publicas, Protocolos del Año 1821, Archivo de la Ciudad de Mérida de Yucatan, Mérida, Mexico). Recollections of Laffite (the sources generally assume it is Jean, but it was Pierre) having a mistress at Mugeres appeared at least as early as 1842, in John L. Stephens, *Incidents of Travel in Yucatan* (New York, 1843), II, pp. 282–83. This source said that she was a widow from Mobile named "Senora del Norte," and was still living in Dzilam de Bravo at that time. A century later the local oral tradition said that the mistress's name was Lucia, and that she died in childbirth at Dzilam de Bravo having a daughter (John Burton Thompson, "The Legend of Lafitte," Baton Rouge, *Morning Advocate*, October 11, 1953). In another twenty years local lore expanded her name to Lucille Allen (Luis A. Ramirez Aznar, "One Answer to the Lafitte Riddle," *Dixie Magazine*, January 2, 1972, pp. 6–7).

13. Joseph Lafitte, son of Pierre and Marie Louise Villarde, born May 2, 1821 Book of free colored. Nolan and Dupont, eds., *Sacramental Records of the Roman Catholic Church of the Archdiocese of New Orleans, Volume 14, 1820–1821*, p. 228.

14. Quoted in Departamento de Historia Naval, *Historia Marítima Argentina* (Buenos Aires, 1994), V, p. 495.

15. Statement of death of Louis Aury, n.d., Aury Papers, CAHUT.

16. Gregory to Secretary of Navy, November 29, 1821, M-148, RG 45, NA.

17. John S. Kendall, "Piracy in the Gulf of Mexico, 1816–1823," *Louisiana Historical Quarterly*, VIII (July 1925), p. 345.

18. Pensacola, *Floridian*, September 15, 22, 1821.

19. Faye, "Privateersmen," p. 1082; Beardslee, *Piracy*, p. 51.

20. Francis Gregory to Secretary of War, October 18, 1821, Letters Received by the Secretary of the Navy from Officers Below the Rank of Commander, 1802–1884, M-148, RG 45, NA.

21. Gaspar López to Martinez, July 1, 1822, Blake, Supplement, VIII, p. 280, Gaspar López to Jose Felix Trespalacios, December 3, 1820, Supplement, XV, pp. 229–30; Francisco Garcia to Martinez, November 11, 1821, Raphael Gonzales to Martinez, January 1, 1822, Blake, Supplement, VIII, p. 258, Béxar Archives, CAHUT.

22. John Sibley to Josiah Stoddard Johnston, June 26, 1821, Josiah Stoddard Johnston Papers, Historical Society of Pennsylvania, Philadelphia.

23. Indictments, July 27, 1821, United States vs. Jean Louis, Ligourgne, Hippolite, Arnould, Difulho, and Cadet, Cases #1728–1733, NAFW.

24. Henry Johnson, James Brown, and Josiah S. Johnston to Calhoun, December 11, 1821, W. Edwin Hemphill, ed., *The Papers of John C. Calhoun, Volume VI, 1821–1822* (Columbia, SC, 1972), p. 564.

25. John Sibley to George Sibley, October 29, 1821, G. P. Whittington, "Dr. John Sibley of Natchitoches, 1757–1832," *Louisiana Historical Quarterly*, X (October 1927), p. 507.

26. New York, *Spectator*, August 11, 1820; Patterson to Secretary of Navy, September 10, 1821, M-125, NA.

27. Pensacola, *Floridian*, March 30, 1822.

28. Patterson to Secretary of Navy, November 24, 1821, M-125, NA.

29. Pensacola, *Floridian*, December 31, 1821.

30. Statement of Miguel Molas, November 4, 13, 1821, Sumaria Instruida contra el ingles don Jorge Schumph, Notarias Publicas, Protocolos del Año 1821, Archivo de la Ciudad de Mérida de Yucatan, Mérida, Mexico.

31. Statement of Thomas Pino, November 26, 1821, Ibid.

32. Statement of Miguel Molas, November 4, 13, 1821, Ibid.

33. Statement of Miguel Molas, November 4, 13, 1821, Interrogation of George Schumph, November 26, 1821, Ibid.

34. See Michael Antochiw, director of the Cultural Institute at Mérida,

Yucatán, to Dorothy Karilanovic, August 22, 1995, Laffite Society Research Collection, Sam Houston Regional Library and Research Center, Liberty, Texas. It is possible that Pierre was wounded, though the documents in the Schumph investigation mentioned by Antochiw do not specify any cause of death.

35. Thomas Duke to Ferdinand Pinckard, May 1843, B[ollaert], "Lafitte," p. 445. On July 12, 1837, S. Rhoads Fisher visited this area and spoke with a Mexican Indian named Gregorio who told him that Laffite died at a place called "Lasbocas," which today is Bocas de Dzilam. S. Rhoads Fisher to Mirabeau B. Lamar, May 1, 1838, Lamar Papers, TSL.

36. Statement of George Schumph, November 10, 1821, Sumaria Instruida contra el ingles don Jorge Schumph, Notarias Publicas, Protocolos del Ano 1821, Archivo de la Ciudad de Mérida de Yucatan, Mérida, Mexico. Schumph does not give the date of Pierre's death, but his arrival in Dzilam on November 10 suggests that the death did not occur more than a day earlier. He also says that Pierre was attended by a woman named "Lucia," which would connect with the later stories of a Lucille Allen. While some have concluded that Pierre was wounded by Molas, López merely says that Pierre was "taken sick" (Houston, *Morning Star*, February 8, 1842), and only Gregorio spoke of fever (S. Rhoads Fisher to Mirabeau B. Lamar, May 1, 1838, Lamar Papers, TSL). Dyer, in the Galveston, *News*, September 3, 1922, said he was told by two men that Laffite died of yellow fever in Yucatán in about 1826, though as usual Dyer carries little credibility.

37. Several versions of Pierre's death survived in local oral tradition, most with some links to genuine recollection. Alice D. Le Plongeon, *Here and There in Yucatan. Miscellanies* (New York, 1885), p. 7, recounted a story of a force of Spaniards—Molas—being sent against him at sea, and Pierre's vessel being run aground, after which he took a handful of men and fled but they were surrounded on a sandbar and all were killed.

38. Statement of Cristobal Carrillo, November 10, 1821, Statement of José Gregorio Cervera, November 10, 1821, Sumaria Instruida contra el ingles don Jorge Schumph, Notarias Publicas, Protocolos del Año 1821, Archivo de la Ciudad de Mérida de Yucatan, Mérida, Mexico; Houston, *Morning Star*, February 8, 1842.

39. Statement of George Schumph, November 10, 1821, Statement of José Trinidad Lisama, November 16, 1821, Sumaria Instruida contra el ingles don Jorge Schumph, Notarias Publicas, Protocolos del Año 1821, Archivo de la Ciudad de Mérida de Yucatan, Mérida, Mexico.

40. Baltimore, *Nile's Register,* XXI, December 22, 1821, p. 258; Information derived [from] James Campbell now residing on the Galveston Bay, 10th June 1855, Lamar Papers, TSL. This account, again a recollection by Campbell of what he was told in 1836 by William Cochrane, matches better with this incident than the earlier recapture of a Laffite prize detailed in chapter 20.

41. New Orleans, *Louisiana Courier,* November 29, 1822. The best account of this episode is Jean L. Epperson, "The Final Years of Jean Laffite," *Laffite Society Chronicles,* VII (October 2001), *passim.* Porto Principe is today Camagüey.

42. Epperson, "Final Years of Jean Laffite," [p. 2].

43. H. A. Bullard to Johnston, February 2, 1822, Johnston Papers, Historical Society of Pennsylvania.

44. New Orleans, *Louisiana Courier,* March 8, April 29, 1822.

45. Pensacola, *Floridian,* March 4, 16, 1822; Salem, MA, *Register,* February 27, 1822. This *El Bravo* is not the same vessel as Laffite's *Le Brave.*

46. Pensacola, *Floridian,* April 6, 1822.

47. New Orleans, *Louisiana Gazette,* June 18, 1822.

48. Pensacola, *Floridian,* March 4, 1822.

49. Logbook of the USS *Alligator,* April 14, 1822, Logs of U.S. Naval Ships, Entry 118, Records of the Bureau of Naval Personnel, RG 24, NA.

50. Pensacola, *Floridian,* June 15, 1822.

51. Logbook of the USS *Alligator,* Entry 118, RG 24, NA.

52. Logbook of the *Belvedere,* May 2, 1822, New Orleans, *Courier de la Louisiane,* May 22, 1822. Logbook of the USS *Alligator,* May 2, 1822, Entry 118, RG 24, NA, makes no mention of the action of May 2 as related in the log of the *Belvedere.* New Orleans *Courier,* May 22, 1822, says the ships USS *Alligator* and USS *Grampus* chased Laffite off Sugar Key, Cuba, along with other pirates.

53. Bogotá, Colombia, *Gaceta de Colombia,* August 24, 1823.

54. Ibid., February 10, 1822.

55. Ibid., December 1, 1822. It is possible that the *General Santander* was Laffite's own vessel, the one that brought him to Cartagena, and that he changed her name to that of a Colombian hero on transferring her to

national service, just as Beluche had changed his *La Popa* to the *General Bolivar* when he entered Bolivar's service in 1816. There is no specific evidence for this, however. The only source bearing on the *General Santander*'s history states that she left Santiago, Cuba, to come to Cartagena, and it seems unlikely that Laffite would have been able to take a vessel out of a Cuban port. Bolívar later claimed that he purchased the *General Santander.*

56. Bogotá, Colombia, *Gaceta de Colombia,* December 1, 1822.

57. Philadelphia, *National Gazette and Literary Register,* September 5, 1822; New York, *National Advocate,* September 5, November 22, 1822; Boston, *Independent Chronicle and Boston Patriot,* January 25, 1823.

58. New York, *National Advocate,* November 22, 1822.

59. Boston, *Independent Chronicle and Boston Patriot,* January 25, 1823.

60. New Orleans, *Courier de la Louisiane,* November 29, 1822.

61. Wilkins and Linton to Johnston, November 26, 1822, New Orleans, Johnston Papers, Historical Society of Pennsylvania.

62. Charleston, *Courier,* November 27, 28, December 22, 1822.

63. New York, *National Advocate,* December 13, 1822.

64. Porter, *Memoirs,* p. 271.

65. Charleston, *Courier,* March 8, November 28, 1822.

66. García to Apodaca, September 23, 1820, Legajo 1900, AGI-Newberry.

67. Bogotá, Colombia, *Gaceta de Colombia,* April 20, 1823. There are several variant accounts of Laffite's death, but only the one in the Bogotá paper is close to an original source, being based on an earlier article in the *Gaceta de Cartajena,* number 63, which has not been found. It would have been a report freshly gleaned on the arrival of the *General Santander* in her home port after the action. An account dated April 10 from Porter's squadron appeared in the Washington, *Gazette,* April 23, 1823, Baltimore, *Nile's Weekly Register,* April 26, 1823, and Portsmouth, NH, *Journal,* April 26, 1823, stating that it was a British warship that took a vessel "commanded by the celebrated La Fitte." He had refused to surrender and instead "the pirate hoisted the bloody flag and cried no quarters, and none were shewd," the slain including Laffite and sixty of his men. It is clearly a garbled account, especially since it says Laffite's ship was boarded and captured off Key

West, Florida. This is probably the source for Ellms, *Pirates,* pp. 79–80, who said in 1837 that Laffite ran into a British vessel. Ellms went on to say that Laffite was hit in the leg and abdomen, but continued fighting even as his ship was being boarded, which did not happen. "Thus perished Lafitte," said Ellms, "a man superior in talent, in knowledge of his profession, in courage, and moreover in physical strength; but unfortunately his reckless career was marked with crimes of the darkest dye" (p. 82).

Meanwhile, in Pratt, *Galveston Island, or, A Few Months Off the Coast of Texas. The Journal of Francis C. Sheridan,* p. 62, Sheridan repeats a story current on Galveston in 1840 that said Laffite was shot in the head in a battle with a Spanish vessel. Manuel López said in circa 1840 that Jean died "of a wound he had received in an encounter with a Spanish vessel at which time he was taken prisoner." In publishing López's story, the editor of the newspaper commented that it was similar to accounts brought back by officers of the United States Navy. Houston, *Morning Star,* February 8, 1842.

68. The article from a March 1823 issue of the *Gaceta de Cartajena* is republished in the Bogotá, *Gaceta de Colombia,* April 20, 1823.

69. Porter to Thompson, March 28, 1823, M-125, NA; Porter, *Memoir,* pp. 279–81.

70. Pensacola, *Floridian,* August 23, 1823.

71. Ibid., May 3, 1823.

72. Logbook of the USS *Alligator,* May 4, 1823, Entry 118, RG 24, NA.

73. Pensacola, *Floridian,* May 24, 1823.

74. Porter, *Memoir,* p. 282; New Orleans, *Courier,* May 12, 1823.

75. Providence, *Rhode Island Republican,* June 4, 1823.

TWENTY-TWO

1. Pensacola, *Gazette,* May 1, 1824.

2. Ibid., September 4, 1824.

3. Thomas Randall to Adams, October 31, 1824, *Message from the President of the United States, Transmitting Information Relative to Piratical Depredations, &c., Furnished In Pursuance of Two Resolutions of 21st and 23d December last* (Washington, 1825), p. 21.

4. Francis B. C. Beardslee, *Piracy in the West Indies and Its Suppression* (Salem, MA, 1923), pp. 55–56.

5. Hollon and Butler, *William Bollaert's Texas*, p. 90.

6. Newark, NJ, *Daily Advertiser*, February 12, 1840.

7. New Orleans, *Times-Picayune*, August 20, 1871.

8. Houston, *Morning Star*, February 8, 1842.

9. Hollon and Butler, *William Bollaert's Texas*, p. 160; Bollaert, "Lafitte," p. 434.

10. Stafford, *Graham*, p. 85.

11. These stories and a host of other nonsense based on spurious findings by Dr. Louis Genella appeared in articles by Meigs O. Frost in the New Orleans, *States* in 1928. See also The Lafitte Cemetery, Louisiana Legends, taken May 1, 1939, Federal Writers Project Collection, NSUL.

12. K. T. Knoblock to Lyle Saxon, n.d., ca 1930s, Melrose Collection, NSUL.

13. Bollaert, "Lafitte," p. 435n.

14. James Dick to Laurent Maire, April 27, 1820, Notary Philippe Pedesclaux, Vol. 15, item 837, NONA.

15. Process verbal of sale, November 6, 1827, Laurent Maire Estate Inventory, September 15, 1827, Orleans Parish Court of Probates, Louisiana Division, NOPL.

16. Dominique You to Nathaniel Jenkins, March 3, 1823, Notary Philippe Pedesclaux, Vol. 26, Act 151; Jenkins to You, April 2, 1824, Vol. 29, Act 164, NONA.

17. New Orleans, *Le Courier de la Louisiane*, November 15, 16, 1830.

18. Jane Lucas De Grummond, *Renato Beluche, Smuggler, Privateer, and Patriot, 1780–1860* (Baton Rouge, LA, 1983), pp. 230–31.

19. William F. Gray, *From Virginia to Texas, 1835: Diary of Col. Wm. F. Gray* (Houston, TX, 1909), p. 170.

20. Pratt, *Galveston Island, or, A Few Months Off the Coast of Texas. The Journal of Francis C. Sheridan*, pp. 54–55.

21. Henry Stuart Foote, *Texas and the Texans; or, Advance of the Anglo-Americans to the South-west* (Philadelphia, 1841), I, p. 196.

22. John H. Lee to Porter, May 12, 1824, Charleston, *Southern Patriot,* July 21, 1824.

23. Stephens, *Yucatan,* II, p. 296.

24. New Orleans, *Times-Picayune,* December 19, 1948; Houston, *Post,* July 10, 1960.

25. Pratt, *Galveston Island,* pp. 56–57.

26. G. Harrison Orians, "Lafitte: A Bibliographical Note," *American Literature,* IX (November 1937), pp. 351–53.

27. Louisville, KY, *Journal,* November 30, 1836.

28. See, for instance, James Rees, "The Gold Chain: A Passage in the Life of Lafitte," New York, *New World,* October 17, 1840.

29. James Rees, "Passages in the Life of Lafitte," clipping in Jean Laffite Vertical File, CAHUT. See also "The Pirate of the Gulf; or, the Hidden Treasure," *Colburn's United Service Magazine 1846,* Part 1 (February 1846), pp. 236ff.

30. Bollaert, "Lafitte," p. 435n.

31. Boutte, LA, *St. Charles Herald,* September 25, 1873.

32. Galveston, *Flake's Daily Bulletin,* November 5, 1871.

33. New Orleans, *Daily Picayune,* January 27, 1895.

34. Ebenezer Allen to Gideon Lincecum, November 10, 1853, Rosenberg Library, Galveston.

35. Boutte, LA, *St. Charles Herald,* September 25, 1873.

36. New Orleans, *Daily Picayune,* January 27, 1895.

37. Galveston, *Daily News,* April 21, 1878.

38. Lake Charles, LA, *Echo,* January 5, 1884.

39. Lake Charles, LA, *American,* April 30, 1909.

40. Clipping from an unidentified Houston, TX, newspaper, in possession of Pam Keyes.

41. Lake Charles, *American Press,* November 15, 1981, November 30, 2002. A substantial number of other treasure stories connected with the Laffites will be found in the Laffite Collection, Rosenberg, and also in the Laffite Vertical File in the Louisiana State Library in Baton Rouge. See also

J. Frank Dobie, "The Mystery of Lafitte's Treasure," *Yale Review*, XVIII (September 1928), pp. 116–34.

42. Interview with Captain J. E. Fehann, August 10, 1939, conducted by Dawn F. Jameson, Folder 554, Federal Writers Project Collection, NSUL.

43. New York, *Spectator*, June 28, 1820.

44. Charles E. Nolan and Dorenda Dupont, eds., *Sacramental Records of the Roman Catholic Church of the Archdiocese of New Orleans, Volume 16, 1824–1825* (New Orleans, 2001), pp. 221, 350. At the birth of Charles Roup, son of Pierre and Catherine Coralie, on November 3, 1827, Catherine Roup is spoken of again as the daughter of "Pierre Lafitte dec[eased]." Charles E. Nolan and Dorenda Dupont, eds., *Sacramental Records of the Roman Catholic Church of the Archdiocese of New Orleans, Volume 18, 1828–1829* (New Orleans, 2003), p. 352.

45. 1830 Census, Orleans Parish, Louisiana, p. 28.

46. Marriages, Free Persons of Color, 1830–1835, Vol. 2, Part 1, p. 35, SAANO. As will be discussed below, the page with the marriage has been torn out but the year can be reconstructed from the volume's index.

47. Nolan and Dupont, *Sacramental Records, Volume 18*, p. 57. No record of Martin's death had been found, but his widow was married to François Leon by 1831, as their first child was born August 8, 1832. LBRI Vol. 4, p. 124.

48. Rieder and Rieder, *Ship Lists*, pp. 29, 41, 68.

49. Marriages S-Free Persons of Color, Vol. 1, Part 2, 1777–1830, p. 79, act #372, SAANO; Mary Louise Christovich and Roulhac B. Toledano, *Faubourg Treme and the Bayou Road: North Rampart Street to North Broad Street, Canal Street to St. Bernard Avenue* (New Orleans, 2003; Vol. VI of Samuel Wilson and Bernard Lemann, eds., *New Orleans Architecture*), p. 22.

50. Baptism Book 35, p. 6, SAANO.

51. Saxon, *Lafitte*, p. 264, says that an 1830 New Orleans directory shows Marie Josephe living with Joseph Sauvinet at 141 Hospital Street. This is apparently pure invention, as there is no city directory known to have been published in 1830, and the 1832 directory shows Sauvinet at 124 Hospital, not 141, and does not list other occupants.

52. Her death is recorded in the LDRI, IV, p. 101, as both Villard and Ramos.

53. Funerals S-Free Persons of Color, Vol. 10, Part 2, 1833–1834, p. 219, entry #1426, SAANO.

54. 1850 Census, Orleans Parish, Louisiana, 1st Ward, 3d Municipality, p. 90; LDRI, Vol. 74, p. 418.

55. LDRI, Vol. 14, p. 538.

56. Funerals S-Free Persons of Color, Vol. 9, 1829–1831, Part 1, p. 317, entry #2015, SAANO, lists the death and burial on October 24, 1832, of Jean Lafitte, aged sixteen, the son of Catherine Villard and a father identified only as "Mr. Lafite." It is just possible that this Jean was a second son of Jean Laffite and Catherine Villard. Jean's brief time in New Orleans in March 1816 prior to his Arkansas trip raises the possibility that he and Catherine conceived another child then, a child born in December 1816 or January 1817, who would thus be just shy of sixteen in October 1832. But far more likely this is the son Pierre born on November 4, 1815, which would make him sixteen as of October 24, 1832, and a perfect fit with the death record, raising the probability that though he was baptized as Pierre, his full name was Jean Pierre. At the moment this can be nothing more than speculation.

57. LDRI, Vol. 14, p. 357.

58. New Orleans, *Times-Picayune,* August 20, 1871; LDRI, Vol. 50, p. 49.

59. Statement of André Tessier, October 31, 1845, Case File 113863, George Renton vs. Miriella Farr, Orleans Parish Civil District Court, Division A, Archives, University of New Orleans.

60. Testimony of Rosalie DuHart, March 29, 1921, Case #25813, State ex rel. Allnet et al. vs. Board of Health of City of New Orleans, March 10, 1924, Supreme Court of Louisiana, University of New Orleans Archives. The testimony of DuHart that mentions the mementos makes it pretty clear that the family had confused the origins of the items.

61. LBRI, Vol. 6, pp. 397, 398, Vol. 10, pp. 225, 565.

62. 1880 Census, Louisiana, Orleans Parish, 7th Ward, p. 596.

63. LMRI, Vol. 14, p. 558.

64. LBRI, Vol. 105, p. 227, 228, Vol. 115, p. 636.

65. LBRI, Vol. 97, p. 738.

66. Statement of Mirielle A. Farr, October 16, 1815, George Renton vs. Mirielle A. Farr, Case #113863, Division A, Civil District Court Archives, University of New Orleans.

67. Petition of George Renton, October 1, 1915, Ibid.

68. Affidavit of Mirielle A. Farr, October 16, 1915, Ibid.

69. In Marriages, Free Persons of Color, 1830–1835, Vol. 2, Part 1, SAANO, this is all quite apparent, and a signed statement by archivist G. Lugano, dated December 21, 1915, attests to his discovery.

70. Testimony of Gaspar Logano, September 30, 1921, June 8, 1922, Testimony of E Joanen, Sr., n.d., Case #25813, Supreme Court of Louisiana, University of New Orleans.

71. Testimony of Rosalie DuHart, March 29, 1921, Ibid.

72. Testimony of Horace E. Farr, May 24, 1921, Ibid.

73. Testimony of Edward Allnet, June 7, 1921, Ibid.

74. Statement of Mrs. Edward Farr, January 17, 1918, Case file #132700, Division E, Edward Allnet et al. vs. Board of Health of the City of New Orleans, Civil District Court Archives, University of New Orleans.

75. Testimony of Marie Gras Gregory, March 21, 1921, Case #25813, Supreme Court of Louisiana, University of New Orleans.

76. Testimony of Rosalie DuHart, March 29, 1921, Ibid. Saxon, *Lafitte,* p. 264, makes this same confusion of the Pierre Lafitte who married Marie Berret being the son of Pierre Laffite the pirate.

77. New Orleans, *Times-Picayune,* November 21, 1922; New Orleans, *Official Daily Court Record,* November 27, 1922.

78. File #25813, Supreme Court of Louisiana, State ex rel. Allnet et al. vs. Board of Health of City of New Orleans, March 10, 1924, Civil District Court Archives, University of New Orleans.

79. Mirielle Farr vs. George Renton, Case #145204, Division F, Civil District Court, NOPL. The actual case file is missing.

80. Saxon, *Lafitte,* pp. 117–18, 264–65, tells this story in substance, but gets most of the details wrong, though he had the transcript of the trials at hand. Subsequently they could not be found again until unearthed in November 2003 during research for this work.

81. Statement of Mrs. Edward Farr, January 17, 1918, Case file #132700, Division E, Edward Allnet et al. vs. Board of Health of the City of New Orleans, Civil District Court Archives, University of New Orleans.

BIBLIOGRAPHY

THE SOURCES ON the Laffites and their world are considerable, and of vastly varying quality. So far as biographies of the principals are concerned, all deal only with Jean Laffite in the main, and only two are of value. Lyle Saxon's *Lafitte the Pirate* is a hodgepodge of legend and lore and some original material, much of which he misused or did not understand, but it has been the standard. Jack C. Ramsay, Jr.'s *Jean Laffite, Prince of Pirates* is a serious effort to do much better, and while it has problems of organization, it is certainly an improvement. Stanley Clisby Arthur's *Jean Laffite, Gentleman Rover* is just a rehash of Saxon laced liberally with unreliable stuff from the collection associated with the spurious Laffite Journal. Arthur did uncover some new material, but generally did not understand it, and so made poor use of it.

The articles of Stanley Faye, Robert C. Vogel, Harris Gaylord Warren, and a number of contributions in the *Laffite Society Chronicles*, along with Warren's *The Sword was their Passport*, represent the bulk of the genuinely original and reliable Laffite publications of the last few generations. For genuinely reliable and new information on the brothers, there is no substitute for the original documents in such places as the New Orleans Notarial Archives, the city and parish records in the New Orleans Public Library, the case files of the Federal district court now at the National Archives Southwest Region in Ft. Worth, Texas, and the records of the Navy, Customs and Treasury, and other branches of government at the

National Archives in Washington. The several collections generally headed as Archives of the Indies, located at Chicago's Newberry Library and the Center for American History in Austin, Texas, are invaluable.

Primary Sources

MANUSCRIPTS

Archives d'Outremer, Aix-en-Provence, France
    Fonds de L'Indemnite de Saint-Domingue
Archivo General de la Nación, Mexico City
    Historia, Operaciones de Guerra, Notas Diplomaticas
Archdiocese of New Orleans, New Orleans, LA
    Sacramental Archives of the Archdiocese of New Orleans
Arkansas County Courthouse, Clerk of Court, DeWitt, AR
    Deed Book B, 1814–1818, Part 1
Ascension Parish Courthouse, Clerk of Court, Donaldsonville, LA
    Conveyance Records, Book 1
    Turner's Acts, Book 2K
Duke University, William R. Perkins Library, Durham, NC
    Jean Laffite Collection
East Baton Rouge Parish Courthouse, Baton Rouge, LA
    Archives of the Spanish Government of West Florida
University of Florida, Gainesville
    Heloise Cruzat Papers
    Greenslade Papers
    Elizabeth H. West Papers
Archives départmentales de la Gironde, Bordeaux, France
    Minutes du notaire Deprat de Bordeaux, année 1771
    Registre de la paroisse de l'église de Saint Seurin de Bordeaux
        année 1771
    Sevie Passeports, 1802
Historic New Orleans Collection, New Orleans
    Coleccion de Documentos del Archivo Nacional de Cuba, Havana
        Asuntos Politicos, Legajo 14, 16, 109, 110
        Comisión Militar, Legajo 5
        Gobierno Superior Civil, Legajo 492
    Carmelite Henry Papers

Pierre and Jean Laffite Collection
Arsené Lacarriere Latour Papers
Edward Nicholls and William H. Percy Letters
G. William Nott Collection
James Stirling, Memorandum by ... Regarding the Condition of
    Louisiana, March 17, 1813
Viaux Carré Commission Archives
Dominic You Papers
Library of Congress, Washington, DC
    Brivezac, Rapport sur Letat et la Situation Exacte des Colonies
        Espagnole de L'Amerique a la fin de 1817
    Department of State Papers
    James Madison Papers
    James Monroe Papers
    United States Department of State Collection, Spanish Affairs,
        1810–1816
Louisiana Division of Archives, Records Management, and History,
    Baton Rouge
    Vital Records Indices
        New Orleans, Louisiana, Birth Records Index, 1790–1899
        New Orleans, Louisiana, Marriage Records Index, 1831–1925
        New Orleans, Louisiana, Death Records Index, 1804–1949
Louisiana State Land Office, Baton Rouge
    Historical Land Title Records
    Records of the Eastern District
Louisiana State Library, Baton Rouge
    Jean Laffite Vertical File
Louisiana State Museum, New Orleans
    Jean and Pierre Laffite Vertical File
    Laffite Vertical File
    Works Project Administration Index to Colonial Court Records
Louisiana State University, Louisiana and Mississippi Valley Collection,
    Baton Rouge
    Charles E. A. Gayarré Selected Papers, 1883–1940
    George Graham Papers
    Miscellaneous Manuscripts Collection
    Alonzo Snyder Papers
Maryland State Archives, Baltimore
    Baltimore County Court Chancery Papers

Minèstre des Affaires Étrangères, Paris, France
    Correspondence Politique, Etats-Unis Supplément, Volume 38
Mississippi Department of Archives and History, Jackson
    J. F. H. Claiborne Papers
National Archives, Washington, DC
    Record Group 15, Records Relating to Pension and Bounty-Land
        Claims 1773–1942, War of 1812
        Campbell, James
    Record Group 21, Records of District Courts of the United States,
        1685–1993
        Minutes of the U.S. District Court for the Eastern District of
        Louisiana, 1806–1814, M-1082, RG 21
    Record Group 24, Records of the Bureau of Naval Personnel
        Entry 118 Logs of U.S. Naval Ships, 1801–1915
            Log of the USS *Alligator*
    Record Group 36, Records of the U.S. Customs Service, New
        Orleans District
        Entry 1627, Records of Customs Houses in the Gulf States,
        New Orleans, LA, Letters Received, 1804–1899
        Entry 1656, Record of Drawbacks, 1795–1849
        Entry 1657, Record of Fees Paid, Cargo Manifests 1809–1821
    Record Group 41, Records of the Bureau of Marine Inspection and
        Navigation
        Entry 143, Vessels Bought, Records of Vessels Bought from or
        Sold to the Federal Government, 1815
        Entry 156, New Orleans Certificates of Registration, 1818–1819
    Record Group 45, Naval Records Collection of the Office of Naval
        Records and Library
        Entry 209, Board of Navy Commissioners, 1815–1842, Journal,
        Volume 3
        Entry 388, Letters from Collectors of Customs Relating to
        Commissions of Privateers, 1812–1815
        Letters Received by the Secretary of the Navy from Captains,
        1807–1885, M-125
        Letters Received by the Secretary of the Navy from
        Commanders, 1804–1886, M-147
        Letters Received by the Secretary of the Navy from Officers
        Below the Rank of Commander, 1802–1884, M-148
        Letters Sent by the Secretary of the Navy to Commandants
        and Navy Agents, 1808–1865, M-441

Area File of the Naval Collection, 1775–1910, Area 8, M-625
Journal of John Landreth on an Expedition to the Gulf Coast,
November 15, 1818–May 19, 1819, T-12
Miscellaneous Records of the Office of Naval Records and
Library Private Letters, T-829
U.S. Navy Subject File 1775–1910, File SG-Pirates
Record Group 49, Records of the Bureau of Land Management
Entry 173: Old Index of Private Land Claims in Louisiana,
1800–1880
Record Group 56, General Records of the Department of the
Treasury
Letters to and from the Collector at New Orleans, LA,
October 11, 1803–April 11, 1833, M-178
Letters Sent by the Secretary of the Treasury to Collectors of
Customs at all Ports, 1789–1847, M-175
Record Group 59, General Records of the Department of State
Miscellaneous Letters of the Department of State
August 1–October 31, 1817, M-38
Domestic Letters of the Department of State, Volume 17,
March 3, 1817–February 23, 1820, M-50
Notes from the Spanish Legation in the United States to the
Department of State, 1790–1906, M-59
Miscellaneous Letters of the Department of State,
June 1–December 29, 1815, M-179
Records Relating to Privateers and Piracy, 1813–1835, Entry 949
Record Group 60, General Records of the Department of Justice
Entry 9, Records of the Attorney General's Office, General
Records—Letters Received 1809–1870, Louisiana 1815–1860
Record Group 94, Records of the Adjutant General's Office
Compiled Service Records, War of 1812
Vincent Gamby
Record Group 98, Records of United States Commands, Army
Commands, 1784–1821
Entry 72, Letters, Division of the South, 1816–1821, Volume 2
Record Group 107, General Records of the War Department
Letters Received by the Secretary of War, Main Series,
1801–1870, M-221
National Archives, Southwest Region, Ft. Worth, TX
Record Group 21, Records of District Courts of the United States,
1685–1993

Entry 21, United States District Court for the Eastern Region
of Louisiana, New Orleans, General Case Files, 1806–1932
Cases 0024, 0217, 0251, 0298, 0312, 0338, 0343, 0344, 0348,
0376, 0377, 0391, 0392, 0393, 0394, 0395, 0399, 0400, 0419,
0439, 0452, 0493, 0509, 0537, 0552, 0573, 0574, 0575, 0596,
0685, 0725, 0730, 0734, 0738, 0743, 0746, 0747, 0750, 0753,
0754, 0760, 0761, 0762, 0763, 0764, 0766, 0770, 0772, 0773,
0774, 0775, 0776, 0777, 0778, 0779, 0780, 0781, 0782, 0783,
0784, 0785, 0786, 0787, 0791, 0801, 0811, 0812, 0814, 0815,
0816, 0817, 0821, 0822, 0823, 0824, 0825, 0826, 0830, 0837,
0844, 0853, 0857, 0858, 0860, 0861, 0863, 0884, 0909, 0912,
0944, 0949, 0957, 0978, 1006, 1026, 1029, 1033, 1035, 1058,
1063, 1064, 1065, 1066, 1067, 1070, 1227, 1437, 1440, 1450,
1509, 1569, 1581, 1588, 1590, 1608, 1609, 1728, 1729, 1730, 1731,
1732, 1733, 1734, 1778, 1779, 1780, 1781
Minutes of the U.S. District Court at New Orleans, 1815–1825,
7RA-119, 1808–1815
National Archives, Kew, West London, England
Foreign Office Records, 72/149, 72/180, 5/123
Records of the Admiralty, and Ministry of Defense, Navy
Department:
Captains' Letters, ADM 1/2346
Ships' Logs, 1799–1974, ADM 51/2791
Master's Log of the HMS Sophie, 1809–1814
Newberry Library, Chicago, IL
Ayer Collection of Transcripts
Historia, Operaciones de Guerra
Notas Diplomaticas
Papeles Procedentes de Cuba Transcripts
Papeles de Estado, Audienca de Mexico
Provincias Internas Transcripts
New Orleans Notarial Archives, New Orleans
Joseph Arnaud Volume
Narcissus Broutin, Vols. 1, 8–12, 20A, 22–28, 32, 33, 58, 60–84, 87
Felix Broutin, Vol. 7
Michelle DeArmas, Vols. 3, 6, 13, 15A, 16A, 18
Eliphalet Fitch, Vol. 3
Marc Lafitte, Vols. 2, 6, 8, 9
Hugues Lavergne, Vol. 2

John Lynd, Vols. 1, 3, 4, 5, 7–12, 15, 16, 41, 42, 43, 88, 89
Philippe Pedesclaux, Vols. 1–4, 6–9, 16, 18, 19, 24, 26, 29
Pierre Pedesclaux, Vols. 43–57, 59, 60, 63, 64, 66, 68, 70–73
S. De Quinones, Vols. 10, 13
Plan de Trois Lots de Terre de La Municipalite No. 1, Plan Book No.
72, Folio No. 27, March 28, 1848
New Orleans Public Library, Special Collections, Louisiana Division
Case Files of the First Judicial Court
Suit Records, #751
City Court Suit Records 1807–1813
#2560 Guilledon Cadet vs. Bellurgey, Robin, Pierre Lafitte, and
William St. Marc
#3117 William St. Marc vs. Lafitte and Garidel
#3395 Antoine Philippe Lanaux vs. Pierre Lafitte
#3486 William St. Marc vs. Peter Lafitte
County Court Records of Civil Suits
#71 Stephen Carraby vs. Peter Lafitte, 1805
First Judicial District Court Records
#10 Paul Lanusse vs. Jean Jeanetty, Vincent Gambi, et al.
#729 William Thomas vs. Peter Lafitte
#751 John Gourjon vs. Vincent Gamby
#1346 Pierre Lafitte vs. Vincent Gambie or Jean Roup
#1701 Henry Coit vs. Jacob Jennings and George W. Morgan
#1702 Henry Coit vs. Christopher Adams
#1727 Henry Coit vs. Christopher Adams
#1730 Pierre Lafitte vs. Estate of Guy Champlin
#3169 Samuel Toby vs. Henry Coit
Orleans Parish Court Civil Suit Records
#300 Paul Lanusse et al. vs. Pierre Laffite
#829 Jean Laffite vs. Joseph Sylvestre
#956 Executors of André Robin vs. Pierre Laffite
#1143 Dominique Youx vs. J. Deglanne
#1971 Pierre Laméson vs. Charles Lallemande
#2289 Jean Laffite vs. Jean Gonzales
Orleans Parish Court of Probates
Succession of Francis Brunetti, April 29, 1846
Will of Francis Brunetti, April 29, 1846, Will Book 8, pp. 240–41
Succession of Pierre Roup, April 15, 1836
Laurent Maire Estate Inventory, September 15, 1827

Orleans Territory Superior Court Suit Records
#2745 Francis Bellestre vs. William St. Marc, Pierre Lafitte et al.
Superior Court Suit Records 1804–1813
#131 Marie Zabeth and infant vs. Pierre Lafitte
University of New Orleans
Civil District Court Archives
Case file #113863, Division A, George Renton vs. Mirielle A. Farr
Case file #132700, Division E, Edward Allnet et al. vs. Board of Health of the City of New Orleans
File #25813, Supreme Court of Louisiana, State ex rel. Allnet et al. vs. Board of Health of City of New Orleans, March 10, 1924
Northwestern State University of Louisiana, Natchitoches
Federal Writers Project Collection
Juanita Henry Collection
James Judge Collection
Melrose Collection
Lafitte Book
Historical Society of Pennsylvania, Philadelphia
Josiah Stoddard Johnston Papers
Princeton University, Princeton, NJ
Edward Livingston Papers
Public Registry Office, Pauillac, Aquitane, France
Birth, Marriage, and Death Registers, 1769–1804
Pulaski County Courthouse, Little Rock, AR
Deed Book A, 1819–1823
Rosenberg Library, Galveston, TX
Ebenezer Allen Letter
J. D. Claitor, "Jeanette: Common Law Wife of Jean Lafitte"
J. O. Dyer Collection
J. O. Dyer Scrapbooks
Felipe Fatio Papers
Anne and Walter Grover Papers
J. Randal Jones, "A Visit to Galveston Island in 1818"
Jean Laffite Collection
Jean Laffite Papers
Ben Stuart Papers
Margaret L. Watson, "Mercedes, or The True Lafitte"
Sam Houston Regional Library and Research Center, Liberty, TX
Jean Laffite Collection

Gene Marshall, "The Languages of the author of Laffite's Journal"
Stephen F. Austin State University, Nacogdoches, East Texas Research
    Center
    Robert Bruce Blake Research Collection, Nacogdoches Archives
        Transcripts
Texas General Land Office, Austin
    Charles Cronea Application, RV 1153, Veterans Donation
        Applications
Texas State Library and Archives, Austin
    Mirabeau Bounaparte Lamar Papers
    Nacogdoches Archives
University of Texas at Austin, Center for American History
    Archivo General de Indias Transcripts
    Louis Aury Papers
    Béxar Archives
    W. T. Block, "A Buccaneer Household in Galveston: Capt. Jim and
        Sabinal Campbell"
    W. T. Block, "'Uncle Charlie' Cronea: The Last of Lafitte's Pirates"
    James Campbell Vertical File
    Alexander Dienst Collection
    Eberstadt Collection
    Stanley Faye, "Commodore Aury" Manuscript
    Stanley Faye, "Privateers of the Gulf" Manuscript
    Jean Lafitte [sic] Scrapbook
    Jean Laffite Vertical File
    James Long Vertical File
    Edward A. Parsons Collection
    Provincias Internas Transcripts
Torch Energy Advisors, Houston, TX
    Torch Collection
Tulane University, Howard Tilton Memorial Library, New Orleans
    William Beer Papers
    Louis DeSoto Papers
    Rosamunde E. and Emile Kuntz Collection
    Albert C. Phelps Collection
    Ernest Sabourin Papers
    Violet Brown Shay Collection
    Robert C. Vogel Papers
Virginia Historical Society, Richmond
    Graham Family Papers

West Feliciana Parish Courthouse, St. Francisville, LA, Act Book 1,
p. 236
Yale University, Beineke Library, New Haven, CT
De Forest Family Papers
Archivo de la Ciudad de Mérida de Yucatan, Mérida, Mexico
Notarias Publicas, Protocolos del Año 1821
Sumaria Instruida contra el ingles don Jorge Schumph

AUTOGRAPH CATALOGS

Anderson Galleries. Catalog Sale Number 2096. New York, 1926.
Edward Eberstadt & Sons. Catalog 161, *Western America in Documents
from the Mississippi to the Pacific 1669–1890*. New York, n.d.

NEWSPAPERS

Baltimore, *Nile's Weekly Register*, 1811, 1812, 1814, 1815, 1818, 1820, 1821
Baton Rouge, *Morning Advocate;* John Burton Thompson, "The Legend
of Lafitte," October 11, 1953
Blakeley, AL, *Blakeley Sun, and Alabama Advertiser*, 1819
Bogotá, Colombia, *Gaceta de Colombia*, 1821–23
Boston, *Independent Chronicle and Boston Patriot*, 1822
Boston, *New England Palladium & Commercial Advertiser*, 1819–20
Boutte, LA, *St. Charles Herald*, 1875
Charleston, SC, *Courier*, 1813–15, 1818, 1821
Charleston, SC, *Southern Patriot*, 1824
Charleston, SC, *Times*, 1817, 1821
Colfax, LA, *Chronicle*, 1962
Galveston, *Daily News*, 1878, 1879, 1884, 1893, 1895, 1919, 1920, 1921, 1924,
1926
Galveston, *Flake's Daily Bulletin*, 1871
Galveston, *News*, 1874, 1881, 1884, 1895, 1909, 1920, 1935
Galveston, *News Sun*, 1921, 1922, 1924
Galveston, *Weekly News*, 1883
Gettysburg, PA, *Adams Centinel*, 1818
Houston, *Chronicle*, 1908
Houston, *Morning Star*, 1842
Houston, *Post*, 1960

Houston, *Telegraph and Texas Register,* 1841–42
Kingston, Jamaica, *Gazette,* 1814
Lake Charles, LA, *American,* 1909
Lake Charles, LA, *American Press,* 1981, 2002
Lake Charles, LA, *Echo,* 1884
Little Rock, *Arkansas Gazette,* 1873, 1937
Louisville, TN, *Journal,* 1836
Natchez, *Mississippi Republican,* 1819
Newark, NJ, *Daily Advertiser,* 1840
New Orleans, *Courier,* 1843
New Orleans, *Daily Crescent,* 1850
New Orleans, *Daily Delta,* 1851
New Orleans, *Daily Picayune,* 1844, 1870, 1871, 1880, 1881, 1891, 1895
New Orleans, *Gazette and New-Orleans Advertiser,* 1814
New Orleans, *L'Ami des Lois,* 1814, 1815
New Orleans, *Louisiana Courier,* 1812–22, 1830; also *Courier de la
    Louisiane* and *Courier of Louisiana*
New Orleans, *Louisiana Gazette,* 1806, 1809, 1810
New Orleans, *Louisiana Gazette and New-Orleans Mercantile Advertiser,*
    1813–15, 1817, 1822
New Orleans, *Moniteur de la Louisiane,* 1802, 1804, 1830
New Orleans, *Official Daily Court Record,* 1922
New Orleans, *Orleans Gazette,* 1819
New Orleans, *States,* 1928; Catherine B. Dillon, "Jean Lafitte's Birth
    Record Finally Found," May 21, 1933
New Orleans, *Times-Picayune,* 1871, 1918, 1925, 1938, 1939, 1948; Robert
    B. Mayfield, "Lafitte Documents Found," August 23, 1925;
    W. M. Darling, "Doubt Expressed as to Piratical Status of
    Jean," August 22, 1937; Meigs O. Frost, "Papers Tell Spying
    Trip of Smuggler," November 13, 1938; Richard Sands,
    "Buccaneer's Signature is Discovered," April 2, 1939; Hal R.
    Yockey, "Tomb Identified by Michigan Professor as Noted
    Pirate's," December 19, 1948
New York, *National Advocate,* 1822
New York, *New World,* 1840
New York, *Spectator,* 1818
Pensacola, *Floridian,* 1821–23
Pensacola, *Gazette,* 1824
Pensacola, *Journal,* 1929
Philadelphia, *American Daily Advertiser,* 1806

Philadelphia, *National Gazette and Literary Register,* 1822
Philadelphia, *United States' Gazette,* 1815
Portsmouth, NH, *Journal,* 1823
Portsmouth, *New Hampshire Gazette,* 1821
Providence, *Rhode Island Republican,* 1823
St. Louis, *Missouri Gazette & Illinois Advertiser,* 1814, 1815
Salem, MA, *Gazette,* 1818
Salem, MA, *Observer,* 1823
Savannah, GA, *Columbian Museum and Savannah Daily Gazette,* 1818
Savannah, GA, *Republican and Savannah Evening Ledger,* 1818
Washington, DC, *Daily National Intelligencer,* 1814–18

UNITED STATES CENSUS

Charleston, SC, 1820
New Orleans, LA, 1810, 1820, 1830, 1840, 1850
Texas, Jefferson County, 1850

LETTERS, DIARIES, MEMOIRS, AND OFFICIAL COMPILATIONS

Adams, Charles Francis, ed. *Memoirs of John Quincy Adams Comprising Portions of His Diary from 1795 to 1848.* 12 vols. Philadelphia, 1874–77.
Annual Register, of A View of the History, Politics, and Literature for the Year 1814. London, 1815.
Barker, Eugene C., ed. *The Austin Papers: The Annual Report of the American Historical Society for the Year 1919,* 3 vols. Washington, 1919–26.
Bassett, John Spencer, ed. *Correspondence of Andrew Jackson.* 7 vols. Washington, 1927.
Bolton, Herbert. *Guide to Materials for the History of the United States in the Principal Archives of Mexico.* Washington, 1913.
Brackenridge, Henry M. *A Topographical Description of Pensacola and Vicinity in 1821.* Bagdad, FL, 1991.
Bradley, Jared William, ed. *Interim Appointment: W. C. C. Claiborne Letter Book, 1804–1805.* Baton Rouge, LA, 2002.
Carter, Clarence Edwin, ed. *The Territorial Papers of the United States, Volume IX: The Territory of Orleans 1803–1812.* Washington, 1940.

————. *The Territorial Papers of the United States, Volume XIV: The Territory of Louisiana-Missouri 1806–1814.* Washington, 1949.

Claiborne, J. F. H. *Life and Times of Gen. Sam. Dale, the Mississippi Partisan.* New York, 1860.

Coker, William, and G. Douglas Inglis. *The Spanish Census of Pensacola, 1784–1820: A Genealogical Guide to Spanish Pensacola.* Pensacola, FL, 1980.

The Debates and Proceedings in the Congress of the United States; with an Appendix, Containing Important State Papers and Public Documents, and all the Laws of a Public Nature. Fifteenth Congress, Second Session, Washington, 1855.

Departamento de Historia Naval. *Historia Marítima Argentina.* 8 vols. Buenos Aires, 1994.

Fayman, W. A., and T. W. Reilly, *Fayman & Reilly's Galveston City Directory for 1875–6.* Galveston, TX, 1875.

Flint, Timothy. *The History and Geography of the Mississippi Valley.* 2 vols. Cincinnati, 1832.

————. *Recollections of the Last Ten Years in the Valley of the Mississippi.* Boston, 1826.

Foote, Henry Stuart. *Texas and the Texans; or, Advance of the Anglo-Americans to the South-west.* 2 vol. Philadelphia, 1841.

Franco, José L. *Documentos Para la Historia de Mexico.* Havana, Cuba, 1961.

Fry, William. *The Baltimore Directory for 1810, containing the Names, Occupations and Residences of the Inhabitants, Alphabetically Arranged; also, A correct List of Streets, Lanes and Alleys Within the City and Precincts. A List of Officers in the General Government of the United States, Government of the State of Maryland, Officers of the Corporation, Custom-House Duties, Banks, Insurance Offices, Turnpike Roads, &c.* Baltimore, 1810.

Furlong, Lawrence. *The American Coast Pilot.* Newburyport, MA, 1817.

Girard, Just. *The Adventures of a French Captain.* New York, 1878.

Gleig, George Robert. *The Campaigns of the British Army at Washington and New Orleans in the Years 1814–1815.* London, 1847.

Gray, William F. *From Virginia to Texas, 1835: Diary of Col. Wm. F. Gray.* Houston, TX, 1909.

Gulick, Charles A., Jr., and Winnie Allen, eds. *The Papers of Mirabeau Bounaparte Lamar.* 6 vols. Austin, TX, 1925.

Heller, John H., comp. *Galveston City Directory for 1870.* Galveston, TX, 1870.

Hemphill, W. Edwin, ed. *The Papers of John C. Calhoun, Volume IV, 1819–1820.* Columbia, SC, 1969.

———. *The Papers of John C. Calhoun, Volume VI, 1821–1822.* Columbia, SC, 1972.

Hill, Roscoe R. *Descriptive Catalog of the Documents Relating to the History of the United States in the Papeles Procedentes de Cuba Deposited in the Archivo General de Indias at Seville.* Washington, 1916.

Hollon, W. Eugene, and Ruth Lapham Butler, eds. *William Bollaert's Texas.* Norman, OK, 1956.

Hopkins, James F., ed. *The Papers of Henry Clay, Volume 2: The Rising Statesman 1815–1820.* Lexington, KY, 1961.

Index to the Archives of Spanish West Florida 1782–1810. New Orleans, 1975.

Kennedy, William. *Texas: The Rise, Progress, and Prospects of the Republic of Texas.* 2 vols. London, 1841.

Latour, Arsené Lacarriere. *Historical Memoir of the War in West Florida and Louisiana in 1814–1815.* Philadelphia, 1816.

Lowrie, Walter, and Walter S. Franklin, eds. *American State Papers. Documents, Legislative and Executive, of the Congress of the United States. . . .: Class I, Foreign Relations.* 4 vols. Washington, 1834.

Lowrie, Walter, and Matthew St. Clair Clarke, eds. *American State Papers. Documents Legislative and Executive, of the Congress of the United States. . . .: Class VI, Commerce and Navigation, Volume I.* Washington, 1832.

Martin, François-Xavier. *The History of Louisiana from the Earliest Period.* 2 vols. New Orleans, 1827.

Memorial of Lawrence Kearny, A Captain in the United States Navy, Miscellaneous Document 207, first session, 35th Congress. Washington, 1858.

Message from the President of the United States, Communicating Information of the Proceeding of Certain Persons who took Possession of Amelia Island and of Galvezton, During the Summer of the Present Year, and made Establishments There. Washington, 1817.

Message from the President of the United States, Transmitting Information Relative to Piratical Depredations, &c., Furnished In Pursuance of Two Resolutions of 21st and 23d December last. Washington, 1825.

Moreau de Saint-Méry, M. L. E. *Description Topographique, Physique, Civile, Politique et Historique de La Partie Française de L'Isle Saint-Domingue.* 3 vols. Paris, France, 1958.

Moser, Harold, David R. Hoth, Sharon Macpherson, and John H. Reinbold, eds. *The Papers of Andrew Jackson. Volume III, 1814–1815.* Knoxville, TN, 1991.

Muir, Andrew Forest. *Texas in 1837, an Anonymous, Contemporary Narrative.* Austin, TX, 1958.

New Orleans City Directory. New Orleans, 1832.

New Orleans in 1805. A Directory and A Census, Together With Resolutions Authorizing Same Now Printed For The First Time From The Original Manuscript. Facsimile: New Orleans, 1936.

Nolan, Charles E., and Dorenda Dupont, eds. *Sacramental Records of the Roman Catholic Church of the Archdiocese of New Orleans, Volume 8, 1804–1806.* New Orleans, 1993.

———. *Volume 9, 1807–1809.* New Orleans, 1994.

———. *Volume 10, 1810–1812.* New Orleans, 1995.

———. *Volume 11, 1812–1814.* New Orleans, 1996.

———. *Volume 14, 1820–1821.* New Orleans, 1999.

———. *Volume 15, 1822–1823.* New Orleans, 2000.

———. *Volume 16, 1824–1825.* New Orleans, 2001.

———. *Volume 17, 1826–1827.* New Orleans, 2002.

———. *Volume 18, 1828–1829.* New Orleans, 2003.

Nolte, Vincent. *The Memoirs of Vincent Nolte. Reminiscences in the Period of Anthony Adverse or Fifty Years in Both Hemispheres.* New York, 1934.

Paullin, Charles O., and Frederic L. Paxson. *Guide to the Materials in London Archives for the History of the United States Since 1783.* Washington, 1914.

Pérez, Luis Marino. *Guide to the Materials for American History in Cuban Archives.* Washington, 1907.

Pittman, Philip. *The Present State of the European Settlements on the Mississippi.* London, 1770.

Pope, William F. *Early Days in Arkansas.* Little Rock, AR, 1895.

Porter, David D. *Memoir of Commodore David Porter of the United States Navy.* Albany, NY, 1875.

Pratt, Willis W., ed. *Galveston Island, or, A Few Months Off the Coast of Texas. The Journal of Francis C. Sheridan, 1839–1840.* Austin, TX, 1954.

Ratchford, Fannie E., ed. *The Story of Champ D'Asile as Told by Two of the Colonists.* Dallas, TX, 1937.

Reid, John, and John Henry Eaton. *The Life of Andrew Jackson.* Philadelphia, 1817.

Richardson and Co. *The Texas Almanac for 1857, with Statistics, Historical and Biographical Sketches Relating to Texas.* Galveston, TX, 1856.

Richardson, James D., comp. *A Compilation of the Messages and Papers of the Presidents 1789–1897.* 10 vols. Washington, 1900.

Rieder, Milton P., Jr., and Norma Gaudet Rieder, eds. *New Orleans Ship Lists: Volume 1, 1820–1821.* Metairie, LA, 1966.

Robin, C. C. *Voyages to the Interior of Louisiana, West Florida, and to the Islands of Martinique and Saint-Domingue During the Years 1802, 1803, 1804, 1805 and 1806.* 3 vols. Paris, France, 1807. Edited and translated by Stuart O. Landry as *Voyage to Louisiana* (Gretna, LA, 2000).

Robinson, William D. *A Cursory View of Spanish America, Particularly the Neighbouring Vice-Royalties of Mexico and New Granada.* Georgetown, DC, 1815.

Robinson, William Davis. *Memoirs of the Mexican Revolution: Including A Narrative of the Expedition of General Xavier Mina.* 2 vols. Philadelphia, 1820.

Rowland, Dunbar, ed. *Official Letter Books of W. C. C. Claiborne 1801–1816.* 6 vols. Jackson, MS, 1917.

Schenck, James R. *The Directory and Stranger's Guide, for the City of Charleston . . . 1822.* Charleston, SC, 1822.

Shackleford, W. *The Directory and Stranger's Guide, for the City of Charleston . . . 1825.* Charleston, SC, 1825.

Shepherd, William R. *Guide to the Materials for the History of the United States in Spanish Archives.* Washington, 1907.

Shinn, Josiah H. *Pioneers and Makers of Arkansas.* Little Rock, AR, 1908.

Ship Registers and Enrollments of New Orleans, Louisiana, Volume 1, 1804–1820. Baton Rouge, LA, 1941.

Smith, Aaron. *The Atrocities of the Pirates, or, A Faithful Narrative of the Unparalleled Sufferings Endured by the Author.* New York, 1824.

State Papers and Correspondence Bearing upon the Purchase of the Territory of Louisiana. Washington, 1903.

Stephens, John L. *Incidents of Travel in Yucatan.* 2 vols. New York, 1843.

Tayloe, Benjamin Ogle. *Our Neighbors on La Fayette Square, Anecdotes and Reminiscences.* Washington, 1872.

Taylor, Virginia H., ed. *The Letters of Antonio Martinez, Last Spanish Governor of Texas, 1817–1822.* Austin, TX, 1957.

Thrasher, J. S. *Galveston City Directory, 1857.* Galveston, TX, 1857.

Walker, Alexander. *Jackson and New Orleans: An Authentic Narrative.* New York, 1856.

Whitney, Thomas H. *Whitney's New-Orleans Directory, and Louisiana & Mississippi Almanac for the Year 1811.* New Orleans, 1810.

Wilkinson, James. *Memoirs of My Own Times.* 3 vols. Philadelphia, 1816.

Wilson, Samuel, Jr. *Impressions Respecting New Orleans by Benjamin Henry Boneval Latrobe, Diary & Sketches 1818–1820.* New York, 1951.

Woods, Earl C., and Charles E. Nolan, eds. *Sacramental Records of the Roman Catholic Church of the Archdiocese of New Orleans, Volume 2, 1751–1771.* New Orleans, 1988.

———. *Volume 3, 1772–1783.* New Orleans, 1989.

———. *Volume 5, 1791–1795.* New Orleans, 1990.

———. *Volume 7, 1800–1803.* New Orleans, 1992.

Works Project Administration. *Synopses of Cases in the U.S. District Court for the Eastern District of Louisiana Cases #1 to #3000 1806–1831.* Baton Rouge, LA, 1941.

ARTICLES

Brown, Everett S., ed. "Letters from Louisiana, 1813–1814." *Mississippi Valley Historical Review,* XI, March 1928, pp. 570–79.

[Brown, John Henry]. "Early Life in the Southwest, No. IV, Captain John McHenry, Pioneer of Texas." *DeBow's Review,* XV, December 1853, pp. 572–84.

Carpenter, Edwin H., Jr., ed. "Latour's Report on Spanish-American Relations in the Southwest." *Louisiana Historical Quarterly,* XXX, July 1947, pp. 715–37.

Dabbs, Jack Autrey. "Additional Notes on the Champ-d'Asile." *Southwestern Historical Quarterly,* LIV, January 1951, pp. 347–58.

Epperson, Jean L. "Testimony of Three Escaped Prisoners from Galveston in 1818." *Laffite Society Chronicles,* IV, February 1998, n. pp.

Graham, George Mason. "Political Occurrences on the Island of Galvezton in 1818." *Tyler's Historical and Genealogical Magazine,* XXVII, April 1946, pp. 255–73.

"Historical Memoir of the War in West Florida and Louisiana in 1814–15." *North-American Review,* VIII, July 1816, pp. 232–66.

"Index to Spanish Judicial Records of Louisiana." *Louisiana Historical Quarterly,* XII, April 1929, pp. 331–58.

Ingraham, Joseph H. "Life and Times of Lafitte." *DeBow's Southern and Western Review,* XI, October 1851, pp. 372–87.

"A Junior Officer's Observations from the Field of Battle." *The Naval Chronicle,* XXXIII, April–May, pp. 385–88.

Karilanovic, Dorothy McD., trans. "Letters from the National Archive of Cuba." *Laffite Society Chronicles,* V, February 1999, n. pp.

———. "Translation Key to 1810 [1816] Map of Galveston Bay." *Laffite Society Chronicles,* II, January 1996, n. pp.

Kuykendall, J. H. "Reminiscences of Early Texans." *Quarterly of the Texas State Historical Association,* VI, January 1903, pp. 243–53.

Marigny, Bernard. "Reflections on the Campaign of General Andrew Jackson. New Orleans, 1848." *Louisiana Historical Quarterly,* VI, January 1923, pp. 61–85.

[McIntosh, James M.]. "A Visit to Lafitte." *Knickerbocker Magazine,* XXIX, March 1847, pp. 254–61.

Owsley, Harriet C. "Travel Through the Indian Country in the Early 1800's. The Memoirs of Martha Philips Martin." *Tennessee Historical Quarterly,* XXI, March 1962, pp. 66–81.

Padgett, James A., ed. "Some Letters of James Brown of Louisiana to Presidents of the United States." *Louisiana Historical Quarterly,* XX, January 1937, pp. 58–136.

Parsons, Edward Alexander. "Jean Lafitte in the War of 1812, A Narrative Based on the Original Documents." *Proceedings of the American Antiquarian Society,* L, October 1940, pp. 205–24.

Prichard, Walter, Fred B. Kniffen, and Clair A. Brown, eds. "Southern Louisiana and Southern Alabama in 1819: The Journal of James Leander Cathcart." *Louisiana Historical Quarterly,* XXVIII, July 1945, pp. 735–921.

Pritchard, Walter, ed. "George Graham's Mission to Galveston in 1818." *Louisiana Historical Quarterly,* XX, July 1937, pp. 619–50.

"Sketch of the Position of the British and American Forces, during the Operations against New Orleans, from 23d. Decr. 1814 to 18th. Jany. 1815." *Naval Chronicle,* XXXIII, May–June 1815, pp. 484–88.

Snow, Elliott, cont. "A Visit to Lafitte." *Louisiana Historical Quarterly,* XI, July 1928, pp. 434–44.

"T." "The Cruise of the Enterprise. A Day with La Fitte." *United States Magazine and Democratic Review.* VI, July 1839, pp. 33–42.

[Tudor, W.]. Review of Historical Memoir of the War in West Florida. *North-American Review and Miscellaneous Journal,* III, July 1816, pp. 232–66.

Vogel, Robert C., ed. "A Louisianian's View of the Mexican Revolution in 1810: Paul Bouet Laffitte's Letter to Dr. John Sibley." *North Louisiana Historical Association Journal,* XVI, Fall 1985, pp. 131–35.

Warren, Harris Gaylord. "Documents Relating to the Establishment of
Privateers at Galveston, 1816–1817." *Louisiana Historical Quarterly,*
XXI, October 1938, pp. 3–26.
———. "Documents Relating to George Graham's Proposals to Jean
Laffite for the Occupation of the Texas Coast." *Louisiana Historical
Quarterly,* XXI, January 1938, pp. 213–19.
———. "Documents Relating to Pierre Laffite's Entrance Into the
Service of Spain." *Southwestern Historical Quarterly,* XLIV, July
1940, pp. 76–87.

WEB SITES

"Afro-Louisiana History and Genealogy, 1718–1820 (Slave),"
http://www.ibiblio.org/laslave/
"Early St. Louis Photographers," compiled by David A. Lossos, based
on city directories, at http://genealogyinstlouis.accessgenealogy.com/
tracylewis.htm.
"New Orleans, Louisiana Death Records Index, 1804–1949," [database
online] Provo, UT: Ancestry.com, 2002. Original data: State of
Louisiana, Secretary of State, Division of Archives, Records
Management, and History. *Vital Records Indices.* Baton Rouge, LA.

Secondary Sources

BOOKS

Alden, Carroll Storrs. *Lawrence Kearny, Sailor Diplomat.* Princeton, NJ,
1936.
Arthur, Stanley Clisby. *Jean Laffite, Gentleman Rover.* New Orleans,
1952.
———. *Old Families of Louisiana.* New Orleans, 1931.
———. *The Story of the West Florida Rebellion.* St. Francisville, LA,
1935; Baton Rouge, LA, 1975 reprint.
Baker, D. W. C., comp. *A Texas Scrap-Book. Made up of the History,
Biography, and Miscellany of Texas and its People.* New York, 1875.
Bancroft, Hubert Howe. *History of the North Mexican States and Texas.*
2 vols. New York, 1884.

Barbé-Marbois, François. *The History of Louisiana, Particularly of the Cession of That Colony to the United States of America; With an Introductory Essay on the Constitution and Government of the United States.* Philadelphia, 1830.

Beardslee, Francis B. C. *Piracy in the West Indies and Its Suppression.* Salem, MA, 1923.

Bell, Caryn Cossé. *Revolution, Romanticism, and the Afro-Creole Protest Tradition in Louisiana 1718–1868.* Baton Rouge, LA, 1997.

Biographical and Historical Memoirs of Louisiana. 2 vols. Chicago, 1892.

Block, W. T. *A Buccaneer Family in Spanish East Texas: A Biographical Sketch of Captain James and Mary Sabinal Campbell.* Nederland, TX, 1990.

Brasseaux, Carl A., and Glenn R. Conrad, eds. *The Road to Louisiana: The Saint-Domingue Refugees 1792–1809.* Lafayette, LA, 1992.

Brown, John Henry. *History of Texas From 1685 to 1892.* 2 vols. St. Louis, 1892.

———. *Long's Expedition.* Houston, TX, 1930.

Brown, Wilburt S. *The Amphibious Campaign for West Florida and Louisiana, 1814–1815.* University, AL, 1969.

Campbell, Randolph B. *An Empire for Slavery: The Peculiar Institution in Texas 1821–1865.* Baton Rouge, LA, 1989.

Cartwright, Gary. *Galveston: A History of the Island.* New York, 1991.

Castellanos, Henry C. *New Orleans as It Was: Episodes of Louisiana Life.* New Orleans, 1895.

Christensen, Roberta Marie. *Pioneers of West Galveston Island.* Austin, TX, 1992.

Christovich, Mary Louise, and Roulhac B. Toledano, *Faubourg Treme and the Bayou Road: North Rampart Street to North Broad Street, Canal Street to St. Bernard Avenue.* New Orleans, 2003. Volume VI of Samuel Wilson and Bernard Lemann, eds., *New Orleans Architecture* (New Orleans, var. years).

Clay, John V. *Spain, Mexico and the Lower Trinity: An Early History of the Texas Gulf Coast.* Baltimore, 1987.

Coggeshall, George. *History of the American Privateers.* New York, 1856.

Conrad, Glenn R., ed. *A Dictionary of Louisiana Biography.* 2 vols. Lafayette, LA, 1998.

Cox, Isaac Joslin. *The West Florida Controversy, 1798–1813: A Study in American Diplomacy.* Baltimore, 1918.

De Conde, Alexander. *"This Affair of Louisiana."* New York, 1976.

De Gerulewicz, Marisa Vannini. *Las Memorias de Agustín Codazzi.* Caracas, Venezuela, 1970.

De Grummond, Jane Lucas. *Renato Beluche, Smuggler, Privateer, and Patriot 1780–1860.* Baton Rouge, LA, 1983.

———. *The Baratarians and the Battle of New Orleans.* Baton Rouge, LA, 1961.

Deléry, Simone de la Souchère. *Napoleon's Soldiers in America.* Gretna, LA, 1972.

Ellms, Charles. *The Pirates Own Book, or Authentic Narratives of the Lives, Exploits, and Executions of the Most Celebrated Sea Robbers.* Portland, ME, 1837.

Erdman, Loula Grace. *Edge of Time.* Ft. Worth, TX, 1988.

Faye, Stanley. *Privateers of the Gulf.* Hemphill, TX, 2001.

Fick, Carolyn E. *The Making of Haiti: The Saint Domingue Revolution from Below.* Knoxville, TN, 1990.

Fields, William, comp. *The Scrap-Book: Consisting of Tales and Anecdotes, Biographical, Historical, Patriotic, Moral, Religious, and Sentimental Pieces, in Prose and Poetry.* 6th ed. Philadelphia, 1890.

Garrett, Julia Kathryn. *Green Flag Over Texas: A Story of the Last Years of Spain in Texas.* New York, 1939.

Gayarré, Charles E. A. *History of Louisiana. The American Domination.* 4 vols. New Orleans, 1866.

———. *History of Louisiana. The French Domination.* 4 vols. New Orleans, 1885.

———. *The Story of Jean and Pierre Lafitte, The Pirate-Patriots.* New Orleans, 1938.

Geggus, David P., ed. *The Impact of the Haitian Revolution in the Atlantic World.* Columbia, SC, 2001.

Hamilton, Charles. *Great Forgers and Famous Fakes.* New York, 1980.

Harvey, Robert. *Liberators: Latin America's Struggle for Independence 1810–1830.* New York, 2000.

Hatcher, William B. *Edward Livingston, Jefferson Republican and Jacksonian Democrat.* Baton Rouge, LA, 1940.

Hayes, Charles. *History of the Island and the City of Galveston.* 2 vols. Austin, TX, 1974 (reprint of destroyed Cincinnati, 1879 edition).

Hempstead, Fay. *Pictorial History of Arkansas from Earliest Times to the Year 1890.* St. Louis, 1890.

Henson, Margaret Swett. *Samuel May Williams, Early Texas Entrepreneur.* College Station, TX, 1976.

Hill, Richard. *The Picaroons; or, One Hundred and Fifty Years Ago: Being A History of Commerce and Navigation in the West Indian Seas.* Dublin, Ireland, 1869.

Hoffman, Paul E. *Florida's Frontiers.* Bloomington, IN, 2002.

Hunt, Charles Havens. *Life of Edward Livingston.* New York, 1864.

Ingraham, J. H. *Lafitte, the Pirate of the Gulf.* 2 vols. New York, 1889.

The Journal of Jean Laffite: The Privateer-Patriot's Own Story. Woodville, TX, 1994.

Keen, Benjamin. *David Curtis DeForest and the Revolution of Buenos Aires.* New Haven, CT, 1947.

Kein, Sybil, ed. *Creole: The History and Legacy of Louisiana's Free People of Color.* Baton Rouge, LA, 2000.

King, Stewart R. *Blue Coat or Powdered Wig: Free People of Color in Pre-Revolutionary Saint Domingue.* Athens, GA, 2001.

Kmen, Henry A. *Music in New Orleans: The Formative Years 1791–1841.* Baton Rouge, LA, 1966.

Lagarde, François. *The French in Texas: History, Migration, Culture.* Austin, TX, 2003.

Lay, Bennett. *The Lives of Ellis P. Bean.* Austin, TX, 1960.

Lemmon, Alfred E., John T. Magill, and Jason R. Wiese, eds. *Charting Louisiana: Five Hundred Years of Maps.* New Orleans, 2003.

Le Plongeon, Alice D. *Here and There in Yucatan. Miscellanies.* New York, 1885.

Mané, J. Ignacio Rubio. *Los Piratas Lafitte.* Mexico City, 1938.

Marshall, Thomas Maitland. *A History of the Western Boundary of the Louisiana Purchase, 1819–1841.* Berkeley, CA, 1914.

McComb, David G. *Galveston. A History.* Austin, TX, 1986.

McIntosh, Maria Jane. *Conquest and Self-Conquest; or, Which Makes the Hero?* New York, 1843.

The Memoirs of Jean Laffite, from Le Journal de Jean Laffite. Trans. Gene Marshall. N.p., 1999.

Monette, John W. *History of the Discovery and Settlement of the Valley of the Mississippi.* 2 vols. New York, 1846.

Mouzon, Harold A. *Privateers of Charleston in the War of 1812.* Charleston, SC, 1954.

Murat, Ines. *Napoleon and the American Dream.* Baton Rouge, LA, 1976.

Nardini, Louis Raphael, Sr. *My Historic Natchitoches, Louisiana and Its Environment.* Colfax, LA, 1963.

Naval History Division. *Dictionary of American Naval Fighting Ships, Volume II.* Washington, 1963.

Owsley, Frank Lawrence, Jr., and Gene A. Smith. *Filibusters and Expansionists: Jeffersonian Manifest Destiny, 1800–1821.* Tuscaloosa, AL, 1997.

Parsons, Edward Alexander. *Jean Lafitte in the War of 1812.* Worcester, MA, 1941.

Parton, James. *Life of Andrew Jackson.* 3 vols. Boston, 1860.

Phelan, Macum. *A History of Methodism in Texas.* Nashville, TN, 1924.

Phillips, Paul Chrisler. *The Fur Trade.* 2 vols. Norman, OK, 1961.

Pickles, Tim. *New Orleans 1815: Andrew Jackson Crushes the British.* Oxford, UK, 1999.

Ramsay, Jack C., Jr. *Jean Laffite, Prince of Pirates.* Austin, TX, 1996.

Reeves, Jesse S. *The Napoleonic Exiles in America: A Study in American Diplomatic History 1815–1819.* Baltimore, 1905. Johns Hopkins University Studies in History and Political Science, Series XXIII.

Remini, Robert V. *Andrew Jackson and the Course of American Empire, 1767–1821.* New York, 1977.

———. *The Battle of New Orleans: Andrew Jackson and America's First Military Victory.* New York, 1999.

Rowland, Eron. *Andrew Jackson's Campaign Against the British, or the Mississippi Territory in the War of 1812.* New York, 1926.

Saxon, Lyle, and Edward Dreyer. *The Friends of Joe Gilmore and Some Friends of Lyle Saxon.* New York, 1948.

———. *Lafitte the Pirate.* New York, 1930.

———. *Old Louisiana.* New York, 1929.

Schwarz, Ted. *Forgotten Battlefield of the First Texas Revolution: The Battle of Medina, August 18, 1813.* Austin, TX, 1985.

Slatta, Richard W., and Jane Lucas De Drummond. *Simón Bolívar's Quest for Glory.* College Station, TX, 2003.

Smith, Gene A. *Thomas ap Catesby Jones, Commodore of Manifest Destiny.* Annapolis, MD, 2000.

Smith, R. P. *Lafitte: or, the Baratarian Chief, a Tale.* Auburn, NY, 1834.

Stafford, George Mason Graham, comp. *General George Mason Graham of Tyrone Plantation and His People.* New Orleans, 1947.

Swanson, Betsy. *Historic Jefferson Parish, From Shore to Shore.* Gretna, LA, 1975.

Taylor, Joe Gray. *Negro Slavery in Louisiana.* Baton Rouge, LA, 1963.

Thompson, Ray M. *The Land of Lafitte the Pirate.* New Orleans, 1943.

Thrall, Homer S. *A Pictorial History of Texas, From the Earliest Visits of European Adventurers, to A. D. 1879.* St. Louis, 1879.

Tregle, Joseph G., Jr. *Louisiana in the Age of Jackson: A Clash of Cultures and Personalities.* Baton Rouge, LA, 1999.

Vogel, Robert C., and Kathleen F. Taylor. *Jean Laffite in American History: A Bibliographic Guide.* St. Paul, MN, 1998.

Warren, Harris Gaylord. *The Sword was Their Passport: A History of American Filibustering in the Mexican Revolution.* Baton Rouge, LA, 1943.

Wells, Mary Ann. *A History Lover's Guide to Louisiana.* Baton Rouge, LA, 1990.

Wilson, Samuel, Jr. *Plantation Houses on the Battlefield of New Orleans.* New Orleans, 1965.

Yoakum, Henderson. *History of Texas from Its First Settlement in 1685 to Its Annexation to the United States in 1846.* 2 vols. New York, 1856.

ARTICLES

Aznar, Luis A. Ramirez. "One Answer to the Lafitte Riddle." *Dixie Magazine,* January 2, 1972, pp. 6–7.

Bardin, Pierre. "Lafitte, Myth or Reality?" *Généalogie et Histoire de la Caraïbe,* Bulletin 64, October 1994, p. 1149.

————. "Laffite ou L'art de la Dissimulation." *Généalogie et Histoire de la Caraïbe,* Bulletin 85, September 1996, pp. 1718–19.

Barker, Eugene C. "The African Slave Trade in Texas." *Quarterly of the Texas State Historical Association,* VI, October 1902, pp. 145–58.

Block, W. T. "A Buccaneer Family in Spanish East Texas: A Biographical Sketch of Captain James and Mary Sabinal Campbell." *Texas Gulf Historical and Biographical Record,* XXVII, November 1991, pp. 77–95.

Bollaert, William. "Life of Jean Lafitte, the Pirate of the Mexican Gulf." *Littell's Living Age,* XXXII, March 1852, pp. 433–46.

Bowie, John. "Early Life in the Southwest—The Bowies." *DeBow's Review,* I, October 1852, pp. 378–83.

Brindley, Anne A. "Jane Long." *Southwestern Historical Quarterly,* LVI, October 1952, pp. 211–38.

Calvet, Louis-Jean. "Barataria: The Strange History of Jean Laffite, Pirate." Trans. Dorothy McDonald Karilanovic. *Laffite Society Chronicles,* IX, October 2003, pp. 3–13.

Camus, Michel. "Miettes et Pistes pour la Saga Laffite." *Généalogie et Histoire de la Caraïbe*, Bulletin 91, March 1997, p. 1917.

"Charles Cronea of Sabine Pass: Lafitte Buccaneer and Texas Veteran." *Texas Gulf Historical and Biographical Record*, XI, November 1975, pp. 91–95.

Cusachs, Gaspar. "The Controversy on Lafitte's Biography." *Louisiana Historical Quarterly*, III, January 1920, pp. 100–11.

———. "Lafitte, the Louisiana Pirate and Patriot." *Louisiana Historical Quarterly*, II, October 1919, pp. 418–38.

Dabney, Lancaster E. "Louis Aury: The First Governor of Texas Under the American Flag." *Southwestern Historical Quarterly*, XLII, October 1938, pp. 108–16.

Davis, William C. "The Laffites—The Early Louisiana Years." *The Laffite Society Chronicles*, X, February 2004, pp. 2–12.

De Grummond, Jane Lucas. "Cayetana Susana Bosque y Fanqui, 'A Notable Woman.'" *Louisiana History*, XXIII, Summer 1982, pp. 277–94.

———, ed. "Platter of Glory." *Louisiana History*, III, Fall 1962, pp. 316–59.

De Sidney, Emery. "Laffite, Frères et Cie, Filibustiers." *Généalogie et Histoire de la Caraïbe*, Bulletin 85, September 1996, p. 1720.

De Suduiraut, Bertrand Guillot. "Laffite Brothers & Co., Buccaneers or, the Impossible Quest." *Laffite Society Chronicles*, III, January 1997, n. pp.

———. "Laffite, Frères & Cie, Filibustiers ou L'enquête Impossible." *Généalogie et Histoire de la Caraïbe*, Bulletin 82, May 1996, pp. 1618–20.

Dobie, J. Frank. "The Mystery of Lafitte's Treasure." *Yale Review*, XVIII, September 1928, pp. 116–43.

Dorman, James H. "The Persistent Specter: Slave Rebellion in Territorial Louisiana," *Louisiana History*, XVIII, Fall 1977, pp. 389–404.

Dureau, Lorena. "Lafitte Won't Rest in Peace." *Dixie Magazine*, November 28, 1967, pp. 55–56.

Epperson, Jean L. "The Final Years of Jean Laffite." *Laffite Society Chronicles*, VII, October 2001, [pp. 2–6].

———. "Flags Flown at Galveston by the Corsairs and Filibusters." *Laffite Society Chronicles*, V, February 1999, [pp. 6–8].

———. "Jean Laffite and the Schooner *Pegasus*," *Laffite Society Chronicles*, VI, February 2000, [p. 10].

————. "The Laffite Family of Bayou Pierre." *Laffite Society Chronicles*, II, July 1996, n. pp.

————. "Mysterious Painting in the Cabildo." *Laffite Society Chronicles*, VIII, October 2002, pp. 8–10.

————. "Where was Champ D'Asile?" *Laffite Society Chronicles*, V, August 1999, [pp. 16–20].

————. "Who was John Andrechyne Laffite?" *Laffite Society Chronicles*, IV, September 2000, p. 2.

Faye, Stanley. "Commodore Aury." *Louisiana Historical Quarterly*, XXIV, July 1941, pp. 619–97.

————. "The Great Stroke of Pierre Laffite." *Louisiana Historical Quarterly*, XXIII, July 1940, pp. 733–826.

————. "Privateers of Guadaloupe and their Establishment in Barataria." *Louisiana Historical Quarterly*, XXIII, April 1940, pp. 428–44.

————. "Privateersmen of the Gulf and Their Prizes." *Louisiana Historical Quarterly*, XXII, October 1939, pp. 1012–94.

————. "Trouble on the Coast." *Southwest Review*, XVI, July 1931, pp. 469–83.

————. "Types of Privateer Vessels, Their Armament and Flags, in the Gulf of Mexico." *Louisiana Historical Quarterly*, XXIII, January 1940, pp. 118–30.

Feuillie, Sylvie. "Dominic Youx and *La Superbe*." *The Life and Times of Jean Laffite*, IX, Spring 1989, pp. 2–3.

————. "Jean et Pierre Laffite, Espions de L'Espagne et Agents de L'Independance Mexicaine." *La Revue Maritime*, No. 423, third quarter, 1991, pp. 76–90.

————. "La Guerre de Course Française aux Antilles Durant la Revolution et l'Empire, I Partie." *La Revue Maritime*, No. 427, third quarter, 1992, pp. 65–74.

————. "La Guerre de Course Française aux Antilles Durant la Revolution et l'Empire, II Partie." *La Revue Maritime*, No. 428, fourth quarter, 1993, pp. 103–12.

————. "La Guerre de Course Française aux Antilles Durant la Revolution et l'Empire, III Partie." *La Revue Maritime*, No. 429, fourth quarter, 1993, pp. 89–100.

————. "La Guerre de Course Française aux Antilles Durant la Revolution et l'Empire, V Partie." *La Revue Maritime*, No. 430, third quarter, 1995, pp. 61–77.

Fretz, Gary. "Laffite's Legacy." *Laffite Society Chronicles*, IX, February 2003, pp. 15–20.

Gardien, Kent. "Take Pity on Our Glory: Men of Champ d'Asile." *Southwestern Historical Quarterly*, LXXXVII, January 1984, pp. 241–68.

Gayarré, Charles. "The Famous Lafittes at Galveston." *Southern Bivouac*, Old Series, II, August 1886, pp. 176–78.

Gracy, David B., II. "Jean Lafitte and the Karankawa Indians." *East Texas Historical Journal*, II, February 1964, pp. 40–44.

"History of Lafitte." *DeBow's Southern and Western Review*, XIII, July 1852, pp. 101–2.

Hodges, Mr. and Mrs. T. L. "Jean Lafitte and Major L. Latour in Arkansas Territory." *Arkansas Historical Quarterly*, VII, Winter 1948, pp. 237–56.

K., W. H. "Lafitte." *DeBow's Southern and Western Review*, XIII, August 1852, pp. 204–5.

Kendall, John Smith. "The Huntsmen of Black Ivory." *Louisiana Historical Quarterly*, XXIV, January 1941, pp. 9–34.

———. "Piracy in the Gulf of Mexico, 1816–1823." *Louisiana Historical Quarterly*, VIII, July 1925, pp. 341–68.

———. "Shadow Over the City." *Louisiana Historical Quarterly*, XXII, January 1939, pp. 142–65.

———. "The Successors of Laffite." *Louisiana Historical Quarterly*, XXIV, April 1941, pp. 360–77.

Keyes, Pam. "Jean Laffite: Catalyst to Jackson's Victory at New Orleans." *Laffite Society Chronicles*, X, October 2004, pp. 2–8.

Klier, Betje Black. "Champ d'Asile, Texas." François Lagarde, *The French in Texas: History, Migration, Culture* (Austin, TX, 2003), pp. 79–97.

Lachance, Paul F. "The 1809 Immigration of Saint Domingue Refugees to New Orleans: Reception, Integration, and Impact." *Louisiana History*, XXIX, Spring 1998, pp. 109–41.

"Lafitte, 'The Pirate'—Early Times in the Southwest." *DeBow's Review*, XIX, August 1855, pp. 145–57.

"Lafitte." *DeBow's Southern and Western Review*, XIII, September 1852, p. 222.

"Lafitte.—Professor Ingraham's Letter," *DeBow's Southern and Western Review*, XIII, October 1852, pp. 422–24.

"Life and Times of Lafitte." *DeBow's Southern and Western Review*, XII, January 1852, pp. 111–13.

Mane, J. Ignacio Rubio. "Los Lafitte, Famosos Pirates y sus Ultimis dias en Yucatan." *Sociedad Mexicana de Geografica y Estadistica*, LIV, 1940, n. pp.

McAlister, L. N. "Pensacola During the Second Spanish Period." *Florida Historical Quarterly*, XXXVII (January–April 1959), pp. 281–327.

Mora, Isidro A. Beluche. "Privateers of Cartagena." *Louisiana Historical Quarterly*, XXXIX, January 1956, pp. 74–91.

Mota, Francisco. "The Adventures of Lafitte and the Pirates of Barataria." *Laffite Society Chronicles*, VI, August 1998, n. pp.

"Mystery of LYNX Visit." *Laffite Study Group Newsletter*, II, Spring 1982, pp. 1–2.

Oertling, Tom. "Historical Comments and Observations on the Map of 'Bahia de Galveston.'" *Laffite Society Chronicles*, II, January 1996, n. pp.

Olson, R. Dale. "French Pirates and Privateers in Texas." François Lagarde, *The French in Texas: History, Migration, Culture* (Austin, TX, 2003), pp. 60–78.

Orians, G. Harrison. "Lafitte: A Bibliographical Note." *American Literature*, IX, November 1937, pp. 351–53.

Perez, Luis M. "French Refugees to New Orleans in 1809." *Publications of the Southern History Association*, IX, September 1905, pp. 293–310.

[Pierce, George A.]. "Life and Times of Lafitte." *DeBow's Southern and Western Review*, XI, October 1851, pp. 372–87.

"The Pirate of the Gulf; or, the Hidden Treasure." *Colburn's United Service Magazine 1846*. Part 1, February 1846, pp. 236–42.

Ramsdell, Charles, Jr. "Why Jean Lafitte Became a Pirate." *Southwestern Historical Quarterly*, XLIII, April 1940, pp. 465–71.

Reeves, Sally K. "Cruising Contractual Waters: Searching for Laffite In the Records of the New Orleans Notarial Archives." February 26, 1999.

Robbins, Fred. "The Origin and Development of the African Slave Trade in Galveston, Texas, and Surrounding Areas from 1816 to 1836." *East Texas Historical Journal*, IX, October, 1971, pp. 153–61.

Sugden, John. "Jean Lafitte and the British Offer of 1814." *Louisiana History*, XX, Spring 1979, pp. 159–67.

Taylor, Joe G. "The Foreign Slave Trade in Louisiana After 1808." *Louisiana History*, I, Winter 1960, pp. 36–43.

"Texas.—A Province, Republic and State." *DeBow's Review*, XXIII, September 1857, pp. 239–69.

Vogel, Robert C. "Jean Laffite, the Baratarians, and the Battle of New
Orleans: A Reappraisal." *Louisiana History*, XLI, Summer 2000, pp.
261–76.

——. "Jean Laffite, the Baratarians, and the Historical Geography of
Piracy in the Gulf of Mexico." *Gulf Coast Historical Review*, V,
Spring 1990, pp. 62–77.

——. "Patterson and Ross' Raid on Barataria, September, 1814."
Louisiana History, XXXIII, Spring 1992, pp. 157–70.

——. "Pierre and Jean Laffite: Going to the Primary Sources," *Laffite
Society Chronicles*, VII (October 2001), [pp. 7–12].

——. "Rebel Without a Cause: The Adventures of Louis Aury."
Laffite Society Chronicles, VIII, February 2002, pp. 2–12.

——. "Some Background Concerning Laffite's Departure from
Galveston." *Laffite Society Chronicles*, V, August 1999, [pp. 7–11].

——. "Who Were These Guys? Some of the Lesser Characters in
the Story of the Laffites." *Laffite Society Chronicles*, IX, February
2003, pp. 6–14.

Warren, Harris Gaylord. "The Firebrand Affair: A Forgotten Incident
of the Mexican Revolution." *Louisiana Historical Quarterly*, XXI,
January 1938, pp. 203–12.

——. "The Origin of General Mina's Invasion of Mexico."
Southwestern Historical Quarterly, XLII, July 1938, pp. 1–20.

——. "Pensacola and the Filibusters, 1816–1817." *Louisiana Historical
Quarterly*, XXI, July 1928, pp. 807–22.

——. "The Southern Career of Don Juan Mariano Picornell." *Journal
of Southern History*, VIII, August 1942, pp. 311–33.

Wellborn, Alfred Toledano. "The Relations Between New Orleans and
Latin America, 1810–1824." *Louisiana Historical Quarterly*, XXII,
July 1939, pp. 710–94.

Whittington, G. P. "Dr. John Sibley of Natchitoches, 1757–1837."
Louisiana Historical Quarterly, X, October 1927, pp. 467–512.

Wilgus, A. Curtis. "Spanish American Patriot Activity Along the Gulf
Coast of the United States, 1811–1822." *Louisiana Historical
Quarterly*, VIII, April 1925, pp. 193–215.

Wilkinson, Norman, ed. "The Assaults on New Orleans, 1814–1815."
Louisiana History, III, Winter 1962, pp. 43–53.

Williams, W. D. "Louis Bringier and His Description of Arkansas in
1812." *Arkansas Historical Quarterly*, XLVIII, Summer 1989, pp.
101–36.

Winston, James E. "New Orleans and the Texas Revolution." *Louisiana Historical Quarterly*, X, July 1927, pp. 317–54.

THESES, DISSERTATIONS, AND LECTURES

Babb, Winston C. French Refugees from Saint Domingue to the Southern United States: 1791–1810. PhD dissertation, University of Virginia, Charlottesville, n.d.

Vogel, Robert. The Galveston Hurricane of 1818. Lecture before the Laffite Society, September 12, 2000.

Warren, Harris Gaylord. New Spain and the Filibusters, 1812–1821. PhD dissertation, Northwestern University, Chicago, 1937.

INDEX

UNITED STATES

Osage
Village
Arkansas R.
Fort Smith
Cadron
Crystal Hill
Hot Springs
Little Rock
Poteau R.
Caddo R.
Pine Bluff
Red R.
Ouachita R.
Arkansas Post
Natchez
Mobile
Pensacola
Canadian R.

Brazos R.
Trinity R.
Sabine R.
Grand Bayou
Natchitoches
Nacogdoches
Champ
d'Asile
Deweyville
slave barracks
New Orleans

COUSHATTA TRACE
San Antonio
de Béxar
ATASCOSITA TRACE
Point Bolivar
Galveston Bay
Galveston Island

Nueces R.
La Bahía
Matagorda Island

Rio Grande

MEXICO

Gulf of Mexico

Dry Tortugas

Straits of Fl

Havana
Regla

Soto la Marina

Yucatán Channel

Cabo San
Antonio

Isla de
Juven

Tampico

Dzilarn de Bravo
Yalahau
Cabo
Catoche
Isla
Mugeres

Telyas
Las Bocas
Isla Cancún

CAY

Sisal
Mérida
Cozumel
Island

Grand Caym

Nautla
Boquilla de Piedras
Veracruz
Campeche
YUCATÁN

Mexico City

Gulf of Honduras
ISLAS DE LA BAHÍA

La Ceiba

Triunfo de la Cruz

Ce

San

PACIFIC OCEAN

0   250 Miles

0   250 Kilometers

INTEMPERANCE

The Lost War Against Liquor

Larry Engelmann

THE FREE PRESS
A Division of Macmillan Publishing Co., Inc.
NEW YORK

Collier Macmillan Publishers
LONDON

The Free Press
A Division of Macmillan Publishing Co., Inc.
866 Third Avenue, New York, N. Y. 10022

Collier Macmillan Canada, Ltd.

Library of Congress Catalog Card Number: 79–7103

Printed in the United States of America

printing number

1 2 3 4 5 6 7 8 9 10

Library of Congress Cataloging in Publication Data

Engelmann, Larry.
    Intemperance, the lost war against liquor.

    Includes bibliographical references and index.
    1. Prohibition--Michigan. 2. Prohibition--United
States. I. Title.
HV5090.M5E53   363.4'1'09774   79-7103
ISBN 0-02-909520-4

For Margo, Marya, and Erika

"Now I lay me down to sleep—
My life and limb may Hoover keep,
And may no Coast Guard cutter shell
This little home I love so well.
May no dry agent, shooting wild,
Molest mine wife and infant child,
Or searching out some secret still,
Bombard my home to maim and kill.
When dawn succeeds the gleaming stars,
May we devoid of wounds and scars,
Give thanks we didn't fall before
The shots in Prohibition's War."

"The Patriot's Prayer"
Arthur Lippman

Contents

Preface

At midnight on January 16, 1920, millions of Americans said farewell to legalized liquor. Old John Barleycorn, destroyer of all that was good and just, had been laid low at last by the Eighteenth Amendment. "Good-bye John," evangelist Billy Sunday cried in an emotional prohibition paean. "You were God's worst enemy. You were hell's best friend. I hate you with a perfect hatred. I love to hate you." Sunday then predicted that "the reign of tears is over. The slums will soon be a memory. We will turn our prisons into factories and our jails into storehouses and corncribs. Men will walk upright now, women will smile and children will laugh. Hell will be forever for rent."

A new age was dawning. A New Era of clean living, felicitous family harmony, full employment, and prosperity was just around the corner. The long war of good men and women against the ravages of intoxicating liquor had been won. John Barleycorn was dead. Tomorrow morning there would be peace without whisky.

But on the next morning there was no peace. It would take much more than legislative majorities, constitutional amendments, and heady visions of a prohibition paradise on earth to destroy the traffic in alcoholic beverages. Laws alone would never quench mankind's age-old thirst for intoxicating liquor. The apostles of prohibition who stirred the masses with heady visions of a world redeemed from alcohol were guilty of a fundamental misconception. The Eighteenth Amendment, they assumed, was a final treaty of peace with the liquor traffic. They were wrong. The Eighteenth Amendment was, in fact, a declaration of war.

And so the war came. Prohibition's paradise was postponed. For thirteen years federal law-enforcement officials fought the illegal traffic in liquor. State and local reinforcements were called up to help. The fight was always frustrating and too often futile. The enemy used guerilla tactics, seldom came into the open to fight, blended easily into the general population, and when finally subdued turned to the United States Constitution for protection. His numbers were legion, his resources unlimited, his tactics imaginative, his friends influential, his cause intoxicating. Men of high resolve and determination were summoned to Washington to direct the federal forces. The enemy was pursued relentlessly on land and sea and in the air. There were an alarming number of casualties on both sides, and, as in all wars, innocent bystanders fell in the crossfire.

Few areas were untouched by the prohibition war. Anywhere liquor was manufactured, transported, or sold was, after all, a potential battlefield. But those directing the federal forces in the conflict had neither the wherewithal nor the desire to confront the enemy with equal energy wherever he appeared. There were obvious strategically important enemy enclaves. There were well-known established supply lines. There were only a few vital centers for the illegal liquor traffic. Saturate one such locality with enforcement officers, cut off supply lines, and root out the wrongdoers and the repercussions would be felt in every corner of the country. Win the war for prohibition on one key front and it might be won everywhere. The government's choice for a Waterloo for liquor was never in question: It was in Michigan.

Michigan had long been a key state in the fight for prohibition. In 1916, four years before national prohibition, Michigan's voters had endorsed a statewide dry measure by an overwhelming majority. The state's surprising conversion to prohibition had sent shock waves across the country. Prior to Michigan's prohibition referendum a solid bloc of northern industrial states had successfully withstood the rising dry winds that swept across the south and the west. In the heavily populated tier of states east of the Mississippi River and north of the Ohio River prohibition made no overwhelming advances. The solidity of those states with their masses of urbanites, Catholics, industrial workers, and foreign-born—all, it was assumed, staunchly opposed to statewide prohibition measures—was a source of comfort and assurance to the brewing and distilling industry.

Acknowledgments

I was aided and encouraged by several individuals and organizations during my work on this book. I would like here to acknowledge my gratitude to them.

A Young Humanist Award from the National Endowment for the Humanities provided me with the funds necessary for a year of research and writing free from the duties of teaching. A small grant from the American Philosophical Society helped defray some of the expenses of research.

The largest part of my research was done at the University of Michigan in the Michigan Historical Collections. Dr. Robert Warner and his staff at the Collections gave me countless helpful suggestions concerning the location and use of manuscript materials.

The Detroit *News* granted me access to both the library and clipping file of the newspaper and consequently saved me an enormous amount of time that would otherwise have been used in searching for materials.

In the Burton Historical Collection of the Detroit Public Library I was granted access to the Correspondence Files of the papers of the Detroit Citizens League. The staff in charge of the Collection also made several helpful suggestions and pointed out relevant materials for me.

Several scholars and friends aided me in my research and writing. I am deeply grateful to John Snetsinger, Mark Shwehn, Ron Mulder, David Katzman, Lee Stone, Donald Rothblatt, Clarke Chambers, John Pamperin, Gerald Wheeler, and Charles Burdick.

The earliest stages of research for this book were done under the direction of Dr. Sidney Fine of the University of Michigan. I was also one of the fortunate students at Michigan who had the privilege of attending Dr. Fine's seminars in American history. As a teacher, research director, and friend, Dr. Fine was always accessible, always helpful, and always compassionate. He remains my ideal as a scholar, a teacher, and a man of the very highest integrity.

Finally, my wife, Margo Morris, provided me with companionship, happiness, and peace of mind while I researched and wrote. Her intelligence, warmth, humor, and instinctive sense of life's proper priorities were a pleasant and solid source of inspiration.

But when Michigan's votes were counted in the fall of 1916 that indomitable bloc was broken. The wet wall had been breached. Now, as the entire nation turned toward prohibition, Michigan led the way.

Michigan's state prohibition law went into effect in the spring of 1918. In the next two years, before national prohibition, that state provided a laboratory for the dry law and presented the rest of the nation with a vivid picture of what could be expected when liquor was illegal. The best and the worst of the new dry world quickly materialized in Michigan. There was defiance of the law on a massive scale. The governor called on the state police to enforce prohibition and requested federal reserves. He declared a state of "limited martial law" in several counties. A shooting war broke out along the Ohio border and many men died for liquor. But with determined state officials and police officers working to enforce the law, the liquor traffic suffered significant interruption.

What difference did that interruption make in the daily lives of people in Michigan? Social researchers in the state were pleasantly surprised. They found that even prohibition's staunchest nonbelievers were soon singing its praises in Michigan. It was a revelation and a salvation. Everything promised by those who worked for the measure seemed to be coming true. Prisons went out of business. Productivity increased. Taxes decreased. There was a dramatic decline in domestic disharmony. There was less divorce and most families seemed happier. Men walked upright, women smiled, and children laughed. The rest of the nation could look forward to flush times if the experience of Michigan was typical. In Michigan Americans saw the future and it worked. Again, Michigan led the way.

By January 1920, those who sought to evade prohibition had two years of invaluable experience in Michigan. In that time they perfected methods of illegal manufacture, transportation, and retail of illegal alcoholic beverages. Canadian liquor was already smuggled across the Detroit River for cutting, distribution, and sale throughout the whole Midwest and beyond that the nation. The advantages of protective constitutional guarantees against unreasonable search and seizure were by now well known. And the integrity of prohibition enforcement agents had been tested and found wanting. Detroit had become an infamous and booming entrepôt for Canadian liquor imports. Planes, boats, trains, and trucks crossed the state bearing illegal intoxicating contraband for marketing in other cities and states. Various gangland syndicates dealing in liquor were forced to come hat in hand to Detroit importers in order to secure their desired booze.

Prohibition made the liquor business good business. The profits proved astronomical. Champions of the dry law appealed frantically to patriotism, religion, common sense, and bullets to stop the flow of illegal liquor. But they failed. Paradoxically, Michigan had the great good fortune in the 1920s to enjoy the best of two contradictory worlds: There were the social and economic advantages of the world of prohibition, as measured by the reports of social workers; and there were the equally enormous advantages of the income from illegal liquor, as measured by the ledgers of lawbreakers.

When the federal government sought a proving ground for prohibition enforcement, then, Michigan was selected. Beginning in early 1920 the state became the "beneficiary" of concentrated drive after drive by law enforcement officials. At one time in the late 1920s the federal government was expending as much as 27 percent of its enforcement budget in Michigan. The southeastern section of the state was regularly referred to in Washington as the "Detroit Front," and orders for men, guns, and ammunition for that front were filled with few questions asked.

Every section of the state became a battleground in the 1920s, a testing place for prohibition enforcement. Police and federal agents pursued their suspects on the highways and waterways of Michigan, under the water and under the streets, across the ice and in the air, through the forests and across the meticulously manicured lawns of the estates of the wealthy. For thirteen years the federal government warred against illegal liquor in Michigan in order to make a point, but by 1933 the point was obvious to all but a few. It wasn't worth the effort.

Michigan, by becoming the first state to ratify the Twenty-first Amendment repealing prohibition, again led the way in 1933. In Michigan intemperance in the use of alcoholic beverages had helped bring prohibition into existence. And intemperance in prohibition enforcement helped take prohibition out of existence. Intemperance, it was discovered, came in more than one odious and destructive form. That was the lesson revealed most clearly in Michigan. And that was the lesson all Americans learned in the 1920s.

Intemperance

Dry Dreams

Do you remember the old saloon days? Do you remember the boisterous crowds inside singing songs and doing things they wouldn't do when sober? Do you remember the old barflies, those broken down men of the gutter who earned their drinks by cleaning out the spittoons and lived off the sausage and crackers on the bar?
                                        Andrew Volstead, 1933

I

Billy Sunday was pleased. Night after night for eight weeks during 1916 he had cursed and castigated brewers, saloons, and alcoholic beverages. Staggering back and forth across the huge stage in a tabernacle constructed specially for his Detroit crusade, Sunday kept his audiences transfixed and hanging on ever word as he melodramatically detailed for them the devastations and sorrows wrought by the traffic in liquors. "If a man says to me, 'I have never been a drunkard,'" Sunday said with morbid solemnity, "I say, God be praised that your wife has never known what it is to see you stagger and vomit and puke and maunder and mutter and blaspheme in her presence; God be praised that your children have never known what it is to walk the streets and have the finger of scorn pointed at them; God be praised that they have never sat around a stove and shivered because they have no money to buy coal because you must drink; that they have never gone to bed hungry for something to eat that you might drink; that they have never known what it is to have the wolf of drink gnaw at your heart and pull at your vitals."

Night after night thousands of people spilled from the tabernacle filled to the brim with prohibition passion and convinced of the truth of Sunday's conclusion: "The saloon must be destroyed."

Sunday was much more than a colorful and effective purveyor of the promise of prohibition. He was an anti-saloon miracle worker. In city after city across the nation he had kindled the spark of anti-saloon sentiment in the hearts of millions of Americans into a roaring fire. Even in John Barleycorn's strongholds Sunday had strutted forth without hesitation to deliver a mortal blow to the sodden giant. And now Sunday's Michigan crusade was the last best hope of the state's drys in their campaign for prohibition. They prayed that Billy would put enough of the Holy Spirit into Michigan's voters to last at least until the election on November 7. And their prayers were answered.

Following Sunday's short foray to the University of Michigan in Ann Arbor, a poll of students in that city showed a large majority in favor of statewide prohibition. Another miracle! And before crying farewell to his Detroit disciples on November 5, Sunday predicted,

"The saloon is going to hell in God's good time." When he asked who was going to vote for prohibition, ten thousand men jumped to their feet with one mighty battle cry. On the next night, in Grand Rapids, standing on the pulpit waving an American flag above his head, Sunday heard seven thousand men roar that they would vote for prohibition the next day.

What was the real impact of the Sunday crusade? An analysis by the prohibitionist Detroit Citizens' League concluded that Billy had added at least ten thousand names to dry voters' rolls in Detroit. "Men previously dry in their conviction were sent forth to aggressive service," according to the study. "Men who were uncertain as to the effectiveness of prohibition as against regulation, are thoroughly convinced. Thousands of working men in manufacturing plants and drained from every section of the city, who for years have not darkened a church door, are inspired with religious fervor and fully convened to the gospel of prohibition."

Sunday sensed all of this himself, of course. And knowing what the result would be on election day, he was pleased. The saloon was doomed!

II

Billy Sunday's impact was substantial because his listeners already knew full well the nature of the enemy—the saloon. Sunday needed neither to fabricate nor exaggerate his descriptions of saloons: The unembellished truth was already bad enough.

The saloon was never just a place where alcoholic beverages were dispensed. It was rather, in the words of Jack London, "a terribly wonderful place where life was different." Another man remembered it as a "mysterious, maleficent, awesome institution, almost flamboyantly wicked." It was an institution created by mankind's need for companionship, leisure, vice, and intoxication—the terribly wonderful things of life.

In the five or six decades before 1920, the saloon was an almost ubiquitous structure on the American landscape. There were more saloons in American than churches, schools, hospitals, libraries, jails, theaters, or parks. More young men grew up to become saloonkeepers than ministers. Every town had its saloons, legal and illegal, open and concealed. They lined the main streets of towns and cities like starlings crowded along a clothesline. For every three hundred Americans in 1909 there was one licensed saloon.

Part of the appeal of the saloon was due to the social services it provided. In saloons files of newspapers in several languages were available along with cigars, mail boxes for regular patrons, free pencils, paper, and mail service for those wishing to send letters, and information on employment. Saloons provided a warm fire in the winter, public toilets and washrooms, card tables, bowling alleys, billiard tables, music, singing, dancing, constant conversation, charity and charge accounts, quiet corners for students, and special rooms for weddings, union meetings, or celebrations. No other institution provided such a variety of necessary services to the public.

The most fondly remembered service of the saloon, however, was the serving of a "free lunch" each day with the purchase of a single five-cent glass of beer. In some cities the saloons were actually required by law to provide a free lunch with drinks, since it was "bad for a man to drink on an empty stomach." Consequently, at noon each day in urban and rural areas alike, workingmen headed for the saloon for lunch. In some parts of the country it was unusual to see a workingman carrying a lunch pail. No need to. The saloon would provide.

Many men later claimed that they actually survived on the saloon free lunch, which allowed them to live quite comfortably on a minimal salary; this was especially true of cub newspaper reporters at the turn of the century. Yet the saloon free lunch was never intended to be a purely philanthropic endeavor. Its goal was to bring in money and provide a profit for the saloon proprietor. Salty food predominated in the saloons, and on top of an American diet that was already thirst provoking, this meant much more business for the bar. In large cities bouncers were hired to discourage anybody who ate more than his money's worth after the purchase of a beer. "In cheap joints where the waiters wore tattoos and could bend a horseshoe with their bare hands, it was dangerous for a ringer to sidle up to the crackers and cheese without doing his devoirs across the way first," Gerald Carson wrote. "Raiding" free lunch counters became a full-time preoccupation for the unemployed and derelicts, and saloons were forced to devise methods of protecting their lunch tables from light drinkers and the penniless. Bartenders became as adept at spotting freeloaders before 1920 as they were at spotting undercover police officers after. In some saloons tickets for the lunch tables were dispensed with each glass of beer, and commonly a "gentleman's agreement" was understood to mean that only a limited quantity of food could be consumed with a fixed quantity of drink. One reporter for the Detroit *Times* early in the century claimed that he had developed his "cold nerve" by staring down bartenders in Detroit's saloons while attempting to eat as much food as possible for a single drink.

The basic democratic spirit that permeated most saloons struck many observers. In the saloon all men with a nickel were equal in the eyes of the bartender and a man was assumed a good fellow until proven otherwise. For men clinging to the lower rungs of the economic ladder this was particularly important. Lack of affluence did not necessarily indicate lack of virtue, intelligence, or self-esteem in the saloon. A special Committee of Fifty that studied saloons at the turn of the century described the saloon as "the most democratic of institutions, appealing to the common humanity of man." "There is nothing to repel. Man is taken as he is and is given what he wants, be that good or bad. The only standard is demand." This unabashed egalitarian spirit was uncommon in churches where members of the respectable middle class often congratulated Jehovah for his wisdom in bestowing the good things of life on the deserving. "Ragged clothes were not a mark of shame" in the saloon as they were in the church. Consequently, the saloon in many areas became "the church of the poor." "It served as a rendezvous for the workers," historian Andrew Sinclair wrote, just as the churches served as a congregating place for the self-conscious middle class. And while religious services provided consolation and reassurance for the fortunate, "the brass rail provided an equal footing with the rest of humanity down at the heel." In *The Jungle*, Upton Sinclair asked, "Where was there a church in which an ill-smelling workingman, with vermin crawling upon his neck could sit without seeing people edge away and look annoyed? He had of course, his corner in a close though unheated room with a window opening upon a blank wall two feet away; and also he had the bare streets, with winter gales sweeping through them; besides this he had only the saloons. . . ."

For millions of Americans the saloon was a kind of club, a "poor man's club."

But the most important function of the saloon was that of dispensing legal opiates to the laborers and the impoverished inhabitants of the city slums and the failing farms, in pouring oil upon the disturbed waters of the American melting pot. The saloon even more than the church served a conservative function by raising the threshold of tolerance among the masses upon whose shoulders the burdens of the industrial revolution fell hardest. During the decades of rapid industrialization and institutional disintegration, when traditional ways of doing things, of working and living and relating to others were rapidly changing, the saloon served as a vital counterbalance to chaos, providing in its gregarious crowds a sympathetic surrogate for group therapy, secular blessed assurance that all would be well, a stable and dependable community like that in the old country in the old days. To anybody with a nickel was available a soothing balm for the brutalizing experiences of work and the humiliating conditions of life in the slums. This might well explain the lack of enthusiasm among industrialists and businessmen for the program of the prohibitionists prior to 1910. Not until the prohibition movement shed its thin-skinned morality and metamorphosed into an appealing economic program did industrialists provide much dry enthusiasm and support. Prior to 1910 industrialists, businessmen, and managers could almost totally disregard the psychological and physical limitations of the laboring masses because the saloon did not. Many of America's industrial empires were built by working good men to death at the rate of twelve or more hours a day, seven days a week. And as historian Sinclair observed, the pace of industry drove many workers to the saloons, "for the shortest way out of Pittsburgh or Birmingham was a bottle of booze." Novelist Upton Sinclair also saw the connection between the popularity of saloons and the increasing pace of American industry and wrote, "If we are the greatest nation the sun ever shone upon, it would seem to be mainly because we have been able to goad our wage earners to this pitch of frenzy; though there are a few other things that are great among us, including our drink bill, which is a billion and a quarter dollars a year and doubling itself every decade." In *The Jungle* Sinclair wrote that the workingmen of Packingtown headed directly for the saloons at the end of each working day. In the packinghouses work was a nightmare for most of the men. Yet for each worker "from all the unending horror of this there was a respite, a deliverance—he could drink! He could forget the pain, he could slip off the burden, he could see clearly again, he would be master of his brain, of his thoughts, of his will. His dead self would stir in him and he would find himself laughing and cracking jokes with his companions—he would be a man again, and master of himself."

Some sensitive labor leaders recognized that the illusion of well-being created by the saloon made the organization of workingmen more difficult. Unionization could make little headway among men whose spirits were dulled by the jovial crowds and glad hands and sentimental doggerel of the saloons. United Mine Workers president Tom Lewis saw that "there is no easier way possible to make the unfortunate man or oppressed worker content with his misfortune than a couple of glasses of beer." During a visit to Detroit, Eugene Debs made the same point and advised the workingmen of the city to buy books rather than beer.

The saloon served similarly as a safety valve for discontent in the urban slums. Frederic Howe saw that any resident of a slum tenement "with three, four or five persons in a room, with cooking and washing, childbirth, sickness, and outside boarders crowded into suffocating and sultry quarters, needs some escape. The saloon and the streets were the escapes the city had to offer." The saloon provided companionship and sympathy for the poor as well as an audience for one to air his feelings about the injustices of American society. It provided a captive crowd to which one might shout his denunciations, a receptacle for rhetorical onanism. And the neighborhoods of the slums were overcrowded with saloons. There was no way for the indigent to escape them—and for most, little desire to. In the slums and the working-class neighborhoods of the cities, one moved with the rhythms of the saloon. To live was to breathe the air of the saloon, to hear its laughter and its music and to walk the streets at night by the glow of its lights. In the neighborhoods of the poor, Upton Sinclair observed, "merely to walk down the street was to be put upon the rack. There was surely a saloon on every corner—perhaps on all four corners, and some in the middle of the block as well; and each stretched out a hand—each one had a personality of its own, allurements unlike any other. Going and coming before sunrise and after dark—there was warmth and a glow of light, and the stream of hot food, and perhaps music or a friendly face, and a word of good cheer."

During the first two decades of the twentieth century hundreds of thousands of Americans changed their attitude toward the saloon. Rather than the church of the poor, the saloon was considered more and more the devil's headquarters on earth. Critics showed quite convincingly that every social service provided by the saloon was balanced by a dozen disservices and every blessing of the saloon by a host of curses. Herbert Asbury concluded that "as an institution the saloon was a blight and a public stench." "It ignored the law," he wrote, "corrupted the police, the courts, and the politicians. It was a breeding place of crime and violence, and the hangouts of criminals and degenerates of every type. It was the backbone of prostitution; in every red light district of the country, the fixer, the big boss, was a saloonkeeper. Usually he also owned brothels, and his bartenders were pimps and panders."

Stories in the daily newspapers at the end of the nineteenth century included in column after column accounts of saloon-related violence and crime. The principal victims of the saloons, moreover, were not the strong and the sophisticated, but the young and the innocent and the poor. Jacob Riis protested that the saloon projected "a colossal shadow" and was an "omen of evil where it falls into the lives of the poor." The Chicago Vice Commission found in 1910 that the saloons of that city were the common procuring establishments for the city's prostitutes. On an average Saturday night in Chicago, according to the commission, more than eighty-six thousand people frequented the saloons; a majority of that crowd consisted of teenaged boys and girls. It is little wonder that reformers hoping to improve the quality of American life should begin with demands for better control of the saloon. Even close associates of the saloon business called for a cleanup. The secretary of the Wisconsin Brewers' Association described saloonkeepers as "bums and beggars not fit to associate with Yellow Dogs." The New York *Wine and Spirit Circular* said editorially that the saloon was "a nuisance and a loafing place for the idle and vicious." "Houses of drunken men, profanity, and obscenity of the vilest possible type," was the *Wholesalers and Retailers Review*'s description of the saloon.

The character of saloons in small towns and villages was no

better. "Americans who lived in the so-called provinces prior to prohibition," Herbert Asbury wrote, "will recall the sidewalks slippery with slops and stale beer, the unpleasant odors, the drunks lurching through swinging doors, the loafers sitting on the curb, and fighting and cursing inside the saloon. They will remember also that respectable women would go blocks out of their way to avoid such a place. . . ."

The anti-saloon campaign that began in the early twentieth century found its most enthusiastic converts in the countryside and focused on solving saloon problems there first. There were as many saloons per capita there at the turn of the century as there were in the cities, and the bright lights and free lunches, the drunkenness, violence, and political corruption connected with the saloon business were intimate acquaintances of rural Americans. On weekends, farmers abandoned the loneliness of the countryside for the optimism and gregariousness of the saloon crowd. Ole Rolvaag recorded the sentiments of settlers along the agricultural frontier when he wrote, "In the town it was cheerful and pleasant. There one could get a drink; there one could talk with people who spoke with enthusiasm and certainty about the future. This was the land of promise, they said. Sometimes one met these people in the saloons; and then it was more fascinating to listen to them than to any talk about the millenium." "In the sod house back there, somewhere along the horizon," Rolvaag wrote, "life got on your nerves at times. There sat a wife with a flock of starving children; she had grown very pale of late, and the mouths of the children were always open—always crying for food." In *Main Street* Sinclair Lewis described the distressing picture of farm wives waiting outside a Gopher Prairie saloon "on the seats of wagons, waiting for their husbands to become drunk and ready to start home." "Saturday was the best day," Brand Whitlock remembered of life in the village of Macochee, Ohio. "The farmers came to town then, and, tying their horses at the tail boards of their wagons in the market, they would drift in and out of the saloons all day long. Now and then you even got a chance to see one of them drunk, a funny sight which made us laugh uproariously."

But the sight that made children laugh uproariously made many grown men wonder. And, like Jack London, many of them concluded that the worst of the evils of the saloon was that saloons

created drinkers and drunks. Saloons were not merely the purveyors of alcoholic beverages, they were also the pushers. They
enticed men to drink. They encouraged men to get drunk. Doing
away with the saloon and its allied interests—brewers and
distillers—would not necessarily end drinking or drunkenness in
America. But it would certainly decrease those evils and enormously enhance the quality of life for the present and for future
generations.

Many good men dreamed of a world without saloons. But only a
few men had the energy, intelligence, and courage to work to make
those dry dreams come true.

III

In 1893, when the political and economic influence of the saloon
and liquor and beer interests were clearly on the rise, the editor of
the *Michigan Christian Advocate* complained that despite the large
number of anti-saloon people in Christian churches, their sentiments seldom made any difference at the polls on election day. He
saw how saloon interests were able to make their demands felt in
government. "Why," he asked, "if the saloons can, can't the
churches." He then pleaded for "some great magnetic leader, some
popular movement or some praying regiment to put in motion God's
reform host that sweeping floods and forest fires may be an illustra-
tion of their rapid and all consuming work." Just two years later his
prayer was answered with the formation of the Anti-Saloon League
of America. "It has not come . . . simply to build a little local
sentiment," a superintendent of the league promised, "or to secure
the passage of a few laws, or yet to vote the saloons from a few
hundred towns. These are mere incidents in its progress. It has
come to solve the liquor problem."

The Anti-Saloon League of America was formed in 1895 by a
group of men interested in a nonpartisan political approach to the
problems of the saloon and of the liquor traffic. The first superintendent of the league and its guiding light for the next decade was
Howard Hyde Russell of Ohio.

The basic grass-roots financial and electoral strength of the league lay with local church congregations. The organization, in fact, called itself "the federated church in action against the saloon." The league worked as a political pressure group, collecting funds from church congregations and independent donors and then spending those funds for anti-saloon publicity, campaigns for local-option prohibition, and for electing political candidates sympathetic to the anti-saloon cause.

The league languished in the 1890s, but then found dramatically fervent support in the first decade of the twentieth century, so that by 1908 only four states were without state league organizations. Bewteen 1905 and 1915 the number of churches cooperating with the league increased from 19,000 to 40,000.

The chief attorney for the league in Michigan explained the reasons for the organization's declaration of war on the saloon: The saloon must be destroyed, he said, "because it contributes so largely to human sorrow." "The men who are fighting through the Anti-Saloon League," he pointed out, "are not 'professional reformers' nor are they men looking for political preferment. They are businessmen, patriotic citizens who recognize the danger in the continuance of the saloon and have set themselves the task to wipe it out of existence. They will do this by a process of education and elimination. When they find a community weary of the saloon the League helps the people be rid of it. . . . We believe that the whole state and the whole nation may come to rid itself of the saloon."

The league was described equally well by its enemies. In 1907, *Bonforts Wine and Spirit Circular* warned that the league was not "a mob of long-haired fanatics, as some of the writers and speakers connected with our business have declared, but it is a strongly centralized organization, officered by men with unusual ability, financial capitalists with very long purses, subscribed to by hundreds of thousands of men, women and children who are solicited by their various churches, advised by well paid attorneys of great ability, and it is working with definite ideas to guide it in every state, in every county, in every precinct."

A league member put it in simpler terms: "The Anti-Saloon League," he said, "is prohibition with the people behind it and in this land of democracy and liberty the people can rule, ought to rule, and are going to rule."

The league began making particularly dramatic gains in its fight

against the saloon in Michigan in 1908. In the spring of that year
eleven counties in that state held local-option elections and eight
voted themselves dry. The next year twenty-one of twenty-seven
local-option elections in the state resulted in dry victories. Twenty-
one of thirty-six local-option elections in 1910 resulted in dry victories, as did eleven of eighteen in 1911 and fourteen of twenty-five
in 1912. In 1910 the league reported that thirty-six of Michigan's
eighty-three counties had gone dry, 750,000 people in the state lived
in saloonless areas, and more than seven thousand saloons and ten
breweries had been forced out of business due to local prohibition
victories.

How did the league so effectively arouse the state's voters? The
standard procedure involved the publication of "cold facts" concerning the social and economic changes that inevitably followed
the suppression of saloons in any community. The league's statistics
were indeed sobering. Temperance societies in the nineteenth century had promised Americans a good deal if their programs were
adopted: upward social mobility, personality development, marital
bliss, healthy children, economic prosperity, and life after death.
Although league publicists believed every one of the traditional
prohibition promises, they couched them in more moderate terms.
The league's vision of a saloonless America incorporated both in-
dustrialism and the free-enterprise system and placed cardinal emphasis upon the economic blessings of prohibition. The so-called
economic argument had long been a useful weapon in the dry
arsenal. Suddenly it was the prime weapon. Basically, the economic
argument contended that alcohol made the workingman, whether
laborer or manager, inefficient and careless. He was likely to make
more errors, and errors were likely to cost time, money, profits, and
lives. New "scientific" studies of the effect of alcohol upon the brain
and nervous system were presented as conclusive evidence that the
consumption of alcohol led to inefficiency in any endeavor. The
argument attracted more and more businessmen and industrialists
as studies indicated the differences in profits that could be made by
a single inefficient worker.

Historian James Timberlake concluded that in the early twentieth century, "economic developments were conspiring to give the
economic argument for temperance an additional boost." As the
pace of industry quickened and specialization, precision, and speed

were demanded on the assembly line, workers who drank, especially those who drank to excess, became more of a risk to employers and fellow workers alike. In later years, in an interview with *Ladies Home Journal*, Henry Ford recalled that "it was not necessary to ask a man whether or not he drank. He always stood out among his fellows who did not drink—he never did his work so well. If he did not show in his work that he had stopped drinking, we simply let him go. More often we did not have to enforce the non-drinking rule. It rather enforced itself; the men quickly found out that they could not drink and do their work, so they either stopped drinking or quit. Thus, gradually we gathered a force in which drinkers were very few and all were transients on the way out. It was because we had such a force that back in 1915 we were able to raise our minimum wage to five dollars a day." Ford concluded that "the tippler has no great interest in his work. We rarely have to discharge the drinkers. They discharge themselves."

The first scientific management studies also placed great importance upon sobriety and gave the industrial temperance movement an important boost. "The thing that temperance fanatics have been unable to accomplish, that a political party has failed to do, that even religion has not been able to bring about, is shortly to come to pass," one writer observed. "Efficiency demands it. Industry calls for it. This is a scientific generation, and we are willing to see things as they are." When workmen's compensation laws were passed, it became doubly important that employers avoid hiring drinkers because courts interpreted the new laws to mean that the employer was liable for employee injuries regardless of whether or not the employee had been drinking. All of this lent credibility to the Anti-Saloon League argument that the best worker was the non-drinking worker. Not because he was honest, frugal, religious, and deserving, as implied in the mid-nineteenth century prohibition propaganda, but because he was efficient, cautious, precise, and punctual.

Since workingmen drank mostly in saloons, employers sought to remove saloons as far as possible from their factory gates in order to discourage employees from patronizing them during lunch periods. Some employers sought even to prevent saloons from delivering buckets of beer for workers to the factory gates. The manager of a large manufacturing firm in Detroit observed that with the disappearance of saloons from the neighborhood of his plant there had been "a wonderful change in our workmen. They are of a higher class in every respect and more efficient." Hundreds of other employers agreed. The Ford Sociological Department visited workers' homes to find which men drank to excess. Heavy consumption of liquor by a Ford worker could bring either dismissal from the job or exemption from the minimum five-dollars-a-day wage. The REO Motor Car Company hired private detectives not only to report workers who drank but also those who smoked and voted against prohibition. A drinker's job in the automobile plants was never a secure one.

But small businessmen throughout the state and nation were not so sure that prohibition was good economics. Each saloon paid a high annual tax which went to the county and, it was popularly held, kept local tax rates down. Also, when farmers came to town they lingered to drink in the saloons. The more often they came to town the more likely they were to spend their money. When their wives accompanied them, the women shopped while the men sought companionship in the saloons. In the larger towns the saloons attracted people to the commercial heart of the city and aided businesses there. Remove the saloon and you remove a portion of the city and county tax base, an attraction to the commercial center of the city, and the lure to the farmer and his family to stay and spend money. Brewers and saloonkeepers insisted that for the small businessman, temperance was bad business, and the small businessman believed them. After all, efficiency was not critical to an enterprise without mass production lines or huge plants or more than a handful of employees. Before 1908, the businessmen of small towns opposed local prohibition because they feared destruction of the saloon would also put them out of business.

A major accomplishment of the Anti-Saloon League was the destruction of the belief that the destruction of commerce in liquors was bad business for small businessmen and merchants. In destroying that belief the league gained the votes of the moderate and cautious sections of the American middle class who soon made up the backbone of the prohibition army.

The league contended that once the saloon was gone the former drinker would spend his money in the same town and would apply money formerly spent on drink to other consumer goods such as furniture, a car, a house, clothing, or groceries. The league pointed out to tax-conscious commercial interests that with the increased sobriety that inevitably was produced by prohibition, there would be less crime, poverty, disease, and disorder and as a result less need for tax dollars to support prisons, police, hospitals, mental institutions, orphanages, and charitable organizations. What made these contentions of the league so convincing was not simply the intense conviction of league speakers, but the hard facts gathered year after year by league workers and by independent social researchers. Wherever prohibition was tried, the widely distributed statistics of the league indicated, it more than fulfilled the predictions of the opponents of the saloon.

Battle Creek, Michigan, provided an early laboratory for the anti-saloon side to demonstrate the effect that local prohibition had on a community. During the dry year of May 1911 to May 1912, 420 people were sent to jail in Battle Creek, an average of 35 each month, costing the city taxpayers $630 each month and $7,560 for the year. During the two previous wet years, 2,232 persons had been sent to the county jail, an average of 93 each month and costing the taxpayers more than $20,000 a year. The added expense to the county from crime alone during the wet year was $12,528, the league indicated. During that year the county received $7,000 in license fees from twenty-eight saloons, but arrests for drunk and disorderly behavior increased nearly 300 percent in Battle Creek with saloons open.

The *Anti-Saloon League Yearbook* for 1911 claimed that in dry Michigan counties in 1909 savings deposits had increased by $3,005,913 and that there had been only 1,351 arrests for drunkenness in dry counties and 2,832 arrests for drunkenness in wet counties. Since the state local-option law did not prevent an individual from importing liquor or beer for consumption in his own home, the statistics revealed to the league's satisfaction that men drank a lot less when the saloons were gone and that business in dry counties was not lost to merchants, saloonkeepers, and brewers in neighboring counties.

Although the brewers in non-prohibition counties insisted that the "evidence" advanced by the Anti-Saloon League was questionable, that there was just as much drinking in dry counties as in wet counties and that their sales records proved this, the annual report of the state attorney general in 1911 clearly supported the Anti-Saloon League contentions. The report showed that in 1910 there had been only 226 arrests for violations of local-option laws in thirty-two dry counties, but there had been 691 arrests for violation of the liquor law in thirty-seven wet counties. The report revealed that in twenty-eight of thirty-two dry counties in the state, drunkenness and crime had immediately decreased with the passing of the saloons, but in five wet counties these same factors had increased as soon as the saloon was reestablished. "It is the excess of drunkenness, disorder, and crime in the five wet counties of the state," the editor of the Detroit *Saturday Night* wrote, "that is forcing men to sit up and take notice. . . . Men cannot turn a deaf ear to such facts as these." Similar statistics inspired the same editor to report that in Michigan men were "conjuring up an inclination" to get rid of the saloon. Even if there was drinking in dry counties, the editor contended, "a little drinking is less dangerous than a lot more."

Reports from throughout the nation were published by the league and by independent journals and papers testifying to the benefits of saloon suppression. In Washington, for example, in the dry years between 1914 and 1916 it was claimed that there were dramatic beneficial changes, including a decline in arrests for public drunkenness and in the costs of law enforcement. Bank deposits increased and tax delinquencies decreased. Major C. B. Blethen, editor of the Seattle *Times*, was converted to the dry cause and explained his turnabout to the nation in *Colliers* magazine: "My paper fought its damndest against prohibition," he recalled. But after seeing the social and economic results of prohibition he concluded that the drier a city became the better it was for business. "It makes me sorry we did not have prohibition long ago," he concluded.

While the battle against the saloon was waged on the local and state level, leading men of science increasingly allied their findings with those of the league. Alcohol, it was discovered, was a depressant rather than a stimulant, as formerly believed. It depressed higher mental functions and muscular control. Physicians began prescribing less alcohol for medicinal purposes, and in their national meeting in 1914 American psychiatrists and neurologists declared alcohol to be a poison.

Along with the men of science, leading figures of the world of sport joined the growing prohibition chorus. Ty Cobb affirmed that baseball players who tippled were usually cut from the major leagues because drinking impaired their skills. Connie Mack attributed the success of his teams to total abstinence. And a close friend of heavyweight champion Jess Willard said that if Jess had it his way, "there would not be a drop of liquor made or sold in America. Even John L. Sullivan, the Boston Strong Boy, went teetotal as an example for others.

By 1911 forty counties in Michigan had adopted local prohibition and the state Woman's Christian Temperance Union declared itself in the fight for a statewide prohibition law. In 1913, immediately after the acceptance of an initiative and referendum law for the state, the Anti-Saloon League announced that it would seek to use the new laws to bring into existence a statewide prohibition law. The league and the WCTU joined forces in a drive to secure enough petitions in the fall of 1913 to place prohibition on the state ballot the next spring.

Fifty thousand signatures were required to place a proposal on the state ballot by initiative, and the drys expected to get two or three times that number. But prohibition sentiment was not as strong as the drys hoped and the necessary number of signatures was not gathered. Michigan began the year 1915 still under the local-option system. The drys, though, were working feverishly to put every saloon and brewery in the state out of business.

The Anti-Saloon League lobbyists had only modest proposals for the 1915 session of the state legislature. The strengthening of enforcement measures for dry counties and the passage of a bill making it illegal to sell liquor within five miles of any state institution would have satisfied the league's demands.

But the league did not speak for all men of good will concerned with the liquor traffic. Its cautious voice was that of the pragmatic and nonpartisan political wing of the anti-saloon movement. Outspoken independent prohibitionists and officers of the state WCTU decided, despite the league policy, to press the 1915 legislature for a statewide prohibition law. In a series of conferences league officials talked with the independents and agreed to support a moderate dry measure in the legislature. The bill, providing for the closing of saloons, distilleries, and breweries in the state but allowing for importation of liquor and beer for home consumption, was introduced in the state senate. While it was being debated, thirteen of fifteen Michigan counties voting on local option approved prohibition. And although the total number of counties voting dry was important, the prohibitionists were more impressed by their victories in counties like Calhoun, Kalamazoo, and Berrien, which contained ethnically diverse populations and sizable urban centers. "If sentiment is making against the saloon at this ratio," the Detroit *Saturday Night* commented, "it is quite easy to conceive the possibility that in another year and a half, dry sentiment will be in control of the state as a whole."

The legislative prohibition measure was killed in the legislature after its oppones tacked on several objectionable amendments intended to make the law "crackling dry" and too extreme for the mass of the public. It was an old and customary tactic of the friends of liquor in the legislature. This time, however, the Anti-Saloon League saw through this approach and had the measure killed. Now the league would go directly to the people with its case. Grant M. Hudson, superintendent of the Michigan Anti-Saloon League, announced a meeting of all state temperance organizations to convene in the late spring to lay plans for initiation by petition of a constitutional amendment providing for "acceptable" statewide prohibition. The drys were now in the advantageous position of going before the voters with the argument that it was useless to try to get a sane anti-saloon bill from the liquor-influenced legislature.

In April, officers of the league met with delegates from the State Grange, Gleaners, State Sunday School Association, Michigan Federation of Women's Clubs, WCTU, Prohibition party, and the State Federation of Christian Endeavor Societies to formulate final plans for the submission of the prohibition measure by initiative and referendum in the general election of 1916. Although the initiatory petitions for the amendment required only 50,000 signatures, the drys were determined to obtain at least 150,000.

Attorneys for the Anti-Saloon League drew up the proposed constitutional amendment for the state of Michigan in May. It provided that the "manufacture, sale, keeping for sale, giving away, bartering, or furnishing of any vinous, malt, brewed, fermented or intoxicating liquors, except for medicinal, mechanical, chemical, scientific or sacramental purposes, shall be after April 30th, 1918, prohibited in the state forever." The amendment mentioned neither the importation nor consumption of alcoholic beverages and so adhered to the anti-saloon tenor of the local-option campaigns.

Summer rallies marked the start of a massive statewide fight for prohibition. A popular front organization, the United Dry Federation, was formed under the leadership of the Anti-Saloon League to spearhead the fight for prohibition. A special steering committee, the Michigan Dry Campaign Committee, headed by Richard Scott, president of the Michigan Anti-Saloon League, was selected to formulate and direct policy. S. S. Kresge, the wealthy magnate of five and ten cent store fame, was named financial chairman of the committee.

Workers for the United Dry Federation gathered enough signatures by midsummer to assure the inclusion of the prohibition measure on the state ballot in November 1916.

Actually, the massive dry propaganda assault of 1916 was quite cautious in tone, and few new arguments or tactics were utilized. The dry leadership was aware that the United Dry Federation was essentially an alliance of convenience, encompassing many divergent views. Too radical a campaign would alienate not only moderate dry voters but also moderate organizations within the federation itself. Accordingly, leaders in the campaign studiously avoided messianic rhetoric and advertised their cause as the paradigm of reason. The principal argument in favor of prohibition thus remained the economic one, and aspects of the economic argument found their way into all other arguments for the dry amendment. Reverend Joseph A. Vance explained to the Detroit Pastors' Union that "the shifting of the prohibition question from moral to economic grounds is what makes the prospect so bright for a dry Michigan. The church has been thundering for years that drinking is wrong. It did no good. When you prove to a man that whiskey is poison to his body and keeps him poor, you set him to thinking." Vance also concluded that the Employers Liability Law had done a lot to awaken big business to prohibition as an economic necessity.

Richard Scott of the REO Company in Lansing agreed that the liability law and the threat to profits were central factors in bringing employers in Michigan to the dry side. The commission set up to administer workmen's compensation in Michigan had interpreted the law so that a worker injured while intoxicated was entitled to full compensation. The admission of a worker to a plant, the commission ruled, was evidence that the employers regarded him as fit to work. Scott concluded that the only way for business to cope with this decision was to weed out the drinkers from their plants and to seek protection against the saloon. Employers "overlooked at one time the fact that liquor slows up their workmen, blunts their brains, and destroys the nice balance between brain and muscles," Scott declared. "They see it now and they cannot afford to overlook it. Business competition has grown so keen that waste simply must be eliminated, and the product of the saloon is wasteful." Scott observed that the wets especially disliked economic arguments because they were unable to respond in similar terms. The liquor interests, he said, knew "that booze never speeded up a single business, that it never made a more efficient workman, and that it has never built prosperity for anyone except themselves."

That most criminals and degenerates were the products of saloons, the league insisted, was beyond dispute. That society paid for these in the form of tax-supported prisons and asylums, and that if saloons were rooted out then crime and insanity would be curtailed and the tax rate reduced, were equally beyond dispute. Statistics cited by the drys in 1916 concerning the human costs of drink were truly staggering. The Wayne County (Detroit) Dry Campaign Committee contended that 82 percent of all crime and 92 percent of all criminals were the products of drink, while 75 percent of all "idiots" were the offspring of intemperate parents. The warden of the Michigan State Prison in Jackson declared that 92 percent of the men confined there admitted to using liquor to some extent while 75 percent of them attributed their downfall directly to drink. Of the men who violated their paroles, he said, "approximately 75 percent do so by frequenting saloons." "Thirty-five and two-tenths percent of the men admitted to the Kalamazoo State Hospital during the last two years presented an alcoholic history," declared Dr. A. I. Noble, medical superintendent of that institution. March Johnson, superintendent of the Michigan Industrial Home for Girls, said that of the 1,276 inmates admitted in the ten years prior to 1915, the fathers of 595 and the mothers of 131 had been intemperate. And after interviewing several prisoners at the Marquette penitentiary, Governor

Woodbridge N. Ferris informed a reporter, "What they told me has more than ever added to my conviction that the liquor business, the saloon if you will, has so many more things against it than all that could be said in its behalf, that it should be put out of existence and kept out. . . . After allowing for all the excuses that men will make who have committed crimes, I am convinced that seven out of every ten men in the prisons of Michigan were started or assisted in the course that led to crime by liquor-drinking associations. I am not a crank on the subject, if I know myself, just a fully concerned observer."

During the last two days of October the dry cause was given another boost when officials of the dry campaign promised to relocate any individual employed by the liquor business who would be displaced from his job should prohibition pass. When Dr. Edward Cantrell asked his audience at the Woodward Avenue Presbyterian Church in Detroit how many of them would give up their jobs to men thrown out of work should prohibition carry, the response was that jobs would be found for 450 men; and the pastor of the church promised to find work for an additional 100 men. The Detroit representative of a large western railroad promised that he would hire 300 men if prohibition passed in Michigan, and a large Detroit employer promised to give work to 50 more men. Henry Ford dispensed further optimism to the drys when he announced at the end of October that his research staff had concluded that denatured alcohol was the automobile fuel of the future, that breweries could be transformed from making beer to making denatured alchohol if prohibition passed, and thus not a single brewery worker need fear losing his job because of prohibition.

No previous vote on the prohibition question attracted the attention of the nation like that in Michigan in 1916. By mid-1916 the drys were claiming that 51 percent of the American people lived in dry areas, while the wets insisted that just under 50 percent lived in such areas. Both sides agreed, however, that America was tottering on the dividing line between wet and dry. Michigan's voters would provide the keystone in the bridge to the future. Would that future be wet or dry? A prohibition victory in the state would give the drys an unquestioned advantage in the popular vote in the nation and would almost certainly signify the beginning of the end for the liquor traffic in the entire country.

Prior to 1916 the prohibition forces had been unable to win a single large manufacturing state east of the Mississippi River and north of the Ohio River. True, Maine had gone dry, but its economic base consisted mainly of farming and fishing, and its population was not much greater than that of the city of Saginaw, Michigan. The wets publicly conceded that the holding of this northeastern bloc of territory, with its large cities, wealth, and voting power, was their principal hope of preventing a swing to prohibition nationally. A prohibition victory in Michigan would make Detroit the first American city with a population greater than 250,000 to go dry. Opponents of prohibition feared the financial loss that would result if one of America's largest cities went dry, since they expected such a development to lead to an immediate curtailment of investments in the liquor industry.

IV

The worst fears of the wets came true on November 7, 1916. The drys in Michigan registered a resounding victory on that election day. There were 353,378 votes cast for the dry amendment and 284,754 against it. The drys carried eleven of the fifteen counties in the upper peninsula, winning over 60 percent of the vote in six of the counties inhabited predominantly by first and second generation immigrants and non-Protestants. In the lower peninsula the drys carried sixty-one counties and the wets seven. In no county did the prohibition amendment win less than 39 percent of the vote.

A most pleasant surprise for the drys was the response of their fifth column—that army of dry voters within the large cities where the wets predicted heavy majorities. The urban centers of Flint and Grand Rapids voted in favor of prohibition, though both had previously rejected prohibition in local-option elections. The Flint *Daily Journal* declared the dry victory in Flint the biggest surprise in the election. The city returned a dry majority of more than six hundred, and the rural townships of Genesee County provided an additional dry majority of over two thousand votes. In Kent County (Grand Rapids) the drys carried twenty-one of the twenty-two rural townships, and in Grand Rapids they won seven of the twelve city wards. In Ingham County the drys carried all seventeen of the rural townships and the city of Lansing as well. In previously soaking-wet Saginaw the drys lost the city by only 561 votes, but they managed to carry half the city wards. The drys fared slightly worse in the rural regions of Saginaw County, carrying only thirteen of the twenty-seven rural townships and losing the area by 326 votes more than they won in the city.

The real surprise, though, for wets and drys both came in Wayne County (Detroit). The wets had predicted that they would carry Wayne by 25,000 votes. They won it by the narrow margin of 1,368 votes.

Prohibition triumphed in Michigan in 1916 because of the votes of the moderates on the liquor issue. The majority for prohibition, it appears, was supplied by men who drank but who voted dry in the expectation that the state would be a much better place to live in without saloons, breweries, and distilleries. The leading scientists, medical authorities, athletes, law enforcement agencies, business and political leaders of the nation and the state had testified to the benefits of prohibition and so the voters responded optimistically. The vote endorsed the brighter future promised for so long by prohibitionists.

The main difficulties of the prohibition campaign appeared only after the November election and involved the maintenance of the moderate tone of the preceding campaign in the face of increasing pressures from both extreme prohibitionists and anti-prohibitionists. There was confusion concerning the specific meaning of the election. What was the real significance of the amendment? What did the voters really want or not want? What legislation was required now by the state legislature? Had the voters spoken out against the consumption of alcoholic beverages as well as against the saloon? Points that were taken for granted during the prohibition campaign suddenly seemed unclear. Several different points of view were expressed on the right of the citizens of Michigan to import liquor and beer for personal consumption. And as the last days of November passed the only point upon which most people could agree in the state was that prohibition remained as perplexing an issue after it had been approved as it had been before.

Four days after the election the editor of the Detroit *Saturday Night* sought to clarify one central point in the debate over prohibition by reminding elated drys that the people had *not* voted against the use of alcoholic beverages, and by closing the saloon and not outlawing either importation or consumption had voted simply against "a way of distribution." "It is for the future experience to say whether we should go further and prohibit the use of alcohol beverages altogether," he insisted. "There is a danger in Puritanism that refuses to recognize the limitation of the law just as there is a danger in a liberalism that knows no law. We hope to avoid both, but we feel impelled to restate our position now lest we be misunderstood in any subsequent discussion." The editor of the *Saturday Night* promised that if prohibition proved ineffective after a fair trial, "we will be among the first to urge its repeal or amendment."

The Anti-Saloon League maintained its moderate position following the election. League spokesmen repeated their belief that the people of the state had voted against the liquor traffic and not against liquor as a beverage. Superintendent Grant Hudson's office was beseiged by telegrams, however, urging the league to lobby in the state legislature for statutory prohibition effective as of May 1, 1917, rather than May 1, 1918, as provided by the amendment. Hudson refused to initiate such action. He also withstood the challenge from opponents of prohibition who hoped for the passage of a very strict prohibition measure by the legislature—so strict that a majority of the state's voters would quickly turn against prohibition. Wets in the legislature proposed the passage of a law prohibiting the importation or consumption of liquor or beer. The Detroit *Saturday Night* was led to observe of the anti-prohibitionists: "So strong is their habit of dictating to the public that they regard it as almost a personal affront for any man to be permitted to buy beer or liquor except in the specific manner they tell him to buy it. Their impertinence approaches humor in condemning as hypocrites everybody who is personally wet and politically dry, while contradictorily extolling as an archangel of intellect everybody who is personally dry and politically wet." Attorneys for the Michigan Bonding Company, as if to prove the point made by the *Saturday Night,* continued openly to plan for bone-dry legislation, ostensibly to "get" drinkers who had voted against the saloons and breweries.

For several weeks the state legislators debated the method by which liquor would be imported into Michigan for consumption in private residences under the provisions of the probhibition amendment. A system of regulation of such imports had to be set up. Both radical drys and wets, at the same time, and for their separate reasons, were outspoken in their demands for cutting off all imports and outlawing completely the consumption of alcoholic beverages. The Anti-Saloon League held the middle ground and supported moderate measures in providing a "wet menu" for the state's drinkers and for having dry provisions go into effect no sooner than May 1, 1918.

As it turned out, however, the course of prohibition in Michigan was not to be determined in Lansing. It was decided, rather in Washington, D.C. On February 16, 1917, a post office appropriation bill in the U.S. Senate was amended to provide for making Michigan and all other states with prohibition laws bone dry, no matter what the specific intentions of the state laws. The Reed-Randall Amendment proposed by Senator James Reed of Missouri, the leading anti-prohibitionist in the Senate, and co-sponsored by Charles Randall of California, the only member of the Prohibition party in Congress, had apparently not been expected to pass. It was offered merely with the intention of defeating a measure before the Senate that made illegal the sending of liquor advertisements in letters, circulars, or newspapers through the mail into dry states. The Anti-Saloon League opposed the measure as a "wet joker," inserted to embarrass the prohibitionists. The act provided that "whoever shall order, purchase, or cause intoxicating liquors, other than for scientific, sacramental, or mechanical purposes to be transported by interstate commerce into any state or territory, the laws of which state or territory prohibit the manufacture or sale therein of intoxicating liquor for beverage purposes, shall be punished" by a prison term or a heavy fine or both. The measure was clearly intended to punish moderates on the liquor question, to hurt the drinking drys. It succeeded in making moderate state prohibition laws, like that approved in Michigan, null and void. Prohibition suddenly became all or nothing at all, thanks to its enemies.

The act was passed by the Senate with most of the anti-liquor members voting in favor of it, and was then passed in the House by a vote of 321 to 72. The prohibitionists in Congress, despite the warnings of the Anti-Saloon League, took Reed's wet joker hook, line, and sinker. In their anti-liquor enthusiasm they seized the opportunity to push ahead in their fight for a dry tomorrow. It was a fateful and fatal burst of enthusiasm.

While the earlier Webb-Kenyon law had extended control over the interstate shipment of liquor to the states, the Reed-Randall Act removed that control from the states and the federal government took it back. The passage of the measure marked the end of Michigan's experiment with moderate prohibition. Suddenly, with both the friends and the enemies of prohibition joining forces in Congress, radical, uncompromising, bone-dry prohibition had won the day. Certainly, few voters in Michigan in 1916 wanted such a measure. But now they had no choice. The passage of the Reed-Randall Act marked the start of a long, confusing, frustrating, and humiliating period for Michigan and for the nation.

After the passage of the Reed-Randall Act, passage of a "real" prohibition statute in Michigan seemed the only alternative left to the state legislators. Following another month of discussion and debate the legislature passed three laws designed to establish and administer bone-dry prohibition in the state. The three measures were signed by Governor Albert Sleeper in late April.

The Damon law was a brief measure that prohibited the importation, or "bringing in," of liquor into Michigan. The legislators inserted the words "bringing in" in an effort to block the private transportation of liquor across Michigan's borders in handbags, wagons, automobiles, and any other type of private conveyance. The Damon law also provided for the suppression of illegal drinking establishments—"blind pigs"—under the state's "abatement of nuisance" law. Upon the furnishing of satisfactory proof, any citizen could cause the condemnation of property used in the sale of liquor. This meant that a building used as a blind pig might be closed for one year, and all the furnishings and fixtures used in connection with the sale of the liquor might be sold or destroyed. Owners could regain the use of their property only by furnishing a suitable bond.

The Wiley law provided the principal machinery to make the prohibition amendment effective in Michigan. Section I of the law acknowledged the primacy of the economic argument in bringing about prohibition and stated that the law was for the protection of (1) the economic welfare, (2) the health, (3) the peace, and (4) the morals of the people of the state. The law prohibited the manufacture and sale of liquor except for medicinal, mechanical, scientific, chemical, or sacramental purposes, outlined the method by which druggists might buy and sell liquor for exempted purposes, and limited the quantity and decided the manner in which liquor could be stored. It also prohibited the sale of medicinal preparations that contained more alcohol than was necessary for the preservation of the drugs or for holding them in solution. It prohibited the sale of patent medicines capable of being used as substitutes for liquor and forbade all liquor advertising or the soliciting of orders for liquor in Michigan. Clubs were forbidden to keep intoxicating liquors in storage. Private homes were exempted from the search and seizure provisions of the law, but places suspected of harboring blind pigs were not. In order to secure a search warrant, laws officers were to provide good reasons for their belief that a house was being used as a place to sell liquor. The destruction or pouring out of any liquid while a search was being made, according to the Wiley law, was to be considered evidence of guilt. All police and peace officers of the state were charged with enforcing the law.

The Lewis law, the third of the three prohibition statutes, made the State Dairy and Food Department a supervisory body. Enforcement of the prohibition law was primarily vested in the hands of local law officers, but the Dairy and Food Department could employ special inspectors to investigate police officials, aid in the enforcement of the law, or supervise prosecutions. The name of the department was changed to the Food and Drug Department.

Following the passage of these measures by the state legislature, law enforcement agencies throughout the state geared up for the new liquorless age. Enforcement was to be carried out concurrently by local law enforcement officials, the Michigan State Police, and agents of the State Food and Drug Department. In Wayne County, where the problem of enforcement was expected to be both crucial and difficult, enforcement was in the hands of the municipal police department, the sheriff's department, and the prosecuting attorney's office.

According to State Food and Drug Commissioner Fred L. Woodworth, there were enough members of the state police force to guard every highway to the south and west of Detroit and thus prevent the importation of liquor into the city. Additional police officers could be stationed on the Michigan-Ohio border in Monroe County to discourage smuggling from still wet Ohio. It was expected that the main supply of illegal liquor would come from Ohio, since Indiana, the other state bordering southern Michigan, passed its own statutory prohibition law early in 1917. Ontario, the Canadian province just across the Detroit River, had gone dry in September 1916 as a wartime emergency measure.

Detroit Police Commissioner James Couzens had little doubt about the ability of his department to enforce the law in Detroit. He announced in 1918 that his men would go after violators of the liquor laws in a vigorous fashion. Drunks would be required to inform on bootleggers, a practice, Couzens predicted, that would be of considerable aid to his men in fighting the liquor traffic. Couzens indicated that he thought prohibition would be "a great benefit" to Detroit. "This being the largest city in the world to try prohibition," he declared, "I believe one man's guess is as good as another's on the effect it should have on crime. It ought to reduce accidents and vice materially, particularly the latter, if the courts will punish persons who sell liquor. And it cannot help but have a beneficial effect on all who then will cut out the use of liquor." Couzens was opposed to the legalization of wine and beer because he believed such a measure would complicate law enforcement. "The reopening of places selling wine and beer would make it very difficult to get evidence for selling anything else," he pointed out, "because men do get intoxicated on wine and beer. It would be very hard to tell when whiskey was used."

As the May 1, 1918, deadline for prohibition approached, there were indications that law enforcement officials throughout the state would be pressured into extreme positions by both the wets and drys. The radical drys insisted that drinkers be given no quarter and that Michigan be made so dry that "folks will crackle when they walk." The wets, on the other hand, wanted Michigan so dry that "people's throats would be parched." The drys thought that unless prohibition were strictly enforced, there would be criticism of the prohibition regime and people would conclude that a controlled liquor traffic was better than an illegal uncontrolled one. The wets, on the other hand, still believed that rigid enforcement would produce a reaction against prohibition and force repeal of the dry amendment. The people of the state, meanwhile, looked forward with optimism and anxiety to the new dry age they were about to enter.

One week before the dry law would close their doors, there were still nearly 1,250 saloons operating in Detroit. Since the final legal wet day was a Tuesday, newspapers expected a large celebration to take place on the last wet Saturday night, April 27. The night, however, produced more sightseers than sights in Detroit. Police Commissioner Couzens prepared for a final bacchanalia and sent numerous police officers into downtown Detroit where the men stood in pairs with clubs under their folded arms. Drunks, however, were not to be seen on the streets and the police had little to do. Liquor stores did much more business than the saloons on Saturday night. These establishments were jammed full and salesmen called out "next" to customers much as barbers did. Few people wanted to drink downtown that night. They all seemed intent on carrying home their booze still in the bottle.

"I believe that a great number of people unconsciously look upon prohibition as a war measure," said the owner of one old established Woodward Avenue bar. "They are taking the matter as a bit of cooperation with the government in its conservation plans. It is not good form to drink and eat lavishly anymore. The food cafe men tell me that this is their belief also. If this were not the case, I am sure that the final days of liquor in Detroit would see wild revelry. Could you have imagined the Detroit of early 1916 or 1917 putting the glass from its lips without a bacchanalian orgy?" The *News* agreed with this judgement and attributed Detroit's restraint to "a sense of national duty."

During Michigan's last wet weekend, reports poured in from all parts of the state that the 3,068 saloons still in operation were closing before the arrival of the last legal wet night. "The better saloon elements of the state" were closing early, it was suggested, in order to avoid possible riots on Monday and Tuesday nights. In the end, though, there were no riots. There were no monster celebrations either. It rained all night in Detroit on Tuesday and this dampened the spirits of those who ventured downtown for a final tipple. At a party in the Hotel Pontchartrain to bid farewell to Demon Rum, "the whole atmosphere reminded one of somebody dying in the next flat," a reporter observed. It was the same wherever one ventured in the rain and the cold. There was little cheer inside or out. In several saloons the supplies of liquor ran out early in the evening. Calls to brewers for more beer brought no response. The family liquor stores did a "night before Christmas in a toy shop" business, but they were the only shops enjoying a business boom. The Detroit Athletic Club was deserted. There was a little draft beer left at the club, but "no one had the courage to withstand the echoes of his footsteps in the grill or dining room." If there was one bright spot in the city it was at the Old Heidelberg. There a large crowd of people forgot themselves in celebration. It was the same crowd seen in Detroit's beer gardens in the summer. In the precinct headquarters of the police department, patrolmen played cards and speculated on where they would eat their lunches after May 1. The police superintendent detailed a few mounted men for the night patrol downtown, but shortly after midnight they were called off duty. Demon Rum was not even given a police escort out of Detroit.

On May 1, the Detroit *News* published a letter from William Allen White, editor of the Emporia (Kansas) *Gazette*, advising Detroiters to put their wet past out of mind because the sooner the dry order became habitual and normal the better. Detroit should not become too proud and look on itself as a pioneer, though, White warned. "Just fill the saloon buildings up with stores and forget that they contained anything else. That's the way we did it in Kansas." "Prohibition isn't a moral question anymore," he reminded his readers. "It's an economic question. That's the real reason for it. When the laboring man works eight hours and spends none of his time at the saloon, he will save up more money and better his economic status. This will lift more and more men from the laboring class to the economic middle class," White predicted. "And the more they attain the more they will want, which is just the condition that ought to prevail. That's why prohibition is a good thing. It's really a part of the inevitable and approaching movement to get for the worker a greater share of the wealth he produces. When the workingman spends his evenings at home or at the library, and has good books and a gramophone and an automobile, society will be better off."

A sobered Ring Lardner was unconvinced. "Goodbye forever to my old friend booze," he wrote. "Dog-gone, I've got the prohibition blues."

2

The Cheerful Spring

Don't Shoot, I'm Not a Bootlegger.
Automobile window sticker popular in the 1920s

I

Prohibition became the law in Michigan on May 1, 1918. That some people would try to evade the new law and postpone the prohibition paradise was not unexpected. There would be a short and perhaps painful period of readjustment as the state moved from wet to dry, to be sure. After nearly thirty years of local-option experience everyone realized that the appetite for drink did not miraculously disappear with the saloons. State legislators had taken this into account and provided for individuals legally to store alcoholic beverages in their homes and consume them there in protected privacy. Many people lacked the financial resources necessary to lay in a good supply of drink for the approaching drought and it was expected that some of them would attempt to import liquor illegally. Surely, many residents of Detroit and other southern Michigan communities would find a short jaunt into nearby wet Ohio to secure booze an irresistible temptation. It was assumed, however, that the offenders would be caught and punished, that eventually the risks would outweigh the advantages of breaking the prohibition law, that bootlegging and smuggling would cease and drinking would gradually come to an end. A whole generation of Americans would then grow up to learn of the evils of beer and whisky and saloons not as their elders had learned, from personal experience, but from history books. Such was the future envisioned by the most ardent prohibitionists in 1918.

Between 1918 and 1920 the entire nation watched a preview of the prohibition future as it manifested itself in Michigan. What they saw was both encouraging and disconcerting. Tens of thousands of citizens dabbled in teetotalism for the first time and found the experience both privately and publicly enriching. But tens of thousands of citizens also dabbled in criminal behavior for the first time and found the experience equally enriching. Prohibition appeared to be the rare kind of statute that benefited both those who obeyed it and those who disobeyed it. The result was a confusing combination of beneficial social transformation accompanied by massive resistance to the new law.

In response to the timely question of whether or not prohibition worked, the resounding response from Michigan's first two years under the dry law was both yes and no. There was still plenty of potable liquor around, and crowds of citizens refused to climb aboard the water wagon. Yet social changes attributed to the dry law led many previous skeptics to embrace prohibition. And given a second chance to express their feelings on prohibition, Michigan's voters gave it an even greater majority in 1919 than they did in 1916.

II

At first the attempts to evade prohibition and secure alcoholic beverages were quite unimaginative. The law allowed doctors to prescribe liquor as a medicine. Any physician might provide a thirsty patient with the prescription necessary to purchase good liquor from a local druggist. Although many liquor prescriptions written after May 1, 1919, were doubtless given in good faith, many more were clearly fraudulent and had nothing at all to do with illness. Hundreds of prescriptions were used to purchase liquor as a "bathing solution," and many more appeared in Detroit prescribing whisky as a stimulant. One prescription turned over to Detroit's prosecuting attorney instructed the patient to "take three ounces every hour for stimulant until stimulated."

Liquor might also quite easily be mailed or shipped to a residence from outside the state in mislabeled containers. When such contraband was discovered and the consigned receiver was requested to appear at the post or shipping office to identify and claim his package, he invariably denied knowledge of its contents in order to escape prosecution. In Detroit alone police seized over twenty-five carloads of liquor that had been shipped illegally into the state in cartons mislabeled as cement, onions, eggs, tar, furniture, violin cases, red peppers, lime, oil, paint, and varnish. This type of smuggling was especially risky, however, since it violated federal law and those apprehended for the offense were usually given jail sentences. As a result, after only a few weeks large-scale amateur bootlegging of this kind largely disappeared. It was replaced by a more direct type of smuggling. In the summer of 1918 Michigan residents rediscovered wet Ohio and short jaunts across the border became more and more popular.

The distance from Detroit to Toledo is only sixty miles. In 1918 there was hourly interurban trolley service between the two cities, numerous passenger trains, and excellent roads, the best being U.S. 25, the Dixie Highway, known popularly as "Avenue de Booze" and "Rummers' Runway." Monroe, Michigan, a city of twelve thousand inhabitants in 1919, lies twenty miles north of Toledo and forty miles south of Detroit. The roads—trolley, railway, and highway— converged in Monroe. It became the center of a rapidly expanding liquor import network. Known as the flower capital of southern Michigan, Monroe was also a stop for Ohio residents who crossed the border to be married quickly and cheaply by a deputy county clerk. After May 1, 1918, travelers passing through Monroe were unconcerned with its flowers or its weddings.

In the early stage of interstate smuggling, law evaders attempted to bring their booze back from Ohio concealed in their baggage or clothing. Because smuggling of this kind was simple and inexpensive, hundreds of otherwise law-abiding citizens from the Detroit area indulged in the practice. What could be simpler, after all, than taking a trolley to Toledo, purchasing a bottle or two or even a case of booze, concealing it in a coat pocket or suitcase, and then returning to Detroit? A bulging pocket or suitcase filled with clanking bottles betrayed hundreds of thirsty travelers to agents of the State Food and Drug Department in Monroe, where checkpoints were established to prevent smuggling. Gradually, however, smugglers showed more imagination and dry agents were forced to work harder. Hot-water bottles filled with whisky were tied to the body or concealed in coat linings. Hollow rubber belts were filled with booze. Liquor was wrapped in baby blankets and coddled by innocent-looking women wishing to evade detection. It was placed inside dolls and in baby diapers. False rubber breasts filled with booze were discovered by one curious border agent. Those who could afford automobiles hid booze under car seats or in the tonneaus. One Detroit mechanic made a small fortune by altering gasoline tanks so that half of the tank could carry gasoline and half could be filled with booze. These and other types of "suitcase smugglers" were classified officially by the police as "casuals" because they were persons endeavoring to smuggle comparatively small quantities of booze for themselves or for their friends.

Droves of casuals were arrested by officers of the Food and Drug Department and by county law officials in Monroe during the summer of 1918. The epidemic of arrests and hearings taxed the judicial and penal facilities of the previously sedate "flower city" but enriched city and county officials. Smugglers and drunks taken from trolleys, trains, and cars were placed in the Monroe County jail and within two months three hundred men were imprisoned in the building constructed to hold only twelve inmates. No record was kept of the amount of money collected by the county sheriff. His job became one of the most sought after in the state in the election of 1918.

Local officials in Monroe objected to the criticism by Detroit newspapers that most of their arrests resulted from illegal searches and seizures. State Food and Drug Commissioner Fred L. Woodworth explained in defense of Monroe officials that citizens were arrested on trolleys and trains for intoxication, were then searched in the county jail, and if liquor was found on them, were charged with possession. Everyone charged with possession of liquor in Monroe, he said, had pleaded guilty. Attorney General Alex Groesbeck ruled that the practice did not involve an illegal search and seizure. Monroe County Prosecutor William Haas also insisted that there was no "promiscuous" search of passengers in Monroe. "Violations are so many that we are not even getting half of the men who are bringing in liquor from Ohio to Michigan via Monroe," Haas complained. "We have honestly tried not to hurt anyone. We are simply trying to enforce the law to the best of our ability and carrying out orders issued by Governor Sleeper."

The Monroe County sheriff employed "spotters" in Toledo to watch the purchase of liquor in saloons and then note which customers boarded the interurban trolleys with suitcases. Conductors on the trolleys also cooperated with law officers in Monroe. In some instances conductors were requested by police officials to assist certain passengers with their luggage to see if it was heavy and if bottles clanked together inside. On the trolleys, many overanxious passengers gave themselves away by taking out bottles and drinking, apparently believing that if they could get all of the evidence inside themselves before they crossed the state line they would be safe. Prosecutor Haas complained that foreigners were the worst violators. Few "Americans" were apprehended, he observed, a misleading and incorrect assertion that would be used again and again to explain resistance to prohibition during the next decade.

By mid-June the illegal liquor traffic between Ohio and Michigan, especially in the Monroe area, had become so heavy that local officials and agents of the Food and Drug Department were unable to cope with it effectively. Following an appeal from Prosecutor Haas, the county sheriff, the Monroe County Board of Supervisors, and several local civic groups, Governor Albert Sleeper ordered Col. Roy Vandercook and twenty-four members of his force of state troopers into Monroe County to assist in law enforcement.

Prior to their assignment in Monroe, Vandercook and his men had policed railway centers, guarded chemical plants, and watched warehouses and stockyards in order to defend them against German espionage. Anxious for action, the state troopers were in no mood to play games of hide-and-seek with violators of the prohibition law. The arrival of Vandercook and his men in Monroe signified an escalation in the state's war against liquor.

The first guns were fired in Michigan's prohibition war in July 1918. An agent of the State Food and Drug Department chased a suspect down the main street of Monroe, firing several shots directly at him before the man stopped. State troopers fired carelessly at cars ignoring their roadblocks. Following the demand by a former Lenawee County circuit court judge for the arrest of two state troopers for shooting at him, Col. Vandercook announced indignantly that his men were justified in what they had done because they were under orders to stop cars in any way that they could and to make special efforts to damage automobiles whose drivers disregarded demands to halt. State Food and Drug Commissioner Woodworth stated his determination to support Vandercook in that policy. He insisted furthermore that the Michigan prohibition law would become a joke if state troopers were deprived of their right to stop and search automobiles.

Protests were lodged in Detroit against the Wayne County prosecutor because his inspectors stopped and searched passengers aboard trains at the Michigan Central Station. The Michigan Central was the first railroad to complain about efforts to keep liquor out of the city. Attorneys for the railroad received complaints daily from passengers who threatened lawsuits because of the inconvenience and lost time resulting from the searches. The Pere Marquette and Wabash railroads, however, invited police officials to search their passengers whenever it was necessary.

By the end of 1918 the state police had seized $689,160 worth of liquor on the Ohio border and had arrested 1,102 persons for violation of the prohibition laws. Woodworth announced that the liquor law was no harder to enforce than any other law. "The people had to be taught first," he moralized. "For many people in different parts of the state living in dry territory was a new experience. But they had to learn how to adjust themselves. Now the great bulk of people are with the department in its efforts to enforce dry legislation. We have the support of 99 percent of the people. Violations now come from professional bootleggers, 80 percent of whom are aliens of the lowest type. These folks constitute about the only problem that is left."

Woodworth's optimistic conclusions and the impressive statistics recorded by the state police concealed the fact that by late 1918 professional "syndicates" composed not of "aliens of the lowest type" but of native-born American citizens, were taking over the illicit liquor traffic in southern Michigan and transforming it into a profitable big business. In the fall of 1918 four brothers of notorious national reputation, the Billingsleys, were arrested for bringing large quantities of liquor into Michigan. Three of the four brothers had arrived in Detroit in November 1917 and had proceeded to lay the groundwork for their bootlegging business. In Seattle, Washington, the Billingsleys had operated a drugstore as a front for a very profitable bootlegging operation. From petty bootlegging in Seattle they moved into bootlegging on a large scale. Their operation mushroomed until it competed directly with that of another large bootlegger in the city; the inevitable result was hijacking, violence, and death.

The Billingsleys hoped to establish their business in Michigan and then to effect a nationwide illegal booze syndicate. As a front to their transactions in the state they opened a grocery store in Detroit and deposited several thousand dollars in a savings account at the Central Savings Bank. The brothers were soon operating an entire fleet of automobiles to import liquor from Ohio. Before long they were selling 100 cases of liquor a day in Detroit. Sherman Billingsley became known as "the man with the black hearse," because of the closely covered black truck in which he delivered whisky to Detroit's blind pigs. When officials of the state police along the border threatened the Billingsley business, the brothers resorted to bribery in order to keep their cars rolling. Two state police officers accepted twenty-five dollars each for every Billingsley car that passed safely through the state police blockade.

The luck of the Billingsleys, however, did not last. First, their operations became so large along the Ohio border and they purchased liquor in such great quantities that liquor dealers in Toledo, fearing the exhaustion of their own supply, began to ration booze sales to large-scale bootleggers like the Billingsleys. Second, their operation practically monopolized liquor smuggling for a short time by freezing out numerous independent operators. The disgruntled smugglers who were forced out of business began speaking freely to the police about the Billingsley enterprise. Third, Logan Billingsley's career was unexpectedly cut short in the early fall of 1918 when he was arrested in Toledo and extradited to Seattle, where a warrant was held for his arrest. And finally, two of the principal drivers for the Billingsley ring were captured by state troopers. Information leading to their arrest and the arrest of the other Billingsleys was supplied by a twenty-two-year-old agent for the State Food and Drug Department who had succeeded in infiltrating the Billingsley syndicate and passing himself off as an experienced driver. At the time of their arraignment in Detroit in September 1918 the Billingsleys were reputedly the largest whisky runners in the United States.

In late 1918 the chief investigator for the State Food and Drug Department was dismissed along with three of his aides because "there is more booze coming into Detroit now than when it was wet." The Detroit police seemed as ineffective as the State Food and Drug agents in dealing with liquor coming into the city. Members of the old underworld were rapidly taking up bootlegging. They were wearing diamond rings and fine clothes and driving expensive new automobiles. Even when they were arrested they paid only a small fine for their transgression before returning to business. There were rumors of payoffs to city and state officials in exchange for "protection." New hope for the enforcement of prohibition in the Detroit area was aroused when John Downey was appointed a member of the county prosecutor's staff and charged with the special responsibility of detecting violations of the liquor law. Downey promised to "wipe out" the sale of liquor in Wayne County and declared that there would be no more "pussy footing or fear that the identity of inspectors is going to be known." He promised to arrest both large and small bootleggers. His promises and threats, however, frightened very few people because already by 1919 promises to enforce the letter of the prohibition law were considered to be little more than campaign rhetoric.

Throughout January 1919, the liquor traffic in Monroe County continued to attract a good deal of attention in the press. State troopers and Food and Drug Department agents came under increasing pressure from both state officials and the state press to stop liquor law violations in the area. The success of big-time bootleggers, along with increasing pressure from state officials, antagonized many enforcement officers in Monroe County. The cold winter nights along the Ohio border were punctuated more frequently now by gunfire. On January 23, state troopers ordered a car to halt on the highway between Ann Arbor and Detroit. The driver, fearing highwaymen, did not obey the command. The troopers opened fire, hitting one of the passengers in the neck. The troopers subsequently failed to find any liquor in the car, apologized to the passengers and offered to drive them to a hospital. Such incidents aroused individuals concerned with violation of civil liberties by law enforcement officers. Governor Sleeper, however, jumped to the defense of the state troopers and took personal responsibility for their actions in southern Michigan. A group of Lansing lawyers, nevertheless, protested that there was no state law sanctioning the use of guns to enforce the liquor law and a member of the attorney general's staff agreed that a police officer had no right to shoot a person trying to escape after committing a misdemeanor. A policeman could shoot, according to the official, only when he suspected that the person attempting to evade arrest had committed a felony. The same official declared that shooting at an automobile for the purpose of destroying the tires was willful destruction of property, and if life were harmed as a result there were grounds for a suit against the offender.

The lawyers also contended that state troopers had no right to search cars, basing this assertion upon the provision of the state constitution which stated that "the person, houses, papers and

possessions of every person shall be secure from unreasonable
searches and seizures. No warrant to search any place or to seize
anything shall be issued without describing them, or without probable cause supported by oath or affirmation." Even the right of the
governor to send state troopers into the border counties for the
purpose of enforcing the prohibition law was called into question.
Governor Sleeper had justified his action by noting that the sheriff
and prosecuting attorney and others had appealed to him on the
ground that the local situation was beyond their control. Sleeper had
thereupon issued a proclamation stating that the border counties
were under "limited martial law." A leading state attorney, however, declared that there was no such thing as "limited martial law"
and that the "Constitution recognizes no martial law in the state, let
alone 'limited martial law.' It says the military shall at all times be in
strict subordination to the civil power." If the governor could enforce limited martial law, the attorney said, he could not do so with
state troopers. Since the federal Constitution declared that "no
state shall without consent of Congress maintain a standing army,"
the very existence of the state troops, according to the attorney, was
of doubtful constitutionality.

While the debate went on in Lansing, so did the conflict in
Monroe County. The Michigan winter, with its snow and freezing
sleet and its long, dark, and sometimes icy nights, did nothing to
increase the patience of state troopers huddling in sentry boxes
beside U.S. 25, south of Monroe. They would step from their tiny
unheated shelters to challenge approaching cars only to have them
disappear in a burst of speed up the highway after the spinning tires
had peppered the troopers with freezing snow. The troopers turned
to more imaginative means of detaining or destroying their prey. In
early February they decided to use a telephone pole as a concealed
barrier across the road. Dividing themselves into two squads, the
first group was to challenge approaching automobiles. If the cars
stopped, they were to be searched. If they sped on, the first unit was
to signal the second, which would then lower the telephone pole
across the highway. The first time the tactic was used the car
involved struck the telephone pole at a speed of seventy miles an
hour, shot thirty feet into the air, and hurled its occupants like rag
dolls into the night sky. Bottles exploded against bottles in the air
and crashed onto the icy highway. The car plunged to the road

again, front down and rear wheels still spinning, skidded forward fifty feet, and then rolled into a ditch. Miraculously, none of the three passengers was killed, but all were seriously injured. Col. Vandercook was pleased with the imagination his men had displayed and tagged the new system "a pretty effective little rum stopper." Higher officials, who had previously sanctioned the shooting out of tires on automobiles, thought the telephone pole caper too dangerous, however, and the word came down from Lansing to cease using the tactic.

Smugglers themselves began using methods as imaginative as those employed by the state troopers. At the same time the troopers were lowering their telephone pole across the highway to demolish one small group of bootleggers, a precarious confrontation developed at the Michigan Central Railroad depot in Monroe between another group of state troopers and bootleggers. When the troopers stopped the train to search the passengers for liquor, a large number of men with drawn pistols and shotguns suddenly appeared at the windows of the cars and atop the engine and several coaches. A score of state troopers and county law officers faced the nearly equal number of armed challengers, but neither side made a move toward the other. The slightest move on the part of the troopers would probably have precipitated a round of gunfire that could have resulted in several deaths. Officers ordered the rumrunners down from the train, but the men refused and said they would kill any police officer who approached them. Neither side made a move for about thirty minutes, and then the troopers and police retreated and let the train go through.

The next day the Detroit *News* reported that the situation in Monroe County was becoming so serious that the federal government would be asked to place special marshals at the state line to accompany state troops and armed state deputies. Engineers and trainmen on the Michigan Central trains running between Toledo and Detroit complained that their lives were constantly in danger, and numerous reports came in of smugglers seizing trains and forcing trainmen at gunpoint to drive straight through Monroe without stopping. In some instances the smugglers cut the engine and first two or three cars from the train, and then the forward units rushed through Monroe. Rumors were rampant. Word was received by the state troopers on January 8 that a caravan of three to four

hundred automobile workers from the Detroit area planned to drive
to Toledo with trucks and guns and return with whisky. According
to confidential sources, the workers were tired of the high prices
charged by bootleggers and intended to bring back their own booze
at more reasonable prices. The State Food and Drug Department
rushed additional officers into Monroe County to meet this new
challenge. And to make matters even worse for enforcement
officers, the state troopers were ordered not to fire their guns directly at automobiles that refused to stop for their roadblocks.

Bootleggers from Toledo were even more audacious than automobile workers from Michigan. On February 8, scouts for the
state troopers learned that the smugglers would attempt very soon to
"shoot it out" with the border guards. The plan, according to informants, was for truckloads of heavily armed rumrunners to pull up
beside a state trooper sentry post, open fire, and wipe it out, and
thus open the road to free enterprise. Although rumors of this kind
may have been primarily for the ears of the state legislature, which
was in session at the time and was to vote additional appropriations
and men for the state troops, some state troopers took the reports
very seriously and began hiding along the highway outside their
sentry boxes, awaiting the bootlegger ambush. At the same time
another group of bootleggers posted a $500 reward in a Toledo
saloon for the names of the state troopers who had pulled the
telephone pole across the Dixie Highway.

State troopers were supplied with automobiles to chase speeding
bootleggers. These proved ineffective, however, since the troopers'
cars could attain a maximum speed of forty miles per hour, while the
heavier rum-running automobiles could travel as fast as ninety miles
per hour. Some rumrunners made sport of the trooper patrol cars by
allowing them to pull alongside and then caustically taunting them
before either forcing them from the road or speeding away. After
agents reported that the rumrunners were preparing for a fight to the
finish by equipping their cars with protective armor plate in order to
stop police bullets, state troopers tried to fill the automobile gap by
obtaining an armored car from their Detroit barracks and, on February 9, running it up and down the main stretch of the Dixie
Highway. The machine, named the "Armor Marue," was filled with
state police officers wielding automatic pistols and rifles. With its

armor-encased turret and bulletproof wheels, the Armor Marue clearly gave the advantage back to the state troopers.

Once the score was evened on the highway, the troopers sought to even it on the railway. Early on the morning of February 12, the troopers made their move. Col. Vandercook took charge of twenty-five heavily armed state troopers who lined up at the depot some time before a freight train was scheduled to arrive. As it approached the station a red light was swung across the tracks and the huge engine screeched to a halt. State troopers leaped from their hiding places. The rumrunners jumped from cars all along the train and dashed into the nearby woods. One overanxious state trooper clambered atop a railway car and attempted to arrest a rumrunner. He was thrown back with such force that both of his legs were broken. The troopers raced around and under the cars and pursued the fleeing rumrunners into the woods. A running gun battle ensued.

The new battle tactic of the state troopers temporarily intimidated the rumrunners. The next evening a large crowd of curious spectators gathered at the Monroe train depot to await the 6:12 from Toledo. Once the train was stopped, State Food and Drug agents failed to find even a single pint of booze aboard. State troopers, awaiting more running targets, were altogether disappointed. A day later state troopers again received a tip that a trainload of liquor was coming through Monroe. They gathered at the Monroe station to await the 1:30 A.M. express, but the rumrunners learned of the troopers' presence, and so they cut the air hose of the train about a mile from Monroe, halting the train, and escaped into the surrounding area to seek other means of transportation.

Just as the state troopers were gaining the initiative in enforcing the state dry law, the state supreme court, which had been considering various sections of that law for several months, declared it unconstitutional, leaving the state troopers with no prohibition law to enforce. That the chief state enforcement officers and state troopers were totally ignorant of the Bill of Rights had been a contention of many legal authorities for several months. After only two months of the dry regime, for instance, enforcement officers requested and received warrants to search private residences. Yet, according to the Damon law itself, no search warrants were to be issued for a private residence unless there was "absolute evidence" that it had ceased to be exclusively a private dwelling. Enforcement officers had become increasingly lax in their pursuit of absolute evidence. In early August, Wayne County Prosecutor Charles Jasnowski authorized a search of the Calf Island summer home, near Trenton, of August Marxhausen, editor of Detroit's *Abend Post*, a leader of the city's German community and an outspoken opponent of prohibition. Reports of wild drinking parties at the Marxhausen estate prompted the warrant and the raid, the first on a private residence sanctioned by Jasnowski. After discovering that Marxhausen was absent, Jasnowski's raiders seized six thousand bottles of beer.

Not wanting Jasnowski's staff to get all of the press coverage, the state liquor inspector for Detroit sent another raiding party to the Marxhausen home and confiscated not only booze but a large portrait of Otto von Bismarck, which was hanging in the Marxhausen living room. The reason for the seizure of the dangerous picture is uncertain. The action, however, clearly underlined the attitude of law enforcement agencies that lack of patriotism underlay the desire of some people to possess and consume alcoholic beverages. When Marxhausen returned on August 10, 1918, from a vacation trip to South Carolina, he was directed to report to the sheriff's office in Trenton. There he was arrested and charged with illegal possession of liquor. Found guilty on the charge, Marxhausen immediately appealed his conviction.

On February 18, 1919, the Michigan Supreme Court ruled against the state in the Marxhausen case. Three questions were involved: whether law officers might search for liquor or seize it without a warrant; whether they might arrest a person for having liquor in his home; and whether liquor obtained without a search warrant could be confiscated. The court answered an emphatic no on each of these questions. Justice Persons of the court was especially outraged at the means used by state troopers to search passengers on trains, trolleys, and in automobiles in Monroe County. "That the end justifies the means is a doctrine which has not found lodgement in the archives of this court," the justice wrote. He contended that there had been an "unwarranted trespass and invasion of the rights of the defendant" in the Marxhausen case. The Damon law itself was declared unconstitutional on a technicality. It had been passed and approved on May 2, 1917, and then the

Wiley Act was approved eight days later. The court held that the Wiley law superseded the Damon law, and since the Wiley law did not prohibit the importation or possession of liquor, the state could not legally prosecute for those actions.

On the morning of February 19, 1919, August Marxhausen arrived at the courthouse in Trenton with a convoy of trucks to supervise the loading of the beer taken earlier from his home. It was discovered at that time that nearly 700 bottles of beer had disappeared since the police seizure.

Word of the supreme court's decision reached southern Michigan at 5:30 P.M. on February 18 and set off what the press termed "The Great Booze Rush." Lieutenant Cosmos Calkins, in charge of state troopers in Monroe, called his men in from their stations and ordered them to make no arrests nor to stop any cars until the legal situation was clarified. In Detroit, Judge Harry J. Dingeman ordered the release of fifty men committed to the Detroit House of Correction for the possession of liquor. A blanket release of fifty others who had provided bail was also ordered. All liquor law violators were released from the Monroe County jail, charges against them were dropped, and they were grudgingly given their booze back.

Temporarily powerless to stop the importation of booze into the state, law enforcement authorities stood back and watched one of the greatest wet processions in American history. By 9 P.M., three and one-half hours after the court decision had been announced, the streets of Monroe were jammed with two lines of cars—one heading for Toledo, the other for Detroit. All night long the procession continued, and in the morning the Dixie Highway was lined in both lanes with cars pressed bumper to bumper. The interurban trolley cars were packed with suitcase-carrying passengers. On the interurbans the only interference with smuggling came from impatient conductors, who ejected intoxicated and disorderly passengers from the cars. Many aboard the trolleys, nevertheless, drank openly and threw empty bottles out the windows. Automobiles with empty rear seats raced toward Toledo and returned loaded with cases of whisky. One reporter compared the streets of Monroe on the morning after the court decision with "a beehive in honey season."

The price of liquor doubled in Toledo, while in Detroit it was cut in half. A Detroit *Free Press* reporter found the scene in Monroe nearly unbelievable. "As far as the eye could reach," he observed, "headlight was beating upon headlight at one o'clock this morning as the unbroken train of liquor-loaded automobiles began to rush on to Detroit, following a tieup of traffic for hours when five cars were shoved off into the ditch about a quarter of a mile apart along the Dixie Highway, a few miles south of Monroe." More than two hundred men, women, and children gathered at the main corners in Monroe, and as each heavily loaded automobile moved precariously at only a few miles per hour around the corner, most of them turned to avoid passing directly in front of the state troopers' headquarters, while the crowd laughed and cheered. The Detroit *News* called it "The Day of Suitcases" because "never was there seen such an array of suitcases assembled publicly at one time and on a common mission; they swarm to the highways and so well advertised is their mission that the very possession in the public street of a suitcase or any kind of baggage is *ipso facto* guilty evidence. Obviously, at this time, any busy suitcase is either going or coming."

Governor Sleeper, Attorney General Groesbeck, state legal experts, and prominent dry leaders met in an emergency conference to determine a course of action. They decided that until the state legislature could enact a new measure to replace the Damon law, the constitutional rights of the citizens of the state could be provided for if the Reed Amendment, the Webb-Kenyon law and the Wiley Act were used as grounds to keep liquor from being imported into Michigan. Meanwhile, according to the Detroit *Times*, an average of eighty cars an hour—more than one a minute—sped into Detroit loaded with liquor.

At noon on February 20 the Great Booze Rush came to an end as Secret Service agents of the federal government arrived on the Ohio-Michigan border prepared to make mass arrests. They were followed by state troopers and agents of the State Food and Drug Department. Most bootlegging drivers, seeing the new faces and uniforms on the border, pulled their cars to the side of the road and then headed back toward Toledo, leaving the job of supplying liquor to Michigan to professionals. Attorney General Groesbeck secured an injunction from Judge Jesse Root of the Monroe County Circuit Court restraining anyone from entering Michigan with liquor, and Vandercook and Groesbeck promised to swear in an army of deputies all across the border counties to stop the inflow of booze. Vandercook posted copies of the injunction at various points along the state line and reminded would-be smugglers that violation of the injunction would mean arrest for contempt of court, confiscation of both liquor and the means of transporting it, and imprisonment without jury trial. "John Doe" warrants, issued by the state of Ohio, empowered Michigan officials to stop and search any person suspected of carrying intoxicants into the state and to confiscate the contraband. Enforcement officials confiscated more than two thousand quarts of whisky in the next few days from cars driving along Rummers' Runway. Federal officials in Ohio made thirty arrests of individuals suspected of conspiring to violate federal law by smuggling liquor into Michigan.

On February 23, 1919, the editor of the Adrian *Telegram* proclaimed that the forecast for Michigan was, ironically, now drier than ever. "If any wet sentiment was reviving in the State, as the liquor forces assert," he wrote, "it is much more than offset by the wave of disgust that spread all over Michigan this week. This last carnival of booze-running drove the last nail in John Barleycorn's coffin, and it can not be pried open. . . ." He failed to state that the rush might also have eased tensions and given state prohibition more of a chance for survival. Those who wanted or needed a drink were suddenly able to satisfy their desire again, after nine months of prohibition. Others were able to lay in ample supplies of booze. For a while longer now, and within the law, the drys could be dry and the wets could be wet. And that, after all, was the intention of the constitutional amendment approved by the state's voters in 1916.

Booze running from Toledo to Detroit was effectively ended by the drying up of Toledo itself at midnight, May 24, 1919, as Ohio's prohibition legislation closed all but a few state liquor outlets. In the last wet week for Ohio, liquor prices rose so high in Toledo that the margin of profit for running booze into Michigan was practically wiped out. Professional bootleggers began looking for greener pastures, and the most enterprising began gazing across the Detroit River toward Canada, which was about to repeal its wartime prohibition act.

III

There were clear indications in 1918 and 1919 that bootleg liquor was not the only kind of booze reaching Detroit's drinkers. Home brewers competed with smugglers in supplying the city's boozers. By early 1919 a large quantity of beer was being produced by thousands of Detroit's incipient brewmasters, many of them living in the finest residential districts of the city. There were no paid gunmen or seedy ringleaders taking part in this early illicit business; instead, "respectable citizens" openly aided one another in the production of alcoholic beverages. Recipes for making home brew with an alcoholic content as high as 12 percent were distributed by dealers in the necessary materials. Friends passed them on to friends. An employee of one of the city's most prestigious clubs charged five dollars for a recipe that he said had formerly been used by a brewery of national repute. An East Side supply house worked its staff overtime putting up packages of hops that were sold with a recipe for making beer disguised by another name. For two dollars amateur brewers could buy a machine to affix patent tops to bottles. Siphons, used for removing brew after fermentation, and isinglass, used for settling the mixture, were sold in five and ten cent stores, including those owned by prohibitionist S. S. Kresge. Drugstores in Detroit and the surrounding communities reported shortages of bottles. The only discouraging aspect of the manufacture of homemade beer was the odor. It took one full day to get rid of the sour smell in the home; the excuse provided most frequently to explain the odor was that it was caused by "salt rising bread." Beer was not the only homemade product in Detroit in 1918 and 1919; brandies, cordials, and whisky were also produced, and peach, prune, and plum pits were in great demand. Local merchants reported an abnormally high demand for raisins, noting that the demand had doubled since 1917.

Police officials tried to close down the home brewing business late in 1919 after John A. Grogan, Internal Revenue collector for the district of Michigan, issued orders that placed restrictions on dealers in the required ingredients. Grogan's orders closed about sixty concerns in Detroit and a large number of other cities around the state. Nevertheless, the home brewing enterprises continued with little interruption. Most Detroit city officials took the position in 1919 that "if a man drinks in his own home until his comparatively limited supply is exhausted, no great harm will be done. The beauty of conditions as they are, even with rum running, is that the saloon is dead, no longer alive, to the boy reaching the drinking age."

Yet disturbing substitutes for the saloon appeared almost immediately after May 1, 1918: they were the so-called blind pigs. In September 1919 the Detroit *Saturday Night* surveyed the illicit retail liquor business in Detroit and discovered that while Police Commissioner James W. Inches estimated that there were only two hundred blind pigs in the city, former saloonkeepers believed there were at least three times that number. One former saloonkeeper told the paper that a "good stand" was no longer a place downtown but was rather an establishment in one of the outlying neighborhoods closed to saloons before prohibition. There, dingy places of the worst kind prospered, he said, since they charged workingmen the outrageous price of fifty cents a shot. Most of these places operated with soft-drink or near-beer licenses issued by the city, but "near beer and soft drinks would not even pay the light bills." Some private residences also operated as blind pigs, and it was extremely difficult for the police to get evidence against such places because of the difficulty of obtaining search warrants. Virtually every blind-pig operator during these early prohibition days owned a telephone and a car, the two essentials for operation. The telephone was necessary for his business because most deals for liquor were made by phone. As early as January 2, 1919, County Prosecutor Jasnowski was tapping telephone lines of suspected blind-pig operators. Several stenographers were employed by the prosecutor to transcribe the telephone conversations, and the information was then used to secure search warrants. The automobile was necessary for blind-pig operators to pick up liquor at storage points throughout the city. The operator usually had to transport his own supply since only a few bootleggers made direct deliveries in these first prohibition years.

IV

The Michigan state legislature ratified the Eighteenth Amendment to the United States Constitution on January 3, 1919. Michigan appeared to have been the sixteenth state to approve the measure, but lost the honor of being listed among the first thirty-six ratifying states because the joint resolution voted upon by the legislators contained an error that changed the meaning of the amendment to such an extent that it could not be legally counted. As approved by the Michigan legislators, section two of the resolution read, "The Congress and the several states shall have *joint* power to impose this article by appropriate legislation"; the Eighteenth Amendment passed by Congress read, "The Congress and the several states shall have *concurrent* power. . . ." Grant Hudson of the Michigan Anti-Saloon League readily admitted that the use of the word "joint" for "concurrent" had been his error. In his haste to have the amendment printed and approved, Hudson had misread the original document and copied it incorrectly. The legislature passed a subsequent joint resolution accepting the amendment, but too late to place Michigan among the first thirty-six states to ratify the document.

The second major task confronting the legislature in 1919 was the drafting of a new state prohibition enforcement law to replace the measure struck down by the state supreme court in its Marxhausen decision. In its final form, the new measure, the Lewis law, prohibited the manufacture, sale, giving away, bartering, furnishing, possessing, importing, or transporting of any vinous, malt, brewed, fermented, spirituous, or intoxicating liquors except for medicinal, mechanical, chemical, scientific, or sacramental purposes. "Intoxicating liquors" was defined by the law as a beverage containing intoxicating properties and all liquors containing any alcohol. The act also forbade clubs and lodges from storing alcoholic beverages. Section 25 of the law provided for the search of any building upon complaint by a citizen that illegal liquors were stored, manufactured, or sold there. If liquor were found, the authorities were to seize it and all the furnishings on the premises. If any "fluids" were poured out or destroyed while police were entering or searching the building, those fluids were to be considered "*prima facie* intoxicating liquor unlawfully possessed." Section 31 of the law allowed any sheriff or any other peace officer to make arrests without warrant of any person suspected of breaking the law. Anyone arrested for intoxication was required to appear before a magistrate and to answer under oath questions relative to the place, date, and person from whom he had secured the liquor that had "contributed" to his intoxication. The refusal to answer such questions was to be dealt with as contempt of court. But by far the most important section of the new law was Section 51, which defined violation of the

Lewis law as a felony (a violation of the 1917 liquor law had been a misdemeanor) and prescribed for first violations a fine of up to $1,000 and a prison sentence of up to one year.

Because a person with liquor in his possession committed a felony, according to the Lewis law, police officers were authorized to use firearms to stop violators of the law. Persons could also be searched without a warrant if police officers suspected them of committing a felony. By making violations of prohibition a felony, the legislative drys believed that they had effectively circumvented the anti-search-and-seizure rules of the courts. The legislature then attached an "immediate-effect clause" to the Lewis law so that it could become operative upon being signed by the governor. The House required only sixteen minutes to pass the Lewis law by a vote of eighty-two to six. Four representatives from Detroit, one from Bessemer, and one from Iron Mountain voted in the minority. There was no debate nor was the bill even read aloud before the final vote was taken. The Senate passed the Lewis law on March 27 and sent it to the governor for his signature. In the Senate, too, the bill was passed without debate, and a roll-call vote showed all thirty senators present voting in favor of it.

The actions of the legislature in 1919 showed the degree to which the lawmakers had been pushed on the liquor question between January 1917 and January 1919. The well-publicized "crime wave" involving liquor smuggling along the Ohio-Michigan border along with the patriotic ardor aroused by the war worked together to produce a prohibition law that even the most radical drys had not dreamed of proposing two years earlier. Enforcing it, of course, would be another thing altogether.

V

Between 1916 and 1920 six states that had previously adopted prohibition by popular vote held a second referendum on the question. In each instance a larger majority was accorded prohibition than it had received in the earlier elections. Michigan was among those states reaffirming their faith in prohibition during these years.

Even before prohibition went into effect in the state, in May

1918, the anti-prohibition forces were at work seeking repeal or revision. The principal scheme favored by the prohibition critics was a constitutional amendment providing for the retail sale of beer, wine, porter, ale, and cider in Michigan. In a final major effort to save themselves, the brewers of the state agreed to sever all ties with the distilling and saloon business and support the proposed reform. Conceding most of the prohibition arguments concerning the social and economic effects of alcohol, the brewers insisted that there existed a fundamental difference between distilled and brewed beverages. Products of brewing, they argued, were "temperance beverages" and should therefore be exempted from state prohibition laws. In an effort to dissociate any connection in the public mind between the interests of the brewers and the proposed beer-wine amendment, the Michigan Hotelmen's Association organized and managed the entire campaign for a referendum on the measure. No brewer was listed as a member of the organization and no brewer was listed as a contributor to the campaign chest of the Hotelmen's Association. But since the securing of a beer-wine exemption was the announced goal of both the United States Brewers' Association and its Michigan affiliates, it is likely that unlisted funding by state brewers supported the wet campaign in 1918 and 1919.

In January 1918, four months before prohibition was even scheduled to become the law in Michigan, Fred A. Baker, a Detroit attorney, submitted to the secretary of state a copy of a proposed beer-wine amendment. Approval by the Department of State and the state attorney general was required before the work of obtaining signatures to an initiatory measure for the amendment could begin. The wets needed to gather the names of 65,152 voters in the state and to file them with the secretary of state at least four months before the date of the election to which the proposition was to be submitted. State officials who made the preliminary examination of the proposal were uncertain as to the possibility of restoring by constitutional amendment liquor laws that had already been repealed by proper legislation, but they gave the measure their approval despite misgivings. The proposal was then taken to the public by the Hotelmen's Association for the necessary signatures. Prohibitionist leaders viewed the efforts of the wets with scant alarm and predicted that the proposed amendment, if submitted to an election, would be decisively defeated.

Despite assurances that the amendment would never pass, the Anti-Saloon League held mass meetings to rally the religious and moral strength of the state against it. But dry leaders knew from experience that religious and moral strength alone could not carry an election. Money was needed to put the cause of prohibition before the Michigan voters. The Michigan Anti-Saloon League and the Detroit Citizens' League sought the funds necessary to oppose the beer-wine amendment from the business establishments in Detroit that benefited most from prohibition. A list of the firms and of personal donations received from executives within those firms by the dry campaign included: Packard Motor Car Company and personal ($1,000); Hudson Motor Company and personal ($3,000); J. L. Hudson and Company and personal ($3,000); D. M. Ferry ($1,000); Ford Motor Company and personal ($5,000); H. H. Rackham ($1,000); Chalmers-Maxwell Company ($500); Anderson Electric Car Company ($500); Timken-D Axle Company and personal ($2,000); Fisher Body Corporation ($2,500); Paige Motor Car Company and personal ($1,500); S. S. Kresge and Company and personal ($3,000); Frank B. Leland ($500); Park-Davis and Company ($1,000); James Couzens ($2,500); Dodge Brothers ($3,000); Briggs Manufacturing Company ($2,000); Studebaker Corporation ($1,000); Cadillac Motor Car Company ($1,000). William Anderson, state supertindent of the New York Anti-Saloon League was brought into Michigan to speak about the congressional investigations of the German-American Alliance and allegations that the United States Brewers' Association had given immense sums of money to finance pro-German propaganda throughout the United States prior to American entry into the war. Grant Hudson of the Michigan Anti-Saloon League also took up the charge that those supporting the beer-wine amendment were friends of the German enemy and predicted, "Should we be forced to make a campaign against the wine-and-beer amendment we will defeat it by not less than a 150,000 vote majority. In other words, the Anti-Saloon League is on the job to route the Hun on every point of the battle line."

On June 27, 1918, C. W. Norton, head of the campaign committee of the Michigan Hotelmen's Association, presented to the secretary of state petitions containing over 100,000 signatures, 28,000 of them from Detroit and the remainder representing voters in every county of the state. The petitions were accepted and a referendum on the issue was planned for the fall elections of 1918.

The drys, however, were successful in postponing the vote on the wet measure until the spring of 1919. All along, attorneys for the Anti-Saloon League had claimed that the wet proposal was illegal because it did not include proper wording for the suggested constitutional alterations. On September 5, 1918, the Michigan Supreme Court ruled that the objections of the Anti-Saloon League that the proposed amendment was incomplete in its wording were valid. The secretary of state should have taken notice of the error in the amendment, the court announced, and rejected it in the spring of 1918. The wets were not vanquished by the decision. They corrected the wording of the amendment and regathered the requisite number of signatures. The secretary of state accepted the signatures and a referendum on the measure was set for the spring of 1919.

Before the referendum took place the wets faced new difficulties. First, Congress passed the Eighteenth Amendment and submitted it to the states. Second, a wartime prohibition act was passed that was to go into effect if no peace treaty had been signed by July 1, 1919. Backers of the beer-wine amendment claimed that the federal amendment and the federal law made no significant difference in Michigan and that beer might still be sold legally. The prohibitionists, however, expressed doubt that the wet measure could ever become legally operative.

Before the 1919 referendum the state legislature extended voting rights to women. The first contest in which women could vote was to be the spring election of 1919. For years the drys had been outspoken friends of the ballot for women and the wets had publicly opposed it. The fact that women could now vote in the state, it was commonly assumed, would fatally affect the chances of the success of the beer-and-wine amendment.

No major public official endorsed the wet amendment in 1919, and in early March the Democratic state convention adopted a prohibition plank in its platform. At the end of the month both the governor and lieutenant governor appealed to citizens of the state to vote against the beer-and-wine amendment. The Michigan Anti-

Saloon League raised a war chest of $50,000 to fight the measure, and Grant Hudson, revising her earlier prediction of the magnitude of the expected dry victory, now declared that the beer-and-wine amendment would be defeated by 300,000 votes. Hudson said that the drys considered a large majority against the measure a necessity because of the impact it would have upon sheriffs and prosecuting attorneys, some of whom paid most attention to laws favored by large majorities.

On April 7, 1919, the beer-and-wine amendment was defeated by a vote of 530,123 to 322,603. Only three counties cast majorities for the measure. The editor of the Detroit *Saturday Night* observed that perhaps the most obvious conclusion to be drawn from the election was that Detroit had developed an attitude on the prohibition question widely divergent from the rest of the state in the years since 1916. In 1916 the city voted wet by a margin of 11,000 votes. It did so in 1919 by 35,000 votes. Except for Wayne County, in the lower peninsula every county increased the percentage of its dry vote over 1916. Kent County, the second largest county in population in the state, defeated the amendment by a vote of almost two to one, while the city of Grand Rapids voted in nearly the same ratio against the amendment. The third largest city in the state, Flint, also became drier. In 1916 Flint returned a dry majority of 600 votes, but in 1919 it had a dry majority of 4,244. Saginaw County also reversed its wet stand of 1916 and voted dry in 1919. Washtenaw County voted dry by over 5,000 votes, and the city of Ann Arbor cast its vote against the beer-and-wine amendment.

Several critical factors worked in the prohibitionists' favor in 1919. For one thing, although an armistice had been signed the previous fall, no peace treaty ending the Great War had been negotiated, and the crusading spirit of the war was still present. Also, Senate investigations discredited the brewing industry by associating brewers with efforts to increase public sympathy for the Germans. As a result of these findings, opponents of the beer-and-wine amendment could campaign against another effort to "Prussianize" the American people. Press coverage of the crimes of smugglers between Ohio and Michigan also caused many voters to turn against any moderation on the liquor question. But most important of all, at a time when prohibition had been in effect for less than a full year, it was claimed and believed by masses of people who had previously been skeptical that what the prohibitionists had been promising all along was true. Prohibition really did dramatically improve the economic status, the health, and the welfare of the people of the state.

VI

The accelerated growth of Detroit after 1890 resulted in great social disorganization that the city government seemed helpless to correct. One result of the growing disorganization was an increase of crime in the city, especially after 1914. The municipal police department seemed both unable and unwilling to deal effectively with the crime problem. A few weeks before the city election of 1916, Mayor Oscar Marx, in a political move, replaced Police Commissioner John Gillespie with James Couzens, formerly of the Ford Motor Company. While a director of the Ford Motor Company, Couzens had supervised private detectives from Murphy's Secret Service who spied on Ford employees and furnished "advice and consultation" to the management. That, however, had been the extent of Couzens's police experience. Nevertheless, Couzens accepted the appointment and launched a personal investigation into crime in Detroit. Mayor Marx blamed the crime increase on "imported gunmen and gamblers." Commissioner Couzens reported, "I found conditions far worse than the public dreamed they were. The real inside conditions were never known to the public. . . . The town was wide open. . . . Gamblers ran as they pleased; hundreds of houses of prostitution were scattered around, and 1,400 saloons ran all day and all night and on Sundays." Couzens worked hard at his new job but was troubled by the lack of cooperation from city officials. "When they asked me to clean up Detroit," he concluded, "they didn't mean it. They wanted me to clean it up and not clean it up. They wanted me to make it nice enough for the reformers and let it stay rotten enough to appease the bums."

Through his efforts, Couzens endeared himself to the influential reform elements of both Detroit and the rest of the state. The task of cleaning up the city, however, appeared to be too great even for a dedicated official like Couzens. Murders in Detroit increased from

27 in 1915 to 59 in 1916, and armed robberies increased from 441 to 647 in the same period. In October 1917, a year after taking office, Couzens announced that Detroit was "the best policed city in the United States," but the Detroit *Saturday Night* complained that the crime wave continued and pointed out that the number of murders in the city had doubled in 1917 and that the number of auto thefts had increased by 400 percent.

In early 1918 Couzens admitted that part of the problem of cleaning up the city resided in the police department itself. In the last half of 1917 nearly three hundred police officers had been brought before the commissioner on various charges, and twenty-nine had been dismissed from the force. Eighty-nine police officers had been charged with drinking or entering a saloon while on duty or being drunk on duty. Couzens began reforming the police department of Detroit and announced his belief that crime in the city was simply part of a national crime wave. Despite all of Couzens's efforts and his optimistic statements, however, the crime wave continued. Fifty-four holdups occurred on the streets of Detroit in the first six weeks of 1918, and the Detroit *News* warned that "if the government cannot restore the good name of the town the people can. And they will." Finally, in mid-February 1918, Couzens employed state troopers armed with shotguns to patrol the streets of Detroit at night. The troopers were given orders to shoot to kill when altercations with suspected lawbreakers occurred.

Soon after the new state prohibition law went into effect in early May 1918, crime began to decrease dramatically in Detroit. Many factors contributed to the decrease, including high employment and high wages, the draft, which removed thousands of young men from the city, and more efficient methods of law enforcement. Leading city officials, however, gave prohibition nearly all the credit for halting the crime wave. In early 1919, when a reporter called on Couzens, now the city's new mayor, to discuss the impact of prohibition on Detroit, the ex-police commissioner said that he had voted wet in 1916 but that if another election were held he would vote dry. He expressed the belief that Detroit would vote dry too. "Prohibition has been a revelation," the mayor said. "It has upset all the alarmist predictions of the wets and more than sustained all the rosiest predictions of the drys." Couzens insisted that prohibition made Detroit a "better town" and observed that the public as a whole was impressed with its results. Petty crime had been reduced by 60 to 70 percent, he announced, and child welfare had received a boost that millions of dollars in appropriations could not have effected. It had become easier for creditors to collect bills. Detroit's merchants reported greater purchases by workers, and banks showed an increase in deposits. Factories reported that prohibition had not brought the predicted labor shortage. On the contrary, reduced tardiness, absenteeism, and accidents in the plants had led to a general increase in production. No large hotels had gone out of business, real estate values had not been impaired, and the theater business was booming. Couzens claimed that there had been no increase in the number of drug addicts in the city, as the wets predicted would occur. He agreed that there was a bootlegging problem, but he also reminded the reporter that Detroit was the largest city in the world to have been voted dry, and, keeping that in mind, there was no more liquor smuggling than had been expected. "When Ohio goes dry," he said, "it should be reduced to a minimum.

Detroit police officials were as happy as Couzens with the results of prohibition. William P. Rutledge, the first deputy commissioner and superintendent of police, said that he was able to spend Saturday evenings at home with his family because of prohibition. In the "old days"—the "booze days," as he called them—he had been forced to remain at the police station at least until midnight on Saturday, and often until late Sunday morning, because of the large number of crimes committed on the weekends. On Saturday nights before prohibition the police station had been as busy "as a department store on Christmas eve," he recalled. "As a policeman up from the sidewalk," he said, "let me tell you that Detroit dry, bootlegging or not, is a better city to live in."

In comparing statistics of Detroit in dry 1918 with those of wet 1917 the Detroit *News* reminded its readers that over 140,000 young men in Detroit had been registered for the draft and that 60,000 of those had left the city by June 1918. Nevertheless, the *News,* too, claimed that prohibition was largely responsible for the decrease in arrests for drunkenness in Detroit from 1,692 in May 1917 to 183 in May 1918. Officials reported that while 20 to 25 percent of the drafted men leaving the city before May 1, 1918, had been intoxicated, there were only two cases of intoxication in seventeen trainloads of draftees leaving the city in June 1918. Dean Marquis of the Ford Motor Company claimed that the ban on liquor had cut the absentee and tardy totals of that company by one half and that personal efficiency had greatly increased on the assembly line. Other Detroit industrialists made similar claims. Prosecuting Attorney Jasnowski stated that crimes reported to his office fell off at least 20 percent after prohibition went into effect. Newspapers noticed that the poor had also benefited from prohibition: in May 1917, 272 people had been sent to the poor farm by the poor commissioners, but in May 1918, only 93 were so sentenced.

The *American Issue,* official newspaper of the Anti-Saloon League, concluded after citing welfare and crime statistics from Detroit's first dry month, "Nobody except a fanatical wet can or will ignore these figures. They cannot be refuted. They prove the blessings of prohibition and bring more clearly into light, the demoralization and death caused by the liquor traffic."

After sixty days of prohibition, the Detroit *News* made another survey of its impact on the city. The findings were as dramatic as they had been after the first dry month. Businessmen still concluded that prohibition had helped business, Mayor Couzens issued a statement acknowledging the dramatic decrease in crime in Detroit, and the number of arrests for drunkenness had decreased from an average of fifty per day prior to prohibition to less than six a day.

In August 1918, Mrs. Mary McGill, of Detroit's domestic relations court, asserted that husbands seemed to be bringing home more money after prohibition than they had previously and that domestic tranquility was descending over many households in which domestic warfare had previously raged. Mrs. McGill observed that there had been a 50 percent decrease in the number of women appearing before the court claiming that they had been beaten or otherwise physically abused by their husbands. The reason for all of this, of course, was prohibition.

Because of the decrease in crime in Detroit, Mayor Couzens relaxed the intensive anti-crime campaign he had initiated. Evidence of the relaxation came in Decemeber 1918 when Couzens appointed Dr. James Inches the new police commissioner. Inches promised "psychopathic treatment" of criminals and modern methods of crime prevention. He remarked that the view that a policeman must knock a man down was obsolete and that psychology would increasingly be used in policing the modern city. There would be a new epoch in the world's history, Inches announced, and an entirely new fabric of society would be constructed. "The man who does not realize that we can never return to exactly the same conditions as existed before the war is blind," the new police commissioner declared.

At the end of the first full year of prohibition in Michigan the Detroit *News* published statistics comparing wet and dry Detroit. The findings were truly impressive:

	WET	DRY
Accidents	5993	4950
Attempted suicides	90	49
Suicides	67	45
Dead bodies found on the streets	77	35
Felonious assaults	361	152
Burglaries	2929	1785
Concealed weapon cases	503	173
Embezzlements	260	166
Larcenies	4721	3225
Homicides	78	38
Robberies	775	295
Drunkenness	7290	3624
Nonsupport cases	767	452
Vagrancy	332	49
Automobile accidents	96	68
Deaths from alcoholism	92	17

Officials statistics of the police department showed that the crime wave had ended in 1918 after reaching a crest in 1917. The dramatic decrease in crime continued through 1919, despite numerous arrests for bootlegging and rum-running and the operation of blind pigs:

YEAR	NUMBER OF ARRESTS	PERCENTAGE OF THE POPULATION
1912	8,855	1.21
1913	10,557	1.72
1914	9,400	1.43
1915	11,365	1.57
1916	15,720	2.14
1917	19,309	2.35
1918	13,469	1.47
1919	6,249	0.6429

The attribution of all major social changes in Detroit after May 1918 to prohibition was a dangerous exercise in which most prohibitionists indulged. For years they had proclaimed that prohibition would bring decreases in crime and accidents, improve domestic realtions, increase industrial production, improve health, and, in short, bring a bright and prosperous new world. The prohibitionists, however, were guilty of a vast oversimplification. It was prohibition, they said, that had produced the desirable social results noted, but they ignored the effects of the war on employment, wages, and consumption. When the war ended and recession replaced prosperity, crime again increased, and the prohibitionists were left defending their simple cause-and-effect assumptions. When things went wrong after 1920, the press and the public were well conditioned to look to prohibition as the causative factor.

VII

The beneficial social changes attributed to prohibition in Michigan communities other than Detroit were even more dramatic than what was reported to have taken place in the state's largest city. Town after town in both the upper and lower peninsulas reported favorably on their dry experience. The *Survey* magazine selected Grand Rapids for a study in depth of the social impact of prohibition, and the findings of the study suggest what may have been occurring in towns all across Michigan in the first two years of prohibition.

During a three-week investigation in Grand Rapids, researchers heard from managers of theaters, amusement parks, factories, boardinghouses, hotels, and other places, that public intoxication had ceased to be an important problem. City officials, social workers, ministers, the chief of police, and the sheriff all agreed that booze was fighting a losing battle. The largest amount of liquor consumed after May 1, 1918, was of home manufacture, local law enforcement officials reported. But police officials believed that home production would be of only temporary significance because people would tire of the process once they discovered it took more effort than they expected and because the product was not always to their liking. In any event, home brewing was not considered to be taking place on a great enough scale to constitute anything like "nullification" of the law. City officials regarded it as an "inevitable incident" in the transition from wet to dry and a practice that young people were not likely to follow.

The most dramatic effect attributed to prohibition in Grand Rapids was the decrease in crime. This phenomenon had been observed in local-option counties in the state prior to 1918, but Grand Rapids had never been dry under local option. Records from the police courts showed a decrease in the number of criminal cases adjudicated as follows:

1916–1917	1917–1918	1918–1919	1919–1920
saloons open	saloons open	saloons closed	saloons closed
3,827	3,666	1,705	2,055

These figures indicate a reduction of 54 percent in criminal case adjudications in the first year of prohibition as compared to the average of the two years immediately preceding prohibition and a 45 percent decline during the second year.

There was also a decrease of 63 percent in the number of prisoners held in the county jail in Grand Rapids during the first year of prohibition. In 1919 the jail was nearly empty several times, a condition unparalleled in the history of Grand Rapids. From 1909 to 1913 the smallest number of prisoners in the jail had been 66 and the largest 106; but in 1919 the smallest number was 9 and the largest 38. Some forty of the one hundred cells in the jail were unoccupied in the two years after prohibition became operative, and Sheriff Viergever remarked, "It is the alcohol bums whom we get now."

In 1917 Kent County had established a work farm for short-term prisoners: drunks, men convicted of petty larceny, and others with sentences of ninety days or less. Shortly after prohibition went into effect, however, the farm superintendent's wife called the police judge to ask for more prisoners. When she was told that there were none available, she concluded that the farm could no longer operate. Six months later it was abandoned, and by 1920 it had been transformed into a government aviation field. Sheriff Viergever reported that a number of sheriffs in counties less populous than Kent had suffered such a reduction in their jail populations since prohibition that they could no longer make a living and would soon be forced to resign. There were 168 police officers in Grand Rapids when the city went dry, and the city commission, anticipating a lesser need for police, reduced the number to 140. Because of the difficulty in obtaining good men, the number of police in the city never exceeded 120 during the next two years. According to the chief of police, this was sufficient for law enforcement under prohibition.

A business upswing in Grand Rapids after May 1918 was attributed by local residents to prohibition. Clothing retailers noticed an immediate increase in the number of buyers who paid their bills promptly. A furniture dealer selling goods on the installment plan observed that the customers were now making larger monthly payments. Collection agencies declared that debts were easier to collect, and insurance agencies claimed that insurance premiums were paid more promptly than they had been before May 1, 1918.

Property formerly occupied by saloons did not remain vacant for long. The value of saloon and adjoining properties, realtors declared, had risen more rapidly than the value of other property. There had also been a change in the character of people frequenting old saloon neighborhoods: "street loafers" disappeared and middle-class shoppers were more in evidence.

Bankers in Grand Rapids testified that prohibition led directly to more and larger savings accounts. Despite both higher real incomes for laborers and the impetus given saving by the Liberty Loan drives of the war, the president of one of the new banks in Grand Rapids remarked, "I am confident that the saving now done by working families in this city, which is far greater than it was two or three years ago, is due to prohibition as a predominant cause."

Employers of Grand Rapids pointed out that Monday morning work absences, the old "Blue Monday," had been greatly diminished since prohibition. Workmanship had improved, they said, and many employees had become more dependable. Surprisingly, leaders of organized labor in Grand Rapids also viewed prohibition favorably. One unionist recalled that before May 1, 1918, whenever the issue of prohibition had been brought up for a test vote before the Central Trades and Labor Council a slight majority against it had usually been recorded due to the influence exerted by some of the strong international unions, like the Teamsters. On the other hand, when the matter had come before the local bodies, where the rank and file expressed themselves directly on the issue, there was nearly always a dry majority. Workers associated directly with the booze business—the coopers who made the barrels, the teamsters who drove the beer wagons, and the brewers, bartenders, and bottlers—had strongly opposed prohibition. The powerful masons union and the building trades in general had been considered friends of booze because the brewers had used union labor almost exclusively in their construction work. If prohibition passed, many union men argued, organized labor in Grand Rapids would receive a blow from which it might never recover. But prohibition did not have a major destructive effect on organized labor in Grand Rapids. Some local unions were weakened—the cigar makers union lost 167 of its 200 members and the bartenders union disappeared—but a soft-drink dispensers union was formed to take the place of the bartenders, and other unions in the city maintained their former membership and strength. Union officials found that after prohibition dues were paid more regularly, and one union leader predicted that labor would show itself more "clear headed" now that the saloons were closed.

Prohibition was also given full credit for dramatic changes in the recreational patterns of the people of Grand Rapids. Pool and billiard rooms and bowling alleys, which increased in number very rapidly after 1918, became social substitutes for the saloon. There was an even greater growth in the popularity of outdoor sports in the city after 1918. Dealers in sporting goods reported that never before had they done such a volume of business. Tennis and amateur baseball grew in popularity. The YMCA furnished baseball equipment for a number of factory leagues, which played evening games. Swimming became more popular, especially among the adults of Grand Rapids, who flocked to the municipal pools in the evening after work. The largest dealer in fishing tackle in the city gave his unqualified opinion that prohibition had caused "a new era in fishing." Unlike more vigorous pastimes, fishing seemed to attract men past middle age, whose complexions gave away the fact that they were former saloon devotees, solacing themselves after 1918 with a line and a sinker. Never within his memory, the dealer said, had fishing been as popular as it had now become. "The golden age of anglers" seemed to have returned, the *Survey* concluded. Observers noted that attendance at Grand Rapids' public parks had increased and that wrestling and boxing matches in the city not only attracted larger crowds after 1918 than they had before but that the crowds now included few people who were either rowdy or intoxicated.

Investigators concluded that by far the most dramatic effect of prohibition was the increased amount of time that fathers spent with their families. One witness advised the *Survey,* "The family is the chief substitute for the saloon." Innumerable men who formerly had spent their evenings and many of their Sundays in saloons now spent them at home. They were seen more often on the front porches of their homes, and they took their families on automobile excursions on holidays and on weekends. Also, after May 1918, the family picnic came into its own, and travelers frequently spotted family picnickers in many parts of the city.

Investigators for the *Survey* warned their readers that many of the changes in Grand Rapids were due to the increased wages paid workingmen, but they nevertheless reported that it was the universal opinion in the city that, had the saloons remained open, most workers would have spent their pay increases on drink. "Prohibition," the researchers concluded, "insured some of the benefit of higher wages by closing one avenue of wasteful expenditure." Wets and drys in Grand Rapids agreed in early 1920 that any politician calling for a restoration of the saloon "would get one of the worst beatings in the history of municipal politics in this country."

VIII

Two weeks after Michigan voters endorsed statewide prohibition, the dry Detroit *News* editorialized that it was "a psychological fact" that once prohibition had been approved at the local level "the naturalness of its happening nationally does not have to be argued." The *News* argued that prohibition was not a county or state issue but a national one. "If prohibition is logical and desirable at all," the *News* concluded, "national prohibition is the most logical and desirable form of it."

"Logical and desirable": The terms are central to the explanations used by the drys in their fight for national prohibition.

Prohibition, they reminded the public, was endorsed by the leading doctors, scientists, law enforcement officers, athletes, and businessmen in the country. Society in general and the individual in particular would benefit from the brave new world produced by the absence of alcoholic beverages. It is not "primarily to make men moral by law," one leading dry wrote of prohibition, "but to establish the social conditions of morality under which men are more likely to be moral than when living under an environment which is conducive to immorality and wrong doing." The most outspoken opponents of prohibition, the drys reminded the public, were those with a vested interest in drinking—the brewers and distillers.

The first dramatic blow in the fight for national prohibition came in 1913 when Congress passed the Webb-Kenyon law to forbid the shipment of liquor into states where its sale was against the law. President Taft vetoed the law, but it was passed over his veto, despite warnings from Attorney General George Wickersham that the law violated the commerce clause of the Constitution.

As soon as the Webb-Kenyon law was safely through Congress, the Anti-Saloon League demanded a constitutional amendment providing for national prohibition. A few weeks later, four thousand league members marched down Pennsylvania Avenue in Washington in a demonstration for prohibition. Five states passed prohibition laws in 1914, another five in 1915, and four more in 1916, bringing the total number of prohibition states to twenty-three in 1917.

In the congressional elections of 1914 the Anti-Saloon League sent fifty thousand speakers into congressional districts at an expense of nearly $2.5 million. League speakers appeared in every congressional contest where there was the slightest chance of electing a dry. A month after the election, a resolution for a national prohibition amendment was introduced in the House of Representatives, and although it failed to gain the necessary two-thirds vote for passage, the measure did win a majority of the votes cast, 197 to 190.

The Anti-Saloon League went to work once again in the congressional elections of 1916, and this time they were more successful than they had been in 1914. "On election night the lights burned late in our Washington office," Wayne B. Wheeler of the league wrote. "Elsewhere our state workers were getting the returns. . . . We knew late election night that we had won. Many hours before the country knew whether Hughes or Wilson had triumphed, the dry workers throughout the nation were celebrating our victory. We knew that the prohibition amendment would be submitted to the states by the Congress just elected."

In early 1917 Congress voted prohibition for Alaska and the District of Columbia and passed an enabling act to allow the people of Puerto Rico to vote on the issue. A resolution providing for the Eighteenth Amendment to the Constitution was favorably reported to the Senate on June 11, 1917, and it passed by a vote of 65 to 20, with both Michigan senators voting with the majority. On December 18, 1917, the House of Representatives approved the measure by a vote of 282 to 128, with Democrats and Republicans dividing almost evenly on the question—62 Republicans and 64 Democrats opposed the resolution and 141 Democrats and 131 Republicans favored it. Eleven Michigan congressmen voted with the majority, and two—both from Detroit—voted against the measure.

Five states ratified the Eighteenth Amendment only four weeks after it had been passed by Congress. Two more approved it in the fall of 1918, and then, suddenly, twenty more during the first fifteen days of 1919. On January 16, 1919, Nebraska became the thirty-sixth state to ratify the amendment, and within two hours two more states approved it.

Congress passed the Volstead Act, a measure to provide for enforcement of the Eighteenth Amendment and for wartime prohibition. The statute allowed for individuals to possess and use liquor acquired before prohibition became effective, provided they consumed it in their own homes. Drinkers were also permitted to manufacture "nonintoxicating" cider and fruit juices for use in their own homes. Provision was made for the sale of alcoholic beverages for medicinal, sacramental, and industrial purposes. The Volstead Act defined "intoxicating liquors" as any liquor containing over 0.5 percent alcohol, a definition taken from an earlier ruling by the Bureau of Internal Revenue that had been adopted with the approval of the brewers as a dividing line between the beverages subject to or exempted from the federal liquor tax.

Following the passage of the Eighteenth Amendment, a writer for the national WCTU newspaper, the *Union Signal*, proclaimed that prohibition was finally as dead an issue as slavery. The wets would be forced to drop their opposition to prohibition, the writer suggested, or be classed as "traitors and Bolsheviks." On the other hand, General Jacob Coxey, who had led a rag-tag army to Washington in 1894, announced that he would call a second army, this time of 10 percent of the population of the United States, to march on the capital to protest prohibition. He did not.

"If in 1919," Frederick Lewis Allen recalled several years later, "you had informed the average American citizen that prohibition was destined to furnish the most violently explosive public issue of the 1920s, he would probably have told you you were crazy."

3

Across the River
and into the Trees

Our aces could drop souvenir post cards from George Creel, assuring the Canadians that we have no quarrel with them as a nation, that all we want is peace without whiskey, and that this is merely a war to make the United States safe for the soda fountains.

Ring Lardner
"Oh, Shoot!"

I

In the last months of 1919 hardly anybody suspected that Canada would shortly provide a major challenge to America's new national prohibition. The expiration of wartime Dominion prohibition throughout Canada on January 1, 1920, thus sent no political shock waves south of the Great Lakes. Control of the retail sale of alcoholic beverages was returned to the provinces, and in all but two of them prohibition was maintained. In Ontario, which shares a long common border with the United States along the Great Lakes from Minnesota to New York, a provincial temperance act of 1916, upheld by a referendum of 1919, prohibited the retail sale of alcoholic beverages after January 1, 1920. Under the Canadian federal system, however, while provincial parliaments controlled the retail sale of alcoholic beverages, the manufacture, importation, and exportation of liquor was controlled from Ottawa. As a result, with the expiration of Dominion prohibition in early 1920, breweries and distilleries, all holding charters from Ottawa, began once again legally to produce alcoholic beverages for interprovincial and international shipment and sale. Ontario residents who could not legally purchase liquor in their own province might legally import it from another province for personal consumption. A resident of Windsor, Ontario, for example, through an express company could order liquor produced in Quebec shipped to his home by common carrier; or he might order liquor or beer produced at one of Windsor's breweries or distilleries exported to Quebec and then transported back to his home in Windsor; but to "short circuit" liquor—ship it directly to his residence from a Windsor distillery a few blocks away—was illegal. Canadian prohibitionists worried over the temptation to criminal behavior inherent in this division of authority, and as dry spokesman Ben Spence speculated, "So long as liquor is legally made, and people have thirsts, and this demand and supply are as close together as in Ontario, it is difficult to keep the liquor and the thirst from connecting up." The liquor and the thirst did connect up, not only in Ontario but in America as well.

Perhaps it was the frightful potential of the power of suggestion that prevented American prohibitionists from publicly commenting on the renewal of legalized liquor production in Canada. With so many American drinkers precariously on the wagon, pointing to the specter of numerous Canadian distilleries and breweries in full production—sixteen distilleries and twenty-nine breweries in Ontario alone in 1920—seemed a little like shouting fire in a crowded movie theater. And in the Detroit area, where the border separating the liquor and the thirst was scarcely a mile wide, prohibitionists waited and hoped for a miracle.

For many years prior to 1920 Canadian liquor and beer had competed successfully for the American drinking market, and the Canadian liquor industry had established a significantly loyal American clientele. Before disruption by Canadian and American wartime prohibition legislation, large breweries and distilleries had moved to the Ontario Border Cities of Windsor, Walkerville, and Sandwich along the Detroit River only one mile from the Motor City. The Detroit River, owned jointly by the United States and Canada, is eighteen miles long and one mile wide, and serves as a commercial link between the two countries, connecting as well as separating their two economies. On maps a dotted line representing the international border runs down the middle of the river and skips back and forth between several islands. But as Prohibition Commissioner Roy Haynes lamented, it is impossible to prevent liquor from dripping through a dotted line. The course of the river between Lake St. Clair in the north and Lake Erie in the south was a natural invitation to smuggling. Heavily overgrown areas on the Canadian shore were broken by sophisticated export facilities at the Border Cities and at LaSalle and Amherstburg. Several large islands in the middle of the river provided landing, resting, and observation posts for smugglers. Hundreds of private homes lined the American shore, particularly near the downriver villages south of Detroit. Private boat wells served many of these structures. High fences surrounded the homes and their docking facilities and special obstructions obscured the view of these homes both from the river and from nearby public streets. None of the homes or boat wells, moreover, could be entered by police authorities without a search warrant. Many of them, consequently, served as relatively secure landing sites for smugglers. Hundreds of fishermen worked the river and Lake Erie daily from the downriver communities and knew exactly how and where to bring in contraband items even before liquor became the most valuable contraband of all. "The Lord probably could have built a river better suited for rum smuggling," Roy Haynes said. "But the Lord probably never did!" A journalist surveying the region concluded that it was "a rum runners' paradise; it is as though a sympathetic creator had fashioned the district expressly for such a purpose."

To keep Canadian booze from crossing to the American shore, American drys expected the cooperation of Canadian authorities. They also expected that a healthy patriotic respect for the law would prevent any significant number of Americans from attempting to smuggle liquor. Unfortunately, Canadian cooperation was not forthcoming (at least not initially); nor did prohibition have any significantly restraining effect on the desire of many Americans for easy fortunes. As the prohibitionists watched, almost helplessly, the worst happened: In the next ten years, along the shores of the Detroit River, the prohibition dream became an American nightmare.

II

On January 2, 1920, Canadian customs officials in Windsor reported an unusual demand for motorboat licenses and warned that liquor smuggling on a considerable scale into the United States was about to be attempted. Large orders for liquor and beer to be delivered at export docks in the Border Cities and in LaSalle and Amherstburg were made. The booze was to be shipped, so the orders said, to Cuba, Mexico, the French Islands at the mouth of the St. Lawrence River, and to several other foreign ports. More than 900,000 cases of liquor were shipped into the Border Cities for "private consumption" during the first seven months of 1920, increasing the per-capita consumption level from a prewar 9 gallons to 102 gallons. Many Ontario residents ordered large quantities of liquor shipped to their homes and then resold it at fantastic profits to those willing to smuggle it into the United States. One Windsor woman, suspected of selling to smugglers, purchased forty cases and nine barrels of liquor during the first half of 1920. When called before a Windsor police magistrate to explain just how she could consume such an incredible amount of alcohol she insisted simply that she had taken up serious drinking since the war, and now downed at least five quarts of whisky daily. The unsympathetic magistrate ordered authorities to confiscate the remainder of her booze cache.

A brisk business appeared in hijacking trucks that carried liquor from the distilleries to the export docks. Ben Spence complained that liquor manufactured in Walkerville "starts out on truck loads, car loads, and boat loads toward every conceivable point on the border, and melts away in transit." Ships bound for foreign ports cleared from the Border Cities with liquor and then landed and unloaded at another point on the Ontario coast. Spence estimated that over a thousand cases of liquor daily were illegally shipped from one point in Ontario to another. Years later, some American smugglers recalled that in the first months of 1920 nearly 25 percent of the population of Ontario within a few miles of the Detroit River was in some way connected with the illegal liquor business. Some Windsor residents even drove to Montreal to purchase their own liquor, then smuggled it back into Windsor in their automobiles. It was illegal for citizens of Ontario to carry liquor in a boat on the Detroit River without the proper export papers, and during the first seven months of 1920 Windsor courts collected nearly a quarter of a million dollars from boaters illegally possessing booze.

For a year and a half after the repeal of Canadian federal prohibition, attempts to smuggle liquor across the Detroit River were hesitant and generally amateurish. The legal status of liquor consigned for delivery in the United States was uncertain, and some Canadian customs authorities insisted that such exports were illegal. To avoid litigation in the dispute, by "gentleman's agreement," the consigned destination of liquor exported from Ontario was usually anywhere but the United States. Large shipments of liquor consigned to Caribbean ports left the Border Cities daily. One observer of the export business recorded that "the country of Mexico has become as rich an El Dorado for Canadian distillers as it ever was for the conquistadores of Cortez." The fact that almost none of the liquor that left the distilleries ever reached its consigned foreign destination did not discourage the "Mexican buyers," who repeated their orders "with dogged pertinacity."

In July 1921, following a special petition by the provincial parliament, the importation of liquor into Ontario from another province was made illegal, and the future of liquor smuggling from the province became uncertain. Then on August 11, 1921, the exportation question was resolved and the liquor export market broke wide open. On that day, in a Windsor court, Police Magistrate W. E. Gundy ruled that shipments of beer and liquor from Canada to the United States were lawful, and declared that the government had no legal powers to prevent such shipments. The decision was made in a test case brought by the British-American Brewing Company involving the seizure by Sandwich police of a shipment of beer consigned to five persons in Wyandotte, Michigan. The court upheld the position of James Haverson, counsel for the brewery, who argued that the company operated under a Dominion charter and thus had an unlimited right to export its product to any other country in the world regardless of provincial liquor laws. E. R. Bond, vice-president of the brewery, said of the case, "We have no knowledge of or interest in the laws of the United States and believe that we are privileged to fill orders for shipments of beer to the United States even if it is illegal for the citizens of the United States to have beer." The president of the Walkerville Brewing Company announced that in the future, "If Sam Smith of Flint orders a carload of beer, the order will go through in the usual way. We will obtain clearance for the beer at the customs office and deliver it to Sam Smith in any boat he sends. We have complied with the law and there our responsibility ends." The only restriction in brewery sales would be to those suspected of short-circuiting booze back into Ontario. "If a boat puts out . . . it cannot return to shore," he warned, "although it may anchor in Canadian waters. If we have any suspicion that the beer might be returned to Canada, we will not fill the order." This position satisfied the legal requirements of the government as well as the economic desires of the brewing industry.

With the announcement of the Gundy decision, large investors began moving into the export business. On August 16, 1921, a charter was granted to the Essex Export Company, Ltd., which was formed to "have liquor for export sale, either in a bonded liquor warehouse or any other warehouse." The charter was only the first of several to be issued in the next weeks to companies set up to sell liquor specifically consigned for delivery in the United States. The new developments shocked American authorities who a few weeks previously had abandoned river patrols to prevent smuggling and had announced that they expected smuggling across the Detroit River to die out with the enforcement of prohibition in Ontario. They now faced an enterprise of ominous and rapidly growing proportions.

III

Years later, in recalling the development of liquor smuggling across the Detroit River, several of the men who first engaged in the trade remembered that it had actually begun on a very limited scale in April 1918, only a few days before Michigan's state prohibition law became operational. Three workers from the Ecorse shipyards took their weekly pay and some savings and traveled to Montreal, where the sale of liquor was legal, and between the three of them purchased twenty-five cases of whisky. They then drove back to Windsor and rowed a small boat back and forth across the river transporting their treasure. It was necessary to make two trips across the mile-wide river, and at the same time to watch for Canadian and American customs inspectors. The smuggling was successful, the liquor was sold in Ecorse in the next days, and the profits were used to finance a second and then a third night trip to Montreal. Another partner was taken in and within a week the small group was purchasing liquor in thousand-case lots.

Following the Gundy decision, Michigan State Police armed with high-powered rifles were mobilized along the river to discourage smugglers. A New York *Times* correspondent in Detroit reported that despite the mobilization, Canadian exporters seemed intent upon setting some kind of record. Hundreds of Americans rushed to do business with the export companies and smuggle booze across the river. Most of the smugglers in the first months of 1920 were nervous and jittery. The smuggling was done mostly at night, and as soon as the sun set smugglers brought their goods to the water's edge. Most of these early operations were simply "mom and pop" enterprises involving hesitant and suspense-filled episodes with amateurish and humorous overtones. "When they first started we'd take it across by rowboat and duckboat, ten cases, fifteen cases at a time," one Canadian smuggler remembered. "You didn't want to

make too much noise over there because you didn't have no out-
board motors at that time and if you had an inboard motor that
would make a bit of a noise."

The London (Ontario) *Times* reported that Canadians and
Americans with secret caches of liquor waited in hiding "like Indians" among the trees and tall grass on the Canadian side of the
river. When boats of smugglers passed by they were signaled with
"pocket torches." The boaters landed and bargaining took place for
the liquor. Once the deal was closed, the liquor changed hands and
was transported across the river and into the trees along the American shore. Those who rowed had the advantage of silence but the
disadvantage of lack of speed when approached by patrol boats.

A system of signals came into use, with each group or family
entering the risky trade adopting its own primitive patterns for yes
and no or stop and go. On clear evenings, as a Canadian customs
boat cruised slowly down the river, the shoreline behind it came
alive with signals from pocket torches and automobile headlights.
One or two quick flashes might mean a small boat was starting
across. A blue light flashed once and then twice quickly meant all
clear. A visitor to the river almost certainly would have concluded
that the Canadian and American shorelines were alive with millions
of colorful fireflies. A large sheet hung on a clothesline meant not
that someone was drying bedding but that police were in the area.
When the sheet was taken down, the coast was clear. A flashing red
light meant "turn back immediately! Police have arrived!" Anyone
with a diabolical sense of humor, a bed sheet, and a lantern might
have brought hours of terrifying confusion to the already jittery
smugglers.

Small independent smuggling operations dominated this early
illegal liquor traffic. Neighbor joined with neighbor to pool money
and form primitive partnerships and temporary minicorporations to
purchase and illegally transport alcoholic beverages. One smuggler
recalled of those early efforts, "It was all common people. They
weren't gangsters. The majority of the guys that were buying the
whisky were all people like us that would go out and buy, invest
their money, to try to make a little bit on it. It was all common
people and neighbors together and one neighbor would land at
another neighbor's place and so forth. They never thought there was
nothing criminal about it." Women participated from the very start

in the smuggling. "Everybody and his brothers and sisters and aunts" helped transport the liquor, a smuggler remembered. "Anybody that had fourteen dollars and his train fare to Montreal would go across the river and buy a case of whisky." There was a kind of democracy in this early criminal traffic. Apparently nobody considered himself a criminal. Hardly anybody packed a gun. People from nearly every walk of life saw a chance to make a profit on a small investment and they took it. Within a few months a new phrase had been coined to describe the outlaw activity—"rum-running."

The Detroit *News* reported in August 1920 that already the business of bringing contraband liquor into the country from Canada had become "intricately organized" by bands of astute operators who realized early in the development of the traffic the tremendous profits to be made from rum-running. Detroit Police Commissioner Dr. James Inches reported in November 1920 that he knew of more than fifty Detroiters who made more than $100,000 each in the first six months of prohibition by transporting liquor across the Detroit River. The increasing effectiveness of police patrols did little to deter the rumrunners, he said. One woman from Sandwich, Ontario, Inches reported, bought a boat for $3,200, had the use of it for less than one month, then lost it to the authorities. Still she succeeded in making a handsome profit in that short period. Boat owners who worked regularly with a small crew from an export dock, it was rumored, could transport about 2,500 cases of liquor each month. The average net profit in that period was $25,000, with the owner himself earning $10,000. Law enforcement authorities reported that many rumrunners made as much as 800 percent profit on a load of liquor. The astronomical profits, as Inches pointed out, made the risks to rumrunners worth taking.

Inches and other law enforcement officials also complained of the Canadian taxation system that provided greater revenues for the government from liquor smuggled into the United States than from liquor exported to countries without prohibition laws. The Dominion government levied a tax of $9 per gallon on all liquors. This amount was refunded upon presentation of a customs receipt from the country to which the liquor was exported. Since rumrunners did not return with receipts from American customs officials, their tax dollars were retained by the government just as though the liquor had been consumed domestically by Canadians. By 1928 the Cana-

dian government was gathering an estimated $30 million in taxes
each year from illegal liquor exportations to America. This amount
did not include taxes on the monumental profits reaped by Canadian
commercial liquor interests due to the inflated prices of liquor in
America. In the 1920s, thanks to American prohibition, liquor became one of Canada's largest industries, and taxes on liquor provided one-fifth of all Dominion and provincial revenues.

At first most of the law enforcement agencies along the border
believed that rum-running would die out, and until that day smuggling could be discouraged by shore patrols that would apprehend
rumrunners at their landing points on the American side of the river.
But as the rum-running trade developed and expanded and it became clear that the policy of the Canadian government would be one
of non-interference and non-cooperation, American law enforcement agencies gradually accepted the necessity of committing patrol boats to the prohibition war. By the summer of 1922 the "Prohibition Navy," consisting of patrol units from the Detroit Police
Department, the Michigan State Police, the Prohibition Border Patrol, Customs Border Patrol, and the United States Coast Guard
daily pursued suspected smugglers up and down the Detroit River.

In early 1920 the Detroit Police Department owned only a single
patrol boat with which to discourage rumrunners. Police Commissioner Inches remembered, "The boats of the rumrunners ran circles around us." As Inches described it, the police boat was "a good
seaworthy scrow that by an effort could overhaul a tugboat." Prior
to 1920 the boat had been adequate for police work on the river.
Then in the fall of 1920 the Detroit police seized the Tennessee II,
the fastest cruiser on the river, while the craft was unloading a
liquor cargo on the American shore. In what would soon become
standard procedure for all law enforcement agencies along the river,
the police confiscated the craft and recommissioned it as a police
patrol boat. The capture of the Tennessee II and the success of the
boat in running down liquor smugglers gradually sent the price of
Canadian liquor in Detroit up by $5 a case. But the Tennessee II
alone could not stop rum-running, and for every smuggler apprehended, literally hundreds of others successfully crossed the
river. In the spring of 1921 two new police patrol boats equipped
with machine guns were commissioned for river duty.

The Michigan State Police began to aid the Detroit police on the river and commissioned their own river patrol in August 1921. Like the Detroit police, the state police at first had only a single ancient craft that could catch only the slowest rumrunners. They sought to overcome this frustrating situation by shooting rumrunners to slow them down, and the river rapidly became a more dangerous place for all boaters. The situation was partially corrected in the spring of 1922 when Patrol Boat No. 1, a two-hundred-horsepower boat with a top speed of thirty-eight miles per hour was launched in Detroit to "inaugurate state marine warfare against the smugglers." The crew of No. 1 was armed with rifles, machine guns, and, for an unexplained reason, tear gas. Two years later, following special funding by the state legislature, four additional heavily armed state police boats were launched. Official announcement of the commissioning claimed that prior to 1924 the state police had been capable only of limiting rum-running, but with the new boats, smuggling across the river would be brought to a standstill.

Despite the fanfare that accompanied the commissioning of city and state police patrols in the river war, the agencies participated only to a limited degree in the conflict. The legal jurisdiction of the Detroit police was limited to a small section of the river, and, like the state police, the city police were responsible for the enforcement not only of the liquor laws but also of hundreds of other important laws. The state police were charged with law enforcement on the state highways and in hundreds of rural townships. As a result, both agencies worked only as auxiliaries to the federal forces primarily responsible for halting international rum-running.

The problem with such division of authority was that the federal agencies were incapable of providing the leadership necessary for a successful campaign against rum-running. Ill trained and poorly equipped, disorganized and uncoordinated, the federal units in the Detroit area were victims of congressional indifference and stinginess. The cause of almost every problem within the federal prohibition enforcement branches, from low morale to high turnover of personnel to widespread graft, could be traced to a lack of funding. Whenever the federal government wished to pare back on the budget, it seemed that the Prohibition Unit was the organization where shortages were most easily tolerated. Federal patrols working the river were constantly plagued with shortages of everything from boats to uniforms. Like a guerrilla army, the federal patrols were forced to wage their war on rumrunners principally through the use of materials captured from the criminals they sought to apprehend. Commanders from each separate branch of the Prohibition Navy complained periodically to Washington to correct critical shortages. But wet congressmen were unsympathetic to the enforcement cause and dry congressmen apparently feared that too large an appropriation for enforcement would be interpreted by the public to mean that prohibition was unpopular and difficult to enforce. To prevent such a misconception, funding for prohibition enforcement was thus kept at a minimum. The actual difficulty experienced by federal forces in their efforts to stop rum-running for nine years was as much the fault of a cheeseparing Congress as of drinkers, rumrunners, and profit-minded Canadian distillers.

Congress was least stingy in funding the United States Coast Guard to pursue smugglers. The Coast Guard had a long and distinguished service record, and its commanders worried openly about the force receiving a tarnished reputation by being assigned an impossible task on an inadequate budget. In 1924, following persistent lobbying, Congress appropriated $13 million to recondition 20 second class destroyers which the Navy transferred to the Coast Guard. By 1928 the Coast Guard had 33 cruisers, 25 destroyers, 243 offshore patrol boats, and 11,000 officers and enlisted men with which to war on smugglers along the ocean and lake borders of the United States.

Spokesmen for the Coast Guard argued effectively from the very start that with more men, money, and ships they could triumph over rum-running. But federal funds always seemed to dry up before booze sources did. Admiral F. C. Billard, commandant of the Coast Guard, testified before a House subcommittee on Treasury appropriations in 1929 that "given sufficient equipment, the Coast Guard could entirely plug up the holes through which foreign liquors came into the United States over the coast lines." Yet no dramatic appropriation of funds followed from Congress.

The Coast Guard was fortunate in having well-trained and experienced personnel to man its patrol craft, so it could use what little it did have effectively. But insufficient funding for the river patrols of the Prohibition Unit and the Customs Border Patrol meant inadequately trained and underpaid, unenthusiastic crews. As a result, numerous government boats were ruined by clumsy handling, burned out engines, twisted propellers, and collisions with buoys and other obstructions in the river. Like Admiral Billard of the Coast Guard, Carey D. Ferguson, Collector of Customs in Detroit from 1927 until 1929, insisted that better funding could completely shut off the liquor traffic. Despite the fact that 27 percent of the total funds allowed for the patrol nationally were spent in the Detroit district, a sum nearly three times that spent in any other district, it was inadequate. In 1928 the patrol succeeded in seizing less than 5 percent of the liquor leaving the Border Cities export docks. "We never had enough men or enough equipment to do the job properly," Ferguson recalled. "At the start we had twenty-five or thirty men, no boats, no bases, and a few old rattletrap cars that had been seized from rumrunners. . . ." Until the summer of 1929, every boat used by the Customs Border Patrol had been seized from rumrunners. Federal forces on the river were not equipped with field glasses until 1926 or with handcuffs to hold their prisoners until 1927. Prior to the summer of 1928 the border patrol had no uniforms and the federal government provided them with caps and badges only. A federal investigation into the Customs Border Patrol in 1927 revealed extremely demoralizing conditions. Although the patrol quota for Detroit was forty-two men, only twenty-four were in the service at the time of the investigation. Only three patrol boats were in use; all of the others awaited major repairs. The commanding officer of the patrol blamed it all on lack of money. Had the full force of forty-two men been employed, Col. A. J. Hanlon warned, the department would have run out of money halfway through the year. A former chief of the patrol bitterly testified after resigning in 1927 that "it's a rotten business and I'm glad to be out of it."

Agents of the Prohibition Unit stationed in Detroit not only worked in a more hazardous location than other agents, but were paid less. Nationally, in 1920, the salary of prohibition agents ranged from $1,200 to $2,000. But outside of the Detroit area a special arrangement had been made by the Treasury Department to supplement the income of the agents. The men were assigned to a duty post in one area, and were then sent to work in another area nearby. They received daily travel allowances from one point to the other, but almost all took up residence where most of their work was done, and thereby succeeded in pocketing the travel allowance. In Detroit, however, there was no such allowance, and agents assigned to work on the river patrol were paid no more than the civilian pilots and mechanics on their boats. Little wonder then that recruiting honest and conscientious agents for prohibition work proved to be an almost impossible task. And, as historian Andrew Sinclair pointed out, bootleggers had more than a hundred times the appropriation of the Prohibition Unit, and they were better organized too. As a result, Sinclair said, "the inadequate were forced by their country to pursue the prepared."

Cooperation between the various enforcement agencies was initiated in earnest in the spring of 1922 when eight speedboats of the Prohibition Unit were added to the seven craft of the city and state police on the Detroit River. At the same time contracts were let out to local shipbuilding firms for the construction of five additional motor launches that would achieve a speed of 35 to 40 miles per hour on the river. The fleet that resulted from this combination of forces was the ragtag conglomeration of boats of all shapes and sizes, most of them captured from rumrunners, manned by crews dressed in various uniforms and armed with every variety of weapon from clubs to machine guns to tear gas. The press saw it as the wackiest navy that ever sailed any body of water, a fleet without admirals or admiration, and dubbed it the "Prohibition Navy." In 1926, in an effort to better coordinate all of the units of the Prohibition Navy, the federal branch of the fleet was placed under the command of the Collector of Customs in Detroit, Carey D. Ferguson. Ferguson sought to upgrade his navy by decommissioning the slowest craft, supplying the crews with field glasses, and promising to apply future government appropriations for enforcement in the area to the purchase of automobiles! Ferguson concluded, logically, that his navy might be more effective against rumrunners if it sneaked up on them from the land and caught them while they unloaded their cargo.

After three years of widely publicized failures to discourage rumrunners by using every tactic from shooting them to running them over and drowning them, in 1925 the government temporarily entertained a promising proposal for sinking the "mosquito fleet," as the rum-running boats were popularly called. Nationally acclaimed speedboat racer and enthusiastic prohibitionist Garfield Arthur ("Gar") Wood was offered the job of Director of Prohibition

Enforcement for the Eastern Judicial District of Michigan, with the specific assignment of shutting off rum-running in the area. The nomination of Wood for the job came from General Lincoln C. Andrews, Assistant Secretary of the Treasury in charge of prohibition enforcement, following Wood's suggestion for the construction of two hundred specially designed speedboats to chase down rum-runners on the Detroit River. Wood's acceptance of the government appointment hinged upon the federal government's appropriating the money to provide him with the equipment necessary for the effective fight against smugglers. Wood suggested that two hundred surplus stock Liberty airplane engines in the possession of the War Department be transferred to the Prohibition Unit. Wood then offered to build the speedboats and install the liberty engines at cost for the government so that a serious effort to swat the mosquito fleet could be made. But like all other practical proposals for effective prohibition enforcement in the 1920s, Wood's plan became ensnared in red tape and the reluctance of federal agencies to request additional congressional expenditures. Also, the War Department was reluctant to transfer the engines at a nominal price to the Treasury Department. Wood insisted that it was useless to accept the job of enforcing prohibition without receiving the material resources necessary to complete the task. His position, of course, was unprecedented in the prohibition enforcement field, and because of that very few federal administrators took his proposal seriously. Within a few weeks, Wood's plan of two hundred speedboats in hot pursuit of the mosquito fleet fell through, and the commanders of the Prohibition Navy reverted to their previous practice of picketing the river and patrolling popular points of entry. Wood went back to boat racing and defending the Harmsworth Cup, and set up his own boat works on the St. Clair River. Some of the boats built by the Gar Wood Boat Works a few years later were used by practical-minded pilots of the mosquito fleet to outdistance slower government vessels.

The task of the Prohibition Navy was made increasingly difficult and frustrating as rumrunners experimented with more imaginative and bizarre methods of liquor transportation in their efforts to evade apprehension. In the 1920s, law enforcement officers pursued boats on the river, planes in the air over the river, submarine cables on the bottom of the river, mislabeled freight cars in the railroad tunnels under the bottom of the river, and ice boats, sleds, and cars on the icy surface of the river in the winter.

In September 1920, Major A. V. Dalrymple, Federal Prohibition Enforcement Commissioner for the Central District, announced that he was considering making a request to the federal government for a special pursuit plane to be stationed in Detroit as an air auxiliary to the regular ground forces. Dalrymple proposed that an Army aviator be selected for the patrol work and that the officer be given the same powers as a regular revenue agent. A second plane, Dalrymple suggested, would be stationed near Chicago for similar patrol work.

Had Dalrymple's request been granted—and it was not—it would have been a simple process for him to find an Army pilot familiar with routes of flying rumrunners, because several Army pilots stationed at Selfridge Field in Mt. Clemens, Michigan, together with a number of civilian pilots in the Detroit area, were already engaged in the transportation of liquor by air from Canada. The ease of air rum-running largely explained the enthusiasm of many officers for flying daily practice maneuvers to Ontario and back. An intelligence officer stationed at Fort Wayne discovered the extent of military involvement in air rum-running during the course of his investigation into the crash of an Army aircraft on August 20, 1921, eight miles from Windsor.

Rum-running by boat was as hazardous as it was profitable, and the dangers discouraged many a potential Ishmael from sailing with the mosquito fleet. Successful rum-running involved coordination and speed as well as bravery, bribery, and luck. Consequently, from the start of prohibition, imaginative would-be rum kings sought safer ways to transport liquor from Ontario to Michigan. By September 1920, nine months after the start of federal prohibition, an alternative method—aerial rum-running—was in use.

The ability to fly over the Prohibition Navy and to carry a cargo deep within the United States for unloading provided a strong temptation for rumrunners to adopt the airplane. The Detroit *Free Press* quoted one flier as saying that although the government could block the river, they could do nothing about flying liquor by air across the river. Airplanes cost less than a good speedboat, he insisted, and loads could be flown directly to Chicago. "They'll have a tough time stopping us," he bragged. "We'll fly right over their heads and laugh at them."

Yet the disadvantages of air rum-running were also significant. The flying was done in the daytime, since night flying was still dangerous, and if a plane were going any great distance, it might easily become lost and be detected by the police. Also, airplanes were still a novelty and people reported seeing them come down. There could be no regular landing place for the aircraft for long without the police tracking it down. But perhaps the greatest disadvantage was the limited cargo capacity and the number of flights that a plane could make each day. Crossing the river by boat with a large cargo took only a few minutes. An airplane carrying a much smaller load, on the other hand, took several hours to transfer its load to a safe landing field. As a result, aerial rum-running functioned best as an alternative method of transport during periods of intensified enforcement "drives" along the river and lakes. Increases in the number of liquor planes flying out of Ontario were noted particularly during the last great enforcement drive in the summer of 1929. By the spring of 1930 authorities estimated that as much as $100,000 worth of liquor was exported from Windsor to the United States by air each month. Yet that total amount of liquor could have supplied drinks for only about forty of the fifteen thousand blind pigs in Detroit.

In order to combat aerial rum-running, in January 1922 federal prohibition agents began using a conficated rum-running airplane for their own air patrol. But the expense of operating the machine along with the belief that aerial rum-running was very limited discouraged the agents, and the idea of a federal prohibition air force was abandoned.

Syndicates tried their hand at air smuggling in the 1920s, but most were quickly infiltrated and broken up by federal agents. In the spring of 1929 several Canadian-American syndicates obtained charters from the Canadian government granting them the right to export liquor by ship, truck, or airplane, and to set up wireless stations. One syndicate allegedly used landing fields in three different Michigan counties. Cars with floodlights aided the pilots in landing, and the pilots themselves were paid five dollars for each case of liquor delivered. A Chicago syndicate headed by Ralph Capone owned twenty rum-carrying airplanes, the largest, a trimotored monoplane that carried fifty cases of liquor. Another Chicago group ran four airplanes, each carrying from fifteen to eighteen cases per trip.

Flying an especially dangerous mission, whether over the Atlantic Ocean to Paris or over the Detroit River to Michigan, captured the imagination of the public. Newspapers therefore devoted a good deal of space to reporting the antics of aerial rumrunners. Only one practitioner of the trade, however, achieved any real notoriety. Irving Schleig, the Lindbergh of Rum-Running, was captured near Kalamazoo, Michigan, in 1925. He had been forced down by bad weather and was detained by the police along with his $1,000 liquor cargo. Schleig was released on bond but never stood trial for rumrunning. A few weeks later his flying career was prematurely and unexpectedly terminated just outside Chicago when somebody shot a bullet into his brain.

A large quantity of liquor was delivered to the United States during the prohibition years by railroad cars routed through the railway tunnels under the Detroit River. Railroad cars, fraudulently labeled or routed for Mexico by way of the United States, were sidetracked and unloaded in freight yards in and around Detroit. In 1923 the New York *Times* estimated that eight hundred cases of beer daily were delivered by mislabeled freight cars to Detroit. Five years later the Detroit *News* insisted that nearly one-half of the liquor imported illegally into the city came by rail. The usual procedure for such smuggling involved shipping a carload of some commodity from one point in the United States, through Canada, and then back into the United States at another point. A trainload of almost any legal product could be shipped from Buffalo through Canada to Detroit. On the American side at its terminal the car was inspected and sealed by customs authorities. In Canada the car was detached from the train, unloaded, and whisky or beer substituted. Counterfeit seals were then affixed to the car, it was recoupled to a train, and hauled into the United States. No further customs inspection took place. Railroad employees who cooperated in the simple process were generously rewarded by rumrunners.

Because it involved extraordinarily large units, the shipment of liquor by rail was done mostly by large syndicates with enough available capital to pay for several boxcar loads of liquor and to withstand the occasional loss of one of them to federal agents. At times as much as a quarter of a million dollars worth of liquor entered Detroit in a single freight car with nothing more than a fraudulent seal preventing seizure by the police. Consequently, seizures made by the authorities of such shipments were quite spectacular. On November 19, 1927, for example, three cars with freight billed as gears, but containing $200,000 worth of wine and whisky for the holiday trade, were seized by prohibition agents at the North Detroit Station of the Michigan Central Railroad.

Stories of electronically guided, liquor-filled torpedoes swishing back and forth beneath the surface of the river between secret terminals and of a liquor pipeline beneath the riverbed circulated throughout the 1920s and after, and haunted the imagination not only of enforcement authorities but also of inquisitive reporters. Neither the reporters nor the bootleggers ever provided convincing evidence that torpedoes were piloted under the river, but one account of a pipeline did receive some interesting notoriety.

The source of the bizarre account, it was said, was a prominent (but, of course, unnamed) Detroit yachtsman. In a story related shortly before his death, he recalled that when he had worked as an agent for a plumbing firm, in the mid-1920s, he had been approached in his office by a man who wanted to buy a pump that could send a liquid through a two-inch pipeline for about two thousand feet. After ordering such a pump the man refused all offers for aid in installing it properly. When he returned a few days later and picked up the pump he again refused offers of assistance. But he came back one more time to complain that he could not make the pump work and requested the help of a pump expert. After an expert was contacted, both he and the agent accompanied the man. The three traveled across the river and headed downstream on the Canadian side until they came to a small shack in a field some short distance from the river. A freshly dug trench, which probably held a pipeline, ran from the shack to the river. The expert prepared to fix the pump, but when he removed a plug from the air chamber of the apparatus, whisky spurted out and over the three men, literally flooding the room. After a few minutes the pump was working and the agent and the expert were taken back to Detroit. Both men were sworn to secrecy concerning the episode, and the agent related his account only several years later. Authorities, however, never discovered evidence that the pipeline existed.

Yet, in light of other nearly unbelievable methods of liquor transportation, the pipeline story cannot be totally discounted. At both ends of the Detroit River cases of liquor were pulled along the river bottom on sleds with the use of pulleys, engines, and long cables. One account even mentioned a diver helping to guide the sled along the bottom of the river. In the fall of 1929 Customs Border Patrol inspectors discovered an apparatus by which liquor was pulled from Mud Island in the middle of the river near Ecorse to a point on the American shore by means of a 500-foot cable. Fifteen to twenty cases of liquor could be pulled along the river bottom at one time by the apparatus. In December 1931, at the north end of the river, Customs Border Patrol inspectors uncovered another cable and sled apparatus running under the river from Peche Island to a cottage at the foot of Alter Road. An automobile engine furnished power for the setup.

But without doubt the most bizarre as well as the most humorous method of running liquor across the river was driving it across in the winter on the frozen surface of the river and the lakes connected to it. Hot pursuit of rumrunners on the cold frozen surface of the Detroit River often took on the look of a Mack Sennett comedy, where the speed and agility of rumrunners tested the skill, daring, marksmanship, foolhardiness, and sanity of the police officers.

During relatively brief spells of very cold weather, parts of Lake St. Clair, the St. Clair River, the Detroit River, and northern Lake Erie freeze over solid. When this happens it is possible to walk or even drive from Canada to the United States across the ice. In January and February of 1925 and 1926, and again in January, February, and March 1930, the ice was solid enough for rumrunners to use ice boats, sleds, and automobiles to transport liquor to America. During the coldest weeks of winter, convoys of cars from Canada crossed the ice daily. Cars on the American shore lined up at night and turned on their headlights to provide an illuminated expressway across the ice. On Lake Erie rumrunners in long convoys drove across the wide stretch of ice at the foot of the Detroit River. This was the most dangerous section to cross, not only because of the thin ice but also because of the close proximity of the South Rockwood State Police Station. Troopers from that station captured a convoy of rum-running cars on the ice in the late winter of 1925. Instead of risking driving away, the rumrunners abandoned their automobiles and ran back to Canada when they saw the state troopers approaching.

The danger of night crossings on the ice was very great because of fishing holes. State police officers complained about the extreme hazard provided by fishermen who cut holes in the ice and went home at the end of the day leaving dangerous unmarked traps. An automobile that happened to drive into one of those holes "would speedily become a submarine with no power for coming to the surface," the *State Trooper* warned. There was also the haunting danger of thin ice breaking up beneath the automobile. Thin ice was difficult to spot, but rumrunners and police were warned to watch for transparent patches in the ice where the water beneath shown through black. A driver came upon such spots usually without any warning of the danger. The ice would suddenly moan and sag as the driver raced desperately for his life. Only the continued speed of the automobile across the sheet of ice held the weight of the driver and his car above a cold grave. The dangers of ice crossing were demonstrated dramatically in February 1926 when rumrunner Norman Willets of Monroe met death in a liquor-laden sedan he was driving across the northern tip of Lake Erie. The car plunged into the open water near the Canadian shore. Willets had left Amherstburg just before daylight to drive liquor across the ice. He was supposed to follow a lead convoy car, but lost his way. Alone and without lights, Willets turned back to the Canadian shore. On his way back in the dark his car broke through thin ice.

Rumrunners took advantage of an extremely cold January in 1926 to bring liquor across the ice in all sorts of vehicles—trucks, automobiles, and sleds. The vigilance of the enforcement officers near the Livingstone Channel caused the runners to take an indirect route across the river. Starting at Amherstburg the route proceeded below Bois Blanc Island to the mouth of the Huron River and then up to the American shore. Police pursuit across this course was extremely difficult. Late one afternoon, police gave chase to two cars after spotting them on the ice. The pursuit up and down the frozen lake lasted far more than an hour. The ice was covered with a thin film of water and every time the police attempted to pull alongside one of the pursued cars, the rumrunners would swerve sharply, drenching the police with icy water. During the chase ten automobiles filled with more bootleggers came out on the ice five

miles below Monroe and drove between the police and their prey.
The blockade was lifted only after the police threatened to shoot
those manning the blockade. Finally, the harried rumrunners made
a break for the shore, and with their cars climbed up to the road and
headed inland. After a short sprint both cars skidded around a
corner into a ditch. Both rumrunners jumped out and ran, but only
one escaped. After a footrace of over a mile, the police apprehended
one lowly rumrunner.

Another long cold spell in January and February 1930 made the
ice thick and inviting on upper Lake Erie and the Detroit River.
Then the long drive by a circuitous route marked by hundreds of tire
tracks was merely an "exhilarating ride of five minutes in the fresh
winds" with handsome profits at the end of the journey. One morning in February 1930 a Detroit *News* reporter counted seventy-five
automobiles leave the Amherstburg beer docks. About ten of them
bore Ohio license plates, and these headed downriver for points
south and east along the Ohio shore. Many others drove to the
Canadian side of Grosse Ile, then drove up on the shore of the island
where the liquor was unloaded into camouflaged trucks to be driven
across the toll bridge to the American mainland. But the largest
number drove from the Amherstburg docks to Bob-lo Park, skirted
the north end of the island, and then headed west for about 2,500
feet to the Livingstone Channel. This reached, they then drove
south for about a mile and there diverged into two trails. One of the
trails led directly to a slip on the lower end of Grosse Ile where,
during the summer, rumrunners took refuge in their fast motor-
boats. The other trail led nearly two miles to a point further north.
As the cars drove, it was about two miles from the upper end of
Bob-lo Park to the Grosse Ile slip, or a five or six minute ride over
the ice. The only dangerous portion of the trip was along the side of
Bob-lo Park, where the ice was treacherous. Rumrunners there
drove with two wheels as far on the shore as possible. But from the
upper end of the island to Gross Ile the path was safe and the ice
solid. No effort was made by the runners to hide their loads. "We
have to take a chance, of course," one of them told the *News*
reporter. "But the law isn't the thing we fear most. What we are
really afraid of is the ice. Any time it may give way beneath and let
one of us through." A car or two had crashed through the ice a few
days earlier, but no lives were lost in the accidents.

Iceboats had many advantages over automobiles on the frozen

surface of Lake St. Clair and the Detroit River. They were lighter, moved faster, and were safer on thin ice. Propelled by strong gusts of wind in their sails, iceboats used by the rumrunners were "phantoms to their pursuers," the state police complained. "A ring of steel clad runners, a ghostly flash of bellying sail and they are gone." The Detroit *News* described rum-running by iceboat as "adventure framed in moonlight, and as grim as the romance of the buccaneers of the Spanish Main." The boats sped across the slick ice of Lake St. Clair in twelve minutes, and simply could not be touched by enforcement officers. They were called, in fact, "the scourge of prohibition enforcement officers." "A gust of flying snow and perhaps now and then a trace of silver canvas stretched taught in the wind," the *News* reported, and the boats were gone. State police used automobiles equipped with tire chains to pursue iceboats, but the fastest patrol car on the lake was slow compared to an iceboat. "Get near the iceboat and there is a sudden tack, perhaps near enough to send an auto skidding for many feet, and the phantom rum smuggler is hundreds of feet away." The police tried to capture the craft by ambushing them at their destination. But if the police were spotted hiding on the shore, the boats quickly reversed their direction and in the wink of an eye were far downriver, leaving the unfortunate enforcement officers freezing in the night, waiting for a less wary runner.

The ingenuity of both police and rumrunners in utilizing the ice was often imaginative. Rumrunners nailed ski runners to boats and pushed them across the lake or towed several behind a car. When police approached, the boats were simply cut loose and abandoned in the middle of the river. In order to aid them in hot pursuit on the ice, federal agents were equipped with "ice creepers," a spiked attachment that fit over the shoe to prevent slipping on the ice. But running with creepers was difficult and progress was safe but slow. Some rumrunners consequently wore ice skates and gracefully escaped the clutches of the creeping cops.

IV

Many river sailors survived to describe to children and friends adventures in purchasing liquor and sneaking it across the Detroit

River past Border Patrol inspectors and state troopers. The press was infatuated with the trade and romanticized the lives of the buccaneers of booze. Yet despite numerous interviews with rum-runners and almost daily spying operations by inquisitive reporters, the newspapers remained hard-pressed in providing specific bona fide heroes of the trade. Rum-running was a tough, often ruthless business, and those who survived in it long enough to gain notoriety were generally not the kind to be held up for public admiration. When some of the most successful rumrunners from the downriver area were indicted and brought into court in 1928 and 1929, they proved to be cowardly, cruel, and dishonest, having more in common with pickpockets and pimps than with sea dogs and buc-caneers.

Yet, now and then a professional rumrunner did gain a certain small degree of public admiration, but these were very rare excep-tions. One such exception was the carefree and colorful admiral of "Peajacket's Navy," John Wozniak of Ecorse. Wozniak, who was in his early twenties during his rum-running years, employed a fleet of twenty-five "sailors" to transport Canadian liquor into the United States. Wozniak's tars were instructed to avoid violence and to outwit enforcement patrols—a task assumed not to be very difficult. The men were unarmed, and Wozniak himself never carried a gun. Whenever a member of Peajacket's Navy was apprehended, Woz-niak stood beside him, financed his defense, and paid the fine if the man was convicted. When Wozniak was jailed in 1928, he was just twenty-two years old. He had succeeded in his business by bribing Customs Border Patrol officials, but had been arrested when a large bribery operation was broken up in 1928. "When I was indicted I was through for good," Wozniak promised in court. "The law was getting too strong. I sold my boats and scuttled the others. I went into the automobile business and have done pretty well." Wozniak's love of sports contributed to the destruction of his navy. He had sponsored a football team representing Peajacket's Navy and his team gained some local fame in the downriver area. Law enforce-ment officers watched the games to familiarize themselves with rumrunners of Wozniak's organization. When he disbanded the navy, Wozniak continued his football team under the name of his new automobile agency.

But those who plied the illegal liquor trade as regularly as Wozniak shared neither his even disposition nor his nonbelligerence. Unidentified bodies discovered floating in the river near Ecorse almost nightly in 1923 testified to the perils of rum-running. Police regularly discovered corpses in and around the river where rumrunners were most active. Some of the victims had been shot, some beaten to death, and some had drowned. Whether their boats had overturned or they had been thrown out or fallen out of their craft, or whether stray bullets from the Prohibition Navy had ended their life was never known. No clues were found. Investigating police officers invariably found that those suspected or rum-running knew "nothing about nothing" involving the cases.

Consequently, rumrunners who survived in the business learned how to live with danger. At first there were the simple mechanical risks—crossing the river at night in a boat overloaded with booze and manned, at times, by amateurs unable to navigate properly. The boats were easily upset or ran aground in shallow water some distance from shore only to be "rescued" by police patrol boats. Losing direction on the river in the middle of the night was a common hazard, especially dangerous during a crossing on the ice, as were collisions between boats. Other dangers became apparent as the years passed. The forty-foot cruiser *Owl* blew up in August 1924 as it was about to start for the American shore with a load of beer. The engine of the $40,000 craft backfired and ignited gasoline leaking from the tank, killing the pilot and seriously injuring the three-man crew.

Even greater dangers were presented by pirates. For if large profits were to be made by "honest" rum-running, even greater profits could be made by anyone unscrupulous enough to rob rumrunners. As early as 1921 pirates were reportedly roaming the river like the English sea dogs of the sixteenth century who sailed the Spanish Main in search of plunder. Because of these individuals, pariahs even of the society of rumrunners, crossing the river at night became even more dangerous than might be expected. Rumrunners therefore not only watched for police boats but also for the boats of masked pirates who pulled alongside and transferred a cargo at gunpoint. "Pullers" crossing the river with cash for large purchases especially feared the pirates. But slower, loaded boats of independent shippers were more likely to fall victim to the pirates. The pirates themselves, known as the "go-through guys" of the river, also plied a precarious trade. Should they make the mistake of attempting to hijack liquor protected by guards of a large rum-running organization or of any of the numerous ruthless gangs that ran liquor across the river, punishment for their error was immediate and final.

But rum-running was not totally lawless. It had its own commandments, its own unwritten constitution, statutes, and code of fair play. Rules were set and appended by the syndicates, the big shippers, and the small independents proud enough to call themselves "legitimate" rumrunners. Legitimate rumrunners learned that the size of their market depended to a great degree upon the ability to supply a product of fairly high quality. A reputation for bad quality or a fraudulently labeled product distributed to those who diluted the imported liquor, undercut the market and hurt all shippers. The ideal business in this respect, and the one to be emulated by aspiring professional rumrunners, was William McCoy of the Atlantic Coast Rum Row, whose product was sold as "the real McCoy." McCoy's reputation clearly enhanced the marketability of his products, which, like those of thousands of other shippers, were "genuine," and drinkers of such beverages needed to fear neither blindness, sickness, paralysis, sobriety, or any other curse resulting from imbibing adulterated liquors. Warnings were issued to all those who would disrupt the liquor market by selling poisoned products. The inviolable commandments for a dependable, smooth-running trade were: Thou shalt not use denatured or wood alcohol in "cutting" or diluting good Canadian liquor; thou shalt mind thine own business; thou shalt not cooperate with police authorities; thou shalt not cooperate with newspaper reporters; thou shalt know nothing about nothing involving crimes on the river; thou shalt not steal from other rumrunners: thou shalt not default on debts because of capture by police; thou shalt not use counterfeit money to pay for liquor; thou shalt not undercut another's market. The rewards for obedience to these commandments was a more abundant, profitable, and safer life. The rumrunners' fair trade commission was simply a boat with a gun-toting commissioner who pulled alongside a commandment breaker and put him out of business permanently. The only review, substantive or procedural, was done by the coroner's office and the police.

The most widely known case of rumrunner flaunting all the

commandments was that of the legendary Gray Ghost (real name unknown) of Detroit. A pirate, extortionist, and counterfeiter, he worked the river as an outcast from both respectable and rum-running societies. The Gray Ghost piloted a gray boat, dressed in gray with a gray hat and a gray mask, carried two gray pistols and a gray machine gun. His favorite practice was to plunder pullers on their way to the Canadian export docks. Intercepting them in midstream, gliding ghostlike in his speedboat, he robbed them of the cash with which they planned to purchase their products. But he incurred the enmity of big shippers when he purchased a large load of liquor in Canada with a bad check. Five wholesalers then pooled $1,000 each and hired a fair-trade commissioner to take care of the transgressor. A few days later the Gray Ghost was shot down on a Detroit street by an unknown gunman in a passing automobile. The case, of course, was never solved.

V

By the mid-1920s large and well-organized export and shipping organizations known as "combines" controlled a significant amount of the transportation and marketing of Canadian liquor crossing the Detroit River, and provided efficiency and rationality to the illegal business unkown in the early twenties when individualism prevailed in rum-running. Although they never came near to monopolizing the traffic, the large organizations on the Canadian side of the river dealt with equally large organizations on the American side of the river in attempts to set prices, control credit, and guarantee shipments of liquor.

In Ontario the first years of rum-running brought competition among exporters, price wars, price cutting, and a fluctuating, uncertain division of the market. In 1926 a group of Windsor exporters sought to alleviate these conditions and combined to form the Bermuda Exporters, Inc. The new organization claimed virtual control of the beer traffic between Ontario and Michigan. It was formed, according to its members, specifically to end price cutting among the hundreds of small organizations trading at the Canadian export docks. The first action of the organization was to raise the price of beer by one dollar per case.

American beer shippers protested against the unfair combination and accused brewers and exporters of the Border Cities of "gouging" and unequalled selfishness in their pursuit of profit. When the trust announced the termination of credit to rumrunners and said that future transactions would be strictly on a cash-and-carry basis, several rumrunners insisted that the policy would put them out of business. Most of the small independent shippers secured their loads on credit. Few of them had enough ready capital to work long if they lost several loads to the police. Several American importers concluded that the combination would hurt Canadian beer sales in America by making "alley beer" a more desirable substitute for the real Canadian product. In other words, price fixing would work to everyone's disadvantage—brewer, exporter, shipper, retailer, and drinker.

Brewers and exporters excluded from the Bermuda Exporters, Inc., formed a second "rum trust," and a competitive battle raged for the next weeks. One exporter dramatized the struggle as a "fight-the-syndicate-or-close-the-docks" battle. A third trust was formed to compete with the first two, and the three groups were forced to negotiate with each other or destroy the export business. Members of the trusts soon recognized that the liquor exportation business was too diversified with too many independents to set prices effectively and to bring the desired degree of regulation. Yet price fixing remained the ideal of the larger Canadian producers and exporters. In 1929, Charles Burns, president of the Carling Brewing Company, called a special meeting of the Border Cities brewers and exporters to discuss plans for organizing and ending price wars. Burns sought some method whereby offenders to price-fixing agreements could be penalized—in effect, a kind of brewers' NRA code. The initial plan drawn up by the brewers and exporters involved the formation of a three-man commission headed by a former Windsor police magistrate to oversee the brewing and export businesses. But coldness of the Ontario government to the plan caused the brewers to lose interest, and they stumbled along through the last years of prohibition with organizations almost helpless in holding the line on prices and in raising profits to the desired astronomical levels.

On the American side of the Detroit River hundreds of independent shippers organized for cooperation in rum-running, and some very large syndicates eventually emerged to bargain more effectively with Canadian exporters. Most American syndicates, however, remained relatively small and operated as "gangs" rather than as legitimate businesses. The East Side Gang, the West Side Gang, the Oakland Sugar House Gang, the Purple Gang, the Little Navy, the Jewish Navy, Peajacket's Navy, and other groups all had large accounts and credit lines with Canadian exporters. But over these organizations grew large syndicates that surprised even government officials in their businesslike efficiency and accounting records. In 1929, following infiltration by federal agents, the government broke up the two largest syndicates, the Pascuzzi Combine and the Miller Combine.

The financial backers of the Pascuzzi Combine owned the Riverside Brewery and the Amherstburg Distillery, both in Ontario. The organization was American, although several of its principal financial backers were Canadians. The Pascuzzi Combine maintained offices and bookkeeping files and business records as complete as those of any legitimate corporation. During the course of the government investigation company records were seized showing fictitious bank accounts, in one case totaling three quarters of a million dollars.

The Miller Combine was formed by six large importers and employed thirty sailors to transport liquor across the river. The organization shipped booze into Detroit, cut it, and then shipped it to New York, Chicago, Cleveland, and other cities of the Midwest in trucks and fraudulently labeled railroad cars. Farmers who allowed the combine to store liquor in their barns were paid $20 a week by the organization. The combine imported four to six hundred cases of liquor nightly before it was broken up by the government.

VI

In order to meet the challenge of rum-running, the federal government organized and carried out several well-publicized enforcement "drives" in the Detroit area, involving the coordination of local, state, and federal law enforcement agencies. Violence accompanied prohibition enforcement, but especially during these regular but only sporadically effective drives. Everyone agreed that some carefully measured use of force by law enforcement officers was necessary. But that used by prohibition enforcers was too often careless and even gratuitous, and many times its victims were not rumrunners but innocent bystanders. Even when rum-running was temporarily interrupted, the assaults on suspected rumrunners, careless gunfire, and rough handling of the public led many citizens to conclude that if such actions were really necessary to prevent drinking, then perhaps it was best to do away with the law rather than the drinking. Bullets of the police, many citizens concluded, were wreaking more havoc on an innocent public than the bottled beverages of the brewers ever did.

At the end of the first year of prohibition only one civilian and one prohibition officer had been killed in the entire country. But after that the body count on both sides grew rapidly. The Wickersham Commission reported in 1931 that 144 civilians and 60 prohibition agents had been killed in altercations involving enforcement of the dry laws. And while many drys worried openly about the rising death toll, others did their cause an injustice in glorying in the shooting. During a Senate debate in 1929, for example, Senator Smith Brookhart of Iowa complained, "When we get senators in this chamber talking sense, instead of all this gush stuff about murders by men who make mistakes once in a while, we will have a better attitude toward the bootlegger question." At another time congressmen applauded when it was announced in the House that a Washington policeman had shot and killed the driver of a liquor truck. But public concern over the violence was more accurately voiced by Jane Addams when she wrote in 1929 that "what the prohibition situation needs first of all is disarmament." Federal agents, she suggested, "should be taught some other methods than those of gunmen. It is their business to bring lawbreakers into court and not to punish them on the spot."

In December 1929, following the shooting of several individuals by prohibition agents and a great public outcry against the violence, Alan G. Straight, the Assistant Federal Prohibition Administrator for Michigan and Ohio, announced new rules of conduct for federal officers operating in Michigan. Straight again appealed to the federal agents to use their guns only in self-defense and specifically ordered them not to fire at fleeing suspects. "Mistaken shootings" must end, Straight insisted. He also answered public criticism of his agents by prohibiting profanity by his men and ordering a halt to assaults on prisoners held for questioning. The Detroit *News* commended Straight for issuing these promptings of "ordinary decency" in police work.

It should be pointed out that the infamous reputation that federal officers received was not entirely their own fault. It was not unusual for river pirates and other outlaws to impersonate federal officers in order to seize liquor in the Detroit River or even on the Canadian shore. There was little the federal government could do except issue denials when reports of seizures under suspicious circumstances came in. In June 1929, for example, charges were lodged in Ontario that federal officers armed with pistols had raided an export dock at Port Lambton five times in one month, seizing more than a hundred cases of whisky and five hundred cases of beer, and had escaped each time to the American shore after laying down a deadly barrage of pistol fire behind them. And to add insult to injury, after one such raid the "officers," upon reaching the American shore, celebrated their good fortune by sitting along the river bank and consuming their entire take. Federal authorities investigating the incidents concluded that the men were criminals dressed in the uniforms of federal agents. To many critics of prohibition, however, the description fit a majority of prohibition enforcement officers.

Despite orders to the contrary, federal agents on the river continued to shoot at suspected rumrunners. Many times their appeals to heave-to were not heard by boaters, and the first sign one had that he was being chased was bullets whistling past his head. A well-publicized accident in 1925 involved federal prohibition agents firing repeatedly at a launch carrying the two sons of Charles F. Fisher, vice president of the Fisher Body Company, and a son of William M. Walker, president of the Walker Brothers Catering Company of Detroit. The boys, out for a ride on the river, passed a federal boat. The men aboard the patrol boat waved at the Fisher launch, and the boys testified later that they thought the men were waving a greeting. Actually, the federal officers later insisted, they had signaled the Fisher boat to stop. The federal officers pursued the Fisher boat and starting shooting. Several bullets were fired, some nearly hitting the occupants of the boat, and one passing through the boat's hull. Charles Fisher denounced the entire episode and complained that it was "an outrage when innocent citizens cannot go out on the river without being molested and placed in danger by these men." He promised to "do something to safeguard the lives of innocent people who use the river."

But by far the most outrageous incident on the river during the prohibition years occurred in May 1927 and involved the murder of an innocent boater and his daughter. James Lee and his eleven-year-old daughter, Mildred, were pleasure boating on the river along with several dozen other boats, and it is easy to understand how Lee's boat might cross the path of a federal patrol vessel in pursuit of rumrunners, as enforcement agents later testified it did. But witnesses agreed that the federal boat, instead of trying to change its course when Lee's boat appeared dead ahead, deliberately rammed it. Both Lee and his daughter were killed in the collision. The little girl, knocked into the water, became entangled in the propellor of the federal boat. The patrol boat ignored this, backed away from the sinking Lee craft, and sped off without hesitating to see if it might help either Lee or his daughter. One eyewitness said the federal officers laughed as they sped away from the scene. The Detroit *News* called the incident "a summary execution" and declared that "no emergency within the scope of prohibition enforcement justified agents making the employment of the Detroit River a hazard of life to the average citizen. No law permits it; no regulation; no special privilege; no order of Col. Hanlon; nothing whatever." The incident, the paper concluded, was only one of several outrages by federal officers, and it "turns the stomach sour for everyone who reads it."

Public lack of confidence in the ability or the good will of the federal enforcement patrols on the river increased daily in the 1920s, and Washington was bombarded with protests against prohibition enforcement practices. The outraged opinion was bipartisan, the Detroit *News* observed, and was "based on the fundamental humanity and sanity of the American heart."

One interesting aspect of the violence in prohibition enforcement was that it seemed to fall especially hard on wealthy individuals who owned their own private docking and sailing facilities along the Detroit River and Lake St. Clair and who pleasure boated regularly. Overly enthusiastic enforcement of the prohibition laws created significant anti-prohibition sentiment along Michigan's

"Gold Coast" in the communities lying north and east of Detroit on Lake St. Clair. In the lakeside communities of Grosse Pointe Shores, Grosse Pointe Farms, Grosse Pointe, Grosse Pointe Park, and Lochmoor, where the estates and summer homes of some of Michigan's wealthiest families were located, prohibition enforcement was an extremely disruptive factor. Originally, most Gold Coast residents had supported the dry laws, on the grounds that such laws promised to clean up city government, bring a new prosperity to capitalist and laborer alike, and to make the rest of the world a little more like the Gold Coast. But the situation that developed along the shore of Lake St. Clair after 1920 seemed almost contrived to alienate the support of the wealthy from prohibition. Daily accounts in the newspapers testified to the non-enforcement of the dry laws in large sections of the state. Yet along the Gold Coast there seemed to be an overabundance of enthusiastic, careless, trigger-happy, and profane enforcement officers. These agents demonstrated an uncanny inability to discriminate between innocent boaters and rumrunners in their never-ending fight to stop smuggling on the lake.

The situation arose because early in the 1920s rumrunners began helping themselves to the hundred of private docking facilities along Lake St. Clair to land cargoes of Canadian liquor. Large boats with several rafts in tow crossed the lake nightly, transporting hundreds of cases of booze. In 1924 a state police patrol intercepted one such flotilla of liquor being unloaded in Grosse Pointe Park in the very shadow of the home of brewer Julius Stroh.

Increasing smuggling activity in the area attracted more and more prohibition agents. Patrol boats soon cruised the lake hoping to intercept rumrunners while prohibition agents lay in wait along the shore prepared to ambush smugglers when they landed with their loads. Hot pursuit, gunfire, hoarse shouts of "Halt!" and "Police!" in the night soon shattered the summer silence of the Gold Coast villages. Complaints were lodged in Detroit and Washington. One Grosse Pointe Village resident, David Rust, was driven nearly to total distraction by the uninvited cops and rumrunners, and pleaded with Congressman Robert Clancy to intercede in behalf of civilization. Rust fretted because it was no longer safe to take his boat on the lake for a cruise. Each time he ventured a short distance from his dock he was stopped and searched by patrolling prohibition pickets. One dry agent not only forced Rust back to his dock, but then chased him on foot into his boat house and there frisked him for liquor. Rust insisted that prohibition had murdered his sleep. Dry agents chased suspects across his lawn in the middle of the night shouting warnings. Late one night a full-fledged gun battle took place just outside Rust's bedroom window, terrifying the entire family. Rust and many of his neighbors could not understand why all of this rowdiness was necessary.

A well-known resident of St. Clair Shores, Henry B. Joy, the former president of the Packard Motor Company, lodged several complaints in Washington about negligent enforcement officers. Joy complained that during 1926 he had been troubled by numerous cars and trucks loading liquor on his lakeside property. "I have thought of putting a gate across my driveway to prevent entrance of automobiles and keeping it locked," he wrote to Thomas H. Brennan, Deputy Prohibition Commissioner for Detroit. "That, however, would be such a nuisance to me that the idea seems impracticable," he concluded. Then prohibition enforcement officers arrived on the scene and violence erupted. "The discharge of firearms by the officers makes it unpleasant to use my premises as a landing for my power boat," Joy complained to Commissioner Brennan. "May I ask if you think my premises are going to be a frequent battle ground? Is the situation under control? Such shooting affrays as occurred on my premises last summer are unpleasant. I would be very glad indeed to have your picture of the situation."

In early December 1928, two Border Patrol inspectors seized a boatload of liquor being unloaded at the Joy dock. Following the seizure the agents maintained a careful watch on Joy's property. Violence followed, and Joy complained to the Secretary of the Treasury about the behavior of the federal agents. Andrew Mellon replied to Joy's complaint. According to Mellon, prohibition agents had spotted smugglers again loading a truckload of liquor near the Joy dock. The agents seized the truck, but one of the men escaped into the Joy boat house. The agents pursued their suspect and broke down the boat-house door. Inside they found only Joy's night watchman. A thorough search turned up no one else.

The incident was only the first of several near Joy's boat house. "My premises continued to be visited by federal officers in their efforts to intercept rummers who would from time to time land a small boat cargo in spite of my watchman," Joy later wrote. Federal agents again visited his boat house and again, without hesitation, kicked the door down. Joy concluded that "conditions were obviously hopeless. While my watchman could keep the small boys away, he could not keep the rummers away. And he was even less capable of keeping the federal prohibition agents out. So I abandoned the idea of a helpless watchman," Joy wrote, "left the premises open and may the best man win. I cannot myself protect my premises against use by smugglers or against marauding federal officers. Of the two I would rather be visited by the smugglers because they have done my premises no damage."

Countless other Gold Coast residents experienced the same sense of helplessness and exasperation and insult as did Joy and Rust. In July 1929, customs agents raided the yacht of Louis Mendelssohn, a Detroit capitalist, and discovered thirty-five cases of wine and liquor. Expecting to duplicate this success, a few days later they raided the yacht of C. F. Smith, a chain store millionaire. Mrs. Smith was holding a tea party on board the yacht when federal agents with drawn revolvers forced their way aboard. The agents "talked rudely and roughly and kept their pistols in their hands," according to Mrs. Smith. When they found no liquor, not only did the refuse to apologize for their intrusion, but insisted that packages of liquor had been thrown out the portholes in order to avoid detection. Mrs. Smith suffered nervous shock because of the raid.

Residents of the Gold Coast were accustomed to deferential treatment by law enforcement authorities, but during prohibition they found themselves unexpectedly thrown into the midst of the anti-liquor war. Harassed, assaulted, and insulted, they discovered that their lives and property were suddenly endangered not so much by lawbreakers as by the crude, rough-talking, rowdy, and rude individuals selected to enforce the law. Arthur Lippman's "The Patriot's Prayer" voiced the sentiments of many citizens of the Gold Coast. Lippman wrote:

> Now I lay me down to sleep—
> My life and limb may Hoover keep,
> And may no Coast Guard cutter shell
> This little home I love so well.
> May no dry agent, shooting wild,

Molest mine wife and infant child,
Or searching out some secret still,
Bombard my home to maim and kill.
When dawn succeeds the gleaming stars,
May we devoid of wounds and scars,
Give thanks we didn't fall before
The shots in Prohibition's War.

When the appeals of Gold Coast residents to Washington for an end to the violence around their communities brought no change, many of them found their way into the class-conscious repeal organizations: the Association Against the Prohibition Amendment, the Women's Organization for National Prohibition Reform, and the Crusaders. Had prohibition enforcement officers been more class-conscious, who can say how little influence the repeal organizations might have had in Michigan or how much longer prohibition might have survived there?

VII

While over-enforcement of the prohibition law irritated residents of communities along the shore of Lake St. Clair, non-enforcement of the same law in communities along the Detroit River produced both an outspoken concern and an unprecedented prosperity.

Residents of Harbor Island, a small river-shore development near the foot of Alter Road and opposite Peche Island, were angered by the scarcity of federal agents near their community. In 1926 the Harbor Island Improvement Association held an emergency meeting to discuss special vigilante action to maintain law and order and to prevent the use of the community's landing facilities by rumrunners. The problem stemmed from the fact that when the island was subdivided a canal had been constructed to provide residents with easier access to the river. But rumrunners from Peche Island to the American shore found the canal a convenient landing facility. "I can estimate truthfully," one resident complained, "that 40 percent of the smuggled liquor in this vicinity comes through Harbor Island because of the advantage afforded by the canal. Yesterday afternoon a forty-foot motor craft unloaded liquor while two patrolmen of the McLellan Station looked on." Another observed, "I have seen policemen take off their caps and coats, assist bootleggers in unloading and then sit down and enjoy a drinking party." Members of the improvement association worried about a dramatic decrease in property values on Harbor Island if rum-running was not stopped. Before long, the association warned, prospective buyers would refuse to purchase a home in a community where their sleep was interrupted nightly by rumrunners unloading a few hundred feet away.

On the other hand, in the communities along the river south of Detroit non-enforcement of prohibition meant unprecedented and widespread affluence. With the passage of prohibition the drys had predicted a new prosperity to be enjoyed by all Americans in the new arid paradise. Nowhere was the promise fulfilled so quickly or so literally as in the "downriver communities" of Ecorse, Delray, Oakwood, River Rouge, Ford, Wyandotte, Trenton, and Slocum. Soon after the passage of prohibition thousands of residents of the downriver communities began participating in rum-running and consequently reaped nearly unbelievable riches from their activities. During the prohibition years, in Ecorse and the other downriver towns, crime paid. Lavishly.

Ecorse became the hub of downriver rum-running. Before prohibition Ecorse was described by the Detroit *News* as "a rather dull and undistinguished community," not unlike thousands of other small towns in America, "and furnishing not a jot of interest, possessing scarcely a single arresting quality." This riverside Gopher Prairie, the *News* concluded, was best described as "a nice place."

But during the prohibition years nobody described Ecorse as a nice place. The Eighteenth Amendment transformed the town. Commercial fishermen, tugboat operators, shippers, and dockworkers gave up their normal occupations and entered the rum-running profession. Rumrunners, because of the wealth they commanded, emerged as influential figures in the downriver villages during the 1920s. The Detroit *Saturday Night* described Ecorse rumrunners as "plutocrats bloated by material prosperity" and warned that they were rapidly becoming "malefactors of great wealth." Journalist F. L. Smith, Jr., recalled that "to have seen Ecorse in its palmy days is an unforgettable experience, for no gold camp of the old West presented a more glamorous spectacle. It was a perpetual carnival of drinking, gambling, and assorted vices by night and a frenziedly business-like community by day. Silk-shirted bootleggers walked its streets and it was the Mecca for the greedy, the unscrupulous, and the criminal of both sexes. When the police desired to lay their hands on a particularly hard customer they immediately looked in Ecorse and there they generally found him." Ecorse's waterfront became known as Michigan's "Barbary Coast." Andrew Volstead, the *Saturday Night* observed, had changed the Detroit River into "a stream of gold" for Ecorse.

Dozens of rum-running boats moored each day at the Ecorse municipal dock at the foot of State Street, which ran through the center of the business district of the village. Rumrunners transferred their cargoes to waiting cars and trucks while residents, police, and politicians "looked on and grinned." Several Canadian breweries set up export docks on the Canadian shore just outside LaSalle, Ontario, directly across the river from Ecorse. Fighting Island lay in the middle of the river between Ecorse and LaSalle and served as a convenient obstruction to hide rumrunners from police patrols. Rumrunners bought large new automobiles with their profits and these were spotted parked conspicuously in the driveways of rundown fishing shacks in the village and residential areas. "Bootlegging is the calf of gold in Ecorse," the *Saturday Night* observed, "and Mammon leads the ball there as elsewhere."

For all practical purposes Ecorse and several other downriver towns were administered by local officials during the prohibition years as though they were extensions of Canada on American soil, and the citizens of those communities, in pursuing their illegal occupations, demanded nothing less than the rights of extraterritoriality. The judicial process in Ecorse was totally corrupted by the demands of rum-running. When arrests were made by state and federal police and cases came before local juries, a verdict of not guilty was assured. Rumrunners served on juries and in at least one case all twelve jurors were known rumrunners. As a result, the only cases from the village tried successfully were those adjudicated in the federal courts.

The police force of Ecorse was not simply inadequate, but was uninterested in enforcing state and federal liquor laws. Very early in the prohibition years the entire force joined hands with the illicit booze business. Instead of seeking a separate peace with prohibition, as did officials and police in Detroit, the police and politicians of Ecorse seemed to make an unconditional surrender to the purveyors of liquor. In 1923, as the illegal liquor business boomed and hundreds of liquor boats slipped up to the Ecorse municipal dock and unloaded, and trucks loaded with liquor rumbled away from the dock down the village streets, the local police made only two arrests for liquor law violations. The lack of arrests, it should be noted, elicited no cries of protest from village residents.

Not only did the police, politicians, boat owners, blind-pig and roadhouse operators, and dockworkers share in the new prosperity, but it spilled over and benefited individuals in nearly every occupation and age group in the village. Even teenaged boys shared the new wealth. As many as twenty-five schoolboys were employed as spies, lookouts, and messengers by Ecorse rumrunners. This condition was uncovered in 1922 after police arrested a fifteen-year-old boy delivering a truckload of liquor to a downriver roadhouse. The suspect insisted that he was only one of several local boys employed in the trade. The boys worked, he said, only on weekends and at night so they would not miss school. Some were employed as drivers and made deliveries, others served as pickets near state police posts. Still others were assigned as lookouts at busy liquor landing points along the river, and some were hired to help unload rum boats. The boys were all aged thirteen to sixteen and their vigilance made it impossible for the police to make unannounced raids on blind pigs and boat-house storage centers in Ecorse. The police were invariably spotted long before they arrived at the destination of their raid, and a warning had long preceeded them. "The boys are spread along the waterfront," a state police officer complained, "and are very awake and diligent. They scatter as soon as a police officer appears. They are well paid and are seen constantly squandering their earnings in poolrooms and playing craps."

Ecorse stood out as the most lawless community in the downriver area, but other towns shared in the benefits of rum-running with less notoriety. The Lincoln Park police force was in league with rumrunners and bootleggers. Whenever a raid was to be made by the state police on the community, the local police were informed first, and they in turn tipped off resort keepers and rumrunners. The police usually escorted patrons of blind pigs to be raided out of the village in patrol cars, and aided rumrunners in stashing their booze before the arrival of the raiding party. Federal and county officials who raided Lincoln Park's blind pigs invariably found them closed and empty, with neither liquor nor customers in sight. Village police officers attempting to enforce the prohibition laws were warned to cease and desist or be squeezed out of the department. Feuds between policemen who wanted to cooperate with rumrunners and those who did not led to the killing of one patrolman and the shooting of another and the sentencing of three Wayne County sheriff's deputies to federal prison. Village officials, on the other hand, proclaimed that ignorance of actual conditions in Lincoln Park on the part of the press and other outsiders had unfairly placed a stigma on the community. Other Lincoln Park residents blamed conditions in their village on conditions in Ecorse, from which the supplies of illegal liquor were transported into their own community, and upon the citizens of Detroit who made up the chief clientele for Lincoln Park's blind pigs and roadhouses.

Ford and Wyandotte were allegedly export centers for Ecorse-landed liquor, and booze from these communities was supplied to big buyers in Detroit. River Rouge, the nearest of the downriver towns to Detroit, was said by its chief of police to be the "goat" of the illicit liquor traffic. "River Rouge is clean," he testified. "There is no bootlegging here. My department will remain honest. But we have to cope with all the drunks and rumrunners and speeders from Detroit and Ecorse, Ford and Wyandotte. We collected $2,000 in fines from liquor violators last month," he claimed, "and 90 percent was paid by Detroiters." The River Rouge police chief received three threatening letters in July 1922 after he refused to discharge a motorcycle officer who had been active against bootleggers. He also discharged a police captain because the man got drunk on the Fourth of July and shared his liquor with prisoners in the local jail.

Trenton's chief of police conspired with rumrunners to land booze in the town with police protection. Rumrunners arrested by county, state, or federal officers and incarcerated in the Trenton jail were released by the police chief, and their automobiles, trucks, and liquor were returned. They were also given assurance of no further interruption in their business while they were in Trenton.

Residents of the downriver villages not only tolerated the illegal liquor trade, but actively defended it against county, state, and federal enforcement officials. As early as December 1920, a pitched battle between agents of the state Food and Drug Department and rumrunners took place in the streets of Ecorse. The enforcement officers surrounded a houseboat rendezvous of the rumrunners, but before any arrests could be made the suspects succeeded in shooting their way out of the police encirclement and escaping. This early success in resisting arrest apparently encouraged other rumrunners in the city to set up regular organizations for cooperative protection and resistance to the police. In the summer of 1923, agents of the Treasury Department seized two hundred small boats in the river off Ecorse, Wyandotte, and Trenton, and affixed customs seals to their engines, thereby preventing their use until the owners explained their failure to comply with government regulations concerning marine equipment. During the action a small quantity of beer was found in a boat well and confiscated by the agents. To prevent the agents from removing the beer, rumrunners and their friends made three incredible efforts to dynamite and burn a small bridge spanning a creek which gave the agents an escape route from the boat well. At one time during the assault, a handful of agents held the bridge against a menacing crowd estimated at two thousand angry men, women, and children. The Detroit *News* reported that the crowd objected to the presence of Treasury agents in the prohibition war and insisted that this was an unfair escalation of the conflict.

Another major altercation between the forces of law and order and the defenders of liquor took place in 1928 in Ecorse's infamous Hogan's Alley. Three boats and several automobiles containing about thirty Customs Border Patrol inspectors converged at the end of Hogan's Alley and waited to ambush rumrunners. When rumrunning craft pulled up to a nearby pier, the agents rushed out and arrested the seven crew members. But no sooner had the arrests been made than the men began shouting for help. Residents from the surrounding neighborhoods came on the run to aid the unfortunate rumrunners. More than two hundred persons arrived on the scene to prevent the agents from departing with their prisoners. Automobiles driven by the customs agents to the scene were destroyed—their tires slashed and their windshields broken. Other cars were pushed across the entrance to the alley and the customs agents were pelted with rocks and bottles. Finally, before their situation became entirely hopeless, the agents formed a wedge, rushed the barricade, and made their escape.

State and federal agents carried out raid after raid in the downriver area, but their successes were always temporary. In April 1921 three van loads of federal agents transported into Ecorse raided several blind pigs and seized a few rum-running boats. The Detroit *News* proclaimed prematurely that Ecorse's boom had been "blotted out." The government proclaimed victory and abandoned the village. The boom continued. In July 1922 Governor Alex Groesbeck ordered the state police, aided by federal agents, to occupy Ecorse, enforce the law, and generally clean up the downriver area. The action was precipitated by the shooting of the chief of police of Ecorse and an appeal to the governor by the Lincoln Park Betterment Association and the Wayne County Prosecutor. The state police first raided blind pigs, roadhouses, and liquor-cutting factories in Ford, thereby giving ample time for bootleggers in Ecorse to get their establishments in order before the police arrived. Protests were lodged from Ford that the police raids were "high handed" and in most cases carried out without the formality of a search warrant. Governor Groesbeck ignored the protests. Most of the bigger establishments on the Barbary Coast, those with expensive chandeliers and other valuable furnishings, disposed of their liquor and temporarily went out of business in order to prevent police raids. Other establishments "used a little diplomacy" when the raiders were near. When asked why Ecorse had not been hit harder by the police raids, Charles Campau, Detroit chief of the State Department of Public Safety, said such raids were useless because Ecorse had received advance warning of the police approach. Campau did not explain why Ecorse had not been raided first. "We shall get Ecorse some time," Campau promised, "but the only way to do it is to come and surprise them."

The fourteen state police raiders left Ecorse on July 12, but soon afterward Governor Groesbeck announced the establishment of a permanent state police post in the area to maintain a close watch on local conditions. Following the announcement Ecorse officials, including the village president and the chief of police, visited local blind-pig owners, warned them that the state and federal officials meant business, and suggested that they destroy their liquor supplies to prevent more raids in the village. A subsequent series of conferences among the leading booze businessmen in Ecorse led to the verbal agreement that the village would be kept liquor-free for thirty days in order to forestall raids. But after that short dry spell, conditions in Ecorse returned to normal.

Business continued to boom in the downriver area. Every time a drive was made on the Detroit front, raiders swept into the downriver communities with success as widely advertised as it was temporary. In the fall of 1931, after a series of brutal murders in the area, Governor Wilbur Brucker sent the state police to patrol the streets of Wyandotte, over the protests of the acting mayor. But no action by the state completely destroyed the illegal liquor business in the downriver area during the prohibition years. Eventually, repeal of prohibition brought a new era of law and order to the infamous communities south of Detroit.

VIII

Various factors made effective prohibition enforcement along the Detroit River difficult. Rum-running developed into a profession, and many of its practitioners were extremely skilled, imaginative, and daring, and would have provided a serious challenge to even the most energetic and conscientious police officers. But the terms "energetic" or "conscientious" were rarely used to describe officers in the agencies charged with prohibition enforcement. Confusion, incompetence, and uncertainty within the enforcement units, particularly those of the Treasury Department, contributed as much to making prohibition enforcement difficult as did the skill of the rumrunners. Federal enforcement groups suffered not only from an almost criminal lack of funding by Congress, but also from disorganization, division of responsibility, inadequate equipment, high turnover in personnel, unimaginative leadership, and general imcompetence. The result was extremely low morale in the enforcement agencies, which in turn influenced a significant number of agents to make their jobs safer, simpler, and more profitable by accepting bribes to cooperate with the criminals they had been hired to apprehend. By the mid-1920s, for many men the most attractive feature of the prohibition enforcement service was the opportunity it presented to become part of the rum-running graft system.

The enforcement branch that suffered most from incompetence, lack of direction, dishonesty, and graft was the Customs Border Patrol. A special investigation into the organization in 1927 uncovered extremely demoralizing conditions. The quota of the patrol in the Detroit area was forty-two men, yet only twenty-four were in active service at the time of the investigation. Only three of the twelve boats at the disposal of the patrol were available for active duty. The establishment of any sense of *esprit de corps* in the Border Patrol was impossible because of the rapid turnover in personnel. The average career of an inspector in the patrol was no more than a few weeks. Many were dismissed "for the good of the service." Others quit the patrol in disgust and went to work for rumrunners. Still others—concluding that two incomes were better than one—stayed in the patrol and worked for rumrunners. Inspector Roland Walter remembered that finding honest men to work in the Border Patrol was his most difficult task. "That took more time than everything else combined," he complained. "Once we put on a drive for men and about three thousand fellows came in for jobs. I examined nearly all of them and I think I hired about eighty altogether. Most of the others were bootleggers, crooks, hijackers, and ex-policemen who had been fired from downriver towns." After one month, sixty of the eighty new men had been fired. "It was a great mess," Walter concluded. "Sometimes an agent would go to work on Monday and on Wednesday or Thursday would be grafting."

Honest, conscientious, and trustworthy agents were hounded from the Border Patrol not only by the dishonest grafters within the organization, but also, ironically, by the "do gooders" in the Anti-Saloon League and the Michigan Law Enforcement League, a citizens group organized to aid the police. "Someone was always trying to get someone else and it was frequently the best agents who were the most likely to be suspected of crookedness," Walter testified. "Somebody was always planting beer in an agent's car or making affidavits about some kind of skullduggery." "The liquor men try to discredit our agents whenever they can," Walter said. "That is natural. But the Anti-Saloon League and the Michigan Law Enforcement League do the same thing whether they know it or not. These organizations hire men to go out and make buys and turn in evidence. Most of these men they hire are discharged federal agents and they have no love for us. They never miss a chance to do us some kind of damage and in a game like this there are a lot of ways. Sometimes we find these fellows in saloons drinking their heads off. A lot of them are fellows that like to drink and they get these jobs because they can get a lot of free liquor."

One of Walter's main criticisms of prohibition enforcement was that to carry out his job efficiently, an agent needed to cut "about a million miles of red tape." Because of this bureaucratic confusion, precise divisions of local responsibility were uncertain. Rumrunners were able to exploit the uncertainty and lack of coordination among the prohibition enforcement branches, particularly in recovering the automobiles and boats taken from them by the government. Automobiles seized by government agents for transporting liquor were periodically auctioned off through the United States marshall's office in Detroit. But before the cars were sold they were simply left "lying around," according to one reporter. No single agency, it seems, had been assigned the responsibility of guarding the cars between the time they were seized and the time they were sold. The public, including rumrunners, had access to the cars, and anything of value—including the engines—was usually removed and carted off before the cars were sold. Although the auction prices of the cars averaged only about $150, most of them were not worth even that. When a good car was auctioned, it was not unusual for the former owner to approach the new buyer with an offer that was hard to refuse, pay him, and drive off.

The government processing of confiscated boats showed an even greater negligence. After impounding, the rum-running craft were moored at a government dock on Lake St. Clair. Incredibly, nobody was assigned to guard duty at the dock, so the boats remained unattended. They were simply towed to the moorings, left there, and forgotten. Many rumrunners, after being deprived of their vessels with all of the solemn legal proceedings of a federal court forfeiture order, drove to the unguarded boat "boneyard" a day or two later and unceremoniously repossessed their craft. It was not unusual, because of this practice, for the Customs Border Patrol to seize the same boat three or four times a year and each time legally forfeit it from the owner. Sometimes a new coat of paint or a new number had been added to the craft. In the summer of 1928, for example, a boat was seized carrying five hundred cases of whisky across Lake Erie. The boat had previously been seized and forfeited three times. Some of the boats were stolen by gangs that made a business of raiding the government boneyard and then reselling the vessels to the original owner. It was common gossip along the river that a good used boat, stolen from the government, could be purchased in Mt. Clemens for as little as $25. At one time, in the mid-1920s, Customs authorities had sold the boats at a public auction. But when it became apparent that the former owners were buying them back for a low bid, the government abandoned the sales and decided to hold the boats indefinitely. In 1928 and 1929 the government seized 366 boats on the Detroit River, legally forfeited them, and tied them to the government dock. All but one of the boats were stolen.

Some critics charged that such incompetence was actually part of an intricately developed plan. A good part of the bungling, it is true, was planned by rumrunners and their friends in the enforcement racket. Several outspoken drys, however, insisted that most of the incompetence and failure in prohibition enforcement was the result of a deliberate plan by government officials posing as friends of prohibition while actually seeking to discredit it. The most articulate spokesman for this point of view was Governor Gifford Pinchot of Pennsylvania. Pinchot concluded that the incompetence, negligence, and corruption that pervaded prohibition enforcement was all part of a conspiracy of national proportions designed to bring back liquor. In an address at Pennsylvania State College in 1933, Pinchot accused federal and state authorities of deliberately encouraging racketeering during the prohibition years. Pinchot pointed out, that in 1920 the Treasury Department had been assigned prohibition enforcement. At the time, the department "had at its command the highly trained, highly efficient, and thoroughly reliable corps of special agents" with an enviable record in enforcing the exise laws. But these men were dismissed, Pinchot said, and "in the place of the invaluable corps of special agents the Treasury Department began installing the scum of the political underworld—men who were totally incapable of enforcing any law, even if they had not been selected, as they were, for the express purpose of nullifying this one. In state after state the federal administrator of the Volstead Act was guilty of breaking the law he was appointed to enforce," Pinchot reported. "In Pennsylvania incompetent after incompetent followed crook after crook. . . . These political nominees were all appointed for the discrediting of the Eighteenth Amendment by wet officials in Washington, many or most of them habitual violators of the law they were ostensibly appointed to enforce."

Pinchot's view is a challenging one. Many state and national prohibition administrators were out of sympathy with the Eighteenth Amendment. Many prohibition enforcement officers were indeed incapable of enforcing any law. Yet the evidence that administrators hired these men *specifically* to nullify the Eighteenth Amendment is entirely circumstantial. That many of these men by their actions did nullify the law is undeniable.

Bribery and graft found its way into every branch of the prohibition enforcement service, but the Customs Border Patrol was distinguished by the pervasiveness of graft in its ranks. Border Patrol inspectors allegedly screened new members for character—or rather, lack of it. Life in the patrol was made unbearable for honest agents. One witness to the Border Patrol graft testified that one inspector, Daniel Shimel, had been offered $50,000 by rumrunners if he would resign from the patrol, "because he was one of the three honest men on the force." Shimel resigned soon after he was threatened with death by other agents for refusing to accept bribes. Eventually, when the full story of the graft among the Border Patrol along the Detroit River was uncovered, nearly the entire force was fired or resigned, and even those "on the take" were surprised by the number of agents accepting bribes.

Bribery was apparently a major fixed cost for bootleggers and affected the price of liquor paid by the consumer almost as much as did taxes before prohibition. George Remus, the "King of the Bootleggers," estimated that he had spent $20 million during his career on payoffs. "A few men tried to corner the wheat market only to find out that there is too much wheat in the world," Remus said. "I tried to corner the graft market only to find out that there is not enough money in the world to buy up all the public officials who demand a share in the graft." In Detroit, however, there was enough money to buy up all the public officials who demanded a share in the graft!

Stories of protected liquor entering the Detroit area led federal authorities to investigate their own agents as early as 1923. One

Border Patrol inspector was convicted of bribery for allowing liquor to pass freely across the river. But not until the end of the 1920s was the graft system broken up by federel investigators. After an investigation that lasted nearly a year, federal authorities were able to break up the "graft trust" within the Customs Border Patrol. A special undercover agent infiltrated the trust and collected $1,700 in bribes in only six weeks. He later described how the system worked. The graft system involved double bribery, according to federal investigators. First, bribery was used to protect liquor transported across the river to "plants" or warehouses near the river where it was temporarily stored. Then a second bribery system was used to provide safe passage for the liquor from the plants to consumer markets in Detroit and other cities of the Midwest. Investigators estimated that as much as 75 percent of the liquor that came across the Detroit River before 1929 was protected by the graft system. The standard method for paying agents differed from month to month and from agent to agent. Rumrunners employed a few "fixers" to arrange payoffs for specific shipments of liquor. The fixer contacted "friendly" Border Patrol inspectors and negotiated for a certain amount of money. Payments to the inspectors were always in cash. Sometimes the fixer met their patrol boat in the middle of the river and passed the money to the inspectors; or he would meet them at other times at a prearranged spot on shore and give them cash and instructions.

A very popular method of bribery involved the "free night." In this arrangement the fixer paid the inspectors to "disappear" for a fixed amount of time, usually three or four hours, on a certain night. During that time the rumrunners could bring as much liquor across the river as they could find means to convey. An imaginative part of the free night involved rumrunners tipping off inspectors as to the location of rumrunners not participating in the payoffs. These "outlaws" were apprehended and their liquor confiscated by the Border Patrol. In some instances, inspectors even "bribed" rumrunners within the graft trust to acquire information on river crossings by rumrunners not involved in the trust. The subsequent arrests sometimes enhanced the reputation of a Border Patrol inspector with his superiors.

The lack of any pretensions of secrecy in the graft trust shocked the Canadian Minister of National Revenue, William D. Euler, when he visited Windsor in the fall of 1928 to observe rumrunning operations. "I could see the United States Customs office on the other shore," Euler recalled, "and I could also see that it was not difficult to detect any boats that left the Canadian shore to go to the American side. . . . I got into a conversation with a man engaged in the business of exporting liquor. I asked him, 'Do you cross in the daytime?' He answered, 'Yes, quite often.' I said, 'How is it they do not get you?' He replied with a smile, 'It just happens that they are not there when we go across.' "

Sumner Sleeper, chief of the Customs Border Patrol in Detroit, said that even with only a few officers accepting bribes, it was impossible to prevent large quantities of liquor from crossing the river. Picket patrols placed on the river could only be effective, he observed, if each of them carried out their assigned tasks. As long as the crew of just one picket boat could be bribed, the rumrunners could use that section of the river and escape the honest agents.

The exposure of the graft trust brought immediate firings and indictments. Federal District Attorney John R. Watkins estimated that nearly the entire force would be indicted and prosecuted. But lack of sufficient evidence in many of the cases against the Border Patrol inspectors meant that the government could go no further than dismissing them for the good of the service.

Along with the grafting customs inspectors, indictments were secured against three of the "Big Four" downriver rumrunners. Frank Schettler, Joseph Rossin, and Norman B. Smith were all convicted of bribery and conspiracy and sentenced to long prison terms in Leavenworth, Kansas. Only James "Buck" Weaver of the Big Four escaped prison in 1928. He fled to Canada. Smith, a reputed friend of the mighty in high political circles as well as in the underworld, promised explosive revelations during his trial because of his suspicion of betrayal by others. He testified that Prosecuting Attorney John R. Watkins had offered him immunity in exchange for information leading to an indictment of Sumner Sleeper. While the deal was being negotiated, Smith said, he and Rossin spent an entire evening in Watkins's office drinking bootleg liquor with the prosecuting attorney. The judge in the case, Charles Simons, said of Smith's story, "I have never in my seven years on the federal bench heard a more malicious and deliberately foul tissue of lies than come from you." Simons sentenced Smith and his codefendants to the maximum prison term and fine for their crime.

Although expulsions, indictments, arrests, and resignations

meant more honest inspectors in the Border Patrol, still stories of bribery and corruption among the inspectors persisted.

But the Border Patrol was not alone in taking bribes from rumrunners. Profits to be made by cooperating with rumrunners provided a heady temptation to the less scrupulous members of the Detroit Police Department. Several of them cooperated in various degrees with rumrunners, and some were even arrested while attempting to smuggle booze across the river themselves. Many officers were dismissed from the force for suspicion of cooperating with rumrunners. Then, in April 1929, in what Police Commissioner William P. Rutledge called "the worst scandal in the history of the Detroit Police Department," Captain Joseph Burkheiser, harbor master and commanding officer of the Belle Isle station, was suspended for conduct unbecoming an officer. Although Burkheiser was never indicted on criminal charges, the Police Department fined him $500, reduced him to lieutenant, and retired him. It seems that as commander of the Harbor Division, Burkheiser had used police boats to convoy liquor from Canada to the American shore and had ordered patrolmen under his command to help unload the liquor once it arrived on the American side. As payment for the help, Burkheiser generously shared his liquor with his men. One load of booze was stored temporarily in Burkheiser's private quarters in the Belle Isle station house.

A few members of the Coast Guard shared in the graft taking also. The entire crew of Coast Guard Cutter 219, working out of Monroe, Michigan, was arrested for illegally disposing of previously confiscated beer, whisky, and wine. The guardsmen allegedly stopped and seized a boatload of booze, then transferred their prize to another rumrunning boat in the presence of the original smugglers. The guardsmen were caught after the original rumrunners complained to Coast Guard authorities.

IX

Soon after taking office in 1929 President Herbert Hoover decided to try to terminate rumrunning from Canada once and for all. In the late spring of 1929 no less than the tenth major enforcement drive in the Detroit area was initiated. The Washington *Evening Star* reported that Detroit had been picked by Hoover as "the laboratory in which to test the noble experiment of prohibition." Through this drive in "the Detroit sector" Hoover hoped to determine whether or not the Eighteenth Amendment could in fact ever be enforced. The *Evening Star* announced that the government had finally declared war upon rumrunners, "war with the full strength of the United States behind it." This drive was to be far greater in importance than any previous drive. "The answer to the 'Prohibition Question' in the tiniest rural hamlet of Texas, California, or Maine; in the largest metropolitan centers of the East and the Middle West is being sought here by Washington," the *Evening Star* reported. In a Detroit dispatch to the New York *Times*, James Young reported that the drive would be "a grimmer war than any of the others that have had the same purpose—an intensive effort to end the rum trade at its principal source."

Actually the most important result of the Hoover enforcement drive of 1929 was the initiation of diplomatic maneuverings between Washington and Ottawa that led eventually to an agreement with Canada concerning cooperation to thwart rumrunning. American officials had argued throughout the 1920s that rum-running could only be controlled if the Canadian government refused clearings to liquor-carrying boats bound for American ports. Although the Canadians had generally resisted such an agreement, the Canadian government did move gradually toward greater cooperation with American enforcement officials. In 1924, for example, the Canadians agreed to an American request extending American territorial waters to twelve miles in order to push rumrunners on the Atlantic coast further from the American shore, and one month later Ottawa agreed to furnish the United States, upon request, information concerning certain shipments across the border. The stern enforcement drive of 1929 and the consideration by the federal government of a proposal for a consolidated border patrol and for the closing of the border with Canada to travel except at a few points of entry to be designated by the U.S. president prompted the Canadian prime minister, McKenzie King, to introduce a bill prohibiting release for export of *any* Dominion-controlled liquor destined for delivery in a country that outlawed its importation (i.e. the United States).

King was to insist that his government had not acted sooner

because it awaited the ripening of Canadian public opinion in favor
of the measure, and in presenting the bill, King based his argument
for passage on moral grounds, stating that Canada simply could no
longer afford to continue a partnership with rumrunners and other
criminal elements engaged in smuggling liquor across the American
border. He insisted that the estimated loss of $9 million in annual
revenue from taxes on exported liquor was not to be weighed against
the preservation of Canadian self-respect. Rumors also circulated in
Ottawa, however, that in exchange for the Canadian action Washington planned to drop immigration quotas for Canadians.

King's bill passed Parliament with very little trouble and took
effect on June 1, 1930. Immediately, seizures were made by Canadian authorities who seemed anxious to demonstrate their intent to
carry out the letter of the law. On June 4, Canadian authorities
seized a barge carrying 1,500 cases of beer off Stoney Point, twen-
tyfive miles east of Windsor. Ten export docks in the Border Cities
were ordered closed by the government. One week later liquor
prices in Detroit increased by 50 percent.

In November two large Border Cities breweries were closed
following the indefinite suspension of their licenses by the Ontario
Liquor Control Board. Nearly seven hundred men were thrown out
of work by the closures. The two breweries—the Walkerville Brewing Company and the Hofter Brewing Company—had previously
been convicted of violating the law forbidding liquor exportation to
the United States and the sale of beer to known blind-pig operators.
Officers of the breweries promised an appeal to Toronto to lift the
license suspensions.

Canadian cooperation in preventing smuggling thus meant that
flush times for rumrunners were gone. Only the bravest and the
most ruthless would dare cross the river between the two fires of
Canadian and American enforcement authorities. Now the well-
organized navies and gangs that formerly coexisted in transporting
liquor began looking for new worlds to conquer. Gang wars broke
out and raged in and around Detroit during the next two years. A
"war" of national proportions raged within the criminal organizations of the Italian-American community. Increases were noted in
kidnapping, robbery, extortion, and murder-for-hire, all involving
individuals formerly employed in the importation and marketing of
Canadian liquor.

In late June 1930, the federal government reported that the Detroit River was free of rum-running. The privately owned boat wells off Ecorse, Wyandotte, and Trenton closed for lack of business. In February 1931 the Detroit *News* noted a dramatic reversion to the old methods of smuggling. Liquor was still entering the United States from Canada, but now it was coming in flasks and bottles concealed in the clothing or in the automobiles of individuals using the Ambassador Bridge or the Windsor and Detroit Tunnel. Such smuggling, however, was more a nuisance than a threat.

In October 1931, W. C. Geagly, the Michigan State Analyst, reported just how effectively the new Canadian law was working. After analyzing whisky, beer, and wine seized by the state police in all parts of Michigan in the previous weeks, Geagly announced that liquor sold in Michigan was unfit for human consumption. "From our examination of these specimens," he said, "it is very evident that legitimate alcoholic liquors no longer can be obtained except for medicinal purposes. Nevertheless, there exists a wide market for intoxicating liquor. To satisfy the market, the business of bootlegging—intrinsically a crooked business—naturally is drawing its supplies from crooked origins. Smuggling, cheating, illicit distilling, redistillation, cutting filthy fermentation, and diversion of industrial materials are furnishing the necessary alcohol for the usual type of alcoholic beverage now being trafficked in," he warned. The situation, he concluded, was "attendant with alarming possibilities."

The fruits of prohibition had all been picked by the summer of 1930. With the death of rum-running the Detroit River once again became safe for pleasure boating. Peace prevailed on the river and on Lake St. Clair, and the waters of the lakes and rivers all along the Canadian border once again flowed unvexed to the sea.

4

A City upon a Still:
Prohibition in Detroit

*Whenever I passed a saloon I sent up a prayer, "O, God,
stop this!" At length God plainly said to me, "You know
how to do it; go and help answer your own prayers."*
                                   Howard Hyde Russell

I

The prohibitionists always expected to face the greatest enforcement problems in the large cities. In this they were not disappointed. They also expected their greatest triumphs in the cities. A dramatic and massive urban conversion to the dry cause was anticipated once city dwellers no longer saw as through the bottom of a glass darkly. The clear bright light of prohibition would reveal in detail magnificent changes and transformations. How long could city dwellers resist the crackling dry peace and prosperity of prohibition? A matter of weeks or months and the last battle for a dry America would be won, the prohibitionists believed.

The conversion of the cities to prohibition was important and imperative because the future of America lay in the cities, the drys realized. Most of their children and grandchildren would some day live and work in or around the nation's great metropolitan centers. Perry Powers, editor of the Cadillac *Evening News,* spoke with dry concern for thousands of Michigan residents when he pointed out that "there is hardly a street in even the smallest Michigan village that has not in it some family that had divided its membership with Detroit." Consequently, the whole effort to create a saloonless and liquorless environment in which men and women would find it easier to do good would be a lost cause if it were relegated exclusively to areas outside the large cities.

And so it was with almost unrestrained joy that the drys read of the changes attributed to prohibition in Detroit in the two years after 1918. But then Detroiters voted against prohibition and in favor of the beer-and-wine amendment of 1919. From that point on Detroit appeared more and more a city in aggressive rebellion against prohibition, a seemingly vast conspiracy of people organized against their own best interests. Neither the churches nor the politicians nor the police nor the federal government nor the outstate drys could make prohibition succeed in the city. Only the residents of Detroit could do that, but they chose not to.

In its persistent resistance to prohibition Detroit was no different than any other metropolitan center in the country. In Chicago, for instance, the *Tribune* published a survey in 1921 indicating that there were at least four thousand speakeasies operating in the city.

The report elicited a sudden burst of police enforcement activity. The chief of police announced an edict ordering the city's 5,300 policemen to "rivet the lid down until it squeaks." He promised to "make Chicago so dry that a sponge can be wiped across it without picking up a drop of liquor." His enthusiasm lasted one week. Then Chicago returned to business as usual. A new mayor ordered another enforcement drive in 1923 and said he would keep the pressure on until he had closed every one of the six thousand soft-drink parlors, which served as fronts for speakeasies. His effort, needless to say, ended without significantly hindering the ability of thirsty Chicagoans to buy an alcoholic beverage.

Philadelphia experienced a more concentrated drive on illegal liquor. Brigadier-General Smedley D. Butler of the U.S. Marine Corps was brought to the City of Brotherly Love to head up prohibition enforcement. Butler had been told that prohibition simply could not be enforced in the large cities. "That is silly," he insisted. "Any law can be enforced precisely as it is written if the men responsible want it done." Butler promised Philadelphia impartial and fearless law enforcement, even if he were "torn apart in the attempt."

On January 7, 1924, Butler became Philadelphia's Director of Public Safety. During Butler's second week on the job two thousand arrests were made in organized police roundups in the city. Eight police lieutenants were suspended for failure to rid their districts of saloons. Butler was invited to head up law enforcement in other large cities after successfully fulfilling his responsibilities in Philadelphia.

But Butler's job in Philadelphia was never completed successfully. Only four months after taking office Butler complained of being double-crossed by members of the police department. One year later he was tired of his job. Enforcing prohibition in Philadelphia, he said, "is worse than any battle I was ever in. . . . The petty annoyances that are piled up on me are worse than the Chinese drip torture." At the end of the year Butler declared his own separate peace with prohibition, abandoned Philadelphia to the drinkers, and returned to the Marine Corps.

From New York to San Francisco, in city after city, the story of prohibition's failure to convert the urban masses was the same. The chronicles of the lost war against liquor in Detroit shed light on the frustration, confusion, and disappointment produced wherever a mass of thirsty urban dwellers confronted prohibition. The prohibition law may have sprung from the soil and the soul and germinated in remote and sacred places where mothers prayed and fathers thought, but it died on the city streets.

II

Detroit prospered because of prohibition. Nowhere else were the dry predictions of impending prosperity fulfilled so literally as in the Motor City. Prohibition made the manufacture and sale of alcoholic beverages illegal, and in so doing created a huge new industry—the illegal manufacture and sale of alcoholic beverages. The criminal liquor traffic in Detroit not only flourished under prohibition but dominated the commercial life of the city. It wasn't what the drys expected or promised, but it was certainly a direct result of their work and their success. In Detroit, the drys discovered, their good law worked in strange ways.

Ten years after prohibition became the law in Michigan, smuggling, manufacturing, and distributing liquor had become Detroit's second largest industry, exceeded in size only by the production of automobiles. Detroit's illegal liquor industry was three times larger than her chemical industry, eight times the size of her stove and heating appliance industry, ten times the size of her cigar and tobacco industry, and about one-eighth the size of her automobile industry. The annual liquor turnover in Detroit, according to the New York *Times*, was valued at $215 million. A survey by the Detroit Board of Commerce revealed that the illegal booze business employed fifty thousand people. Another study two years later set the actual retail value of illegal liquor sold over the bar in Detroit at $219 million. Wine and beer accounted for another $30 million. When shown this estimate, however, one knowledgeable and outspoken bootlegger insisted that it was too low and declared that the real annual value of the liquor business in Detroit was closer to $400 million.

In the spring of 1918, just before Michigan went dry, there were 1,534 licensed saloons and 800 illegal unlicensed saloons in Detroit, a total of 2,334 retail liquor establishments. A survey by the police department in 1923 recorded 3,000 blind pigs in the city, but according to another survey in 1923 by the Detroit *News* there were 7,000 additional blind pigs unknown to the police, or a total of 10,000 retail liquor outlets in the city. In certain areas of Detroit, the *News* reported, "every house is either a bootleg stand or a blind pig." One newspaper investigator found 150 such places on one block; and in one twenty-block neighborhood there were 500 blind pigs. Over $2 million a week was spent in these places, the *News* reported. Subsequent estimates of the number of blind pigs in Detroit indicated a steady increase in their numbers. In 1925 the police department estimated the number of blind pigs to be at least 15,000. Three years later the *News* revealed that 16 to 25,000 blind pigs did business in the city.

The quality of the blind pigs and the ease with which a drinker might secure an alcoholic beverage in one varied from place to place. "It was absolutely impossible to get a drink in Detroit," journalist Malcolm Bingay remembered of the 1920s, "unless you walked at least ten feet and told the busy bartender what you wanted in a voice loud enough for him to hear you above the uproar." In 1925, A. B. Stroup, deputy administrator in charge of prohibition enforcement in Detroit, complained, "I can say without reservation that Detroit is the wettest city I have been assigned to. I have worked in several parts of the country and observed conditions carefully, and I can say without hesitation that nowhere else is the law so openly violated as it is here. Since coming to Detroit I have been constantly amazed at the open flaunting of the law by resort keepers and others who profited in the illicit sale of prohibited beverages. I cannot understand this, for I have sensed during my stay here a demand on the part of better citizens for effective law enforcement. Yet defiance of the liquor statutes goes on, and I am puzzled."

Blind pigs ran into very little legal trouble if they were adept at distinguishing undercover police officers, WCTU matrons, Anti-Saloon League crusaders, federal prohibition agents, and state troopers from serious boozers. And they were extremely talented in making such distinctions. Hundreds of blind pigs operated in the city as soft-drink parlors and near-beer saloons. Licensed annually by the city to dispense non-alcoholic beverages, these institutions, were required by law to obey most of the pre-prohibition saloon ordinances, including requirements that there be no obstructions in windows and that the full length of the bar be visible from the street. Brawling and disorderly conduct were forbidden, and the places were required to close by 2 A.M. It was well known, however, that soft-drink and near-beer retailers who dispensed only legal beverages could not make enough profit even to pay their rent. The relatively high retaining fee demanded by local attorneys for handling the securing of soft-drink licenses indicated that something more profitable than soda was being dispensed. Yet proving law violations by such establishments was surprisingly difficult. Soft-drink and near-beer retailers commonly divided an open front bar from other sections of their establishment by illegal screens or curtains. Strangers were served only legal beverages at the front bar and were carefully scrutinized by the bartender and paid spotters before being admitted to an inner sanctum. In most soft-drink parlors if you were not known to the "private man" you actually drank soft drinks. In this way, hundreds of plainclothes law officers were effectively kept from purchasing alcoholic beverages. In establishments serving working-class clientele, prospective drinkers were asked where they worked, who their foreman was, and to identify some of their fellow workers. Many retailers protected themselves by maintaining a "rogues gallery" photo album behind the bar containing pictures of local and federal law enforcement officers. Even this, however, was not complete insurance against mistakes. In 1923, Federal Prohibition Agent No. 1, Izzy Einstein, paid a visit to Detroit in order to aid local police in a crackdown on the booze business. In one Woodward Avenue blind pig the bartender refused to serve him because, he said, pointing to a black-draped photograph of Einstein, "Izzy Epstein's in town." "you mean Einstein, don't you?" Izzy asked. When the bartender insisted it was Epstein, Izzy bet him a drink. The bartender poured him a shot of booze, Izzy emptied it into a secret funnel sewed to his breast pocket and connected by a long rubber tube to a concealed flask he used to gather evidence. Then Izzy announced in his usual plaintive manner, "There's sad news here. You're under arrest." But Einstein was an exceptionally adept dry agent. Countless prohibition cases were thrown out of court in Detroit after police chemists showed that arrests had been made after police undercover agents had been served near-beer or soda pop or non-alcoholic cocktails.

Unlike the retail liquor business in pre-prohibition years, downtown establishments did not dominate the booze trade in the 1920s. The downtown liquor retailers complained constantly during prohibition about the "small fry" operators who opened places of business almost anywhere in the city. These were the neighborhood pigs, apartment pigs, back-room pigs, front-room pigs, basement pigs, attic pigs, and garage pigs. Since legal licensing of the liquor traffic no longer existed and only supply and demand regulated the market, anybody could set up his own blind pig in any place if he had the necessary nerve and money. One downtown blind-pig proprietor complained that "any bird that has enough dough to buy a bottle of whisky and a case of beer is going into the blind pig business." The result, he said, was that competition was as intense as it had been before 1918, and many respectable places had been forced out of business. By 1927 some blind piggers lamented the fact that they were without customers at night. "The reason," one said, "is that the little birds have opened up places wherever they can find a roof to cover them in the residential district, and the crowd won't come downtown. They're sort of becoming a gang of apartment drinkers." One of the more important results of the growth of the illegal liquor traffic was that there was no longer any restriction as to where a retail liquor outlet might open. Wards and neighborhoods that were free from saloons before 1918 were now inundated with entrepreneurs who came to the customers rather than wait for them downtown.

Neighborhood pigs in prosperous outlying residential areas found it necessary to disguise themselves elaborately in order to avoid the wrath of many non-drinking local residents who did not hesitate to apply political pressure in order to have blind pigs raided and closed. The result was that undertaking establishments, Turkish baths, barber shops, candy stores, drug stores, near-beer saloons, and soft-drink parlors were often blind-pig fronts. The police tried to regulate some of these places, directing them to remove screens and partitions and other view-obstructing devices, but the regulations were difficult to enforce, and not enough citizens were sufficiently concerned to encourage the police to pursue such a policy over a long period of time.

In 1924 Police Comissioner Frank Croul proposed the "tip-over raid" as the most effective weapon to control illegal retail liquor establishments in Detroit. The tip-over then became a controversial and effective police tactic and served as an ingenious vehicle for public authorities to circumvent restraints on search and seizure limitations of the state and federal Constitutions. County and federal courts insisted that law enforcement authorities show some proof that an establishment was a blind pig before they were issued a search warrant to enter the premises. But since blind-pig doormen were uncannily adept at recognizing plain-clothes police officers, it was difficult to secure such evidence. The tip-over policy was consequently employed whenever the police had "definite knowledge" that the prohibition law was being violated, but did not have enough hard evidence to secure a legal warrant—or, in the words of Police Commissioner Croul, when the police were "morally certain" that a place was breaking the law, but not "legally certain." In such instances a "strong arm squad" of policemen, armed with axes and sledge hammers—police officers called a sledge hammer "the big key—swooped down on the offensive blind pig, smashed open the door, and destroyed all the property in sight until the floor of the establishment was a mixture of glass, kindling wood, and booze, and nothing over two-feet high remained intact. Clocks, pianos, expensive mirrors, and Tiffany lamp shades were all fair game for the tip over. The tip over was used by every Detroit mayor in the 1920s despite the fact that it was clearly illegal. Since the policemen involved in the raids carried no legal warrant, they could make no arrests, but Police Commissioner John P. Smith declared, "In this case we are dealing with law violators and we have to break the law to enforce it." Smith complained that if the city police were compelled to operate exclusively with legal search warrants "there would be a blind pig on every corner." Both Croul and later Commissioner William P. Rutledge regarded the tip over as the police department's "most effective weapon." As Croul explained it, "It is the exceptional case in which we are able to get evidence enough on which to obtain a search warrant or a criminal warrant, but by constantly harassing the bootlegger, by raiding him again and again without discouragement, by making life miserable for both him and his patrons, you can drive him out of business. And when the blind pigs are gone a considerable part of the underworld will go with them."

The tip over remained, nevertheless, an extremely controversial tactic. One year after tip-over raids were initiated, Police Superintendent Rutledge admitted that the tactic often made his officers look "ridiculous." The Police Department had been forced to resort to "rowdyism and lawlessness," he complained. "We have virtually been outlaws." The raids were illegal, he concluded, "and in smashing furniture and seizing liquor where we have no right to do so, we are merely following the example set by hijackers who prey on blind-pig operators in much the same way.

The most articulate defender of the tip over was Wayne County prosecuting attorney Robert Toms. According to Toms, courts interpreted the search-and-seizure clause of the Consitiution in liquor cases "so that it is a shield for liquor law violators." Detroit was inundated with blind pigs, Toms said, because the courts tied the hands of police officers. "The greatest obstacle to the attainment of prohibition," he pointed out, "is the Constitution of the United States, the instrument which decreed its birth." "If the Constitution could speak," Toms imagined, "it would say, 'thou shalt not possess nor traffic in intoxicating liquor, but if you do I shall lend my best efforts to prevent its being proved.' " The Constitution had been composed and passed for the purpose of protecting individuals from tyrannical monarchs and oppressive autocracies, Toms explained, "passed in the days when individual freedom was endangered, when great complex communities were unknown, when social contacts were few and infrequent, and when apartment houses and autos and blind pigs were unknown. These same laws are now invoked by the individual to furnish license and immunity for him in breaking other laws." "The time has come when society needs a few constitutional guarantees against the tyranny and oppression of lawless individuals," he said. "The courts have interpreted the search-and-seizure clause of the Constitution in liquor cases in the light of antiquated and obsolete precedents and have strained and twisted the law and have split technical hairs in a frantic effort to make this clause of the Constitution, which was originally passed for an entirely different purpose, a sword and a sheild to the person who, by the very invocation of this clause, is admittedly a violator." Until the courts changed their interpretation of the law, Toms said, it would be necessary to break the law to enforce it.

As the blind-pig business grew in Detroit during the 1920s it incorporated certain features that had been outlawed in pre-prohibition saloons. The "free lunch," a central attraction of the old-time saloon, had become so elaborate and expensive in pre-prohibition Michigan that brewers and saloon interests pressured the state legislature to outlaw it, thus making competition less costly. Once liquor was outside the law, however, and blind-pig proprietors operated as they wished, the free lunch returned to become a standard competitive feature of the booze business. Connoisseurs of the old-time free lunch counters were delighted at the elaborate nature of the lunches served in many blind pigs during prohibition. One Detroit *News* reporter found in a busy downtown blind pig "juicy red beef, presided over by a white-aproned functionary with a long knife, who sold you a sandwich plus trimmings for 10¢." When the reporter asked a patron of the place why he didn't eat in the restaurant next door, he was asked in turn, "Can I get a sandwich there like this one for 10¢? You should ask such a question! The pigs may be selling food below cost and all that, but I should worry. I'm going where I can get filled up on the smallest expenditure." In another blind pig the reporter found long tables bearing liverwurst, salami, bologna, ham sausage, garlic sausage, anchovies, sardines, herrings, green onions, celery, dill pickles, head cheese, veal loaf, Swiss cheese, American cheese, Roquefort cheese, rye bread, and pumpernickel bread. Beside the table stood a workingman on his lunch break, a glass of beer in one hand and a sandwich three inches thick in the other. "The man bore a look of triumphant rapture in his eyes."

The city's restaurant owners, not unexpectedly, complained about the free lunches. "Nearly every restaurant in the city is losing money as the result of free lunches and meals served at cost or below in blind pigs," one restaurateur complained. According to the association of restaurant owners, more than three hundred city restaurants went out of business in 1925–26 because their trade had been stolen by the "unfair competition" of the blind pigs. As a result, in the summer of 1926, two hundred restaurant men in the city formed an association to oppose the blind-pig lunch. The names of association members were kept secret in order to protect them from retaliation by irate blind-pig proprietors. "Because they get bigger tips there, our waitresses and cooks are finding work in the pigs," one restaurant manager complained. "Yet the pig, in most instances, being an unlicensed restaurant, operates with little cost.

Their alley rent is little or nothing, their kitchens are not equipped with hot water, they have no expense for sanitary provisions and their profits are excessive. This, we want the public to realize, is unfair and unclean competition." Members of the National Restaurant Association and the Restaurant Men's Association announced that they would "fight to the last" to bring a halt to the blind-pig free lunch.

Association members met with Police Commissioner William Rutledge and city health commissioner Harry Vaughan to discuss a strategy for the elimination of blind-pig free lunches. Rutledge proposed that precinct police captains thoroughly investigate every application for a city restaurant license to insure that blind pigs did not receive such licenses. Rutledge and the Restaurant Association knew very well, however, that such a measure would be of only limited effectiveness since most blind pigs operated without a restaurant license. The Detroit *News* pointed out the absurdity of the entire situation and asked why the Restaurant Association did not simply swear out warrants against known blind pigs, forcing the police to raid them and close them all down.

When the Restaurant Association resolved to hire private detectives to gather evidence against the blind pigs unless they promised to eliminate the free lunch, the blind pigs, at the end of the first week of September 1926, capitulated. The restaurants began winning back the noontime crowds. Rutledge's warning that he would use Department of Health rulings to close the blind pigs that served food also intimidated many blind-pig proprietors.

As with most agreements in illicit business, the decision of the blind-pig proprietors to abandon the free lunch was in the form of a "gentleman's agreement." The trouble was that there was no way to provide uniform enforcement, and so while most of the pigs abandoned the free lunch, a few continued the practice. Enough blind pigs dropped out of the food business, however, to satisfy the Restaurant Association. After the onset of the depression in 1929, however, the free lunch again became a primary consideration in determining where a man would drink—particularly if he was unemployed—and the free lunch came back to the blind pigs, in a more elaborate form than ever before. The president of the Detroit Caterers Association declared in 1932 that "those old free lunches were chicken feed compared with the food the blind pigs are now giving away." Steaks that sold for $2 in hotel restaurants were free in numerous blind pigs, and turkey and caviar were not unusual items on the new free lunch counters. Once again the restaurants were hard pressed, and once again their association decided to take action. Before truly effective steps could be taken, however, the repeal of prohibition put all but a few of the blind pigs out of business.

The blind pigs went out in a glorious way. Not only were their lunches free and elaborate in the depression years, but price wars drove the retail price of beer and whisky down in late 1931. Beer dropped from 24¢ to 15¢ a glass, while whisky dropped from 50¢ to 35¢ a shot. Free Friday fish fries or frog-leg dinners were offered in some blind pigs, and pinochle contests and door prizes were featured in others.

Because they were illegal, blind pigs were supplied by elaborate underground liquor agencies employing ruthless and brutal men, and the pigs themselves were often haunts for racketeers and gangsters. As a result, many people feared that anyone who entered a blind pig took his life in his hands. This, of course, was part of the attraction of the blind pig—the thrill of engaging in something forbidden and dangerous. Sometimes the dangers were manifested in unexpected ways. In 1926, for example, four University of Michigan students danced their way into the hearts and pocketbooks of the patrons of one blind pig. The students danced a wild Charleston with girls in the blind pig to the delight and applause of the patrons of the place. Then they suddenly drew guns and turned on the appreciative audience, shot two men and fled with $2,000 worth of jewelry. The students were arrested in Ann Arbor a few days later. Because of similar episodes, the Detroit *News* commented that when a man entered a blind pig, "he knows that he has crossed the border between the things of his decent home and things not to be spoken of in the hearing of his family." The courts, however, thought differently. In 1929 the Title Guaranty and Casualty Company of America refused to pay an insurance policy claim of $1,000 to Mrs. Lula Anders of Detroit after her husband, Bert, was shot to death in a downtown blind pig. Anders, according to the company, had exposed himself to unnecessary danger by entering a blind pig. Mrs. Anders sued for the money and won her case before Judge John Brennan in Recorder's Court. Brennan concluded, in a revealing decision, that "prohibition in law is not prohibition in fact," and that liquor was served not only in blind pigs and kindred establishments but was also at times illegally possessed, served, and consumed "in almost every sort of place where human beings foregather, in large cities in this country, with the exception possibly of religious edifices, court rooms, cemeteries, schoolrooms, prisons, reformatories, and WCTU headquarters." Brennan conceded that blind-pig customers were "occasionally disturbed by gunmen," but, he declared, "so are clergymen, policemen, and judges. If the contention of the defendants in the case are sound," the judge noted, "then Bert Anders' widow would also have lost her insurance had her husband chanced to have been shot while attending a debutante's party, a football game, a banquet of Senators, a poker game, or had he been on a fishing trip or celebrating New Year's Eve. The policy would have been voided had he entered the private office of a stock broker, the average kitchenette, or the cloakroom."

And yet while a large proportion of the public and police observed an anxious tolerance toward most illegal retail liquor outlets, there was one type that was not suffered so easily: the so-called school pig. The problem of the school pigs first emerged in 1924 after the publication of a front-page story in the Detroit *News* dealing with "horrifying revelations" of drunkenness among grammar school students. The story described the plight of fourteen-year-old Kenneth Nestell, who, according to his mother, had become a hopeless alcoholic. Several bootleggers in the Nestell neighborhood supplied the boy with large quantities of moonshine, his mother complained. He became addicted to the stuff and was able to attend school only infrequently, and even then was so stupefied with booze that he fell asleep over his books. When police took young Nestell into custody he pointed out a blind pig where children were regularly sold booze. The publication of Nestell's story brought a barrage of complaints and pathetic pleas to city hall to do something about blind pigs that exploited schoolchildren. Edith Shaw, principal of Lyon School charged that blind pigs in the school neighborhood served as "liquor traps" for slow learners in the school's special grades. The school, located in a low-income working-class neighborhood, included in addition to regular students in grades one through four, fifty special pupils from fourteen to seventeen years old, who were lured into the five blind pigs located on the same block as the school. Police investigating Miss Shaw's complaint discovered that young children in the neighborhood could tell anyone on the street where beer or cheap whisky might be purchased. In mid-March the principal of Franklin School complained directly to Acting Mayor Joseph Martin that blind pigs operated in the neighborhood of his school and made it a regular practice to sell liquor to students. School officials appealed to the mayor and the police for protection from the school pigs as well as from the taxi drivers who picked up young girls and delivered them to the blind pigs. Wayne County's prosecuting attorney was told that at least 10 percent of the students of Franklin School, aged fourteen to sixteen, were victims of blind pigs and bootleggers. Martin was so upset by the complaints that he ordered the police to "knock off the head of any bootlegger appearing over the parapet." Seven men and one woman were arrested during the 1924 investigation into school pigs. What most surprised investigators was that the young girls they found frequenting the school pigs were "not even of the flapper type," but "just little schoolgirls."

The school pigs scandal quieted after 1924 only to be revived again in 1927 when yet another crusade against them was initiated. In mid-October of that year police received complaints of the existence of school pigs in the upper middle-class residential areas, and charges were made at a meeting of the Board of Education a few days later that many new blind pigs in residential areas were having a bad influence on school children and should be eliminated. Because of the fear of school pigs, students of Cass Technical High School were required to bring their lunches or to purchase them in the school cafeteria, but under no circumstances were they to leave the school premises during the noon hour. Bishop School was closed because of the abundance of blind pigs nearby. A spokeswoman for the Florence Crittenden Home announced that blind pigs serving teenagers were the principal contributing cause for a 300 percent increase in the number of delinquent cases handled by the home since 1921. The school board demanded that the police maintain "safety zones" for children in school neighborhoods.

In late November 1927, Superintendent of Police James Sprott initiated a vigorous campaign against the school pigs. Sprott was provided with the addresses of blind pigs in the neighborhoods of various schools, and police officers visited those places, informed the proprietors that the police were establishing safety zones around the schools, and "suggested" that they close or move. If the proprietors hesitated or refused to follow the police suggestion, they were raided. Twenty-three places had closed by early December. By the end of the year fifty-six blind pigs near schools had discontinued business, and Sprott reported to the Board of Education that the safety zones had been established. With the onset of the depression, however, the school pigs reappeared. Once again complaints from the Board of Education to the police commissioner brought investigations, pressure on the pigs, and, eventually, raids. In the end, repeal solved the problem of the school pigs just as it solved the problem of the free lunch.

The blind-pig proprietors themselves worried not only about the police policies, the Board of Education, federal agents, private detectives, organized criminals, the Restaurant Association, and other blind-pig proprietors, but also about their own employees. In the spring of 1931 the unionization of blind-pig employees precipitated a very embarrassing situation in Detroit.

The Hotel and Restaurant Employees and Beverage Dispensers International Alliance, affiliated with the Detroit Federation of Labor, began to organize blind-pig cooks and waiters in the spring of 1931. Louis Koenig of the Waiters and Waitresses Local 705 placed a picket line of union members around a Detroit blind pig at that time to protest the establishment's postponement of salary payments to its employees. Koenig objected loudly to "illegitimate places" in Detroit—"fly-by-night places that don't even bother to get restaurant or beverage licenses. They open up dirty and unsightly place," Koenig complained, "and serve poisonous beer and liquor. They don't pay fixed wages of any kind." Frank X. Martel of the Detroit Federation of Labor explained that because of the depression, many former union members—cooks, waiters, and waitresses—had been forced to work in non-union blind pigs, and the federation, he declared, felt an obligation to protect these workers. Mayor Frank Murphy, who enjoyed a close friendship with Martel, denied any knowledge of the unionization efforts and announced to the press that if an attempt were made in Detroit to organize an illegal business, he wanted it stopped immediately. "If such an organization were permitted to operate," Murphy worried, "there is no telling to what lengths it would go. The whole illegal liquor industry from brewers and distillers down to the lowly porter in a saloon could become fraternalized under one leader." Murphy, nevertheless, did nothing to halt the campaign of Local 705, which continued to increase its membership despite the deteriorating conditions of the liquor industry.

Complete unionization of the illegal blind-pig business never materialized. Some blind-pig proprietors conceded to union demands, others did not. An investigation into the affair by Wayne County prosecuting attorney Harry S. Toy revealed no illegal practices by Martel, Koenig, or the union. In the end, the problem of organizing blind-pig employees was solved by repeal.

III

Supplying blind pigs with alcoholic beverages became an extremely profitable enterprise during prohibition. In Detroit a main supply of imported Canadian liquor was supplemented by domestically produced products. Throughout the prohibition years a local liquor industry flourished in Detroit, and several thousand city residents found profitable employment either directly in the brewing and distilling trades or in the various ancillary services that fed into them, such as the production and distribution of brewing and distilling apparatus, bottles, labels, corks, caps, wooden cases, and other materials necessary for the production and bottling and distribution of alcoholic beverages. In destroying the legal brewing and distilling industries without destroying public thirst for beverages with a "kick," the government created opportunities for thousands of local entrepreneurs who rushed forward to share in prohibition's prosperity.

Wine, beer, spirits, and various exotic alcoholic concoctions were produced in large quantities in Detroit throughout the prohibition years. Legally, brewers could continue to operate only if they produced dealcoholized near-beer. Since the market for that product was very limited, most large commercial breweries went out of business when prohibition came in. A few, however, continued to make legal as well as illegal beer. To produce near-beer, strong beer first must be manufactured and then dealcoholized. It was quite simple for any unscrupulous brewer to market some strong beer because of the inadequate number of federal and state inspectors available to supervise the brewing industry. The Anheuser-Busch company protested that prohibition had made valueless a plant worth $40 million. The company expended $18 million to convert its brewing facilities to the production of legal near-beer only to discover that the product did not sell well because of the continued availability to the public of real strong beer. Anheuser-Busch spokesmen complained that "those who are obeying the law are being ground to pieces by its very operation, while those who are violating the law are reaping unheard-of rewards. Every rule of justice has been reversed." One of the most notorious brewers reaping the "unheard-of rewards" was the Auto City Brewing Company on McDougall Avenue in Hamtramck, which produced illegal beer until 1925. Brew from the plant was shipped by boxcar and truck throughout Michigan and the Midwest. Several large, well-disguised underground brewers were established in Detroit and the surrounding area and produced a palatable product for the blind pigs of the Motor City. Detroit police officers, during prohibition, located and wrecked more than a thousand illicit breweries in the city, including one subterranean establishment that included an intricate system of interconnecting tunnels and passageways and occupied an entire city block of basements only a few feet off Woodward Avenue.

Home brewing, generally for personal consumption, also prospered in Detroit in the 1920s. In the last years of prohibition the state government began taxing the raw materials used in home brewing. In the first six months of 1932, according to the Michigan state taxing agency, about fourteen million gallons of homemade beer were brewed in Detroit, or enough to provide every man, woman, and child in southeastern Michigan with six gallons of beer.

Wine was also produced for private and commercial consumption in Detroit during the prohibition years. The Volstead Act permitted an individual to ferment wine for private consumption, but selling the product was a violation of both state and federal laws. California grape growers shipped dehydrated grape bricks throughout the country labeled with warnings that if certain things were done to the bricks they would ferment and become wine. The warnings provided the necessary recipe for initiating such a process. Grape juice and grape flavorings were also marketed in kegs suited for fermentation. In Detroit, anyone could order for delivery to his front door "in strict compliance with the law," several gallons of port, sherry, claret, Tokay, Riesling, or Catawba flavorings and set up an intoxicating home fermentation process for fun and profit. Wine was available across the counter in nearly every blind pig in the city.

But by far the largest and most important aspect of the production of illegal booze in Detroit during prohibition was the distillation of raw alcohol. In thousands of warehouses, garages, vacant factories, attics, basements, and even in one case in an abandoned church, heated corn mash produced hundreds of thousands of gallons of Detroit "white lightning." For as little as fifty cents a gallon home stills produced alcohol which was then sold locally for three or four dollars. One still operating at full capacity could usually pay for itself completely in only four days of production, and by 1928 at least five thousand Detroit stills bubbled forth alcohol to slake the city's thirst. Many of these distilling enterprises were large-scale operations producing several thousand gallons of alcohol per day, but most were smaller setups in family basements, living rooms, closets, and attics, and these served as units in a large network responsible in the end for the production of tens of thousands of gallons of alcohol each week. Distilling syndicates set up an individual or a family in business—usually providing a house, a still, and the materials necessary for distilling. An agent or middleman supplied the instructions, legal and technical advice, a lawyer in case of arrest, payoffs to prevent arrests, and money if a fine were assessed in court. The compensation for running a still for a local syndicate was generous, and all a family needed to do was tend their still day and night, keep the fire burning, the mash boiling, and the alcohol running. The product from the still was collected several times each week by a regular pickup and delivery man who could be seen lugging large steel milk cans back and forth between his truck and the house where each still was located. The syndicates were efficiently organized from the purchase of the still apparatus to the distribution of the final "Canadian whisky" to the blind pigs or to nationwide distributors. Supplies of corn sugar and fuel were secured from wholesalers who did business exclusively with a certain distilling syndicate. Some syndicates even maintained a staff of experts who installed the stills, furnished technical advice, and made regular house calls to inspect, adjust, and repair the devices.

There were dangers, however, for the operator of the home still as well as for the consumer of his product. First there were the legal dangers. Police and federal agents carried out daily raids on large and small distilling operations, and thousands of distillers were fined or sent to jail. It was difficult to disguise the home distilling operation perfectly, and some aspects of the operation were likely to arouse the suspicions of either jealous or law-abiding neighbors. The regular delivery of fifty-pound bags of corn sugar to a home was a sure sign that something was amiss, as was the regular arrival and departure of a man lugging several dozen large milk cans to and from a basement door, particularly if one did not own a herd of dairy cattle. Some stills produced pungent odors and caused steam to rise through a roof in the summer and snow to melt very quickly from the roof in the winter. The mash left over from the still operation, if dumped in a sink or toilet, after a few weeks clogged the drainage. Any of these signs was likely to indicate to police where distilling operations were in progress and to bring closer scrutiny of a suspicious neighborhood. Between 1920 and 1933 the Detroit police seized nearly three thousand stills, more than half a million pounds of corn sugar, and over two and one-half million gallons of mash.

Mechanical dangers were often more a threat than legal dangers for home distillers, especially for the unwary amateur. Proper ventilation and regular adjustment for a still were absolutely essential. The danger of a constant flame on a boiling container in a closed space is obvious. Throughout the 1920s stories appeared in the local papers about families asphyxiated, homes, garages, and warehouses burned down or blown up, boiling mash scalding children and adults, and other destruction produced by home distilling. Despite these dangers, however, enough private distilling continued so that if at any one moment all industrial and traffic noises in Detroit could have been silenced, a listener with a good ear would have been able to hear the heavy percolating sounds of hundreds of hidden stills bubbling away producing booze and profits.

Consumption of some of the locally distilled beverages was infinitely more dangerous than their production, first, because bottles were mislabeled and one could never be certain whether bottles labeled as Canadian liquor contained any part Canadian liquor or just plain water or some liquor vaguely resembling rat poison. A combination of ignorance and greed was responsible for many of the dangers of consuming home-distilled booze. Prior to prohibition illegal distilling had generally been in the hands of those who understood the mechanics and chemistry of their chosen profession. But after 1918 amateurs flooded the market who neither understood nor cared for anything other than the profits of their racket. Mechanical ignorance could hurt only the producers and their families and their property. But ignorance of the chemistry of a home still was a problem for the unsuspecting consumer. Many home distillers were unaware that a still produced not only what they wanted—that is, ethyl alcohol—but also various "doublings," including amyl alcohol, butyl alcohol, and other compounds. These doublings were drained off and disposed of by distillers concerned with the toxicity of their product, but a significant number of home distillers simply lit the lamp under their still and left it on until the mash was dry, unaware that the first and last drops produced were quite different from ethyl alcohol. All the still products were then left together, and the resulting product was much more unhealthy for the drinker than anything dispensed by pre-prohibition saloons. Some distillers even used lead rather than copper coils for their stills, and the resulting product contained lead acetate, a deadly but slow-working poison. Some bottlers and blind-pig owners added methanol or wood alcohol to drinks in order to produce an additional "kick" for the drinker. Still others added dead rodents or pieces of rotten meat for a pungent and mysterious flavor. The results produced by these various ingredients were both devastating and tragic.

But most drinkers survived to tell about it. Most drinkers enjoyed the company in the blind pigs, enjoyed the risks, downed their drink, felt good, and survived. Their stomachs suffered, their livers deteriorated, their noses reddened, and their cheeks became a bit more flushed, but they did survive. Some domestically concocted drinks may have been bad, but most were not, and the risks were not great enough to produce droves of teetotalers. And the chances one took with a bootlegger or moonshiner or blind-pig owner were certainly better than those one took drinking "condensed heat," jamaica ginger, shellac, perfume, or the various other products consumed by a few desperate drinkers in the 1920s. Despite warnings to hurry up and drink the gin before it ate through the bottom of the cup; despite annual warnings that the government had added a new and more deadly denaturant to industrial alcohol to prevent its diversion to the beverage market and then to insure the death of anyone who might swallow it if it were diverted; despite warnings of the horrifying effects of lead poisoning, producing everything from purple gums, severe cramps, and partial paralysis of the forearms to coma and death; despite the warnings of Dr. David Clarke of the Detroit College of Medicine and Surgery that anyone who drank "doublings" would "think at one minute he is in the hospital surrounded by doctors and the next believe himself with the Common Council in City Hall"; despite all these warnings and stories and more, the manufacture and consumption of alcoholic beverages not only survived, but prevailed in Detroit in the 1920s. Booze was manufactured, imported, exported, marketed, bottled, rebottled, and consumed in Detroit, and it continued to please, soothe, sedate, upset, render unconscious, stupify, intoxicate, paralyze, blind, and kill. And although the friendly salutation "What's your poison, mister?" did not originate in the 1920s, it certainly might have been used quite appropriately in many of Detroit's blind pigs in that decade.

IV

An unforeseen result of prohibition was the widespread assumption by the underworld of many branches of the illegal liquor business—from brewing and distilling to rum-running and blind-pig management. Once the legal liquor business was terminated by state authorities, the free marketplace in booze had been thrown open to fearless, enterprising, and visionary men in the cities who were not averse to risking prison and death for profits.

At first the men attracted to the illegal liquor business were little more than daring adventurers, and their plans and schemes were easily disrupted by the police. But very quickly the independent adventurers were replaced by well-organized gangs that not only reaped large profits and eluded apprehension by the police, but also in the process became minor folk heroes.

To the public the best-known gang operating in Detroit by the mid-1920s was one with quite limited influence: the Purple Gang, a loose coalition of two different groups of young Jewish hoods—the Oakland Sugar House Gang and the original Purple Gang. Harry Fleisher, Henry Shore, Eddie Fletcher, Irving Milburg, Harry Altman, Harry Keywell, and Morris and Phil Raider—the original Oakland Sugar House Gang—grew up together on Detroit's East Side and attended the same high school. As teenagers in 1920 the boys had gone into business manufacturing alcohol for bootleg liquor. They gained hundreds of regular customers and before long became suppliers of dozens of blind pigs in the Detroit area. Another group of petty thieves on the East Side gathered around Samuel Cohen, known as "Sammy Purple." In the early twenties the leadership of this "Purple Gang" was assumed by the three Bernstein brothers, and like the Oakland Sugar House Gang, the group turned from shoplifting and extortion to distilling and brewing. Eventually, instead of competing, the two groups joined forces under the leadership of Abe Bernstein and branched out into the business of importing the marketing liquor.

The Purple Gang remained loosely organized. Instead of concentrating on a single racket, as did other gangs the individual members of the gang were generally "for hire": they entered into numerous activities, going wherever the price was highest but always falling back on the liquor business for a regular income. As a result, they were too often overextended and careless in their work—careless in whom they double-crossed, careless in selecting which jobs to take or not to take, and careless in carrying out their work. This, in the end, contributed to their demise. For several years, however, the Purples managed the prosperous business of supplying Canadian whisky to the Capone organization in Chicago. The Purples furnished Capone with Old Log Cabin, an expensive Canadian whisky. Despite its high price the brand could be sold easily because of its well-established reputation. It was the hijacking of a shipment of Old Log Cabin by the Moran gang of Chicago that led to the St. Valentine's Day Massacre in 1929.

During 1927 members of the Purple Gang exacted thousands of dollars in tribute from Detroit businessmen in a series of incidents that became known as the "Cleaners and Dyers War." The mainstay of the gang remained, nevertheless, the liquor traffic.

They muscled their way into the downriver booze traffic, but instead of transporting liquor across the river themselves, they arranged for the Jewish-dominated "Little Navy" gang to bring it across for them. Operations on the Michigan side of the river under this arrangement were managed by the Purples. The Purples also pushed their way into some of the downriver blind pigs and gambling joints, either operating them outright or simply exacting protection" money. The gang organized a phony Detroit business, the Art Novelty Company, to facilitate the important interstate shipment of their Canadian booze. Liquor transported to Detroit from Canada was brought to the Art Novelty Company, where it was packaged under false labels and then shipped by train or truck to New York, St. Louis, Toledo, Chicago, and other cities.

In the late 1920s the Purples branched out into minor fields to secure additional money: they hijacked prizefight films and forced movie theaters to show them for a high fee, defrauded insurance companies by staging phony accidents, kidnapped and accepted contracts for "rubbing out" enemies of this or that thug who did not wish to commit a particular murder himself. Because they were flamboyant and well known in the city's night spots, and because many of them liked to dress fashionably and be seen in public and live in fine houses, a romantic aura surrounded the Purples and distinguished them from other gangs that were operating in the Detroit area.

The power of the Purples evaporated rapidly in 1929. In the summer of that year four of the leading gang members—Axler, Milburg, Sutton, and Fletcher—were sentenced to terms of twenty-one months in Leavenworth for conspiracy to violate prohibition. In November 1929, Morris Raider was sentenced to twelve to fifteen years in Jackson State Prison for shooting a boy he suspected of spying on members of the gang. This disaster was followed by a dispute between the Purples and the Little Navy, which led several Purples to ambush three leading members of the Little Navy at the Collingwood Manor apartments in Detroit and to shoot them to death in what the press called the "Collingwood Massacre." In November 1931, Ray Bernstein, Irving Milburg, and Harry Keywell were found guilty of first-degree murder in the case and sentenced to life imprisonment.

Remaining members of the Purple Gang were methodically

preyed upon by better-organized elements of the underworld. In July 1929 young Irving Shapiro was dumped from a speeding auto near downtown Detroit; his head had been shattered by four bullets fired from behind at close range. In November 1933 the bodies of Abe Axler and Eddie Fletcher were found in a car on an isolated Oakland County road. Each man had been shot several times directly in the face from close range with a high-caliber weapon. Their deaths marked the end of the Purple Gang in organized crime in the Detroit area.

As early as 1919, while many of the future Purple Gang members were still students in East Side high schools, Sicilian rumrunners in Detroit and downriver districts grouped themselves around two families, the Giannolas and the Vitales, and fought for control of the already illegal liquor market. The Giannola-Vitale war ended in late 1920 with the deaths of all the leading members of both family groups. Peace was declared among the surviving Sicilian families and a business agreement was negotiated. According to that agreement each of the feuding Sicilian groups was to be allotted a district in the Detroit area in which to carry on the illicit liquor business. Competition and warfare were thereby eliminated, and profits consequently were enhanced. The most enterprising of the groups under the cooperative agreement formed the Pascuzzi Combine and began importing Canadian liquor across the rivers and lakes into Michigan. Under Joseph Moceri members of the combine became owners of the Riverside Brewery in Riverside, Ontario, and major stockholders in the Amherstburg Distillery in Amherstburg, Ontario. The organization was so successful in bribing Customs Border Patrol agents that they were able to ship liquor without fear of federal interference. The organization also bribed public officials in Detroit and included a number of city police officers on its payroll. Whenever anyone "crossed" the group or stumbled onto their operations it was the usual procedure to have that unfortunate individual killed. The police on numerous occasions arrested prominent members of the organization, particularly the suspected executioner of the group, Peter Licavoli, but convictions were extremely rare.

The business agreement among the Sicilian groups in Detroit was presided over by Samuel Catalonotte, who personally resolved and adjudicated differences among the numerous enterprising factions. Catalonotte worked so effectively behind the scenes patching up differences and assigning areas of operations that few people outside the Sicilian community even knew of his role. When he died of natural causes in late 1930 the coalition of the early 1920s again disintegrated into several competing and hostile factions. Each group was ambitious and impatient and demanded a bigger share of the illegal liquor business in the Detroit area. At this moment of upheaval, Chester LaMare, a close friend of the Catalonotte family, made a fateful bid for power.

The Catalonotte agreement had delegated areas in Hamtramck and northeast Detroit for LaMare to engage in the liquor business. In the late 1920s, however, LaMare was arrested for violation of prohibition, found guilty, and sentenced to a year in prison and a $1,000 fine. It seemed for a short time that LaMare had been put out of business permanently. But instead of serving his time in prison, LaMare worked out a deal that testified to his influence and his business drive. He arranged to have an additional $500 added to his fine and was in return placed on probation. LaMare promised the judge in the case that he would go straight. He was awarded a lucrative job with the Ford Motor Company supplying fruit for the food wagons that served workers during their lunch period. His income from this source was estimated at $100,000 a year. LaMare's contract with the Ford Company was terminated in 1929, however, following constant complaints to Ford concerning LaMare's continued criminal activities.

In late 1930 LaMare called a meeting of the heads of the various Sicilian factions in the Detroit area in order to discuss the selection of a successor to Catalonotte. Some of those invited to the meeting sent instead two intermediaries to talk with LaMare. But when the intermediaries stepped from their car outside a fish market on East Vernor Highway, where the meeting was to take place, they were cut down at close range by several shotgun blasts. It was all a mistake; LaMare had meant to execute the leaders of the independent factions and to make himself head of the entire liquor racket in the Detroit area. The punishment for LaMare's transgression was death. The other factions united in the effort to punish LaMare, and in that union Joseph Zerilli emerged as a persuasive leader and successor to Catalonotte. In early February 1931, LaMare was murdered in the kitchen of his own home by two of his former close friends. His death marked the renewal of peace among the Sicilian groups of Detroit, now under the effective leadership of Zerilli.

As the prohibition years drew to a close the future continued to look very bright for the gangs that had been organized in Detroit to supply liquor to thirsty citizens. The Sicilian factions of the city in particular were tightly and effectively organized, had accumulated a good deal of liquid capital, and under Zerilli's leadership were flexible and imaginative, prepared to move into new areas of business endeavor. Prohibition would end, but when new public demands arose that could not be supplied legally, the gangs organized in the 1920s would be there to serve as suppliers. For organized crime, prohibition had been a blessing, serving as a midwife, a teacher, and a rich uncle; and with the end of prohibition, many former rumrunners and gangsters moved with relative ease from rum to riches and respectability.

V

The prohibition law worked in strange ways in Detroit, and to at least one man it brought a shattering revelation. In the fall of 1927, nine years after state prohibition went into effect in Michigan, an unidentified man walked up to the information desk at Detroit police headquarters and asked where he could purchase a permit to buy some beer for a party.

"I don't know," replied the surprised officer behind the desk.

"Well, can I get a permit to make and sell a little beer?" the man asked.

"Hey," responded the police officer, "how long have you been in this country?"

"Ten years."

"Did you ever hear of the prohibition law?"

"No. What's that?"

The police officer explained, and the confused and disappointed pilgrim wandered away.

5

Prohibition in Action

Grayson Murphy: "Personally I do not know a man—I
   want to make this clear: I may know a man, but I
   cannot remember him if I do—I do not know of a single
   leading banker in the United States, I do not know of a
   single leading industrial executive in the United
   States, I do not know a single important railroad
   executive in the United States, that I can think of who
   does not break this law and who does not drink."
Mr. Michener: "Henry Ford?"
Grayson Murphy: "I do not know him."
(Laughter)

House of Representatives Hearings on
   the Prohibition Amendment, 1930

I

In the spring of 1925 President Plutarco Elias Calles of Mexico told an American reporter how he had enforced prohibition while governor of Sonora. "As soon as the law was announced I blew up all the breweries and distilleries with dynamite," he explained. "Then I arrested a few smugglers who were taking contraband across the border from Arizona near the Cananea Pass. I had them all shot the next morning. After that, the law was generally observed." Calles suggested that the American government would experience less trouble enforcing prohibition if it, too, used "a little executive firmness."

By 1925 there were doubtless many Americans receptive to Calles's suggestion. After five years of national prohibition, an enforcement problem of overwhelming and apparently insoluble proportions loomed in the United States. This condition was entirely unexpected by doctrinaire dry spokesmen who had insisted in 1919 that the Eighteenth Amendment was a logical evolutionary outgrowth of nearly a century of agitation for temperance reform. Initial enforcement problems would melt away, they assumed, once the enormous and pervasive benefits of the new cold-water culture materialized. But that illusion faded rather rapidly. In the face of praise for the social advances attributed to prohibition, disregard for the measure in many localities made it appear to troubled drys that some communities had become involved in vast illegal conspiracies against themselves. And with the fading of the easy-enforcement myth, Calles's suggestion of "executive firmness" to many erstwhile dry idealists seemed not an undesirable alternative to explore.

Several factors contributed to the enforcement dilemma. Among the most important of these was the financially tight-fisted stance of prohibition's friends both in Congress and the state legislatures. Notwithstanding oceans of evidence to the contrary, ardent dry legislators were reluctant to acknowledge that a major enforcement effort was necessary. Massive funding for enforcement, they feared, would involve acknowledging massive problems resulting from a reluctance of the public actively to support the dry laws, and would consequently fuel the fires of prohibition's critics. Funding for enforcement was, as a result, both inadequate and inconspicuous. The friends of prohibition in Congress acted as if generous doses of prayers, good wishes, optimistic pronouncements, and denunciations of law-breaking would serve as substitutes for cash in the effort to enforce prohibition. Until very late in the 1920s, congressmen sympathetic to the dry cause generally remained unmoved by regular appeals for dramatic increases in financial support for the Prohibition Bureau. Their counterparts in the state legislatures, on the other hand, actually outperformed them in prohibition penny-pinching, spending less for enforcement of the dry laws than they did to maintain their parks and public monuments.

A budget-minded Congress consequently dispatched agents of the Prohibition Bureau to the states to enforce dry statutes "concurrently" with state law officers dispatched by similarly budget-minded state authorities. The federal agents found themselves almost immediately in an unfortunate dilemma. They were denied adequate resources. Understaffed and underpaid, their jobs were not classified under the civil service system. They were thus vulnerable to attack by prohibition critics who derided them for being political appointees with neither the proper qualification, training, or intelligence for their jobs. They pursued the often unpopular task of detaining and prosecuting liquor-law violators in the face of ill-defined constitutional constraints, an indifferent public, an impatient Congress, well-financed and organized criminal organizations, and wary-eyed critics of the dry law. The dangers facing them were great, and the temptations for accepting payoffs, bribes, and other gratuities were often irresistible. Eventually the Prohibition Bureau listed "bribery, extortion, theft, forgery, perjury, and other causes" among the reasons for releasing from the force nearly one agent in twelve; Congress was receiving only as much quality prohibition enforcement as it paid for.

In 1927, in a belated effort to strengthen prohibition enforcement, Congress approved a measure requiring all federal prohibition agents to pass a civil service examination. Those failing the examination were to be replaced. Although the purpose of the law was to improve the quality of federal agents, it served simply to demoralize them further. Fewer than one-half of the federal agents stationed in the Detroit area in early 1928 passed the examination and retained their positions, and some very good agents lost their jobs because of their performances on the examination. In one case, a bartender in a blind pig qualified for a position with the Prohibition Bureau because he scored high on the examination. The agent who had arrested him a few days earlier failed the test and was released from the force.

Had competent, enthusiastic support from state and local law enforcement agencies been forthcoming, the task of the federal agents would have been enormously easier—even perhaps manageable. But the story of state and local enforcement efforts was also one of balanced budgets and faith in the miraculous. Agents of the Prohibition Bureau in Michigan were aided in their pursuit of lawbreakers by troopers from the state police force. Like the federal agents, the state police patrolled both high-crime metropolitan areas and unincorporated rural districts in Michigan. During the prohibition years they were twice ordered by the governor to occupy the city of Hamtramck and at other times were dispatched to both Detroit and various downriver communities. Soon after state prohibition went into effect in 1918 the state police discovered that their limited resources were inadequate to discourage significantly the illegal manufacture and transportation of alcoholic beverages in Michigan. That did not mean, however, that they were exempt from trying to discourage such activity. Consequently, in rural areas and small towns, urban centers and suburbs, from Monroe to Negaunee and from Lake St. Clair to Lake Michigan, by automobile, airplane, locomotive, speedboat, canoe, on foot and on ice skates, in the water, over the ice, and across the land, the state police pursued suspected prohibition violators. After five years of such pursuit, Roy Vandercook, commander of the state police, concluded that his force had been assigned an impossible task. Even massive funding would not solve the problem of prohibition enforcement, he declared. "We could not enforce the prohibition law in Michigan," he complained to a reporter, "if we had the United States standing army. As long as the people maintain their present attitude toward prohibition, the law is unenforceable.

Among the most frustrating of the unenforceable enforcement tasks of the state police, Vandercook had learned, was stopping the liquor traffic that moved across southern Michigan each day toward Chicago. Liquor transported across the Detroit River from Canada was of little value unless it could be marketed. As a result, each day and night of the prohibition years, dozens of liquor-laden cars raced

west on U.S. 112 across Michigan toward Chicago. In Chicago one
bottle of pure Canadian whisky would be cut into three bottles and
the product relabeled and sent on to Minneapolis, St. Louis, and
other liquor-marketing centers throughout the Midwest. In the
mid-1920s police officials estimated that at least fifty loads of liquor
each day left Wyandotte, Ecorse, and Detroit for Chicago by way of
U.S. 112 through Ann Arbor, Jackson, Kalamazoo, and Benton
Harbor, while an average of fifteen cars were daily routed through
Lansing and points further north. The ordinary load per car was
fifteen to twenty cases of whisky. Some large Chicago buyers operated fleets of cars on a daily schedule, paying their drivers as much
as sixty dollars for each safe delivery. Many of the drivers were
women, often accompanied by other women and by children in
order to give their venture an appearance of innocence. Some liquor
runners preferred to drive at night in groups of two or three cars
bunched together for protection from hijackers and dishonest law
enforcement officials. A scout car usually preceded such a caravan
and another followed at some distance. A few cars were equipped
with smoke-screen devices to ward off pursuing state police motor-
cycles, and at least one car emitted deadly mustard gas.

In their attempts to disrupt the cross-state liquor traffic, state
police officers found themselves as often arresting as cooperating
with local law enforcement officials. For when the opportunity to
share in liquor profits appeared, public officials in small towns and
rural areas of the state proved themselves to be as morally malleable
as officials in Detroit or in the notorious downriver settlements. The
outstate areas may have foisted bone-dry prohibition in Detroit, but
when it came to dividing the profits from the illicit liquor traffic,
outstate law enforcement officers demanded their fair share of the
wet windfall profits.

The most widely publicized of the cross-state liquor shipping
scandals involved the liquor conspiracy ring of Jackson County.
Drivers transporting carloads of booze from Detroit to Chicago via
U.S. 112 passed through Jackson County. Their automobiles, heavily loaded and squatting low on their frames, were easily spotted.
Sheriff Warren Stoddard of Jackson County at first arrested many of
the rumrunners and confiscated their cargoes. Before long, however, the rumrunners succeeded in negotiating an agreement with
the sheriff whereby Stoddard, through his deputy "toll collectors,"

was paid thirty dollars for every load of liquor passing through the county. Drivers who did not pay the toll received no protection, and Stoddard was quite successful in detecting such "offenders" and confiscating their booze as well as their automobiles. He sold the automobiles back to them at a bargain rate, but the booze was provided to Jackson County blind-pig managers at wholesale prices. Stoddard eventually branched out into bigger enterprises and began levying a regular toll on blind pigs in the county, charging according to their volume of business, the usual fee being fifty cents for every case of beer sold.

Like thousands of other Michigan residents, Henry Ford fretted over the often futile efforts of the state and federal prohibition enforcers. The only permanent solution to the enforcement problem, Ford concluded, would come through education. "We must educate the people," he said, "and after a time just as in other social problems, when the truth is known the liquor law will be enforced." But until the truth was known, Ford recommended that "we turn enforcement of our laws over to the army and navy and get it done right."

But Henry Ford was an impatient prohibitionist, and he did not wait for the army and navy to step in and enforce the dry laws. In the early 1920s he personally set out to show the country how prohibition could be enforced. Ford's principal concern was with the "moist" environment of Highland Park and Springwells where the principal Ford production plants were located. He issued a mandate directing that any employee who reported to work with liquor in or on his person be promptly fired. Ford further directed that any worker discovered with liquor in his home be dismissed by the company. Politics had interfered with enforcement of the dry laws, Ford complained, but he reassured everyone who listened to him that "so far as our organization is concerned, it is going to be enforced to the letter."

After several years of unhappy effort to enforce prohibition, Ford concluded that there was a villainous conspiracy behind the law-breaking. It was neither human nature nor drink itself, but rather the big-money interests of New York that were frustrating prohibition. He charged that the moneyed interests were concentrating their illegal retail outlets near his factory in Dearborn because they knew he was a leading prohibitionist and they sought to discredit him. Ford reported that the assiduous efforts of the liquor interests had, nevertheless, failed to convert Dearborn from dry to wet. But when newspaper reporters visited the city to observe an area where prohibition was supposed to be working perfectly, they found only "the usual wide open speakeasy-ridden factory town." Coffee houses in Dearborn usually had large back rooms, not accessible or visible from the street, where liquor could be obtained. Boarding-house operators made money on the side by distilling booze and selling it at a special rate to their boarders. Among the workers of Dearborn, contrary to the pronouncements of Ford, a reporter for the New York *World* observed, "No more attention is paid to prohib-ition than if it had never been heard of."

In April 1930, in an effort to enforce prohibition in Dearborn, Harry Bennett, chief of the Ford Service Department, concluded an agreement with Carl Brooks, chief of police of Dearborn, whereby the Ford Service Department would aid the police in "keeping" the city dry. Brooks raided suspected blind pigs and gave the names of Ford workers apprehended in them to Bennett, who then arranged for the men to be dismissed. Bennett declared that exceptions to the rule would be made only when the family of an offender was desti-tute.

In mid-June Bennett and Brooks announced that the Ford Motor Company and the Dearborn Police Department had transformed Dearborn from a moderately wet factory town to "perhaps the driest industrial community of its size in the country." Bennett proclaimed that numerous small speakeasies and beer kitchens that formerly operated among the boardinghouses rented to Ford employees had disappeared entirely, and Brooks noted that no blind pig could be found anywhere in the city. "If there is any liquor in the city at all," Brooks said, "it is in private homes behind closed doors and is not being sold or used openly. We are looking as hard for evidence, but are unable to find any to speak of." Near the end of June 1930, Ford announced that the idea that prohibition could not be enforced was "utterly ridiculous." The liquor traffic could be stopped whenever the police wanted to stop it, he pointed out, just as it had been stopped in Dearborn.

But beyond the city limits of Dearborn the enforcement problem persisted. It did so not because a relatively small conspiracy had determined to discredit the law, as Ford believed, but because tens

of thousands of otherwise law-abiding citizens were casually breaking the liquor laws without much motivation beyond the desire to
secure alcoholic beverages for themselves. Detroit may have received the most national attention as a wet spot in the state, but
newspaper and police reports from throughout Michigan indicate
that no area or county escaped the problem of liquor law violators.
Even in the countryside, in areas where it had been demonstrated
that local-option prohibition had worked well, there were commercial and casual liquor-law violations on a grand scale. In the Upper
Peninsula, for example, the village of Keldon had presented a general appearance of poverty and shiftlessness in the years before
1918, with most of the local buildings in disrepair and lacking even
paint. But soon after prohibition passed, sleepy Keldon woke up and
became a boom town. Owners of buildings repaired and painted
them, and farmers appeared in town with new automobiles and sent
their children to good schools in Sault Ste. Marie. Uncritical prohibitionists might have pointed to Keldon in order to demonstrate
the dramatic benefits of prohibition. But the state police were suspicious of the town's prosperity. Within a short time they discovered the source of Keldon's wealth: the woods around the village
had become a veritable forest of illegal stills which were the chief
source of liquor for the thirsty populace of Sault Ste. Marie. In 1924
one of the largest stocks of contraband liquor ever taken from
private premises in Michigan was confiscated from a farm home
near Indian Town in Saginaw County. In Adrian a twenty-year-old
girl was arrested for transporting liquor in her car. An investigation
revealed that she had earned $30,000 a year driving liquor from
Monroe to Fort Wayne, Indiana. In Alma, Michigan, Mrs. Ellen
Crow informed her neighbors that she could tell them a thing or two
about liquor violations in the village; a few days later she was found
strangled to death in a field near her home. A local bootlegger was
convicted of her murder. In Mount Clemens, Reverend Thomas
Sykes, a preacher and prohibition crusader, was poisoned, allegedly
because of his determination to dry up the village. In Owosso
bootleggers sold poisoned liquor to high-school students. James
Oliver Curwood, a novelist residing in the town, gave public notice
that he would hunt down and kill any bootlegger who tried to furnish
liquor to his twelve-year-old son. Washtenaw County, according to
the bootleggers grapevine, was a "safe" county for the booze busi-

ness whether one sold it or simply transported it across its plush farmlands. When Ernest Hemingway married Hadley Richardson in Horton Bay in 1920, representatives from the Italian consulate in Detroit brought a supply of wine to the wedding and everybody present got roaring drunk. Hemingway and his bride honeymooned at a cottage in Bayview, where in sylvan surroundings they produced their own wine. In July 1922, Flint police swooped down on the Fairview district of that city's north end in a clean-up drive. Over three hundred still operators, blind-pig owners, and drinkers were arrested in this first series of raids. Yet despite periodic enforcement drives the liquor traffic in Flint prospered. On March 29, 1926, four hundred angry citizens stormed the city council chambers to protest against laxness in liquor-law enforcement. Investigators in Lapeer arrested Elmer Holman, secretary of the Lapeer chapter of the Anti-Saloon League, for possessing and selling liquor. According to testimony from undercover agents, Holman sold three kinds of whisky, two kinds of beer, and four kinds of wine, as well as a bucolic concoction that was called "carrot champagne." Holman protested that the use of undercover agents was "unfair."

The above incidents are simply samples from the thousands of cases of prohibition violations reported each year in Michigan in the 1920s. They indicate that in Michigan's small towns and rural areas significant amounts of liquor were produced despite prohibition laws.

The most publicized failure of prohibition in a Michigan city outside of Detroit occurred in Hamtramck. The state's seventh-largest city, Hamtramck lies entirely within the borders of Detroit, north and east of downtown Detroit. Only eight thousand of the city's eighty thousand inhabitants were voters in the 1920s; the remainder, although of age, were aliens. By far the largest group of aliens in the city were the Poles, who comprised over 50 percent of the city's population, and who in 1922 helped elect the first Polish mayor, Peter C. Jezewski, a local druggist. As candidate for mayor in 1922 Jezewski was able to win the support of some of the city's formerly irreconcilable ethnic groups and succeeded in defeating the incumbent mayor. According to the Detroit *Saturday Night*, the Poles of Hamtramck "wanted a chance to prove they were law abiding and to accept the responsibility for their success or failure in this line," but the campaign was so violent and so many rallies ended in brawls that the state police were called in on election day to guard the polls.

In power, Jezewski maintained a wide-open town, regulating rather than prohibiting vice. A split developed between the mayor and the city council over this policy, and in December 1923 the council appealed to Governor Groesbeck to send in the state police to enforce the law of Hamtramck. After a short investigation, Groesbeck complied and sent in the state police. Even the worst stories leaked to the press had told only a part of the truth of what had been happening in the city. State police officers found nearly four hundred "soft drink" parlors in Hamtramck that served as fronts for saloons, and they discovered that liquor was sold in candy stores, restaurants, pool rooms, brothels, private homes, and from automobiles that cruised the main street. One factory in Hamtramck installed frosted-glass windows so that stenographers would not be distracted by the goings and comings in a busy brothel just across the street. The mayor, state police learned, was financially interested in the local brothel circuit, and he had urged the justice of the peace to lighten fines on women convicted of soliciting. Paul Kleba, a member of the city council, testified that women walked the streets of Hamtramck and that automobiles were sometimes parked for blocks around popular night spots.

During a four-month occupation of Hamtramck, the state police carried out nearly two hundred raids, seizing about seventy-five stills, closing two breweries, and destroying nearly twenty thousand gallons of moonshine liquor. Disorderly houses were put in order. The state police also made raids into neighboring Macomb County, closing gambling resports, roadhouses, and blind pigs.

In their efforts to clean up Hamtramck the state police received no cooperation from the local police department. No sooner had the state police brought in those arrested in raids than they were released by local authorities. The chief of police of Hamtramck was arrested for drunkenness by the state police but was released without bond. In order to get to the bottom of the scandal, Governor Groesbeck called the mayor of Hamtramck before him for a hearing. For nearly six hours Groesbeck listened to testimony concerning conditions in Hamtramck. Following the hearing Groesbeck warned Jezewski that he would have to fire his chief of police and that the laws would have to be enforced in Hamtramck or the state police would return to enforce them. Groesbeck refused to remove Jezewski from office, however, after he learned that a federal grand jury was about to launch an investigation into the conditions in the city, and he was assured that the investigation would yield more conclusive results than his own hearing provided. Shortly thereafter, Jezewski and thirty-one other defendants were indicted by a federal grand jury for conspiracy to violate the prohibition law. Found guilty, Jezewski was sentenced to two years in Leavenworth prison.

The removal of Jezewski and his fellow conspirators did not end the problems of corruption growing out of the liquor traffic in Hamtramck. In the spring of 1928 another Polish-America, Dr. Rudolph Tenerowicz, took office as mayor amid praise from the state's liberal press. The Detroit *Saturday Night* concluded after four months of the new administration that Hamtramck had at last been made an unwelcome refuge for crooks and grafters. Tenerowicz, according to the *Saturday Night,* had cleaned up the city without the full cooperation of the city council, but with the aid of a local newspaper publisher whom the mayor had named police commissioner.

But soon after his reelection, Tenerowicz was indicted by a state grand jury for conspiracy to violate the prohibition and vice laws of the state. Rather than cleaning up the vice dens of the city, Tenerowicz had taken control of them and subjected them to regulation under his personal protection. The much-lauded reform mayor, it seems, had transformed Hamtramck from a city of uncontrolled to controlled vice. For success in that endeavor, Tenerowicz was sentenced to federal prison.

II

During prohibition just about any citizen might easily discover who manufactured, sold, and consumed liquor at any township or municipality in the state. Only law enforcement officers seemed to experience any difficulty in carrying out such research. And even if some wary dry-law enforcer might stumble across information on prohibition law-breaking, he could do little about it until he gathered good hard evidence. Then he would need to secure a search warrant, and that depended upon the sympathy of local judges. Indictments and convictions by local juries were additional concerns of those hired to uphold the law, and the well-publicized widespread violation of prohibition seemed to indicate clear public hostility toward prohibition enforcement. Yet if disenchantment with prohibition is measured by the rate of arrests and convictions for violations of the dry laws, there is, ironically, little evidence for such sentiment in Michigan outside Wayne County. Although the conviction rate was consistently below that for other serious crimes, once he entered the courtroom, a person charged with violation of state or federal liquor laws could never be assured of either leniency or sympathy. In the eleven and one-half years after June 1918, practically the entire time that prohibition was the law in Michigan, 54,007 persons were prosecuted in the state for violation of the liquor laws, and 36,327 of those persons, or 67 percent, were convicted. Wayne County convicted 10,772 of 20,589 indicted, a conviction average of 52 percent. The rest of the state did better, convicting 25,555 of 33,418 prosecuted, or 76 percent. The conviction rate in Wayne County fell off at the end of the decade, but this did not happen in other counties. In the last six months of 1929 Wayne County convicted only 23 percent of the defendants on trial for liquor-law violations, but the conviction rate in the remainder of the state in the same period was 73 percent. From the beginning of 1920 the conviction rate outside Wayne County was fairly consistent—always between 70 and 80 percent—except for the half year ending June 30, 1926, when it rose to 85 percent. Wayne County's conviction rate, on the other hand, fluctuated greatly. For the first six months of 1920, 80 percent of those indicted in liquor cases in Wayne County were convicted, but after that time the conviction rate fell dramatically.

The volume of prohibition cases was great enough to put a serious strain on the state and federal prison and jail facilities. By 1930, for example, one-third of the twelve thousand long-term federal prisoners were serving sentences for prohibition violation. Such statistics made the ardent prohibitionist appear to be not his brother's keeper, but his brother's jailer.

The type of arrests, moreover, was bothersome to many citizens. As in the case of other laws, justice was not blind to prohibition prosecution, but only nearsighted. The big-time law violators, those able to accumulate money and power, too often escaped the clutches of the law, while the small-time violator was frequently arrested and successfully prosecuted. A federal grand jury in Detroit took note of the fact in 1930 and issued a statement protesting that 75 percent of the cases before the grand jury involved only "small-fry crooks." "We feel that the prohibition department is catching only the minnows and letting the big fish get away," the report read. "The matter that impressed us was that the big bootleggers who hang around the court know all the officers and keep them in check." No member of the grand jury volunteered to explain exactly how the identity of the "big bootleggers" was known.

Many of the "minnows" were, nevertheless, able to display a remarkable sense of humor in the face of both their arrest and jailing. Prohibition violators sentenced in federal court in the Upper Peninsula were transported to the Detroit House of Correction to serve their sentences. The arrival every few months of such prisoners in Detroit aboard the "Moonshine Special" train was a troublesome reminder that many individuals refused to obey the law and refused to be penitent for their disobedience. The arrival of the May 1922 Moonshine Special was a case in point. The train pulled into the Woodward Avenue Michigan Central Station at 9:00 A.M. The *News* reported that fifty-two prisoners aboard the train, despite the fact that they faced jail sentences of three to six months, "acted like school boys out on a lark." With laughs and cheers, the prisoners, watched closely by twenty U.S. marshals, tumbled from the last cars on the train. Most of the men smoked cigars and carried large parcels of lunch. One bore a giant cribbage board. They were loaded into buses for transport to the jail, and as the buses pulled away from the depot someone began singing a hearty "Hail, Hail, the Gang's All Here." Most of the prisoners took up the refrain, later swinging into "Merrily We Roll Along." According to delighted reporters, "windows were flung open as the procession passed and children came running for blocks."

III

Even after the passage of state and national prohibition legislation, the debate over the merits of the dry measures continued. It is unlikely that any other issue in American history was discussed by so many people so intensely over so long a period as was prohibition. The 100-year war of words seemed to intensify in the 1920s, leading the editor of *Survey* magazine to observe that "emotions are gun powder and words are bullets" when discussions of prohibition took place. Despite the passion of the debate, *Survey* asked its readers to remain objective and to support enforcement of the prohibition experiment so that it might be given a fair trial. It would take at least one full generation for the experiment to be given a fair test, *Survey* cautioned. In the intervening "twenty-five or fifty years," social workers should collect data so that when "a judicial frame of mind has been restored to the people, real evidence may be weighed and a permanent decision may be reached; a decision which, being the judgement on the efficiency of a method, will bring the greatest good to the greatest number of human beings."

Both sides in the wet-and-dry debate in the 1920s seemed more concerned with quantity rather than quality of the figures they could marshal to their support, as if, indeed, each statistic were a military unit equal in strength to each opposing statistic. Eventually, some serious debaters on the subject agreed to use no statistics, since one set of numbers seemed just as good or bad as the next. Looking back over the prohibition controversy, historian Herbert Asbury concluded that the 1920s were the "Era of the Big Lie." "The drys lied to make prohibition look good," he wrote. "The wets lied to make it look bad; the government officials lied to make themselves look good and to frighten Congress into giving them more money to spend; and the politicians lied through force of habit." To historian Andrew Sinclair, the dry years were the period of "the half truth, the half truth, and nothing but the half truth."

The drys maintained a clear advantage in the wet-and-dry debate until about 1923. In the honeymoon atmosphere of those early prohibition years, the public and the press seemed willing to give bone-dry prohibition the benefit of the doubt. The dry barrage of statistics associating prohibition with "the great god of boom times, business," either convinced or intimidated potential critics of the dry establishment. By connecting prohibition with prosperity, the drys were successful in forcing their critics to argue with a "condition" rather than an idea. Prosperity was the proof of prohibition, the drys insisted. And in the 1920s building and loan assets tripled,

the number of students in school doubled, real wages of workingmen increased, the automobile business boomed, and the country actually seemed every day in every way to getting better and
better. All of this, the drys had no doubt, was directly due to
prohibition. Prohibition Commissioner Roy Haynes concurred in the
opinion that most of the beneficial social and economic developments of the early 1920s were brought about by the dry laws.
Prohibition was not the "exclusive" factor in producing the beneficial results, he wrote, but it was "the most dominating and determining force."

Beginning in 1923, however, insistent dissenting voices regularly
interrupted the dry propagandists. The incipient critics of prohibition included many newspaper and magazine editors, politicians,
businessmen, and other pillars of middle-class respectability. The
increasing proliferation of illegal drinking establishments, the easy
access to illegal liquor, more liquor-associated crime, and the refusal of leading dry spokesmen to face up to prohibition's unexpected results all troubled the new critics. Many of the new critics
carried credentials claiming membership in the 1916–1919 dry coalition which had provided a double endorsement for state prohibition
in Michigan. They usually attacked the National Prohibition Act
rather than the Eighteenth Amendment or the state prohibition
laws, emphasizing the need for a redefinition of the term "intoxicating liquor" rather than an outright repeal of prohibition itself.

In Detroit, a first indication of the dramatic shift in public
opinion came in a report issued by an ad hoc Committee of Eleven,
representing civic and religious organizations concerned with disintegrating social conditions in the city. The committee sent communications to the general public and to clergymen in Detroit dis-
cussing the results of prohibition. Basically the committee disagreed
with the use of statistics by the drys. Arrests for violation of the
prohibition laws had decreased, the committee insisted, not because there were fewer violations of the law, but because nobody
was very interested in prosecuting drinkers any more. The exercises
of the Anti-Saloon League, the WCTU, and the Methodist Board of
Temperance and Morals in attempting to measure the amount of
drunkenness by the number of drunks arrested was meaningless,
the committee claimed. All that could be measured by such figures
was the policy of the local police department.

Following the publication of results from a survey of Detroit by the Methodist Episcopal Church attributing increased bank deposits and other economic and social advances to prohibition, a group of city businessmen joined former police commissioner Frank Croul in denouncing the study. Croul and his associates picked the report apart point by point. To the contention that crime had decreased by 60 percent in Detroit due to prohibition, Croul showed that crimes of violence such as murder, serious assaults, and other felonies directly attributable to liquor had increased. Chester Culver, secretary of the Detroit Employers' Association, claimed that while prohibition might have caused more regular habits among workingmen, bootleg liquor was having the same bad effects that legalized liquor had had previously. The president of the Central Savings Bank indicated that he could not attribute a great amount of the increase in savings accounts to prohibition. Benjamin Vernor, vice-president of the Merchants National bank, concluded from a study of the weekly changes in bank clearances and deposits for a year that there was absolutely no way of proving that increases were traceable to prohibition. While prohibition was responsible for a little increase in savings, a comparison of savings deposits and the figures of the Employers' Association in regard to employment and unemployment in the country led to the conclusion that the increase in employment was more directly responsible for the increase in savings, Vernor observed. Whether prohibition was the cause of the increase in employment was another question, he contended, but he believed that the direct and immediate cause of the increase in savings and commerical deposits between 1917 and 1922 was the increase in employment. He also asserted that business was booming primarily because the dollar had decreased in value, and he denied that labor was more efficient because of prohibition. "Employers are complaining to me every day that liquor is being sold to workers outside the factory gates and sometimes in the factory," Vernor explained. "And it is well known that large numbers of workers are leaving the factories to become bootleggers." That the Methodist Episcopal study group could find no hospitals in the city devoted to the treatment of alcoholics was not surprising, according to Croul. "I don't suppose a hospital treating alcoholics today would advertise the fact," he noted. "These people ought to visit Receiving Hospital Saturday nights, when they have all the tables and floors littered with unconscious drunks suffering from acute alcoholism."

The most noteworthy single defection from the cold-water army in 1923 was Michigan's United States Senator James Couzens. In November 1922, Republican Truman Newberry resigned from his Senate seat, and Republican Governor Alex Groesbeck appointed Couzens, Detroit's dry Republican mayor, to serve out the remainder of Newberry's term. Couzens had voted against statewide prohibition in 1916, but soon after his election as mayor of Detroit in 1918 he announced his conversion from wet to dry and declared that he would vote for prohibition in the spring of 1919. Sometime between his 1918 statement and the summer of 1923, however, like tens of thousands of other Americans, Couzens changed his mind about prohibition. In June 1923, during a vacation trip to Canada, the senator was asked by a newspaper reporter to comment on the liberal Quebec liquor laws. He praised the statutes and intimated that the United States would be wise to adopt similar measures. "If our Constitution were easier to amend," Couzens said, "I believe the Volstead Act would be repealed" (a strange confusion, since the Volstead Act was not part of the Constitution). The senator's views were wired to newspapers in the United States on the same day that President Harding defended prohibition in a speech in Denver. Consequently, Couzens was roundly denounced by prohibitionists throughout the country.

James Couzens was not a man to sit back and take criticism calmly. He clarified his beliefs on the liquor question and struck back at his critics. In early July he publicly urged the revision of the Volstead Act in order to allow the manufacture and sale of beer containing no more than 5 percent alcohol. Couzens announced that he believed such a revision would be in the best interests of all of the people, that beer of 2.5 to 5 percent alcohol was not intoxicating, and that it was a beverage most people wanted. Nobody would be injured by such revision, Couzens claimed, and it would go a long way toward eliminating bootlegging and the desire for beverages of higher alcoholic content. "I do not wish under any circumstances," Couzens cautioned, "to violate the law or to encourage violation of the law. . . . My record in Detroit has been strictly for law enforcement, and strictly for adherence to the Constitution. I may differ with some as to the interpretation of the Eighteenth Amendment, but I have a perfect right, both as a citizen, first, and as a senator, second, to have my own viewpoint on the matter."

Couzens received hundreds of letters both praising and condemning his stand. Lieutenant Fred Clark of the Detroit Police Department informed Couzens that rumrunners, bootleggers, and operators of blind pigs in Monroe and Wayne Counties were unanimously arrayed against him because of his stand for moderation—a program that might deprive them of most of their business. R. N. Holsaple of the Anti-Saloon League, on the other hand, accused Couzens of being a victim of a "brainstorm" and charged that he had turned a "mental handspring" since his appointment to the Senate. In 1924, despite enthusiastic efforts by the Anti-Saloon League to remove Couzens from the Senate, he defeated his bone-dry opponent in the GOP primary and in the general election carried every county in the state. His success haunted the state's drys throughout the remainder of the prohibition years.

Gradual erosion from the prohibition coalition in Michigan continued until 1926, when the drys received another shocking setback. Prior to 1926 the social workers of the country had quite enthusiastically supported prohibition. In the wet-and-dry statistical war some of the most encouraging prohibition data presented had been carefully gathered by social workers. The study of Grand Rapids by *Survey* in 1920 was one long hymn of praise for prohibition and was typical of the numerous studies undertaken by social workers. Thus ardent drys were both shocked and outraged by the conclusions concerning the effects of prohibition drawn by a conference of social workers in Detroit in 1926. Two facts emerged clearly from the information presented at the conference: first, from 1918 when the state went dry, through 1920, there had been a sharp decline in the incidence of alcoholism, insanity, dependency, and delinquency; but, second, after 1920 there had been a steady increase in all categories. The significance of the statistics from the 1918–1920 period was not, however, considered as conclusive as the statistics from the later period because of the absence of nearly 100,000 young men under arms during the war and because of the great prosperity and ardor of the people during the national crisis in the earlier period. The statistics presented at the conference, *Survey* observed, were quite disappointing. They were accurate yet they were either inconclusive or were qualified in so many instances that they could be interpreted in any of several ways.

A leading physician from the Pontiac State Hospital for the Insane, for instance, presented statistics to the conference indicating that a decline in admissions to the hospital after 1917 was attributable to causes other than prohibition. He contended that the increase in admissions of alcoholics to the hospital after July 1, 1920, indicated that prohibition legislation was not sufficient to curtail alcoholism in his district. A statistician for the Detroit Board of Health, on the other hand, noted a decrease in the death rate in the city and concluded that while this decrease might be attributed in part to the coming of prohibition, extreme caution should be exercised in drawing such a conclusion because factors other than prohibition were involved. Edward Pokorny, "friend of the court" who acted in the capacity of domestic relations adjuster for the Wayne County Circuit Court, presented a study of the part played by alcohol in 250 cases of divorce for 1915 as compared with the same number of cases for 1925 and concluded that in neither year could one detect the influence of liquor upon divorce. Pokorny's conclusion was that one could make no valid deductions at all from the available statistics.

Superintendent William P. Rutledge of the Detroit Police Department presented statistics to the conference that were "startling if not unexpected." According to Rutledge, 23,385 quarts of liquor had been confiscated by his department in 1918. The quantity was less in 1919, but then it steadily increased until it reached a total of 3,138,242 quarts seized in 1925. In 1918, 1,275 persons had been arrested for liquor law violations in Detroit; in 1925, 27,183 such arrests were made. Chalkey S. Slack, manager of the Cooperative Department of the Studebaker Corporation, reported the results of an inquiry among employment managers of the largest factories in the Detroit area. Six factories reported a greater labor turnover since prohibition had gone into effect, nine reported less turnover, and ten were in doubt. Eleven firms reported greater regularity of attendance at work, thirteen worse attendance, and one was in doubt. Seven factories reported more tardiness since prohibition, eleven reported less, and twelve were in doubt. Seven factories reported better health among their workers since prohibition, eleven reported worse health, and six were in doubt. Eleven factory managers thought the worker a better producer since prohibition, twelve thought that he was not, and two were in doubt. Six factory managers reported fewer appeals for charity from workers since prohibition, three reported more appeals, and thirteen were in doubt. Seven thought that there were more homeowners as a result of prohibition, ten thought that there were fewer, and five were in doubt. Slack's conclusion was that prohibition was too new an experiment to make possible any valid conclusions regarding its benefits to industrial workers. He observed that a general impression prevailed among employers that prohibition had been useful to the workingman but that the evidence to support such an impression was unavailable.

Dr. Clarence Cook Little, president of the University of Michigan, announced to the conference that the delegates should seek to maintain open minds on the question of the effects of prohibition, and he noted that he himself was confused by the information presented. He pleaded for more research aimed at uncovering additional facts about prohibition's results. Bishop Thomas Nicholson, who summed up the evidence of the convention for the dry side, accused Little of raising "jelly-fish scholars with no morals or settled convictions" and described him as "a man trying to balance water on both shoulders." Judge Vincent Brennan, who made a summation for the wets, also disregarded the evidence presented to the conference and instead made a partisan attack upon the defenders of prohibition and a spirited defense of Dr. Little's reservations.

In 1926 the National Federation of Settlements launched an investigation of the impact of prohibition in order to more clearly inform Americans concerning the muddled wet-and-dry allegations. Lilian Wald became chairwoman of the study and Martha Bensley Bruere, a frequent contributor to *Survey*, was appointed director. After organizing a staff including wets, drys, and doubters, Miss Bruere set out on a field trip across the country to examine social conditions under prohibition. In her final report, *Does Prohibition Work?* (1927), Bruere wrote that "all through the American Belt . . . wherever Americans from earlier immigration are still in control, our reports show prohibition works." But wherever significant settlements of the foreign-born were located, she reported, prohibition was least observed. In Detroit Bruere found very little cause for optimism. One social worker there replied to a survey questionnaire that intoxicating liquors could be obtained by anyone in the city who wanted them and that drunkenness in Detroit was common. The same social worker concluded, nonetheless, that Detroit was no worse off than it had been before prohibition. The former head of Detroit's Franklin Street Settlement reported that the neighborhoods of foreigners had improved after 1918 because of steady employment, higher wages, and the abolition of the saloons, but another worker at the Franklin Street Settlement wrote that middle- and upper-class drinkers patronized the bootleggers and home brewers in ethnic neighborhoods and drove up profits and thus were responsible for encouraging the foreign-born to break the law. A general belief among residents in the ethnic neighborhoods in Detroit, the Bruere study found, was that prohibition was both an unwise and an unworkable method for controlling drinking.

The records of the Child Caring Department of the Society of St. Vincent DePaul in Detroit indicated that desertions had increased in the years since the adoption of prohibition and that there had been a great increase in the numbers of mothers who deserted husbands and children. The percentage of cases of drunkenness among women also increased, the spokesman for the society noted. In both relative and absolute terms the number of children removed from their parents had increased after prohibition. Workers in the Bureau of Domestic Relations reported to Bruere that 98 percent of their cases involved drunkenness on the part of either the mother or the father. Bruere's researchers found that the number of adult residents of Eloise, Detroit's poorhouse, had increased from 1,607 in 1914 to 4,137 in 1925. According to Eloise workers, in 1914 the cases admitted for habitual drunkenness were about 25 percent of the total, but in 1925 this percentage had nearly tripled. Records of Eloise also indicated that before 1918 men under the age of fifty-five were seldom committed to the institution, but after that date there were frequent admissions of men between the ages of twenty-five and fifty.

Despite all of the above information, social workers contacted for the Bruere study in Detroit agreed that prohibition was desirable. A condition of complete prohibition would be difficult to attain, they admitted, but it was nevertheless attainable. Education was the most important element in achieving real prohibition, the social workers insisted, and since they believed that booze would die with all the old drinkers, they reaffirmed their faith that education was preparing a new generation to grow up in a better nation without either alcoholic beverages or saloons.

While the Bruere study reserved most of its praise for what could happen under prohibition, the Methodist Board of Temperance, Prohibition, and Public Morals continued to praise what was happening under prohibition. In 1927 spokesmen for the board announced that crime had decreased dramatically in Detroit thanks to prohibition. But H. N. Nimmo, editor of the Detroit *Saturday Night*, disagreed. True, crime had recently declined in the city, he conceded, but it was also true that Detroit was only under prohibition of a sort. The dry period, moreover, was also marked by the bobbing of women's hair, a progressive shortening of skirts, the spread of radio broadcasting, a wider popularity for motion pictures, and a greatly increased use of cigarettes. The decrease in crime might be attributed equally to any or all of these factors, Nimmo contended, or it might have nothing to do with them. As to the decrease in arrests for drunkenness in Detroit, he said, this too could be meaningless. Individuals were arrested for drunkenness only when they became obnoxious on the streets to an extent exceeding the tolerance of the police, who were notorious for never arresting common drunks. A man drunk in a taxi could easily escape arrest. "Perhaps Detroit's police are more tolerant," Nimmo suggested. "Perhaps our citizens can afford more taxis." The chief criticism of prohibition was that it had driven drinking into the home, Nimmo pointed out. Everyone knew that this was true, but nobody, not even law enforcement officials, could break into the home of a suspected boozer, nor could enforcement officers even search the premises for whisky. "Probably there is less crime," Nimmo concluded. "There is also less clothing on women, less travel by horse and buggy, and less water in the Great Lakes. No doubt all this is due to prohibition."

Throughout the late 1920s critics of the dry law, like Nimmo, continued to point out prohibition's shortcomings. All that prohibition had accomplished, they claimed, was to deprive the public treasury of tax revenues from the liquor traffic and to make drinking more attractive, particularly to youth, by giving it the tinge of romance since it had become an illegal activity. Frederic Meyer, the

state superintendent of Lutheran schools in Michigan, complained
that before prohibition German children had consumed beer only at
family dinners and celebrations but that after prohibition many of
them began to drink whisky "because it's prohibited." "Now men,
women and children indulge in that hellish stuff," Meyer lamented.

Yet despite vociferous insistence by the critics of prohibition
that anyone who opened his eyes could see quite clearly that there
was a good deal more drinking in America under prohibition than
there had been before, careful analysis does not support their contention. In fact, under prohibition there was a substantial decrease
in the per capita quantity of alcohol consumed in the United States.
Concerning this matter, historian John C. Burnham concluded in
1968 that prohibition had successfully cut liquor consumption and
produced favorable social results until about 1923. Burnham pointed
to the dramatic decrease in the number of patients with alcoholic
psychoses admitted to mental hospitals in the early twenties, a
decrease, he contended, that indicated a drop in alcohol consumption generally. (James V. May, an eminent American psychiatrist,
wrote in 1922 that "with the advent of prohibition the alcoholic
psychoses as far as this country is concerned have become of little
more than historical interest.") Of the journalists who insisted that
under prohibition "everyone drank, including many who never did
before," Burnham concluded that those writers reported honestly
what they observed; they seldom if ever observed the working
classes, however, and knew very little about pre-prohibition drinking habits of the masses. The "everyone" who was reported to be
drinking more heavily, Burnham concluded, did not include
working-class families, and he pointed to a careful study by Clark
Warburton in 1932 which indicated that "the working class is consuming not more than half as much alcohol per capita as formerly,
and the expenditure of this class upon alcoholic beverages is probably one billion dollars less than it would be without prohibition."
Burnham concluded that "even in its last years the law, with all its
leaks, was still effective in cutting down drinking among workers,
which was one of the primary aims of prohibition." The panacea of
the Anti-Saloon League had also succeeded, Burnham observed, in
destroying the old-fashioned saloon, which had long been the main
target of its campaign. The new-fashioned saloon, however, the blind
pig, was something else again.

In another recent study, sociologist Joseph Gusfield, utilizing Warburton's data, found credible the contention that drinking decreased under prohibition. Gusfield noted that prohibition succeeded in curtailing the heavy drinking that had characterized early twentieth century America. Available statistics, Gusfield contended, support the conclusion that per capita alcohol consumption in America during the 1920s was 30 to 50 percent less than in the pre-prohibition 1911–1915 period. The law worked best among workers and in rural areas, he concluded. It worked least well among the upper classes.

Such evidence, then, indicates that the prohibitionists were not totally incorrect in their insistence that prohibition did prohibit. But all too often the drys and their critics were, as Sinclair noted, guilty of telling a half-truth. Everyone did not drink under prohibition; and everyone did not stop drinking under prohibition. A decrease in drinking by 30 to 50 percent, after all, still left 50 to 70 percent of the previous consumption level. The association made by the drys between soaring prosperity and the eradication of drinking was based more on faith than fact. The association made by the wets between a soaring crime rate and increased drinking was likewise based more on faith than on fact. In the 1920s there was, until late 1929, prosperity; there was also less drinking. The actual connection between the two was never convincingly explained. It is doubtful that it ever can be convincingly explained. Prohibition's true believers found almost any statistics favorable to their position convincing. The proof of prohibition, they proclaimed, was in the pudding. Had they examined the pudding carefully, however, they would have discovered that it still contained a disturbingly high alcoholic content.

IV

Prohibition's critics often pointed to the alleged behavior of college-age youth in the 1920s to illustrate the failure and dangers of bone-dry laws. The fiction of postgraduates like F. Scott Fitzgerald, along with sensational newspaper and magazine reporting, lent credibility to the allegations. Yet surveys taken during the prohibition years lead to other conclusions: Both on campuses in Michigan and the rest of the nation prohibition worked better and decreased drinking to an even greater extent than it did in the non-campus communities. Prohibition, ironically, may have obtained some of its greatest success in the very locations from which it got its worst press—on the college and university campuses.

The publication of a *Literary Digest* poll in 1926 surprised and reassured many Americans who worried about reports of college drinking. According to the testimony of more than two hundred college and university heads, the *Literary Digest* reported, "prohibition is winning the colleges." The replies to questionnaires concerning the effect of prohibition on the campus were nearly unanimous in indicating that drinking in colleges and drinking by the younger generation as a whole had decreased in the 1920s, and it was agreed that the student body of the dry decade was of a much higher moral and intellectual caliber than any generation had been in the days of legal liquor. The academic presidents concluded that there were even fewer drinkers on campus in 1926, when there were three times as many students, than there had been in the years just prior to prohibition.

An interesting conclusion of the *Literary Digest* poll was that student drinking as it existed in 1926 was largely an imitation of elders, especially of the returning graduates who "seek to restore their youth and pristine enthusiasm by recourse to highballs and beer kegs," and also reflected a student desire to do something forbidden by the law. The novelty of illicit conduct, however, appeared to be wearing off by 1926, the college and university presidents agreed. "Hip flasks, if they are as numerous on campus as they are said to have been," the *Literary Digest* concluded, "are tabu in most institutions; uproarious cocktail parties are not generally a favorite form of celebration. For this condition of affairs much credit is given to the fraternities, some of which impose a penalty on bibulous brethren and warn returning brothers that high revelry is no longer the fashion." The study noted that "one drunk does not make a village or campus spree any more than one swallow makes a summer."

At the University of Michigan, according to President Little, there was less habitual and "vicious" intoxication than there had been under pre-prohibition conditions. What drinking did take place by members of the student body, Little observed, was largely motivated by a spirit of "daredeviltry" from which no student body in any generation had been entirely free. Officials from other colleges in Michigan were even more enthusiastic than Little about the change in the campus atmosphere. President K. L. Butterfield of Michigan State College of Agriculture and Applied Sciences agreed that "the amount of drinking had declined greatly since prohibition became effective." From Alma College, President H. B. Crooks replied to the survey that "drinking among students has not been increasing in the prohibition era. I am able to say that I travel much over the state of Michigan," Crooks said, "and see very few evidences of liquor, except in Detroit, which is, everyone knows, perilously near the source of supply in Canada."

President W. O. Hotchkiss of the Michigan College of Mines reported that student drinking there had decreased also and that not a single discipline case for student drinking had come before the faculty in 1926. There were still some student drinkers, he remarked, "but it is chiefly confined to that small group possessed of the naughty boy's spirit who think it proves them to be 'men of the world' if they do something devilish." President Paul Voelker of Battle Creek College wrote that "the stories of students' use of the flask the country over is very greatly exaggerated. Our young people have better sense than some of their elders. . . ." Battle Creek College, he said, was united behind the Eighteenth Amendment and the Volstead Act. President John L. Seaton of Albion College arrived at the "mature judgment that college life is incalculably safer and better since prohibition became national law." In two years only two students had been found guilty of drinking at Albion, he noted, and drinking now was among the least worries of a college president. "The students of today are stronger in mind and body, cleaner in habits and more responsible to the call of service than other students of twenty-five years ago," Seaton thought. "They are so in spite of the great changes made by war, the world-wide unleashing of ugly passions for a period of ten years, and the varied reactions which are loosely described as 'the revolt of youth.' There is no real revolt, but there is a strong and orderly movement toward social justice, economic equity, international reason, and a warless world."

One week after polling the college presidents, the *Literary Di-*

gest published the results of a poll of 100 editors of college newspapers across the country. The student editors agreed with the presidents that there was much less drinking on campus than there had been prior to the passage of the Eighteenth Amendment. Students, however, were somewhat more critical of the Volstead Act, stating that they believed it was too drastic in its definition of intoxicating beverages. Modification, they indicated, would ultimately achieve "absolute abstention." Norman R. Thal, editor of the *Michigan Daily,* wrote that conditions at the University of Michigan were almost ideal from the prohibitionists' point of view. He concluded that since 1918 drinking had "undoubtedly decreased, though the drinking that does go on receives more publicity than that of former years, due to some college students' misunderstanding of the collegiate." Thal was critical of the Volstead Act, however, and concluded that it had produced "a distinctly harmful effect as presently enforced." He made it clear, though, that he was not indicting prohibition but only "paper enforcement," as he called it. Professor John B. Waite, of the law school, agreed with Thal and reported that "both drinking and drunkenness are today but a very small fraction of what they were prior to prohibition." President Little agreed with Thal's criticism of paper enforcement of the law; in May 1926 he reported to a special conference on prohibition that the problem of student drinking in Ann Arbor could not be solved as long as the law remained unenforced all around the university. When University of Michigan students were asked if the Eighteenth Amendment should be rigidly enforced, 84 percent of those questioned answered yes. When asked if the Eighteenth Amendment should be repealed, 82 percent answered no.

It would be extremely misleading to infer from the above testimony that there was no drinking problem among students at the University of Michigan in the 1920s. There was. What was unique about student drinking during prohibition was that the principal drinking establishments for students became the fraternity houses on campus instead of the downtown saloons. Almost every year during the 1920s, officials of the university were forced to discipline fraternities for allowing drinking at parties, and many visitors to fraternity functions found the drunkenness among both male and female students shocking and reprehensible.

In early 1927, however, the Michigan Alumnus reported that

fraternity drinking was not entirely the fault of the students. "It is up to the fraternity alumni before it is up to the present generation of men at Ann Arbor to rid the fraternity houses of drinking in accordance with the demands of President Little," the journal reported. "There are plenty of cases where fraternity alumni have come in for the big games with not only bottles but cases and proceed to stage a 'party' in their fraternity houses. In other cases the rules have been evaded by keeping the liquor in a car just outside the door." The *Alumnus* noted that there had been a time when the rules against having liquor in the fraternity houses were obeyed and enforced. It was the alumni now who were most responsible for violations of the liquor laws and for the embarrassment of the fraternities. The Detroit *Saturday Night* reported of fraternity alumni that "it is not uncommon for the old gentlemen to appropriate so much of the accomodation of the fraternity house during their visit to the University and to stay so long, that the fraternity students are delighted to see them go and dread to see them come." In 1926 the *Michigan Daily* branded as "incomprehensible stupidity" a suggestion by the president of the University Alumni Association that campus fraternities set aside one room in each house "so that returning alumni may indulge their cravings for liquor far from the madding crowd of thirsty undergraduates." The suggestion was made during a special conference to consider a solution to the problem of alumni drinking in fraternity houses. And although the suggestion was never acted upon by university authorities, it did serve to underline the fact that the problem of student drinking was very often a problem of alumni drinking.

Local law enforcement authorities were, nevertheless, kept busy by student prohibition law violators in Ann Arbor. In 1927 three university students were arrested at the Windsor ferry terminal for attempting to smuggle nearly two dozen bottles of champagne and whisky across the Detroit River. One of the students, Howard C. Kresge, was the son of Anti-Saloon League financial angel S. S. Kresge. In the fall of 1929, the Ann Arbor Police Department raided Fletcher Hall, a student dormitory, and confiscated a small amount of liquor and arrested three students for violation of prohibition. And in early 1931 the police broke up the "Ethyl Ring" of student bootleggers on campus, and then, acting on information secured from members of the ring, the police raided five fraternity houses, arresting eighty-four students, including the captain of the Wolverine football team, James O. Simrall, and confiscated small amounts of whisky, beer, and rum. The university reacted by padlocking all five fraternities and placing them on special probation for one year.

Following the release of the students arrested in the fraternity house raids of early 1931, a special committee of the dry Michigan House of Representatives investigated the policies of the Ann Arbor Police Department and the problem of student drinking. The committee reported that drinking by students on campus did not constitute a serious problem. Commenting upon the raids by the Ann Arbor Police Department, however, the committee wrote, "It is the opinion of the committee that the police officers who actually raided the fraternity houses were indiscreet and overzealous, or were quite willing to embarrass the students needlessly." The committee found that drinking among students at the university was actually decreasing. "Drinking is not a common practice among students," it reported. "Conditions are materially better than they were five years ago and there is less drinking on campus by students than there was before the adoption of prohibition. The committee finds that conditions at the University of Michigan are better than at most colleges and universities."

The committee cautioned that the fact that liquor was found in five fraternity houses on campus should not constitute an indictment of the entire membership of those fraternities. In each instance, it reported, only a few students possessed liquor, and no large amount of booze was found in any single room of the houses. The time at which the raids were conducted, moreover, according to the committee report, was "a period of general relaxation and celebration"—final examinations had been almost completed and the Junior Hop was in the offing. "The committee finds that general conditions at the University with reference to discipline are excellent," the report concluded.

In a 1930 poll of the University of Michigan student body, 33 percent of the nearly five thousand students interviewed indicated that they never drank, while 67 percent indicated that they did. Of those who did drink, 86 percent indicated that they never got drunk, while 14 percent said they did. A separate poll of campus coeds indicated that 587 of them never drank while 305 did occasionally.

Only 33 of the 902 coeds interviewed admitted that they "got under the influence" of liquor occasionally. A simultaneous poll of student opinion on the prohibition law found that 60 percent of the student body favored modification of the Volstead Act, 16 percent favored repeal of the Eighteenth Amendment, and 24 percent favored strict enforcement of the existing laws. The wet New York *Times* grouped the modificationist and repealist sentiment together and reported that the University of Michichan was three-to-one "wet." President Alexander G. Ruthven of the University of Michigan objected to the poll and said that he had never believed in straw votes and thought that they seldom represented real opinion on any controversial issue. The "anti's" always rushed out to vote, he contended, while only a small part of those satisfied with the measure responded. "I know from my own observations that conditions at the University of Michigan are better since prohibition than they were before," he announced.

A traditional appeal of the drys involved benefits that prohibition would bring to young Americans. The attractiveness of that appeal should not be underestimated. Scott Fitzgerald, an alumnus of Princeton University, insisted that youth of college age were among the first Americans to reject the dry laws. The evidence, however, suggests that the older generation, many of them like Fitzgerald addicted to drink, rejected prohibition first and then frantically "beat on, boats against the current," as they attempted to restore their youth and the romantically remembered pristine enthusiasm of the old saloon days.

V

While millions of Americans either gave up drinking or drank less under prohibition, millions of others, to be sure, continued their imbibing. Eventually, after personal stores of pre-prohibition liquor were exhausted, the continuing demand for drink could be provided for only by the illegal manufacture and sale of alcoholic beverages. And it appeared in the 1920s that so long as drinkers drank, manufacturers of liquor would manufacture, and enforcers of the prohibition laws would enforce. Yet while the manufacture, sale, and consumption of liquor was relatively simple, trying to prevent such activity was often absurdly difficult. And the difficulties stemmed not just from the law breakers, but from the laws themselves. The numerous legal confusions surrounding prohibition at times nearly paralyzed the law's enforcers. Among the troubling qualifications, exemptions, and assignments of the federal dry laws were those providing for the legal production of "non-intoxicating" cider and fruit juices for home consumption, the licensed production of industrial alcohol, and medicinal liquor, sacramental wine, and near-beer, the allowance for intoxicating liquor in a private home, the exemption of a liquor purchaser from prosecution for conspiracy, and the assignment of vaguely defined "concurrent" enforcement responsibilities to both federal and state governments. All of these along with preexisting constitutional constraints on search and seizure provided a monumental headache for law enforcement officials. The editor of the Detroit *Saturday Night* complained in 1921 of the "Chinese puzzle" that had resulted from differing and sometimes contradictory prohibition laws of state and federal governments. "Who is the prohibition boss, the state or the federal government?" the editor asked. "If both, where does the jurisdiction of one end and the other begin? Is home brew permissible for private consumption, or is it not? and who has the say, Washington or Lansing?" "The first requisite for respect for law is that the law shall be clear and specific," he insisted. "Today we have rulings from supreme courts and petty courts, from commissioners and collectors of internal revenue, from secretaries of the Treasury, from federal prohibition officers and state prohibition officers, all of them contradicting each other as often as the newspapers go to press."

Exactly how important a reasonably rapid resolution to the legal confusions and contradictory interpretations of prohibition might be became apparent a few weeks after the Eighteenth Amendment became operative. In February 1920 a series of incidents occured in the vicinity of Iron River in Michigan's upper peninsula that were described in the newspapers as the Iron River Rum Rebellion. In Iron River, differences of opinion concerning prohibition and police rights of search and seizure very nearly resulted in a shooting war.

The trouble in Iron River involved "Dago Red," a zinfandel wine produced by local Italian-Americans for personal domestic consumption. Section 29 of the Volstead Act specifically exempted the domestic manufacture of "non-intoxicating cider and fruit juices" from the prohibition-law restraints so long as it was neither sold nor delivered for consumption purposes. Because of Section 29, national and state prohibition had no effect at all upon Dago Red production and consumption in the Iron River Area.

In mid-February, however, state police officers raided three homes in the Iron River area and confiscated several barrels of Dago Red. The local state's attorney, Martin A. McDonough, ordered the wine returned and warned the state police that their raids had been illegal. A few days later, nevertheless, members of the state police force accompanied by prohibition agents from Chicago raided the same homes and seized the same Dago Red. This time McDonough intervened vigorously. Accompanied by several local law enforcement officials, he contronted the state and federal officials outside one of the raided homes. McDonough ordered the Dago Red returned, called the state police officer in charge of the raid a "tramp," and advised all local wine makers to arm themselves and to shoot any federal officer who might in the future attempt to enter their homes. Not only was a man's house his castle, McDonough proclaimed, but under Section 29 of the Volstead Act, it was also his wine cellar. McDonough again insisted that the major law enforcement problem in Iron River was not prohibition violation by local residents but illegal searches and seizures by non-local law enforcement officers.

McDonough's defiance of the federal agents was reported to Major A. V. Dalrymple, the supervising prohibition director for the Central Division, which included Michigan. Dalrymple, a man completely devoid of any sense of proportion when it came to prohibition enforcement, informed United States Attorney General A. Mitchell Palmer that Iron County, Michigan, was in "open revolt" against prohibition enforcement. To Palmer, this Dago Red Scare on the heels of the Big Red Scare was a serious matter indeed. He immediately authorized Dalrymple to raise an armed force and to invade Iron County. The Iron River rebels had to be taught a lesson. Palmer said he regarded the rebellion as a matter for the State Department or perhaps the War Department to handle, but he boldly accepted the task and delegated full authority for action to Dalrymple. Dalrymple then solemnly told newspaper reporters that he would take as many men as necessary from Chicago, and, reinforced by the Michigan State Police, "I shall put respect and fear of the law into Iron County, cost what it may." Despite the fact that the "rebellion" involved only the actions of a single state's attorney, Dalrymple insisted that "this is a showdown between the Federal Government and those who would defy the Constitution." "I am going to enforce prohibition," he warned, and "I do not want bloodshed, but if the state authorities stand in the way, and they are backed by their political cohorts, I am going to shoot."

Dalrymple and his invaders, armed to the teeth, caught the next train for Iron River. Dalrymple was unsuccessful, however, in securing search warrants for his venture. The U.S. district attorney, it seemed, would not issue such warrants without sound evidence of law-breaking. Dalrymple could produce no such evidence.

Panic swept through Iron County as the raiders advanced. Hundreds of frightened families, in an effort to satisfy the angry federal god from Chicago, rolled their barrels of Dago Red into the streets and emptied them. A wild rumor swept across the snow-covered slopes of the county insisting that McDonough was drilling miners and lumberjacks in order that prohibition could be fought "to the last ditch."

McDonough was not raising an army of opposition. Rather he was on the telephone speaking with federal prohibition officials in Washington demanding that the invasion be halted before somebody was hurt. But before orders from Washington could be relayed to Iron River, Dalrymple and his army rolled in. The prohibition enforcers made a few raids—without warrants—and destroyed a small amount of Dago Red. Prior to Dalrymple's doing any permanent damage, however, he was ordered back to Chicago by the federal prohibition commissioner. A subsequent federal investigation ruled that Dalrymple had acted both illegally and injudiciously. Dago Red, in the home, the investigation pointed out, was indeed legal. And Dalrymple's raids were indeed illegal. The failure of the raiders to secure the requisite warrants had been an irresponsible oversight. As a result of the investigation a large number of prohibition violation cases initiated by Dalrymple's agents in Chicago were thrown out of court because arrests and seizures had been made without due process—duly sworn and authorized warrants. To prevent further federal law violations, Attorney General Palmer announced that in future prohibition cases, arrests and seizures without warrants were to be considered unconstitutional.

The New York *Times* editorialized that the entire bizarre Iron River episode had been "ridiculously exaggerated." "There will probably be many 'revolts' in the country," the paper predicted. "They will arise from honest differences of opinion about interpretations of sections of the prohibiton law, State authorities more or less sensitive about their rights and powers refusing to submit to Federal agents until the matter in dispute can be adjudicated. On both sides is to be expected cases of officials and agents with more zeal than discretion who will provoke exhibitions of independence and get themselves into trouble." The *Times* concluded, "The National Prohibition Act is going to be enforced, and in the process there may be some tragedies but there will be more comedies and farces." One of the farces, unfortunately, involved the fate of Major Dalrymple. The Iron River fiasco by no means hurt his career. He continued to rise within the Prohibition Bureau until All Fools' Day, 1933, when U.S. Attorney General Homer Cummings appointed him to head the agency.

The Iron River episode pointed out dramatically one of the central dilemmas of prohibition enforcement—procedures for legal search and seizure. Both federal and state constitutions protected citizens against "unreasonable" search and seizure. Nevertheless, more than six hundred cases involving search and seizure procedures in prohibition cases were reported in the *American Law Digest* during the first six months of 1920 alone. Gradually the courts clarified the meaning of "unreasonable" search and seizure in cases of prohibition law violations, expanding police powers in some areas, restricting them in others. The Michigan Supreme Court, for example, ruled in 1921 that the hip pocket was immune from investigation under search-and-seizure provisions of the state prohibition law: The court ruled that officers who had searched the home of a Bay City man with a search warrant exceeded their authority when they examined his clothing. The next year the court took a significant step in aiding the enforcement of the dry laws by ruling that police officers had the right to search an automobile for contraband liquor without a search warrant. Yet three dissenting judges in the case warned that the majority decision rendered the Bill of Rights a "scrap of paper." The Detroit *News*, on the other hand, observed that the decision would go down in legal history as one of the most important ever handed down by the court, since it recognized for the first time that the automobile was a distinct factor in modern society. Because of the advantage given criminals by the automobile, the court contended that an automobile did not have the same immunity from search without a warrant that a man's home did. In another 1922 decision the court ruled that a dwelling could not be searched for liquor, even with a proper warrant, unless it was first proven to be a public resort, the property to be searched was designated in the warrant, and the search warrant was based upon written affidavits only.

In a 1923 landmark decision the court confirmed that an individual might legally produce his own liquor in his own home for his own use. It thus set aside the conviction of an Ottawa County man who had a stock of home brew in his basement because "it was not alleged that his home was used as a place of public resort, or for illegal manufacture or sale of liquor."

In 1924 the court ruled that in order to secure a search warrant policemen could use both their sense of smell and evidence of heavy pedestrian traffic in and out of a dwelling. Such evidence was deemed sufficient to suspect that such a dwelling was indeed a place of public resort. The Detroit *Saturday Night* editorialized concerning the decision that "men with long and sensitive noses and perhaps women with longer and more sensitive noses will presently be in demand by the prohibition forces. Amateur detectives with olfactory nerves dedicated to the salvation of humanity may even whiff their neighbor's breath from afar and tear him from the bosom of his family." But when the state legislature passed a law in 1927 making the sense of smell of a law officer sufficient ground for the issuance of search warrants for private homes, Governor Fred Green vetoed the measure. "At its best this act would result in the arrest of a few home brewers," Green said. "At its worst it would prove a steady instrument for the gratification of private spites and instrumentalities for police inquisition." He also warned that such measures would certainly arouse public opinion against prohibition and would lend credibility to the allegation that "prohibition cannot be enforced except by methods that smack of Czarism." Green told the legislature that prohibition laws would never be made effective simply by strong enforcement measures. "Our greatest problem," he observed, "is to obtain the cooperation of the public in their enforcement. This can be done by education and continuation of the campaign that made prohibition possible. We need stricter enforcement of our present laws rather than more laws."

Throughout the 1920s, while the courts sought to clarify enforcement procedures, the state legislature sought to make enforcement more effective by providing increasingly severe penalties (and presumably deterrents) for prohibition violators. In 1927, guided by what it took to be public sentiment, the legislature adopted a revised state criminal code that included one of the most controversial and misguided legal provisions of the dry years. The measure provided mandatory life imprisonment for individuals convicted of four felonies—"four-time losers," as they were known to the press. The new criminal code defined such offenders as "habitual offenders." Some enthusiastic prohibitionists, led by R. N. Holsaple of the Anti-Saloon League, approved of the provision because violation of Michigan's prohibition law was a felony and recividism in the case of prohibition violators would thus lead to their imprisonment for life. Since an individual who had committed three previous felonies could be arrested and imprisoned for possession of as little as a pint of alcoholic beverage under Michigan law, the provision of the new criminal code dealing with "habitual criminals" became known as Michigan's "Life for a Pint" law.

A controversy over the new law developed in the fall of 1927 after Lansing police officers arrested Fred M. Palm for the alleged possession of two pints of liquor. Palm was released on bail but did not appear for his hearing. Police officers armed with a bench warrant went to his home to arrest him, and although they had no search warrant, entered the premises and discovered a partially filled bottle of gin. Palm was charged with felony possession of liquor—fourteen ounces of dry gin—pleaded guilty, and was sentenced to life imprisonment at hard labor. The sentence brought a national outcry against the severity of the Michigan criminal code. The *New York Times* attacked the sentence on its editorial page. In the spring of 1928 Palmer won an appeal hearing before the state supreme court on the grounds that the "habitual criminal" code section was unconstitutional in that it violated federal and state constitutional provisions against "cruel and unusual punishment." He also pointed out that the arresting officers had no right to seize the gin without the evidence first having been submitted to a grand jury. Despite what appeared to be a good case, Palm lost his appeal, and in January 1928 his conviction was upheld.

In the fall of 1928, Alonzo Noyes, an Ionia farmer, pleaded guilty to a charge of possession of liquor. The crime was Noyes's fourth felony, but his first liquor law violation. He was sentenced to life in Jackson State Prison. A month later in Flint, Channie Tripp, a bootlegger, was sentenced to life in prison as a habitual criminal. All four of Tripp's violations involved breaches of the state liquor law. The greatest outcry against the Michigan law came in mid-December 1928, when Mrs. Etta Mae Miller, forty-eight years old and the mother of ten children, was sentenced to life imprisonment for a fourth violation of the state liquor law. Mrs. Miller's husband, Alvin, was already in prison, serving a term for prohibition violation. Mrs. Miller's case was appealed, and while the appeal was still in the courts there was renewed controversy over enforcement of the dry laws. The arresting officer in the Palm and Miller cases, Frank Eastman, confessed that the liquor found in the Miller home had been planted there by a fellow police officer. As a result of this and other charges concerning questionable procedures in the arrests of "habitual criminals," Governor Green, in Janury 1930, commuted the sentences of five persons serving life sentences for violations of the state prohibition law from life to from seven and one-half to fifteen years. Green asserted that it had not been the intention of the framers of the criminal code that persons whose fourth offenses were violations of the prohibition law should be punished by life imprisonment. In commuting the sentences, Green said, he was actually carrying out the intention of the framers of the law. In March the state supreme court reversed the conviction of Mrs. Miller and she was released from prison.

When the state legislature convened in 1929 the battle lines were drawn over the issue of whether or not liquor law offenders should be exempted from the state criminal code's "habitual criminal" definition. A bill was initiated to exempt 120 "minor felonies" from the "habitual criminal" definition. Under the new provisions only felonies that called for a maximum sentence of at least five years for the first offense were to be included in the accumulation of felonies that determined if one was to be defined as a "habitual criminal."

The bill, drafted by Attorney General Wilbur Brucker at the request of Governor Green, was rushed through the Senate under a suspension of the rules, no member speaking a word in opposition. The House also passed the measure by a lopsided majority. The adoption of the law was considered a major defeat for the Anti-Saloon League and its allied organizations, which had campaigned throughout the state in opposition to changing the criminal code provisions for "habitual criminals."

Governor Green signed the new bill into law on April 2, 1929, and a little over one month later signed a new liquor measure, the Cuthbertson law, which increased penalties for first offenders of the prohibition law to not less than a $500 fine and a prison term of not less than one year. Penalties were increased for each succeeding offense until a fourth offender was to receive ten to fifteen years in prison. A legislative conference committee inserted a clause into the measure stating that the intent of the legislature was for the courts, in imposing sentences under the act, to discriminate between casual or slight violations and habitual or commerical violations of the law.

Judges in Detroit's Recorder's Court immediately expressed fear that juries, lenient with offenders under former provisions of the prohibition law calling for a fine of no more than $500 or thirty days in jail, would be even less likely to convict law violators under new and more stringent laws. Because of the difficulty of getting convictions in prohibition cases, the Wayne County prosecutor's office had adopted a policy of accepting nominal fines if offenders would waive jury trials and plead guilty, thereby clearing up the docket. Under the new law, the judges said, offenders would surely call for jury trials and in most cases would be found not guilty. Two Detroit attorneys who had often represented bootleggers and rumrunners expressed the opinion, on the other hand, that because of the severe federal Jones law and the state Cuthbertson or "Little Jones" law, bootleggers would fight it out with police rather than submit to arrest. And if arrested, the attorneys claimed, prohibition law violators would plead not guilty and would fight and appeal their cases rather than submit to the penalties prescribed by the new laws. The Cuthbertson law, consequently, became a major factor in the rapidly decreasing number of convictions for violation of prohibition in Wayne County at the end of the 1920s.

VI

Although it appeared throughout the 1920s that the state legislature was interested in strict enforcement of the prohibition laws, there were also disturbing indications that many legislators regarded stringent dry statutes as measured to be applied to the common citizenry of the state and not to the public servants. The knowledge or at least the suspicion that this attitude existed among lawmakers helped undermine public support for the dry laws. A correspondent for the Grand Rapids *Herald* verified certain suspicions concerning state legislators when he reported from Lansing in 1921 that he was shocked by violations of the prohibition laws by solons. "Each new arrival in Lansing brings it," he reported of liquor in the capital city. "He may be a member of the legislature. He may be a lobbyist, but he brings it with him. The Lansing bootlegger is not getting fat off this legislative session. He can only stand on the streets at night and sadly sigh as he hears the shrieks of joy coming from the rooms of the hotels where the lobbyists and members of the legislature are enjoying parties such as were never put on in the old days. . . ." The reporter was amazed because no attempt at concealment was made: Booze was served openly to the legislators in the hotels of the capital.

It was even intimated that Governor Fred Green, who had defeated incumbent Alex Groesbeck in the gubernatorial race of 1926, was himself a violator of the prohibition laws. Green, like Groesbeck, was an outspoken supporter of prohibition and a contributor to the state Anti-Saloon League. In March 1930, nevertheless, a national magazine created a scandal by reporting that Green had participated in a wild party at the Allen Gardens roadhouse in Wayne County on the evening of October 15, 1929. According to the magazine *Plain Talk*, liquor had been served in the dining room and in the side rooms of the roadhouse, a bar had been set up in the basement, and the party had degenerated into a drunken revel. Six girls, it was alleged, had been brought in near the end of the party and had danced naked before Green, four circuit judges from Detroit, the chief of the Michigan State Police, a former Detroit police commissioner, a former Wayne County sheriff, and Green's campaign manager. Several well-known bootleggers and gangsters had also been present at the party with Green, according to the article.

Plain Talk also reported that a large part of the $25,000 that the state legislature had appropriated for the entertainment of visiting executive officers during the National Governors' Conference on Mackinac Island in July 1927 had been used to purchase liquor for the convention. Commissioner Olander of the state police, according to the article, unwrapped the liquor bottles personally, handed them to Governor Green, and encouraged the guests to drink publicly. Some of the Michigan officials present at the conference had incurred heavy "bar bills," and these, *Plain Talk* said, had been turned over to the state auditor to be paid from state funds. When the editor of the Michigan *State Digest* attempted to investigate these charges, he discovered that the detailed expense vouchers had disappeared and that the total amount recorded for expenditures at the conference had been altered as compared to what had appeared on documents previously prepared. Governor Green had personally paid $1,414.10 of the "bar bills," *Plain Talk* reported.

Stories of this kind clearly undermined efforts by the state legislature to make the prohibition laws more effective. At the same time they certainly also weakened the morale and resolve of law enforcement officers who were asked to risk their lives in efforts to make prohibition work. The stories furthermore encouraged bootleggers and rumrunners to envision themselves as legitimate suppliers of a real public need. Thus, in the end, Governor Green and the inbibing state legislators played no small role in undermining the entire idealistic prohibition experiment. When prohibition's critics charged that the dry laws were making America a nation of hypocrites, they needed to look no further than the Michigan state legislature to substantiate their allegations.

6

Prosperity, Liberty, and Lower Taxes: The Story of Repeal

Prohibition has made nothing but trouble—trouble for all of us. Worst thing ever hit the country. Why, I tried to get into legitimate business two or three times, but they won't stand for it.

Al Capone

The Convention wants Repeal. I want Repeal. I am confident that the United States of America wants Repeal. I say to you now that from this date on, the Eighteenth Amendment is doomed.

Franklin D. Roosevelt, 1932

I

Dry crusader Andrew Volstead told a national convention of the Anti-Saloon League in 1921 that there was no question at all in his mind regarding the permanency of prohibition. "They can never repeal it," he said. Senator Morris Sheppard of Texas asserted that "there is as much chance of repealing the Eighteenth Amendment as there is for a hummingbird to fly to the planet Mars with the Washington Monument tied to its tail." Evangelist Billy Sunday added his assurances and contended that there was no more chance of repealing the Eighteenth Amendment "than there is of repealing the Thirteenth Amendment and restoring slavery." No more chance, he said, "than you can dam Niagara Falls with toothpicks."

The dissenters, nevertheless, were not silenced with the adoption of national prohibition. For ten years critics called for revision of the Volstead Act and a redefinition of the term "intoxicating beverage," with the goal of legalizing beer and wine. The U.S. Brewers' Association was one of the most outspoken champions of such revision. The spokesman for the organization, Hugh Fox, contended that beer containing 2.75 percent alcohol was not in fact intoxicating. In 1923 Fox praised 2.75 percent beer as the salvation of the prohibition experiment. Dissatisfaction with prohibition was increasing, Fox warned, and all indications were that bone-dry prohibition was unenforceable. Bring back beer and once again Americans would have an inexpensive, palatable, and harmless beverage. Legal beer, Fox predicted, would undermine the bootlegging business and bring much greater compliance with the prohibition laws. Fox's position was shared by Michigan's Senator James Couzens and by tens of thousands of concerned Americans who hoped by revision to preserve the prohibition experiment. The dry leadership, however, refused to budge on revision. Prohibition, they insisted, must be total—bone dry. The legal lid stayed on.

From the early 1920s on, national and local opinion polls indicated a good deal of dissatisfaction with bone-dry prohibition. As early as the summer of 1922, in a national survey conducted by the *Literary Digest* that included more than one million responses from individuals listed in telephone directories throughout the country, 61.5 percent of those polled favored either modification or repeal of the Eighteenth Amendment. A separate poll of women showed them to be about 55 percent in favor of revision. A poll of workingmen indicated that they favored revision of the Volstead Act by more than nine to one.

The portion of the *Literary Digest* poll conducted in Michigan indicated that 11,207 of those who were contacted favored the Volstead Act and the Eighteenth Amendment in their existing form but that 14,374 favored either the legalization of wine and beer or the outright repeal of the Eighteenth Amendment. A separate poll of Michigan women indicated that a majority favored the dry laws as they stood. On the other hand, a poll of Michigan workingmen showed them to be in favor of revision by 16,251 to 13,390. A 1926 poll conducted in Michigan by the Newspaper Enterprise Association revealed overwhelming sentiment in favor of revision of the Volstead Act.

The champions of prohibition gave little credence to the findings of the public opinion polls in the 1920s. "The newspapers take straw votes and the wets vote early and often," the president of the Michigan WCTU explained in 1926. "We who believe that prohibition is the only solution of the liquor problem, who know that all of the talk about light wine and beer, all of the straw votes and the differently worded referendums submitted in the last election, are simply entering wedges to pry the Eighteenth Amendment from the Constitution, are not blind to the fact that enforcement has been made a political football."

A turning point of sorts in public opinion occurred in 1923. New York repealed its "Baby Volstead Act" that year and an increasing amount of criticism welled up in the mass media. In the fall, the Detroit *News* published a series of articles describing the association of organized crime and the illegal liquor business in Detroit and concluded that prohibition had produced at least as much crime and corruption as had the saloon before it. Several prominent Detroit clergymen began speaking out in favor of revision of prohibition in late 1923.

In the spring of 1925 the Detroit *Free Press* came out in favor of revision. "Reluctantly," the editor observed, "this newspaper arrives at the conviction that the Eighteenth Amendment was a fearful error, and that the most pressing domestic problem before the U.S. today is how to get rid of prohibition in its present extreme form and substitute for it moderate but effective liquor legislation that will have the support of public sentiment."

Growing public dissatisfaction with bone-dry prohibition was accompanied by a propaganda campaign spearheaded by the Association Against the Prohibition Amendment, an organization founded in late 1920. In its publications and pronouncements, the AAPA insisted that the promises of the prohibitionists had not been realized because in their fanaticism the drys had outrun both public opinion and common sense. Temperance was a good thing, a desirable virtue, AAPA speakers agreed. Even prohibition was good for some people. But prohibition and temperance did not necessarily require the bone-dry type that had triumphed with the passage of the Volstead Act. Because of the unreasonableness and the blindness of the prohibition leaders, the AAPA contended, the Eighteenth Amendment had produced a plague rather than a paradise.

The most interesting facet of the anti-prohibition campaign before 1930 was the way in which it resembled the earlier prohibition campaign. This was understandable, since the leadership for the anti-prohibition campaign was drawn increasingly from the ranks of former dry crusaders who had seen the light and changed their minds. The anti-prohibitionists insisted that they were not disillusioned with either the social or economic ideals of the drys, but rather with the actual results. The anti-prohibitionists, consequently, managed to portray themselves as the true temperance force of the nation, the genuine anti-saloon league. One early circular of the AAPA, for example, listed the following as ideals of the organization: (1) a contented citizenry; (2) very little drunkenness; (3) no "thou shalt nots" to perpetually challenge young people; (4) no expensive enforcement, hence no patronage and of course no graft; (5) better, safer highways, the sanctity of the home protected, and the police left free to pursue their regular duties of protecting life and property; (6) no clogging of the courts and jails. Spokesmen for the AAPA insisted that a major change in the administration of the liquor laws was necessary in order for the nation to be redeemed. "We look forward now to the day when prohibition with its brood of speakeasies, home-brew kitchens, bootleggers, bomb throwers, and snoopers will follow the saloon system out of the nation's back door. This will be accomplished by extricating our country from the tyrannical grip of the prohibition amendment," Henry Curran, president of the AAPA, testified.

AAPA officials alleged that a primary danger of the Eighteenth Amendment was the misguided, even dangerous overextension of the powers of the federal government and the consequent weakening of the federal system. The traditional balance between the states and the central government and the built-in responsiveness to local conditions in a truly federal system had been breached by the passage of national prohibition. Whether this had occurred by accident or design was debatable (many members of the AAPA, however, believed it was part of a conspiracy on the part of the Antisaloon League and the Methodists). AAPA officials warned that the overextension of governmental police powers brought with it the destruction of traditional American liberties. And the harder the government tried to enforce the prohibition laws, the more individual freedom was sacrificed. Repeal, on the other hand, would restore the federal system, reduce government bureaucracy and expense, allow for more reasonable democratic decision making, and revive the golden past when the individual had been freer to assert his own will and make his own choices.

Throughout the 1920s the AAPA supported critics of prohibition for public office. When elected, however, the AAPA-supported politicians were advised to cooperate with the dry majorities. William Stayton, president of the AAPA for most of the 1920s, believed that the AAPA would undermine its own position if it supported obstructionist tactics and fought appropriations for prohibition in Congress and the state legislatures. Stayton explained to Henry B. Joy that the drys would probably move more and more to the border position of "give us twenty-five more years to try the experiment." "We, of course, do not want any such nonsensical thing," Stayton said, "but if we, the wets, throw any obstacles in the way of the drys so far as organization and appropriation are concerned, they will have some excuse and say that their law has not had a fair show and after consultation with a good many of our friends in Congress the Association has taken the attitude that we will not try to defeat at the present time any appropriations and that we will not object to any form of organization the drys ask for. We will give them, in short, all of the rope they want to take and we will be careful not to let them accuse us of obstructive politics." Of course, Stayton concluded, "when the time comes that we can win, we shall expect to give open battle."

The Michigan chapter of the AAPA was organized in late 1921. Under the direction of Dr. John Slevin, the state branch worked throughout most of the 1920s to revise the state prohibition laws. Slevin declared that his organization hoped to secure the enactment of a law legalizing light wine and beer by "organizing the unorganized majority, by crystallizing the anti-prohibition sentiment and directing it into channels which will bring about the enactment of the law for which the majority clamor." He said that the principal activity of the organization would be voter education. No lobbies would be maintained by the state AAPA, he promised. There would be no lavish expenditure of money, no bribery, and no "star chamber methods." Money was to be expended by the organization, Slevin explained, only to tell the public who was for and who against the AAPA programs.

Despite its moderate program, the AAPA was fiercely denounced by dry spokesmen. Congressman Louis Cramton described the organization as a group "opposed to law enforcement, promoting, thriving upon, and rejoicing at the triumph of crime and disorder over law and order. It brazenly proclaims by its title its opposition to a part of the Constitution of the United States, the fundamental law of the land." Cramton asserted that the country had little to fear from organized bootleggers and criminals, but a real danger was posed by men in high places "fitted for and insisting upon leadership" who lent their names and their influence to a direct attack upon the Constitution and sought to justify its nullification. "Then lovers of law and order had better pay due regard," he warned.

In their intemperate criticism Cramton and other prohibitionists misread the conservative nature of the AAPA. The organization did not endorse nullification of the Eighteenth Amendment or any other law; in fact, the AAPA was very strict on the law and order issue. The primary difference between the law and order of the wets and that of the drys in the mid-1920s lay in the fact that the AAPA believed that so-called bone-dry federal prohibition was unenforceable and thus undermined all efforts at law enforcement and bred public contempt for all law. Law and order could be established and maintained only when control of the liquor traffic was returned to the states, which were more responsive to the sentiments of local communities. The drys, on the other hand, believed that law and order could only be maintained in a country in which there was no liquor traffic and in which bone-dry prohibition was enforced by the federal government, uniformly and on a national level.

The transition of Henry B. Joy of Detroit from dry to wet, from Anti-Saloon League contributor to leading member of the Michigan division of the AAPA, was typical of the path followed by many leading AAPA members in the state. Before the passage of the state prohibition amendment in 1916, Joy contributed to local campaigns of the Michigan Anti-Saloon League, but he was not so much averse to drinking as he was to the evils of the saloon, which, as he saw it, destroyed organized social patterns. Joy believed that Michigan was on the way to achieving reasonable and realistic liquor control when, as he later recalled, war intervened, bringing with it an intemperate and impatient spirit. From this wartime spirit, Joy thought, "impractical and fanatical prohibition resulted."

At first, however, Joy, like most later AAPA converts, was willing to give bone-dry prohibition a chance; but the longer the experiment lasted, the clearer it became to him that prohibition was doing more harm to the country than had the saloon. As a result, Joy turned against prohibition and became one of its most outspoken critics. He joined organizations working for revision and then for repeal of prohibition, and in 1926 he became treasurer of the state division of the AAPA.

Joy explained that it was useless for the state and federal governments to attempt to make the population bone dry when at least one-half of the people of the country would never accept such a condition. As a result, he said in 1925, "We have a condition of civil war going on in the United States. The best of the people, Republicans and Democrats, are divided in this civil war," he remarked, but "some of the broadest minded on both sides of this bitter controversy are in favor of seeking to accomplish a more practical situation, in which reasonable unity of sentiment can exist."

Emory Clark, president of the First National Bank of Detroit, explained his conversion to the AAPA as similar to that of Joy's: "I voted for the Eighteenth Amendment," Clark recalled, "and have supported it consistently. But when I find the bootleggers of the country making no move to oppose the law, I conclude that either the law is wrong or the bootlegging business is right. I am convinced the law is wrong." Clark believed that the evils of prohibition could be corrected only by repealing the Eighteenth Amendment and substituting for it a law that had the backing of all law-abiding people in the country. "When outstanding men in most communities of the country are actually evading the law there can be little doubt that there is something wrong with the law rather than with representative citizens," he said. "The anti-amendment association does not aim to make it any easier to get liquor," he explained. "There is plenty of evidence that it is easy to get if one wants it. But the Association proposes to do what it can to correct a law which had a bad effect on the morale of citizens."

Neither Joy nor Clark offered economic arguments for supporting the revision or repeal of the Eighteenth Amendment. After 1929, critics of the AAPA pointed an accusatory finger at the AAPA and insisted that the primary motive of individuals in the organization pressing for repeal was selfishness. It was assumed that AAPA members believed that repeal would lower their taxes, and so they supported repeal because they believed it fiscally wise. Long before the depression made economic arguments central to the repealist cause, however, wealthy businessmen like Joy and Clark joined the AAPA for conscience's sake. The Eighteenth Amendment weakened the social fabric to a greater degree than the saloon did, they believed, and it threatened the traditional American value system by bestowing wealth and prestige on the lawbreaker, the bootlegger, and the rumrunner. Unlike the free enterprise system that they idealized, members of the AAPA believed that the Eighteenth Amendment rewarded hypocrisy and punished honesty, and this greatly disturbed them.

The first efforts of the AAPA to revise the state prohibition law came in 1923. Robert Wardell of Detroit, secretary of the Michigan chapter of the AAPA and director of the Michigan Modification League, led the fight for revision. In the fall of 1923 Wardell sought to increase AAPA membership in Michigan in order to launch a massive campaign aimed at placing a prohibition referendum on the ballot. In late September, Wardell claimed that his organization included members in sixty-three of the state's eighty-three counties and had a total membership of nearly twenty-seven thousand. He explained that this massive organization would not only support Senator Couzens but would launch a drive to place a modification proposal on the state ballot in November. Each of the twenty-seven thousand members was sent a petition with space for twenty-five names on it. Since only sixty-three thousand signatures were required to place a referendum measure on the state ballot, if each of the AAPA members secured only three names, the measure could go before the voters.

For several weeks the AAPA and the Michigan Modification League gathered signatures to petitions requesting that the electorate be allowed to vote on a measure providing for the sale of alcoholic beverages that did not exceed legal U.S. government standards, prohibiting the consumption of those beverages on the premises where the sale took place, taxing the production and sale of alcoholic beverages, and applying the resulting revenues to the retirement of the state's bonds and the construction and maintenance of county and state highways and institutions. In this effort Wardell combined the twin appeal that eventually became central to the revisionist-repeal movements: The success of his measure would not only mean the return of mild booze, but also revenue for state and county treasuries that would facilitate a reduction in taxes.

Wardell successfully gathered the necessary number of signatures on his petitions, but the state Anti-Saloon League raised the question of the legality of the action. The state constitution provided that every petition should include the full text of any amendment proposed for a statewide referendum, and Wardell's petition did not meet this requirement. The state attorney general upheld the league's contention and informed Wardell that his measure could not be placed on the state ballot in November 1924. Wardell immediately petitioned the state supreme court for a reversal of the attorney general's ruling, but the court refused to issue even an order to show cause, thereby bringing to an end the 1923–24 effort to revise the state prohibition law.

In March 1927, Wardell introduced a resolution in the state legislature calling for a November 1928 referendum on an amendment to the state constitution providing for the sale, under state control, of beer and wine for use in the home. Wardell announced that if the legislature would not act on his proposal, he would launch another petition drive to force the placement of his measure on the ballot. He believed that the two major advantages of his 1927 bill were that it assured against the return of the saloon in any form and

that it would "terminate hypocrisy." His proposed resolution, however, was never reported out by the hostile House prohibition committee.

As he had promised, Wardell set to work on another petition
drive. A few days before the final deadline for presenting his petitions to the secretary of state, Wardell filed 5,000 of the necessary
63,076 signatures. He promised to file the remainder later, but when
the July 5, 1928, deadline passed, Wardell had still not filed them
and all chances for a referendum on prohibition in the fall of 1928
passed. Wardell offered no explanation for his failure. Whether he
found it impossible to gather the required number of signatures or
whether he was convinced that such a measure would be easily
defeated is unknown. In the spring of 1929 Wardell again introduced
a measure in the state House of Representatives to allow for the
manufacture and sale of strong beer and light wines for private
consumption in the home, but once again his measure was not
reported out by the House prohibition committee.

As of late 1929 all but two of Michigan's congressmen were bone
dry, the state legislature was dominated by the drys, and the
greatest hope of the wets, the AAPA leadership believed, lay in a
revision of the state constitution to allow for the manufacture and
sale of wine and beer. There was a good deal of dissatisfaction with
prohibition, yet the drys remained securely in control. The idea that
prohibition was a failure had simply not caught on. Then, suddenly,
the entire situation shifted dramatically, and the plans and expectations of both drys and wets were completely changed.

II

"If you wished to be set down as the craziest of prophets by any
of the men whom you have watched going about their affairs in the
glaring sunlight of September 3, 1929, you would have only to tell
them that within two months they are to witness the greatest financial panic in American history, and that it will usher in a prolonged
and desperate economic crisis," Frederick Lewis Allen recorded in
Since Yesterday, a study of America in the 1930s. Yet on that very
day, the Great Bull Market peaked. The next day it declined, and by

the end of October it was racing downward, destroying millions of dollars in investments. With the crash of the stock market in the last months of 1929 and with prosperity fleeing, "Americans were soon to find themselves living in an altered world which called for new adjustments, new ideas, new habits of thought, and a new order of values. The Post-War Decade had come to a close." Prohibition, along with countless other fads and ideals of an earlier America, was very soon relegated to the scrap heap of outdated illusions.

The deflation of the economy had an immediate impact in Michigan. Unemployment increased rapidly in the last three months of 1929; in September about 56,800 workers in the state were unemployed, but the number rose to 111,800 in October, 212,500 in November, and 249,400 in December. During the next three years unemployment in Michigan averaged 34 percent of the non-agricultural work force, as compared with 26 percent for the entire country. After only two years of depression, the number of dependents on Detroit's relief rolls was equal in size to the entire population of Grand Rapids.

Numerous schemes were proposed for relieving the distress of the depression, ranging from the humanitarian to the absurd. One panacea that quickly gained public attention was the repeal of the Eighteenth Amendment. For many years prohibition had been associated closely with the economy. After 1919, champions of prohibition had attributed the economic prosperity of the nation almost exclusively to the dry laws, but with the depression, the economic propaganda of prohibition toppled backward onto its proponents. Now opponents of the Eighteenth Amendment asked Americans to remember how many workers had been employed in the breweries before prohibition, how many had been employed as bartenders, how many had been employed in the allied trades of the booze business, and how much money came into the government coffers as a result of the licensing and taxation of the booze business. The saloon need never return, the wets said, but if the production and sale of liquor were legalized, more people could be put to work, the government would gain revenue, unemployment would be alleviated, and the depression could be reversed.

As the depression deepened, the anti-prohibitionists began to place almost exclusive emphasis upon the economic advantage of repeal, and their speeches began to echo more and more the dry rhetoric of the early years of the century, with repeal replacing prohibition as a panacea. After 1929, wet spokesmen argued not only that their measure would bring law and order, a restoration of the proper distribution of power between the federal government and local governments, and true temperance, but also an end to the depression, the undermining of radical movements that had sprung up among the unemployed, and a new industrial Eden as perfect as that promised years earlier by the prohibitionists. For an American public searching for simple solutions to the depression, the wets provided very attractive answers.

The economic case for repeal was detailed carefully in Leslie Gordon's *The New Crusade*, in 1930. An introduction to the book by "S. R." stated that "before prosperity can return to this country the budgets of local and national governments must be balanced." The easiest way to accomplish this, the writer continued, was to legalize liquor and then tax it. "If the liquor now sold by bootleggers was legally sold, regulated, and taxed, the excise income would pay the interest on the entire local and national bonded indebtedness and leave more than $200,000,000 for other urgently needed purposes. And while the government treasuries were being revived the power of the bootlegger would be broken and our country could once more become the law-abiding land of security that the forefathers of this country intended that it should be." With proper sharing of liquor revenues, "the tax assessments on the farms and on the small communities will be reduced to that point where the farmer, the small home owner and the small businessman will see daylight again."

Addressing a crowd of thirty-five hundred enthusiastic wets a short time before the election of 1932, Jouett Shouse of the AAPA explained the economic benefits of repeal. Under prohibition, Shouse claimed, the federal government had lost about $1 million annually, an amount that could have been applied to the national debt throughout the twenties. If liquor were marketed under government supervision, Shouse contended, the resulting revenue would provide major relief for the individual taxpayer, who would also benefit because the government would no longer have to spend money to enforce prohibition since there would be greater respect for law and order, which should result in lower costs for law enforcement.

In the depths of the depression the Detroit *Saturday Night* pointed to the economic results of liquor control in Quebec. In that Canadian province the liquor commission provided nearly $10 million annually in profits from the sale of liquor, much of it purchased by Americans visiting Canada. It followed, the *Saturday Night* reasoned, that if booze were legalized, the same profits could be realized in America. Establishing that repeal would yield an annual profit of not less than $800,000, the *Saturday Night* concluded that this "could relieve the pressure of the present depression and perhaps start a business revival that could crack it for keeps."

Robert Wardell estimated that an excise tax on liquor in Michigan would significantly decrease the real-estate taxes that had become a serious burden in the depression. During pre-prohibition days, Wardell pointed out, Michigan levied about $15 million in taxes on real estate each year, but by 1930 that figure had doubled. Wardell predicted that an excise tax after repeal would restore the property taxes to their original level and reduce the state's deficit by $10 million. Wardell estimated that as much as $75 million spent annually on liquor by Michigan visitors to Canada could be returned to the domestic market, creating jobs and bringing "a general improvement in economic conditions."

The economic aspects of repeal were given credibility by the results of a state tax on malt. In the closing days of the 1929 legislative session, legislators passed the malt-tax measure in the hope of returning over $2 million to the state treasury for the relief of depressed school districts. The statute provided for a tax of five cents per pound on malt syrup and extract and a small tax on wort, a basic ingredient of beer. Since these products were used almost exclusively in the production of home-brewed beer, the state, for all practical purposes, had decided to tax the illegal booze traffic. In 1931 the legislature passed a similar measure over the veto of dry Governor Wilbur Brucker, who asserted that the taxation of an illegal product was "wrong in principle and vicious in practice." In a single year the tax raised over $500,000 in Detroit alone. Since the measure so successfully produced revenue, many people concluded that the economic arguments of the anti-prohibitionists were sound.

Mayor Frank Murphy of Detroit soon became an outspoken advocate of the economic benefits of repeal. Like other leading critics, Murphy was not disagreeable to the initial goals of prohibition. "What was sought by prohibition was nothing but commendable," he wrote in reply to a dry inquiry in mid-1932. But an "unreasoning attitude crept into prohibition legislation and its enforcement," he contended, and "made it impractical in great areas of the country." "We both want the same thing," Murphy concluded, "good government and, as a consequence, a well-governed and happy people. There will have to be a correction in the prohibition law if this is to be brought about."

Although he warned against making prohibition "a dump heap for all our economic ills," he also pointed out that "we cannot avoid the fact that a reasonable tax on beer alone would bring $700,000,000 a year into the public treasury." Such a tax would also be equitable, Murphy asserted, since it was paid "only by those who chose to make themselves subject thereto." "Every citizen with the welfare of suffering humanity at heart, should give earnest consideration to the economic aspect of this proposal," Murphy believed.

In the spring of 1932 Mayor Murphy became a member of the Executive Committee of the Michigan Civic League Repeal Parade Committee in Detroit. The group organized a giant repeal parade and rally in Detroit. The slogans on banners carried in the parade testified once again to the miracle repeal was expected to bring. Among the slogans were: Better Business By Brewing; This Procession to End Depression; Bring Back Beer to Bear the Burden; Bring Back Beer and Better Business; Dry Failure or Wet Prosperity; Billions Spent or Billions Saved; Taxes Tell the Tale; Prohibition and Poverty or Beer and Business. The letterhead of the organization read: "Which Shall It Be, Poison Liquor or Everybody in Health and Happiness. Repeal the State Prohibition Law, Bringing Back Prosperity, Liberty and Lower Taxes."

But many people worried over the morality as well as the logic of the economic argument for repeal. "I think 'Soup' comes ahead of beer," one man wrote to Murphy, "and I am opposed to weakminded men spending money for beer which should go for food and clothing for their families." "We are living in the days when the prophets foretold that satan would be doing his stuff," the writer warned, "but I do not propose to help him along with it, even if he would pay a tax for the privilege."

But the repealists had other arguments in favor of their cause too. They linked prohibition to the rise of radicalism during the depression and suggested that repeal would undermine this disturbing development. Before a special committee of the House Judiciary Committee in 1930, Congressman Robert Clancy of Detroit warned that "this is a rather dangerous time, with the people in the cities, which hold 60 percent of the population of this country, in great discontent because of prohibition and also in great discontent because of the unemployment situation." Clancy noted that just a few days previously a mob of unemployed in Cleveland had attacked city hall and battled the police. "They have announced meetings, the 'red' workers and the socialists and communists, to stir up discontent in Cleveland, and I now hold in my hand a 'red' placard, announcing the big meetings in Detroit sponsored by the communists, socialists and bolshevists, who are taking advantage of the unemployment situation, which is very serious. They issued a statement saying that there are 6,000,000 unemployed in the United States now, and that there will shortly be 10,000,000 unemployed." The radicals of Detroit demanded that the blacks be organized for the socialist and Bolshevik cause, Clancy warned, and their appeal was being given a hearing because many blacks were unemployed and suffering. The reds were also trying to organize the foreign-born, many of whom were also out of work. All of this was extremely dangerous, Clancy said, "because in my city 80 percent of the population are very much dissatisfied with the government because of its stand on the dry question, and that is true in Cleveland, and as you know, in large cities of the United States, and there is also quite a bit of discontent in the rural communities." Clancy assured the committee, nevertheless, that America would be "safe" as long as there were officials "who are fair and statesmanlike, and allow free discussion of grievous wrongs like Eighteenth Amendment."

Two years later, at a Senate hearing on the prohibition amendment, Matthew Woll, vice-president of the American Federation of Labor, followed Clancy's lead and blamed radicalism in the United States on the Eighteenth Amendment. Former Governor Fred Green voiced concern over the violation of the Eighteenth Amendment and the continued existence of the United States as a free country. To Green, the very survival of the Republic hinged on nothing less that the immediate repeal of the Eighteenth Amendment.

The repeal cause eventually marshaled an impressive array of scientific statistics to its side just as the drys had done in their earlier prohibition campaign. Findings were published indicating that moderate drinkers lived longer than total abstainers, alcohol was important in treating disease, beer in the diet of pregnant women helped build strong teeth in their children, and 4 percent beer was indeed non-intoxicating. All of these figures and more were circulated throughout the 1920s in middle-class-oriented magazines and were somewhat effectively used by the AAPA and other repeal organizations. But the day of scientifically gathered statistics swaying public opinion was passing now, and the public was much more interested in simple arguments, like those equating repeal with prosperity. For as long as most adults in 1930 could remember, thousands upon thousands of numbers and dollar signs and percentages had been listed to demonstrate this truth or that truth about liquor or prohibition, and the war of numbers continued to rage throughout the 1920s. And the more statistics there were, the clearer it became that the situation was hopelessly unclear. For every objectively drawn conclusion of the wet-and-dry issue there were ten qualifications and counter-conclusions to be drawn. The dilemma was illustrated most depressingly by President Hoover's specially appointed Wickersham Commission, which was to present the facts and figures of prohibition and law enforcement and thereby clear the air for Mr. Average American. Yet when the commission report was issued in January 1931 it simply added to the existing confusion. While the main body of the report contained very explicit evidence indicating that prohibition was not working, the eleven commission members came to eleven separate conclusions—two for repeal, four for modification, and five for further trial of bone-dry prohibition. Then, to add further to the confusion, the commission as a whole came out for further trial of bone-dry prohibition. Frederick Lewis Allen drew perhaps the most common conclusion from the activities of the commission and wrote that "the supposedly enlightened device of collecting innumerable facts and trying to reason from them to an inevitable conclusion had been turned into a farce." What just about anybody could understand was that the economy of the United States was rapidly coming undone. At the same time, if breweries and distilleries and liquor stores opened, people would be put to work. It was simple logic.

The repeal forces sought the endorsement of leading public figures in order to add prestige and luster to their cause. Before 1932 in Michigan, however, they were disappointed in their efforts along this line. Businessmen of national repute were reluctant to speak out on the repeal issue in Michigan because of the policies of Alfred P. Sloan, Jr., of General Motors and Henry Ford of the Ford Motor Company. When the wet-and-dry debate intensified with the deepening of the depression, Sloan forbade any member of the General Motors Corporation in Michigan to express any opinion whatever on prohibition. Ford, on the other hand, stood 100 percent behind prohibition and decreed that no member of the Ford organization should speak out in behalf of either modification or repeal. "The attitude of these two men," Henry Joy wrote, "sets the pace for the general businessmen, industrial leaders, and men in the banking world in our community. Bankers will not speak out on either side for fear thay may lose Ford deposits or General Motors deposits, or the deposits of those allied with those respective companies. And so on down the line, throughout." Joy said that many of Detroit's leading businessmen told him that they would like to see the dry laws repealed but that they were opposed to making "a public issue" out of the question. Some of them contributed anonymously to the repeal organizations, Joy claimed.

A major breakthrough for the Michigan wets finally occurred in June 1932, when Sloan announced that he favored repeal of the Eighteenth Amendment and strict government control of the liquor traffic. Like other wet converts, Sloan couched the reasons for his conversion in terms of his concern for temperance. Sloan announced that he was "definitely content that the road toward greater temperance with a resulting better standard of ethics in our country is through repeal." He cited increases in the liquor traffic, lawlessness, and racketeering, as well as economic loss from prohibition as the main factors influencing his change in sentiment. Sloan asserted his belief that with repeal "lawlessness will no longer be subsidized and as a very important and vital economic consideration, industry will be relieved from part of the heavy burden of taxation through an increase in Government revenue made possible by placing the sale of liquor under governmental auspices instead of as now conducted. It is my belief," he concluded, "that our whole social and economic structure will in this manner be greatly strengthened and the real foundation built for renewed prosperity."

The wets won important organizational announcements of support also. The American Federation of Labor had favored revision of the Volstead Act throughout the 1920s, and in early 1931 the Michigan Federation of Labor adopted a resolution demanding the total repeal of the Eighteenth Amendment. The principal reason given for the MFL's championship of repeal was that prohibition "had failed utterly in its avowed purpose and was largely responsible for the present economic conditions."

The national convention of the American Legion met in Detroit in 1931, and members of the state's repeal organizations worked assiduously to secure from the legionnaires a resolution favoring modification or repeal of the Eighteenth Amendment. Previously the legion had avoided what it considered to be controversial political subjects, and at the national convention in 1930 the national commander had ruled out of order a resolution presented on the floor calling for the repeal of the Eighteenth Amendment. There was, however, outspoken sentiment at the 1931 convention in favor of repeal. The growth of anti-prohibition sentiment among the legionnaires was striking in view of the fact that the strength of the legion was concentrated in the small towns and rural districts of the country. The decline of sentiment for prohibition in the countryside was an extremely dangerous signal for the drys.

The repealists at the legion convention, led by Col. Fred Alger of Detroit, were successful in securing a resolution stating that the Eighteenth Amendment "has created a condition endangering respect for law and the security of American institutions, therefore be it resolved that the American Legion in this thirteenth annual convention assembled favors the submission by Congress of the repeal or modification of the present prohibition laws to the several states with a request that each state submit this question to the voters thereof." The measure was reported out by the special resolutions committee after a prolonged session during which advocates of the declaration for outright repeal argued stubbornly with prohibitionists, who sought to keep the issue from being submitted to the delegates at all. Alger wrote to Henry Joy during the convention, "In the whole history of the Legion there has never been such a bitter fight. . . ." The resolution was adopted by a vote of 1,008 to 394.

Yet rapidly increasing repeal sentiment after 1929 did not bring a rush of new members into the AAPA. Ironically, the organization was in a very precarious situation in the fall of 1930. After financially overextending itself in crucial congressional campaigns, the AAPA found itself over $120,000 in debt.

The AAPA was laboring under such difficulty in late 1930 that its directors decided upon a major reorganization of the body. Henry Joy and Col. Alger were asked by the national directors to consider how the state organization could be made more economical and effective. The two men concluded that the AAPA should cooperate more closely with other repeal groups so that the finances of all could be closely coordinated and duplication of effort avoided. It was decided that the Michigan AAPA should not aim at a large membership, as Wardell had done in the mid-1920s, but should rather be composed of only about 150 "influential men" of the state. This small membership was to be scattered throughout the key counties of Michigan, with the nucleus in Wayne County. It was hoped that the AAPA could thus play a directing role for organization and provide financial management for the entire repeal movement.

In early 1931 the state AAPA was further centralized and control of the organization passed into the hands of three directors—Joy, Alger, and Sidney T. Miller. These three were authorized by the national leadership of the organization to make policy decisions without conferring with other members in the state, because the others, according to Alger, were "not active, and are somewhat difficult to move." This triumvirate was called the Michigan Committee of the National Association Against the Prohibition Amendment.

Following the reorganization, Stayton informed Joy that it was necessary for the AAPA to overcome the popular impression that leading business executives and industrialists favored repeal simply for economic reasons beneficial to themselves. Joy was accordingly authorized to recruit "men of large affairs to take a stand definitely and publicly on the prohibition issue" on other than economic grounds and to offer them membership in the AAPA in return for the use of their names. Names of prospective members were forwarded to Stayton who then arranged to contact them through other prominent members of the AAPA.

Despite the emergence of hundreds of grass-roots repeal organizations after 1929, effective control of the repeal movement remained in the hands of the AAPA and its two subsidiaries, the

Crusaders and the Women's Organization for National Prohibition Reform (WONPR). The Crusaders was founded in Cleveland, Ohio, in 1929. The organization soon spread across the country by forming local chapters in major cities, its initial aim being to establish a chapter in every American city of over twenty-five thousand population. Fred G. Clark, a Cleveland oil executive, became the first commander in chief of the Crusaders, and the first executive board consisted of fifty prominent citizens from the northern and eastern states. Despite efforts to recruit large numbers of members, however, the Crusaders, like the AAPA, depended upon the wealth and prestige of its membership rather than its size.

In 1930 the Crusaders began to organize divisions of young men under the age of thirty in Detroit. At that time one of the Michigan organizers explained to the *Free Press*, "We are a temperance, not a wet organization." The *Free Press* endorsed the calm approach of the Crusaders toward the liquor problem and described them as "a middle-of-the-road movement, composed of reasonable and reasoning people who will look at facts as they are and proceed accordingly. If the Crusaders prove to be pioneers of such a movement they will deserve the name they have adopted."

Leslie Gordon's *The New Crusade* (1930) explained further both the concern of the members of the organization and their program of action. The book reads like a pre-1919 WCTU tract. The Crusaders were outraged by the corruption in politics and law enforcement accompanying prohibition. The Crusader "warms under the collar when he hears the rumble of whiskey trucks on the highway and realizes that it is the neutrality of corrupted police officers that permits them to travel," an introduction to the book explained. Yet the Crusader understood that the blame for the flagrant law violations did not lie with the average police official. "He believes that under normal conditions all of these police agencies would take the bootlegger by the neck and vigorously give him his just desserts." But the power behind the police officer was the one corrupted by payoffs from liquor sellers. Echoing exactly the earlier dry propaganda, the Crusader recognized that "the corrupt liason between the king bootleggers and the ward heelers and leaders of local political machines is the most dangerous factor now facing the public. Ward-heeling politicians protect ward catering speakeasies and bootleggers." Corruption existed also when liquor was legal, and in both cases it was founded upon unscrupulously acquired profits from liquor sales. As a result, "the Crusader intends to use all his individual and organized strength to take the profit from the liquor traffic."

According to Crusader founder Clark, members of the organization "interested in the salvation of society" believed that "actual temperance is so vitally necessary to the future welfare of this country that he is going to fight for it with every law-abiding power at his command." The Crusader, Clark wrote, "respects to the point of veneration the legions of silver-haired women and gray-haired men who gave the best part of their lives in placing the Eighteenth Amendment on the statute books. He thrills to the idealism that prompted the great temperance movement of fifty years ago, of thirty years ago, and twenty years ago." Clark assured those Americans who remembered the saloon that the Crusaders would fight hard to prevent that institution from ever being reestablished. "He is determined that the licensed saloon must stay closed—the speakeasy saloon must be closed and the power of greed and profit must be removed from the traffic in alcoholic beverages." Clark concluded that the Crusader "believes that when sincere temperance people understand his motives, they will back his Crusade, since the principles he stands for are practically the code of principles the WCTU adopted when present day gray-haired mothers were children in short dresses."

In Michigan the Crusaders announced that their members could either be wet or dry and had only to agree that existing conditions were intolerable. Clark described the group as "neither dreamers or fanatics," but as simply men who had "had enough lawlessness, bootlegging, hijacking, poison-whiskey selling, shooting innocent citizens, gin parties attended by innocent high school girls and boys and rum parties attended by dry agents and other hypocrites; of whisky flasks on the hips of college and high school men at gatherings of all kinds; . . . of huge sums spent futilely in vain attempts to control men's appetites by legislation and of absolute disregard for the distinction between drunkards and temperate users of liquor."

Michigan's Crusaders were drawn almost exclusively from Republican ranks; and although the organization claimed nonpartisanship, it was Republican in its political activities. Indeed, what the AAPA, the Crusaders, and the WONPR hoped to accomplish before the fall of 1932 was to make the Republican party wet rather than to bring the already wet Democratic party into power. Accordingly, their principal political effort was to defeat dry candidates in Republican primaries.

The dilemma of the Republican wets was illustrated in 1930 when Alger, prominent in both the AAPA and the Crusaders, endorsed the dry Republican gubernatorial candidate, Wilbur Brucker, over the wet Democrat, William A. Comstock. In supporting Brucker, Alger rationalized his position by claiming that, if elected, Brucker would be "governed by the will of the people" with regard to prohibition. Frank A. Picard, Comstock's aide and one of the few leading Democratic Crusaders, protested that Alger was trying to delude the electorate to believe that Brucker was potentially wet. Picard pointed out to Alger, "You are not in favor of the State of Michigan being wet. You are in favor of the Republican party being wet. If that will bring about prohibition in the state you are in favor of prohibition but you won't look at the big question because of your firm belief that if anything is to be done in this state the Democrats—though they help pay taxes, though they help support our government—cannot be expected to perform any political good."

Two other Democratic congressional candidates complained bitterly about the failure of the Michigan branch of the AAPA to support Comstock in the gubernatorial race: Edward Frensdorf of Hudson and Michael J. Hart of Saginaw publicly criticized the two-faced policies of both the AAPA and the Crusaders. In response to an AAPA questionnaire, Frensdorf replied that he had concluded that "both wet and dry organizations in our state are strictly adjuncts of the Republican Party." Hart observed, "The general impression seems to be that the AAPA is the left wing of the Republican Party the same as the Anti-Saloon League is the right wing of the Republican Party. Just looking from the side lines," he wrote, "I would say that it is the purpose of this association to do just enough work, and create enough sentiment, to cause a change in the Republican Party's attitude towards this question of prohibition and then join them."

Another major repeal group was the WONPR, founded by Mrs. Charles Sabin in the spring of 1929 following meetings of several "society leaders" in New York and Chicago. The group first called

itself the Womens' Legion for True Temperance, but later changed
its title to the Womens' Organization for National Prohibition Reform. The first Michigan WONPR chapter was formed in Detroit in
December 1929. One year later effective chapters were meeting in
Kalamazoo and Battle Creek, and by the end of 1931 there were
WONPR locals in nearly every sizable community in the southern
half of the lower peninsula. According to an early historian of the
WONPR, the Michigan branch of the organization recruited most of
its members by canvasing rural districts of the state. The leadership
and membership lists appearing in the press at the time, however,
include almost exclusively women from urban and suburban areas.

The WONPR membership consisted of women from the upper
social stratum, many of them wives of officers in the AAPA. The
Michigan WONPR, headed by Mrs. Fred A. Alger, carried on a
struggle for goals strikingly similar to those sought earlier by the
WCTU. Mrs. Alger made this clear when she explained, "One thing
I would like to emphasize is that those working for the repeal of the
Michigan dry law are not trying to make it easier to obtain liquor.
We are trying to make it more difficult; we are trying to regulate and
control the sale of liquor; trying to wipe out the dives that infest
Detroit and the rest of the state; trying to bring liquor from vile
resorts that lure and ruin our young people into the sunlight where
we can at least see what is going on and apply intensive restrictive
measures." Mrs. Alger said she believed that the majority of the
people in the state accepted the view of the WONPR and favored
true temperance rather than prohibition, "which did nothing except
cause intemperance." The pledge card for the organization read,
"Because I believe that prohibition has increased crime, lawlessness, hypocrisy and corruption; because I believe that the cause of
real temperance has been retarded and that sumptuary laws have no
place in the Federal Constitution, I enroll as a member of this
organization, which is working for some change in the law to bring
about a sane solution of the problem without the return of the
saloon."

Like the AAPA and the Crusaders, the WONPR was reluctant
to actually practice the anti-prohibition nonpartisanship it
preached. The women who made up the WONPR leadership were
from wealthy Republican families. When Democratic candidates
endorsed repeal, the WONPR was hesitant to support them. It

required a heated seven-hour session in July 1932 for the national executive committee of the WONPR to produce a resolution "urging" members of the WONPR to support the national Democratic ticket, which was committed to outright repeal of the Eighteenth Amendment. The use of the word "urge" was significant—the vote of the members was not to be used as an acid test of their loyalty to the WONPR. Sixty-two prominent members of the WONPR repudiated the action of their executive committee by signing a statement that advised each member to vote for the presidential candidate "who is best qualified to lead the nation, regardless of the prohibition issue." "To make the position of the candidate towards control of the liquor traffic the sole test of his fitness for the office of president," the rebel group stated, "is the very negation of our responsibilities as citizens." Mrs. Alger ignored the rebels and, following the instructions of the national executive committee, urged the Michigan WONPR members to vote for Roosevelt and Garner because they were pledged to repeal. In the congressional races, Mrs. Alger said, "We will endorse any candidate who openly favors repeal of the Eighteenth Amendment, Republican or Democrat." WONPR regulars hoped to make it impossible for any political candidate in 1932 to straddle the repeal issue. "It has turned into a barbed wire fence between two camps," a WONPR member warned dry Congressman Earl Michener, "neither a safe nor a dignified seat for any candidate."

In the fall of 1932, the AAPA, WONPR, and Crusaders formed the Michigan Repeal Fund Committee to coordinate the financing of all the major repeal organizations. The committee set out to raise $70,000 to finance the campaigns of repeal candidates in the November election. The anti-prohibition campaign of the repeal groups came to a head in November 1932.

In early 1931 Robert Wardell had initiated another petition drive to amend the state constitution and repeal prohibition. Wardell's 1931 initiative measure, like all of his previous petitions, provided simply for the legalization of beer and wine under supervision by the state. But after ten months and the gathering of only twenty-two thousand signatures, Wardell gave up his drive. Then, in January 1932, the Crusaders and the WONPR began a new public petition drive—the Red, White and Blue Petition—which, unlike Wardell's proposals, provided for the repeal of the state prohibition law and the establishment of a state liquor control commission to regulate the alcoholic beverage traffic in the state and to set the standards regarding the legal percentage of alcohol in beverages. A major effort by the Crusaders and the WONPR resulted in the gathering of petitions containing 202,480 signatures by early April 1932. The petitions were presented to Secretary of State Frank Fitzgerald on the steps of the capitol building.

In a last-ditch effort to block the repeal referendum, the dry organizations in Michigan formed a joint Board of Strategy. The executive secretary of the board, Walter J. Hoshal, filed a petition with the state supreme court for the issuance of an order to prevent the proposed amendment from being placed before the voters. Hoshal's suit alleged that the state could not adopt the substitute amendment because it would violate the spirit and letter of the federal Constitution. Hoshal insisted at the same time that the drys were willing to go to the polls at any time to vote on an out-and-out wet-and-dry referendum that was legal. "We are fighting the present proposed amendment because it is illegal and defies the Constitution of the United States," he explained. The state supreme court, however, refused to act on Hoshal's petition, which meant that the state electorate would be given the opportunity of expressing itself on the repeal issue in the fall election.

As they prepared for the showdown with the forces of repeal, the state's leading dry organizations found themselves in even more difficult straits than the repeal groups. Also, when the Anti-Saloon League and the WCTU sought to mobilize the voters of Michigan in defense of prohibition, it became apparent how much they had alienated many of their former supporters. The two organizations proved so ineffective in the emergency that special ad hoc dry campaign committees were organized to fill the power vacuum created by the decline of the established dry organizations.

The most dramatic loss of influence by a dry organization was that suffered by the Anti-Saloon League. Immediately following the passage of the Eighteenth Amendment there had been a sharp decrease in the pledges to the national league, resulting, its officials concluded, from the common belief that the prohibition battle had been won once and for all. In the five years between 1920 and 1926, funds of the Anti-Saloon League of America decreased drastically, until by the end of the decade the financial position of the organization was desperate. When league fund raiser Howard H. Russell sought the usual large donation from Detroit businessman Joseph Boyer in 1928, he was turned down. "I am sorry to come to the conclusion that there is something incompatible with man's relation to prohibition," Boyer wrote at the time. "I am thoroughly discouraged over the outlook. I do not mean that you are on the wrong side, but it does appear to me that you are on the losing side, and what is the use of playing a losing game knowingly?" Three years later, Ernest Cherrington, a leading national officer of the league, wrote that he had been "hoping for weeks that . . . finances would improve, but our financial situation seems to be rapidly getting worse instead of better. . . . I have never found conditions quite as bad as they are and many of our best friends are in such position they cannot even pay their old subscriptions past due, to say nothing about giving any special help. . . . As you probably know, the salaries of many of the men . . . are back for several months. In some cases they are back for a year. . . . Frankly, I have never known a more difficult time from the financial point of view . . . and the prospects for the future are not very bright."

Michigan Anti-Saloon League Superintendent R. N. Holsaple, in the midst of this crisis, optimistically announced plans to restructure the state league in order to increase its effectiveness in the struggle with the forces of repeal. Yet, while he was publicly mouthing optimistic predictions, he was privately struggling to keep the state league solvent. In January 1931, Holsaple sent a confidential letter to various large contributors to the league stating that "the negative business situation has reacted disastrously to our work." He disclosed that over $100,000 was past due the league in unpaid pledges and that in December 1930, for the first time in the history of the league in Michigan, the organization had lacked the necessary funds to publish the monthly Michigan edition of the *American Issue*. "We have gone to the limit in economizing," Holsaple warned. "Much needed workers have been let go and expenses cut wherever possible." Now, Holsaple said, "something heroic has to be done or the Michigan Anti-Saloon League will have to shut up shop." He asked those who had made pledges to pay the promptly. If the entire pledge could not be paid, he asked that at least some portion of it be forwarded immediately. "Nothing but the greatest need would prompt me to write this letter," he concluded, "and I trust you will accept it in the spirit of helpfulness and generosity."

About the time of Holsaple's appeal, F. Scott McBride, general superintendent of the Anti-Saloon League of America, told a league convention in Detroit that the growing popularity of the wet organizations had actually helped the dry cause by bringing many former members back into the fold. "Our organization," he lied, "finds itself in a better position today than ever before. Despite the financial depression, our financial statement is favorable and in general we are in about the position we were just before prohibition was enacted." McBride predicted that in November, "if I'm any judge, we're going to win back every one of those lost districts and give the wets such an answer as will stand for all time."

Yet the future of prohibition continued to look grim. Billy Sunday's 1932 Evangelistic Crusade in Detroit, instead of firing up voters in favor of prohibition simply demonstrated how enthusiasm and prestige had fled the dry camp. Sunday's 1916 crusade had not only been the high point of the prohibition drive but also one of the most exciting events in the city's history. By 1932, however, the mood of the city toward the evangelist had changed drastically. No large crowds greeted Sunday at the train depot in 1932, and no special tabernacle was built to house the meetings of the old-time preacher of the old-time gospel. A more restrained Sunday spoke at the Metropolitan Methodist Episcopal Church, his sermons lacked the fire and timeliness that had characterized them earlier, and the crowds were neither very large nor enthusiastic. Sunday reassured his listeners, nevertheless, that "the people of this country are going to knock the liquor traffic straight to hell, where it belongs," and he insisted, "you'll never see the Eighteenth Amendment repealed on God's earth. All we got to do is hold twelve of our forty-seven [sic] states to keep America dry," and that, he said, would be simple. The real trouble with prohibition, Sunday reasoned, was that "a bunch of low-down crooks in official positions . . . don't want to enforce the law." He predicted that Hoover would be reelected and would carry Michigan by a large majority. Sunday closed by calling the repealists "the worst crowd of God foresaken cut throats this side of hell, and if I was God for half an hour they wouldn't be this side." But who was listening to this kind of rhetoric now? The evangelist's bullying made little impression in a depressed world, and his preaching illustrated that the dry cause was in danger of being smothered by the illusions of its most outspoken supporters.

The WCTU stood by the Anti-Saloon League and promised to

fight the good fight for bone-dry prohibition. The organization, however, had lost both members and influence during the depression,
and it no longer had the power and prestige that it enjoyed before
1916. The state president felt compelled to ask WCTU members in
1932 to "quit feeling poor and quit putting off subscribing to the
Michigan Union and the *Union Signal!*"

The summer of 1931 witnessed the emergence of two new important dry organizations—the Allied Forces and the Allied Women.
Leaders of these groups declared that they did not wish to divide the
dry crusade but wanted simply to conduct a prohibition campaign
along the lines they thought most effective. Some leaders of the
Allied Forces were so confident that prohibition would win in a
public referendum that they pushed for a showdown with the wets
by endorsing the state referendum. Among the nationally prominent
sponsors of the new organizations were William G. McAdoo, Gifford
Pinchot, Thomas Edison, and Jane Addams.

The most active and vibrant dry organization formed in the last
months of the fight against repeal was the Michigan Youth Council
on Prohibition, made up of students from high schools and junior
high schools in the state. The Youth Council was formed by Mrs.
Truman Newberry in early 1932 to aid in the November election.
The Youth Council petitioned the Detroit Board of Education for a
reintroduction of textbooks that pointed out the physiological dangers of alcohol consumption, but the board refused even to consider
the request, explaining that the texts had been distorted in their
presentation of the facts. In the fall of 1932 the Allied Youth held a
mammoth rally on the steps of the state capitol in Lansing and
pledged support for the Constitution, the Eighteenth Amendment,
and the prohibition laws. Over seven thousand members of the
organization gathered in front of the capitol and took a temperance
pledge administered by the prohibitionist lieutenant governor,
Luren Dickinson. The Youth Council also introduced something
new into the prohibition camp in 1932—humor. The Youth Council
put on skits in which they mocked the excesses of both wets and
drys, but at the same time urged their audience to support prohibition and the Eighteenth Amendment.

In addition to revitalizing the old prohibition organizations and
establishing new ones, the drys, like the wets, sought endorsements
by leading public figures. The best-known businessman to lend his

prestige to the prohibition cause at this time was Henry Ford. In an interview with Samuel Crowther of the *Ladies Home Journal* in 1930, Ford contended that prohibition was a moral issue "because it is economically right. We know that anything which is economically right is also morally right," Ford reasoned in his sometimes peculiar manner. "There can be no conflict between good economics and good morals; in fact the one cannot exist without the other." Ignoring the fact that the illicit liquor industry was the second largest enterprise in the state, Ford restated the hackneyed dry argument that prosperity was built upon the abolition of the liquor traffic. "Our present industrial system simply cannot work with liquor," Ford said. "We must choose between drink and poverty on the one hand and prohibition and prosperity on the other." Ford seemed oblivious to the reality that the nation had prohibition and poverty in 1930.

When Crowther appeared before a special House Judiciary Committee in the spring of 1930 he read messages from both Ford and Thomas Edison strongly supporting the Eighteenth Amendment. While Ford's statement predicted that "the sane people of the nation" would never let the Eighteenth Amendment be repealed or be weakened by "any dangerous modification," it was Edison's opinion that "prohibition is the greatest experiment yet made to benefit man. My observation is that its enforcement generally is at least 60 percent and is gaining, notwithstanding the impression through false propaganda that it is a lower percent. It is strange to me that some men of great ability and standing do not help remove the curse of alcohol."

III

The Democratic state convention met in September 1930, just two weeks after the primary elections in which two leading dry Republican congressmen of the state had been defeated by wets. Never before had it been so clear that public sentiment on the wet-dry issue was shifting. Prohibition was the issue upon which the Democrats might ride to victory. With the promise of victory, the drys within the state party were silenced. The assembled delegates unanimously adopted a platform calling for a nationwide referendum on the Eighteenth Amendment. "The Democratic party in Michigan," the resolution stated, "recommends as a direction to Congress and the states a nationwide referendum on repeal of the Eighteenth Amendment in a separate election dealing with the question alone."

The state Republican party, on the other hand, remained staunchly behind the Eighteenth Amendment and the existing prohibition laws. The bone-dry state attorney general, Wilbur Brucker, was nominated as the party's gubernatorial candidate. Fred Green told the party convention that prohibition was a social and not a political question and should therefore not be discussed by the party.

After receiving the Demcoratic party's gubernatorial nomination, William A. Comstock went beyond the party declaration in favor of a referendum and endorsed outright repeal of the Eighteenth Amendment. In an address before the Exchange Club of Warren, Comstock confessed that he had never been in favor of national prohibition, and called for control of the liquor traffic by the states. "It is something that was put over on the people," Comstock said of national prohibition, "and should never have been permitted to get into the Constitution." Unlike state prohibition, he declared, national prohibition had been forced upon the people of Michigan after they had already eliminated the saloon. "The situation is ten times worse than it ever was in the wet days," he contended. "Yes, hundreds of times worse." Comstock promised, if elected, to request the legislature to petition Congress for repeal of the Eighteenth Amendment and to seek state and national referenda on the issue.

In the general election in November, Comstock carried only three counties. Brucker was elected governor, and Dickinson, the outstanding political prohibitionist in the state, was reelected lieutenant governor. The voters of the state, clearly, were not yet ready for Comstock and his bold stand against prohibition.

The repealists, nevertheless, continued their agitation, and following the election, dissident wet voices were heard even within the ranks of the victorious Republican party. The Wayne County Women's Club went on record in favor of the repeal of the Eighteenth Amendment, and a few weeks later the North End Republican Club of Detroit adopted a resolution favoring repeal of prohibition as an incentive to prosperity and a curb on crime. Republican repealists became more and more outspoken in their fear that if the party did not endorse at least a popular referendum on prohibition, it would be defeated in 1932. As a result, after months of debate and maneuvering and bargaining, in the spring of 1932 the state GOP endorsed a national referendum on the Eighteenth Amendment.

Repeal sentiment intensified within the Democratic party also. At the state party convention in Flint in 1931 the Democrats reaffirmed their 1930 stand in favor of a nationwide referendum on prohibition. In December 1931 the Detroit Democratic Club unanimously endorsed a resolution assailing prohibition and adopted "Roosevelt and Repeal" as the club's slogan.

The midsummer national party conventions in 1932 added to the continuing drama of the wet-and-dry battle. The Democrats wrote a repeal plank into their platform and nominated Franklin D. Roosevelt of New York, a repealist. Following his nomination, candidate Roosevelt announced that "from this date on, the Eighteenth Amendment is doomed." The Republicans, on the other hand, endorsed a moist plank, calling for resubmission of the Eighteenth Amendment to the states and maintenance by the federal government of the power to protect dry territory and prevent the return of the saloon. The Detroit *Free Press* commented that the Republicans, at best, offered only a modified form of national prohibition. Despite their endorsement of a referendum on the prohibition question, the Michigan Republicans renominated bone-dry incumbent Brucker to oppose the wet William Comstock in the gubernatorial race. In the campaign of 1932, both nationally and locally, the Republicans were the party of the drys, and the Democrats the party of the wets.

The election of November 8, 1932, resulted in a resounding victory for the Democratic party and for repeal. For the first time since 1852 Michigan gave its electoral vote to the Democratic presidential candidate, and the entire Democratic slate for state office was swept into power. Lieutenant Governor Dickinson was defeated by the wet Allen E. Stebbins by nearly eighty thousand votes.

In the gubernatorial race, Comstock, who had joined the Crusaders in January 1931, and who had the endorsement of both the AAPA and the WONPR, triumphed over the incumbent Wilbur Brucker by 190,637 votes and carried forty-three counties to Brucker's forty. Comstock's victory came because of his majority in the most populous industrial counties of Wayne, Kent, Genesee, Saginaw, Oakland, St. Clair, and Macomb. In fact, Comstock's majority in Wayne County gave him the election: While Comstock carried Wayne County by 190,727 votes, Brucker carried the rest of the state by 90 votes.

On the question of the establishment of a state liquor control commission and the repeal of state prohibition, Wayne County gave repeal a majority of 309,364, while the rest of the state voted repeal by a majority of 237,879. As the repealists pointed out following the election, had Wayne County's vote not even been counted in 1932, repeal would still have carried Michigan.

It is impossible to separate the influence of prohibition and depression upon the behavior of Michigan voters in 1932 or to draw any concrete conclusions regarding which of the two was more important in determining the outcome of the election. To do so would be to ignore the principal thrust of two and one-half years of repeal propaganda in the state. High employment, low taxes, and repeal had been welded together into a winning combination by the wets. A vote for repeal was a vote for recovery, a vote for a new deal in liquor as well as in politics. Try as they might, the drys had been unable to pry these issues apart.

In viewing the wreck of his beloved dry cause following the election, R. N. Holsaple of the Anti-Saloon League concluded that the drys had faced an impossible task in 1932. "All the psychology was against us," he said. "The voters were in an unreasonable and unreasoning state of mind. Whatever is, is wrong, was their slogan. That feeling defeated us," he insisted, "just as it defeated President Hoover and Governor Brucker." Holsaple contended that had the drys remained true to the bone-dry cause and not considered modification, they would have received more votes. Because many of them adopted a moderate stand, he thought, the entire dry cause lost both the respect and the votes of many former prohibitionists. Later, Holsaple remembered November 8, 1932, and concluded, "It was a sad day for the 'ins.' We were 'in,' therefore, we suffered." Henry Joy, on the other hand, concluded that prohibition had indeed been the major issue of 1932. "Prohibition totally broke the back of the Republican party," he wrote to Senator Arthur Vandenburg following the election. "If we had had good times," he concluded, "my opinion is that the Republican party's attitude on prohibition would have broken its back and thrown it out of office."

IV

Within a few days of taking office, Governor Comstock initiated action to revise the prohibition laws of Michigan in accordance with the expressed wishes of the voters. On January 23 he appointed a special bipartisan committee of seventeen persons drawn from all parts of the state to advise him regarding liquor legislation. While the governor and his advisory committee deliberated, Congress submitted the Twenty-first Amendment, which repealed the Eighteenth Amendment, to special conventions in each state. On April 3, 1933, Michigan voters went to the polls to select one delegate from each state legislative district to attend a convention on April 10 to consider ratification of the Twenty-first Amendment. The inordinate rural representation in the legislative districting of Michigan was of no aid to the prohibitionists, and the election resulted in an overwhelming majority for the wets, who won ninety-nine of the one hundred seats at stake. Eugene Davenport of Hastings was the single dry delegate elected to the convention.

On April 10, the delegates convened in Lansing and elected Mrs. Mary Alger of Detroit president of the convention. Davenport did not vote in the selection of the president. After a short address by Governor Comstock, the delegates voted ninety-nine to one to ratify the Twenty-first Amendment. By this action Michigan became the first state to vote for the repeal of the Eighteenth Amendment.

On April 4, following the wet victory of the preceeding day, Governor Comstock sent the legislature a bill to make 3.2 percent beer and wine freely available in all parts of Michigan except in those counties that exempted themselves under new local-option provisions. The bill defined 3.2 percent alcoholic beverages as non-intoxicating. In addition to imposing substantial license fees on manufacturers and dealers, the bill set a tax of $1.25 a barrel on all beer or wine manufactured or sold in the state. Part of the revenue was to be distributed among local governments. In an attempt to prevent the return of the old-time saloon, the bill forbade the use of bars, the serving of persons not seated at a table, and the giving away of either food or drink. The measure provided not only for the sale of 3.2 percent beer and wine in restaurants, hotels, clubs, dining cars, and the dining rooms of passenger ships, but also for the establishment of something new in Michigan—the beer garden. The word "garden" was defined simply as a retail establishment partly enclosed, selling beer to persons seated at tables. The gardens were authorized to dispense food as well as beer.

While the Senate debated the Comstock bill, legal beer returned to nineteen states and the District of Columbia. Finally, after increasing pressure was exerted by the governor, the Senate passed the beer bill in mid-April and sent it to the House, which approved the measure on April 20.

The legislature set May 11 at 6:00 P.M. as the day and hour when beer and wine could once again be sold legally in Michigan. A special exemption provided for the sale of beer at a victory celebration of the American Legion in Detroit on the night of May 10. At the legion celebration, nearly three hundred half barrels and five hundred cases of beer were consumed by ten thousand celebrants in eight hours. The Stroh Brewery of Detroit provided the brew, Julius Stroh poured the first glass of legal beer in Michigan in fifteen years, and police officers on duty outside the celebration reported that all the drinkers were good-natured. The next evening beer went on sale to the general public throughout the state. In Detroit large crowds attended special celebrations arranged by many of the downtown hotels and restaurants and the new beer gardens. The press was surprised to find that the celebrants were restrained and that the New Year's Eve atmosphere that marked many celebrations in the dry twenties was absent. Reporters noted that Detroiters, like drinkers in the rest of the state, seemed to be taking legal beer in stride.

The legalization of 3.2 beer and wine was only a temporary measure, however, and within ten months the Comstock administration had legalized strong beer and distilled spirits. The state legislature approved laws establishing a state liquor monopoly and provided for special state liquor stores to make all original sales of hard liquor and wine at a maximum gross profit of 40 percent. Although the new measures provided for the legal sale of strong beer and hard liquor beginning December 15, state liquor stores did not open until December 30. The first whisky to be sold out in Detroit's liquor stores on the evening of December 30 was the cheapest— Snug Harbor—at seventy-five cents a bottle.

Repeal was successful in returning legalized liquor to the drinker, but none of the temperance and anti-depression promises of the repealists were realized. The year 1933 witnessed the darkest days of the depression, and during the winter of 1933–34 thousands of the state's unemployed were saved not by booze production but by CWA jobs. Reviewing changes in Michigan since the advent of legal hard liquor, the Detroit *News* in August 1934 found little ground for optimism. Repeal had provided jobs for only twenty-five thousand persons in the state, and indirectly probably for several thousand more, the paper estimated. It had meant at least $50 million worth of business annually and provided more than $17,800,000 in taxes and public revenue. Although the blind pig had been driven further underground, bootlegging had been reduced by only 20 percent, according to the *News*. And everywhere there appeared disturbing signs. The paper pointed out that traffic accidents attributed to drunk drivers or drunk pedestrians had more than doubled during the first year of hard liquor in Michigan, and it complained that liquor prices were too high and that the quality of booze dispensed by the state liquor stores was poor. The drys, as expected, contended that conditions after repeal "eclipse the darkest days of the old saloon." The wets answered that the statistics were unreliable indications of the success of repeal because the wave of excessive drinking would gradually subside as the novelty of legalized liquor wore off. The battle of statistics continued down through the thirties, but the public had lost interest after a quarter of a century of debates on the subject. The public did not lose interest in liquor, however, as the repealists suggested they might.

Lewis L. Bredin of the Crusaders was severely critical of Comstock's liquor measures and characterized the first year of repeal in Michigan as a mess. The legislature had carelessly passed a "hodge-podge law," Bredin contended, and he complained that the personnel who staffed the State Liquor Control Commission were political appointees unqualified for their jobs. According to Bredin, Michigan was getting low-quality liquor at high prices. The commission was supposed to encourage the drinking of beer and wine to offset consumption of distilled liquor, but it was impossible to get good wine in the state liquor stores. Moreover, Bredin said, the 40 percent markup in the state liquor stores played into the hands of the bootleggers, who could supply a better quality of booze at lower prices.

Many of the initial problems of the new liquor control system in Michigan were the product of the emphasis upon revenue and recovery rather than upon temperance—a legacy, in other words, of the repeal campaign of 1929–1932. State employees in the new state liquor stores, like the much-criticized prohibition agents in the mid-1920s, were handpicked by politicians and were dependent for their jobs on good sales performances. They were exempt from civil service examinations. Because liquor prices were high, bootleggers and rumrunners again found it profitable to carry on their Canadian-American trade. It sounded like the mid-1920s all over again when Frank Picard, chairman of the Liquor Control Commission, announced a six-point "extermination campaign" against bootleggers in 1934. He appealed to President Roosevelt, federal authorities, and the state police to assist him in his campaign. Secretary of the Treasury Henry Morgenthau stated in the same year that Detroit topped all other American cities in the sale of illicit bootleg liquor. He estimated that two thousand cases of fraudulently labeled Canadian whisky were sold each week in Detroit. Morgenthau increased the number of federal revenue agents in Detroit from twenty-four to sixty and authorized numerous wiretaps to gather evidence against rumrunners. When questioned about the complaints concerning the wiretaps, Morgenthau reminded reporters, "You can't get these people in a sissy manner." The activities of Picard and Morgenthau, as the drys pointed out, were clear evidence that repeal was not working. The public, however, seemed uninterested in the whole mess.

Eventually, by a slow process of trial and error, the problems of the Liquor Control Commission were resolved—but the problems of liquor persisted. Prices of booze went down, quality went up, and the state monopoly proved financially profitable. By 1955 the state's liquor operations had become a $200 million a year business. Once again, booze was second only to automobiles in the commerce of Michigan.

V

The Anti-Saloon League of Michigan never recovered from the depression and repeal. On November 17, 1934, the organization went into receivership in Circuit Court in Lansing. The league listed fifty-four creditors with claims totaling $16,184.00, and its only assets were pledges of doubtful legality totaling $9,055.66. Yet the organization lingered on as a haunting reminder of what it had once been. In late 1934, Howard H. Russell sent out hundreds of letters to former Anti-Saloon League contributors, requesting financial aid again because "evidence from all directions indicates that the tide is beginning to turn." "A Second Dry War Is On," Russell believed. The next year the general superintendent of the league, F. Scott McBride, predicted that prohibition would be back within ten years. But the Michigan league couldn't wait that long. In September 1941 the Anti-Saloon League went out of business in Michigan and was replaced by a new and equally impotent organization, the Michigan Temperance Federation.

Ironically, the league was preceded in death by the organizations that had led the fight for repeal—the AAPA, the Crusaders, and the WONPR. Since the AAPA had been founded primarily to effect the repeal of the Eighteenth Amendment, it seemed logical that it should be dissolved with the realization of its objective. Several AAPA leaders, however, had different ideas. In October 1933, William Stayton, founder of the AAPA, wrote Henry B. Joy that it seemed to him that the personnel of the organization should not be permitted to disband, "but just how we ought to keep them together and what we ought to say is our ultimate purpose, or how far we ought to be specific and how far we ought to be indefinite are matters that concern me deeply—and these are matters on which, old Harry, I need your careful thought and earnest advice." Stayton thought that the campaign pursued by Joy throughout the 1920s stressing loyalty and the separation of church and state might be taken up by the organization, but he thought there was a more important issue to which the AAPA might address itself—the New Deal. Roosevelt was sure to attempt an extension of the National Industrial Recovery Act, Stayton thought, and perhaps the AAPA could be held together through opposition to the NIRA and other New Deal measures. Despite Stayton's desire to keep the AAPA going, the board of directors at a meeting on November 16, 1933, authorized the president of the organization to take all steps neces-sary for the immediate dissolution of the AAPA. Accordingly, on

December 31, 1933, the AAPA went out of business and sent its files to the Library of Congress.

In August 1934 a new organization, the American Liberty League, was formed from the remnants of the AAPA and the Crusaders in order "to defend and uphold the Constitution, to teach the necessity of respect for the rights of persons and property as fundamental to every successful form of government . . . to teach the duty of government, to encourage and protect individual and group initiative and enterprise, to foster the right to work, earn, save, and acquire property, and to preserve the ownership and lawful use of property when acquired." The American Liberty League formally adopted as its primary political goal the defeat of the man who had presided over the repeal of the Eighteenth Amendment, Franklin D. Roosevelt. The failure of the organization to defeat Roosevelt in 1936 led to its decline and eventual dissolution in 1940.

During the repeal campaign, Fred Clark, founder of the Crusaders, had assured his followers that "the biggest job confronting the Crusaders will begin when the Dry Law ends." "Continuous agitation for temperance is the price we must pay for a sober nation," Clark believed. And for a short time after the successful ratification of the Twenty-first Amendment Clark and his group did make half-hearted efforts to see that "sane" liquor legislation was passed in state legislatures and to convince Americans that intemperance was harmful to individual as well as to social health. But the Crusaders were hurt by the same type of apathy that eroded dry groups after 1920: With the triumph of the immediate objective, most of the enthusiasm and sense of crisis and crusade escaped the movement, and its followers sought new campaigns or rest. Clark, on the other hand, saw looming on the horizon a danger to the American Way of Life far greater than intemperance. The incipient monster called itself the New Deal. At first Clark feared that the New Deal's abandonment of the gold standard would lead shortly to socialism. "Inflation flies in the face of economic law as much as prohibition did in the face of moral law," he warned. The Crusaders forgot about temperance preaching and merged with the American Liberty League to defeat the New Deal menace. When this failed, Clark continued carrying on his mission of saving the nation. In late

1939 Clark organized the American Economic Foundation, and characterized the work of the group as "the job of selling to all Americans the system that made them the most productive and prosperous of peoples." When Clark died in 1973, at the age of eighty-two, the foundation was still on the job.

The WONPR ineffectively assumed many of the tasks undertaken earlier by the WCTU. At the annual meeting of the WONPR in 1934, a special resolution was passed committing the organization to pursue a program of temperance education, with a new approach based on modern scientific research and "character building" as its major objectives. The national organization of the WONPR disappeared, but the Women's Organization for Non-Partisan Reform, headed Mrs. Fred Alger, carried on temperance work in Michigan. This WONPR pledged itself to "work for proper liquor control and the eduction of the people of the state for temperance." But the necessary enthusiasm and crusading spirit were gone. The organization disappeared in the early 1940s.

VI

Personalities associated with prohibition continued to haunt Michigan for many years. In July 1933, for example, Fred Palm was paroled from prison. He told reporters that he hoped to open a small barbershop somewhere and to make something of his life.

Detroit's last prohibition case was not formally removed from the Recorder's Court docket until June 4, 1952. Until that time, Daniel Hines had been more or less a fugitive from justice since he had jumped bond in 1931 following an arrest for illegal possession of a pint of liquor. In 1952 Hines was arrested for assault and battery, and a routine fingerprint check revealed that he was wanted on a warrant issued on July 2, 1931. Recorder's Court Judge W. M. Skillman dismissed the prohibition charge against Hines.

Memories of the dry decade were revived once again on June 1, 1957, when planking from the Canadian steam tug Maude, believed to be more than eighty years old, was retrieved at the foot of West Grand Boulevard, where marine contractors were contructing a new city dock. Crane operators doing the dredging and piling work were unable to lift the remains of the tug, which was buried in silt under fifteen feet of water. The tug had sunk in 1923 with a load of Canadian beer aboard; some of the beer aboard the tug was now brought to the surface and helped to slake the thirst of several dockworkers.

Then, in the summer of 1967, it became glaringly apparent once again that many problems involving the sale and consumption of liquor were still unresolved. In March of that year a blind pig opened for business on Twelfth Street in the Virginia Park section of Detroit. The proprietors of the pig named the establishment the "United Community League for Civic Action." The Detroit police were advised of the activities in the establishment by an informant, and on the morning of July 23, 1967, decided to raid it. After a plainclothes officer was admitted to the pig and succeeded in making a buy, four uniformed police officers using sledgehammers pounded down the door, announced a raid, and placed nearly eighty patrons under arrest. A crowd gathered outside the pig as the police escorted the customers into several paddy wagons and squad cars. As the last police car was pulling away, somebody hurled a beer bottle through its window. That was the signal for the start of four and one-half days of burning, looting, and killing in Detroit. One of the first actions taken by Governor George Romney in the crisis was the closing of all bars and liquor stores in Detroit and the surrounding area, a step with which the old prohibitionists—if there were any still around—would heartily have agreed, and one that indicated that many of the arguments of the prohibitionists against liquor were true. The day, however, when the state would concern itself more with the problems than with the profits of liquor lay in the distant future. Until that day arrived, the concerns and hopes of an earlier generation—a generation that voted for a better world through prohibition in 1916 and 1919, and then for a better world through repeal in 1932 and 1933—would remain embarrassing reminders of human aspiration and failure.

Sources

INTEMPERANCE: THE LOST WAR AGAINST LIQUOR

General

The most useful manuscript source for this study was the "Temperance and Prohibition Papers" of the Michigan Historical Collections (MHC) located at the University of Michigan in Ann Arbor. The papers include reports of numerous organizations active in the fight for and against prohibition along with the private papers of dozens of individuals engaged in the dry struggle. "The Michigan Union," official organ of the state Women's Christian Temperance Union, is available for the years 1895–1934 in the MHC as are the volumes of the *Michigan Manual*, the annual reports of the Michigan State Legislature.

The Graduate Library of the University of Michigan has a complete set of the yearbooks for both the Anti-Saloon League of America and the United States Brewers Association. The complete set of the monthly periodical *State Trooper*, a periodical for the Michigan State Police, is also available in the university's Graduate Library.

In Washington, D.C., the papers of the United States Coast Guard and of the United States Treasury Department were made available to me at the National Archives. In the Library of Congress the papers of the Association Against the Prohibition Amendment and of Senator James Couzens proved valuable sources of information.

In Evanston, Illinois, the national library of the Women's Christian Temperance Union made available to me the annual reports of both the national WCTU and the state branches of the organization. I was also given the use of the rich collection of rare temperance and prohibition books preserved in the library.

The Burton Historical Collection in the Detroit Public Library includes the *Annual Reports of the City of Detroit, 1920–1930* and the papers of the mayors of the city for the prohibition years.

For the day-to-day developments in the war against liquor I relied very heavily upon the major newspapers of Detroit. The clipping file of the Detroit *News* was made available to me and proved to be very useful in tracking the course of the anti-liquor movement in Michigan after 1933. The Detroit *Saturday Night*, a weekly in the 1920s and 1930s is available on microfilm as are the complete files of the *News* and the Detroit *Free Press*. In places in this study I also relied upon the Detroit *Times* and on several outstate papers listed in subsequent chapter divisions.

There have been dozens of books of high quality dealing with the prohibition experiment in general or with personalities from the prohibition years. The first good analysis of the prohibition phenomenon was *The Dry Decade* (New York, 1932) by Charles Merz. The facts provided by Merz are still very useful for researchers digging for facts about the war against liquor. John Allen Krout, *The Origins of Prohibition* (New York, 1925), provides a history of the anti-liquor movement through the adoption of the Eighteenth Amendment. Ernest Cherrington (ed.), *The Standard Encyclopedia of the Alcohol Problem* (Westerville, Ohio, 1924–1928), 6 volumes, is a massive gathering of facts on the origins and the final victories of the temperance movement. The study reflects the opinion of its sponsor, the Anti-Saloon League of America.

The best of the more recent general studies of prohibition include Andrew Sinclair, *Era of Excess: A Social History of the Prohibition Movement* (Boston, 1962); John Kobler, *Ardent Spirits: The Rise and Fall of Prohibition* (New York, 1973); J. C. Furnas, *The Life and Times of the Late Demon Rum* (New York, 1965); Norman Clark, *Deliver Us From Evil: An Interpretation of American Prohibition* (New York, 1976); and a lively biographical approach to prohibition, Thomas M. Coffey, *The Long Thirst: Prohibition in America* (New York, 1975). Herbert Asbury's *The Great Illusion: An Informal History of Prohibition* (New York, 1950) also remains a useful source of information.

Sections from the following books also provided important information and interpretations of prohibition: Frederick Lewis Allen, *Only Yesterday: An Informal History of the 1920's* (New York, 1931); Frederick Lewis Allen, *Since Yesterday: The Nineteen Thirties in America* (New York, 1940); Paul Carter, *Another Part of the Twenties* (New York, 1977); Paul Carter, *The Twenties in America* (New York, 1968); William E. Leuchtenburg, *The Perils of Prosperity, 1914–1932* (Chicago, 1958); John Braeman, Robert H. Bremner, and David Brody (eds.), *Change and Continuity in Twentieth Century America: The 1920's* (Columbus, Ohio, 1968); David Burner, *The Politics of Provincialism: The Democratic Party in Transition, 1918–1932* (New York, 1968); Kenneth Allsop, *The Bootleggers and Their Era* (Garden City, N.Y., 1961); and Isabel Leighton (ed.), *The Aspirin Age, 1919–1941* (New York, 1949).

Various state studies are also available and provide a source of comparison with events in Michigan during prohibition. The best of these studies are: Gilman Ostrander, *The Prohibition Movement in California, 1848–1933* (Berkeley, 1957); Norman Clark, *The Dry Years: Prohibition and Social Change in Washington* (Seattle, 1965); Paul E. Isaac, *Prohibition and Politics: Turbulent Decades in Tennessee, 1885–1920* (Knoxville, 1965); Lewis L. Gould, *Progressives and Prohibitionists: Texas Democrats in the Wilson Era* (Austin, 1973); C. C. Pearson and J. Edwin Hendricks, *Liquor and Anti-Liquor in Virginia, 1619–1919* (Durham, 1967); James B. Sellers, *The Prohibition Movement in Alabama, 1702 to 1943* (Chapel Hill, 1943); Daniel J. Whitener, *Prohibition in North Carolina, 1715–1945* (Chapel Hill, 1945); William Elliott West, "Dry Crusade: The Prohibition Movement in Colorado, 1858–1933" (Ph.D. thesis, University of Colorado, 1971), and G. K. Kenner, "Prohibition Comes to Missouri, 1910–1919," *Missouri Historical Review*, LXII (July 1968), 363–97.

Two recent articles providing new interpretations of prohibition are J. C. Burnham, "New Perspectives on the Prohibition 'Experiment' of the 1920'," *Journal of Social History*, II (Fall 1968), 51–68; and Joseph R. Gusfield, "Prohibition: The Impact of Political Utopianism," in John Braeman, Robert H. Bremner, and David Brody (eds.), *Change and Continuity in Twentieth Century America: The 1920's* (Columbus, Ohio, 1968).

Chapter 1: Dry Dreams

Books

Donald Barr Chidsey, *On and Off the Wagon: A Sober Analysis of the Temperance Movement from the Pilgrims to Prohibition* (New York, 1969); Malcolm Bingay, *Of Me I Sing* (New York, 1949); Raymond L. Calkins, *Substitutes For the Saloon* (Boston, 1919); George Ade, *The Old Time Saloon: Not Wet, Not Dry, Just History* (New York, 1931); Chase S. Osborn, *The Iron Hunter* (New York, 1919); Jacob Riis, *How the Other Half Lives: Studies Among the Tenements of New York* (New York, 1914); Lilian Wald, *The House on Henry Street* (New York, 1915); Upton Sinclair, *The Jungle* (New York, 1906); Matthew Josephson, *Union House, Union Bar: The History of the Hotel and Restaurant Employees and Bartenders International Union AFL-CIO* (New York, 1956); Melvin G. Holli, *Reform in Detroit* (Chicago, 1969); Jane Addams, *The Second Twenty Years at Hull House: September, 1909 to September, 1929* (New York, 1930); John C. Lodge, *I Remember Detroit* (Detroit, 1949); Sinclair Lewis, *Main Street*

(New York, 1920); F. P. Weisenberger, *Triumph of Faith: Contributions of the Church to American Life* (Richmond, 1962); O. E. Rolvaag, *Giants in the Earth* (New York, 1927); Brand Whitlock, *The Little Green Shutter* (New York, 1931); Lewis Atherton, *Main Street on the Middle Border* (Bloomington, 1954); Donald Elder, *Ring Lardner* (Garden City, N.Y., 1956); Annie Wittenmyer, *The Womans' Crusade* (Philadelphia, 1878); J. S. Smart, *The Whiskey War in Adrian or the Trials and Triumphs of Prohibition in Lenawee County, Michigan* (Detroit, 1870); Stanley Baron, *Brewed in America: A History of Beer and Ale in the United States* (Boston, 1962); Thomas C. Cochran, *The Pabst Brewing Company: The History of An American Business* (New York, 1948); James Timberlake, *Prohibition and the Progressive Movement* (Cambridge, 1963); Peter Odegard, *Pressure Politics: The Story of the Anti-Saloon League* (New York, 1928); Glen Niemeyer, *The Automobile Career of Ransom E. Olds* (1963); Keith Sward, *The Legend of Henry Ford* (New York, 1948); William Allen White, *The Autobiography of William Allen White* (New York, 1946); Louis A. Banks, *Ammunition for the Final Drive on Booze: An Up to Date Arsenal for Prohibition Speakers* (New York, 1917); Reynold M. Wik, *Henry Ford and Grass Roots America* (Ann Arbor, 1973); Oscar G. Olander, *Michigan State Police: A Twenty Five Year History* (Lansing, 1942).

Articles

Larry Engelmann, "Billy Sunday: 'God, You've Got a Job on Your Hands in Detroit,' " *Michigan History*, LV (Spring 1971), 1–23; Jon M. Kingsdale, " 'The Poor Man's Club,' Social Functions of the Urban Working-Class Saloon," *American Quarterly*, XXV (October 1973), 485; Gerald Carson, "The Saloon," *American Heritage* (April 1963), pp. 24–31; Paul A. Carter, "Prohibition and Democracy: The Noble Experiment Reassessed," *Wisconsin Magazine of History*, 56 (Spring 1973), 192; George Kibbe Turner, "Beer and the City Liquor Problem," *McClure's Magazine*, XXXIII (September 1909), 531; Floyd B. Streeter, "Michigan Prohibition Legislation," *Michigan History*, II (April 1918), 302–4; John Fitzgibbon, "King Alcohol, His Rise, Reign and Fall in Michigan," *Michigan History*, II (October 1918), 768–73; Joseph Gusfield, "Social Structure and Moral Reform: A Study of the Women's Christian Temperance Union," *American Journal of Sociology*, LXI (November 1955), 221–32; Elmer Houser, "Wet or Dry?" *Michigan History Magazine* XIV (Spring 1930), 276–85; A. D. P. Van Buren, "Our Temperance Conflict," *Michigan Pioneer and Historical Collections* (Lansing, 1888), XIII, 388–407; Samuel Crowther, "Prohibition or Poverty: An Interview With Henry Ford," *Ladies Home Journal*, XLVII

(April 1930), 35, 225–26; "The Full Dinner Pail Takes a Crack at the Flowing Bowl in Lansing, Michigan," *Everybody's* XXXII (May 1915), 633; Harvey G. Furbay, "The Anti-Saloon League," *North American Review,* CLXXVII (September 1903), 437.

Newspapers

Detroit *News;* Detroit *Free Press;* Detroit *Times;* Detroit *Saturday Night;* New York *Times;* Detroit *Peninsular Herald;* Detroit *Advocate; The Center;* Grand Rapids *Press; Michigan Christian Advocate;* Lansing *State Journal;* Flint *Daily Journal;* Ann Arbor *Daily Times News;* Hastings *Banner.*

Documents

"The Election in Detroit: Billy Sunday," November 7, 1916, Detroit Citizens' League Papers, Correspondence Files, Box 3, Burton Historical Collection; "Digest of the Common Council," Burton Historical Collection; Detroit Temperance Society Papers, Burton Historical Collection; MS scrapbook, 1873–1876, Mrs. W. H. Turner Papers, Michigan Historical Collections; U.S. Congress, Senate, Subcommittee of the Committee on the Judiciary, "Brewing and Liquor Interests and German and Bolshevik Propaganda," 66th Cong., 1st Sess. (1919); James Couzens Papers, Library of Congress; Howard Hyde Russell Papers, Michigan Historical Collections.

Other

Nuala M. Drescher, "The Opposition to Prohibition, 1900–1919: A Social and Institutional Study" (Ph.D. thesis, University of Delaware, 1964); Samuel Unger, "A History of the Woman's Christian Temperance Union," (Ph.D. thesis, Ohio State University, 1933); Norman Harding Dohn, "The History of the Anti-Saloon League," (Ph.D. thesis, Ohio State University, 1959).

Chapter 2: The Cheerful Spring

Books

Francis Russell, *The Shadow of Blooming Grove: Warren G. Harding in His Times* (New York, 1968); Harry Barnard, *Independent Man: The Life of Senator James Couzens* (New York, 1958).

Articles

Frank B. Elser, "Keeping Detroit on the Water Wagon," *Outlook,* 121 (April 2, 1919), 560–67; "Michigan's 'Great Booze Rush' and Its Suppression by State and Federal Action," *Literary Digest,* LX (March 15, 1919), 85–90; "Michigan Stays Dry," *Survey,* 42 (May 10, 1919), 245–6; Winthrop D. Lane, "Prohibition: What Elimination of the Liquor Traffic Means to Grand Rapids," *Survey,* XLV (November 6, 1920), 138–238; Larry Engelmann, "Booze: The Ohio Connection, 1918–1919," *Detroit in Perspective: A Journal of Regional History* 2 (Winter 1975), 111–28.

Newspapers

Detroit *News;* Detroit *Free Press;* Detroit *Saturday Night;* Lansing *State Journal;* Grand Rapids *Press;* New York *Times;* Ann Arbor *Daily Times;* Adrian *Telegram; American Issue.*

Documents

James Couzens Papers, Library of Congress; Detroit Citizens League Papers, Burton Historical Collection.

Chapter 3: Across the River and into the Trees

Books

Gerald A. Hallowell, *Prohibition in Ontario* (Ottawa, 1972); Albert B. Corey, *Canadian American Relations Along the Detroit River* (Detroit, 1957); Alistair Moray, *The Diary of a Rum Runner* (London, 1929); Reginald W. Kauffman, *The Real Story of a Bootlegger* (New York, 1923); Robert Carse, *Rum Row* (New York, 1931); Merrill Donison, *The Barley and the Steam* (Toronto, 1955).

Articles

" 'Shooting' Detroit Bootleggers—With a Camera," *The Literary Digest*, LXXIX (December 29, 1923), 34–36; Richard DeBrisay, "Canada Turns Against Prohibition," *The Nation*, CXX (April 22, 1925), 460–62; "Canadian Press on Halting Rum Running From Canada," *The Literary Digest*, LXXIX (October 6, 1923), 20–21, 81–85; Morrow Mayo, "Rum Running on the Detroit River," *The Nation*, CXXIX (September 4, 1929), 42; Richard N. Kottman, "Volstead Violated: Prohibition as a Factor in Canadian American Relations," *Canadian Historical Review*, XLIII (June 1962), 108–20; Walter Liggett, "Michigan—Soused and Serene," *Plain Talk*, VI (March 1930), 270; Walter X. Brennan, "Rumble on the River," (n.d., n.p.): Arthur J. Tuttle, "Prohibition Enforcement from the Viewpoint of the Bench," *The Si-De-Ka Quarterly*, XI (April 1923), 297–304; Ben H. Spence, "Prohibitory Legislation in Canada," in T. Henry Walnut (ed.), *Prohibition and Its Enforcement* (Concord, N.H., 1923), pp. 260–64; Cyril D. Boyce, "Prohibition in Canada," in T. Henry Walnut (ed.), *Prohibition and Its Enforcement* (Concord, N.H., 1923), pp. 225–29; F. L. Smith, "War on the River," *Outlook and Independent* (July 24, 1929), pp. 507–9; *Living Age*, CCVI (August 28, 1920), 547–54.

Newspapers

Detroit *News*; Detroit *Free Press*; Detroit *Saturday Night*; Detroit *Times*; New York *Times*; Windsor *Star*.

Documents

Canadian Broadcasting Corporation, "Prohibition Broadcast," October 8, 1968; National Commission on Law Observance and Enforcement, Report on the Enforcement of the Prohibition Laws of the United States (Summary and 5 vols., 71st Cong., 3d Sess., 1931); James Couzens Papers, Library of Congress; Earl Michener Papers, Michigan Historical Collections; Henry B. Joy Papers, Michigan Historical Collections.

Chapter 4: A City Upon a Still: Prohibition in Detroit

Books

Malcolm Bingay, *Detroit is My Own Home Town* (New York, 1946); Izzy Einstein, *Prohibition Agent Number One* (New York, 1932); Charles Fenton, *The Apprenticeship of Ernest Hemingway: The Early Years* (New York, 1954); Kenneth Jackson, *The Ku Klux Klan in the City* (New York, 1967); Cash Asher, *Sacred Cows: A Story of the Recall of Mayor Bowles* (1931).

Articles

Sidney Glazer, "The 225th Anniversary: A Detroit Profile of 1926," *Michigan History*, 35 (June 1951), 151–60; Walter Liggett, "Michigan—Soused and Serene," *Plain Talk*, VI (March 1930), 257–73; Larry Engelmann, "A Separate Peace: The Politics of Prohibition Enforcement in Detroit, 1920–1930," *Detroit In Perspective*, I (Autumn 1972), 51–73; "Bootlegging and Murder in Detroit," *Literary Digest*, LXXVIII (September 29, 1923), 52; *American City Magazine*, XXII (January, 1925), 61.

Newspapers

Detroit *News;* Detroit *Free Press;* Detroit *Saturday Night;* New York *Times;* Detroit *Times.*

Documents

James Couzens Papers, Library of Congress; William A. Comstock Papers, Michigan Historical Collections.

Other

Maurice M. Ramsey, "Some Aspects of Non-Partisan Government in Detroit, 1919–1940" (Ph.D. thesis, University of Michigan, 1944); Gordon W. Davidson, "Industrial Detroit After World War I—1919–1921," (M.A. thesis, Wayne State University, 1953); Norman F. Weaver, "The Knights of the Ku Klux Klan in Wisconsin, Indiana, Ohio and Michigan" (Ph.D. thesis, University of Wisconsin, 1954).

Chapter 5: Prohibition in Action

Books

Frank Woodford, *Alex J. Groesbeck: Portrait of a Public Man* (Detroit, 1962); Constance C. Montgomery, *Hemingway in Michigan* (New York, 1966); Arthur Evans Wood, *Hamtramck: Then and Now: A Sociological Study of a Polish American Community* (New York, 1955); Clark Chambers, *Seedtime of Reform: Americal Social Service and Social Action, 1918–1933* (Minneapolis, 1964); Martha B. Bruere, *Does Prohibition Work: A Study of the Operation of the Eighteenth Amendment Made by the National Federation of Settlements Assisted by Social Workers in Different Parts of the United States* (New York, 1927); Clark Warburton, *The Economic Results of Prohibition* (New York, 1932); Charles Goshen, *Drink, Drugs and Do Gooders* (New York, 1973); Bruce Catton, *Waiting for the Morning Train: An American Boyhood* (Garden City, N.Y., 1972); Lewis Reiman, *Between the Iron and the Pine: A Biography of a Pioneer Family in a Pioneer Town* (Ann Arbor, 1951); Willis Frederick Dunbar, *Michigan:*

A History of the Wolverine State (Grand Rapids, 1965); George N. Fuller
(ed.), *Messages of the Governors of Michigan* (Lansing, 1925); Nicholas
Gage, *The Mafia Is Not an Equal Opportunity Employer* (New York, 1971);
Peter Maas, *The Valachi Papers* (New York, 1968); Ramsey Clark, *Crime
in America: Observations on Its Nature, Causes, Prevention and Control*
(New York, 1970); Samuel Marquis, *Henry Ford: An Interpretation* (Boston, 1923).

Articles

Ring Lardner, "Oh, Shoot!" *Colliers*, LXXXIV (August 10, 1929), 15;
"College Student Drinking Since Prohibition," *Literary Digest*, XC (July
10, 1926), 30–31; Larry Engelmann, "The Iron River Rum Rebellion,"
Mid-America, 55 (January 1973), 37–53

Newspapers

Detroit *News*; Detroit *Free Press*; Detroit *Saturday Night*; New York
Times; Escanaba *Daily Mirror*; *The Daily Mining Gazette* (Houghton and
Calumet).

Documents

National Commission on Law Observance and Enforcement, *Enforcement of Prohibition Laws of the United States* (Summary and 5 vols.), 71st
Cong., 3d Sess., 1930; U.S. Congress, House of Representatives, Committee of the Judiciary, "The Prohibition Amendment," 71st Cong., 2nd Sess.
(Washington, 1930); U.S. Congress, House of Representatives, "Amendment to the National Prohibition Act as Amended and Supplemented,"
68th Cong., 2d Sess. (Washington, 1925); U.S. Congress, Senate, Subcommittee on the Judiciary, "The National Prohibition Law," 69th Cong.,
1st Sess. (Washington, 1926); U.S. Congress, Senate, Subcommittee of the
Committee on the Judiciary, "Bureau of Prohibition" (Cramton Bill), 68th
Cong., 2nd Sess. (Washington, 1924); Lewis Cramton Papers, Michigan
Historical Collections; Earl C. Michener Papers, Michigan Historical Collections; Roy C. Vandercook Papers, Michigan Historical Collections;
William A. Comstock Papers, Michigan Historical Collections; James
Couzens Papers, Library of Congress; Iron River Junior Historical Society,
"The Rum Rebellion"; Canadian Broadcasting Corporation, "Prohibition
Broadcast," October 8, 1968.

Chapter 6: Prosperity, Liberty, and Lower Taxes: The Story of Repeal

Books

T. Henry Walnut (ed.), *Prohibition and Its Enforcement* (New York, 1923); George Wolfskill, *The Revolt of the Conservatives: A History of the American Liberty League, 1934–1940* (Boston, 1962); Leslie Gordon, *The New Crusade* (Cleveland, 1932); H. A. Brink, *The Michigan Plan of Federal, State and Local Liquor Regulation, Including State Internal Control* (Grand Rapids, 1932); Grace C. Root, *Women and Repeal: The Story of the Women's Organization For National Prohibition Reform* (New York, 1934); Joseph Lash, *Eleanor and Franklin: The Story of Their Relationship Based on Eleanor Roosevelt's Private Papers* (New York, 1971); Yandell Henderson, *A New Deal in Liquor: A Plea for Dilution* (New York, 1932); Al Kaufman, *A Special Report on the Michigan Liquor Control Commission* (Lansing, 1956); Michigan Liquor Study Committee, *Liquor Control or Chaos* (Lansing, 1940); William E. Leuchtenburg, *Franklin D. Roosevelt and the New Deal, 1932–1940* (New York, 1963); Van Gordon Sauter and Burleigh Hines, *Nightmare in Detroit: A Rebellion and Its Victims* (Chicago, 1968); Ernest Gordon, *The Wrecking of the Eighteenth Amendment* (Francestown, N.H., 1943); John Starr, *The Purveyor: The Shocking Story of Today's Illicit Liquor Empire* (New York, 1961); J. O. Monroe, *The End of Prohibition* (Collinsville, Ill., 1929); William G. McAdoo, *The Challenge: Liquor and Lawlessness versus Constitutional Government* (New York, 1928); James A. Reed, *The Rape of Temperance* (New York, 1931); Walter S. Foster, *The Saloon or So-Called Beer and Wine Amendment* (1919); Edgar Kemler, *The Deflation of American Ideals: An Ethical Guide for New Dealers* (Seattle, 1941).

Articles

Samuel Crowther, "Prohibition or Poverty: An Interview with Henry Ford," *Ladies Home Journal*, XLVII (April 1930), 56; Louis Hacker, "If Beer Returns," *Current History* (January 1933), pp. 385–92.

Newspapers

Detroit *News;* Detroit *Free Press;* Detroit *Saturday Night;* Detroit *Times;* New York *Times; Christian Science Monitor;* Pittsburgh *Christian Advocate;* Chicago *Herald;* Ann Arbor *Daily News.*

Documents

U.S. Congress, Senate Subcommittee of the Committee on the Judiciary, "Lobby Investigation," 71st Cong., 1st Sess. (1930); U.S. Congress, Senate, Senate Subcommittee of the Committee on the Judiciary, "Modification or Repeal of National Prohibition," 72d Cong., 1st Sess. (1932); State of Michigan Liquor Study Commission, "Report," (January 21, 1943); Michigan Convention Record Repealing the Eighteenth Amendment Ratifying the Twenty First Amendment of the United States Constitution, April 10, 1933; Henry B. Joy Papers; Lewis Cramton Papers, Michigan Historical Collections; Frank Murphy Papers, Michigan Historical Collections; Clarence Burton Papers, Burton Historical Collection; Howard Hyde Russell Papers, Michigan Historical Collections; Detroit Citizens' League Papers, Burton Historical Collection; James Couzens Papers, Library of Congress.

Other

Norman Harding Dohn, "The History of the Anti-Saloon League" (Ph.D. thesis, Ohio State University, 1959); Dayton Heckman, "Prohibition Passes: The Story of the Association Against the Prohibition Amendment" (Ph.D. thesis, Ohio State University, 1939); Louise P. Duus, "There Ought to Be a Law: A Study of Popular American Attitudes Toward 'The Law' in the 1920's" (Ph.D. thesis, University of Minnesota, 1967); Richard T. Ortquist, Jr., "Depression Politics in Michigan, 1929–1933" (Ph.D. thesis, University of Michigan, 1968).

Index

Index